HANDBOOK OF
MULTIVARIATE EXPERIMENTAL PSYCHOLOGY

CONTRIBUTORS

Harry E. Anderson, *University of Georgia* • Carl Bereiter, *University of Illinois* • R. Darrell Bock, *University of North Carolina* • David H. Brand, *Systems Research Laboratories* • Sir Cyril L. Burt, *University of London* • Raymond B. Cattell, *University of Illinois* • Richard W. Coan, *University of Arizona* • Jacob Cohen, *New York University* • Malcolm A. Coulter, *National Institute for Personnel Research, Johannesburg* • Karl H. Delhees, *University of Zurich* • John M. Digman, *University of Hawaii* • Benjamin Fruchter, *University of Texas* • Louis B. Guttman, *The Hebrew University and the Israel Institute of Applied Social Research* • Harold W. Hake, *University of Illinois* • Chester W. Harris, *University of Wisconsin* • John L. Horn, *University of Denver* • Paul Horst, *University of Washington* • Lyle V. Jones, *University of North Carolina* • Roy B. Mefferd, *Baylor University and Houston Veterans Administration Hospital* • Murray S. Miron, *Syracuse University* • John R. Nesselroade, *University of Illinois* • Charles E. Osgood, *University of Illinois* • Kurt Pawlik, *University of Vienna* • Joseph R. Royce, *University of Alberta* • Saul B. Sells, *Texas Christian University* • William R. Thompson, *Wesleyan University* • Bien Tsujioka, *University of Kansai* • Ledyard R. Tucker, *University of Illinois*

HANDBOOK OF MULTIVARIATE EXPERIMENTAL PSYCHOLOGY

Edited by **RAYMOND B. CATTELL, Ph.D., D.Sc.**
RESEARCH PROFESSOR OF PSYCHOLOGY
UNIVERSITY OF ILLINOIS

RAND McNALLY & COMPANY
CHICAGO

RAND McNALLY PSYCHOLOGY SERIES

Lloyd Humphreys, Advisory Editor

Dedicated to those fellow reformers who initiated the Societies of Multivariate Experimental Psychology in the U. S. A. and Europe.

Preface

A preface is a heart-to-heart talk from writer to reader conveying what might seem too personal or human for the austere content of the text. As such, if frankly given, it can be as helpful as a hundred pages of text in enabling the reader to focus, follow, and evaluate the rest. Then, like a good autobiography, such as that of Cellini, Rousseau, or Wells, it permits us to click our tongues at the questionable social taste while enjoying the uniquely truthful gift of the artist! At once I must confess that I shall disappoint the reader on this score, though a minor novel could be written on the group production of this work, with its interaction of creative ideas with the quirks, unusual sensitivities, and solid virtues of the contributors—not to say much of what the editor regarded as the pathological dilatoriness of a few. (But of the majority let me say at once that I view them as Wellington did the splendid companions who won with him the battle of Waterloo.)

This last allusion is perhaps not entirely inapt, for as the substance and spirit of the chapters will clearly show, the book, in addition to its creative purpose, has also militantly to attack the dictatorship of a too rigid, outmoded view of experimental psychology, in order to produce freedom for a new growth. And it is already socially evident that the more traditional of bivariate psychologists, on the one hand, and of psychometrists, on the other, have initially reacted to the field of multivariate experimental psychology (and to the Society of Multivariate Experimental Psychology) as an unnecessary declaration of independence. Modern societies grow by new syntheses and specializations, but it is a law of group dynamics—illustrated in the American War of Independence—that established groups are quite automatically hostile to newborn groups. Consequently the new methodological developments of multivariate experimental psychology have been forced explicitly to defend themselves. This accounts for the challenging tone of some of the following pages, and hopefully the same spirit has increased the originality of attack on old problems. Further, one may venture to guess that in the perspective of psychological history this movement, far from appearing as a splinter group, will be seen as the creator of an important synthesis combining within a new conception those scientific values which brass-instrument psychologists on the one hand and psychometrists on the other, have served in separation. If, in this attempt at a union, some onlookers have reacted like rival in-laws at a wedding, we can only say sadly with the historian that time, distance and decease alone can take care of things.[1]

The notion of attempting to present this synthesis in a book, helpful to students and others, was conceived in 1960 in a bedroom at Allerton House (where the University of Illinois offers hospitality to its Visiting Conferences) where two dozen members of the newly formed Society of Multivariate

---

[1]It is a reflection on our scientific motivation and training that an eminent historian and methodologist of science (Thomas Kuhn, *The Structure of Scientific Revolutions)* feels it realistic to write: "Today it has become a truism to say that a major scientific theory triumphs, not by converting its opponents, but by their deaths."

Experimental Psychology had secluded themselves for intensive discussion. The dedication of the book so conceived to SMEP in no way makes it an official product of the Society. Similarly, ONR, to which all are grateful for arranging the conference where, incidentally, both SMEP and this book thus began, is not to be considered an official parent, though it gave its blessing.

There has been some little disagreement among the contributors as to how enthusiastically it is permissible to write about revolutionary aspects and intentions. The editor's view, as his chapters will indicate, takes the position that the most revolutionary transitions in sciences have usually occurred through methodological innovation rather than grand and bookish theories. A new direction and power is usually given by *devices* — as by the microscope, the telescope, and the electron tube, or more subtly by stereochemistry or the differential calculus — by the light of which all can see emerging new theories. These methodological inventions solve new kinds of problems and do so, moreover, with altogether more exact standards of what constitutes a solution. The more exact theories readily enough follow, because they are made possible by the new vision. It is this instrumentation — this capacity to approach old problems in new operational terms, and to open doors before which bivariate methods have monotonously marked time — that multivariate experiment now brings. Unfortunately, it is often the nature of textbooks in science, especially those designed for the student, to picture a smooth transition of reasonable viewpoints, denying the frequently rather violent change of gears and shifts of leadership from one field to another which actually occur in scientific advance. The importance of recognizing and preparing for such methodological revolutions is thus not understood and conveyed.

In consequence, perhaps an insufficiently recognized social problem today is the need at times to stir up and break that smooth cycle of teachers followed by students in the image of their teachers, which so silently achieves the dreadful momentum of a Juggernaut. This procession gains its momentum from the ordinary occupational feedback of supply upon demand, and also, if awkward truths may be uttered, from the tendency of less creative heads of departments to fill their time and obtain their consolation from simple empire-building. The problem as far as a new methodology is concerned is to get teachers with a radically new approach into university departments which have a completely blank face as far as these developments are concerned. For in 1966 it is still possible for a clean and powerful solution to a vital theoretical or practical question in almost any area in personality, learning, clinical, social, and even comparative and physiological psychology — to be sent back by an editor with the comment that it is an excellent article but that his readers would not understand multivariate methodology. At first it may seem a simple solution to this ludicrous situation in a growing science (as suggested by the formation of more quality-restricted scientific societies than the APA in psychology in the last few years) to label some journals "popular psychology" and others scientific journals. Unfortunately, this is not the whole solution, for unless we attend to graduate education there may still be many "qualified" men so one sided as to operate at a popular level in important fields.

The present Handbook is primarily written for the graduate student and the independent researcher. For every graduate student who has professors who will guide him through its pages there will be two or three other psychologists who have to find their own way, with the inevitable rough times of adventurers, by their own resources. While it is good thus to learn to read, a readable book demands a better job than I have probably done to enable the independent reader easily to find his way. If

Contents

List of Tables

my fellow contributors are correct in believing that every graduate student in psychology should be familiar with multivariate methods and concepts, since these experimental designs are indispensable to *every* specialist content area, then something better adapted than this book to the limited time of graduate courses must in time be produced. It would probably be premature to aim at a smoother, condensed, pedagogically-oriented text, however, before the often radically novel concepts here have been shaken down by specialists and turned over by five or ten years of discussion and experience in their application. For it must be pointed out that whereas some chapters and themes, e.g. those of Anderson, Bock, Burt and Horst, deal with highly developed and authoritatively settled issues, others, such as the present writer's development of the data box, Coulter and Tsujioka's work on patterns, or Cohen's survey of multivariate findings in clinical, raise more questions than they can settle, and necessarily aim at a more speculative treatment, offering fertile ideas for further attack rather than exact solutions.

One major problem of study orientation which will plague some readers is an uncertainty as to whether this is a book on statistics and mathematics or one on experiment and the associated psychological concepts and theories. It can only be said that the same has plagued the writers. The book is for a new species of psychologist — the mathematician experimenter — and there are not enough representatives yet in existence to decide how the book should either be read or written. The ideal author — a highly competent mathematical-statistician who has spent most of his life deeply immersed in scientifically productive work in some branch of psychology, is — except for a few instances — a figment of the editor's imagination. This figment the editor has nevertheless painted and held up before the eyes of his contributors to remind them of the future man. On

behalf of this still scarce "balanced psychologist" the contributors in Part I, dealing with abstract method — have constantly been reminded of Part II, which deals with substantive psychological concepts and laws from the application of such methods. Similarly those writing in Part II have been reminded to keep an eye on the more abstract disciplines set as standards in Part I. The result, one hopes, is that relatively few contributors in Part I have written presentations that are statistical chapters uninspired by experimental reference. It is happily more certain that those experimentally engaged writers in Part II have been unable to proceed without relating their psychology to Part I. Indeed, they have often had the editor's encouragement to be critical of the mere models of Part I, as well as to orient their own presentations to experimental realities rather than to mere mathematical elegance of statement as such.

The defect remains that the chapters deliver their wares at very different levels of difficulty. The atheist who defended his position by claiming he found the world in such a mess that it could only have been created by a committee surely had in mind especially those books, so popular with publishers nowadays, which are not written by a single author — and which seem to receive negligible guidance from any single editor. The editor here had an initial agreement with his contributors that the work would not be just a collection of unrelated chapters held together only by the binding, but that he would really edit, demand integration of designs, insert cross-references from chapter to chapter, and even add introductory chapter sections evaluative of each chapter's viewpoints vis-a-vis other existing viewpoints.

Certainly one owes this degree of integration to the graduate student reader, and probably to *every* reader in such a new field. One wonders, in reading current symposia, how sensible it really is to help a reader with the simpler, more specific questions while leaving him to form his total perspectives — requiring the widest knowledge and experience — quite alone? Too often the student is given a set of readings of widely uneven quality, and grossly conflicting conclusions, while the editor or his teacher — in the interests, they claim, of avoiding value judgements — maintain an unearthly silence. In this vacuum, all too frequently the student's interest ceases to breathe. In the present book the editor's wish to help the reader has had to be restricted, in only one or two instances, by the nervousness of a contributor who wished critical cross-references, and the clear illumination of points of difference, to be omitted. But the majority of contributors have expressly welcomed insertion of reference to other chapters and recognized that an introductory paragraph or page by the editor of explicit and calm debate of vital differences is part of the spirit of science.

The only respect in which the editor is regretfully aware of having done more than was planned lies in his having had to step into the breach at the last moment to write two chapters when, through illness and other causes, contributors, after some years, were holding up the Handbook for lack of their chapters! In apology for this second-best, one must point out that the book was planned essentially as a *collection of areas and concepts,* not as an outlet for a transient or fortuitous company of individuals; and to leave gaps in these areas would have been serious. (There are still some slighter gaps, for which the qualified multivariate experimenter author simply did not exist.)

Probably the greatest problem from the standpoint of the psychological reader is the demand here, in places, for a degree of mathematical education which in our present arrangements of psychological course work he does not automatically acquire. It cannot be denied that a few of our contributors can go further than any other living psychologists in covering a blackboard in ten minutes with a shower of completely bewildering but highly meaningful formulae. In some cases, since they

indicate the standard background reading in statistics by which their *tour de force* becomes duly comprehensible — and, indeed, vastly entertaining — it has not seemed practicable to me to ask them (with little hope of success) to forgo their mathematical elegance. In others I have succeeded in obtaining some helpful concessions to "writing down," by introducing words, and by the meaningful relation of statistics and models to actual research and conceptual issues — a style at which I strongly feel more writers should aim in this field. Although logic required general methodology to come in Part I, I believe the reader would do best to begin with his natural area of interest in Part II, and, later, if he encounters a chapter in Part I which proves too abstract, to withdraw and return to it after patiently studying some of the preparatory reading suggested.

I am greatly indebted to those contributors who contributed promptly and waited two years with me patiently for the last of their fellows, and especially to Dr. Sam Hammond, of Melbourne University, who carefully helped edit chapters for press over the last six months and then compiled most of the bibliography. He has agreed to share with me the responsibility for any errors that may be discovered — and for this I cannot be too thankful to him! His perspective, from a different psychological culture, became especially valuable where real surgery was needed. I am also much indebted to my research associate, Mr. Malcolm Coulter of Johannesburg, for a final run over the style of mathematical expositions. Finally, I wish to express gratitude to numerous non-academic helpers in this large undertaking, notably to Mrs. Deborah Skehen who retyped the final versions of the chapters and Mrs. H. Ponleithner who attended to those editorial matters which no author seems to be able to handle alone.

RAYMOND B. CATTELL

Urbana, Illinois, 1965

List of Diagrams

CHAPTER 1

Psychological Theory and Scientific Method

RAYMOND B. CATTELL
University of Illinois

1. THE ROLE OF METHODOLOGY IN SCIENCE

Psychology is young as a systematic study and still younger as a true science. For many reasons its growing pains have been unusually severe and its progress fitful. The three most baffling difficulties have arisen from (1) the intangible and fluid quality of its subject matter — behavior — compared with that of older sciences; (2) the unique situation created by the scientist studying his own mind; and (3) the fact that scientific writing has found it almost impossible to disentangle itself from semi-scientific, popular terminology, modes of reasoning, and "theories," since "psychology" is such an enormous daily preoccupation of all mankind.

We cannot stop here to view historically the various maneuvers, some foolish, some wise but desperate, by which psychology has sought to extricate itself from these difficulties. The abandonment of introspection for behavior, the turning from human life, which cannot be controlled, to manipulatable animals, the periodic retreats into physiology, the "salvation in sociology" movement, the final, determined facing of measurement prob-

lems and their occasional conversion into an obsession — all these and many other vacillations of strategy and tactics have marked and sometimes marred the history of an unusually difficult but adventurous science. Yet it is our belief that as of the mid-point of the twentieth century, the ship of psychology has perhaps at last cleared the rocky coast of popular illusions and the peril of false landmarks and has set out, well provisioned with new methodological resources, on the true bearings for the first stage of its ultimate voyage.

Curiously enough, as arguments here may perhaps substantiate, one source of a malign compass deviation in the early days has been the very eagerness to assume a true scientific status. For this led to premature regimentation, and indeed slavishness, in following the rules of the older, established sciences when the need was really for invention of methods and trial-and-error exploration of the scientific quality of a new area. For psychology had to move toward a methodology suited to a science different in some fundamental, unperceived ways from the physical sciences. In any case, both to extirpate this erroneous mode of thinking, and to overcome the difficulties due to the unusually complex

subject matter, it is now essential for psychologists to become unusually explicit and sophisticated about methodology.

Yet, although the situation absolutely demands that psychologists become explicit and imaginative about their methodology and their processes of concept formation, there are dangers in this too. In any field of human enterprise it is possible to become so self-conscious about methods and instruments that all energy is absorbed in the preparatory rituals and no real discoveries are made. Every child knows that hours of instruction in the theory of how to ride a bicycle are less important than a few minutes of bold trial-and-error. And alike in science and religion the spirit and the capability of performance are readily lost once pundits and pharisees entrench themselves as the guardians of pure method and traditional wisdom. Let us never forget that some of the best work in science has been done by inspired men who knew nothing and cared less concerning what philosophers of method were pontificating about in their lecture rooms. One thinks of Faraday devising, amid the amusement of pure mathematicians, his "tubes of force" (later to become respectable field theory), of Liebig substituting chlorine atoms for hydrogen when everyone knew the absurdity of trying to substitute a negative for a positive valence, of Banting fooling with the pancreatic juice of diabetics despite the opinions of medical authority, of Harvey banished from respectable medical texts for his theories of circulation, and of Einstein going right outside the pillars of the Newtonian reference system. Art and literature, of course, are equally aware, in retrospect, of the deadening effect upon creativity of too self-conscious an approach, and too great a dependence upon purely conscious reasoning, and too great a respect for classical tradition. Michelangelo would have bequeathed us less if he had had to justify every brush stroke to a committee of leading lecturers on art. Method, ritual, and traditional authority are prone to seek each other's company. The

danger of retreat into such company is particularly great in a difficult science like psychology — difficult as shown by the rarity of discovery of real laws and substantiation of clear theories. In such a situation there is great danger of being left with few players and presented with a great escape of self-styled pundits to the sidelines and the grandstand. "Those who can, do," said G. B. Shaw, "and those who cannot, teach."

Despite these dangers of compulsive methodological and theoretical ritualism, psychologists urgently need to climb to a new plateau of methodological self-awareness. They will do so more wisely if they recognize quite frankly from the beginning that this plateau has crevasses of punditry and pedantry where some will stay forever entrapped. We need subtle and sophisticated methodologists who are also seasoned in productive research work. It is for this reason that the main plan of the present book is not that of the typical pure method textbook, but has two equal parts, one on method, as such, and one showing the relations of concepts to methods across the whole field of substantive psychology.

2. DESIGN OF THE PRESENT BOOK

With an eye open to the above demarcated dangers, we plan to ask the reader to begin with methodology in the abstract in Part I, and to proceed in Part II to recognize its enrichment by interaction with important psychological research and theory development. The importance of sound and adequate theory development, if psychology is to take its proper place among the sciences, is recognized by all psychologists. Yet if we are realists, we must surely recognize that as of the middle of the twentieth century, nine-tenths of the voluminous writings on "clinical theory," "group dynamics principles," "personality theory," and "learning theory" were highly questionable constructions if examined by the standards of theory in other sciences. Even when one has set aside the popular and pompous verbiage — vague, unexperi-

mental, unmeasured, and unoperational — which many textbook writers still serve up as theory, there remain some sincere theoretical attempts at organization which are fruitless simply because the writers have failed to recognize the necessary symbiosis of method and theory. For the precision and fruitfulness of theoretical constructs are no greater than that of the methodology of experiment and observation from which they derive and by which they are checked.

Most researchers in psychology — though they may once have had courses that familiarized them with a variety of experimental and statistical methods — actually have a rich experience and competence only in the restricted methods they habitually employ in their own field. For it is still possible, e.g., in reflexological learning theory, or in test theory, to get along without comprehensive and integrated use of a variety of designs. By contrast, our purpose in this chapter is to take an overview of *experimental designs generally,* and then in subsequent chapters of Part I, to focus on their particular advantages, shortcomings, and relevances. In so doing, we shall at first pay attention not only to the inherent and logical character of methods, but also to the historical garb in which teaching has accustomed us to perceive them. For inasmuch as our own lives are part of the stream of history, and insofar as we have to recognize the priority of ideas that have come to roost in our minds in our susceptible formative years, we know that few psychologists move much beyond their graduate education. Those who do 'realize that a relatively painful self-scrutiny has to be made if one is to achieve independent' emancipated thinking. Parenthetically, it is dismaying to realize the extent to which even the selected minds of graduate students prove to be imprisoned for life in the particular patchwork of emphasis and ignorance of their immediate teachers. For wide and free reading is as effectively cut out by our crowded course time tables as if it were explicitly forbidden. In some American universities, and in some whole countries,

e.g., Russia and Germany, until recently, it happens that multivariate experimental methodology has suffered from these influences. Free, adequate, and systematic exposition in this area is lacking because of a series of historical, and political accidents. It is as important to recognize these cultural and emotional fixations in our lives, in reacting to the following pages, as to recognize the difficulties from the cognitive and intellectual complexities themselves.

Just because our theme is centered on multivariate experimental methods there is no reason to assume that we depreciate in any way the importance of bivariate methods. Both share the virtues of experimental as opposed to non-experimental theoretical development. Our contention, indeed, is that psychology will make its greatest advances through a two-handed, flexible, and appropriate use of what we shall soon define more precisely as multivariate and bivariate experimental designs. Nevertheless, it is also our duty to bring home the fact that insufficient teaching and research development has been bestowed on the former, in relation to its extreme importance and usefulness at the present juncture in psychological theory development. To what extent this alleged neglect needs to be, and can be remedied in the next few years the reader may form an opinion as he proceeds. It is at any rate certain that countless volumes exist on experiment defined narrowly as bivariate experiment, whereas this book is one of relatively few aiming to provide instruction on multivariate experiment. However, our first two chapters are concerned with a total perspective over both divisions of experimental design. They concern methodological principles and theory development in the widest possible sense.

For the sake of guidance in reading, a word or two on the design of the book as a whole is desirable right here, at the beginning. The lecturer with relatively specific course objectives will naturally make his own special choices and recommendations as to chapters and sequences. But for the self-directing reader, granted he has some initial research experience, the editor would suggest: (1) That he begin with the first four chapters, which are consecutive and panoramic, and thereafter move to individual chapters, according to his area of interest; (2) That with *any* chapter the reader should first peruse it for general sense and content and then read once again for more exact meanings and inferences. For condensation and complexity in this book are in general of high degree; (3) That the reader keep in mind the general design, which is to present methods in Part I and resulting findings and concepts in Part II. This may often suggest the desirability of reading first, in Part II, the substantive area in which he is most directly interested, and then following back the references to chapters in Part I which enlarge on the methods employed.

The editor has considered and rejected the proposition that Parts I and II should be published as separate volumes. One reason for rejecting this has already been stated, namely, that method discussions are only half alive when separated from the active research applications by which methodology grows and reveals its true role. This reason also points to the hollowness of the frequent claim that method principles are eternal, or at least may expect to stand, for a decade or two, with little need of change, whereas the meaning of results and concepts in any theoretical framework will begin to "date" within a shorter period. There is some ground for this distinction, but methods also grow out of date unless linked with new research, in which they grow to new capacities. An equally cogent reason for keeping both parts together is that a Handbook of Multivariate Experimental Psychology would be a dull, theoretical abstraction, as far as most true psychologists are concerned, without the psychological content. Indeed, the only argument with any weight for separating the parts, is the physical weight of the single-volume book!

Hopefully, it will be evident from the above comments and actual reading that the editor has *not* aimed merely at a collection of rather disconnected chapters by distinguished authors in the form now common in many "symposia." First, there has been the above indicated design in terms of a proper balance of areas, and of a best logical sequence. Here, nevertheless, distinguished writers, unfortunately, do not distribute themselves precisely according to the coverage requirements of the subject, appearing miraculously where most needed. As confessed above the editor has himself had to step into the breach with a less inspired treatment in two instances, namely, the neglected methodological area of identifying and measuring processes, and the substantive area of social and political culture pattern dynamics. Second, the book has exemplified the above discussed aim of producing more integration than commonly exists in such handbooks, and this has been achieved by regular insertion of brief editorial comments. These are made recognizable by an editorial signature, so that the individual writers need not be held responsible for any opinions or evaluations expressed in these connecting links.

In a book of this kind, a substantial index is particularly needed, and can do much to assist the integration. The chapter by chapter bibliography is awkward for the reader though easier for writer and publisher. At the cost of considerable effort we have organized at the end a single bibliography which enables the reader to work with the far more convenient and less distracting single number placed in the text as reference to bibliographical source. As part of the plan for integration of terms and concepts we have also provided an extensive index which the reader may find it advantageous to use freely.

3. SOME MAJOR HISTORICAL SPRINGS OF METHODOLOGICAL TRADITION

Books on psychological method and experimental design are rapidly on the increase. This is beneficial in its promise to reduce ill-designed and inconclusive research and theorizing, but not, as indicated above, if it breeds a sterile, would-be elite of scientific lawyers, or blinds the student to the fact that research is in the last resort an art.

Above all, if a raised standard of education in methods is to be achieved, it is necessary to engender, beyond any knowledge of particular skills and formulae as such, a *perspective* as to what methods are most appropriate to various areas and occasions. The lack of this perspective is undoubtedly still widespread, and responsible for much of our fruitless beating upon Nature's closed doors. Because, say, a talented agricultural statistician puts forward designs for agricultural research which evoke the admiration of statisticians, it does not follow that they should be the automatically preferred tool for all psychological experiments. The opposite kind of misperception, in which different disciplines stick to different methods when, in fact, each would benefit from what has been developed in the other, is equally common. For example, economists and psychologists have built up substantially different techniques for analyzing time series and trends (see Chapters 11 and 12), though each would gain new concepts and make better progress by incorporating the insights of the other. Or, again, medicine, which lagged for fifty years in the use of more powerful statistics, but reached sophisticated levels at least a generation ago in the use of analysis of variance, has failed to make adequate use of partial and multiple correlation. This neglect of multivariate designs is completely at variance with its philosophy that diseases are multiply determined! And psychologists themselves, if arguments by the present writer and colleagues over the last twenty years are correct, have failed to make much theoretical advance in such areas as drives, personality learning, clinical taxonomy, etc., through failing to pick up the tools of factor analysis, discriminant functions, and anal-ysis of variance and covariance in the right order.

Perhaps, before psychologists make the effort necessary for this advance in perspective, two realizations are necessary: (1) That relative to the man-hours applied, the real progress of psychology has sadly little to boast about, and (2) That in the way we equip our students with research designs, we are the victims of a quirk in our psychological culture. The first is for others[1] to

[1]However, although this realization is unpalatable, few mature psychologists who have watched many torrents of fashion pass over the dam will dispute it. Argument on the intrinsic merits of the host of theories constituting our stock in trade must be bypassed here, for it would be endless. But first one may simply count, asking: "How many useful and dependable laws have we actually unearthed in psychology so far?" Second, one may apply the well-known, realistic, but rough touchstone: "What body of technology has followed from our alleged basic theoretical advances?" The latter test rapidly brings cloudy theories to reality, for certainly more than half the elaborate and pretentious theories which now inflate textbooks vanish in our hands when we attempt to give some practical technical help, e.g., in school or clinic. Learning theory, large in *academic* schools, looks very small when judged by the advances it has generated in the *public* schools. Even the recent teaching machines were known in principle to the country schoolteacher. And it is hard to find much that a successful advertising man owes to the thousands of published "experiments on perception."

In the current public trial of psychotherapy as a possible impostor, e.g., through the challenge by Eysenck, it does not matter whether we conceive it as a failure of learning theory or of personality theory, for in either case, practitioners have been guilty of excessive claims for theory as such. Actually, personality theory comes out of the examination better, for, with psychometrics, it can claim some genuine gains in effectiveness in clinical diagnosis, counseling, and guidance. But these gains are not so vast and beyond question that every ambitious culture is determined to acquire them. By contrast, one observes from Saskatchewan to Singapore, operating effectively in radios and automobiles, vaccines, and antiseptics, the scientific laws and potent theories of Faraday and Hertz, Liebig and Mendeléef, Pasteur and Curie.

Doubtless, as Thurstone, McDougall, Hull, Lashley, and others have said in turn, psychology happens to present unusually complex problems. And we have the excuse that until quite recently it has been poorly financially endowed in research compared with the biological and physical sciences. But when all due allowance has been made for these, ought we not in all

examine; the second will be attacked in this section.

It is a commonplace of history that catchwords and stereotypes have often deflected people for considerable periods from the logically required solution to a problem. In psychological method just such an instance — and an important one — faces us in the widespread teaching that "experimental" and "correlational" methods are two distinct approaches. Automatically, in some universities, the student is taught that the former is largely applicable to process (perception, learning, maturation) and the other to structure (psychometrics and individual differences). A reasoned account of why these academic labels overemphasize and mislead with regard to what is really a comparatively small and irrelevant aspect of design will soon be given.

But first let us take a quick backward glance at history. For if we are to disembarrass ourselves of unseen prejudices in this matter, we must learn to go with the clinician, at least to the point of recognizing the therapeutic value of reliving an early, twisted phase in the history of our science which produced this strange dissociation! To recognize the birth trauma which produced the rigidity of what is still popularly called the "experimental," brass-instrument tradition, one has to go back to the second half of the nineteenth century. There we encounter the real beginnings of experimental psychology, in the traditional sense, in a movement extending from the approach of (and principally represented by) Wilhelm Wundt to that of Ivan Pavlov. This movement rightly insisted on its distinctness from the mounting floods of literary and popular, speculative psychology which threatened to engulf it. Pavlov's contribution gained additional respectability from its close association with physiology, of which, indeed, Pavlov considered it a branch. (Indeed, physiological response has provided a solid shore to the bewildering

ocean of behavior, one to whose safe harbors the discouraged perennially retreat.) This early form of "experimental psychology" became still more attractive to the scientist intolerant of the ambiguity and complexity of total behavior, by reason of its very simple formulations. In the extremely mechanical, penny-in-the-slot paradigm of the conditioned reflex, it provided so jejune a formula that, like Freud's sexual symbolism, it would fit everything. The fact that personality learning theorists feel that for twenty years it has controlled a field beyond its true scope as a model to explain, and has rested on unjustifiable assumptions, need not bother us as far as its early history is concerned. Regardless of its possible flaws, this movement constituted an attempt at a purely scientific, precise treatment that could be easily and widely appreciated. Because of this ease of appreciation the mainstream of research in perception, the special senses, learning etc., grew up within it.

Meanwhile, a very different movement began with the versatile and non-academic genius of Sir Francis Galton. To be reminded of the scope of his creativeness, one has only to think of his discovery of the cyclone-anti-cyclone structure in meteorology, of his ethnological and pioneer, geographical exploration of West Africa and of his invention of the correlation and regression concepts. Galton did not enter psychology with the physiological and animal emphasis of the Wundt-Pavlov tradition, but through observation of living people and interest in finding laws in the totality of human behavior, from sensory to social. His approach comprehended the clinical interests of the more numerous medical psychologists, of whom Kraepelin and Bleuler were becoming outstanding representatives, but he viewed clinical method only as a subsection of a far broader and newly developing quantitative, statistical methodology. Although Galton's explicit and finished contributions ended at behavioral measurement, the normal distribution curve, and devices such as the

---

humility to ask ourselves if there may not be something basically deficient in our methodological resources?

correlation coefficient, Sir Cyril Burt has pointed out (172) that the embryo of factor analysis and other multivariate techniques is foreshadowed and exists in his writings. There is little doubt that Galton's vision included in embryo the refined methods of analysis of behavior *in situ* and undisturbed which psychologists now view as the vital tool of individual and social psychology.

Galton's interactions with such statisticians as Karl Pearson generated, through a widening interplay of the work of such men as Quetelet, Spearman, Fisher, Stern, Burt, Hotelling, Thurstone and many others, what is now easily recognizable as the second main stream of psychological methodology and theory-building. Without historical research it would be difficult to say now whether the challenge of actual scientific problems, as, for instance, Spearman's wrestling with the problem of general ability, and Thurstone's attack on the basic problems in attitude scaling, or the development of mathematical and statistical models as such, as in the mathematician's work on latent roots and vectors, or matrix algebra, has done more to give vigor to this movement. Certainly the interplay of experiment and mathematical thinking was timely and powerful in opening up, for those who had eyes to see, an altogether new and effective methodological approach to analyzing, conceptualizing, and predicting behavior. More recently, indeed only in the last decade, a second powerful stimulus has been given to the development of multivariate experiment by the complex programing possibilities in electronic computers. Alas, one must also recognize that this has brought dangers of magnifying mistakes, of spreading vulgar abuses and favoring uninspired collection of data. However, this is not too much to pay for the gain to basic research which results from bringing certain ideal, intricate treatments into the realm of the actual.

What one must not forget in thus contrasting the essence of the classical and the multivariate experimental designs and traditions is that both the Galton-Spearman and the Wundt-Pavlov movements stand out very clearly, by a common regard for scientific rigor, from a more rank growth of non-scientific or quasi-scientific schools of psychological "research" which have flourished then and since. Naturally, one finds certain developments less disciplined than these which were nevertheless deserving of scientific respect. Today, certain experimentalists of both the Wundt-Pavlov and the Galton-Spearman (as we may for symmetry call this movement) traditions wish explicitly to deny the status of scientific psychology to the writings of Freud, James, Adler, Jung, and to theories of various anthropologists and sociologists of a generation ago. As a multivariate experimentalist, the present writer would prefer to say that several of the latter were at least scientific in intent and in their espousal (though with poor operational expression) of certain subsets of scientific methodological principles. The best of these methodologically looser contributors approached the empirical carefulness and honesty evident in, say, a Darwin, a Humboldt, or a Linnaeus. It must be recognized that such more casual psychological methodologists perceived, though dimly, a truth which has been denied to some in the doctrinaire brass-instrument, Wundt-Pavlov tradition. For they perceived that many of the problems of psychology are not those in which one can hope to find sufficiently determining laws so long as one attempts to adjust the complexity of nature to the narrow limits of our minds merely by the old, familiar process of biting off a bit at a time. The atomistic, bivariate, piecemeal approach must often fail when thus inappropriately applied. And these early explorers, including the Gestaltists, realized that it needed to be replaced by a method capable of a wholistic, multivariate regard for the totality of relations and patterns.

Let us therefore recognize that zeal for a narrow interpretation of "experimental psychology" can go too far when it rejects in toto the essence of the rough concepts emerging from general observational and clinical methodologies. If such early concepts, or something much like them, receive verification and formalization from more precise operational methods, it is nothing but a kind of intellectual snobbery to deny one's scientific ancestry by ignoring the connection. This snobbery is shown, for example, by those "experimentalists" in personality who have a pharisaic aversion to attaching terms like ego strength, super ego strength, etc., to the essentially similar structures confirmed for instance, by later factor analysis. In some matters, doubtless, both the Wundt-Pavlov and the Galton-Spearman traditions do well to make a clean break between what Thurstone called "a quantitative, rational science" and the jargon of the numerous quasi-scientific schools which led to that scholastic Tower of Babel whose sights and sounds still confound us.

4. WHAT IS AND WHAT MIGHT BE IN PRESENT DAY RESEARCH METHOD CONCEPTS

Although what we may thus briefly call the Wundt-Pavlov and Galton-Spearman traditions stand out, bearing certain true hallmarks of science, from the wrack of semi-scientific and downright bogus and expedient writings on psychology, they have nevertheless long been regarded as mutually conflicting, or, at least, as highly divergent. Our aim here is to show that they are in fact just two out of a more numerous but little recognized array of possible and essentially integratable experimental designs. An emancipation from the current cat-and-dog concept of these two traditions may be better achieved, however, if we pause to see what the nature of the mistaken accretions has come to be.

By historical accident the multivariate Galton-Spearman tradition has been more developed at the hands of educational psychologists and psychometrists than by those in traditional laboratories. Conse-

quently, many casual observers add to the confusion in the first place by assuming that this methodological approach is merely synonymous with psychometrics, though psychometric methods actually include both more and less than is in this development. Second, in the thinking of many psychologists it has become associated with non-manipulative treatment. Certainly it has been successful in extracting scientific law and order from social, educational, and clinical data which could not be brought alive into the laboratory and manipulated by the Wundt-Pavlov methods, but there is no need to restrict it to this. However, because of these failures of perception, it transpired that in many departments in America and Germany, and to a lesser extent in England, France, and Australia, its experimental and law-revealing possibilities were scarcely recognized. Among these it was misperceived as "the study of individual differences" or in some similar shrunken and static role.

In the same period, say, from 1880 to 1950, one sees that the bivariate method likewise settled down to certain areas, mainly the areas of what we shall call process study, as instanced in perception, the special senses, and learning. By the nature of this methodology the process concerned tended to be studied "in the abstract," suitably isolated from the complexity of the total organism, and with the individual differences therein omitted. The fact also gradually became evident, to the dissatisfaction of many psychologists, that important classes even of process phenomena themselves were also being omitted — or, at least, not caught — by these manipulative methods. In particular, it has a relatively fruitless record in attempting to cope with the nature of the emotional and dynamic processes of human adjustment. Such areas eluded the manipulative bivariate method for the purely practical but sufficient reason that human subjects and human ethics will not stand for manipulation of deep dynamic values and the creation of intense emotional experiences in a laboratory experiment.

The result has been that the bivariate brass-instrument method has fallen away from what most psychologists consider to be the fundamental problems of psychology. This swerve from facing the main issues has been most criticized by the clinicians, who are but little hypnotized by the academic "prestige" of the laboratory back room. The failure of the Wundt-Pavlov tradition to cope with these problems, which, as we now see, require for their solution that we climb to new and difficult methodological summits, is evidenced by a falling away on three different sides. First, the method has constantly slipped back, when actually claiming to study fundamental dynamics, into treating purely cognitive, emotionally superficial, perceptual and learning issues instead. To keep in the laboratory, it retreats to problems that are humanly trivial, as well as unrepresentative of most behavior in actual life. Second, it has retreated time and again into physiology (the direction of the psychology department of an old university was not long ago given to an embryologist!). Third, it has had to substitute animals for humans in any serious attack on motivation and total behavior. No matter how it succeeds in animal psychology, it then must stand frustrated when later faced by the almost impossible task of translation into terms of human personality.

Meanwhile, the newer multivariate, analytic approach has gained headway in these same areas, for it takes human life in its natural setting. What it cannot achieve by direct manipulation, it teases out by more subtle designs and more sophisticated statistical analysis, not attempting to isolate by manipulative control *alone*. The multivariate method is noncommittal and open-minded about the dependent-independent variable relationship. It can use it or leave it. Moreover, it watches and measures the natural, ongoing events without risk of distortion or contamination by the experimenter's manipulative interference.

Unfortunately, in spite of these fairly obvious advantages, the average psychologist's grasp of its potentialities lagged. One can see in retrospect that this followed partly from the staffing of psychology departments, partly from prejudicial stereotypes, and partly from a failure of proponents of the method to exploit its inherent birthright. As pointed out above, it became identified especially with individual differences and psychometry and was almost entirely neglected in the study of process. Where the preoccupations of the reflexological tradition lost the organism, this sheep-like concentration of the intellectual descendants of Galton upon psychometrics lost connection with the processes of response, motivation, and learning (see Chapters 16 and 17 below). It is small wonder that such one-sided categorizations as Spence's "stimulus-response" and "response-response" psychology had appreciable acceptance by methodological classifiers.

How small and inadequate a fraction of the full possible range of experimental research designs was in use by *either* tradition — Galtonian or Wundtian — in this period can be more fully realized when we reach the comprehensive analysis of possible experimental designs in Chapter 2, or grasp the logic of the Basic Data Relation Matrix in Chapter 3. In retrospect, it appears as if only the wandering gypsy fringe of academic psychology, as seen in the freely operating research clinicians and social psychologists, courageously kept up in the wilderness that study of the full range of human behavior from which the brass-instrument and psychometric purists had gradually withdrawn. From the standpoint of the effect of method upon theory, it is interesting to note that such theoretical constructs as instinctual drive, the self sentiment or ego structure, the process of repression, and many other concepts which are today again recognized as important, then found their only shelter and development among these errant, substance-directed researchers. Actually, as we must increasingly recognize, it is the Galton-Spearman tradition which truly holds the potential of coming to grips, in a scientifically rigorous way, with the wholistically-structured and multivariately-determined phenomena of the clinician and the social psychologist. It is a sad reflection of the seductive power of the misleading stereotypes which have grown up around the two more rigorous methods that generally when a clinician in that period felt the need to be "scientifically precise" he promptly set up a classical, bivariate, "brass-instrument" experimental design!

In short, in the actual historical outcome, these two traditions settled into an equilibrium of mutual supplementation, each predominating in a field where its use could most easily be recognized. Yet this temporary resting place does not actually express or recognize their inherent natures and potentialities. What was overlooked primarily in these stereotypes was that the Wundt-Pavlov tradition represents essentially a sedulous copying of scientific method as it was then recognized in other sciences, whereas the Galton-Spearman movement was a new and creative adaptation to methodological needs in psychology itself. Born in response to the intrinsic challenges and new horizons of the behavioral sciences, the multivariate methods soon showed that they were destined to spread, with important developments, into other complex life sciences. While history must be regarded as something more than a summation of personalities and personal attitudes, one can detect definite attitudes in the brass-instrument tradition, from Wundt to Boring, expressing a professional academic competitiveness which coveted the respectability of the physical sciences, and consequently imitated them. Wundt, and many others in that tradition, in fact drilled their assistants on the barrack square of the physical sciences, as such. Such intense concentration on emulation,

as usual, impoverished free-ranging creativeness and adaptation, in this case to the methodological needs of a new subject. On the other hand, the brilliant amateur Galton, economically secure, and like Cavendish, Humboldt, and Lavoisier, untrammeled by any academic professionalism, simply asked what the subject needed. Like Darwin, Spearman, Freud, and others gifted with the same spiritual freedom, he made no assumption that Victorian physics had plumbed the depths of methodology or perfected the philosophy of scientific enquiry. He saw the highly multivariate nature of the interactions, the need for probability thinking in place of thinking immediately in terms of infallible, unitary causalities, and the dangers of manipulation in upsetting the very phenomena we want to study.

Nevertheless, the lack of any abrupt upset of academic tradition in the Wundt-Pavlov approach led to its being regarded as "experimental psychology" — at least in Germany, and in such early psychological schools as those at Harvard and Yale, and in Russia to this day. Elsewhere, e.g., in Britain, Australia, Holland, and Scandinavia, the Galton-Spearman movement in psychological experiment has become one hand — even the right hand — of a two-handed view of scientific investigation and method. Insofar as the bias of personal upbringing impels the Montagues and Capulets of psychology to assert that one tradition deserves the name of experimental psychology and the other does not, we may be tempted to say, like the poor victim, Mercutio, "A plague o' both their houses." But perhaps we may, instead, hope to show how they can be united in a far more effective understanding of the full resources of experimental psychology.

5. THE NATURE OF THE INDUCTIVE-HYPOTHETICO-DEDUCTIVE (IHD) METHOD IN SCIENCE

The preceding brief and therefore necessarily simplified glance at historical trends is required here simply in order that we may step out in a more enlightened way from what now is to what might be. Any current discussion in this area of experimental design abounds with stereotyped expressions such as "uncontrolled," "independent variable," "psychometric," "brass-instrument," "experimental," etc., which obviously have different meanings to the speakers, often rooted in historical accidents and misconceptions. Consequently it is necessary to escape at once from these entanglements by defining the terms more cleanly. In the next chapter we shall therefore move ahead on the basis of a naturalistic examination of what the term *experiment* can mean. That is to say, we aim to begin with a comprehensive taxonomic overview of experiments as they are performed, to set out descriptive parameters of experimentation, and to use terms correctly covering its varieties. In so doing, we shall see that there is much more to the domain of experiment than the above duality. But here we should first take stock of the fact that an *experiment* is only a subdesign within the larger design of a total *scientific investigation*. In this last section, prior to the next chapter on the varieties of experiment as such, we therefore propose to recognize the main concepts and landmarks in the process of scientific investigation as a whole.

Science is concerned with establishing general laws which can be empirically tested and which lead to deductions extending our theoretical understanding and practical control. The expression *"general laws"* will be understood, in expansions below, to include both generalizations on *process* and generalizations on *structure* (including taxonomies) in any domain of observable phenomena. The latter—the structural laws—appear especially when dealing with the early "natural history" phase of a science. Chapter 2 (Section 4) will examine more thoroughly this notion of generalization as such and such concepts as law, postulate, etc., and their role in the investigatory process, especially in relation

to theory development. But here we need to describe and define the investigatory process only to the point where we can sufficiently recognize and define the *setting* of the unit of experiment later to be analyzed.

What are we going to accept as scientific method? In psychology, especially, one hears claims for all sorts of methods which are vaguely implied to be either special forms of scientific method or somehow "legitimate alternatives" to scientific method. In Germany, for example, there still lingers a claim that psychology belongs methodologically to the *Geisteswissenschaften*. Since the methods used in the latter, though applied to behavioral science data, are patently *not* the methods of science, it is semantically confusing to retain the term *Wissenschaft,* and we reject this as a form of scientific method. In Australia and Britain the writer has encountered enthusiastic exponents for a "method of history" (even Toynbee may be counted among them) which extracts social psychological laws *without* the organized and generally quantitative methods of analysis (together with that replication and checking of findings) which any scientist in neighboring fields, say a social psychologist, would require. Almost anywhere in psychology and medicine one will encounter, additionally, claims for a "clinical method" of research which additionally, denies that it need face up to the statistical checks and experimental measurements plainly demanded by the inductive-deductive method of science.

Without pursuing the particular nature of each of these maverick forms, let it be said that they often hide (seemingly even from their practitioners!) some real but implicit use of the same sound tenets that hold in scientific method generally. When this is not so they are in fact *not* part of the inductive-hypothetico-deductive method. For example, sometimes under "historical method" the speaker is really aiming at an aesthetic rather than a scientific goal. Again, by the "clinical method" the speaker sometimes obviously means a treatment method rather than an investigatory method. At other times he is claiming investigation but by use of the "pragmatic proof" of experience. Unfortunately, much pragmatism hides, under this philosophically respectable term, from the hard work of proving that "experience" *is* experience. But in yet other cases the exponent of the clinical method is indeed *implicitly* using scientific method, though venturing to substitute his erratic memory for dependable scientific records, his vulnerable personal perceptions for measurement, and his intuitive judgment for statistical computation. Nevertheless, in this last sense of clinical method it is in principle a true scientific method.

Indeed, let us in this connection recognize, as stated above, that when the clinician is thus truly applying the procedures of scientific method (though in implicit form and with the roughness of poor instrumentation), he may actually be proceeding more wisely than his far more exact bivariate experimentalist brethren. The important point is that he is attempting to bring into a single experimental field of reference *all* the variables necessary to detect and define the concepts that need to be employed for scientific understanding and without which it may not be possible to arrive at any lawful relationship. By contrast the bivariate experimentalist often starts out with such a meaningless fragment of the totality that it is impossible to encompass any lawful relation or construe the conceptual sentence. There is no particular reason *why* one should expect to find a simple and clean lawful relation between any two of the two thousand variables that could be measured in a given situation. The lawful relation is more likely to exist between two or more abstracted *concepts,* each of which could be an underlying factor representable and measurable *only* by perception of a weighted combination of many variables. Weak though much clinical and literary observation has been, in its lack of operational measurement and

exact calculation, clinicians as a whole have had a sure instinct when they rejected brass-instrument, bivariate methodology as inapt and powerless for their wholistic, multiply determined, and unmanipulable data.

In rejecting controlled experiment, unfortunately, they failed to see those other methods for *exactly* handling their "gestalt" problems which a multivariate experimentalist could have brought to their assistance. The methods of Freud, Jung, and others were, in fact, implicitly multivariate, and can be criticized only insofar as they substituted, and were content with, non-metric observation and fallible memory in place of the experimental test and the computer. Unfortunately, the probability of obtaining a psychological research with the vision of both a good mathematician and a good clinician is far, far smaller in the products of our present graduate schools than that of getting individuals whose vision is adequate to navigate within these single alley-ways.

However, beyond these easily disposed of misunderstandings about alleged varieties of scientific method there remain fairly prevalent misunderstandings also of the central nature of the hypothetico-deductive method itself. Perhaps that which does most damage to the advance of psychological research is the authoritative, cut-and-dried academic textbook account of the "model research procedure" now so frequently imposed upon the student. In the first place, it demands of the student researcher, as a matter of course, that he appear with a fully developed and finished hypothesis, before he gets into his research at all. This he has usually had quite insufficient time and experience to generate. To say that he can safely borrow it from his instructor is not good enough, first because this denies him the most important part of research activity and secondly because psychology as a whole has not yet gathered enough measured data to generate an adequate crop of those regularities which lead to fruitful hypotheses. A further source of misunderstanding of method is that his training commonly leads to a testing of the given hypothesis by nothing but some simple t test of difference of means. This whole pedantic approach has two cardinal shortcomings as a training for research. First, it fails to teach the student anything about research as exploration and the process of initially generating hypotheses from experiment. Second, it gives the impression that the establishment or support of a hypothesis can happily be allowed to rest on some single measurement difference, referring to a single cause, instead of keeping in mind all the possible sources of variance, and keeping in perspective the relative importance of multiple causes.

Research need not begin with a hypothesis at all, and in its true life setting, a finished hypothesis is rarely the real germinal point of research action. It can begin with noticing a curious and intriguing regularity, as when Oersted found a compass jerking oddly in the neighborhood of an electric circuit, or when Hertz noticed the photo-electric effect, or Becquerel found fogged plates by his uranium desk drawer, or when the engineer Berger noticed the unaccountable "galvanic skin response" in unpowered circuits, which psychologists have been so busy with ever since. A statistical count of fruitful researches of any really frankly written history of science will show that the real turning point in major scientific theoretical advances, in a quite substantial and noteworthy proportion of cases, has been the noticing of just such intriguing regularities or irregularities as these in observed phenomena or tables of data gathered for some other primary purpose or out of sheer curiosity.

By contrast, the textbook often asserts, or magnifies the importance of the hypothesis, the theory, and subjective intellectualism in the history of scientific advance. This is a mistake which can be made quite sincerely in looking backward from a time when the idea in the hypothesis has become accepted and all important. One forgets all the other puffed-up intellectualisms which merely distracted and misled at the time, but are now heard of no more. Further, alas, one must not forget that theories often flourished merely because of that less sincere "political" importance of an hypothesis or grand theory in getting a thesis plan accepted, attracting a grant, or merely capturing the conference limelight! When Columbus spent his two years begging for funds before the court pundits of Isabella and Ferdinand, he made much of the hypothesis that China was ninety degrees west of Madrid. But one may well doubt that he was so far out in his reckoning of where China really lay. More likely adopting what we may later call a "representative design" in experiment, he believed that with land masses randomly distributed over a globe, he could simply sail west (with good navigation!) and sooner or later reach a substantial land mass. At any rate, his discovery of America actually required no more elaborate an "hypothesis" than that "by exploring westward, one has a good chance of finding land."

When the champion and emphasizer of the primacy of the hypothesis in the scientific "hypothetico-deductive method" is challenged with historical and contemporary realities, he generally retreats to the logically unassailable position that *any* action implicitly contains some hypothesis. To start eating my dinner implies the hypothesis that I have a stomach to receive it. But this is a weasel use of words for what a faint caricature of what we normally mean by an hypothesis is! It certainly does not support the argument that a precise hypothesis is necessary because "without it no one would start out on an investigation." It is important to note this final confession of even the most theory-worshiping researcher that the hypothesis can effectively be of "the most vague and tenuous kind." Let us further assert that in the last resort this "hypothesis" ceases to be a single, rigid, cognitive structure at all. It suffices in fact, if it is nothing but an ebullition of alternative ideas and a pure emotion—a consuming speculative curiosity about a certain aspect of the world. When an hypothesis becomes, as in our analysis of Columbus, nothing more than a statement that "there must be something there," or "there must be some order in the universe," it is surely better described as pure, disinterested curiosity—the most important of all ingredients in scientific method. If this is correct, some of our universities, as far as the graduate students are concerned, have become, as suggested above, a poor place in which to learn the true spirit and method of scientific research. For they provide no time or opportunity for the true apprenticeship in "inspired exploration" when a degree deadline stands a few short months ahead. Within this straitjacket, the thesis *can* actually only operate with a cut-and-dried hypothesis. Indeed, in the process of his research, the student must put on intellectual blinkers to shield him from any new, intrusive relations which may appear, even though they are likely eventually to prove theoretically and statistically more significant than any pale evidence for his shop-soiled hypothesis.

It may be desirable to reiterate at this point that an emphasis on the powerful hypothesis-creating qualities of multivariate methods should not be taken as any reflection on the degree of their hypothesis-testing utility. As Chapters 4, 5, 6 and 10 in Part I, in particular, set out, and as virtually all chapters in Part II illustrate, the various multivariate experimental designs are capable of exactly testing a great range of hypothesis structures. For, at the appropriate stages of scientific investigation, the clean-cut testing of a single hypothesis, which we have said scarcely belongs to the creative stage of research, becomes finally a vital necessity. It is an essential part of research, and one must not mistake that the point of the above criticism of it is only that

we do the student a disservice when we teach him that this is the whole story. In other words we should avoid making a virtue out of the necessity dictated by timetables and other circumstances to keep him to a one-shot test of a cut-and-dried hypothesis. If most Ph.D. research has to run within this groove (and other grooves, such as that which compels the neglect of all long-term developmental issues), let us at least not fool the student further by telling him that what he is doing is the ideal prototype of all research. Let us, instead, with an apology for circumstances, give him a true perspective, such as he may gain for example, by working as a research assistant apprentice with a mature researcher in long-term "programmatic" research.

Let us recognize also another artificiality in his working on a thesis for a whole committee, namely, that the most inspired research cannot be done in the public limelight of constant committee exposure, where half-clad ideas are afraid to appear, and where a committee's schedule is as imperative as a railroad timetable. Instead, a researcher must have time—and inclination—to wander through the wilderness of phenomena, watching and listening. Advance begins with dim, fleeting, and far-flung hypotheses, gleaned from the faint movement of straws in the wind. Such an hypothesis is checked and certain new expectations are drawn from it, which, again quickly checked against facts, lead to a still more formed and adequate hypothesis. The hypothesis spirals out of the dust of many observations, and it is checked and tried many times. There is rarely a one-step, final confirmation of *the* thesis hypothesis.

The standard cliché of textbook scientific method thus commonly misrepresents to this extent the living psychological process of hypothetico-deductive research and does so in two major respects. First, it chops out a single link—the testing of a specific hypothesis—from what is truly a chain, or more exactly, a spiral. Second, it speaks of *the* hypothesis. It may do so in a third respect too, in that it fails to recognize the existence and special qualities of applied research where there is much deduction from an already established principle to a specific application or device, the functioning of which is examined by some standard of efficiency whereas in basic research the effectiveness of inductive, hypothesis-creating steps are surely more important than the relatively automatic check. As to the emphasis in the textbook on studying a single link, we have conceded that the normal research process does indeed begin in some sense with an "hypothesis," but that it can be initially no more specific than curiosity. The initial surmises grow, through a long series of inspired guesses — checking against facts, deducing further properties, and checking again — into a *series* of links which eventually come to consist of well-structured hypotheses in a sort of organic growth. Somewhere in that later series comes the demand for a more "legal" specification of the deductions to be exposed to the next experiment. In other words, before the written hypothesis, specific, complete, and immaculately stated, comes the intuition, the hunch, and the "working hypothesis," and these hold the field for several spirals before the typical "thesis hypothesis" check can realistically be employed.[2]

Even though the textbook's "single-link structure" sometimes becomes a facsimile of actual hypothesis and experimental procedure if taken at this late stage, it still has to make a more arbitrary choice of

[2]Against the insistence on the immaculate hypothesis made by the writer of scientific method and philosophy textbooks, one may set the frank comments of countless productive researches. As a recent example, Linus Pauling (1137) commented: "A popular idea is that scientists apply their powerful intellects in the straightforward logical induction of new general principles from known facts, and deduction of previous unrecognized conclusions from known facts, and principles. This method is, of course, sometimes used; but the advances in knowledge that are made by it are less significant than those that result from . . . subconscious processes."

where the link or cycle is to begin than is commonly admitted. Should one begin the formal, public process with the experiment that is to generate a hypothesis or the hypothesis that is to generate an experiment? The linked cycles run on, one after another. Thinking inductively over experimental data, the researcher generates a new hypothesis. Thinking over the hypothesis, he generates deductively a new experiment. The data as it appears may call for a modified and amended hypothesis, or a close scrutiny (or accidental observation) of data containing new relations may inductively generate something so different that it is scarcely the same hypothesis at all. Robert's Rules of Order demand that we vote either on a motion or on an amendment, but science proceeds more creatively than committees or courts of law, and may at any stage generate entirely different hypotheses — a third and fourth alternative — to that originally put up in an experiment for a verdict of guilty or innocent.

It is for this reason that the traditional term "hypothetico-deductive method" is so misleading. For this describes only one part of the cycle — the legalistic and disputative rather than the exploratory and more scientifically creative part. If there is any part of the spiral which can be called the scientific beginning, it is in the induction rather than the deduction. But what we can be certain about is that the complete cycle is an inductive-hypothetico-deductive-experimental-inductive one, no matter where we decide to cut it.

Since a name can perpetually mislead, and the difference here is important, let us henceforth speak of the inductive-hypothetico-deductive method — or IHD method for short. Even with this correction to IHD method, let us never forget that the scientific process is a spiral, as shown in Diagram 1-1. The penny-in-the-slot concept of scientific method as testing the deduced consequences of a single, miraculously-produced-from-nowhere hypothesis by a single, final, experimental verdict must give way to the more realistic concept of the IHD spiral.

In this IHD spiral, nevertheless, there is a steady change of emphasis from inductive activity, which emphasizes the personality qualities of an explorer and a detective, in the first stages, to deduction, which emphasizes the qualities of the lawyer, in the later stages. The mistake of much research description is to bring the case into court and dwell on the skills of the lawyer too soon.[3] In a good detective story, the advent of the police court, as when Sherlock Holmes hands over the case to Inspectors Gregory and Lestrade, signals the end of the really exciting part of the story. There is admittedly much good intellectual exercise still be had in the courtroom, but the skills of the explorer and detective are more essential and characteristic of scientific research than the skills of the lawyer.[4] These are most involved in the formative stage of hypotheses. And, as psychologists, we must by no means overlook the substantial role of unconscious processes in the generation of hypotheses, especially at the stage of the intuition and the hunch. To demand that all shall be as explicit as courtroom procedure is to sterilize the spirit of science, which is born in mystery.

At the risk of some repetition let us examine more closely the second feature of the museum-pickled specimen of the scientific process, with which we have already taken issue above, namely, the textbook's constant reference to *the* hypothesis. (The didactive device of repetition may perhaps be excused when we attack a fallacious habit so deeply ingrained.) For the fact is that most graduate students emerge with the notion that the only approved research

DIAGRAM 1-1. The Inductive-Hypothetico-Deductive Spiral

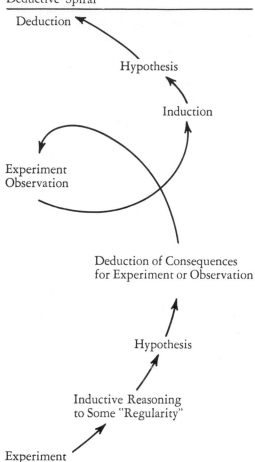

is that in which a single hypothesis is tested by a single experiment. The alternative suggested above is that an exploratory scientist has as many hypotheses at hand as there are small pieces in the pile usually standing beside a half-solved jigsaw puzzle. A diversity of hypotheses hovers in his mind like a flock of seagulls waiting to dive on a dimly seen school of fish. Such high fertility of possible ideas is essential, for the sufficient reason that a very small percentage of humanly conceived ideas and models can turn out to be true. By the nature of

---

[3] "Ask an archaeologist," says Blackler, "what he is digging for, and he will tell you he does not know—he will tell you when he has found it." Exaggerated though this may be—since the digging at least begins with rumor or legend—it contains an important truth.

[4] For those interested in cultural milieus, it is noteworthy that Rome, which gave the world law, gave it precious little science—compared, say, with Greece.

autism they will systematically err in the direction of fitting the conformation of our minds and wishes rather than the intractable complexities and peculiar ingenuities of Nature as she is.

The infant mortality of generated hypotheses is thus very high indeed. The vitality of science, like that of a nation, is not great when there is too much fond concentration on "only" children. Consequently, it is good for scientists to "spread" their attacks, and to revert constantly and vigilantly to the data itself, to catch the last hint from Nature of what new hypotheses may better fit the data. Unfortunately, there is a sense in which the social organization of science works against this need for a richly varied, individually creative and data-directed approach. The noise of conventions and congresses, not to mention social competition, tends to bring a bandwagon concentration on particular theories. Only the free, individually thinking scientist in "the small back room" tends fluently to produce and turn over a great many possibilities, each flexibly tried out for fitting the hints of Nature.

Where mature research is concerned, in research institutes and university laboratories, rather than in the qualifying theses of students under pedantic regulations and schedules, the array of hypotheses tentatively kept in view is very great. There the expected rejection of the greater part of the array of hypotheses occurs through less formal experiment than is commonly recognized, and can be informally based even on "casual" observation. Formal experiment is reserved in the end for only a few hypotheses. But even here, the "ideal" of a single experiment for a single hypothesis is rarely accepted as ideal. Most experiments are designed to be capable of throwing light simultaneously on more than one hypothesis. The single hypothesis puristically tested by a single experiment may indeed come into its own in certain final tidying-up processes, but the economics of research make such procedure too wasteful to

become typical. Any experiment is intended to throw light on the relative promise of a variety of possible hypotheses. The experimental demonstration, for example, that intelligence tests scores of higher social status children are higher than for lower socio-economic status children is relevant to at least half a dozen different hypotheses in such diverse fields as sociology, genetics, the nature of intelligence, nutrition, learning theory, etc.

These and related issues of method and design will be treated more fully in the next chapter, when more precise definitions have been given to theory, hypothesis, postulate, etc., and when the varieties of experimental design have been systematically studied. There also, we can better pursue the above suggestion that a single t test of a difference—or indeed any single empirical "check" on a hypothesis—is of limited value, and ask with a more sophisticated background, about the degree of probability assignable to alternative hypotheses and theoretical structures.

6. SUMMARY

(1) The quality of theory in psychology has been extremely uneven—and in the main unhelpful—compared with that in the older sciences, particularly the physical sciences.

(2) Up to a century ago, most attempts at generalizations about behavior belonged to a literary and philosophical stage of the subject. A second, clinical phase supervened which was productive of the bulk of theory in the half century after 1870, though it was confined largely to personality and dynamic theory.

(3) The third phase, based on measurement and experiment, has gained momentum since 1890. However, it began in two distinct sources, which have been called the Wundt-Pavlov and the Galton-Spearman traditions, and which have remained egregiously distinct because of failure to realize their joint potentialities.

(4) The Wundt-Pavlov methodology is a direct imitation of the physical sciences, undertaken partly in reaction against the diffuse, non-operational, and frequently irresponsible theory-building of the persisting literary-philosophical and clinical phases. It is bivariate and manipulative ("controlled"), but, except in perception, the special senses, and a learning theory that avoids human personality learning, it has not equalled in psychology its effectiveness in the physical sciences.

(5) The Galton-Spearman experimental tradition has been multivariate and non-manipulative, and has developed more directly as a response to the inherent needs of the behavioral sciences, whence it has spread to other life sciences. It enables wholistic real-life action to be analyzed without manipulative control. For too long, it was regarded and used as a method for psychometrics and the study of abilities, but it actually admits of manipulative experimental control and has been the main contributor more recently to personality and dynamics, and, potentially, to learning.

(6) A certain artificiality has prevailed in textbooks of theory and scientific method wherefore it is proposed to treat them here in closer relation to substantive findings and concepts and the natural history of science. The student is commonly taught a notion of scientific method as essentially hypothetico-deductive, and the constraints in routine academic theses encourage the "one-shot" test of a cut-and-dried, second-hand hypothesis. Actual scientific research is an *inductive-hypothetico-deductive* spiral, in which a good array of alternative hypotheses are in constant development.

(7) The following chapter pursues further the meaning of experiment and theory, but this introduction suffices to bring out that: (a) The quality and reality of theoretical growth are closely tied to the properties of the methodology. For example, clinical theories are actually those derivable from a multivariate, wholistic, Galton-Spearman method, but in the absence of measurement and formal mathematical models, they remain vague and their quality has been poor. There is no scientific method which can be called "the clinical method," the latter being a degenerate (or undeveloped) form of the multivariate method. (b) Experiment is part of a broader process of scientific investigation by the IHD — inductive-hypothetico-deductive — method. The properties of an experiment, to be studied in experimental design in the next chapter, can be appreciated only in the context of the IHD method. (c) Multivariate and bivariate experimental designs are equally important to the advance of psychology, but a more enlightened conception of their interrelations and their special advantages and disadvantages is urgently needed at the present juncture in research.

CHAPTER 2

The Principles of Experimental Design and Analysis in Relation to Theory Building

RAYMOND B. CATTELL
University of Illinois

1. THE SIX BASIC PARAMETERS OF EXPERIMENTAL DESIGN

The frame of reference on which we now focus is that of general psychological research, within which we propose to define the varieties of experimental design. For it is necessary to get into such a perspective that multivariate experimental design which we have so far briefly historically introduced but with which later chapters are extensively concerned.

What is an experiment? If we take a "naturalistic" approach, by surveying the varieties of procedures which people call "experiments," we become aware at once that the views of individual psychologists and often of whole schools are both narrower and more diverse than one would expect. A contrast of usage becomes apparent, for example, between the publications of members of the Society of Multivariate Experimental Psychology and those of the Society of (Bivariate) Experimental Psychology. Or again, what a clinical psycholo-gist calls an experiment is something remote from what some social psychologists (especially an "action-researcher") may consider an experiment.

Among those trained in classical bivariate, dependent-independent variables methods there exist some older brass-instrumentalists who hesitate to call anything an experiment which takes place outside the sacred four walls of a laboratory! Others, again, consider that manipulative control is the hallmark of an experiment — a definition that would deny the term "experimental science" to such a science as astronomy, since astronomers (even in this rocket age) do not control the movements of stars and planets. The so-called action-research concept would give the word "experiment" to starting a riot or any other unique and incomparable but observed and manipulated historical event, such as Hitler's precipitation of World War II. Some historians, who call themselves social scientists, would consider a whole culture to be an experiment, leading to definable deductions and conclusions for further testing. Among these there are large and vague differences of implicit definition, but a clear though still broad chasm opens up between those who consider *measurement* essential to an experiment and those who demand neither measurements nor records. This chapter therefore has many questions to ask.

If an experiment is to play the role which we have just discussed for it in the total inductive-hypothetico-deductive process of science, it must certainly be defined for psychology more broadly than, for example, the local prejudices of the brass-instrumentalist would admit. But at the same time it needs more rigor than the action researcher's vague conception of research or some historian's erroneous view that the *Geisteswissenschaften* provide scientific generalizability.

Let us get into discussion by taking a stand with a definition, namely, *an experiment is a recording of observations, quantitative or qualitative, made by defined and recorded operations and in defined conditions, followed by examination of the data, by appropriate statistical and mathematical rules, for the existence of significant relations.* It will be noted that the ambiguous term "controlled," as in, e.g., "under controlled conditions," is deliberately avoided here, as also is the question of whether we are using the relations to create or to test an hypothesis. Unfortunately, "controlled" sometimes means "manipulated," sometimes "held constant," and sometimes just "noted and recorded." Only the last is essential to an experiment, as indicated by "defined and recorded operations and . . . conditions" above.

The present definition of experiment is thus designed to include observation and measurement both of *a naturally occurring event* (like an eclipse, an hysterical paralysis, or the change in magnetic variation), or of *an event abstracted from its natural setting* and manipulatively repeated in the laboratory. For if one is examining the change of variable *A* with variable *B,* say, the change of blood pressure with loss of atmospheric oxygen, it is basically quite immaterial whether an "act of God" or an act of man has arranged the series of events under observation. As a secondary matter, it is true that some phenomena can be more readily arranged and observed by manipulation, e.g., the bringing together of two specific chemicals, while for others it is better to wait upon nature, e.g., the effect of a shock of earthquake magnitude upon geological strata or the effect of still-births upon the mother's body chemistry. The choices here are subsidiary, depending on ethical, economic and other considerations, e.g., of convenience, which do not affect the essential relationships under study.

By this definition, what one can only regard as some laboratory dwellers' somewhat parochial view of experiment (as "what I do in the laboratory") may better be defined as a special and miniature subvariety. It is but one of many ways of recording observations, in planned conditions to yield evidence on specific relations, which we have just defined as an experiment. All experiments give us that desired specific empirical check which it is the function of an experiment to give, within the IHD (inductive-hypothetico-deductive) procedures of science.

If the species of event which we call "an experiment" is thus defined by a specific role in the IHD process, we can shake ourselves free of traditional perceptions and misperceptions of its nature and proceed to ask, from first principles, what procedures will meet this requirement. We now propose in fact to look over the variety of data-gathering and data analysis procedures employed by psychologists which meet this criterion, and observe the parameters with regard to which the design of an experiment can be varied. Such a set of dimensions could both (1) provide us with a framework within which to understand and arrange in order the familiar varieties of experiment, and (2) help us to transcend the present range of existing species of experiment and perhaps create varieties not yet utilized. Thus experiment itself now becomes the object of scientific study, with the object of arriving at a taxonomy. Whether the dimensions or parameters we describe will appeal to everyone as being immediately self-evident and "fundamental" remains to be seen. Actually, the classes proposed below are exhaustive in the sense of representing virtually the only dimensions one can find, short of such trivialities as "performed on week days vs. weekends," or "under a laboratory roof-vs.-outside"! Nevertheless, it would be good to have some debate on the exact definition of certain of the dimensions.

Let us therefore briefly define and illustrate the six parameters we can locate, leaving to a later section any fuller discussion of their properties, advantages, aptnesses, and disadvantages.

Dimension 1. The Number of Observed or Measured Variables Included in the Experiment. In subsequent notation we shall symbolize this as the N *dimension,* with a bipolar symbolism, *b-to-m,* for "*bivariate to multivariate.*"

At one extreme we have an experimenter who, as in the classical, traditional experiment of the physical sciences (or the Wundt-Pavlov tradition in psychology), works with *two* variables. (The identification of one as dependent and the other as independent is, however, an additional step, which need or need not be made in the design, which must not be confused, and which will therefore be considered specifically below.) On the other hand, especially when a later statistical analysis by factor analysis, canonical correlation, or multivariate analysis of variance is contemplated (see Chapters 4, 5, 6, and 7), the experimenter will generally plan to observe many variables simultaneously. This defines a multivariate experiment. Parenthetically, the number of *people* (or other subject entities), or the number of *occasions,* or the number of *observers,* etc., also come under

this rubric of *b-to-m,* for, as will become more evident when one can consider the Basic Data Relation Matrix in Chapter 3 a pair of occasions, or an occasion and some observers, or a set of situations could constitute the "variables" instead of what we traditionally call variables. Variables lie along any edge of the Basic Data Relation Matrix (Chapter 3), the choice of which will vary according to our experimental purpose. But that "mutation" is a special extension for later study, and initially *m* means many variables, while a *b* experiment has only two.

In this definition we assume there will *always* be also a sufficiency of "cases" for the two variables or the many variables, regardless of whether the cases are occasions or people or states, etc. Unless we accept the doubtful or extreme proposition that two cases each measured on one of two variables can decide the fate of an hypothesis, there must always exist a sufficient "sample" of cases (more than two with the minimum design of two variables) regardless of whether we are conducting a bivariate or a multivariate experiment. In other words, the issue of size of *variable* sample, i.e., whether bivariate or multivariate (considering variables as something which, like people, can be sampled), and the issue of size of "case" sample should not be confused, though one may have some implications for the other.

The real alternative here is whether we set out *to examine the relation between just two variables or to examine simultaneously all possible relations existing among many (more than two) variables.* To remind the reader from the beginning of the broader perspective we must eventually reach, let us repeat that what he customarily calls "variables" are not the *only* possibilities of variables, regardless of whether we are talking of bivariate or multivariate designs. One has freedom to choose "the variables" from people, stimuli, occasions, etc. However, this extension will be systematically considered in Chapter 3 and it will become apparent that it "rings the changes" in a way which multiplies the dimensions of experiment to produce many more possible varieties of "design plus analysis" patterns, within either the bivariate or the multivariate design.

Obviously this *b*-to-*m* parameter is the main, though not necessarily the only one to distinguish the two approaches we have been historically defining as the Wundt-Pavlov and Galton-Spearman traditions. One should explicitly recognize, both here and in later parameters, that these parameters of experiment are not dimensions of *statistical analysis,* but of data-gathering. They do not inevitably commit one to specific forms of analysis. One does not choose a multivariate design merely because multivariate statistical methods exist to analyze the results, but for good reasons in the experiment itself. A multivariate experiment could, indeed, have all connections examined in bivariate pairs, and an accumulation of pairs of relations from a bivariate experimental design data-gathering could conversely be analyzed by a multivariate mathematico-statistical model. The consideration of *analysis methods* will come later and it can be shown that their dimensions are largely independent of those of experimental observation.

Dimension 2. Presence or Absence of Manipulation ("Control" or "Interference"). Denoted as the *M* — manipulation — dimension with the dichotomy defined as *i*-to-*f*, meaning *"interfered with"* to *"freely happening"* —(*m* cannot be used for manipulated as *m* is used as a dimension symbol in Parameter 1). The terms "manipulated" or "interfered with" define the situation where the experimenter physically produces changes in the variables or specific instances to be measured (patterns and their *associated* levels or *values* on this or that scale). He manipulates the values on one (or more) variable (or variables) while he observes the values for some other variable (or variables). This manipulation may, as a secondary conse-

quence, produce some artificial selection of range, or some artificiality and disturbance of the relation itself. However, such possibilities and the occurrence of range selection are best considered below as separate parameters. For selection *can* occur without manipulation, e.g., by choice of the group to experiment on, and manipulation *can* deliberately be carried out to avoid selection on range or, usually, disturbance of the intrinsic nature of the relation.

Dimension 3. Presence or Absence of Known Time Sequence Between Measurement: Succession-vs.-Simultaneity. Denoted by *T* (for time relation dimension), the dichotomy being (*d*-to-*s*) — *dated to simultaneous.* This is considered contiguously to Parameter 2 because they are sometimes confused and do in fact interact. If the value of the variable *B* is measured *later* than that of the variable *A* (regardless of whether we manipulate or are dealing with a freely happening "natural" event), then part of the "score" on *B may* be considered "caused" by the value of *A,* but not vice versa. Successive or "dated" measurement so frequently occurs as a by-product of a manipulative design — manipulating and measuring *A* is *followed* by measuring *B* — that succession and manipulation are widely, and mistakenly, considered to be synonymous. A little reflection will show that though manipulation with absolutely simultaneous measurement is virtually impossible, successive measurement without manipulation is quite common. One can relate, for example, the amount of sunshine and the size of the resultant crops, barometer reading now and wind force six hours later, or in behavioral science, recorded strictness of parental discipline ten years ago and extent of compulsive behavior among children measured now.

The concept of causality is, of course, an extremely important one in science, and it is discussed at two main points in this book (pages 22, 90 and 179) and noted at several others. At this point it is necessary to digress into causality as such sufficiently to clear up at least the issue of the relation of experimental design to possible causal inference. This is necessary both for the sake of a clear distinction between the *M* (manipulation) and *T* (time relation) parameters of experiment, and also because several prominent writers in the Wundt-Pavlov tradition have assumed that causal influence and inference are peculiar to the brass-instrument form of experiment and that they lie outside the scope of the non-manipulative form of the multivariate experiment, i.e., the Galton-Spearman design. It *happens* that most multivariate researches up to 1950 did not include causal, or dependent-independent variable, relationships, but in introducing the *condition-response design,* and other designs since we (324) have made clear that causal inference is as natural and integral to the one as to the other, and that only conventional failure to use the full potential of multivariate experiment has excluded it. In putting forward the condition-response and similar new designs involving manipulation it was also pointed out that multivariate designs can retain the advantages of the non-manipulative approach (which have been so frequently associated with them) and still include causal conclusions, by using known time sequences or succession designs.

To see how inferences about causal laws enter into either multivariate or bivariate designs, and to justify the conclusion that manipulation is not essential but time sequence is, let us make a brief but thorough analysis of the concept of causality as such. Parenthetically, we should recognize that, semantically, dependent-independent is not today necessarily identical with *cause-consequence.* Often one finds that an investigator variously means by "the independent variable": (1) the one he thought of first, (2) that which he chooses to manipulate, or (3) that which he chooses in later statistical analysis to place on the right of the equation or to be regressed upon instead of being the regressed variable. Dismissing (1) as naïve

absent-mindedness, we are still left with four possible interpretations when someone says "dependent-independent." Confusion could be avoided by calling them instead: (a) the *manipulated* variable and the *reacting* variable; (b) the *regressed* and the *regressor* variable (or abscissa and coordinate), implying direction of mathematico-statistical analysis dependence; (c) the *causal* and the *consequent* variable; (d) the *prior* and the *subsequent* variable. Of these we have made (a) and (d) distinct parameters of the experimental design, symbolized respectively as *M* and *T,* while (b) does not belong to design but to a choice in the subsequent statistical analysis. Whether the conceptual (c) shall be considered identical with the operational (d) is a matter for further, more philosophical discussion, but, anticipating that it *is* essentially identical, there evidently still exist three distinct possible meanings when we speak of dependent and independent variables.

Let us therefore come to grips with the issue of whether the conceptual notion of *cause* and *consequence* can be identified with what is inferable from the *prior and subsequent* relation in experimental design, i.e., whether (c) is (d). We shall endeavor to show at the same time that this has no necessary connection with the *manipulative-vs.-freely happening* parameter, i.e., the distinction between the manipulated and the reacting variable. (Note that we avoid manipulated-vs.-"responding" [psychologically] variable.) For although "responding" does not mean only behaviorally responding, reflexological schools have all too often fallen into the habit of speaking as if stimulus-response were the only causal connection in psychology.)

In a subsection of a chapter subsection it is naturally very difficult to do justice to the theme of causality, which has so frequently occupied whole volumes. The very term "cause" has been given countless meanings, starting with Aristotle's four types of cause: material, as when marble is the cause of a statue; formal, as when the artist's idea is the cause; the efficient cause; and the final or teleological cause. John Stuart Mill reminded thinkers that in natural situations there is usually a plurality of causes and therefore spoke of a range from sole causes to equipotent causes. What modern philosophers of scientific method can do with it can be seen in such careful works as Cohen and Nagel's (367), Braithwaite's *Scientific Explanations* (136), the writings of Carnap (190), and Feigl and Brodbeck (497), Feigl and Sellars (498), and many other volumes. Our concern in science is, of course, with efficient, not final causes, and we must from the beginning recognize Mill's point that an event may have a plurality of causes (both marble and artist are necessary preconditions to the statue), as well as the fact that one cause may have a plurality of consequences.

The desire of the scientist for causal laws (where the mathematician is content with an equation of relationship) has its ultimate root in the desire to implement "understanding" with the capability of controlling and producing changes by manipulation. This admission of manipulation as a goal by no means implies that we can *obtain knowledge* of what manipulation will do *only* by manipulative experiment. Since the future can never control the past, what the scientist means by a cause is an *invariable predecessor* and it is to this definition of causality as invariable sequence that most philosophers have gravitated. However, this definition has to be operationally qualified insofar as we have admitted plural, mutually substitutable, and jointly necessary causes. Water may be discovered as the invariable predecessor of plant growth, provided earth and sunshine are held present. For this reason the operational indicator of causal action is that an appearance or increase of R, a result or effect, is found to be preceded (even if only by an infinitesimal fraction of time) by the rise of C, a cause. With the typical plurality of causes and effects, the relation will be

statistical rather than absolute, according to the expectations of Diagram 2-1.

Therein a rise of R will not literally be invariably preceded by a rise in C, but we shall find only a correlational probability of such a rise, since rises in B and D will sometimes be the only predecessors of a rise in R. Only if B and D are held constant will the relation of R to C be invariable. Tales told by parents to young children, or by lovers to irate parents notwithstanding, the bulk of humanity believes that intercourse is the cause of pregnancy. More closely examined, the fact that pregnancy

DIAGRAM 2-1. Plurality of Causes and Consequences

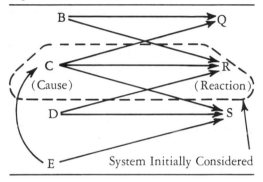

is invariably preceded by intercourse, but intercourse is not invariably followed by pregnancy, implies that other joint causes as in B and D are at work. In a community practicing artificial insemination, the search for correlated antecedents and the explanation of the full variance in R in a wider range of equipotent causes would have to be continued.

The causes of an event R are therefore the antecedent but mutually independent events that can fully account for its variance. By this definition causal inferences can be made only if the experimental observations are made at different times and we *know* those times. (It is not necessary that they be *gathered* at different times: I may gather information *today* about children's current behavior and their parents' behavior ten years ago.) To be able to check on the causal correlations it is obviously necessary that one be able to include cases where both the antecedent and the consequence are sometimes present and sometimes absent, and where possible antecedents are combined in various ways—in fact in a factorial or Latin-square type of design. One must also be able to check, when C apparently causes S, whether a more acceptable alternative is that some second-order influence, E affects *both* C and S.

Without pausing for any comprehensive discussion of what the above means in terms of statistical analysis, we can take as our main paradigm the multiple correlation coefficient in which the predictors are all antecedents, in time, of the criterion measure. Any predictor with a significant correlation with the criterion is one of several causes (Mill's plurality), and the size of the correlation indicates the magnitude of its role in that general situation. However, except for special conditions, it could account fully for the variance of the effect when other causes are held constant. The special cases may be illustrated by the *permissive* relation (discussed in factor analysis, Chapter 6) in which one factor is impotent without the action of another, and the situation in which a *particular constellation* of causes at certain levels, rather than any simple addition of causes, alone can produce the effect, as discussed in Chapters 9 and 13 below. But the simplest model is one in which the magnitude of the consequent variable is some simple function of the magnitude of mutually substitutable causes.

In view of the complexities and difficulties which often arise in finding and assessing causes (when measured simply as a set of antecedent variables in relation to a set of consequent variables) by correlational and probabalistic, stochastic methods, e.g., when dealing with a field of merely natural, unmanipulated observations, it is easy to understand why so many experimenters prefer to resort to manipulative designs (varying, one at a time, various antecedents which might be causes). It is less defensible that they fall into the habit of believing that manipulation is the only possible approach.

In short, causation can be established by proving significant covariation (1) where the sequence of events is known, and (2) where instances of all kinds of sequences can be observed and tagged. And since the interference of manipulation is sometimes either impossible, e.g., in astronomy, and in emotionally important psychological matters (e.g., the effect of family bereavement), or else unavoidably adds disturbances other than that intended (e.g., removing an organ by physical operation), there are real advantages of the dated event (the d or dated observation design) over the manipulated event design. These can be discussed in their appropriate place.

Dimension 4. Degree of Situational Background Control, i.e., Manipulation of the Unmeasured Variables. Denoted by C, for the control dimension, the dichotomy and range being (c-to-u), maximizing the *constancy of control* as opposed to *uncontrolled, permissive variation.*

We can assume that even the multivariate experimenter must leave *some* of the large number of *possibly* involved variables in the environment unobserved and unmeasured. Whether these, or the still larger number left unmeasured by the bivariate experimenter are, as far as is practicable, held constant, i.e., controlled at fixed values, or allowed to change and differ as they will, is for the designer to decide. In many experiments in physical science, experimenters have customarily decided that it is better and worth the effort, to control them, but the physical scientist usually has a simpler, less numerous set of possibly influential variables and it is not hopeless to aim at "controlling," i.e., holding constant, the whole environment. We propose to specialize the adjective in "controlled" experiment—which indeed has frequently meant nothing more than an experiment of explicit and definite design—*to mean specifically this kind of "control."* Control is, in the sense of involving "interference," a form of manipulation. But it is by definition not concerned with manipulating the focal variables. Mainly it is "negative manipulation" practiced only in the sense of "holding to normal," often when we would not know how to manipulate positively even if we wished. For example, a half-hour learning experiment can be performed with the subjects "controlled" to normal breathing, but not with the breathing manipulatively stopped!

There may be good reasons at times for *not* wishing to control the non-measured variables, but even if one wishes to control them—usually to reduce random "error variance"—success cannot always be guaranteed, partly for mechanical reasons but largely because one does not *know* all the relevant variables. Sometimes this "experimental control" can be so inefficient—in terms of not having recognized many sources of the variance, and not having measured them to check that the supposed control and constancy were achieved—that it might as well not be claimed in the experiment! Galileo, noting the time of swing in relation to length of pendulum, held constant the mass of the bob (initially), which is irrelevant, but not the temperature and pressure of the air, the distance from the earth's center, etc., which are relevant, since at that time he was not clearly aware of their relevance. *Through fortunate circumstances, partly inherent in the nature of our universe, the physical sciences have usually found it possible to hold constant more of the relevant background variables, but in the life and behavioral sciences the possibility of so doing often becomes remote.* For example, in sociology the attempt to predict changes in population intelligence levels from intelligence and birth rate measures proved impossible because of the importance of uninvestigated variables which were known (223), but could not be held constant or estimated.

In connection with this parameter one can conceive of a quasi-independent or intermediate parameter of design consisting of the number of non-focal variables actually *measured* (regardless of being held constant). However, if they are measured and included in the analysis, the design is simply a multivariate one. If they are measured but *not* included, their use is simply to check on the reality of the control. Consequently, it seems best not to complicate our framework by adding this unimportant parameter.

Dimension 5. Degree of Representativeness of the Choice of Relatives.[1] Dimension symbolized by R, the dichotomy being (a-to-r), for *abstractive* to *representative*.

It is important to distinguish this from selection on Parameter 6, which deals with *referees*. The present form of selection is illustrated typically by choosing a set of tests when the referees are people. The referee selection would be illustrated by selecting people at particular values to give a particular distribution on a test variable. The question of design here is: "Are we aiming at a representative array of variables truly to explore and evaluate the given domain of phenomena, or are we abstracting in some way with respect to a subjective and perhaps unconscious concept or limited hypothesis? In the abstractive case the experimenter is most commonly making his choice according to a specific hypothesis about relations among a set of variables or concepts in which, for adequate or inadequate reasons, he happens to be interested. In the representative case there can still be said to be a hypothesis, but a very general one, namely, "That significant structure exists to be found in this domain."

---

[1] To make this clear we must anticipate the distinction made in Chapter 3, on the data box, between the set of entities among which we find relations, and therefore called the *relatives,* and those which are used to determine the relation and therefore called the *referees*. We are so accustomed to relating tests or responses that we often forget that one can correlate people occasions, etc. However, in the traditional experimental record, with tests across the top and people down the side, we are talking about selection of tests, though, more generally, they are the *relatives*.

Representative design belongs either to the basic, exploratory stage of research or to some final stage in which the relative importance of various naturally distributed influences need to be exactly defined and compared, e.g., the relative importance of various causes of neurosis in our culture.

Hypotheses can be thus involved at *both* ends of the "abstractive (or preconceived) to representative," (a-to-r), continuum. Moreover, a particular selection, or restriction of variables is not necessarily the consequence of anything so deliberate as a hypothesis. It frequently occurs as a result of dearth of resources (unobtainable variables) or accidentally, through unawareness of the real extent and nature of a domain. Accordingly, in introducing representative design by the *personality sphere* concept (213), the writer did not (as Brunswik [152], subsequently did) define its opposite as *systematic* or hypothesis-directed. As a true operational description of an experiment, free of incorrect surplus meaning, "abstractive" is a better opposite.[2] For *abstractive* points out that a conscious *or* unconscious abstraction of a "biased" subset of variables has been made

in the experiment, i.e., this term describes the actual structuring operation in the experimental choice of variables—which is what is important for definition—without commitment to particular and perhaps accidental reasons for the abstraction.

Until a generation ago representative designs were quite uncommon and their purpose little appreciated. Probably the most extensive uses of representative design that can be recorded today are in Osgood and Suci's (1128) work on semantics, and in the notion of the personality sphere—a total realm of behavioral variables—used by Allport (18), Cattell (213), Digman (419), Tupes (1469), Norman (1100, 1101), and others. The theory of representativeness in experiment has been more systematically set out by the present writer (213, 240) and by Brunswik (152), while Sir Cyril Burt demonstrated cogently its neglected importance in the special realm of Q technique and Q sort (158) (see Chapters 6 and 8 below).

Interaction does exist between this R dimension (Representativeness) and the N dimension (multivariate to bivariate) in that it is difficult, in terms of any sampling law, to speak of a *single* bivariate experiment as being deliberately representative, i.e., as to the relatives! Usually it is deliberately non-random. However, a bivariate experimenter sometimes states the intention, and sometimes actually succeeds in implementing it, eventually, by a series of experiments, to sample representatively all variables and connections in a domain.

Dimension 6. Representativeness of Distribution of Referee (Population) Entities. Denoted as the D or distribution dimension, from k, keyed to a biased sample,[3] to n, normal, representative sampling.

Just as Parameter 5, R, refers to the representativeness of the *variables whose covariation (association) is to be examined,* so

---

[2]The idea that the opposite to "representative" is "systematic" is patently absurd and misleading—if by systematic we mean "made according to some systematic theory and hypothesis." To bring home this small role of theory in non-representative studies, one needs to instance only the "magpie" research design, in which the investigator's attention is caught by the glitter of a particular novelty, or an exciting fashion, or even a fondness for a particular instrument or gadget. For example, journals were packed for a decade with articles relating this or that psychological variable to sets of scores on the Rorschach or Szondi. Or again, social psychology seemed 90 per cent concerned with racial attitude (prejudice) studies after the close of the Second World War. Hypnotism, again, is a hardy perennial fascinator of students determining their interest in variables in undergraduate essays, while the authoritarian personality variables are a constant personal preoccupation of adolescents at most ages. These choices have *anything but* a true, theoretical-systematic background. There are journals—not a few—in which what one must frankly recognize as fads in choice of variables predominate. Such emotional choices are non-representative but they are far indeed from being examples of selection for systematic theoretical reasons; yet they may have made a severely *abstractive* choice of variables!

[3]In the interests of avoiding overlap of symbols for designs, methods, etc., a rather "far-out" phrase—such as "keyed" here—must occasionally be used. It seems best, however, to keep a symbol with some mnemonic reference, and "keyed" suggests an arbitrary non-representative sample.

this refers to the distribution of the "referee" sample, providing the measurements on the variables. This means a selection on (from) the set, e.g., of people, in the most familiar case, over which the variables are measured.

The deliberate selection or biasing of samples with respect to some measured variable, as when an experimenter selects, for comparison and association on certain other variables, the top and bottom 10 per cent of occasions in a learning rate study, or a group of delinquents versus normals on a character test, etc., is an extremely common feature of experimental design and needs no further explanation or illustration here. Its implications *do* need underscoring, however, for certain of them are seldom fully realized. As later discussion will bring out, many experimenters get a totally distorted perspective about the general importance of certain influences when they use *Design b* experiments; but it must be recognized that such a design is sometimes chosen precisely because it magnifies associations in this way!

Selection or bias is thus sometimes deliberate, in which case it is important to know just how severe it is, but accidental bias is also quite common. Accidental bias, or lack of check on similarity of sample distribution to a natural distribution of stimuli, etc., has been very common, for example, in perception and learning experiments and whenever manipulation of variables occurs. Often the manipulated independent variable is made to assume values that would never occur in a natural setting. By contrast, obtaining results on a true random or stratified, natural sample has been characteristic of much careful research, e.g., in educational psychometrics, in evaluating factors in achievement.

The six dimensions above and their polar labels are summarized in Table 2-1. It is to be hoped that correct use of these symbols to denote any experimental design tersely and exactly will be aided by their phonetic reference. Other dimensions of design can probably be suggested as possibilities, but probably these six would be commonly agreed upon as the most fundamental.

2. THE LOGICALLY POSSIBLE AND PRACTICALLY VIABLE TYPES OF EXPERIMENTAL DESIGN

When Chapter 1 raised the question "What is and what can be in experimental

TABLE 2-1

THE SIX BASIC DIMENSIONS OF EXPERIMENTAL DESIGN

Symbol for Dimension	Parameter Title	Polar Dichotomy	Polar Notation
N	Number of Variables	Multivariate to Bivariate	$m-b$
M	Manipulation	Interfered with (Manipulated) to Freely Occurring	$i-f$
T	Time Relation	Dated to Simultaneous Observation	$d-s$
C	Situational Control	Controlled (Held Constant) to Uncontrolled	$c-u$
R	Representativeness of Relatives (Choice of Variables)	Abstractive to Representative	$a-r$
D	Distribution of Referees (Population Sampling)	Keyed to a biased sample (selected or "unrepresentative") to Normal or true	$k-n$

design?" it foreshadowed a "what might be" now implicitly contained in Table 2-1. For if these dimensions are exhaustive of the important parameters of experiment, all possible varieties of experiment can be produced by their mathematically possible combinations. No longer need we stay in the rut of a Wundt-Pavlov — vs. — Galton-Spearman antithesis; we can instead recognize many more varieties in a comprehensive perspective of six dimensions. Indeed, as suggested at the outset of our search, this exhaustive framework should enable us not only to gain perspective on historically familiar designs, but also to conceive and create entirely new designs. A combination of six dimensions, each dichotomous, in all possible ways, logically can yield $2^6 = 64$ *types* or patterns of experimental design. Whether *all* of them are viable, in the sense of being useful, practicable, non-contradictory combinations, is, however, still to be examined.

What stimulates creative design immediately is that this analysis releases us from the shackles of partly accidental, socio-historical schools and their rule-of-thumb restrictions. The Wundt-Pavlov and Galton-Spearman — or "brass-instrument" and "psychometric" — dichotomies are seen to be only one special case of the up to 32 possible bivariate-vs.-multivariate dichotomies. Actually, they are the cases which might be written in our notation — Table 2-2 — as *bidc* and *mfs* respectively. (The latter has only three terms because the Galton-Spearman approach is not restricted to either *c* (controlled) or *u* (uncontrolled) on the unmeasured variables. Neither extends to a six-parameter definition because neither tradition has anything to say on the specific *R* and *D* dimensions.) The notational formulae which extend over and describe the bivariate and multivariate possibilities also remind us, as we have indicated in the condition-response design (measuring both stimulus and responses in the same factor analysis) (229), that multivariate methods

are *not* restricted to non-manipulative, *f* (free), designs any more than the bivariate designs are restricted to the opposite (*i,* interfering) pole. If after examination and debate we conclude that the six parameters above are indeed the most fundamental dimensions of possible experimental design, we shall find ourselves set up with a system which should enable us (1) to appraise the qualities and properties of any given experiment, (2) to keep in mind all possibilities in designing a new experiment, and (3) to discuss experimental advantages and disadvantages in more expert and functional terms.

In surveying these bases for classifying experiments, in Tables 2-1 and 2-2, however, the reader will almost certainly notice that no definitions are provided for classifying the subsequent mathematico-statistical treatment employed. Now the method of statistical analysis, and its implied mathematical model, must be organically related to the experimental design, and is ordinarily planned at the same time, but *design* and *analysis* are appreciably independent. The operation of carrying out the experiment is one thing; the statistical analysis made later is another. They belong to different realms of discourse, and one is often free to use any of a variety of statistical methods, and certainly a great variety of mathematical models, in analyzing the data gathered by one type of experimental design.

Accordingly, and because of their very different parameters, we shall consider the statistical methods in a fresh, distinct taxonomic system in the following section. Indeed, Chapter 3 makes it clear that any total *research* really has not one, or two, but *three* substantially independent domains of parameters necessary for its definition, as follows:

(1) What we have just called experimental *designs,*

(2) That which in Chapter 3 we shall call relational analysis *systems,*

(3) The kinds of statistical *methods* used

for analyzing and examining the fit of data to theory. (For the present we may consider the form and nature of the theoretical *model* to be contained in this last.)

The triadic combination formed by choosing an alternative type from each of these three — design, system, method — to put in tandem with the others defines the nature of the total research. Some meaning can also be given to the three combinations of any two of them (see page 51). For example, the unique combination of a particular experimental design with a particular mode of mathematical-statistical analysis we can commonly call a *technique,* as in *P, Q,* and *R* techniques, and so on. The thinking which initiates the total research plan may begin with theory, experimental design, or preference for an analysis method — most probably with the first. However, we are not concerned at the moment with the progressive development of the researcher's attitudes and interests, but with the *possible* logical descriptions and classifications of the three main parts of any research plan open to him.

Returning from this brief overview to the problem of classifying designs, we ought next to ask if the number of practically made, finally usable *designs* may not be fewer than that logically obtainable by mathematical combinations, simply because some combinations are internally inconsistent. When this is done we have fewer *available* designs since some instances of the mathematically possible 64 are eliminated. Among the practically incompatible and non-viable we may note the following chief losses. First, bivariate, *b,* with representative, *r,* is impossible as noted above; second, manipulative, *i,* with simultaneous, *s,* can rarely exist since the act of manipulation commonly precludes simultaneous observation; third, controlled, *c,* with representative, *r,* is probably to be eliminated, since if one is already taking all the possible existing variables to represent a domain, no others are left to hold constant. The last instance can be debated, and there are

possibly one or two other borderline possibilities which diligent search by the reader may reveal to be of questionable practicality. Thus the total number of types of available design is actually in the neighborhood of 29, which is a small enough number to be set out, with names for some of them, in Table 2-2.

It is readily seen that most fall under a smaller number of familiar, or, at least, recognizable, experimental designs or traditions. Thus the four designs 17 through 20 are the traditional "classical" bivariate designs, with and without control of unmeasured variables, and representativeness. The first five, 1 through 5, cover what was described in 1952 (229, 324) as the *condition-response* experiment design (because conditions (treatments) and responses are intercorrelated in the same matrix). The five in 6 through 10 and in 21 through 25 are respectively the multivariate and bivariate forms of "naturalistic-sequential" designs common in social psychology, sociology, physiology, and personality-family investigations, or, indeed, wherever some antecedent but unmanipulable independent variable is related to its possible consequences.

The five designs in 11 through 15 (multivariate) and the four 26 through 29 (bivariate) are commonly thought of as psychometric, in that they correlate (or examine by analysis of variance) variables between which no direct causal dependence is necessarily inferred. Such designs are thus more frequently conceived of as "structure-finding" than "law-finding" approaches. However, when factor analysis is brought to bear on the 11 through 15 designs, causal influence can be inferred with a certain probability — by simple structure — without using information on sequence, as explained in Chapter 6. So these also become designs aimed to reveal causal laws.

Although these familiar areas and design names can thus be assigned to these 30 or more possible designs, what is perhaps

TABLE 2-2

Types (29) of Usable Experimental Design

Code Number	Possible Label	Polar Combinations
1	Multivariate (experimental) condition-response design (a)	*midcak*
2	" " " " " (b)	*midcan*
3	" " " " " (c)	*miduak*
4	" " " " " (d)	*miduan*
5	" " " " " (e)	*midurn*
6	Multivariate naturalistic-sequential design (a)	*mfdcak*
7	" " " " (b)	*mfdcan*
8	" " " " (c)	*mfduak*
9	" " " " (d)	*mfduan*
10	" " " " (e)	*mfdurn*
11	Psychometric simultaneous controlled (a)	*mfscak*
12	" " " (b)	*mfscan*
13	Psychometric simultaneous uncontrolled (a)	*mfsuak*
14	" " " (b)	*mfsuan*
15	" " " (c)	*mfsurk*
16	" " " (d)	*mfsurn*
17	Classical (experimental) controlled (typical)	*bidcak*
18	" " "	*bidcan*
19	" " uncontrolled (typical)	*biduak*
20	" "	*biduan*
21	Bivariate naturalistic sequential (a)	*bfdcak*
22	" " " (b)	*bfdcan*
23	" " " (c)	*bfduak*
24	" " " (d)	*bfduan*
25	" " " (e)	*bfdurk*
26	Bivariate naturalistic simultaneous (a)	*bfscak*
27	" " " (b)	*bfscan*
28	" " " (c)	*bfsuak*
29	" " " (d)	*bfsuan*

Key: *m* multivariate   *b* bivariate
    i interfering   *f* free, natural
    d dated, sequential   *s* simultaneous
    c controlled background   *u* uncontrolled background
    a abstractive   *r* representative on variables
    k biased on population   *n* normal on population
(From the 64 possible combinations, 35 are dropped, namely, those containing *b* with *r*, *i* with *s*, or *c* with *r*.)

more important is that this analysis of parameters demonstrates that many of the designs have uses well beyond their traditional uses, as in the instance above of what have previously been called "psychometric research designs." We cannot pause here to explore and list the various new applications but it would be a rewarding exercise for the student and would enable him to see old designs in new perspectives. The functions of Table 2-2 are, in fact, (1) to see familiar designs in the light of a fundamental comparative analysis, (2) to recognize the totality of possible designs, asking which have perhaps been used insufficiently, (3) to understand the relatedness of various designs, and (4) to increase appreciation of the meaning and implications of the six parameters. The discussion in Section 6 of this chapter on advantages and disadvantages of various designs should extend our conceptions of the last. But before that, it is necessary to discuss the varieties of method of mathematico-statistical analysis with which designs of any kind can be linked.

3. THE MAIN METHODS OF MATHEMATICO-STATISTICAL TREATMENT

As noted above, the methods of mathematico-statistical analysis of experimental data are to a substantial degree independent of the experimental design by which the data are gathered. Although no one in his right mind would proceed to the final experimental design without thinking ahead to the mathematico-statistical analysis to which it is to be adapted, and the theoretical mathematical model which is being tested, the fact remains that one has a fair range of choice of method of statistical analysis for a given data-gathering design. Indeed, nowadays we need more and more to avoid the rough habit of defining an experiment merely by the statistical analysis form and hence such solecisms as talking of an "analysis of variance" design of experiment, or a "discriminant function" experiment, etc. Admittedly, these last two analysis method expressions, for example, would tend to imply that the basic experiments must be bivariate and multivariate respectively, but the five (effectively four) remaining dimensions of experiment are left in the air. Consequently, with this much freedom, we shall speak of mathematico-statistical *analysis methods* as a realm distinguishable from experimental *designs,* as stated earlier, above.

Nevertheless, because of the organic connections just indicated, one might at first, in a taxonomy, be tempted to make "method of analysis" a seventh parameter of experimental design. The result would be a very cumbersome set of classificatory concepts, for method of analysis is a very substantial world in itself needing as many parameters for its description as the realm of experimental design. Furthermore, the analysis method opens up, so to speak, into the farther realm of model and theory. With this third realm, which affects both design and analysis, to consider, we do best to discuss each separately before considering their integration.

For the sake of perspective in reading it would be helpful to pause at this point and take stock of the way in which we are dividing the totality of the research process. What happens when one thinks one's way to a research design is one thing; and what a logical, objective, taxonomic examination of the possibilities in a given case would actually present is a second; and the way in which one might pedagogically best set out to teach about these parts is probably yet another. Setting aside the first—the history of what happens in a researcher's mind as he feels his way to a research design from certain observations and theories—and confining ourselves to the logical and pedagogical, one may well conclude that the *logical* order of exposition here would be to begin with Chapter 3 below, i.e., *relational systems.* For it simply describes the possible varieties of relationship which *can* exist among data, in the Data Box, and is therefore prior to the experimental design issues of how one gets the data, or the statistical method issues of how one tests the relationships.

Being more concerned with ensuring clear assimilation, we have followed neither the logical sequence, nor the opposite, psychological one, which would have begun with the structure of theory, and even particular psychological theories dear to the contemporary psychologist. Instead, our compromise of logic and interest has been to begin with an experiment, a common reference point for all interested in theories, and to defer consideration of the stark and abstract framework of *possible data relationship systems,* which needs quite a lot of specialized thinking and treatment, to Chapter 3. Also we have taken the statistical analysis as a distinct issue, separating its difficulties from those of the experiment per se. All these are interrelated however, and the mathematico-statistical treatment lies at the center. It is a crossroads where the data relations, the experiment, and the theory transact their business.

It is possible to speak of a *t* test, or of a correlation of given magnitude and significance, or of some other statistical evaluation, without reference to any particular theory, yet the mathematico-statistical analysis of data always has within it and is determined by some sort of theory, capable of mathematical model formulation, however simple. The statistical analysis is to test the significance of agreement of data and model, and whereas models are almost infinitely numerous, types of statistical test are few. What all methods have in common is a determination of the degree of relationship of two quantities and a comparison of that relation with chance expectations. This is true of the simplest analysis of variance test, on the one hand, when we make merely an *"F"* or *"t"* test to see if the mean of persons on variable *B* is to be considered higher among those already selected as high on variable *A*. It is true of the most sophisticated factor-analytic method, on the other, where we ask if second-order factor *X* is really oblique to (correlated with) factor *Y*. Sometimes, as Chapter 3 brings out more clearly, the relationships tested are between things categorically differing in quality, kind, or type, as when we ask whether boys are more frequently delinquents than girls; and sometimes they are between variables or parameters, as when we ask if rate of learning is a function of strength of motivation, or if persons low on the 16 P.F. Scale C (Ego strength) are lower in G.S.R. to threat stimuli.

Theoretically, a type or entity can always be represented as a particular pattern, vector, or combination on a set of parameters or coordinates: the two systems are not in different worlds. However, this difference of types (vector) and scale or trait (scalar), together with the difference between chi-square and correlational statistics has perhaps obscured the fact that fundamentally we are capable of translating these into the same kind of conclusion—a conclusion about relationship between two variables in a population. Even the lesser difference between examining the relation between two variables on the one hand by analysis of variance and on the other by correlation has been magnified (through the first having been the favorite tool of the Wundt-Pavlov group and the latter of the Galton-Spearman group) until many no longer recognize that both are concerned simply with relating two variables (or a type and a variable).

Table 2-3 has been set out simply to remind us that whether we examine the difference of two means by a *t* test (or of more than two means by an *F* test in analysis of variance) or correlate the two series by some kind of correlation coefficient, we are, up to a point, getting evidence on the same issue—the degree of concomitance of two phenomena. Incidentally, Coan (350) (see also Chapter 24 below) has recently used *concomitance* and *correlation* to distinguish these modes of examination of association; but the former term is perhaps better used in the broader sense in which John Stuart Mill used it, as the common "statistical" meaning in his five canons of scientific method for arriving at natural laws and structures. That is to say, it is any kind of significant *going together* of phenomena in nature. Such *concomitance* or *covariation* is what we are fundamentally testing regardless of whether we ask a simple question like "Are younger children less anxious than older children?" or a complex one like "Are the parameters of motor learning at an advanced level related by these particular hypothesized functions to those at a less advanced level?" (Chapter

16 below). Our different methods — correlation coefficients, mean differences, curve fitting, etc. — differ chiefly in asking such a question with different assumptions and with different complexities of specification, e.g., simply linear or complexly curvilinear, to clear up an obstinate assumption in the statistical field that multivariate methods necessarily work with correlation coefficients and bivariate methods with analysis of variance (in the broadest sense). This is a historical, not a necessary or logical, con-

TABLE 2-3

THE FUNDAMENTAL SIMILARITY OF ANALYSIS OF VARIANCE AND
CORRELATION METHODS IN TESTING THE EXISTENCE OF
A RELATIONSHIP (CONCOMITANCE COVARIATION)

| | Entities | Attributes or Patterns | |
		A	B
	1	a_1	b_1
	2	a_2	b_2
	3	a_3	b_3
	.	.	.
	.	.	.
	.	.	.
	k	a_k	b_k
X			
	$k + 1$	a_{k+1}	b_{k+1}
	.	.	.
	.	.	.
	.	.	.
	$n - 1$	a_{n-1}	b_{n-1}
	n	a_n	b_n

The *Entries*, a_1 through a_n and b_1 through b_n, are scores of the corresponding entities respectively on the A and the B attributes or aspects of patterns. The entities must be assumed to be ranked with more than chance order with respect to A before the calculation begins.

By analysis of variance or group mean comparison methods we cut the entities into two groups, as at X, with respect to their characters on A (which may be bimodally distributed or categorical) and then ask if the groups differ significantly on B.

By correlational methods we correlate the A with the B values. A biserial correlation clearly brings out the common nature of the two methods of analysis.

in the answer about the mode of association. And these differences in the simple, mathematical "model" — linear, curvilinear, etc. — being tested have obscured for many the fundamental fact that in any case we are testing the existence of a relationship between the same attributes.

Since our concern in this book is with multivariate experiment, in contrast to bivariate experiment, and since we have already had to dispel certain biases associated with the historical Wundt-Pavlov and Galton-Spearman traditions, it is desirable

nection. Thus, if one simply asks if there is any concomitance or covariation (*not* covariance, a more specific concept) between variables A and B in Table 2-3, we have, as every statistics course points out, a considerable choice of particular expressions, including a variety of correlation coefficients. For example, one might use Pearson's contingency coefficient (from chi-square), Yule's coefficient of association, O, and the sorting into subgroups on A followed by an examination of their differences of means and sigmas on B, by t test from analysis of variance methods, and so on. Some, e.g., a simple *t*-test comparison of two means, throw away possible information relative to others, e.g., the correlation coefficient. What has been indicated in Table 2-3 by way of alternatives in comparing two single parameters can be extended into the combinations of parameters, as when we separate "types," and to categorical, qualitative differences.

This dissolution of some possibly interfering, too readily accepted daily habits of thought is perhaps necessary to clear the ground for getting a fair perspective on the classification of available methods of statistical analysis. Such an undertaking is not going to be an easy one on which to obtain general agreement, in any case, because there is little existing discussion as to what may be considered major and minor features[4] of methods and also because mathematical statisticians are apt to have a decidedly different value system within their "pure" subject from that which scientists need in applying statistics within a scientific framework.

Consequently, without space to go into fundamental discussion our taxonomy may seem more arbitrary, and is certainly put forward more tentatively than were the classificatory principles for experimental design. In nomenclature, the term "mathematico-statistical" is retained to remind us that the statistical test is sometimes closely enough determined by the mathematical model to require some regard for the mathematical form of the model. Nevertheless, there is on the whole considerable freedom to chose diverse statistical methods in investigating any given theo-

retical model, consequently we are considering theory separately in Section 4.

Dimensions of Mathematico-Statistical Methods

Dimension 1. Degree of "Power" of the Statistical Significance Test Adopted. (Symbolized by E for extent of measurement-property assumptions. Ranging from e, extended in assumption, to v, vacant of assumption.)

A typical instance of this is the use of parametric — vs. — non-parametric statistics, or distribution-assumed — vs. — distribution-free statistics, but, more generally, it means the particularity of assumptions one is prepared to make about the quality of the original measurements, their scaling, their behavior in distribution, the mathematical processes to which they can be subjected, etc. If one is prepared to assume and assert many known properties of the measurements, then any general species of test of significance can be correspondingly more sensitive and powerful.

Naturally, this parameter could be split into several subparameters. However, the use of a method which either ignores or uses *available* information (as distinct from assuming that it does or does not exist) should probably be distinguished, and is made a separate dimension 4. It is one thing to say that one does not *know* the scaling or distribution properties and quite another to elect to use a method which simply does not avail itself of them, e.g., by coarse grouping, failure to use known distributions, etc.

Probably the main relevance of this dimension for most psychologists is in connection with scaling, from nominal (non-parametric in one sense) through rank and equal interval to absolute scales. It can therefore be considered a graded, polar parameter.

Dimension 2. Degree of Mathematical Complexity of the Model to Which Fit Is Examined Immediately by the Statistical Method. (Symbolized by B, for built-in complexity of the

---

[4]For example, the distinction between finding associations between "types" (kinds, qualities, defined groups) on the one hand, and between variables (traits, parameters, scales) on the other is a very obvious and practical one. But because entities or types can be represented as vectors, and because mixed relatives — types and traits — can also have their associations determined, we have not included this — perhaps wrongly — among the major descriptions of statistical analysis treatments below.

model in the statistical test, and ranging from *j*, jejune, to *h*, highly resolving or structuring.)

One must distinguish at once between the complexity of the mathematical model as it is involved in the researcher's ultimate theory, on the one hand, and as involved in the kind of fit evaluated in the *immediate* statistical test, on the other, as here. The simplest, most jejune statistical model is illustrated by testing the significance of the difference of two means. Being simple, it is also universal, in the sense that almost any mathematical model *could* have its fit examined, piecemeal, by many single differences tests, though it might be unnecessarily laborious. A somewhat more complex level on this parameter would be instanced when the fit of a curve, involving perhaps a dozen means, is examined. A distinctly high degree of complexity again is involved when a hypothesis is stated in terms of (1) a given number of factors, (2) their intercorrelations, and (3) their loading patterns, and the fit examined by pattern fitting with complex distribution assumptions.

If one considers Diagram 2-2 he will note that analysis (a) fits a whole variety of possible "laws" or "explanations," e.g., curves 1, 2, and 3, whereas analysis (b) fits very few. If the continuous curves (1) and (1') are the hypotheses being tested in the (a) and (b) analyses, then (a) is making slower research progress toward the ultimately correct hypothesis. In general, greater complexity of the mathematico-statistical model means that the same data will be examined by a more exacting significance test, i.e., will less often be significant, but it will provide more information when they meet the test. If my statistical model is "that when subgroup *x* is higher on *A* then it will also be higher on *B*," many explanations are possible (1, 2, and 3 for example in Diagram 2-2). On the other hand, when a factor analytic question is put to the data, the answer is given in a highly structured form. It is as if we asked on the one hand, "Is there a sound beyond

DIAGRAM 2-2.   Differences in Mathematical Complexity of Model to Which Statistical Fit Is Immediately Tested

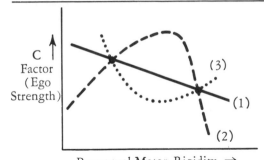

(a)   Hypotheses tested by dividing rigidity range into only two groups.

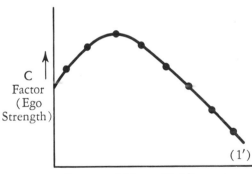

(b)   Hypotheses of more complex curvilinear relation tested by dividing into eight groups.

this wall?" and on the other, "Is Sarah singing an aria in the bathroom?"

Statistical methods are increasingly being developed, with the aid of computer programs, which will permit obtaining this immediacy of an answer to a highly structured question. For example, when using factor analysis one does not have to test separately (1) How many factors, (2) How large, (3) What form. The answers are part of the total solution. Thus if one adopts the high "resolving power" possible in this model, one may ask only, "What structure is there?" Of course, if the built-in model for perception is wrong, one gets nothing (as for instance, in applying Q technique, which gives dimensions, in an attempt to locate types); but if the statistical test applies the appropriate model, one gets answers without having to ask the part questions. The human perceptual apparatus does this all the time. It does not explicitly ask "Is it near or far?", "Is it large or small?", "Is it brown or black?", but gives the goodness of fit immediately to certain built-in models, saying "There are two brown cows ten yards away." Of course, the flexibility of the human computer enables a new model to be substituted rapidly if expectations are wrong. If one expects to encounter armed knights, but instead a couple of windmills stand on the horizon, one does not, unless he is a Don Quixote, persist with the wrong perceptual model and continue to ask the wrong questions.

Except with methods of very high resolving power, however, the distinction made above between the scientific mathematical model and the immediate statistical testing method stands. This possibility of considering statistical method apart from scientific model resides in the fact that the total theoretical model with which the investigator is working can be far more complex than the analysis method and its simple model which he employs at each step. For example, his model may contain and express the hypotheses that four mean values will fall into a particular rank order or complex curve. However, he may, on the one hand, test that rank order by a series of paired comparisons each employing a simple t test (granted a significant F test, with allowance for multiple comparisons). Or he may, on the other, hypothesize that a complex cubic function expresses the plotted curve of relation of x and y, and use a method of analysis which yields an answer on the significance of agreement of the plot with the hypothesized rank order or

function straightaway in a single verdict.

At one extreme of this B continuum — that which we have symbolized by j, for jejune or empty of model assumptions — is a simple examination of the difference of two values, commonly means. At the opposite extreme — symbolized by h for highly resolving — is such a method as Q' technique or factor analysis, which yields respectively the number and nature of type groupings in a population, and the number and nature of dimensions or influences operating on the given individuals. In these latter cases a lot of structure is built into the method itself, so that *seemingly without entering with any developed hypotheses, e.g., that x number of factors are at work having the natures, a, b, . . . k, etc., we are given a developed answer,* in terms of a created hypothesis for the next round. The word "seemingly" is introduced because *a considerable hypothesis statement lies in the specific model development implicit in the method itself.* The hypothetical questions it asks are in terms of entities and relations factors and linear relations — build into the method of analysis. Any clearly significant answer implies that the model to that extent fits the data. However, when gaining the advantages of using such a built-in structure "high resolving" method we always have to ask the prior question indicated above: "Does it fit this kind of data?"

The built-in model can acquire its increased structural complication in several ways, but notably (1) by assuming multivariate relations and (2) by involving ever more complex functional relationships between variables, instead of, e.g., a simple linear relation or a relation to be tested by the difference of two means. Regarding the latter, the more complex built-in relations inevitably demand analysis with a larger number of results than are shown by two points only, so an incompatibility or, at least, an inconvenience, arises early in any attempt to use bivariate experiment with high resolving statistical methods.

When we turn to consider the advantages

and disadvantages, aptnesses and inaptnesses of various statistical methods, instead of confining ourselves to descriptive
taxonomy as here, we shall recognize the
important difference between statistical
methods useful at exploratory stages and
methods more apt for "cleaning up" an
area, or for research with emphasis on the
inductive rather than the deductive phase
of the IHD process. By a seeming paradox,
the more complex structuring and resolving methods are better for the former,
whereas a single difference of means may
suffice to decide, or rather, to give an
infallible lead, between two complex hypotheses in a well-structured field. Thus in
fresh fields factor analysis has advantages in
terms of the creativity and precision with
which it generates new hypotheses within
its model.

*Dimension 3. The Number of Relationships
Simultaneously Handled.* (Symbolized by S,
and varying from "only," single relations, o,
to multiple and general relationships, g.)
Examination of single relations is the only
thing possible in a bivariate experimental
design, though multiple analysis methods
could be applied to an *accumulation* of
bivariate studies. Multivariate experimental
results, on the other hand, can be analyzed
either piecemeal, e.g., in pairs, or by some
multivariate analysis method.

The simultaneous analysis of several relationships has naturally developed hand in
hand with the development of multivariate
experimental designs. An increase along
this "multiplicity" parameter of a statistical
method, however, actually implies something more than a simple increase in the
number of variables. It brings with it
possibilities of new orders of analysis,
notably of examining various interaction
effects, e.g., of comparing the relation of x
and y when z is high with that when z is
low (see Chapter 15); of higher-order
factoring; and of dealing in general with
complex emergents from several variables
(Chapter 9).

Dimension 4. Degree of Utilization of

Information. (Symbolized by I, and ranging
from p, plenary to l, limited.) This is the
parameter which was initially recognized
under Parameter 1 above as being similar
to, but distinct from, richness of assumptions made. For, regardless of the analyst's
readiness to assume properties, a method
may use or fail to use all available information, as when one uses a rank correlation
formula with data assumed to be scalable,
or employs a linear correlation coefficient
with data which admits of non-linear plots.

The analysis of parameters of statistical
analysis methods made in this section is
admittedly brief and pioneering. The upshot is four major dimensions—E, extent
of assumptions or "power"; B, degree of
built-in complexity; S, number of simultaneously examined relations; and I, information utilization—while such issues as
type (categorical) versus trait (continuous)
data, and certain more abstract mathematical statisticians' subclasses, have not been
considered to be of the same order of
importance. Since these four parameters
are substantially independent, they can give
sixteen method varieties or types as shown
in Table 2-4. It may be noted that the
symbols, by suitable choice of "labels," have
been deliberately kept non-overlapping
with those used for experimental design, to
avoid confusion when design and method
are brought together in a single total
indexing of a research plan.

To illustrate the notation: analysis of
variance as commonly used is an *ejol*
method; factor analysis an *ehgl* or *ehgp*
method (according to the correlation coefficient used), while application of the
Mann-Whitney test to differences of two
groups is a *vjol* method.

Any lack of independence in conjugating
statistical *methods* with experimental *designs*
lies principally in the inapplicability of h
(high-structuring) and g (generality of relationships among variables) methods to
bivariate designs. Thus 18 of the possible
34 designs can be conjugated with only 4
methods, but 16 of the experimental de-

signs can each use any 16 methods. Consequently there are 328 possible types of design-method linkages, which we have called research *procedures* (Section 6, below).

section by examining theory *in itself,* to look at the socio-historical influences in the next, and then to return to the relation of procedure and theory.

TABLE 2-4

THE 16 MAIN TYPES OF MATHEMATICO-STATISTICAL METHODS OF DATA TREATMENT

Dimensions:

E Extent of measurement property assumptions ("power"); *e* extended to *v* vacant
B Built-in complexity of model; *j* jejune to *h* high-structuring
S Number of simultaneous relationships; *o* only to *g* general
I Information utilization; *p* plenary to *l* limited

1. *ejop*	5. *ehop*	9. *vjop*	13. *vhop*
2. *ejol*	6. *ehol*	10. *vjol*	14. *vhol*
3. *ejgp*	7. *ehgp*	11. *vjgp*	15. *vhgp*
4. *ejgl*	8. *ehgl*	12. *vjgl*	16. *vhgl*

4. DEFINITION OF THEORY, LAW, POSTULATE, HYPOTHESIS, AND REVERSIBILITY-IRREVERSIBILITY

When the experimental design and the method of mathematico-statistical analysis have been defined, one has essentially fixed the operational side of an investigation. This operational totality of a research we shall refer to as a *research procedure.* As it stands, however, it is virtually a plan of behavior without a teleological explanation. It is a plan of battle without any purpose assigned to victory. It lacks, except implicitly, a definition of its relation to theoretical goals, or, at least, to the questions being asked in the given domain. As pointed out earlier, this sectioning into straightforward and independent taxonomic analyses of parts of a research—experiment, analysis, etc.—is part of a deliberate plan. But it is now appropriate to study the structure of theory, also in taxonomic fashion, in order finally to examine intelligently the ultimate linking of procedure to theory in a purposeful whole. In studying structure of theory it helps if at the outset we recognize that the purely cognitive philosophical conception of theory is one thing, while its development as an individual and social historical process is another. We propose to begin in this

Discussion often arises as to whether theory is a tool and stimulus for research, or whether it is the very goal and consummation of research. Although both of these organic purposive connections operate, the scientist at heart will probably give priority to this second view, in which gaining a complete theoretical system is the meaning of science itself, for sheer curiosity would suffice to stimulate him to scientific experiment regardless of the existence of this and that competing theory; but theory is the sum total, at a given time, of our organized understanding and predictive power—our capacity to explain—in the given area. It also shapes and stimulates research, as a strategic "tool" and as a provocation, in the sense that any unfinished building is a provocation to criticism and the construction of extensions.

Even with scientifically sophisticated readers it seems necessary to make a brief survey—in this section—of the meaning to be assigned to the parts of a theoretical system such as postulate, law, hypothesis, model, etc., and, of course, to theory itself. For such terms as postulate, intervening variable, and model have changed—often merely oscillated—even over the past decade. And the uses and abuses of these terms made by particular individuals and schools lead to a continual possibility of misunderstanding. For example, theory is seen as the ultimate expression of science by some scientists, whereas the general public and more fundamentalist logical positivists (possibly Stevens [1347] and Skinner [1328] in psychology today) may use "mere theory" to refer to masses of loose and profuse speculation, which unfortunately exist but should not be called theory. Granted the existence of extensive scientifically undisciplined writings using the name of "theory of motivation," "personality theory," "learning theory," etc., the statements of such positivists are perhaps semantically and pragmatically justified. But "theory" will be used here in a much more restricted and classical sense.

Let us, therefore, start with definitions,— a statement of our syntax of science— which may not be complete, but which, for those who wish, can be further tied down by consulting the references cited.

By a *law* we mean a statement of a regular relation (Cohen & Nagel, 367) or possibility of prediction (simultaneous *or* successive) from either (1) one observable variable to another or (2) one concept to another, each concept being of a kind definable operationally in empirical variables. Many difficulties in discussions in this area arise from people treating as "types" or Aristotelian ideas, concepts which are more accurately described by dimensions, because in reality they grade one into another. In any such situation in scholarship it is really more important to recognize the dimensions than the local, ill-defined patches of ground or apparent groupings of types and species existing within the dimensions. The present task of defining a "law" runs into the difficulty of arbitrary boundaries, because a law among concepts comes close to being a theory, since theories are concepts connected by explanatory, lawful principles. The line has to be drawn as it is drawn between a loop of string and a fisherman's net. That is to say, theories usually grow, or can best grow, from integration of collections of laws, and at some point a collection of explanatory

laws—maybe only two or three—becomes appropriately renamed a theory. Madsen (978) states that a hypothesis that is of such high probability that it has been accepted as true by most scientists for some time constitutes a law. But this is where a law begins to shade into theory.

What is perhaps more important to the definition of law is that we recognize—as we do elsewhere in this book (pages 64, 242, and 358)—that science is concerned to discover both what are sometimes called *laws* and what are sometimes called *structures*. The generalization that cells have nuclei with certain internal structures is as important as the generalization that cells are born by fission and die. Yet in roughly nine out of ten writings by psychologists on theory, this second sense of a law—as a generalization about structure—is not mentioned. Nevertheless, regard for the second sense of law is as essential to our theoretical "bearings" as recognizing latitude in addition to longitude is to a good navigator. Most of the difference between the two kinds of law can be properly covered by the statement that the first is a *process law* whereas the second is a *structural law*. Operationally, this virtually amounts to the former being defined by a prediction of *succession,* and the latter by a prediction of *simultaneous* appearance. For some people an aura of "explanation" clings to the former, and they may want to use "descriptive" for the latter; but when examined more closely—though a systematic difference in the form of prediction undoubtedly exists—it is highly questionable whether the notion of "understanding" or "explaining" is any more properly linked to the first than to the second. For example, the old sailing ship law that wind preceded by rain is likely to develop into a gale is no more explanatory than the law that the doldrums is an area characterized simultaneously by light airs and heavy showers. Or, in psychology, the law of conditioning is no more explanatory than the law that catatonia tends to appear with hallucinations.

Yet another way of recognizing the

fundamental kinship of these two forms of law will appear in Chapter 3. There the study of possible relationships among observations in the data box reveals the process law as dependent on relations along one axis of the box and structural law as derived from relations taken in an axis orthogonal to the first. If we are to preserve the term "law" for both kinds of generalization, as would seem most economical and enlightened, then it would be best to adhere to a division of observable natural regularities into *structural laws* and *process laws*. As to the disposition to append "explanation" to the latter, we shall take the position already implied above (1) that this depends on the more precise meaning to be assigned to "explanation," about which a more sophisticated position has to be taken, and (2) that insofar as the layman thinks he means two different things by "describe" and "explain," closer analysis shows that we deal with a continuum. An explanation merely has more top-hamper of theoretical concepts, but these in turn are bedded in facts, so to explain is merely to bring in a wider area of description of lawful connections. Only a child is (sometimes!) satisfied with an "explanation"; the philosopher recognizes that most explanations create a need for more explanations than that we felt need of at the beginning, in an indefinitely widening circle.

Having accepted "breadth of reference" as the true nature of the hidden parameter, which in popular thought distinguishes "explanation" from "description," let us consider next the less acceptable notion above that a "causal" (process) explanation or description is more explanatory than a "simultaneous" (structural) explanation or description. To say that X shows telegraphic speech because elated, manic individuals generally do, is a structural explanation, which may leave us wanting more, but so also do most sequential process "explanations." The issue is subtle enough to need more space than we have, but let us say (1) there may be a *systematic* tendency of succession laws to embrace wider reference systems than structural laws do and thus to be more explanatory, in the true "breadth of reference" sense, and (2) the difference may be a sheer prejudice due to our human liking to "control," since, as we have seen in examining the concept of cause, a process law implies a chance to control, whereas a structural, simultaneous law does not, and hence we tend to feel that the former is a superior type of explanation. Thus description-versus-explanation is somewhat positively correlated with structural versus process law, but they are basically different dimensions, since "explanation" is really breadth of reference.

The second most used concept in theory construction — the hypothesis — we mainly distinguish from a theory as a "working conjecture," about relationships, sometimes specific in character and reference even to one experiment, and temporary or contingent in its nature. It may be derived deductively from a larger theoretical system, or inductively from whatever scanty previous empirical signs existed. Frequently, its real origins are more humble, in that it comes as much from nowhere as does an hypnagogic image! Since theories also come and go at the verdict of experiment, the difference between hypotheses and theory is one of degree — degree of duration, of probability, of extent of organized relations, of immediacy of the tie to empirical observations.

A *postulate* is a slyer affair. It should be a formal and explicit assumption, usually tied to the basic definition of a component variable or relationship in the system, but the fact that the experimenter forgot to state it does not make it disappear. It *may* be a pervasive part of a model or theory, and therefore is generally wider and less temporary than a specific hypothesis. At the same time, it is less complex than a hypothesis often is and is usually tested indirectly by its implications. It is sly in the sense that its presence is apt to be overlooked. For example, if I postulate that operational measurement x is a linear function of the magnitude of concept y, and on this basis carry out tests of a lot of hypotheses about y's relation to various other things, the tendency is to overlook, in any failures or successes of these individual hypotheses, the role this early assumption may be playing, since attention is focused on the hypotheses.

By a *model,* we refer to a theory reduced to some mathematical, physical, or symbolic essentials in which the relations of parts are completely determined by accepted rules. All theories are, of course, explanatory systems couched in symbols, but verbal symbols are much looser than others. Consequently it is not uncommon to find that when some psychological theories are stripped of their elaborate verbal clothing, they tend to disappear altogether (Lachman, 897)! In the interests of meaningful research it is therefore always a good plan to demand that a theory be stated as a mathematical or mechanical model, even though certain qualities may be superfluous to the model.

Although the scientist's skill lies in choosing or inventing the rare model that best fits the empirical facts, the model and its properties can be defined independently of and externally to the observational system. It is commonly mathematical, enjoying the firm, conventional definition characteristic of mathematical operations, as in Estes' probability calculus in learning (468) or the linear factor-analytic model in personality; but it can be mechanical or physical as in the reflexological theories of learning, using the analogy of the neurological reflex arc, or in dynamics, in the hydraulic model (Cattell, 242, 246) of the dynamic lattice. It can even be chemical, as in the catalytic theory of factor action, or merely pictorial, as in the alleged topological theories, or in the sketch with which any lecturer tries to get an idea clearly to a class.

The advantage of a model is that it is precise, and clear in its testing implications. Only in some form of model can certain aspects of a theory be sincerely tested. Furthermore, its very explicitness and internal consistency may forcefully bring to our awareness additional testable attributes of the theory. The disadvantage of a model is that its abstractness does not permit it, in some cases, to represent everything in the theory. In addition, its chances of having the inappropriateness and inaptness of any sort of "imported theory," when it is imported wholesale as discussed below, are higher than its creator commonly recognizes.

Finally, in our condensed formulation here, it remains to make the distinction between a *concept* and a *construct* — or what can be more elaborately named "a theoretical construct (or concept)" and "an empirical construct." An empirical construct is an idea constituted by directly perceivable relations among empirical (sensory) fundaments and by the relations immediately built on those relations. Thus in Diagram 2-3 the perception of four legs to one body may give us, at A, the notion of cat, and at B, with the relations of smaller legs, the notion of kitten. Between A and B we observe the relation $- X -$ of birth, i.e., that of parent to offspring. Independently, as shown in the center, we may perceive woman C, and child D, and a somewhat similar construct, Y, may arise.

Naturally, the complexity of the relations in the mind of an individual who first forms such empirical constructs is vastly simplified by using four legs as the basis for cat, two legs as the basis for woman, and seeing a kitten born as the basis for "offspring." If now we "educe," as Spearman defined it (1339), the relation of similarity between the cat-kitten and woman-child, our concept of cat-kitten is enriched by "surplus meaning." (So, for that matter, is the woman-child construct by reciprocal importation.) One might surmise, for example, that the cat teaches the kitten, as a woman does a child. Such surplus meaning may or may not be correct. At this point we are generating, through the relation, Z, of similarity between X and Y, the more general, cross-species concept of parent and offspring. Then one may carry this over

DIAGRAM 2-3.   Basis of Distinction of Theoretical Concept and Empirical Construct

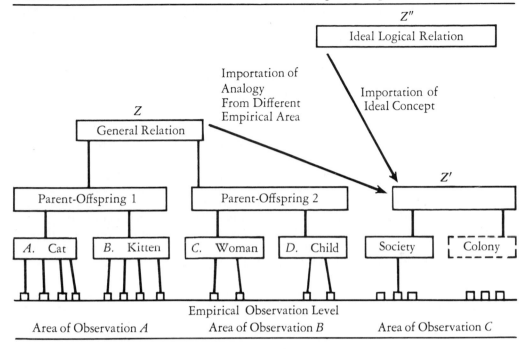

from areas of observation *A* and *B*, to an entirely new area, at *C*, by carrying over *Z* to *Z'*. Here we may ask whether the parent-offspring relation, as a "theory" or "model," helps to explain what one can see happening, say, among amoeba, or two branches of a business, or motherland and cultural colonies, or even more remote analogies.

What is frequently overlooked in regard to the "surplus" meaning, or better, the *imported meaning,* in a model or theoretical concept is that its newness may have two quite distinct origins. First, it arises from degrees of "distance" defined by the remoteness of the new empirical construct realm from which it is borrowed, and, second, it arises from degrees of deductive abstractness in the way it is derived, on allegedly logical, inferential grounds, from some allegedly self-evident general postulate. The trouble with this latter derivation — which we may call an "ideal importation" as contrasted with an "analogue importation" — is that in fact the properties often turn out to be vague and ill-defined, since what seems "logical" and "self-evident" to the creator of the model often turns out to be loosely metaphorical and subjectively vague and indefinable in the eyes of others.

To evaluate a few common psychological concepts in these terms, let us note that the reflex concept in behavior (*S-R,* reduced to classical and operant conditioning) does not come from far — indeed it is borrowed from the closely related physical neurological arc, in connection with which neurologists first developed the term. The hydraulic analogy in explaining the dynamic lattice (explaining interest relations) (240) is, on the other hand, a far cry, as also are some computer-simulator models, e.g., of extra-version-introversion. However, none of these is vague, and what is being imported can be precisely stated as an analogue model. On the other hand, "dissociation," "masculinity component," "cerebrotonia," "life style," and even seemingly precise analogies such as "defensive behavior," "approach-avoidance," "negative valence," conflict, and inhibition are commonly nebulous as to the operational basis elsewhere, needed to define the analogue from which they spring, or as to the model itself which they import. Sometimes, as in approach-avoidance and positive and negative valence, they seem to import a very simple geometrical or algebraic model—which is precise enough—but the way of fitting it to operations in the observed data has never been worked out and thus remains metaphorical. For example, fear is called avoidance behavior, but fear may often cause a person to approach the feared object, e.g., to deactivate a bomb. And this uncertainty is still greater in logical structures from ideal considerations which have never been accurately translated from verbal to operational meaning. The degree of *complexity* of the importation is, of course, a different dimension, and would apply as a parameter of theory regardless of its origin.

Both greater distance of borrowing and greater "ideal" vagueness of surplus meaning generally impair a theory's chances of survival. The vagueness of psychological theory has almost always been the result of stopping with merely verbal definition and leaning on metaphorical usage without mathematical formulation. Today, with methodological sophistication rapidly becoming more widespread, most psychologists realize that a worthwhile theory requires a model clear in its implications and, preferably, capable of mathematical formulation. Nevertheless, editors still accept and classify under the heading of theory a lot of stuff that merely discourages psychologists from taking theory seriously. This phase, it is hoped is nearing its end.

This notion—that various kinds of empirical *constructs* are separate from theoretical constructs and *concepts* along at least two major dimensions—enables us to approach current discussions of such expressions as intervening variable ("varia-ble" is unfortunate) in relation to hypotheses (or "hypothetical constructs") with less danger from common pitfalls. Even apart from the limited nature of recent discussion, due to "interesting variable" having been born in the narrow intellectual alley of the reflexological model, one may wish that Tolman had used instead the notion "immediate construct," or some term similarly implying a concept one step *lower* on the scale, i.e., toward the data, than the simple *empirical construct*. An excellent, succinct treatment of the present standard position on this issue, presented against a background of interests of psychologists, can be found in Henrysson (720).

Let us consider more closely the dimension or continuum that we have called *imported meaning*. It is a dimension of perception beginning at uninterpreted sensory data, passing next through the perceptual constructions we call "observed variables," and so progressing through what Tolman called "intervening variables" (and which we suggest might be called "immediate constructs") to full empirical constructs. The latter are inductive generalizations, of which many "working hypotheses" are instances. The dimension continues on from these to concepts (theoretical constructs), then to theories, and ultimately to purely logical, mathematical models, which show the highest degree of abstraction from concrete facts. Indeed, some philosophers think $2+2=4$ is independent of empiricism, either ontogenetically or phylogenetically, i.e., independent of the evolution of the human brain towards enabling it to mirror its space and time environment. But the dismay of modern physicists with the "illogicality" of a new world, which man has never had time to get adapted to, should cast doubt on this classical reification and, almost, deification, of pure logic.

The question one must ask, of concepts, theories, and models alike, as he moves further out on this continuum, is whether the meaning being imported is a good-quality import, from legitimate empirical constructs elsewhere, having precisely defined properties, or whether it is brought in by those slips toward animism, reification of words, vagueness of verbal meaning, and emotionality of attachments, to which the human brain so readily reverts. Even the most abstract conception is scientifically safe and effective if its surplus (imported) meaning derives from other areas of real observation and not from a Never Never Land peopled by the regressions, false short-cuts, and slips to which, as Francis Bacon showed, the human mind is liable (48).

A quite different issue in theory development in the biological and social sciences concerns the degree of generality at which a theory can appropriately aim in a given area or period. The physical scientist has a serene idealism in this respect; he wishes to reach laws about chemical properties, electrical action, etc. which are true at *any* time and place. The social scientist, on the other hand, may seem to have to be content with a law that migration selects for intelligence in the 1920's but not the 1960's; or that extraversion has such and such a factor pattern in behavior in the U.S. but another in Greece; or that learning curves follow this law with species of monkey *A* and another with species *B*. The behavioral scientist is often baffled in his attempt to carry his generalization further, whereas a physical scientist, when he recognizes that uranium deposits at *X* have more of a certain isotope than at *Y*, is willing to leave this fact to the applied mineralogist or geographer and to pass on to more basic findings.

The temporariness and parochialism of such behavioral laws cannot be altogether set aside as a feature of a young and immature science. *All* growing sciences have to move from local to general laws. There is a pyramid of generalizations built on ever larger aggregates of what were local laws. What is different in behavioral and social sciences, however, is a change in the very data itself. If the observer looks back a

few thousand years, he sees that the human societies about which he seeks to establish laws did not exist. And it is no escape to turn to physiology, for it also needs only a million years to make the immediate physiology that the researcher would study a structurally and chemically different set of phenomena. There is an emergent and irreversible process—an evolution if we wish—in the subject matter of the science itself. Closer inspection shows, however, that physical science is not actually free of the same problem. The astronomical scene changes, and, possibly, the universe expands. The astronomer differs from the physicist in being concerned about particular stars, and, initially, even in the "geography" of specific galaxies. The physical scientist, looking for eternal laws, hopes that the basic properties of basic particles remain the same, and that all the apparent change is to be explained by rearrangements and trends in organization. However, even the physicist and chemist *may* find the properties of elements, gravitational laws, etc. to have some local inconstancy or emergent change.

Without further discussion or illustration, perhaps we may conclude that the difficulty is not that there is any greater inherent problem in the social sciences in passing from local to general laws. It lies in the presence of an irreversible and perhaps evolutionary process, which exists to some degree in the data of physical as well as biological and social sciences. A theory or law about a neuron is not more "basic," and of very little greater permanence, than one about the behavior of a particular organism or culture, for neurons also evolve. Science has to search not only for basic "elements," their properties and elemental laws, but also for the laws that govern the emergent features as they become aggregated and structured. Moreover, as we admit emergence, we are compelled to recognize that the actual course of history may not supply us with all the logical possible combinations we would need to study to detect universal laws, i.e., apart from emergence (Chapter 9) there is a sampling problem.

Admittedly, an alternative view is possible — that history, as Bismarck said of politics, confines itself to the possible. Purple sparrows do not exist perhaps because the combination of color and body chemistry is intrinsically impossible or because Nature could not find its way by small mutations to this physically possible combination. If for either reason Nature failed to supply us with the material for a "balanced design" or Latin square, it becomes an argument for the methodologist to put more emphasis on manipulative experiment in order to produce the necessary "unnatural" combinations. Not that he can go far. He still cannot employ in his combinations new species which Nature has scheduled for the next generation or era. Thus we have to recognize in theory and natural law a third dimension; one describing the extent to which the generalization is tied to a changing and irreversible process, as opposed to a reversible process, unlocalized in time.

5. SOCIAL AND PSYCHOLOGICAL INFLUENCES IN THE NATURAL HISTORY OF SCIENTIFIC THEORY

After this glance at the structure of theory in general and of behavioral science in particular, we are still not quite ready to bring them into relation to research procedures, because the structure of theory is one thing and its use by psychologists — or any other scientists — is another. To be realistic, it is necessary to take almost a clinical look at some of the stagnations, the excesses, the individual quirks, and the swings of fashion which have powerfully affected the application of known research procedures to known theoretical needs.

A word has been said above about the dangers of something analogous to an obsessional neurosis or even a schizophrenic disease developing within model-making itself. An historian of science, looking specifically at psychology, would, moreover, be bound to conclude that, over the last thirty years, the construction of "theory" has been generally premature, rank, and unduly pretentious, seemingly more motivated by dressing to "keep up with the Joneses" (our fellow sciences) than by intrinsic, realistic needs and possibilities in our observations. The factors that have contributed to this spawning of theory have been the social prestige of "theory"; the absence from psychology of that clear majority of scientifically disciplined followers which curbs such untoward growths in other sciences; the ease of stating a theory compared with the difficulty of finding a law; and the similarity of psychological language to popular language and ideas.

As a result of such influences, psychological theory approaches Voltaire's definition of metaphysics. "When he who speaks is not sure what he is saying and he who listens is even less sure; they are talking metaphysics."[5] A warm glow of intellectual intoxication in debate is no substitute for sincere and exact thinking. The recent result has been, as Marx (994) points out, a strong reaction against "theory" and an "increase in strictly positivistic and empirical types of scientific work" among the more serious investigators.

A substantial contribution to the difficulties of healthy theory development in psychology has come from its being concerned too long and too extensively with verbal, non-metric, non-experimental approaches, as in clinical and social psychology. As suggested above, it is hard to overestimate the degree to which these difficulties have been augmented by the fact that exactly the same phenomena are the daily concern of popular media and popular language. Belatedly, one may re-

---

[5]In rough translation of: "Quand celui à qui l'on parle ne comprend pas et celui qui parle ne se comprend pas, c'est de la métaphysique."

cognize that the main sources of error latent in scientific development in such a field could easily have been anticipated from Francis Bacon's writings on "the error of the market place" etc. Indeed, his *Novum Organum* of 1600 is still timely. If one asks why the postponement of measurement and experiment was so prolonged in these areas of psychology, the responsibility is perceived to lie partly with the very people who wished to be scientific. It lies substantially with the brass-instrument tradition, unimaginatively clinging to the classical bivariate experimental design, which has been impotent to measure the things with which a clinician, for example, or a social psychologist, must deal.

But one must also recognize that psychology has for some reason had a substantial following of verbal theorizers, temperamentally averse to using measurement, and even to sober empirical observation. For them the word created the concept, and they have been most likely to start theory construction with the big postulate, followed by a chain of deduction which is supposed to develop logical inferences, but which unfortunately is rarely logical in any exact sense. (Much of the work on "rigidity," for example, and Otto Gross's "secondary function" has been of this type.)

To engineer a clear escape from the mere popular connotations of terms, which drag their erroneous and unseen assumptions into every discussion, one can, as the present writer has tried to preach and practice, shift to new technical terms, or even to symbols and index numbers, for each newly demanded empirical construct. For example, in personality research, the factors that clearly confirm existing clinical concepts, such as ego strength, superego strength, etc., can be so named, but other indubitable, constantly replicated patterns, unknown to the earlier clinical methods, have been given new names, such as surgency, premsia, and autia, rather than popular terms like sociability or enthusi-

asm. These new terms of exact reference are derived from acronyms or classical language roots describing the pattern's properties. And in the objective, laboratory-test, personality patterns, it has proved a great gain for precise discussion to proceed even to universal index numbers, U.I. 16, U.I. 17, etc. The fact that U.I. 17 appears to be the general inhibition factor, U.I. 22 activation level, and that U.I. 24 is clearly general anxiety, will appear in due course. But meanwhile, all kinds of premature, misleading interpretations have been avoided as well as the aura of social values and personal top-hamper which many individuals apply differently to popular terms. Without such deliberate disinvolvement, scholars all too frequently get caught by that bugbear of verbal "theoretical constructs" — the debate which has nothing to do with science, but, which, caught in accidental verbal implications, runs in exasperating, purely semantic circles.

Our essential position regarding healthy theory development is that theory should arise largely from the Inductive-Hypothetico-Deductive spiral summarized in Diagram 1-1 earlier. That is to say, one should begin, not with the big word, or even with the tight but abstract mathematical formula, but with the *small observed regularity or law*. From this one must cleverly build hypotheses at the *immediate construct* ("intervening variable") level, and then at the level of hypothetical, empirical constructs. Just how the "small observed regularity" is to be most effectively spotted will be discussed a few paragraphs below. From empirical constructs growing up simultaneously in *several* areas, one can either pass, by a creative generalization, to a higher-level theoretical construct, as shown at Z in Diagram 2-3 above (page 43) or one can import a theoretical construct or model from either (1) some remote field (as at Z' in Diagram 2-3) or (2) as a deduced system from a chosen postulate, as at Z''. Whatever the origin of the theoretical construct, one must at once attempt to fit it to what is now the broad array of empirical constructs.

The creative syntheses of a theoretically broader model from a series of initial empirical constructs has often been observed in good scientific work, e.g., Darwin's theory of evolution, Maxwell's electro-magnetic synthesis, Mendeléef's periodic table, etc., and requires no comment except commendation. The importation of the model from some remote field, (1) above, or as a logical derivative of a postulate drawn from thin air, (2) above, on the other hand, is subject to the troubles of any *tour de force*. The history of science is littered with instances where this maneuver has excessively and inaptly applied. Its excessive attractiveness springs from several sources. First, there is a real sense in which, like other kinds of "cheating," it is at once a lazy and a bold procedure. It is easier to borrow from a neighbor than to build up a new theoretical construct in one's own field. Second, it brings prestige, like an imported wine. Third, it has the dramatic quality of a conjuring trick, which excites the imagination even though it demands less real imagination than does creation of a model directly from empirical constructs. And last (particularly in this last wave of fashion), it has given scope, if models are made from postulates rather than taken from other sciences, to the compulsive disease of model-making as a form of scientific solitaire.

To think of and to import just the right theoretical construct is a feat of imagination and shrewd judgment for which science can never be too thankful. But real success is very rare, and the experienced researcher is justifiably suspicious that his time will be wasted by the "theoretical constructs" arising from the uninspired and ill-judged importations of amateurs, in cases where the development upward from empirical constructs might better have been undertaken. Probably we have tended in science to carry the principle of specialization, so useful in many cultural fields, too far, if and

when we set out to recognize a researcher and a theorist as two different specialists. For whether the theoretical construct is generated *in situ* from empirical constructs or imported, the development or the choice can be effectively made only by a person deeply immersed in all the available findings. Let us recognize that only a few individuals, combining something approaching the mental scope of a Leonardo, a Darwin, or an Einstein, with an occupational freedom for total research concentration, can simultaneously be deeply immersed in substantive data while successfully reaching out for the model to be fitted.

Most attempts in psychology, so far, at highly formalized theoretical constructs have been obviously premature, based on too little foundation in empirical constructs, and therefore lacking sympathetic feeling for the required complexity in the model. Hullian theory, for example, began with what were probably too few elements and postulates for the kind of phenomena that had to be explained. This has happened in science with unhappy regularity. The notion of four elements—fire, air, earth, and water—which had the authority of Thales and classical and medieval philosophers generally, for centuries held back the recognition by alchemists and chemists of the necessity for at least a hundred elements. The whole reflexological development in learning theory, in fact, can be accused, as indicated more fully below (and in Chapters 15, 18, and 20), of setting out to explain too much, with this simple gadget or model, before it had studied fondly enough the gamut of actual learning phenomena, especially integrative personality learning (Cattell, 226), to be explained. The result in this field, over the last few years, has been, as Marx (994) well points out, "a drastic decline in . . . highly formalized theory, particularly of the Hullian hypothetico-deductive variety."

To those who stress the value of theories — especially of the "imported model," or, worse, the "verbal intoxication" variety—as a tool in advancing science, one must point out that this value is discounted by the frequency with which prematurely formulated theory has been an obstruction or a gigantic waste. Boring has said that microscopes did not reveal cells until the cell theory taught people to see them, implying that the theory was the means of advance. Of such an evaluation one can only say that it is unfortunate that creative scientists are too busy making history to have time to write history. Historians and method writers naturally tend to see only the successful theories, which came down to them after having survived the period of strife. They know little of the far more numerous, contemporarily vigorous, fashionable but incorrect theories which blinded honest natural observation at the time and led the scientific pack away on diverse wild goose chases. Or, alternatively, like Hegel, they see the illusion of an orderly and stately movement from thesis to antithesis, in which a legalistic argument settles issues between successive pairs of contenders, whereby science progresses with the pedestrian and dull certainty of one leg being moved past the other!

What most commonly happens in scientific exploration may be illustrated by an experience of the writer when sailing. Approaching Narragansett Bay with the wind astern in a thick, swirling fog, we had two vigilant comrades in the bow peering for the landfall. Lookout No. 1 believed it would be Point Judith and No. 2 Brenton Point. As the first dark rocks loomed up dangerously close, each recognized a verification of his theory. It was a third lookout, with no theory at all, who recognized the point as Sakonnet, and saved us from a dangerous maneuver. Undoubtedly, comparatively late in the game, when mere obstinate conservatism has to be overcome, there *are* occasions when a legal battle between two theories is the appropriate conduct. (Incidentally, the prolonged wave-corpuscle light theory debate is an unusual, atypical instance in science.) But in the creative, exploratory phases this paradigm is misleading, for then it is better to have not two but a well-stocked armament of many theories, "subliminally" held, in touch with a wide array of data. The model must be kept as the servant, not the master, of the data. This relation ceases when the emotionally involved investigator, and premature crystallization of opposed views in public debate, make the theory master of the investigator as well as of the data. A liking for debate is a poor substitute, in the task of advancing science, for a love of nature.[6]

Doubtless the grand theory, marching with a flourish of verbal trumpets and social banners, will continue to mean theory to many. But the creative and scientifically useful role of theory emerges in the tentative play of ideas in the minds of men in love with the data, pondering it in the laboratory back room. However, there is another disorder of theory-making, which also prevents an affectionate give-and-take with the data, but has nothing to do with social prestige and theoretical posturing. As indicated earlier, it is the quite sincere but somewhat obsessional invention of models as a fascinating game with inexhaustible pieces. For although the possible models are infinite, those which will survive as having a good fit for science (for a time, at least!) are extremely few. Since such a severe natural selection is to operate, the only good excuse for giving birth to a model is that it is begotten from such close attention to empirical nature that its adaptation and survival are reasonably assured. The history of mathematics, it is true, is very different, with numerous instances of "models" created for nothing at all, some of which fitted in very well in some much later scientific development. But such a spawn-

---

[6]Newton and Darwin, who both found debate distasteful and left it to others, e.g., Huxley, had much in common with the poet Landor: "I strove with none, for none was worth my strife. Nature I loved and next to nature, art."

ing of models in psychology, by those remote from experiment and observation, has mainly produced models less general and precise than those found in any branch of mathematics. Above all we need to remember that wholesale model construction as such, divorced from science, yields an extremely small number of naturally applicable permutations.

Finally, in regard to the degree of "distance" (Diagram 2-3) from which models are imported, it is interesting to note some cultural differences and their consequences. It has been pointed out that in general, continental European writers have tended to evaluate a theory by how well it hangs together in a purely logical, deductive, internal consistency, whereas the empiricism of British and American philosophy (characterized, for example, by writers from Locke and Hume to James and Dewey) demands far more frequent checks by bringing the theory into contact with the earth. An elaborate, internally consistent theory may be built up *de novo,* (as a postulate system) or it may be borrowed from a construction already developed in

some remote substantive area, e.g., as in psychology, when Spearman tried to borrow "the law of diminishing returns" from economics, or, in optics, the wave theory was borrowed from mechanics. Any such borrowing, incidentally, is precisely what the man in the street warily stigmatizes as "reasoning by analogy." Its defects are, first, that, as stated above, the chances of a remote importation fitting are very small. When the engine falls out of my car, it is just *possible* that if I put the grandfather clock under the hood, the car will go. I may even discover that it goes better than before. The few triumphs of this kind, which are known to every historian of science, have the appeal of miracles, and the number increases encouragingly if we count the use of analogies that have been reasonably trimmed and modified to the new field. Second, going out on a long limb sustained by purely logical connections, without putting a foot down to empirical evidence at reasonable intervals, is more likely to be done by philosophers with an exalted idea of the infallibility of logic and a certain doctrinaire blindness to the mis-

TABLE 2-5

Dimensions of Theory Structure

---

1. *Extent of Formulation in a Strict Model. Dimension F,* from *q* (qualified as a model) to *w* (word based). (This need not be a mathematical model, but may be any model from a region of known and fully defined properties.)
2. *Degree of Dependence on Imported or Postulate-Derived, as Opposed to Local, Empirically Derived Properties. Dimension L,* from *x* (xenoid, i.e., strange) to *y* (yielded locally).
   (A single dimension is made of two discussed in the text. The imported and the postulated alike import from the non-empirical.)
3. *Number of Inductively and Deductively Connected Empirical Construct or Law Areas. Dimension W* (for width of base), from *z* (zetetic, i.e., seeking all proof) to *t* (tied to little, or transcendent).
4. *Degree of Intricacy or Order of Complexity of Relations Involved. Dimension O,* from α, simple to ω, remotely complex.

   (This is a self-evident dimension not discussed in the text. It is different from *B,* built-in complexity, in the statistical methods (Table 2-2), for it refers to the complexity of the model itself, not to the amount of this complexity carried over to the statistical method used to test it.)

Note—If there appears to be some far-reaching for the terms to describe the polar opposites here, the reader is reminded that it is because we have adhered to the plan of not using the same symbol twice, across the experimental design, method, and theory codes. This has brought us to the end of the alphabet! Treating the taxonomy as all possible combinations of four dichotomous dimensions, our analysis points to 16 types of theory structure, *qxzα, qxzw,* etc., which need not be spelled out or examined further here.

takes that humans can make with their alleged "logic."

Although the last two sections have looked fundamentally at the structure of theory, the rounding-off of our conclusions in a codified taxonomy, similar to that for experimental design, must be even more tentative than in the case of the dimensions of statistical analysis, for space has precluded as exhaustive an examination as would be required ideally. However, the dimensions that obviously have some potency are listed in Table 2-5.

6. THE TOTAL PLAN: ADVANTAGES AND DISADVANTAGES GUIDING THE CHOICE AMONG VARIOUS RESEARCH PROCEDURES

The choice of a research procedure begins with the choice of a theory or hypothesis, though, as one must never forget, this hypothesis may be no more than that "some regularity exists in this area in which I am interested." For example, Galton began with the hypothesis that "there is some significant relation between wind strength and barometric pressure, or its change," and Faraday with "There is some connection between magnetic and electrical phenomena."

From the hypothesis one perceives what *kinds of relationship* need to be studied. Consequently, a taxonomy of relational systems possible in psychology is our next need. This constitutes the substance of Chapter 3. In any case a systematic study of relations is rewarding because it opens up views of relations needing to be studied which might otherwise escape the theorist. Relational analysis may also enrich one's conceptions of the hypothesis and avoid misinterpretation of results found in a relational system. As the next chapter brings out more adequately, a total research plan proceeds, therefore, through *four* phases: from a choice of a theory or *hypothesis,* to a choice of a *relational system*

for study, and so to devising an *experimental design* to get data on the relations, and thence to a *statistical analysis method.*

Each decision may be affected by anticipation of the next. It is no use employing a *hypothesis* for a theory or model which has not been adequately worked out in a relational system, i.e., in terms of relations of such and such responses on such and such occasions or persons or stimuli, according to the relational system needed. The choice of a system may in turn be affected by the practicability of some experimental *design* to collect data in that system. Again a more or less ambitious design may be worked out according to the availability of suitable computer-aided *statistical methods* to handle it. All four phases cast a vote in the total research plan.

Since it will be convenient to be able to make precise reference to various combinations of these four parts, we shall adhere to the terms set out in Diagram 2-4. Thus an *investigation* is the broadest term of all, and includes both the theoretical *theme* and the *research design* to handle it. The *research design* has to do with the specification of all rationales and procedures short of the original theory or hypotheses. It includes definition of three things (lines following through to bottom row of Diagram 2-4)— the *relational system* to be examined, the *design of experiment* to get the data, and the *mathematico-statistical method* to analyze the data.

Any apparent complication in Diagram 2-4 is due to the simultaneous representation of terms and concepts for certain other groupings of the four primary parts. For it is indeed convenient to be able to designate the relational system and the experimental design as a subunity called the *data-gathering plan;* while the *design* and the analysis *method* comprise a unity which can be called the *operational procedure;* indeed its unity is evidenced by the fact that it is sometimes handed over as a whole to someone in charge of a laboratory other than the main investigator. Again, the combination of the *relational system* and the

DIAGRAM 2-4. Interdependence of Four Essential and Other Definable Parts in a Scientific Investigation

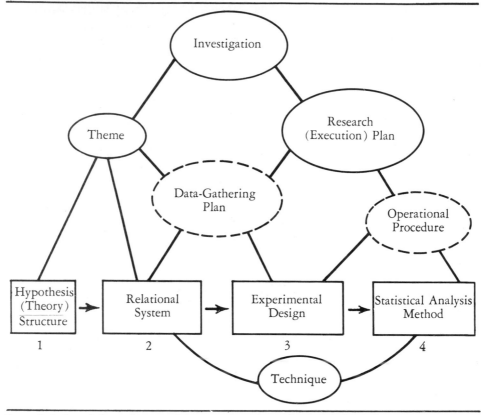

Parts 1, 2, 3, and 4 are the essential parts of any investigation and it is for these that dimensions have been assigned in Tables 2-1, 2-4, and 2-5 and Table 3-2. The remaining headings are organizational conveniences in distinguishing aspects of the total investigation.

statistical method constitutes an entity which is often called a *technique* (as in *P* technique, *Q'* technique, discriminant function technique) and which is something for methodologists to conjure with. The combination of hypothesis structure worked out in a relational system, which has lacked a name, we have termed *a theme*. A theme is a *pre*-procedural part of an investigation which sets out the relational systems by which a theory or hypothesis is defined and expressed, prior to any consideration of the data gathering or the statistical method by which the relations are to be evaluated.

At the beginning of any investigation, all these parts have to be considered, and the advantages and disadvantages of the alternatives in Tables 2-1, 2-4, and 2-5 evaluated singly and in conjunction. To take a small example from the personality field, it has been known for a decade that there exists a trait independent of, for example, intelligence, anxiety, extraversion, etc., which has been called cortertia (240, 796) and expresses itself in rapid reaction time, rapid flicker fusion rate, rapid ideomotor performance, etc. (see Chapter 19), but not in fluency, quickness of intelligent decision, etc. The theory has been entertained that this is partly a temporary state (as well as a relatively permanent difference of trait level) and that it corresponds to "activation level" as studied by Duffy (435), Lindsley (937), and others in animals.

The expression of this *hypothesis* in a relational *system* shows that one needs to investigate covariance of the variables over time, possibly in one person initially, but ultimately in several. An experimental *design* to apply to the first part of this *theme* might be that of testing the several variables in the cortertia pattern, along with additional variables chosen to be applicable to humans from activation-level research, every hour for 200 successive hours (apart from sleep periods). Alternatives would present themselves in design, e.g., to introduce stimuli, drugs, etc. to bring about changes in cortertia and activation level, or to let natural changes provide the variance. Moving from *design* to statistical *method,* we would have to ask whether a bivariate analysis, testing if cortertia (indexed U.I. 22, see Chapter 19) measured as a single variable (battery score) is higher (by *t* test) when some activation stimulus or response is higher, or a multivariate method, (factoring by *P* technique), would check more adequately on our hypothesis.

In such a study the choice of *theme* — of the relations that best express and define the hypothetical concepts — might be carried out by a different group of specialists from that which speaks with most authority on the *technique*. And the advice on experimental *design* would again invoke more specialists on instrumentation and kindred problems, though all would need ultimately to be cooordinated by the chief investigator. Sometimes the gap between the theorists at one end and the statistical specialists at the other is so great that the investigator has difficulty spanning it!

Yet, far more than appears to have been recognized before, the choice of *method* of statistical treatment needs to be decided jointly with consideration of hypothesis, type of analysis, and experimental design in mind. For although some slight restriction is introduced by the choice of experimental design, e.g., one cannot use an *m* method (multivariate analysis) on a single univariate experiment, or a *p,* parametric analysis method, and an *h,* highly structured, model analysis very well with only a couple of gross observations, there is in the main much independence of experimental design and statistical method. What the mathematico-statistical method harks back to most closely is the original hypothesis and it is the model in the *theme* which really should determine the experimental design and the method simultaneously. What investigators most frequently talk about when describing a planned research, however, is that which has been described as operational procedure in Diagram 2-4. For the critic and evaluator of researchers, this at least has the advantage of describing *exactly what the researcher is going to do,* in terms of data-gathering and its analysis. And since the probable goodness of alternative theories and hypotheses before testing is often almost a matter of taste — and certainly a matter of flair — advantages and disadvantages, aptnesses and inaptnesses are better discussed in the realms of *design* and *method.*

Let us therefore consider the aptness of various types of operational procedures, within research design to the construction and testing of theoretical development. No attempt is possible here to go systematically through all possible (34×16) *design* and *method* combinations, and in any case, the implications of some have already been discussed in the original introductions in Sections 1, 2, and 3 above. Brief further comments will be useful, however, in regard to the Dimensions of Design *m-b* (multi-to-bivariate), *i-f* (interfering to free), and *a-r* (abstractive to representative) and to those Dimensions of Method whose poles are *j-h* (jejune to highly resolving) and *o* to *g* ("only" to general relationships). The chief concentration in this book must naturally be on the multi-to-bivariate design and the "only" to "general" relationship methods of analysis; but it is to be hoped that some scholar will give to the systematic relation of design and method combinations, i.e., to procedures, the book-length treatment that it deserves in the light of its role in theoretical advance.

Advantages lie on both ends of the M (Manipulation) continuum (*i*, interfering to free, *f*) design. There are important areas where manipulation is impossible. Theoretical development has stood still in some areas of physiological psychology and social psychology, however, because of lack of realization that significant causal relations can be established *without* resort to manipulation. We need not permit ourselves to be persuaded by an "action researcher" that it is necessary to provoke wars in order to study their causes; since factor-analytic and multiple regression investigations (Chapter 26) have already shown themselves capable of giving a specification equation assigning weights to predictors. By recording time sequences one can also establish causal laws in physiology, and one advantage here of the "free" design is that the organism does not have to be upset by manipulative interference. If, as seems certain, the operation of "organic" principles, i.e., of adjustive actions by the total organism, is an important part of physiological theory, it is less likely that vital aspects of theory will be overlooked by such experimental multivariate and non-manipulation studies of natural action undisturbed by surgical operation, etc. In ordinary psychological experiment there is even more reason to be sensitive about interference, for here even the subject's *knowing* that he is part of a laboratory experiment may powerfully disturb generality of inference.

On the other hand, the manipulative experiment has an advantage in that combinations of events can be arranged which might never be discoverable if we waited for the ideal, free, detached observational experiment. Certainly Nature fails to provide some possible combinations of its parts, such as one might need for statistical treatment in a balanced experiment. For example, the reaction of potassium with water was not to be observed (at least for many million years) before Humphry Davy. Theory is supposed to mirror the essence of Nature, but at times Nature offers an unnatural, or at least, incomplete picture of its own potentialities! We have manipulatively to fill in some cells of the table.

Concerning the abstractive-vs.-representative continuum (*a-r*), one needs again to recognize advantages at both ends, and, especially, to correct for the widespread prejudice of subjectively guided—not to say intellectually bigoted—investigators that abstractive designs alone advance theory. There is a quality of personality (probably factor M) which causes a person to be convinced not so much of a *particular* theory—where facts and insights do sometimes justify strong convictions—as of *any* theory he entertains. That is to say, subjective formulations, whether verbal or mathematical, easily hide from him the fact that he is engaged in trying to force a limited perception upon Nature, instead of waiting for Nature to reveal a pattern to him. This has happened a good deal in the imposing of "mosaics" (Chapter 6) upon correlation matrices. To such a person it seems axiomatic that one can only enter an experiment with what he would call a "clear" abstractive design, i.e., with variables which ask only that question which he believes exists, and to him the representative design seems no design at all. Yet with Nature as with society there is often more to be learnt by listening.

Regardless of the temperamental tendencies of the investigator, one way or the other, to make a more representative or a more subjective choice of variables in design, there do exist certain objective indicators of which pole is likely to advance theory more effectively in any particular situation. The indicators come from our information about the origins of the theory that has favored the abstractions. Whence, in fact, *do* people get their theories? The next section considers the psychological nature of theory more closely but already we have argued that a theory gets into a man's mind, far oftener than is commonly admitted or accepted, by a more slovenly and dubious thought procedure than he realizes. Certainly the beginnings of a good theory must very often be vague, but this is very different from being arbitrary, casual, or prejudiced.

In Chapter 1 it was pointed out that an especial difficulty of psychology in its theoretical development is its need to pull itself up out of the viscous mass of popular ideas. Today, psychological hunches can come from two levels: the premetric, observational level, present in popular and much clinical generalization on the one hand, and the tables of reported experimental and psychometric data relationships on the other. The latter is more honored in public acceptance than in the private generation of theory. For example, nine-tenths of what is written under the title of "personality theory" still comes from clinical and "observation" or anecdotal report— and this despite there being substantial evidence of lawful relations at an altogether more precise and subtle level (in the extensive correlation tables of objective tests, for example) for effective theory generation. Indeed, when examinations of the natural history of "theory" adoption are made, it will probably appear that the basis is often not even good qualitative "clinical" and popular observation, but semantic hypnotism by a word, by hypnagogic imagery, by a magpie attraction to some glittering gadget needing a theory for its respectable use, by an accidental personal contact, or by the social contagion of a fad at a convention. Very commonly today, therefore, there is a dislocation between the poor level of quality in the thinking from which a theory is taken and the level of professional methodological skill at which it is later examined.

If "theory" were theory, there would be some justification for using the abstractive design with the frequency and flourish with which it is now used. But the "theories" are often bogus in their pretensions of springing from well-assembled and examined information, regarding the regularities in Nature on which worthwhile hypothetical hunches should be based. In the clinical and popular fields one is often building on ideas that are really based on the most casual observation, distorted by stereotypes, and riddled by errors of human memory. Either we should be turning to abstractive theories, based on inspection or statistical analysis of the many 150×150 correlation matrices of actual behavior measurements now available, or initiating frankly and explicitly representative designs. There are very few fields indeed where we should not benefit today from returning in all humility to a representative and extensive array of variables, to seek afresh, at the new experiential level of experimental breadth and accuracy, what may be the suggestive regularities and relevant connections and variables for the formation of theory and the initiation of a new IHD spiral.

7. CREATIVE SCIENTIFIC THINKING IN RELATION TO MULTIVARIATE AND BIVARIATE PROCEDURES

Our account of *hypothesis structure, relational system, design,* and *method,* so far, may be accused of presenting the play without Hamlet. For what happens in the actual scientific investigation is an interaction of these logical possibilities with historical perceptions and habits of thought, which we have already discussed, as well as with the mind of the researcher, which we have not discussed.

In recent years much has been unearthed about the personality and activity of the researcher as such, as summarized in, for example, Kretschmer (887), Taylor and Barron (1386), and in the researches of Cattell and Drevdahl (283, 427). The latter show, for example, that creativity has much the same personality pattern, regardless of field, and that it is an unusual combination of genetic "extraversion" (H factor) with environmentally imposed introversion, together with some other curious personality contributions. Drevdahl (427) has also shown, on the same primary personality factors, some significant differences between clinical and bivariate experimental psychologists (not a sample especially selected for creativity, but random APA members) which might account for some properties of research in these areas.

This whole subject of "the psychology of research" and zetetics, as defined by Tykociner, is too vast and too new to be effectively brought into contact with our presentation except tangentially. However, possibly zetetics should never be considered purely in terms of possible scientific procedures divorced from human behavior, but rather realistically related to personality dynamics. Obviously, there are personality differences in the readiness to re-orient one's thinking, and in general, the effectiveness of the greatest scientists has been shown in their capacity to transcend the limitations of existing scientific methods, as illustrated by Galton and Spearman and, in a narrower sense, by Pavlov. Perhaps it will prove to be the bolder spirits in this generation who will recognize the need for a much stronger emphasis on multivariate thinking and on multivariate teaching in psychology.[7] On the other hand, in one sense personality traits of fortitude and patience may influence one to follow the bivariate trail, since keeping one's eye

on the main theoretical objectives through as long a maze of trial and error as the use of successive pairs of variables requires, is no mean feat. Personality differences probably enter also into serendipitous research, i.e., into the ability to see significant side connections despite preoccupation with a main theory.

Doubtless many connections of personality with preferences for designs could be interestingly discussed. Since space precludes this being done comprehensively, we shall concentrate on the associations of the dimension most important to this book — the multivariate-bivariate dimension. Many special attachments can be understood through circumstances extrinsic to logic, e.g., the irrational historical omission of manipulative procedures from multivariate designs or the inclination of bivariate experimenters to favor abstractive rather than representative designs because of the labor involved in being representative (a goal obtainable in bivariate work only by a long succession of studies).

For brevity's sake the advantages of the multivariate approach brought out at various places (Chapters 2, 3, 4, 5, 6, and the substantive chapters) must be simply summarized here and left to expansion in other writings. They are: (1) A very great economy in the number of relationships brought under consideration by a given amount of experimental work. (2) The intellectual gain of revealing where most of the rest of the variance of a focal variable has gone, instead of having blindly to regard that residual variance as lost in the limbo of error variance. (3) A more dependable, exact evaluation of the relative importance of various influences, as a result of establishing all their connections on the *same* sample, instead of on a succession of non-comparable bivariate experimental groups. (4) A more fertile creation of new concepts having high viability, because enduring concepts depend generally on a whole pattern of relationships becoming apparent, and this occurs more readily

---

[7]As a recent writer, T. Kuhn, has rather uncompromisingly expressed it (page vii above), erroneous methods and theories often only pass with the passing of those individuals, schools and departments which have long held them. This is certainly true of the rank and file of scientific workers. Hopefully, modern education is doing something to make flexibility of thought more widespread.

when many variables are studied together. (5) A more adequate testing of hypotheses about concepts, because *whole* concepts are usually poorly represented, in dependent-independent or any other kind of experiment, by a *single* variable and really require a weighted composite of the variables through which the concept is expressed. (6) A more successful avoidance of misleading indications, inasmuch as in the bivariate controlled situation the variation of concept *A* with concept *B* may fail to show its typical form and range in the artificial situation where other variables are held constant.

Let us begin here with No. 4, the creation of concepts, since the others are more obvious, and our main concern here is with theory development. Regardless of where it occurs or by what statistical instruments the perception or proof of covariation is made, the inference of a unitary entity or concept depends on demonstration of covariation of the parts alleged to belong to the functional unity. Multivariate experimentalists may use both correlation clusters and factors to recognize this covariation. But bivariate psychologists have sometimes objected to a full-dress factor analysis being demanded before proof of a unitary concept is accepted. Thus Leeper (917) says, quite correctly, that "the factor analytic approach has by no means a monopoly on interest in learning to identify the fundamental factors involved in personality,..." (p. 399) and he instances that the basis for grouping things can also be their having "similar functional properties or that all may be described by the same laws." This penetrating comment, however is followed by the suggestion that a sleuthing by bivariate and arbitrarily abstractive, non-representative methods is virtually as effective in achieving this goal.

The scientific record of wasteful, trial-and-error search, by bivariate methods, and the ensuing hopelessness — or resort to fantastic, unnecessary intellectual contortions — in such fields as motivation (the search for drives), Gestalt psychology (the attempt to calculate Gestalt effects), and in the attempted application of atomistic reflexological learning principles to clinical personality change, scarcely supports his position. Also such statements as Leeper's, frequent in bivariate texts, overlook the fact that factor analysis can handle functional *response* patterns, i.e., processes and laws having to do with sequences, additional to the individual difference structures we call "traits." As an instance of the bivariate capacity to locate important connections, Leeper cites the discovery of the connection between fluorides and tooth decay. I am aware that this was tested and *checked* by a bivariate design but I know of nothing in the record which points to it not being *discovered* by a multivariate design — operating, of course, at the informalized, "in one's head" level.

The contention is not that bivariate experiment on hunches will not find connections, or even that most existing connections have not been found by bivariate designs — since multivariate researches are too recent to have had their chance to contribute in a major way. The infinite roving of an infinite number of investigators will uncover anything, just as enough men with garden spades could dig a new Suez Canal. But if efficiency of scientific discovery and use of funds is a consideration, the planned multivariate and representative experiment is superior. If the hundred remedies for scurvy had been tried in a representative and recorded design, instead of in a series of confident, disconnected bivariate hypotheses, it might have taken two years instead of two hundred, to discover the potency of citrus fruits, and the finding would not have been lost or disputed for a further two hundred years during which countless victims perished.

A second result of insufficiency of exploration, and of widespread comparison of variables, is the tendency, often repeated in the history of bivariate experiments, to settle on a certain variable having *some* degree of statistical connection, and to consider it *the* cause, whereas a wider search would have shown it to be several causal links removed, and at a lower degree of statistical association, than many other variables. Thus malaria was considered, as its name still indicates, to be due to "bad air" — the night air of marshes — and it was centuries before the closer association with a mosquito, a particular mosquito, and a germ which it carries, became understood. In the search for statistically higher and causally closer possible connections, the present writer has had occasion (244) to point out to certain *Bulletin* survey article writers the extreme lopsidedness of their alleged surveys. For actually there were more connections with the variable they were specifically writing about in *one* published multivariate representative research (which they had overlooked, since multivariate article titles cannot arrest the skimmer's eye with the name of every variable used) than in *all* the bivariate articles they had included in the survey bibliography.

During the last century of psychological theory building, we have actually suffered from a piece of poor timing. For somewhere in the twenties there began a healthy and disciplined revulsion against vague, vast, and unprovable theoretical elaborations together with a heightened regard for operational definitions. Unfortunately the opportunity was missed for combining this step with its logically necessary adjunct — a regard for multivariate definition of concepts and multivariate methods. For Spearman and Thurstone and a tiny group of advanced thinkers were voices crying in the wilderness then, and the laboratory "scientist" saw science only in the Wundt-Pavlov tradition. A fuller understanding of the philosophy and techniques of multivariate experiment has come only in the last fifteen years, and, of course, has received considerable impulse fortuitously from the mechanical advances in computers and programs in the last ten. Meanwhile, the new, hard-headed theory development unfortunately got tied to the limited capacity for definition in the bivariate designs.

Let us next pursue the multivariate-bivariate methodological difference beyond the issue of effectiveness in discovery of connections to the more complex issue of generating and checking hypotheses. First let us distinguish between the popular usage of "concept" as an idea in some form in someone's mind and the more restricted and disciplined "concept" as an *operationally unitary entity,* which is also an idea, but one bound to operations. It is clear that the former type of concept need have no counterpart in natural operations. It could be a psychotic idea, part of a nightmare, or a piece of disconnected verbal symbolism. A concept beginning in this subjective fashion *may,* eventually, be brought to definition by a set of operations, but they can remain a set of operations or conditions which refuse to make sense in Nature and, for instance, leave the concept either imaginary or, at the least non-unitary.

For example, $\sqrt{-1}$ is operationally defined, and so is the group of people standing with top hats at 5:00 PM within forty feet of the clock in Grand Central Station, but neither need have a counterpart in reality. Putting aside such purely imaginary concepts, we must next recognize that in the remainder — those actually capable of some fit to the real world — a lot of entirely logical and operationally expressed concepts may lack the useful property of corresponding to *single* structures or functionally unitary entities. For most scientific purposes a concept which does not have the property of corresponding to some functionally unitary or reliably repeating pattern is either useless and meaningless or of only temporary applicability. As Chapters 3, 6, and 9 show, the most central and common instances of operationally definable concepts which also have operationally demonstrable unitariness appear statistically as *factors* and *types* (in organisms or processes) and, to a lesser extent, in such statistical patterns as correlation clusters, etc. Each and all of these exist as *patterns* of observables (patterns of attributes or patterns of organisms or entities). And since one can define a pattern of any of these kinds by a *single* element only in the limiting case of a single element pattern, the definition of a concept is normally a multidimensional operation.

Both logically and metrically therefore, the attempt in experiment to define a concept by a single variable must be a failure (unless the variable is the sum of several observable variables). It is no escape from this judgment to say "I state the clean postulate that the activation (or anxiety or other concept) level is expressed and measured by the operation of measuring electrical skin resistance." For this defies a more universal postulate: that no concept or universal is capable of being wholly expressed by a particular. (In statistical terms, not all the variance of a particular variable can be accounted for by a factor concept, or indeed, by a multiple correlation from any other set of variables.) Thus let us consider Table 2-6 as a brief reminder of a typical factor-variable correlation matrix. Then variables 1 and 2 are the clearest manifestations of concept 2; while 3, 4, 5, and 8 (reversed) represent concept 1; and 7 and 6 (reversed) are manifestations of concept 3. However, even with .7 correlations available (as for variables 3, 6, and 7), *in no case does a single*

TABLE 2-6

TYPICAL VARIANCE REPRESENTATION OF
CONCEPTS BY OPERATIONALLY
DEFINED REPRESENTATIVES

Variable Manifestation	Factor Concept 1	Factor Concept 2	Factor Concept 3
1	.0	.6	.1
2	−.2	.4	.3
3	.7	.0	.0
4	.4	.0	.3
5	−.6	.2	.2
6	.0	.0	−.7
7	.0	.0	.7
8	−.4	.1	−.2

variable represent as much as 50 per cent of the variance of the concept which a bivariate experimental design might presume that this variable "operationally represents." Informal surveys of experimental findings show that as a rule no single variable comes anywhere near to representing a concept, and, conversely, that no single concept accounts for more than a fraction of the variance in any given observable. A concept has to be "estimated" as a *whole pattern* of inferred or empirically known associations. Except in quite unusual "control" conditions, experimental investigation of the presence and action of the concept involves its representation by some combined function (at times a precisely statable mathematical function) of the whole pattern of observables. Thus the typical bivariate experimenter constantly falls (especially in his conclusions) into what we may call the *error of inefficient reference*.

A second danger of error to which bivariate designs are particularly liable is that of *the confounding of postulates with hypothesis structures*. Let us illustrate this by an investigation in which the research question asked is: "How much is anxiety level related to speed of conditioning?" Let us suppose (as has in fact occurred) that a bivariate experimenter has postulated hand tremor (represented by variable *a* in Diagram 2-5), as his operational definition of anxiety (independent variable), and rate of eye blink conditioning as the dependent variable, *b*. Let us suppose that anxiety (unknown to investigators at this research stage) happens to be a single factor affecting variables *a, c, e,* and *d*.

Now if the bivariate experimenter gets a null result when he seeks a significant relation of *a* and *b*, he does not know whether his hypothesis—that anxiety is related to conditioning—has failed, or whether his postulate—that *a*, tremor, is a measure of anxiety—has failed (or that both have failed). The possibility that *a* is *not* a measure of anxiety is represented in the same diagram by putting it, alternatively, outside the circle of the anxiety concept, at *a'*. The multivariate experimenter, on the other hand, will first (or in the same experiment) have factored variables *a, c, d, e, f, g, h,* and *i,* and will then know whether *a, c, d,* and *e* do or do not share one factor. If *a* does *not* share their company (as shown in the alternative *a'* position) but all other things semantically called manifestations of anx-

illustration (see Chapters 19 and 22), *a,* tremor, does load the anxiety factor, but it also loads the distinct stress factor (325) — as in the ellipse in Diagram 2-5. However, let us next suppose that the bivariate experimenter has been cautious enough to check that *a* falls into the anxiety factor (by first intercorrelating *a, d, c,* and *e*) but then proceeds to use *a* alone as his

DIAGRAM 2-5.   Possible Misleading Conclusions From Operationally Defining a Concept by a Single Variable

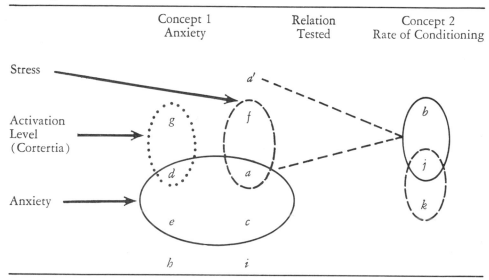

| Concept 1
Anxiety | Relation
Tested | Concept 2
Rate of Conditioning |

Variables: *a* = tremor magnitude; *b* = eyelid conditioning rate; *c* = tendency to agree; *d* = many reactions to false signals; *e* = lack of confidence in untried performance; *f* = motor-perceptual rigidity; *g* = irregularly forewarned reaction time; *h* = fluency of association; *i* = decision speed on cursive miniature situation test; *j* = g.s.r. conditioning rate; *k* = finger movement conditioning rate.

iety in our society factor out in company with *c, d,* and *e,* then he concludes that there exists an anxiety factor concept, but that he made a mistake in counting *a* in it. Here we assume *a* joined *c, d,* and *e* in a single anxiety factor. Also we shall not question that *b* is fairly representing rate of conditioning, though, to follow through systematically, one would also question this as a single concept until variables like *j* and *k* have been correlated with it.

To admit actual research findings as

anxiety reference measure. He may next find a positive statistical association of tremor with, say, low motor-perceptual rigidity, *f,* and would then conclude that anxiety is productive of low rigidity (or vice versa). This introduces a third type of error to which bivariate studies are prone and which we may call the *error of the surplus (or counterfeit) concept,* for the correlation with rigidity is due to *a* and *f* sharing a stress factor. (Alternatively, as Diagram 2-5 reminds us, he might have taken for anxiety variable *d,* many reactions to false reaction time signals. He would have a variable instead substantially loaded in U.I. 22, cortertia or persistent activation level, and could again be deceived.)

Thus there is at this point a radical difference of conceptualization and procedure in the bivariate and multivariate approaches. The former makes at least two assumptions where the latter checks them as hypotheses one by one. The assumption that an operational definition is enough causes endless mischief from the assumption's being dangerously hidden at the postulate level. The two hidden postulates are that anxiety is a single entity and that operation *a* (or, alternatively, perhaps operations *a'*, or *f*) measures it. The bivariate experimenter may even confound his difficulties by postulating that *two* arbitrarily chosen variables together, say *a* and *g,* measure anxiety, and thus have a foot in each of two different factors. The multivariate experimenter will make no assumption either that anxiety or a person's rate of conditioning are single concepts, but will check on both hypotheses and choose variables appropriate to the structure that he finds. (The circles on the right of Diagram 2-5 remind us, incidentally, that we also have to consider the existence of these possible independent forms of conditionability.)

It is not contended that these errors are irretrievable or that they put the bivariate experimenter "out of business." For if he recognizes his failure and patiently persists, trying one variable after another (and assuming, for argument's sake, that U.I. 24, anxiety, is related to conditioning whereas activation and stress are not), he will in time find that *a, c, e,* and *d* behave in the same way in relation to the dependent variable, whereas *g, h, i,* etc. do not. This is what writers like Leeper (917) mean when they state that unitariness can also be recognized and established by looking for common functional properties by bivariate sequences. But since multivariate methods, including factor analysis, also recognize and use evidence of functional unity (correlating to discover common effects, common fate over time, etc., as covered in Chapter 2), the real issue between the methods is, as stated above, one of economy. Is one to find this unitariness at an early stage, by efficient multivariate methods, or by a long succession of more or less disconnected and questionably comparable bivariate steps? All too frequently the bivariate experimenter operates at the end of too long a chain of "ifs." And limited and faulty human memory tries to piece together the clues from many bivariate studies, which in a multivariate study the computer would positively and precisely consider together. Parenthetically, it should be understood that when we speak of correlational methods and factor analysis as being tests, of conceptual unitariness, the reader should not restrict his thoughts to factor analysis as it has been conventionally understood, in what has hitherto happened in the Galton-Spearman tradition, but in the senses developed in Chapter 6. That is, it inspects unitariness not only in the individual difference, cross-sectional sense but also in longitudinal, functional senses. However, in most pursuits of concepts it makes good sense to check on the cross-sectional, across-person, factor structure before going to manipulative and time-succession designs.

In viewing the wastefulness of approaches which risk the *error of confounding* of assumptions, the reader may yet say, "An investigator is quite free to postulate that *any* subset of operational variables, provided they have unitariness in correlation, constitute some concept he is talking about." Thus he might surely call *a* and *f* in Diagram 2-5 anxiety (or stress, if he knows of the latter's conceptual existence). The issue here is purely with dictionary-makers, though, like most semantic problems, it can masquerade all too insidiously as a real problem. When a field is first studied scientifically there already exists a set of dictionary symbols which, because of their lack of any organic, scientifically proven connection with the operations we shall simply call a *semantic facade*. *Facade* is better than *surface* because its conventional structure is usually a strong, but from the scientific standpoint, false (and not internally consistent) one. For example, the semantic facade might be that a whale is a fish. (Educational psychologists have even gone so far as to take this facade pretty seriously, hesitating to disturb popular communication, and using the ideas of "content validity" and "face validity" for tests, but the scientist cannot afford these social compromises with the PTA!)

For behind the facade there exist some true and probably different structures, which can be revealed by the methods of science, primarily that of experimentally observing the true covariations. For example, semantics has the term "depression," but factor analysis shows six to eight distinct, independent factors in the area of manifestations roughly covered by the word "depression." Similarly, what we popularly designate by the single concept and expression "intelligent behavior" may well be due to two functionally very different factors or influences. The scientist has to insist that if he finds two concepts he must employ two terms, but it is nevertheless good scientific manners to avoid unnecessary confusion such as would arise from arbitrarily labelling a factor found in what is popularly, semantically, called *anxiety* manifestations an "intelligence factor." A researcher is free to postulate what he likes and use what term he likes for his postulate. But in the interest of not planting traps to generate purely semantic disputes, we owe to the dictionary the duty of calling our factors and concepts, say, anxiety 1 and anxiety 2, if we find *two* entities in the realm of phenomena popularly called anxious behavior. Alternatively, as in the personality and motivation realm (Cattell, 240; French, 549, 550), we do well to use defined index systems rather than to launch into premature and therefore misleading interpretive connotations.

Apart from the convenience of retaining for concepts the terms that existed in the general area of their observable manifestations, the more clearly we recognize that the scientific structure is one thing and the semantic facade another, the better. Failure to realize this causes some misunderstandings. For example, the present writer has asserted that the limit in conceptual bankruptcy is reached in the pre-factor-analytic nadir of test theory: "intelligence is what intelligence tests measure." But Marx (994, p. 27) apparently considers this a satisfactory operational construct definition. It is satisfactory in its respect for the semantic facade, but otherwise it stumbles over most of the bivariate errors: the "error of confounding," the "error of the surplus concept," and considerable "error of inefficient reference." It leads nowhere except to arbitrarily, subjectively designated "intelligence tests."

Space permits discussion of only one or two other angles of the relation of design to theory construction. Turning to disadvantages of the multivariate design, we recognize, especially when the *experiment* as such is combined with a general *simultaneous method* of analyzing all relations at once, that the method compels one to use the same mathematical function, e.g., a linear correlation, over all relations, whereas a bivariate design might leave one free to try different forms for different relations. On the other hand, if a *controlled* (Dimension *C*, pole *c*) bivariate design is used, one will miss the possible interaction and superordinate relations which, as indicated earlier, may exist in the freer situation when all things are allowed to vary together, and to do so over full natural ranges.

Some extensions and refinements should also be considered on this introductory proposition, that multivariate experimental results lead more quickly to the shaping of a scientific concept toward a realistic fit to the whole realm of data. That construction of theory which we have called "importing" analogues casts an intellectual spell but, as we have seen, is also extravagant, in the sense that it seldom "comes off." The multivariate definition of a theory, e.g., by factor patterns, discriminant function weights, etc., is a powerful safeguard against the vulnerabilities and excesses inherent in this approach. For it far more quickly rejects the false graft, i.e., it reveals the situations where "surplus meaning" is incorrect.

Finally, in evaluation of concepts and theories, one must remember (as developed more operationally in Chapters 6, 17, 18, and 24) that the meaning of a concept always derives from inspection not only of what is *in* it, but also of what is *out* of it. For example, positive relations in a set of puzzle-solving performances might lead one to conclude that he is dealing with intelligence, until he finds that a whole set of verbal and numerical problems have *no* systematic relation to this group, whereupon he recognizes that he us dealing instead with some special primary ability in the total intelligence realm. Such exposure of a pseudo concept, and the bringing of a concept into perspective, is far less likely to happen when one is dealing with only two or three variables. The automatically broader sweep in multivariate studies is a built-in corrective for parochialism of conception.

The rapid growth of computer size and complex program construction in this generation is going to overcome many of the obstacles of sweat and cost which for years have kept many fairly energetic psychologists rationalizing against multivariate designs. Inevitably it may also cause much pointless tossing about of masses of data by uninspired researchers; but this is less important than the encouragement it will give to correct and potent uses. Notably we can expect a richer flow of well-born hypotheses, with a healthy and realistic aptness to the data, from the beginning. There will also be an increase in the power and expedition of testing hypotheses that are high on the method parameter of "mathematical complexity of model tested." As in the game of "Is it living or dead?", "Is it animal or vegetable?", etc., there will quickly be a transition to the questions "Does it consist of three ripe apples?" In what is not a very remote metaphor, we may say that the bivariate experimenter is compelled to look at his world through a narrow slit, moved now to this and now to that part of the field. By properly adjusting the view we can thus, in a well-known field, answer fairly major questions. It can be placed horizontal at a certain height and we can answer the question "Is the third bookshelf full or empty?" But if we know nothing of the room, the grating formed instead by the multivariate slits, running in all directions, alone will permit us to form a developed hypothesis about the room as a whole, and whether indeed it contains a bookcase.

Not unnaturally, it is sometimes asked why, if multivariate designs are so superior in certain respects, the physical sciences did not adopt them earlier. Part of the answer is that the methods did not exist for the three hundred years in which the physical sciences were struggling through their exploratory stages. A second reason—not always immediately accepted—is that the physical sciences have simpler problems! This may sound a little absurd because, at the present stage of behavioral science, the physical sciences can obviously boast far more complex, established formulae between two or three variables on either side of an equation. But the *number* of variables operating in a biological or behavioral science problem is far greater than it usually is in physical science (partly because it is harder to get manipulative control). And it is this sheer number and complexity which demands the proper application of multivariate methods. In other words, it would require more of a genius to find the relevant variables in the vast chaos of the life sciences. Which means that with our present supply of geniuses we can hope to get further sooner by having them operate with developed multivariate methods.

If this is correct, the proposition must be seriously entertained that one reason why adequate accumulation of demonstrated laws and theories has eluded the tireless efforts of psychologists is the fact that in the past a very small proportion of psychologists have been trained in multivariate experiment relative to the needs of the subject. But proper recognition of the urgency of the over-all supply and demand situation must not lead to any denial that each design and method has its appropriateness for particular areas and stages of advance. Thus viewed, the multivariate methods have a special, indeed indispensable function at the first, *exploratory* stages, to find the underlying influences ("relevant variables") and concepts and the valid ways of measuring them. Once found, they can also be used as the concepts in bivariate experiments with manipulative control. Nevertheless, it is not *necessary* to go to bivariate experiment for manipulative designs, or for sequential designs, etc., since, as independent parameters of design, they can be combined with either pole of the multivariate bivariate dimension. The advantage of the bivariate design at this stage is that it permits non-linear and complex relations to be hypothesized and tested. Multivariate procedures, however, belong as well to the very last (and to some extent the applied) stages in a field, in that they lead to a final comprehensiveness in determining the relative importance and interaction of the totality of theoretical concepts or influences in some complex phenomenon. Obviously, without a sufficiently broad base of variables the higher-order interactions cannot be examined. It is for these reasons that a thorough education in multivariate research designs is at least as important to the psychologist as that training in bivariate methods alone which in many universities hitherto has been his sole acquaintance with experiment.

8. SUMMARY

(1) The first half of this book deals with experimental design and analytical method per se; the second illustrates them by problems, discovered laws, and developed theories gained by applying multivariate experimental approaches in the important, commonly recognized divisions of psychology.

(2) Progress in psychology has been difficult because of three conditions more prominent in it than in other sciences, namely, the taxonomic elusiveness of the data, the continuous entanglement with popular amateur discussion, and the slowness to achieve measurement. The first reaction, to these problems, that of seeking scientific discipline in imitating the experimental designs of older sciences, which expressed itself in the Wundt-Pavlov tradition, solved some problems but missed others. Fortunately, other psychologists responded creatively to the unusual problems of psychology in what became the Galton-Spearman or multivariate experimental approach. The development of this methodology on its own, and in company with the more classical tradition, now offers better hopes of progress through a strategic "two-handed" attack.

(3) In their current form, however, these two traditions actually present only a limited perception of the full possible range of experimental designs. Their historical rivalry is as obsolete as the idea that together, in their present form, they cover the ground.

(4) An experiment is defined as *a controlled gathering of data aimed to discover significant relations*. As such, it is one phase in the inductive-hypothetico-deductive (IHD) spiral of scientific investigation. Whether it occurs within the walls of a laboratory or not is irrelevant to the definition.

(5) The laws that are first established are about either *structures* or *processes*. Theories rest on empirically checked laws, but the actual order of establishment of laws, hypotheses, and theories in the scientific process varies.

(6) Experimental designs can be more usefully classified and evaluated by parameters (dimensions) than by types. Most varieties are covered by six parameters:

1. Dimension N (Number of variables) Bivariate to Multivariate (b to m)

2. Dimension M (Manipulation degree) Interfered with to Freely Happening (i to f)

3. Dimension T (Time relation dimension) Dated to Simultaneous (d to s)

4. Dimension C (Control of non-focal variables) Constant to Uncontrolled (c to u)

5. Dimension R (Representativeness of "relative" variables) Abstractive to Representative (a to r)

6. Dimension D (Distribution of "referees," i.e., population sample) Known Bias to Normal Representative (k to n)

Except for a few impossible, non-viable combinations, the parameters can be combined in all ways, yielding at least thirty varieties of experiment, of which the historical Wundt-Pavlov "classical" (A.P.A. Division 3) and the Galton-Spearman "multivariate" (A.P.A. Divisions 4, 5, 6, 8, etc.) cover only a minority.

(7) Mathematico-statistical methods of analyzing data are to a degree independent of design and offer a distinct taxonomy. They can likewise, but perhaps more arbitrarily, be classified according to four parameters:

1. Dimension E (e to v) (Power of significance test)

2. Dimension B (j to h) (Degree of mathematical complexity of the model)

3. Dimension S (o to g) (Number of relations simultaneously evaluated)

4. Dimension I (p to l) (Degree of utilization of information)

With some obvious exceptions, each of the 2^4 possible combinations ("types" of method) can be combined with the thirty or so experimental design possibilities, though there will be certain naturally greater congenialities. A combination of an experimental *design* with a statistical *method* will be called an *operational procedure,* since it defines what is actually done in the research.

(8) Theories are both ends and instruments in scientific investigation. Definitions are given for law, postulate, working hypothesis, model, and theory. The difference between theoretical concept and empirical (working) construct is defined in terms of the imported or surplus meaning in the former, which can be classified by the distance from which the analogy is brought or, alternatively, by the ideality of its origin. A dimension of imported meaning exists in which an *immediate construct* (formerly "intervening variable") is lowest, a hypothetical construct middling, and a theoretical concept highest. Theory in the behavioral sciences is affected more than theory in other areas by the limits to timeless generalization imposed by the incompleteness of the irreversible emergent process in Nature in any given era.

Tentatively, dimensions for a taxonomy of theory can be stated as (a) Degree of strictness of expression in a model, (b) Extent of role of imported or postulate-derived concepts, (c) Breadth of base, defined as the number of areas of observation inductively and deductively tied to the theory, and (d) Degree of complexity of internal relationships.

(9) The complete description of an investigation requires definition of (a) hypothesis *structure,* (b) relational *system,* (c) experimental *design,* and (d) mathematico-statistical analysis *method.* In conducting research it is useful also to consider these in various couplings, such as *procedure,* covering design and analysis method, *technique,* covering relational system and statistical analysis, etc. Each of these combinations normally involves emphasis on the work of a different kind of specialist in an investigatory team.

(10) Understanding the structure of theory, and the best sequences for theory construction, assists, but does not insure, healthy development. Outside the logical structure are the personality of the researcher and the values and prejudices arising from socio-historical accidents. Since theories exist only in the minds of men, their historical development has suffered from partisan excesses and educa-

tional prejudices, from being exploited as status symbols, from being less easily separable, in psychology, from popular verbalizations, from the greater ease of stating a theory than finding a law, from the proliferation of oversimplified models out of touch with observation, and from fixation on conflict within pairs of alternative theories, encouraged by legalistic debate and emotional overvaluation of theories.

(11) In the light of the intrinsic structure of theory, and in catering to the perversions to which its development has proved historically susceptible, different scientific *procedures,* (i.e., *designs* plus *methods*) have characteristic advantages and disadvantages. The multivariate procedures have the greatest potential for generating concepts, and suffer only from the inconvenience of the large demands they make on experimental time and the restriction that relations have to be first examined in a simple linear form. In generating theoretical concepts, their advantages are great but in theory-examination, as distinct from theory-construction, the gain is smaller. However, checking a whole pattern still usu-

ally offers a more significant conclusion than checking a correlation or difference of means using only two variables. Moreover, the simultaneous multivariate procedure offers opportunities to analyze higher-order interactions and relations commonly missed in bivariate and atomistic experimental steps.

(12) Advantages and disadvantages of manipulative-vs.-non-manipulative, abstractive-vs.-representative, and other parameters of designs and method have also been examined more briefly. Such advantages are never "absolute," but generally relative to a strategic or tactical situation in research. For example, multivariate methods are vital to getting movement in the early, structuring, exploratory stages. Bivariate procedures have advantages in transcending the present limitation of multivariate methods largely to linear relations. Multivariate methods have a second role again at late and applied stages, when perspective is needed on the relative quantitative importance of various influences, interactions, and laws.

CHAPTER 3

The Data Box: Its Ordering of Total Resources in Terms of Possible Relational Systems

RAYMOND B. CATTELL
University of Illinois

1. RELATIONAL SYSTEM, HYPOTHESIS, DESIGN, AND METHOD AS THE FOUR PANELS OF THE INVESTIGATORY PLAN

After a glance at the relatively accidental, historical grouping of features in the Wundt-Pavlov and Galton-Spearman research traditions, we have embraced in the last chapter a new and more comprehensive view of the taxonomy of possible research designs. Therein we have recognized three "panels" — or separate areas of decision that contribute to the total planning of an investigation — namely, hypothesis *theme* (theory), experimental *design,* and analysis *method,* each with a set of four or more definable parameters.

Although these three panels are what experimenters most discuss when they get together, they tend to think of the first as "definition of hypothesis" rather than "theme." For theme, as pointed out in Table 2-4, is both hypothesis structure and relational system. That is to say, it contains

in addition to hypothesis, a set of real, observable relations in terms of which its meaning can exist. This environmentally embedded set of possible relations, necessarily a sub-set of all possible relations in the universe, is often taken for granted by the planners of hypotheses much as architects take the firm earth for granted. As a consequence, an experiment may either neglect a proper relational statement of his hypothesis or at least fail to realize that his study is not taking into account all the possible relations among entities which are relevant to the full expression and recognition of the theory in the given field of observation. Obviously it pays to turn frequently from the subjective logic of the theory to its phenomenal relational expression. But there has been little attention in methodology hitherto to clarifying a scheme whereby the researcher can quickly and comprehensively recognize what the totality of the relationships can be in which he is free to operate.

Possibly implicit in this neglect is the

67

assumption that to attempt to encompass these relations is to enter on a journey that will extend to the infinite! But we shall hope to show that there is a sense in which this fear will prove quite incorrect. For, properly conceived in taxonomic classes, the array of relationships is by no means boundless, and there are substantial gains to be made in the actual and practical design of investigation by studying their structure.

In the first place, if one thinks further on what we have defined in barest essentials as "the theme of an investigation" (Diagram 2-4, page 52), it becomes eventually clear that a theory is inevitably constructed out of a set of relationships. However metaphorical or cloudy or verbally bound a theory may be in its first visit to the experimenter's mind, it must eventually have its precise statement only in the flesh and blood of actual data relationships. The actual later experimental gathering of data on the relations, and their quantitative analysis, belong to what we have called *operational procedure* (i.e., design and method). But the nature of the pure scientific understanding—the conceptual structure of the theory itself—is already ultimately couched in the *theme,* i.e., in the model and the set of relationships in nature which express the model and match any verbal statement of the theory. The model may be a formula expressing a particular relationship of time to distance (in a simple theory) so that time and distance are the relatives, and although they are necessary for expressing this particular model they are also the "medium" for other models. What we are asserting as an important point in hypothesis definition is that when these relations are systematically kept in view, one finds that most experimenters notice and operate upon only a small and arbitrary selection from the total system of relational possibilities necessary to defining or proving their theories.

The chief gains in studying a taxonomy of Nature's possible relational combinations—apart from the scientific-esthetic value of a previously unperceived vista of knowledge—are:

(1) A check on whether the experimenter has indeed chosen to study the best relationships to test his theory.

(2) An assurance that the theory has been expressed in real relations and is no meaningless, superfluous literary fiat.

(3) Such an explicit recognition of the relations to be examined that the experimental design can be confidently, insightfully planned to quantify and examine them.

(4) Again in that listing of the relations and their expected role in the model aids in proceeding to mathematical formulations of the model and the choice of proper statistical tests to check on them. Incidentally, it will be recalled (Diagram 2-4) that we have defined this *relation of mathematico-statistical methods to particular relational systems* as the development of *techniques* (such as R and P techniques).

(5) The expression of a theory in terms of the relational systems it employs and within which its working appears, provides not only a check on the internal consistency of the theory, as in (1) and (2), but also a provocative invitation to extend its natural development in ways which might otherwise be unperceived and unsuspected.

2. THE PURPOSE OF DEVELOPING THE COVARIATION CHART INTO THE BDRM OR DATA BOX

The question of how far the different entities and observations in different sciences preclude a single common scheme of relational systems is something we must set aside, except to comment that these differences are far smaller than at first appears, and that the present treatment would probably suit other sciences with little modification.

In psychology, the germ of relational systems analysis began in 1946 with what was first called the Covariation Chart (213), which systematically set out the totality of relations open to observation upon people, tests, and occasions or conditions. This we shall expand from a three- to a ten-dimensional system; but it is helpful to refer back to the simpler treatment at a number of points. First, a brief historical reference may suffice to illustrate that collecting and classifying the varieties of relationship open to psychological study is something more than an academic diversion, something indeed, that is indispensable to good research strategy and the enrichment of theory. The Covariation Chart was introduced primarily as a means of classifying and extending the possibilities of *correlational* researches, but it was stated that in principle it was applicable to any other kind of statistical analysis of concomitance, as demonstrated here. It is useful to refer to the Covariation Chart, primarily (1) as a "nursery example" of learning to think multidimensionally in research planning, and (2) historically as illustrating the manner of birth of new factor analytic techniques (*P, O, S,* and *T* techniques) which demonstrated the utility of relational systems.

This utility has been shown in the Covariation Chart's helping to bring a proper realization of the true relationships of various systems of statistical analysis, e.g., of the "error" in one being the "true" variance in another. However, Coan (350) may be right in suggesting that, more than this gift of perspective over variance, its "major virtue ... is that it can suggest forms of valuable research which might otherwise be overlooked." Other writers, however, object to the original three-dimensional Covariation Chart being relegated by the present writer to the status of a mere pedagogical stage on the way to the mature use of the ten-dimensional *Basic Data Relation Matrix* (or BDRM), which we shall develop in the next section, and wish to treat the three-way matrix as still the most practically useful model for the bulk of actual researches. For persons with simpler

tastes the BDRM concept may well have "priced itself out of business" by going to ten dimensions! However, the present writer's view is that although the ten-dimensional treatment may often be more than is needed, (1) it should be kept in mind as representing the true dimensionality, and (2) there is nothing sacred about

DIAGRAM 3-1. Possible Techniques of Relational Analysis Shown in the Simpler Context of the Three-Axis Covariation Chart

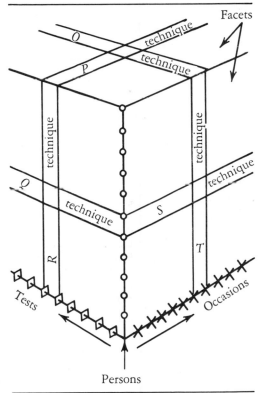

three dimensions, and if abridgment is desired, then four, five, or six may often be the more apt simplifications for particular purposes.

Nevertheless, for those who find it convenient to teach the collapsed three-dimensional BDRM let us briefly recapitulate the essence of the original Covariation Chart. It sets out three Carte-

DIAGRAM 3-2. The Six Correlational or Relational Matrices and Techniques Obtainable from the Three Facets of the Three-Axis Covariation Chart

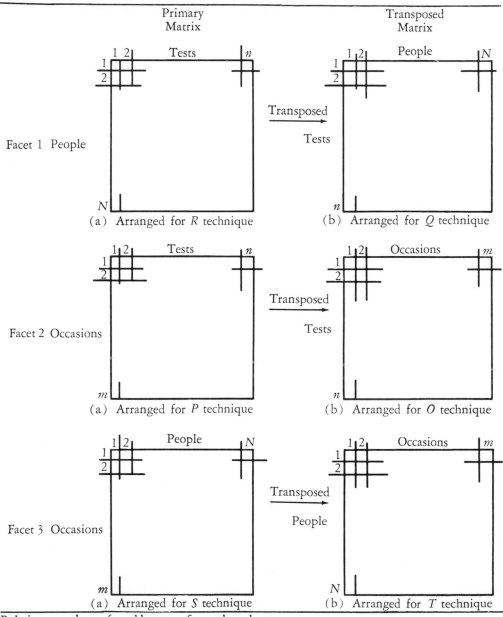

Relations are always found between figures by columns.

sian coordinates: for *persons,* for *tests* (defined in more general terms as situations-cum-responses), and for *occasions* (conditions, present and prior, internal and external). The numerical entries made in the cells, bounded by these row and column entities, are commonly magnitudes of responses. Thus a_{ijk} is the act (response) magnitude by person i to test j on occasion k. The original six basic correlational (and ultimately, factor-analytic) techniques are illustrated by pairs of parallel lines in the data box, showing the correlated series, i.e., each showing the score column (or row) which is to be correlated with its neighbor. If all members of a set, instead of the two at the ends of the parallel lines, are correlated, we have six score matrices, as shown in Diagram 3-2. From these, six corresponding correlation matrices can be obtained and six corresponding factor-analytic techniques used.

The role of the Covariation Chart in theory development may perhaps most easily be illustrated by reference to Spearman's theory of "g" as general mental energy. From 1903 to 1943 (approximately) this was investigated in terms of individual differences, i.e., by R technique. However, if "g" is a unitary energy, theory would require also that the pattern vary within one and the same person, with changing physiological and other conditions, from day to day. That is to say, it should be possible to gather data on this theory from an additional set of possible relationships. The Covariation Chart shows us that these are definable as those of a P-technique research, i.e., taking one person's measures on several cognitive and other variables and correlating over many occasions.

Again, in such a concept as that of anxiety or of general autonomic reactivity, shown by Scheier (325) and others (240, 796, 484, 1516) to be a general factor by R technique, further theoretical issues have been raised. They have been raised by Endler, Hunt, and Rosenstein (464) in terms of a difference in intensity versus extensity across situations, by Lacey and Lacey (895, 896) in terms of idiosyncratic modes of expression, and by Cattell (325) in terms of the difference of a pathological, characterological anxiety on the one hand, and a healthy temporary reactive state of anxiety on the other (Chapter 22). These theories are given operational expression, for experimental testing, comparatively easily and clearly when the Covariation Chart is before one to indicate the possible systems of relationship. Again, when one considers in learning research the analyses of factor parameters in the learning curve made by Tucker (see Chapter 16 below), or of the changing compositions of skills made by Fleishman (531), the Covariation Chart is useful even at the stage of exposition in avoiding confusion in communicating the specific kind of covariation pattern about which one is theorizing.

Our purposes, therefore, in this chapter are:

(1) to ask more fundamentally and answer more explicitly the question of *how many* dimensions are finally needed in setting up a comprehensive, and, indeed, exhaustive system for recognizing the possible data relations that can be made the basis for psychological theory;

(2) to explore the *number and possible varieties* of analysis technique which become available in such an n-dimensional Covariation Chart or Basic Data Relation Matrix, and to agree on a standard nomenclature and notation by which the varieties may be intelligently and reliably handled in discussion;

(3) to bring out the *mutual relations* of the various possible relational analyses, and the properties of the latter when brought into conjunction with experimental designs and mathematico-statistical methods, as well as with different score-scaling methods.

Such explicitness, it is hoped, may save some initial blundering by "trial and error" in research design; may suggest, by its

orderliness, various new mutually supporting attacks on a theoretical problem; and
may give broader vision in planning, as well
as richer interpretation and perception of
implication in emerging theoretical constructs.

3. TWO PROTO-CONSTRUCTS: PATTERN ENTITY (VECTOR) AND ATTRIBUTE SCALE (SCALAR)

Before we can proceed to expand and
organize the Covariation Chart, however, it
behooves us to ask a still more fundamental
question regarding the rules by which
entries into the coordinate and cell system
of the Chart may be chosen. How, indeed,
do we conceive *data,* when we speak of it as
a system of "facts and relationships"?

One might wish to go back through
centuries of philosophical cogitation on this
question, but it is more practicable to start
comparatively recently with the formulation of a psychological methodologist,
Spearman, who himself surveyed these
centuries (*Psychology Down the Ages,* 1936).
In his laws of noegenesis, and elsewhere, he
referred all cognitive structure—all conceptual maps of the real world—to (1)
fundaments and (2) *relations* among fundaments. Without digressing into the phy-
logeny and ontogeny of perception, or into
epistemology, we may conclude that fundaments arise as sensory data or unitary
patterns of relations among sensory data,
and that the point in a hierarchy of relations
at which we recognize and split off a
fundament is a matter variously decided by
cultural convention, learning, and immediate purpose.

For example, a photographer may perceive as "the entity to be photographed"
the group, or the full-length person, or the
head only, for each of which we have a
word and for each of which there is some
degree of functional unity.

Now, in one sense or another, we can
consider the data of all sciences as sets of
such unitary *"objects"* and the *relations*
among these objects—the relations often
being generalized as "attributes" or properties of the objects. Thus a chemist may
deal with such *fundaments* (entities) as
chlorine and alcohol, and such *attributes* or
relations as solubility and smell. (An attribute is usually a generalization or abstraction from a variety of actually observed
relations.) A physicist may deal with elec-
trons and such relations as velocities, and a
psychologist may talk of entities such as
"neurotics" and attributes such as "popularity" or "speed of response." These two
constructs with which scientific fact-finding
must necessarily begin we shall call
proto-constructs, because they are pragmatically accepted universally and taken as
the natural basis of perception in scientific
observation. Entities and relations (or the
attributes distilled from relations) are thus
the primary perceptions or proto-constructs
out of which more refined constructs and
scientific concepts are derived and elaborated. Defining them for their greatest
generality of use, we shall refer to the
"objects" as *pattern-entities* and the "properties" as *attribute-scales* (or "patterns" and
"scales" respectively), for reasons soon to
be explained.

Incidentally, the recognition of these two
basic classes of external "fact" is woven into
all languages, namely, in nouns (for objects)
and adjectives, or initially verbs (for attributes and relations). Some adjectives derive from direct sensory effects—hot,
green, smelly—and others from relations
originally given in verbs. This direction of
change continues Locke and Hume's
primary division of attributes into primary
and secondary. Another way of viewing the
structure is in terms of reference points
between which relations exist and upon
which attributes are consequently hung, as
derivatives of the relations. A relationship
—"The dog chases the cat"—becomes, with
additional congruent evidence, the assignment of an "aggressiveness" *attribute* to the

dog, and a score on a "timidity" scale to the cat, and so on.[1]

Although the issue of defining these self-evident proto-constructs at the base of scientific observation has existed in all sciences, it has remained, curiously enough, for a latecomer, the psychologist, to develop the most explicit reasoning and methodology for locating them, namely, in the voluminous writing on "types" and "scales." This obviously arose because he was challenged more than the physical scientist or the biologist by the peculiar intangibility, in his science, of "type" or "trait," and by the boundless possibilities of disagreement thereon.

In accordance with these developments we shall recognize a "type" (see Chapter 9) as a particular *modal pattern* of quantitative values, occurring on a dimensional system extending across the genus in which such a species type belongs. An individual entity is similarly a unique (but not modal) pattern in the common dimensions that extend within the species type. So defined, the individual entity is a pattern or *vector* quantity, to the mathematician, and the attribute is a scalar. But this mathematical abstraction represents only one part of the truth. For instance, the "person entity" in the Covariation Chart is not defined *only* by those scales which are included in measurement entries in the given score chart. The latter may cover only psychological behavioral scales, but he is defined fully, as a "vector," also by his physical appearance measurements and many others beyond the given score matrix, such as the price of the suit he is wearing.

An unexpected point which the tyro in this field *must* keep in mind here is that the axes of the Covariation Chart or BDRM are *not* the quantitative axes he is accustomed to in the ordinary graph. They are constituted by *a series of entities* — people, tests, occasions — each a pattern or vector in a known but not usually an ordered sequence. (The individuals could be ordered in as many different ways as they have attributes.) The "intersection" of any two individual entities bounding the matrix (or facet, in Diagram 3-1) results in a cell (See Diagram 3-2, or *a, b,* etc. in Diagram 3-3.) which contains a quantity referring to some agreed attribute or relation of one or both of them. The pattern-entities arranged along any one coordinate of the Covariation Chart must belong to some one type (psychologically), species (biologically), or set (mathematically). Accordingly, to set up such a matrix we must know enough to distinguish the different "sets" into which individuals are to be gathered. Thus in the familiar chart we must be able to distinguish a person from a test, and a test from an occasion.

In summary, we begin at this stage by operating at a common-sense level, accepting the natural division of proto-concepts into two kinds: (1) objects, organisms, entities, or, more generally, *patterns,* or, in simplest mathematical form, vectors. These are recognizable by being particular combinations of measurements (vector quantities) on many attribute scales or dimensions, and by their retaining of these individual configurations with useful stability across place and time. (2) An *attribute* or *relation,* on the other hand, is something differentiating objects in the set, and along which they can be at least ranked (and possibly parametrically quantified) by a specified measurement operation. It is one element in the pattern. Parenthetically, we use *scale* for *any* variables, and do well to reserve the term *dimension* for a certain restricted set of scales with particularly important properties among variables, e.g., those which prove to be mutually mathe-

---

[1]Some will be disposed to go off here into the question of which has priority — the object or the attribute. Whether we pursue this phylogenetically and logically with the epistemologist, or ontogenetically with the gestaltist or perception theorist, it remains, for our present purposes, no more relevant than "Which came first, the chicken or the egg?" and admits of the same answer.

matically independent or recognized as unitary source traits, and which will be much less numerous than variables (scales) generally.

4. THE TEN COORDINATES OF THE HYPERSPACE BDRM

Reverting from generalities across all science to the particular needs and stock in trade of psychology, we note that three or four types of pattern-entities, according to area, have been generally recognized in psychology so far. The general experimentalist has thought of four, as follows:

(1) Organisms (people, animals, organized groups),

(2) States (inner transient drive conditions, mood patterns, motivational configurations),

(3) Stimuli or particular external situations,

(4) Particular patterns of response or of discrete recognizable processes in the continuous, ongoing behavior process.

The last two were originally combined in the Covariation Chart as "tests"—a particular stimulus and particular permitted response. The corresponding *scale* scores entered into a record of experiment, or a score matrix, for calculation are then seen as measurable attributes of (and relations among) such person, process, stimulus, etc., patterns.

Now, it has just been indicated that we do not consider the three sets of the original Covariation Chart—persons, tests (or stimuli and response types), occasions— as truly exhaustive of the sets needed in a more advanced treatment. Let us, therefore, ask what additional sets are indispensable, and let us discuss the criteria by which a non-arbitrary choice of the number and nature of sets of patterns can be made.

Doubt about the adequacy of only three kinds of set begins when one considers the *test* axis or set and recognizes that a test is itself a stimulus-response pattern, i.e., a conjunction of two patterns. Consequently,

one could obviously give separate consideration to the properties of stimulus situations on the one hand and response patterns on the other. For a stimulus and a response are not to be considered as bound in eternal wedlock. Only in certain artificial laboratory experiments and psychometric textbooks is there one and only one type of response to be made to a stimulus. Among these marriages are those we call "tests," but more widely, e.g., in personality and social research, we recognize that the tie is not indissoluble and that quite a variety of different response patterns, each scorable along its own continuum, often can be made to one and the same stimulus. Consequently, we must first split the "test" axis into a stimulus series set and a response series set.

Similarly, an "occasion," state, or condition can be defined by two very different things: the internal state of the organism, e.g., hunger, rage, sleep, on the one hand, and the background situation surrounding the focal stimulus, e.g., the room temperature, illumination, visibility of the observers, etc., on the other. Parenthetically, let us at once set aside the misconception of identifying an "occasion" merely with a score *point* on a *time axis*. Time and space axes are scalar attributes—part of the measurement of the pattern of an occasion —but psychologically often its least important attributes. (Moreover, time and space are attributes equally used in defining the organism and other entities.) "Occasion," therefore, is primarily defined by *conditions*. And since the conditions at a given moment are independently variable inside and outside the organism we need independent series or sets for each. Accordingly, what was allowed to fuse into a single total pattern—"an occasion" in the original covariation chart—must now be recognized as a conjunction of two patterns distinct in kind and independently variable: the internal conditions or the state, and the external conditions or the environment. The distinction of (1) this background condition of the environment from (2) the focal stimulus in the environment is something we shall have to discuss further.

At this point in exploration, especially as one ponders on the claim for independence of focal stimulus and background condition one may begin to wonder if there are not just four or five pattern-entity sets as so far considered, but as many sets as one can have concepts of, in the whole of psychological theory. However, to reject this wider, looser, subjective, non-operational scheme, it is necessary first to remember that we are so far dealing with the number of basic possible types of experimentally observable variables out of which the superstructure of psychological theory and its concepts can be built rather than with the concepts themselves. The derivable concepts are infinite, but behavioral science, founded on the observation of behavior, must initially concern itself with whatever can be operationally independently varied. It is not concerned merely with what can be independently conceived, for the latter will depend on each individual's private furniture of ideas. To fix the bounds to the number of sets of entities, therefore, we need to be guided by the definition of experiment in Chapter 2 (which includes, for example, both manipulated and unmanipulated situations). Within this framework of action we now see that a pattern entity is defined as something that can change or be changed without compelling any change in the entities of all the other sets with which it was combined. The changing of an entity, however, does not necessarily have to be under the command of the experimenter's will, i.e., be manipulable. It qualifies as a representative of a discrete set if at least it is capable of naturally varying independently of other entities. This can be recognized by, for example, the fact that it can be independently recognized and measured, as it creates its fresh "behavioral event" combinations. That the response to a test A can be made by either Bill or Harry,

and that either can respond to a test B instead of A suffices to give people and tests status as separate sets.

The distinction of sets which at first glance is more suspect of subjectivity than the others is that between focal stimulus and background environmental condition. It may be objected that we do not know which is stimulus and which background until we have pursued experiment long enough to find the regularities in the organism's response which solve this problem. This is true, but the fact remains that without any dependence on perceptual introspection we can arbitrarily locate a stimulus and vary it operationally in independence of the background. Another objection might be that one is going thus arbitrarily to cut off a part. It is possible to vary not just two parts of the external environment but many. Perhaps one needs a whole series of sets to represent external environment. The most cogent answer seems to be that it is the universal nature of mind to focus on, and give response to, one part of the environment. The duality of stimulus and background is deeply rooted in the nature of perception and an experimenter can vary them independently.

A few critics have objected to the distinction of the person and the state of the person. However, it should be evident that the behavioral event of John Smith, sitting at home, responding by laughter to a joke presented as a stimulus by his friend Bill, will be a different kind of behavioral event depending on whether he is in (1) an irate mood, or (2) a genial mood. Internal condition (or the history of previous treatment which produces it) is, therefore, a discrete observable entity — a state — capable of varying independently (even though it is rarely fully manipulatable).

A fifth set which must be added — especially in view of the recent work on instrument factors and image factors by Becker (85), and Campbell and Fiske (183), and Cattell and Digman (281) in the measurement of personality—is the *observer*. The motion and action of the observer are now recognized to be important matters for record even in physics (as in the Heisenberg indeterminacy principle) and indeed were first recognized in astronomy, as the "personal equation." The observer—as the psychiatrist projecting his own interpretations into the behavior of the patient, or simply as the unreliable scorer—as well as his personal states, is obviously even more important in psychology. One may, indeed, anticipate in the next decade a considerable development in psychological relativity. Hopefully, the needed allowances will prove to be small in laboratory experiment, but in social and clinical data, by the *in situ* methods, very systematic correction, according to new laws, by observer characteristics of observer observations, may be necessary in obtaining true data on subjects per se. Undoubtedly, therefore, any complete account of a psychological experiment should include a record of the observer and his relations to the other entities.

Finally, since every one of these five entities (person, stimulus, response, background, and observer) can vary with time and circumstance—in its own peculiar modes of variation—there should be five additional "occasion" terms, one for each of them, defining the *condition* in which each stands. Since, in Shakespeare's phrase "every fair from fair sometimes declines," any entity has to be represented both by its standard or mean condition—its *traits*—and by its pattern of deviation at any given moment—its *states*. This variation is more traditionally recognized in some of the five —a person's mood, an observer's standards, a climatic shift in the "background"—than in others, namely, the stimulus and the response. However, the response of, say, a man kissing his wife goodbye to go to work, is different in kind (pattern) from time to time, and though one might measure some fixed aspect of it, he might have to recognize several distinct "types" (patterns) best

placed on series of their own. Similarly for the stimulus: it is likely to admit of distinct phases: no two dawns that wake us are alike.

A ten-dimensional BDRM (or, to be precise, one bounded by ten sets) will undoubtedly strike some psychologists as an appalling complication of the original three-dimensional analysis. However, if these are the true dimensions of independently operating sources of variance in any observed psychological event, the needs of science dictate that we recognize and accept them. After all, as will be seen below, the number of dimensions can be restricted to three or four for particular purposes, and, properly handled by clear terminology and notation, they are not cumbersome.

Indeed, the only likely misgiving of the thoughtful psychologist is that perhaps an eleventh and twelfth set might need to be added—namely, a sixth pattern and its varieties of "state." In much research we are contrasting and comparing scores where antecedent conditions are different. The person has been exposed to this or that conditioning, or family background, or prior instruction or medication. Where does such a series or dichotomy of levels enter? Our answer is that this is already taken care of either by "the subject" or by the "condition of the subject" set, since the present person or condition is properly regarded as containing whatever influences have been applied before the experiment. Many other manipulatable or independently varying conditions and patterns will doubtless need to be discussed, but our contention is that the ten types of pattern here chosen are in a real sense more fundamental than any others that might be considered, and that they *suffice* to define a behavioral event.

To say that they are the most fundamental and necessary, however, is not to say that they are simply coordinate and "on a par" in importance or frequency of usefulness. In the first place, there is obviously a two-class structure of sets, dividing them broadly into fixed "trait" and transient "state" patterns — the five types of inter-individual patterns and the five corresponding sets of state variants. Second, few psychologists will take the recording of the observer as seriously as the recording of, say person, stimulus, and response. To include him is likely to remain an ideal "custom more honored in the breach than in the observance." The internal condition of the subject, except where hunger, previous learning, special instruction sets, and other "modulators" (259) have been deliberately manipulatively arranged, is likely to go unrecorded.

These differences of accepted emphasis will be commonly admitted, but probably the greatest issue of doubt and debate will be the separation we have just critically discussed of the former "outer condition" environment or occasion into what we may more accurately call a focal stimulus and an ambient stimulus[2] (259) or environmental background condition. The split has recently been questioned by Coan (350), for example. Certainly a duality here may remain for a time scarcely comprehensible to those accustomed to handling environment under that doctrinaire monolith "the stimulus." The contention above has been that the separation is based on (1) consistent difference of the organism's perceptual reactions, (2) their independent variation either manipulatively or non-manipulatively. It must nevertheless be admitted that fractions of the background can also be manipulatively handled independently. Actually locating the boundaries of focal and ambient stimulus, by experiment and not by fiat, may be a relatively difficult

matter. But, as pointed out above, there is in principle always the "attended to" and the "unattended to" and they can be clearly distinguished and independently varied. Incidentally, focal stimulus, background stimulus, and response were, of course, all three tied together in a single entity — a test — in the original person-test-occasion Co-variation Chart.

Accordingly, we finish with ten sets — five relatively permanent kinds of pattern and five covering the transient states in each. And although we recognize that the BDRM *can* at any time have its coordinates collapsed to revert to some simpler desired treatment, yet to correspond to the realities of possible independent occurrence it requires ten dimensions.[3] With the ten sets constituting the *coordinate system* of the data box thus defined, let us now ask about the nature of the entries. These are scalar values — measures on continua — and thus differ from the *patterns* (in the simplest, linear sense vectors) which bound the matrix. But *what kinds* of continua (or alternatively polar dichotomies or non-parametric series) are admissible for these attribute entries?

The typical experimental data matrix is a slab or facet, such as would come from cutting a one-pattern-thick slab from the box in Diagram 3-1, as shown in Diagram 3-2, but which we have reproduced in more general form in Diagram 3-3. In order to enforce and maintain some generality of thinking, we have not here designated Set 1 as some particular kind of entity as was done in Diagram 3-2. The set might be persons, states of the environment, observers, and so on through each of the ten possible coordinates. The slab or facet is bounded by n patterns of the X or Set 1 kind and m of the Y or Set 2 kind and is, of course, only

---

[2]For lack of space, the reader must be referred elsewhere (259) for a fuller defense and operational realization of this distinction. Although always unstable, because it hinges on the subject's play of attention, the division into classical "stimuli" and other "conditions" affecting the subject (other than by direct, conscious psychological response), is, one must conclude, a very important one.

[3]For the sake of brevity, let us from this point on refer to the Basic Data Relation Matrix as BDRM, or, colloquially, as the data box, for it is indeed the scientist's complete box of data — of all facts and relations available for study.

TABLE 3-1

COMPREHENSIVE COORDINATES OF THE
BASIC DATA RELATION MATRIX*

Proto-Types
   1. Person or organism.
   2. Focal stimulus, associated with instruction to attend.
   3. Environmental background other than stimulus (non-focal stimulus).
   4. Response or unitary ongoing process.
   5. Observer.

Variants
   6. *State* of the organism (including adoption of a role and exposure to specific learning experience).
   7. *Variant* of the stimulus.
   8. *Phase* of the environmental background.
   9. *Style* of the response.
   10. *Condition* of the observer.

---

*It has been suggested by Coan (350) that these coordinates be regarded as nominal scales. Such an idea may help to emphasize the distinction from the attributes, which are true interval scales, but it perhaps does not sufficiently draw attention to the fact that they consist of a series of patterns or vectors, not single values.

one pattern entity thick on Set 3, i.e., all the entries in the XY matrix of "scores" apply to one fixed entity in the Z set, e.g., one observer, one state of the stimulus.

Psychologists are so accustomed to writing response measures as the only cell entries that it is necessary now to become explicit in stating that the attribute quantity (let us henceforth talk in parametric terms) entered may refer to a score on position on attribute scales other than some aspect of a response. For example, when the bounding sets are persons and stimuli the entries could be measures on attributes of observers — at the mode or event when person, stimulus and observer come together, of course. These varieties possible in entries we shall call *modes* of entries. Commonly psychologists deal with response modes, but also with modes of persons, states, conditions, etc. This matter will be discussed from various angles at various points in

this chapter, but essentially we can recognize the following possibilities for entries.

Possible Cell Entry Modes in the BDRM

Broadly, there are two kinds of modes:

(1) A *relation*. The entry at a (Diagram 3-3) may simply represent the magnitude of a relation between the entities X_j and Y_t, e.g., their distance apart, the number of times X_j meets Y_t in a month, etc.

(2) An *attribute* of either X or Y. In principle an attribute is an abstraction from the relations of pattern entity X_j to most other kinds of entities. But this must be an attribute that changes as X comes into conjunction with different Y's (or Y with different X's). For otherwise, we can make no relational calculation. A second point to keep in mind about the attribute is that merely naming the pattern entity does not tell us or define what attribute is considered in the cell. For example, I may correlate responses of trying to solve various mechanical puzzles, over a set of people. But naming the puzzles and responses does not say what attribute of the response is measured. It might be speed, number of errors, etc. For any single entity, X_j, or its set, X, has a great number of possible attributes. Consequently the attribute is something needing to be defined apart from and in addition to the coordinates, with which it is associated. The facet requires two sets and an attribute measure designation to define what it is about.

Either a relation or an attribute can be defined as *the same* over the whole face of the facet score matrix, e.g., if X's were *stimuli* and Y's were *people,* the entries could be everywhere — at a, b, c, and d — *frequencies* of the person's past encounters with the stimuli, or *speeds* (in seconds) to respond to them. Alternatively, also for *both* relations and attributes, the nature of the entry can be peculiar to one column or one row, e.g., the X_j column might be speed of response to the stimulus X_j, and

DIAGRAM 3-3. *A Typical Facet with Relatives, Referees, and Attribute Entries Indicated*

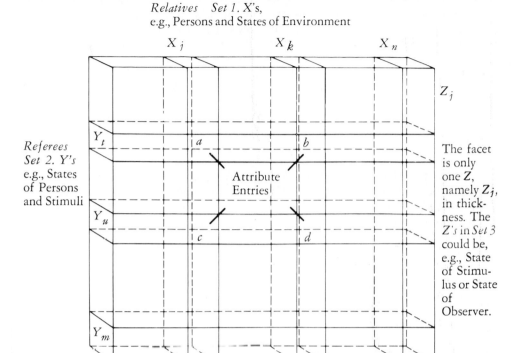

Relatives   Set 1. X's,
e.g., Persons and States of Environment

X_j X_k X_n

Z_j

Referees Set 2. Y's e.g., States of Persons and Stimuli

Y_t a b

Attribute Entries

Y_u

c d

Y_m

The facet is only one Z, namely Z_j, in thickness. The Z's in *Set 3* could be, e.g., State of Stimulus or State of Observer.

The terms "relative" and "referee" are defined more completely in the text. They do not define positions in the matrix — either rows or columns can be the relatives — but only the direction of analytic operation upon the matrix. Thus correlations, *t* tests, chi squares, etc. look for relations *among the relatives,* and *over* the referees, e.g., correlations of tests over persons.

the X_k column number of words recognized in stimulus X_k. This is particularly frequent in bivariate experimental designs. Consequently, these measures are independent of the entities X_j and X_k at the head of the column, and not defined by them. For one can imagine them attached reciprocally the other way around.

As a result, to describe the data box completely requires also that we define the attribute entries (or "indicators," as they may be called in some broader sense), as well as the bounding sets. Furthermore, in what may be called a *unimodal uniform entry matrix,* the definition need not be be peculiar in nature to particular entities, whether relatives or referees. But in a *multimodal* matrix it is necessary to state which attributes or relations are appropriate to which relative. (From the explanation at the bottom of Diagram 3-3, it will be evident that indicators, as quantities, are defined for [tied to] relatives only, not referees.) Thus a unimodal matrix might have entries which are all reaction times to various stimuli, whereas if one column were reaction time indicators, another distance in a maze, another words recognized, etc., we would have a matrix of multimodal entries.

Having defined the coordinate *sets* and the *entries,* let us deal with the frequent suggestion that time and space coordinates beyond the ten listed in Table 3-1 should be added to the data box. Clearly, however, they are not entities in sets like the ten classes of patterns, but *continua*. As descriptive *attributes* of patterns in a set they clearly fall in the class of *entries* and can be used for either relations or attribute entries. Further, they belong to the class of possible *uniform* entries or attributes, in that all sets and all entities in all sets have a location in space and time. Indeed, these attributes are of a peculiarly universal quality, which is shared only with a limited class of broad and sometimes metaphorical attributes, e.g., ripeness, strength, age. (It is not our purpose to make a taxonomy of attributes and relations, but one can recognize that there are some which cut across all sets, some of them negotiable across a single set, e.g., intelligence across people, cost across stimuli, and temperature across environments, and some which apply only as special attributes of one entity.)

Besides this universality, shared with a few attributes, there is, however, a second and more absolute peculiarity of a time measurement, namely, that entities can move only one way along this continuum. And this is an unescapable and important quality to the psychologist. It affects, for example, the meaning of learning and development scores, and sometimes makes the sequence in test scores of importance. When test scores go into a matrix we may choose to consider them approximately simultaneous in recording, but true simultaneity is practically never attained. Stimulus and response occur only at *approximately* the same moment, and so on.

Time must also be considered in its relation to the five *variant sets* — P', E', A', S', O' — which we called variants of the five entities P, E, A, S, O (Table 3-2, page 86 below). Almost necessarily, these variants imply a variation in time, and belong to the axis called "occasions" in the original Covariation Chart.

A special symmetrical relation of two kinds of sets has been noted in Table 3-1.

The second five coordinate sets "repeat" the first five in the sense of being particular types of state pattern deviations from the mean pattern of the corresponding entity in the first five. The deviations occur from the mean not of a single variable, but of a whole vector — a whole pattern of deviation. It is important in an experiment whether the animal is or is not hungry; whether the environment — say, Monday morning — is a cheerful or a rainy Monday morning; and whether the observer is alert or fatigued. These unavoidable, or even deliberately engineered, variants need representation in the data matrix; hence the need of axes both for the persons and the states of the persons, and so on for the other four sets.

But although these variations almost always imply occurrence at different times, we may in analysis *not* be concerned with time sequence but only with *the differences in and of themselves.* For example, it is interesting to find that people make more errors in anxious states than in unanxious ones, regardless of sequences. On the other hand, if relations to time sequences, etc., *are* to be investigated, it will be largely through using the time attribute as the entry in the score matrix on these variants. For example, the generalization that rigidity increases with fatigue (hours since sleep) was made by correlating, for single individuals, such a state attribute score as time of day with a state attribute score of rigidity (P technique). Time is therefore just another attribute score, but one with some special properties and some particular involvement with the five variants axes.

The use of the deviational conditions or variants (called for clarity by different names for different entities — state of a person, style of a response, condition of an observer, etc.) perhaps deserves a little more justification and description. It is perhaps not sufficiently recognized in research design that only in extreme conditions of laboratory control is the stimulus really constant. Such a stimulus as the child's mother (changing emotionally), the environment (changing as to temperature, atmosphere, etc.), a particular stipulated kind of response (changing as to style) will vary for the same person and observer from day to day. And since the basic data matrix aims to take account of all sources of variance, it must include the possibility of a coordinate set expressing the actual variants on a given defined stimulus, response, etc. Indeed, so long as these variants can be separately recognized and measured, it is appropriate to have separate axes for them. There is only this much difference between the series constituted by a lot of different stimuli and the coordinate series constituted by the variants on a stimulus: the former range across species, genera, and orders, whereas the latter are variants of a species, i.e., as patterns they vary in some absolute sense *less,* about a central pattern.[4]

In conclusion of this phase of exposition let us anticipate debate of the statement that (a) all ten sets are necessary, and (b) that they are exhaustive, i.e., that no more than these are necessary. Since the present writer had already extended the 1946 Covariation Chart in 1957 to include all of the above but the *observer* and his *condition,* these last two sets will probably occasion most debate. To exclude these would be the equivalent in psychology of operating in a Newtonian rather than a relativistic framework. And, as the recent work on the phenomenon of "instrument" and "observer" factors (250, 281) shows, the effects of the relativity of an observation to the observer are much grosser in psychology than in physics. Nevertheless, it may often be a defensible simplification in certain discussions here and elsewhere to deal with eight axes only, taking the perfectly reliable observer for granted.

Naturally, it is possible to think of coordinate sets beyond these ten that could be added, but they are always in some sense subdivisions or derivations of the basic ten. For example, as mentioned earlier, the environmental situation could be subdivided further, beyond "focal stimulus" and "ambient stimulus or environmental background," while the observer could be usefully divided in some special studies into the "observer as a person" and the "instruments of observation," since these could be independently varied. If one wishes to do this the necessary extensions of the following generalizations on the basic ten will be self-evident.

At this point we may note that there is some danger, in almost any taxonomic system, of becoming involved in the spent arguments covered by the scholastics regarding nominalism-vs.-realism. The recognition and labeling of sets do not, however, involve us in any greater "reification" than occurs in any other concepts we use. The patterns or entities exist, as such, in the minds of the investigator, but he can give operations for recognizing them. Nor does such classification of species of objects, e.g., people, tests, deny certain other possible classifications. However, our arguments do claim that the present sets combine maximum operationalism of definition, with independence of natural action, and aptness to theoretical concept development. Chief among the alternative patterns which can be recognized, are those constituted by special *combinations* of these more elementary constituent patterns of person, stimulus situation, and response, e.g., a test, but also one can conceive a few new patterns or sets at the level of these ten constituents.

There is always one sense in which the pure theorist can claim that the sets of entities are arbitrary, namely, that he can mathematically conceive far more varied combinations of the attribute elements than appear in any of the sets of patterns he is asked to deal with. However, this

---

[4]It will be noted that in the simple Covariation Chart all variants are really lumped together, in a series of single composites of variants, in the occasions axis. That is, an occasion is a particular state of the person accidentally (but not necessarily randomly) combined with some variant of the stimulus, phase of the environmental background, style of response, etc.

is a fact of nature not of subjective selection and can perhaps be kept in mind by calling it the *principle of selective natural realization*. According to this, when any system of dimensions, attributes, predicates, parameters, or whatever we wish to call them, already obtains in a given area, not all the mathematically possible quantitative or qualitative combinations thereof will be found to exist. In the biological realm this is clearly due to natural selection for survival, whereby certain combinations would be inefficient, e.g., legs and gills, and presumably, the same is true in the social world and even the physical world. This accounts both for all "possible" species not appearing in a genus and for the gaps that make genuses quite distinct and separable. Our contention is that the properties of, say, a test stimulus (instruction, test materials, score key, etc.) and of a person (physical organs, nervous system, etc.), although they possess some common parameters such as those above (e.g., spatial size, age), are such that no intermediates can arise. That is to say, the choice of sets such as people, stimuli, etc., is to that extent non-arbitrary and inevitable.

So much for the legitimate basic questionings of the philosophers. Critics from the opposite side, mainly robust applied psychologists unsympathetic to abstractions, have doubted not so much the distinctness and discreteness of the ten sets, as our right to consider them coordinate and equivalent in any single system. Chiefly under fire here is the contention to which the present writer (213), as well as Burt (158, 160), Brunswik (152), and Guttman (651), has contributed, that the notions of "population" and "sampling" developed for people are applicable also to the other sets, under certain circumstances. The present writer's concept of the personality sphere in 1946 (213) and Brunswik's (152) representative sampling of variables in 1951 explicitly developed the notion that a "population" of responses, stimuli, tests, etc., can be said to exist, from which one may take a random sample, or a stratified

sample or a biased sample (240, p. 808) just as with people. The notion is fully implicit in the "R dimension" (representativeness) of experimental design in the last chapter, according to which we deliberately make a selection *of* the variables in addition to making selection *on* the variables (Dimension *D,* distribution) over people, etc.

Several other equivalences and comparabilities of the ten sets have been mentioned and could be explored with more space; but this question of equivalence for statistical operations deserves especial discussion. It is true that in most current experiments people are of one species, whereas the tests or stimulus sets contain entities that appear as disparate as cats, cabbages, and kings. The question of just how uniform a "set" of responses, stimuli, states, etc., are in comparison to people must be decided empirically. They may differ appreciably in the number of subspecies and the normality of distributions, etc. Some sampling laws, notably those on such simple statistics as means and variances, make no demands on assumptions about normal distribution or belonging to a single species. Others, in more complex statistics, such as those connected with factor analysis, are more sensitive to distribution conditions. So far, no adequate arguments have been presented against treating the other sets of the BDRM by any different sampling assumptions from those we have customarily applied to people.

As the picture of the Basic Data Relation Matrix or data box now finally shapes itself, we see that it contains all possible elements of data: the *ids* (see below) or entities in the sets and, potentially, all modes of attributes and relations among them. Thus "data" in the broader sense covers sets and the attributes or relations among them observable in experiment and susceptible to quantitative examination. The only question that remains is whether the person "patterns" or entities, stimulus entities, response patterns, etc., which constitute the bounding coordinate sets of the box are (1) required each to meet the conditions merely defining a mathematical set, as such, or additionally to conform to the properties of a single "species," and (2) mutually interchangeable, one set with another, for purposes of mathematical treatment and the meaning of analysis.

As to the first question, the difference is that a mathematical set can be quite arbitrarily defined or indicated, whereas a species implies that the members are in some sense an organic type, meeting the measurement condition of being all more like each other than they are like some other patterns in a larger universe of varying patterns. Basically our model has no restriction to use only of species, but deals with sets in the standard mathematical sense. However, further restrictions are often added in actual usage in behavioral and life sciences and mostly we do deal with species. However, often with a broad species or genus, e.g., of person, responses, or stimuli, we work with fairly arbitrary sets. This arbitrariness, sometimes apparently expressive of a theoretical uncertainty about method, has shown itself especially in the studies where the entities are groups. In some of the group dynamic correlation studies of Gibb (593), Cattell and Stice (329), Hemphill and Westie (717) and Lawson and Cattell (907), or nations (Adelson, 265; Cattell, 224; Gibb, 593; Rummel, 1241; and Guetzkow, 620), no preliminary demonstration has been given that the entities are of one species. One must begin somewhere, and it is permissible to begin with what might be a mixture of species, provided one is clear that until further analysis has been made the conclusions refer only to that mixture.

This consideration of the nature of sets brings us a distinction which is very important in the actual score matrix or facet, namely that between the set which may be called the *relatives* and the set which constitutes the *referees*. As one ordinarily thinks of a score matrix the entities (their attributes to be exact) across the top play the role of relatives — the things that are to be related. The set down the side plays the role of constituting the referees — those entities to which the relationship refers. When we correlate, or do statistical *t* tests, with respect to relatives, we are asking how the relatives are related (over the referees). Commonly, in *R* technique we relate response measures across people. If we are not sure that our people constitute a single species we may, beginning with a sample of responses for referees, use *Q'* technique to find whether in fact we have a reasonably uniform species of people. For before proceeding to ask how tests are related there is some logic for restricting the set of referees to a species.

Parenthetically, the term "mode" has sometimes been used for *set,* notably by such a leader as Tucker, but after careful consideration, we find this term less satisfactory. It is derived from the Latin "modus," a measure, and this is precisely what a set is not. The measure goes into the cell of the matrix as a scaled "attribute" or "relation" entry. Any single entity we shall henceforth for brevity refer to as an id (Latin "it") for an *individual* in a set. Any id, as we have said, is always a pattern or organism (and mathematically a vector). The term mode has a useful role, as shown above, in describing varieties of measures that go into the cells and for this we shall reserve it here. For example, when correlating responses as relatives over people as referees, one might do so with three different modes of attribute: of responses, of people, or of stimuli. In summary, then, the coordinates will be systematically and consistently defined as *sets* (of ids). The data box is thus a ten-set matrix of ids.

In regard to the interchangeableness of the sets in any analytical treatment, it is difficult to argue that they are in all respects equivalent and coordinate. Principally, we have to recognize the inevitable time sequence relation of the stimulus and the response, which puts them out of line with the other sets. Incidentally, it would be incorrect to claim some unique belonging of the response to the organism, for it "belongs" also to the stimulus, the environment, the state, etc. The observer-experimenter set might also be claimed to lack some equivalence with the others, since he stands further outside the behavioral event. With these exceptions, however, the implications of which for interchangeability of sets will gradually be clarified, the data box may be rolled over for analysis in any direction with essential equivalence of the types of conclusion possible.

Let us finally consider the attributes and their modes. The attribute value written in a cell is part of the description of a total event at which the bounding ids have all come together. The person, the stimulus, the state, the observer, etc., have come together in a unique event, and they are the "signatures" (or subscripts) which uniquely locate that measurement of the event, as follows: $a_{sapeos'a'p'e'o'}$, the subscripts each indicating one id from one set, and a being the chosen attribute of the event or part of the event. The measurement, a — or, to be precise, the attribute or relation on which it is made — is only one of a vast number of possible dimensions. In the most familiar case, a person has met a stimulus and reacted with a certain type of response pattern. The cell entry in the score matrix is typically a dimension of the response, e.g., its speed, its correctness, an electrical resistance change, a degree of fear, etc. In talking about *the* response measure it is seemingly often forgotten that a particular response can be measured across hundreds of different aspects, constituting different sub-modes. It is still less realized that the mode of entry in a person set-response set, a person set-state set, a stimulus set-state set matrix could be *any* relation of the two ids, e.g., the age of the subject when he made the response, the frequency with which the average man encounters the stimulus when in that state, and so on. It does not need to be a mode (attribute, relation) of the bounding sets of that particular facet (score matrix). In the broadest sense, the entry is a relation or quality in the total pattern of the event. It could be the color of the stimulus, the

temperature of the environment, the intelligence of the observer — all at the moment the event (node) occurred which bound together the various ids (one from each set) involved. The numerical value of the mode is peculiar to the *node*, i.e. it is some attribute or relation in the ten-id unique event, not just of the two kinds of set chosen for the given score matrix.

This somewhat abstruse issue must be pursued further below, after we are more accustomed to its setting. But at this point, let us recognize that the entries could be predicates (attributes) of any of the ten bouding id sets that are peculiar (in identity) to that event. From analyses of the various kinds of measurements possible in such entries, we arrive at a desired fuller knowledge of the characteristics and structure of not just one but all the bounding sets. For example, response measures are the raw material from which we infer knowledge about persons, states, responses, and situations. Stimulus relation measures would also throw light on the characters of all sets, e.g., the frequency with which a man meets a stimulus is part of the observational basis both for knowing something about the man and something about the cultural ecology of stimuli. The *meaning* of all sets therefore resides in all the possible modes of entries that can be inserted into the cells between them.

What we commonly use as concepts in employing verbal attributes are derived, implicitly, from such entry measures. In any one BDRM, although normally there are many different modes of entry (one kind for each column, e.g., responses on test A in column 1, on test B in column 2, etc.) — defined by information in "footnotes" additional to the BDRM itself — they far from suffice to define all the attributes of all the sets. Conceivably an infinite data box — infinite in columns and rows on all sets and repeated for an infinite variety of entries — would do so. But from any given entries in a data matrix the number of qualities of the set entities that are inferable constitutes only a small part of what is necessary to define the objects.

Another way of looking at the id-entry relation is to recall that scores can be represented by placing people in a space (sometimes called the "test space," but actually a response-attribute or entry space) by projections representing their magnitudes on each kind of relative entry. Alternatively, one can place people as orthogonal axes and represent the attributes by positions corresponding to scores — called the person space. This is a mode of representation often employed in handling the *R*-technique-*Q*-technique transpose problem.

Regardless of mode of representation, the meaning and description of any entity (pattern), on the one hand, or of any attribute dimension (entry) on the other, comes from the magnitudes of relations (of all modes) used as entries and referred to entities (patterns) in the data matrix. A person of wide methodological interest may at this point want to ask how far the BDRM is applicable beyond psychology to all the sciences. This we have no space to pursue, but with slight removals of restrictions, it looks as if it would be applicable. The chemist or physicist, for example, deals similarly with entities and relations. He would speak of the "reaction" of sodium when it meets the stimulus of water, but, except that he will find different properties for organismic and non-organismic entities, his paradigm of observation is very similar. Presumably the design fits the investigatory acts and conceptual needs of all sciences. The psychologist manifests the biases of his craft only in spending more time in that area of the BDRM concerned with interactions of organisms with stimuli!

5. THE NATURE AND DEFINITION OF A BDRM FACET

The foregoing can be summarized by saying that an observable "experimental" event may be regarded as a *node* or knot at which one of each of the above ten sets intersects or comes into a combined event.

An event may be viewed as an integral *total* pattern-entity — absorbing the ten individual patterns — the uniqueness of which is definable and recordable by a particular person, a particular stimulus, a particular observer, etc., tagged to the particular attribute measurement we choose to operate upon.

To proceed to further analysis of the possible relations, we must now agree on a notation system. Although a mathematician is free to use whichever symbols he chooses, there are substantial advantages (as illustrated further in Chapter 5) in using a notation which is (1) mnemonic, reminding us easily of the names for the referents, (2) non-overlapping with other accepted psychological symbol uses,[5] and (3) stable. It is particularly important to ensure that the psychologist does not encounter confusions and contradictions in going from one area, e.g., personality theory, to another, e.g., learning theory or group dynamics. Accordingly, an attempt has been made throughout this book where possible to bring contributors to a common system. However, where a practice is not explained, we must ask the reader to believe that there *are* good reasons for the choice of a particular symbol (which the reader may well find in the morasses encountered when he departs therefrom!).

To begin with, let us symbolize the ten coordinate sets of the Basic Data Relation Matrix as described in Table 3-1 (page 78) by the code given in Table 3-2. As a mnemonic aid it should be noted that the symbols for the five primary coordinates make the word *SAPEO*. These symbols are repeated with primes, $S'A'P'E'O'$, for the

---

[5]In a period when experimenters complain about the waste involved in scientists learning several foreign languages, it is a little inconsistent that some prima donnas among statisticians follow the whim to change their symbol system every time they write! For mathematics is a language and for the student, and the person who is primarily a scientist, there is a great deal to be said, in terms of convenience and comprehension, for settling down to a standard language of symbols in his area.

TABLE 3-2

Proposed Symbol Code for Coordinates of BDRM

Nature of the Pattern Element or Id in the Set	Symbol for Set and Number of Ids	Symbol for Attribute Scales (Modes) by Entry Measurements on Which the Given Pattern (Id) May Have Its Dimensions Described
1. Focal Stimulus	S_1 to S_Q	s_1 to s_q
2. Variant on Stimulus	S'_1 to $S'_{Q'}$	s'_1 to $s'_{q'}$
3. Acts, Responses, or Behavior Process	A_1 to A_n	a_1 to a_n
4. Stage of Behavior Process	A'_1 to $A'_{n'}$	a'_1 to a'_e
5. Persons (or Organisms)	P_1 to P'_N	p_1 to p_N
6. States (Modulators, roles, learning)	P'_1 to $P_{N'}$	p'_1 to $p'_{N'}$
7. Environmental Backgrounds (ambient stimuli)	E_1 to E_V	e_1 to e_v
8. Phase of Environmental Background	E'_1 to E'_V	e'_1 to $e'_{v'}$
9. Observer	O_1 to O_F	o_1 to o_f
10. Condition of Observer	O'_1 to $O'_{F'}$	o'_1 to $o'_{f'}$

Total number of attribute measurements $= G \times G' \times n \times n' \ldots \times F \times F' = T$.
The N, D, etc., are the total numbers of ids. But any single id will henceforth be represented by a general case symbol thus:

    i is *any* individual, or, more fully P_i

    h is *any* stimulus, or, more fully S_h

    j is *any* response, or, more fully A_j

    l is *any* environmental background condition, or more fully E_l

    w is *any* observer, or, more fully O_w

(Primes in these are variants, e.g., i' is state of an individual.)
The reason for not using R as symbol for response lies in its long-accepted use as symbol for a correlation matrix. (Besides, act or performance often better describes its prolonged nature.) The reason for breaking the rule of capital subscripts for ids here is the traditional use of n for the number of response (test) measurements.

five transient conditions, to remind the reader of this special relation.

As the writer has suggested elsewhere (240), we may apply the term *facet* or face to the score matrix formed by any two of the above mentioned coordinate sets. (Strictly, when all ids in a set are of the same species we should speak of coordinate subsets; but for simplicity "sets" will in general be used for the coordinate ids.) Of the possible facets formed by combining pairs of the ten sets above, the most familiar to the reader are probably the two shown in Table 3-3. The first matrix (a) might be the scores of a set of children upon a set of personality tests, the entries being, perhaps, a constant minus the num-

ber of errors. Such a facet of scores forms a frequently employed basis for personality research. On the other hand, a process investigator, e.g., a learning theorist or perception researcher, would be more familiar with the second facet, (b) in which a set of stimuli or background conditions is brought into relation with a set of states.

Pursuing a precise nomenclature, we shall henceforth call a series of patterns of the same identical class a *set* of *ids* (as explained above) releasing *pattern* generically for each and all of the members in the ten diverse sets of ids. Thus each id in the person set (which becomes a coordinate) is a person, and each id in the stimulus coordinate set is a stimulus. A facet is thus formed when two sets of ids are arranged to border a rectangle. The numbers that go into the cells of such a facet will, of course, be called "entries," of various modes.

Attention must now be called to certain basic characteristics of a facet. From early mathematics we are accustomed to two coordinates or axes representing *dimensions,* on which positions may be assigned according to numerical values thereon.

person, a test, and a state or occasion. Let us postpone for a couple of paragraphs further discussion of the issue already opened above about the exact scope of the *entry,* and where it is obtained, and agree merely that it is an associated value placed in that cell. As pointed out above, the score number is finally to be tagged by *ten* ids, each a subscript to the entry. (For it is the score of a particular person,

TABLE 3-3

Two Possible Facets

(a) Facet for Personality Research						(b) Facet for Process Research					
(P) Persons	(S) Stimuli or "Tests"					(E) Environmental Background	(P') States in the Organism				
	S_1	S_2	...	...	S_g		P'_1	P'_2	...	...	$P'_{N'}$
P_1						E_1					
P_2						E_2					
P_3						E_3					
.						.					
.						.					
.						.					
P_N						E_D					

Entries are magnitudes on some response parameter.

Entries are magnitudes on some produced state.

Consequently, as pointed out above, we may overlook the vital fact that the Cartesian coordinates in this case are not dimensions but simply a series of *discrete* pattern-entities or ids. A simplified and three-dimensionally representable drawing can be used for reference here by reducing the ten sets to the three of the old Covariation Chart; this has been shown visually in Diagram 3-1 (page 69). The numerical entry that goes into a cell of this three-dimensional score matrix is a value associated with the conjunction of three things — three pattern-entities or ids — namely, a

in response to a particular stimulus, with a particular background, in a particular state of the subject, etc.) But here, in a *facet,* only two tags are immediately evident and recorded, though the rest exist and are implied.

Any *single behavioral event* to which one score is thus attached (and to which thousands of scores, as we have said, could potentially be given) we shall call a *node,* for it belongs as we have said to a "knot" formed by the conjunction, in a unique combination, of ten ids. The value given in any entry belongs to a node, and is in some lawful, scientific sense, a function of all ten of the involved ids, though only two may be explicit in the facet. Consequently, as we shall see, various analytic operations performed on these entry numbers contribute to understanding the attributes and dimensions of all the ten kinds of ids. However, the ids are, of course, defined by many measures which cannot enter any one matrix. We enter with, say, the subject's response magnitude, but he is defined also by his weight, his age, his number of relatives, his fingerprints, and many other things we should be unlikely to enter in a psychological matrix. What age a person has when he enters a certain situation does, however, happen to have relevance to sociological and economic analyses, and could, therefore, be entered in a matrix relating people and situations. The individual id or pattern is thus described and identified, in the case of the person set, ultimately by an indefinitely long profile of scale scores on age, intelligence, popularity, etc., and a stimulus may be described by weight, area, attractiveness, memory value, etc. And so on for the ids in other coordinates. Obviously, however, they cannot be entered into a finite matrix, no matter though it be the Basic Data Relation Matrix with all ten coordinates. One must imagine, therefore, that as many BDR matrices exist as there are modes of attributes to be measured, and that from analyzing all of these we should get the dimensions necessary to describe and structure all sets of ids.

A second important feature to keep in mind is that a facet is only one id thick. For example, it may relate scores of a set of people over a set of stimuli each made on *one* occasion; or those of a set of states over a set of people for *one* stimulus. Actually, we have two options in defining what might be called the off-facet ids (or simply the off-set ids or off-ids). First, when the entry applies to one of the bounding sets, and eight sets are, therefore, free to vary, we can assume that they *do* vary. For example, the score of Smith on response to stress (a $P \times S$ facet) may be assumed to be different in its occasion, observer, etc., from that of Brown. (Whether these differences are *recorded*, even though permitted, depends on the C dimension of experimental design.) The statement that a facet is one id thick must therefore be qualified by the comments (1) that it is one id thick on each of all eight of the off-sets, (2) that it can be the same id, for all entries, on the given off-set or many different ids on that off-set. For example, all people may be tested for a given response to all of a set of stimuli, on one background condition (occasion) only, but it need or need not be the *same* occasion, (3) that we must distinguish between (a) uncontrolled-vs.-controlled, and (b) unknown-vs.-known, off-id values (identities). Combinations of the latter give four possibilities.

As we typically use the term "controlled" (see page 22, Chapter 2), we mean both held constant *and* possessing a known value. To avoid proliferating terms for all combinations we shall speak of a *constant* or *fixed facet* when the single id on any off-set is not only known but held at the same fixed identity and value over the whole facet. This gives a neater experimental design and is statistically easier to handle, but it is actually very seldom attainable!

In the great majority of score matrices comprised by such a one-id-thick facet, the signature on the off-sets is different for every entry. Indeed, it is not only uncontrolled, but commonly unknown. For example, we have the response scores of persons on attitude test A in terms of a memory measure, but may not know what sort of a day it was given on or who gave it, or what state of hunger the person was in at the time. All that is assumed, apart from, say, the person and the attitude, is that the kind of response measured is the same, usually for one column, sometimes for a whole facet.

To recapitulate, the term off-sets (and off-ids) will henceforth mean those not directly represented and recorded in the coordinate sets bounding the facets. And two alternative recording possibilities are recognized for these unstated, unrepresented off-sets: they can each be held at a fixed id value, or they can be allowed to vary across all ids.[6] For exact reference, we shall call the former an off-set *fixed facet* or simply a *fixed* facet, i.e., where all off-set ids are held each at one fixed id value, and the latter an off-set *varied or mixed facet,* i.e., when they are allowed to vary over all possible members of those sets. In either case, a facet is formed by a two-set Cartesian coordinate system in which the remaining eight sets are visually unrepresented.

6. PRINCIPLES GOVERNING "ENTRIES": ASPECTS AND SHIFTS

One of our objectives in systematizing the data matrix is, as stated, to become aware of the possible number and nature of relational matrices within which theories may be defined. Merely to designate and list the number and nature of the possible pairs of sets which can form coordinates for homogeneous facets is an elementary exercise in calculating combinations. Ten sets two at a time make possible 45 kinds of score matrix, and since each can be analyzed in two directions (normal and transpose) we have 90 kinds of relational analyses. However, two further possibilities of relational treatment complicate and expand this taxonomy of relations.

First, one can form matrices in which one or both sets are mixed sets. For example, one can relate a stimulus id to a state id or an observer id (over people — organisms — as referees, for instance) as when one correlates the frequency with which rats have encountered a stimulus with the intensity of their anxiety state (measured as avoidance behavior). Thus, if we confine

ourselves to the set of relatives only, we can have a mixed set or a uniform set facet.

Second, with the ids thus fixed, one is still free to do a variety of things about entries. For the entry is only one of many possible attributes of a given id and is not defined by putting the id at the top of the column, e.g., a person might head a column, but whether his weight or his degree of hunger is to be entered opposite the environments in the rows is still to be defined. Psychologists have become so thoroughly accustomed to "measuring a response" to provide their variable and inserting the measure at once in the score matrix, that the statement in our introductory assertion that there are logically many other psychological experimental possibilities may evoke some incredulity. It may even have upset common assumption somewhat to assert that we are commonly not even measuring *the* response, but getting figures for only *one* continuum or dimension out of a very large number of possible attributes or aspects of the unique response pattern being studied.

Let us therefore undertake a more systematic examination of the nature of the entry and the ways in which it may be entered in the basic record of an experiment. Some five principles emerge, as follows:

(1) *An entry is either a relation or an attribute.* This has been sufficiently discussed above. The figure entered can express a *relation* between the two bounding ids, e.g., the frequency with which they meet, their distance (psychological or physical), which belongs no more to one than the other, or an *attribute magnitude* for any id in the node, along an attribute left undefined by the original definition of the two sets. *However, this must be an attribute which changes its immediate value for each relation to the other ids* and is to that extent a kind of relation. A true relation, however, can be regarded as an attribute immediately applicable to ids of both sets.

(2) *The specific value of the attribute of an*

[6]For example, we measure each of a set of persons on one response to each of a set of stimuli. But are the persons all held in one dynamic state, observed by one and the same observer, etc., or is there variance in these?

id on Set 1 can differ for each id on Set 2 either as a changing "aspect" or as a "shift," response, or reaction occurring in the immediate bringing together of these ids in the node. The former is illustrated by the changing visibility of a stimulus in different environments, the differing acquaintance-ship of a rater (observer) with different subjects, the differing mood states of a person as he is called upon to make different responses, etc. The latter is illustrated by the differing response magnitudes to different stimuli, the change of an environment occasioned by the person entering it, the effect of an observer upon a subject's state, etc. Generally, a shift value, for the pattern concerned, is considered to be what takes place during the brief or virtually instantaneous nodal event that is the object of observation. Normally, the other patterns in the node are considered to stand at fixed aspect values, or they can be tagged at their initial values. Of course, if the attribute or aspect remains the same over all referees, on all data box coordinates, it has no variance and no useful relations can be found. Assuming, for example that the IQ does not alter over a year, it would be no use trying to correlate it within a year-long *P*-technique study, but it would in an *R*-technique study in relation to, say, score on arithmetic. A *shift* is a *creation* of the node; an *aspect* is only an *accompanying part* of its definition. Since both attributes and relations can be either fixed, inherent aspects or shifts happening at that node, we actually have a fourfold classification of entries.

As pointed out above, the concentration on behavioral response entries, any instance of which constitutes a typical *shift* entry, has tended to obscure two facts, (1) that shift entries that are *not* responses can generally be conceived and measured also for the remaining nine kinds of id sets, and (2) that *aspects* as well as shifts are widely usable as entries. To exemplify the first: one could enter a change in the stimulus, a mutation in the condition of the background situation, or a shift in the condition of the observer. Consideration of this issue precipitates some more specialized discussion of that larger issue of inferring causality which was undertaken in Chapter 2. The fact is that the psychologist thinks of the stimulus as the *cause* of the response, though some other aspect of the person's personality, or of his state, or of the background ambient environment, etc., can and must also be considered what we called in Chapter 1 an equipotent or sufficient cause of the response. Furthermore, changes in ids other than the responses also have a right to be reckoned as causal consequences. Consequently to set out with the idea, as many reflexologists do, that stimulus-response is the only observational basis for causal laws in psychology is, to say the least, a somewhat dim and restricted perception. It may perhaps be objected that the particular shift or change at the nodal occasion which we call a response differs from change in other sets, e.g., the decline of a stimulus, a rise in temperature in the background environment, the nodding of an observer, etc. This illusion would be less prevalent if such psychologists recognized that, especially in natural situations, behavior responses are overlapping and continuous. In behavior patterns, as in any other patterns, the *shift* measurement has the same property of being a change—a first differential on an existing output rate or velocity which is thought of as the fixed aspect. Another way of considering the shift is as a difference matrix between two immediately successive aspect matrices.

Thus, in summary, sets other than responses *can* yield *shift* measurements, and much causal inference in physical science is based on such observations. And, complementarily, behavioral responses, as when a boy whistles continuously, or a workman grumbles all day, or an animal gnaws constantly at an obstruction, can be measured to yield *fixed aspect* measures. There is more symmetry in this respect among the ten sets than may at first appear. The question of when causal influence can and cannot be inferred must be decided for *both* fixed aspect and shift measures on the basis of the time sequence and manipulation conditions of the experiment, as discussed already in the previous chapter. The sequence need not occur in the moment of experiment. Correlation of the fixed aspects of deceased parents and of living children also justifies causal inference. Normally, there will be rich relationships among shift and aspect measures which initially can be treated simply as statistically significant relations, and only later analyzed into structural and causal laws. And, of course, it is within the scope of these relations to throw light on all id sets, not only on the nature and structure of persons. One wonders if the false uniqueness given to "the response" in the thinking of classical bivariate experimenters might achieve some degree of correction by the semantic aid of speaking more frequently of "the behavior *process*," and of "states and environments," and other entities and attributes of interest to psychology besides "stimulus and response." In asking for greater consideration of, for example, a more prolonged "response process," or a maturational course, we are not negating the general concept of the distinctness and separability of responses, as response *processes*, from the other nine entity patterns — people, environments, stimuli, states, etc.

(3) *On-set (or "proper") and off-set (or "off-id") attribute entries can both be used in relational analysis in a given facet.* So far it has been customary to expect that the entry (or "the element" if one thinks as a matrix algebraist) is a relation or attribute *immediately* tied to the two bounding ids of the entry cell. But, as argued above, it is possible to make both mathematical and psychological sense of an entry drawn from a wider resource.

For example, in a facet bounded by people and stimuli the entries might be attributes of stimuli encountered by people, or relations such as the frequency with which person *x* encounters stimulus *y* in daily life (a "sociological" matrix). This we may call an *on-set or proper entry*. But it might also be a relation or attribute in terms of an attribute of an id on some off-set, i.e., some coordinate orthogonal to those of the facet. For example, in the above person-stimulus facet the entries could be attributes of responses, of states, or of environments. If, for instance, the temperature of the environment were entered, in a rat-stimulus matrix, the analysis by columns (as relatives) would reveal the similarity of two stimuli in regard to the background temperature in which they tended to be encountered by the rats.

This use of off-set attributes is possible because, as stated above, an entry applies, not to one id or pair of ids, but to the *node* or event in which all ten particular ids came together, one from each set. This is brought out more effectively by the total data box than the usual two-coordinate facet "score sheet," in which one is in constant danger of forgetting the remaining eight ids that are peculiar to the entry. In a comprehensive view, therefore, the nature of the attribute or relation in the entry can refer to any one of the ten sets. Thus a facet of persons and stimuli can be written *PS.a; PS.p; PS.s; PS.e; . . .* etc., according as attributes of acts, people, stimuli, or environments are made entries. Incidentally, the possibility exists, especially with aspects as contrasted with shifts or response, that an *a* entry for, say, *S,* though varying over *P* (people) will not vary with respect to the off-ids, and in that case off-set entries could not be used.

(4) *Further varieties of facet arise for (a) the above-described mixed-vs.-fixed reference to off-set ids, (b) homogeneous-vs.-heterogeneous attribute entries, and (c) uniform-vs.-cross-set ids.* The entries to be related can also differ according to the variety admitted on entries and on sets. In the first place, the entries in a facet can be made, as stated earlier, either (a) to stand at those found for the same

"controlled" id value on all off-sets, e.g., a response to a stimulus is controlled for all to the same state of the subject, the same background, the same observer, etc. This we have called a constant set facet or simply a *fixed facet.* Alternatively, (b) we have no control or record of the off-sets and the entries include random variance on these, and we then have a *mixed facet* (uncontrolled off-set values). Incidentally, one can recognize degrees in mixed facets. As Diagram 3-4 (2) (b), page 93, shows, the facet can be set up in which each stimulus is held on all its values at a fixed off-set — though stimuli differ among themselves as to the off-id involved. This we can call a staggered facet.

A mixed facet may be actually necessitated by the non-viability of certain combinations or the unavoidable absence of certain combinations, e.g., one completes the facet only by projecting upon it various off-facet values, as in Diagram 3-4. Later we must also take up the question of the unconsidered selections on off-sets upon conclusions drawn from any score facet which may be appropriately sampled on the on-sets.

However, there are two additional respects in which the content of a facet can be varied. Namely, (a) with respect to the homogeneity, or non-uniformity, of the *entries,* from column to column (regardless of mixed or fixed off-ids), and (b) with respect to the uniformity or otherwise of the relatives themselves. At first, it may not seem to make sense to correlate an observer with a stimulus, or both with a person, with respect to response magnitudes. But it can be done if the attributes used are different.

In regard to the first — entries — the attributes can be all the same, e.g., reaction time speeds, to different stimuli, or they can be quite different, e.g., reaction times in one column, maze distances in another, and so on. There is indeed *some* lack of independence of homogeneity and uniformity, since homogeneity of attribute entries may be impossible if the relatives themselves become too different. In general there is increasing difficulty in getting homogeneity of attribute entries as relatives become more diverse. Such attributes as space, time, color alone remain common to cabbages and kings. In any case, depending on whether the score entries in successive columns are for the same or for different attributes, we can have either a *homogeneous* or a *heterogeneous* attribute entry facet. For example, the usual *PS.a* matrix could measure responses homogeneously to all stimuli in terms of reaction time, or heterogeneously in a reaction time attribute of the first, a galvanic skin response to the second, a frequency of errors to the third, and so on.[7] Actually, heterogeneous entry facets are decidedly more frequent than homogeneous ones, and this places restrictions on the things one could otherwise do mathematically with facets, as well as on the scaling treatments (see Section 11 below).

Related to this last dichotomy (in the sense of not being entirely independent) is the difference between a *uniform* and a *cross-set* facet, which concerns the non-uniformity of relatives — their choice from different sets — as just described. When all columns, for example, are stimuli, we have a *uniform set* and a *uniform facet.* But a facet could be made up of categorically diverse stimuli or one could even, at the cost of some possible confusion as indicated above, correlate across sets and have, for example, stimuli and states (as relatives) with people (as referees), or have environment and person ids on the relatives coordinate and stimuli on the referees. In the first instance one would plot (or correlate), say, frequency of encountering a certain stimulus in the past with motivation state toward it in the present, or, in the second instance, frequency of appearance of a stimulus in an environment with a person's recognition certainty.

---

[7]In biology it may be absurd to try to enter a score for running speed for fish or in psychology a score on, say, physical temperature for, say, certain tonal stimuli.

It will be noted that the cross-set facet is perhaps the most common of all in the realm of bivariate experiment. There we typically have two columns, one of which could be the brightness of a particular stimulus and the other the magnitude of a particular response, the referees being people. But when we take a cross-set which (unlike Diagram 3-4 [1]) has several columns for each of the different kinds of set

DIAGRAM 3-4.   Cross-Set, Mixed, and Staggered Facets

(1) Cross-Set Facet

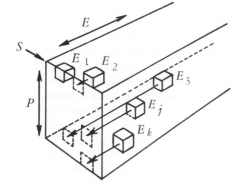

(2) Mixed Set Facet
   (a) Simple Mixed Facet

Projection of single
cell values onto a facet
to give a *mixed facet*.

in the relatives, e.g. several stimuli, several responses, several observers, we have done something which violates the simplicity of the data box as so far understood.

How can the attribute of stimulus S_h be related to one of stimulus S_g and to one of response A_j and of response A_k? No longer are we speaking of a single node at which one id from each and every set is a single knot. Instead we now have a supernode in which several responses, e.g. action, heartbeat, galvanic response are recorded as simultaneously tied in to a single situation in which several stimuli may also come together. The justification for correlating or comparing them can only be this juxtaposition in a supernode. One can thus bring to an experiment several people, stimuli observers, acts, and conditions, but is limited as to variants (several variants or states at least cannot appear simultaneously in the same person: one is free on $SAPEO$ but not on $S'A'P'E'O'$). The data box would thus have many empty entries and is best considered a coalesced DB, i.e. one in which people, stimuli, etc. have

DIAGRAM 3-4 (continued)

(b) *Staggered Facet*

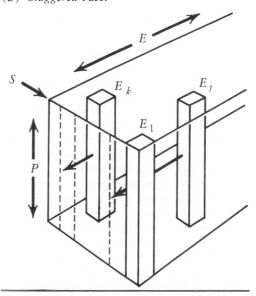

coalesced in certain blocks on the bounding edges. A cross-set matrix having from $n = 2$ to $n = 9$ different relatives can be within the frame of the ordinary data box and is what we shall commonly refer to henceforth when speaking of a cross-set facet; but beyond this we run into the special conditions of super-nodes. Indeed, because of this the majority of multivariate designs which we shall commonly discuss will be considered to operate treatments are on uniform set matrices. However, in the condition-response experimental design (page 31), and the super-set matrices discussed at the end of this chapter, an effective multivariate experiment can be performed with cross-set matrices. Diagram 3-4 illustrates cross-set and mixed facets.

(5) *The range of sets and entries possible in the BDRM generates relational systems which extend to academic and research areas usually considered beyond psychology.* As already briefly mentioned, the choice of the full roll of sets necessary to cover all psychological topics creates the possibility of subsets of relations in the data box which lie outside behavioral science. (Indeed, the whole data box could be adapted readily to any science.) If we omit the sets constituted by subjects and their states and responses and their variants, the relations among the remainder are in fact those relations among stimulus conditions, background environment, and observers which belong to the study of ecology and even, in the broader sense, to sociology, geography, economics, and physical science. In other words, the subset of relations comprised by the pairing of stimulus, environment, etc., with the *person* constitute psychology, but the relations among the environment, stimulus, observer, etc., sets *themselves* belong mostly to other sciences.

Consequently, when the BDRM is broken down into facets, some of them will yield relations and laws no more immediately interesting to the psychologist than the physics of stage scenery and lighting systems is interesting to an actor-producer.

The existence of these "irrelevant by-products" of some coordinate set combination must be recognized in comprehensive BDRM operations, though a psychology of the future, in embracing ecology, may regard them as less alien.

It may help in remembering the above terms to note that fixed-vs.-mixed and uniform-vs.-cross-set refer to id arrangements, but homogeneous-vs.-heterogeneous to modes of entry regardless of sets.

7. THE NUMBERS AND VARIETIES OF FACETS, AND ASSOCIATED TECHNIQUES

As stated earlier in this chapter, our aim in introducing the BDRM is first to explore the *possible relational analyses* upon which all psychological theory has to be built. As we do so, it helps to keep in mind that on the flanks of this purely relational study stand (1) *the method of mathematico-statistical analysis,* to check the significance of agreement of the observed relations with a particular quantitative model or formula, and (2) the *design of experiment,* to procure the relational data appropriate to the analyses to be made. In short, it is agreed that, logically and operationally, *design* and *method* are distinct from *system*, but it is important to keep an eye open for inevitable organic connections. Thus, although the choice of sets in the relational analysis and the complexity of the relations invoked do not bind the experimenter immediately to any particular statistical method of evaluating the relations, the same ideas of hypothesis structure as led to the choice of relational system may also lead to a statistical method. At any rate we tend to find certain methods preferentially attached to certain relational systems and to these conjunctions there have been given the name "techniques." (See Diagram 2-4, page 52.) We have reached the point where enough has been defined to permit us profitably to look systematically at techniques.

The previous chapter defined as the *relatives,* those ids among which relations, significant or null, are being tried and evaluated. By contrast with the *relative* set, the *referee* set or the *instances* describe the set and its ids *over* which the relation is to be established. Thus stimuli might be relatives, and people instances, or vice versa. Basically, mathematically, we are free to find relations between numbers in any two parallel arrays, and these arrays may be either rows or columns. (For the moment we speak of arrays being related only two at a time, for simplicity, as in bivariate analysis. But in multivariate analysis, we extend this to *all* column combinations.) Most commonly, when we relate by correlation, we correlate two *columns,* i.e., the relatives are placed along the top of the matrix. But psychologists are by now thoroughly familiar with *Q* technique in which, instead, we correlate two rows — or what were rows before we transposed the matrix. It is simplest to speak of this as *transposing* the matrix, i.e., putting people along the top, now in the role of relatives, and the set of stimuli, etc. down the side, as the referees. (For a time the literature in this area suffered from a misnomer. At variance with the standard meaning of matrix algebra the faulty expression "inverse factor technique" was unfortunately sometimes used for what is correctly called "transpose factor technique.") Below, incidentally, we propose that the referee set always be named first, exactly as in the standard way of naming the order, e.g., $N \times n$, of a matrix, so that, with people and stimuli, "PS technique" identifies the standard "R technique," and "SP technique" what was previously ambiguously called "Q technique." Indeed, the new nomenclature for techniques conveys not only the direction of analysis, but indicates simultaneously the particular pair of sets involved.

It was the introduction of the Covariation Chart actually that opened up the perception of the *P, O, S,* and *T* techniques, lying beyond the *R* and *Q* then alone known and discussed. For it showed that we could exhaustively arrive at the possible techniques by asking what could be encompassed by three sets combined two at a time. Our task in systematizing here requires not only that we extend the derivation of techniques from the six out of the Covariation Chart to the larger number derivable from ten sets, but also that we point out that their labelled techniques — *R, Q,* etc. — can have a wider reference than to factor analytic techniques alone. Already in this direction, the reader may be familiar with the increased precision of usage which distinguishes an analysis of the same relations by correlation cluster search rather than factor analysis. One then adds a prime — *R', Q',* etc. techniques — to indicate correlation cluster analysis methods rather than factor analysis of the same correlations. Thus *Q'* technique is seeking for clusters — *types* — of persons where *Q* technique is seeking for factor dimensions. Here, retaining this prime distinction we should write it in the new dual letter designations as illustrated in the following varieties of the *PA* (person-act or response) matrix, by:

(1) *PA* technique, correlating and factoring responses (*A*) over persons as referees;

(2) *AP* technique, correlating and factoring people (*P*) over responses as referees;

(3) *AP'* technique, correlating and clustering by types among people;

(4) *PA'* technique, clustering responses, was frequently done with tests before the time of factor analysis.

Next, recognizing as a third general method of analysis of the same relations the statistical treatments in the class of analysis of variance, let us symbolize this by a *double* prime applied to the designation of the sets. Thus we have:

(5) *PA''* technique, evaluating associations of responses by grouping people by their level on one and applying a *t* test or anovar to the means and sigmas on the other.

(That is to say, unprimed is factor analysis;

primed is cluster analysis; double-primed is analysis of variance.)

Since the Covariation Chart and the R and P, etc., techniques are more widely familiar at the moment than the complete ten-set data box, we would suggest that the terms P, Q, R etc. be retained for the combinations in the simple three-set Covariation Chart, while the new, more systematic notation and terminology is being introduced. Indeed, in our initial discussion of important combinations of system and method, i.e., of techniques, it may be helpful to pause and look at the general problem of techniques first in these simpler, more familiar terms. Moreover, for psychometrists' purposes only, much use may remain for the simpler Covariation Chart. In any case the reader is advised to pause here and see that he understands the six original techniques in relation to Diagrams 3-1 and 3-2 above (see pages 69 and 70).

With this nursery run completed, let us next examine what the total possibility of techniques becomes in the complete (ten-set) data box. From the reference to just three sets, as coordinate axes in Diagram 3-2 (page 70) we have seen how the data source for a single correlation (or, indeed statistical method used in a relational analysis) appears in each facet and in its accompanying transpose. We realize also that in multivariate analysis, *all* possible pairs among the relatives, e.g., of stimuli, appearing along the test coordinate shown would be correlated in such a facet. This procedure yields the square correlation matrix with which a multivariate analysis typically deals. It will be noted from Diagram 3-1 that any two transposes always lie in one facet. Thus R and Q technique lie in a "slab" or "slice" corresponding to one occasion (in the ten-axis BDRM the slice corresponds to *one* observer, *one* environment, *one* state, etc.). Let us now see how this operates in ten dimensions.

In the present wider treatment we recognize that the three dimensional covariation chart is one particular simplification — one

of several possible abstractions — from the vaster relational system presented by the BDRM. Let us pause to notice how that simplification was made. First, two coordinate axes are collapsed into one by combining stimulus and response into "test"; second, it is collapsed by phase of environment, and, indeed, collapse of all "state" axes, including the "state of subject" into a composite "occasion" axis; third, it completely omits the "observer," and last, it omits observer conditions from consideration. As indicated above, the omitted patterns in this or any other simplification of the total data box may either be considered held constant in a fixed "constant facet," at the same id value on the offsets, or admitted to be uncontrolled in a varied facet. However, a combination of a stimulus and response in a "test" is obviously a particular stimulus bound to a particular response. The Covariation Chart, moreover, (1) accepted only response measures as cell entries, and (2) omitted any systematic naming (but not consideration [see Cattell, 213]) of what we shall call *staggered and cross-set techniques.*

The expansion resulting from recognizing ten sets in place of three, and from allowing entries to represent scores on *any* attribute of *any* set of id patterns, can be readily followed. The introduction of cross-set or staggered relations, on the other hand, requires brief description. In an ordinary facet, all column headings on the one hand or all row designations on the other consist of ids of one class. Frequently, however, one may wish to seek relations among relatives from different sets (hence cross-set) which, however, must be over the same referees. For example, one may wish to relate the response to a stimulus with the mood state of the same set of subjects. In all such cases, while adhering to one coordinate (in this case the people set) to represent the referees, one is taking the two columns of entries chosen for comparison — the relatives — from *different* sets among the remaining nine. This is shown visually in a simplified three-dimensional Covariation Chart setting, in Diagram 3-4 (2), but it will be recognized that three dimensions allow cross-sets relations to only one additional set, whereas the full BDRM would permit nine. However, it demonstrates the meaning of a cross-set *facet* or technique in which each column is assembled from a different "depth."

Incidentally, the difference between a homogeneous facet technique and a cross-facet technique has been one of the conceptual distinctions most habitually and inveterately associated with the difference between the Wundt-Pavlov study of processes and the Galton-Spearman study of individual differences. Bivariate experiment has worked largely within cross-set techniques, relating stimulus measures to response measures, environmental condition measures to state measures, etc., in a *t*-test examination of relations in a single pair of columns. Psychometry, on the other hand, has related stimuli or responses within themselves (homogeneous facet) but over many columns (relatives) in one set.

At this point we must recognize that the symbolism in the Covariation Chart no longer suffices to cover the richer world revealed by the full ten-set data box.[8] For that matter it is defective in not properly designating the way in which the Covariation Chart—or any other "collapsed" version of the DB—is in fact collapsed. The new symbolism must be terse, because there are now many more facets and techniques to be designated. It has been recognized that there are now $^{10}C_2=45$ homogeneous facets alone. And since each of these relational systems admits of two transposed analysis methods, there are 90 techniques—for which an alphabetic extension of "*P, Q,* and *R* techniques" will no longer suffice! However, each of these can be filled with modes of entries consisting of attributes from any one of ten kinds of sets and also of relations between sets, so the total number of techniques is beyond $90 \times 10 = 900$. Furthermore, for certain purposes, a facet needs also to be set up between two coordinates of the same class. For example, one could have a stimulus-stimulus facet with entries giving the frequency with which they occur together, or a person-person facet, with entries giving strengths of attitude ties between the persons. Since there will be ten of these, each capable of having its cells fitted (even without cross-sets) with ten different kinds of entries (attributes and relations), the basic total is $900 + 100 = 1,000$ usable facet techniques (even without cross-sets, heterogeneous facets, etc.)!

With such large numbers it is perhaps less important to work out the exact total than to develop a means of proceeding systematically through the varieties and of designating each by a formula. To begin with, it should be realized that we are designating only the varieties among *facets*, i.e., analyses of simple score matrices, for there are other types of matrix still to be studied. To designate a given facet technique it is necessary only to mention (1) the bounding coordinates, (2) the direction of analysis which the technique uses, and (3) the nature of the entry. Thus a *PS.a* facet is one bounded by people and stimuli with response measurements as entries. The entry—*a*—is written in the lower case to remind us (Table 3-2) that it is an attribute or scale continuum, not a pattern or id. Since it does not matter, as far as indicating a facet is concerned, which axis is named first, the convention of putting the alphabetically earlier letter first *could* be followed. However, when one comes to speak of *techniques*, whereby an actual *mode of analysis* of the facet is implied, the two transpose analyses must be distinguished, which can best be done (as one does in indicating matrix orders) by putting the row symbol first. Thus a *PS.a* analysis is one that relates stimuli (with respect to response

---

[8] Let us henceforth more regularly substitute data box or DB for the more descriptive but extended "Basic Data Relation Matrix" or "BDRM."

similarity) as relatives over people (as referees), whereas an $SP.a$ analysis is one which explores the resemblance of people, still with respect to response similarity, over stimuli as referees. Thus the *second* symbol always states what is related or correlated, i.e., it defines the relatives, while the first fixes the referees.

The notation just introduced in simplest form needs tightening, however, to indicate the alternatives discussed above regarding the extent to which the off-sets are controlled, by being attached or unattached to one such off-set pattern only (fixed or mixed facet) and also to make reference to the cross-set matrix possible. For example, in the above $PS.a$ analysis should we assume that facet is on *one* particular off-set only, e.g., the one same occasion of state, on the *state* off-set? And does "fixed" mean on *all* the coordinates other than P and S? Thus, in regard to the P coordinate, should we assume a constant facet in which all persons are in *one* state, all stimuli in *one* variant, all response measures on *one* type of response, and all scores recorded by *one* observer? Or because these are unspecified, do we assume that, in a mixed facet, states, observers, etc., are uncontrolled and therefore random samples from their populations, randomly associated with P, S, and A attributes?

Because this control and recording of off-set ids is a "custom more honored in the breach than in the observance," it is probably more economical to use a notation which *says nothing when nothing is controlled,* but which adds specific symbols only when the more strictly regulated "constant facet" is known to be in use. Thus $PS.a$ is a person-row stimulus column facet with response attribute measures as entries, but with the particular state of the person, observer, etc., admittedly different from one entry to another and possibly unknown. If the off-set ids are known to be uniform for all people, stimuli, etc., i.e., if we have a fixed facet design, then up to

eight additional symbols should be added for particular ids on particular sets. Thus $PS.a.O_jE_kS'_e$ designates a facet fixed on observer, environment, and state of the stimulus, respectively at the ids j, k and e. For a mixed facet, where each entry may not be by one observer, O_j, but ranges over O_j, O_{j+1}, O_{j+2}, etc., nor for one environmental condition, E_k, but many, and similarly for all other off-sets, we have agreed to the simplest notation, $PS.a$. There remains the case, however, where the off-sets, though mixed, are at least known and recorded, and probably following certain sampling intentions. This can be indicated simply by writing O, E, S, etc.; thus $PS.a,OES$ in the case of a facet with known but varied values on O, E, and S, i.e., a known mixed facet. Thus $PS.a$, $PS.a,OES$, and $PS.aO_jE_kS'_e$ represent three degrees of increasing precision and control with respect to the off-sets, O, E, etc., and the last represents reduced variance on the entries relative to the first.

Beyond the fixed and mixed facets, we have the cross-set-vs.-uniform facet, but because of the varieties and particularity of the cross-set facets the powers of *any* notation system would be strained to represent them. Consider a typical experiment in perception or learning, where people (or rats) are the referees and correlations (or t tests) are examined between magnitudes of certain stimuli, on the one hand, and attributes of certain responses, on the other. The relatives are S's and A's and the entries are no longer, as in a constant or mixed matrix, of the same class. The notation can begin as before with the referees, P, and can be followed by the relatives, each with its special attribute class. Thus $P.S''s$, $A''a$ indicates a t test analysis (double prime) of the relation of attributes of stimuli to attributes of responses, over people as referees. The $''$ indicates an analysis of variance treatment, as $'$ indicates correlation (leading no further than cluster analysis), and no prime a factor analysis.

8. THE NUMBERS AND VARIETIES OF FACES, FRAMES, AND GRIDS

An adequate survey of the relational systems and techniques of analysis encompassed by *facets* is a proper beginning to the study of the data box because most of our score data matrices from experiments come as facets. It is to be hoped that the notation for facets developed here, though not pursued to all exhaustive possibilities, will be helpful in precision of communication and the avoidance of confusion. After this introduction by way of the facet we must

will average subgroups of people in order, for example, to give each point stability, in, say, a learning curve. In that case, he is using what we shall call a *face,* not a facet, to get his plotting and calculating values. Pictorially one can define a *face* as a score matrix formed by collapsing several parallel (and generally adjacent) facets into one, thus putting the total or mean of the several corresponding cells into a single cell. In matrix algebra it is simply the addition (and maybe averaging) of conforming matrices. This is illustrated below in Diagram 3-5.

DIAGRAM 3-5. Deriving a Face from Several Facets

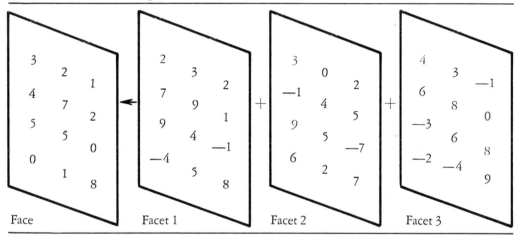

next recognize, however, that the facet is only one of four possible abstractions from the full data box that one may need to deal with at one time or another. The remaining three, which also belong to the class of score matrices in a broader sense, we shall call the *face,* the *frame,* and the *grid.* All admit of being treated eventually as two dimensional score matrices.

To recognize the importance of a *face,* we need to remember that many psychological experiments, e.g., one requiring determination of the form of a stimulus response curve, the experimenter will not operate on entries for single people, but

Naturally, the summation in a two-coordinate matrix can be across any and all of the remaining eight coordinates, and the notation for a face, and for the individual entries, will need to designate which and how many of these coordinates are thus "collapsed."

For a notation to designate a particular face, it suffices to use the symbols already introduced for homogenous facets, e.g., *PS, PA, EO,* etc., since the coordinates and entries must be the same if addition is to occur. The only new feature to be defined is the number and nature of off-sets (and also the number of ids in each) on which collapse (averaging) has taken place. This can be done by putting a line under the letters, thus, e.g., $\underline{ESAOP'}$, representing the off-sets, over which averaging has occurred. For example, a face from the above $PS.a$ matrix would be defined as $\underline{PS.a}\,P'E$ if it were the mean response over all states of the person and all background environment conditions. These "barred" symbols could run up to eight in number. Subscripts can be added, as in P'_{20} and E_{65} to indicate the size of the samples (20 and 65, respectively) over which addition has taken place. If one wishes to designate entries, rather than the character of the whole matrix (face) as above, then lower-case letters can be barred, thus $a_{ih \cdot p'es}$ would be a response of a person i to a stimulus h averaged over states of the people, the different environments, and the variants of that stimulus. (It might in other contexts be written $\overset{p'es'}{\underset{o}{\sum}} a_{jk}$.)

The number of possible homogeneous faces will be the number of possible facets, i.e., 1000, with the assumptions above, multiplied by the number of possible combinations of collapsed sets available among the eight "off-id" sets, i.e., $^{8}C_2 + {}^{8}C_3 + {}^{8}C_1$, etc. The number of possible techniques will obviously be very great, especially when we consider that each can be analyzed both by the direct and the transposed technique. Furthermore, one can have *cross-sets* faces in which, say, the magnitudes of the stimuli given to the various people, averaged over, say, several states, are compared with the magnitudes of responses, also averaged over several states.

In considering all such derived faces, as distinct from the facets from which they are derived, it is necessary to keep one's conceptual handling of the problem in line with the relational and statistical-analytical handling. Thus, the "proper ids," i.e., the on-set ids actually bounding the face matrix, or bounding a facet when its entries are mixed, are no longer the simple and uniform entities they once were. For example, a $PS.a$ face has people (rows) no longer

at one particular occasion, e.g., in state $P'_{i'}$ or environment E_e, but, if it is collapsed over states (P') and environmental backgrounds, E, at "people over many states and backgrounds." Similarly, in a mixed facet a bounding entity is person $P'_{y'}$ in state P_x, person $P'_{u'}$ in state P_z, or other quite specific combinations. Indeed, in facets, faces, and the frames and grids yet to be described, it is always important to pause and ask just what the character and degree of definition of the individual set members (ids) may be. In any sort of restricted facet or face, i.e., cut out of the total data box, the bounding id for the matrix (the "proper" as distinguished from the "off" id) has properties on the off-sets which need to be defined. Such an id is usually not just, say, a person, P_i, or a stimulus, S_h, but a person averaged over all moods, a person meeting a stimulus in a particular background, a person as viewed by a particular set of observers, and so on. A common instance of failure to recognize this is that of the educational psychologist, e.g., Vernon (1489), Guilford (622), who uses a single-occasion facet of people and tests to discover "ability traits" where occasion-to-occasion (P', E', etc.) variance (which could be largely eliminated by a face technique) clearly enters so that the factors found could just as easily be states as traits.

To complete our taxonomy of faces we should note various *composite faces* combining cross-set with mixed entry averaging. For example, a particular person in a stated known condition might constitute the typical id of one set and a particular stimulus with a particular background condition the typical id of another, each being averaged across the same samples of the other sets. Insofar as a notation is needed, it could be an extension of that for cross-set facets. Thus $P.S\underline{sEO}.Aa\underline{EO}$ would be cross-set in that stimulus attributes are related to response measures, and a face in that averaging takes place over E and O axes.

Under the term *"frame"* we approach the possible score matrices having *more* than the two coordinates so far used in the *facet* and the *face*. Such "solid" score matrices are parallelopipeds in three-space or more. Mathematicians have used the expression "tensors" for such solid matrices, but since we wish to remain free to handle them for psychologists' objectives, we shall continue to call them "psychological score frames," though the applicability to them of tensor methods must be explored. The *total* Basic Data Relation Matrix is, of course, a frame — the *ultimate* frame if we are correct in saying that ten sets is exhaustive. Resort to a frame generally betokens an experiment carried out with more comprehensive vision than is often indicated by the single-sheet, facet score matrix commonly employed (which is not to say that the latter does not have many appropriate and legitimate uses.) Indexing the nature of a particular frame can be carried out by extension of the notation used for facets, since a facet is a special case of a frame, namely, one reduced to one id length along one set. Thus data obtained on the responses of a set of people, each measured in all of a set of states, on all of a set of possible types of response, to all of a set of different stimuli, would be designated a $PP'RS.a$ score frame, the nature of the entry always being represented, as in faces and facets, by the lower-case letter. This could be called a four-set homogeneous entry frame, since it has four sets. The possible techniques of analyses of such a typical total frame are so complex that they need special discussion, which is relegated to Section 9 below, but meanwhile we can assume that the prospective referees are indicated by the first symbol, i.e., people are the referees in the example given.

In regard to entries in a frame, the possibility exists, mathematically and experimentally, of having different modes for each id of any set over and above the first two set coordinates. Indeed a different entry could occur either on each set or on each id (of each set) beyond the first two coordinates. That is to say, we have again the possibilities described for facets and faces as the fixed-vs.-mixed and uniform-vs.-cross-set alternatives. For example, in the instance above, the person and state facet first on the stimulus axis could have response measures, the second might have observer shift measures, and so on. There are probably extremely few experiments, however, in which it would make sense to carry out analyses with such a constellation of data. Nevertheless, these rarer types need designation, and one could again use the code for cross-set facets given in Section 5 above, i.e., add the type of entry in parentheses after each additional coordinate.

Since a frame does not, except in the limiting DB instance, occupy all the space of all known sets, it can always, like a face, contain figures that represent an averaging over the neglected off-sets. Such a frame can usefully be designated a *faced frame,* and in notation can be indicated by a combination of frame and face symbols from above. Thus the four-frame $PP'RS.a$ above, if averaged over observers and states of observers, would be written $PP'RS.a\underline{OO'}$. Frames can also be fixed or mixed on their off-sets, so that, again like a facet or frame, one can either leave the off-sets unspecified, when mixed, or assign the particular fixed value when fixed. Thus $PP'RS.aE_eO'_{m'}$ is not a faced frame, but a frame fixed on the off-sets at E_e and $O'_{m'}$.

The number of possible simple frames obtainable out of the total data box is obviously $^{10}C_3 + {}^{10}C_4 \ldots + {}^{10}C_9$. The limiting instances of a "two-set frame" $^{10}C_2$ and a ten-set, $^{10}C_{10}$, actually constitute, respectively, single facets and the data box itself. Some of the intermediate frames will perhaps acquire names because of special interest. A subclass of particular interest is that which we may designate a *composite frame* because it has composite sets, each member of which is a particular combination of an id from one set with an id from another. For example, a "stimulus situation" composite set may consist of ids, each of which represents a particular stimulus linked with a particular background. (The linking may be deliberately randomized, or fortuitous, etc., according to further definition.) The Covariation Chart is an outstanding instance of such a convenience, and, in accordance with the agreed notation of representing composite ids by brackets, this particular frame would be written:

$$P(SAA')\ (EE'P'S').a\ .$$

(The observer and his state, O and O', are not in because not recorded.) Herein we recognize that a "test" is both a stimulus (S) and a response (A), fixed at a particular response style (A'), i.e., it is always a particular type of response, according to instructions, tied to a particular stimulus. An "occasion" is a still more composite set, consisting of a particular environmental background, $E,$ a particular state in the subject, P', etc.

A type of frame likely to occur with especial frequency is one with composite sets each constituted by *an entity and its present state:* for example, the composite PP', "person in a given state"; EE', environment in a certain phase; RR', response at a particular stage; SS', stimulus in a particular variant; and OO', observer in the condition he happens to be in. Some fairly frequent confusion might be avoided by calling these composite coordinates respectively *individuals* (persons who may differ also in states), *environments* (ambient stimuli differing in phase), *reactions* (response acts not all fixed at the same style), *presentations* (stimuli with variable variants). A five-frame (i.e., a frame with five coordinate sets) built from these coordinates should actually find rather prevalent use because it is an intermediate between the Covariation Chart and the full complexity of the data box, and also because it avoids many of the experimental difficulties of keeping ids of one set all in the same state at the moment of measurement. It would however, be largely confined to psychometry of individual differences, owing to the absence of occasions.

Although the calculation just given of the number of possible simple frames is straightforward, calculation of the various composite frames, and the faced frames, etc., is too elaborate to justify our time here. All we need to note is that it leads to very large numbers.

In summary, a frame, just like a facet or face, can vary in type according to the treatment on the off-sets. If off-set values are each held at one particular id, uniformly over the frame, we speak of a *fixed frame* and indicate it by, e.g., $PSOaE_lA_j$ (l and j being the fixed E and A ids). Alternatively, without any postscripts to A and E, it would be a *mixed frame.* If the entries are collapsed over some off-sets, as in a face, we write $PSO_1a_1\underline{OR}$, and refer to a *faced frame.* There is also the possibility of a *cross-set frame* on the off-sets, and the special case which we have called the *composite frame,* where the composite coordinates are denoted in parentheses, e.g., $P(SAA')\ (EE'P'S')a,$ which defines the Covariation Chart.

The last of the available data matrix forms to be considered is the *grid.* The grid is a two-coordinate matrix, normally one id thick (and, therefore, up to that point in its definition, a facet). However, it is formed by "unrolling" a frame, as shown in Diagram 3-6.

In fact, its peculiarity, if it were viewed as a facet, would be that one coordinate (S in Diagram 3-6) repeats itself several times along what we shall call, in distinction from the ordinary referee coordinate, the *extended* or *combined, balanced referee coordinate* (top in Diagram 3-3). This excluded coordinate contains the balanced, randomized id combinations from the two sets, and though it appears in Diagram 3-6 as the relatives, it can in transpose appear as the referees, relative set. The information set out in the entries is, of course, no different in the grid from that in the frame from which it was unfolded. But by setting this same total of information in the grid form we have now implied *a technique of analysis*—or rather, two transposed techniques of analysis—which are a selection

DIAGRAM 3-6.   Unrolling of a Frame into a Grid

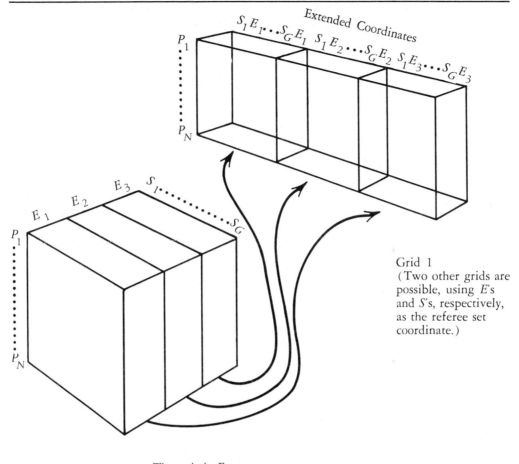

Grid 1
(Two other grids are
possible, using E's
and S's, respectively,
as the referee set
coordinate.)

Three-Axis Frame

from among those which can be made in the frame. Along one edge — the top edge — of the grid, we now have the S series repeating itself, its id members attached in cyclic order to a different E id each time. Thus the extended "relatives" coordinate is similarly a balanced set constituted by all possible combinations of stimuli and background stimuli (See Diagram 3-6). To show which is the referee set, P is placed first, and to show the special nature of the extended coordinate in the grid the notation puts the sets in brackets, as for a composite set (which this is). However, it also puts a bar over them to indicate the *balanced* completeness of combinations among them, as in an analysis of variance with two or more effects. Thus, if response attribute magnitudes are the entries in Diagram 3-6, that example would be written $P(SE).a$. Psychologically, the difference between an analysis of a single $PS.a$ facet, taken out of the frame shown, and of the grid from the same frame is that the latter includes, in this example, relations that exist also through the variance among background conditions, E. Parenthetically, one can also conceive a grid in which the sets are *not* combined in a balanced design but left separate. (The edge would then have, say, $G + N + F$ cases instead of $G \times N \times F$.) But this "unbalanced" grid is not a true grid and does not encompass all the entries in the corresponding frame.

The number and variety of possible grids is a function, first, of the number and variety of the possible frames from which they are derived, and this has been indicated above. Given one frame, the number of grids derivable from it is determined first by the number of coordinates of the frame. For each set or combination of sets can in turn become the set of referees, to be combined with various possible extended coordinate sets of relatives. With ten coordinate sets the relatives can be made of 1 to 9 sets, and if that number of relative sets is k, the referees will consist of 10-k sets. There are thus 9 degrees of oblongness for the grid, including the square 5(relative) by 5(referee) grid. If we consider only the first, with one set only in the relatives, the number of extended coordinates is thus the number of combinations of two sets and more in n-1 sets, n being the number of axes or sets to the frame. For example, in a five-dimensional frame, the total number of grids is $4(^4C_2 + {}^4C_3 + {}^4C_4) = 44$. In other terms, the 5-frame has $n \times N \times G \times D \times F$ entries (see Table 3-2), and various facets (grids) can be made by variously combining the product terms, e.g. $(n \times N)(G \times D \times F)$ or $(n \times G \times F)(N \times D)$. The number for the full data box can be worked as an exercise but is obviously very large. However, additional variations can occur if the grid is allowed to include mixed and cross-set matrices.

9. THE TOTALITY OF POSSIBLE DIRECT AND DERIVED RELATIONAL ANALYSES AND TECHNIQUES

The argument up to this point has been that there is a finite number of possible kinds of relational systems among psychological data and that they can be studied and classified in terms of ultimate techniques of analysis of facets, faces, frames, and grids. Having been familiar in the past with just a few techniques — R technique, P technique, and certain anovar and covar designs — we find the sheer number of possibilities reached somewhat overwhelming. However, we are rather less interested in the total magnitude than in recognizing the various types and varieties and their uses. For again, as in the relatively crude three-dimensional Covariation Chart of 1946, the important point is that the data box not only informs us on a definitive limit to possible research designs, but also (1) gives us perspective on the relations of conclusions from different analysis systems, and (2) reveals whole regions of possible relational analysis which hitherto psychologists have never perceived as a useful battleground for theories. These "regions Caesar never knew" — these new worlds of conceptualization and theory — will be found to reside particularly in the spaces bounded by such blocks of coordinates as $P'ESO, PSOO', AEE'SE,$ etc., using, especially, entries from response, person, stimulus, and observer attributes. However, since we have further objectives to pursue here, the hunting in these new domains must be left to individual researchers.

Before proceeding to what we may call higher relational systems, a quick backward glance can be taken at the essential concepts emerging from what has now been covered. Rough calculations have been made of the total number of possible *facets, faces, frames* and *grids,* respectively, in the total ten-coordinate data box. In some cases, it is possible to be definitive in a few words. For example, the possible number of facet systems is the combination of ten things two at a time, i.e., 45. Each system is susceptible to using ten modes of score entry, each entry being a *shift* score, absolutely peculiar to the event, not an *aspect* score, which as we have seen, would give scores peculiar to each cell only in special circumstances, which we shall discuss. Thus we have initially 450 possible kinds of facet, each designatable by three letters, e.g., *PS.a*, or *EA.p*, etc. Each of these, however, can be either a fixed or mixed, uniform or cross-set, or heterogeneous or homogeneous facet with regard to the relatives and off-sets. The combinations of holding constant and allowing to vary on the eight off-sets are ${}^{8}C_1 + {}^{8}C_2 + \ldots {}^{8}C_8$, i.e., 2^8 or 256, so that our total is now $450 \times 256 = 115{,}200$. Each of these can be analyzed in two ways, i.e., by two different techniques, namely, as the matrix or its transpose, e.g., as *PS.a* or *SP.a*, so that the total of different possible kinds of techniques from the 115,200 relational analysis systems, with facets alone, is 230,400!

Without pursuing arithmetical exercises, with similar astronomical numbers, for the possible faces, summed over two to eight off-sets, and the possible grids from each of the possible frames, one can easily see that the number of alternative matrices and ultimate techniques must be very roughly in the neighborhood of some millions. Every one of these distinct possibilities of associating one thing with another operates basically on a two-dimensional matrix — the columns and rows representing people, test stimuli, mood states, observers, conditions of ambient environment, etc., and combinations thereof; and the entries some continuum or dichotomy in a relation or attribute. Since the latter can be chosen to refer to a considerable variety of the sets, it is evident that the types of possible relational analysis are still further expanded.

Finally, when one turns from relational analysis to techniques, i.e., to combinations of the relations with possible statistical methods to analyze them, the number expands yet again. For simplicity we have spoken above of factor analysis, correlational analysis and analysis of variance, and assigned — notation-wise — a prime and a double prime to distinguish the two last from the first. This is a concession to the grossest simplicity of practical discussions of method, for, as the dimensions of method in Table 2-4 (page 39) remind us,

there could be $2^4 = 16$ types, and even at a simple descriptive level one can reel off such methods as analysis of variance, of covariance, non-parametric methods, chi square, correlation, curve plotting, etc. The combinations of relational analysis with mathematico-statistical methods thus yield an enormous number of techniques. And even here we are not at the end, for we have dealt only with what might be called the *direct* relational analysis systems. It behooves us to look — at the risk of vertigo — also at the difference, ratio, etc., relational systems which arise when we no longer operate on a single data box but on entries expressing the relation of an entry in one box to an entry in another. For it is possible to operate on entries that are *relations among relations* (or among attributes) and on "derived" data boxes obtained by subtraction (or other relation) of one data box from another. These further "score" matrices we shall call the higher order data boxes or *derived matrices*, because their values are always derivable from values in matrices already described above. By derived score matrices we mainly refer to formally similar matrices built up by arranging conforming matrices side by side and obtaining for the cell in the resulting similar matrix some function of the scores in corresponding cells in the conforming matrices. An obvious example would be where the new derived matrix contains *learning* scores obtained as differences between two scores in the corresponding cells of the conforming matrices. Another instance would be the use of "adjustment process analysis" matrices by Cattell and Scheier (325) to calculate outcomes in clinical personality learning; yet another occurs in the study of psychological states and moods by differential R technique. Let us consider the last in a little more detail.

In what has been called (240) *differential or incremental R technique* (called in Chapter 11 *dR* technique, for differential R technique), one measures a sample of people on, say, an array, *A*, of hypothesized anxiety, extraversion, and intelligence measures on occasion x (like any "occasion," a combination of P', E', S', and O' ids). One measures the same set of A response variables again after an interval of hours or days, either manipulatively introducing anxiety, by producing stimuli in between, or leaving the shifts to be produced by life happenings. One then subtracts, for each variable, the score on the first occasion from that on the second. These "differential scores" (usually with a constant added to eliminate negative numbers) are then intercorrelated and factored. Such a *differential R-technique* design will yield the *dimensions of change,* showing the pattern of anxiety as a state and revealing whether intelligence has daily changes as a whole.

What we are doing in this case is obviously to subtract facet X from facet Y and generate a new score facet on which to operate in any of the usual ways. Another familiar instance — the study of learning, as when we plot a learning curve for a group of animals on a dozen successive occasions, and use a dozen increment scores correlated with some absolute score on another set and id, e.g., number of repetitions, or strength of motivation. Such research designs operate on a whole class of derived matrices which may be called *sum and difference matrices* (usually a single difference between two, and a sum of two or more, but also a difference of two summed matrices, etc.). What we have called a *face* is really already one of these derived matrices. We could therefore expand the meaning of "face" to include *sum faces* and *difference faces* but it seems best to speak generally of derived matrices, with a face as a special case in the other series. But one could, of course, also have product and quotient derived scores and, indeed, any mathematical function of two or more numbers. Indeed, corresponding to every facet analysis, and to most grid analyses so far described and included in the system, there are derived score forms.

In pursuing the ultimate complexities (which, however, we do not propose to do here), one would need also to consider combinations of cross-set matrices, e.g., correlating stimulus with response or with environment, each on its own type of entry, over the same set of referees, with "staggering", i.e., taking the subjects, for example, each at a different state. For example, one might take response scores as entries over a set of stimuli, the individual, John Smith, having them all taken in mood p_1, Sally Jones all the while in mood p_2, and so on. Uses of such data, though not common, will occur to the reader. Such staggered facets can be regularly (Diagram 3-4, page 93) or irregularly staggered. They differ from mixed facets (page 98) in that all of p_1's measured are at the same value y; when they are irregularly staggered we may call them mixed facets (Section 5).

Studies of interviewing and rating in which O the observer (interviewer) is himself observed by another experimenter (involving the possibility of infinite regress!) illustrate design possibilities in which entries are relations among conforming matrices. So also do Osgood's (1129) semantic studies in which words (stimuli) are scored for differences of meaning between people with regard to the relations of words to certain concepts. Doubtless many more experimental designs of such degrees of complexity will be employed when systematic familiarity with the DB enables investigators to perceive more reliably the structures and implications of such designs.

From the standpoint of scientific concept development it is important to note that what we are doing in most of these derived matrices is to find relations among relations instead of among simple scale measures. For example, in Chapter 26, a design is presented in which each referee is no longer a single organism but a *difference* between two organisms. It is for example U.S.A.-Britain; U.S.A.-Germany; Belgium-Bolivia, etc. The relative attributes are "geographical distance apart," "amount of trade exchange," "frequency of involvement in war." (It is true that in the ordinary facet the entries can be relations as well as attributes, but they are relations between

DIAGRAM 3-7. Sum and Difference Faces and Regularly Staggered Facets

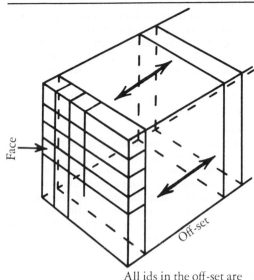

All ids in the off-set are collapsed between arrows to the face cells.

Here each cell in the facet comes from a different off-set column.

2. A super-
in which
in a bal
e.g., *SA*
eneous
which r
the hor
other. 7
or repe
Designs in
coordinate
(Chapter
data box
not group

Note—N
are repre
remaind
trations.

high ar
say, an
cation
selecti
ment
butior
a cono
on the

10. S
COV

INH

O
simp
kinc
ami
syst
poi
bee
a p
ma
ysi
sch
ma
wh
fra
so
ov

relative and referee, whereas here they occur between two referees.) The factors emerging from such a technique are *dimensions of national relations,* not *dimensions of nations* (see Chapter 26). And so one can proceed to extra relations of relations, mathematically, in a hierarchy which corresponds to an increasing hierarchy also of conceptual abstraction. However, comparatively few examples exist yet for such techniques, i.e., that take relationships among the sets in a matrix to create "higher-order sets" for further analysis.

With this we may close our study of possible varieties of relational systems and techniques—except for certain treatments of the total data box yet to come—and summarize the total taxonomy we have covered in Table 3-4.

In concluding this survey of basic *techniques,* i.e., of relational systems per se, and the directions and methods of mathematico-statistical analysis, with which they may be more or less freely combined to produce techniques, it is appropriate to ask something about the sampling and distribution properties of the various sets and entries. Space forbids any exhaustive treatment, but some approaches will be made in the next section. However, the main point here is that sets can be selected and sampled either on a *single* attribute or on their *total vector* or type properties, but that the latter is so difficult that it is rarely done. In this respect the typical use of anovar (analyses of variance) is far less controlled than most multivariate methods. The experimenter using anovar throws the first set into subgroups, e.g., divides people into more and less delinquent groups, and looks for significant differences among them on some id-attribute of the second set, e.g., responses on tests. Frequently the real magnitude of the differences among groups on the first set (the "independent variable") is never meaningfully stated. For example, delinquents may be shown by the anovar design to differ from non-delinquents at the $P<.01$ level on measured endomorphy. But no measure is given of the severity of the delinquency (independent variable). Or

discussed in Chapter 2 are necessary. Incidentally, an arbitrary subset of actual variables has sometimes been claimed to be identical with an ideal concept, indeed, a factor, as in Guttman's use of the term "facet analysis." But factor (see Chapter 6) is not to be identified with a literal cluster, which is formally only a surface trait. (Incidentally, Guttman's use of "facet" should not be confused with the more general use of facet made here. His use might perhaps more lucidly be called cluster analysis or correlation "order" or *correlation "mosaic" analysis,* as in Chapter 14 below.) However, the issue of variance on these ideal constructs and its relation to variance on observables is best left to Chapters 5, 6, 7, 9, 12, 13, and 14. Except insofar as we use general conceptual terms, the consideration of variance here will be restricted to the division of variance in the DB in terms of observables, or, at most, such "immediate constructs" as error, function fluctuation, etc. Similarly, we shall concentrate only on variance and distribution problems in entries, leaving questions of distribution of ids in various sets to the discussion of types in Chapter 9.

The kind of questions we will ask are: "With a frame of uniform entries, how much of the variance is associated with each set?" "How much of this remains as we collapse the frame to various faces and facets?" And, "What happens to the concept of error variance?" Answers to these affect, for instance, our current conceptions of standardized scales, and the setting out of the problems requires definition and notation to fit a broader conception of scale standardization. Answers about the sources of variance also affect our conceptions of what we get out of covariation analysis.

Any coordinate "set" bounding the Data Box corresponds, as pointed out earlier, to one possible class of "tag" for any single measurement. As we now turn our attention to entries (attributes), we shall continue to designate them by lower-case letters, as shown in Table 3-2, with capitals

for the ids by which they are tagged. Thus, in full dress, an entry will have ten tags, thus:

$$a_{P_i P'_{i'}, S_h S'_{h'}, A_j A'_{j'}, E_l E'_{l'}, O_w O'_{w'}}$$

or, if we are familiar with the symbols for each general id, thus

$$a_{ii'hh'jj'll'ww'}.$$

This defines the measure of a response (act) attribute, a, in response to stimulus S_h, in the particualr variant form $S'_{h'}$, for the type of response A_j, by the person P_i, in the general environment E_l, recorded by the observer O_w, etc. As with the facets, etc., it will be assumed that if set subscripts are not given, the values are *not* known, so that:

$$a_{ihj}$$

(dropping the capital subscripts by the simplification indicated) is the response attribute score j of person i, to stimulus h, the i', h', j', l, l', w, and w' ids being unknown.

Now just as the data box has functioned hitherto to remind us what sets need to be considered and what totality of relations among them exist, so now, with regard to the entries, it reminds us of the sources of variance, and needs to be brought into relation with analysis of variance concepts. In order to make any comparatively simple generalizations here it is necessary at first to avoid reference to cross-set facets, etc., and consider only the uniform data box in which the same attribute, a_j, is measured as the "dependent" variable (using this not in the causal sense but in the statistical sense of the reference variable).

Let us then consider the variance of the real variable, a (rather than that of any abstract ideal variable underlying a, etc.), and also the operationally possible divisions of this variance (into the ten sets) rather than divisions according to some concepts the investigator might entertain but have no operational way of applying. Then just as the total variance in analysis of variance may be divided into variance of subgroup means on various "effects," the interaction variance and error variance, so here we can find the amount of variance of the attribute associated with people, stimuli, states of persons, environmental background, etc., and their interaction and error.

Thus the typical expression for a three-set sum of squares — in this case let us take p person, t test, and o occasion as in the original Covariation Chart — becomes:

Sets $\Sigma^p\Sigma^t\Sigma^o(a_{pto}-a)^2 = PO\Sigma^r(a_t-a)^2$

Variances $+ PT\Sigma^o(a_o-a)^2$
$+ TO\Sigma^p(a_p-a)^2$
$+ P\Sigma^t\Sigma^o$
$\cdot(a_{to}-a_t-a_o+a)^2$
$+ T\Sigma^p\Sigma^o$

Interaction $(a_{po}-a_o-a_p+a)^2$
$+ O\Sigma^p\Sigma^t$
$\cdot(a_{pt}-a_p-a_t+a)^2$

Triple Interaction $+ \Sigma^p\Sigma^t\Sigma^o$
$\cdot(a_{pto}-a_{pt}-a_{po}$
$-a_{to}+a_p+a_t$
$+a_o-a)^2$

where p, t, and o are the numbers of people, tests, and occasions respectively; a_p is the mean for a person across all tests and occasions (similarly for a_t and a_o); a_{pt} is the mean for each person and test combination across all occasions (and equivalently for a_{po} and a_{to}); and a is the grand mean.

It must not be forgotten that with only one attribute score in each cell, as is typical of the data box, it will always be necessary to have data on one more set than the number of sets being examined if one is to examine for the statistical significance of the highest level of interaction. Thus in the three-set DB above one does not have an error term and an independent triple interaction term. That is to say, one can examine for significance of the variation among people, among tests, and among occasions as well as the first-order interactions among these. To examine also the second-order (or triple) interaction it would be necessary to have a new set — say an array of observers — added, from whence an error term could be derived.

A full ten-set data box should thus enable us to examine the significance (and relative magnitude in the given sample) of the variances contributed by all ten sets, and also the significance of any interaction effects up through the eighth order. The inferences to relations in the general population rest on the usual degrees of freedom, for, of course, a complete data box does not mean a complete population.

It is helpful to look at a number of elementary statistical concepts afresh in the context of the data box — concepts such as correlation, interaction, and error. For example, the correlation of two relatives will *generally* be different in a face from that in a facet or grid. For as we range over more off-sets we introduce more sources of variance, generally without adding similar degrees of covariance. For example, reading and arithmetic are positively correlated over people, but this is no particular reason for them to be correlated over states of people, environmental backgrounds, etc., which introduce error and attenuate the correlation. In this connection we are familiar with the fact that in general as we hold more of the other variables constant, the correlation of two variables will rise, eventually to unity. When we say that superego strength, G (Chapter 19) is correlated $+.3$ with school achievement, we recognize that if we could hold constant all other variables that contribute to school achievement, this correlation would rise to a perfect predictive relation, $r = 1.0$. In many cases the fixed facet or face with which we start out will, on the other hand, contain fewer sources of covariance than reside in the off-sets, and then going to the entries in mixed facet or grid will *raise* the correlations obtained. Parenthetically, it should be noted that the facet contains as many sources of set variance and covariance as the full ten-set grid entries, from which it is a random sample. In short, correlations within the data box need always to be considered and evaluated with regard to the restrictions on the face, faced grid, or facet one is operating upon.

To consider error in relation to the DB one must begin as usual by distinguishing between experimental error and sampling error. Any filled data box is, of course, only a sample, though it contains complete evidence on that sample. (Population inferences from it will be considered in a moment.) But as far as experimental error is concerned, we may note that the DB offers opportunities for more precise definition. For "experimental error" of measurement as commonly used (1) covers the variance over different numbers of off-sets in different researches, commonly without recognition of what they are, (Hence the saying that error is the variance the experimenter has chosen not to be interested in!) and (2) is often confused with the error term in analysis of variance, i.e., with the statistical sense of error.

As to the first, some experimenters may include the variation over environmental conditions, E, in error, others the variation over states of the subject, the P' set, in addition, and so on. The situation is the same as that in psychometrics when some test users call the stability coefficient (which is lowered by trait "function fluctuation") a "reliability" coefficient. Parenthetically, the distinctions made elsewhere (260) among dependability coefficient, stability coefficient, equivalence coefficient, etc. can be expounded most easily by use of the DB. With the aid of the DB notation it should be possible quickly and clearly to indicate what is meant by "error variance" in a given experiment. Thus the designated measurement: $a_{P_iS_hA_jE_l'}$, or $a_{ihjl'}$ in general, shows that "error" is the variance on the remaining, and therefore uncontrolled and unstated, six sets P', S', A', E, O, and O'.

If "error of measurement" is to be strictly applied habitually to any *one* source of variance it should be to O and O' — the differences with different observers and measuring instruments and their temporary states. It may be objected that this is not sufficient because the operational definition of true measurement which then follows — namely, that estimated by averaging across all observers and states of observers — ignores the possibility of a constant error among all

of them. However, the proof of such a constant error, if it exists, can only be made by indirect evidence, and, unless such evidence is introduced, our only available evidence of what the true score may be has to be what remains when observer variance is eliminated.

As far as experimental error is concerned, therefore, the DB offers some better definition than just "disregarded sources of variance" or "variation due to those influences which the experimenter is not interested in recognizing, measuring or controlling," which changes in an unstipulated way in every reference. It permits a limiting definition and a formula for every case. It also has a bearing on the meaning of "statistical error" when the error term is used in analysis of variance to provide an F ratio whereby the significance of certain mean variances is examined. If, for example, we examine the significance of variance over people and over tests, with appropriate degrees of freedom, the variance over states, environmental conditions, observers, etc. remains the basis of the error estimate with which these are compared. Typically the variances within the DB will be very different for different sets. For example, with personality measures the differences of means of persons will be greater than differences of means of environmental backgrounds. There is a sense in which the differences of two people can be evaluated against the variance in people generally, as well as against the error variance of states, observers, conditions of observers, etc. The analysis of variance significances in fact take on additional meaning when viewed in terms of the sets contributing to the error variance.

As to sampling error, we must assume, first, that if two data boxes were taken with exactly the same persons, stimuli, states, observers, backgrounds, etc., the entries on the chosen attribute would also be exactly the same. For if we have been truly exhaustive in our determining sets there are no other influences that could cause change. The difference from one experiment to another — the sampling error — is therefore due to a sampling of people, states, observers, etc., not to a sampling of entries as such.

Now much expert statistical comment has appeared on sampling of people, but the recent pioneering in P technique and other fields has revealed that statisticians have uncertain ideas about sampling of occasions, tests, stimuli, etc. The present writer's position on sampling of "time" is given below (Chapter 11), and in regard to stimuli and tests was stated long ago (213) in the *personality sphere* concept. In this latter field an essentially similar position has since been taken by Guttman (651) and by Kaiser (840) in the notion of "psychometric sampling." However, there seems no need to consider psychometric sampling as *essentially* different from "statistical sampling," for this implies an acceptance of the parochial horizon of statistics as applying only to populations of persons. Of course, it may be convenient in discussion to use such terms. The present writer's position, however, is that statistical sampling laws apply equally to all ten DB sets; but *that in all of them preliminary taxonomic work is necessary to make clear when one is sampling within species and when across them.* In terms of subjects we know what we are doing, and do not put men and monkeys in the same sample; but in regard to tests and states such solecisms occur every day. Insightful and correct use of sampling principles in other sets can come *only as we come to know more about their taxonomies.* In any case, the chief criticism of experiments not planned with the aid of the DB is that though they take acceptable samples of people, they have been very negligent in taking *sufficient* samples on other sets to justify the conclusions commonly drawn. It would certainly help to designate any measurement with sample sizes on the subscripts. Thus $a_{iP'_{20}S_{30}O_2}$ might be a measure of anxiety for person i, averaged over 20 states, over 30 stimuli for the given anxiety reaction, and again on repetition over two observers.

The sampling of ids in any given set must be carried out in regard to a recognized, indicated population, and if it aims at a stratified sample, it is at a multivariate stratification of profile patterns that it must aim (see Multivariate Distribution, Section 6, Chapter 13). It has been argued above that prior taxonomic studies can give as much meaning to "population" and "sample" in stimuli, responses, states, conditions and observers as in the common situation of a set of subjects. On closer inspection of much classical, bivariate experiment one is astonished to find how frequently the conclusions are stated without any reference to the populations of stimuli, responses, states, etc., to which they apply. Consequently, especially in manipulative types of experiments, inferences on degree of significance of associations have often been misleading. If a law of relation of response to stimulus or learning situation is being investigated, it is important to know that it holds, for example, when the manipulated stimulus range is twice or ten times that encountered in everyday life, and not necessarily in the normal range. Also in many interview-type investigations and studies with behavior ratings the extent of the origins of variance in different sets are seldom realized or quantified.

When it is contended here that the use of the DB has importance in experimental design in reminding us to take stock of the diverse sources of variance, and in permitting us to make variance analyses according to each of the sets, one must nevertheless be wary that variance analysis does not necessarily mean that one can simply apply the assumptions and procedures of standard analysis of variance. Especially is it doubtful that the assumption of homogeneity would be met by the variance across the different sets. The DB also reminds us that analysis of variance is commonly set up with an artificial, unrepresentative sample, in which the effects (influences) are made to be uncorrelated when in the total population they are usually correlated. (That is to say, in a stratified sample of the population according to demographic characters persons would not occur in all cells of a balanced design with equal frequency, but according to frequencies expected from the natural correlation of the effects.) For example, when the two effects are, say, positively correlated, one has difficulty in getting enough cases to fill the cells high on one effect and low on the other. Thus one takes all available cases for these cells and uses only a small selection of variables for the cells high or low on both. The distribution of entries then shows no correlation of the two effects, whereas in the stratified sample DB, representatively selected on the sets, the entries will have a normal rather than rectangular distribution and their covariance will be evident in the plot. This also reminds us that we should allow in various relational analyses for the fact that not all DB cells will necessarily contain entries, in a random or stratified (on other variables) sample.

Finally, in this glance at sampling and possible selection effects revealed in the data box, we must pause to note something hitherto passed over lightly, namely, the selection of *kinds of attributes* for entries. All too often, the experimenter proceeds to conclusions as if the particular attribute chosen to measure members of a particular set, say, a given response id, is its only attribute and is sufficient to define or represent it. A response, however, is a pattern with many attributes and only one has been taken for the entry measured. Just as the scientist is under an obligation to sample the ids appropriately from the various sets in drawing general conclusions representative of a given field, so he is obligated to attend also to the sampling of attribute and relation modes from each id when arranging for entries in the matrix. For example, the meaning of intelligence structure from correlating test stimuli over people becomes complete only to the extent that factorings over several kinds of response, e.g., speed, errors, effort, etc., are compared.

So far we have been reminding the reader principally that an attribute variance can be considered as broken down into: $\sigma^2 a_{SAPEOS'A'P'E'O'} = \sigma^2{}_S + \sigma^2{}_A + \sigma^2{}_P + \ldots + \sigma^2{}_{O'} +$ interaction terms and that each of these contributory variances depends on certain sampling assumptions. But it remains briefly to comment on the variances of the abstract or latent concepts which investigators may choose to use as alternatives to the literal, "real," operationally arrangeable sets. For example, Cartwright divides the variance of a stimulus-response variable into personality and ability factors, state and mood factors, aspects of the test instruction, e.g., what is actually said, what is perceived as being said, and, finally, into certain subdivisions of errors of measurement.

In general, the variance on any concept can be subsumed under (expressed by) the variances on the observed sets. But mutual translation and estimation is likely to be limited by (a) the fact that not all entry modes necessary to adequate definition have been tried, and (b) the likelihood of low "efficacy" (pages 44, 199) for many concepts, so that they predict largely only neither certain set and facet variances. However, this is where the sets function to help us look for missing concepts. The variance on any abstract scientific concept must be resolvable into some function—commonly simply a weighed composite—of the variances of the observed variables. For example, the personality factors are weighted composites of the response attribute measures over a set of stimuli. The variance contribution of an abstract or latent variable is therefore a function of variance on the variables we have been discussing. Commonly these concepts will arise from two sets, as in a facet. The possibility of concepts from three, four, and higher set analysis is discussed in Section 12 below.

In summary of Section 10, the value of the ten-set DB in adding meaning to discussions of variance, covariance, interaction, significance, as well as to conclusions in the form of laws is (1) its reminding us of the totality of sources of variances and interaction; (2) its offering of a basis of real variance sources into which operationally to analyze proposed conceptual sources of variance; (3) its suggestion of fresh conceptual resources; (4) its definition of error in a number of alternative ways; (5) its offering of a perspective on the relative importance and meaning of a variety of variance sources.

11. SCALES AND STANDARDIZATIONS: NORMATIVE, IPSATIVE, ABATIVE

The numbers and kinds of relations that can be encompassed in behavioral science have been set out, and we have further considered how the variance on any uniform entry score, in any given sample, can be totally resolved into the variance contributed by each of the ten sets, plus interactions up to the tenth order. (Though significance can be tested only up to the ninth.) It can alternatively be resolved into contributions from conceptual entities which are themselves functions of the parameters of sets.

An understanding of relations in the data box, however, is not complete so long as the relations and attributes are expressed in raw scores only, as they have been considered to be up to this point. Psychologists rightly question whether much value can be attached to relations and laws expressed in raw scores, because the latter are obviously arbitrary and accidental. And in some cases scientists can conceive units that better express increments in the concept or dimension being measured. Accordingly, we cannot complete our overview of data and its relations in the Data Box without facing the vexing question of behavioral measurement scales and the meaning of units.

As the present writer has reasoned elsewhere (240, 254), there are fundamentally only two ways in which we can hope to climb the ladder from ranking, to equal interval, or to absolute scales. They are: (1)

to assume that either the single sets of the data box (and/or their totality over all sets) comprise such a variety of patterns that we can assume for them a tendency to a normal (or some other known) distribution with respect to virtually any attribute we are using as entry; or (2) to adopt the *relational simplex theory,* which, stated most tersely, assumes that the true scales are such as will give the greatest mathematical simplicity of relationship over all variables with respect to the universe of scientific laws (254, 255).

The relational simplex theory (254) is too new to have received sufficient critical discussion and experimental illustration to permit us fully to lean upon it here, though Lingoes (939) has made a valuable contribution to solving its problems by the computer. Consequently, our considerations in this section will deal with the more modest objective of getting rid of the patent absurdities of raw scores by bringing measures into at least a recognized distribution. In fact, we may take the limited aim of obtaining common meaning in the data box by a definite distribution of attributes in the population for each given set separately. This process of bringing scores to a meaning in relation to a population distribution is broadly called *standardization* of raw scores. Within *standardization,* it is our purpose now to define and recognize *normatization,* across "columns" of a matrix (traditionally people), *ipsatization* across "rows" (traditionally tests), and *abatization,* across "files," i.e., at right angles to rows and columns, commonly across occasions or conditions.[9] (See Diagram 3-8 below.)

---

[9]The terms *ipsative* and *performative* were suggested by the present writer a decade or so ago to mean standardization across responses to one stimulus, and across stimuli (tests) respectively for one person. The term *normative* was already restricted to standardization across people (the social norm). The concept of *ipsative* standardization has generated an interesting and valuable literature, notably concerning the effect of ipsatization on factor analysis and on type search (e.g., Broverman, 149, 150; Clemans, 349; Ross, 1226; Tucker, 1462). The distinction between performative and ipsative, however, has not "caught on," perhaps because it is seldom needed. The distinction intended was that the scores averaged to give an ipsative mea-

In developing this useful beginning (the normative and ipsative concepts) to a comprehensive and, indeed, exhaustive definition of possible standardizations of psychological measurements one has the choice of (1) anchoring the various terms and meanings to the nature of the particular *sets*, e.g., people, stimuli, or (2) referring them to particular directions of standardization *relative to the facet, face or grid under examination*. Both have their usefulness, but the former can be handled by so simple a reference that no new nomenclature or notation is necessary. One simply refers to a person-standardized, or an O or an S standardized matrix (face, facet or grid). But the more abstract case, where one no longer refers to the concrete nature of the set, but is concerned with various directional standardizations of any facet or grid with which one is dealing, could be handled more intelligibly and clearly with a developed notation and terminology. As just pointed out, "P normatized, S normatized, etc." is sufficient and precise for the concrete set. But we would now propose that the alternative and general use of *normatized* be applied to "standardized over columns," regardless of the nature of the set of ids in the columns. This more general use seems far more useful and important and will be explored further here. Thus the reader should be on guard to recognize that normatization is not over *people*, but over whatever constitutes the column set population of a facet. It is always a standardization of a relative across *referees*.

All three directions of standardization — normative (over referees — columns), ipsative (over relatives — rows), and abative (over off-ids — files) — of course involve bringing raw measures to a mean of 0 and a standard deviation of 1. (*Normalized* standard scores by contrast to *normatized* are

DIAGRAM 3-8. The Standardizations Over Sets Which Produce Normative, Ipsative, and Abative Scores

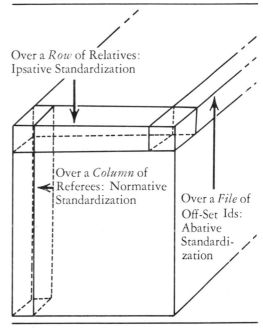

Over a *Row* of Relatives: Ipsative Standardization

Over a *Column* of Referees: Normative Standardization

Over a *File* of Off-Set Ids: Abative Standardization

raw score transformations which *bring the standard scores to a normal distribution.* Zero is then the raw score *median,* not only the mean.) *Abative*[10] scaling — using values in a facet which are standardized over the off-sets — though not yet much exemplified in psychological practice is valuable in many settings, e.g., in motivation test scoring. In any case, it is always important to know whether the entries in a matrix have or have not already been standardized with respect to the off-sets, which are always implicit when we are considering

---

sure were assumed of uniform response form, e.g., reaction times to the different stimuli represented by the columns, whereas the performative measure might (and must) employ the same units but could come from different kinds of tests (stimuli), e.g., errors in a sorting test, in response to an intelligence test, in a calling out names response, etc., i.e., from a heterogeneous facet. Because of the questionable correctness of adding and averaging scores from such diversity of tests, we propose that performative now be restricted to the adding and standardizing across rows of scores which have first been standardized by columns, as discussed below, i.e., to double-standardized scores. For ipsative itself a broader frame of reference is now suggested, as developed below.

---

[10]Abative is, of course, from "ab" — away — meaning standardization over sets of variances away from those in the main score matrix.

the two on-sets bounding any facet. For example, in the most common person-stimulus matrix, with response magnitudes as entries, i.e., a *PS.a* facet, the alternative conditions of the entries having or not having first been standardized over mood states of the subject, or over these and observers too, and so on, would make a great difference to either factor analysis or analysis of variance results.

One should note, however, that since psychologists are always operating in principle with a ten-set data box any two-dimensional score matrix always has no less than eight file sets running orthogonal to it. Consequently, it is necessary to say whether abative scaling represents a standardization across all at once, or some one only or some combination. This might be handled by designating a 1-abative to 8-abative standardization.

This choice of a *generalized* meaning for normative, ipsative and abative — relative to any score matrix for which relatives and referees have been defined — seems justified by (1) its lining up with the equally general distinction of direct and transposed matrices; (2) its permitting, later, statements about the relation and cumulative effects of normative, ipsative, etc., standardizations, regardless of the concrete nature of the sets involved, and (3) the fact that matrix analyses are performed in so many different ways nowadays that confusion quickly results from tying, say, normatization to people as referees. For example, what one experimenter, dealing with tests, is calling an ipsatized matrix is the same as that which another, concerned to type people, is calling a normatized score matrix, and is the same again as what someone working with *P* technique would call an abatized matrix.

In notation, if we stand consistently by our practice of putting the referee first and the relative second, an ipsatized *PS.a* matrix is understood at once to be standardized across stimuli (the relatives). Similarly, an *OS* normatized matrix is understood to refer to stimulus-associated entries of some

kind standardized across all observers, for each stimulus.

In the extensive discussion and debate regarding the effect of ipsatization on factor analysis (the corresponding problem has scarcely been raised in analysis of variance, or with respect to abative scaling), it has become evident that further definition of some varieties of standardization is necessary to avoid confusion. For whereas Burt and the present writer have used "double-centered matrix" to mean a matrix both normatized and ipsatized, Tucker, for example, has written of ipsatization and "double-centering" as a process in which only the *means* of rows and columns are brought to the same values.

There are actually three main possibilities in this area of what may roughly be called "double-standardizing" of matrices. Since their effects on the outcome of statistical calculations which employ them are very different, they should be explicitly recognized, along with the labels for the matrices which employ them singly or combined. (1) *A fully normatized or fully ipsatized* (or fully abatized) raw score series is one that has the same mean (0) and sigma (1.0) as another. (2) *A semi-normatized or semi-ipsatized,* etc., series is one brought to a mean of zero, but left at its original (or some irregular) sigma. (3) A third, less widely "standard," statistical treatment is what will be called a *fund-ipsatized* or fund-normatized, etc., series. It is one in which each original score, $a_1, a_2 \ldots a_n$ is divided by the sum of all scores, i.e., by $(a_1 + a_2 \ldots + a_n)$. Thus all such series add to unity and have a mean of $1/n$, but the sigmas are variable, equalling the original raw score sigma divided by $(a_1 + a_2 \ldots + a_n)$. Fund ipsatization, incidentally, gathers its name from and has its greatest use in motivation measurement. Here, for certain purposes, notably in employing the solipsistic theory of interest (202), the "total fund" of interest is required to be the same for all subjects while individuals are still allowed to "disperse" their interests little or highly. Incidentally, fund-ipsatized scores, despite their special properties and effects on correlations, factoring, and analysis of variance, have long been used in psychology, e.g., in most studies using preference judgments among all possible pairs and even in some multiple-choice data, without adequate recognition of those properties.

When one views scaling in the context of the data box, it is evident that besides over-all treatment by any one kind of transformation, one must also consider many combinations of normative, ipsative, and abative treatment. (Also keeping in mind, with ten dimensions, the above mentioned possibilities of abative 1, abative 2 ... abative 8 scoring.) This whole question of *multiply standardized matrices* has barely been touched in regard to its implications for conclusions from classical experiments. On the other hand, in psychometry there has been more discussion and we now distinguish *double-standardized* (Burt, 158; Cattell, 228, 230; Stephenson, 1346) facets when they are both fully normatized and fully ipsatized both ways, and *double-centered* (Tucker, 1462) when semi-normatized and semi-ipsatized. Apparently abatized matrices have been used so far only on *P*-technique data. However, we stand at the moment in a curious position in that although writers happily refer to truly double-standardized matrices, and theoretically they can easily exist, no one knows how to derive them immediately from raw scores!

Double-centered matrices can be obtained easily enough; one simply adds to every value in a row the constant necessary to bring its mean to some agreed value (commonly zero) for all rows. This can be repeated for columns without making the row means unequal. On the other hand, in double standardization each normatization (by columns) throws off the previous ipsatization (of rows) and vice versa. Nesselroade and the present writer have shown that a cycle of repeated treatments *does* ultimately converge on a stable double-standardized matrix. However, the nature of the converged matrix differs according to whether one starts with rows or

columns! It has long been obvious that, say, any two or three single successive row-column standardization cycles will leave one with different final scores, depending on the order in which they are done; but we must now also recognize that any *ultimate* stable convergence position will also be affected by the order. Such a score matrix will have the equal mean and equal sigma property of the matrix which, say, Burt theoretically starts off from in his proof of equivalence of R- and Q-technique principal axis, unreduced matrix factorings. But from any set of actual score data one can obtain two distinct double-standardized matrices (depending on which foot one first stands on in the normative-ipsative-normative-ipsative iteration) from which to begin.

The issue of double-standardized matrices must be left to further specialized inquiry. But the effects of simple normatization, ipsatization, or abatization can be pursued to ultimate conclusions and have importance for a variety of experiments in motivation, perception, etc. currently being debated. Ipsatization, for example, will affect the clusters found among variables, the results of analysis of variance, and crucially, the outcome of a factor analysis, compared with the factor analysis from the raw data.[11]

Standardization is concerned, of course, only with eliminating the non-comparabilities of raw scores, but *normatization* is something more and will be considered as one of the two avenues (the relational simplex is the other) for producing meaningful equal interval scaling. It assumes that any set of ids presents a multivariate normal distribution when measured with

---

[11]This will be discussed in Chapter 6. But briefly one may note that since, in the ipsatized score matrix, there can now be no mean difference between the total for any one person and the total for any other, whatever would have appeared as the first centroid or principal axis factor tends to be destroyed. However, this first unrotated factor is not a single meaningful factor, but a composite of several, so the net effect is a distortion of the variance and form of the *rotated* factors, and of their interaction as shown by their intercorrelations.

proper scaling on the various attributes. This assumption is safer when the score can be considered the outcome of addition of a relatively large number of diverse influences. Provided we first have evidence from type studies (Chapter 9) that we have essentially a single species, this may be justified as the best *brief* approach to equal interval scaling. The more fundamental approach lies in the simplex theory (254), which says those transformations of the raw scale which give the simplest lawful relationships among variables yield an equal interval scale. That the normalization procedure moves in this direction is suggested by the repeated finding of a clearer simple structure factor analysis when raw data is normalized than when it is not.

The classification of standardization procedures suggested for the data box is summarized in Diagram 3-9.

12. SUPERORDINATE RELATIONAL AND INTERACTIONAL ANALYSIS TECHNIQUES:

INCLUDING SUPER-SET AND INTER-SET FACTOR ANALYSIS

A parting glance at the data box is now called for in regard to the promise it holds of extracting relations and information over something more complex than a two-set facet. To the abstraction of such further relations we shall give the general designation of *superordinate relational analysis and techniques*. Indications of higher orders of analysis have already been given in such directions as operating on differences (or other functions) of scores in two conforming DB matrices; in the more familiar processes of calculating higher stratum factors; in the possibility of continuing

DIAGRAM 3-9.   Possibilities in Rescaling to Standard Scores

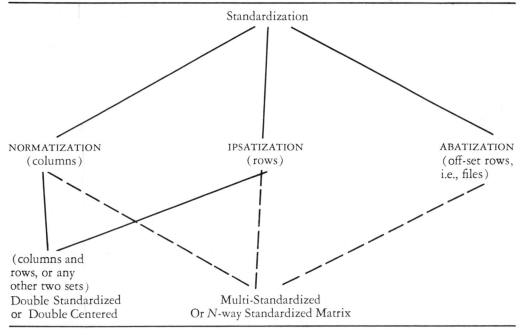

Always relative to a defined matrix, e.g., a *PS.a* normatized facet.

variance analysis to a nine-set interaction, and in the preliminary discussion of correlations over grids and frames in which the relatives have their relations studied over more than one set of referees, in fact, over a balanced composite set.

Yet these are only a few special instances of the dawning possibilities of analyzing in various ways relations built upon relations, with the accompanying development of more abstract and far-reaching concepts. Since a whole book would be needed even to clarify the necessary constituent concepts and to give just a skeletal outline of systematic possibilities, the present section can hope only to take glances along a few vistas. Perhaps this restriction can be justified by the fact that the experimenter who has kept us company thus far already has enough to think about and apply in the relational analysis possibilities defined. Consequently this section is unfinished and intended largely as an orientation to likely future developments. One must recognize, of course, that any investigator, in the usual processes of developing his concepts, already piles relation upon relation. But he does so in the spirit and with the resources only of a lone prospector personally and subjectively bringing evidence from one facet analysis into relation with that from another. What needs to be studied in an adequate expansion of this section concerns the development of systematic concepts of further relational hierarchy systems, and the development of mathematico-statistical methods, using computer resources, to carry out much of this piecemeal intuitive, trial and error exploration with the guidance of concepts and methods as systematic as those so far discussed for simpler relations.

Superordinate DB analyses of the factor analytic type require centrally a simple structure, a confactor or other rotational resolution method capable of recognizing the same factor influences when they appear in different facet or grid analyses. Mostly the efficacy of factors is such that they appear only in one or two facets. (For example, state factors, such as anxiety, appear

both in *PSa* and *ESa* facets.) When the former holds we need only an *addition* of all separate facet specification equations to produce the *grand specification equation* necessary to predict any entry in the total data box. But in addition to *additive superordinate analyses* it is possible to imagine *interactive superordinate* models using, for example, product terms.

A conspicuous recent example of progress in interactive models is the three-way (three-set) factor analysis discussed by a number of psychologists, e.g., Horst (763, 766), but brought to clearest form and expression by the work of Tucker (1467). (He has called it three-mode analysis, but since mode has been adopted here for a species of entry, we shall, consistent with other uses, call it three-set — or, eventually, *n*-set — factor analysis.) Naturally one thinks of generalizing — once two-set factor analysis is transcended — to the *full* ten-set factor analysis indicated by the full data box. But to proceed with sufficient regard for the meanings of the model in terms of empirical data, and to adjust it appropriately as we proceed, it may be best to forgo the mathematician's leap to the full logical possibilities and confine ourselves awhile to the quite sufficiently complex three-set treatment.

Let us begin by recognizing (Tucker, 1467) that any uniform entry in a three-set frame is considered to be resolved as follows:

$$a_{jkl} = \Sigma_{F_P}\Sigma_{F_S}\Sigma_{F_E}P_{i_{F_P}}.S_{j_{F_S}}.E_{k_{F_E}}.g_{F_PS_FE}$$

where $P_{i_{F_P}}$ is the projection of any individual i on a matrix F_P of abstract ("idealized") stimulus-factors, in a matrix F_P, and so on. The matrix g is a three-set frame, bounded by the idealized F_P, F_S, and F_E dimensions and showing their relations one to another. (This could be extended to the ten-set Data Box, i.e., to a ten-set g.) The meaning of g is at present that of a relating of the ideal constructs from each of several sets, and for this reason we call such techniques *interactive* or *inter-set* factor analyses, from three-way to ten-way inter-sets. It remains for psychological use to bring out its meanings in terms of behavioral concepts. An initial application of three-set inter-set analysis to actual data has been carried out by Levine (927). With this designation of its role, n-set factor analysis will not be pursued further here because it belongs more specifically to factor analytic methods in Chapter 6.

As to the exploring of the higher-order relations of the data box in terms of interaction effects, at second, third, and higher orders (discussed in Section 10 above), and perhaps best named n-set analysis of variance, only isolated instances of research treatments going up to the third or fourth order exist apparently, and the reader must be referred to these in the writings of Digman (Chapter 15), Saunders, Guttman, Jones (Chapter 7), and others. He will also find an interesting substantive example, at only first or second order of interaction, in the recent work on dynamics (Horn, Chapter 20). Therein he will notice that motivation component factors are recognized as largely absent from correlation of attitudes over people, with vehicles constant, or from correlation of vehicles over people, with one fixed attitude, but appears when attitude strength variance and vehicle strength variance are allowed to occur together. Such relations should make themselves quickly evident either by analysis of variance or by factor-analytic methods.

A third movement into superordinate relation analyses occurs in what we may call *super-set factor analysis*. By this we mean factor analysis going beyond the use of a simple two-set facet, as will be shown below, and generally involving the relating of factor resolutions from these diversely chosen super sets, but not in the sense of n-way factor analysis mentioned above. In super-set analysis either the relatives or the referees or both include joint variation over two or more sets, in a balanced arrangement, e.g., all subjects over all observers. "Higher-order factor analysis" would be a misleading term, implying that we are dealing with higher-order factors, and "super-matrix analysis" is also not quite suitable because although the grids we are to deal with *are* strictly super matrices, the treatment is only one aspect of the possible super matrix treatments. A certain parallelism exists between n-set analysis of variance and super-set factor analysis, the difference being the usual one between the two methods (see Chapter 8), namely, that the former asks about relations of ids in sets to a dependent variable, the entry, whereas the latter seeks relations among the ids (relatives) in terms of the entry. In both the entry is, of course, the "indicator" of whether a relation (of the first or the second kind) exists.

In super-set factor analysis we can recognize a series of possible analyses within the data box which may be said to show, for lack of a better term, increasing "depth of reference" in taking in (a) the variance from more types of referee as one goes from facets to grids, or (b) the relations among more kinds of relatives, as a grid with "combined relatives" (see below) is used.

As to super-set analysis with combined referees, let us remember that in a fixed facet, referees are held at the same fixed values (ids) on all off-sets so that no variance of the relatives is being compared and analyzed except that on the single set. A face comes next to this in simplicity, for there, having averaged over the off-sets, we have eliminated most off-set variance. It is the grid, therefore, and especially that unfolded over eight sets from the ten-set data box, which gives the greatest variability on the referees—indeed a total possible variability. The number of entries in any such grid will be the total $N \times n \times G, \ldots$ etc., product of totals in each set, but the referees ("cases") over which correlation occurs will be this total, T, divided by the number of relatives. Diagram 3-10 illustrates this on a small scale. This calculation of the total referees as the product of the numbers on the non-relative sets holds, of course, only

DIAGRAM 3-10.   Illustration of a "Homogenous Relative" Grid from Unfolding a Three-Stimulus, Four-Environment, Five-Person Frame

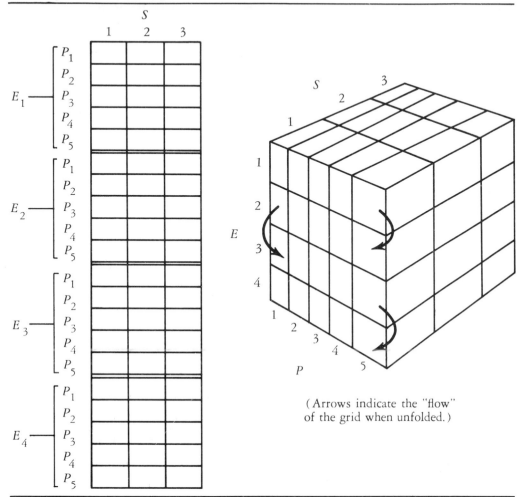

(Arrows indicate the "flow" of the grid when unfolded.)

in the completely combined, randomized design, where every id one on set is combined systematically with every id on the others.

Each of the ten different "homogeneous (one-set) relative" (see Diagram 3-10) analyses (grids) possible from the full data box (each hinging on a different set of referees) will in fact contain the same *information* (same entries). But the analysis will be with respect to ten partially different sets of relatives, and, as we have seen in inter-set factoring, the abstractions ("ideal dimensions") are relatable through a central ten-dimensional matrix "g," though in additive super-set analyses they will be simply additive factor matrices. Regardless of which model is used, our concern in super-set factor analysis is with the relations among the factors found from various factorings of any one set of relatives, when, instead of using one (constant) facet and factoring over one set of referees, one factors over several referee sets (hence "super-set") at once, e.g., comparing stimuli simultaneously over people, states, environmental backgrounds, observers, etc. Let us consider an illustration restricted for simplicity to a three-set grid — P, S, and P' (state of person) being the sets. Using stimuli as relatives, we are now "confounding" (in a statistical sense, though compounding might be better) state variance with person variance. If we had analyzed relations separately over people as referees and states as referees, we should have obtained respectively trait and state factors. The super-set analysis will yield both together. If our example had been the full data box, then our answers would have included also instrument "perception" factors for the observers, environment modification factors for the stimuli, etc. The super-set factor matrix when combined referees are used will thus normally be the sum of the factor matrices from the single-set, fixed-facet analyses, unless there are interaction effects as discussed below.

Now, even if one should fall short of balanced design (which would involve stratified sampling not only on each set but also on the combinations among sets), certain scientific advantages can be claimed for super-set analysis. First, it is true of all "control" designs, which hold non-analyzed variables at fixed values, that the relations we find among the analyzed variables from such experiments may be regarded as proven only for the quite specific fixed control value held on the other sets. When we come to apply the conclusions in the normal, freely varying totality, there is a certain artificiality about these results and a definite doubt about their applicability. States of the individual, recognized as factor patterns (dimensions), defined across *many* differing individuals, have a different loading pattern from those found at a control position fixed by one individual or one type of individual only. Each pattern has its meaning and use, but the meaning of the former has wider utility. Second, in a constant facet, as contrasted with a grid, we miss whatever interaction effects — in the usual statistical sense of interaction — may

exist. It is possible that certain variances and covariances are associated with, say, people over stimuli, taken when state variance exists, which are not evident when it does not exist. The superordinate grid analysis over several sets can include most of the interaction possibilities described above (page 111). For each variance and covariance obtained is due both to the variance on the ten sets and their interactions in twos, threes, fours, etc.

An important instance of new factors appearing in super-set analysis occurs, for example, in the anxiety field, where inclusion of a variety of environments as well as a variety of responses seems to bring out certain specializations to environment. It is probable, as Cattell and Digman (282) suggest, that super-set analysis of personality responses and observers can reveal instrument factors leading to better understanding of formerly puzzling irregularities of rating results. The proper separation of motivation component and dynamic structure factors in human motivation study may also (Horn, Chapter 20) turn on this, and Table 3-5 presents a schema for this.

The second main conceptual possibility in a super-set analysis as designated above (beyond what we have just described as homogeneous relative super-set analysis) is that in which the *relatives*, not the referees, are made to present all possible combinations of the sets. Obviously this is a variety of what we called a cross-set analysis, but it is a very special variety in that it is complete. Further a third, hybrid form can be considered in which we not only correlate across systematic combinations of referees but simultaneously use this new systematic combination of the remaining sets to constitute the relatives. Such a hybrid operates on the kind of grid we discussed earlier (page 104) representing the various possible flat unfoldings of the total DB. Incidentally, the sum of the relative and referee sets must be no more than 10 because if the same set were incorporated in referees and relatives there would be square "holes" in such a matrix, running as a diagonal, because it is scarcely possible

TABLE 3-5

SOURCES OF VARIANCE IN A THREE-FRAME ILLUSTRATED IN MOTIVATIONAL RESEARCH

Score Component	How to Remove	Putative Psychological Content
Over-all between-vehicle mean differences.	Subtract vehicle mean.	Irrelevant and likely to be artifactual.
Over-all between-vehicle variance.	Above and take standard scores within each vehicle lamina.	Irrelevant. Do not analyze.
Over-all between-persons mean differences.	Above and subtract mean of over-all persons laminae.	General individual differences in response tendencies which summate within persons. Particularly second-order trait factors. In this sense "like" a "first-factor centroid" but not necessarily the same as one.
Over-all between-persons variance.	Above and take standard scores within each person lamina.	General individual differences in discrimination between attitudes irrespective of vehicles. Likely to involve traits such as (B) Intelligence, (N) Sophistication.
Person-vehicle mean effect.	Above 1, 2, 3, and subtract mean of person-vehicle file.	Traits that are particularly evoked by this vehicle, and averaged effects of person-vehicle-attitude interaction.
Person-vehicle variance effect.	Take standard scores within person-vehicle files.	Scale size of personal discrimination between attitudes within each vehicle. Would appear as a vehicle factor on some faces.
Attitudes within person-vehicle files.	A remainder.	Attitude discriminations purified of the influences above so that different vehicles become simply occasions for expressing variability or consistency of a person's attitudes.

(or meaningful) to give entries for a set with itself. However, this does not prevent, say, using five sets as relatives over the other five sets as referees, in a square but non-symmetrical matrix, as shown in Diagram 3-11. Incidentally the reader will remember that the agreed mode of representation of such super-set analyses is instanced by $\overline{PSS'.AEE'O}.a$ or $\overline{ES'OP.SE'}.s$, in which the capital letters cannot exceed 10 or be repeated.

Whichever of the eight possible degrees of combined relative super-set grids are used (*beyond* the homogeneous relatives grid, and systematically combining relatives on two up through nine sets) the factors which normally emerge may be difficult immediately to relate to those which come out from a homogeneous set. For example, they will not load simply tests, but tests on a particular occasion as measured by a particular observer, etc. Again, in a broad sense, requiring more careful statistical expression in relation to scales and total variance, the super-set result should be a sum of the single homogeneous-facet factor-pattern matrices resulting from the same referees. Such a matrix would be expected to have as many factors as the sum of non-identical factors from the separate homogeneous relative facets, and to be a convenient way of predicting, say, a person's score on the composite type of relative. It offers additional information in giving the correlations among the factors from the different sets of relatives.

Obviously space cannot be taken either here or in Chapter 6 on factor analysis to work out the many relations between different kinds of additive super-set analyses or between these and interactive, product models. For example, a whole series of relations exist to be worked out between the factors from the series of grids just indicated as going from a homogeneous (one-set) relative grid up through the various systematic randomized combinations of 2, 3, etc. sets of relatives—and their transposes. All that needs to be said is that a full conceptual understanding of the sources of influence, and a full capacity to estimate a given entry, can be reached only when these various analyses are related. Meanwhile we have to point out

DIAGRAM 3-11. A Super-Set Matrix with Persons, States, Stimuli, Environmental Back - grounds, and Responses

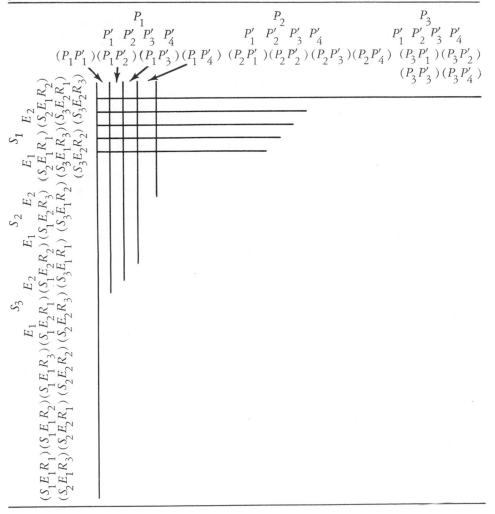

that our objective here is to state comprehensively the possible relational systems in which any theory may have its being, and to leave statistical analysis methods and problems for later treatment.

13. SUMMARY, GLOSSARY, AND NOTATION

(1) Explicit focusing of the relational systems available in behavioral science data for the discovery, representation and testing of theories has the advantage of adding precision and enrichment to theories. Of equal importance is the fact that it gives concrete help in working out experimental designs and choosing statistical analysis methods. Further, it permits new possibilities of relational analysis to be seen, as well as the relation of one analytical approach to another.

(2) What began a score of years ago as the Covariation Chart can now, with years of experience in its use, be made a more adequate Basic Data Relation Matrix or data box (DB), extended to ten coordinates, each corresponding to an independently variable class of entities or ids, designated *sets*.

(3) The data box is constituted by the two proto-concepts with which science and logic have concerned themselves — entities (patterns, ids, vectors — in sets) and relations (attributes, dimensions, predicates) among them. The ids (individual members of sets) bound the box as Cartesian coordinates, while the relations and attributes, defined for the matrix, enter the cells as dimensional quantities in "entries."

(4) Each cell value measures an attribute of a single unique event or *node* (or constituent thereof). The signatures (subscripts) of this attribute measure of this node are those of the unique ids from the ten sets — organisms (P), stimuli (S), environment backgrounds (E), responses or acts (A), etc. — which meet in the node. The entries can be of different modes according to the sets of which they are attributes. But ultimately they are either measures of rela-

tions or of attributes (which can again be either aspects or shifts). In general it makes sense to attach a measure of an attribute of any part or set of the node to any pair (bounding the matrix) of ids out of those uniquely combined in the node.

(5) Within the main theme of this chapter — relational *systems* — one can speak further of relational *analyses*. For any one system of relations can be analyzed, using exactly the same data, in different *directions*, as one sees in matrices and their transposes, or in normative and ipsative standardizations. A relational analysis can be considered to exist independently of the statistical method used, but a *technique* is a combination of a relational system and a statistical analysis method. All methods — bivariate or multivariate, analysis of variance or factor analysis — begin with comparing two relatives, with respect to a series of attribute values, over a series of ids belonging to another set — the referees. Any such mathematico-statistical comparison, regardless of its particular form, treats the two ids so related as the *relatives* (indeed the whole set to which they belong is to be called the *relative set*), and the sets over which they are compared as the *referees* or instances. (The question of establishing which is dependent and independent belongs to the later stage of experimental *design* or in another sense of dependent and independent, to the *method* of analysis, and has no relevance here.) Relatives may be related in one pair, as in most analysis of variance designs and some correlation studies, or in large numbers, as in factor analysis, multiple discriminant function methods, etc. Later discussion in this book is couched more often in the form of the latter, multivariate methods because their conclusions are comprehensive of the former too.

(6) Efficient discussion of this complex realm of relational analysis requires a compact and unambiguous nomenclature and notation. For this purpose it does not suffice simply to take over the terms of matrix algebra, because science involves more considerations than mathematics.

However, the suggested notation uses traditional algebraic symbols and psychological terms without doing violence to standard mathematical usage. In particular, a notation is needed for the rich variety of submatrices and their modes of analysis which can be arranged within the total data box. The following is a brief glossary of main terms; others are defined in tables in the text.

A set: the group of entities of similar type forming a bounding coordinate.

An id: an individual member of any set.

A facet: a two-coordinate score matrix, each entry corresponding to an attribute or relation of a relative, a referee, and only one id on each of the off-sets.

A face: a two-coordinate score matrix with entries expressing values (usually means) condensed from a whole series of off-ids.

A frame: a score matrix of more than two coordinates — a prism — with the data box as the limiting ten-frame.

A grid: an unrolled frame which, though two-dimensional, differs from a facet or face in having either a single set as one coordinate (a "homogeneous relative" grid) but confounded sets over the other, i.e., a repeating series of ids of one set paired with successive ids on the other sets, or mixed sets over both relatives and referees.

(7) According to the combinations of sets and entries used, a facet can be classified as: (a) a mixed or a fixed (set) facet. The latter has the off-set ids fixed at the same value for all entries; the former does not. (b) A homogeneous or heterogeneous entry facet. The former uses the same entry for all relatives; the latter defines a different entry for each relative (column), regardless of the state of sets. (c) A uniform or cross-set facet. The former has all ids in the relatives belonging to the same set. The latter has "staggered" entries from across the data box, so that columns represent ids from different sets.

(8) The notation suggested consists in using $P, E, A, S, O, P', E', A', S'$, and O' for the ten sets, and p, e, a, s, o, etc., for the entries, when attributes, indicating thereby the set of which they are an attribute measure. However, a is used also as a general unspecified entry symbol. The nature of a facet or face, and of the direction of analysis, can be indicated by such a notation as: $PS.a$, $\underline{EP'O}$, which indicates people and stimuli as the bounding sets, the placing of S second showing that it is the relative and P the referee, i.e., that one is going to correlate stimuli over people. The entry has the lower-case letter, e.g., a. The line under $EP'O$ indicates that E, P', and O are being held fixed (the remainder, by omission, not being so fixed), i.e., all measures have the same background environment, internal state, and experimenter (observer). For frames this can be extended, e.g., $OPS,s,\underline{ER}$ indicates a three-set faced frame, bounded by $O, P,$ and $S,$ and averaged over E and R ids.

The notation can be extended to define all relational systems and relational analyses, and one can determine the exact numbers of each possible relational system, which are considerable.

(9) The concepts of sampling used for people or organisms need to be extended to the other coordinates of the data box if we are adequately to interpret results of experiments. In a homogeneous entry matrix the variance of the attribute or relation is the sum of the variances due to each set separately, plus the various orders of interaction. What is often called error variance would commonly here be recognized as *off-set variance*. Error of measurement is error over the observer and observer condition sets, O and O'. Sampling error remains, in inference from every finite data box.

(10) It is suggested that the terms for standardized scores over sets be attached to *directions relative to the facet to be analyzed* rather than attached to particular set contents, e.g., people, stimuli, states of people. Then, arrays being of three kinds, one can speak of *normatized* scores when *columns* are brought to standard scores, *ipsatized*

scores when *rows* are treated, and *abatized* scores when *files* (i.e., arrays on sets perpendicular to the facet) are standardized.

(11) Discussion of relational systems begins with those in simple facets, faces, and grids. However, the complete data box calls attention to higher orders and hierarchies of possible relations among relations. First, there are the derived score data boxes in each of which the entries are functions of simple entries in two or more conforming data matrices. Second, there are analyses of higher-order factors and higher-order interactions among sets. (The data box, by analysis of variance, permits estimation of up to the ninth order of interaction.) Third, there are superordinate analysis possibilities, using interactive models, as in n-way factor analysis or additive models, as in super-set factor analysis. A considerable variety of super-set analyses (able to use super-matrix methods) exist, principally in the classes of combined relative and combined referee designs. The aim of factor analysis in these settings is to achieve a description of the influence concepts operating across all set sources of variance, and to calculate from these by either additive or interactive models.

CHAPTER 4

An Overview of the Essentials of Multivariate Analysis Methods

PAUL HORST
University of Washington*

1. INTRODUCTION
(BY THE EDITOR)

Up to this point we have concentrated on the rationale and planning of scientific investigations in the most general sense. We have asked, systematically, what kinds of relations are to be examined, how they give substance to theory, and by what general kinds of statistical methods the theories may be examined through these relations. What we have called the panels of theoretical *theme,* relational *system,* and experimental *design* ending in the obtaining of data on the stipulated relations have been examined in detail. But the ensuing use of *statistical methods* has only been evaluated in a taxonomy of essentials. From this point on we begin to give detailed technical attention to the statistical analysis methods as such. And whereas the treatment up to this point has dealt with all kinds of research designs, being equally

*This study was supported in part by Office of Naval Research Contract Non R-477 (08) and Public Health Research Grant M-743 (C5).

relevant to bivariate and multivariate methods, it will now concentrate on the multivariate half of research activity. For the purpose of this Handbook is to advance multivariate designs and to clarify the conceptual advances in psychology which have resulted from their use.

However, in scientific research, a comprehensive knowledge of the taxonomy of theory structure, of relational systems, of design and method is only half the story. Any experienced perspective on the available research alternatives — of the whole taxonomy of investigation — needs to be supplemented by a shrewd appreciation of the relative *effectiveness and aptness* of different designs for the various kinds of undertakings a researcher normally encounters. In a broad sense the study of aptness has already begun above in regard to considering the fitness of designs for various theoretical purposes — notably as to the relative power of bivariate and multivariate methods — but this approach to "fitness" has so far been much less complete than has the study of taxonomy as such.

Doubtless a general, scientific, methodological treatise for psychologists and others will be written before long, one that will be as exhaustively systematic on the utilities, properties, and strategic and tactical felicities of designs as the above may be on their taxonomic description. However, it would perhaps be best to postpone such an undertaking for a while because, unlike taxonomy, it cannot be developed from logic alone. It must be bought partly with experience. The potentialities of a new method, like those of a new weapon in war, frequently turn out to be very different from those initially predicted. At this stage, therefore, the reader is invited to a considerable degree to form his own opinion on the strategic and tactical utilities of the above, by observing the methods in action in the remainder—especially the second part—of this book.

Some of the writers in Part I (though not those in Part II) have conceived their task as applying only to the *method* panel of the four panels we have described. As leading psychological statisticians, they have quite correctly written where they have most to give. However, even these specialists have generally kept their statistics well oriented to research—and specifically to psychological research—and at the same time have made substantive contributions to psychological work. Consequently their expositions show either a sensitiveness to the experimental design and theme issues, or an actual linking of the statistical method with the theory construction and experimental design panels. However, if the reader should feel that any method described in Part I stands in too puristic a mathematical isolation, he can seek a remedy in Part II.

It is appropriate to begin the study of multivariate statistical method with a survey chapter. For a broad and deep understanding of the natures and relationships of the chief methods it would be difficult to find a better authority, more experienced in the needs of psychologists, than Dr. Horst. In one point only has an editorial change from the treatment in his other books been suggested, namely, in the trivial semantics of *entity* and *attribute,* because his original use might cause confusion in the light of a slightly different usage systematically made in the first three chapters and elsewhere. Dr. Horst's original use is very straightforward—the signatures of rows are entities and of columns attributes, in any matrix. However, in the broader sense, which goes outside the realm of matrices and matrix algebra as such, both the signatures that mark the rows *and* those that mark the columns are entities, as pointed out in Chapter 3. For example, they may be tests, people, occasions, observers—and every one of these is a pattern entity, not a dimension or abstracted attribute. We have in fact called them *entities* or *ids,* falling in *sets* or *species. It is the values in the cells which refer to defined attributes of these entities.* For example, if, in a *Q*-technique experiment, the rows are objective test situations and the columns people, the attribute measured in the cells is some one aspect or dimension of the total relation between the situation (entity to us, entity to Horst) and the person (entity to us, attribute to Horst). When the measured attribute is a relation it belongs as much to the row as to the column entity. The attribute (our sense) might be the speed with which each person reacts to each of the situations. The attribute or relation is thus a single continuum (or dichotomy or quality), whereas the entities or ids have each the form of a total pattern-entity or individuality, as defined at some length in Chapter 3.

However, although the data box matrices are actually bounded by Cartesian coordinate sets consisting of entities, or ids as we have called them, it remains operationally true that columns often coincide with attributes—usually *one possible attribute* of the object or id at the top. For practical matrix purposes, therefore, when this chapter uses the term "attribute" it remains the same as attribute or relation in Chapter 3. We shall also continue in this and other chapters the use of the term "relatives" for the ids in the set among which relations are being found — by correlation, analysis of variance, or what not. Tests or stimuli are the most common sets for relatives, but a different technique can use people, or observers, or states of people, as relatives. The ids over which relations are being evaluated will continue to be designated the *referees*. They are the field of instances or the "population" over which the relations are said to hold.

The use of relatives and referees, of course, supposes nothing more than a direction of analysis, namely, that comparisons are made *among* columns and *over* rows (by correlation or analysis of variance over rows). It assumes nothing about the scientific roles of the two entities in a theoretical model or theme though a distinction *is* possible between the "active" entities, subjects, and observers, who come to "passive" situations, environmental conditions, etc. which could be paralleled by analyzing as statistically dependent and independent "variables." All such distinctions are for most purposes, however, initially outside statistics and belong to inferences from experimental design. The only distinction of entities necessary in the method stage is in terms of the operations in mathematical analysis, and this distinction is exactly described by the terms referee and relative (or "rees" and "rels," if we wish, for short) defined earlier.

It is not easy to make a comprehensive list of the totality of multivariate analysis methods, because they fall at very different levels of comprehensiveness. However, one may mention: (1) Multiple regression, the joint relating of many variables to one; (2) Canonical correlation (and such problems as the most predictable criterion), in which a function of many variables is related to a function of another plurality; (3) Factor analysis, the resolution of many variables into fewer; (4) Multiple analysis of variance, looking for significance of relation of several independent and several dependent variables; (5) Differential prediction, magnifying differences of prediction and selection rather than concerning

oneself with absolute prediction; (6) Multidimensional scaling, a relative of factor analysis; (7) Multiple discriminant functions, maximizing the separation of individuals on pre-assigned groupings; (8) Configural and type analysis, *discovering* naturally existing segregations of entities in groups by various dimensional properties, including measuring the "distance apart" of individuals; (9) Latent class analysis, a further form of "typing" with special restrictions; (10) Study of the action of modifier variables and modulator action, i.e. the change in relations of two variables according to level on a third, etc.

Obviously, these methods differ widely in their positions on the four-dimensional analysis scheme for analyzing the properties of statistical methods presented above (page 36). The methods differ in the parameters, such as strength of assumptions, complexity, relative utilities, and aptness for purposes of discovery as contrasted with hypothesis checking, etc., but they also differ in more specific ways. The following presentation begins with certain concepts, e.g., matrices, common to most multivariate designs, and then proceeds to the individual methods, pointing out special areas of substantive application only incidentally at this stage. Unlike the more technical expositions in subsequent chapters, Dr. Horst's presentation almost completely avoids formulae — except to summarize the essential form of each method — and depends more on a logical, verbal presentation, in the interests of less mathematically trained readers, who may have planned to confine themselves to these four introductory, survey chapters.

2. ESSENTIAL AND GENERAL MULTIVARIATE CONCEPTS

To begin at the beginning, it is necessary to ask about the fundamental features of any collection of multivariate experimental data and to consider what possible operations can be done on such a set of data. Since such questions have been asked in a basic and comprehensive sense in Chapter 3, this section involves some slight repetition, but mainly it involves further refinements oriented to the special purpose of this chapter.

The Matrix of Experimental Data

It is difficult to conceive of any kind of scientific experiment which does not involve observation on one or more things. The things may be persons or substances or intervals of time, or spatial or geographical areas or volumes. They may be white rats, fragments of organic tissue, smears of blood, psychological tests, or attitude test items. For the sake of generality, let us call these things merely objects or entities. With this broad definition, it should not be difficult to agree that any experimental design or in fact any scientific experiment must involve objects of some kind. We use the plural advisedly because if only one object is involved, then we have the anecdotal rather than the scientific method.

Having established that any scientific experiment must involve objects, it should not be difficult to agree that one cannot consider objects without considering some aspects of those objects. One cannot have a scientific experiment with a person, or point in time, or a blood smear, without being concerned with some specified aspects of them such as test scores, prices of stocks, or red blood cells. For convenience, let us call these *aspects* of the entities attributes or relations.

While it may be easy to agree that any scientific investigation must involve entities (ids) and attributes, it may not be so obvious that the attribute of an entity must be capable of being expressed as a number or numerical index. It is obvious that if the first entity is a person and the second set entity a test, then the attribute can be a response of a particular kind to the test stimulus and to this we can assign a number. Also, for the blood smear and the red blood count we have a number. For the period of time and the closing price of General Motors on Friday, September 3,

we also have a number. If the entity in the first set is a person, and the entity in the second an eye, with the attribute of eye-color, how do we specify numerically that person's eye color? Several alternatives are available. We may specify color in terms of wave length corresponding to the color. This may not be useful for our purposes. More likely we should establish a set of dichotomous variables such as brown-eyed, blue-eyed, grey-eyed, etc. If anyone wishes to argue that this procedure for quantifying descriptive words or phrases is far-fetched and in many cases can be handled much more simply without quantification, we may well challenge the objector to show that he is not indulging in literary rather than scientific activity.

Next let us consider a third category in addition to that of entities and attributes. This we shall call replication. We may have repeated evaluations for given attributes or entities. The concept of replication is important in connection with the role that error of measurement plays in some of the multivariate analysis techniques. It is also important because replication may be considered either as of entities or of attributes in certain designs, such as those of some learning experiments. However, in terms of the Data Box of Chapter 3, the "replications" are always "off-sets," i.e., extensions of a two-dimensional matrix or facet in directions orthogonal to itself.

In this chapter we shall have little occasion to go into the ten-set data box of Chapter 3; most points can in fact be made simply with the three-coordinate Covariation Chart, from which two-set slabs or facets can be cut. In our present terms these are entities, attributes, and replications of these over occasions. Actually, very little attention has been given to the role even of this third dimension, let alone additional dimensions. Professor Cattell (213, 229), however, has explored its possibilities in at least one type of multivariate analysis, namely, factor analysis. Here I should merely like to point out that there is nothing in the multivariate model of entities and attributes alone which prevents us from regarding replications of an attribute as distinct attributes. That is, we may regard repeated tests or alternative forms as separate attributes along a new set dimension, as pointed out in Chapter 3.

Most of the multivariate analysis techniques are based on some sort of a priori classification system of the attributes. This we shall consider next.

Classification of Attributes

Chapter 3 has dealt with the classification of entities and attributes in the broadest sense, finishing with ten sets for the former and ten corresponding classes of entries for the latter. However, in the context of psychometry, especially, there are more specific systems. We may partition a matrix by columns when the relatives, or their attributes which we have chosen as relevant aspects of them, in some sense go together in subgroups. That is, in the sense of Chapter 3, we have a cross-set collection of relatives or a heterogeneous set of attributes. However, in the simplest case we have homogeneous attributes (*a* in the symbolism of Table 5-1) because we have no a priori reasons for classifying the variables into subgroups and hence require no partitioning of the matrix by columns. The conventional factor analysis models are of this type.

Perhaps the most common type of classification for multivariate analysis purposes occurs when one subset of variates is regarded as socially more significant than the other set and in some way is thought to be dependent or related to the other set. Here, of course, we refer to *predictor* and *criterion* variables, or *dependent* and *independent* (in the restricted statistical, not the causal, sense) variables. (Incidentally, we may henceforth use the more general term "variable" for the attribute defining a column [or row] of score entries.) In this case the matrix of observations would be partitioned by columns into two submatrices, namely, the submatrix of predictor variates and the submatrix of criterion variates. The simplest case of the parti-

tioned data matrix has only one kind of predictor and one kind of criterion entry.

Another type of attribute may be called the disturber variable. We may consider two different types of disturbers, one related to the predictors and another to the criterion. We shall refer to the first as suppressor variables and to the second as contingency variables. With this model, the predictor subset may be partitioned into two sets, namely, the suppressors and the predictors. The criterion set may also be subdivided into two sets, namely, the criterion and the contingency variables.

Another type of attribute classification consists of two or more subsets where each subset is regarded as coordinate with every other. A special case is a two subset system with only a single partitioning which does not involve assumptions about directional relationships.

The system chosen for classifying the variables is important primarily as it relates to the appropriate method of analysis. Usually, the hypothesis to be tested or the particular model chosen for the analysis will determine how the variables are grouped.

Classification of Measures

A great deal has been said and written about the nature of measurement. For our purposes, however, it is enough to consider only two types of numerical indices which are of major importance in characterizing specific multivariate designs. First, we consider all types of measurements or numerical indices that involve more than two numbers. In characterizing multivariate models it is not necessary to distinguish between discrete and continuous variables. Whether the indices are obtained by counting or by other non-digital procedures is irrelevant for multivariate analysis operations. The methods by which we arrive at the numerical indices may be important for the objectives of a specific research project, but the operations involved in a multivariate analysis are independent of these methods.

The other kind of measure that plays an important role in multivariate analysis is the dichotomous measure. Here we have only two possible values. Without loss of generality these values may be taken as "zero" and "one." For most of the multivariate analysis models, attributes must be so defined that for given entities one of these two kinds of indices is applicable. Perhaps the most common example of dichotomous variables is sex. If we have a group of entities, namely, persons, we can give a score of one to female and zero to male or vice versa. Not quite so obvious is the case of other kinds of group membership. If we have a total group of entities and we have some way of subdividing them into a number of subgroups, then we may regard each subgroup as a variable. A person gets a score of one if he belongs to a particular subgroup and zero if he does not. The t test has as its underlying model a two-attribute matrix in which one of the variates is usually multivalued and the other dichotomous. For the simplest case of chi square we have the multivariate model of two kinds of entries, both of which are dichotomously measured.

3. GENERAL MULTIVARIATE PROBLEMS OF METRIC AND LINEARITY OF RELATION

The Problem of Metric

In psychology and in the social sciences our units and origins of measurement are in general quite arbitrary. So are the particular functions in terms of which we express our measures. It is common in psychology and other social sciences to use origins of zero and standard deviations of unity for particular samples. Some of the multivariate analysis procedures are independent of unit and origin of measurement, or of linear transformations in general. One of the most important roles of metric is in the factor analysis models. One reason various types of factor analyses do not give the same results is because the methods of handling

unit and origin are not consistent. Factor-analytic variations (R and Q, or O and P technique) which interchange relatives and referees yield different results according as arbitrary metrics are imposed on the system.

In general, the multivariate analysis techniques assume linear relationships among the variables involved. This assumption may be gratuitous in view of the arbitrary scaling procedures involved in most of the multivariate analysis techniques. Our measures of attributes are dependent on the operations used in arriving at them. For example, a test score may be taken as the number of items correct. We know very well that the shape of distribution obtained depends not only on the distribution of difficulties of the items for the particular group but also on their covariances. These arbitrary methods of defining measures of the variables may result in all sorts of nonlinear relationships among the variables in a multivariate analysis experiment. (See Chapter 15 by Digman.)

There are several methods of making non-linear transformations of simple variables. One of these is with transcendental functions such as logarithmic, trigonometric, or exponential. Another method uses area transformations that may convert arbitrary distributions to rectangular or normal form. The transformation to normal form is commonly accomplished directly from tables, but it may sometimes be more appropriately carried out by a polynomial transformation.

Non-Linear Relations

Typically the multivariate analysis operations involve linear combinations of variables. Since our scaling procedures are in general arbitrary and since, in some cases, we know that the relationships cannot be linear, we need linear operations for handling non-linear relationships. We may distinguish two types of non-linear relationships involved in multivariate analysis techniques. The first of these concerns the relationships among the observed or experimental measures themselves. The other concerns the parameters of a particular multivariate analysis design. Although the relationships among the measured variables may appear to be substantially linear, the model may be non-linear in its parameters.

We have suggested that one method of transforming a single variable is a polynomial transformation. This method of transformation is of particular interest because the new variable is a linear transformation of a set of observed variables, namely, successive powers of an experimental observation. These powers are linearly combined with coefficients determined in some appropriate manner. Ordinarily, this form of transformation, while it involves additional variables, does not reduce the number of degrees of freedom in the system, since the procedures for determining the linear combinations are independent of the other variables in the system.

We may, however, adopt a more generalized method of handling non-linear relationships among the observed variables in a multivariate analysis that does involve more than one variable at a time. Suppose that non-linear relationships are assumed among variables in a multivariate experiment and we have no hypothesis as to the general nature of these interrelationships. We may set up a generalized multivariate polynomial model which includes not only the observed variables themselves but also any specified number and order of product terms involving the original measures. These higher-order terms may then be treated as new variables in the system, and the linear operations which characterize most multivariate procedures may be carried out in a straightforward manner.

This is a purely empirical procedure for handling non-linear relationships and amounts in effect to assuming that any multivariate model that is non-linear in the variables of the model may be expressed as a higher-order multivariate polynomial. The assumption is probably justified in most cases of experimental data. The obvious limitation of such a procedure for handling non-linear relationships is, however, the enormous rapidity with which higher-order variables are introduced into the system. This proliferation of variables without an appropriate increase in number of cases does, of course, reduce the degrees of freedom in the system, and the number of variables or attributes can well exceed the number of cases or entities.

So much for non-linear relations assumed to exist among the measured variates. We have shown that procedures exist for extending the set so that linear operations may be applied to the new system. Some of the multivariate models, however, are not linear in the parameters of the model. Two general methods for handling such situations may be considered. Both of these general procedures proceed by successive approximations or iterative techniques.

One of these procedures uses a Taylor's expansion of a function of several or more variables where the parameters of the model rather than the observations are taken as the variables of the function. In this general procedure, only the first-order differentials of the expansion are retained. Such a procedure always permits linear solutions to additive adjustments of first approximations to the parameters. Using second approximations, linear solutions are obtained for a second set of corrections. This procedure is continued until no further corrections are indicated. The computational model is always linear even though the number of operations cannot be predicted in advance. When and under what conditions this general approach will be convergent has not been treated comprehensively so far as I know. Such a systematic analysis would be extremely valuable for some of the multivariate analysis designs.

The second approach to models involving non-linear parameters may not be sufficiently specific to justify calling it a method. Here also first approximations are taken to the parameters in a model, but instead of solving for corrections to the parameters, each stage consists of solving for new approximations to the parameters. In general, the method consists of writing the equation of the model so that on the right side we have a vector of the parameters while on the left we have the more mathematically complex function of the parameters. First approximations to the parameters are substituted in the left side to get a second approximation on the right and so on.

Frequently, in these more complex multivariate models there may be several methods of writing the equation so that the right-hand side will be a vector of the parameters; but one cannot say that in general all of these methods will give convergent solutions, as each new estimate of the parameters on the right is substituted in the non-linear form on the left. Again, I know of no systematic discussion of convergence of multivariate non-linear systems of this kind. By experience and insight born of a great deal of trial and error, one may discover empirically procedures that are convergent. In any case, however, the operations involved in these procedures are again linear because the left-hand side of the equation involving non-linear functions of the parameters can usually be expressed as linear functions of numerical values.

4. MULTIVARIATE OPERATIONS: THE USE OF MATRICES

Multivariate Analysis Operations

Next let us consider the basic kinds of operations involved in all the multivariate analysis techniques. Some of the multivariate analysis models may require scalar operations on individual numerical values. However, the large-volume computational operations in multivariate analysis solutions may in general be outlined more efficiently in terms of simple matrix operations.

Two operations are important in matrix algebra which are not relevant to scalar algebra. One of these is known as *partitioning* of the matrix. In many multivariate analysis designs the partitioning operation is important in defining the particular model and for programing the numerical computations. When partitioning is appropriate for an analysis, among the ids that are relatives (to be exact among their attributes) the partitioning is usually by relatives rather than by referees. The concept of partitioning a matrix into submatrices seems so simple as to be almost trivial, but it can greatly facilitate not only the discussion and development of multivariate analysis procedures but also the actual computational operations.

A second operation commonly used in matric operations is that of *matrix transposition.* When we transpose a matrix of numbers or elements we simply write its rows as columns or its columns as rows. It is convenient to say that the operation of transposition reverses the orientation of the matrix. In programing multivariate problems for solution on high-speed electronic computers, it is easy to make errors with reference to orientation of the matrices involved, and one may throw away hundreds of dollars worth of computer time because of transpositional errors. I emphasize the importance of the concept of transpositional operations in multivariate analysis because even in the most elementary texts on matrix algebra the notion of transposition is handled only briefly.

Very little needs to be said about the operations of addition and subtraction in the multivariate analysis of data matrices.

These are usually straightforward, provided errors in orientation are avoided. (See Chapter 5 by Anderson.)

The commonest operation in most multivariate analyses is that of matrix multiplication. The major part of most iterative-type solutions in multivariate analysis involves primarily matrix multiplications. Although on some of the slower electronic computers matrix multiplication is not rapid, it can be easily programed. Solutions of multivariate analysis problems can be designed so that most of the operations are those of multiplication.

The operation of matrix inversion is common in the solution of multivariate analysis problems and although the most commonly used computational procedures require scalar operations for square roots and reciprocals, most of the computations in these procedures are those of matrix multiplication. Many matrix inversion programs are available for electronic computers.

The preparatory operations, then, of partitioning and transposition and the computational operations of addition, subtraction, multiplication, and inversion are common to many multivariate analysis techniques. There is, however, a class of multivariate analysis designs which is essentially different from these and requires a more complicated type of solution. This type of solution actually involves one or more of the operations already considered. It consists in finding the latent roots and vectors of certain matrices. Usually these latent roots and vectors involve symmetric, positive, definite matrices derived from data matrices. However, some of the matrices may have negative roots, while in a few special cases the matrices whose latent roots and vectors are required may not even be symmetric.

Some of the more involved models require the solution of latent roots and vectors of matrices which in themselves contain unknown parameters to be solved for. In any case, the solution of the latent roots and vectors problem means that one cannot lay out in advance the numbers of operations of various kinds that must be applied to the matrix. Usually, however, matrix multiplication occupies the bulk of the computational time.

The Transformation of Matrices

Most, if not all, of the multivariate analysis models require or imply the linear transformation of a matrix of experimental data into another matrix, or the multiplication of the data matrix by another matrix. Some models require the transformation of the entire matrix of experimental data according to some model or hypothesis, while others require the transformation of submatrices of the original matrix partitioned in accordance with certain hypotheses. In any case, the notion of the transformation of matrices of data to other matrices is fundamental to most of the multivariate analysis designs.

The models may vary not only with reference to the number of submatrices involved in the transformation but also in the orders of the transformed matrices. For example, a matrix might be multiplied by a vector to yield a vector, or it might be multiplied by a matrix to yield a product of a higher or lower order. Also, the matrix by which the data matrix is multiplied may be of lower rank than its lower order.

One important respect in which the various multivariate analysis models vary with regard to the transformation of matrices is the restrictions which are put on the transformed matrices and the transforming matrices. The more common models are concerned with conditions to be satisfied by the transformed matrices. However, some of the models require also that restrictions be placed on the transforming matrices.

The types of restrictions placed on the transformed matrix are usually of two kinds. First, the transformed matrix shall resemble some other specified matrix as closely as possible according to some criteria of congruence, and second, the transformed matrix itself shall satisfy certain conditions within itself.

Matrix Approximation and Residuals

We have said that most multivariate analysis designs require or imply the transformation of an entire matrix of one or more submatrices so that the transformed matrices satisfy certain conditions. One of these conditions is that the transformed matrix or submatrix shall resemble as closely as possible, according to some specified criterion, another matrix or submatrix of the original data matrix, or one derived from it.

Let us now consider several kinds of criteria for determining the degree of approximation of one matrix to some other matrix. One criterion is that the sum of the absolute values in the residual matrix shall be a minimum. This criterion is not very frequently used and has definite limitations. The computational procedures for obtaining a minimum are not well defined or straightforward and the solution may not be unique.

Another criterion, which may be regarded as a special case of minimizing the sum of absolute discrepancies, should be mentioned because it is implied in some of the standard multivariate analysis designs. This criterion assumes that the matrix to be approximated is a zero-one matrix. The object is to transform the original matrix in such a way that when its elements are dichotomized and compared with corresponding elements in the zero-one matrix, the sum of the absolute discrepancies will be a minimum. This criterion is even more difficult to handle than the previous one.

By far the commonest criterion of similarity between two matrices is the sums of the squares of the differences of their corresponding elements. For convenience we may call this the minimum residual variance or MRV criterion. This criterion is preferable to the other two in that it lends itself more readily to analytical solutions and to tests of significance. The chief objective in most multivariate analysis designs is to minimize residual variance among two or more matrices. Even when the residuals are taken from dichotomous matrices, the model can usually be cast in the MRV form.

Operations with Residual Matrices

For some of the multivariate designs, interest centers in certain residual matrices upon which further standard operations may be performed. These designs assume that certain residual matrices may have been obtained from operations with submatrices of the data matrix and that one or more residual matrices are subject to linear transformations which will be optimally congruent, say, in the least-square sense, with some other submatrix derived from the system. Variations and elaborations of this procedure are available depending on the rationale according to which a data matrix is partitioned and the particular model being investigated.

The Incomplete Data Matrix

I shall mention briefly a topic which is of fundamental importance in many multivariate analysis procedures and techniques. Adequate solutions for some of the most important multivariate problems cannot be provided without satisfactory solutions to what I have called the matrix of incomplete data. In many important multivariate applications it is in the nature of the case that not all of the values for a data matrix can be available. The general problem is the estimation of missing elements in a data matrix. The pattern of missing elements may vary according to the experimental design. In designs with predictor and criterion submatrices it is usually the criterion submatrix which is fragmented. In a special type of incomplete data matrix which involves only the criterion submatrix, data are available for each entity on only one of a set of criterion attributes.

5. EVALUATING SIGNIFICANCES IN MULTIVARIATE ANALYSIS

Significance Tests

I shall comment briefly on significance test but these comments will be largely non-technical. In general, tests of significance for any of the multivariate analysis models or for any statistical model must depend primarily on three things: the number of parameters in the model, the number of entities, and some function of total and residual variances. These are the necessary but by no means sufficient requirements for deriving estimates of significance. Unfortunately, adequate tests of significance are not available for all important multivariate designs. In Chapter 7, Jones presents tests for some examples of complex multivariate problems.

We may have tests that show statistical significance and yet the results may not be practically significant. In general, this is true when we have a very large number of entities. On the other hand, with few degrees of freedom the confidence level may be very low. Yet if decisions must be made, and the cost of accepting the null hypothesis when it is not true may be very great, then such tests are not of much practical value.

In practical situations, we must often make decisions at certainty levels much less than .99 or .95. In many cases it would be useful if we could evaluate confidence levels readily which are less rigorous than the .05 level. It is no answer to say that the .01 and .05 levels have come to be accepted as the standards. The reason they have come to be accepted as the standards is, of course, that such values have been tabled, not because these are the most useful standards under all conditions. It is important to distinguish between a high degree of scientific certainty per se and situations where practical decisions have to be made on the basis of scientific investigation.

In any case, research models in general should not be restricted to those for which easy derivations of significance tests are available. The models should be developed according to the needs of science and society, and mathematical statisticians should be urged to develop the best available approximations to adequate significance tests for such models.

Cross-Validation

One method that has come into considerable use for checking the accuracy or reliability of conclusions based on particular models is what is known as cross-validation. Here the results obtained from one experiment are applied to another to see how well they hold up. This is a purely empirical approach and has certain weaknesses. We cannot argue that just because the results did not hold up on a second set of data, they would not have held up on a third or a fourth set. Neither can we argue that because the results held up fairly well on a second set of data, they would also hold up well on subsequent sets of data.

Over the years my enthusiasm for the cross-validation techniques has progressively waned. But the reason for this waning enthusiasm is not that the techniques are purely empirical or that they lack statistical or scientific sophistication; neither is it because discrepant results from a second experiment do not necessarily invalidate the results of the first, nor that concurrence of a second experiment does not necessarily validate the results of the first.

The real reason for my lack of enthusiasm for the cross-validation techniques is even more fundamental. In these techniques we require that our available experimental sample of objects be divided into two parts. For one of these, some optimizing transformation is developed, and on the other it is verified. As a matter of fact, the data can be fractionated into more than two parts and several or more cross-validations can be carried out. But for most of the multivariate analysis designs we never have enough cases. We know that other things being equal, the more cases we have, the more stable and reliable our results will be. Therefore, for purposes of both application and generalization, our procedures must be developed on the largest sample available. If we develop a procedure and then cross-validate it, we have *ipso facto* not developed the best procedure possible from the available data.

We have considered some of the essential characteristics of multivariate analysis models. Let us now consider briefly some of the more commonly used types of multivariate analysis designs and see how they fit in as special cases of the generalized model.

In considering individual multivariate methods in the following sections it will not be possible to consider all of the commonly used or proposed types of multivariate analysis or to discuss them in detail. One can doubt even whether the selection I have made is the best or the most representative. However, a discussion of some of these may show how special types can be identified in terms of the characteristics already discussed.

6. MULTIPLE REGRESSION AND FACTOR ANALYSIS

Multiple Regression Analysis

Perhaps the most common type of multivariate analysis is what is commonly called multiple regression analysis. Here we begin typically with a data matrix of relatives, related on certain attributes over a sample of referees. The indicators are partitioned into dependent and independent or criterion and predictor variables. If X is the score on a criterion variable and Y_1, Y_2 ... are predictor variables, then X is treated as a weighted sum of predictor variables.

$$(1)\ X_1 = W_1 Y_1 + W_2 Y_2 + \ldots W_m Y_m.$$

In the simplest case, we may have only one predictor and one criterion variate. The general solution or model makes no restrictions on the kind of measures used. They may be discrete, continuous, or dichotomous for either type of variable. In general, for this model the unit and origin of both sets of variables is irrelevant. The experimenter may introduce non-linear combinations of observations as new variables into the predictor system. The transformation matrix is determined only for the predictor submatrix. It is determined in such a way that the sum of squared residuals between the transformed predictor matrix and the criterion submatrix is a minimum. In its standard form, the multiple regression problem is not in general concerned with operations on residuals. Significance tests for standard multiple regression analysis results are available. The matrix computations required in these models are those of addition, subtraction, multiplication, and inversion. Latent root and vector solutions are not usually required. Examples of such work are given in Chapters 5, 7, and 26. In Chapter 5, Anderson provides the basic formulae for multiple prediction work.

Factor Analysis

Another well-established multivariate model is that of factor analysis (see Chapter 6). Actually, factor analysis includes a family of models. In general, factor analysis is concerned with determining the dimensionality or non-error rank of a set of variates. It may involve any two of the ten general multivariate model dimensions (Chapter 3), depending on the particular interest of the investigator. The method of analysis may make either coordinate set the relatives and the other the referees, and the attributes may be preserved as those of the relatives or altered to be those of the set that was originally the referees. In factor analysis models, both dichotomous and discrete measures on entries may be used. The results depend on the metric chosen for the more common models. This is true particularly with reference to how the entity and attribute dimensions of the model are specified.

Factor analysis solutions may be independent of scale. Lawley's maximum likelihood solution (903) is independent of scale, not because it is a maximum likelihood solution but because of the particular model chosen. It is also possible to construct other models which are independent of scale. With current methods of factor analysis, non-linear or higher-order product terms of the observations may be introduced into the original data matrix and into the covariance or correlation matrix derived from it. The operations involved in factor-analytic solutions ideally require the determination of latent roots and vectors. Approximation methods such as the many variations introduced by Thurstone are available; the best known of these is the centroid method.

A typical factor-analytic solution requires for the transformation matrix one which when applied to either the data matrix or matrices derived from it, yields another matrix of lower rank but as nearly equal to the original matrix as possible. Therefore the transformation matrix is singular (that is, some of its roots are zero). The ideal solution gives minimal residual variance between the original and the transformed matrix.

In factor analysis the matrix to be transformed may in itself involve unknown parameters to be determined, as in the case where communalities are assumed. Here we have a latent roots and vector problem with additional parameters to be deter-

mined. Whether unknowns are to be assumed in the matrix to be transformed or not, the number of operations is not predictable in advance. The number of iterations may be considerable if unknown communalities in the diagonal are to be solved for. However, various rule-of-thumb approximation procedures that greatly reduce computational time have been proposed by Thurstone and others (1420).

In this initial stage of a factor analysis the raw score on each indicator is treated as the sum of a series of independent (uncorrelated) components from the various factors. This may be written

$$(2) \quad a = b_1 F_1 + b_2 F_2 + \ldots . b_g F_g$$

where a is the raw attribute score, the b's are weights, loadings, or "behavioral indices" when behavior is being predicted, and the F's are common factors.

7. SOME SPECIAL DEVELOPMENTS IN FACTOR ANALYSIS

Rotation in Factor Analysis

Next I want to consider a multivariate analysis design that is part of the factor analysis models. This is the simple structure transformation problem. Actually, the rotational problem is formally quite different from models that concern themselves primarily with the systematic dimensionality of a data matrix. It is only because the two models are usually applicable in a given experimental setting that they are usually associated with each other.

Let us see how the rotational model can be characterized in terms of the differentiating characteristics of multivariate analysis models in general. Typically we begin with a matrix of data whose dimensions may be characterized by entities and attributes in the conventional manner. However, the matrix is not an experimental data matrix but rather the arbitrary factor loading matrix obtained from a correlation or covariance matrix. In this case, what in the primary data matrix served as attributes now serve as entities in the factor loading matrix. The attributes of the factor loading matrix are now the factors themselves. The measures are the loadings or saturations of the variables on the factors. The factor matrix may have been obtained by any of the various procedures such as principal axis, multiple group, centroid, etc. It is irrelevant from the point of view of the model we are now considering whether or not specificities were assumed in the original factoring procedures. The characteristics of the simple structure model are very closely related to those of the optimal classification model.

In the model as it has been developed by Thurstone (1420), we consider the matrix of arbitrary factor loadings as a submatrix of predictor or independent variable data. We then hypothesize a submatrix of criterion or dependent variable data. This hypothetical criterion matrix is a zero-one matrix. As a special case it may be regarded as a classification matrix where we have only a single "one" in each row. Unlike the optimal classification model, the simple structure model in general makes no assumptions about the number of ones in each column. One may, of course, have hypotheses about the number of ones but this is another matter. Thurstone has specified certain restrictions on the pattern of ones in the simple structure hypothesis matrix, and a slightly different definition of simple structure is given in Chapter 6.

Analytical methods of rotation which have been developed are in general attempts to approximate a matrix of dichotomous measures with the restrictions specified by Thurstone. Theoretically, one considers the covariance characteristics of a simple structure hypothesis matrix together with the moment characteristics of the individual columns within it. One then attempts to find a transformation matrix for the arbitrary factor matrix such that the transformed matrix exhibits as closely as possible the covariance and moment characteristics of the simple structure hypothesis matrix.

If one has an a priori simple structure hypothesis matrix consisting of zero-one elements, that is, if one has any other a priori hypothesis about which tests have high and low loadings for each factor, then the rotational solution becomes a straightforward multiple regression model with the arbitrary factor matrix constituting the predictor submatrix and the hypothesis zero-one matrix the criterion submatrix. The Procrustes program for getting the closest fit to this solution is given in Chapter 6.

One may put an additional restriction on the transformation matrix, namely, that it shall be orthonormal. This introduces the controversy between correlated and uncorrelated or oblique rotations as well as that of higher-order general factors. This important issue is dealt with more thoroughly than is possible here by Cattell in Chapter 6.

Dimensional Characteristics of Factor Models

While discussing the subject of factor analysis, I should like to remind you of the distinguishing features of the so-called R, Q, and P techniques. These techniques are distinguished primarily by their dimensional characteristics. The R technique considers people as referees and measures or tests as relatives. The Q technique regards people as the relative attributes and tests, etc., as referees, by transposing the score matrix (hence "transpose technique"). The P technique introduces the third-dimensional characteristics of the model, namely, replications or occasions. The replications can serve also as relatives, in what Cattell has called O technique, the transpose of P technique.

Since Cattell was the first to explore systematically the possibilities of the three-dimensional model, I shall defer to his system of (R, Q, P, O, S, and T-technique) analysis, without attempting to improve upon it, referring the reader to Chapter 6. What I want to emphasize is that these multivariate models differ primarily with respect to the dimensional characteristics of the general multivariate model and the orientation of the data matrix for a particular pair of dimensions. The choice of metric is important. If one sticks with the same metric, he gets the same results with a latent roots and vectors solution irrespective of which orientation he chooses (as Burt, 158, has shown), provided specifics are not assumed in the system. A special case of a consistent metric is given by the doubly-centered data matrix (see page 118, Chapter 3).

Models with Residual Matrices

I mentioned earlier that we may be interested not only in working with submatrices of the data matrix but in performing further operations on residual matrices obtained by some of the methods previously described. In general, models of this sort involve variations or elaborations of partial covariance and regression techniques. For example, suppose we are interested in predicting the adjustment of patients discharged from mental hospitals. We may have several different criteria of success such as length of time outside the hospital, number of times patient returns to the hospital, and so on. For predictor variables we have ratings of various measures such as personality tests, physiological measures, and items of personal history. We may wish to see how well success could be predicted provided certain contingency factors such as kind of supervision outside the hospital, economic status, and other factors are taken into account. Here the model would be to estimate the criterion variable from the contingency variables, then to use the residual matrix as a second-order criterion matrix to be estimated by conventional transformation methods from the original submatrix of predictors.

A recent example of one of the residual models involves two formats of a personality schedule, one a forced choice and the other a rating format, so that the data matrix is partitioned into submatrices involving scores or measures from the two formats for the same group of persons (Karr, 846). Suppose we are interested in testing whether the rating form measures some variables that the forced choice does not and vice versa. The computational model is different from that of the canonical correlation or most predictable criterion model. In that model we attempt to transform each submatrix in such a way that the two transformed matrices will be as nearly the same as possible.

In this model we begin with the general multiple prediction model. We let one set, say the rating set, be the predictor set and calculate a residual between the transformed predictor matrix and the criterion matrix. We then get another residual matrix in the same way by letting the forced choice be the predictor submatrix and the paired rating the criterion matrix. We now have two residual matrices which can be independently analyzed by factor-analytic methods to determine the dimensionality of the residual matrices. If we have reasonably accurate estimates of the non-error variance of the measures, we can also calculate the reliability of the residuals and therefore determine the non-error or systematic rank of these residuals. By appropriate rotational procedures we can then investigate the factors in one format not measured in the other.

The Single Case

Next I should like to consider the application of multivariate models to the single case. Here the single case constitutes an entire universe. The case is the universe. One could invent a model utilizing the three dimensions of the generalized model that applies to the single individual. For example, one might segregate regions on the body surface so that each region would represent a single entity. At a given instant one could measure electrical potential, temperature, perspiration rate, and perhaps other variables as well, for each region. These would constitute the relatives and their attributes. If such measures were taken repeatedly we would also have replications.

One type of model with the single case regards the replications over a period of time as entities measured with respect to a set of attributes. Such a model might be used for predicting certain behavior attributes of a single individual on the basis of other measured variables. This can be done simply by leading the predictor variables and lagging the criterion variables in the data matrix. One may systematically lead a variable for each of a specified number of temporal units and regard each of these leads as a new variable. In this way one may generate a multivariate model from a single variable. It is possible then to apply any of the multivariate models to such a system. The problem of incomplete data because of missing data in opposite corners of the data matrix would be encountered in this model.

Another example of the multivariate model for the single case is of considerable interest. A person is asked to respond to a list of statements or attitudes. He may be asked to rate the list of statements as they apply to him, as they apply to either or both parents, to siblings, etc. The general model requires that the individual respond to the statements as they apply under each of a number of different conditions. Each of these conditions represents an attribute of the data matrix, whereas the individual statements represent the entities in the data matrix. The entire data matrix then comes from a single individual. Such a matrix could be analyzed by the general multiple regression model where certain of the attributes are regarded as dependent and others independent. It could be designed to yield two or more submatrices representing attributes that are different or of the same type. The measures could be discrete or dichotomous or both. In general, various methods of analysis would be available, depending on the objectives of a particular

experiment. This perhaps will serve to indicate how multivariate models may be applied to a single entity functioning as a universe, and the varieties of possibilities available for research in clinical situations. The single case is taken up again in Chapters 6, 10, 11, 12, and 20.

8. SOME DESIGNS USING A PRIORI CLASSIFICATION OF VARIATES

Relations Among Sets of Variates

Another multivariate model has been called "the most predictable criterion" problem. It was first solved by Hotelling (772). It is not quite appropriate to call it the most predictable criterion problem because formally the model does not require the categorization of variables into predictor and criterion sets. It requires only a single partitioning of the entity-attribute matrix into two sets of attributes. The model will accept both dichotomous and discrete measures. The solution is not independent of metric. In addition to the standard operations, the solution for the latent roots and vectors is required. This model calls for the transformation of each submatrix so that the residual variance between the two is a minimum. The transformation matrices must be the same width for both submatrices but cannot be of greater width than the submatrix of smaller width. As Hotelling first presented the problem, these transformation matrices consisted of single vectors corresponding to the largest latent root of a matrix. It has been convenient to put restrictions of orthonormality on the transformation matrices. This model has been used to compare two factor matrices for similarity. The model can be solved formally much as a factor analysis problem. In Chapter 5, Anderson deals further with this technique under the heading of Canonical Correlation.

A generalization of the most predictable

criteria problem has recently been presented in which we start with a data matrix partitioned by attributes into more than two sets (Horst, 760). Each submatrix is presumed to represent essentially the same factors as the others. The multitrait multitreatment problem is a special case of this model where we have measures on a set of traits provided under several different conditions. For example, we may have a personality test administered to a group of individuals under three or more different sets of instructions. We may wish to see to what extent the different sets of measures are independent of the particular instructions. The general model here requires the transformation of each submatrix to another matrix such that all of the transformed matrices are as nearly alike as possible. In general, the total residual variance among all of the transformed matrices should be a minimum.

The solution of this problem is not independent of metric and in general, restrictions may be applied both to the sets of transformed matrices and to the sets of transformation matrices. The type of solutions obtained will depend on these restrictions. While a number of different kinds of restrictions give the same solution for the two-set case, the solutions may be quite different for the general case. In general, the various solutions are fundamentally latent root and vector models. In some cases, however, the matrices whose roots and vectors are required are functions of parameters to be solved for. The solutions are iterative and somewhat more involved than solutions for the conventional latent roots and vectors problems. Further discussion of interbattery methods in factor analysis is to be found in Chapter 6 by Cattell.

Analysis of Variance Designs

Next let us consider the analysis of variance models as represented by the typical Fisherian designs. Here the experimental data matrix is typically concerned with entities and attributes. It is important to note that the term replication as used in analysis of variance and covariance experiments is essentially different from the sense in which we have used it in describing the categorical characteristics of a multivariate system. In this model the term replication refers to the introduction of several or more entities with the same vector of predictor elements. The model calls for partitioning of the attribute columns into dependent and independent variables. The dependent set may involve discrete or dichotomous measures but the independent submatrix is always a matrix of dichotomous elements. Typically this submatrix is made up of variables that represent treatments. The entities are systematically chosen or manipulated so that the predictor submatrix will exhibit a specified pattern of zeros and ones according to the experimental design chosen.

An important characteristic of these models is that they typically involve non-linear relationships among the independent variables and include higher-order product terms as separate variables. These are what are referred to as interaction terms. This is a special case of the use of the general multivariate polynomial with dichotomous measures.

If a represents the raw score on a dependent attribute variable and Y_1, Y_2 .. are independent variables, then in analysis of variance

$$(3)\quad a = W_1 Y_1 + W_2 Y_2 + W_3 Y_1 Y_2 + \dots.$$

It should be noted that unlike formula (2) above for factor analysis this includes terms for interactions.

The criterion or dependent variable submatrix may consist of a single column, in which case we have the analysis of variance model, or it may consist of several or more columns in which case we may encompass also the analysis of covariance models. Formally these models call for a transformation matrix applied to the dichotomous predictor matrix to yield a transformed matrix as close to the dependent variable matrix as possible in the MRV sense. Certain problems of non-singular matrices are involved in such a solution but they are soluble.

Curiously, however, the analysis of variance procedures have not led to emphasis on these aspects of the model. Rather, workers have been preoccupied with testing the significance of various sets and subsets of residual variances. Some few have objected that the kinds of questions answered by these tests have not been the most useful kinds of questions to ask in psychology or the social sciences. This point I shall not pursue for it is possible that even less than fifty million statisticians and researchers are not likely to be wrong. For further discussion of analysis of variance approaches, see Chapter 7 by Jones and Chapter 28 by Bock.

The Eta Coefficient

Next I shall consider a rather specialized multivariate model from which the eta coefficient may be derived. We begin with a two-dimensional model of entities and attributes. As a special case we have only one predictor attribute and one criterion indicator, although the number of criterion attributes is irrelevant. The predictor variate, however, is known to have a non-linear relation with the criterion when measured in terms of a discrete or continuous series. The predictor variate is then subdivided on the basis of class intervals, each class interval being regarded as a separate predictor variable. A new submatrix of predictor measures is then established. Each person has a "one" for the class interval attribute in which he falls and zero for all the others. This means, of course, that there is only a single "one" in each row of the predictor submatrix and that the total number of "ones" in each column is the number of people in that particular class interval. If now we apply the multiple

regression techniques to this matrix, the multiple correlation calculated by conventional methods comes out to be the classical eta coefficient.

9. METHODS CONCERNED WITH DIFFERENTIAL PREDICTION AND OPTIMAL CLASSIFICATION

Differential Prediction

A model that has aroused interest in recent years is the differential prediction model. Here the data matrix consists of entities and of attributes partitioned by predictor and criterion submatrices. The model, so far as it has been explicitly defined, begins first with a transformation on the criterion submatrix. This transformation in its simplest form is a row centering operation. In its most general form, it consists of a singular transformation. In its simple form, it amounts to transforming the criterion variables to ipsative variables. Each of a person's criterion scores is measured from the mean of all of his criterion scores. The transformation matrix is then found for the predictor submatrix to yield a transformed matrix with minimal residual variance between it and the transformed or ipsatized predictor matrix.

A typical characteristic of the differential prediction model, since it is a special case of the generalized multiple prediction model, is that the criterion matrix is usually fragmented or mutilated, since, in general, criterion data are not available on all people for all criterion activities. The problem of how to handle such cases is a major one and in itself requires special designs.

Predictor Selection

A general set of multivariate models of considerable importance is that involving predictor selection. Here we have a special case of the multiple regression model. We seek a transformation matrix of the predictor submatrix which has zero elements corresponding to certain predictor variables. The problem is to find where these should be placed, once it is determined how many of the predictors are to be zeroed out of the system. There are two types of predictor selection models. In one of these, predictors are selected one at a time so that the one added to the subset yields a lower MRV with the criterion submatrix than any other not in the subset. This is known as the accretion method (Horst, 757, 758). The second model begins with all available predictor measures and eliminates in turn those which cause less increase in the residual variance (Horst & MacEwan, 768). This is known as the elimination method.

So far there is no satisfactory solution to the predictor selection problem unless one knows in advance how many predictors he wants. The solutions that have been proposed have been primarily for the predictor accretion techniques and give lower bounds to the number of predictors to be included. I suspect these bounds may be much too low.

Optimal Test Length

An interesting multivariate model is concerned with optimal lengths for tests in a battery (Horst & MacEwan, 767). This model assumes that parts of variables may be eliminated or that they may be fractionally increased. Obvious examples are increasing or reducing the number of items or testing time for a test. We assume that the over-all amount of test material or testing time is a prespecified amount. For this prespecified amount of over-all testing time, the transformation matrix for the predictor submatrix, when the variables have been adequately readjusted, gives an MRV between it and the criterion submatrix. This concept introduces replications into the model in addition to entities and attributes, but the replications are not necessarily integral. Furthermore, the replications are not treated as a separate

dimension of the multivariate model but are included with the attribute dimension as a special kind of attribute.

Optimal Classification

An important model related to the discriminant function models and also to the differential prediction model is the optimal classification model. Here the data matrix consists of entities and attributes where the attributes may be considered as criterion variables. We regard them as criterion variables because as the model is usually conceived, it is concerned with activities of a socially significant nature. The problem is to subdivide the ids (entities) in such a way that a prespecified number will be assigned to each subgroup within a total group so that the sum of the criterion measures corresponding to the subgroups to which persons have been assigned will be a maximum.

Another way of putting it is to assume that we have a matrix of estimated criterion measures on each of a number of criterion activities. We then conceive of a zero-one matrix of the same order. This matrix has a one in each row and all other elements are zero. We do not have information as to the location of these ones in the matrix. We do, however, specify the number of ones in each column of the matrix. The problem now is to determine the position of the ones in each column so that the trace of the product of the two matrices is a maximum. Theoretically, then, each person is assigned to the activity indicated by his score of one in the dichotomous matrix.

This problem as stated has not been closely related to the general multivariate model. Traditionally, only by linear programing techniques can such solutions be found and even then many ambiguities may arise.

A more elegant way of looking at the problem is to assume we have an estimated criterion matrix and that we know the number of people to be assigned to each classification or group activity. We may then consider a transformation matrix for this estimated criterion matrix such that the transformed matrix will satisfy the characteristics of the classification covariance matrix and specified moments of zero-one vectors, and will be, in some MRV sense, as close to the original classification matrix as possible. This means, of course, that we restrict only the number of elements in a classification matrix column without any specification of their position. The problem has recently been formulated in this way, which admits of an analytical solution, rather than the trial-and-error approach characteristic of linear programing procedures (Horst, 760).

We wish now to formulate what is the outcome with respect to an individual's response. Clearly his score is not partitioned as in factor-analytic or analysis of variance procedures, but it is assigned (on an MRV basis) to one or another of the criterion classes. In this sense it resembles latent class analysis where assignment is made on a probabilistic basis. Most generally, if X is the individual's score, k_1 and k_2 are the two criterion classes, and p stands for some measure of fit between the score X and the criterion group score, then we arrive at values for

$$p_1 X \text{ for } k_1$$
$$p_2 X \text{ for } k_2$$

and assign X by comparing p_1 with p_2.

Perhaps just a word with reference to the estimated criterion matrix is essential. Discussions of the optimal classification problem usually assume the availability of an estimated criterion matrix. This assumes that previously we have had a data matrix on a cross-set sample of ids which includes cases from both predictor and criterion variate sets, so that the conventional multiple prediction solution has been available. The availability of such a data matrix implies all of the problems with a criterion submatrix of data with missing elements.

10. METHODS CONCERNED WITH GROUPING AND SEGREGATING ENTITIES IN TYPES

Most of the methods so far discussed are concerned with handling attributes as dimensional continua or dichotomies. Psychology is also substantially concerned, however, as Chapters 9 and 26 below remind us, with recognizing persons, nations, etc. as classifiable into "type" (occupations, culture areas, psychiatric syndrome groupings, etc.) for various practical and theoretical purposes.

Two very different approaches and purposes must be recognized here, namely, (1) to find natural groupings and (2) having agreed on a classification of entities, to find out relations among their attributes — especially to weight those attributes to make their distinction greater. In the pursuit of this second aim the next set of multivariate analysis models we shall consider are the multiple discriminant function designs. These designs start with a data matrix where the attributes are partitioned into two parts. Typically, one of these consists of measures that may be either discrete or dichotomous, but usually they are discrete. The other sub-matrix consists of dichotomous measures. The purpose of the discriminant function models is to determine, on the basis of a set of measures, into which of a number of possible groups or classifications an entity belongs.

In spite of all the theory and rationale that has been developed for the two-group case, the computational procedures are precisely those for classical multiple regression analysis where we have discrete predictor measures and a dichotomous single criterion. A transformation matrix is determined for the predictor matrix of observations so that the resulting vector when subtracted from the dichotomous vector yields the MRV. Minor modifications may be introduced into the computational scheme but essentially we have a simple multiple regression model with a dichotomous criterion.

The more general case for the multiple discriminant function model involves not only several or more predictor or independent attributes but also several or more criterion or dependent attributes measured in dichotomous terms. It should be emphasized that in the multiple discriminant function model, although we are generally concerned with the problem of classification of a sample of entities into one of a number of different groups, the only distinguishing feature of the data matrix from that of the general multiple regression model is that the criterion submatrix is always dichotomous. Furthermore, each row of the criterion submatrix contains only a single one for the class to which the individual has been assigned and zeros for all other classes or criterion attributes.

We shall now consider several different kinds of methods for handling the data matrix in the multiple discriminant function model that has more than one dichotomous criterion vector. One of these is simply the standard multiple regression model (Horst, 759). It requires the determination of a transformation matrix for the predictor submatrix. This transformation matrix is determined in such a way as to yield the minimum residual variance matrix and the dichotomous criterion submatrix. Further restrictions, however, are put on the transformed matrix. These are that means and variances of columns for the transformed matrix must be equal to the means and variances of the corresponding columns of the dichotomous matrix.

Two other models are available. One of these implies first a transformation of the predictor submatrix. The next step is to dichotomize the elements in the transformed matrix according to some prespecified rule, for example, such that the largest element in each row for an entity shall be called one and all other elements in the row zero. This dichotomized transformed matrix should then have a minimum sum of absolute differences when subtracted from the criterion submatrix of dichotomous measures. In simple words, the sum of the misclassifications or the total number of misclassifications should be a minimum. It must be emphasized, however, that we have no satisfactory way of mathematically handling solutions that minimize the sums of absolute discrepancies. Solutions are even less adequate when we imply dichotomization of the transformed matrix.

In a third model we wish to find a transformation vector for the predictor submatrix. The resulting vector shall be such that when partitioned according to the subgroups, the ratio of the within-group variance to the total-group variance shall be a minimum. This model calls essentially for the transformation of both the predictor and criterion submatrices so that some function of the residuals between the two matrices is minimized. The solution requires the finding of latent roots and vectors, and the solution is independent of the metric chosen.

Latent Class Analysis

A special type of scaling and grouping technique is a model introduced by Lazarsfeld and known as latent class analysis (910). An elaborate body of theory has been developed, but basically the model is rather straightforward. In the latent class model we begin with a data matrix where rows are usually people, and the columns are items or stimulus elements to which all-or-none responses have been made, resulting in a matrix of dichotomous measures. The latent class model extends the data matrix of attributes not only to the original items or subcategories within items but to higher-order or non-linear functions of these elements. These higher-order terms are also dichotomous elements since they are products of ones and zeros. This is a special case of the general multivariate polynomial for dichotomous measures. Although the computational procedures for the latent class model have not been efficiently worked out, the assumption is implicit that the extended data matrix is of much smaller rank than its order.

The essential relation has been formulated by Gibson (596) in matrix form

(1) $R = L'VL$ and
(2) $R_k = L'VD_kL$

where R is the sample joint proportions matrix bordered by the manifest marginals; R_k is the sample triple proportions matrix for item k bordered by the joint proportions involving item k; L' contains the latent marginals for all items and has its top row filled with 1's; V is a diagonal and contains the relative class sizes in its diagonal cells; and D_k is diagonal and contains the entries from row k of L' in its diagonal cells.[1] The order of R and R_k is n +1, n being the number of items involved, and the rank of all matrices in (1) and (2) is m, the number of latent classes needed to account for the manifest data.

Configural Analysis

Another multivariate model is referred to as configural analysis, configural scoring, or pattern analysis (see Chapter 9 below). Configural or pattern analysis is usually discussed in terms of the pattern of a person's responses to a set of items (Cattell, 220; McQuitty, 1016). Only in recent years have more analytical approaches to the pattern or configural analysis problem been emphasized (Horst, 756; Lubin & Osburn, 965). It can readily be shown that the general multivariate polynomial model will completely identify all possible patterns of item responses to a set of items. The general configural model may then be taken as the general multivariate model

---

[1]All diagonal cells but the first in R and R_k and all cells in row and column k of M_k are empty, and would have to be estimated if those cells were directly involved in the solution.

considered in latent class analysis where the entities are not only the items but all or any number of desired higher-order terms. Here as in the latent class model, all of the elements are dichotomous.

What one does with these now depends on his particular interest. One may apply a simple factor-analytic model to the multivariate polynomial data matrix, and attempt to find a minimal rank transformation matrix which will give an MRV solution to the observed data matrix. One may further proceed to partition the matrix as in the case of the latent class model, and consider transformations of submatrices that shall, with appropriate restrictions, yield MRV results for the transformed submatrices. I suspect that there is a very close relationship between the latent class and the configural analysis model. So far as I know, however, this has been only recently suggested (Lunneborg, 970).

The general configural analysis model has aroused interest most recently and frequently in connection with prediction problems. Here the data matrix includes also a criterion submatrix of data that may be either dichotomous or discrete. In this case the problem is to find an appropriate transformation for the dichotomous submatrix which will give an MRV solution between it and the predictor submatrix. However, except for a very small number of items, one soon runs out of degrees of freedom.

11. SCALING AND SAMPLE SELECTION

Multidimensional Scaling

Next I shall discuss briefly what may be called the multidimensional scaling model. The developments in scaling procedures, particularly the paired comparison and the successive intervals approaches, have not been entirely satisfactory because of the large amount of information thrown away. The basic model common to most scaling techniques begins typically with a data matrix of objects and indicators. The objects are usually persons or judges and the indicators are stimulus objects to be judged. From the point of view of the general model, it is not important whether the indicators are single or pairs of elements. Typically, the measure is dichotomous.

In the traditional procedures the subject is asked to judge or react in an all-or-none fashion to each stimulus element. The stimulus element can usually be readily defined so that the reaction is dichotomous. It would appear that the most obvious approach to the scaling of such a set of data is a factor-analytic approach. The direct factor-analytic approach to the multidimensional scaling of items was first suggested some years ago (Horst, 753). Somewhat later Guttman again revived the factor-analytic approach to multidimensional scaling but abandoned it for less elegant methods (Horst, 755). The factor-analytic approach has surprisingly enough not been followed up extensively. One consequence of this position is that in multidimensional scaling it is possible to make assertions about the scale values of items but difficult to make a factorial specification of the responses of a given subject. This is true also in latent class analysis.

Sample Selection

I shall mention one more rather broad area of multivariate analysis designs. These have to do with non-random sampling. I refer to the effect of sample selection on variances, covariances, and means. For special cases and special assumptions, the procedures have been quite adequately worked out. There are, however, many important cases where the assumptions may not be assumed to hold. In certain multivariate designs such as the multiple regression models, the problem of selection is not as crucial as it is sometimes thought to be. One of the chief advantages

in the concept of simple structure in factor analysis is that results may be relatively independent of the particular samples chosen. If the assumptions of rectilinearity of regression and homoscedasticity of arrays are satisfied, then sample selection does not affect matrices of regression coefficients.

However, where the individual is free to select his criterion activities, such as jobs or courses in college, sample selection is a problem. The assumptions involved in the conventional methods may not in general be assumed to apply. It is in these areas where more generalized solutions of the incomplete or mutilated data matrix problem are required.

One of the difficulties in developing such general solutions is that of their dependence on metric. In general, the solution of the randomly mutilated matrix problem requires optimization of functions of the roots of a covariance matrix. For example, one might specify that the missing elements should be estimated in such a way that the remaining elements in the matrix would be approximated by a matrix of specified lower rank. But here again the problem of metric would enter in, for in general the elements of matrices of experimental data are based on arbitrary origins, units, and functions of measurement.

It is probably not necessary to go on adding to the list of applications and specific examples of multivariate analysis techniques. I should like to close by suggesting that the essential characteristics of multivariate designs which I have outlined are adequate for most of the traditional experimental problems in psychology, and that if these characteristics are kept clearly in mind, new and fruitful approaches for the design and execution of research projects might be developed.

12. SUMMARY

(1) With this chapter the book turns from the most general treatment of scientific investigation—in terms of obtaining a

correct combination of theory, relational systems, experimental designs, and mathematico-statistical method parameters — to concentrate on the last — statistical methods as such; and specifically on multivariate statistical methods.

(2) Multivariate statistical methods require, and proceed most elegantly with the aid of, matrix formulations. The matrix is the central means of formulating multiple data observations. The discussion on the data box and its facet, face, and grid submatrices of the previous chapter is thus continued and developed more specifically for a three-coordinate system and in relation to statistical concepts concerning entities, attributes, and replications.

(3) An introduction is given to the general multivariate problems of metric and linearity, or otherwise, of mathematical relations.

(4) Tests of significance in the multivariate field in general depend on three things: the number of parameters in the model, the number of entities, and some function of the total and residual variances. Cross-validation is a possible practical aid but it involves severe loss of efficiency.

(5) A very common multivariate problem is that of estimating a designated criterion from a designated group of predictors, in multiple regression.

(6) The basic problems involved in deriving a set of common factors can be solved by a variety of methods, some of which are independent of scale. These methods usually involve operations on residual tables.

(7) Rotational techniques are independent of those used for factor extraction. They allow us to transform the original matrix so that its entries conform more closely to some configural criteria such as those involved in simple structure.

(8) Psychological problems that involve differences or change are shown to be soluble using the residual matrices left after making a general multiple prediction from the original set. The most predictable criterion model is discussed for data divided into two sets.

(9) Some formal properties of analysis of variance designs and the special case of intraclass correlation are presented in matrix terms.

(10) Predictor selection, test length, and problems of optimal classification are special cases of the multiple discriminant function. This leads to an extended discussion of types and their differentiation.

(11) Finally some attention is given to latent class analysis, configural analysis, and multidimensional scaling.

CHAPTER **5** Regression,
Discriminant Analysis,
and a Standard Notation
for Basic Statistics*

HARRY E. ANDERSON
University of Georgia

1. THE NEED FOR A
STANDARD GENERAL NOTATION
(BY THE EDITOR)

With the brief but comprehensive survey of multivariate statistical methods by Dr. Horst in the preceding chapter, the reader is ready to concentrate on more detailed accounts of particular methods, according to his interests. A word therefore becomes necessary regarding the plan, order, and interdependence of the statistical method chapters that now stand before the reader in Part 1.

Because of the central importance of *correlational methods* in multivariate designs (where more powerful superstructures of analysis can be built upon them than on bivariate designs), it has seemed desirable to begin with this chapter, asking about the basic meaning of regression calculations. On this basis the present chapter follows

the formulation of correlation into partial, part, and multiple correlation, canonical analysis, and the use of discriminant functions of combinations of variables. Chapter 6 then follows with a study of that specialized but highly important superstructure developed in correlation methods which we call factor analysis and component analysis. Thereafter, in Chapters 7 and 8 (Jones and Burt) we turn to analysis of variance—the main complement to correlational procedures—studied here especially in its multivariate developments and its relations to correlational procedures. Through the remaining chapters—9 through 14—the sequential dependence is less important and the reader may turn at will to problems of defining "type" and "process" entities (Tsujioka); measuring change in multivariate observations (Harris); studying modulation and interaction (Digman); carrying out multivariate hypothesis-testing (Fruchter); and, as an intellectual sauce, to non-Euclidean "ordering" of correlation matrices

*This study was supported in part by a research grant from the Vocational Rehabilitation Administration.

153

(Guttman), and the study of games theory (Brand).

From this point on, however, the chapters are likely to bristle with formulae. Consequently, from the angle of good instruction, one must consider what can be done to avoid that mental paralysis which grips many good psychology graduate students — quite unnecessarily, we would claim — on encountering a page full of equations. The somewhat intemperate passion that most mathematicians have for elegance of formulation makes them notoriously unwilling to meet the equally justifiable demands of pedagogical elegance. The latter requires, among other things, that one look to the reader's own line of interest, be unashamed to introduce a concrete example, and link up what is being said with what other contributors are saying. Where such treatment is missing, all that can be said is that the editor used his persuasion against what turned out to be better arguments (sometimes his own arguments as a contributor, in some parts of Chapter 6!). However, there is another way in which an editor can perhaps assist. Let us recognize that half the goose pimples caused by formulae are due to the sheer strangeness of the symbols, for the identical relation stated in words is often digested without a tremor.

If mathematics is a language, why should we not do the commonsense thing by standardizing the symbols and providing a handy dictionary by means of which the mathematical foreigner can begin to feel at home? To some extent the mathematician regularly does this, with π, and e; χ^2 and i, etc., and at least one reason for his not doing more — apart from his precious freedom to let anything represent whatever he chooses at any moment — is the absurd discrepancy between the size of the alphabet and the astronomical number of concepts he needs to represent.

However, in one science, such as psychology, and in one branch of it, such as multivariate experiment, the possibility of agreeing on a limited set of symbols that everyone can use in the same way is less hopeless. There is no doubt that for the psychologist — whose job is psychology, and whose excursions into mathematics occur mainly in one field — it would mean a great gain in intelligibility and ease of discussion if a symbol always meant the same thing. If in a psychological article, instead of saying that he obtained an r of $+0.7$ on an N of 320, the writer used π for r and j for N (and perhaps ϕ for a plus sign!), there would be justifiable gasps of indignation. If this much annoyance is caused by an odd use of single terms, how much more justifiable is the reader's irritation when forced to stare in dismay for ten minutes at some lengthy equation that proves later to be as familiar as his own front door?

Accordingly, the system in Table 5-1 has been proposed on the basis of research and teaching experience and consideration of the main textbooks. The editor hopes that it *looks* so simple that it will also create the impression it *was* simple to derive and set down. But one must confess it actually required much hammering out of explicit principles and a good deal of cross-reference among uses by the principal writers in the field to see where contradictions and obscurities need eliminating. Ultimately, the following principles were followed:

(1) The letter symbols should as far as possible derive from the initial letters of the words we commonly use in speaking of these entities, so that the representation seems natural and is easily recollected. This means that the notation should have the mnemonic advantage of a set of acronyms. For example, V is a variable-dimension matrix; C is a covariance matrix; s is a standard deviation (sample); P is a person; N is a number of referees; etc. This procedure can be extended to make the symbol fit not only a mathematical meaning but preferably also the more common meaning of the concept among psychologists. Thus a factor loading is b for *behav-*

ioral situation index, rather than *w,* for weight, the latter being used here instead for statistical weights generally.

(2) Since the twenty-six letters of the alphabet are altogether too few for all that needs to be represented, one must be reconciled from the beginning to the use of specifying subscripts. In any case, the only drawback to using subscripts is that it adds to the labor when a great deal of manipulation of equations has to be done — and psychologists rarely need much manipulation. They use rather than manipulate. (When it is necessary to "strip down," for a lot of algebraic acrobatics, it is quite simple to drop from the present notation the subscripts, which are then taken care of by the immediate, understood context of the manipulation. Thus r generically is any kind of dyadic *relation* coefficient, i.e., it can be r for correlation, r_p for pattern similarity coefficient, r_{jk} for correlation of two variables j and k. Similarly, among the V's (variable-dimension, sometimes variable-factor relations), the distinct matrices are V_{fp} (factor pattern), V_{rs}, (reference structure), etc.

(3) One should avoid Greek or other special letters not readily available on the typewriter (or even in some pronunciations), the use of which would limit suitability in manuscripts and discussion. (The only exception occurs in deference to the convention [Fisher] of putting sample statistics in Roman and population values in Greek, which use is restricted to mean, sigma, and a few other parameters.)

(4) Capitals and lower case should be related in a systematic way. Generally, a capital stands for a matrix, the lower case being used for the entries in the corresponding matrix. Thus A is a raw score matrix of attribute — a — scores. C is a covariance matrix — of c's — covariances. R is a correlation matrix, etc. However, the capital–lower-case relation can also be used, without confusion: capitals to represent a set (Chapter 3) and lower case the particular kind of attribute that applies to

members of that set; thus P is a set of people and p_i a particular attribute of a person; A a set of acts (responses) and a_j a particular response-attribute measurement. But these uses of capitals necessarily both for matrices and sets should occasion no confusion because the set and the matrix are of a different order. For example, A is a set of responses, but A is also a shorthand in the statistical context for an entire score matrix, which in the previous chapter we have written less concisely but more specifically as *PS.a* or *EO.a,* etc.

(5) *Absolute* avoidance of overlap within the alphabet is not essential. Very restricted overlap can be tolerated provided the symbol enters into two quite different areas of discourse in its two senses. To instance two unavoidable examples, one may mention s_j, which is a particular stimulus attribute, and s, which is the standard deviation in a sample (but these practically never come in one equation), and F for a factor and F for a variance ratio.

(6) Symbols should be such that they are also unambiguous to the ear in discussion. N, n, and m for people, variables, and factors is a nightmare ("Did you say an n by m or an m by N matrix?"). The choice of k (instead of m) for number of factors (despite its use for groups also) was settled for us by the opportune use of g by some leading writers for number of groups in analysis of variance, leaving k free to refer to numbers of factors.

(7) Some anomalies in an otherwise rational system must nevertheless be accepted because some usages are fixed, if not hallowed, by tradition to such an extent that change is impractical, e.g., N for size of referee sample and n for size of relative (attribute) sample. Or again z and Z for standard score and standard score matrix, despite the fact that these symbols lack any suggestion of the verbal meaning.

The editor is indebted to several colleagues, notably Henry Kaiser, Sam Hammond, Ledyard Tucker, and John Hundleby, for discussion of the notation problems.

2. PROPOSED STANDARD NOTATION FOR MULTIVARIATE EXPERIMENTAL ANALYSES (BY THE EDITOR)

The suggested notation, followed through as consistently as possible in the rest of this book, is presented in Table 5-1. Although the table covers the main areas, e.g., multiple correlation, type study, factor analysis, and analysis of variance, it does not repeat the everyday accepted symbols such as chi square, eta, etc., and gives its most detailed consideration to the matrix symbolism of factor analysis, where a standard "language" has been most needed. In this last area, a further translation from the notation here to that of Thurstone and of Harman, in the minority of instances where it is needed, can be readily derived by referring to their books (688, 1420).

The plan of Table 5-1 is to move from raw data at the top to more complex derivatives at the bottom, and (at least in the factor area) from lower order at the left to higher order at the right.

3. INTRODUCTION TO BASIC MATRIX OPERATIONS IN MULTIVARIATE METHOD

The present chapter has as its main aim the outlining of various aspects and properties of classical prediction and discrimination, which are fundamental in multivariate analysis. For convenience and simplicity of presentation, the predictor variables will be assumed to be scaled continuously, though most models will admit discrete cases for the criterion variable or variables. The topics, therefore, are first the multiple correlation problem for the single continuous criterion, and second the canonical correlation problem for the case of two or more criterion variables. The discriminant problems are then considered, for two groups and then g groups, where the criterion variable is not continuous but rather a discrete one broken up into two or more a priori units.

Basically, the problems of prediction and discrimination in multivariate analysis

TABLE 5-1
PROPOSED GENERAL NOTATION SYSTEM FOR MULTIVARIATE ANALYSIS

Relation to Data Box Notation

The system in Chapter 3 proceeds to greater specification than is needed or desirable in operational manipulations. Thus, data facet (score matrix) was there written, for example, *PS.a*, to indicate attributes (to responses) of a set of *stimuli* (relatives) made by a set of *persons* as referees. We suggest simplifying this matrix to *A*, designating a set of $N \times n$ scores written as *a*'s (attributes). However, the present notation, for the rest, has to be compatible with either condensed or expanded symbols, and for that reason we shall recapitulate the *main* data box notation.

1. Data Score Matrices

It will be recalled that each entity (id) is considered a *pattern*, and, therefore, mathematically a *vector* matrix (Chapter 9) representable by a capital. However, the matrix necessary to describe an id completely is far larger than any *one* in which it appears as a bounding entity for column or row. (Presumably its nature would be defined only by the DB's covering an infinite variety of types of entry.) There is thus no contradiction in representing a matrix of scores as *A*, while using capitals for the bounding ids. The entries, on the other hand, refer to a defined attribute, and in lower case, e.g., a_{ij}.

The ten sets of ids (entities, patterns) are therefore represented, in accordance with the Data Box, Chapter 3, as follows:

1. Any Stimulus by S_h $h = 1,2 \ldots j, k \ldots q$
2. Any Variant of a Stimulus $S'_{h'}$ $h' = 1,2 \ldots j',k' \ldots q'$
3. Any Response or Act A_j $j = 1, 2 \ldots c, d \ldots n$
4. Any Particular Stage of Response $A'_{j'}$ $j' = 1, 2 \ldots c', d' \ldots n'$
5. Any Person or Organism P_i $i = 1, 2 \ldots i, y \ldots N$
6. Any State of a Person $P'_{i'}$ $i' = 1, 2 \ldots i', y' \ldots N'$

TABLE 5-1 (Continued)

7. Any Environment Condition E_l $l = 1, 2 \ldots g, t \ldots v$
8. Any Phase of an Environment $E'_{l'}$ $l' = 1, 2 \ldots g', t' \ldots v'$
9. Any Observer and Instrument O_w $h = 1, 2 \ldots h, w \ldots f$
10. Any Condition of an Observer $O'_{w'}$ $h' = 1, 2 \ldots h', w' \ldots f'$

The corresponding *attributes* measured for the ids that are relatives are s, s' (attributes of stimuli), a, a' (attributes of responses and response stages), and so on through $p, p', e, e', o,$ and o'. However, in any simplified use from here on, a can also comprehensively stand for *any* measurement on any attribute.

Matrices	Designation of Matrix	Order	Entry	Subscripts
Raw score variable data matrix	A	$N \times n$	a	j and d
Standard score variable data matrix	Z (or Z_o)	$N \times n$	z	j and d
Estimated score (from standard scores on variables) common factor data matrix*	$A_{F(\mathrm{I})}$	$N \times k$	$F_{(\mathrm{I})}$	j and d
Standard true score common factor data matrix	$Z_{f(\mathrm{I})}$	$N \times k$	$f_{(\mathrm{I})}$	j and d
Raw score unique factor data matrix	$A_{u(\mathrm{I})}$	$N \times n$	u_{I}	j and d
Standard score unique factor data matrix	$Z_{u(\mathrm{I})}$	$N \times n$	U_{I}	j and d
Estimated score second-order common factor data matrix**	$A_{F(\mathrm{II})}$	$N \times 1$	$F_{(\mathrm{II})}$	j and d
Standard true score second-order common factor data matrix	$Z_{f(\mathrm{II})}$	$N \times 1$	$f_{(\mathrm{II})}$	j and d
Standard score second-order unique factor data matrix	$Z_{u(\mathrm{II})}$	$N \times k$	$U_{(\mathrm{II})}$	j and d

Naturally, the subscripts can be reduced where context is understood, so subscripts I, II, III, etc., will commonly be dropped. Similarly, the o can be dropped from Z_o, the variable standard score matrix.

These formulae assume n variables, k factors (first order), and o factors (second order).

2. Multiple (and Simple) Analyses of Variance
N = number of individuals
g = number of groups
m = number in each group (If groups are of same size, then $\dfrac{N}{g} = m$.) Variables are separately designated for independent and dependent, thus:
Independent variables are $t_1, t_2 \ldots t_n$ ("treatments")
Dependent variables (sometimes considered as criterion variables) are $q_1, q_2 \ldots q_p$. (This use of t and q for a group of predictors and a group of criteria is preserved in canonical correlation, etc., below.)
Group means $\dfrac{\overset{m}{\underset{1}{\Sigma}} q}{m} = \bar{q}_j$
Grand mean $M = \bar{q}$
Number and nature of *levels* on treatment and dependent variables:
  Independent: Second subscript 1 to 1, through j and k, e.g., $t_{11}, t_{12} \ldots t_{1j}, t_{1k} \ldots t_{11}$
  Dependent: Second subscript 1 to s through j and k, e.g., $q_{11}, q_{12} \ldots q_{1j}, q_{1k} \ldots q_{1s}$

3. Relations (Immediate, Lower-Level) Among Data, Singly and in Matrices
(Omitting reference to distribution statistics, which have their adequate symbolism, e.g., χ^2.)
  (a) Singly:
  M = mean
  d = difference of ids or means, according to subscript, on attributes
  p_f = cumulative frequency, hence p and q as proportions in a total frequency
  s and s^2 = standard deviation and variance in a sample

HARRY E. ANDERSON

TABLE 5-1 (Continued)

σ and σ^2 = standard deviation and variance (true) in a population

$\hat{\sigma}$ and $\hat{\sigma}^2$ = estimates of standard deviation and variance in a population

(Illustrative of general principle of Greek letters for population parameters and $\wedge$ for estimate.)

m_1, m_2, m_3, etc., = sample higher moments (than s) around mean (m'_1, m'_2, etc., when around origin)

μ_1, μ_2, μ_3, etc., = population higher moments around mean, with primes — μ'_1, etc. — when around origin

t = Student's t (approximately, the "critical ratio")

v = a coefficient of variation

F = variance ratio

df = degrees of freedom

r = correlation coefficient, subscripts x and y

r_p = pattern similarity coefficient, subscripts x and y

$r_{1.23}$ = *multiple* correlation of 1 with 2 and 3 (Since R is needed for the general correlation matrix, and the subscripts sufficiently distinguish a multiple r, there is no real point in continuing to use R for multiple r.)

b = *standard* partial regression coefficient (This use of b instead of β is consistent with reserving the latter for a population parameter, as well as with the use of b for any loading [which is a standard partial regression] in the factor specification equation. The former use of b, as a *raw* score weight, can be expressed by b_r [and the third use of b, as weight for a *deviation*, by b].)

$r_{12.3}$ = *partial* correlation of 1 and 2 with 3 subtracted

$r_{1(2.34)}$ = *part* correlation of 1 with residuals in 2 after variance associated with 3 and 4 has been taken out of 2 (only)

(b) In Matrices:

Title	Matrix Designation	Order	Entry	Subscripts
Simple correlation matrix, 1's in diagonals	R	$n \times n$	r	b and c
Reduced correlation matrix ($R - U^2$) communalities in diagonals	R_o	$n \times n$	r	b and c
Raw score product matrix	P	$n \times n$	t	b and c
Variance-covariance matrix	C	$n \times n$	c	b and c
Pattern similarity matrix	R_P	$n \times n$	r_p	b and c
Angular cosine matrix	R_c	$n \times n$	o	b and c
Linkage (1's for a connection,*** 0 for no connection) matrix	R_1	$n \times n$	1	b and c
Diagonal Matrix of Communalities	H^2	$n \times n$	h	1 to n

4. Variable-Dimension Matrices

(a) Common factors:

	Matrix Designation	Order	Entry	Subscripts
An orthogonal "extracted" matrix (principal axes, centroid, square root) starting with *unreduced* (R) matrix, i.e., unities in diagonal and taking n factors	$\underline{V}_o$	$n \times n$	r	(variables b and c and factors f and g)
Orthogonal "starting position" matrix, from *reduced* (R_o), or with communalities, as in maximum likelihood	V_o	$n \times k$	r	(variables b and c and factors f and g)
Rotated matrix from V_o (to simple structure, confactor, hypothetical Procrustes position, etc.). Oblique	V_{rs}	$n \times k$	r	(variables b and c and factors f)

TABLE 5-1 (Continued)

with freedom to go orthogonal. Left in reference vector structure form (i.e., r's with RV's)

				and g)
Reference vector pattern matrix	V_{rp}	$n \times k$	b	(variables b and c and factors f and g)
Factor structure matrix (Oblique; orthogonal as special case)	V_{fs}	$n \times k$	r	(variables b and c and factors f and g)
Factor pattern matrix	V_{fp}	$n \times k$	b	(variables b and c and factors f and g)
Factor estimation matrix (conventional)	V_{fe}	$n \times k$	w	(variables b and c with factors f and g)

(Note: This means b is the weight of a factor estimating a variable; w the weight of a variable estimating a factor.)

Factor estimation matrix treating factors as the non-fallible variables (see page 183)	$\underline{V}_{fe}$	$n \times k$	$\underline{w}$	(variables b and c with factors f and g)

[Factor estimation from $(\underline{V}_{fe} = (V'_{rs}V_{rs})^{-1}V'_{rs})$]

Matrix of common error factors (in sample)	V_e	$n \times k$	b_e	(variables b and c with factors f and g)
Matrix of "common-specific" factors (in sample)	V_s	$n \times k$	b_s	(variables b and c with factors f and g)

(b) Unique, Specific, Error Factors:

	Matrix Designation	Order	Entry	Subscripts
Factor loadings (correlations) of unique factors (assumed orthogonal in population) Diagonal matrix	U	$n \times n$	b_u	j or k
Corresponding specific factor loadings (assumed orthogonal in population)	S	$n \times n$	b_s	j or k
Corresponding error factor loadings (assumed orthogonal in population)	E	$n \times n$	b_e	j or k

5. Operating Matrices

	Matrix Designation	Order	Entry	Subscripts
Matrix of latent vectors (prior in computation to V_o or $\underline{V}_o$)	L	$n \times n$	v	b and c with f and g
Diagonal matrix of latent roots	D_L	$k \times n$	λ	f and g

TABLE 5-1 (Continued)

Transformation matrix (V_o to V_{rs})	L_r (or rs)	$k \times k$	l	f and g
Transformation matrix (V_o to V_{fp})	L_f (or fp)	$k \times k$	$\underline{L}$	f and g
Diagonal matrix of sigmas of scores for converting from correlations to covariances (by pre- and post-multiplication)	D_s	$n \times n$ or $k \times k$	s	b and c or f and g

6. Other D-V, Variable Dimension Matrices

	Matrix Designation	Order	Entry	Subscripts
Any non-factor matrix of multiple regression weights for estimating several criteria (q) from several predictors (t)	V_{qt}	$q \times t$	w	j and k
A factor matrix — the *associated factor contribution matrix* — for calculating multiple r's of factors on variables	V_{afc}	$n \times k$	v	b and c with x and y
The dissociated factor contribution matrix (Schmid-Leiman only at variable level)	V_{dfc}	$n \times k$	r	b and c with x and y
Variable contribution matrix for calculating multiple r's with F's, in estimation of factors	V_{vc}	$n \times k$	$\underline{v}$	b and c with x and y

7. Matrices for Factors of Higher Orders and Strata

	Matrix Designation	Order	Entry	Subscripts
Square matrix of intercorrelation of k reference vectors (steppingstone from L_{rs} to R_{f1})	R_{rr}	$k \times k$	r	x and y
Matrix of intercorrelation of k factors (pure factor intercorrelation derived from $R_f = L'_f L_f$)	R_f or R_I	$k \times k$	r	x and y
Matrix of intercorrelation of estimated factors (derived from correlations of factor score estimates in a sample)	$R_{F(I)}$	$k \times k$	r	x and y
Variance-covariance of k factors (Employing factor score estimates)	C_F	$k \times k$	c	x and y

(Note: This abandons use of C for the factor correlation — or cosine — matrix, and uses $R_{f(I)}$, $R_{f(II)}$, etc., for correlations of successive orders of factors, consistent with R_o for variables. C is thus similarly used for covariance matrix at levels C_o, $C_{f(I)}$, $C_{f(II)}$, etc. Just as the common factor matrices at successive orders are V_o, $V_{f(I)}$, $V_{f(II)}$, etc., so the unique factor matrices are $U_{(I)}$, $U_{(II)}$, etc.)

Supermatrix of correlations of first-, second-, and higher-order factors, common and unique, directly upon variables
 (a) Orthogonal (Schmid-Leiman) $V_{fu(I...o)}$ $n \times (n + k) + (o + k)$, etc. $\underline{b}$
 (b) Oblique (Cattell-White) $V_{fu(I...o)}$ $n \times (n + k) + (o + k)$, etc. b

---

[*] A_F would suffice but as we come to higher-order factors later, a (I) is added to indicate primary factors.

[**] Symbols for number of factors are k first order, l second order, m third order, etc.

[***] Sometimes called by mathematicians and *incidence matrix*. In psychology the link might be an r_p above an agreed value, or a sociometric tie.

are one and the same. If a high relationship is obtained between the predictor and criterion variables, then prediction, or discrimination, will be efficient. The sophistication of such portmanteau methods, however, though they permit full exploitation of predictor-criterion relationships, do not increase the degree or accuracy of the fundamental relationship of the variables. The efficiency of the methods, in general, is optimum for the extant relationships among the variables.

The operations of multivariate analysis can be presented quite succinctly by the use of matrix algebra. This has already been indicated by Horst (Chapter 4) and prepared for by Cattell's use of experimental data matrices (in Chapter 3) and survey of matrix notations in the section above. However, the use of matrix methods is now so universal in multivariate methods that a further introduction to simple, relevant matrix notation, definitions, and operations is desirable before proceeding further.

To the mathematician a matrix is an orderly array of numbers arranged in columns and rows. In this paper, the discussion will be limited primarily to the types of data and statistical matrices used in the behavioral sciences. Moreover, for simplicity of notation, a capital letter, such as A, will be used for reference to an entire matrix with the corresponding lower-case letter representing elements, a_{ij}, where the first subscript refers to a row and the second subscript refers to a column of matrix A.

There is no restriction on the order of a matrix. If there are n rows and k columns, then the matrix is said to be of order n-by-k or simply $n \times k$. It may consist merely of one row or one column with a number of elements; these are called, respectively, a row or column vector. Quite generally, the matrix is rectangular, and in particular it may be square, where $n = p$.

Square matrices are of particular interest in many analytic methods, especially those of a symmetric type wherein the ith row and the jth column have identical elements $(i = j)$. In a square matrix A, the set of diagonal elements extending from the upper left-hand corner to the lower right-hand corner, a_{ii}, constitutes the principal diagonal of the matrix. A square matrix with zero values entirely above or entirely below the principal diagonal, but with values different from zero elsewhere, is said to be triangular. A square matrix with values different from zero in the principal diagonal but having zeros elsewhere is said to be a diagonal matrix, and a diagonal matrix containing unities throughout the principal diagonal is said to be an identity matrix.

As mentioned in the previous chapter, matrices are subject to arithmetic operations that allow us to write extensive calculations in short-hand form. The operations of addition and subtraction can be carried out with matrices, providing they have the same number of rows and the same number of columns, by adding or subtracting the corresponding i, j elements in each matrix. In the example below, A is added to B and the result is matrix C, or simply, $A + B = C$, and C has the same number of rows and columns as A and B. If B had been subtracted from A, the resulting matrix would be the same as C except that the plus signs in the elements of C would be replaced by minus signs.

$$\begin{vmatrix} a_{11} & a_{12} \\ a_{21} & a_{22} \\ a_{31} & a_{32} \end{vmatrix} + \begin{vmatrix} b_{11} & b_{12} \\ b_{21} & b_{22} \\ b_{31} & b_{32} \end{vmatrix} = \begin{vmatrix} (a_{11}+b_{11}) & (a_{12}+b_{12}) \\ (a_{21}+b_{21}) & (a_{22}+b_{22}) \\ (a_{31}+b_{31}) & (a_{32}+b_{32}) \end{vmatrix}$$

$$A \quad + \quad B \quad = \quad C$$

Matrices can be multiplied but the order of multiplication is important. For the operations of addition and subtraction, the commutative law of algebra holds so that $A + B = B + A$, but such is not generally the case for multiplication. If matrices R and V are multiplied such that $RV = A$, then one may say that R is post-multiplied by V or that V is pre-multiplied by R. In general, $RV \neq VR$. The multiplication op-

TABLE 5-2

EXAMPLE OF MATRIX MULTIPLICATION

$$
\begin{vmatrix} r_{11} & r_{12} & r_{13} \\ r_{21} & r_{22} & r_{23} \\ r_{31} & r_{32} & r_{33} \end{vmatrix} \times \begin{vmatrix} v_{11} & v_{12} \\ v_{21} & v_{22} \\ v_{31} & v_{32} \end{vmatrix} = \begin{vmatrix} (r_{11}v_{11} + r_{12}v_{21} + r_{13}v_{31}) & (r_{11}v_{12} + r_{12}v_{22} + r_{13}v_{32}) \\ (r_{21}v_{11} + r_{22}v_{21} + r_{23}v_{31}) & (r_{21}v_{12} + r_{22}v_{22} + r_{23}v_{32}) \\ (r_{31}v_{11} + r_{32}v_{21} + r_{33}v_{31}) & (r_{31}v_{12} + r_{32}v_{22} + r_{33}v_{32}) \end{vmatrix}
$$

$$R \quad\quad \times \quad\quad V \quad\quad = \quad\quad\quad\quad\quad\quad A$$

eration requires, moreover, that the number of columns of the pre-multiplier and the number of rows of the post-multiplier be equal; the resulting matrix will then have the same number of rows as the pre-multiplier and the same number of columns as the post-multiplier. As in Table 5-2 above, elements (first, second, third, etc.) in the ith row of the pre-multiplier are multiplied with the corresponding elements (first, second, third, etc.) in the jth column of the post-multiplier; these individual elemental products are then summed to yield the corresponding i, j element of the resulting matrix.

Another important matrix operation, as noted by Horst in Chapter 4, is the transposition of a matrix. We can obtain the transpose of a matrix, which will be denoted by a prime, merely by writing its rows as columns, or vice versa. Thus, the elements in the ith row of matrix A will be identical with the corresponding elements in the jth row of its transpose, A', providing that $i = j$. This operation is particularly useful for many analytic methods. Consider a set of n tests given to N persons and the score matrix, A, with N rows and n columns. The multiplication $A'A$ will yield an $n \times n$ matrix of sums of squares and cross-products over the n tests. If the matrix A contains deviation-from-the-mean scores divided by N, the product $A'A$ will produce an $n \times n$ matrix with variances in the principal diagonal and covariances elsewhere; moreover, if A contains standardized scores (with mean zero and unit variance), the $\dfrac{1}{N} A'A$, where each element of $A'A$ is divided by N, results in the correlation matrix R containing ones throughout the principal diagonal and elements r_{ij} as the product-moment correlation between tests i and j.

The multiplicative properties of matrices provides for two operations that are of major interest in multivariate analysis. The first operation of interest is one of factoring. Any square matrix, such as $R = V_0 V'_0$, can be factored, providing that it is definite and non-negative or in general Gramian, into two or more other matrices. The mechanics of factoring matrices, however, is somewhat complex since it involves breaking down a whole system into component vectors. The second operation of interest is that of inverting a matrix. Recall that the multiplication of a single number by its reciprocal is equal to unity, such as (8) $(8^{-1}) = 1$. The same is true of square matrices or determinants; if A is an $n \times n$ determinant, its inverse A^{-1} is composed, or derived, as an $n \times n$ matrix so that the multiplication $AA^{-1} = A^{-1}A = I$, where I is the conventional identity matrix. The inverse of a matrix will exist, providing that the determinantal value[1] is not zero (which would be comparable to $\frac{1}{0}$, which is undefined mathematically), but in general the procedure is a fairly complicated one because again the entire system must be considered simultaneously. For large matrices, it is convenient to use Fisher's auxiliary statistics (Fruchter, 563, pp. 28-30), or by factoring V into a triangular root matrix such that $V = TT'$, then by the rules of

---

[1]The determinantal value of many statistical matrices can be determined easily through a factoring process. If an $n \times n$ triangular root matrix, T, is derived from an $n \times n$ correlation matrix, R, such that $R = TT'$, then the determinantal values Δ_R and Δ_T have the relation $\Delta_R = \Delta_T \Delta_{T'} = (\Delta_T)^2 = (\prod_{i=1}^{n} t_{ii})^2$ because the determinant of a product is equal to the product of the determinants.

matrix algebra $V^{-1} = (T^{-1})'(T^{-1})$ (Anderson & Fruchter, 27, 29, p. 71; Durand, 440), and the inverse of a triangular matrix of any order is simple and straightforward (e.g., Fruchter, 562).

The matrix operations presented herein are sufficient to provide the basic arithmetic language of multivariate analysis. Most of the matrices of interest in multivariate analysis are rectangular observation (score) matrices or determinants containing sums of squares and cross-products, variances and covariances, dispersions or correlations. These types of determinants will almost invariably be non-negative and definite, unless "corrections" are made in the elements, so that algebraic equations can be used quite freely. If an equation is written, for instance, in the form

$$CB = A$$

where C is a square variance-covariance matrix, then by pre-multiplying both sides by the inverse, C^{-1}, we get

$$B = C^{-1}A.$$

Likewise, if dimensionalities are consistent, we can add or subtract matrices in equations; from above, for instance, we can obtain the determinantal equation,

$$B - C^{-1}A = 0.$$

For slightly more extensive work in matrix algebra in multivariate analysis, the reader is referred to Fruchter (563), Harman (688), and Thurstone (1420), or for more complete works, see Horst (763).

4. THE MULTIPLE CORRELATION PROBLEM

The multiple correlation problem is one of the most fundamental problems in multivariate analysis. The method of multiple correlation is employed to predict a single criterion variable from two or more predictor variables with the minimum amount of (squared) error. The amount of variance in the criterion variable can be determined empirically, and the multiple correlation technique is used to maximize the amount of the criterion's variance predicted, or accounted for, by the predictor variables, which is another way of saying that the technique seeks to minimize that amount of variance in the criterion variable which is unpredicted and hence ascribed to error in the immediate problem.

If n predictor variables were statistically uncorrelated in and among themselves (i.e., if they were orthogonal), then the squared individual predictor-criterion zero-order product-moment correlations, r^2_{ic} ($i = 1, 2, \ldots, n$), would represent separate and distinct proportions of the criterion's variance accounted for by each of the predictors, and we could simply sum these values to determine the proportion of the criterion's variance that is accounted for by all of the predictors. The condition of orthogonality among the predictor variables, however, does not in general exist. Usually the predictors are found to be significantly correlated so that their separate predictor-criterion correlations (and predictable variances) will overlap. The problem, then, is resolved to one of "partialling" out the overlapped predicted variances in the criterion's variance.

For the basic mathematical model, we consider that a value, or score, in the dependent criterion variable, X_c, can be written as a function of the effects of scores in the independent predictor variables plus some random error, ϵ: explicitly,

$$(1) \quad X_c = \sum_{i=1}^{n} b_{ri} X_i + \epsilon$$

where the b's are the weights for the raw scores in the predictor variables (see Table 5-1) and ϵ is assumed to have mean zero and unit variance. This standard model in (1) is actually a univariate model (Kendall, 865, pp. 68-69), but we will not consider this aspect of the model in detail here. If we seek to minimize the squared error, $(x^*_c)^2$, in the criterion variable as taken from a linear compound of the n predictor variables, then we write, with the variables in deviation-from-the-mean form,

$$(2) \quad (x^*_c)^2 = [x_c - (b_{r1}x_1 + b_{r2}x_2 + \ldots + b_{rn}x_n)]^2.$$

Summing over the N observations, taking the partial differentials with respect to each of the b_{ri}'s ($i = 1, 2, \ldots, n$) weights and setting these n equations equal to zero leads to, in matrix form,

$$(3) \quad CB_r = V_c$$

where C is the $n \times n$ sums of squares and cross-products matrix for the predictor variables, B_r is the $n \times 1$ column vector of partial regression weights, and V_c is the $n \times 1$ column vector of predictor-criterion sums of cross-products. Division through the ith rows by $\sqrt{(\Sigma x^2_i)(\Sigma x^2_c)}$ gives,

$$(4) \quad RB = V_r$$

where R is the predictor variable intercorrelation matrix, B is the column vector of standard partial regression weights, and V_r is the column vector of predictor-criterion (validity) correlations; here, $b_i = b_{ri}\sqrt{(\Sigma x^2_i)/(\Sigma x^2_c)}$. The b_r coefficients in (3) are the coefficients for use with raw or deviation scores, while the b's in (4) are the coefficients for the variables in standardized form with mean zero and unit variance. These coefficients indicate direct, or independent, changes in the independent variables as changes occur in the dependent criterion variable.[2] The multiple correlation, $R^2_{c.1,2,\ldots,n}$, is obtained from

$$(5) \quad r^2_{c.1,2,\ldots,n} = b_1 r_{1c} + b_2 r_{2c} + \ldots + b_n r_{nc}$$

which is the least-squares maximum proportion of variance predictable in the criterion variable from a linear combination of the predictor variables.

The significance of the multiple correlation coefficient's departure from zero can be evaluated by a conventional variance ratio test,

$$(6) \quad F = \frac{r^2_{c.1,2,\ldots,p}(N - n - 1)}{p(1 - r^2_{c.1,2,\ldots,n})}$$

where the F table is entered with n and $(N - n - 1)$ degrees of freedom. The same evaluation can be made of the b_{ri} and b_i coefficients; the estimates of their respective standard errors are

$$(7) \quad \sigma_{b_{ri}} = \sqrt{\frac{s^2_c(1 - r^2_c)}{s^2_i(1 - r^2_1)(N - n - 1)}}$$

and

$$(8) \quad \sigma_{b_i} = \sqrt{\frac{(1 - r^2_c)}{(1 - r^2_i)(N - n - 1)}}$$

where s^2_c and s^2_i are the respective variances in the criterion and i^{th} predictor variables, r^2_c is the squared multiple correlation between the criterion and the n predictor variables, and r^2_i is the squared multiple correlation between the predictor and the $(n - 1)$ remaining predictor variables. The t table, with $(N - n - 1)$ degrees of freedom, is used to evaluate the significance level of the values and $t = b_{ri}/\sigma_{b_{ri}}$ and $t = b_i/s_{b_i}$. The values r^2_i may be difficult to obtain, but if the b's, for instance, are obtained by inverting the predictor variable intercorrelation matrix, the r^2_i value may be obtained as $r^2_i = 1 - (1/r^{ii})$ where r^{ii} is the principal diagonal value in the ith row of the inverted matrix (see Anderson & Fruchter, 29, p. 72).

The presentation of the multiple correlation problem herein has been limited to the case of linear relationship. As indicated by Horst in Chapter 4, however, logarithms, powers, or other scale transformations could be carried out on the variables prior to their inclusion in the model, and the resulting relationship would be dependent on these non-linear transformations. For a more systematic treatment of non-linear analysis, the reader is referred to Hartley (696) and Monroe (1066).

The multiple correlation formulas herein,

---

[2]Because the fit is by the method of least squares, some of the b_r's or b's may have negative values. Lev (925) presents a method for multiple correlations with the restriction that all weights are positive.

together with the various methods for arriving at the coefficient, can be depicted in the observation, or person, space. Though the geometric presentation is by necessity limited in dimensionality, a simple illustration with two predictors will serve to give the principles. Consider the three-dimensional hyperplane in Diagram 5-1. The test vectors extend from the origin of an N-dimensional hyperplane defined by N orthogonal vectors, each representing an observation, and here scaled in standardized score form. The end-points as well as the directions of the vectors representing the criterion variable, **OC**, and the two predictor variables, **OX** and **OY**, are determined by the score values on the N orthogonal vectors; the angular cosines between each pair of these vectors is equal to the correlation between the two variables. All of the vectors, **OX, OY, OR,** and **OY′** (to be explained later), lie in the same plane; **OC** is not in this plane but **CR** is perpendicular to it. The length of the vector **OR** is easily shown to be equal to the multiple correlation between the criterion and the two predictor variables, while **CR** represents the error variance. Moreover, the oblique projections of **OR** onto **OX** and **OY**, respectively, O_{b_x}, and O_{b_y}, represent the magnitude of the regression weights for the predictor variables. Schweiker (1279)[3] presents these relationships, as well as others, in detail.

Most methods of linear least-squares approaches to multiple correlation, such as the Doolittle method (Dwyer, 443), arrive at the measurement of the estimate vector, **OR**, in Diagram 5-1 (Fruchter & Anderson, 564). One of the most widely used methods is the square-root method anticipated by Horst (752) and Roff (1207), and developed in detail by Dwyer (444), by Summerfield and Lubin in a predictor-

DIAGRAM 5-1. The Multiple Correlation Model in the Observation Space for the Case of One Criterion and Two Predictors

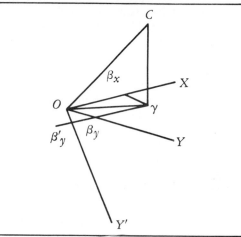

selection paper (1366), and in great detail by DuBois (431). The method involves factoring the $n \times n$ predictor variable intercorrelation matrix, R, into a triangular matrix, T, such that $R = TT'$; the criterion variable is then computed into T as the last row and the value of $r^2_{c.1,2,\ldots,n}$ is simply the sum of the squared elements in the criterion's row vector of T. In the geometric sense, orthogonal components of the predictor vectors are constructed, such as the vector **OY′** in Diagram 5-1, which is orthogonal to the vector **OX**, and, by the Pythagorean theorem, the vector **OR** is determined as the root of the sum of its squared orthogonal projections on these mutually orthogonal component vectors, such as $O\beta'_y$ in Diagram 5-1. Mathematicians know the principle of the method as the Gram-Schmidt method of orthogonalization, and the basis of the methodology has been used for many purposes (e.g., Horst, 757, 758). The method is efficient as a step-wise predictor-selection technique, but other methods, such as the one presented by Elfving, Sitgreaves, and Solomon (459), appear to be more promising in this respect.

---

[3]It is somewhat disappointing that this work has not been made more widely available in some published form since it is one of the most complete presentations of the geometry of statistics in the N-dimensional observation space.

The latter method allows for the selection, either totally or fractionally, of the optimum 2, 3, etc., predictors from an entire set as they fall outside of specified regions defined by parallel hyperplanes in the latent factor structure underlying all of the variables; the method requires knowledge of the underlying latent factor structure and there is some question as to the practical use of these methods in their present form, but, in general, the approach of selecting predictors from a latent factor structure seems reasonable (Anderson, 26).

Two problems related to multiple correlation are the partial and semi-partial correlational techniques. A first-order partial correlation such as $r_{12.3}$, is the correlation between two variables with the effects of a third variable extracted from the relationship, a third-order partial correlation, such as $r_{12.34}$, is the correlation between two variables with the effects of two other variables extracted from the relationship, and so on. With p predictor variables, the multiple correlation $R_{c.12 \ldots p}$ has the relationship

$$1 - R^2_{c.12 \ldots p} = (1 - r^2_{c1})(1 - r^2_{c2.1})$$
$$\cdot (1 - r^2_{c3.12}) \ldots (1 - r^2_{cp.123 \ldots (p-1)});$$

actually, this relationship holds for $R_{c.12 \ldots p}$ regardless of the order the coefficients in terms of the variables involved. The semi-partial, or part, correlation is similar to the partial correlation except that the denominator carries only one of the error terms, and hence, higher-order semi-partial coefficients are likewise available. In fact, the columns of the triangular T matrix, where $R = TT'$, contain successively higher-order semi-partial correlation coefficients. The multiple correlation is again related to these coefficients; explicitly,

$$R^2_{c.123 \ldots p} = r^2_{c1} + r^2_{c2,1} + r^2_{c3,12}$$
$$+ \ldots + r^2_{cp,12 \ldots (p-1)}.$$

The reader is referred to Roff (1207) and particularly to DuBois (431) for further details of the semi-partial coefficients, and almost any standard text for the ordinary partial correlation coefficients.

5. THE CANONICAL CORRELATION PROBLEM

The canonical correlation problem arises when we have more than one predictor variable *and* more than one criterion variable, on which we have N observations. We might have, for instance, a set of scores on achievement tests for students in a course that we wish to predict from a set of scores on aptitude measures. The canonical correlation is, then, the generalized model of the relationship between predictor and criterion variables of which zero-order and multiple correlation are special cases. For predictors and criterion variables, we consider the matrix R partitioned such that

$$R = \left| \begin{array}{c|c} R_{11} & R_{12} \\ \hline R_{21} & R_{22} \end{array} \right|$$

where R_{11} is the $t \times t$ intercorrelation correlation matrix of the t predictors, R_{22} is the $q \times q$ intercorrelation matrix of the q criteria, and $R_{21} = R'_{12}$ (the prime denoting transposition) is the intercorrelation matrix of the predictor and criterion variables. If $t = q = 1$, then R is the conventional 2×2 zero-order correlation matrix. If $q = 1$ but $t \geq 2$, then R_{11} is $t \times t$ dimensional, R_{12} and R_{21} are respectively column and row vectors with t elements, R_{22} is a scalar of unity, and the problem is one of multiple correlation. If $t \geq 2$ and $q \geq 2$, then R is of $(t+q) \times (t+q)$ dimensions and the problem is one of canonical correlation.

For canonical correlation as developed by Hotelling (773), we consider again the linear case, and the problem is reduced to finding linear combinations of the predictors *and* criteria that will maximize the relationship between the two sets of variables. This is the same process used in multiple correlation except that there is only one possible significant relationship in multiple correlation because there is only one criterion variable. As t and q take on greater dimensions, there exist more possible independent significant relationships between the two sets of variates, although the number of possible independent relationships remains restricted to the smaller of the dimensionalities, t or q.

Basically, the problem in canonical correlation is to determine a vector made up of a linear combination of the t predictor variables in x, $\gamma = \sum_{i=1}^{t} a_i x_i$, $(i = 1,2, \ldots, t)$ and a vector made up of the q criterion variables in y, $\zeta = \sum_{i=1}^{q} b_j y_j$ $(j = 1,2, \ldots, q)$ such that the correlation between γ and ζ is as large as possible. It makes no difference computationally which set are predictors or criteria and for convenience we will consider $q < t$. There will be, then, q sets of independent linear combinations, γ_i and ζ_j $(i = j = 1,2, \ldots, q)$ so that a given γ_i is independent of all other γ's, a given ζ_j is independent of all other ζ's, and the correlations between a given γ_i and ζ_j will be ρ_{ij} when $i = j$ and zero otherwise; and in general, successive independent correlations are determined such that $\rho_{11} > \rho_{22} > \cdots > \rho_{qq}$.

Let A_1 be a $t \times N$ raw score matrix for the predictor variables, A_2 is the corresponding $q \times N$ raw score matrix for the criterion variables, B_{21} is the $q \times t$ matrix of regression coefficients, and $A_{2.1}$ the residual part of A_2 in the regression; then, similar to the multiple correlation model,

(9) $A_2 = B_{21}A_1 + A_{2.1}$.

Defining $C_{11} = A_1 A'_1$, $C_{21} = A_2 A'_1$, $C_{12} = A_1 A'_2$, and $C_{22} = A_2 A'_2$, the problem is reduced to finding the q roots, λ_i $(i = 1,2, \ldots, q)$, which are the squared canonical correlations (i.e., $\lambda_1 = \rho^2_{11}$) in the determinantal equation (see Danford, 402, pp. 96-99).

(10) $| C_{21}C^{-1}_{11}C_{12} - \lambda_i C_{22} | \, b_i = 0$

where b_i is the column vector of criterion variables' weights associated with λ_i. The equation has a non-trivial solution when

(11) $| C_{21}C^{-1}_{11}C_{12} - \lambda C_{22} | = 0$.

The solution is derivable (Anderson, 26, Chapter 12) also in terms of the submatrices of the previously presented partitioned matrix, R;

(12) $| R^{-1}_{22}R_{21}R^{-1}_{11}R_{12} - \lambda_i I | \, b^*_i = 0$

where b^*_i is the column vector of weights to be used with the standard scores of the criterion variables as they are combined in the canonical vectors of λ. The canonical roots are obtained from

(13) $| R^{-1}_{22}R_{21}R^{-1}_{11}R_{12} - \lambda I | = 0$

and for each canonical root λ_i, the corresponding canonical vector of weights for the predictor variables' standard scores is determinable from

(14) $a^*_i = (R^{-1}_{11}R_{12}b_i)/\sqrt{\lambda_i}$.

The elements in the vectors a^*_i and b^*_i for the ith canonical correlation can be converted for use with raw or deviation-from-the-mean scores by dividing each element by the standard deviation of the corresponding variable.

The test of significance for rejecting the null hypothesis as to whether the t and q variates are related in the canonical correlation problem is presented by Bartlett (65, 66). We use the canonical roots, λ_i $(= \rho^2_{ii})$, and compute

(15) $\Lambda = (1 - \lambda_1)(1 - \lambda_2) \ldots (1 - \lambda_q)$

$$= \prod_{i=1}^{q} (1 - \lambda_i)$$

or, in general, after the extraction of any number of $m(<q)$ significant roots,

(16) $\Lambda = (1 - \lambda_{m+1})(1 - \lambda_{m+2}) \ldots$

$$(1 - \lambda_q) = \prod_{i=(m+1)}^{q} (1 - \lambda_i)$$

the value of Λ can be evaluated prior to the extraction of successively smaller roots after $m(=0,1, \ldots, q)$ roots have been extracted by a χ^2 approximation.

$$(17) \quad \chi^2 = -[N - .5(t + q - 1)] \log_e \Lambda$$

with $(t - m)(q - m)$ degrees of freedom.

The canonical correlation model can be illustrated with test vectors in the person space similar to that in Diagram 5-1 (see Schweiker, 1279, pp. 54-57). Consider the simplest case of two predictors, x_1, and x_2, and two criteria, y_1, and y_2. The plane x_1, x_2 is inclined to the plane y_1, y_2 because of the relationships among the variables. The set of all linear combinations of y_1 and y_2 form a circle in the y_1, y_2 plane, but the trace of such combinations in the x_1x_2 plane is an ellipse; the first or largest canonical correlation between the two sets of variables corresponds to the half-length of the major axis of this ellipse, while the second canonical correlation corresponds to the half-length of the minor axis of the ellipse.

The similarity between canonical correlation and principal component factor analysis is evident by analogy. In principal component factor analysis, we consider the internal relationship among n variates and determine an orthogonal transformation of their intercorrelation matrix, $Q'RQ = \lambda$, where Q is an $n \times n$ orthogonal matrix of directional cosines, R is the $n \times n$ intercorrelation matrix, and λ is an $n \times n$ diagonal matrix of roots, $\lambda_1 > \lambda_2 > \ldots > \lambda_n$. The person points in the test space form a hyperdimensional ellipsoid of n dimensions. With the scores in standard form, $\sqrt{\lambda_1}$ is the half-length of the longest axis through the ellipsoid, $\sqrt{\lambda_2}$ is the half-length of the next longest axis orthogonal to the first, $\sqrt{\lambda_3}$ is the half-length of the third longest axis orthogonal to the first two, and so on. The similarity of the two analyses has led to reference to principal component analysis as internal factor analysis, and canonical correlation analysis as external factor analysis (Bartlett, 67).

Moreover, if a canonical correlation is computed between the set of principal component factors and the set of original variables, the first canonical correlation can be shown to correspond to the first principal axis, the second canonical correlation to the second principal axis, and so on (Danford, 401, pp. 110-112).

The method of canonical correlation has not, in general, been used widely by researchers, a fact lamented by Kendall (865, p. 81). Several extensions of the methodology might serve to enhance its utility. Tucker (1463) used the method to compare factor structures across samples and Horst (761) extended the theory and methodology to the relationship among more than two sets of variates. Moreover, simple and straightforward presentations and computer programs, such as that presented by Cooley and Lohnes (381, Chapter 3), should provide the methodology at an operational level for researchers.

6. THE DISCRIMINANT PROBLEM: TWO GROUPS

Discriminant analysis, in its general form, is used for examining differences among an a priori classification of groups, for instance, on the basis of t measurements. The simple case with two groups is fundamental to the analysis. The more generalized case with $g > 2$ groups will be discussed in the next section of this paper.

The circumstance often arises in psychology and throughout the behavioral sciences where we take t measurements, $x_1, x_2, \ldots, x_t$ on two samples of sizes N_1 and N_2, and the experimenter seeks to determine if the two samples are different on the basis of the t measurements (e.g., Anderson & Leton, 30). One approach might be to consider each of the t variates separately and to perform ordinary t tests, t in number, between the samples. This approach lacks efficiency in two respects: (1) the approach ignores the interrelationships (viz., covariances) among the variables, and

(2) it does not allow for an assessment of the relative power of each of the t variates in determining sample differences. The t test was developed in a more general form by Hotelling (770) for the case of determining the significance of the differences between two groups on the basis of t correlated variates, and some examples of its use are given by Bock in Chapter 28. The general problem as a discriminant function was developed by Fisher (520), and in terms of the generalized distance function, D^2, by Mahalanobis (979). Nonlinear forms of the function were studied by Lubin (961), but we will restrict consideration herein to the linear case.

We will assume that we have t measurements on two groups of individuals, of sample sizes N_1, and N_2, and we seek some linear combination of the variables that will maximize the "between"-group difference relative to the "within"-group differences. The multivariate samples will then be reduced to the univariate case, and maximum distinction between the two groups will be afforded as their scale values are computed on the single discriminant variate. The linear function can be specified for the x_i variables and the weights λ_i,

$$(18) \quad z = \sum_{i=1}^{t} \lambda_i x_i$$

and the difference between means of z for the two groups is

$$(19) \quad S_b = \sum_{i=1}^{t} \lambda_i d_i$$

where d_i is the difference in the two groups' mean on the ith variate, while the variances within groups on z is

$$(20) \quad S^2_w = \sum_{i=1}^{t} \sum_{j=1}^{t} \lambda_i \lambda_j S_{ij}$$

where S_{ij} is the $t \times t$ matrix of within sums of squares and cross-products. The ratio to be maximized is S^2_b/S^2_w. If we take the partial differentials of this ratio with respect to each λ_i, and set these equal to zero, the result is a set of t simultaneous equations in which the solutions are proportional to, in matrix form,

$$(21) \quad \lambda = W^{-1} d$$

where λ is a column vector of t elements, W^{-1} is reciprocal to, or the inverse of, the $t \times t$ within dispersion matrix with elements defined by

$$(22) \quad w_{ij} = \frac{1}{(N_1 + N_2 - 2)}$$
$$\bullet \left[\sum_{c=1}^{N_1} (x_{i1c} - \bar{x}_{i1.})(x_{j1c} - \bar{x}_{j1.}) \right.$$
$$\left. + \sum_{c=1}^{N_2} (x_{i2c} - \bar{x}_{i2})(x_{j2c} - \bar{x}_{j2.}) \right]$$

the first subscript denoting the variate, the second the group, and the third the individual; similarly, d is a column vector with elements $d_i = (x_{i1.} - \bar{x}_{i2.})$. It is conventional to test the significance of the difference between the two groups, which we can do with the D^2 statistic,

$$(23) \quad D^2 = d' W^{-1} d$$

using a conventional F ratio

$$(24) \quad F = \frac{N_1 N_2 (N_1 + N_2 - t - 1)}{t(N_1 + N_2)(N_1 + N_2 - 2)} D^2$$

with t and $(N_1 + N_2 - t - 1)$ degrees of freedom.

If the F test is significant at a suitable level, it is reasonable to use prediction equations that will allow for the optimum assignment of sampling observations to group 1 or group 2. We use the discriminant weights λ_i for this purpose and first compute for group 1, for equation (18),

$$\bar{z}_1 = \lambda_1 \bar{x}_{11} + \lambda_2 \bar{x}_{21} + \ldots + \lambda_t \bar{x}_{t1} = \sum_{i=1}^{t} \lambda_i \bar{x}_{i1},$$

then for group 2,

$$\bar{z}_2 = \lambda_1 \bar{x}_{12} + \lambda_2 \bar{x}_{22} + \ldots + \lambda_t \bar{x}_{t2} = \sum_{i=1}^{t} \lambda_i \bar{x}_{i2}$$

For future observation with scores, x_i, on the t variates, we would then use,

$$s_z = \lambda_1 x_1 + \lambda_2 x_2 + \ldots + \lambda_t x_t = \sum_{i=1}^{t} \lambda_i x_1$$

and assign the observation to group 1 or 2 depending on whether s_z is closer to $\bar{z}_1$ or $\bar{z}_2$ respectively.

The discrimination afforded by the above procedure is maximum with the variables in the immediate problem. As with multiple correlation, the deletion or addition of any variable from the analysis would reduce or increase, respectively, the distance function and the consequent efficiency of the prediction equations. Various tests for the significant effects of deleting or adding variates in the analysis are given by Rao (1178, pp. 249-255). For assessing the effects of deleting a single variate, the statistic to be evaluated is

$$(25)\quad U = \dfrac{1 + \dfrac{N_1 N_2}{(N_1 + N_2)(N_1 + N_2 - 2)} D^2_t}{1 + \dfrac{N_1 N_2}{(N_1 + N_2)(N_1 + N_2 - 2)} D^2_{p-1}} - 1$$

where D^2_t is the distance function with t variates and D^2_{t-1} is the new one with one variate deleted from the analysis; then

$$(26)\quad F = U(N_1 + N_2 - t - 1)$$

can be referred to an F table with 1 and $(N_1 + N_2 - t - 1)$ degrees of freedom. The statistic, U, in fact, is useful in two other instances. If q variates are added to the analysis, then their effects on discrimination can be assessed for significance by substituting the new D^2_{t+q} for D^2_t in the numerator, and the original D^2_t for D^2_{t-1} in the denominator, then

$$(27)\quad F = \dfrac{N_1 + N_2 - t - q - 1}{q} U$$

can be referred to an F table with q and $(N_1 + N_2 - t - q - 1)$ degrees of freedom. Finally, an arbitrary discriminant function with weights $\lambda_1, \lambda_2, \ldots, \lambda_n$ (for instance, unit coefficients) can be tested to determine if discrimination afforded by this function differs significantly from the maximum; the resulting distance, D^2_a, from the arbitrarily assigned function is substituted

in the denominator of U and, retaining the original D^2_t in the numerator, the value

$$(28)\quad F = \dfrac{N_1 + N_2 - t - 1}{t - 1} U$$

can be referred to an F table with $(t-1)$ and $(N_1 + N_2 - t + 1)$ degrees of freedom.

The foregoing discriminant function, as a classification system, assumes symmetry in the two populations under study, and this may indeed be the case in many studies in the behavioral sciences. The error of classification may be calculated on the basis of the discriminant variate, z, and its standard deviation,

$$(29)\quad \sigma_z = \sqrt{\sum_{i=1}^{t} \lambda^2_i}$$

Assuming $\bar{z}_1 > \bar{z}_2$, the classification system above takes the middle value between these means,

$$(30)\quad M_z = \dfrac{\bar{z}_1 + \bar{z}_2}{2}$$

and assigns individuals to group 1 when $s_z > M_z$, and to group 2 otherwise. The error of classification, e, is the same for both groups:

$$(31)\quad e_1 = \dfrac{\bar{z}_1 - M_z}{\sigma_z}$$

and

$$(32)\quad e_2 = \dfrac{\bar{z}_2 - M_z}{\sigma_z}$$

which can be evaluated from a table as a normal deviate with mean zero and unit variance. If the two populations are not equal in number (i.e., $N_1 \neq N_2$), or even sample sizes for present observations, then the optimum separation value between the two groups is

$$(33)\quad M^*_z = \dfrac{z_1 + z_2}{2} + \log_e \pi_2 - \log_e \pi_1$$

where $\pi_1 = \dfrac{N_1}{(N_1 + N_2)}$ and $\pi_2 = \dfrac{N_2}{(N_1 + N_2)}$.

Then observations are assigned to group 1 if $s_z > M^*_z$, and group 2 otherwise.

Errors of classification for both groups can be evaluated by substituting M^*_z in (31) and (32).

7. THE DISCRIMINANT PROBLEM: g GROUPS

The more general form of the discriminant problems arises when we have several (g) groups of individuals, events, things, etc., and we seek a determination of the differences among the groups on the basis of t measures. We may have several kinds of achievement scores, for instance, and try to determine relative grade-level differences on the basis of these scores (Leton & Anderson, 924). The problem is similar to the canonical correlation problem, then, and much of the methodology will appear the same. There have been many other approaches to the problem of discrimination and classification procedures (e.g., Cattell, 220; Cronbach & Gleser, 396; DuMas, 436), but the methodology herein will in general follow the outline of Anderson and Fruchter (28), which is based on work by Rao (1178) and Rao and Slater (1179). Computer programs, as well as brief presentations, for these methods are presented in Cooley and Lohnes (381, Chapters 4, 6, and 7).

The initial problem is the same as the two-group case. We seek a linear function of the t variates,

$$(34)\quad \gamma = c_1 x_1 + c_2 x_2 + \ldots + c_t x_t = \sum_{i=1}^{t} c_i x_i$$

such that the ratio of the variance among groups to the variance within groups is maximized; the ratio is, in matrix form,

$$(35)\quad \lambda = \frac{C'AC}{C'WC}$$

where C is a column vector with t elements, A is the $n \times n$ among-groups sums of squares and cross-products matrix with elements

$$a_{ij} = \sum_{b=1}^{k} N_b (x_{ib.} - \bar{x}_{i..})(\bar{x}_{jb.} - \bar{x}_{j..})$$

using the first subscript for the variable, the second for the group, the third for the individual, and N_b as the sample size of the bth group; likewise W is the $t \times t$ matrix of sums of squares and cross-products within groups with elements

$$w_{ij} = \sum_{b=1}^{k} \sum_{t=1}^{N_b} (x_{ibt} - \bar{x}_{ib.})(x_{jbt} - \bar{x}_{jb.}) .$$

Taking the partial derivatives of the ratio and setting these equal to zero leads to the determinantal equation

$$(36)\quad |A - \lambda_i W| \, C_i = 0$$

or

$$(37)\quad |W^{-1}A - \lambda_i I| \, C_i = 0$$

which has a non-trivial solution when

$$|W^{-1}A - \lambda I| = 0.$$

The over-all test to determine if there are differences among groups, and consequently if we can make any discrimination at all on the basis of the t variates, can be made with the m canonical roots, where m is the lesser of $g - 1$ or t.

$$(38)\quad \Lambda = \left(\frac{1}{1+\lambda_1}\right)\left(\frac{1}{1+\lambda_2}\right) \cdots \left(\frac{1}{1+\lambda_m}\right)$$

$$= \prod_{i=1}^{m} \left(\frac{1}{1+\lambda_i}\right)$$

which is the same as the multivariate analysis of variance test.

$$(39)\quad \Lambda = \frac{\Delta_w}{\Delta_T}$$

where Δ_w is the determinantal value of the matrix W and Δ_T is the determinantal value of $T = A + W$. The value of Λ can be tested for significance by referring

$$(40)\quad V = -\left(N - \frac{t+g}{2}\right) \log_e \Lambda$$

to a chi-square table with $t(g - 1)$ degrees of freedom; here N is the "total" degrees of freedom, $N = N_1 + N_2 + \ldots + N_g - 1$, and, of course, g is the number of groups and t is the number of variates. A more powerful F test is available when the factor $\left(N - \frac{t+g}{2}\right)$ is small: define

$$y = \Lambda^{1/s}$$

then,

$$(41) \quad F = \left(\frac{1-y}{y}\right)\left(\frac{ts + 2u}{2r}\right)$$

is used as an F ratio with $2r$ and $(ts + 2u)$ degrees of freedom; here

$$q = g - 1$$

$$s = \sqrt{\frac{t^2 q^2 - 4}{t^2 + q^2 - 5}}$$

$$t = N - \frac{(t + q + 1)}{2}$$

$$u = (tq - 2)/4$$
$$r = tq/2.$$

The significance of each canonical root can be evaluated with the chi-square distribution; each root $\lambda_1, \lambda_2, \ldots \lambda_m$, has degrees of freedom equal, respectively, to $(t+g-2)$, $(t+g-4), \ldots, (t+g-2m)$.

If there are significant differences among the groups, then the t-dimensional space can be partitioned into regions so that the misclassification of observations is minimal (Rao, 1178, pp. 307-316). For the purpose of classification of observations, a linear discriminant equation is constructed for each of the g groups, the jth one being

$$(42) \quad \gamma_j = \sum_{i=1}^{t} c_i x_i - \frac{1}{2} \sum_{i=1}^{t} c_i \bar{x}_{ij} + \log_e \pi_j,$$

where x_i is an observed score on the ith variate, $\bar{x}_{ij}$ is the jth group's mean of the ith variate, π_j is the relative group size of the jth group (viz., $N_j/[N_1 + N_2 + \ldots + N_g]$), and the c_i values are computed, in matrix form, from

$$C = B^{-1}M$$

where M is a $t \times 1$ column vector containing the t variable means of the jth group and B^{-1} is reciprocal to the "within" dispersion matrix, the within dispersion matrix

being obtained by dividing each element of W by the degrees of freedom associated with that matrix, $N_1 + N_2 + \ldots + N_g - g$. If one can assume equal populations, which may often be the case in the behavioral sciences, then the quantity, $\log_e \pi_j$, can be eliminated in predicting group membership of future observations on the variates; in deciding group membership for a new individual, for instance, with scores on the t variates, we enter his scores in each of the g equations in (42) and assign him to that group for which his γ-score is largest.

If all of the group centroids actually lie in a straight line in the t-dimensional space, then a single discriminant function will exhaust the variance in their differences. If they are co-planar, then two discriminant functions may be required, and so on, and it may prove helpful to plot the several groups in the discriminant space to determine group constellations. The variates' angular cosines, 1_i, with the jth canonical vector are obtained, in matrix notation, from

$$(43) \quad |B^{-1}A - \lambda_j I| L = 0$$

where B^{-1} is reciprocal to the within dispersion matrix, A is the among-groups sums of squares and cross-products matrix, λ_j is an $t \times t$ diagonal matrix with λ_j entered throughout, and L is a $t \times 1$ column vector of cosines. The result is a set of simultaneous equations in the ones, and setting one of them equal to unity (arbitrarily), the other $t - 1$ are determined. The ones are then standardized by division by the square root of their variance,

$$(44) \quad \sigma^2_1 = L'BL$$

and the resulting t values are used as coefficients for the corresponding means of each group, so for the ith group on the jth canonical vector, λ_j, using

$$\zeta_{ij} = \frac{1_{1j}}{\sigma_{1j}} \bar{x}_{1i} + \frac{1_{2j}}{\sigma_{1j}} \bar{x}_{2i} + \ldots + \frac{1_{tj}}{\sigma_{1j}} \bar{x}_{ti}$$

and the canonical scores, ζ_{ij}, serve to define coordinate values on the canonical vectors for the groups. A second method for examining group constellations would be to compute ordinary distance function, D^2, values and collect groups together on the basis of proximity of distance. Both methods are covered substantially by Rao (1178, pp. 357-378). See also Chapter 9 below for a fuller treatment of grouping by r_p.

In this section and the previous one, the discriminant and classification procedures were presented without consideration for cost or loss functions involved in mis-classification (see Rao, 1178, Chapter 8). Moreover, the analysis was advanced on the implicit assumption that the group within dispersion matrices are the same; Cooley and Lohnes (381, pp. 62-63) present a test of this hypothesis, and Kendall (865, pp. 157-158) and Rao (1178, p. 289) give an example of analysis with two groups having different dispersion matrices. If the results of the Norton (1104) study are generalizable to multivariate analysis, however, as might be indicated from Lohnes' (943) study, only marked departures will have an appreciable effect on the results; Lohnes also compared classification methods from the discriminant space and the test space.

8. SUMMARY

(1) A great many multivariate relations can be handled as if they were linear; indeed this model has been found to work well, as an approximation, over a wide range of substantive problems.

(2) Multiple regression covers what are commonly called multiple, partial, and part correlations, but proceeds into canonical correlation, component analysis, factor analysis, discriminant functions, etc. The present chapter stops short of factor and component analyses as such, but handles the general problem of multiple prediction by linear procedures.

(3) Since these procedures can all be most economically handled by matrix algebra, an introduction is given to the kinds of matrix algebra most commonly used in multivariate psychological research.

(4) The multiple correlation model is discussed for the case of linear relationships and a geometric representation is offered. The comparative advantages of making the multiple correlation analysis on the basis of a knowledge of the latent factor structure underlying all the variables are shown.

(5) With several predictor and several criterion variables, we have the canonical correlation problem — the generalized model of the relation of predictor and criterion variables. The method is presented with appropriate significance tests. Several interesting correspondences between canonical correlation and principal component factor analysis are pointed out.

(6) Discriminant problems are discussed first for the case of two groups and then for more than two groups.

CHAPTER **6**   # The Meaning and Strategic Use of Factor Analysis

RAYMOND B. CATTELL
University of Illinois

1. ITS ROLE AND RELATIONSHIPS AMONG STATISTICAL METHODS

The general surveys of multivariate analysis methods by Paul Horst in Chapter 4 and of regression by Anderson in Chapter 5, have already given some idea of the relation of factor analysis to other methods in a mathematical sense. However, factor analysis differs also in a wider, experimental, strategic sense, from, for example, both multiple correlation and discriminant functions, in not *arbitrarily* choosing a criterion variable or criterion group, but in arriving at a reduced number of abstract variables and a weighting of observed variables according to structural indications in the data itself. It is thus a means of *creating* concepts, not merely of employing them or checking their fit to new data.

These special qualities have led to factor analysis playing a unique, major and sometimes misunderstood role in the theoretical development of psychology in the last generation. With the new refinements of technique here to be described, it is likely to play an even more potent role in the future, not only in psychology, but in sociology, biology, medicine, and wherever causation is complex and multivariate and basic concepts have been elusive. Since, in addition to the present writer's introduction to factor analysis (229), which was designed for experimenters and couched in a research setting, there are now several excellent books on the mathematico-statistical formulations per se (Burt, 160; Harmon, 688; Henrysson, 720; Horst, 80; Lawley and Maxwell, 906; Thurstone, 1420; Thomson, 1393), this chapter will simply state the mathematico-statistical framework with maximum economy, referring the reader to these books for expansions of the main formulae and mathematical derivations. This will permit concentration here on the logic, the investigatory strategy, and the necessary perspective in interpreting results.

Obviously, the central aim of factor analysis is to represent or explain observed covariational relations among many experimental variables in terms of linear dependencies on, and relations among, a much reduced number of "ideal," "intervening,"

174

or "abstract" conceptual variables. Since substitution of a reduced number of concepts and laws (relations) for a vaster set of particulars ("chaos") is the aim of all science, factor analysis is one of the most direct, universally applicable, and representative of scientific methods. It is not surprising therefore that in many fields one can point to what factor analysis would normally do as being already accomplished, historically, by the industry of the freely-operating researcher's mind and the expenditure of a great deal of time. Instead of making a factor analysis he has observed this change of mean with that change of influence, or compared this, that and the other single correlation, finally putting a whole lot of relational inferences together. But factor analysis has advantages where (1) the number of variables to be watched over and thought about is bewilderingly large, (2) there has been little success after several years in reaching agreement on the major concepts, and (3) there is good reason to expect complex interactions, which are not easily experimentally separable by manipulation or control, notably when most phenomena are multiply determined. An open-eyed observer must soon admit, however, that these conditions apply over most of the life sciences.

Historically, it happened, as the opening chapters indicated, that (with the germ in Pearson's writings) factor analysis was stimulated to its first growth by the Galton-Spearman struggle with psychometric problems. Here an explanation of multifarious individual differences — in ability areas — was sought in fewer concepts and particularly in a theory of intelligence. But our considerations above of the relational system of the data box make it immediately evident that factor analysis *could* be applied to far more scientific data than these. It needs to be applied especially to learning and perceptual processes, and to all that has to do with deriving and testing causal concepts in change over time and situation, as discussed in Chapter 11 below.

2. THE BASIC MATHEMATICAL PROPOSITIONS AND FORMULATIONS

Before viewing the strategic use of the method, let us proceed to some precise statements about its mathematical and statistical form. Typically the experimenter will have measured (regardless of his field of work) n response attributes (variables) on N people or organisms ($N > n$), though, as the Basic Data Relation Matrix has pointed out, n could also refer to other sets of relatives, e.g., states, stimuli, etc., and their attributes, and N could be the number of conditions, observers, etc., and so on through referees in other alternative facets. Wishing to find the relations among these n variables (relatives) over the N referees, he will next correlate them to produce an $n \times n$ square correlation matrix (commonly symbolized as R) containing the same $\dfrac{n(n-1)}{n} r$'s on either side of the diagonal (Diagram 6-1, page 178).

In search of possible determiners of the observed correlations, the psychologist accepts the mathematician's demonstration that the relations among n variables can be represented alternatively as generated by the relations of n variables to k factors. The computational process of "extracting" these factors from the correlation matrix values can be readily studied by the student elsewhere (229, 688, 1420, 1393) since here we are concerned only with the ultimate relation of correlations to factors. The principal axes method presents them mathematically as latent roots and vectors, obtainable from a computer thus:

(1) $R_v = L_V D_L L'_V$

in matrix terms, where L_V is the matrix of unit length latent vectors and D_L the diagonal of latent roots. The (square roots of the) successive latent roots tell us the "sizes" of the factors, and the correlations (loadings in the orthogonal case) of the variables with the various factors are given by the columns of the V_o "unrotated factor loading" matrix, thus:

(2) $V_o = L_V D_L^{1/2}$

In accordance with the general notation system adopted in Chapter 5 above (page 156), V_o will always refer to the orthogonal, original, unrotated matrix as it appears from the extraction,[1] and various other subscripts will be used for derived factor matrices.

The above equations imply that the orthogonal factor matrix can restore the correlation matrix (Equation 4 below). This exemplifies the basic proposition in any single correlation that the correlation between the two variables is the product of the correlation of each with the factor common to them:

(3) $r_{ab} = r_{ag} r_{bg}$

where a and b are variables, and g is a factor common to both of them.

3. ALTERNATIVE MODELS: COMPONENTS AND FACTORS

Although the resolution of a set of variables into "factors" occurs basically as shown in equations (1) and (2) above, there are two main alternatives, and some subsidiary ones, as one proceeds to further

specialization and developments of the model.

A first differentiation is between a model (1) which considers the variance of each variable wholly accounted for by common factors, and another (2) which considers it partly accounted for by common factors and partly by a factor specific to each variable. A second alternative is to (1) take out as many common factors as there are variables, or (2) take fewer common factors than variables. A third dichotomy, one less important mathematically, but equally important psychologically is (1) to rotate, or (2) not to rotate, from the original extraction position. The combinations of these three pairs of alternatives would yield eight models; but excluding the rotation alternative and the inherent incompatibles, we finally have three:

Model 1. The variance of variables is wholly accounted for by common factors, which are as numerous as variables. This uses the principal axis extraction method putting unities in the diagonal of the R_v matrix, and yields what mathematicians and psychologists have begun to agree to call a *component analysis,* as distinct from a *factor analysis.* Scientifically it is the *closed model.*

Model 2. The variance is accounted for by n (correlated)[2] common and n uncorrelated specific factors. This involves using communalities in the diagonals of R_v. We may call it the flexible *free general factor analysis* model, since several of the n common factors may be negligible, and it then ends in (3), as follows, as a special case.

Model 3. The variance is accounted for by k (correlated) common factors ($k > n$) and n specifics. This might be called the *approximating factor analysis model,* since it involves some statistical or other agreed approximation whenever it is applied to empirical data. Models 2 and 3 are scientifically *open models,* because they are specifics to be explained by future broad factors.

The components model must be rejected for general scientific investigation, because

---

[1] In the extraction process, although the mathematicians have certain reasons for preferring the principal axis (Burt's "weighted summation") to the centroid (Burt's "simple summation") method, psychologists are in a doubtful position if they concede that the latter is "less accurate," and should perhaps be more grateful to Thurstone for the centroid contribution to the saving of computation time. Moreover the centroid makes it possible to handle more variables with a computer of given size. As far as the psychologist is concerned, the fact that the former takes out the variance more efficiently *earlier,* is irrelevant if he is going to take out the full number of factors. And if he is taking out fewer than there are variables the gain is trivial, for the earlier and later factor variances get redistributed in rotation. Nevertheless, with modern large computers the principal axis is probably to be preferred, notably for mathematical properties and for practical reasons such as yielding a test of number of factors, e.g., by the scree test.

[2] Correlated means "free to be correlated." They may be uncorrelated, as a special case.

it would be most unlikely that n variables would contain within themselves *all* the causes for accounting for their own variances. To do this, they would have to lie in a completely self-explanatory subuniverse, self-sufficient as a system entirely isolated from the rest of the universe. The components model, as far as the great majority of real data are concerned, must be considered a mere mathematical figment. The factor analytic models in (2) and (3) with which we shall proceed must, however, be further defined as including rotation, because the initial position at extraction depends on accidents of the extraction process and the choice of variables. And if by factor analysis we mean a search for scientific, conceptual factors or determiners, the procedures must be completed by a rotation to a unique position, still to be discussed.

The distinction between (2) and (3) is perhaps over-nice. For while (2) has a mathematical completeness which appeals to mathematicians, it is scientifically *still* an approximate model. For, as we shall see below, there are generally more influences (factors) at work, though each probably in very small degree, than there are variables — n. Thus both n and k are alike approximations to the number of factors truly needed to represent nature. In either case they are made to account for *all* the variance on the variables by a piece of mathematical violence in the interests of an elegant but workable model.

Since the great bulk of factor analyses are done with model (3), which is the best approximation practically, we shall continue with formulae appropriate to it. (Further, it *may* be considered to include [2] in the limit that k equals n.) The notation will be that recommended in Chapter 5. Therein the typical factor analytic regression equation — the *specification equation* — for estimating a variable from a set of common and unique factors will be:

(4) $\quad a_{ji} = b_{j1}F_{1i} + \ldots + b_{jk}f_{ki} + b_j U_{ji}$

where the b's (behavioral involvement indices) indicate the weight or loading

(involvement) of the given factors F and U (unique factor) in the given behavior act a_j.

As is well recognized by most psychologists, U is a temporarily convenient mathematical fiction representing what is left over, in terms of variance, after subtracting what is due to the (meaningful) common factors ($u^2 = 1 - h^2$). It presumably is a reservoir for the variance of as yet undiscovered common factors. But even before we consider that some specific factor variance may be unknown common factor variance, we must recognize that in the existing matrix the unique variance has to be split into possibly several uncorrelated specific factors and error factors, thus:

(5) $\quad U_{ji} = S_{ji} + E_{ji} = S_{j1l} \ldots + S_{jxi} + E_{j1i} \ldots$
$$+ E_{jyi}$$

That is to say, the model need not, but ought in the interests of realism to consider U to be *several* scientifically real, independent, uncorrelated specific and error factors. However, there is usually no means of immediately checking on this. The unique factor has to remain, generally, "a confession of ignorance." However, the reliability coefficient enables us at least to distinguish S from E (or the series of S's from the series of E's). It should be noted that when we come to the *sample* as distinct from the *population,* these specific and error factors (not only the common factors) will *also* be correlated (i.e., *free* to be correlated or orthogonal). Parenthetically, there is something to be said for the model which considers them also correlated in the population!

Thus it will be seen that this model deals with common factors, common to several variables, specific factors peculiar to one variable, and error factors (which may also, at least in any *sample,* because of their correlation, result in factors both common and specific). The expressions "general factor" (loading *everything*) and "group factor" (loading two or more variables) have sometimes been historically used to designate two kinds of common factors, but this is a relatively unimportant subdesignation since in the great majority of well rotated analyses there are *only* "group" common factors, so that "general," in the above sense, is just an accident of choice of variables. Most people therefore speak generically of *common factors*,[3] though this also brings confusion when we want to distinguish factors common to all people (R technique) from those unique to one person (P technique) and it would actually be best to speak of factors common to several *variables* as *broad factors* (opposed to specifics).

using a transformation matrix L_{f_p} to move to the unique position x as yet to be defined, thus:

$$(7) \quad V_{f_p} = V_o L^{-1}{}_{f_p}$$

(This V_{f_p} has thus to be reached by first finding L_{f_p} through $V_{rs} = V_o L_r$, which provides L_r and so to $L_{f_p} = DL^{-1}{}_r$.) The nature of the process in (6) will be seen more easily in Diagram 6-1, which arranges it as a matrix chart. It should be noted that $R_{v.o}$ in (6) — and which for short we shall write R_o

DIAGRAM 6-1.   The Matrix Multiplications Relating the Reduced Correlation Matrix to the Factor Pattern

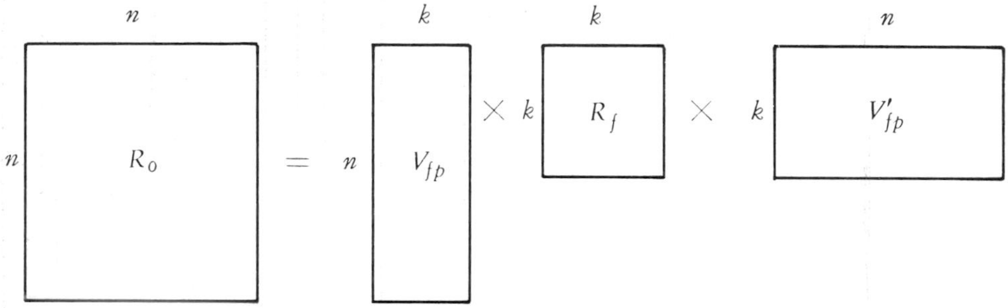

$$R_o = V_{fp} \, R_f \, V'_{fp}$$

In matrix terms the relation of these specification equations (which constitute rows in V_o or V_{f_p}) to the (reduced) correlation matrix may be stated:

$$(6) \quad R_{v.o} = V_{f_p} R_f V'_{f_p}$$

where V_{f_p} is a rotated factor pattern matrix from the V_o of equation (2) obtained by

in most formulae — has this subscript to show it is reduced from R_r by substitution of communalities for the unities which would initially appear in the diagonal of R_v.

The reader should note that here and throughout all later formulae, unlike some formulations he may encounter elsewhere, the V matrices are always kept upright, in the familiar form, as in Diagram 6-1, i.e., they are written as $n \times k$ not $k \times n$ matrices. Similarly the formulae are always arranged so that the score matrix is in the familiar upright form (people down the side) in $N \times n$ or $N \times k$ form.

The R_f in (6) is the correlation among the first-order factors and could be more fully written R_{f1} to indicate that it refers to first orders. If they should happen to be orthogonal, R_f would become an identity matrix and would leave $R_{v.o} = V_o V'_o$. (In the past

---

[3] Parenthetically, some confusion arises when the mathematical use of common and unique — which applies to *relatives* — comes into contact with the psychological use of common and unique factor traits (Allport, 18; Cattell, 213), which applies to *referees*. This can be avoided by using *specific* for a trait *specific* to a variable, as S in (5) above, and *unique* for a trait specific to a person, as proposed elsewhere (240). A *unique* trait is *common* to several variables (or other relatives) as in a P-technique factoring of one person. However, unique factor has come firmly into mathematical usage as applying to "specific plus error" and unfortunately must be so retained.

C_F has been used for this correlation among factors, but as studies progress to second- and third-order factors, it is more elegant to preserve R for *all* correlation matrices, from variables to nth-order factors, indicating the order reference by a subscript. In a complete description the V's would similarly have ones, twos, etc., as subscripts to indicate the factor order involved for factor patterns and structures.)

Similarly to $R_{v,o}$ above, when the first-order factor intercorrelation matrix, R_{f1}, is reduced to communalities for higher-order extractions, confusion may be avoided by writing it $R_{f1.0}$.

An aside is in order here on the above parenthetic comment that if the model assumes the possibility of oblique common factors it should also, in the name of a scientifically consistent picture, admit oblique specific factors, i.e., oblique to one another and the common factors in the population. The standard mathematical presentations present them as orthogonal, although statisticians must recognize that if they are orthogonal in the population they are still not orthogonal in the sample. If what is written as a single specific is the *sum* of *a lot* (Equation [5]) of small specifics, the total of all of them — S_j in equation (5) — is unlikely to be significantly oblique to another similar composite. But if, as in the second part of (5), we refer to various simple specifics, each is best considered (i.e., in the most likely model) as oblique *ideally in the population* and practically in the sample. (Common factors among these oblique specifics should in a scientific model stand at the same level as second orders among the common factors.)

However, since there is absolutely no mathematical possibility of extracting $2n$ factors (n common and n specific) from n variables, we must accept the fact that in any actual sample some of the real oblique specific factor variance will normally be falsely incorporated in the common factor space. (In the *components* model, on the other hand, this real specific factor variance, which is at least kept initially specific in the *factor* model, is incorporated "wholesale" with spurious specific variance into the common factor space, by putting ones in the diagonals). It is just possible to think of assumptions by which operations could be developed to recognize the degree of obliquity of a specific factor, but in all ordinary practice the totality of variance of what in the model is considered an influence specific to one variable is treated mathematically as orthogonal to the common factor space.

4. PROPERTIES AND FORMULAE FOR THE FULL FACTOR MODEL

Laws in science have been described in Chapter 1 as either structural or causal. In this chapter so far, factor analysis has been mainly described as a scientifically parsimonious way of accounting for the behavior of many variables by introducing "ideal" intervening variables or concepts. Let us consider more closely the additional restrictions or conditions that are necessary to ensure that factors preserve their identities across different experiments and correlation matrices and thus acquire the conceptual *status* of determiners (in the case of structural laws) or of influences (in the case of causal laws). If time sequences are known, and have a form demonstrating the factors in that experimental design to be the *necessary predecessors* of variable changes, we can call the factor a *cause*. But otherwise our model will give factors the slightly different and more generic status of *determiners,* though if simple structure is an added condition it argues for a high probability of causal status.

Incidentally, it will be noted that we are proceeding to a conception of the method very different from that which calls factor analysis "a technique for classification, and investigating taxonomy." It is true that variables, people, etc., may be "brought into groups" as a secondary development *after* factor analysis. The scientific model we are now developing as an extension of the preliminary mathematical model, and which will have additional restrictions and properties, aims to find dimensions of common variation, which may further be recognized as *sources* of observed variance and therefore as underlying determiners or causes. The finding of types and species is quite a different aim, pursued, for example, by cluster analysis (Tryon, 1454) and by methods in Chapter 9 below. They may use factor analysis as an intermediate step, to get the best dimensions in which to look for taxonomic spatial clusters of individuals and organisms, but factor analysis is by no means primarily a taxonomic instrument, and it is poor and misleading teaching to present it as such.

The full properties of the scientific model can be appreciated only after we have discussed the rationale for definition of simple structure, of confactor rotation, and of higher-strata resolutions. But it is already evident that the scientific model cannot tolerate unities in the diagonals, or orthogonal rotations pledged to keep all scientific influences completely unrelated to one another! If we pursue the oblique model, we quickly discover the mathematical implications that loadings, correlations, and weights of variables in estimating factors become three instead of two different things, as in the orthogonal model. In the orthogonal matrix, V_o, the weight of a factor, b, in the specification equation for estimating a variable, is the same as r, its correlation with the variable. But in the oblique case, a true reciprocity of estimation arises between factors and variables. Just as in any multiple correlation prediction of a criterion (see Anderson's Chapter 5), the weights that would be derived from the correlations with the criterion are modified again by the correlations among the predictors. This obviously holds if we are "predicting" a variable from a set of factors or a factor from a set of variables, since in both cases the predictors are

mutually oblique. (Such reciprocity fails in orthogonal factors.)

Thus among the Dimension-Variable relation matrices we now recognize V_{fs}, a *factor structure* matrix of *correlations* (r's) with the factor, V_{fp}, a *factor pattern* matrix of *weights* (b's) of factors to estimate variables, and V_{fe}, a *factor estimation* matrix of variable weights (w's) to estimate factors. Equation (5) above expressed the restoration of the reduced correlation matrix from the V_{fp}, but with suitable rearrangements we could use any of the D-V (dimension-variable) matrices. For example:

$$(8) \quad R_{v.o} = V_{fs} R^{-1}_f V'_{fs}$$

It follows that the correlation matrix can also be resolved thus:

$$(9) \quad R_{v.o} = V_{fs} V'_{fp}.$$

Just as the oblique model thus requires a difference, for example, between *structure* and *pattern*, so it also calls upon us to recognize a difference between a *factor* (sometimes less happily called a primary factor, since it confuses the issue with primary, secondary, tertiary, etc. factor *strata* or *orders*) and a *reference vector*. In factor analysis what we normally first locate (and sometimes temporarily call a "factor") is the *reference vector* (rv), which is the normal axis erected *perpendicularly to the hyperplane* discovered in the rotation. The factor (f), on the other hand, is the axis formed by the *line of intersection of all hyperplanes other than that on which the given factor has its zero loadings*. In three-space, in an attic with sloping walls, the rv is a perpendicular to the floor at the corner, and the factor is the non-perpendicular line of intersection of the sloping roofs. As far as this can be shown in two dimensions (which has the peculiarity that hyperplanes are merely lines), the relation can be shown in Diagram 6-2.

Let us continue our investigation of the scientific model we are accepting by following the ways in which the various interconnected values are obtained in any given

DIAGRAM 6-2. Relation of Loadings, etc., on Reference Vectors and Factors, in Two Dimensions

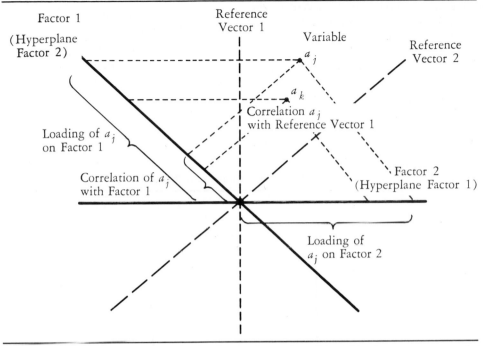

From this it will be seen that the loadings of a series of variables, a_j, a_k, etc., on the factor (f's) are proportional to their correlation with the corresponding **RV**'s.

factor analysis. Having got the orthogonal, unrotated V_o factor matrix from the computer—equations (1) and (2)—and rotated it to the best (probably simple structure) resolution (see Section 5 below), we find ourselves with an empirical transformation matrix, L_{rr}, or, briefly, L_r, which rotates the V_o to the position found, thus:

(10) $V_{rs} = V_o L_r$.

The entries in L_r are the direction cosines, here correlations, of the rotated rv's with the original orthogonal reference frame. From this L_r we can get also the correlations among the reference vectors, thus:

(11) $R_{rv} = L'_r L_r$

At this point we have all the information necessary for any transformation we wish to make within this system. For example:

(12) $R_f = DR^{-1}{}_{rr}D$

when D is a diagonal matrix consisting of the reciprocals of the square roots of the diagonal values in R_{rr}. A sample of these transformations into equivalents can be indicated by:

(13) $V_{fp} = V_o L_r D^{-1} = V_{fs} D^{-1} R_f D^{-1}$
$\qquad = V_{rs} D^{-1} = V_{rp} R_r D^{-1} = V_o L_f^{-1}.$

Of particular interest is the calculation of the total communality of a variable, referred to above as *its variance from all the common factors together*. This can be computed from the accepted factor resolution position using the *loadings* in V_{fp}, thus:

(14) $b^2{}_j = \sum_{f=1}^{F=k} b^2{}_{jf} + 2(b_{j1}b_{j2}r_{f1f2} + \ldots$
$\qquad\qquad + b_{j(k-1)}b_{jk}r_{f(k-1)fk})$

the r_{fjfk} values being the correlations

among the various factors. With orthogonal factors, the second term in (14) vanishes, whence it is convenient to calculate the communality simply as the sum of squared loadings from the original V_o, *before* rotation.

The main transformations remaining to complete this view of the model are those which go to the estimation of scores.

The estimation of test scores from factor scores goes, of course, by the specification equation (3) above, which in matrix terms, for all variables at once, is V_{fp}, including an $n \times n$ section for specific loadings. Then:

(15) $\hat{Z}_t = Z_f V'_{fp}$ (or, for variables in general, $Z_r = Z_f V'_{fp}$),

where Z_t is the matrix of estimated standard test scores and Z_f is that of standard factor scores, including the specifics. It is well in general to regard the V_{fp} and the Z_f as covering also the specific factors, as shown in Diagram 6-3, which sets out the matrix multiplication in visual form, and adds

DIAGRAM 6-3.   Matrix Operations for Obtaining Factor Standard Scores

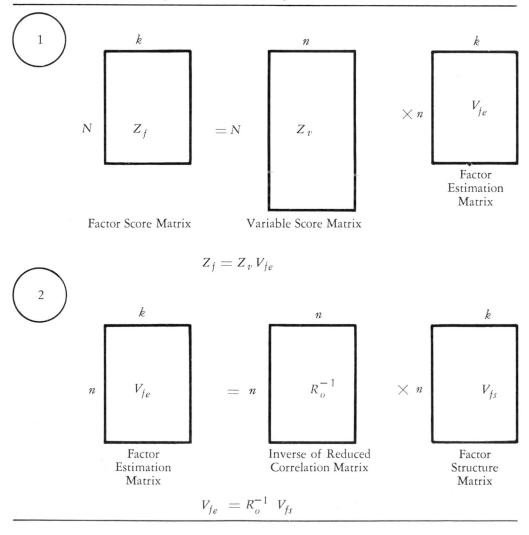

$$Z_f = Z_v V_{fe}$$

$$V_{fe} = R_o^{-1} V_{fs}$$

the matrices for specifics. Nothing is actually gained by this, because we have no good means of estimating the specific factor, but without it the variance of the test estimates will be less than that of standard scores.

In ordinary procedure one would first estimate factor scores from test scores, because it is the latter that we actually possess. To do this, we must first calculate the factor estimation matrix, V_{fe}, as follows:

(16) $V_{fe} = R_v^{-1} V_{fs}$.

This is precisely equivalent to calculating beta weights for a multiple correlation, where V_{fs} gives the correlations with the criterion.

Whence,

(17) $\hat{Z}_f = Z_t V_{fe}$ (or, for variables in general, $\hat{Z}_f = Z_v V_{fe}$).

Formulae (16) and (17) represent the traditional approach which regresses factors on tests, i.e., it assumes the tests to be the real and dependable entities and the factors as abstractions to be *derived* by regressions from them. However, it would be more consistent with the scientific model we have adopted here, which views the factors as real determiners or influences, to consider instead that the factor structure matrix represents the regression of tests on factors. Accordingly, other ways of estimating factors have been set up by Bartlett (67) and suggested by Tucker and by the present writer. The resulting formula in our present symbolism is:—

(18a) $V_{fe} = V_{fp} (V'_{fp} V_{fp})^{-1}$

which, in terms of going directly from test to factor scores becomes

(18b) $\hat{Z}_f = Z_v V_{fp} (V'_{fp} V_{fp})^{-1}$

Horn has shown (747) that the factor estimates from this formula differ somewhat from those by (17), so that this reversal of the model, making factors influences of tests, is not a purely academic issue. A comparison also of certain approximate and more exact methods of factor estimation is given by Baggaley and Cattell (496).

A related development is found in the model by Lawley and Maxwell in which any selective process operates directly on the factors, and therefore only indirectly on variables. Actually, they show that this model, for reasonably large samples, permits a more sensitive test of the correspondence between the two covariance matrices of two samples drawn randomly from the same population. This greater sensitivity comes from the fewer degrees of freedom for error variation in the sampling of a few, k, factors rather than many, n, variates. The degrees of freedom for a chi-square test of a comparison of matrices based on variables is $\frac{1}{2}(n[n-1])$, whereas the corresponding test based on the assumption of sampling of factors has only

$\frac{k}{2}(k+1)$ degrees of freedom.

5. UNIQUE RESOLUTION AND THE TESTS OF ITS ATTAINMENT

Let us now turn to the problem of obtaining the unique resolution—contained in the L_r transformation matrix above—which gives the V_{fp} on which all the above system of interchange between variables and factors depends. In order of computing procedure, one would first, of course, have to have solved the problems of the number of factors and the communality estimation. We shall assume this question solved as in Section 7 below, and keep to the rotation issue. Let us assume that the experimenter has reached a V_o, with defined communalities appropriate to the decided number of factors. This V_o, when multiplied by its transpose, exactly or very closely restores the original correlation matrix, $R_{v.o}$.

An infinite number of either orthogonal or oblique transformations are, of course, possible from any V_o, corresponding to the innumerable possible positions of coming to rest after spinning the axes. To the mathematician, each is equally satisfactory because each is equally capable of restoring the V_o. Scientific meaning, on the other hand, has no use for this intellectual roulette and requires some particular resolution that will satisfy additional conditions, and bring scientifically useful properties, i.e., factors that will give invariant concepts across different experiments, maximum reliability, and parsimony in psychological predictions and calculation, etc. Since in science, two or three alternative models will occasionally give, for a time, equally good "meaning" in these respects, e.g., the wave and corpuscle formulations of light, it should be understood that our search for the unique resolution may, for a time, entertain different principles. And even the use of one principle may possibly lead to one or two almost equally "explanatory" positions, with quite special properties out of the infinite possible number.

Incidentally, one must distinguish this rotation for *general scientific meaning* from the spurious imitation that some psychologists invoke when they "rotate for special psychological *meanings.*" Rotation for a particular set of psychological meanings, most easily done by the Procrustes method (Hurley & Cattell, 800; Schoenemann, 1276), is legitimate and useful in the applied field, using well-established factor concepts. It will work even in basic research if one can check fit to the "meaning" hypothesis used, by a statistical test (see Chapter 10), but most "rotation for meaning" is merely intellectually chasing one's tail. Research is undertaken to obtain *new* knowledge. Paying attention in rotation to *general conditions and criteria* which will ensure a scientifically meaningful resolution is quite different from adapting the rotation to one's own particular conceptual prejudices.

Broadly, there are three possible rotational principles, two based on *general scientific meaningfulness,* which are thus devices for creating new concepts, and one to *check specific hypotheses,* by the usual application of statistical tests.

In listing essential rotational principles here, we have omitted what are sometimes called criterion rotation, canonical correlation, and rotation to the most predictable criterion, as well as rotation with shift of the origin, which has utility, in a complex sense, in special circumstances. Criterion rotation involves first locating type groups, e.g., imbeciles, neurotics, or occupational groups, and rotating so that each factor maximally distinguishes one group from another. This proposal, introduced by Eysenck, apparently for the satisfaction of psychiatrists, appeals to those concerned with an immediate, simplified intelligibility, and a set of weights, in a particular applied problem, e.g., neurotic diagnosis. But, unfortunately, there is every reason to expect that one group will differ in general from another in *several* factor concepts at once, e.g., neurotics are more ego-weak, desurgent, guilt-prone, anxious, etc. (325), and there is no single general factor of neuroticism. Moreover, social and biological subgroups are far more numerous and arbitrary than psychological dimensions — they are almost infinite. Similarly, we set aside canonical correlation and most predictable criterion resolutions on the grounds that convenience for any particular criteria prediction is less important than invariance and maximum scientific negotiability, as described below; *these* are for applied psychology, in special instances; but basic science must be universal. Thus we have left (apart from Procrustes, for *hypothesis testing*) two scientific rotation principles, as follows: —

(1) *Simple Structure.* This is a specific application of the general principle of hypothesis-choice stated by Newton, in his *natura est simplex,* or by Occam, in a wider context as "Entia non sunt multiplicanda sine necessitate." One view of this idea of "simplest explanation," as it affects the present aim of explaining a configuration of variables, is that it is reached when each factor has loadings extending over (affecting) only a few variables, i.e., that it loads or

correlates with the smallest possible number. In common-sense terms we may say that *given a wide sample of variables, we should expect any true natural influence to affect only a few of them, rather than all* indiscriminately. The "wide sample" demanded in this definition, i.e., the representativeness of a population of variables, is important and should never be overlooked in using the principle. In terms of a plot like that in Diagram 6-4, this means that there

edly occur in real data, and, in two-space, appear like the blurred lines (blurred from a true Euclidean line by intrusion of measurement error) shown in Diagram 6-4. Indeed, Cattell and Gorsuch (288) have shown that simple structure does not exist in random, artificial correlation matrices, but only in organic, natural data in which separate and real underlying influences may be assumed to be at work. On finding such nebulae of points, one rotates until the new

DIAGRAM 6-4. Two Empirical Examples of Simple Structure

(a) From Objective (Laboratory) Personality Measurement Data
(Japanese — 13 Year Old — O-A Battery)

(b) From Objective Motivation Data
(American Adults on the MAT Test).

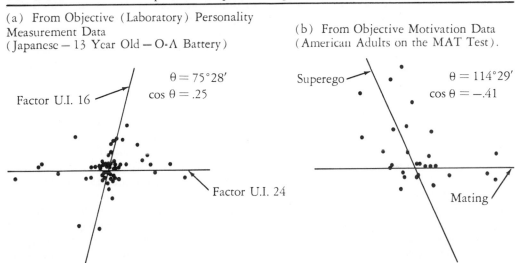

should be possible rotation positions for each factor in which a *majority of the variables have zero projections* upon it. (Whether these projections should be correlations or loadings we can discuss in a moment). In three-space, for example, we should be able to find planes (discs) of variables (these planes, of course, become *hyper*planes in the general, hyperspace case, and *lines* in the present two-space example) which can be perceived as crystallizing from the random distribution of points.

Experience verifies that these undoubt-

"factors" (technically "reference vectors") can be placed as perpendiculars to these planes, as shown at A and B in Diagram 6-4, which represents real data from two kinds of factor analysis. At that point the factors obviously affect (correlate with) fewest variables. This amounts to maximizing the number of zero entries over all columns of the V_{fp} (or the V_{rs}, since it is proportional by rows to V_{fp}) specifically chosen from the possible V_{fp}'s from the V_o.

The whole meaning of a factor-analytic solution can be changed by comparatively slight modifications in the rotational resolution. This means that no matter how carefully the original measurement, correlation, and factor extraction have been carried out, the meaning can easily be lost in the last stage of the study. Issues of great theoretical import can turn on rather abstruse technical points in evaluating the correctness of a simple structure. For this reason, no apology is needed for a brief digression here on attaining and testing a correct simple structure. Considerable saving of labor has been achieved by electronic computer methods. Formerly, a large factor analysis might take a month's calculation for two clerks, and the rotation to simple structure four or five months. Nowadays the former time can be reduced to minutes, and the latter to perhaps a month but not, as some imagine, to a moment. And it remains true that three-fourths of published factor analyses are demonstrably nowhere near simple structure (editors having no standards or resources to check this) and constitute no contribution (except confusion) to the field they are intended to clarify. What these casual and unworkmanlike studies have actually done in the last decade is to create an atmosphere of pointlessness and disillusionment by accumulating a junk heap in which factors can rarely be matched from any one research to another.

To meet the great need for increased efficiency in reaching the primary goal of simple structure rotation, previously pursued by an exhausting process of trial and error graphical rotation, quite a number of computer programs have been written. We shall distinguish here between an *automatic* program and an *analytical* program. Both are objective, i.e., they proceed without human judgment once the program is written, but the latter is restricted to aiming at some single mathematical analytical function, e.g., maximizing the ratio of fourth powers to third powers, while an automatic program is broader and open to all kinds of devices and combina-

tions of conditions, one subdivision being the analytical programs and another the topological programs.

The pioneer contribution to analytical simple structure programs was Wrigley's quartimax (1592) and, like most pioneer efforts, it had crudities (mainly failure to get away from the "pull" of the first centroid or principal axis). Kaiser's varimax (835) followed, but was still restricted to an orthogonal solution and had some of the same tendency to be unable to "spread the variance."

It needs to be said clearly at this point — despite the fond theories on which the hopes of orthogonal rotators are invested — that orthogonality and simple structure are contradictions. Only in very rare cases do factors happen to be orthogonal (theoretically they are never perfectly so). Hence the pursuit of maximum simple structure with the restriction to orthogonality is an impossible goal, a worshipping of two gods, and must end in some odd compromise (see Diagram 6-5 below). To create further orthogonal programs, e.g., the equimaxes[4], which spread the variance evenly, is merely to concentrate on suppressing a symptom while leaving the disease unchanged. However, a number of automatic *oblique* programs, good within the limitations of their "analytic" assumptions, discussed below, have since been devised, such as oblimax (Pinzka & Saunders, 1168), oblimin (Carroll, 195), and binormamin (Kaiser & Dickman, 841). If by an "analytical solution" we mean that subset of "automatic" computer solutions which find a limit to some single mathematical function of *all*

---

[4]It is sometimes helpful before applying a good automatic program, like oblimax or maxplane (or varimax if for some unusual reason an orthogonal restriction makes sense) to spin the original centroid or principal axis V_o to comparatively equal distribution. A transformation for this is available by Landahl (898); but the simplest is Eber's program which rotates midway between the 1st and the nth factor, the 2nd and the $(n-1)$th, and so on, and then repeats this with the n factors so derived, which usually suffices to give a very even spread.

loadings—usually a maximizing of the sum of the fourth power of the loadings over all factors at once—then all *present* analytic solutions fail because they are not working with the criterion rightly demanded by the model. The maximizing function that analytical programs use commonly maximizes the *dispersion* of factor loadings. It is

DIAGRAM 6-5. Simple Structure, Obtained Obliquely, Unobtainable Orthogonally (Data from Cattell-Dickman Ball Behavior [Five-Factor] Problem, 280)

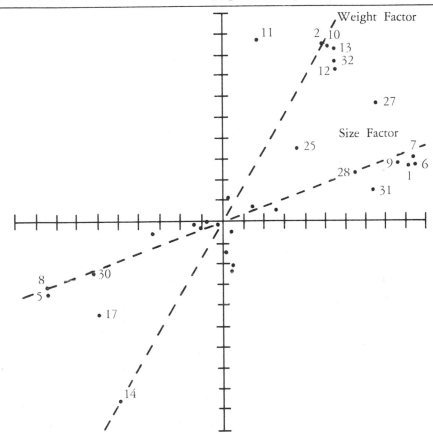

Identification of Variables by Number:

1. Diameter
2. Weight
5. Rotations rolling
6. Distance from eye to cover circle
7. Diameter of shadow cast
8. Rotations to one rotation of tire
9. Number of squares covered by ball

10. Distance of weight from ball
11. Collision displacement
12. Paddle wheel rotations
13. Springboard depression
14. Angular momentum
17. Croquet blow up in inclined plane
25. Inclined plane carpet friction
27. Weight of splash

28. Inclined plane impulse distance
30. Winding necessary to use up string
31. Size of eclipse shadow
32. Impact displacement by pendulum

satisfied when as many as possible are either high or low. But thus indirectly maximizing the number of those that are "low" *is not the same thing as maximizing the number in the hyperplane* (say within ±.10), which is the real objective.

One must not forget in evaluating the soundness of analytical approaches, that one is dealing not with an exercise in geometry but in psychological geography. A single mathematical expression for finding the Rocky Mountains or the Panama Canal would yield a line merely caricaturing the true shape of the Sierras or the canal bed. The position that gives merely "a lot of low loadings" is different from the exact one that "maximizes the number of *zero* loadings" (i.e., those within ±.10, if that happens to be the standard error of a zero loading). In fact, the two criteria in practice probably correlate only about 0.7 (as to loading patterns), and in some cases the position found by the analytical program (even if oblique) is demonstrably remote from a demonstrably attainable maximum simple structure position — corresponding in known cases to the known meaning.

To aid the search for the desired single goal of maximum simple structure as such two main automatic or semi-automatic programs have been developed, maxplane (Cattell & Muerle, 304; Eber, 446), and rotoplot (Cattell & Foster, 286). The first is a completely automatic but not analytic-function program. It searches, by trial and error, until it has maximized the total hyperplane count, and experience shows that it finishes, in practice, with higher counts than the analytic programs.

It is, mathematically, a topological program, in that it locates and separates zones of high density of variables. However, an analytical program recently suggested by Harris and Kaiser (693c) operating directly on the latent vectors has been shown by Digman, in our laboratory, almost to equal the goodness of simple structure obtainable by maxplane. They might be used "in tandem" with some saving of machine

time, but our routine use has been maxplane alone. As a "finishing" device after these, rotoplot is an automated film (fluoroscope) or paper output of graphical plots which enables the experimenter to see his rotations (without the tremendous previous plotting labor). Thus one makes visually, but far more rapidly and easily than formerly, those final "polishing" adjustments without which maximum simple structure is never attainable. (Hammond, Forster, Eber and others have made a rotogram version, printing on paper, for those lacking an oscilloscope to give the photo plot.) Laboratories producing well-finished researches have typically used a program such as oblimax, oblimin, or maxplane (or oblimax followed by maxplane, which gives one a still more advanced jumping-off point) and made the final adjustments in half a dozen rotoplot sequels, which can be done very rapidly by the above automatic plotting and which remain indispensable (especially if one wishes the angles accurately determined for a higher order).

The goal of a single "push button" rotation to final simple structure is naturally so seductive that many proceed as if it existed, but the resources at present claiming to do this are theoretically and practically misleading. After all, a theoretical mistake incorporated in a quick and efficient computer program is merely a bigger and quicker mistake. The logical error that because resolutions are untouched by hand they must be "objective" and precise haunts many of the arguments about objectivity of rotation resolution. The result of pushing a button to start a runaway train or watching where lightning strikes in a thunderstorm would also "give the same result for different investigators," but neither has any consequence of universal significance. The objectivity of a resolution resides *in the statistical significance check on the position finally reached* regardless of the instrumentalities which led to the assumed point of completion. That evaluation consists of

(1) a plot of successive positions tried (in terms of hyperplane count) to show that the curve reaches a plateau from which no new rotational attempt succeeds in producing anything but a drop, and (2) a statistical test of significance of simple structure, such as that of Bargmann (59),[5] applied just as with any other conclusion, (3) a third but less objective test which can be roughly applied is a count of the *percentage* of variables attained in the hyperplane. This will differ with domain and with representativeness of variable sampling, but in most careful studies and for most domains it lies between 55 and 85 per cent. (For example, in the various questionnaire researches leading to the 16 P.F., it has stood around 65 per cent, but in several other alleged solutions in this realm of Q data that have been published it falls to counts of 40 to 48 per cent which are demonstrably still far from simple structure.)

The question of hyperplane "width" (standard error), and considerations of whether any distribution of zeros other than a general maximizing is desirable, are taken up in another connection below. Meanwhile, a very different principle must be considered.

(2) *Confactor Rotation.* It is crucial that in the definition above of simple structure we include the notion of "a wide sample of variables." For if the experimenter's choice of variables in his design is not foresighted or fortunate in its representativeness, simple structure necessarily fails. And it is unhappily true that few experimenters plan enough markers for factors, and enough variables which *should* lie in the hyperplane of those they are principally interested in, to form a "background." For it is this background which reveals the "pattern" of the factor, and *locks* the given research into the framework of past research. For instance, factor studies have been done on mechanical aptitude with nothing but mechanical aptitude measures, and on neurosis, anxiety, and depression with nothing but items concentrated in this general area. But long before this degree of failure is reached, the simple structure principle, even properly applied, begins to show defects. For example, if a factor is naturally very pervasive in its action, e.g., the second-order anxiety factor in the 16 P.F., it will tend to have a poor hyperplane, and there will then be a risk of actually rotating into its hyperplane certain variables which properly belong slightly outside it (see also geometer's hyperplanes, below).

The alternative principle of rotation now to be described avoids these weaknesses. This confactor principle, incidentally, did not arise as an attempt to overcome drawbacks in simple structure, but developed as a new basic principle in its own right. As we shall see, it is theoretically independent of simple structure but consistent with it, in the structures it is likely to yield. It should be pointed out from the beginning, however, that certain technical difficulties still remain to be overcome before it can be used routinely.

Confactor rotation rests on the principle (Cattell, 208) that if factors are determiners, then certain relations will hold between factor-loading patterns of such determiners in two experiments using the same variables, in samples and situations where the determiners would operate with different magnitudes (variance contributions). When confactor rotation was first proposed (Cattell, 208), it was assumed that when a factor *x* thus operates with different power in two experiments, its loadings in experiment A should all be proportional to its loadings on the corresponding variables in experiment B. That is, the loadings would be multiplied by the same constant *d,* though *d* would naturally be a different value for different

---

[5]Bargmann's test has also been modified by Cattell and Pawlik to accept the fact that variables of low communality should more frequently fall in the hyperplanes, and thus to evaluate the probability of a particular specific set of variables falling into one hyperplane. But any estimate of probability based on which particular variables fall in the hyperplane proves, computationally, to be very costly.

factors, i.e. (where D is a diagonal matrix of such d's),

(19) $V_{f_{p_{(A)}}} = V_{f_{p_{(B)}}} D.$

It was then shown (208, 272), that (1) this position can be found analytically, without trial and error (if the relation exists at all), and (2) that if it does exist, it is unique (at least in the restricted orthogonal case), so that no other pair of positions in A and B exist with this property. As with a combination lock, there is just one combination of the positions of the two cylinders that unlocks the door. If this had to be found in psychological experiments of any magnitude by trial and error it would be an impossibly long job, but fortunately a later contribution (272) was able to find a general analytic solution, demonstrated to work on made-up examples (plasmodes). Nevertheless, with real experimental data, which typically admits oblique factors and error variance, the solution is not clear and unambiguous, largely because uniqueness is lacking when factors are allowed to go oblique.

As the present writer has recently pointed out (272) this theoretically most satisfactory of all resolution methods may perhaps be made to work in practice by two extensions: (1) Keeping the absolute size of variance (covariance matrices) and even differences of means (cross-product matrices—see page 375) in the analysis, since two experiments would be expected to vary on both means and absolute variances of factors. That is to say, the two analyses to be compared should be made in terms of cross-products, not correlations, which lose this information. And (2) keeping in mind that the proportionalities will hold at *all* factor order levels, not merely at the first. This takes care of the obliquity problem, for the proportionalities of factors at the higher order define the obliquities at the lower order. Consequently a solution has been proposed (272) which solves simultaneously for the proportionalities of loadings existing between the two

experiments at all factor stratum levels. An alternative solution might be to start with some approximate estimate of the correlations at the first order to make a basis to discover the dimensionality of the second order space, within which a rotational solution giving the required proportionalities could perhaps be iteratively found. Thus the complexities of obtaining an analytical solution simultaneously over all possible factor orders presents an as yet unanswered challenge to programmers of this scientifically more ideal resolution (than simple structure) by the confactor principle.

It should be noted that confactor rotation begins as does simple structure with the assumption that factors are determiners, and then deduces a certain type of invariance across researches. However, it does not produce invariance across researches as an inferred *by-product,* as simple structure does, but *requires* it directly.

An important distinction should be noted also between confactor rotation and the interbattery matching or unified factor procedures of the Procrustes method (792), Ahmavaara's method (10) and the methods of Tucker (1460, 1464) and of Kaiser (836), though all of these have certain formulae in common. The vital distinction is that these methods seek either (1) (Procrustes, Ahmavaara) to state a hypothetical or experimental rotation position and to bring a second unrotated matrix as close to it as possible, or (2) (Tucker's interbattery, Kaiser's method, Cattell's configural matching method, [263]) to bring two studies to a common position which produces maximum (least squares fit) alignment. (After this they can be rotated in lock-step to any desired criterion position.) Confactor rotation, on the other hand, (1) asks for a very special kind of "similarity" (proportionately of factor sizes as shown by their variance contributions) and (2) uses this only as a means to an end—that of finding the unique position of the real influences—not as an end in itself (a convenience).

(3) *Rotation to Test Hypotheses*. As pointed out earlier, factor analysis is both a hypothesis-generating and a hypothesis-testing statistico-mathematical model. In hypothesis testing the hypothesis can be drawn from some earlier factor analysis, possibly using a different technique, e.g., from *P* or *T* technique to suggest an *R*-technique pattern, or from "out of thin air," or in cross-disciplinary ways by borrowing (Chapter 2). In any case, if the theorizer is serious, his hypothesis must literally state (a) the number of factors, (b) their loading patterns, and (c) the correlations among the factors, to be expected. Having set out the prescribed particulars of the hypothesis in this form, the psychologist proceeds (provided the number of factors turns out to be reasonably congruent in the first place) to rotate the empirical V_o to it as closely as possible and asks how good the match is, by some test of statistical significance of match. Various aspects of hypothesis-testing by factor analysis are discussed by Fruchter in Chapter 10 below.

The rotation of the V_o toward the hypothesized pattern involves the same procedure as for any other prescribed position. The Procrustes program (800) is perhaps the simplest in its assumptions, for one solves therein for a least-squares fit as follows:

(20) $L_x = (V'_o V_o)^{-1} V'_o V_{rs}$

Here one asks for the best (least-squares) fit for the factor "pattern" (actually in the V_{rs} or structure) and leaves angles to fall as they will. Other, future developments of Procrustes might involve improvements such as indicating angles also, which sometimes come out at rather excessive values if uncontrolled. (See Schoenemann's Oblisim program [1276] and White's Promax [1539].) As pointed out elsewhere (800), there is much pressure to abuse Procrustes, by using it as a short cut to avoid the more difficult simple structure search, and by concluding that a given study has been made to fit the hypothesis without any test of goodness of factor match having been employed.[6] (As indicated, if angles are allowed to go to any extreme obliquity almost any V_{fs} can be matched.)

6. FACTOR INVARIANCE, IDENTIFICATION, AND INTERPRETATION

Any rotation process aiming to generate scientific meaning necessarily includes the

---

[6]The possible rotational practice of rotating to put a factor vector through the center of a cluster has *not* been discussed here, because it mixes factor analysis with cluster analysis. It is in many ways unfortunate that the conceptual distinction between *surface traits* (clusters) and *source traits* (factors) (Cattell, 213) is still insufficiently recognized to obviate much confusion. Clusters can be either more or less numerous than the factor dimensionality. Usually there are decidedly more clusters (Chapter 9) than factors, and such methods as Tryon's (1454) are reduced to an arbitrary selection of some clusters as more important than others—if one is to choose just as many clusters as the dimensionality of the space.

An equally vital objection to rotating to clusters is that they can be artificially made. One needs only to repeat a test or test item with slight modification of meaning to create a whole correlation cluster where there was previously only a lone vector. In some *highly* generic sense a hyperplane, by which one rotates a factor, can semantically also be called a cluster, but actually it is very different. A hyperplane must have variables loading substantially on many *different* factors, and no one could create it simply by repeating some pattern of tests until enough are created in contiguity to produce a cluster artificially. It represents the footprint of a natural influence.

A supreme piece of artificiality in the guise of science occurs when psychologists set up a theoretical scheme requiring clusters at such and such points, as in Guilford's (or anyone else's) subjective schema for abilities. For the investigator can then proceed, with some trial and error, to make up tests that will so correlate that they fill these spaces. Here one is not finding out about nature, i.e., testing an hypothesis, but creating nature to fit the hypothesis, which in this case is any subjective set of categories one likes to make. In the little artificial world of the school psychometrist it is easy to "create nature," but this has nothing to do with the structures which naturally arise from biological and sociological realities in the broader sense, and which must be found by experiment. According to anything we know at the moment, the pattern of

aim of some kind of *invariance* of the factor properties from experiment to experiment. The present writer would claim that there is now sufficient empirical support for considering oblique simple structure to succeed far better than most alternative methods in achieving this. But confactor rotation guarantees it (at least for experiments in pairs) from the beginning. The third principle, rotation to test hypotheses, argues and implies invariance to the extent that any hypothesis continues to be exactly verified.

At this point the technical questions present themselves: "In terms of what factor manifestations is the invariance to be expected?", and "By what statistical tests, of matching, etc., can the significance of the degree of invariance attained be evaluated?" Regarding the first, we must recognize that in any given factor analysis the relations of *variables* to *dimensions* (using the term "dimension" to cover such underlying entities as reference vectors and factors) admit of at least eight different expressions, in eight distinct D-V (dimension-variable) matrices (251). These have been given in the notation in Table 5-1 above and are repeated in isolation in Table 6-1.

Three of these are relatively new and require description. First, we may note that the V_{dfc} ("dissociated factor contribution") (251) represents the loadings of each factor on the variables *in dissociation from the effect of any higher-order factors,* whence it might be regarded as the purest statement of the meaning of that factor. The Schmid-Leiman formula (Schmid & Leiman, 1272), incidentally, produces these values for the primary factors, but not for the second- and higher-order factors in their typical loadings on the next lower-order factors. (To

TABLE 6-1

THE MORE IMPORTANT D-V MATRICES

1. The V_{rs} (Reference Vector Structure) Correlations of reference vectors with variables.
2. The V_{rp} (Reference Vector Pattern) Loadings of reference vectors on variables.
3. The V_{fs} (Factor Structure) Correlations of factors and variables.
4. The V_{fp} (Factor Pattern) Loadings of factors on variables.
5. The V_{dfc} (Dissociated factor pattern matrix).
6. The V_{afc} (Associated factor matrix).
7. The V_{fe} (Factor estimation matrix) Beta weights of variables in factors.
8. The V_{fm} (Factor mandate matrix).

anticipate the later discussion on higher-order factors, we must simply say that higher-order factors are found by factoring the correlations among the oblique lower-order factors. Thus, second-order factors come from factoring $R_{f1.o.}$) The values in columns on the V_{dfc} (*dfc* for "dissociated factor contribution") are obtained for each column by multiplying down the corresponding V_{fp} column by a constant less than one. Thus it is by defining its total variance contribution more accurately, and not by any change of the essential pattern (the only change being multiplication by a constant), that the V_{dfc} may be said better or more uniquely to express the nature of a factor than does the V_{fp}.

The V_{afc} (*afc* for "associated factor contribution") which represents the loading ("beta weight") of each variable multiplied by its correlation with the factor, indicates the extent to which a factor contributes to the multiple R (the h^2 or communality) obtainable from all factors for that variable, in the specification equation. Finally, we must introduce the V_{fm} or "factor mandate matrix" (251), which is an "incidence matrix" with only ones and zeros in it and reminds us that any discussion of the meaning of a factor involves recognizing that a factor really either affects a variable totally or leaves it untouched. All apparent

clusters required by any logical, subjective schema could be "found" by first setting up test items and contents to fit the categories and then applying correlations. This is not science, but a parlor game of skill in making up tests to fit any prescribed constellation.

intermediate values, i.e., between zero and one (or more, for loadings), found in the other six matrices (Table 6-1, excluding V_{fe}), may be considered as unities reduced as a result of the intrusion of other factors in helping to determine the total variance (or communality) of a variable.

The first question that will arise in perusing these matrices is whether the zeros sought in simple structure, and the proportionalities sought in confactor rotation, when used in finding a unique rotational resolution, should be sought in the V_{fp} (identical in this respect with V_{rs} and V_{dfc}), in the V_{fs} (equivalent to V_{rp}) or the V_{fe}. If we are consistent with our model of the factor being an influence, both should be sought in the V_{fp} (or the V_{dfc} which derives from it) for it is zeros in this matrix which indicate zero influence of the factor upon the variable. With a test of significance for loadings, to permit separation into zeros and unities, we could also logically use the factor mandate matrix for matching, employing the salient variable similarity index, described below.

Incidentally, the reader is reminded that in the orthogonal case all the first six matrices in Table 6-1 are the same (not the V_{fe}, however), i.e., loadings and correlations, for factors and reference vectors are the same. The *differences* of these matrices, in the oblique case, however, now offer an additional guide to finding simple structure, one not previously exploited. For the absolute size of the percentage in the hyperplane depends too much on accidents of variable sampling to be a sure standard in itself. However, in general, when a factor influences fewer variables, there is also some tendency for fewer variables to contribute to the factor estimate. The number of variables making a significant contribution in the V_{fe} to the average factor is a better general evaluation of the effect of variable sampling (expressed as a factor-variable ratio) in the given field than any other, and thus it becomes a fair standard by which to evaluate the goodness of simple structure. Operationally, this means that for each of, say, six alternative and competitive resolution positions for simple structure, we should work out the ratio of zeros (meaning, say, $\pm.10$'s loadings) in the V_{fp} to zeros in the V_{fe} and accept the position for which this, or some function of this ratio and the total of V_{fp} zeros, is largest. We have in effect said, in what may be called this *one-way definition of simple structure,* that Thurstone's definition should be modified to ask *only* for the greatest number of zeros in columns, not rows. But arithmetically in the V_{fp} or V_{rs}, the average number in rows is bound to bear a simple ratio to the average number in columns. Meaning can be given to the primacy of the columns, i.e., to the model of factors as causes of variables, only by comparing the column zeros in the V_{fp} with those in the V_{fe}.

The above defines the setting and operational and statistical meaning of simple structure. Yet one must recognize that though this can be stated in seconds, there are arts and strategies in the use of simple structure which require months of apprenticeship to research to acquire. One can merely glimpse the latter in this space. If one rotoplots from an analytical solution like oblimax or oblimin, he will find that each program has its characteristic vices, which can be most quickly corrected if explicitly recognized. For example, oblimax tends to require rotoplot systematically to "open" (enlarge symmetrically) the factor angles, and oblimin to reduce them, to move into simple structure. Shifts, of a factor, A, made simultaneously, on several factors speed convergence on simple structure, but the total of tangent values in the shift matrix for A should be kept low, for the same variables can be moved toward the hyperplane twice over (and overshot) in different plots. Large shifts, over 0.4, can rarely be safely combined from different plots, especially in the early stages. These arts are incorporated in the construction of maxplane.

As far as possible, though orthogonality must never be a fetish, the whole reference frame should be kept marching "in step" in the shifts, to move the whole coordinate system around while keeping it *approximately* orthogonal. In shifting a hyperplane, the direction given by a whole lenticular mass is more important than single far-out variables. However, one must not be seduced by "geometers' hyperplanes" (page 209). When the latter can be brought in with little loss on the least-squares fit to the main lenticular mass, all well and good. But in the last two or three of the dozen to a score over-all rotations, after the first "analytical" position, one may have to recognize that even a far-out variable is factorially complex. At the last, one must also let factors go as oblique as is required by the hyperplanes which are now clearly crystallized. It is valuable to plot, in the course of any rotation, a "history of the hyperplane," giving the total hyperplane count with successive trial-and-error shifts. (The plateau shows when one has "arrived.") The width of hyperplane to guide visual shifts may vary from $\pm.25$ at the beginning to $\pm.05$ at the end. Typically, with the "history of hyperplane" one counts progress at $\pm.10$. The question of how the true zero values in the hyperplane become distorted by sampling is debatable (but see page 235).

The disappearance of a superfluous "over-estimated" factor in rotation can occur by either (1) rotation leading to a factor with virtually no variance in its hyperplane, or (2) the correlation of two factors becoming high until they collapse into one. Conversely, a clear *new* hyperplane, as a third line in the two-dimensional plot, will appear quite late in the rotation, and require insertion of a new column in the L matrix and use of an additional previously rejected factor in the V_o. More important than the risk of losing a factor by collapse is the danger of splitting a factor into two factors on essentially the same hyperplane, which ruins interpretation (see page 208). Rotation of a matrix of many

factors (say > 25) will occasionally (and more easily than in a small matrix) lead to a singular (uninvertable) R_f. It is reassuring to find that if simple structure is more persistently and single-mindedly pursued, the better simple structure attained will automatically clear up this trespass of one factor into the plane of two others.

Granted that a unique position has been obtained in any study (by confactor rotation, or by simple structure defined in the V_{fp} (V_{rs}, V_{dfc}) or V_{fp}/V_{fe} ratio), how are we to test the invariance of this structure from study to study? This is a complex issue for brief discussion, for there is, in the first place, some difference between matching one factor in one study with one factor in another, and matching the whole resolution, i.e. over all factors, including higher-order factors. However, even if a single factor only is to be matched, it is better to take the whole resolution into account. The term "matching" is used here because the problem is essentially one of asking, "What is the likelihood of the given degree of resemblance occurring between these studies, on the assumption (of course) of certain distributions?" This divides into (1) expressing the degree of resemblance, and (2) evaluating its significance. Naturally, we are talking about (a) studies on different subjects (since the matching requires no discussion — being a matter of correlating factors or estimated factors directly — if the measures and factors are on the *same* subjects), and (b) studies using the same variables — possibly among others. (With *totally* different variables — and of course different subjects — obviously no match is possible.)

Of course, no serious difficulty exists in matching when clusters of high loadings — 0.8 to 0.9 — are found. Perhaps it is this which has caused Tryon and others to prefer cluster analysis to factor analysis. But even with this temptation one must never forget that their objectives are the entirely different ones of surface trait description on the one hand contrasted with ours of source trait measurement on the other. Characteristically there are decidedly more clusters in an area than there are factors, e.g., the MMPI has some five factors but many more syndrome category clusters. Rotation to put axes through clusters is an entirely different—almost opposite—principle to rotation for simple structure. Frequently a hyperplane found in simple structure will have only loadings of 0.3 to 0.4 among the highest loaded variables upon it. Usually, in laboratory data, one may hope to locate in time the nearly pure factor variable by producing a variable with a truly high loading. But in natural data, *in situ*, it will usually be true that *every observable variable is normally complexly determined.* We should not be at all surprised that important factors never have loadings above 0.3 to 0.4. Does the chemist doubt the existence of silver because no natural rock or ore on the surface of the earth contains more than 30 per cent?

Matching methods must cope with low loadings. But which of the several variable-dimension matrices should we use in matching? If we are concerned to match single factors, the V_{dfc} is somewhat better than the V_{fp}, since it reliably expresses variance *level* as well as shape of pattern. But matching of a whole resolution requires the attention to the V_{fp} and the angles among the factors, R_f, or preferably the complete resolution into second- and higher-order factors. (See [251] for complete designation of identity of a factor.) Since reliabilities of experimental measurement of variables may vary independently from study to study, it is preferable to work with loadings, etc. corrected for attenuation.

Existing matching techniques are of three types: (1) non-parametric tests, such as the hyperplane variable similarity or *s* test (Cattell & Baggaley, 268), (2) tests of similarity of factor loadings (sometimes adding weight for agreement of the factors also in their correlations with other factors), and (3) tests that project the compared studies into a common variable space and then examine correlations of alleged matching factors (and, consequently, their loading similarity and intercorrelations simultaneously). (1) and (3) are not conceptually but only methodologically independent; they both depend in part on similarity of loading magnitudes.

The first, as exemplified by the *s* index (221, 268) has the advantage of at once yielding a *P* value, but the disadvantage of all non-parametric methods of possibly throwing away some information. It requires that we group loadings into classes, such as *salients* (variables above some significant loading value which puts, say, only 10 to 20 per cent of variables on each factor into the "salient" class), leaving the rest as hyperplane variables. If, say, six out of eight of the salients on Factor X, Study 1, are identical with six in the eight highest on Factor Y on Study 2, for a given total of common variables, the *s* tables would tell us that this match is, say, beyond a $P = .05$ level. The *s* index as originally designed has proved reasonably reliable (240), but is on the conservative side, tending to underestimate in certain known cases. However, more recently it has been improved by resorting essentially to the factor mandate matrix. Here it does not "throw away information," because in fact we must accept that a factor either affects a variable positively, or negatively, or not at all (see page 203). Ignoring the *modification* of this incidence matrix—in the detailed loadings—is, from this point of view, not losing information but ignoring error. By the Harris test of significance (see below) variables are divided into three classes—significantly positively loaded (+1), significantly negatively loaded (−1), and hyperplane variables (0). The modified *s* index or chi square is then applied to the incidences in the two columns to be compared in the factor mandate matrices. This avoids the distortions which occur in evaluation by the congruence coefficient through variations produced in the magnitude of significant loadings by alterations in variables of factors other than the two being compared.

The second technique—determining loading pattern similarities—has to face the problems of all pattern similarity evaluation. The too commonly used procedure of correlating the columns of the factor matrices is the poorest, because it ignores the difference between the origins (in the plot of the two) and the differences of mean loading, and takes no account of difference of level in the two patterns. A better index for this purpose is Burt's *coefficient of congruence, r_c* ($r_c = \dfrac{\Sigma XY}{\sqrt{\Sigma X^2 \Sigma Y^2}}$ where X and Y are loadings—not deviations of loadings—of the same variables). Its defect is still that it can give unity for patterns of identical shape but different levels. Also the meaning (by distribution) of a numerical value is not that which we are accustomed to in correlation coefficients. The pattern similarity coefficient, r_p (see Chapter 9), would avoid this difficulty, indicating high congruence of loadings only when the level as well as the shapes of the patterns are similar; but its assumptions have not been examined in this context.

Since we have recognized above that the actual magnitudes of loadings will be quite fluctuant (even when corrected for attenuation) owing to the variations of contributions from other factors in the two studies, a non-parametric test of pattern similarity, along the lines of the s test above, is almost certainly preferable. A very simple possibility, though it ignores the valuable hyperplane versus salient distinction, is to take only the *sign* of the loading. With, say, thirty variables, and a 1 in 2^{30} chance of a particular overall sign pattern being repeated, one is justified in feeling that a non-parametric test of this kind should be sufficiently sensitive.

The identification of factors by loading (preferably V_{dfc}) pattern sizes, as just discussed, has proved only tolerably effective in studies up to this point—effective-

ness judged by agreement with what factors are known to be put into a study. (The s index for the known general intelligence factor, for example, has yielded P values from .01 and .04 for subjects of the same age, etc., to as low as .50 (50/50) across child-adult and psychotic groups (240, p. 826). Doubtless, with attention to the above points, especially the carrying of better samples of marker variables from study to study, s or chi square applied to the pattern will become a more powerful aid. In itself, however, either s or a pattern similarity contains the Achilles heel which causes it to stumble over *cooperative factors* (229). By cooperative factors we mean two factors (possibly entirely orthogonal) which have considerable similarity as to the variables they load highly (naturally no one loading can be above $\sqrt{.5}$, however). There are natural reasons why two factors sometimes act cooperatively in this way, e.g., the sympathetic and parasympathetic (sign reversed) autonomic factors (226, 240) are cooperative because they affect the same target organs, for different purposes (see Chapter 22, Section 5). By loading pattern matching methods one could easily confuse two such factors, and we have argued in Chapter 22 that this has in fact happened in a big way in the writings about theories of "autonomic balance" (Chapter 21). Without supplementation by evidence on correlation among factors (below), profile matching evidence can be inadequate and its use requires an alert eye for cooperative factors.

The third main method—and the best—is that of obtaining a common variable configuration space and finding how closely factors from the two studies align themselves in this common space. This simultaneously takes note of loading pattern and correlations among factors. The computing problem is closely akin to the confactor rotation specification (263, 272), but has been developed in its own right in contributions from Tucker's interbattery method (1464), Kaiser's solution and the present writer's configural matching[7] paper (263). The essential calculating steps are, first, to obtain a $k \times k$ matrix K from,

(21) $K = V'_{OA} V_{OB}$,

where V_{OA} and V_{OB} are the *un*rotated

---

[7]What may perhaps best be called the configurative method of testing the degree of agreement between independent resolutions from two experiments with different people but enough of the same variables, derives from the Procrustes method (275), its shaping to an orthogonal solution by Schoenemann (1276) and a paper by Kaiser (836). It permits evaluation of a single factor pattern with proper regard to the total resolution as discussed above; i.e., the angles to variance contributions by the other factors. Parenthetically, one should notice the distinction of the confactor principle, which brings factors in two studies on different people or a special relation (as also does the interbattery synthesis method of Tucker (1464), on the one hand, and the *configuration alignment* method here, which first brings the identical *test vectors* in the two experiments as closely to agreement as possible, not the factors.

The basic problem is to find the transformation matrix L_{AB} in the estimation (where V_{OA} and V_{OB} are the two unrotated matrices)

(a) $V_{OA} L_{AB} = V_{OB} + E$

under the conditions that E, the error matrix, is minimized (least squares) and L_{AB} is orthogonal. Let us call K a matrix such that

(b) $K = V'_{OA} V_{OB}$.

By the usual latent roots and vectors program in factor analysis one obtains the latent vectors L_x and L_y from

(c) $KK' = L_x D^2_x L'_x$ and $KK' = L_y D^2_y L'_y$

Then, as Schoenemann shows:

(d) $L_{AB} = L_x L_y$.

The $k \times k$ triangular matrix of correlations between the factors as resolved in experiments A and B can then be found by:

(20) (e) $R_{AB} = L'_{fsA} L'_{AB} L_{fsB}$

where L_{fsA} is the usual transformation matrix for the factor structure.

In this, the test vectors are kept at their proper lengths, as required by their communalities. An alternative program by Kaiser and Bianchini extends them to unit length; but since the length of the vector is part of the description of the factor space being dealt with, the present writer prefers the above form of the configurational alignment test of factor identity. Some improvement might be possible by weighting tests according to their reliabilities or communalities as Nesselroade has suggested. The more difficult problem of evaluating the significance of a given angular agreement has received only a partial answer from the work of Coulter and the present author.

matrices, $n \times k$, from the two experiments to be compared. Next one obtains the latent vectors L_x and L_y, by the usual latent roots program used in factor analyses, from the matrices KK' and $K'K$, thus

(22) (a) $KK' = L_x D^2_x L'_x$
     (b) $K'K = L_y D^2_x L'_y$.

The required transformation matrix for going from V_{OA} to V_{OB} is:

(23) $\lambda_{AB} = L_x L_y$,

and the $k \times k$ triangular matrix of correlations between the resolved factors of experiments A and B is:

(24) $R_{AB} = \lambda'_{fsA} \lambda'_{AB} \lambda_{fsB}$,

where λ_{fsA} is the transformation matrix for factor structure used in the A resolution, and similarly λ_{fsB} for B. It has been programmed for the computer by Bianchini and by Schoenemann (1276).

Like profile matching, the configuration alignment test requires a *sufficiency* of marker variables to be common to the two studies. The above formula aims at getting the configurations of these variables to fit, vector for vector, as closely as possible. Mathematically there is a certain artificiality about the common space in which these two configurations are brought to the best possible fit. If the relative variance of the same identical factors differs appreciably from one study to the other, there may be appreciable disagreement at this first step, in that the two configurations of variables cannot themselves be made to agree very well. Like the loading profile similarity method, it has its special weaknesses: in this case that two factors might have only a small angle between them and yet be different factors, because distinct factors *can* sometimes be correlated as high as, say, 0.7. At the same time two factors that are really versions of one and the same influence in the two samples could correlate *less* than, say, 0.7, because the obliquities are different owing to differing amounts of influence of second-order factors. Finally one has the problem of finding the significance of a correlation between two matched factors in a given k space, and this presents difficulties, as Coulter and the present writer have shown.

At this stage of research, no *single* pair of experiments can give convincing evidence of the general invariance and reality of a factor concept. There is absolutely no way to arrive reliably at our basic scientific factor concepts except by (1) independently rotating each research blindly, and far more exhaustively than has been fashionable, to maximum simple structure, (2) matching, and (3) repeating this on not just a couple of coordinated researches, but a dozen. By putting these side by side, one must show that a series of matches, each perhaps not at a very high level of significance, center consistently on a particular pattern, i.e., one looks for a sort of general factor in the matrix of pattern correlations of the same putative factor from, say, a dozen studies. With errors being what they are — and variations are still inevitable in even the best simple structure rotated factor systems — the only proof of factor identity must come thus from the weight of a series of systematically and emphatically interlocked (by markers) researches. Actually, though the ability field is older, the evidence gathered by Hundleby and Pawlik (796) over twelve to twenty researches in the personality field, defines some twenty personality factors (Chapter 19) with higher proof than yet exists for ability factors!

In the last resort, as the present writer has pointed out in more detail elsewhere (221), the matching of factors must depend on the joint evidence of (1) loading profile, (2) size, (3) angles, to other identified factors, and (4) reaction under applied experimental influences. In other words, though s, r_c are useful indications and formula (24) above, the only really satisfactory matching, even for a single factor, is that which simultaneously takes into account the context introduced by *all*

factors. For if two factors were indeed identical, they would *not* have identical V_{fp} profiles (even within experimental error) in two distinct populations. Their loadings would be expected to change in complex but quite predictable ways, with changes in the magnitudes and correlations of other factors that enter into the determination of the variables. The issue cannot be pursued in detail here, but if we imagine k factors affecting n variables, and the variation from one experiment to another to arise primarily from changes in the factor variance, then, dealing with an equation in covariances, an experiment (and population) (1) has the relation to one with different factor variances, in (2) as follows:

$$(25) \ (a) \ C_{o_a} = D_{\sigma_a} R_{o_a} D'_{\sigma_a} =$$
$$D_{\sigma_a} V_{fp_a} R_{fa} V'_{fp_a} D'_{\sigma_a} = V_{c_a} R_{fa} V'_{c_a}$$
$$(b) \ C_{o_b} = D_{\sigma_b} R_{o_b} D'_{\sigma_a} =$$
$$D_{\sigma_b} V_{fp_b} R_{fb} V'_{fp_b} D'_{\sigma_b} = V_{c_b} R_{fb} V'_{c_b}$$

where the σ's are the (raw score) standard deviations of the variables in the two cases. If we now suppose the *factors* have changed in variance from (a) to (b) by values in the diagonal matrix, D_{ab}, then:

$$(26) \ (a) \ V_{c_b} = V_{c_a} D_{ab}$$

and an expression can be worked out for the V_{fp_a} implied by the experimentally given V_{fp_b}. It is on this basis, not the experimentally given V_{fp_b}, that the search for matches between experiment (a) and experiment (b) should begin. The configurative method of matching, as expressed in equation (24) comes the nearest, as a single test, to meeting the requirements just discussed, but experience shows that unless it is performed with enough common variables, of sufficient communality — say 3 times as many, at $>.50$ communalities, than there are factors — its results are unstable.

This whole matching treatment is, of course, consistent with the model of factors as determiners, and with the idea brought out by the *factor mandate matrix* that a factor either operates fully upon a variable or leaves it entirely alone, and that the fall from a unit loading is therefore purely a function of the other factors that happen to be operating. That is to say, when we talk of a lower factor loading implying "a smaller effect on a variable" we are really recognizing that in this situation other factors are more intrusive. The mere mechanical pursuit of literal "invariance of factor loadings" is not enough. We must not forget that basically we are in pursuit of scientific meaning, and "invariance" is secondary in the sense of being one manifestation of a scientific entity, and even so, it needs to be evaluated with regard to these principles showing what kind and degree of matrix to matrix *variation* is really the evidence for the highest degree of invariance.

The interpretation of factors, i.e., the inferring of their natures as scientific determiners, is closely tied to the problems of pattern matching and identification. (For interpreting a factor that has appeared in only one study would not be profitable as a rule.) In the process of inference, from the emerging pattern as matched across experiments, reasoning must work on (1) Contrasting significant with hyperplane loadings, i.e., affected with unaffected variables. This includes asking if other variables expected on hypotheses to be affected or unaffected are *available* in the studies. (2) Contrasting the pattern with that of other factors in the same studies and elsewhere. In particular, would the hypothesis fit other factors as well as this one? (3) Are the differences of the V_{fp}, the V_{dfc}, and the V_{fe} for the factor what the interpretation would lead one to expect? (4) Are its correlations with other factors, and therefore its pattern of influence by second-order factors, what would be expected? (5) Does it modify its V_{fp} as would be expected from hypothesis with sampling selection, etc.? The last brings us toward two further aids outside the factor analysis itself, namely: (6) Does its level change as expected in manipulative experimenta-tion? (7) Does its level change with age, amount of learning, sex, etc., as would be hypothesized? (These are expanded in 221.)

Interpreting a factor in some particular sense cannot be undertaken wisely, of course, without analyzing concepts of what factors may be *in general*. While there has been neglect to explore this on an empirical basis by applying factor analyses across a sufficient variety of sciences, the basic position has been defended in Chapter 2 that a simple structure (or confactor) factor is an influence. With further attention to analysis we would state here that it is either: (a) a single cause, i.e., some influence which can be seen over time to bring about a change in several dependent variables, (b) a substantive determiner, by which we mean a substance which determines the consistent appearance of several properties (the marble permitting the statue) or a dimension which determines other dimensional properties (as the radius of a circle determines its circumference, area distance covered in rotations, etc.). Here, incidentally, we must accept a factor as the product of many small influences affecting the same property, as a set of genes affecting "g" or a number of leaves determining the diameter of piles of leaves. Or (c) an emergent process by which we mean an ongoing process generating a set of relationships to variables. An example of the last is probably the second order anxiety factor in Q and L and T data (318) where the primaries which go together seemingly admit no simple causal order or effect from any known single ulterior cause. Instead, the best theory is that they mutually interact with positive feedback and it is this process of mutual interaction which generates anxiety as a new emergent dimension.

No single narrow definition of an influence thus seems appropriate to cover the influences that may be unearthed by factor analysis.

In any discussion of the nature and conceptual status of factors the notion of *factor efficacy* (Cattell, 229, 232) is generally helpful. Nowadays, the use of strategically interrelated factor analyses often seeks the same conceptual entity in different populations, as well as by different R, P, etc., technique experiments (cutting in different directions across the data box). Some factors can be found only in a certain population, others turn up across several, and others continue to appear simultaneously in R, differential R and P technique, etc., and despite different instrumentalities of measurement. Any scientific concept — mass, pressure, intelligence, metabolic rate — of high generality and usefulness should transcend a particular matrix, data box facet, etc. While it is not correct to say that a factor is just "real" or "not real" (as Table 6-6 reminds us), it *is* appropriate to speak of the *degrees of efficacy* of a factor concept. Efficacy can be given operational meaning as the number of different sampling situations and forms of analysis in which the given factor (as an inferable influence) reappears.

7. DECIDING THE NUMBER OF FACTORS

Although this topic might be clearer if less had been written on it, the number of papers is a tribute to its complexity and its many aspects. However, to cut a long story short, reasons have been given elsewhere (243, 264) for rejecting some widely accepted practices, such as (1) treating it as a purely mathematical problem of finding the "exact rank" (there is no such thing as "the exact rank" of a real, experimental, *reduced* correlation matrix), (2) seeking to insert communalities[8] that will bring the correlation matrix to the *minimum* or *maximum* possible limit of rank, (3) indeed, the very assumption — in the mimimum rank procedure — that there are fewer factor influences than there are variables in the matrix (unless it is an artificial rather than natural matrix), (4) the notion that true variance *only* is extracted in the first factors taken out, and that error variance begins "after the true number of factors have come out," (5) the statement that what are really zero hyperplane values in the population will depart from zero in the sample because of sampling errors, and (6) the notion, encour-

communalities trivial. As a starting point "Guttman's lower bound", i.e., the squared multiple correlation of the given variable with all others, is excellent. Humphreys incidentally has argued that the value should be the multiple r *corrected for shrinkage*. This may be defended whether one is arriving at the factors in the sample — including the error factors — or in the population, and, as argued below, we are often concerned with factors in the sample. But one should always keep in mind that this is a *lower* bound and one should beware, for example, of throwing out from an R matrix variables which happen not to have a significant multiple R with others. After iteration, the off-diagonals may bring a significant communality to such a variable. As a comment on this, let us consider four variables loaded on four factors as shown here. Calculation of the inner products will show that the correlations, and therefore the squared multiple R's, are zero everywhere.

	F_1	F_2	F_3	F_4
a_1	.4	.4	−.4	−.4
a_2	−.4	−.4	.4	.4
a_3	−.4	.4	−.4	.4
a_4	.4	−.4	.4	−.4

This is not a "trick matrix," for a great variety of V_O's can be set up such that $V_O V'_O$ produces zeros except for the diagonal. When a set like a_1 to a_4, i.e., a zero intercorrelating set of variables, is added to a set of substantially intercorrelating variables, there is appreciable chance that they will acquire substantial communalities and appreciable loadings as the rotated factors come to span the F_1 to F_4 space and the space of the other variables. This comment is both an argument for keeping variables of low initially estimated communality and for not taking the loadings of random number variables as finally indicative of the lower limits of significance.

---

[8]It will be noted that comparatively little discussion has been given here to "the communality question" which looms large in many texts. The reasons will be apparent as the framework develops, but two reasons for considering that no major problem exists here are: (1) that theoretically we are prepared to let the decision on number of factors be prepotent, determining the communality, and (2) iterative procedures nowadays make differences in the estimation of

aged by some verbal formulations of Guttman's image analysis, that by taking a large number of variables *in any one domain,* one can hope to account almost wholly for the communality of the variables in a matrix from within that domain. (The weakness in leaning on the Guttman position is that approach to a unit communality requires an infinite set of variables in *the* universe, not merely in *a* domain).

The positive propositions alternatively presented and followed here are:

(a) That one cannot speak of the exact or true number of factors to take out (except in artificial, specially manipulated cases) as anything less than the number of variables. For example, in a fifty-variable problem in which, say, twelve factor influences are quite large, the factoring of ten of these variables will still require twelve factors (assuming all ten variables originally affected by all factors) though we could not know this mathematically. Normally, in typically complex scientific fields there will be *more* real influences at work than there are variables, counting all quite small influences, e.g., the influence of temperature and a passing jet plane on examination responses. But for purely mathematical reasons we obviously cannot determinately take out *more* than n. The insoluble problem in mathematical-statistical terms has been that to fix the number of factors, we needed first to know communalities, and to get communalities, we needed first to know the number of factors. If now we accept that there is no true number of factors $< n$, this issue is irrelevant.

(b) The common and specific factors in the system will consist both of what are sometimes called real factors (but which we shall more operationally call substantive or subject-behavior-tied factors) and error factors. It should be made clear that by error factors we mean something quite different from the *sampling effects on the real factors.* By errors we mean strictly errors of measurement, and in terms of the data box, according to the model we

prefer, we can define them (as there proposed) as the variance connected with individual differences (and states) of observers. Or, more inclusively, we can define it as observer variance plus the variance over occasions in the observed ids (P, A, S, and E). If we accept the latter, then an error factor, common or specific, is operationally defined as one that does not repeat itself in any two studies, whereas "real" factors do.

(c) Where the present writer's exposition differs sharply from the classical one is in asserting that these error factors are real influences and not to be equated with the common (or specific) factors generated by correlating random numbers. If one takes the position of scientific determinism, then there are no such things as random factors. Errors of measurement, or specific factors "uncorrelated in the population but correlated in the sample" do not become correlated in the sample by chance, but as a result of some real influence—though that influence may be so transient and peripheral that we *call* it error, because we are not substantively interested in it, and it is a "nuisance."

(d) A further point, not of difference from the classical position but at least from a widespread popular misunderstanding, is our explicit reminder that in the extraction process one does not begin to extract only substantive ("real") factors until one suddenly gets to "error" factors, but that some degree of error variance is present from the beginning. If the transient ("error") factors, as usual, are smaller, then, with most methods of factor extraction (principal axis, centroid) there will be a tendency for the later extracted factors to contain *more* (relatively, not necessarily absolutely) of the transient, "error" variance.

Thus (1) in Diagram 6-6 shows the typical successive latent roots in extraction, while (2) and (3) show common alternatives after rotation: error factors as big as real (substantive) factors and error factors of a smaller order of size.

Consequently, if one extracts only as

DIAGRAM 6-6.   Extracted Distributions of Factor Variance Before and After Rotation

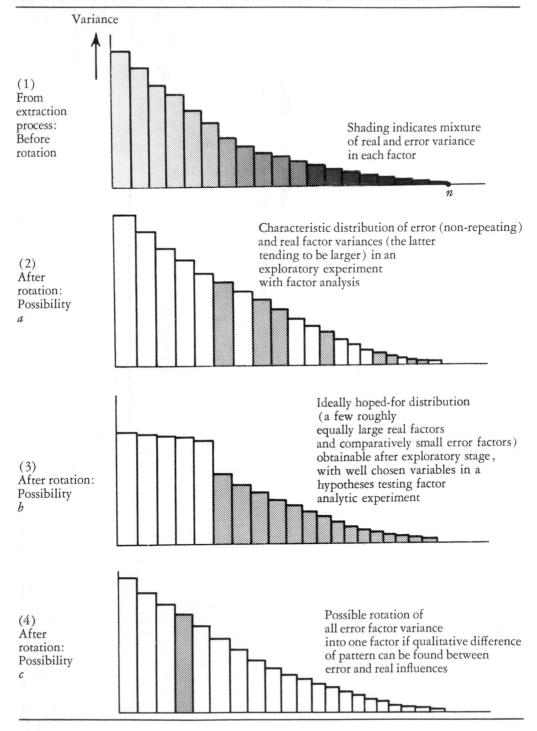

Variance

(1)
From
extraction
process:
Before
rotation

Shading indicates mixture
of real and error variance
in each factor

n

(2)
After
rotation:
Possibility
a

Characteristic distribution of error (non-repeating)
and real factor variances (the latter
tending to be larger) in an
exploratory experiment
with factor analysis

(3)
After rotation:
Possibility
b

Ideally hoped-for distribution
(a few roughly
equally large real factors
and comparatively small error factors)
obtainable after exploratory stage,
with well chosen variables in a
hypotheses testing factor
analytic experiment

(4)
After
rotation:
Possibility
c

Possible rotation of
all error factor variance
into one factor if qualitative difference
of pattern can be found between
error and real influences

many factors as are "substantive," i.e. of permanent importance and major size, some of the error variance (which should have gone into further, "error" common factors) will tend to get rotated into the substantive factors and hyperplanes will be blurred, e.g., to about ±.10. (The salients will also be slightly off their true positions.)

(e) Where the writer is again asserting a principle novel to the traditional statistician's position is in stating that if all factors could be taken out (by going to $>n$ factors), then and only then would rotation leave *unblurred* (exact) hyperplanes for the substantive factors, because the superfluous error variance, which formerly blurred those hyperplanes, will now be collected in the error factors. Our position involves the apparently paradoxical assertion that although *non-zero* loadings will suffer from sampling variation (according to the usual statistical laws) with the changing contributions of and correlations among factors, *the hyperplane loadings will exhibit no standard error,* but will stay at zero in all samples. What is zero in the factor mandate matrix will stay at zero in the sample. What is unity in the mandate matrix, on the other hand, will be reduced *variously* in different samples and contexts, i.e. will show standard error variation.

Since to some this statement seems paradoxical in terms of classical statistics, it must be justified by reference to the factor influence or determiner model from which it derives. Imagine, say, 200 flasks, in each of which 30 objects of different substance are exposed to sunlight, moisture, oxygen pressures, and two or three other factor influences, differing in strength from flask to flask. The variables are measures on the 30 objects, such as the weight of rust on iron objects, the amount of gas absorption in charcoal, the conduction in a piece of platinum wire, the rate of growth of a mold, etc. Each factor will leave some variables untouched. Let us assume conduction in platinum wire is affected by the warmth of sunlight and the amount of moisture, but

not by the oxygen pressure. Or that the growth rate of a plant is affected by oxygen pressure, sunlight, and moisture, but not by the changes in the magnetic field. This zero correlation of magnetic field strength and plant measurements, or oxygen pressure and conduction in platinum, will remain zero in *any* sample of flasks, because it is a law of Nature.

The variable "conduction in platinum" lies *exactly* in the hyperplane of the oxygen pressure factor, because scientific laws operate as infallibly in the sample as in the universe population. What we call sampling error arises from the unevenness or heterogeneity of interaction of influences in the universe, not of its laws themselves, which are immutable. Sampling of any objects at different times and places will give different means and variances, and different observed correlations, because when several influences operate together, any correlation is affected by their various variances. The statement that "if a zero correlation exists in the population, one can always pick a sample subgroup with a non-zero correlation" misses the point. Sampling affects numbers, not the laws, e.g., multiplication, applying among numbers. The statement that hyperplane variables have *exactly* zero loading in *all* samples means, of course, that the factor is in its true position when we *make* it exactly normal to these same hyperplane variables in all samples. If this cannot be done exactly, i.e., if all cannot simultaneously be brought to zero, it is because of error of measurements, *not* sampling error. And if the common error (and "common specific") factors that arise among error measurements (uncorrelated in the population, correlated in the sample) can somehow be rotated clear of the real factors, the real factors should stand on exact hyperplanes. Only the non-zero loadings of subject-tied ("substantive") factors will change with sampling.

(f) The possibility may be entertained that instead of waiting for a second experiment to tell us which factors are error "transients,"—the only sure way—something in their intrinsic appearance will enable them to be recognized and set aside even in one experiment only. Earlier (243) it was speculated, for example, that error factors might not show a true hyperplane but only a normal distribution of loadings with most at the central median. If we assume, as here, that *common* error factors, though not "real" in the sense of substantive, are real in the sense that some influence entered into the observer's observation of two or more different variables (instead of assuming the artificial model that "random numbers correlating zero in the population correlate in the sample") then such factors could, as observer-situation factors, have characteristic properties and loading distributions (even if not this speculated normal distribution).

One property they are likely to have is a smaller variance, and a variance which gets less as the reliability computed for the variables gets higher. Another might be a relation to the variables covered by a certain instrument of observation, since error attaches to instruments. Research may therefore yet open up ways of picking out error common factors with some degree of certainty even before their "transience" is established by comparison with a second experiment. Incidentally, one may also speculate whether it might not be possible to avoid taking out all error factors but to stop earlier and rotate all error variance into a single convenient "garbage" factor, as shown at (c) in Diagram 6-6. This would be an approximation of the total error because it would be projecting several dimensions upon one, but if it could be done it would then leave the substantive patterns uncontaminated.

(g) A final principle which needs to be asserted in contrast to common assumptions, is that there are normally more hyperplanes existent in the hyperspace than are represented by the number of factors we take out, i.e., than the dimensions we choose to rotate on. The reason is that for every real factor at work in a system of varying variables there exists a hyperplane configuration, i.e., a "deposit" or crystallization in the factor space of unaffected variables. This structure appears as a conspicuous density of representation of variable "points" in the factor space. But since there are admittedly generally more than n factors in an n-variable problem, there will usually be more discoverable hyperplanes than the smaller number, k, of factors commonly taken out. (This has been shown empirically by Bargmann (58) and by the present writer (243).) Many of these hyperplanes will correspond to factors of quite trivial variance (except where the number of factors extracted is grossly short of that required). For example, where appreciable variance exists for ten rotated factors and only three are taken out, ten smeared, inflated hyperplanes (projections from ten to three space) will be discoverable in the three space.

The practical procedure deriving from the five propositions above involves three principles: (1) Since one can never take out all factors $-n+-$ that exist, it is necessary to have a clear policy on taking out some arbitrary reduced number. That number should give maximum representation to the substantial and real factors while cutting off as much as possible of the error variance as will not simultaneously carry away too much real variance. Such an open eyed compromise is the only realistic approach possible to the number of factors problem. It can be most quickly designated by saying that we substitute for the question "What is the true number of factors?" the more operational question "Where do we stop factor extraction?" Our aim is to take what we shall call the *comprehensive non-trivial common variance,* and we do not wish in this term to indicate merely some vague, question-begging concept. Rather it is something which, though not definable by a single cut-and-dried mathematical formula, is yet definable with some precision—enough for the decision to be precise—by application to each case of a set of clear principles.

The comprehensive non-trivial common variance can be defined either (a) independently of any inherent signs in the data by taking some conventionally agreed, *arbitrary* but exact value, say, 99 per cent of the common factor variance when communalities are assigned for *n* factors, or (b) stopping according to signs in the data of the onset of what we shall call *formless* or *scree* factors. (2) After this, at a later stage the exact number of *significant and meaningful* factors to be considered has finally to be decided by a purely *rotational verdict,* and (3) In this last step, for reasons now to be developed, the principal practical problem is avoiding *factor fission,* in what we have called a *degenerate solution.* Let us consider these three procedures.

1. Obtaining the comprehensive, nontrivial common variance. Approach (a) by taking the largest variance possible without being forced to an excessive number of factors, say, 98 per cent where 99 per cent would require doubling the number of factors extracted. In this, one may (with small samples) be taking in an appreciable amount of common error factors, to be sorted out in the rotation later, but one is also making sure of a very adequate (98 per cent?) representation of the true factors. However, there is some difficulty in defining the per cent because one cannot define the whole, since the communalities for taking *n* factors out of *n* variables are not uniquely determinate. We advocate taking out *n/2* factors, which *do* have determinate communalities, discoverable by iteration, and entering with these for *n* factors and stopping at the communalities reached after ten iterations. Taking this as an extremely close estimate of the true total common factor variance, one can then find from the plot of successive factor contributions where to stop for the 95, 98, or 99 per cent one agrees to consider worthwhile. (Note that the usual "Percentage of variance" print-out reported in articles is not this figure but the rela-

tively meaningless figure of the percentage, at the given factor number, of the variance included at some other number, the latter being an already completely arbitrary number of factors (that at the stopping point dictated to the machine by the experimenter.)

Approach (b) by taking signs inherent in the data, in order to reach some cutting point between the comprehensive and the trivial variance has been most systematically pursued in terms of finding a (still arbitrary!) statistical significance point. From a practical standpoint this generally saves some work, relative to the arbitrary 98 per cent (or 99 per cent) criterion, because it tends to stop one sooner.

The purely statistical approaches to the number of factors have been numerous and have worked on several principles of which perhaps the two most important[9] have been:

(i) The maximum-likelihood method as set out by Lawley (903) and Rao (1179). This amounts to independently varying the number of factors and the sizes of trial communalities to arrive at a combination that restores (by $R_o = V_o V'_o$) the correlation matrix to an acceptable statistical likelihood standard. Its defect is its heavy cost in computer time.

(ii) A variety of tests of the standard error of a factor loading and of a factor have been suggested by Burt (169), Saunders (1253), and in earlier cruder forms by McNemar and Coombs. By these one can stop extraction when the size of the factor being extracted is that of the larger (or of the average) common error factors. The practical procedure proposed by Sokal (1333) rests on standard error and seems to work well in practice, as witnessed by

---

[9]Note that we are not including the already rejected *mathematical* (page 200, (b) above) solution of getting communalities to *minimize* rank (Guttman) or to maximize or to minimize unique variance (Butler Lawley), which are ingenious but irrelevant to most experimental work.

plasmodes (made-up examples with known factor structure).

However, a problem arises in all statistical approaches, namely, whether we wish more to avoid a type 1 or a type 2 error of inference. In this case, are we more concerned to avoid including error variance in our rotation or to avoid loss of true factor variance by cutting error variance out too completely? The present writer has argued for avoiding the Type 2 error, on the grounds that error can be rotated out into separate error factors, as pointed out above, in the rotation process.

Most of these statistical tests are cumbersome and time consuming; but fortunately

from the term for the straight slope of boulders and debris at the foot of a mountain.)

When successive roots extracted begin to fall in this regular way one is dealing only with common factors due to a large number of random small influences. In classical theory these could be due to two sources: (1) correlations among specifics orthogonal in the population and (2) errors of measurement. In large samples, there are usually clear representations of *two* not one, successive straight scree slopes. In this case one takes the line of the upper slope. But in strata theory (264) the scree is differently explained as random correlation across domains.

DIAGRAM 6-7.   Ideal and Empirical Diagrams of the Scree Test

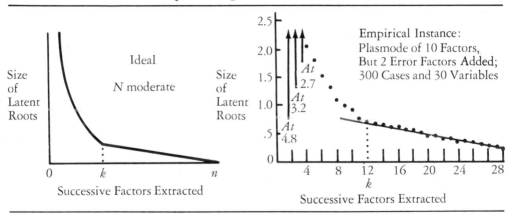

a quick and convenient approach, unfortunately not entirely worked out in its theoretical statistical basis, has appeared in the present writer's *scree test*. To use this one takes the unreduced R matrix (unities in the diagonal) and extracts n latent roots plotting them as shown in Diagram 6-7. (Alternatively one can first take some estimates of communalities, such as Burt's (160) for a slightly greater accuracy.) Typically, the curve falls in a curvilinear fashion and then becomes absolutely straight (except, sometimes, for minor, irregular departures) in a "scree" of small factor debris, as shown in Diagram 6-7. (Hence the term scree test,

Incidentally, one must not forget that the distribution of the rotated resolved factors may actually be anything from that shown at (b) to that in (c) and (d) in Diagram 6-7, depending on the nature of the data and the sample size, whereas the extracted factors will be pretty well as at (a) (see also Diagram 6-5).

Another factor number check which, because of its extreme convenience (it may be built into a single program package) has been widely used is that proposed by Kaiser, of plotting the curve (or examining it by machine) of latent root sizes when unities have been put in the diagonals. Thus far this test proceeds like the scree test, but in the final decision, instead of stopping at properties indicated in the curve, one cuts off sharply *at the last latent root above one.* It has the rationale that this marks the last factor with significant alpha[10] coefficient homogeneity (392). This is not entirely satisfactory, theoretically, for if one wishes to estimate a factor one generally uses only the variables correlating highly with it, and these will continue to give satisfactory homogeneity for factors beyond those rejected on the alpha criterion. Moreover, one is really concerned with the significance of the smallest factor *after* rotation. Since rotation "evens up" size, almost invariably, this test stops extraction too soon. Extensive experience with the Kaiser test convinces the writer that it cuts off too soon when variables are few ($n < 20$), and too late when they are many ($n > 50$). Indeed, it is essentially arbitrary in that it stops factoring when the contribution of a factor is no more than that of the average variable — a not too logical basis for decision. It has appreciable parallelism in results to Guttman's lower bound, using

squared multiple r's as communalities, which therefore suggests that in addition to the above distortions it is systematically underestimating (except with large n's) the number of factors.

A number of methods have been proposed, which like the scree test depend on relations among successive roots in the curve. They are empirical, but in the case of Tucker's test (Thurstone, 1412), they have worked pretty well. Now that latent roots can be readily calculated, the *scree test,* which has some rationale in a statistical basis as pointed out above, is probably the most convenient, requiring only a simple computer calculation and the laying of a ruler on the plot. Empirically, as distinct from theoretically, it stands on a very substantial basis indeed. It has been tried on more plasmodes (numerical examples made up according to the model) than any other factor number test and has proved again and again to issue with the correct number when other tests, e.g., the Kaiser unity test, have been somewhat misleading. However, it remains true that any research which claims in publication to have made an adequate examination of the number of factors should check by two or three independent tests. Routinely our own laboratory has used some two of the scree, the Kaiser, the Sokal, the Lawley-Rao and the Tucker test. Most often we have used the two first, even while recognizing that the Kaiser is likely to be too conservative (making Type 2 errors); but the agreement of the different methods has been very good, tying down the factor number typically to within two or three. For example, the different approaches in a certain clinical field have said 16 to 18 factors very clearly, with 17 central when on theoretical speculative grounds alone workers like Becker, Eysenck and Peterson have wanted to settle for 3 or 4. Our troubles in this area are not in lack of agreement of good methods.

In any case, having the number of factors indicated for the *comprehensive non-trivial*

---

[10]The elegance offered by Kaiser in this justification by alpha factor analysis rests, as indicated, on the proof that the last factor with a latent root size of greater than unity is the last factor with significant internal homogeneity. In other words, the estimation of a factor beyond this will not satisfy Cronbach's alpha coefficient of homogeneity; the separate estimations of any two halves will not correlate. However, this assumes that *all* variables are used in the estimation — those in or near the hyperplane as well as those with appreciable loading.

We often hear of a multiple R "capitalizing on error"; this is the opposite procedure of unnecessarily going bankrupt by a special accumulation of error. In any typical experimental situation we would estimate the factor only from the three to six high loaded variables and would not "accumulate error" and reduce the degrees of freedom of the multiple R, by bringing in all these more or less irrelevant variables. The fact remains that the "proof" is misleading, since one can still get a consistent estimate of a factor beyond this cut-off point of unity. Even if one could not, as Tucker points out, the existence of the factor and our ability to estimate it, can in some respects be considered two distinct things.

TABLE 6-2

The Degenerative Process of Factor Fission as Revealed by the Rotational Test for Number of Factors*

	4 Factors Insufficient Number for the Substantive (Physical) Factors				5 Factors Number According to Scree Test					6 Factors First Extraction of Definitely Excessive Number of Factors					
	1	2	3	4	1	2	3	4	5	1	2	3	4	5	6
1				.65				.59	−.11					.36	−.11
2		.56				.62					.60				
3	.81	−.23		.10	.85					.43					
4			.99				.98					.96			
5				−.50				−.38	.47					.48	
6		−.12		.67				.60	−.11				.37		
7				.64				.59					.37		
8				−.50		.11		−.39	.48					.49	
9		−.12		.62	.10			.63	.10				.48		
10		.56				.61			.11		.59				
11		.75		−.30		.63		−.35			.62		−.30		
12		.50				.41			−.19		.39			.17	
13		.52				.54					.51				
$V_{fp's}$ 14		−.56				−.61			−.11		−.59				
15	.71	−.15			.77				.22	.43					
16	.81	−.23		.11	.84	−.10		.13	.10	.42					
17	.59	−.16		−.34	−.56	−.20		−.31		.26	−.13		−.29		
18	.86				.86										.37
19	.85	.16		−.14	.83	.11		−.17							.38
20			.98	−.11		.97					.96				
21			.97	−.13		.96					.94				
22			.98			.97					.96				
23			−1.00			−.98					−.97				
24				−.94		−.95					−.93				
25	.54	.25			.48				−.37		.15		−.31	.42	
26	.80			.12	.80					.31					
27		.19		.39		.22		.33	−.12		.22		.12		
28	.52			.36	.54			.31					.27		.28
29	.78		.11		.75				−.15						.44
30			.58	−.39			.54	−.25	.35			.54		−.36	
31		−.13	−.42	.54				−.43	.47			−.42	.31		
32	.14	.47	.32		.16	.47	.29			.44	.28				
No. in Hyperplane	21	15	22	14	20	20	23	18	15	27	22	23	22	26	28

	1	2	3	4		1	2	3	4	5		1	2	3	4	5	6
1	1.00				1	1.00					1	1.00					
$R_{f's}$ 2	.31	1.00			2	.34	1.00				2	.44	1.00				
3	−.06	−.03	1.00		3	−.10	−.17	1.00			3	.17	−.03	1.00			
4	−.37	−.81	.03	1.00	4	−.29	−.56	.11	1.00		4	−.40	−.41	−.08	1.00		
					5	.22	.60	−.13	.03	1.00	5	−.24	.26	−.14	.65	1.00	
											6	−.88	−.27	−.23	.40	.40	1.00

variance (CNTV) and having, if it indicates less than $\left(\frac{n}{2}+1\right)$ factors, iterated to convergent communalities), we are in a position to apply the second procedure — namely, the more exact rotational verdict on factors to "respect" in the solution. Some basic propositions on rotation must first be stated:

(1) If fewer factors than k are extracted, when k are indicated by the CNTV the sets of unaffected variables which lie almost *exactly* in the hyperplane in k space will be scattered more broadly — in what we have just called a smeared hyperplane — in their projections in space of less than k dimensionality. Usually, these blurred hyperplanes are still clear enough to be located, but the variables both in them and in the salient, high loaded cases are out of place. As one takes out more factors, the hyperplane width steadily drops and reaches a minimum when the main factors have been taken out.

(2) In addition to the true hyperplanes of the primary factors, there exist in the factor space: (a) pseudohyperplanes, of the error factors, (b) pseudohyperplanes created by the second or higher order factors, and (c) geometers hyperplanes. As to (b), it can be shown that though the higher order factor hyperplanes upon lower order *factors* do not generate exact hyperplanes in *variables,* they *tend* to produce a band of near-zero loadings in the variable space. Let us look at (c), the artificialities which have been called *geometers'* hyperplanes. It can be shown from solid geometry that with n variables in k space $(k\text{-}1)$ variables can always be found lying exactly in a plane — indeed there are $\frac{n!}{(k-1)!}$ such planes. The danger of confus-

ing these with the $n+$ true hyperplanes is small so long as k is not greater than $\frac{n}{2}$ and $(k-1)$ is below 50 per cent. For the percentage of variables in the true hyperplane is *well* above 50 per cent in most well-planned studies. However, if we proposed to take out all n factors, which would be a possible procedure of perfection according to anything yet discussed, we should actually get into difficulties. For the percentage of variables in the geometers' hyperplanes as we approach n will exceed that in any true hyperplane. Indeed, as we know in practice, the pursuit of maximum simple structure with n factors will end with each individual variable becoming a factor, planted in a geometer's hyperplane of $(n-1)$ variables. (Then the factor correlations, R_f will be those of the original variables R_o, except for the correction necessary for communalities of variables being short of unity, i.e., the cosines will be the same.)

Long before this ultimate debacle is reached, a change which has been called "factor fission" (Cattell, 229) will have spread among the factors. This is illustrated in Table 6-2, where the Cattell-Dickman ball problem (280), known to contain five influences, is rotated again on a basis of four and then six extracted factors. It will be noted that as an extra false (though small) dimension is added by factor 6, a true factor — factor 1 — tends to split, as if it were trying to retain the same hyperplane and hinge two factors upon it. These two factors are necessarily highly correlated (.88), because the new dimension adds little amplitude in which to swing the vectors apart. (To follow this more closely, see diagram in [243].) Also, algebraic laws

---

*Only loadings greater than .10 are shown.

Note — In going from the 5 to the 6 factor extraction we have first definite evidence of factor fission. 1 has split its variance between 1 and 6 (and slightly in 5). 4 has split between 4, 5, and 6. At the same time the cosines among 1, 4, 5, and 6 rise far above the median (.21) of the original matrix, totalling $.40 + .65 + .24 + .88 + .40 + .40$, and having a median of .40. A composite index of splitting, hyperplane count and angle, properly weighted, would thus show a sharp change between the 5th and 6th factor extraction.

require that they be correlated in order to be able to restore the correlation between variables that previously shared loadings on one factor and are now on different factors.

The result is that as one rotates for simple structure on k, $k+1$, $k+2$, etc., factor solutions, where k is the CNTV number of factors (or the true number in an artificial example with an exact number of factors), a degenerative process occurs. It is this which is the real and fatal obstacle to the otherwise ideal procedure of taking out n factors and letting most of them rotate to trivial variance. And it is one reason for removing the practical shortcomings still remaining in confactor rotation; for confactor rotation would encounter no difficulty in rotating with n factors. Since the final solution is likely to be based, in most theoretically important experiments, on simple structure, one naturally asks if there is any way of avoiding this factor fission and degeneration of resolution while using the full[11] variance of n factors, instead of the, say, 98 per cent of their variance proposed in the alternative of stopping at "worthwhile" variance above, compressed into $\frac{n}{2}$ factors or less.

Preliminary work with plasmodes indicates considerable promise for a test of onset of fission which is a joint function of: (1) Width of hyperplane (count within $\pm.05$, or $\pm.03$ with large samples), (2) Number of high angles among factors, and (3) Number of factor pairs with high coefficient of congruence between patterns. (Fission produces very similar patterns.) No one of these is reliable alone, but together they seem dependable.

The nature of *the rotation test for the number of factors* is, therefore, to take for rotation a number, c, well below the CNTV

number, k, and rotate to maximum simple structure. Repeat with $(c+1)$, $(c+2)$, etc., to $(k+1)$, calculating the function indicated above at each number. (The factors placed on coarse hyperplanes at the earlier stages should remain on those hyperplanes as they narrow, becoming increasingly true in loading pattern, and this stability in consecutive analyses and rotations is itself proof of the resolution, and indication that any sudden change is a degenerative fission.) At the point where the calculated total function above shows degeneration to have set in, one stops and takes the last rotated number of factors, recognizing that this is the best resolution possible for the number of factors approached in the Comprehensive Non-trivial Variance approximation. The rotational test may in fact show that one more or one *fewer* rotatable factors exist than the first approximation indicated.

The mathematical statistician's training causes him to prefer some single, "clean" index to the step-by-step, trial-and-error solution by the rotational test. But there as in some other scientific situations, the elegance is meretricious, for no simple, practicable mathematical expression will recognize the existence of a mountain range or decide in non-arbitrary fashion when a mountain is really a hill. The rotational basis of solution tells us both how many factors above a certain agreed trivial size can be located, and what their location is. It says, "This is the structure here: cut it off at whatever point suits your purpose." But it recognizes that error factors, whose size depends on the reliabilities, are part of the structure, and it does not allow the experimenter to cut off an important part of the picture beforehand, until he has seen what it is. From this, it follows, incidentally, that different experiments on the same variables, in studies with the usual fluctuation of factor variances, will not match all the way down the series. For, toward the end of the series, first this factor and then that will have slipped into triviality and another will have stepped up

---

[11]The reader is reminded that even this "full" variance remains slightly inexact because we have had to fit communalities for n factors when there are really more than n, and strictly speaking, we should be rotating in more than n dimensions.

or down into its place. The smallest 10 per cent or so of factors will finally get replicated only over a few researches, as their hyperplanes are sporadically located and lost. Confactor rotation may someday rescue us from these trial-and-error procedures.

8. THE RETICULAR AND STRATA MODELS FOR HIGHER-ORDER FACTORS

The use of orthogonal factors appeals to the mathematician per se — or to anyone who wishes to be engaged only in the simplest computations. This meretricious appeal has all too frequently been allowed to disrupt progress toward the more fundamental scientific goal of reaching invariant, maximally efficacious factor concepts. The arguments for oblique factors are (1) that even if factors were, in some special case, correctly conceived as orthogonal in the population, they would not so fall in any actual sample, (2) that if factors are oblique no orthogonal solution, e.g., Varimax, can obtain the true position of maximum simple structure. The theoretical principle that simple structure and orthogonality are incompatible (except in the rarest of cases) is demonstrable by numerous experimental instances, where the simple structure hyperplane count improves greatly when the orthogonal restriction is removed (see Diagram 6-5), (3) any oblique rotational resolution will permit orthogonality as a special case, but the converse is not true, (4) all research on second and higher order factor structures — which often greatly illuminate our scientific concepts — is cut off, as completely as circumnavigation of the earth by belief in a flat world, when we insist on the mathematical habit of orthogonality, and (5) there is no reason why factor influences, interacting in the same universe, should be expected to be orthogonal, i.e., independent.

The last and most philosophical argument is surely entirely adequate to dispel recourse to orthogonal factors except in truly odd situations. However, we are concerned here more with point (4), and our aim now is to look at the world of higher-order structures appearing when first-order factor resolutions are guided by simple structure or confactor rotation. Obviously, if we have a number of oblique, correlated factors, it is possible to proceed to a factoring of factors, which can be symbolized thus:

$$(27)\ R_I = V_{fpI} R_{II} V'_{fpI}.$$

In accordance with the standard notation proposed in Chapter 5, R_I is used for correlations among first-order factors, R_{II} among second orders (consistent with R_o among variables), and so on, though the subscript f has here been dropped to avoid cluttering. Similarly, V_o is now the D-V matrix of primaries on variables, V_I of secondaries on primaries, etc., i.e., the V subscript refers to the order of the row entries. The extra subscripts, f, fp, rs, etc., indicate whether correlations are factors or reference vectors, and whether the D-V (dimension-variable relation matrix) numbers are loadings, correlations, weights, etc. This system seems likely to have the widest convenience.

As to the nature of second-order factors — and therefore the rotational principles to be followed in giving them unique resolution — there are two possibilities to consider. First, if we are to be consistent with all that has so far been said about factors, a mechanical arbitrary orthogonal rotation is out of the question. A factor would still be considered an influence, and, as such, it should have simple structure on the primary factors — *not* on the variables — and a third order should have simple structure on the secondaries. That hyperplanes appear under these conditions, corresponding to known influences, is empirically generally well supported. Sometimes, although the hyperplanes are clear, the percentage of variables in them runs noticeably lower than for primaries on variables. It is easy to see why these hyperplanes should be more scanty, for the requirement of a comprehensive, well assorted sample is naturally less often met in going from lower- to higher-order factors than in going from variables to factors. For factors from a fairly diverse domain of variables are nevertheless, as factors, likely to be largely of one family. A more diversified choice of original domains is necessary to give good simple structure on higher-order factors. This has been shown, for instance in the work on fluid and crystallized general ability, where proper rotation of higher-order ability factors was missed for thirty years, because of failure to go well outside the ability domain in the search for "hyperplane stuff" (258).

However, surveys of results in this new experimental domain also suggest that an alternative to the *influence* model, namely, the *emergent* model, must also be considered at higher orders. Specifically the cases of the anxiety and exvia-invia factors in the 16 P.F. have suggested the likelihood that a second order dimension may sometimes be "generated" among primaries by mutual positive feedback in some fairly complex circular causative pattern. Although the primaries might here be called "causes" of the secondary it seems better to distinguish this relation by calling the secondary an "emergent," implying that it is not a causal product of any primary but of interaction among them. However, since such interaction would be expected to arise only among members of a limited subgroup the effect on configuration would still be that of simple structure.

As several orders in succession come into experimental view we should anticipate causal and emergent (interactive causal) model possibilities which never concern us at the first order. It is quite possible that factors will act both on orders below them and above them. This requires a conceptual distinction between *order* and *strata,* the latter being a new concept and

the former retaining the operational meaning it has always really had—namely that second orders are what you get by factoring first orders, and so on. These lead also to concepts of reticular models and strata models.

Before discussing these we may pause to note that even at the lowest order a surprising amount of discussion has been given to particular possible interaction stereotypes, orders, mosaics, or patterns. A brief designation of them is a useful preparation for the higher-order concepts. At the lowest order these patterns, such as the bifactor, the simplex, etc., are not even models, in the scientific sense, but examples of visual patterns or orderly forms in the correlation matrix or in the factor matrices. Parenthetically, Chapter 14 (Guttman) below uses "order" in this sense of an ordering of correlations in a pattern, not in the general sense of factor order— first, second, third, etc.—so necessary in describing the realms of factor structure which research is now discovering and which are represented by the successive factor strata matrices V_o, V_I, V_{II}, etc. Here, before proceeding to scientific models connected with the operational levels of factors we call factor order, we shall briefly glance at the history of ordering matrices in descriptive *mosaics,* as these stereotypes are perhaps best called. The difference between a model and a mosaic is that a model implies a full scientific model of concepts and causal mechanisms, probably mathematically expressed, whereas by mosaics we mean a "model" restricted to *patterns hypothesized to appear in a matrix.* A mosaic is a statement about a pattern of significant positive and negative entries appearing in a matrix. Some mosaics, like Guttman's simplex, are statements about a correlation matrix, others, which we are about to consider, are about the dimension-variable $(D\text{-}V)$ matrices and yet others could be about transformation matrices and so on.

Obviously, at the simplest, lowest $D\text{-}V$

order (variable-to-factor) the factor matrices can show factors standing in various mutual relations with regard to their patterns of effects upon variables. These will often have implications for the mosaic of relations of variable to variable in the *R* matrix. Many theories in the history of ability concepts have been expressed in a variety of possible mosaics of loading patterns on variables (in the *D-V*'s). These have been given various names, and some have been somewhat obsessionally followed for no particular reason as a "necessary ideal" in factor resolution, regardless of the necessary priority of isomorphism to nature as given by simple structure requirements. Taking a sample of four factors only for illustration, we have set out in Table 6-3 Burt's *bipolar* pattern, Holzinger's *bifactor*, Guttman's *simplex*, and the most general pattern of all—simple structure factors overlapping without restriction —which the present writer has called the

multiplex. Other mosaics can be suggested almost indefinitely, including the circumplex, radex, etc. They are useful as taxonomic descriptive terms, provided we recognize they are seldom found very exactly represented in Nature, except for the multiplex; the bipolar (as a necessary consequence of principal axis or centroid extraction); the simplex (in time-staggered measurements); and the bifactor mosaic in some ability data.

Conceived more broadly than in mosaics, namely, in terms of scientific models, the principal possibilities are shown in Diagram 6-8. This deals with relations of (1) primaries to variables, (2) primaries and secondaries to variables, and (3) factors to factors. Among factors we have principally to consider (Models I through VIII) the more discussed alternatives of the pyramidal hierarchy (Spearman's monarchic model), the non-pyramidal hierarchy or one-way strata model, the two-way strata

TABLE 6-3

SOME MAJOR MODELS FOR THE RELATIONS AMONG FACTORS: *D-V* MOSAICS

	Unrotated ("Genealogic") Resolution							Bifactor ("Staircase") Resolution		
	With Reflection (Bi-polar Pattern)			Without Reflection						
	1	2	3	1	2	3		1	2	3
1	+	+	+	−	−	−		+	+	
2	+	+	+	+	+	+		+	+	
3	+	+	−	−	−	+		+	+	
4	+	+	−	+	+	−		+	+	
5	+	−	+	−	+	−		+		+
6	+	−	+	+	−	+		+		+
7	+	−	−	−	+	+		+		+
8	+	−	−	+	−	−		+		+

	Simplex				Multiplex, Complete with Higher Stratum						
	1	2	3		1	2	3	4		1	2
1	×			1	×				1	×	
2	×	×		2	×				2		
3	×	×		3		×		×	3	×	×
4	×	×	×	4					4		×
5	×	×	×	5		×	×				
6	×	×	×	6	×			×			
7	×	×	×	7		×					
8	×	×	×	8			×				

DIAGRAM 6-8.   Some Major Models for the Relations among Factors

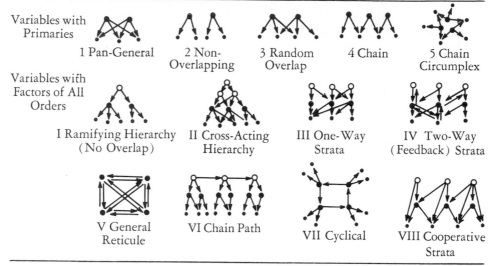

Variables with Primaries

1 Pan-General   2 Non-Overlapping   3 Random Overlap   4 Chain   5 Chain Circumplex

Variables with Factors of All Orders

I Ramifying Hierarchy (No Overlap)   II Cross-Acting Hierarchy   III One-Way Strata   IV Two-Way (Feedback) Strata

V General Reticule   VI Chain Path   VII Cyclical   VIII Cooperative Strata

(1)   A variable is shown by a •, a primary factor by a •, and higher-order factors by a ○.
(2)   An influence, as a contribution to the variance, is shown by an ——→. Unless a sign is attached it can be assumed the correlation can be + or −. Models or patterns concerned with magnitudes, e.g., cooperative factors, cannot be represented in this all-or-nothing symbolism.
(3)   The actual numbers of factors shown here has no significance; only enough factors or variables are used to make the necessary pattern clear.
(4)   These type patterns are models of actual influence instead of factor loading only. However, the earlier patterns should be given their place here. Thus, among *Variable-Factor Models,*
     (a)   Burt's Bipolar, "Genealogical" Pattern (Centroid or Principal Axis) is No. 1, the Pan-General factor model, with a specific ("genealogical") sign pattern imposed on the successive general factor loadings.
     (b)   Holzinger's Bifactor and Burt's Group Factor Patterns are a hybrid of (1) and (2) above, in which a general factor and non-overlapping factor are combined.
     (c)   Guttman's simplex, radex, and circumplex are sub-forms of the chain and circumplex models in (4) and (5). In the chain the factors overlap on the variables, sequentially by one variable, as shown for illustration, or on two or more as could be drawn in on (4). When this sequential or chain pattern is joined up in a ring, we have what is here defined as a circumplex.
     (d)   The random overlap model, in (3), is by far the most common and generally applicable, and one of which all the others may, of course, be considered special derivations.
(5)   The two-way (feedback) influence is potentially applicable to all models, but when it is quite general, as in the reticule, No. V, it abolishes the difference of factor order and the significance of simple structure. As indicated in the text, present factor-analytic techniques are capable, without ancillary evidence, of discovering specific structure only in models of the type (1) through (5) and I through III.

model, and the reticule, as well as some more specialized forms discussed elsewhere (261). The distinction we are beginning here between order and strata is that the former simply represents an operation — whatever factors emerge from a matrix are by definition higher in order than those in the matrix. The latter represents a more substantial, "real" difference of level of action, derived from consideration of

several matrices and other evidence, and referred to a model as discussed below.

In the strata models, it is assumed that all first-order factors have a mutual peer status, all second-order factors another peer status, and so on, in the sense that they load on (affect) the same strata of factors (or variables) below them. The first two models in Diagram 6-8 deal with influence in only one direction, the second two admit it in both directions. Although the hierarchical model has been very popular (Burt, 160; Humphreys, 794, among contemporaries), the present writer has reasoned (261) that it is little more than an artefact, owing to the mathematical mandate that at any step *one must take out fewer factors than there are variables.* Thus, if after arriving at a single monarchic factor at the head of a hierarchy, one were to broaden the base of variables, afresh, it would *generally* transpire that the "head" is only one of several peer factors. What factor analysts, and others, perhaps need to pursue further, as an alternative concept with wider applicability, is the reticule or network. This supposes that once we have left the level of variables, the entities we find as factors are influences that can act upon one another in *all manner of directions* (including, therefore, feedback effects). Strata are then only concentric shells widening out from the center or level of observation where we happened to begin correlating and factoring. If the structure is thus seen as having no real beginning or end, our model becomes that of a network or reticulum. This broadest of all models — the network or reticule — permits the ultimate freedom of inference needed in using factor analysis in basic research. For if the technical difficulties about making inferences in a network can be overcome, factor analysis can become the most general of scientific methods. It becomes a general multivariate, computer-programmable method for getting at structural and causal relations (with only a linear restriction) in scientific research of all kinds. Parenthetically, it may be asked why variables cannot also be both causes and, like factors, consequences. The answer would seem to be that they can be, but with lower probability. For example, speed of repartee in conversation might be a variable which is a function of factor 1, general intelligence, and factor 2, exuberance (U.I. 21) or cortical metabolic rate. In turn it might be the cause of the individual's taking up politics and being divorced by his

wife. But in general, one specific piece of behavior will be less wide, less common over people and less systematic in its action so that a substantial variance and clear hyperplane would be less probable for it.

Unfortunately for any programmed, immediately systematic use of the reticulum model, we do not yet have the means of rotation, etc., either in simple structure or confactor rotation, to handle resolution of such possible complexity in a single experiment (see section below on models). Among the *simpler stereotyped influence* models, therefore, that which can be taken as most representative of present possibilities in stratoplex models is the one-way strata matrix at (b) in Diagram 6-8. We propose now to put the general reticular model "on the shelf" for more advanced study, and to concentrate on the stratoplex models and in particular on the *one-way stratified model.*

At this point let us explain a little further why it is necessary to introduce the idea of *strata* as well as the earlier, more familiar notion of *orders.* The answer is that "order" is correctly used in terms of *operations specific to one experiment and matrix,* whereas "stratum" conveys and refers to a general scientific structural status. For example, it is a possible, and, indeed, a not infrequent happening, for an investigator accidentally to begin factoring together a set of variables (factor battery scores) which, *in terms of some other experiment* are already regarded as representing a mixture from more than one factor order. Or he may *knowingly* begin factoring measures which, in terms of other experiments, are suspected of being *mixed* in order. For, as Table 6-4 illustrates, the proper test of whether a supposed primary factor is really a primary is to factor it with many other primaries. If it still stands out on its own, as a single factor specific, at the second order, or if it loads a second-order factor unity, we know it was really a second stratum factor from the beginning. If by accident the choice of variables *a, b, c, d, e,* etc., for factoring contains a variable, d, that is already at the first-factor (primary) stratum, then in the analysis where factor A covers $a, b, c,$ and B covers variables, $e, f, g,$ etc., variable d will reappear as a factor D essentially loading *only* d (i.e., a specific). When this pattern appears, as in the first factoring in Table 6-4, one does well to try again with a higher

The tactical considerations in putting together the immediate information on *orders,* from different experiments, to produce inferences about *strata,* can be most concisely shown by a sketch, as in Diagram 6-9. Therein the three rows of circular dots represent the real structure of strata, expressed in the directions of causal action

TABLE 6-4

RECOGNITION OF FIRST-STRATUM FACTOR
ACCIDENTALLY INCLUDED AS A VARIABLE

	A	B	C	D		A	B	C	D		X	Y
a	.5		—.4	—.1		.5		—.4	—.1	A	.6	
b	—.6		.4			—.6		.4		B	—.2	
c	.3					.3				C		.8
d				.5					.9	D		.6
e		.8	.4	.1			.8	.4	.1			
f		.4	.8				.4	.8				
g		—.7					—.7					
		—.2	—.1				—.2	—.1				

First Factoring	Factoring with Adjusted Communality for d	Second-Order Factoring

or further iterated communality for d, whereupon the true nature of d is likely to appear as in the second matrix in Table 6-4. The strata thus represent what we may think of as *real* orders among the factors; the *orders* refer to the result of a single experiment. The example above indicates how strata are recognized from observation of orders.

(arrows). Four possible experimental situations are here considered, the scope of each being shown by the variables or factors within one enclosure of dotted or continuous lines.

In the first, a second stratum (primary factor) measure (No. 3″) has unknowingly been included with first stratum variables. As Table 6-4 has shown, there is no prob-

DIAGRAM 6-9. Relation of Operations Revealing Factor Order to Inferences About Factor Strata

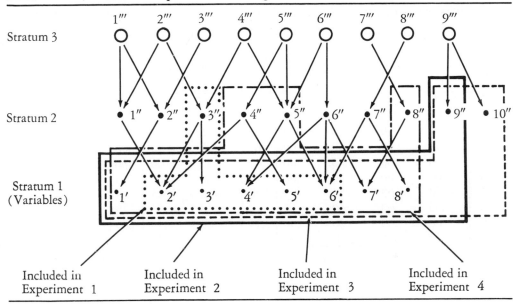

lem, provided it has some quite minimal loading on "another" variable (No. 3'), since it takes its stand with the other second stratum (primary factor) members, Nos. 4", 5" and 6". In the next case, however, a second stratum measure (No. 9") is similarly included but lacks any representation whatever among the variables. Its nature will not be recognized and it will simply be a "specific factor." In case 3 another measure like No. 9", namely, No. 10" is included and these will yield together what will at first be mistaken for a primary factor (second stratum). Only in later, second stratum factorings will its behaving like 3" in the first example, (first stratum) factoring reveal that it is really a third stratum factor, No. 9'". In the last case we consider the possibility of two or more primary factor measures (actually three: Nos. 4", 5", and 8") being included when they *do* have some representation in other variables used. They will be recognized for what they are, but factor 5'", which is really a third stratum factor, will appear as a second stratum,

primary factor. These four cases are the most common and important, but are not exhaustive of other possibilities, which the reader may wish to work out on Diagram 6-9 or an extension.

In any real data we cannot, of course, assume that everything can be accounted for by such a stratoplex model. It may be necessary to give a trial to the more complex reticular model. The working out of inference there cannot be pursued here, but obviously "split levels" must then be considered. Calculations required by factoring through different orders will therefore be considered here only for the stratoplex model.

The main calculations with which one is concerned in the stratoplex model are (1) the estimation of scores of people on variables directly from all the higher factor scores, (2) the converse estimation of higher-order factor scores from variables or lower strata factors, and (3) calculating loadings of higher-strata factors *directly* on variables.

TABLE 6—5

CONTRAST OF CATTELL-WHITE AND SCHMID-LEIMAN LOADINGS OF HIGHER-ORDER FACTORS ON VARIABLES

By Cattell-White Formula

	First Order				h^2	Second Order		h^2	Third Order	h^2
	1'	2'	3'	4'		1"	2"			
1	.00	.00	.00	.50	.25	.00	.30	.09	.21	.04
2	.00	.50	.00	.00	.25	.00	.00	.00	.00	.00
3	.00	—.50	.60	.00	.61	.36	—.30	.09	.09	.01
4	.50	.60	.00	.00	.61	.25	.00	.06	.21	.04
5	—.50	.60	.00	.00	.61	—.25	.00	.06	—.21	.04
6	.60	.00	.50	.00	.70	.60	—.25	.24	.33	.11
7	—.60	.00	—.50	.00	.70	—.60	.25	.24	—.33	.11
8	.00	.00	.60	—.60	.79	.36	—.66	.28	—.16	.03
9	.00	.00	.00	.50	.25	.00	.30	.09	.21	.04
10	.00	.00	.00	.60	.36	.00	.36	.13	.26	.07

Intercorrelations of First-Order Factors (Cattell-White)

	1'	2'	3'	4'
1'	100	00	15	18
2'		100	00	00
3'			100	—08
4'				100

Intercorrelations of Second-Order Factors (Cattell-White)

	1"	2"
1"	100	60
2"		100

By Schmid-Leiman Formula

	First Order				h^2	Second Order		h^2	Third Order	h^2	Σh^2
	1'	2'	3'	4'		1"	2"		1'''		
1	.00	.00	.00	.40	.16	.00	.21	.04	.21	.04	.25
2	.00	.50	.00	.00	.25	.00	.00	.00	.00	.00	.25
3	.00	—.50	.52	.00	.52	.19	—.21	.08	.09	.01	.61
4	.43	.60	.00	.00	.55	.13	.00	.02	.21	.04	.61
5	—.43	.60	.00	.00	.55	—.13	.00	.02	—.21	.04	.61
6	.52	.00	.43	.00	.46	.32	—.18	.13	.33	.11	.70
7	—.52	.00	—.43	.00	.46	—.32	.18	.13	—.33	.11	.70
8	.00	.00	.52	—.48	.50	.19	—.47	.26	—.16	.03	.79
9	.00	.00	.00	.40	.16	.00	.21	.04	.21	.04	.25
10	.00	.00	.00	.48	.23	.00	.25	.06	.26	.07	.36

The relation of scores between any two successive strata, x and $(x + 1)$ is given by:

$$(28)\quad Z'_x = V_{fp(x+1)}Z'_{(x+1)}$$
$$+ U_{(x+1)}Z'_{u(x+1)}$$

where U is the unique (specific) factor pattern matrix and Z_u is the unique factor (standard) score matrix. The estimation of factor scores may be illustrated by a two-strata gap, from x to $(x+2)$, by computing V_{fe} weights directly across two strata as follows:

$$(29)\quad V_{fe_{(x:x+2)}} = R_x^{-1}V_{fs_{(x:x+2)}} = R_x^{-1}V_{fp_{(x:x+2)}}$$

The value of $V_{fp(x:x+2)}$ in (29) requires some discussion. This is our required loading of a higher-stratum factor *directly* on variables or lower-stratum factors. Hitherto the most familiar treatment of this problem has been by the Schmid-Leiman (1272) formula. This has the peculiarity, by no means universally desirable, that each higher factor loading pattern is first reduced to its V_{dfc} (dissociated factor contribution) form (page 192 above). That is to say, it expresses the loadings on variables only of the *unique* part of the primary factor —the part remaining orthogonal to whatever higher-order factors are taken out of *it*. The alternative of adhering strictly to the higher-order factor *just as it stands* in its oblique position, has been proposed as a generally more meaningful solution by Cattell and White. The Schmid-Leiman and Cattell-White matrices are set out for comparison side by side for a small three-strata example in Table 6-5.

It will be recognized that the Schmid-Leiman values have simplicity in one respect, in that squaring and summing along a row leads directly to the total factor communality on each variable, whereas the Cattell-White values have the less simple relation of oblique factors. However, the latter have the advantage of permitting us to see at a glance the real nature of each factor in terms of its variable loadings. (For

it may be objected that the Schmid-Leiman does not present factors in their true order of size, in terms of magnitude of contribution to variables.) Moreover, the Cattell-White matrix can *end* with a top stratum of still correlated factors, whereas the Schmid-Leiman achieves formal consistency only by the probably artefactual arranging of a pyramid to lead to a single general factor to head a hierarchy. The Schmid-Leiman formula is given elsewhere (Schmid & Leiman, 1272), while the Cattell-White formula, i.e., the formula required in (29) above, and elsewhere, to express directly the loading of an oblique higher-order factor on the variables is:

$$(30)\quad V_{fp1.d} = V_{fp1} \cdot V_{fp2} \cdots \cdot V_{fpd}$$

where V_{fpd} is the dth-order factor pattern matrix, i.e., of d on $(d-1)$, and $V_{fp1.d}$ is the loadings directly of the dth-order factors on the first stratum.

As pointed out earlier, the simple structure of higher-order factors directly on lower-order variables, especially at several removes, is distinctly poorer than on that stratum to which the higher-strata factors are actually direct influences, i.e., that immediately below them. This follows from formula (30) above, for the loadings at order $(x+1)$ are, for each factor, a weighted combination of those for two or more factors at x order, and the latter are unlikely to have zeros opposite the same variables. But this lack of simple structure of a higher stratum factor directly on variables has also been shown empirically (261). Partly for this reason and partly for others, the simple structure of the spurious "higher-order factors" sometimes sought (Becker, 87; Peterson, 1152; Eysenck, 472) by *directly* taking out as few factors at the first order as one believes there are higher-order factors at a higher order, is so defective as to yield increasingly misleading pictures of factor structure at the higher order. One cannot find the rotational position of a higher stratum factor directly on the variables. Rotationally this "short cut" gives nothing really like the true primary simple structure, and, in terms of defining factor variance, it is no substitute for carefully proceeding to the higher orders through reliable definition of the lower-order foundations.

9. SOME MODIFICATIONS, DEVELOPMENTS, AND CONDITIONS OF THE MAIN FACTOR MODEL

Every mathematician recognizes that the additive, linear factor-analytic model is one of a family of more or less related models, some of which, like *non-Euclidean* factor analysis (Chapter 14) are obvious *possible* mathematical alternatives, while others, like the *permissive* and *expending* models, are not only possible alternatives, but may be improvements from a scientific point of view. A brief glance at these should now be taken, together with a perspective on relation to adjacent models.

Gibson (597) has pointed out that among adjacent models (see Chapter 4 above) that of *latent class analysis* is essentially formally similar, and some further comment on this is made in Coulter, Tsujioka and Cattell's chapter on types. Multidimensional scaling is also essentially similar, differing mainly in that whereas factor analysis sets up dimensions and generates expressions for distance functions, multidimensional scaling begins with information on distances and generates dimensions, though not such dimensions as individuals can be given scores upon. There is also the practically important difference that the framework of multidimensional scaling rests on nothing better than the unreliable single item and possibly only on "subjective" distance judgments, whereas factor analysis normally depends on measured behavior, with respect to whole tests and scales as variables, and yields scores for individuals.

The relation of factor analysis to analysis

of variance has been brought out in an introductory way in earlier chapters, and will be pursued in the following chapter, though its main treatment is in Sir Cyril Burt's Chapter 8 below. Its relation to canonical correlation and multiple discriminant functions has already been clarified in Professor Paul Horst's Chapter 4. What especially needs to be kept in mind in regard to multiple discriminant and canonical correlation is the fundamental difference from factor analysis in fixing dimensions, groups, and weights by relatively arbitrary decisions, in the latter through the efficiency of a particular prediction and in the former through a prior assignment of people to subgroups. They thus have greatest use in applied psychology, in applying discoveries rather than in making basic discoveries. However, canonical factor analysis has a role in matching two researches, in that the Tucker interbattery method of synthesizing two researches described above (page 196) has the same effect of producing maximum correlation of two sets of factors derived from common variables.

If we consider variants which essentially have the same aim as factor analysis, and might be considered as variants within a broader family, our attention must be given to latent type analyses by Lazarsfeld and Gibson; to non-linear factor analysis by McDonald; to analysis beginning with raw scores, as proposed by Saunders, Tucker, and others; and to special models of interrelations among factor effects as proposed by Coombs and Kao (384) and the present writer (250, 261).

Let us consider first what happens if we start with direct score factoring, using other products than the correlation coefficient, which has hitherto been most commonly treated as the basis for factor analyses. Actually, some four degrees of removal from raw scores can be employed, as Ross (1225) has reminded us: —

1. Making the "co-relation" matrix from

simple *sums of cross-products of raw scores*, i.e., the matrix entries are $\frac{\Sigma_o^N a_j a_k}{N}$.

2. Making a *covariance* matrix, i.e., the matrix entries are $\frac{\Sigma_o^N (a_j - M_j)(a_k - M_k)}{N}$.

3. Using the ordinary correlation matrix, i.e., with each entry being $\frac{\Sigma_o^N z_j z_k}{N}$.

4. Using the correlation coefficient over rows which have first been ipsatized.

It is obvious that these four steps successively abandon information present in the original data. Thus (2) loses the means of the variables and (3) loses both the means and the sigmas, while (4) loses the differences of individuals as they exist on a total of all variables. It is commonly agreed that (3) and (4) are often justified by psychological assumptions — (3), the correlation coefficient, by the fact that absolute means and sigmas are mere scaling artefacts, and (4), ipsative scoring, by psychological situations in which it does not make sense to think that one individual can be higher than another on everything.

However, in proportion as our scales become more meaningful, the covariance and cross-product factorizations become superior. They retain factors that tell us more in describing each individual, because they have not thrown information away. And when we come to compare the results of direct with *transpose factorings* of the same score matrices we shall find that matchings of the two series of factors become increasingly false as we proceed from system (1) to system (4), because (see page 228) what is thrown away affects the direct and transpose analyses differently.

As pointed out above, psychological and substantive arguments nevertheless sometimes indicate that we should use system (4), with its ipsative scoring (page 115). For example, in the factoring of culture pattern dimensions (Chapter 26), it makes sense to speak of real income per person,

murders per 100,000, etc., and in motivation research (Chapter 19) it is reasonable to divide the G.S.R. reaction magnitude to this and that stimulus by the average size of the individual's G.S.R. responses generally, i.e., we standardize across the rows. When unities are entered in the diagonals of an R matrix from ipsatized data, then each row and column sums to zero. With communalities the sum is therefore slightly negative. In any case we have lost essentially the first general factor that would have appeared had we not ipsatized. (In geometrical terms we have shifted the origin. See Broverman [149, 150], Ross [1225] relative to where it would have been.) However, this does not usually imply that we have lost a single meaningful factor, for in the process of rotation the variance of the first factor would generally be "spread around" among the meaningful factors. It implies, therefore, that all later, meaningful factors, relative to a complete, unipsatized factoring of the same data, will have lost some of their variance, and will assume different angles, analogously to the effect of a univariate selection (1420).

The computing procedures are essentially the same at all four levels. For example, covariance factor analysis (to be distinguished, of course, from covariance analysis, which is a modification of analysis of variance) proceeds by essentially the same series of processes and formulae as factor analysis, but substitutes a matrix of covariances (Σxy terms, where x and y are in *raw* score deviations) for correlations. The result is that the factor loadings are affected by the standard deviation of the raw scores of each test. To obtain covariance expressions the formulae usually used now need to be pre- and post-multiplied by diagonal, Δ, matrices representing the standard deviations of those raw scores. Thus the covariance matrix we begin with, C, is:

(31) (a) $C = \Delta R_o \Delta$ whence,

(b) $C = (\Delta V_{fp}) R_f (V'_{fp} \Delta)$,

where V_{fp} has the usual meaning of the factor pattern obtainable from R_o. (Assuming n factors extracted: for k factors another term appears derived from the communality in the factor analysis.) The inescapable objection to covariance factor analysis is that as psychologists we can assign no particular meaning to the sigma of arbitrary raw scores. On the other hand, covariance factor analysis has advantages regarding different *absolute factor variance* contributions as in confactor analysis, or to deal with factoring difference scores as in differential R technique (section 11 below).

The *permissive* model represents a greater deviation from the simple model, in which the condition is introduced (Cattell, 229; Coombs & Kao, 386) that factor A cannot operate *at all* until factor B has reached a certain absolute level. This model is one definitely suggested as desirable by some psychological laws and scientific situations. For example, we realize that a person's numerical ability factor could not come into operation on an arithmetic test in a foreign language until his language ability reaches a certain level, or that intelligence (B factor) could not operate in leadership activities until sociability (A factor) reaches a high enough level to gain acceptance for the individual socially. The *expending* model is one suggested in psychodynamics (Cattell, 246) wherein, unlike the usual model, the investment of a factor in variable x reduces its potential investment in variable y. That is, the factor tends to expend itself by its action. Here the sum total of investments for one individual must remain constant. This has been successfully handled to some degree by ipsative scoring (Chapter 3). However, a clear and adequate presentation of the *expending model* in factor analysis remains to be made. An important modification for development in the near future is the *modulator model,* required in the study of roles and moods (259). Probably an essential model for moods and a useful alternative for roles is one in which a situation modifies a factor level (thus chang-

ing a whole series of behavior) as well as determines the expression of the factor. Thus, we must speak of a *focal stimulus, j* or k, determining expression, and an *ambient stimulus, m,* determining factor level. Then for two different focal stimuli with the same global stimulus background, we have:

$$(32) \quad (1) \ A_{ijm} = b_{j1}(b_{ml}T_{1i}) \ldots + b_{jg}(b_{mg}T_{gi})$$
$$\quad\quad (2) \ A_{ikm} = b_{k1}(b_{ml}T_{1i}) \ldots + b_{kg}(b_{mg}T_{gi}).$$

This comes close to assuming that part of the stimulus (the focal part) operates directly on the first-order factors and part (the ambient part) on second-order factors.

New models can be thus introduced on grounds of psychological theory or simply on grounds of obvious mathematical alternative possibilities, and, in the end, they must all be stated in mathematically clear form. Saunders' work (1256) on moderator variables or moderator factors belongs somewhat more in the "mathematical alternatives" class (see Digman's Chapter 15 below) in that it simply supposes that the regression of factor A on variable x changes at extreme values of factor B. The multiplicative and non-linear models are also primarily mathematical possibilities, though psychological considerations at times suggest non-linear relations of factors to variables, and that a performance might be the resultant of multiplying one factor endowment by another, rather than of adding it. The fact that interaction is found to be significant fairly often in analysis of variance suggests that there must also be occasions when interaction effects occur among factors. Such interaction might take the form of a multiplicative relation or the appearance of a factor raised to a certain power, and so on. Incidentally, the undoubted phenomenon of cooperative factors (229) could be due to multiplicative effects. For in a multiplicative relation a factor would not affect a variable at all when its co-factor is loaded zero, and this could account for the parallelism of zero entries between two factors, as observed in the phenomenon of cooperative factors.

The recent work of McDonald, referred to above, promises actual computer programs for non-linear factor analysis. Space precludes adequate treatment here of this important development, but the essential idea is that various derivatives are tried of the orthogonal factor scores from an ordinary factor analysis to see, in the "person space" (i.e., the scores of persons plotted on the factor derivatives) whether the scores best fit a first-, second-, third-order, etc., curve. It remains a trial-and-error procedure in that one must try various relations, and it operates at present only on orthogonal factors. But both the laboriousness of the first, and the theoretical unsatisfactoriness of the latter may in time be overcome.

The legion of possible modified models which even a few hours of reflection by an experienced psychologist can easily suggest obviously cannot be more than sampled here. Normally, except for strong a priori indications, one proceeds with the ordinary factor-analytic model. When it fails to fit, then is the time to seek to modify it. What do we mean by failure of fit? Obviously, this is many things, but largely lack of internal consistency of results and lack of efficiency of prediction. For example, if the communalities we obtain constantly fall short of what would be expected, in a certain area, on *other* grounds, we may suspect that what is happening scientifically, e.g., the presence of diverse source trait (factor) structures in different persons or subgroups, is departing from the model. Or again, if experimentation by other methods, e.g., stimulation of factor increase, produces inconsistent results, one model or the other may be wrong. Incidentally, it is sometimes said by applied psychologists that pure factor tests have failed to do as good a job of criterion prediction as would be expected if the model were correct. This particular comment by some allegedly practical men can be completely discounted because, in the first place, applied psychology has simply not yet given adequate testing to pure factor tests; in the second, the batteries used to estimate factors have not yet reached very high validity of estimate, and third, the percentage of criterion hits from the relatively few experiments where factor batteries have been used has actually been much higher than for unfactored measures (329, 485).

Although we must look for improved fit of the model to actual data by developing it definitely in certain directions, as by McDonald's programmed curvilinear factor analysis, the improvement of factor-analytic practice is most likely to come through intensive research application to particular areas, where modified action is strongly suspected and in which the first results of the factor-analytic model become shaped through specific modifications by the usual hypothetico-deductive, trial-and-error procedures. For example, in abilities and learning factor analysis may yield results of tolerably good fit in terms of a linear model. One may then either experiment with the general non-linear program or take the *individual* factors and relate them to variables, trying various non-linear formulae (and at the same time experimenting with different factor estimation formulae) to reach the highest degree of prediction of the variable. One approach proposed in exploring non-additive relations has been the factor analysis of logarithmic values. Incidentally, it is well known that *in general* the weights for the best estimate of a factor will be different in the higher and lower ranges of the population endowment on that factor than in the middle ranges. It is by such specific explorations that we can hope best to find what modifications of the factor-analytic model need to be made.

A device which has proved useful both in exploring the fit of the factor model and in computer exercises, as described in the next section, is the *plasmode*. It is important to distinguish between a plasmode and a model. A plasmode (from plasm = form, and mode = measure) is a set of particular numerical values which meet the formal requirements of the model. The best plasmode is one not generated by pencil and paper alone, but by some physical model with known formal properties akin to those of the mathematical model, but, of course, subject to errors in the measurements and having other physical realities not present in a purely abstract mathematical "mock-up." Instances are the Cattell-Dickman ball problem (280), the Coan egg plasmode, the coffee cups (331), and, with error introduced, the Thurstone boxes (1420), the Bargmann data (58), and the recent "complete plasmode" (306).

In these particular plasmodes — the only substantial ones yet available — factors are made to be determiners of variables, and we thus know the "backstage" structure with certainty even as we measure the variables. The use of plasmodes where the relation is made to depart in various degrees from the exact additive linear model has shown that factor analysis is indeed capable of reaching the essentials — the number and nature of factors at work — even when such marked departures as multiplicative instead of additive relatives exist (58, 280). In these cases it is surprisingly potent in giving the good first approximation one might hope for on mathematical grounds, and thus offers a reliable take-off point for the experimental modifications of model to give a better fit as just discussed.

Even when using the standard factor model in psychological research, it is wise to remember that the factors one obtains are likely to include not only those corresponding to definite scientific hypotheses or constructs already focused in the experimenter's interests. They will also include unexpected factors corresponding to what have been called *perturbation* factors — e.g., artefactors and instrument factors (250), which have to do with modes of observation and measurement, and with which the experimenter would rather not be bothered. However, a mature experimental design will insert variables for marking

these more clearly and will take special precautions in rotation for sorting these out. A general scheme for keeping in mind the varieties of possible factors is given in Table 6-6.

Matrix-specific factors can be identified with those due to lack of (or variation in) experimental control in the widest sense. In Table 6-6 we have listed the three main sources that are practically important, namely, (1) errors of observation and measurement extending across several variables during the experiment, (2) errors of recording, scoring, and computation after the experiment, and (3) (a) uncontrolled variations of conditions which bring out a new source of common variation in the subjects themselves, e.g., an uncomfortably high room temperature might bring out a factor of ability to resist discomfort, and (b) sampling variation so great as to bring in persons having dimensions of variation simply not present in previous samples. It is perhaps unlikely that (3) would introduce a new dimension *absolutely* absent in another experiment. However, it would appear to do so in that with small samples and ill-controlled experiments, the effect would raise a factor from an imperceptible to a perceptible (non-trivial) magnitude.

On the right-hand side of Table 6-6 we have perturbing factors, which are "error" in a sense, because they are unwanted factors which thrust themselves among what the experimenter is trying to measure, but which strictly should not be thought of as error. They may, indeed, be real personality or other factors, accidentally interacting with instruments, and, like dirt, are only "matter out of place."

Elsewhere, Cattell and Digman (282) have listed seven influences responsible for perturbation factors — common test scaling procedures; demands on some specific (narrow) ability across all responses; a single stimulus affecting all behavior in the test situation; testing a personality factor in one role only; having different densities of

TABLE 6-6

A TAXONOMY OF POSSIBLE VARIETIES OF COMMON FACTOR SOURCES
(In a Simple Structure or Confactor Resolution)

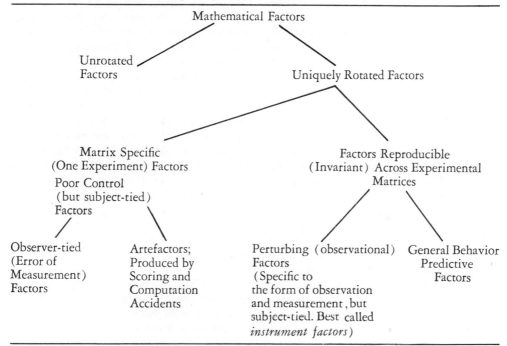

variables in different media of observation; having *areas* of observation peculiar to a set of behaviors; and influences upon perception of factors x, y, z, etc., which are functions of other factors in the rater and self-rater. Thus, instrument factors are a major class of perturbing factors which spring from variance in the data box associated with observers and their instruments. The line between a personality factor and an instrument factor is therefore often one of purpose only—many instrument factors are often (narrow) personality factors "out of place." Nevertheless, these very narrow, instrument-bound factors, or factors projected by an observer through a particular medium of observation, need particularly to be watched because of the systematic contamination they often add to estimates of theoretically more important factors or practically important source traits. Although Table 6-6 presents a categorical treatment of these contaminators, there is a sense in which they form a continuum from a highly specific error factor to a substantial common instrument factor.

A partial approach to perturbation factors—and to instrument factors in particular—is that represented by the phrase "multi-method—multi-trait" proposed by Campbell and Fiske (183). Its weakness, like that of Guttman's "facet analysis," is that it assumes that the experimenter can recognize by inspection what is a method factor subset ("facet"), whereas actually the real instrument factor may not simply correspond with a type-of-test subset, or appear simply as a correlation cluster (surface trait). This semantically attractive "multi-t multi-m" phrase is actually a semantic trap. For trait boundaries cannot be decided by inspection of the superficial nature of variables. For example, more than one instrument factor may actually be at work, as simple-structure resolution will show, in what the experimenter, if naive, has designated his subset of "method" (instrument) markers. Furthermore, instances are not infrequent (282) where the instrument factor does *not* really sit on the instrument variables only but goes beyond and straddles other subsets. Simple structure is the only criterion of what we really have in the region of instrument factors. The term "method" is also objectionable as inviting confusion with broader experimental and analytical methods, as defined in Chapter 3. Multi-trait—multi-device (or instrument) would be more clear, but the formulation *trait and instrument-factor analysis* is best, as indicating the above determination of boundaries independently of the experimenter's subjective concepts.

Finally, in glancing at the main modifications and special conditions of use of the basic factor model, one should consider the modifications of sampling and other inferences occasioned by using the method across different sets in the data box. These have been sufficiently indicated in Chapter 3. Incidentally it is well to distinguish terminologically between *n-way* factor analysis (at present exemplified in Tucker's 3-way [or 3-mode] analysis, page 120) and *n-set* analysis, in which one carries the correlation over a grid of 2 to 9 sets of relatives (assuming a 10-way data box). The expected results and properties of *n-set* factor analysis have been discussed briefly in Chapter 3. In this connection one must consider also the relations to be expected between factoring of facets and faces. As illustrated by the motivation field (Chapter 20 and Cattell, 261), valuable additional information about the nature of factors can be gained by watching the changing variance of certain factors as we factor first a facet, which includes the full variance associated with the off-set ids, and then a face, in which, by collapsing many off-set ids, we have greatly reduced the off-set variance contribution.

Finally one must consider the gains possible from factoring not the id values themselves but values which are the differences, or other relations among ids. One of the possible developments here is well illustrated by Rummel's factor-analytic studies in political science, in which he factors, instead of traits (relatives) over nations (referees), the *relations* between nations over all possible pairs (referees). This (sometimes called) *dyadic* analysis is a special case of taking single relations instead of attributes which are inferred from many relations. For example, a dyadic approach might, instead of scoring each nation for bellicosity, score it for frequency of war in a hundred years with each of eighty other nations. There are thus obviously differences of level of abstraction at which data can be fed into a factor analysis. If space permitted we might consider the interpretation of factors in terms of entries from different levels of a Spearman hierarchy of relations (*not* the factor order hierarchy). Or, starting with variables of any given relational abstraction, one could seek a systematic epistemology dealing with relations between meaning at various factor strata and various relational levels.

10. STRATEGIES IN THE PRACTICAL USE OF FACTOR ANALYSIS

Some miscellaneous but nonetheless important matters remain to be discussed. They can perhaps best be coordinated in a single theme by considering them alternative practical techniques deriving from the main accepted model above. They also concern, however, expressing the experimental design for any technique; the methods of creating and checking hypotheses; and the arts of coordinating the computer with factor analysis.

The absence of a mathematically "tight" solution to the communality problem causes statisticians constantly to return to the attack with the devotion of a dog to a particularly irritating flea. Our argument from a scientific model, leading to a percentage concept of "non-trivial variance" and a best possible solution by a rotational criterion, fixes (by an act of accepting a known approximation) the number of factors and, thereby, the communalities. With the large numbers of variables in most modern factor analytic experiments minor uncertainties as to the sizes of communalities are the least likely source of error in the final conclusions.

Nevertheless two approaches offering a more definitive solution to communality and related problems—in an elegant if not always practically acceptable theoretical framework—deserve brief exploration. The first—image analysis—is due to Guttman (651) and has been set out very clearly by Kaiser (839). An exact factor space can be fixed by taking as communality the squared multiple correlation of each variable with all others. We have rejected this in our general treatment because it is the lowest bound, not the most likely value. But as the number of variables increases, if combined with a principle of sampling from a universe of variables (as proposed in the personality sphere concept), this bound asymptotally approaches what may be considered the true communality value. The "image" of a variable is its projection on the space of the remaining $(n-1)$ variables and the principles of image analysis (see 651, 839), factoring the G matrix of image covariances, therefore provides a basis for an exact factor analysis (as Guttman has shown) in the limiting case ("total image") where $n \to \infty$.

In this connection Kaiser points out a very illuminating convergence brought about by Harris (691) in relation to Rao's canonical factor analysis (1179) and Lawley's maximum-likelihood solution (903). Further, his work with Hanka on 64 empirical matrices using what he calls the Guttman-Rao-Harris rule, shows the k (number of factors) value to be typically $n/2$, which we have adopted as the limit in our routine proposal (with the scree test) above. The relation of the ordinary factor extraction matrix, V_o, to the image analysis factor matrix, V_g, becomes simply,

$$(33)\quad V_g = V_o D$$

where D is the diagonal matrix, $I - D^{-1}{}_L$, D_L being the diagonal matrix of eigenvalues from R (Equation 1 above). (Note the formal similarity to equations [19] and [26] above.) The factors in V_g are invariant under changes in the original metric.

A second development relevant to increased precision in factor extraction is Kaiser and Caffrey's (840) alpha factor analysis hinging on the application of the alpha coefficient of homogeneity as a test of number of factors, which we have discussed above. Having stopped the extraction at the point indicated one calculates, from $V_o V'_o$, a new $R_{v.o}$ matrix, and factors this once again, again applying the alpha homogeneity test to decide on the number of factors to retain, and so on iteratively to a stable number of factors and converged communalities. According to our arguments above this should give a conservative rather than a most likely estimate, because rotation commonly "evens up" factor variance, so that the homogeneity of the last extracted factor is likely to be deficient when that of the last rotated factor is not. However, the iterative principle could probably be advantageously applied to a number of other tests of when to stop factoring.

We next approach certain principles of design and interpretation of factor analytic experiment which are concerned with stages beyond factor extraction and which have high generality of reference across the 45 facets of data box analysis (and their transposes, succeeding the limited $R-Q$, $P-O$, $S-T$ transposes of the covariation chart) discussed in Chapter 3. Three problems of highest generality to all kinds of facet and face factor analysis design concern: (1) Recognizing the effect of introducing time sequences among the observations, (2) Recognizing the relations of the factor analytic solutions from transposed techniques, and (3) Planning and recognizing the effects of selection of variables. The first was examined initially in Chapter 2 on experimental design (and again in Chapter 3), where it was pointed out that introduction of known time sequence is essential for experiments designed to reveal causality. On this issue we shall merely point out the importance of asking whether variables, people, and other sets have been measured in any particular order, including time order, of the ids. Also we must point to the special problems in P technique and differential R technique associated with causal inference. Because of its complexity and great importance for factor analysis, however, further study of this realm will be pursued separately in Chapters 11 and 12.

The second issue — the relations between factor resolutions obtained from transpose techniques — has been the subject of a considerable literature (Burt, 158; Cattell, 230; Overall, 1131; Ross, 1226; Stephenson, 1346; Tucker, 1462; and others) and has been already commented upon at appropriate points above. However, since Burt's 1937 proof (158), it has been commonly recognized, as Horst points out above (page 143) (but perhaps with insufficient warning of the restrictions) that "one gets the same results with a latent roots and vectors solution irrespective of orientation." What is often overlooked, however, is that this simple conclusion must be watched warily, for it is hedged about with special conditions, rarely met in factor analyses, and not necessarily fitting our basic model. Notably it supposes that (1)

we use unit communalities, thus accepting no specific factors and forfeiting our most likely scientific model; (2) we use a double-standardized score matrix; and (3) we use covariance or cross product factor analysis. Consequently, it is certain that the *customary* practical uses of R and Q technique will *not* yield any such simple relation between the transpose solutions. Moreover, as Chapter 5, Section 11, has pointed out, the double-standardized matrix is to some extent an unattainable fiction, for attempts to reach it result in not one double-standardized matrix, but two, depending upon the start in the iterative procedure being made respectively with columns or rows.

It is perhaps helpful first to handle the issues on a common-sense, experimental level, and then in more abstract terms. If one uses correlational rather than covariance analysis, i.e., proceeds as usual, the main consideration is that the R-technique results lack a first (unrotated) factor which is found in Q technique, and the Q technique begins without the first factor obtainable in R technique. And since the ultimate meaningful factors are obtained from the unrotated by rotation, the probability is that the missing variance from these different first factors will spread as two different deficiencies showing over all rotated factors, whence there could be *no simple equivalence of meaningful factors from ordinary* R- *and* Q-*technique results.*

On the other hand, it is possible that the conditions of measurement and selection of variables will be such that as it stands, the first factor from each transpose will already be virtually in a meaningful position. What this missing factor means can be realized most quickly by noting that the correlation of tests (relatives) over people (referees) automatically normatizes (standardizes) test scores, while correlation of people over tests similarly fully ipsatizes, i.e., removes any difference of means and sigmas among people. Q technique, therefore, can recognize no general size factor among people, since all have the same average, etc. Thus the equivalent in Q technique of Spearman's general ability factor in R technique among cognitive tests is lost for Q technique can recognize no difference of behavioral level of the human species on different test situations. If we were using physical measures, R technique, reciprocally, would lose the "species definition" factor. For the first general factor in Q technique is a "human species" similarity, recognizing that men are longer in the leg than the nose, etc. The person most highly loaded on it is he, or probably she, who shows the most perfect typical human form.

The transformation from R to Q technique results can be viewed in several ways: (1) It amounts to shifting the origin of the plots with respect to essentially the same set of points. (2) It is equivalent to the transformation from factoring raw scores to factoring ipsatized scores (approximately) (see Chapter 5, Section 11), since ipsatization also removes a first general factor. (3) It also presents antitheses having some similarity to those from using different correlational indices in the matrix. (The intra-class correlation, r_c and r_p, respect differences of level, where r ignores them, and covariance also behaves differently from correlation as indicated.) (4) They may be regarded as potentially handling the same common factors (with the special conditions indicated) but with different specifics — specifics in persons and tests respectively. No. (1) amounts to saying that the first factor in one gets lost in the other.

There is only one condition under which transposition can occur without any of the above distortions, and that exists, as Ross (1226) has clearly shown, in the limiting, unreduced case (No. 1) of the four steps in "treatment" of the data matrix listed on page 220 above. Thus, if we keep the raw score matrix, i.e., complete with its differences of column and row means and variances, and use cross products instead of r's or covariances, and proceed (principal components) to take out all factors, then the

relational matrix loses no information, and R- and Q-technique results become exactly mutually translatable. Unfortunately, this is at the cost of using an unlikely model and one for which the meaning of factors in which is still insufficiently understood.

In Chapter 9, page 301, it has been pointed out that using r, or even r_p, to get the resemblance of two people requires a weighting correction on the variables unless they are uncorrelated. A statistician may assert that reciprocally, the correlating of two tests requires the assumption of uncorrelated people. But decisions here depend on what information we want to keep in our factors. Incidentally, it seems likely, though it has never been tried, that if we correlated people, weighting tests according to their initial correlation, and then correlated tests, weighting people according to the obtained correlation, iteration would eventually converge on a correlation matrix equivalent to that from a double standardized matrix, as in Burt's proposition (158). (Chapter 5, Section 11 points out that attempts to obtain double standardization yield two solutions, not one.) But the first R and the first Q factors would presumably be missing when this matrix is factored.

One needs, to avoid poorly determined specifics, to keep an oblong score matrix (say, at least at 3:1). The decision between R and Q could[12] consequently be tactical, depending on the comparative ease of getting more relatives or more referees. Except under the rare conditions where R and Q will give the same factors, there is more to it than this. R technique is, in fact, generally then preferable, for loss of the species factor (we know our species) is unimportant, and we do not encounter the questionableness of applying simple structure to people.

Though complex, transpose factoring has the virtue of bringing us face to face with the

---

[12]The reader is reminded that we use the term "Q technique" strictly for a factor analytic technique, using "$\bar{Q}$ technique" for what stops at searching the correlation matrix only for clusters (Chapter 9).

problems of "test space" and "person space," which we shall briefly discuss in virtue of its theoretical interest. We need to recognize that in these alternatives we are taking one and the same score matrix facet and in one case following the convention of placing any two tests as orthogonal axes with persons as points in the test space and, in the other, placing persons as orthogonal axes with the tests as points projected on them in a person space. If now the tests are allowed to assume angles with cosines defined by their intercorrelations, the persons cease (in the case of a significant correlation) to form the usual elliptical scattergram and become evenly distributed in space. From such test vectors we can define (page 141) a common factor space, in which each person has no longer an exact projection on a test because part of it is outside the common space. Nor does he have an exact position in space defined by his factor score (because he has only an "estimated score" thereon. Again we find the person space (Q technique) and the test space (R technique) no longer exactly mutually negotiable, for the test specificity is something outside the common space, just as, in the transpose, the specificity of the person is outside the common space. Person and test space only partly overlap.[13]

In view of the difficulty of transition between transposes it is an unfortunate fact of life that the preferred R-technique approach is sometimes definitely denied to the experimenter. For example, in factoring countries for culture pattern definition (Chapter 26) one can obtain decidedly more variables than countries. If one is to use the recommended excess of referees over relatives[14] one must either switch to Q technique or cut the matrix up into several small vertical oblongs, each with, say, 60 more referees than relatives, and piece the separate R-technique factorings together later by one of the well known devices (229, 237).

Other decisions in the strategy of factor analysis concern the alternatives in research design symbolized as the M, T, R, D, and C alternatives in Chapter 2, i.e., (1) manipulation-vs.-non-interference, (2) simultaneity or time sequence in observations, (3) abstraction or representativeness of variables, (4) selection-vs.-representativeness of sampling, and (5) allowing or not allowing variability in the unmeasured variables.

The two last are essentially the alternatives of factoring a fixed facet, on the one

---

From this he shows that the angular cosines between person and test vectors in the same hyperspace are obtained as the product of their respective projections on the common orthogonal reference frame.

$$(30) \quad \frac{R'}{n \times N} = \frac{V_{ot}}{n \times k} \frac{V'_{op}}{k \times N}$$

where V_{ot} is the test factor matrix and V_{op} the person factor matrix (R is a set of angular cosines).

If now we consider a super matrix:

$$(31) \quad \frac{V_{os}}{p \times k} = \left[\frac{V}{n \times k} : \frac{V}{n \times k} \right]$$

where p = total population of ids = $N + n$. Then:

$$(32) \quad \frac{V_o}{p \times k} \frac{V'_o}{k \times k} = \left[\begin{array}{c|c} \dfrac{R}{n \times n} & \dfrac{R'}{n \times N} \\ \hline \dfrac{R}{N \times n} & \dfrac{Q}{N \times N} \end{array} \right]$$

which Overall considers enough to define the joint test-person configuration.

[14]See note below, page 237, on the number of variables in relation to the number of referees.

---

[13]A number of imaginative attempts have been made, by Cardinet, Ross, Overall and others, to bring person and test space into alignment by adopting a convention to bring persons and tests as oblique vectors into the same space. Although it has been rejected by editors it may stimulate others to see the lines along which Overall's argument proceeds. He begins with an equation (29) for an individual score ($a_{ij} = a_{ij} - \bar{a}_i - \bar{a}_j + \bar{a}$, where a_{ij} is the original score and the $\bar{a}$'s the row, column, and total mean) on orthogonal axes from the double-centered score matrix.

(29) $a_{ij} = b_{i1}b_{j1}\sigma_i\sigma_j\lambda_i^{-1} \ldots + b_{ik}b_{jk}\sigma_i\sigma_j\lambda_k^{-1} + U_{jk}$

when b_i's are the angular cosines (regressions, loadings) between the ith person vector and the k factors, and the b_j's the angular cosines of the jth test vector and the same k factors. The sigmas are those of the jth test over the N persons and the ith person over the n tests respectively. λ^{-1} is the reciprocal of the latent root (the square root of the variance of the n tests accounted for by the given factor, multiplied by $\sqrt{n}$).

hand, or a super matrix or grid on the other (see Chapter 2 above). In general, the argument stands that allowing variance on more sets leads to factors of wider meaning and negotiability though on the opposite side it may be argued that restriction of sources of variance makes a factor more interpretable. If the intelligence factor is measured on persons all in the same motivation state, at the same instant and with the same environment we get a readily recognizable pattern, but if on a set of people at different occasions and different environments we may find some additional loadings on the general ability factor, which nevertheless belong to the concept of intelligence in its widest meaning, e.g., that it is something lower when humidity-temperature is higher.

In regard to manipulation-vs.-non-interference, the pros and cons already discussed (page 22) apply to factor analysis as to other methods. Sometimes interference will itself produce disturbing secondary results, as in surgical interference or social interference. The alternatives are to factor *without* interference and, having found the factors, subject them, when deliberately measured as dependent and independent variables to manipulative experiment, or to introduce manipulations of conditions as balanced influences, correlated into the matrix of variables and to then factor as defined in the *condition-response* design (229). Each has its advantages and conveniences.

Factor analysis has an especial sensitivity to the issues bound up with the next dimension of experimental design, namely, that of a planned abstraction-vs.-planned representativeness of variables. Since its purpose is often to bring initial structure into a new domain, factor analysis often definitely needs to enter with a very deliberate and effective representativeness of variables. Indeed, before Brunswik (152) had called the attention of bivariate experimentalists to representative designs, both Burt (158) and Cattell (213) had enunciated the *representative principle* in multi-

variate experimental design and worked out operational procedures, such as the *personality sphere* (213, 240, 211, 237) to enable representativeness of variables to be planned. The truly representative factor analytic design is still not used as much as it needs to be in many areas of psychological, sociological and medical research. On the other hand, an explicit use of abstraction is also needed, when clearcut, final hypothesis testing is involved and in the use of what have become known as *marker variables* to give a recognizable factor background as one spreads into new areas.

As to the last, the factor analyst who plans skillfully will always carefully choose a minimum of two good marker variables for each common factor relevant to his research. They will be variables that previous research has shown to load highly on the factor being considered though sufficiently different in other respects, and lacking much loading (at least jointly) on any other factor. The expressions "relevant" and "being considered" deserve comment here, for it is a common mistake to assume that only variables in the area of the principal hypothesis and topic or focus of research are relevant. Judging by blatant failures in current research to heed this feature of design, it cannot be too strongly emphasized that factors "under consideration" must include both the *background* and the *focus* or pattern factors.

The background markers have two functions. First, far too many factor analyses—roughly two-thirds of all those published between 1950 and 1960—are practically lost to science because they operate in "private universes." They have no exactly reproduced markers from other prior researches which would show whether some factor now appearing is an old factor in new guise. In short, they have no means, generally, of tying the new construction intelligently into the fabric of existing scientific knowledge.

Insofar as a contribution to the recognition of the meaning of a factor (page 191 above) lies partly in its correlations with other factors and its belonging to certain second-order factors, additional support is given to argument for extending the representation of variables in every factor analysis beyond that of the researcher's immediate interest. These correlations, moreover, tend to be more accurately determined in the context of more variables and more factors. In an ideal "theoretical" sense, this is not true. If, for example, twelve variables yield six factors and an additional twelve variables give a matrix which yields a total of nine factors, then rotating the original six factors for simple structure in the nine space yields exactly the same angles among them — in fact the same transformation matrix — as in the six space. For the six rotated factors are still defined by the original six space and have no extension into the three new orthogonal factor space, i.e., zeros appear in the transformation matrix opposite these new factors. But *in fact,* there is some likelihood that the original six space may not have been completely exhaustive — the last one or two small factors were perhaps lost in error. Consequently, the search for the six hyperplanes in, say, eight space, may result in slightly more precise hyperplanes and slightly better determination of the true correlations among the original six factors.

In the abstractive (hypothesis-directed) design, as contrasted with the representative design, the choice of variables will be continuously guided by what we defined in Chapter 2 as the hypothetico-deductive spiral. A hypothesis about each factor will be formed on the inductive comparisons of the empirically given salient and zero loadings, interfactor correlations, etc., and new stimuli and response measurements will be introduced on the next round. The whole strategy of research in such settings hinges on the repeated distillation of meaning in successive, carefully planned, factor-analytic experiments.

This aspect of the choice of variables

involves the desirability of moving gradually and regularly from mapped to unmapped areas of behavior. The statement that the addition of new variables does not upset the simple structure in existing variables is true in principle and generally in fact. But insofar as extremes of sampling *do* affect invariance of simple structure, more integratable and clearer results are obtained by keeping additions at each step smaller than the number carried over. Where invariance is sought the argument is all in favor of an *ample* sampling in any factor analysis. Consider, for example, the extreme instance where an experimenter attempts to define a factor X in only a two-factor system, with one more factor Y. By placing Y in the hyperplane of X, he has really defined X very poorly indeed. The true reference vector for X could actually be in an infinite number of positions, though all are orthogonal to Y. *The addition of each new factor dimension to the system gives increasing certainty that we are dealing with* X *and not a mixture of* X *with other, unknown factors.*

Thus, the choice of variables in a strategic factor-analytic experiment is guided not only by the need for good abstraction in the interest of deciding among certain definite hypotheses, and the relating of the factor to already known factors, but also by a need for representativeness. This holds even when one is beyond the exploratory period and concentrating on hypothesis testing. It follows that considerations of good design persistently demand a larger number of variables in a factor analysis than do the first thoughts — and sometimes the last casual acts — of too many experimenters. This demand, however, runs into more inherent obstacles than those presented only by the limited fortitude of the experimenter, namely, by the fact that with inexorably limited *subject time,* any increase in number of variables *means a decrease in length and reliability of the individual test.*

To be concrete, one meets the criticism

expressed by superficial research in the personality field that any experimental work must be "sloppy" which uses a majority of tests of no better than an average 0.6 reliability. They overlook the shrewd strategic choice which has been made in deciding to apply, for the reasons given above, no fewer than 120 carefully chosen kinds of personality test. When these have to be applied to 250 to 500 subjects, reaching 15 hours of testing per subject—an amount rarely granted from school time—one has reached the upper limit of reliability attainable and must be content with it. Yet it is far better thus to "block in" all twenty or so of the chief factors in the area, to avoid confusion of factor identity, to "know where one is" by many landmarks and cross-checks, and to permit broad examination of second-order realms, than to cut down the number of tests in the interest of "show case" high reliabilities (but not necessarily large loadings) for a few variables.

This advocacy of the five-minute test and the 0.5-0.7 reliability supposes that one is not interested in applied research, where a factor score must be estimated, but only in basic, investigatory research, in which the number and nature of factors is to be recognized from their total patterns. Low loadings (absence of high clusters) do not, incidentally, prevent the correlations of factors one with another (and therefore the structure of the second order) being accurately determined by hyperplane fits, nor do they, in the balance of gains, reduce accuracy of factor matching. For if the latter is done with the non-parametric approach —the Cattell-Baggaley salient variable "s" index—then mere signs (+ and −) of loadings suffice, and if with what we have called (page 196) the configural alignment method (for which programs by Kaiser, Bianchini, Schoenemann, and the present writer have been developed), then there are advantages in having more variables to obtain the agreement of configurations. In this and other matching, incidentally, there is much to be said for correcting all studies to the same reliability of variables before beginning this matching process by:

$$(34) \quad b_e = \frac{b_o}{\sqrt{r_r}}$$

(where b_e is the estimated corrected loading, b_o is the observed, and r_r the reliability).

In summarizing these considerations on selection of variables, we would remind the reader also of (1) choosing with an appropriate and even density of variables to give factors not scattered over different strata,[15] (2) choosing crucially to permit recognition and separation of instrument and perturbation factors (see especially motivation device factors in Chapter 20), and (3) wherever possible, using variables most likely to have a linear relation to the factor (at least for *marking* it), over a good range of variation.

In factor analysis, strategic errors are made more frequently in the selection of tests than in the selection of persons, but some comment must also be made here on the latter. The fundamental theorem in this area was stated by Thurstone (1420) to the effect that choices of person sample which produce selection along one variable (and its associated variables, i.e., along one dimension) do not change the factor pat-

---

[15] The concept of "density of variables" in an area cannot be adequately covered here (see 240, p. 735). However, unless some concept of natural density is used, the investigator can inflate specific factors (in a psychological sense) into common factors, and reduce common factors to specifics. Psychology has indeed the peculiarity among the sciences that the researcher may deform the universe according to his subjective choice of variables. He can work in a corner of a corner and still multiply variables enough to believe he is dealing with a universe. Whole branches of psychology might be invented and artificially maintained in this way if we had no sense of perspective or concept of natural density. The factors in which most scientists are likely to be interested, and which they will finally call common or general factors, are, however, those with predictive power across everyday life behavior.

tern (nor, therefore, the simple structure) but only the relative contributions of the various factors, i.e., selection is really on factors not just variables. Empirical findings, as the present writer can witness, support this, at any rate up to extreme limits, one of which is when selection on one factor is so strong that it virtually disappears.

On this basis it may be advantageous, when one's interest is some particular factor, to choose persons varying markedly upon it. On the other hand, obtaining large variance sometimes means mixing people of different types, and here a different problem arises from that handled above by ordinary sampling theory. Where we mix several types, as Chapter 9 brings out, the nature of the correlations in the between-group and within-group variances may differ considerably. The dimensions among types may be different from those within types and those within one type from those within another. It is not unusual when a person has two types, e.g., delinquents and neurotics, to do an analysis of covariance within each and make a weighted addition of the two to get a single covariance matrix which is then factored. This gets rid of disturbances from between-group variance, but not of any due to the structure in neurotics and delinquents being possibly different. It is true that one may say, "I am interested only in the generic dimensions — those generalizable across several types." But, even so, except when it is imperative to score the different types exactly on the same factor, it is likely to give a clearer solution if we do not blur by superimposition of patterns, but obtain each separately and then cross-identify factors. A gross average may ignore differences of hyperplane and angle, for example. For the rest, the effect of person (or occasion) selection follows the usual statistical formulae for the effect of selection on size of r's, etc.

A special problem in the person-sampling area concerns what to do about people for whom scores for some variables are missing. One thing is certain — that if correlations are inserted in this same R matrix from different N's, the sampling error differences are in danger of producing non-Gramian matrices, and in fact quite often render factor analysis impossible. Data must go into the score matrix itself, either as non-committal mean scores, or, better, as estimates by multiple regression from the other variables on beta weights from the subgroup which is complete. (See Jasser on regression estimates of missing data.)

Finally, in the strategy of factor analysis, we need to comment more definitively on hypothesis testing. As pointed out in Chapter 2, the fact that factor analysis has exceptional powers among available methods in exploratory *hypothesis creation* must not blind us to the fact that it is also an exceptionally comprehensive and sensitive method for *hypothesis testing*. The practice of so using it has developed at two levels: (1) At the correlation matrix level in hypothesizing that certain clusters or *mosaics* (see section 8 above) will appear there. Guttman's simplex, etc., mosaics are the most widely publicized of these, and Spearman's hierarchical structure of the correlation matrix — the test for his "g" hypotheses was the original prototype. (2) At the factor matrix level. In the latter the approach most frequently used now is to write out a factor pattern expressing with the greatest possible accuracy the nature of the factors required by the hypothesis and then to apply the Procrustes formula and program (page 142) to one's experimental matrix to see how closely it will reproduce the hypothetical structure. As the present writer was careful to point out in first publishing the Procrustes program (800), there is grave danger of its abuse (because, as its name indicates, it can go far to make any body of data fit any hypothetical bed), and it should not be used without (a) requiring the hypothesis to state not only the patterns but also the number of factors, and the *expected correlations among them,* for without some restriction on the latter particularly, Procrustes can go far to stretch data to fit, and (b) requiring a statistical test, in terms of the standard errors of loadings, to express the goodness of fit achieved. A statement of correlations, in (a), can alternatively be achieved by requiring the experimenter to state the second stratum pattern.

In general the testing of hypotheses by mosaics at the R-matrix level seems to the present writer too crude. (It does not even require that the simple structure condition precede the attempt to match.) Several interesting instances of hypotheses listing at the factor matrix level have been published by Bechtoldt (81, 82, 83), and such approaches have been used extensively in the survey of conclusions on personality structure by Hundleby, Pawlik, and Cattell (796). The testing by the Procrustes method may be given the extra condition of meeting simple structure, and the writing in of this should be mandatory in most studies with good choices of variables.

11. QUESTIONS OF STATISTICAL SIGNIFICANCE AND USE OF COMPUTER PROCEDURES

Considered only in regard to its properties as a statistical analysis method, factor analysis is fairly high on the E dimension (Chapter 2, Table 2-4), i.e., the "measurement property assumptions," and very high on B, "built-in complexity of model"; high on S; and high on I, "information utilization." The advantage of high capacity to structure data bestowed by B has, however, until recently been offset by a comparatively poor development of significance-testing formulae. Such formulae naturally concern (1) the evaluation of departure from chaos, i.e., of significant departure from "no relation at all," e.g., no factor, no loading, and (2) evaluating the relative acceptability of two alternative structured interpretations (hypotheses — patterns).

In the course of handling other issues, we have had occasion to refer to testing

significance in regard to matters such as the number of factors, the significance of a factor and a loading, the significance of correlations among factors, of a communality, of a factor score, and of the agreement between a stated and an obtained factor pattern. Adequate discussion of the rationale of any one of these would require much space, and the reader must be referred to other sources. The Lawley-Rao test for significance of a factor by a chi-square criterion has already been mentioned (906, pp. 24-84). This will allow testing for such a hypothesis as that three factors are present, correlated by such amounts, and with loading patterns as designated (op. cit., p. 98).

Burt (169), Whittle (1540), and others have also contributed alternative evaluations of the significance of a factor. The significance of a loading has encountered more debate. As to the standard error of an unrotated loading, when corrected for attenuation, Saunders (1254) has suggested:

$$(35) \quad \sigma b_{jk} = \frac{(1 - r_{rj}{}^2)\hat{b}_{jk}}{2r_{rj}\sqrt{N}}$$

(where r_{rj} is the test reliability, $\hat{b}_{jk}$ the loading of variable j on factor k, and N the number of people). Henrysson (720) suggests investigating the significance "by studying the sum of the square of the differences between empirical loadings and loadings from a specific hypothesis." Implications for the standard error of a loading exist in Lawley (904, 906) and McNemar (1014); but the most direct and satisfactory proposal is that of Harris (C. W. Harris, Personal Communication), which is consistent with our position on factors as influences in that it treats a factor loading (in oblique setting not the same as the correlation) as a partial correlation. That is to say, the loading is the correlation in the common factor space when the other factors are partialled out. Thus, applying standard multiple regression theory for predicting the observed values for variable

j from the (fixed) factor scores, for factors $f = 1, 2 \ldots k$, we have that

$$\frac{a_{jf}}{\sqrt{\dfrac{(1 - h_j^2)dff}{N - k - 1}}}$$

is distributed as t. Where dff is the diagonal element in the fth row and column of R_f^{-1} and other symbols have usual meanings. We may choose α and determine a critical value of t for $N - k - 1$ degrees of freedom. Call this t_x. Then, using a two-tailed test, any loading such that

$$(36) \quad |a_{jf}| > t_x \sqrt{\frac{(1 - h_j^2)dff}{N - k - 1}}$$

is significantly different from zero.

In practice a difficulty arises in drawing safe inferences because a certain amount of "experimental error" (or "analytical error" if the term may be permitted) exists in every attempt at unique rotational resolution. Depending on the rotation method and the "personal equation" of the rotator, the distribution of error for loadings on rotated factors is decidedly more dispersed. If we could estimate the sampling variance of rotational positions and add it to the above variance we should more closely approach the variance by which to estimate the significance of a rotated loading.

An important significance test in this connection is a test of the significance of an obtained simple structure. At present, Bargmann's test (59) is the only fully worked-out formula. Theoretically it is tolerably sound (except for the arbitrariness of width of hyperplane) but in practice it seems to make severe judgments. At a rough estimate perhaps four-fifths of resolutions claiming simple structure published between, say, 1940 and 1960, would be non-significant by this test! Pawlik and the present writer have suggested a modification, which takes into account the particular variables entering into each hyperplane, but computation time has so far been prohibitive. Granted, however, that one has some significance—say $P < .05$ on the Bargmann test—one can perhaps conclude

that one is in the hyperplane position and then assess the significance of any individual loading from that position.

It is because of this as yet little investigated magnitude of error in rotation that most investigators rightly feel that the only satisfactory proof at present of the reality of a factor is that after it has been obtained *by blind rotation to simple structure in each experiment,* it yields a significant invariance, i.e., significant matches of pattern over repeated studies. Curiously enough, the more recent realm of *personality* factoring (see Chapters 19 and 20) contains more instances of successful replication—across as many as fifteen researches—than the *ability* field. Because of that interaction of factors within each study which we emphasized above, it would be best to apply the Bargmann and other significance tests to *studies as a whole* rather than to individual factors, and to assign significance to factors that continue to be parts of significantly matchable total studies.

While in the context of significance tests, it is appropriate to discuss that aspect of experimental design which concerns the choice of a number, N, and a kind of subject (or of occasion or whatever kind of set constitutes the N referees in a data matrix). The choice of a suitable N is indicated partly by the considerations of factor loading significance just discussed—on which basis one would hesitate to use factor analysis with fewer than 80 to 100 subjects,[16] and partly by the considerations connected with the number of variables.

---

[16]It may be objected that we have implied above, in the discussion on simple structure, that since one is always primarily concerned with *recognizing* the factors and their loadings in the sample, the smallness of a sample should be no deterrent to a factor analysis. It is true that the step of inferring loadings in the population is a distinct and later interest, and that the simple structure is theoretically still as clearly obtainable in a small as in a large sample. *But,* (1) one *is* interested in the population values, when it comes to factor matching and also general interpretation, and (2) the size of *common error factors* becomes substantial and intrusive with fewer than 100 cases, e.g., one can

Regarding the relation of number of referees, N, to number of relatives, n, a useful rule of thumb has grown up which states that the ratio of persons to tests (occasions to tests, and so on) should not be less than about $2\frac{1}{2}$ to 1 (some favor a 2 to 1 lower bound, others go as high as 5 to 1). Admittedly, a ratio of at least 2 to 1 is helpful as a rough guide; but closer examination indicates ways in which exceptions are permissible under pressure of circumstance. Perhaps the two main considerations relevant to "the oblong matrix" are the increasing role of specific factors as one approaches a square matrix, due to vanishing degrees of freedom and the failure to be able reliably to estimate the factors found. (See Kaiser [840] on alpha factor analysis.)

When one gets close to a square score matrix (in fact to $n = N - 2$) the degrees of freedom vanish; one has insufficient information to define the correlations, or, in spatial terms, to place the n axes determinately by the projections of the N individuals. One can do R technique on an oblong matrix with referees much more numerous than relatives, or Q technique when the same relatives are decidedly more numerous than referees; but at the transition point of a square matrix the analysis passes, so to speak, through a sound barrier, where everything is unstable. (Before that the specifics are in tests; after it, in Q technique, they are in people.)

The present writer would suggest as the firmest rationale for determining the limiting relation of N to n for a satisfactory analysis that one consider the ultimate purpose of a factor analysis to be the estimation of factors. If one considers a factor as a criterion to be estimated by variables, the standard error of a multiple R is a function of the *difference* of n and N. It is this $(N-n-1)$ rather than any ratio of n to N

get random variables loading 0.3 and 0.4 comparatively easily, and in practice this upsets simple structure rotation and factor recognition.

which must be kept adequate, e.g., a factoring of 200 variables on 350 people should be reasonably satisfactory. In the case of factoring with nations as referees, where the total population was (Chapter 26) no more than about 70, and one could easily choose 60 variables needed to give structure, the present writer has made refactorings on selections from a 5 to 1 to a 1.1 to 1 ratio without any marked change in the rotated solution, but this may be an unusual domain.

There remains the question of whether the sample should ideally show a normal distribution. Factor analysis makes no assumption of normality, but it is a fact that simple structure is clearer when scores are normal than when rectangularly or unevenly distributed. This, we have argued elsewhere is due to better scaling. In the interests of bringing out certain factors in magnified form, one may, as is done analogously in bivariate studies, as Thurstone advocated, choose to employ a sample of unusually large range on the variables suspected to mark the factor, e.g., a mixed set of clinical cases and normals to clarify neuroticism factors. However, unless a factor is of such escape detection, such departure from a normal distribution and an ordinary range is questionable tactics. This is especially so, as pointed out above, if extending the range brings in essentially different *types* of individuals. For example, a study in the writer's laboratory which mixed students, neurotics, and criminals (in order to bring in class criterion evidence) showed poor and distorted definitions of factors as previously well known. If factors are actually of structure A in the first group and structure B in the second (as, say, with abilities in two widely different age groups), then factoring them together may give a blurred structure, like a composite photograph, which misses the clear and particular dimensionality of each. Such designs increase all the difficulties of subsequent matching, in ways mentioned above. Factoring across several subspecies at once, e.g., students, middle-aged general population, and psychotics, may be regarded as dragging in interspecies differences, and curvilinearity; and the between-group factors (genus dimensions) may be very different from the dimensions within species, so that serious distortions of factors can then occur. One best avoids this by factoring separately within each well-defined subspecies, though this provides no direct basis for comparing the levels of the subgroups on the same factors. For this latter, one must either use a more complex design of a series of factorings, or equate factors conceptually.

Granted that the emerging factor patterns are considered in the context of the aforementioned dimensions of experimental design, as chosen in the given experiment, the interpretation of a factor, as pointed out above (page 198) depends on at least half a dozen kinds of evidence — high variables, variables unaffected, size of total variance contribution and its change with sample and technique, correlation with other factors, evidence of factor score changes with manipulative experimental influences. Such being the case, the point to bear in mind from the standpoint of designing factor-analytic experiments is that one is always engaged in an "iterative" plan, in the broadest sense. The emerging meaning at experiment A must suggest new variables — both those which should load the pattern still more highly and those which should be in the hyperplane for experiment B. The outcome of experiment B should distil the meaning still more clearly and again suggest better measurement variables, correlations to other factors to be tested, and manipulative influences to which the factor should respond, in, say, a condition-response experimental design. After this strategically planned succession in factor analysis itself there remain, of course, ancillary experiments of almost any type. Thus, as far as significance testing is concerned, each experiment needs to be designed, by choice of N referees and n relatives, to give maximum and acceptable significance on number of factors, soundness of rotational resolution, etc. Yet at present we still lean most on the cross-experiment, cross-sample verdicts of congruence for our conclusions in factor analytic research.

No overview of the practical desiderata in factor-analytical experimental procedures would be complete today without a brief note on effective use of the computer. Any aloof theorist, psychological or mathematical, who claimed that nothing basic can be altered by a mere mechanical contrivance, would be missing some fundamental experimental and social organizational truths. The computer has done more than alter the ease, speed, and scale of analysis. It has made whole new procedures and designs possible. For example, no instance of iterating to unique communalities existed in the literature prior to the computer. Because of the labor of inverting a matrix of correlations of ten or more reference vectors, no one, as far as this writer can find, had gone to a second-order analysis on ten or more primaries (and how inadequate a study is likely to be on fewer is shown when we recall that even Thurstone at first reached only one general factor and missed others among his primary abilities). The computer's introduction of maximum likelihood methods to real data has been mentioned as bringing a decided reduction in doubts about the number of factors with which to begin the final rotational test. But perhaps the greatest contribution, in scientific values, has been the effect of the computer in advancing factor identification and interpretation. As pointed out above, the identification and interpretation of factors requires, first, adequate *representativeness*, by markers, of the main "continents" of factor knowledge, to aid rotation and to see if we are really in new space. Second, it provides sufficient opportunity for comparing *in the same experiment* the highs and lows, the present and the absent variables *in factors which might otherwise be confused.* (Intelligence, for example, is not the only factor with substantial loadings on certain intelligence subtests.) In this and many other ways, an increase in scale has brought more than bigness.

On the other hand, socially, as so often happens, the abuses of this invention have disfigured its gifts with many nuisances. Attracted by the ease (and indeed the prestige) of computers, many have entered multivariate research who have not really acquired the perspective, the skills, or the scientific techniques and disciplines to use them properly. Push-button factor analyses and slick use of allegedly objective analytical rotations (without examining whether their principles may be fundamentally wrong) have placed our journals in grave danger of a flood of essentially ill-planned and misleading correlational studies. Fortunately, there is an increasing society of highly competent multivariate experimentalists — those to whom this book is dedicated — who are now enabled by the computer to plan, and to execute in a few years, well-articulated and systematic researches formerly beyond the scope of a lifetime.

From the standpoint of graduate teaching and research formulation, the computer has hastened the introduction of that matrix algebra which would in any case have become apt at this point. In the case of matrix algebra, as with factor analysis itself, the psychologist will benefit from a treatment and emphasis in many ways different from, and better adapted than, that of the standard mathematics course; such a treatment has recently been provided by Horst (763). A knowledge of matrix algebra would help in adequately formulating theory in many fields other than that of individual differences, e.g., learning theory (Cattell & Scheier, 325).

The editing (by Vandenberg in *Behavioral Science,* Hallworth in the *British Journal of Mathematical and Statistical Psychology,* and Michael in *Educational and Psychological Measurement*) over the past six years of articles on necessary programs, as well as the organization of programs by Wrigley and others, has provided psychologists with a rich description of programs in factor analysis. Probably the essential programs in the field of this chapter (beyond the correlation and covariance matrices) are:

(1) A principal axes (or centroid) program for not less than 120 variables (a) with unities in the diagonal, (b) iterating from estimated communalities to a fixed number of factors.

(2) An automatic rotation program of an oblique kind to maximum simple structure, e.g., oblimax (1168), oblimin (195), and, especially, maxplane (304).

(3) The rotoplot program (Cattell and Foster, 286) for maximizing the hyperplane count by fine visual adjustments after automatic rotation programs have done their best.

(4) A matrix inverse program capable of inverting both R_r, to get factor correlations, and R_v, to get factor estimates. A factor score estimation program is a "must" nowadays, when all kinds of further experimental and relational studies remain to be done with the factors obtained.

Besides these essential routine programs, which should include, of course, the ordinary matrix multiplication programs, it would be useful to have the Procrustes program for rotating to pre-stated or hypothesis-expressing positions, the orthogonal varimax rotation, an r_p matrix program for finding factor profile similarities (D^2 derivative) among persons, and the taxonome program (Cattell & Coulter, 327) for finding types by systematic cluster search through the pattern similarities. If certain difficulties are solved in the confactor rotation method in the near future, this also would be an essential. Most current tool racks for computer factor analysis instruments especially lack the three or four rotation programs in (2) and (3) above, and many published studies spoil much excellent experimental data by patently falling short of maximum simple structure. A dozen over-all rotoplot rotations is average for a thorough study and 20 is not uncommon. Obviously, correct rotation is vital for final meaning and the meaning can be completely lost at the last step by a slovenly rotation.

If the considerations above may be summarized in a brief cookbook recipe, we would offer the following reminders for design of a factor-analytic experiment:

(1) Inclusion of the necessary two or three markers for each of all known factors that may be relevant.

(2) Use of some 100 or more subjects than there are variables.

(3) Two or more independent tests of the number of factors, e.g., maximum likelihood, the Kaiser unities test, the Sokal test, or the scree test, or fixing the factors for rotation at 95 per cent or 99 per cent of the variance present when all n factors are abstracted. Usually there is reasonably good agreement (e.g., to within $k \pm 1$) among the last two of these.

(4) An iteration of communalities to third decimal place stability on the agreed k factors.

(5) Rotation to simple structure (or, with two studies, the confactor position), which except in some specific hypothesis-testing design *must be carried out blindly,* i.e., without the rotator knowing the meaning of the variables. This can be done by an automatic (preferably non-analytic but topological in principle, as in, e.g., maxplane) program followed by a single plane, e.g., rotoplot, shifts to maximize the hyperplane count. (Here we would emphasize again that among the vast variety of automatic rotation programs available today, there is a fundamental difference between those like varimax, oblimax, verisim, etc., which work analytically, but with a wrong function and those like maxplane, which actually count the variables in the hyperplane. Only the latter can give that really tight fit to hyperplanes necessary for exact

factor description and the determination of factor correlations for higher-order structure.) This rotation should be repeated on solutions from a $(k - 2)$ to $(k + 2)$ factor extraction, to check that over the $(k - 2)$ factors common to the five rotations, the same essential positions are reached, except for the slightly broader hyperplanes in the $(k - 1)$ and $(k - 2)$ factorings.

(6) Application of a test of statistical significance to the simple-structure position reached. Because variables are rarely representatively sampled, and for other reasons connected with the Bargmann significance test stated above, this may tend consistently to be too severe. From empirical data with known factor structure, we would conclude that a Bargmann $P < .05$ or better is to be considered acceptably significant.

(7) Any statement about a hypothesis being supported, or a match being found to previous factors, must be supported by actual indices of goodness of matching, such as the s index for individual factors, or the configurative matching procedure (263) for the total resolution, as discussed above.

12. SUMMARY (AND RATIONALE OF NOTATION)

(1) It is necessary to distinguish between *component* analysis, which resolves all the variance into common factors, and *factor analysis* which, using communalities, recognizes common and specific factors. Although rotation *can* be carried out with either, it is indispensable to, and a more integral part of, the purpose of finding *one unique resolution,* which is proper to the latter only. Component analysis might be called the *closed model,* because it claims to contain all explanatory variance within the closed circle of the given set of variables. The rotated factor-analytic model is an *open model* because it leaves the specifics, as confessions of temporary ignorance, to be explained by common factors yet to be

located through variables not in the given experiment.

(2) The basic equations have been set out in Sections 2, 3 and 4 above. Most central are those relating test scores to factor scores, and relating the correlation matrix to the factor pattern matrix along with the factor intercorrelation matrix. In this complete oblique factor system (of which orthogonal factors are a special case), a whole set of D-V matrices is required to express the relations of variables to dimension, including the factor structure, reference vector structure, factor pattern, factor estimate, etc., matrices.

(3) The notion of unique resolution presupposes an explicit postulate that one seeks in factor analysis the set of underlying determiners or influences. Factor rotation to a unique resolution can be carried out either (a) to discover underlying influences, in which case we depend on the tried principle of blind rotation to *simple structure* or the still developing principle of *confactor rotation,* or (b) to certain a priori pre-specified meanings, notably to test preferred hypotheses, in which case the Procrustes principle is available.

(4) In either case, one is using principles aiming at subsequent invariance of scientific meaning in the factors located. However, invariance has to be confirmed by matching with factors from other experiments or with hypothetical factors. Single factors can be roughly matched by the salient variable similarity index, s, best applied to hyperplane members, or by the coefficient of congruence; but the only satisfactory matching is one that takes into account *all* factors simultaneously, employing the configurative matching procedure, resting essentially on the same formulae as in the interbattery and confactor rotation principles. The principles for interpreting factors are discussed. Ultimately a factor either affects a certain variable or leaves it completely untouched. Consequently, its influence pattern is best expressed by an incidence matrix called the *factor mandate matrix,* in which the simple structure is as in the factor pattern matrix. This, and five other features (size, correlation with other factors, etc.), are the basis for factor identification and interpretation.

(5) Decisions as to the number of factors can be made on a mathematical model (lowest rank), on a statistical limit, or on rotation properties based on a CNTV (Comprehensive Non-trivial Variance) estimate. The statistical decision should not be concerned with sampling error on the real factors — one is prepared to accept the factors as they stand in the sample — but with their size relative to common error factors arising from measurement error. Stopping factoring by statistical considerations always involves throwing away real with error factor variance.

The decision by rotation beginning with the scree test, on the other hand, accepts that there are at least as many common real and error factors as there are variables, though most will be trivially small. It seeks to take out all variance, with a best communality estimate, and by rotation, to separate substantive and measurement error factors. However, owing to the existence of "geometers' hyperplanes," both factor fission and a degeneration of the true simple structure accompany the search for maximum simple structure when as many factors as variables are used. An empirical formula, based on hyperplane widths, and on increase of angles and congruences among factors, exists whereby the point of onset of degenerative solutions can be detected, and correct positions found for the factors of worthwhile size.

(6) It must be obvious from the above that the idea of "accepting those psychological concepts which are common products of different methods of analysis" — component analysis and factor analysis, orthogonal and oblique rotation, R and Q technique, etc., extractions of two factors and of ten, etc., — which one sometimes

hears seriously advocated, is methodologically absurd. If anything should ever survive analysis on these different assumptions, it would be so obvious as to need no experiment and so vague as to be computationally useless. On theoretical grounds, invariance is to be expected only with (a) factor analysis, (b) verdicts from the best tests of number of factors, and (c) unique simple structure or confactor resolution, checked for significance, etc.

(7) If the model of factors as influences is retained, second-order factors must be regarded as influences on primaries. However, if possibilities are freely pursued, one recognizes (a) that a second-order factor may be an emergent, alternatively to a cause, (b) that a number of alternative "mosaics" and factor influence stereotypes exist for causal models, which are natural extensions of those discussed for patterns of primaries on variables. Among these we recognize *one-way strata, two-way strata,* and *reticular* models (hierarchies being rejected as, in general, artefacts). Only the first is simple enough for present general use. Therein we must distinguish between second-strata and second-order factors, the latter being merely the result of immediate operations, but the former a cross-experiment reality.

Formulae are given (Cattell-White) for calculating loadings of higher-strata factors directly on variables, and of truncated, orthogonalized higher-strata factors (Schmid-Leiman) on variables, as well as for score transformations. It is shown that hyperplanes of higher-strata factors counted directly on variables are not clearly evident and that rotation of second-strata factors depends on hyperplanes on the immediately lower stratum. For this and other reasons the attempt to find the small number of higher-strata factors by taking out only a small, inadequate number of factors at the primary level and rotating is misleading.

(8) Modifications and developments of the factor model are to be considered both in terms of mathematically indicated variations and psychologically suggested improvements. They include image and alpha analysis, models with non-linear relations, interactions, multiplicative relations of factors, and especially, the *permissive* and *expending* models. The model also needs to be considered in relation to neighboring models such as latent class analysis, canonical correlation, multiple discriminants, etc. Plasmodes are useful devices for exploring the fit of any model and they show that when the postulates are not well met, the standard factor model generally still locates influences to a first approximation, beyond which special experiment can locate the non-linear, etc. departures. In the general use of factor analysis it is useful to recognize true factors, error factors, artefactors, and perturbing factors, each with distinctive properties and the last including the important class of instrument factors.

(9) Factor analysis is a multivariate method; but otherwise it can be employed with use of either pole of the five remaining dimensions along which basic experimental designs can be varied. An examination is made of the advantages and disadvantages of manipulative-vs.-non-manipulative, time sequential-vs.-simultaneous, variable representative-vs.-variable abstractive, person selective-vs.-normal sample, etc., uses of factor analysis, and certain properties and limits are indicated for each. A glance is also taken at techniques, which, beginning with $R, Q, P,$ etc., now extend to 45 transposes, plus incremental techniques. The relations of factors found from any two transpose techniques is shown to be moderately complicated, except when component covariance analysis is used, when they become identical.

A definite set of conditions necessary for an ordinary, adequate factor-analytic experiment is suggested.

(10) Throughout this chapter a notation has been used which has appealed to many

psychological users of factor analysis, and which departs from the varied notations of mathematicians in the direction of (a) reminding the user, by mnemonic derivation of the symbol from the corresponding words, of the entity of which the symbol is representative, e.g., f for factor, V for variable-dimension matrix, R for correlation matrix, C for covariance matrix; (b) using in some cases, symbols and terms which also keep in mind the *psychological* meaning, e.g., b, for behavioral index (a loading) since this is what a loading represents; (c) adapting symbols to several directions of development of formulae, e.g., preserving similarity of form over first-, second-, and higher-order factor analyses.

CHAPTER 7   Analysis of Variance
in Its
Multivariate Developments*

LYLE V. JONES
University of North Carolina

1. INTRODUCTION
(BY THE EDITOR)

To many psychologists the method covered in the last chapter—factor analysis—and that in the present—analysis of variance—stand at opposite extremes in the researcher's tool kit of statistical analytical methods. The present chapter, however, will show that analysis of variance also has multivariate uses, while Sir Cyril Burt's Chapter 8 will bring them into a common perspective.

Nevertheless, it is undeniable that analysis of variance has functioned largely as the supreme court of appeal in classical, bivariate experimental decisions. Consequently factor analysis has been the queen of the correlational, multivariate designs, and they differ in ways that should be brought clearly into focus if the best is to be

obtained from both. Typically, in analyses of variance there has been a dependent and an independent variable, such as may not or need not be in correlational procedures. However, as Chapters 2 and 3 have shown, this now goes by the board, as an inessential, as far as *causal* dependence and time sequence are concerned. Mathematically, however, we need to retain "dependent" and "independent" for clarity concerning direction of analysis.

In regard to the independent variable, analysis of variance has always been a multivariate method, since several "effects" can be examined with respect to significant relation to one dependent variable. The present development by Professor Lyle Jones elaborates methods for analyzing more than one dependent variable. From being semi-multivariate or *unilaterally* multivariate, it becomes *bilaterally multivariate*. In practice, it is true, the number of independent variables used has seldom exceeded two or three, because the complications of experimental design and computation of higher-order interactions have discouraged investigation. It thus achieves multivariate status in principle,

*This paper reports results from a research program at the Psychometric Laboratory, University of North Carolina, supported by the National Science Foundation, Grant G-5824. I am indebted to R. Darrell Bock for his substantial contributions to the program, including those phases reported here.

but scarcely performs some objectives of multivariate method, such as comprehensively sampling large domains of behavioral manifestation.

The differences that remain deserve clear focus. First, analysis of variance is commonly used to determine whether there is a significant difference, i.e., whether one may "believe" in an observed difference, whereas in, say, factor analysis, one is more concerned to discover the magnitude of an association by estimation. However, it may be said that the significance test is made only to find evidence that estimates may be safely considered.[1] Second, factor analysis is more used in hypothesis-creating activities, and analysis of variance more in hypothesis-testing; though as pointed out in Chapter 2, each is useful for both; for factor analysis may test a hypothesis, and the demonstration of a single difference of means may contribute to forming a hypothesis. Third—and this is most overlooked—when there is more than one independent variable, analysis of variance allows no examination of the relation between them—they are made orthogonal, by "balancing," in the experiment regardless of their typical relation in nature. The method spotlights the relation between what have been called the dependent and independent variables and has no regard for the relations among members of each of these classes—except to eliminate them.[2] On the other hand, it permits recognition of independent variables having interaction effects in affecting the dependent, which correlation misses.

It is not the function of this chapter to guide the student on analysis of variance in general. Many textbooks do an excellent job of this. Professor Jones' contribution is in the analysis of "bilateral" multivariate analysis of variance and its illustration that the gaps between the two approaches can be narrowed by psychological experiments designed for its use. He will show that this development has some of the greater power to suggest hypotheses and interpretations which the perspective given by other multivariate methods typically has, and also some of the dangers inherent in those methods.

2. MULTIVARIATE ANALYSIS OF VARIANCE

Multivariate analysis of variance, like the more familiar univariate analysis of variance, focuses upon differences between groups or between experimental conditions. In this sense, it may be contrasted with correlational methods, which apply to within-group inter-individual relations. In analysis of variance, the matter at issue is that of systematic differences in performance between groups of subjects, with groups defined by the levels of classification of one or more independent variables. For illustration I shall discuss three distinct research studies, each of which was designed for multivariate analysis. Each will serve to illustrate unique advantages of using a multivariate design as contrasted with alternative procedures either of repeated univariate experimentation or of arbitrary consolidation of the several dependent variables into a single measure.

While the form of analysis which I shall discuss does not vary from one example to the next, this feature is not nearly so restrictive as it may seem, owing to the intrinsic generality of the form of analysis utilized. In its most general sense, that form is multivariate analysis of variance. More specifically, we combine with multivariate analysis of variance certain valuable features of discriminant function analysis.

I shall preface discussion of the experimental work with some general discussion

---

[1] Thus, the "contrasts" and the discriminant functions that receive attention in this chapter represent estimates of population effects, which are made and interpreted subsequently to a finding of significant mean vector differences.

[2] Analysis of variance is not free from the assumption of linearity of relation of dependent and independent variables, but only among members of each.

of the method of analysis which is employed. The purpose of the preface shall be to clarify the nature of the problem and to present in some detail the statistical tools appropriate for the solution.

Consider a t-dimensional analysis of variance design, with q dependent variables, i.e., q scores obtained from each subject. Let a be the number of levels or treatment conditions along one dimension, b the number of levels or treatment conditions along the second dimension, etc. Assume that the classifications are completely crossed and that the total number of subjects is the sum of the numbers over all cells of the table. The design is thus a q-variate t-classification factorial design.

Clearly, where $q = 1$, we have a familiar univariate analysis of variance design. When $t = 1$, as well as $q = 1$, we have a univariate one-way analysis of variance. The situation $t = 1, q > 1$, when treated as multi-variate analysis of variance, generates an l-sample discriminant analysis solution, where l is the number of levels of classification. (See, for example, 825.)

The empirical examples to be considered later will involve $t = 2$, $q > 1$, a two-way multivariate analysis of variance. The mean vector of observations for every cell in this two-classification case is displayed in Table 7-1. Each entry in the table represents a $q \times 1$ column vector, the mean of m_{ij} observation vectors, one for each subject.

The intermediate results of a multivariate analysis of variance may be displayed in a summary table such as Table 7-2. For convenience in specifying the entries of Table 7-2, assume an equal number m of observations (subjects) in each cell. It is easily seen that the computation and decomposition of total sums of products, as displayed in Table 7-2, is directly analogous to that of sums of squares in univariate

TABLE 7-1

MEAN VECTORS FOR A TWO-WAY MULTIVARIATE ANALYSIS OF VARIANCE

	1	2		j		b	Row mean
1	$\underline{X}_{11\cdot}$	$\underline{X}_{12\cdot}$	$\cdots$	$\underline{X}_{1j\cdot}$	$\cdots$	$\underline{X}_{1b\cdot}$	$\underline{X}_{1\cdot\cdot}$
2	$\underline{X}_{21\cdot}$	$\underline{X}_{22\cdot}$	$\cdots$	$\underline{X}_{2j\cdot}$	$\cdots$	$\underline{X}_{2b\cdot}$	$\underline{X}_{2\cdot\cdot}$
	$\cdot$	$\cdot$		$\cdot$		$\cdot$	$\cdot$
	$\cdot$	$\cdot$		$\cdot$		$\cdot$	$\cdot$
	$\cdot$	$\cdot$		$\cdot$		$\cdot$	$\cdot$
i	$\underline{X}_{i1\cdot}$	$\underline{X}_{i2\cdot}$	$\cdots$	$\underline{X}_{ij\cdot}$	$\cdots$	$\underline{X}_{ib\cdot}$	$\underline{X}_{i\cdot\cdot}$
	$\cdot$	$\cdot$		$\cdot$		$\cdot$	$\cdot$
	$\cdot$	$\cdot$		$\cdot$		$\cdot$	$\cdot$
	$\cdot$	$\cdot$		$\cdot$		$\cdot$	$\cdot$
a	$\underline{X}_{a1\cdot}$	$\underline{X}_{a2\cdot}$	$\cdots$	$\underline{X}_{aj\cdot}$	$\cdots$	$\underline{X}_{ab\cdot}$	$\underline{X}_{a\cdot\cdot}$
Column Mean	$\underline{X}_{\cdot1\cdot}$	$\underline{X}_{\cdot2\cdot}$	$\cdots$	$\underline{X}_{\cdot j\cdot}$	$\cdots$	$\underline{X}_{\cdot b\cdot}$	$\underline{X}_{\cdots}$

Each cell entry is a mean vector

$$\underline{X}_{ij\cdot} = \sum_{\alpha=1}^{m_{ij}} \underline{X}_{ij\alpha} / m_{ij}.$$

We assume

$$E(\underline{X}_{ij\alpha}) = \underline{\mu} + \underline{\beta}_i + \underline{v}_j + \underline{\gamma}_{ij}.$$

(All underlined symbols represent vectors of order $q \times 1$.)

analysis of variance. Analogous to each $q \times q$ sum-of-products matrix of Table 7-2 is a sum of squares in the univariate case. Carrying the analogy farther, a mean-product matrix is defined for each source of variation, corresponding to a mean square in univariate analysis of variance. All sum-of-products matrices and mean-products matrices are, of course, symmetric.

As a descriptive device the computations of Table 7-2 may be performed in any

hand, are not so easily secured. Further, here, unlike the situation in univariate analysis, we have no evidence that the distribution functions required for multivariate statistical inference are insensitive to these assumptions, that the test statistics are "robust." In fact, failure to meet the assumptions may be very disturbing. This is a question that should be systematically investigated by Monte Carlo methods. Even with high-speed computers, however,

TABLE 7-2

GENERATING MEAN PRODUCT MATRICES FOR TWO-CLASSIFICATION MULTIVARIATE ANALYSIS OF VARIANCE

Source	df	Sum of Products	Mean Product
A	$df_{h_A} = a - 1$	$S_A = bm \sum\limits_{i=1}^{a} \underline{X}_i \ldots \underline{X}'_i \ldots - abm\underline{X} \ldots \underline{X}' \ldots$	$M_A = S_A/(a-1)$
B	$df_{h_B} = b - 1$	$S_B = am \sum\limits_{j=1}^{b} \underline{X}_{.j.} \underline{X}'_{.j.} - abm\underline{X} \ldots \underline{X}' \ldots$	$M_B = S_B/(b-1)$
$A \times B$	$df_{h_{AB}} = (a-1)(b-1)$	$S_{AB} = S_C - S_A - S_B$	$M_{AB} = S_{AB}/(a-1)(b-1)$
Between cells	$ab - 1$	$S_C = m_i \sum\limits_{i=1}^{a} \sum\limits_{j=1}^{b} \underline{X}_{ij.} \underline{X}'_{ij.} - abm\underline{X} \ldots \underline{X}' \ldots$	
Within cells	$df_e = ab(m-1)$	$S_e = S_T - S_C$	$M_e = S_e/ab(m-1)$
Total	$abm - 1$	$S_T = \sum\limits_{i=1}^{a} \sum\limits_{j=1}^{b} \sum\limits_{\alpha=1}^{m} \underline{X}_{ij\alpha}\underline{X}'_{ij\alpha} - abm\underline{X} \ldots \underline{X}' \ldots$	

problem without necessitating any distributional assumptions whatsoever. However, in order to generate results that allow inferences to a specified population, assumptions must be made, analogous to those of univariate analysis of variance. In particular, it is assumed that the within-cell residuals have the multivariate normal distribution with a common covariance matrix, and that observations on different individuals are uncorrelated. The latter condition may be assured by experimental design. Assumptions of normality and homogeneity of covariance, on the other

the study is formidable, since assumptions may be violated in such a great number of ways, some of which may prove critical, others of which may be relatively innocent. In any case, for the present, serious attention must be given the status of the assumptions in order that conclusions from the analysis may be viewed as valid generalizations.

Once the data have been summarized as shown in Table 7-2, it is desirable to test certain hypotheses concerning the interaction and the main effects in the population. It should be noted that this step of hypothesis-testing is not viewed as an end in itself, but only as an intermediate procedure preparatory to an estimation approach outlined below. This is consistent with recent criticisms of traditional uses of psychological statistics (e.g., 616, 1238), criticisms with which I have long been sympathetic (822, 823).

Several competing principles are available for effecting significance tests in multivariate analysis of variance. These include (1) the maximum likelihood criterion, proposed by Wilks (1543), (2) the trace criterion proposed by Hotelling (775) and systematically considered by Pillai (see 1166), and (3) the largest root criterion proposed by Roy (1227).

All three criteria may be considered to apply to the roots of a characteristic equation of the form

$$|M_h - \lambda M_e| = 0$$

where M_e is a $q \times q$ matrix of error mean products and M_h is a matrix of mean products for a classification variable or an interaction. The numbers of non-zero roots of this equation can be shown to equal df_h, the number of degrees of freedom associated with M_h, or q, the number of dependent variates, whichever is smaller. For the characteristic equation to yield a solution, it is necessary that M_e be non-singular, which in turn demands that the number of variates, q, be no larger than df_e, the number of degrees of freedom associated with M_e.

Most treatments of this topic present the characteristic equation to be solved as

$$|S_h - \gamma S_e| = 0,$$

where S_h and S_e are sums-of-products matrices associated with hypothesis and with error. We have found it useful to utilize

$$M_h = \frac{1}{df_h} S_h,$$

and

$$M_e = \frac{1}{df_e} S_e,$$

where df_h and df_e are degrees of freedom for hypothesis and error respectively. This convention serves to scale the elements in the matrix so as to make them comparable with mean squares in univariate analysis of variance, and has the advantage of providing a scaling basis already familiar to most experimenters. It also provides a partial remedy for the problems of scaling in a computer program, presuming that one uses fixed-point arithmetic.

The three possible criterion functions are defined in Table 7-3. Note that when $df_h = 1$, we have only a single root; in this case the largest root, the trace, and the likelihood ratio criteria are essentially equivalent, for, when $df_h = 1$,

$$\Lambda = \frac{1}{1 + \tau} = 1 - \theta.$$

To test hypotheses concerning equal subclass mean vectors, a number of alternative procedures are available. First, note that when $df_h = 1$, an exact test is available.

$$F = \frac{df_e - q + 1}{q} \tau$$

has the F distribution with q and $(df_e - q + 1)$ degrees of freedom. Since, when $df_h = 1$, τ, θ, and Λ are simply interrelated, this test applies equally to each criterion. In the examples to be presented here, whenever $df_h = 1$, this statistic will be used to test the hypothesis of equal subgroup mean vectors.

We might note parenthetically that where $df_h = 1$, the criteria also are equivalent to Hotelling's T^2 (775), for $T^2 = df_e \tau$.

When $df_h > 1$ (and $q > 1$), no longer are the three criteria equivalent. The test procedures which may be employed thus also are distinct.

(1) For the likelihood ratio
    (a) when $df_h = 2$, use the exact test

$$F = \frac{1 - \sqrt{\Lambda}}{\sqrt{\Lambda}} \frac{df_e - q + 1}{q},$$

with $2q$ and $2(df_e - q + 1)$ degrees of freedom;

TABLE 7-3

Outline of Multivariate Test Criteria

The characteristic equation is

$$| M_h - \lambda M_e | = 0,$$

where M_e is a $q \times q$ matrix of error mean products and M_h is a $q \times q$ matrix of "between-subclass" mean products, associated with a main effect or interaction hypothesis.

(1) The likelihood ratio criterion is

$$\Lambda = \prod_{k=1}^{s} \left(1 + \frac{df_h \lambda_k}{df_e} \right)^{-1}.$$

(2) The trace criterion is

$$\tau = \frac{df_h}{df_e} \sum_{k=1}^{s} \lambda_k .$$

(3) The largest root criterion is

$$\theta = \frac{df_h \lambda_1 / df_e}{1 + df_h \lambda_1 / df_e}.$$

When $df_h = 1$, λ_1 is the only root of the characteristic equation. When $df_h = 1$,

$$\tau = \frac{1 - \Lambda}{\Lambda} = \frac{\theta}{1 - \theta} = \frac{T^2}{df_e}.$$

(T^2 is Hotelling's T^2.)

    (b) when $q = 2$ (for any df_h), use

$$F = \frac{1 - \sqrt{\Lambda}}{\sqrt{\Lambda}} \frac{df_e - 1}{df_h}$$

with $2df_h$ and $2(df_e - 1)$ degrees of freedom;

    (c) when $df_h > 2$ and $q > 2$, two approximations are available. The more familiar, due to Bartlett, is

I $$\chi^2 = -\left(df_h + df_e - \frac{df_h + q + 1}{2} \right) \ln \Lambda,$$

with $q(df_h)$ degrees of freedom. Alternatively, an even more accurate approximation is given by

II $$F = \frac{1 - \Lambda^{1/k}}{\Lambda^{1/k}}.$$

$$\frac{k(2df_e + df_h - q - 1) - q(df_h) + 2}{2q(df_h)},$$

where

$$k = \sqrt{(q^2 (df_h)^2 - 4)/(q^2 + (df_h)^2 - 5)}.$$

This F has the F distribution with $q(df_h)$ and

$\frac{1}{2}(k(2df_e + df_h - q - 1) + q(df_h) - 2)$ degrees of freedom. (The latter quantity need not be integral.)

(2) For the trace criterion, when $2 \leq s \leq 4$, .05 and .01 points of the distribution of t have been tabulated by Pillai and Samson (1166) with arguments

$s = $ (the smaller value, df_h or q),

$$l = \frac{|q - df_h| - 1}{2};$$

and $$m = \frac{df_e - q - 1}{2}.$$

(In [1166], l and m are denoted m and n, respectively.)

For $s > 4$ and large m, one may utilize an approximation

$\chi^2 = df\tau,$

approximately distributed as χ^2 with $q(df_h)$ degrees of freedom.

(3) Roy has determined the null distribution of θ, and nomographs for the .05, .025, and .01 points on this distribution have been prepared by Heck (707) for $2 \leq s \leq 5$.

Power functions for these statistics depend upon values of all the population roots. No one criterion is known to be uniformly most powerful for all possible alternatives. When more than one population root is large, i.e., when there are several prominent orthogonal dimensions of between-group differences, the power of the likelihood ratio criterion clearly approaches its maximum, while the power of the largest root criterion approaches its minimum. The power of the trace criterion is independent of the relative distribution of roots.

The likelihood ratio criterion exhibits the considerable advantage of yielding exact tests for a rather large class of problems, whenever either df_h or q is no larger than 2. Further, the approximate tests provided in other instances appear to be excellent approximations, in contrast to those for the trace and for the largest root. Also, the tables available for the latter two criteria are of severely limited applicability. For these practical reasons, the likelihood ratio criterion probably should be preferred in current empirical usage. The two other criteria are not without some virtues, however. The largest root criterion has the prominent advantage of providing simultaneous confidence bounds for several important parameters. Important work along these lines has been begun by Roy (1231). The trace criterion has an advantage in that the test may be performed even without knowledge of the values of the separate roots. This is the case since the sum of the roots $\Sigma\lambda$ is precisely the sum of diagonal elements in the matrix $M_h M_e^{-1}$.

For each example cited here, I shall present all three statistical criteria. One means for learning more of the behavior of each is the comparison among them over a variety of empirical applications.

I have noted that the basic statistics for testing equality of mean vectors are the roots of the characteristic equation

$$| M_h - \lambda M_e | = 0.$$

Associated with each non-zero root is an eigenvector $\underline{a}$, determined by the matrix equation

$$\underline{a}_p (M_h - \lambda_p M_e) = 0.$$

For any hypothesis matrix of mean products, the latent vector $\underline{a}$ represents a species of discriminant function, which may be inspected as an aid in the interpretation of a significant result. The relative size of the elements of $\underline{a}$ characterize the relative contribution of each of the q dependent variates to the significant difference between subgroup mean vectors. Further,

given the weights that are the elements of a, we may compute discriminant scores for each subject. Then a plot of discriminant scores of subjects in the several subgroups portrays the extent and direction of differences reflected by the significant root.

With single-classification designs ($t = 1$) it is generally recognized that the eigenvector $\underline{a}$ specifies a discriminant function. When t exceeds 1, the vectors still are discriminant functions in the sense that they could be used to assign or classify subjects optimally into the subgroups of one dimension of the design when membership in groups of the other dimensions is known, and where there is no interaction among classification dimensions. Of course, the aim of this use of discriminant functions is not to classify subjects but rather to understand the nature of differences that do appear among the pre-established subgroups, to go beyond a mere statement that differences are significant in an attempt to understand their origin and to suggest more refined hypotheses for further empirical investigation.

3. AN EXAMPLE OF SCHOOL GRADE DIFFERENCES FOR SEVERAL MEASURES OF LANGUAGE DEVELOPMENT

Zigler, Jones, and Kafes (1600) have reported a study designed to determine the nature of differences (if any) in basic language skills among boys in first, second, and third grades of elementary school. Forty-four boys served as subjects, students at eight elementary schools in Hampden, Connecticut. Subjects were selected from available male students so that five boys at each grade would represent low, medium, and high levels of anxiety, as measured by the Test Anxiety Scale for Children,[3] except in Grade 1 where only four subjects

---

[3]S. Sarason, K. Davidson, F. Lighthall, R. Waite, and B. Ruebush, *Anxiety in elementary school children: A report of research.* New York: Wiley, 1960.

represent the low anxiety level. Anxiety scale scores of 0 to 3 are "low," of 7 to 9 "medium," and of 16 or greater are "high." A 3×3 factorial design is appropriate for data analysis, having adopted three school grades and three anxiety levels.

Dependent variates are six selected subtest scores of the Language Modalities Test for Aphasia.[4] While designed for assessing language skills of adult aphasia patients, this test was also considered to be appropriate for measuring language skills of young elementary school children. The six subtests chosen for the analysis are defined in Table 7-4, and are seen to measure a variety

TABLE 7-4

DEFINITION OF THE SIX TEST VARIATES, EXAMPLE 1

Variate No.	Items Which Define the Variate
1.	Writing names of pictured objects
2.	Oral reading of printed sentences
3.	Matching printed sentences to pictures
4.	Writing aurally presented words
5.	Oral repetition of aurally presented sentences
6.	Matching aurally presented sentences to printed sentences

of abilities which demand use of visual and auditory stimulus modalities and of speaking, writing, and gestural response modalities; included also are measures of comprehension of language symbols.

Form 1 of the LMTA was individually administered to each subject. Each subtest is represented on Form 1 by six items. As a convenience for data analysis, each correct response was scored 1.5, and each incorrect response was scored -1.5, yielding possible scores on each subtest of -9, -6, -3, 0, 3, 6, and 9.

The analysis of these data was performed on an LGP-30 computer, using a program written by Johnson (810) for the programming system designed by Bock (121). To accommodate the unequal subclass numbers, use was made of the method of unweighted means (Anderson & Bancroft, 32, p. 279). Analysis is carried out directly on the means of the subclasses as given in Table 7-5, but the error mean product is obtained by dividing the within-cell mean product by the harmonic mean of the subclass numbers. (The computer program utilized allows as an option a solution of this form.)

For each main effect and for the interaction, we construct a 6×6 mean-product matrix M_h; a 6×6 error mean-product matrix, M_e, also is obtained. The mean-product matrices are presented in Table 7-6. In Table 7-7 are shown the roots of the three determinantal equations, two roots for each main effect and four for the grade $\times$ anxiety interaction. Also in Table 7-7, the roots are evaluated for statistical significance. All three alternative criteria are in agreement in showing both interaction and anxiety mean differences to be nonsignificant. These are desirable results for allowing clear interpretation of the remaining main effect, that of grade classification, which clearly is significant.[5]

The analysis does not terminate with the tests of significance shown in Table 7-7. Location of a significant effect is important primarily as providing incentive to investigate both the nature of the difference, i.e., the way that grades differ, and the source of the difference in terms of the variates which contribute to it.

To determine the source of the difference, we consider that linear function of

---

[4]J. M. Wepman and L. V. Jones, *The language modalities test for aphasia.* Chicago: Univer. of Chicago, Education-Industry Service of Industrial Relations Center, 1961.

[5]Whenever df_h exceeds unity, there is a possibility that significant discrimination between levels of a classification may remain after adjustment for between-group variance attributable to the largest root. In this study, roots other than the largest are small and obviously nonsignificant. In Section 5 an example is discussed for which two significant dimensions of discrimination are discovered.

LYLE V. JONES

TABLE 7-5

SUBCLASS MEANS, EXAMPLE 1

Grade	Variate	High	Medium	Low	Means
1	1	−6.00	1.80	0.75	−1.29
	2	−4.80	0.60	−3.00	−2.36
	3	−1.20	0.60	−1.50	−0.64
	4	−4.20	−1.20	−2.25	−2.57
	5	6.00	7.80	6.00	6.64
	6	−3.00	2.40	−1.50	−0.64
2	1	2.40	4.80	4.80	4.00
	2	1.80	3.60	3.60	3.00
	3	4.20	6.00	7.80	6.00
	4	−0.60	2.40	3.60	1.80
	5	7.20	7.80	7.80	7.60
	6	0.60	4.20	4.20	3.00
3	1	7.20	7.80	7.80	7.60
	2	4.80	5.40	6.60	5.60
	3	6.60	8.40	6.60	7.20
	4	7.20	6.60	6.60	6.80
	5	6.60	6.00	8.40	7.00
	6	6.00	7.20	6.00	6.40
Means	1	1.20	4.80	4.71	3.54
	2	0.60	3.20	2.79	2.18
	3	3.20	5.00	4.71	4.30
	4	0.80	2.60	3.00	2.11
	5	6.60	7.20	7.50	7.09
	6	1.20	4.60	3.21	3.00

the dependent variates which maximally discriminates, in a least-squares sense, scores of students from the three grades. That function is the discriminant function for which coefficients are provided by the latent vector associated with the significant latent root for the grade effect. The function is given by the coefficients listed in the final row of Table 7-7. Coefficients are here presented in standard-score form, each row discriminant coefficient having been multiplied by the within-group standard deviation of the corresponding variate. As a consequence, coefficients for the variates appear in comparable units, lending themselves to direct interpretation as the relative influence of the dependent measures regardless of their disparate variances. In the context of these six variates, by far the best discriminators of school grade are Variate 3 (matching printed sentences to pictures) and Variate 4 (writing words aurally presented). The mean differences between ages show Variate 3 to distinguish first graders from second and third graders; Variate 4 better separates the third grade from the other two.

The nature of the difference is shown in Diagram 7-1, a frequency distribution showing scores, V, for all subjects in the sample, organized by school grade. The sharpest discrimination is seen to be between grades 1 and 3, with scores for subjects in grade 2 more similar to those in grade 3 than in grade 1.

Considering simultaneously mean differ-

TABLE 7-6

MEAN PRODUCTS, EXAMPLE 1

Between grades:

290.113					
267.925	249.800				
267.875	256.250	271.850			
305.538	278.225	272.525	328.363		
16.225	17.600	22.850	12.725	3.800	
233.550	214.050	212.400	248.700	11.250	189.150

Between anxiety levels:

59.112					
38.725	26.600				
25.750	18.050	12.350			
31.187	19.925	13.100	16.663		
11.725	7.100	4.550	6.425	2.600	
45.900	33.150	22.950	22.950	7.650	43.350

Interaction:

20.337					
9.025	10.400				
−1.100	1.550	7.850			
7.000	4.625	5.375	9.462		
2.275	6.500	−.250	1.325	5.600	
8.025	7.650	5.700	8.700	3.450	9.750

Within cell:

22.398					
8.351	22.094				
5.576	5.497	12.104			
12.619	9.673	2.511	19.121		
.317	2.801	2.325	−.159	6.977	
5.470	10.095	6.871	8.695	2.590	21.195

DIAGRAM 7-1.   Distribution of Discriminant Scores by Grade, Example 1

Score	Grade		
	1	2	3
54-65			1111
42-53		1111	11111
30-41		111	11111
18-29	1	111	
16-17	1	111	1
−5- 5	1111	1	
−17 to − 6	1		
−29 to −18	1		
−41 to −30	111	1	
−53 to −42			
−65 to −54	111		

TABLE 7-7

TESTS OF SIGNIFICANCE, EXAMPLE 1

$q = 6$	Effect		
	Grade	Anxiety Level	Interaction
df_h	2	2	4
df_e	35	35	35
λ_1	33.50	3.93	2.30
λ_2	2.66	.59	.86
λ_3	. . .	. . .	.72
λ_4	. . .	. . .	.18
Likelihood ratio Λ	.2979	.7900	.6527
F	4.16	.62	1.189
df	12/60	12/60	24/127
prob.	$p < .001$	$p > .50$	$p > .50$
Trace τ	2.066	.258	.464
Tabled prob.	$p < .01$	$p > .05$	$p > .05$
Largest root θ	.657	.183	.208
Tabled prob.	$p < .01$	$p > .05$	$p > .05$
Parameters for evaluating τ and θ:			
s	2	2	4
l	1.5	1.5	.5
m	19	19	19

Discriminant function for grades:
$$V = .019x_1 + .145x_2 + .730x_3 + .526x_4 - .119x_5 - .080x_6$$

ences, discriminant function coefficients, and significance tests, several general conclusions may be entertained. The ability to read sentences with comprehension (Variate 3) matures rapidly between grades 1 and 2, and the ability to write simple words to dictation (Variate 4) develops dramatically over the first three school years, particularly from grade 2 to 3. Increases also appear in the abilities for writing names of pictured objects (Variate 1), oral reading of sentences (Variate 2), and matching of aurally presented to printed sentences (Variate 6). But these skills do not increase independently of the more dominant changes in reading comprehension and writing to dictation. (The mutually positive covariances are shown in the within-cell product matrix of Table 7-6). Variate 5, repetition of aurally presented sentences, fails to discriminate be- tween grades, and fails to yield a regular improvement from grades 1 to 3; at grade 1 students are already proficient in this skill. There is no evidence that anxiety level, as measured, is related to performance on the language tasks.

4. AN EXAMPLE OF SPEAKING STYLE DIFFERENCES RELATED TO EDUCATION AND SEX OF SPEAKERS

This second example is selected from a dissertation by Elizabeth Niehl at the University of North Carolina.[6] One aim of this study was to explore possible differences in grammatical usage among groups

[6]E. W. Niehl, Grammatical classes characterizing speech differences. Unpublished Ph.D. dissertation, Univer. of North Carolina, 1966.

of adult English-language speakers who differed in sex or in educational level.

Data had been collected by J. M. Wepman and L. V. Jones by tape recording responses from each of 54 adult speakers to the 20 cards of the Thematic Apperception Test. Recordings were transcribed, and each word spoken was classified into one of a set of 19 mutually exclusive grammatical categories, based upon a system presented by Jones, Goodman, and Wepman.[7] For each speaker there was determined the relative frequency of words produced in each category. These proportions (after arcsine transformation, $X = 2$ arcsine $\sqrt{p}$), for a subset of seven categories, constitute the seven dependent variates in this study. Categories used are defined in Table 7-8.

TABLE 7-8

DEFINITION OF THE SEVEN DEPENDENT VARIATES, EXAMPLE 2

Variate No.	Grammatical Class
1	Personal subject pronouns
2	Personal possessive pronouns
3	Nouns (excluding highly frequent nouns)
4	Prepositions
5	Indefinites (something, everywhere, anyplace, etc.)
6	Quantifying modifiers
7	Conjunctions

A 3×2 factorial design is determined by three levels of education and two sexes. Classification of the sample is displayed in Table 7-9. Subclass means are shown in Table 7-10.

Analysis was performed on mean-product matrices of order 7×7. The correlation matrix which corresponds to M_e, the within-cell mean-product matrix, is reproduced in Table 7-11.

[7]L. V. Jones, M. F. Goodman, and J. M. Wepman, The classification of parts of speech for the characterization of aphasia. *Language and Speech,* 1963, 6, 94-107.

TABLE 7-9

CLASSIFICATION OF SUBJECTS, EXAMPLE 2

Education	Sex		Total
	Male	Female	
Failed to complete high school	8	10	18
Graduated from high school	11	8	19
Two or more years of college	9	8	17
Total	28	26	54

Results of the analysis of variance appear in Table 7-12. Once again all three criteria, the likelihood ratio, the trace, and the largest root, yield the same conclusion. (For the Sex effect, since $df_h = 1$, the three criteria are identical.) While the Education by Sex interaction is nonsignificant, significant differences are found for both main effects. (After removal of effects associated with the larger root for Education, no significant discrimination remains.) The finding of significant main-effect differences allows consideration of the source of the differences in terms of discriminant functions associated with each significant root. Standardized discriminant coefficients for Education and Sex appear as the final two rows of Table 7-12.

The discriminant function for Education shows that differences between educational levels depend largely upon x_2, the proportion of spoken words which are nouns, a variate considered to indicate relatively rich vocabulary usage. We observe from Table 7-10 that mean noun usage increases markedly with increasing education of the speaker. Indefinites, x_5, are represented by a positive discriminant coefficient in V_E, even though mean usage tends to *decrease* at the highest educational level. An explanation resides in the sizeable negative within-group correlation, $-.54$, between use of nouns and indefinites (Table 7-11). Due to this negative relation, the prominent positive weight for nouns implicitly weights

LYLE V. JONES

TABLE 7-10

SUBCLASS MEANS, EXAMPLE 2

Education	Variate	Sex		Mean
		Male	Female	
Failed to complete high school	1	.572	.592	.583
	2	.209	.138	.170
	3	.453	.417	.433
	4	.701	.678	.688
	5	.188	.220	.206
	6	.356	.338	.346
	7	.523	.533	.529
Graduated from high school	1	.489	.563	.520
	2	.212	.147	.185
	3	.535	.489	.516
	4	.727	.694	.713
	5	.193	.237	.212
	6	.359	.312	.339
	7	.494	.520	.505
Two or more years of college	1	.466	.518	.490
	2	.213	.174	.195
	3	.594	.537	.567
	4	.756	.699	.729
	5	.174	.180	.177
	6	.351	.327	.340
	7	.508	.574	.539
Mean	1	.505	.560	.532
	2	.211	.152	.183
	3	.531	.476	.504
	4	.729	.689	.710
	5	.185	.213	.199
	6	.356	.327	.342
	7	.507	.542	.524

TABLE 7-11

WITHIN-CELL CORRELATIONS BETWEEN VARIATES OF EXAMPLE 2

Variate	1	2	3	4	5	6	7
1. Subject pronouns	(.068)*						
2. Possessive pronouns	−.042	(.038)					
3. Nouns	−.619	.257	(.063)				
4. Preposition	−.475	.324	.165	(.054)			
5. Indefinites	.152	−.299	−.541	.112	(.045)		
6. Quantifiers	−.263	−.071	.134	−.050	−.025	(.038)	
7. Conjunctions	.064	−.024	−.039	.035	.036	−.157	(.046)

*Within-cell standard deviations appear as diagonal entries.

TABLE 7-12

TESTS OF SIGNIFICANCE, EXAMPLE 2

	Effect		
	Education	Sex	Education × Sex
$q = 7$			
df_h	2	1	2
df_e	48	48	48
λ_1	23.828	45.283	6.086
λ_2	3.826		1.846
Likelihood ratio Λ	.433	.485	.741
F	3.12	5.66*	.97
df	14/84	7/42	14/84
prob.	$p < .01$	$p < .01$	$p > .50$
Trace τ	1.152	.943	.331
Tabled prob.	$p < .01$		$p > .05$
Largest root θ	.498	.515	.202
Tabled prob.	$p < .01$		$p > .05$
Parameters for evaluating τ and θ:			
s	2	1	2
l	2	2.5	2
m	20	20	20

Discriminant function for Education:
$$V_E = .006x_1 - .025x_2 + 1.149x_3 + .109x_4 + .461x_5 - .297x_6 - .060x_7$$

Discriminant function for Sex:
$$V_S = -.220x_1 + .807x_2 - .067x_3 + .026x_4 - .084x_5 + .386x_6 - .251x_7$$

*Since $df_h = 1$, this test applies equally well to τ and θ.

indefinites negatively, and more negatively than is warranted by the main-effect difference associated with Education. The explicit coefficient for x_5 in V_E serves to correct for this phenomenon.

Univariate F-statistics for each of these seven variates show both nouns and personal subject pronouns to differ over educational level beyond the .005 significance level. Noun usage increases with education, while pronoun usage decreases. The within-group correlation between nouns, x_3, and pronouns, x_1, is $-.62$; this helps to explain why differences between educational groups in pronoun usage can be accounted for completely by noun use. The discriminant coefficient for x_1 is essentially zero.

Multiplication of the 54×7 matrix of

dependent measures by the 7×1 vector of raw discriminant coefficients associated with Education yields a 54×1 vector of discriminant scores. When these scores are organized by educational level of speakers, the result is the frequency distribution of Diagram 7-2. Differences between educational level are striking; the discriminant function is particularly effective for separating speakers who failed to graduate from high school from those at higher educational levels.

The Sex effect, also significant beyond the .01 level, results largely from differences in x_2, possessive pronouns and x_6, quantifying modifiers (which include numerals, whether or not used in modification). For both variates male speakers exceed females, and for both, the discriminant coefficients are positive. Results also suggest that use of personal subject pronouns (x_1) and use of conjunctions (x_7) contribute to discrimination between the sexes, independently of the effects of x_2 and x_6. For personal subject pronouns and conjunctions, discriminant coefficients are negative, and means for female speakers are consistently higher than means for male speakers.

DIAGRAM 7-2. Distribution of Discriminant Scores for Educational Level, Example 2

Score	Education		
	Low	Medium	High
12.3-12.8			1
11.7-12.2			1
11.1-11.6		1	111
10.5-11.0		1	
9.9-10.4		111111	111
9.3- 9.8	1	1111	11111
8.7- 9.2	1111	11111	11
8.1- 8.6	111	11	11
7.5- 8.0	1111		
6.9- 7.4	111		
6.3- 6.8	111		

The univariate F associated with sex of speaker for noun use, x_3, is significant at the .01 level (with male speakers using more nouns than females). However, the discriminant coefficient for x_3 is near-zero, showing that nouns contribute little to differentiation of the sexes, independently of the other variates.

Scores on the discriminant function for sex are shown in Diagram 7-3. The distribution of scores for male speakers is substantially higher than that for females. (Some caution should be exercised in interpretation of this difference between the sexes. It is overestimated in this study, since the 7 grammatical classes had been selected from the set of 19 available classes on the grounds that they displayed large differences between means for men and women. In the absence of this selective influence, discrimination between educational levels

DIAGRAM 7-3. Distribution of Discriminant Scores for Sex, Example 2

Score	Sex	
	Male	Female
5.6-6.0	1	
5.1-5.5		
4.6-5.0	1	
4.1-4.5	111	
3.6-4.0	1111	
3.1-3.5	11	
2.6-3.0	1111111	111
2.1-2.5	111111	1
1.6-2.0	11	1111
1.1-1.5	11	11
.6-1.0		1111111
.1- .5		111111
−.4- 0		111

is appreciably greater than discrimination of sex, based upon relative frequencies of grammatical categories in speech.)

5. AN EXAMPLE OF THE EFFECT OF LEVEL OF AUTHORITARIANISM ON SEMANTIC DIFFERENTIAL RESPONSES

The third and last example is taken from a study by William S. Jones, which was part of his dissertation research at the University of North Carolina (831). Jones was interested in possible relations between an authoritarian-personality dimension and the nature of judgments offered concerning the behavior of others in an interpersonal situation. Sixty subjects were selected from a pool of 250 male students of introductory psychology on the basis of scores obtained on the California F scale. Twenty subjects were selected representing the highest, middle, and lowest 10 per cent of F scores in the initial sample and these three groups of twenty subjects define one classification variable.

Available for presentation to subjects were four sound moving pictures which portray a therapist-client relationship. The films are briefly described in Table 7-13. Each subject viewed one of the films. Immediately following the presentation of a film, subjects were asked to rate the patient portrayed in that film on a specially selected form of semantic differential rating device. From a total of 20 dimensions rated by subjects a subset of six was selected a priori to serve as dependent variates for this study. The six are identified in Table 7-14.

In the experimental design, film and authoritarianism classifications were completely crossed, as displayed in Table 7-15.

In Table 7-16 appear the subgroup means. The mean-products are in Table 7-17, and Table 7-18 summarizes results from the generalized analysis of variance.

It may be seen from Table 7-18 that the interaction mean differences fail to reach significance. Both the χ^2 and F tests on the likelihood ratio yield p-values greater than .50, as does the approximate χ^2 test on the trace criterion. With six variates and six degrees of freedom under the hypothesis, there is no convenient way to test the largest root; however, even if df_h were five rather than six, a θ-value of .375 would be required for significance at the .05 level. The observed θ of .2337, considerably smaller than .375, clearly is non-significant.

Since the interaction effect fails to reach significance, we may turn directly to the main effects. Let us first consider the authoritarian-personality dimension. Whether evaluated by the largest root criterion, the trace criterion, or the maximum likelihood criterion, the differences among mean vectors associated with the authoritarianism dimension appear to be significant, at least at the .01 level.

To interpret the source of this significant effect, we may determine the discriminant function associated with the larger root. It is given in Table 7-18 as

$$V_A = .116X_1 - .066X_2 + .013X_3 + .061X_4 + .058X_5 - .293X_6,$$

where $X_1 \ldots X_6$ represent the six semantic

TABLE 7-13
BRIEF DESCRIPTION OF FILMS, EXAMPLE 3*

Film A

The patient is a young college-educated unmarried woman, about 20 years old, who feels that others object to her masculine mannerisms and homosexuality. She has previously seen two psychiatrists and states that because of this she is "anti-psychiatry" and is now coming in "against her will," that she does not want to give up her homosexuality but only to rid herself of the more obvious mannerisms.

Film B

The patient is a young man in his early twenties who is intelligent, college-educated, verbal, and seemingly well-to-do financially. He had previously been in treatment with a psychiatrist in another city, and feels that he benefited from this contact. The presented problem is one of becoming a "more complete person" rather than any symptomatic complaint and he spends the greater part of the interview describing his relations with women, his need for love and security from them, and his feelings of rejection by them.

Film C

The patient is a 34-year-old married woman with three children, who complains of intense anxiety, conversion symptoms, and phobias. Her strong dependency needs were frustrated first by her mother and later by her husband, whom she sees as both weak and rejecting. She is unable to express or admit openly the hostility she feels and instead has developed a variety of symptoms which have increased in intensity over the past 12 years.

Film D

The patient is a middle-aged man of low socio-economic standing. He complains of anxiety and persisting gastrointestinal pain, apparently psychogenic.

*Films A, B, and C were produced by the University of North Carolina Communication Center according to specification of Dr. Hans Strupp. Each represents an initial psychotherapeutic interview of about 18 minutes duration; roles were enacted by professional actors. Film D, produced by the United States Veterans Administration, depicts an *actual* therapy session of 50 minutes duration.

TABLE 7-14

SEMANTIC DIFFERENTIAL RATING DIMENSIONS USED IN EXAMPLE 3

good	____ : ____ : ____ : ____ : ____ : ____ : ____	bad
friendly	____ : ____ : ____ : ____ : ____ : ____ : ____	hostile
cooperative	____ : ____ : ____ : ____ : ____ : ____ : ____	obstructive
strong	____ : ____ : ____ : ____ : ____ : ____ : ____	weak
active	____ : ____ : ____ : ____ : ____ : ____ : ____	passive
sincere	____ : ____ : ____ : ____ : ____ : ____ : ____	deceitful

TABLE 7-15

CLASSIFICATION OF SUBJECTS, EXAMPLE 3

F-group	Film				
(Authoritarianism)	A	B	C	D	
High	5	5	5	5	20
Medium	5	5	5	5	20
Low	5	5	5	5	20
	15	15	15	15	60

TABLE 7-16

SUBCLASS MEANS, EXAMPLE 3

		Film				Mean
		A	B	C	D	
High F	1	−1.2	1.2	−3.6	−2.4	−1.50
	2	1.8	1.8	1.2	6.6	2.85
	3	4.8	−2.4	0.6	3.0	1.50
	4	2.4	4.2	6.6	5.4	4.65
	5	−2.4	1.2	5.4	0.6	1.20
	6	3.6	0.0	2.4	1.8	1.95
Med F	1	−1.8	−1.8	−2.4	1.2	−1.20
	2	1.8	−4.8	−3.6	5.4	−0.30
	3	3.6	−3.0	−4.8	−0.6	−1.20
	4	−0.6	4.2	7.2	4.2	3.75
	5	−7.2	1.2	4.8	2.4	0.30
	6	−5.4	−3.6	−3.6	−0.6	−3.30
Low F	1	−1.2	−1.8	−4.8	0.0	−1.95
	2	1.8	−5.4	−1.2	7.2	0.60
	3	1.2	−3.0	−3.6	0.6	−1.20
	4	0.0	3.6	6.0	6.6	4.05
	5	−4.2	1.2	6.0	4.2	1.80
	6	−2.4	−2.4	−4.2	−2.4	−2.85
Mean	1	−1.4	−0.8	−3.6	−0.4	−1.55
	2	1.8	−2.8	−1.2	6.4	1.05
	3	3.2	−2.8	−2.6	1.0	−0.30
	4	0.6	4.0	6.6	5.4	4.15
	5	−4.6	1.2	5.4	2.4	1.10
	6	−1.4	−2.0	−1.8	−0.4	−1.40

TABLE 7-17

MEAN PRODUCTS, EXAMPLE 3

	1	2	3	4	5	6
M authoritarianism						
1	2.85					
2	−2.02	52.65				
3	1.35	48.06	48.60			
4	−0.75	14.85	13.50	4.20		
5	−5.55	9.45	2.70	3.00	11.40	
6	0.82	92.47	90.45	25.80	8.40	169.35
M films						
1	30.55					
2	39.95	245.35				
3	24.30	121.90	127.90			
4	−21.15	−4.55	−80.30	100.95		
5	−40.50	−36.90	−142.00	161.90	263.40	
6	7.60	42.80	18.60	1.80	2.40	7.60
M authoritarianism × films						
1	12.25					
2	8.37	20.05				
3	−6.45	−1.70	8.60			
4	1.35	−3.05	−0.80	6.00		
5	5.55	−1.05	−2.50	5.90	12.00	
6	2.72	−8.42	−1.05	2.10	8.10	13.75
M within-cell						
1	12.75					
2	4.01	23.02				
3	0.33	9.15	17.70			
4	3.78	5.85	2.36	11.92		
5	3.30	0.60	0.48	3.93	17.92	
6	4.30	4.23	5.36	5.24	3.52	13.80

differential scales specified in Table 7-14. It is readily seen that discrimination among high, medium, and low authoritarian respondents is primarily due to X_6, ratings on the sincere-deceitful scale. Subjects with high scores on this function tend to view the patients portrayed in the films as more sincere; those with low scores tend to view patients as more deceitful. The discriminant scores are plotted for high, medium, and low authoritarian subjects in Diagram 7-4. Clearly the best discrimination is between the high authoritarian group, with a negative mean score (indicative of "deceit-ful" ratings) and the low authoritarian group with positive means (indicating confidence in the sincerity of the patients). The means among authoritarian groups, Table 7-15, show several sizable differences in addition to that of the sincere-deceitful dimension. The high authoritarian subjects tended to rate subjects not only as more deceitful but also as more hostile, more obstructive, and weaker than did medium and low authoritarian groups. It would seem plausible that the high authoritarian subjects are displaying considerable rejection of the patients, possibly reflecting a

TABLE 7-18
Tests of Significance, Example 3

	Effect		
$p = 6$	Authoritarianism	Film	Interaction
df_h	2	3	6
df_e	48	48	48
λ_1	16.203	27.384	2.440
λ_2	.965	10.064	1.770
λ_3	– – –	2.174	.821
λ_4	– – –	– – –	.330
λ_5	– – –	– – –	.138
λ_6	– – –	– – –	.016
Likelihood ratio	.5739	.1993	.5401
F	2.29	– – –	– – –
df	12/86		
prob.	$.001 < p < .005$		
χ^2 (eq. I, Table 3b)		74.20	29.27
df		18	36
prob.		$p < .001$	$p > .50$
F (eq. II, Table 3b)		5.21	.80
df		18/122	36/192
prob.		$p < .001$	$p > .50$
Trace τ	.7153	2.476	.6806
Tabled prob.	$p < .01$	$p < .01$	not tabled
χ^2	– – –	– – –	32.67
df			36
prob.			$p > .50$
Largest root θ	.4030	.6312	.2337
Tabled prob.	$p < .01$	$p < .01$	not tabled

Discriminant functions
    Authoritarianism
$$V = .116X_1 - .066X_2 + .013X_3 + .061X_4 + .058X_5 - .293X_6$$
    Film
$$V = -.023X_1 - .049X_2 - .096X_3 + .178X_4 + .139X_5 - .056X_6$$

Tests after deletion of largest root

	Effect	
	Authoritarianism	Film
df_h	1	2
df_e	48	48
Likelihood ratio Λ	.9803	.6460
F	.14*	3.65
df	6/43	6/43
prob.	$p > .50$	$.005 < p < .01$
Trace τ	.0201	.5099
Tabled prob.		$p > .05$
Largest root θ	.0197	.2954
Tabled prob.		$.025 < p < .05$

Second discriminant function, film:
$$V = -.001X_1 + .216X_2 - .040X_3 - .022X_4 + .074X_5 - .001X_6$$

*Since $df_h = 1$, this F test applies equally to Λ, τ, and θ.

general intolerance toward those persons unable to adjust readily to the demands of life. In the study their attitude is best indicated by the sincere-deceitful dimension, partly as a consequence of the covariance structure present among the variates.

In this study we have at least two characteristic roots associated with each experimental effect. When, in such a case, the test criteria reflect significant differences among levels of a classification, there arises the possibility of a second significant dimension of discrimination, orthogonal to the first. We would conclude that a second dimension is involved if, after removing effects of the first discriminating dimension, i.e., after removal of the largest root, the test criteria were significant.

Distribution theory has not been fully worked out for the set of eigenroots remaining after removal of the largest. However, a sufficient (although not necessary) condition for concluding that one or more further discriminating dimensions remains is the apparent significance of criteria on the remaining roots when tested by the same procedures utilized for the full set of roots.

In Table 7-18, these tests are illustrated for both authoritarianism and film effects for which one discriminal dimension was shown to be significant. Note that the degrees of freedom for the hypothesis have been reduced by one in each case, since one root now has been removed.

For the authoritarianism effect, there clearly is no evidence for further differences among mean vectors after extraction of the larger discriminant function. The F test applicable to all three criteria when $df_h = 1$ clearly is non-significant. For the film effect, note that results suggest that a second dimension of discrimination is at least marginally significant. Remembering that this test procedure is "conservative" in the sense that it lacks maximal power, the significance of the criterion probably is sufficient to indicate the existence in the population of a second discriminant function.

Returning to the earlier section of Table 7-18, it is seen that differences among the mean rating vectors for the four films clearly are significant, as evaluated by all three criteria. The discriminant function associated with this effect is

$$V_{M1} = -.023X_1 - .049X_2 - .096X_3 + .178X_4 + .139X_5 - .056X_6.$$

The rating dimensions strong-weak (X_4) and active-passive (X_5) best discriminate among mean ratings assigned the four moving pictures. The function associated with roots remaining after deletion of the largest, for the film effect, appears in Table 7-18.

$$V_M = -.001X_1 + .216X_2 - .040X_3 - .022X_4 + .074X_5 - .001X_6,$$

where the friendly-hostile X_2 ratings are most effective for intermovie discrimination.

The two functions can perhaps best be understood by a bivariate plot of discriminant scores such as that presented in Diagram 7-5. The first discriminant function serves to distinguish Film A sharply from Film C with Films B and D falling between. The patient of Film A is a rather domineering homosexual girl with negative first discriminant scores; she tends to be viewed as relatively strong and active, in sharp contrast to the housewife of Film C. Ratings from subjects who viewed the male patients of Films B and D tend to be considerably less extreme with respect to this strong-active vs. weak-passive dimension.

The second discriminant function serves best to distinguish Film D, with consistently positive scores, from the other three films. That discrimination is primarily in terms of the hostility rating is apparent from the high weight of X_2, friendly-hostile, on the second discriminant function; this is consistent with the discrepant mean hostility rating assigned Film D as seen in Table 7-15. While the distribution of scores on this function for raters of Film D overlaps with scores of raters of the other

DIAGRAM 7-4.   Distribution of Discriminant Scores for Authoritarian Groups, Example 3

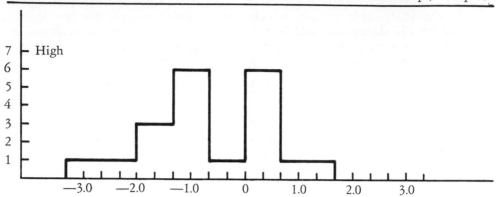

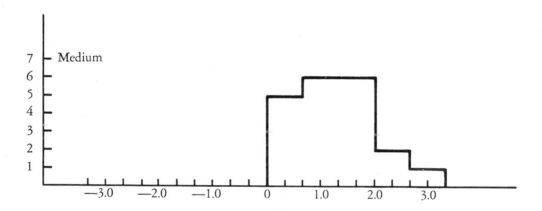

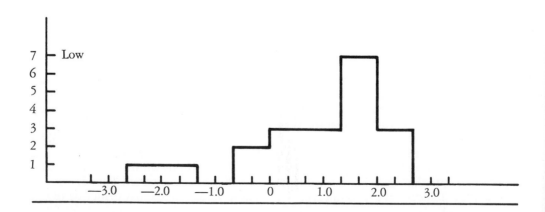

films, nevertheless the plot portrays a definite, possibly an interpretable, differentiation among films.

While in this study the differences among authoritarianism groups may be intrinsically more interesting, differences among films illustrate the method of analysis and interpretation when more than a single dimension of discriminability is discovered to be significant. There is seldom a priori assurance that more than one discriminant function will be interpretable even when more than one appears significant. However, two-way plots with the form of Diagram 7-5 will be helpful in the determination of an interpretation if one is possible.

6. DISCUSSION AND SUMMARY

The three studies I have cited as examples are in no way meant to be prototypical. They do represent studies that have profited

DIAGRAM 7-5. Distribution of Discriminant Scores for Films, Example 3

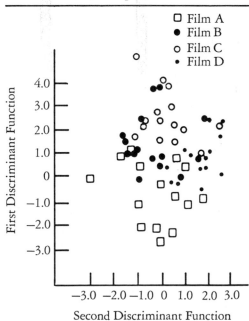

as a direct result of utilizing multivariate statistical analysis.[8]

It would seem that the innovation in such studies is less in the experimental laboratory than it is in the laboratory of data analysis. The limitations that have hampered work along these lines are not those of the experimenter; he is perfectly able to design multivariate studies. The limitations rather have been in the technology of analysis—and happily these limitations most definitely are on the wane. On the one hand, statistical advances continue to be made. For valuable summaries of the statistical framework for multivariate analysis I would mention representative texts of Wilks (1544), Kendall (863, 865), Rao (1178), Roy (1228), Anderson (33), and Williams (1545). In addition, and of at least equal importance, computer technology has provided the tools essential for application of the statistical methods (e.g., 122, 381, 615).

All three examples cited here illustrate use of a fixed-effect analysis of variance model. Were a mixed model to be appropriate, i.e., were levels of a classification to be randomly sampled from a universe to which conclusions pertain, this would influence the choice of an appropriate error mean-product matrix. In direct analogy to univariate designs, for testing a fixed effect M_e would be replaced in the determinantal equation by the mean-product matrix representing interaction between that fixed effect and the random effect. (Green & Tukey, 616, provide a helpful discussion of these issues for analysis of variance designs.)

Within the scope of this paper, it has not proven possible to delve thoroughly into the area of speculative interpretation of results from multivariate analyses of the

[8]Additional evidence regarding the value of multivariate analysis of variance in empirical studies may be found in Bock (117, 120, 123), Fillenbaum and Jones (518), and Jones and Bock (825), as well as in Chapter 28 of this handbook.

class discussed. Enough has been said, however, to suggest that the proposed procedures have interpretive value, and also that they have many of the attendant risks familiar to critics of factor analysis. As is the case in factor analysis, interpretations should be viewed as hypotheses to aid in the design of further experimental research rather than as substantiated principles. While the statistical model provides evidence for the existence of differences and suggests possible explanations thereof, it does not allow evaluation of the degree of credence of such explanations. This function is served only by further empirical study designed so as to manipulate or control the factors that are the terms of the explanations.

A basic feature of discriminant function analysis is the concern with between-group covariance structure rather than within-group structure which is at issue in factor analysis. The analysis which I have illustrated is seen to be a direct extension of analysis of variance, for the simultaneous treatment of q dependent variates. There remain serious unresolved problems pertinent both to theory and application of the procedures discussed. Yet, even at this relatively early stage of the development of these procedures, and granting their limitations, certainly their wider adoption should be urged. The alternatives are repeated, disjointed univariate studies. In comparison, the multivariate approach pays substantially higher dividends in terms of the rate of convergence of knowledge gleaned from experimentation in psychology.

CHAPTER 8

The Appropriate Uses
of Factor Analysis
and Analysis
of Variance

SIR CYRIL BURT
University of London

1. INTRODUCTION
(BY THE EDITOR)

The theme of this chapter has already taken a prominent place in the historical introduction, in the Wundt-Pavlov and Galton-Spearman antithesis, and in Chapter 2 on general principles of experimental design. In the latter the important point was made that whereas statisticians are prone to talk of experimental design as if it were an appendage, or even a simple expression, of the form of statistical analysis to be employed, experiment really has more parameters of planning than those in statistical methods only.

Undoubtedly, as Chapters 2 and 3 have tried to bring out, preoccupation with the choice of statistical analysis method has played a larger role than it should have in dictating the optimal method of data-gathering in many historical instances. Certainly the rigid adherence to the classical, bivariate, analysis of variance design, because of its familiarity and simplicity, has kept many psychologists tied down to fruitless frontal attacks on problems in which at least the initial exploratory advances could have

been made more rapidly by a more resourceful use of multivariate methods. On the other hand, it is true that even with more flexible and imaginative thinking on experimental design one is committed to certain broad features of design as soon as he adopts one or another of the two main analysis methods.

As Chapter 6 on factor analysis, and Chapter 7 on analysis of variance, attempt to show, the modern conception of both of these methods is very different from the narrower earlier conceptions. For example, factor analysis (as Chapter 10 also brings out) is hypothesis-testing as well as hypothesis-generating, and can readily be used in manipulative dependent-independent experimental designs, while analysis of variance can employ more than one dependent variable. Nevertheless, although the hunch for a hypothesis to be tested by factor analysis can, as Sir Cyril Burt points out, come from some significant mean difference indicated on a dependent variable in an analysis of variance design, it is more likely, and a better strategy, for one first to locate certain concepts, measurable by defined weighted composites, by factor analysis, and then to employ them in an analysis of variance design.

The different functions and effective two-handed use of these broadly distinct approaches have been defined in first essentials on pages 140 through 148 above. It is also very important, however, to understand the precise *statistical* relations and translations between these two methods. Writing on Sir Cyril Burt's eightieth birthday, one is perhaps justified in saying that he has unrivaled claims to giving a ripe judgment on this issue. His experience has been of the active type; he has not only known Galton, Pearson, Spearman, and Fisher personally, he has contributed very substantial clarifying and integrating conceptions to the movement in which he and they have been central. It is a commonplace among well-informed multivariate experimentalists that on several occasions important new ideas which have swept the psychological world have very soon been found tucked away in some article footnote by Sir Cyril twenty years before—and often without some of the errors of the modern "rediscovery." This is an argument, perhaps, for reading more carefully in bibliographical depth—or, at least, for sometimes reading a quite old book by a writer of demonstrated genius when one is about to read what the publisher's banner informs us is the very latest. Perusal of the fundamental and well-weighed ideas in this chapter may well suggest such supporting reading.

The algebraic symbols used by the author in this chapter and in his quotations from earlier British work have been adapted to bring them into line with the notation used in the rest of the book.

2. GENERAL CHARACTERISTICS: AIMS OF THE TWO METHODS

In the first half of this chapter I have, so far as possible, avoided technicalities and algebraic formulae and, by taking a typical but exceedingly simple numerical example, have sought to make the arguments intuitively obvious to the general reader. In the second, which is addressed rather to the research worker and the specialist, I have endeavored to give formal proofs for the conclusions reached.

At first sight it might seem that almost any set of data which could be subjected to an analysis of variance could also be studied by factorial techniques, and that almost any problem which could be answered by factorial techniques could be solved just as well by an analysis of variance. Indeed, in the past the choice of procedure often depended not on the nature of the issues raised or the material available, but on the personal habits and preferences of the investigator. Statistical psychologists who had been trained in the correlational methods developed by Karl Pearson and his followers nearly always preferred some form of factor analysis; those brought up on the techniques introduced by Fisher quite as resolutely chose an analysis of variance. Often the more ardent champions of either procedure maintained that the solutions reached by the two procedures would be different, and that one solution would be right and the other wrong.

Further experience, however, has shown that, save in somewhat exceptional cases, these various assumptions are not borne out in practice. The particular issues—or the particular aspects of the general issue— with which the two techniques are primarily concerned are by no means the same. They answer different questions, and each is suited to its own special type of problem and its own special brand of data.

3. GENERAL CHARACTERISTICS: FACTOR ANALYSIS

Factor analysis was originally concerned with the classification of a group or population of persons, or with the determining of the best classificatory scheme. Karl Pearson

(1145), who developed in 1901 the "method of principal axes" and so set the whole movement going, was interested in classifying criminals according to their bodily measurements. Most of the factorial work carried out by the earlier psychologists dealt with the classification of school children according to their mental abilities. To discover the most suitable classificatory scheme for persons is tantamount to discovering the most suitable classificatory scheme for traits. And the researches of Spearman and his followers treated the problem as essentially an analysis of mental qualities, particularly those which could be measured by cognitive tests.

Thus it appears that the primary aim of factor analysis is exploratory. It seeks to *discover* principles of classification; it is these that constitute what have come to be called, somewhat inappropriately, "factors." Indeed, many research students have rather naïvely supposed that factor analysis is, as it were, a self-guided, self-regulating technique for making such discoveries: take any pile of individual measurements, no matter for what purpose they were collected, correlate them and factorize the correlations, and (they assume) you will automatically discover the essential components.

But few successful efforts at exploration have started from a position of utter ignorance. If you are trying to discover something, you must at least know in what directions to look. Before you can formulate a problem with scientific precision, you must have some antecedent notions, however vague and tentative, about the most likely answers. These notions will form the *hypotheses* you desire to test; and your experimental inquiry must be planned ad hoc, with those specific hypotheses in view. The statistical analysis will then take the form of a verification or refutation of one or more of the hypotheses proposed. If the procedure is a factorial analysis, it will very probably modify the nature of the hypotheses which it tends to confirm, and often, in addition to the factors which have

been envisaged, it may reveal one or more factors hitherto unsuspected.

4. GENERAL CHARACTERISTICS: ANALYSIS OF VARIANCE

In an analysis of variance there is no thought of *discovering* new schemes of classification. The classification is already given as part of the data. We have, let us say (if I may take one of Fisher's early studies), figures for the yield of half-a-dozen different varieties of barley—Manchuria, Peatland, Velvet, and the like. The primary object of the analysis is simply to determine whether the difference between the mean yields for each class or variety is statistically significant or not. However, the figures for the yields, as they are given to us, may also very possibly be cross-classified according to the places in which the crops were grown and according to the year in which they were harvested. In all there might thus be three main sources of variance, or "factors"; and their effects might either be independent of each other or display a certain amount of "interaction," i.e., correlation. And the statistical significance of each of these different types of influence would be formally tested.

5. GENERAL CHARACTERISTICS: COMPARISON OF THE TWO METHODS

The relation between the two alternative modes of approach may be most readily understood if we think first of a single dichotomous classification in terms of discontinuous "attributes," e.g., sex. We might, for example, inquire whether girls are better at tests of reading than boys. Here every investigator would compare the difference between the two means (i.e., the "between-class" variance) with the standard error of the means (based on the "within-class" variance). Early investigators adopted much the same procedure to determine the influence of continuous "variables," e.g., intelligence. They selected a group of exceptionally bright and a second group of exceptionally dull children, applied the test of reading (or whatever it was) to both, and then compared the two averages. Such a procedure shows whether the group-difference is statistically valid (i.e., not attributable to sampling error); but it does not show the amount of influence exercised by the presumable cause or "source."

Accordingly, after Galton had introduced the notion of "correlation," it became more usual to calculate the correlation coefficient, which was taken to measure the strength of the alleged influence, and compare the value obtained with its "probable" or "standard" error. This became almost the invariable practice in psychology when dealing with continuous variables, like intelligence, but less common in the case of discontinuous attributes — though both Pearson and Yule devised modified coefficients (or "correlation," "association," "contingency," or the like) to deal with special types of cases.

Now it should be noted that in deducing his formula for the coefficient of correlation, Galton (573) in 1886 proceeds, not by deriving the product-moments, but by what is virtually an analysis of variance. Thus, in calculating "fraternal regression," which in the case of adult brothers is also the "fraternal correlation," he reaches the expression $c^2/(c^2 + b^2)$ — a fraction which in modern notation would be written $\sigma^2_g/(\sigma^2_g + \sigma^2_s)$, where $c^2 (=\sigma^2_g)$ in effect denotes the variance attributable to the common or "general" factor and $c^2 + b^2 = \sigma^2_g + \sigma^2_s$ denotes the total variance. Thus we can regard the formula so reached either as measure of correlation or as a ratio of the variance of the common factor to the sum of the two variances into which the total variance has thus been subdivided.

Fisher himself, in introducing the whole subject, actually starts with "the intraclass correlation as an example of analysis of variance" (519, sec. 40), and discusses it with reference to the correlation between n pairs of brothers. "The interpretation of inequality of variance in terms of a correlation," he says, "may be made clear as follows. ... Let a quantity be made up of two parts, normally and independently distributed; let the variance of the first part be A and that of the second part B ...." Then the total variance will be made up of these two components — namely, A (the variance of what has been called above the "common factor") and B (the remainder); and "in the infinite population from which the sample values are drawn, the correlation between pairs of members of the same family will be $\rho = A/(A+B)$." Thus "the intraclass correlation will be merely the fraction of the total variance due to that cause which observations in the same family have *in common*." Here, it will be noted, the expression reached by Fisher is virtually identical with Galton's.

The familiar applications both of analysis of variance and of analysis into factors are essentially the result of extending the foregoing principles from bivariate problems to multivariate problems. With the former method, instead of comparing the means for *two* groups, we apply the same procedure to compare the means for a *series* of groups. Thus, after asking whether girls differ from boys in their average reading ability, we might go on to ask whether children from the different social classes — higher and lower professional, clerical, skilled, semi-skilled, and unskilled — differ in average reading ability; and instead of answering piecemeal by testing the significance of the *differences* between all possible pairs, we could answer it more generally by testing the significance of the *variance* of the means of the several groups. Or again, as in one of the earliest psychological researches in which Fisher's procedure was systematically applied, we may want to know whether matched groups of children, taught by phonic, visual, kinaesthetic, and alphabetic methods respectively, differ in their mean performances at suitable tests of reading (cf. Burt & Lewis, 176): once again we can test the variance "between groups."

Similarly with factor analysis: instead of correlating the heights of brothers only, we might include in our data the heights of sisters, male and female cousins, nephews and nieces, and so on, and then inquire whether there is evidence for a "general" factor influencing all members belonging to the same stock, and possibly group factors affecting in different fashions the female members and the male.

So far as analysis of variance is concerned, the advantages of this extension are clear. (1) It is more economical: instead of testing six or more differences in succession, we carry out only a single test of statistical significance. (2) It can be far more precise: with a suitably planned and randomized arrangement we can at once refine and reduce our estimates of error. (3) It can be more comprehensive: by allowing known subsidiary factors to vary (e.g., choosing children from different schools and studying the variance for the classification by schools), we can increase the breadth of our induction. (4) The conditions are more natural: to try eliminating or controlling these subsidiary factors by experimental means would inevitably entail artificial restrictions. (5) Above all, by allowing several factors to vary concurrently we can study their mutual interactions, and their joint effects may turn out to be quite different from the sum of the effects taken in isolation.

We could of course proceed by an entirely different mode of attack. In comparing the methods of teaching children to read, an enthusiastic factorist would doubtless prefer to start with a large and representative sample of the school population, calculate the relevant correlations, factorize the correlations, and then inquire whether the factors obtained confirmed our hypothetical assumptions. But in this type of case such a procedure would be extremely circuitous, and in all probability fail to answer the specific questions we had in mind.

Evidently then, an analysis of variance forms the more effective procedure where we are dealing with factors that are already known and identifiable — different sexes, different schools, different teaching methods, and the like. Where we are concerned with sources of variation that are as yet unidentified, or at least known or suspected only in the vaguest way, a multiple factor analysis obviously provides the more promising line of approach.

6. A WORKED EXAMPLE

So far we have described the similarities and differences between the two techniques in plain common-sense terms. But, when the techniques are essentially mathematical, a merely verbal formulation can never be sufficiently exact. Let us therefore take a specific numerical example and compare and contrast the two methods by examining results as expressed in arithmetical or algebraic form. I shall choose the type of problem for which multiple factor analysis was first developed, and for which, in the early days at any rate, it was principally used — namely, the classification of school children according to their mental abilities and aptitudes. At that date one of the chief problems that exercised psychologists whose function it was to aid or advise British education authorities was (1) how to select those pupils who were sufficiently bright to be recommended for some form of higher education, and (2) how to distinguish (a) those suitable for an academic type of education such as was provided by so-called "grammar schools" and (b) those suitable for a technical type of education such as that provided by so-called "trade schools" or "technical institutes." A common practice was for the headmaster to set an examination for those of his pupils who had reached the age of eleven, covering the main subjects of the elementary curriculum, e.g. (to take an instance from an actual group of London schools), papers in (1) Problem Arithmetic, (2) English Composition, Reading and Spelling, (3) Drawing, and

(4) Handwork. The examination was spread over two days, Arithmetic and Drawing being taken on the first day (Monday), English and Handwork on the second (Tuesday). To simplify the calculations, I have limited the number of pupils to six boys from a single school, and have selected them so as to illustrate the commoner types and to yield much the same correlations as the entire group. Their marks are shown in Table 8-1.

best (a poor best, it must be admitted) on the second day; and as a matter of fact the master actually reported that on the first day Henry was "suffering from a touch of stage fright": George, on the other hand, was said to have been at his best on the first day and to have become stale or fatigued on the second. These are instances of what in analysis of variance are termed "interactions." If we want to measure the varying effects of these subsidiary factors more

TABLE 8-1

MARKS FOR SIX BOYS IN FOUR TESTS

Tests	Day	Persons						Average for Subject
		John	James	Hugh	George	Ralph	Henry	
Academic								
(1) Arithmetic	Mon.	16	11	8	6	7	0	8
(2) English	Tues.	15	14	9	5	6	5	9
Manual								
(3) Drawing	Mon.	17	8	10	16	8	1	10
(4) Handwork	Tues.	20	11	13	13	15	6	13
Average for Person		17	11	10	10	9	3	10
Average as Deviation		+7	+1	0	0	−1	−7	0

7. ANALYSIS BY SIMPLE SUMMATION

It is evident at a glance that John is the brightest of the lot, and that the names are arranged in order of merit. To assess the general ability of each child the ordinary teacher would calculate the total marks scored by each boy or calculate his average, as shown in the last line but one. To indicate more clearly which of the boys are above and which are below the mean of the whole batch, it will be more convenient to express the averages as positive or negative deviations from the general mean, as shown in the last line of all.

If we allow for the rather generous marking that subjects like handwork and drawing commonly receive, it would appear that James is much better at the academic subjects than the technical, while George is better at the technical. Moreover, it looks as though Henry was at his

precisely, it will be natural to average the relevant deviations of each boy's marks about his own average, or, what amounts to the same thing, calculate the differences between the various pairs of subjects.

Before doing so, however, it will be well to allow for the varying standards adopted by the specialist teachers who marked papers in their own particular subjects, and start by reducing each of the raw marks to deviations about the mean for each subject. The results[1] of this conversion are shown in the top panel of Table 8-2.

[1]The inclusion of a boy who obtains zero marks in every test and every factor imparts a somewhat artificial look to the table. But any random sample, no matter how small, will usually include one or more individuals who obtain *approximately* average marks in every test. And, as I have everywhere rounded off the actual marks to make the illustrative calculations simpler, the consequence is that one boy gets *exactly* average marks throughout. The inclusion of such a case also reminds us that the marks actually reported

TABLE 8-2

OBSERVED MARKS IN DEVIATION FORM:
ANALYSIS AND RECONSTRUCTION BY EQUAL WEIGHTS

Test	John	James	Hugh	George	Ralph	Henry	Sum of Squares
(1) Arithmetic	+8	+3	0	−2	−1	−8	142
(2) English	+6	+5	0	−4	−3	−4	102
(3) Drawing	+7	−2	0	+6	−2	−9	174
(4) Handwork	+7	−2	0	0	+2	−7	106
Total Square							524

Test Weights				Analysis into Factor Measurements						
	(1)	(2)	(3)	(4)						
I	$\frac{1}{2}$	$\frac{1}{2}$	$\frac{1}{2}$	$\frac{1}{2}$	+14	+2	0	0	−2	−14	400
II	$\frac{1}{2}$	$\frac{1}{2}$	$-\frac{1}{2}$	$-\frac{1}{2}$	0	+6	0	−6	−2	+2	80
III	$\frac{1}{2}$	$-\frac{1}{2}$	$\frac{1}{2}$	$-\frac{1}{2}$	+1	−1	0	+4	−1	−3	28
IV	$\frac{1}{2}$	$-\frac{1}{2}$	$-\frac{1}{2}$	$\frac{1}{2}$	+1	−1	0	−2	+3	−1	16
Total Square											524

Factor Weights				Reconstruction of Test Measurements						
	I	II	III	IV						
(1)	$\frac{1}{2}$	$\frac{1}{2}$	$\frac{1}{2}$	$\frac{1}{2}$	+8	+3	0	−2	−1	−8	142
(2)	$\frac{1}{2}$	$\frac{1}{2}$	$-\frac{1}{2}$	$-\frac{1}{2}$	+6	+5	0	−4	−3	−4	102
(3)	$\frac{1}{2}$	$-\frac{1}{2}$	$\frac{1}{2}$	$-\frac{1}{2}$	+7	−2	0	+6	−2	−9	174
(4)	$\frac{1}{2}$	$-\frac{1}{2}$	$-\frac{1}{2}$	$\frac{1}{2}$	+7	−2	0	0	+2	−7	106
Total Square											524

8. MATHEMATICAL FORMULATION: ANALYSIS OF VARIANCE

The process of calculating averages and average differences for each pupil can be expressed most succinctly by forming a matrix of weights to be applied to the tests. The weights will have the same numerical value throughout but will differ in the pattern of positive and negative signs. Adding John's marks for each of the four subjects and then dividing by four is equivalent to dividing each mark by four and then adding these reduced values. If, however, we then square the averages and then sum the squares, we should find that the "total square" (131) is only one quarter the value of the "total square" as computed from the initial data (524). This is because

(Table 8-1, column for "Hugh") may be misleading unless first related to the averages for the group.

each of the squared averages occurs four times over in the initial sum of squares (once in each of the four tests). We can allow for this by dividing the sums (or summed differences) of each pupil's marks by two (as shown in the middle panel) instead of by four. The entire process is thus equivalent to pre-multiplying the initial matrix of marks (in deviation form) by a 4×4 orthogonal matrix.

Accordingly, in place of the summation notation customary in the textbook exposition of analysis of variance, let us substitute the more succinct notation of matrix algebra. Then, if A_T denotes the matrix of test marks, L' the orthogonal matrix of unstandardized test weights, and A_F the matrix of factor measurements, the whole process can be expressed by the simple matrix equation

(1) $A_F = L'A_T$.

From the hypothetical factor measurements so obtained we can, if we wish, recontruct the observed test marks by pre-multiplying the former by a matrix of factor weights, which is the inverse of the matrix of test weights. Since this latter matrix was orthogonal, its inverse must be identical with its transpose; and, owing to the way it was constructed, its transpose here turns out to be identical with itself. We thus have

(2) $LA_F = LL'A_T = A_T$

since, $LL' = I$: (see third panel of Table 8-2).

The interpretation of the larger factors is fairly obvious. The first factor, for which all the weights are positive, is plainly what in factor analysis is termed a "general factor"; it represents the underlying ability common to all four tests. The remaining factors, obtained with weights that are partly positive and partly negative, are "bipolar factors"; they correspond with what in analysis of variance are termed "interactions."[2] The

second factor distinguishes boys who are superior in the tests of academic aptitude from those who are superior in the tests of technical aptitude. The third factor apparently distinguishes those who were at their best on the first day from those who were at their best on the second. We might perhaps suppose that the fourth factor also represents some further difference in aptitude, e.g., that it contrasts those who are superior in subjects involving numerical calculation and quantitative measurement (arithmetic and handwork) from those involving some kind of aesthetic appeal (English and drawing). But, when there are n tests, the figures obtained for the nth factor are merely the averages of the residuals left after deducting the other three weighted averages from the original marks. Consequently, with the procedure we have adopted it would seem more logical to regard them as furnishing the best available measure of the amount of uncontrolled variation in the empirical assessments obtained for those individual differences that are presumed to be due to the three main controllable causes. Certainly in planning the examination there was no thought of assessing any *further* aptitude such as the former interpretation would imply. In any case they seem to represent the effects of irrelevant influences, and as such may best be treated as measuring "errors."

Before we attempt any more refined type of analysis, it is worth noting three or four fairly obvious points that emerge from the elementary procedure we have so far employed. First, the effect of the "loadings" in the "weighting matrices" is not so much to *weight* the tests as to *classify* them — or rather to provide a means of testing all the available types of classification. Second, the classification is dichotomous or "bipolar." It

---

[2]The reason for identifying "bipolar" factors with "interactions" is obvious if we bear in mind the implications of each term. So far as the type or difficulty of certain subjects tends to be the same for *all* pupils, we regard the type or difficulty as a "main" source of variation; and so far as a given type of ability tends to affect the pupils' performances in *every* subject, that too is regarded as a "main" source. But when the type of certain subjects renders them hard for *some* pupils and easy for *others,* while the opposite (relatively speaking) holds good for the rest of the subjects, we say there is an "interaction" between the type of subject on the one hand and the abilities of the pupils on the other. When there is no such interaction, we should be able to predict a pupil's mark by adding the average mark for the type of subject to the average deviation for the pupil, e.g., the average mark for "academic" subjects is $8\frac{1}{2}$, and the average deviation for John is $+7$. Hence we may expect John's average mark for such subjects to be $15\frac{1}{2}$, as indeed it is (see Table 8-1). Similarly for his average mark in "manual" subjects. The same holds of Hugh. But it does not hold of James, whose average mark for academic subjects is $12\frac{1}{2}$ instead of $9\frac{1}{2}$. Nor does it hold of George (average $5\frac{1}{2}$ instead of $8\frac{1}{2}$). The question therefore is — are these various discrepancies statistically significant or not? And in analysis of variance this is answered by testing the significance of the "interaction" itself as a source of variation. If they are significant, then we should expect that, when the influence of the general factor has been partialled out,

the residual correlations between marks for each academic subject and those for each manual subject will be negative, while the intercorrelations within each group are positive; and this pattern of negative and positive residuals will yield a "bipolar" factor when the whole table is factorized.

is effected by the use of positive and negative signs: as students of logic will know, such a classification is always formally valid, and it has the further merit of arranging the classes according to a regular hierarchical scheme. Third, all the subclasses are equally balanced: except for the first, the weights in each row and each column add up to zero. For exploratory studies, in fields where the principles of classification are but vaguely known or suspected, this type of dichotomous classification seems undoubtedly the safest to adopt, at least in the earlier stages. But it also implies that the initial variables that we measure or test should themselves, so far as possible, be selected with this balanced classification explicitly in view. Fourth and finally, perhaps the most striking result in the table of figures we have computed is the wide difference between the amount of variation which the different factors contribute. This is indicated most clearly by the sums of squares. With the four initial tests the differences between the square-sums were comparatively small; with the four factors they are enormous. For the first and largest factor the square-sum is 25 times the size of the square-sum for the smallest. It accounts for over 75 per cent of total variation. The next largest accounts for only 15 per cent. From a practical standpoint this result makes possible a great simplification. More than 90 per cent of the total variation displayed by the four tests can be accounted for by two factors only; and thus very close approximations to the different measurements for the several individuals could be estimated from, or predicted by, these two factors alone.

Tests of Significance

The procedure I have described is virtually the same as that adopted by the practical teacher in dealing with the same sort of problem, except that he seldom carries it out so systematically or so completely; and he probably looks upon it as an application of the principles of common sense rather than of mathematical analysis. As a scientist, therefore, what the psychologist wants to know is the validity of the results which such a procedure yields, and in what ways, if any, it could be refined or improved. How far can we trust the classification and the individual factor measurements to which we are thus led? These are questions for which the analysis of variance claims to provide an answer.

Our initial data, it will be remembered, consisted of twenty-four observations, namely, the marks scored by six boys in four tests. We are, however, concerned only with variations, i.e., with deviations about the general mean. The mean for the whole sample (10) has to be calculated from the data. That reduces the total number of degrees of freedom to 23. On squaring the 24 deviations and summing the squares, we obtain for the total square-sum a figure of 608.

To account for it we have, to begin with, three obvious sources of variation—the differences in general proficiency shown by the six persons here tested, the difference in type of subject (academic vs. technical), and the difference in day (first day vs. second). These three main sources, however, may very possibly give rise to "interactions," viz., three first-order (between persons and type of subject, between persons and day, and between type of subject and day), and one second-order (involving all three main variables). This last, being the interaction of the highest order, will be used to furnish our estimated sampling error. With this scheme of classification, the requisite square-sums, mean squares, and variance ratios can be calculated in the customary fashion. The final analysis of variance can therefore be tabulated in the ordinary way, as shown in Table 8-3.

To determine whether or not these possible sources of variance are indeed genuinely operative, we must examine the statistical significance of their apparent "effects." There is clear evidence that the differences in general ability between indi-

TABLE 8-3

ANALYSIS OF VARIANCE
(With Unstandardized Marks)

Factor	Source of Variation	Degrees of Freedom	Sum of Squares	Mean Square	Ratio of Variances	Probability
I	A. Persons	5	400	80	25.00	0.001 − 0.01
—	B. Type of Subject	1	54	54	16.87	0.01
—	C. Day	1	24	24	7.50	0.01 − 0.05
II	AB. Persons and Type of Subject	5	80	16	5.00	0.05 − 0.20
III	AC. Persons and Day	5	28	5.6	1.75	< 0.20
—	BC. Type of Subject and Day	1	6	6	1.87	< 0.20
IV	ABC. Residual	5	16	3.2	—	—
	Total	23	608	—	—	—

vidual pupils, as assessed by the examination taken as a whole, are statistically significant. It seems plain too that the tests for the two academic subjects were decidedly more difficult, or at any rate more severely marked, than the tests for the two technical subjects. It also looks as if, generally speaking, the boys improved somewhat as time went on: on the second day they had apparently gotten over the initial qualms that such an ordeal tends to arouse, and warmed up to their work, although here the statistical evidence is not quite so strong. Thus we may regard the three *main* sources of variation as definitely established. On the other hand, with the present sample, none of the second-order interactions is statistically significant. The test is to determine how accurately the mark actually obtained by a particular boy in a particular test can be predicted from the averages for (1) the boy, (2) the type of subject, and (3) the day. There will of course usually be at least a small discrepancy or "residual." On calculating the sum of squares for all such residuals we find that the figure obtained is quite devoid of significance. (In the entire sample of 250 from which these half-dozen boys have been selected, the first of the second-order interactions *was* in fact statistically significant.) When the second-order interactions are non-significant, and we therefore decide

to accept the null hypothesis, the proper procedure would be to recalculate the error variance by pooling *all* the non-significant square-sums: (cf. below, page 284). It is, however, hardly necessary to pursue this modification of the basic procedure here.

Now it was not the intention of the examination to compare differences in the difficulty of the subjects or in the standards of marking which their teachers adopt, nor yet to investigate differences arising from the order in which the tests were taken or the days on which they were set. Indeed, before carrying out our first attempt at analysis (see page 272), we eliminated these influences by reducing the raw marks to deviations about the mean for each of the four subjects. That, of course, will abolish variations due to "type of subject" and to "day," as well as their interaction. We can therefore delete from Table 8-3 the rows so designated. We are then left with the four rows labeled factors I, II, III, and IV respectively. With this reduction the total sum of squares is altered to 524 (as in Table 8-2). The variance ratios for the four remaining components, and the probabilities deduced from them, are left unchanged.

Unitary Standard Measure

There is one further adjustment that the theoretical psychologist would probably prefer to make. So far we have treated the observed variances for the several tests as if they and their differences possessed objective validity. But with mental measurements (as distinct from physical) such an assumption is scarcely justifiable. On looking back at Table 8-1 we see that for Arithmetic and Drawing the range of variation was 16, whereas for English it was only 10. A knowledge of the actual tests and of the habits of examiners suggests that these differences are the result of differences not in the pupils' abilities, but in the way their performances were marked. Galton, when he first attempted to turn individual psychology into a rigorous and quantitative science, began by proposing that the mental differences between persons should be measured in terms of the same scale for every ability or trait; and the unit he suggested was in effect the average range of individual variation. For inquiries such as the present, the most convenient type of scale is what may be termed "unitary standard measure," i.e., a scale for which the mean is zero and the standard deviation (and consequently the variance) unity.

Table 8-4 shows the effect of the rescaling. The figures are given to four decimal places, so that the reader can, if he wishes, check the subsequent calculations. The averages for each pupil are given in the last row but one; and in the last row of all they are themselves reduced to unitary standard measure.

From a practical standpoint these adjustments evidently make little difference.

Thus, if we multiply the fractions in the last row by ten (to bring the variance back to 100 as in Table 8-2), we have a set of figures which differ hardly at all from those obtained in Table 8-2, line 5. I leave the reader to recalculate the values needed for an analysis of variance. Since not only the means but also the standard deviations have now been derived from the observed data, the degrees of freedom both for "persons" and for the three "interactions" are reduced to 4. The ratios of variances, however, are scarcely changed at all. There is a slight diminution in each. But the final results — the various probabilities — remain unaffected.

9. MATHEMATICAL FORMULATION: FACTOR ANALYSIS

So far we have assumed that all the measurements for our "hypothetical factors" can be derived by simple summation, that is, by averaging, without any attempt at differential weighting. And this, as we have seen, is also the assumption on which our analysis of variance is implicitly based. We have now to inquire how far this assumption is really justified and whether our results could be improved by introducing some form of differential weighting.

The General Factor

The first question that we naturally ask is whether there are any grounds for postulat-

TABLE 8-4

Marks Reduced to Unitary Standard Measure

Test	John	James	Hugh	George	Ralph	Henry
(1) Arithmetic	.6713	.2517	.0000	−.1678	−.0839	−.6713
(2) English	.5941	.4951	.0000	−.3961	−.2970	−.3961
(3) Drawing	.5307	−.1516	.0000	.4549	−.1516	−.6823
(4) Handwork	.6799	−.1943	.0000	.0000	.1943	−.6799
Average	.6190	.1002	.0000	−.0273	−.0846	−.6074
Average in U.S.M.	.7054	.1142	.0000	−.0310	−.0964	−.6922

ing a hypothetical "general ability" common to all four tests. Unless there are, we have no warrant for averaging the results of the tests to measure such an ability. If all four tests have indeed some component in common, then each of the tests should exhibit a positive correlation with every other. Were there no correlations between any of the tests, then in the long run the averages for all the pupils should be approximately the same. Let us therefore correlate the tests and investigate the significance of the coefficients so obtained. Since the test measurements have already been reduced to unitary standard measure, the product-moment correlation for any pair of tests will be identical with the product-sum. It will in fact be a covariance. The complete set of correlations is shown in Table 8-5.

In passing, however, let us notice that, as a result of the way they have been calculated, the total of all the correlations in a matrix such as Table 8-5 is necessarily equal to the total of the squares of the sums of the several columns of figures from which the correlations have been calculated. This can readily be demonstrated by a little algebra. If x_{ij} denotes i's marks in the jth test (expressed in unitary standard measure), then his total mark in all the n tests will be $\Sigma_j x_{ij}$; and the square-sum for all such totals will be $\Sigma_i(\Sigma_j x_{ij})^2$. Multiplying out and summing, we find that this is identical with the sum of all the n^2 correlations in the correlation table, the self-correlations being taken as unity. Thus, the sum total of all the sixteen values in Table 8-5 (12.3206) is sixteen times the sum of the squares of the averages for the several boys (.7700), as

TABLE 8-5

CORRELATIONS BETWEEN TESTS AND CALCULATIONS
OF FIRST FACTOR SATURATIONS BY SIMPLE SUMMATION

Test	Arithmetic	English	Drawing	Handwork	Total
(1) Arithmetic	1.0000	.8808	.7125	.8477	3.4410
(2) English	.8808	1.0000	.3753	.5193	2.7754
(3) Drawing	.7125	.3753	1.0000	.8247	2.9125
(4) Handwork	.8477	.5193	.8247	1.0000	3.1917
Total	3.4410	2.7754	2.9125	3.1917	12.3206
Saturation	.9803	.7907	.8298	.9093	3.5101

Note.—Saturation = Column total ÷ ($\sqrt{12.306}$, i.e. 3.5101).

It will be seen at once that all the correlations are positive. If we proceed to test each coefficient in isolation, then only the two largest would be regarded as statistically significant by Fisher's criterion. What we have to consider, however, are the joint implications of the whole system of intercorrelations. Unfortunately for this purpose, there is as yet no universally agreed test of significance: that is one of the main problems with which factor analysis has to contend. Judged by all the empirical methods hitherto proposed, the joint effect of the correlations taken together appears to be fully significant.

shown in the last line but one of Table 8-4. This square-sum forms the basis of the "mean square for persons" as calculated in the analysis of variance; so in testing the significance of the variance for persons (with standardized marks) we are in effect testing the significance of the total correlation.

First Factor

The factorist's chief reason for calculating tables of intercorrelations, however, is the need to know which of his tests is most highly correlated with the postulated general factor, i.e., which of them can be expected to furnish the best measure of it. In the present case, where the number involved is quite small, we can calculate the pupil's measurements for the general factor by the method of simple summation already described, and then correlate the factor measurements with the marks for each of the four tests in turn. But in a full-scale research, where the number of persons tested will probably run to well over a hundred, such a process would be both lengthy and laborious.

There is, however, a short-cut. Instead of summing the observed marks, we can sum the observed correlations. The legitimacy of this procedure can readily be demonstrated algebraically. Let Z denote the matrix of marks (in unitary standard measure), and let us pre-multiply this matrix by a vector (or one-rowed matrix), w'_1, consisting solely of units with positive signs throughout, in short, by the "summation operator." We then obtain $w'_1 Z = A'_{F_1}$, a one-rowed matrix containing the unstandardized factor measurements. Accordingly, the correlation between the factor measurements and the several tests will evidently be

$$(3)\quad A_F Z (A'_F A_F)^{-1/2} = w'_1 ZZ' (w'_1 ZZ' w_1)^{-1/2}$$
$$= w'_1 R (w'_1 R w_1)^{-1/2}$$

where $A'_F A_F = w'_1 R w_1$ is a scalar.

Changing from matrix notation to the more ordinary formulation, we have

$$(4)\quad r_{jg} = \frac{\sum\limits_{k} r_{jk}}{\sqrt{\sum\limits_{j} \sum\limits_{k} r_{jk}}}$$

where r_{jk} denotes the correlation between any two tests, j and k, and r_{jg} denotes the correlation of test j with the hypothetical general factor g.

In other words, the correlations between the general factor and the several tests (the "factor saturations" or "factor loadings," as they are variously termed) can be obtained by simply summing the columns of correlations for each test, and then dividing by the square root of the grand total of all the figures in the correlation matrix. The results of the calculation are shown at the foot of Table 8-5. It will be seen that in the present case the correlations of all the tests with the general factor are fairly high, the correlation of Arithmetic being highest of all, and the correlation of English being the lowest.

Second Factor

To estimate and study the second factor we can proceed in much the same fashion as in estimating and studying the first. A few obvious modifications will be needed in the working procedure because, like all factors except the first, the second is necessarily bipolar. As before, the first question to ask is whether the evidence for the existence of a further factor is statistically valid. As we have seen, bipolar factors represent "interactions"; hence in the analysis of variance this question was answered by examining the residual *variance*. In factor analysis we answer it by examining the residual *correlations*. Accordingly we first calculate for every pair of tests

$$(5)\quad r_{ij.g} = r_{ij} - r_{ig}.r_{jg}.$$

Whether or not, in accordance with the full formula, we then allow for the reduction in the two standard deviations by dividing each residual by the product of $\sqrt{1 - r_{ig}^2}$ and $\sqrt{1 - r_{jg}^2}$ will depend on the type of problem we have in view. If the problem is practical, the division will probably be desirable; if theoretical, it will not. The residuals obtained by the above equation must next be tested for statistical significance. As before, the familiar test applied to each partial correlation taken singly is likely to be too severe. We need a test for the joint significance of the entire system of residuals. And in principle this is the same as that for testing an interaction of the first order. However, when factors are calculated by the rough and ready method of simple summation, the conditions requisite for an analysis of variance are not strictly fulfilled.

How these shortcomings can be remedied so that an analysis of variance is strictly applicable, we shall see at a later stage (page 281 below). It may be observed that the foregoing procedure is much the same as that adopted by Pearson in calculating and testing the significance of a multiple contingency table (see Pearson, 1146, and Kendall, 862, I, p. 319, equ. 13.28).[3]

would be wrong to infer (as is so frequently done) that the reversal of signs is *merely* a device to avoid this self-stultifying outcome; it is, as the underlying theory clearly implies, a method of *weighting* the several tests.

The complete set of factor saturations obtained in this way is shown in Table 8-6. It will be seen that the first factor contrib-

TABLE 8-6

FACTOR SATURATIONS OBTAINED BY SIMPLE SUMMATION

Factor	I	II	IV	III	Sum of Squares
(1) Arithmetic	.9803	.1829	.0548	.0501	1.0000
(2) English	.7907	.6077	−.0548	−.0501	1.0000
(3) Drawing	.8298	−.4828	−.2755	.0501	1.0000
(4) Handwork	.9093	−.3078	.2755	−.0501	1.0000
Sum of Squares	3.1016	.7306	.1578	.0100	4.0000
Contribution to Variance (as a percentage)	77.54	18.26	3.94	0.26	

To calculate the saturations (or "loadings") for the second factor we proceed much as before. The matrix of residual correlations is pre-multiplied by a one-rowed matrix consisting solely of units but with the same pattern of positive and negative signs as was used in calculating the factor measurements: in calculating the latter, it will be remembered, the marks for Drawing and Handwork were subtracted from those for English and Arithmetic. Accordingly, when we turn to the table of residual correlations we must reverse the signs of the coefficients for Drawing and Handwork before summing the several columns. Evidently, if we summed each column of residuals just as it stands, the total in every case would be zero. But it

utes about 77 per cent of the total variance—almost exactly the same proportion as in the analysis of variance with standardized marks; the second factor contributes 18 per cent—a slightly larger proportion than that contributed by the interaction between persons and tests (classified into academic vs. technical). The relative amounts contributed by the last two factors is reversed (this is typical of the changes that may ensue from taking into account the differences in the predictive values of the several tests). If it were significant, we should have to regard our former factor IV as indicative of an interaction between the persons and the tests when the latter are reclassified into quantitive vs. aesthetic subjects. However, the actual variances contributed by factors IV and III are much too small to be significant with this tiny sample. And in both cases the equalities revealed by the saturations strongly suggest that they are artifacts produced by treating specific error factors as common factors.

[3]It was this analogy that suggested the chi-squared test for the significance of factors (see Burt, 160, p. 339 and ref.). The above formula for calculating the factor saturations (equ. 4) and the procedure for calculating the residual correlations (equ. 5) were first described and used in the report on the "Distribution and Relations of Educational Abilities" (Burt, 157, p. 53 and Tables XVIII-XX).

TABLE 8-7

FACTOR SATURATIONS OBTAINED BY WEIGHTED SUMMATION

Factor	I	II	IV	III	Sum of Squares
(1) Arithmetic	.9791	.1908	.0275	.0610	1.0000
(2) English	.7850	.6126	−.0869	−.0376	1.0000
(3) Drawing	.8310	−.4897	−.2640	−.0085	1.0000
(4) Handwork	.9148	−.2851	.2851	−.0252	1.0000
Sum of Squares	3.1021	.7328	.1593	.0058	4.0000
Contribution to Variance (as a percentage)	77.55	18.32	3.98	0.15	

10. MATHEMATICAL FORMULATION: FACTOR ANALYSIS BY WEIGHTED SUMMATION

It will be remembered that, in undertaking an analysis of variance, whether we worked with standardized or unstandardized marks, we assumed that the factor measurements could be adequately estimated by taking simple sums or averages. But, as we have already seen, the correlations between the several tests and the first factor (the so-called "factor saturations") differ in their magnitude; and the differences are still more striking in the case of the second factor. That being so, it becomes difficult to defend a method which gives each test an equal weight. A natural suggestion is that we should recalculate the factor measurements by weighting the tests differentially in accordance with their factor saturations. The theory of regression would suggest that it might be better still to use regression coefficients calculated in the usual way by pre-multiplying the vector of factor correlations by the inverse of the correlation matrix. But whichever method we adopt, it is evident that the alterations in the factor measurements will produce an alteration in the factor correlations; and to allow for this we ought to recalculate the factor measurements yet again with the weights modified accordingly.

At first sight it might seem as if we had started going round and round in endless

circles. But with each iteration the changes become less and less; and eventually we reach a stable set of factor measurements whose correlations with each test are identical with the figures used as weights.

Now it is not difficult to show, by the same type of reasoning as was outlined above, that these final values can be reached much more simply by applying the iterative procedure, not to the large $n \times N$ matrix of test measurements (Z), but to the smaller $n \times n$ matrix of correlations or covariances (R). As so applied, it is in fact the stock procedure for finding the "latent roots" (or eigen-values) and "latent vectors" (or eigen-vectors) of any symmetric matrix. Thus, let R be the matrix of correlations with units in the leading diagonal. Any such matrix can always be reduced to a canonical form

$$(6) \quad R = LD_L L',$$

where L is an orthogonal matrix consisting of the latent vectors and D_L is a diagonal matrix containing the latent roots; since R is an empirical matrix, the number of latent roots, and consequently of factors, will be the same as the number of tests, i.e., n. Then, since by definition $R = ZZ'$, we can write

$$(7) \quad Z = LD_L^{1/2} Z_F = V_o Z_F \text{ (say)}$$

where Z_F now denotes the standardized factor measurements (a facet of an orthogonal matrix), and forms the $n \times N$ matrix of hypothetical factor measurements, and V_o

is a matrix of "factor saturations" (or "loadings") indicating how far each test is "saturated" (or "loaded") with each of the factors. On pre-multiplying both sides of this equation by $D_L^{-1/2}L'$, $=W'$ (say), we have

(8) $W'Z = D_L^{-1/2}L' . LD_L^{1/2}Z_F = Z_F.$

It will be seen that

$$(9) \quad Z_F Z_F' = D_L^{-1/2}L'ZZ'LD_L^{-1/2}$$
$$= D_L^{-1/2}L'RLD_L^{-1/2}$$
$$= D_L^{-1/2}L'.LD_LL'.LD_L^{-1/2}$$
$$= I,$$

the identity matrix. Hence, as thus calculated, all the factor measurements will be in unitary standard measure, and the measurements for any one factor will have zero correlation with each of the others. It further follows that, since

$$V_o'R = D_L^{1/2}L'.LD_LL' = D_LV_o',$$

(10) $V_o' = D_L^{-1}V_o'R$ and

(11) $D_L^2 = V_o'RV_o.$

Moreover, because L is an orthogonal matrix, analogous equations hold good of the several factors taken singly. If, for example, v_1' is the row of factor saturations for the first factor, then

$$v_1' = d_1^{-1}v_1'R, \text{ and}$$
$$d_1^2 = v'Rv.$$

Now by applying one of the stock (but somewhat lengthy) proofs of convergence (cf. Frazer et al., 546, pp. 40 f.) it is not difficult to show that, if we take a set of trial estimates for the factor saturations $(_1v_1'$, say), and obtain $_2v_1' = d_1^{-1} . _1v_1'R$, then $_2v_1'$ will be an improved estimate of v_1'.

In passing, it may be noted that, if there are more tests than persons, it would be more economical to factorize the product-sums for persons rather than for tests. Instead of the $n \times n$ correlation matrix for tests (R), we then obtain the $N \times N$ product-moment matrix $(R_p$ say) for persons. We have

$$(12) \quad R_p = Z'Z = Z_F D_L^{1/2}L'LD_L^{1/2}A_F$$
$$= Z_F'D_LZ_F,$$

and on factorizing this we shall evidently reach the same set of factors as before. It should be observed, however, that, unless the initial measurements are restandardized by columns, the new product-moment matrix is not a matrix of covariances or correlations in the ordinary sense. The analogous character of the alternative formulae brings out the so-called "reciprocity" of persons and tests (using the term "test" to cover whatever traits or items are measured).

The foregoing method of factorization has been termed the method of "weighted summation" to distinguish it from the less accurate method of "simple summation": this yields a matrix of factor saturations which nearly always show slight correlation. In terms of normal correlation theory, the factors obtained by weighted summation represent the principal axes of the correlation ellipsoid, and are therefore uncorrelated. The method itself was originally suggested in 1901 by Karl Pearson (1145); and the later method of "simple summation" was proposed as a simplified and convenient means of approximation, sufficiently accurate for the purposes of most psychological inquiries (Burt, 157).

The results of factorizing the above correlation matrix by the more elaborate procedure are shown in Table 8-7. It will be seen that there is very little change in the first factor; rather more in the second; and still more in the next. In the last factor even the sign-pattern has undergone a change, and its contribution to the total variance is still further reduced. The method can claim two further advantages. First, the initial matrix of test measurements can be reconstructed with perfect exactitude from the factor measurements, and second, since the inverse of an orthogonal matrix is simply its transpose, the matrix of factor weights required for reconstructing the test measurements is identical with that used for calculating the (unstandardized) factor measurements from the test measurements, except that the rows are rewritten as columns. This is illustrated in Table 8-8. The formulae used for this purpose are $L'Z = D_L^{1/2} A_F$ and $LD_L^{1/2} A_F = Z$.

themselves that call primarily for such a test. Now with the method just described the analysis into standardized factors is, as we have seen, effected by an orthogonal matrix of factor saturations, and the measurements for each factor are also orthogonal to the measurements for every other

TABLE 8-8

ANALYSIS AND RECONSTRUCTION OF TEST MEASUREMENTS WITH
DIFFERENTIAL WEIGHTS OBTAINED BY WEIGHTED SUMMATION

Test	John	James	Hugh	George	Ralph	Henry	Sum of Squares
	Observed Marks in Unitary Standard Measure						
(1) Arithmetic	.671	.252	.000	−.168	−.084	−.671	1.0000
(2) English	.594	.459	.000	−.396	−.297	−.396	1.0000
(3) Drawing	.531	−.152	.000	.455	−.152	−.682	1.0000
(4) Handwork	.680	−.194	.000	.000	.194	−.680	1.0000
Total							4.0000

	Test Weights				Analysis into Factor Measurements					
	(1)	(2)	(3)	(4)						
I	.556	.446	.472	.519	1.242	.188	.000	−.055	−.150	−1.225	3.1021
II	.223	.716	−.572	−.333	.045	.562	.000	−.581	−.209	.184	.7328
IV	.069	−.218	−.662	.714	.051	−.129	.000	−.226	.298	.006	.1593
III	.798	−.492	.112	−.330	−.040	.038	.000	.010	.032	−.040	.0058
Total											4.0000

	Factor Weights				Reconstruction of Test Measurements					
	I	II	IV	III						
(1)	.556	.223	.069	.798	.671	.252	.000	−.168	−.084	−.671	1.0000
(2)	.446	.716	−.218	−.492	.594	.495	.000	−.396	−.297	−.396	1.0000
(3)	.472	−.572	−.662	.112	.531	−.152	.000	.455	−.152	−.682	1.0000
(4)	.519	−.333	.714	−.330	.680	−.194	.000	.000	.194	−.680	1.0000
Total											4.0000

11. MATHEMATICAL FORMULATION: ANALYSIS OF VARIANCE APPLIED TO FACTOR MEASUREMENTS

In the past most of the suggestions put forward for testing what the psychologist calls "factors" have been applied either to the residual correlations or (less frequently) to the factor saturations. But in point of fact it is the factor measurements

factor. Moreover, the last factor, which represents error, is reduced to a minimum —a minimum in the sense of the "least-squares" principle. All this would seem to indicate that we have now fulfilled, and indeed improved upon, the conditions ordinarily considered requisite for a valid analysis of variance along the lines described at the outset. It remains to decide how the available degrees of freedom are to be partitioned among the several factors. Since in standardizing the initial test measurements we calculated both the means and the standard deviations from the data, those measurements now provide only $n(N-2)$ degrees of freedom—in the present case (as we have seen) only $4(6-2)=16$. The factor measurements themselves are also in unitary standard measure. Hence, of the N measurements for the first factor only $N-2$ are determined from the data: the other two can then be deduced from the twofold requirement that the mean must be zero and the standard deviation unity. The measurements for the second

weights must add up to unity, and this implies that one of the weights can be determined from the other three. In the present case the result will be that only three of the weights are determined from the data. But the three degrees of freedom that this represents must be added to the total number of degrees of freedom which that factor absorbs. Only two of the weights for the second factor are determined from the data; but once again these two degrees of freedom must be added to those which the second factor absorbs. And so on, much

TABLE 8-9

ANALYSIS OF VARIANCE
(With Factors Obtained by Weighted Summation)

Factor	Source of Variation	Degrees of Freedom	Sum of Squares	Mean Square	Ratio of Variances	Probability
I	Between Persons	7	3.1021	.4432	4.49	0.01 − 0.05
II	Between Persons and Subjects (Academic vs. Manual)	5	.7328	.1466	(3.55)	0.05 − 0.20
IV	Between Persons and Subjects (Quantitative vs. Aesthetic)	3	.1593	.0531	(9.16)	0.05 − 0.20
III	Residual	1	.0058	.0058	−	−
	Total	16	4.0000	−	−	−

factor have to be orthogonal to the measurements for the first factor: this imposes yet another restriction: hence, with this factor only $N-3$ measurements are determined from the data. The measurements for the third factor have to be orthogonal to the measurements for the first *two* factors: hence, with this factor only $N-4$ measurements are determined from the data. And so on. Thus, in the present case, out of the twenty-four factor measurements only $4+3+2+1=10$ are determined from the data. But in calculating those measurements the orthogonal weighting matrix is itself determined from the data. For the first factor, n weighting coefficients are required: but, since the matrix is orthogonal, the sum of the squares of the several

as before. The row of weights for the last factor owes nothing at all directly to the data: all of them can be calculated from the other rows of the orthogonal matrix. It thus appears that, in all, seven degrees of freedom are absorbed by the first factor, five by the second, three by the next, and only one by the last. This makes up sixteen degrees of freedom, which corresponds to the number of degrees available in our initial data. The sums of squares and mean squares calculated on this basis are shown in Table 8-9.

Owing to the artificial character of our simplified example—a study based on half-a-dozen persons only—it must again be emphasized that the discussion is merely intended to illustrate the procedure. We begin by calculating the variance ratio ($.00531 \div .0058$) for the interaction between persons and numerical vs. aesthetic subjects. Here, as we might expect, it proves to be completely devoid of statistical significance. As it happens, this variance ratio was also non-significant with the complete sample of 250 persons from which our artificial example is drawn. For this particular interaction, therefore, we must accept the null hypothesis. That being so, we may regard the mean square for this factor, like that for the residual factor, as providing an estimate for the "error variance." We can therefore pool both the two sums of squares and the corresponding degrees of freedom; and in this way we secure a new and improved estimate for the error variance. The mean square so obtained is $.1651 \div 4 = .0413$; and the variance ratio for factor II thus becomes $.1466 \div .0413 = 3.55$. With our present small sample this ratio is also non-significant: (with the larger sample the value obtained was fully significant). Accepting the null hypothesis (as we should have to do if the small sample comprised the whole of our data), let us now go on to pool the sums of squares for all three bipolar factors. We then obtain a critical ratio of 4.49, which, with seven and nine degrees of freedom respectively, proves to be fully significant at the .05 level.

In following this procedure, it must be noted, the partitioning of the degrees of freedom and of the total variance is carried out after the observed data have been transformed by weighting equations derived from the data themselves. Hence, the technique employed in Table 8-9 can be described as an "analysis of variance" only in a somewhat extended sense. Under the conditions formulated in the matrix equations on page 281 above, it appears to be a valid procedure. But my purpose here is not to recommend it as a routine technique for testing the significance of the factors derived by ordinary factor analysis, but

merely to demonstrate the similarities and dissimilarities between the two methods by examining a specimen case in which the alternative techniques seem to approach each other most closely.

Specific Factors

In the commoner applications of factor analysis within the field of psychology, the conditions formulated above are seldom completely fulfilled. When we are concerned with mental tests, and with psychological measurements of almost any kind, there can be little doubt that (save perhaps for a few dubious exceptions) we must always allow for a unique or specific factor, peculiar to each test. Since these specific factors are usually irrelevant to the purposes of the research in which they appear, a good many statisticians and several psychologists have held that their variance can safely be included within the "error variance" — interpreting that term in its broadest sense. However, when this course is followed (as in the method we have so far adopted here) the effects are apt to get spread over the more important bipolar factors and so distort their characteristic features. Hence, most psychologists prefer to treat each specific factor as a statistically independent component and eliminate it at the outset by substituting reduced self-correlations or "communalities" for unities in the leading diagonal. When that is done, either the method of "simple summation" (the "centroid method") or that of "weighted summation" can still be used. But the conditions requisite for an analysis of variance are no longer strictly satisfied. In many cases, if not in most, the method would still give a reasonable answer to the problems of statistical significance. But for most practical purposes it is in my view better to use the chi-square test, applied either to the residual correlations (after transformation to Fisher's z: cf. Burt, 160, p. 339) or to the latent roots (cf. Bartlett,

69, p. 79, who uses it for our Table 8-9).

12. SUMMARY AND CONCLUSIONS

(1) Both factor analysis and analysis of variance seek to investigate, by suitable statistical techniques, what are variously termed the "components," "factors," "dimensions," or "sources" of a complex set of variations. That means that both are essentially concerned with problems of classification of variables. In factor analysis we *end* by determining what the "factors" are, i.e., what the appropriate classification appears to be, and we seek to measure the relative importance; in analysis of variance we *begin* with a knowledge of what the factors presumably are, and we test their statistical significance.

(2) In order to extract the component variances, the analysis of variance adopts a procedure which is in effect equivalent to pre-multiplying the matrix of observed measurements by a quasi-orthogonal weighting matrix containing equal weights but different signs; and from the components themselves the observed measurements can, if necessary, be reconstructed by applying the inverse of this weighting matrix. The procedure is thus formally analogous to the use in factor analysis of a matrix of regression coefficients to calculate the factor measurements from the observed measurements and a matrix of factor saturations (or "loadings") to reconstruct the observed measurements from the factor measurements.

(3) When the signs of the weights are all positive, the component obtained represents what is commonly termed in analysis of variance "a main source of variation" and in factor analysis a "general factor"; in an analysis of variance the procedure itself is tantamount to simple averaging. When half the signs are positive and half negative, the components obtained represent what are commonly termed in analysis of vari-

ance "interactions," and in factor analysis "bipolar factors." This analogy confirms the view that bipolar factors may have a meaning as they stand and involve a "reciprocity" between tests or traits and persons. For calculating these interactional components the procedure is equivalent to simple averaging, with the signs reversed for certain of the classes. In factor analysis the weights and the loadings differ not only in sign but also in numerical value.

(4) Factor analysis as a rule contemplates only one general factor. A complete analysis of variance, however, usually takes account of several other "main sources of variation" which in factor analysis are ruled out in advance as irrelevant to the problem investigated. On the other hand, a complete factor analysis will often include far more supplementary factors than are dealt with in the corresponding analysis of variance.

(5) With analysis of variance the weighting matrices are orthogonal, but the factor measurements are not. With factor analysis by simple summation the weighting matrices are not orthogonal, but the factor measurements are. With factor analysis by weighted summation both the weighting matrices and the factor measurements are orthogonal; and, as in analysis of variance, the weighting matrix used to reconstruct the observed measurements from the factor measurements is simply the transpose of the weighting matrix used to obtain the factor measurements from the observed measurements.

(6) Factor analysis involves the calculation, not only of square-sums, but also of a complete matrix of product-sums or intercorrelations. This of itself provides the psychologist with additional information which is of interest for its own sake. But, where a system of differential weights reached by successive approximation is required, it also furnishes a convenient short-cut. The special merit of differential weighting is twofold: first it enables us to take into account the differing values of the various test measurements as aids to esti-

mating the hypothetical factor measurements; second, it enables us to draw the sharpest possible distinction between the relative importance of the various independent factors which thus emerge. We begin by extracting the factor which is responsible for a maximum proportion of the total variance; and with weighted summation we endeavor to maximize that maximum. With each subsequent factor in turn, we adopt a similar principle. For in factor analysis it is an axiom of the method that we refrain from postulating any further factors unless it is clearly shown that the factor or factors already extracted fail to account (within the limits of statistical significance) for the entire amount of variance presented by our data. Finally, with factor analysis we can if we wish also allow for the specific factors peculiar to each test.

Each of the two main techniques thus has its own advantages and its own limitations. Each is suited to deal with the complex problems confronting the investigator from a slightly different aspect or angle. And in considering the lines which any given research is to follow he will always do well to decide in advance which particular technique he intends to apply to the data he collects and to plan his experiment accordingly.

CHAPTER 9

The Taxonometric Recognition of Types and Functional Emergents

RAYMOND B. CATTELL
University of Illinois

MALCOLM A. COULTER
National Institute for Personnel
Research, Johannesburg

BIEN TSUJIOKA
University of Kansai

1. THE SCIENTIFIC HISTORY OF TYPE CONCEPTS

Psychological description begins (as Chapter 3 brings out), with entities and attributes. Much could be written about their co-development, in physical, phylo-genetic and other percepts, in semantics, and in concept formation. But perhaps it suffices to say in these connections, as with the hen and the egg, that no one of them came first. Id (total pattern) and attribute (behavior response, on a continuum or categorization) are alternative abstractions from the same phenomena.

As a fact of Nature, patterns rarely come singly but more often in distinct "sets" — people, responses, cabbages, and kings. For the initial purposes of defining the data box all sets were kept logically on a par; but it is also a factor of Nature that there are sets among sets. Thus the taxonomic schemes of naturalists recognize species, genus, order, class, phylum, etc. For when Nature hits on a successfully functional pattern it is apt exuberantly to multiply sub-varieties thereof. The dictionary, fol-lowing Nature, gives us, after the word "dog," the further reference indicators Alsatian, spaniel, bulldog, etc.

In the first great attempt, by Aristotle, to build a system for seeing order in our world, the emphasis on taxonomy and types led to a system of "explanation" which is nowadays referred to as "Aristotelian." Its explanation is contrasted with the "Gali-lean" system, which analyzes and explains in degrees of attributes. It is natural that having achieved a recognition of types, men took pride in using them, and it sufficed to place an individual in a type in order to "explain" why he had such and such properties. "He is a dog; therefore, you may anticipate that he will bite." It fitted naturally the syllogistic form: "All men are mortal. Aristotle is a man. Therefore, Aristotle will die." The gain in prediction here comes with the act of first recognizing to what type the given individual belongs.

Typing has suffered a transitory unpopularity in our generation,[1] as a result of a distaste for the limitations of ancestry in particular — and perhaps for limitations and laws in general! Nevertheless, people continue to behave thus and so because they are so-and-so's, and animals continue to reproduce and die because it is the nature of animals, as distinct from mountains, seas, and stars, to reproduce and die. However, there are more reasonable reasons for being somewhat dissatisfied with typing, and for leaning, instead, to the principles of Galileo. These are contrasted with those of Aristotle in that essentially, as just stated, they consider the attribute and measurable degrees of the attribute. (Our "entity" and "attribute" division in the data box is thus historically referable to the apostle of each — Aristotle and Galileo.)

A first objection to explanation by species is that few individuals perfectly fit a type, and that *additional*, functional, explanatory laws can be invoked when one knows something about the natural history of a given attribute. For example, we can explain Mr. X's behavior by docketing him as a paranoid schizophrenic, or by pointing to his extremity on this and that primary personality or dynamic trait. The latter may give us some additional control, but, to give type its due, a recognition of belonging thereto may also give us some prediction

that is lacking from attribute prediction — because of interaction and emergent effects connoted in a pattern. One of our tasks is to try to understand these special pattern effects as mathematical functions of continuous trait scores.

Our discussion of types here will be oriented to types in those data box sets which we call subjects (people, organisms) — P — and observers — O — but most generalizations will apply also to recognizing types in stimuli, responses and processes, states and environmental (sociological and physical) patterns. Types — at least as types of people — have a long history in psychology, becoming respectably scientific in the brilliant recognition by Kraepelin, Bleuler, and others of psychiatric syndrome types, such as schizophrenia and manic-depressive psychosis, and profusely scholarly in Jung's writings on the introvert and the extravert.

2. THE VARIETIES AND UTILITIES OF TYPE MODELS

Here, as in so many fields of psychology, it is necessary first to eliminate some confusions of a semantic nature inherited from an undisciplined use of words. In terms of mathematico-statistical models one must recognize three or four clear and distinct conceptions of type, and of these we shall find most use in what we may verbally call the "species type" concept. But, as the senior author here has set out elsewhere (240), one can find no fewer than 45 semantic usages of type! Of these there are perhaps two that have really come to stay, because they can be equated with exact models, as follows:

(1) *The Polar Type.* This takes the opposite extremes on a normal distribution of some defined trait and calls them types. Extraversion-Introversion is an example. Usually the dimension is a broad one, e.g., a higher-order factor, as in the Exvia-Invia dimension derived from the 16 P.F. (which defines extraversion-introversion for the first time as something more than an

---

[1] An instance of psychologists' "advance in thought" is given in M. A. Merrill's (1046) quotation of Towle: "Yesterday we said this is a thief. What do we do with thieves? Today we say this is a person who steals and try to understand why he steals." This illustrates the lack of capacity to embrace trait and type descriptions in a single comprehensive intellectual schema.

arbitrary cluster). When type is thus applied, it is usually implied also that the dimension affects simultaneously a great deal of behavior. But it can be, and is, used for poles on a quite specific trait, e.g., the type of golfer that slices and the type that hooks. Probably it would help *not* to use type for poles on (a) a specific and (b) a *surface trait* (cluster) as contrasted with the uniquely, objectively definable *source* trait or factor, by which, for example, Exviants and Inviants can be defined.

(2). *The Modal Type.* This can be on a single dimension or simultaneously on many dimensions. In either case, the type is defined by a high "modal" *frequency at a certain point* in the distribution or distributions (or frequency in a certain *category,* in the case of a non-parametric "distribution"). Obviously, it is possible to have modes also in a *total* pattern, *even when there are no modal discontinuities on each constituent dimension.* For example, many distinct breeds of dogs overlap on length, color, head size in such a way that distinct modes would not occur in the single traits but only in their patterns, ratios, etc. These two senses of type are shown diagrammatically in Diagrams 9-1 (a), (b), and (c).

Among the popular uses of type which are confusing is "the Napoleonic type," etc., where a single individual is made a type, although there is no accumulation of cases at a mode there. There *are* occasions when one wishes to refer to an arbitrary pattern as a "type" for some theoretical reason but it would be less confusing to refer to this as a particular "profile" or "reference point" in a coordinate system. For typing people it is a barren concept, because there are no people (except the one) to be put into the type! Type connotes a distribution property.

In what follows we shall make no further reference to these earlier semantic uses, such as polar types[2] or arbitrary reference points, i.e., to these last or to the first use above, because they are much more easily handled simply by reference to single or multiple trait measurements as such; we shall confine ourselves to the *species type* defined as: *the central profile tendency found in a defined subgroup of a population, which is measurable on certain dimensions. The subgroup is not arbitrarily defined but recognized by its constituting an unusual modal frequency of occurrence and segregation in the*

DIAGRAM 9-1.   Basic Uses of Type

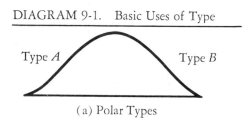

Type *A*   Type *B*

(a) Polar Types

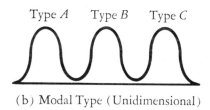

Type *A*   Type *B*   Type *C*

(b) Modal Type (Unidimensional)

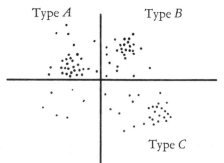

Type *A*   Type *B*

Type *C*

(c) Species Type (Modal Multidimensional)

---

[2]There is a verbal *convenience* in being able to describe a person with, say, a high anxiety score as "an anxious type," but perhaps the term *egrege* (pronounced "egrēēj") would be better for a mere extreme deviant or eccentric on a dimension.

general population on a dimension or combination of dimensions.

While defining terms for later use, it is desirable also to distinguish and set out precise uses for the terms *pattern, profile* and *configuration,* which we shall need henceforth to employ in careful discussion.

(1) *Pattern* will be used as a generic term to include both profile and configuration.

(2) *Profile* will be used as a particular combination of measurements or categories on a set of designated elements or aspects of a population. It is mathematically, in parametric data, a vector, and can be represented on Cartesian coordinates as a specific point in space.

(3) *Configuration* or *constellation* is used for a combination of measurements or categorical designations in which the *order* of elements as well as their size is relevant to their description and their effects. The same designated profile elements in a different stated sequence would now mean a different thing. A man's *profile* on a set of physical measurements, on the other hand, can be stated in any order with equal correctness provided we are given the key to the order for purposes of recognition. A typical *configuration* occurs in defining a *process,* a life history, a melody, a learning experience, a maturation process, etc. in all of which order is important.

The pattern resemblance by which individuals, processes, and other patterns are recognized to fall in modal types should include both *profile* and *configuration* resemblance. But for economy most discussion in this chapter must first be given in terms of profiles, leaving the special developments in configurations to Chapters 11 and 12 on process.

For the psychologist, if not the mathematical statistician, it may help further thinking to take a brief glance at the areas where recognition of types and use of type concepts is likely to be most useful. In general, multimodal, non-normal, distributions seem to arise either through (a) complex adjustment processes, as in bio-logical evolution or in fitting into complicated societies, in which some niche or special function has to be fitted, or (b) in disease processes, where the normal adjustment characteristic of all members of a species is upset in some specific way, producing definite deviations simultaneously on several functions. Thus, in more detail we can recognize three main areas.

(1) *Sociological Patterns.* Whereas most primary personality traits seem to be normally distributed, there are many specific cognitive and dynamic traits which are not. Most learning patterns which reflect the form of a social institution (church, school, suburbia, social class) or role position (occupation) are such that many individuals do not possess them at all. Where there is affiliation or non-affiliation, civilized specialization, and specific situationally determined personal histories, there will be non-normal and discrete distributions of single traits and patterns of traits — in short, *species types.*

(2) *Genetic Patterns.* Patterns also arise as a result of influences at the opposite end of the basic continuum of influences in psychology — from nurture to nature — namely from *constitutional* traits. Here we may expect a discrete pattern to arise either from the pleonasm of a single gene, or from the segregation of certain groups of genes. Races, for example, are definable as particular collections of genes, and insofar as some psychological traits are genetically determined, patterns may arise from particular natural selections of gene combinations. However, very few of these logically possible and scientifically expected outcomes have yet been verified by demonstration of true type patterns in quantitative terms, except in physical features or in pathological constitutional pattern, which are considered as a special subclass in (3).

(3) *Patterns Created by Response to Specific Disease Agents.* In abnormal traits in physical medicine, very definite exemplifications of a species type are offered by various physical diseases. In such *syndromes,* a

unique pattern of many parts appears and disappears as a whole. Mental disease presents almost equally clear illustrations. Such syndromes we have defined (Chapter 18) to a first approximation as surface traits (correlation clusters), but they often also involve non-linear and discontinuous distributions. The curious profile of elements, in, say, Huntington's chorea, presents an example, incidentally, both of the abnormal and the constitutional. Indeed, psychopathological syndromes actually provide the area in which typological concepts have hitherto had their greatest use in psychology. So long as everyone is not to some degree ill with the same disease, discrete species types will be exemplified by diseases.

Origins (1) and (2) above imply a special functional advantage for the particular combination of measures, but origin (3) implies only certain inherent laws of decline from functioning.

If we raise the question of the utility of the type concept here and elsewhere, we ask not only, "Is it useful in the sense that many examples can actually be found in nature," but also, "Will it enable us to make predictions and scientific generalizations that cannot be made without it?" Now one of the basic common-sense reasons for an Aristotelian use of all-or-nothing species types is that by assigning an individual case correctly to a type, our decisions are enriched because we are able to draw on *all* the information that exists about the type — both as to what it does and what you should do about it. If I recognize this as "a dog" I know it may bark and bite, whereas if I recognize it as "a cat" I can expect it to meow and scratch. Or I may feel that the former needs my company more. Or, in the more complex area of psychological types, the classification of a person as a depressive or as an anxiety hysteric will not only give me more understanding of what he is likely to do, e.g., "Is he a suicide risk?", but also of what treatment I should try, e.g., EST will improve the former but not the lat-

ter. This value of types has set thinkers, from Aristotle to Linnaeus or Kraepelin, to undertake a searching logical treatment of scientific problems of type taxonomy.

Even so, it may be asked what one gains by assigning an individual to a type that could not just as easily be attained by measuring him on dimensions and predicting therefrom. The answer is that with the *egrege,* or "type extreme" use of type, and any other use but that of species type, there is positively no advantage in going away from attribute prediction. Where species types exist, on the other hand, (a) we must recognize that their existence as non-linear emergents often causes the Galilean prediction from dimensions alone to become complex and inconvenient, because the regression whereby a performance is predicted from a dimension almost certainly changes sharply as we go from *between-species to within-species* (see below) measurements. (Incidently, part of the meaning of species is that, unlike random groups in analysis of variance, within and between variances will not estimate the same population variance.) Prediction from attributes becomes embarrassed by complex derivatives, interaction effects, or even entirely unpredictable "emergents." (b) By contrast, the prediction from type —if we are content to ignore the within-species variance as trivial— is very simple and quick. It is economical so long as there are not too many species types to store in memory, and when plenty of people occur at each type position. (c) Prediction from dimensions alone, even if simply linear, has the complication of involving two systems of dimensions (see below), namely, those *between*-species and those *within*-species. These systems, even when they employ similar variables, are likely to regress differently on any criterion, and require some complex handling. It may be better, therefore, first to recognize "He belongs to this type" and then use only the within-species regressions. This is what we commonly do as psychologists when we apply one law to learning in humans and another in rats.

3. DEVICES FOR MEASURING THE RESEMBLANCE OF PROFILE PATTERNS: d^2 and r_p

There are two main problems to be handled with types: (1) finding them, and (2) using them (descriptively, predictively, or in contributing to scientific understanding). This section is concerned with the first problem, without which a solution for the second cannot be pursued. Obviously, in many fields, types *can* simply be "seen" immediately and, unfortunately, many behavioral scientists, at least in sociology and anthropology, seem content to leave their methodology at this unsubtle level. As to this process of designating "types" by immediate perception, one should recognize that there are biases inherent in its very facility. It seems likely that many animal species are even innately predisposed to pick out entities of certain types more readily as perceptual objects, while social discussion and early upbringing incline us unconsciously and naïvely to see particular wholes, rather than others with equal claim. With risks arising from this predisposition, it is all the more important to put objective scientific type recognition on an explicit basis.

The modal concept of a type implies that the members of it resemble one another much more than they resemble persons classified as outside the type. When a single dimension is concerned, this is visibly demonstrated by their heaping up at the same modal score level but when several dimensions are involved, there is no simple way of representing and scanning the distribution visually. Then we ask instead for statistical means of answering the questions: (1) "How much does any one member of our population sample resemble any other?" (2) "What and how many are the groupings of persons with high mutual resemblance?" and (3) "How do we express exactly the modal measurement (central tendency) of each of these groupings?"

Essentially, there are two ways of locating dense spots or multi-dimensional modes in a distribution of people in a factor coordinate space: (1) the inter-id relational approach, and (2) the systematic space-density search. In the former one begins with the ids, e.g., people, and finds some distance function value among all possible pairs. That is, one finds the "bunchings" first and their positions later. This operates in matrix terms always from what we shall generically call a Q matrix, i.e., a square matrix bounded by all the ids, and with resemblance terms in the cells. In the space-density search method, on the other hand, one takes convenient intervals on the coordinates, for chopping the total space into (multi-dimensional) "squares" by "latitude and longitude," and sets a computer systematically to counting the number of cases in each.

With either method the further problem arises of fixing limits to decide when a density is significantly high. In what follows we shall pursue only the inter-id relation method, because its concepts have use in other connections also, and because the space-density search procedures are self-evident. As to any technical difficulties in the latter, it need only be said that they lie in the very large number of cubes to be counted. (For example, with 16 factor dimensions each cut into six intervals (say units of standard deviation, to cover the population span), there are $6^{16} = 2,830,000,000,000$ [approx.].) On the other hand, with a large enough sample of ids properly to cover a multidimensional space the number of paired person comparisons is no less formidable.

Unfortunately, in the inter-id relational approach one has to disencumber current practice and theory of some deeply rooted erroneous practices before a clean dissection can be made. Thus we must pause very briefly to set aside certain fashions in determining the degree of resemblance of one person to another. First, Q technique, which is properly a method of determining dimensions (Chapter 6, page 229), has been used (Rogers, 1213), in an attempt to determine person resemblance. Even as Q' technique (cluster search only) it fails if the correlation coefficient is used to determine resemblance of people, or if any measure of profile resemblance is applied to scores on correlated variables instead of independent factors, as elements. Certainly Q technique (factor analysis, as contrasted with cluster search in Q technique) is quite wide of the mark in classifying people on total type.

Any two profiles may be viewed as having separate degrees of resemblance in (1) shape, (2) level, and (3) accentuation (steepness of profile) of shape. If we speak of *configurations* instead of *profiles*, we must also add (4) order or sequence. The correlation coefficient, canceling means and sigmas, ignores differences in (2) and (3) and is affected by the accidental circumstance of the direction (see Cattell 230; Howard & Diesenhaus 777b) in which a variable happens to be called positive. (As an *intraclass* correlation coefficient it is distinctly better but still poorer than r_p to be described). Various indices to avoid these limitations are discussed below. The objection to applying almost any index that gives equal weight to the profile elements when these are substantially correlated is obvious. If they are given equal nominal weight, as is often done, they will in the end not have equal actual weight. If we envisage the independent, orthogonal dimensions in the space, then that which happens to have several single variable profile elements much correlated with it will be over represented while other dimensions may be bare of variables. On such a basis, as in Q-sort, there is no meaning to the statement that "These two people resemble each other to such and such a degree." With different choices of variables the resemblance (though sometimes worked out as a correlation with three decimal places!) will stray all over the range from + 1.0 to − 1.0.

Some of the above objections unfortun-

ately apply to the otherwise excellent applications in biology of Sokal and Sneath (1334). Among inadequate type approaches we must also classify the use of Holzinger's B coefficient (688) because it does not first locate clusters objectively; many uses of latent class analysis (596) because not applicable to continuous data and not permitting unambiguous assignment of individuals; and certain uses of the multiple discriminant function, because this is a means of emphasizing group differences, *not* of finding them.

To begin with a systematic study of appropriate means for finding the degree of resemblance of two profiles, let us start with people measured on a set of continuous variables among which approximately linear relations exist. This, or something very close to it, is the situation with which most psychologists are most commonly concerned in practice. Many conclusions and calculations from this model are readily transferred, with slight change, to the neighboring case of dichotomous categorical variables. On the other hand, complex non-linear (and some non-parametric) models are a different story, but they can best be tackled after we have solved the problem of recognizing and using types within the linear model.

Let us begin by assuming that we know from some source a set of orthogonal coordinates representing the dimensionality required to represent all the variables. For simplicity we can assume they are principal components, not factors, so that there are no specific factors to be considered and every person can be *exactly* represented by a point in the space. Then what we have defined above as a type (species type)—a modal frequency in a distribution of multi-element profile measures—can be most readily recognized as a particularly dense swarm of points (among more attenuated distributions) in this k dimensional space, each coordinate corresponding to a profile element. Diagram 9-1 (c) (page 290) shows this, of course, for two dimensions only, as also does Diagram 9-2, on which we shall now work out indices of resemblance.

A priori coordinates of the space in which people are placed can be either tests, or components or factors. The reasons for rejecting tests as orthogonal coordinates have just been given, namely, that by giving equal nominal weight to all tests, even though some have high mutual correlation, it overweights certain domains and to an (initially) unknown degree. The restriction on coordinates composed of common factors, rather than components, is that a person cannot be *exactly* placed, because we have only factor estimates—unless our framework includes both common and specific factors. However, we shall come to common factors in the end because their psychological meaningfulness more than outweighs their being only estimates. Meanwhile, let us ignore the question of whether our coordinates represent tests, components or factors, and consider them simply as unit variance coordinates with respect to which we want to work out an expression for the resemblance of two people, granted we know their scores on the coordinates (a) when the coordinates are truly orthogonal, as in our diagram, but also (b) for the case where they are oblique and we want to correct or allow for their obliquity.

Initially we shall talk of the simpler situation of giving *equal weight* to all dimensions. However, our general solution must obviously permit unequal weights to be given, and view equal weights as a special case. For in many psychological situations differences on some dimension could be more important than on another, e.g., in recognizing a type of political outlook, what we call a "radical-conservative" continuum of attitude scores may be more important than differences of intelligence in views expressed.

The problem of measuring the resemblance of two persons therefore becomes essentially the calculating of their distance apart in a defined factor space, and as Diagram 9-2 will remind us, this becomes, by Pythagoras' theorem, a computing of the square root of the summed squares of their distance apart, i.e., of the difference of their several projections, on the various factors.

$$d_{f(iy)} = \sqrt{(a_{1i} - a_{1y})^2 + (a_{2i} - a_{2y})^2}$$

where $d_{f(iy)}$ is the factorial distance between persons i and y, and the a's are their scores on factors 1 and 2. (Alternatively, this could be written $d_{a(iy)}$, if for variables instead of factors.)

This can be written as a "generalized distance function" for k *dimensions,* thus (j being any dimension):

$$(1) \quad d_{\underline{k}(iy)} = \sqrt{\sum_{j=1}^{j=k} (a_{ji} - a_{jy})^2}.$$

DIAGRAM 9-2. Basic Calculation of a Distance Function

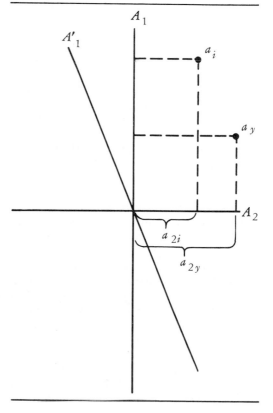

The dimensionality $\underline{k}$ is underlined to indicate it is the special case of k *orthogonal* coordinates (k being reserved for the general case of *any* coordinate angles). It will be noted that k is kept as a subscript for the distance function because the distance apart of i and y would differ in some other system with dimensions other than these $\underline{k}$ dimensions chosen.

The *resemblance or likeness* of two people, i and y (which we can write "L"$_{(iy)}$) can then be written:

$$(2)\quad L_{\underline{k}(iy)} = |\, E_{\underline{k}} - d_{\underline{k}(iy)} \,|$$

where $E_{\underline{k}}$ is some constant expressing the *expected* distance apart of two people, on chance alone, in $\underline{k}$ dimensions and d is their actual distance apart, from (1).

If we wish to make the generalized distance function still more general by considering the orthogonal case as only a special instance of the general obliquity of axes, we can rewrite (1) thus:

$$(3)\quad d_{k(iy)} = \sqrt{\sum_j^k \sum_m^k (a_{ji} - a_{jy})(a_{mi} - a_{my})r_{jm}}.$$

(The expression under the radical on the right can most easily be written in matrix form as a variance-covariance matrix C.)

Now the objections to leaving the resemblance of two persons expressed as in (1) or (3) above, i.e., in simply using the distance function as an inverse expression for degree of resemblance, as is done in many published researches, are:

(a) The magnitude of the d is not comparable across different scaling metrics for variables or factors (without the standardization advocated in our later r_p formula). For example, if reaction time in one experiment is in milliseconds and in another in tenths of a second, the result will be quite different; d is thus meaningless as it stands and unsuitable for comparison across experiments.

(b) As used or advocated by several writers, it makes no distinction between results based on orthogonal factors (Equation [1]) and on the oblique variables or factors (which we have distinguished by Equation [3]).

(c) The value of d ignores also any allowance for the *number* of dimensions involved. This can be achieved only by bringing it into relation with the *expected d* value and its distribution with different numbers of factors and kinds of factor score distributions.

These limitations were pointed out by Cattell (220) in proposing the pattern similarity coefficient, r_p, as an expression for measuring distance in entirely general and comparable terms. (When Osgood and Suci [1128], Cronbach and Gleser [396], Gaier and Lee [see Cattell, 240], and others wrote on this issue in the following decade, however, they discovered d^2 again, apparently unaware of the advantages pointed out earlier in going *beyond d²*.) The choice between Mahalanobis' original (979) straightforward definition of distance by d^2 (often written D^2, which incidentally, we avoid because it would conflict with matrix symbolism) and Cattell's r_p is essentially that the latter (1) takes account of the "metric" and "number of dimensions" incomparabilities mentioned above, (2) compares the d with the magnitude to be expected by chance, and (3) provides a convenient function which behaves, e.g., as regards distribution, in essentially same general way as r, varying from 1 for complete agreement of profiles, to 0 for no relation, and to -1 for completely inverse relation. Consequently, the usual mental habits in appreciating the meaning of the magnitude of a numerical correlation relation can be retained. Its formula (for continuous variables, in the orthogonal case) is:

$$(4)\quad r_{p(iy)} = \frac{E_{\underline{k}} - \sum_j^k d^2_{(iy)}}{E_{\underline{k}} + \sum_j^k d^2_{(iy)}}$$

where k is the number of dimensions involved in the comparison, d is the difference, in standard score units, between the individuals i and y on each of the successive dimensions, and E_k is twice the median chi-square value for k degrees of freedom, i.e., $E_k = 2k$, where k is the median chi-square.

The choice of the estimate of *the chance (expected) magnitude of difference* could be made in various—mainly two—ways. The logic of the adopted choice for r_p is as follows: The difference between a randomly chosen case x on one normally distributed standard score dimension and a case y on a similar uncorrelated dimension, has a variance of 2. For:

(5) $\sigma^2_{a-b} = \sigma^2_a + \sigma^2_b$.

The distribution of a series of such differences, taken for each of k pairs (i.e., over k profile elements) is, however, skewed, particularly when k is small. Since the number of elements in a psychological profile is likely to be small—say 10 to 30—the distribution of chi square strongly suggests that the median rather than the mean chi square be taken as the most likely value. Thus the value we need for E_k with which to compare the obtained value, is (twice) the median χ^2 for k degrees of freedom when we have k profile elements. This value, E_k, can be changed in the formula, for each new number of profile elements. (A χ^2 table can be kept in the computer program. The programming of r_p for the computer is very simple.) The further properties of r_p, the profile similarity coefficient, are discussed in connection with its use in the following section.

4. EVALUATING THE SIGNIFICANCE OF ORTHOGONAL r_p FOR INDIVIDUALS AND GROUPS

The meaning of an r_p of $+1.0$ is that two persons or patterns have exactly the same profiles and fall on the same point in a multidimensional space (as represented for two-space in Diagram 9-2.) A value of 0 means that they fall as far apart as one would (on an average) expect for any two points taken at random. A value of -1.0 means that they are at opposite ends of the distribution. Since the ends of a distribution are ill defined and asymptotic, the value -1.0 is in actual practice approached but never quite reached, and there is in consequence a small asymmetry (positive skewing) in the distribution of r_p about its median value of 0 (derivative from the skewed chi square distribution).

Since one cannot long effectively employ a statistic without more precise knowledge of its distribution, a much needed contribution was made here when Horn (742) showed that the probability P of obtaining a value up to (and including) the given r_p when the true value is zero is:[3]

(6) $P = \int_{2x_k^2\left(\frac{1-r_p}{1+r_p}\right)}^{\infty} \frac{e^{-\frac{\chi^2}{2}} (\chi^2)^{\frac{k}{2}-1}}{2^{k/2}\, \Gamma\left(\frac{k}{2}\right)} \, d\chi^2$

where k is the number of profile elements.

The higher-order moments of r_p are given by:

(7) $\mu_t = \int_a^{\infty} \left(\frac{k-x}{k+x}\right)^t \frac{x^{\frac{n-2}{2}} - c^{\frac{x}{2}}}{2^{\frac{n}{2}}\Gamma\left(\frac{n}{2}\right)} \, dx$

Table 9-1 is a useful reference source for reading off the significance of any r_p. It was calculated by Horn from (6). The slight asymmetry will be noted, requiring that separate parts of the table deal with positive and negative values. Similar reasoning can be used to evaluate the significance of a

---

[3] The reader may wish to compare this with the earlier expression by Cattell (220) for the moments of r_p around the origin:

(7) $\mu_t = \int_a^{\infty} \left(\frac{k-x}{k+x}\right)^t \frac{x^{\frac{n-2}{2}} - c^{\frac{x}{2}}}{2^{\frac{n}{2}} \Gamma\left(\frac{n}{2}\right)} \, d_x$

given *difference* of r_p. (What is the likelihood that Smith, whose r_p is .5 with Jones and .4 with Roberts, is really more like Jones?) Horn advocates going back to the Σd^2 term and using the following variance ratio expression given by Rao (1178):

$$(8) \quad \frac{N_1 + N_2 - k - 1}{k - 1} \left\{ \frac{1 + N_1 N_2 \Sigma d^2{}_i}{1 + N_1 N_2 \Sigma d^2{}_y} - 1 \right\}$$

with $(N_1 + N_2 - k - 1)$ and $(k - 1)$ *df*. Here, as usual, k is the number of elements, i and y are two individuals, and N is the size of sample on which the estimation of sigma is based.

Comparisons of r_p with other similarity indices have been made by Helmstadter (see Cattell, 240), regarding time of computation and accuracy of placement (according to known resemblance). Among the various indices of profile resemblance tried were: the intraclass correlation; r_p; the discriminant function; and r. The results show r_p to hold the advantage over all when equal weight is given to the above

TABLE 9-1

THE SIGNIFICANCE OF r_p FOR VARIOUS NUMBERS OF ORTHOGONAL ELEMENTS
(From Horn (742))

P is the probability of exceeding a given (absolute) value of r_p
corresponding to k degrees of freedom (Number of profile elements)

k	Positive r_p $P = .01$	.02	.05	.10	Negative r_p .01	.02	.05	.10	Median χ^2
2	.971	.943	.862	.736	−.738	−.699	−.624	−.537	1.386
3	.907	.855	.741	.604	−.655	−.612	−.535	−.451	2.366
4	.837	.773	.650	.519	−.596	−.553	−.477	−.397	3.357
5	.774	.705	.583	.460	−.552	−.509	−.436	−.360	4.351
6	.720	.650	.532	.416	−.517	−.475	−.404	−.331	5.348
7	.673	.605	.491	.383	−.489	−.447	−.378	−.309	6.346
8	.634	.567	.458	.356	−.465	−.424	−.357	−.291	7.344
9	.600	.534	.430	.334	−.444	−.405	−.340	−.275	8.343
10	.570	.507	.407	.315	−.426	−.387	−.324	−.262	9.342
11	.544	.483	.387	.299	−.410	−.373	−.311	−.251	10.34
12	.521	.462	.369	.285	−.396	−.359	−.299	−.241	11.34
13	.501	.443	.354	.273	−.383	−.347	−.289	−.232	12.34
14	.482	.426	.340	.263	−.372	−.336	−.279	−.224	13.34
15	.466	.411	.328	.256	−.363	−.335	−.271	−.217	14.34
16	.450	.397	.317	.245	−.352	−.318	−.263	−.211	15.34
17	.437	.385	.307	.237	−.343	−.310	−.256	−.205	16.34
18	.424	.374	.297	.230	−.335	−.302	−.250	−.200	17.34
19	.412	.363	.289	.223	−.327	−.295	−.243	−.195	18.34
20	.401	.354	.281	.217	−.320	−.288	−.238	−.190	19.34
21	.391	.345	.274	.211	−.314	−.282	−.233	−.186	20.34
22	.382	.336	.267	.206	−.307	−.277	−.228	−.182	21.34
23	.373	.329	.261	.201	−.302	−.271	−.223	−.178	22.34
24	.365	.321	.255	.197	−.296	−.266	−.219	−.174	23.34
25	.358	.314	.250	.193	−.291	−.261	−.215	−.171	24.34
26	.350	.308	.245	.189	−.286	−.257	−.211	−.168	25.34
27	.343	.302	.240	.185	−.281	−.253	−.207	−.165	26.34
28	.337	.296	.235	.182	−.277	−.248	−.204	−.162	27.34
29	.331	.291	.231	.178	−.273	−.245	−.201	−.159	28.34
30	.325	.285	.227	.175	−.269	−.241	−.197	−.157	29.34

requirements. A "ready-reckoner" for computing r_p on $k = 16$, 14, and other numbers of orthogonal profile elements is given in the Handbook to the 16 P.F. test (Cattell & Eber, 1966).

One must distinguish among the uses of r_p to determine the degree of resemblance (a) of two persons, (b) of two groups, and (c) of a person and a group. Only the first has been discussed so far, because it alone is relevant to the typing of individuals as such. But (b) becomes relevant when we extend to typing groups, e.g., occupations, and (c) is of constant importance in applied (clinical and personnel section) practice.

The same r_p formula (and standard error thereof, etc.) may be used for comparing group mean profiles with one another, provided we use d scores appropriate for the sigma of group means instead of individuals. Thus a standard score of unity is now defined by the sigma of the group means and all raw score differences must be expressed in those units. However, we cannot usually assume that the sigma of the group means estimated for a total population of groups, e.g., occupations, on any factor is $\sigma/\sqrt{N+1}$ (σ being that of the population of individuals and N the typical size of the groups being compared). For when we deal with occupations, clinical groups, etc., one must realistically assume that selection has occurred in entering them! Consequently, the within group variance must be smaller than would be expected from random assignment to sub-groups and the null hypotheses in analysis of variance does not hold. In accurate work, therefore there is no escape from the necessity of obtaining new, *empirical* evidence as to the sigma of the group means. This is an unexplored field, but presumably our surveys should not mix, say, occupations and clinical groups, but should find the sigma typical of the *species* of group with which we are dealing. At any rate the meaning of the r_p will be different if we define it as "the relative resemblance of anxiety hysteria and conversion hysteria *among clinical syndrome types*" from that when it is defined

as "the relative resemblance in regard to all known types of human grouping." When this empirical evidence is not available it may be *faute de mieux* procedure to substitute $\sigma/\sqrt{N+1}$ for the intergroup mean variance, but it will generally result in a systematic underestimate of the similarity of two groups. (In our experience this underestimate has turned out to be appreciable.)

Quite apart from the selection effect within the groups (whose profiles are being tested for resemblance) one must keep in mind the ordinary effect from a statistical point of view of the size of the occupational samples, etc., from which the group mean sigma is estimated. The true variance among subgroup means (for the population) is augmented in our observations by the error of estimate, due to the sampling smallness of the subgroups. Generally, we would want to estimate resemblance in terms of the true, population sigma of these means, so the variance of means for groups of the size taken must be subtracted from the empirically estimated variance of all group means to get an unbiassed estimate of the population variance of these means.

In the third use, (c), of r_p, e.g., in the frequently encountered problem of asking how similar a given *individual* is to a diagnostic or occupational *mean profile,* one must revert to the use in the r_p calculation of the sigma for *individuals* in the population. However, we may wish to interpret the significance of the given answer in a variety of perspectives. In vocational guidance it would suffice to take the individual's r_p to each of several occupational mean profiles and rank them in suitability, though the need to calculate the significance of a difference in r_p's may still remain. Alternatively, we might want to go further and compare the *fraction of persons in the occupation* with *the fraction of the general population* which reach or exceed a given r_p value to the occupational mean profile. This could be called a "chances of success" ratio, and an r_p cut off could be named at some familiar probability, e.g., 95 out of 100.

Yet another approach is White's proposal that for comparing group profiles, as above, we depart from the directly interpretable r_p and use Mahalanobis' expression. As given by Rao (1177, p. 246), this is $d^2_n = \Sigma_i\Sigma_j w^{ij}d_id_j$, where the elements w^{ij} are the elements of the matrix reciprocal to the dispersion matrix; d_i and d_j are differences on any two elements i and j, n is the number of elements, and summation is over both i and j from 1 to n. To test the hypothesis that there is no difference in mean values in this expression, Horn (741) suggested the variance ratio given by Fisher (519):

$$(9)\quad \frac{N_1N_2(N_1+N_2-k-1)}{n(N_1+N_2)(N_1+N_2-2)}\sum_1^n d^2$$

with k and (N_1+N_2-k-1) df, the N_1 and N_2 being the size of the two groups.

The pattern similarity coefficient can readily be adapted from continuous to categorical variables and in the typical case of items (provided they are orthogonal and 50-50 in cut) as used in McQuitty's (1015) pattern analysis, the resemblance over k dichotomous items, where disagreement occurs on d items is:

$$(10)\quad r_p = \frac{E_k - d}{E_k + d}$$

Since one fairly often encounters comparisons, as above, between properties of d^2 and r_p, it is appropriate to bring out here more explicitly the advantages and disadvantages of d^2 in relation to the whole class of coefficients of which r_p is only the principal representative. All of these coefficients are functions of the observed inter-id difference (sometimes distance) compared to an expected difference. The advantages of the profile similarity coefficient are, as indicated above, its abstraction from particularities of metric and number of dimensions, and its possession of an immediate meaning through having a distribution approximately as for the familiar r. Its disadvantage — if non-Euclidean space is a disadvantage — is that the inter-id similarities cannot be handled by Pythagoras'

theorem. The relation of d to r_p is, of course, parabolic, but over the middle range of r_p values the departure of the curve from linearity is comparatively slight (278).

The parabolic relation implies that in, say, calculating the similarity of two persons to a criterion profile, each is "penalized" according to the *square* of his distance from the criterion, and without regard to direction. In other words the value at the criterion is regarded as an optimum. This is inconsistent with the usual linear factor specification equation, in which performance goes on improving with any increment (or decrement) of factor score throughout the whole range of the dimension. Some further aspects of this relation will be taken up in Section 6 below on "pattern effects." But meanwhile it may be noted that other members of the family of profile similarity coefficients are available, with different properties in some of the above respects. Thus in what may aptly be called the *coefficient of nearness, r_n,* because it handles distance in virtually a Euclidean fashion, the nearly linear relation of d and r_n extends further than for r_p (278). Thus:

$$(11)\quad r_n = \frac{\sqrt{2k} - \sqrt{\Sigma d^2}}{\sqrt{2k} + \sqrt{\Sigma d^2}}$$

(The symbols are the same as in [4]. Strictly, the expected value of $\sqrt{\Sigma d^2}$ is $\sqrt{2k}\,(1 - 1/4k + 1/32k^2 - 1/128k^3 + \ldots)$, but $\sqrt{2k}$ is close enough if k is not too small. r_n has a distribution which approaches -1.0 more slowly than r_p, being approximately at -0.6 with a 5 sigma difference on all elements.) Other possible members of the family are indicated in Section 6 below.

5. THE FORMULA FOR r_p WITH DIFFERENT CORRELATIONS, WEIGHTS AND VALIDITIES AMONG THE PROFILE ELEMENTS

Before showing how the calculated similarities of people by r_p can be used as the means of locating naturally existing type clusters, there is need to expand the applicability of the similarity measure itself. For the r_p of the last section is only an introduction and an approximation, when used, as it often is, with somewhat correlated factors but using a formula strictly developed on the assumption of orthogonality.

Indeed, the majority of meaningful source traits are (a) oblique, and we need to be prepared also for the possibilities (b) that for some psychological reason, e.g., their importance after some age transformation, we shall need to give special arbitrary weights to the traits, other than the arbitrary equal weights, and (c) that source traits may be measured with unequal validities (arising partly from unequal reliabilities) which require again some difference of weights.

Three kinds of modification have therefore to be applied to formula (4) above. Our aim here is to develop an entirely general formula for r_p such that formula (4) can be considered as a special case, assuming orthogonal angles, unit weights and equal validities of measurement, while other special cases of unusual utility, e.g., equal unit weight without orthogonality, can be singled out for a more simplified statement.

Since most practical situations will present the psychologist with a series of differences $-d_1$, d_2 . . . d_k- between two people on the k elements of a profile, regardless of correlations, further weights to be applied, or validities $-$ but in standard scores $-$ our derivations should begin with the assumption that he starts with k standard score differences, d_1 to d_k, between two people x and y (and of course for any number of other pairs of people).

The main problem now is to find what the distribution of the distances apart of such people will be $-$ in terms of orthogonal, Euclidean space $-$ when d, the required distance, no longer equals $\sqrt{\Sigma d^2}$ as in the orthogonal equal weight, etc., situation. For from this distribution we need to find the average expected distance $-$ the equivalent in the general case of E_k in the

particular case of equation (4). As we shall see, the new formula calls both for a different way of calculating the distance apart of each pair of individuals and a different expectation of distance, E_k.

To calculate the distance in Euclidean (orthogonal coordinate) space between two people x and y when given a vector (matrix) $Z_{d_{(xy)}}$ of differences on the oblique factors we must use:

$$(12) \quad d^2_{(xy)} = Z'_{d_{(xy)}} R_f Z_{d_{(xy)}}$$

$$(\text{or } d_{(xy)} = \sqrt{Z'_{d_{(xy)}} R_f Z_{d_{(xy)}}}),$$

where $d_{(xy)}$ is the required distance and R_f is the square matrix of correlations among the factors.

To calculate next the effect of any special weights we may wish to give the dimensions (oblique or orthogonal) let us set up a diagonal matrix W of the chosen weights. (Incidentally, for simplicity of symbolism we drop the subscripts xy, f, d, etc., since they can be assumed. We will also deal in d^2, reverting to d only at the end.) The covariance among the weighted Z's is no longer R but is $WZZ'W' = WRW'$. So we have:

$$(13) \quad d^2 = Z'W'WRW'WZ$$

If next we consider the validities of the available scales or batteries, i.e., the multiple correlations of their items with the pure factors, to be r_{v1} to r_{vk}, then the variance of the measured factors will be only a fraction (r_v^2) of the true factor variance. Consequently we can allow for this by introducing what is virtually another diagonal matrix of weights, which we will call V (for validities). Thus WVZ must now replace Z and the covariance becomes $WVZZ'V'W' = WVRV'W'$. The distance, calculated on elements thus reduced in variance on the true factors, by our inability perfectly to estimate the latter, becomes:

$$(14) \quad d^2 = Z'V'W'WVRV'W'WVZ$$

To the practical issues involved in most conveniently calculating this distance (the root of the above) for any given pair we shall return. But the larger theoretical problem has first to be solved of determining the distribution of such d values over a population of persons, and thus calculating the typically expected (mean or median) value with which a given pair's d can be compared (as done for the simple case in Section 4 above). To do this we are going to condense the terms between Z' and Z in (13) into a single expression A. And to show how this A may be used a digression of a page in length is necessary into a number of purely formal mathematical propositions and transformations.

Let G be any general non-singular matrix such that $GCG' = I$, where C is the covariance matrix of Z and I is the conforming identity matrix. In practice we may not know the population value of C and must use an estimate, but this is an additional complication which we will not consider further. Further let Y be a matrix related to our given Z above by the relation $Y = GZ$, i.e., $Z = G^{-1}Y$. Then C_Y (the covariance of Y) $= GZZ'G' = GCG' = I$. Whence we can conclude that, since Z has the multivariate normal distribution with zero means and covariance C, i.e., $N_k(O, C)$, Y has the multivariate normal distribution $N_k(O, I)$, and

(15) $d^2 = Y'G'^{-1}AG^{-1}Y$

where A is some symmetrical matrix which can be the general symbol, as stated above, for a whole block of products such as $(V'W'WVRV'W'WV)$ in (14) above.

Now, by the principal axis theorem there exists an orthogonal matrix T such that:

(16) $T(G'^{-1}AG^{-1})T' = (\lambda_i \delta_{iy}) = \Lambda$

The last is, of course, a diagonal matrix whose elements are the latent roots λ_i of $(G'^{-1}AG^{-1})$. Now let $X = TY = TGZ$ so that $Y = T'X$. Since T is an orthogonal transformation we have that X is also distributed $N_k(O, I)$ and

(17) $d^2 = X'TG'^{-1}AG^{-1}T'X$
     $= X' \Lambda X = \Sigma \lambda_i x_i^2$

Thus we have shown that each element x_i of the vector x has a normal distribution with mean zero and unit variance and hence we have the well known result that each x_i^2 has a chi-square distribution with one degree of freedom. Thus the expected value (mean) of x_i^2 is 1.

So the expected value, E_k, of Σd^2 is, in the most general case, with which we are now dealing

(18) $E(\Sigma d^2) = E(\sum_i \lambda_i x_i^2) = \sum_i \lambda_i E(x_i^2) = \sum_i \lambda_i$.

We have now obtained the important result that the value of E_k to be used in equation (4) is simply the sum of the latent roots of the matrix product $G'^{-1}AG^{-1}$ where A is *any* symmetric matrix.

We have the further simplification that

(19) $\sum_{i=1}^{k} \lambda_i = \text{trace}(G'^{-1}AG^{-1})$

i.e. the sum of the latent roots is simply the sum of the diagonal elements of the matrix.

The problem now remains to find the matrix G. Fortunately this is quite easily done. We can resolve the known matrix C into its latent roots and vectors, a process readily accomplished on a modern computer. Then we have

(20) $C = LDL'$

where L is a matrix whose columns are the latent vectors of C and D is a diagonal matrix whose elements are the latent roots of C.

Suppose we take $G = D^{-1/2}L'$ then G is non-singular and

$GCG' = D^{-1/2}L'LDL'LD^{-1/2} = I$

so $D^{-1/2}L'$ is a G matrix as required in the above derivation, and we now have that the λ_i are the latent roots of

$G'^{-1}AG^{-1} = (LD^{-1/2})^{-1}A(D^{-1/2}L')^{-1/2}$
           $= D^{1/2}L'ALD^{1/2}$

which together with (18) and (19) gives

(21) $E_k = \text{trace } (D^{1/2}L'ALD^{1/2})$

This is the required general formula for the expected mean distance in any pair chosen at random. We can now return to formula (14) from which we take the equivalent of A in terms of the correlations, weights and validities among our factor scales.

(22) $A = V'W'WVRV'W'WV$

Since both V and W are diagonal matrices we may write (22) as

(23) $A = D_{WV}^2 R D_{WV}^2$

where $D_{WV} = (w_i r_{vi})$, a diagonal matrix whose elements are the products of the "a priori" weights and the validities.

So we get

(24) $E_k = \text{trace } (D^{1/2}L'D_{WV}^2 R D_{WV}^2 LD^{1/2})$

which can readily be determined given R, W and V.

Of course, the simple r_p considered in section 4 above had an E_k which is one special case of (24). For, with uncorrelated factors ($R=I$) equal weights ($W=I$) and unit validities ($V=I$), (24) collapses to:

$E_k = \text{trace } (D^{1/2}L'LD^{1/2}) = \text{trace } (D) = 2k$

since trace (D) = trace (C) = sum of variances of the Z_i, each of which is a difference score between two standard scores and thus has variance 2.

Another simple case of special practical interest is that given in equation (12) above where we have equal weights and unit validities, but the factors are correlated. This gives us

$E_k = \text{trace } (D^{1/2}L'RLD^{1/2})$
$\quad = \text{trace } (\tfrac{1}{4}D^{1/2}L'CLD^{1/2})$
$\quad = \text{trace } (\tfrac{1}{4}D^{1/2}L'LDL'LD^{1/2})$
$\quad = \text{trace } (\tfrac{1}{4}D^2)$

so E_k is one fourth of the sum of the squared latent roots of C. Or, if we deal with R (correlations) rather than C (covariances), E_k is simply the sum of the squared latent roots of R.

So far we have assumed the most psychologically meaningful case, in which the elements of the profile are known source traits, i.e. *factors*, orthogonal or oblique. There is, of course, no point in considering *variables* as elements, if we are to allow profile elements to stand on an essentially equal footing. However, the experimenter may have nothing but variables given to him and wish to proceed from these, *with a factor analysis implicit in the ensuing calculations*, i.e., he is still to give comparable influence only to factors. For the variables he is given can be only a sample (and with so few, a poorly representative sample) of the variables that might ideally be chosen to represent the factors in the given domain. Furthermore, each variable has associated with it specific and error variance which can only distort the distances we derive from them between people. To minimize this distortion therefore it is desirable to go back to the factor analytic model. If C_n^* is the observed covariance matrix we consider instead C_n, the *reduced* covariance matrix which has the specific and error variance removed from the diagonal. We will suppose that C is of rank $k < n$, i.e. we have k common factors.

Then we have $C = LD_kL'$ where D_k is a $k \times k$ diagonal matrix of the non-zero latent roots of C and L the matrix of associated latent vectors. We can then estimate the principal factor scores

$$Z_f = D_k^{1/2} L'R^{-1} Z = 2D_k^{1/2} L'C^{-1}Z$$

or for general orthogonal factor scores

$$Z_f = 2TD_k^{1/2}L'C^{-1}z$$

where T is any orthogonal transformation. Then the covariance of Z_f is

$$\begin{aligned} Z_f Z_f' &= 4TD_k^{1/2}L'C^{-1}ZZ'C^{-1}LD_k^{1/2}T' \\ &= 2TD_k^{1/2}L'C^{-1}LD_k^{1/2}T' \\ &= 2TD_k^{1/2}L'LD_k^{-1}L'LD_k^{1/2}T' \\ &= 2I \end{aligned}$$

so the Z_f are uncorrelated and

$$d^2 = 1/2 Z_f' Z_f$$
$$= 2Z'C^{-1}LD_k^{1/2}T''TD_k^{1/2}L'C^{-1}Z$$
$$= 2Z'C^{-1}Z$$

So the A of equation (20) is $2C^{-1}$

so E_k = trace $(2D_k^{1/2}L'C^{-1}LD_k^{1/2})$
= trace $(2D_k^{1/2}L'LD_k^{-1}L'LD_k^{1/2})$
= trace $(2I)$

where I is the $k \times k$ identity matrix
so $E_k = 2k$

It will be noted that in the model most likely to be used—oblique factors equally weighted but of differing validities of estimation—the calculation of the central A term by (23) above is comparatively simple. However, the calculation of r_p for *every individual case* (pair) can no longer be done simply by computing Σd^2, which can be done in one's head or on a desk computer for the ordinary restricted r_p. Instead the vector of differences must pre and post multiply a square matrix (equation (14)), a task which makes it desirable to have a computer program on hand for handling any series of individual cases.

The profile nearness coefficient (r_n in equation (11) above) can correspondingly be expressed for oblique and weighted factors.

$$(25) \quad r_n = \frac{E_k - (Z'_{d(xy)}D_w^2 R_f D_w^2 Z_{d(xy)})^{1/2}}{E_k + (Z'_{d(xy)}D_w^2 R_f D_w^2 Z_{d(xy)})^{1/2}}$$

Here, to a first approximation:

$$(26) \quad E_k = (\text{trace } (D^{1/2}L'D_w^2 R_f D_w^2 LD^{1/2})^{1/2})$$

where D and L are respectively the latent roots and vectors of the score covariance matrix.

6. DIFFERENCES OF TYPING BY PATTERN NATURE AND PATTERN EFFECT (ON CRITERIA)

The main mathematical problems for a general handling of similarity measures,

with diverse assumptions, have been solved in Section 5, but a number of statistical and even philosophical issues remain. Before applying similarity measurement to the discovery of types in Section 7, the present section will discuss these issues.

First there is the relatively trivial issue that in previous use of r_p, confined to the orthogonal case, we have used as the expected distance, E_k, the *median* value of the distribution, by taking the median chi-square value for k degrees of freedom. The reason for thus resorting to the median chi-square instead of taking the mean is that the distribution is skewed for a small number of cases and profiles commonly have only a small number of elements. However, with the 16 P.F., with which much profile research has been done the difference between the mean and the median chi-square is only $16 - 15.34$ which is 4%. And if applied psychology proceeds as it should, with, say, at least six primary abilities, sixteen personality factors and, say, ten motivation factors, to cover the main aspects of personality, the difference $(32 - 31.34 = .66)$ the difference is even less (2%). In either case r_p cannot have an *exactly* symmetrical and normal distribution, but, as theory would require, empirical data (224) shows that it is very close, even with 16 elements, to symmetry and normality. If we desire to take median chi-square with the oblique or weighted case it is necessary to know the distribution of

$$y = \sum_{i=1}^{i=k} \lambda_i x_i^2$$

where λ_c's are constants and x_i has a univariate distribution, and to know the median value for various values of k. However, for reasonably large profiles it is a matter of little importance whether mean or median is taken, provided one keeps to one system.

A second issue concerns the weighting matrix, W. Although we have thus preserved the freedom to weight source trait profile elements in any way we wish, by what rationale do we introduce weights?

Intuitively we have a sense of giving unequal weights in our everyday type classifications. For example, though women are usually shorter than men, and do not usually have beards, a tall woman is not judged as masculine as one with a beard. Furthermore our weights apparently alter from purpose to purpose, so that at this moment we see a group divided into men and women, at the next into graduates and undergraduates, at the next into Democrats and Republicans, and so on. Again it must be said that the discriminant function is not an answer to this weighting problem, because it presupposes that we know the groups we want to separate whereas we are saying that the weights, by altering the distances among people and groups of people, *give* us the groups we see.

Earlier (220) the senior author argued for a *pattern effect similarity index,* saying that the weights given to elements should depend on their *effects* with regard to some criterion or group of criteria. There are statistical problems here arising from possible confusion of the usual linear with the present quadratic, parabolic relation of score to criterion, and to these we shall turn in a moment. But first, at a more philosophical level let us note that some psychologists react adversely to this idea that types depend on purpose, believing in a sort of Kantian "Dinge an sich," and admittedly we commonly assume that the difference between a cat and a dog resides in properties which have their natural weights and do not depend on our purpose or mood of perception.

If the dimensions of an id are transformed into some single criterion prediction, by no matter what kind of mathematical function, then the distribution of those ids in multi-dimensional space will be projected upon some single continuum. In the case of a linear function, as instanced at wx in Diagram 9-3, the grouping will be simplified. Thus types 1, 2, 3, 4 and 5 become Type I and Type II, as shown by the histogram of projections there. In the case of a non-linear, polynomial expression as in the yz line (but still more complex) the number of types need not apparently be reduced (since one type might equal two "effect" types) but it would be *different.* The important point is that each classification by "effect," i.e., in terms of some specific function of the individual's primary dimensions, is different from every other. In these distorted derivative lines or spaces we seem to have an infinity of arbitrary classifications compared with what appears, at any rate at first sight, to be a unique and stable resolution in terms of the *equally* weighted *primary* dimensions.

However, it may be argued that though we do not classify objects according to a single purpose — and therefore see them differently re-classified with every change of purpose — we *do* have a certain collection of purposes in mind — our usual life purposes — and that (except for space and time which are universal) the weights we give to dimensions are a function of their classificatory relevance to the sum total (or average) of our purposes. The distinction made by such writers as McQuitty (1021, 1022) in his pattern analysis, between relevant and irrelevant properties for grouping people in patterns is a special extreme (non-parametric) case of this general weighting principle, and we shall meet it again in connection with "core" and "peripheral" variables for typing.

Nevertheless, a distinction between the person as he *is,* i.e. on some properties having nothing to do with purpose and effects, and what he *does,* i.e., his performances, is particularly doubtful in psychology, where our inference about structure of the object is based entirely on behavior. If for a moment we accept the distinction between a test measure and a criterion measure as apparently supporting this dichotomy, then, in any truly broad concept of personality and the personality sphere (213), we are soon compelled by mathematical and statistical logic to recognize that the dimensionality of the personality-ability measures and of the criterion measures is not only equal but applies to the same space. (The need for canonical correlation procedures is a confession of incomplete psychological grasp of our problem.) Consequently, classification by particular criterion, "effect" performances, is like classification by single traits or variables. Any generally meaningful typology has to classify by *all* dimensions, and the only question which remains portance or desirability, to "getting on well with a group," "being honest as a company treasurer," or "writing a profound novel," but the psychologist will then have to refer these weights back to the personality factors which produce them, redistributing the weights essentially by the factor estimation matrix. And from a suitably stratified sample of criterion performance values one could arrive at meaningful personality factor weights.

DIAGRAM 9-3. Regrouping and Reduction of Modal Types when Specific Effect (Criterion) Functions Are Used

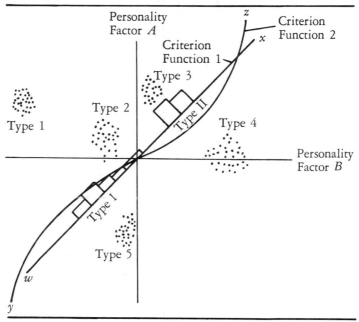

Histogram drawn of Criterion Function 1 shows two modes (types) replacing the five modes (types) on the profile elements themselves. The projections on Criterion Function 2 are too complex to be readily drawn.

is whether we get our weighting system from some direct appreciation of the traits or indirectly from values assigned to a lot of criterion performances.

If we are to assign weights or values to factors in a profile it is probable that we ought not assign them directly, but that our operational weightings should begin with what we usually call criterion variables. Society, e.g., by a vote, can assign im-

In principle, the weights which we have agreed could be applied to source trait profile elements could originate in four ways: (1) By transfer (through, say, a linear transformation) from value weights which an occupation, or society, has first attached to criterion performances predictable from the source traits, (2) By their efficacy, in terms of a discriminant function or other statistical test, in separating members of one group from another. An objection has been lodged to this above, namely, that we need to use r_p (weighted or unweighted) to find the natural groupings, so we cannot assume before using it, that we *know* the groups. But an iterative approach is discussed below (page 321) which does not so literally "beg the question" of what the groups are. (3) By some more intrinsic, immediate evaluation, having nothing to do with the functional statistical basis in (1) and (2). (4) By weighting factors (from the V_{fp} matrix) by their contributions to the variance of a standard personality sphere of variables. A combination of this with (1) is probably the most objective and theoretically sound procedure.

Without the above reflections, many psychologists have evidently proceeded on the assumption that the two paths—(a) calculating a criterion score for two people and taking their distance apart on it, and (b) calculating their distance apart directly on the (weighted) profile axes—will lead to the same result. But a little algebra will show that this is not so. In Diagram 9-4 (a) profiles x, y and z are very different and do not agree by r_p, but their criterion scores, assuming unit positive weights for A, B, C, and D are identical.

The earlier discussion above pointing out that r_p is thus itself a weighted, or, at least, not a simple linear function of the dimension should perhaps again be illustrated in Diagram 9-4 (b) where a non-linear relation is supposed between any one factor and a criterion. In a linear regression a given d will make the same absolute contribution to r_p no matter at what range it occurs, but, as we have just seen, because its sign is ignored, the specification (criterion) distances will bear no single ratio to the r_p similarity. When a non-linear relation is involved, as in Diagram 9-4 (b), or in any complex factor-criterion function, the discrepancy will be worse. For now not only the sign but also the quantity of criterion increment from a given d varies, as will be seen by comparing the criterion difference

for $f(x_1 - y_1) = c$ and $f(x_2 - y_2) = c$. This holds no matter what weights, exponentials or signs are involved.

The exception, as pointed out above, is when there is some optimum value of each factor for criterion performance and when the specification relating each factor to the criterion is approximately $c = a - bf^2$ (a and b being constants, f the factor score, c the

DIAGRAM 9-4. Projection of Persons onto Criterion Hyperplane

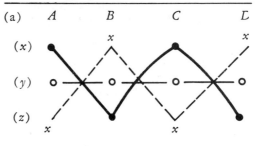

(a)   A   B   C   D

(x)

(y)

(z)

(b)

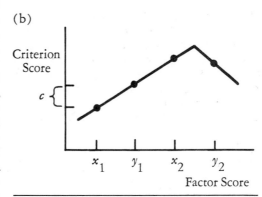

Criterion Score

criterion score). If one is to accept an optimum—and many social psychologists and personnel psychologists argue for this—then the best simple approximation is the quadratic relation and r_p is the most convenient formula for "fitness" of an individual to the occupation. Where, however, an optimum exists and we use r_p for the distance between two people over any part of the range, it will not give accurately meaningful results because (Diagram 9-1 [b]) the same d's are not equivalent at different levels. Thus, using the r_p of individuals from an ideal doctors' profile, z, we can say that if the value for $r_{p(xz)}$ is larger than for $r_{p(yz)}$ x is likely to make a better doctor (psychological assumptions being correct), but we cannot say that the mutual resemblance of x and y is greater than that of two other people a and b, *in terms of "doctor-fitness,"* simply because $r_{p(xy)}$ is greater than $r_{p(ab)}$. However, it is doubtful if anyone would want to ask this question!

7. THE GENERAL THEORY OF TYPE HIERARCHIES AND FUNCTIONAL EMERGENTS

Let us suppose for the moment that we have applied r_p in all possible combinations (pairs) of people in a population and that on the basis of the distances found among them — in the space fixed by the factors incorporated in our profiles — we see them as swarms of points variously separated as in Diagram 9-1. Further let us suppose — though the quite complex technical concepts and computing basis for this has still to be set out on page 316 below — that we have recognized g distinct subgroups or types in the total population of N persons and thus already know who belongs to which.

Our purpose in this section is first to look in rather general terms at the nature and origin of types, and at the concepts necessary to handle the phenomena which now appear. Obviously one set of useful concepts will be those of analysis of variance, or at least, of the notions of within group variance ("in-type variance" henceforth here), between group mean variance ("cross-type variance") and total population (or large sample) variance.

First we need to look at the meaning of the factor concepts with which we are usually operating in a population which

admits of a type breakdown of this kind. The main factors, forming the very coordinate system within which we see these types is that from factoring the total population. The fact that this is not homogenous *may* not imply that the distributions are *not* multivariate normal. With a large number of type groups well distributed a multivariate normal distribution on the factors could be obtained. On the other hand, with few types, this might not hold and, in any case, an obliquity of the factors, such as normally obtains, could be due to the massing of dense types in certain quadrants. Further, the existence of massive type groupings, and the generation of non-linear relations go together.

Another way of stating the existence of non-linear relations is to say that the factoring of the same variables on within type samples and across type samples is likely to yield factors somewhat differing in obliquities and possibly in patterns. Indeed, as soon as an investigator has used population factors to set up profiles whereby he has gained a preliminary separation into type subgroups he would be likely to (a) redetermine dimensions within groups, and (b) to begin changing his variables, noticing that the dimension most suitable for his previous task of locating types are no longer necessarily the best for maximally distinguishing individuals within types.

In the great naturalistic classification systems, such as those of Linnaeus and Darwin, this shift quickly became evident. For example, the features by which one best distinguishes the many local varieties of thrushes or snails are very different from those most useful in distinguishing thrushes from other birds or birds from snails. In fact, naturalistic classification recognizes not merely two levels as above, but a whole hierarchy of levels, in which individuals are first typed as species (if we omit local varieties), species are typed into genuses, and so on through families, orders, classes, and phyla. Within the class of fishes the representatives of the various orders differ in size of gills, arrangement of fins, etc., but within the phylum chordata the most typical fish differs from the most typical reptile, bird, mammal, amphibian, and other class representatives specifically in measures on nature of covering, body temperature, division of the body cavity, hollowness of bones, and many other dimensions that have little meaning for differentiating among fish.

Regardless of whether type groupings appear as sporadic isolates, or in some dendritic or hierarchical structure, what needs to be explained is the fact that *no* individuals appear at certain possible combinations of dimension values, whereas a mode of high frequency of "duplication" occurs at others. A brief digression to focus the natural origins of types might do more to improve models and methods for type isolation and use than any amount of mathematico-statistical virtuosity as such.

Earlier it was suggested that empirically one observes types to occur from genetic or sociological adjustments or from laws governing patterns of breakdown in a functioning organism. The two first imply special advantages in certain combinations of measurements, in terms of "criterion" performance. One way of looking at this is in terms of the principle of "emergents" which in one form or another has had a role in biology since the time of Lloyd Morgan. However, to be comprehensive, one must recognize that certain combinations may not exist at all, not because no useful emergent suddenly appeared at that combination, but because Nature never succeeded in finding the combination. This could hold for both genetic types (in which intermediate mutations to reach a very advantageous mutation might be disadvantageous) and of social types. (It took a long time to produce mathematics students who were also interested in psychology!)

That certain combinations of measures on basic dimensions are much more functional than others is evident both in organic and inorganic structures. The long legs of the giraffe function with a long neck; a spade needs a stronger handle than a spoon; a camera with an f1.0 lens needs to be combined with a shutter of faster speeds than one of f8. The multiplication of ids at certain combinations only implies generally that the relation of any one factor to the criterion cannot be linear, and that certain new factor dimensions are likely to appear when factoring within the modal type which do not appear between types, i.e., which are likely to be lost when a total population sample is factored. By "functional emergents" we refer both to the sudden accesses of criterion performance which occur at certain factor combinations, in factors themselves meaningful over the whole population, and to the new factor dimensions of variation which occur at modes on the distribution plotted over the population factors.

If this is the general nature of the origination of types, certain characteristics other than the primary one of sheer high density of cases should contribute to the location of types, notably certain historical sequences (if we *have* any history of genesis) and especially, *a sudden increase in the loading (contribution) of the cross-type factors relative to a number of useful criterion performances.* Secondarily, we shall usually find that where this replication of persons (a multi-dimensional mode—multimode for short) occurs a number of new adaptive habit skills, personality behaviors, etc., will appear which have no existence (and therefore, originally no variance) in the general population. These secondary, in-type traits will, of course, henceforth have an extremely skewed distribution in the population as a whole.

Naturally we have held to linearity as long as we can, and in practice we may continue to do so even when we know it is only an approximation, provided the convenience is not offset by *too* crude an approximation. However, in this general theoretical overview we must consider what is necessary when linear weighted functions no longer suffice or fit at all, and when emergents require more complex functions. The present chapter cannot ambitiously set out to handle the whole problem of non-linear, complex relations of variables. However, since the issue of non-linear, "emergent" effects has become tied up in psychological discussion with the concepts of "pattern effects" and "gestalts" and since the existence of a discrete type argues, as stated above, for some special *non*-linear, functional relation of profile elements to the criterion, we must at least treat that aspect of complex functions which has to do with pattern *effects*. (Though not the more complex issue of the implication of complex effect relations for pattern (type) *discovery,* as such.)

Unfortunately, the whole issue of "pattern effects" upon criteria has been handled either in a spirit of gestalt mysticism or in a grossly empirical "hole and corner" fashion —e.g., by regarding a particular effect as arising in some quite mysterious fashion from a particular "wholism." The empirical and "applied" approach has experimented with thousands of psychometric item combinations blindly trying to tie certain patterns with certain criterion performances. In theory, the important generality to keep in mind is that a formula can always be found which simply substitutes for the linear weighted or unweighted equation an exponential polynomial of any required degree of complication, thus:

$$(27) \quad a_{ji} = b_1 f_1^n + b_2 f_1 f_2^p + \text{etc.}$$

Some first steps in drawing attention to these possibilities have been taken by Lubin and Osburn (963, 964), Meehl (1029), Horn (746), Horst (756), and others (e.g., Cattell in the notions of interactive, permissive, and catalytic effects [240, p. 387]). It is perhaps unfortunate incidentally, that educational measurement statisticians have considered combinational, pattern effects most in regard to patterns of single "items," instead of meaningful source

trait elements in a profile, each yielding a continuous score. For it is not necessary to reduce our treatment to the empty assumptions necessary when the elements have all the instability, unreliability, and meaninglessness of single items. What this area most needs is a generalization in terms of source traits, thus expanding equation (27) into models consistent with the general properties of source traits now being discovered.

However, accepting the item level merely for illustration, the issue is at any rate embodied in some psychological cases. Thus there is Meehl's "paradox" that combinations can predict effectively when the elements which go to make them have no predictive value. For example, instances can be cited where yes on No. 1 or on No. 2, is unpredictive but where the answers being the *same* or *different* is predictive of something. Horst (756) shows that this is just a particular case of the general kind of equation in (27) above, which he particularizes for such a dyad, involving items x_1 and x_2, as follows:

$$(28) \quad (a) \quad a_1 = 1 + x_{1i} + x_{2i} + 2x_{1i}x_{2i},$$

or more generally,

$$(b) \quad a_1 = b + b_1 x_{1i} + b_2 x_{2i} + b_{12} x_{1i} x_{2i}$$

For a triad, as in Stouffer's use, this becomes:

$$a_1 = x_{1i}x_{2i} + x_{1i}x_{3i} + x_{2i}x_{3i} - 2x_{1i}x_{2i}x_{3i}.$$

Lubin and Osburn (965) point out that for the dichotomous element profile, the general equation (for three items) is:

$$(28) \quad (c) \quad a = b_0 + b_1 x_1 + b_2 x_2 + b_3 x_3 \\ + b_{13} x_1 x_3 + b_{23} x_2 x_3 + b_{123} x_1 x_2 x_3$$

and, since $2^3 = 8$, this requires experimental determination of mean criterion scores (a) for persons with each of the eight profiles, followed by solutions for the weights (b_1, b_2, etc.) by means of the eight equations. They point out also that the linear multiple regression equation for n elements would normally not achieve a validity equal to these more complex functions, but that certain special conditions, e.g., that one finds only $n + 1$ separate criterion values exist for the n elements, would simplify the polynomial to a multiple regression.

Horn (746) points out that there is a serious problem of loss of degrees of freedom in use of an equation like (28) if the b weights are obtained by use of what he calls "empirical search" techniques, i.e., procedures which involve scanning through all possible profiles in search of weights which will raise the reliability or validity of the scores implied by (28). With an n of only 10 dichotomously scored profile elements, there are no less than 2^{10} possible profiles. Thus, if a degree of freedom is lost in considering each of these possibilities, an N of 1024 is used up and an N larger than 1024 would be needed to establish stable b weights. Of course, ordinarily not all possible profiles would be regarded as reasonable. Still, the possibility of considerable loss of degrees of freedom in research aimed at finding profiles must be clearly recognized if the results from such research are to contribute to our understanding.

However, over most of this field of prediction of criterion performances from treating the elements of a profile in a way more complex than a linear regression we are today reduced to theoretical discussion only. There is extremely little psychological data firm enough to have demonstrated an indubitable need for any prediction of effects through more than a linear or, at most, a quadratic expression such as is involved in r_p. But where one wishes to pursue this approach, the necessary procedure is to start with approximate unitary source traits, and with individuals having independently measured endowments upon them. By successive purification of the trait patterns, and by obtaining enough instances of measured performance on a particular criterion in a plot against factor scores, one may then seek to solve the polynomial.

8. TAXONOMIC PROCEDURES FOR FINDING TYPES AND CLIQUE STRUCTURES

Let us remind the reader that we have discussed the properties of modal types but that, except for indicating the alternative *id relation,* and *systematic space search* approaches, we have postponed the technical discussion of how they are to be found. One reason why psychologists have hitherto been totally unsuccessful in finding and agreeing upon clinical and social types is that they have failed to define what formal entity they are looking for. Even when fully defined it is no easy task objectively to locate types, as we shall see. But the major principle to keep in mind is that the modal type notion actually hides two distinct operational concepts, which we shall call the *homostat* and the *segregate.* The first emphasizes that the members are all alike; the second that they are isolated from others.

The term homostat, meaning "standing similarly," is defined as *a group of ids such that every member resembles every other beyond an agreed limit of high resemblance* (on the profile similarity or d measure). In the spatial representation the members of such a group will stand within a multidimensional sphere of diameter d, corresponding to the r_p agreed upon. In Diagram 9-5, which is a two-dimensional representation, the ids in circles 1, 2, 3, and 4 constitute four homostats.

The term segregate (or "ait," for short, indicating an island, aptly of an elongated shape as in Diagram 9-5) is defined as *a group of ids in which each resembles (to a defined degree of resemblance) more ids in the group than out of it.* In Diagram 9-5, $A, B, C, D, E,$ and F are segregates, and $A_1, A_2, B_1, B_2, B_3,$ etc., are still higher resemblance levels of aits within these. The ait is thus defined by its isolate nature. Its exact operational definition involves more detail than the above, requiring the use of the term *phenomenal cluster,* not yet defined.

However, it is easy to see that aits and homostats are very different things. For example, a property of homostats frequently unrecognized is that the ids with which they begin and end are arbitrary, so that all kinds of overlaps may exist among them, as between 3 and 4 in Diagram 9-5. For example, if we imagine ids *a, b, c* and *d* arranged in a square whose side is just within the stipulated *d,* then we have the arbitrary alternative of homostats *ab* and *cd* or *bc* and *ad.* There is a little-realized subjectivity about a homostat, in that, like the circle of light thrown by a flashlight, it creates a unity wherever the experimenter cares to direct it. The number of ids within the circle will, however, be high or low, according to the data, and by fixing that limiting number the investigator can restore some objectivity and meaning to his search. However, he will still encounter the fact of series of overlaps, as in 3 and 4 in Diagram 9-5, and

to this we shall address ourselves by the concepts of *phenomenal* and *nuclear clusters.*

From this point on we shall be simultaneously describing a set of concepts defined by operations and a computer program, *Taxonome* (278), which successfully embodies them. It has the aim of finding both homostats and aits, but must begin by finding homostats on the way to aits. One begins with a Q matrix, i.e., a square matrix with the same people repeated along each boundary, any cell in which will have an entry representing the resemblance of the id at the top of the column with the id at the end of the row. This is the usual beginning of all $\overline{Q}$ technique cluster search procedures. The entry will normally be r_p or r_n, either on total dimensions or as a specific "effect" resemblance, but it could be d or some other index. Indeed, one should stress that from here on the model and procedure we are describing has quite

DIAGRAM 9-5.   Segregates ("Aits") and Homostats Illustrated in Two Dimensions

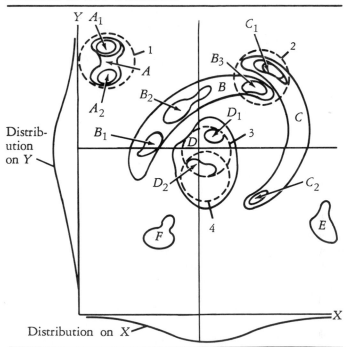

a high generality, for it applies both to finding types and to finding clique and communication network structures. In the latter case the Q-matrix entries will represent degrees of "social tie" attitudes, contact frequencies, or degrees of communication, instead of degrees of resemblance.

From this first Q matrix one proceeds to a Q incidence matrix, in which entries above a certain value are transformed to 1's and those below to 0's. Modifications of the present procedure will be evident in which "degrees" of linkage can be envisaged and adaptations made to the notion of continuous variables, but in this complex field it has seemed best to experiment first with the "all or nothing" linkage of the incidence matrix. Some consideration must, however, be given to principles for choosing the cutting level on r_p above which high or significant resemblance may be said to exist.

Most psychologists have been content with some arbitrariness about the limiting cut — say, an r_p of $+0.5$ — but this is scarcely satisfactory. One suggestion has been to employ Holzinger's B coefficient (Holzinger & Harman, 740). Therein we start with a substantially related pair and go on adding other persons, one at a time, working out the mean r_p or r for the set at each step, and stopping when an addition threatens to produce a significant drop in the mean. But what is "significant" and how arbitrary is the starting point? This approach, also, amounts to saying that the mean must not fall below an arbitrary point, instead of the lowest inter r (or r_p) as in the simple arbitrary definition. In the end, the only escapes from arbitrariness are either to say (1) one will recognize only the *highest* x per cent of clusters as clusters in a given domain — this is a hidden arbitrariness; it amounts to defining those covering n per cent of the total variables, or (2) one will take the *mean r_p* obtaining in that area as one's cutting point (or some function of the mean and sigma, e.g., $+1$ sigma).

The relativity to the correlation level in the given domain, as implied in both (1) and (2) has much common-sense support. Ten men meeting in the Sahara constitute a noteworthy crowd, but not in Times Square or Piccadilly. The density of points has meaning, directing that we apply the word *type* or *cluster* only in relation to the general density of points (people) across the whole plot of that domain.

How can this relation to the general density best be expressed? One possibility is to take the average r_p. This value, when calculated on the median chi square formula (13) above is very close to zero (slightly positive, about .005 with $k=16$ and about 100 cases); and can be shown to alter only trivially with the size of sample. Such a cutting point would merely exclude negative r_p and would include roughly half of the people in clusters. Another promising value suggested is the mean of all positive r_p's. With random samples this runs from roughly 0.1 to 0.2 with more than a dozen elements in the profile. The square root of the mean positive r_p has also been proposed. Trials are being carried out on a variety of known taxonomic structures to decide empirical practicabilities, but a significant positive r_p, say 0.25, might be a good baseline, since one wants most individuals to fall in some group. An r_p taken arbitrarily at $+0.4$ worked very well in grouping nations, on a 12 factor profile, in culture pattern types (224). It should be noted that except for sampling variability a given r_p value will cut off the same *percentages* of the sample. Clusters will be larger in large samples, but the percentage correctly indicates the density of representation in an area.

Taxonomic investigations should in any case normally check an analysis by repeating it at two or three levels of cutting point. It must be recognized that the number and forms of clusters found will vary with the cutting point. As the tide drops in some estuary strewn with sandbars, the map of island areas which we see appreciably changes. Two islands become one and new islands appear. This parallels what happens as we alter the limiting value for "belonging" to a cluster type, except that it is happening in a multidimensional instead of a three-dimensional topography. Whatever persists in some form despite moderate r_p cutting point level changes would receive the greatest confidence.

possible pairs, exceed the cutting point. However, two such phenomenal clusters may, and frequently do, overlap, as these do in the nuclear cluster c, d, and e. It may be necessary to point out here that "nuclear" conveys no value judgment of greater importance or stability; it is simply an operational statement of a necessarily distinct

DIAGRAM 9-6.   Phenomenal and Nuclear Clusters

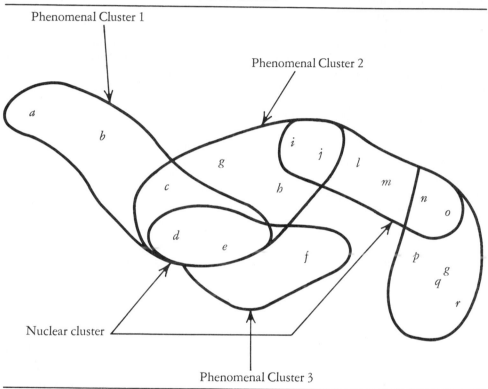

Granted the incidence matrix, the task is now to find homostats. Actually, the term homostat is probably best reserved to cover both *phenomenal* and *nuclear* clusters, for both fit the homostat definition above. Diagram 9-6 most quickly shows the meaning of these two entities: a phenomenal cluster, as its name indicates, is simply a statement at the level of observation of phenomena, that certain ids, e.g., a, b, c, d, and e, or c, d, e, g, h, and i "go together" in the sense that all r_p's among them, in all

concept. Both phenomenal and nuclear clusters meet the definition of homostat, but the latter adds a restriction.

Now an algorithm called the ramifying linkage method was proposed years ago by Cattell (229) for objectively combining Q matrices for clusters. It proceeds down the first column, noting the incidence entries, and then proceeds systematically down the columns corresponding to these entries, deleting from the accumulating group those which prove not to be linked to any earlier addition. For effective use of this algorithm it is necessary to introduce a Boolean multiplication. The whole cluster search process can be briefly illustrated by beginning with a simple Q' matrix, as in Table 9-2 (which it is always more convenient to set up with symmetrical repetition across the diagonal of unities, as shown). The ramifying linkage method starts us down column 1 of Q'_o, and each time we come to a 1 we must decide if this person belongs in the group or not. He will belong if he is linked with everyone already in the group, that is, if for every 1 entry above him in P_1 there must be a corresponding entry 1 in his row (or equivalently, column) or Q'_o. (P symbolizes phenomenal cluster matrix, and it is written P_1 because the first sweep does not include all, and successive P's are necessary.) So, from Q'_o of Table 9-2, we see that 5 is linked to 1. Then going down the column to the next 1 entry we find that 7 also belongs to the group, since when we look along the 7 row there are 1's in columns 1 and 5, the two persons already included in the group. Going on to column 2 we find that persons 2 and 6 form a group, from column 3 that 3 and 7 form a group. Column 4 contains a single 1 and need not be considered. Working down column 5 we include 1 and 5, but on examining person 6 we find a 0 in the 1 column of row 6, so 6 does not belong in the group and the 1 corresponding to person 6 in P_1 is changed to 0. Seven is related to 1 and 5, and so is included. However, the group now found is identical to group I and so we do not include it in P_1. Similarly, we work through columns 6 to 10, finding in all the five distinct groups listed in Table 9-3 as the columns of P_1.[4]

Actually, the ramifying linkage method is best regarded as a first extraction step and the whole procedure has a formal analogy to factor analysis in that it resembles the first step in a multiple factor extraction. Indeed, the formal similarity is considerable, for our procedure is to set down a first phenomenal cluster matrix, P_1, from the ramifying linkage "extraction" process, and make therefrom a product matrix, Q_1, which, subtracted from Q_o, leaves a first residual, Q_2. Thus, step 2 in Table 9-2 is:

(29) $Q'_1 = P_1 \cdot P'_1$

where the prime denotes transposition and the period denotes Boolean matrix multiplication, i.e., matrix multiplication with arithmetic addition and multiplication replaced by logical addition ("or") and multiplication ("and").

If P_1 contains all phenomenal clusters, then we must have

$$Q'_o = Q_1$$

since a link (other than a diagonal one) in Q_o indicates that two persons are related and so they must appear together in at least one phenomenal cluster. The operation $P_1 \cdot P'_1$ simply determines which persons appear together in phenomenal clusters. Table 9-2 gives Q_1 for the example. Zeros in Q_1 corresponding to ones in Q_o have been denoted by x's, indicating that in this case not all phenomenal clusters have been found. Now a new "residual" incidence matrix, Q_1, is formed from the x's of Q^*_1 plus any element in their columns that was a one in Q_o and for which there is also an x in its row of Q^*_1. Such an element might form a phenomenal cluster with the x's and so needs to be included. Table 9-2 gives the Q_1 for the example. Using the ramifying linkage method we now find additional phenomenal clusters — in this case one, No. VI — which we include with those already found to form P_2.

---

[4]Two points must be noted about the ramifying linkage method. Firstly, some of the clusters found may be subsets of other clusters. This presents no problem. Secondly, due to the sequential nature of the procedure, not all clusters may be found, at least where certain unusual configurations exist. Thus in Table 9-2 the group consisting of persons 5, 6 and 7 is not found. We do not include phenomenal clusters of only one person, which correspond to a column with only a diagonal element that is non-zero, e.g., columns 4 and 8 of Table 9-2, Q_o.

Then,

$$Q^*_2 = P_2 \cdot P'_2,$$

and,

$$Q^*_2 = Q_1$$

if all phenomenal clusters have been found. We proceed in this way until we find a P_n such that $Q^*_n = Q_{n-1}$ except possibly for

some diagonal elements. In the example, Table 9-2, $Q^*_2 = Q_1$ except for the (4,4) and (8,8) elements, so P_2 contains all the phenomenal clusters in Q_0.

How is one to represent the results of such an analysis? Up to this point they refer only to homostats, and can be ex-

TABLE 9-2

SEQUENCE IN THE PHENOMENAL CLUSTER SEARCH PROCESS

	1	2	3	4	5	6	7	8	9	10
1	1	0	0	0	1	0	1	0	0	0
2	0	1	0	0	0	1	0	0	0	0
3	0	0	1	0	0	0	1	0	0	0
4	0	0	0	1	0	0	0	0	0	0
5	1	0	0	0	1	1	1	0	0	0
6	0	1	0	0	1	1	1	0	0	0
7	1	0	1	0	1	1	1	0	1	0
8	0	0	0	0	0	0	0	1	0	0
9	0	0	0	0	0	0	1	0	1	1
10	0	0	0	0	0	0	0	0	1	1

(1)

$$Q'_0$$
(a)

P_1:

	I	II	III	IV	V
1	1	0	0	0	0
2	0	1	0	0	0
3	0	0	1	0	0
4	0	0	0	0	0
5	1	0	0	0	0
6	0	1	0	0	0
7	1	0	1	1	0
8	0	0	0	0	0
9	0	0	0	1	1
10	0	0	0	0	1

P'_1:

	1	2	3	4	5	6	7	8	9	10
I	1	0	0	0	0	0	1	0	0	0
II	0	1	0	0	0	1	0	0	0	0
III	0	0	1	0	0	0	1	0	0	0
IV	0	0	0	0	0	0	1	0	1	0
V	0	0	0	0	0	0	0	0	1	1

= Q'_1:

	1	2	3	4	5	6	7	8	9	10
1	1	0	0	0	1	0	1	0	0	0
2	0	1	0	0	0	1	0	0	0	0
3	0	0	1	0	0	0	1	0	0	0
4	0	0	0	x	0	0	0	0	0	0
5	1	0	0	0	1	x	1	0	0	0
6	0	1	0	0	x	1	x	0	0	0
7	1	0	1	0	1	x	1	0	1	0
8	0	0	0	0	0	0	0	x	0	0
9	0	0	0	0	0	0	1	0	1	1
10	0	0	0	0	0	0	0	0	1	1

(2)

$$P_1 \qquad\qquad P'_1 \qquad\qquad = \qquad\qquad Q'_1$$
(b)

Q_1:

	1	2	3	4	5	6	7	8	9	10
1	0	0	0	0	0	0	0	0	0	0
2	0	0	0	0	0	0	0	0	0	0
3	0	0	0	0	0	0	0	0	0	0
4	0	0	0	1	0	0	0	0	0	0
5	0	0	0	0	1	1	1	0	0	0
6	0	0	0	0	1	1	1	0	0	0
7	0	0	0	0	1	1	1	0	0	0
8	0	0	0	0	0	0	0	1	0	0
9	0	0	0	0	0	0	0	0	0	0
10	0	0	0	0	0	0	0	0	0	0

(3)

$$Q_1$$
(c)

TABLE 9-2 (Continued)

Sequence in the Phenomenal Cluster Search Process

		I	II	III	IV	V	VI		1	2	3	4	5	6	7	8	9	10
	1	1	0	0	0	0	0	1	1	0	0	0	1	0	1	0	0	0
	2	0	1	0	0	0	0	2	0	1	0	0	0	1	0	0	0	0
	3	0	0	1	0	0	0	3	0	0	1	0	0	0	1	0	0	0
	4	0	0	0	0	0	0	4	0	0	0		0	0	0	0	0	0
(4)	5	1	0	0	0	0	1	5	1	0	0	0	1	1	1	0	0	0
	6	0	1	0	0	0	1	6	0	1	0	0	1	1	1	0	0	0
	7	1	0	1	1	0	1	7	1	0	1	0	1	1	1	0	1	0
	8	0	0	0	0	0	0	8	0	0	0	0	0	0	0	x	0	0
	9	0	0	0	1	1	0	9	0	0	0	0	0	0	1	0	1	1
	10	0	0	0	0	1	0	10	0	0	0	0	0	0	0	0	1	1

P_2 Q^*_2

(d)

TABLE 9-3

Phenomenal Clusters Discovered

Raw Size	Identifying Number	Instances	Size, if Cluster, as Percentage of Sample	Frequency Distribution
6	(2) $a\,b\,c\,d\,e\,i$		60	$16\frac{2}{3}$
5	(1) $a\,b\,c\,f\,g$	(3) $a\,b\,c\,d\,h$	50	$33\frac{1}{3}$
4	(4) $k\,l\,n\,o$		40	$16\frac{2}{3}$
3	(5) $j\,k\,n$	(6) $l\,m\,o$	30	$33\frac{1}{3}$
2	None		20	0

haustively set out in two (potentially three) kinds of table, as follows:

(1) A listing of phenomenal clusters by size, from 2 membership upward, and recording the individuals involved (see Table 9-3).

(2) A listing of nuclear clusters, which requires a tabulation according both to size *and* the number of phenomenals involved in the overlap (see Table 9-4).

It may be rightly objected that (1) the resolution does not present a particularly simple picture and indeed seems to offer alternative nuclear and phenomenal concepts, (2) that it may be dependent on the level of cut-off for r_p. Furthermore, we have still not reached the statement concerning segregates. But the reader has at least been forewarned above that we are necessarily out to describe something complex, not resolvable, as are factors,

into a *simple* end result.

Nowhere is the futility of oversimplified and abstract mathematical models (already encountered in the components-vs.-factors debates) shown so clearly as in cluster search. Clusters are a matter of topography, and this topography, like, say, that of the Isles of Greece, simply will not yield the neat, distinct, exactly comparable entities which some mathematical psychologists see

TABLE 9-4

Account of Nuclear Clusters

Size	Phenomenal 2	Clusters 3	Involved 4
4	$a\,b\,c\,d$		
3	$e\,a\,b$		
2	$c\,d,\,k\,n,\,l\,o,$	$a\,b$	
1	e		

in their mind's eye. Clusters and types in nature are as untidy as a tangled skein of wool, or the cloud masses in a stormy sky. Our system of representation and recording must recognize this (as does Sokal and Sneath's [1334] mathematical treatment of biological data, though in factor, not cluster terms). At best the taxonomic search can end (1) in a list of phenomenal clusters,[5] or (2) in a list of nuclear clusters arranged in a hierarchy according to (a) size (number of variables involved) and (b) the number of phenomenal clusters which overlap in them, (3) in a list of segregates, and (4) in what may be called a general statement about the *texture* (see below) of type distributions in the domain (analogous to the meteorologist's cumulus, cirrus, etc., descriptions).

Before proceeding to "aits," two incidental points should be made here. First, one cannot reflect a person as one reflects the sign of a test, e.g., by scoring "sociable" as "unsociable." The latter procedure is commonly followed, and is quite permissible, with *correlation coefficients and with variables,* as in reflection for the centroid analysis, or any other arranging of variables to have "consistent" signs in a cluster. But this cannot be done in proceeding to the simplified Q matrix (incidence matrix) with r or r_p, as it can in the R matrix, because a negative r_p or r means that

the persons are as far away and unlike as possible. There is no guarantee that an anti-person exists, as one can assume that an anti-trait does. The existence of God is no longer taken as proof that there must be a Devil. It may also be true that in a logical sense opposites are more alike than randomly unrelated things, and theology recognized this by insisting that Lucifer was a fallen angel. In short, there *are* perhaps special psychological purposes in which it would make sense to consider diametric opposites as in some way belonging to the same type, and in that case the Q matrix can have its entries reflected in sign to maximum positiveness before forming the simplified Q matrix, i.e., the *tie matrix*. But usually one must accept Nature as it stands, and only *positive* r_p's give entry to a cluster.

A second incidental observation concerns the relation of clusters to factors. There is *some* probability that the largest nuclear clusters found by $\bar{Q}$ technique above will have a moderate tendency to line up with factors found by Q technique. But it will be only a casual similarity of essentially different concepts, for (1) Q technique produces dimensions, *not* types, (2) Q technique reflects people and $\bar{Q}$ technique (Taxonome) does not, and (3) factors are rotated by hyperplanes, not clusters, and (4) clusters are usually much more numerous than factors.

As for tidying up and reaching some statement at the level of phenomenal and nuclear type clusters, one can proceed to the most complete definition of homostats possible by·

(1) Choosing again some arbitrary cutting point—if, as usual, clusters are altogether too numerous at the phenomenal level—in terms of taking only nuclear clusters existing above a certain membership size and hierarchical overlap. This yields what may be called the major important types, for, as pointed out earlier, the "size" of a cluster in terms of id count is really a statement about *density* of representation. If one takes the three or four

---

[5]It should be realized that when people are placed in multidimensional space and the distributions are approximately normal on all dimensions, a sufficiently low limiting cut (say an r_p equal to half the mean of positive values of r_p) will be likely to yield the average man as the largest type—as indeed he is. For in such circumstances the greatest density of people will be at the origin. This, however, is no artifact but a statement of the fact that the "typical average person" is the most numerous and most surrounded by people like himself. As yet, insufficient knowledge has accumulated, through empirical use of the Taxonome method, to say how prominent among detected types this central type will be in the usual batteries of psychological tests. As Chapter 19 indicates, attitude and occupational skill measures are likely to be less dominated by this central type than are general personality measures.

largest clusters one is locating the three or four instances of highest modal density.

(2) Calculating the average central profile of that subset of people (or other ids) which is allocated to a type. This amounts, in the spatial picture, to defining the centroid of each cluster. This vector, plus the standard deviation of r_p among those in the type, plus the percentage of the total population in the type, defines the chief parameters of the type.

(3) Calculating the relations and resemblances (distances apart of the centroids in (2) among the various types in the whole system, by a new Q' matrix of r_p's.

If the texture of the domain happens to be such that just a few highly distinct, well-defined segregates exist, some trial and error with the r_p cutting point *may* yield, as at cluster 1 in Diagram 9-5, homostats which are also segregates. But otherwise — by the flashlight circle analogy — we are merely listing the densities as the circle moves mechanically along an overlapping series of snapshots. It may be true, for example, that persons a through j constitute an unusual dense mass, but it is also truly reported that b through k do the same. If we are interested not only in high densities but also their boundaries, as modes, we must proceed to locating aits.

Objective and mechanical procedures to reveal the boundaries of segregates can be conceived in two approaches: (1) The Density Ratio Method. Here the diameter (d, or r_p) of the homostat is enlarged by successive equal steps, yielding a succession of incidence matrices. Each should bring a proportionate increase in the number of ids appearing in the largest phenomenal clusters, but this regular increase should fail as the circle of the homostat reaches the boundary of the segregate. However, this will work effectively only where the aits are roughly circular (n-dimensional spherical). (2) The Cluster Contiguity Method. Here one chooses initially an r_p (or d) cut that will place roughly a half of the ids in phenomenal clusters of, say,

size four or more. This assumes that 1, 2, or 3 (or the percentage which corresponds thereto) is the average density of the ground, from which the segregates stand out. Consequently it will be difficult in the ground area to find pairs of phenomenal clusters which overlap by more than 1 or 2 ids, whereas in segregate all phenomenal clusters will typically overlap by much more.

The size (r_p or d) of phenomenal clusters used is important. For as phenomenal cluster 2 in Diagram 9-5 shows, if the diameter is large such a homostat will succeed in spanning across two aits, failing to give evidence of the gulf between them. As in photography, a halftone picture, or television, there is a problem here of choosing a "grain" size in the mechanical process appropriate to the picture to be recognized. Homostats of the size of the four shown in Diagram 9-5 would be too large, and would probably already be rejected by the condition above that they do not collect more than 3 or 4 cases in the ground. To locate, separately, the segregates A, B, etc., shown there, one would need homostats of approximately a fourth of that diameter.

Having made the best estimate of the r_p and listed the phenomenal clusters as in Table 9-3 above, the Taxonome program now builds a cluster contiguity matrix as shown in Table 9-5(a), which is bounded by clusters as the original Q' matrix was bounded by people (or ids of any kind). Analogously, when the degree of overlap needed to establish "contiguity" for homostats of that diameter is agreed upon (2 ids or more is the value taken here, 1 being assumed too unstable under sampling), an incidence matrix can be substituted, as shown in Table 9-5(b).

The search through this contiguity incidence matrix is, however, not analogous to the ramifying linkage method, because something different from the compact homostat now needs to be recognized. As the aits in Diagram 9-5 are deliberately

TABLE 9-5

(a) Phenomenal Cluster Contiguity Matrix

Phenomenal Cluster Identifying Numbers	1 (6)	2 (5)	3 (5)	4 (4)	5 (3)	6 (3)
1 (6)	6	3	4	0	0	0
2 (5)	3	5	3	0	0	0
3 (5)	4	3	5	0	0	0
4 (4)	0	0	0	4	2	2
5 (3)	0	0	0	2	3	0
6 (3)	0	0	0	2	0	3

(b) Incidence Matrix among Phenomenal Clusters

Phenomenal Cluster Identifying Numbers	1	2	3 PQ	4	5	6
1	1	1	1	0	0	0
2	1	1	1	0	0	0
3	1	1	1	0	0	0
4	0	0	0	1	1	1
5	0	0	0	1	1	0
6	0	0	0	1	0	1

(c) Segregates Discovered by Segregate Search Algorithm Applied to (b)

	S_1	S_2	
1	1	0	
2	1	0	
3	1	0	
4	0	1	$S_1 = a\ b\ c\ d\ e\ f\ g\ h\ i$
5	0	1	
6	0	1	$S_2 = j\ k\ l\ m\ n\ o$

planned to illustrate, a segregate may be a straggling affair. Chains and amoeboid multi-pods may also need to be discovered. Accordingly, in what we may call the *segregate search algorithm,* any connection encountered as one descends a column is pursued to a tracing of its connections with all clusters.

Stated in logical terms one proceeds, starting with column 1, systematically through the columns, accruing the groups in a column to the segregate being considered, if the intersection of the segregate and the column is not null. One continues thus until no new segregates appear. Thus in Table 9-5(b), columns 1, 2 and 3 form a segregate

but the intersection of this with 4, 5, and 6 is null. Starting again with 4, the first remaining column, one finishes with 4, 5, and 6. Illustrated in Boolean terms, if the columns were as in (a) the Boolean product would be zero, and we should proceed no further. In (b) on the other hand, it is not null, so we proceed as in (c) to Boolean addition to form the new segregate, in the last column of Table 9-6 below. One may also try the limit of having each cluster show contiguity with *at least two* clusters in the segregate which is being accumulated.

Taxonome has been tried on a culture pattern typing of a 12-factor profile on each of 69 countries, as described in Chapter 26 below. In this case the ramifying linkage method yielded groups of phenomenal clusters each closely knit around a distinct nuclear cluster. These ten or so nuclear clusters agreed well with the "civilizations" of Toynbee, i.e., the culture pattern groupings on historico-anthropological bases. Applied to thirty ships known to fall in six types (measures from *Jane's Fighting Ships*), it yielded homostats of no immediate exhaustiveness, but aits which fell fairly neatly into recognized classes of warships. It is being tried now on biological material.

TABLE 9-6
SEGREGATE SEARCH ALGORITHM

(a)			(b)			(c)		
0	1	0	0	0	0	0	0	0
1	0	0	1	1	1	1	1	1
$1 \cdot 0 = 0$			$1 \cdot 0 = 0$			$1 + 0 = 1$		
0	1	0	0	1	0	0	1	1
0	1	0	0	1	0	0	1	1

As Diagram 9-5 reminds us, a segregate has "continuity" among its members, but not homostat properties. Thus individuals at the upper end of ait C, e.g., those in $C1$, could have zero (or even negative!) resemblance (r_p) to those at the lower end, e.g., those in $C2$. The concepts of homostat and ait are quite different, and the experimenter must decide which he wants. But the boundaries of a homostat (which experimenters seem hitherto to have wanted for a "type") will depend partly on where the experimenter first starts looking!

One of the pieces of information which the investigator can gain from Taxonome, and which is probably as important as the finding of particular homostats and aits, is about the "texture" of the domain. Does it consist of compact nuclear clusters of roughly equal size? Or segregates, still well knit, but of unequal size? Or of chains and straggling sets such as might appear in a bacteriologist's microscope? And what is the ratio of ids in and out of the eventually designated segregates? A certain amount

of trial and error, iterative procedure with adjusted r_p cutting points and cluster size cut-offs will always be part of investigation in this field. Effects of sampling will almost certainly have to be explored for some time yet purely by Monte Carlo methods. For example, how broad must an "isthmus" between two "islands" become in order that they cease to be considered segregates? Taxonome is fitted with adjustable parameters to permit such adjustive use.

9. TYPES IN RELATION TO HIERARCHIES, VARIABLES AND THE ITERATIVE MDF PROCEDURE

Among the further issues which arise from the above concepts are (1) the relations of types to sampling of variables and people, (2) the recognition of type hierarchies, and (3) the possibility of using the taxonome principles above jointly with multiple discriminant function methods in an iterative cycle.

As to the first one may note:

(a) With the relatively small samples (say 200 to 300 people) which can be handled in Q matrices (even with large computers), and the undoubtedly low percentage incidence of certain types, e.g., Huntington's chorea, color blindness types, typing procedures of any kind are always going to be peculiarly vulnerable to poor sampling of ids.

(b) There will be strong interaction consequences between sampling of people and sampling of variables. As part of the general principle that attributes and ids are reciprocally related, it will follow that certain variables are incapable of revealing certain types. The procedure of basing r_p on factors instead of any odd set of variables is an advance toward elimination of false typologies to the extent that the profiles approach coverage of a comprehensive totality of factors. But the location of subtypes which agree with a major type on a majority of dimensions and differ systematically only on two or three will never be easy. Spatially they will be an appendage cluster to a nuclear cluster. Types will sometimes show no different distribution from the general population on some sets of dimensions and a modal grouping only on others. After the main structures are found, based on similarities and groupings over *all* profile elements, these additional subgroupings will be found only by experimenting with variations on the level of the r_p cut-off point and variations on the sets of dimensions included. The effects of such selection for relevance (though one may not agree with his subjectivity in assigning "relevance") is brought out clearly by the work of McQuitty (1021, 1022).

(c) The distinction made earlier, in speaking of emergents, between *in-type* and *cross-type* factors, needs to be followed up in regard to its implications for the sampling of variables and the distributions of variables. By the nature of investigation anyone exploring the types within a population is compelled to begin with those variables (and therefore dimensions) which are operationally measurable across the whole population concerned. Certain variables simply cannot be measured for certain entities. Space, odor, temperature, etc., in biology; speed, number of errors, warming up ratios, etc., in psychology are among the few universals. One cannot measure the length of tail feathers in worms or the length of time given to preparing sermons in a group of stevedores. Within species, the profile measures are often upon factors which have no reliable application to another group. For example, head size is a distinct factor in man (364, 365) but there is almost certainly no comparable factor in measures on oysters.

The only possibility of measurement across the larger population is on factors which transcend subspecies (cross population factors, page 292), and to get these one must first find variables which transcend subspecies. These will often be of a very "gross" nature and the problem will arise

whether the proper answer is that the length of a periwinkle's leg is (a) unmeasurable or (b) zero. A measurement operation can generally be given to the experimenter, but it makes a lot of difference to subsequent computing when he decides that score on "reaction to the first grade teacher" is zero or unmeasurable for grandpa compared to his six year old grandson. If, as seems safer, we conclude that despite being able to go through a measurement operation, we find many variables are logically unmeasurable across the larger population, then we can straightway make a useful distinction between *universal* variables and various degrees of *localized* variables. Upper hierarchy types will *have* to be defined in terms of differences on relatively localized variables.

Secondly, decision on type hierarchy and other distribution properties of single variables, before we encounter any evidence from covariation or know what the type subgroups will be. A variable which shows near zero score on most cases and high score on a few (skewed) is likely to be a species differentiating variable and to be of promise for differentiating the further subtypes within one species. A normally distributed variable, suggesting an ordinary relation of within and between species variance, can be useful both in higher and lower type differentiations. A distribution with several modes suggests a small within-to-between variance ratio (though type groups are still not known) and therefore a good variable for differentiating and locating the higher order type structure.

Consequently, the search for types has in some degree begun even before one starts factoring and applying taxonome search procedures upon the factor profiles. Nevertheless, the systematic procedure must hinge mainly on the taxonome approach, in that one must first find a set of variables measurable (with some non-zero score for most individuals) across the whole collection of ids one has agreed to call one's main population. When the homostats and segregates emerge therefrom it is time to look for variables which may be measurable on these alone.

Both these new in-type variables and the original cross-type variables now go into a fresh within-species type of factor analysis, whereupon the factor patterns and the regressions for the cross-type variables will almost certainly be different from what they have been in the total populations. The curvilinearities of relation observable in the total population become simplified into a combination of (perhaps approximate) across-type linearities and within-type linearities. At the same time factor dimensions entirely unique to the within-type variables will emerge. Thus one fulfills the original aim of (a) assigning an individual on a first gross set of measurements to a type and (b) continuing one's prediction to a refined conclusion by using the in-type factors and standard scores for an in-type criterion estimate. The cross-type factors predict the mean criterion scores for the type: the in-type factors predict the individual's deviation from this mean.

As we have pointed out above, the "texture" of a segregate structure may be almost anything, and preliminary descriptive terms for kinds of texture have been suggested. A hierarchical or dendritic structure is only one possibility, but it is one which interests psychologists and biologists a good deal, especially because this texture obviously predominates in biology, with the tendency of several species to congregate in a genus, and several related genuses in a family, and so on to order, etc. What then are the operational procedures by which one objectively and without conscious perception prejudice recognizes and establishes the existence of a hierarchy? For example, does one begin at the top or the bottom? Following the factor model, and many other empirical procedures, it might seem that one does best to start at the bottom, first establishing the group "floor" and working up. This is possible, but it would be a sporadic procedure, hit

and miss with regard to landing on suitable variables. According to the arguments above, one would do better to begin at the top, discovering first what variables give a range of scores across our whole population. With physical objects, e.g., animal species, these would be such universal variables as length, breadth, color, length of life, body temperature, pack or isolate behavior, etc. Only as groupings appear on these would one go to the in-type variables, e.g., in mammals to length of hair, time of weaning, number of ribs, size of optic lobes, etc.

As to classifying and determining the dendritic structure within the hierarchy as such the main procedure must surely be the same as that for upper strata factors, namely, by locating clusters, abstracting the central vector for each of many clusters, and performing a taxonome program cluster search upon them (to get the "genuses" among "species"), and so on if indicated to a higher order.

However, a second computational approach may also work here. Although persons a through l may form one group with high positive r_p's and m through t another group, these two distinct groups may be near each other in space, so that if we descend to an r_p cutting point of half the original level all a through t cases will satisfy the condition for a single cluster. Thus the lower and higher groupings in a hierarchy could be checked by observing the ways in which groupings founded on a lower r_p comprehend groupings made on a more exacting r_p. Related to this is the possibility on which we are awaiting empirical evidence, that *nuclear* clusters may prove to be the genus patterns and *phenomenal* clusters the species.

The above discussion of type hierarchies hinges on the familiar fact that by shifting the range of variables included in the analysis we shift the type groupings obtained. It progresses beyond this observation in so far as it points to a deliberate strategy in deciding on the variables and coordinating the shifts of variable groups with shifts of person groups in the interests of discovering a systematic type hierarchy. When a subgroup or type begins to emerge on the universal variables it suggests that we begin to include local variables on which that group has significant mean and variance and the rest score zero, to see which among them help the emergence of the group by r_p standards.

Coming to the third and last topic of this section we raise the possibility that although multiple discriminant function techniques are only used mistakenly at present — if they are used to "confirm" the types which an investigator has already subjectively decided exist — yet they might be assigned some more logical role in relation to the taxonome procedures. When the Taxonome program has done its best to define segregates we shall normally be presented with, say, three or four closely similar but different alternatives. They will be equally "objective," but derived from different (a) cut-off points in r_p or d in making the Q'-contingency matrix, and (b) different "percentage of the population" sizes in recognizing phenomenal clusters and their minimum overlap in producing the cluster contiguity matrix for reaching aits.

At this point of convergence it would be logically defensible to apply the multiple discriminant function to these alternatives and accept that which gives the clearest separation of type groups. The argument would be that structure is not accidental, and that the action of accident and error is always, on an average, to blur structure rather than to produce it. Consequently, if an index of clarity of structure can be derived in terms of completeness and unambiguity of assignment of individuals to groups — and there should be no difficulty in this — the final decision among the taxonome process alternatives would rest on their value on this index after the multiple discriminant function is applied to them.

Indeed we would propose what might be called the iterative multiple discriminant function, or IMDF, technique, in which Taxonome is followed by the MDF, and one then reverts to the taxonome procedure after weighting the dimensions (in the r_p calculation) with the weights found in the MDF, and so on to some iterative convergence. At present this would be laborious but it might be worth while for establishing important biological and psychological basic type systems. For completeness of presentation let us remind the reader how this would be done in the simplest case of two aits emerging from Taxonome. It compares the main difference on each variable with the sigma of that variable for each group and gives greater weight to such a variable when the mean difference is large relative to the sigmas. A weighting system is thus reached to give a single total score on which the groups will be more different than on any other possible function of the profile elements. Parenthetically, this brings out a very important fact about types, namely, that they may show no significant difference in distribution on any *one* of the variables on which they are measured, and yet be completely distinguishable on the total pattern. (This is the limitation on inference under [2] above.) If non-linear functions are permitted, such as we see applying to certain criteria and configurational derivatives, this separation can be very great. It is easy to see that this could be true of a simple ratio score, even with two variables. If Group A members are lower than Group B members, but not significantly, on x, and higher, but not significantly, on y, the distribution of the ratio (or, for that matter the difference) of x and y could be significantly different for A and B. This fact that patterns, shapes, configural functions, etc., can be significantly different when no single attribute score is significantly different has never been sufficiently taken into account in the social psychology of social status, race, and occupational difference, and perhaps not in the clinical psychology of syndrome types.

As Horst points out (page 148, Chapter 4), the computational procedures for discriminant function work are in a sense not new, for they are "precisely those for classical multiple regression analysis where we have discrete predictor measures and a dichotomous single criterion." What is needed in general taxonometric typing, however, is not the maximum separation of *two* groups but the more general solution of reaching a weighting system which will give maximum separation (accentuation) simultaneously of *all* groups on a common set of variables. Horst discusses three models for handling this problem (page 148, Chapter 4). For practical guidance we refer back to Chapter 5 where Anderson treats this discriminant problem for two groups and then for g groups using t predictor variables. His treatment "seeks" a linear function of the t variates,

$$(30) \quad \gamma \, c_1 x_1 + c_2 x_2 + \ldots + c_t x_t = \sum_{i=1}^{t} c_i x_i$$

such that the ratio of the variance among groups to the variance within groups is maximized; the ratio is, in matrix form,

$$(31) \quad \lambda = \frac{C'AC}{C'WC}$$

where C is a column vector with t elements, A is the $n \times n$ among groups sum of squares and cross-products matrix with elements

$$(32) \quad a_{ij} = \sum_{b=1}^{k} N_b (\bar{x}_{ib.} - \bar{x}_{i}...)(\bar{x}_{jb.} - \bar{x}_{j}...)$$

using the first subscript for the variable, the second for the group, the third for the individual, and N_b as the sample size of the bth group; likewise W is the $t \times t$ matrix of sums of squares and cross-products within groups with elements

$$(33) \quad w_{ij} = \sum_{b=1}^{g} \sum_{t=1}^{N_b} (\bar{x}_{ibt} - \bar{x}_{ib.})(\bar{x}_{jbt} - \bar{x}_{jb.})."$$

This approach yields a determinantal equation and an appropriate test to determine if we can make any discrimination between groups.

Even with computers, the procedure with a large number of groups is laborious, and one must regard research of this kind as something to be done well, once and for all, on sound data from an experiment with a very good choice of ability, personality, and motivation factors as profile elements — not something for isolated forays with arbitrary and temporary sets of variables. Granted this, the *taxonome-guided iterative multiple discriminant method* is describable as one which starts off with the guidance given by the phenomenal or, better, the aits, nuclear clusters yielded by the Taxonome program from the Q' matrix. It then submits the obtained groupings to the multiple discriminant procedure and drops, say, the 10 per cent of variables (or factors) which contribute least to the separation of the groups (or, in broader terms, reweights the factors). The profile similarities of persons in the Q' matrix are then recalculated on this reduced list of variables (or factors) and thrown afresh into more precise type groups by the Taxonome program. Probably some borderline types will by then either have become accentuated or dispersed, while the membership of the stable type groupings (nuclear clusters) may have altered somewhat. A fresh weighting system can now be determined by the MDF, and a few further irrelevant variables dropped on the basis of low weights. (It will be noted that "irrelevant" is no longer an arbitrary decision by the experimenter, nor is it based only on separating two groups, without regard to the sense of the *total* population of type groups.) A possible addition to the procedure would be also to drop individuals at each cycle who do not fall into any type category. It is not yet known whether this iterative alternation of the Taxonome program and the MDF will produce convergence to a point where a further cycle produces no significant change, but such a termination is reasonably possible.

No account has yet been given here of the role of Latent Class Analysis in typing, because it stands apart from procedures applicable to continuous variables. It begins with dichotomous variables and commonly with frequencies of response on each. It then sets out joint frequencies of each in the cells, for the total population, with people as referees, i.e., it "correlates," or, at least relates, variables, not people. It then asks how many and what kinds of subgroups could produce this final effect, each subgroup consisting solely of individuals who respond in exactly the same way. It is this last condition which, to the present writers, makes it a somewhat improbable model for wide use, since natural subgroups almost always show some variation *within* themselves (see pages 149 and 220 for discussion of the method) and for this reason we set it aside earlier in this chapter.

The ultimate goal of the guided iterative MDF method above is to arrive at a grouping which is (1) objective, i.e., such that any investigator would arrive at the same grouping, beginning with the same population of variables and persons; (2) comprehensive, through starting with a stratified sample of people and variables; and therefore (3) as invariant as possible with further additions of persons or variables, except when one deliberately extends inquiry up or down the hierarchy. It should achieve the recognition of the numbers and nature of "concentrated swarms of individuals in a less densely populated space" depicted in Diagram 9-1, the dimensions, and their obliquities being those of the total population. (Obviously, these dimensions will "bend" as we run into the denser clusters, i.e., the variance and obliquities and loadings of these factors will be different if founded on some one cluster rather than on the total space. Similarly the discriminant function weights will alter as we look at two groups or some other subset of the total set of all groups.) These differences probably correspond to what the human cognitive apparatus automatically does in its ordinary perceptions. We

have one system of emphasis in recognizing types of objects in general, another when concentrating on distinguishing two types, say, men and women, and yet another as we predict and form judgments on, say, men among men alone, or trees among trees alone, and so on.

As briefly outlined above, once the types are recognized, we can finally seek a fresh set of in-type dimensions, factor analytically, to predict criterion, etc., performances within groups. We shall then have two distinct systems of factor dimension: (1) *cross-type* for maximally defining the central profile vector of each type, and (2) *in-type* for maximally defining an individual within his type. However, it will still be possible to predict many individual performances by cross-type dimensional measurements, i.e., neglecting our knowledge of the belonging of the individual to a species type. However, this is bound to be a relatively inefficient procedure, because of (1) the real relations being curvilinear, especially as one reaches type concentrations, as indicated above, and (2) the phenomenon of emergents or configurational effects, whereby the in-type dimensions are indispensable for more exact individual predictions. Mathematically there may be two alternatives upon abandoning this rough method of predicting from cross-type measures, namely, (1) the assignment of the individual simply to a group or type (all or nothing) on the basis of the cross-type measures, followed by a criterion prediction from his in-type profile source trait scores, or (2) the combination of linear in-type and cross-type specification equations in some single complex function specification equation. This latter has not been worked out or tried. Either presents a suitable way in practice of approximating complex relations, through successive use of two sets of simple linear equations — especially since the second set can include variables which have no place whatever (except 0 and 1) in the cross-type variance measurement. For example, Smith proves to have the education, age, family background, etc., of a college student, so in further prediction we assign him to this category and use the specification equations found most apt to that category.

10. SUMMARY

(1) The term type has been very loosely used in psychological literature. Of some 45 discernible possibilities of meaning two are considered important: (2) a bipolar type — the "egrege" types constituted by individual deviating to a stated degree at opposite ends of a defined dimension, and (b) a modal type — constituted by the individuals clustering at a distinct mode, either on one dimension or simultaneously on many. When this occurs in a multivariate distribution it is aptly called a species type. Modal types again permit of being conceived in two ways: (1) as homostats, i.e., sets of ids all having high mutual resemblance, and (2) as segregates or "aits," i.e., sets of ids isolated from others.

(2) Modal accumulations on one or many dimensions could be found by (a) "space frequency counts" taken laboriously at regular intervals on variables and combinations of variables, or (b) "inter-id resemblance methods," taking distance measures among all possible combinations of individuals, recognizing high concentrations (modes) as "correlation clusters" in the distance function used in the matrix and noting the position (the vector combination of mean scores) of the central type formed by each such group. The second is pursued here as more practicable and in certain ways more definite.

(3) Measuring the similarity of persons in pairs is thus the first necessity for proceeding to species types. Persons or other ids (patterns) can have their score profiles matched by shape, level, and accentuation of shape aspects of a profile, or ideally by all three. Correlating persons by

r ignores level, and the pattern similarity coefficient r_p which considers all three, is the most useful instrument for most purposes in this field.

(4) Calculating resemblance of two persons in this way is related, geometrically, as determining their distance apart in a space of Cartesian coordinates. For this purpose Mahalanobis' d or d^2 is less satisfactory than r_p especially when the latter is used with factors instead of the variables commonly used in the former. For r_p (a) by using factors avoids giving unknown inequalities of weight to the various domains of psychological variables included, (b) is not rendered non-comparable by different metrics, and (c) allows for the different number of orthogonal axes in use in different studies, so that comparisons can be made of similarity of one pair of patterns and another despite different numbers of elements in the two pairs.

(5) The profile similarity coefficient r_p is commonly used in three situations where degree of similarity is to be quantified: (1) person with person, (2) group with group, and (3) person with group. Care must be taken to use the appropriate expected distance function (E_k for k profile elements) with each. It has the advantage (additional to those in [4] above) over simple distance measures of distributing from -1 to $+1$ with "no relation" expressed by a value virtually of 0. Significance tables are available for evaluating r_p.

(6) The simple, commonly used r_p formula which assumes orthogonal factors and equal weights is developed here to meet the perfectly general case of (a) any degree of obliquity, (b) assigned different importances (weights) for different source traits, and (c) differing concept (factor) validities of the batteries used for the different source traits. Use of r_p with these adaptations is best pursued by computer since both the expected distance function, E_k, *and* the individual pair's distance score, requires matrix multiplications. An addi-

tional index in the family of profile similarity coefficients is offered, namely, the profile nearness index, r_n, which more closely approaches Euclidean distance properties.

(7) A distinction is drawn between *similarities of profiles* and *similarities of profile effects*. A linear or more complex function can always be applied to a profile of scores (pattern) to recognize more complex pattern effects upon a criterion. Indeed it is part and parcel of the concept of types that there will be complex nonlinear relations of elements to criteria. For the development of high modal frequencies at certain combinations reflects the appearance of *emergents,* i.e., products of particular combinations which have especial value for adaptation (high criterion scores). Consideration is given to these complex "pattern" functions, and it is pointed out that people can be classified in types by modes on these single resultant functions.

(8) Any single criterion, like any single personality variable, will show different modal groupings than any other, and, in general (and absolutely in the linear case), fewer modes than in the multidimensional space. However, "effect" (criterion) variables, and "inherent nature" (personality) variables will tend to occupy the same space. The main virtue in taking account of effect variables is that society's values are commonly attached to criteria. From there they can be mathematically projected backward upon the traits, for weighting purposes. The weights given profile element traits in (6) (b) will commonly be derived from (a) the Σb^2 (loadings) for the factors over a personality sphere of variables, (b) the social importance or values weights just discussed, and (c) the potency in separating types, in Section 9 above.

(9) A model and a corresponding computer program called Taxonome have been constructed objectively to discover species type clusters in a (Q') matrix of r_p's or any other relations between people, e.g., clique ties, expressible finally in a unit or zero "incidence matrix." The cutting point for assigning 1's or 0's is probably best taken as the mean of positive r_p's in the matrix, since a modal high type density has meaning usually only in regard to the general density in the domain. Granted the incidence matrix, taxonome applies the ramifying linkage search method (229) emerging first with phenomenal and second with nuclear clusters, classified by size clusters, classified in both cases by size (the sample percentage in the group is an expression of *density*) and in the latter also by number of phenomenals overlapping.

The location of segregates (aits) involves a further step in Taxonome, in which a cluster contiguity matrix is subjected to a Boolean analysis. The aim of a type search is not only to locate and describe homostats and aits, but also to reveal the *texture* of a domain. Homostats, aits, and texture will vary somewhat with the "grain" of the perception grid, fixed by the r_p cut-off points, etc., which are adjustable parameters in the Taxonome program.

(10) Remaining problems concern the effect on type perception of sampling variables and ids, the methods to bring out the particular texture we call a type hierarchy, and the logic of combining multiple discriminant function methods with taxonome technique. Although the types found in any data will vary with the sample of variables, the sample of people, and, especially interaction between these, one can avoid subjective decisions on the "relevance" of variables (and people) and at the same time recognize the hierarchies of species, genus, order, etc., by (a) exploring to see which *variables* are universal and which local, by observing the distribution of single variables, and (b) starting analysis with common variables and adding variables unique to types as the latter are located. Hierarchies can be checked by (a) applying r_p to the central vectors of the lower order clusters, and (b) experimenting with differ-

ent levels of the cutting point or r_p in relation to phenomenal and nuclear clusters. A final clarification of clusters is possible by a process defined as an iterative multiple discriminant function procedure which reweights the r_p elements in the taxonome calculations and accepts maximum possible structuration as true structure.

Individuals can be represented, and their scores used in criterion prediction, either in the universal variable, cross-type dimensional system, or by being assigned to a type on the basis of cross-type dimensions and employing the in-type dimensional system. The value of type methods is that they make the latter, more accurate system possible and lead to a combination of cross-type and in-type criterion specification equations.

CHAPTER 10

Manipulative and Hypothesis-Testing Factor-Analytic Experimental Designs

BENJAMIN FRUCHTER
University of Texas

1. INTRODUCTION (BY THE EDITOR)

As Chapter 2 has pointed out, there is a great difference between the stilted use and limited stereotype of multivariate experiment in certain popular notions on the one hand, and, on the other, its real range of possible fulfillment in intelligent designs. The task of several of the chapters has been to clarify developments that may lead to better education of students, and, in research, to the application of new experimental designs, where traditional designs have left some scientific concepts halted before a road block.

Nowhere has this Wundt-Pavlov—vs.—Galton-Spearman stereotype been so obstructive as in the notions that (1) only bivariate designs can employ the dependent-independent variable relation, and (2) multivariate designs, especially factor analysis, are "only" exploratory and hypothesis-creating, and not fitted to hypothesis-testing, as for example, is the familiar analysis of variance design. Chapter 2, Section 7,

has already dealt broadly with the unusually creative role of multivariate methods in concept formation, hypothesis-testing, and the advance of scientific theory. It was also shown that there are some advantages in the multivariate "global" approach and others in the bivariate, "step-by-step" approach, at different phases of research. Chapter 6, Sections 6 and 9, have discussed within the factor-analytic field the technical implementation of these strategies, in a way that will be illustrated further here.

In regard to general experimental design and the six fundamental parameters therein discussed in Chapter 2 (Table 2-1, page 28) it was pointed out that the expression "dependent-independent" has been used ambiguously to mean (1) the order of variables that is chosen in the experimental procedure, to ensure causal relationship, and (2) the order chosen in the statistical analysis, often according to quite arbitrary value judgments of "importance" or "preference," determining the direction of regression. Confusion has been further heightened by the still widespread belief that in (1) the causal dependent relation can arise only through manipulation, whereas actually it depends on another design dimension, namely, demonstrated sequential time relation.

How extensive are the varieties of designs in experiment which permit verdicts on *causal* dependence? Table 2-2 shows a total of 34 usable distinct types of general experimental design, of which 18 are bivariate and 16 multivariate. Of the latter, 5 are both manipulative and time-sequence-involving, and 5 are only time-sequence-involving. The reader may see for himself how the half-dozen illustrations in this chapter scatter across these 10 possibilities of causal scrutiny designs, but what has been called the *condition response* design at once covers 5 of them—those which involve actual manipulation.

As Professor Fruchter points out, one of the characteristics of factor analysis (in the true sense of uniquely rotated, simple structure or confactor resolutions) contrasted with other multivariate methods, e.g., multiple correlation, discriminant functions, pattern analysis, etc., is that it produces and isolates by its intrinsic power the concepts that one expects to find genuinely generalizable across studies. Even so, one is as much obligated to test this fit across new studies when using factor analysis as one is to test in such new studies a concept or hypothesis which comes from some quite distinct source.

This testing is sometimes spoken of as "the factor matching problem," but that is only a specific form of the general hypothesis-testing problem, and, as Professor Fruchter well points out, the hypothesis-testing, even within factor analysis, may easily take other forms, such as inquiring about the significance of this and that loading, or a difference of loadings.

What has delayed a more regular and routine use of hypothesis-testing in factor analysis, even among those intelligently aware of the powerful hypothesis-testing functions inherent in the method, has been

the long debate and uncertainty among mathematical statisticians about expressions for significance of loadings, factors as a whole, and differences of loadings (Burt, 169; Bartlett, 69; Lawley, 904; Rao, 1179; Saunders, 1253; and recently Harris, 492a). This is taken up by Professor Fruchter in Section 3.

It is, to say the least, self-evident that one can only test a hypothesis if the experiment includes the necessary variables in the first place. Without this, no statistical finesse is of any avail! By "necessary" one means either to an *interpretive* hypothesis—in which case some hard thinking has to be done about how a concept should be expressed—or to a *descriptive* hypothesis, in which case it is indispensable to include literally the same variables as in the study whose factors are the hypotheses for the checking study. In spite of Professor Fruchter's stress on "marker variables," and the pointing out of the same elsewhere by other writers in this volume (as well as by the editor—almost *ad nauseam* as far as he is concerned!) journal editors still accept every year dozens of alleged factor-analytic researches which operate in "private" subjective worlds, failing either to link up in an exploratory way with researches in the same area, or else to have statistically enough markers from "reference batteries" or reference concepts to make a test of congruence of results possible. Perhaps the cogent arguments of the present chapter will help to drive home this requirement in testing descriptive and interpretive hypotheses.

2. THE PROBLEM OF "GENERALIZING" FACTOR-ANALYTIC RESULTS

One of the claimed advantages of factor analysis, as compared with multiple correlation and other multivariate analyses, is the possibility of generalizing the resulting concepts over studies and, it is to be hoped, over investigators, laboratories, and instruments. Factors are concepts that, though they arise in specific studies, frequently indicate functional unities that can be verified across a wide variety of studies and situations. There is no assurance, however, that a factor found in one study is general. Criteria are needed for establishing the limits of the generality of a factor.

An apparent contradiction to the idea that the results from factor analyses can be generalized is the seeming difficulty of applying tests of significance to the results of factor analyses. Two of the areas for which tests of significance, or other criteria of generalization, are needed are the matching of factors and the determination of whether factor loadings, or the differences between factor loadings of variables, are significant. Recently Kaiser and Caffrey (840) have applied the distinction between statistical inference and psychometric inference to factor analysis, the basic notion of the latter being that the number of discernible factors is dependent on the number of variables rather than the size of the sample.

The generalization of factorial concepts over studies, experimenters, instruments, and other sources of variation is the area in which factor analysis can be most useful in multivariate research. Instead of using a single measure, arbitrarily selected, to represent a concept, as is done in many bivariate experimental investigations, two alternative procedures are available. One of these is to use marker variables that have been shown in several exploratory analyses to mark the location of given concepts for a specified population, under specified conditions, in the test space. The other approach is to compute indices of agreement, such as those developed by Ahmavaara (9, 10), Kaiser (836), Cattell (221), Cattell and Baggaley (268), Tucker (1450), Wrigley and Neuhaus (1573), and others, to the matching of factors derived from different studies using the same variables.

The importance of tests of significance for the matching of empirically derived factors with hypothesized factors has been

pointed out by Hurley and Cattell (800), and some of the bases for recognition and interpretation of factors have been extensively considered by Cattell (251). These issues are discussed by Cattell in Chapter 6.

In his book on factor analysis Cattell (229, pp. 58-59) has pointed out:

The entities which the investigator with the broad approach most frequently wishes to relate as dependent and as independent variables are themselves generally abstractions from a considerable set of operational variables. For those workers in biology and the social sciences who are not acquainted with factor analysis this has proved a baffling problem, which they have generally sought ineffectually to solve by taking a single symptom of the abstract concept in question, attempting to claim that if this behaves as predicted the hypothesis about the concept is correct. Nothing could be more misleading. The variance in any single, operationally defined symptom (dependent variable) is usually determined by many influences. The part due to the concept in question can only be determined by typing the latter down as a factor, by the other variables through which it is expressed. Thus, writing of some social consequences of the Oedipus complex, Winch exclaims: "Because they consist of high order abstractions, the major concepts of Freudian theory lack observable referents." But in his later work he recognizes that the problem is one of collecting and weighting the referents, not one of lack of referents, and the former is achievable by factor analysis. It has well been said that psychoanalysis can be scientific, not by experiment, but by becoming a branch of factor analysis. Generally speaking, it is a poor hypothesis — of the cheap variety formally imported because it is nowadays socially respectable to be clothed in a hypothesis — which can be tried out by appeal to one variable. A rich, well-thought-out concept, founded on patient observation, will generally be rooted in several variables and permit inferences as to combinations of relationships among them. Factor analysis is ideally adapted to testing theories extending to simultaneous relationships (patterns) among several variables.

The pursuit of intensive studies on single pairs of variables, even if guided by good hunches as to their conceptual reference, can seldom confirm a theory. At least in the social sciences the history of failure justifies designating this approach as "muddling" rather than "muddling through." The latter has sometimes been derogatorily attached to factor analysis in its groping for wholes. But an incisively designed analysis is far less in the realm of blind trial and error than is the practice of getting precise relations between two variables which are each complex in their factor constitutions and probably not very significant from the standpoint of the factor one is really interested in (as loadings of later factorization sometimes show). But the real failure of the classical controlled experimental approach in these circumstances is not the lack of significance in the particular pairs correlated: it is the absence of all the other pairs of correlations which are indispensable to giving meaning to the first relation.

The best way to select standard reference variables has been a perennial problem. One possibility is to have a committee of experts agree on standard reference variables in a substantive area. This approach has been used in the *Kit of Reference Tests for Cognitive Factors* put out under the editorship of John French, *et al.* (550). While this approach has the advantage that different investigators will have a common source of marker variables and that there is some standardization, possible disadvantages are that the marker variables may not apply equally well to all populations with which they are used, and the introduction of new improved marker variables may be slowed down unless provision is made for periodic review and revision of the recommendations.

Another approach to the use of marker variables is to select reference variables either from the *Kit,* or from other sources, and to establish their factor content in the reference battery for the sample on which the study is being conducted. In this approach, confirmation of the factor content of the marker variable is obtained on the sample, and it is possible to observe the relationships of other reference variables to the marker variables.

One of the areas in which tests of significance are needed is tests of hypotheses concerning dependent variables. The variables used in many correlational studies may conveniently be classified into two broad categories. One of these categories represents the independent or reference variables, and the other represents the dependent or criterion variables. In factor-analyzing the intercorrelations among sets of such variables, two alternative approaches present themselves for consideration. In one of them (interdependency analysis), all variables, regardless of type, are treated as equal in status. They are placed in a single intercorrelation matrix, and the entire matrix is factor-analyzed.

In the other alternative (dependency analysis), the independent variables are separated from the dependent variables and the intercorrelation matrix for the independent variables only (indicated as matrix R_{11}, in Table 10-1) is factor-analyzed. A further step, then, is to estimate the loadings of the dependent or criterion variables on the factors resulting from the

TABLE 10-1

Schema for the Factor Regression and Other Independent-Dependent Variable Designs

	Independent, Predictor, or Reference Variables	Dependent, Criterion Variables
Independent Variables	R_{11}	R_{12}
Dependent Variables	R'_{12}	R_{22}

analysis of the independent variables by means of linear regression techniques using the correlations in matrix R_{12} in Table 10-1. In this latter design, in which dependent variables are considered separately from the reference variables, the intercorrelations among them (represented by matrix R_{22} in Table 10-1) do not enter into the determination of the reference space.

One of the reasons it is advantageous to analyze the reference measures separately from the criterion measures is that the interpretation of the reference measures is not affected by imperfections, unique variance, or shifts in factor content due to learning or experimental manipulation in the dependent measures. If linear dependence, experimental dependence, or other sources of spurious relationships are biasing the correlations among the criterion measures, the factor structure of the reference variables is not affected by these sources of error or bias.

3. REQUIREMENTS AND POSSIBILITIES IN MANIPULATIVE DESIGNS (BY THE EDITOR)

The study of experimental designs in Chapter 3 has brought out two principles of importance for the present chapter. First, that *independence-dependence,* besides its arbitrary mathematico-statistical designation, has meaning as (1) manipulative dependence-independence, and (2) causal independence-dependence through having a known time sequence in the data. Second, that multivariate designs, though they have historically neglected such opportunities, can intrinsically be used with either of these basic types of dependence-independence of variables. The following section will therefore consider the (2) type and the present section the manipulative (1) type.

In a multivariate design the possibilities of manipulation are much greater than in a bivariate. The entry—the attribute value for a relative—is necessarily the dependent, unmanipulated variable, but the referees which can be manipulated to new values are now many—stimuli, S, background environments, E, the condition of the person, P', and the condition of the observer, O'. A simple instance—the condition-response design—is illustrated in Section 8 below, in which the stimuli are manipulated. Therein each of three stimuli are introduced at each of two levels, and a considerable variety of potentially dependent variables are correlated with the stimulus levels and factor-analyzed. (See Diagram 10-1.) But many more complex manipulative designs can be considered, depending on the introduction of further manipulated conditions.

A formal relatedness must be noted between the condition-response design first proposed by Cattell in 1952 (229), as well as other multivariate manipulative designs, and analysis of variance, specifically with the multivariate analysis of variance developed by Jones in Chapter 7. For the *conditions* are, of course, essentially "effects," which, in one form—the factorial, balanced form—of the condition response design, are introduced in a balanced fashion. The difference, as any student will recognize, is that the dependence of the attribute or attributes upon the conditions or effects is examined by the correlation coefficient instead of by F and t ratios. In regard to any single correlation coefficient, this is no difference at all, for the significance of a difference by "t test" and of an r employ identical principles and values; but, of course, an F test examines a wider set of relations. It is argued that the condition response design is preferable in those cases where the loss of the scope of the F-ratio examination is less important than the gain from discovering the factor structure among the many dependent variables. By the condition-response design one issues ultimately with the (biserial) correlation of the effects (conditions) with the dependent *factors* instead of only with the dependent *variables*.

An alternative to this approach would be first to factor the response region (Variable

1-5 in Diagram 10-1) and then to set up batteries for each factor and treat these as single dependent variables in a multivariate analysis of variance, as in Chapter 7. Another is to factor the stimuli alone and the responses alone and determine the regression of the first upon the second set of factors, as in the factor regression analysis model (Section 6 below). Favoring the present design are the facts that (a) two steps are carried out in one, and (b) one has access also to the higher-order factors among the responses.

However, the C-R design itself can benefit, in some cases with few response variables, from rotating for simple structure on the responses themselves, so that the stimuli, which might help blur a hyperplane, are not in the picture. It would be almost the same to factor the stimulus part of the matrix as a Dwyer extension to the response part. In either case the particular D-V matrix one will eventually want will be the V_{fs} (factor structure), to examine the *correlation* of factor response magnitudes and *stimulus* magnitudes.

In the balanced C-R design one manipulates the stimuli or independent variables to mutual independence as in the usual factorial design. However, if they are naturally occurring stimuli, as in many social situations, one is throwing away information available about the natural structure of the stimulus world in so doing. This defect of the manipulative C-R design may cause one, in circumstances where this loss would be important, to revert to the non-manipulative C-R; but the present chapter concerns manipulation. A useful compromise is that in which, having already explored the structure of stimulus conditions, one enters the C-R design with

DIAGRAM 10-1. Arrangement for a Simple Manipulative Condition-Response Design Experiment: *R* or *P* Technique

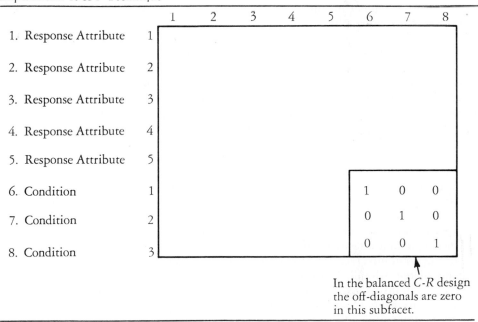

		1	2	3	4	5	6	7	8
1. Response Attribute	1								
2. Response Attribute	2								
3. Response Attribute	3								
4. Response Attribute	4								
5. Response Attribute	5								
6. Condition	1						1	0	0
7. Condition	2						0	1	0
8. Condition	3						0	0	1

In the balanced C-R design the off-diagonals are zero in this subfacet.

On C1, C2, *and* C3, half the subjects may be subjected to high and half to low conditions (for a biserial *r*) or they may be divided into more grades (ordinary *r*). The response attribute measures will generally be continuous.

known *factors* as the manipulated "variables."

In any broad array of variables it will naturally happen that certain factors will appear, e.g., constitutional temperamental factors in the subjects, which have nothing but chance correlation with the manipulated variables. This background of unrelated factors is in any case informative and a further contribution to evaluating the magnitude of the dependence (correlating) of the factors in responses upon the manipulated stimuli.

As described so far, a single measurement is made of all subjects on all variables, the conditions (effects) being manipulated to give the required combinations. But a second design, comparable to the dR (differential R), is possible in which everyone is measured twice. The *changes* on the conditions, from first to second testing, will then be randomized manipulatively in a factorial design. This has the advantage, as in analysis of covariance, of eliminating much of the error variance in the response measures. For example, the temperament factor contribution mentioned above would fall out of the determination of the variables, because on largely temperament measures there would be minimal difference from first to second occasion.

A second broad area of manipulative design in multivariate experiments is that discussed as stimulus-controlled P technique under P and O techniques in Chapters 11 and 22. Just as in the above, if one is to manipulate the stimulus values introduced from day to day there will usually be no point in having them correlated, and the experimenter will need to work out from the beginning a factorial design over time, for all contemplated sessions, among the manipulated stimuli. Occasionally, of course, one will instead want to arrange the stimuli also to have relations or lack of relations to unmanipulable variables, e.g., weather, and some nice techniques could be worked out in games theory to finish with such and such correlations after such and such a series of occasions. The especial

value of manipulation in P technique is that it permits checks on causal connections inferred from factor-lagged P-technique analyses of unmanipulated data (Chapter 11).

Manipulation, of course, may also be regarded as forcibly holding constant. Normally a facet with stimuli as relatives, people as referees, and response attributes as entries, will not be fixed on the off-sets. That is to say the people may be in various states (the P' set), and the stimuli backed by changing environments (E and E' sets). What we have called in Chapter 3 a *fixed facet,* in which all people are brought to one state, e.g., hunger, and all background environments to, say, a given temperature and social atmosphere, involves an intrusion of manipulation, in the sense of manipulating for constancy. Of course, analysis of covariance can commonly achieve without manipulation what is here achieved; but there are situations where manipulative control appeals more.

Further areas of manipulated multivariate designs which need exploration are those in which—as is uniquely possible in multivariate work—different sets of the data box are simultaneously manipulated. For example, the nature of stimuli and their levels, S and S', background environment and levels, E and E', and conditions of the subject, P' (e.g., hunger or drug conditions) admit of simultaneous change. (Indeed, all primes, S', A', P', E', and O' connote manipulability.) This could be done simply in the interest of giving greater variance over a single set of the DB, or of producing sequential conditions for causal inference. However, all these developments lie in the future as far as any check or experience from empirical feedback is concerned.

4. REQUIREMENTS AND POSSIBILITIES IN HYPOTHESIS-TESTING

Interdependency factor analysis can be done at two levels, exploratory analysis and confirmatory analysis (Tucker, 1461).

The former is used to generate hypotheses and the latter is designed to test them. The purpose of an exploratory analysis, as stated by Thurstone (1415) is "... to discover the principal dimensions or categories ... and to indicate the directions along which they may be studied by experimental laboratory methods."

Since the interpretations of factors in an exploratory factor analysis represent "raw" hypotheses, they need to be evaluated by comparing the results with those obtained on new samples from the same population. Also predictions concerning changes in inter-relations and in factor loadings which result from planned modifications in the reference variables need to be verified on new samples as a check on the validity of the factor interpretations (Guilford, 626).

In many studies involving hypotheses, a distinction is made in the statements of hypotheses between the set of reference or independent variables and the set of criterion or dependent variables. This is a departure from the more traditional interdependency factor analysis design in which all variables are treated as coordinate or equal. For hypotheses expressing one or more dependent variables as functions of the set of independent, reference variables, the usual interdependency factor analysis model is inappropriate. Such non-factorial hypotheses include those dealing with factors as sources of variance in tasks not used in the definition of the factors.

Since factors represent inferred, unobserved variables, one way to study the functions they represent is to define them in such a way that they may be represented in explicit, objective form. The definitions may take the form of reference variables of previously established factor content in a given population, or combinations of such variables. This operational method of defining factors helps to bypass the possibilities of certain semantic and empirical confusions which may arise concerning identification of factors derived from different studies and determination of whether the factor space occupied by two or more test batteries is a common factor space (Bechtoldt, 81). The scores on the explicitly defined factors may be used in the same ways as any distribution of test scores, but there is the special advantage that they represent factorially defined variables.

Where a status distinction is made between independent and dependent variables in the hypotheses of an investigation, the dependent variables can be projected onto the space of the explicitly defined factors representing the independent variables. The explicitly defined factors may be used in combination as predictor variables and the linear regression model is applied to determine the beta weights for estimating the loadings of the dependent variables on the independent variables (Fruchter & Jennings, 566). Objective procedures for the conduct of such studies, if they are properly designed, are available, together with some of the desired statistical tests of significance (Bechtoldt, 82).

In selecting a method for matching factors across batteries, two issues to be considered are (1) whether the match should be for similarity of profile, or level, or some combination of the two; and (2) the level of measurement that may appropriately be assumed. With regard to the latter, Cattell and Baggaley (268) proposed the following possibilities:

Scale	Technique
Nominal	Salient variables similarity index
Ordinal	Tau coefficient
Interval	Product moment correlation
Ratio	Coefficient of congruence.

The first two techniques may be classified as non-parametric. The salient variable similarity index (s_c) is a probability value, indicating the probability that a given number of coincidences between the salient variables (i e., those with high loadings) common to two factors are expected to occur by chance. A computationally convenient formula for the index is as follows:

$$S_c = 1 - \sum_{x=0}^{c-1} p_x.$$

Where p_x is the expected probability of exactly x coincidences for the pair of factors being matched, and c is the number of coincidences observed for the pair.

A table containing values of s_c, for selected values on n (the total number of variables common to two studies), g (the number of common salient variables), and c is given by Cattell and Baggaley (268).

Where the interval level of measurement can be assumed, a number of comparable indices are available that have been proposed by Ahmavaara (9, 10), Burt (166), Tucker (1464), Wrigley and Neuhaus (1591), and others.

Let us now turn to the statistical issues in hypothesis-testing. Among the procedures to be considered are those for testing hypotheses by matching factors across batteries, matching an obtained factorial solution with an hypothesized factor structure, and determining the rank of the correlation matrix and the significance of factor loadings.

Ahmavaara (9, 10) calls his procedure "transformation analysis" and obtains a matrix L which contains estimates of the loadings of the factors of the second study on the factors of the first study. The formula, in matrix notation, is as follows:

$$L = (F'_1 F_1)^{-1} F'_1 F_2.$$

The rows of matrix L are then normalized to adjust the factor of F_1 to the space of F_2. The normalized matrix is designated L_n and is the "comparison" matrix. The matrices F_1 and F_2 contain only the variables that are common to the two studies. "Transformation analysis" is similar to Cattell s earlier Procrustes solution (page 191 above), which is the basic development incorporated in the later Kaiser-Schoenemann Procrustes matching procedure for *comparing* two solutions (Procrustes and "transformation analysis" *synthesize* two studies to maximum agreement.)

Wrigley and Neuhaus (1591) compute the scalar products of the normalized vectors of factor loadings over the p tests

common to the two batteries that may be obtained from:

$$e_{jk} = \frac{\sum\limits_{i=1}^{p} f_{ij} g_{ik}}{\sqrt{\sum\limits_{i=1}^{p} f_{ij}^2 \sum\limits_{i=1}^{p} g_{ik}^2}}$$

where f_{ij} is the loading of the ith variable on the jth factor of F_1, and g_{ik} is the loading of the ith variable on the kth factor of F_2. In matrix notation, the formula for calculating the indices for the m_1 factors in F_1 with the m_2 factors in the F_2 is as follows:

$$E = D_{F_1}^{-1/2} F'_1 F_2 D_{F_2}^{-1/2}$$

where D_{F_1} and D_{F_2} are diagonal matrices consisting of the principal diagonals of $(F'_1 F_1)$ and $(F'_2 F_2)$. Either orthogonal or oblique factors may be used, and the matchings may be made either between those pairs of factors which have the highest indices, or so as to maximize the sum of the indices over the matched pairs.

In evaluating factor matching coefficients, several considerations need to be taken into account. A high coefficient between two factors does not necessarily indicate that they should be matched. They may represent what Cattell (251) has termed "cooperative" factors, i.e., factors that have similar profiles of loadings but represent two distinct, and often quite uncorrelated, influences that affect a set of dependent variables similarly.

On the other hand, two factors that should be matched may have a low correlation for any one, or a combination, of the following reasons: (1) attenuation of correlation and hence size of factor loadings and communalities of some of the variables due to low reliability; (2) differences in factor variances due to population or sample differences; (3) using a set of reference axes for factor representation that is not optimal for factor matching; (4) insufficient common variables in the two studies; (5) non-congruent rotational solutions for the two batteries. (For a method for maximizing the congruence of two factor matrices, see Tucker, 1460.)

Another type of hypothesis that may be tested in factor analysis is the rank, r, of the correlation matrix of n variables, i.e., the number of independent factors. Among the more systematically proposed tests of factor significance, or completeness of extraction, are those of Bartlett (69) applicable to a principal components solution; Burt (169), using a chi-square test based on z differences; Coombs (382), appropriate for the positive-manifold situation; Lawley and Maxwell (904), involving the standard error of a partial correlation; Rao (1179), involving canonical correlation; and Tucker, which has been widely applied (cf. Fruchter, 563).

Most of the above methods are concerned with finding the minimal rank of the correlation matrix or the standard error of a factor loading from a statistical viewpoint. As Burt (169) has pointed out, "none . . . is completely immune from objection on either theoretical or practical grounds or both."

A procedure which may be contrasted with the statistical inference approach is the psychometric inference approach (840). It is concerned with determining those factors which have maximum generalizability in the Kuder-Richardson, or "alpha" sense. It is based on the principle that those common factors are to be retained which have maximum correlation with the corresponding universe of common factors. The number of factors retained is a function of n, the number of variables, rather than N, the number of observations. The psychometric inference approach emphasizes the common variance in contrast to the statistical inference approach which emphasizes the error variance.

Once the decision concerning the number of factors has been made, another type of hypothesis, which it is sometimes desirable to check, concerns the fit of an empirically derived factor matrix to a hypothesized factor matrix. The hypothesis matrix, stated in terms of the hypothesized pattern of factor loadings, may be based on considerations external to and independent of factor analysis, such as theory, or the results of previous exploratory factor analyses.

One of the methods for obtaining the least-squares fit of an empirically derived factor matrix to a hypothesis matrix has been proposed and programmed by Hurley and Cattell (800) in what has become known as the Procrustes formula. Another possible approach to testing hypotheses is through the configural matching (263) and salient variable similarity (268) tests of congruence, and the use of Burt's congruence coefficient (160). In the case of the Procrustes method the formula for the transformation matrix (λ_x) which transforms the orthogonal, unrotated factor matrix (V_o) toward the hypothesis matrix (V_{rs}) is as follows:

$$\lambda_x = (V'_o V_o)^{-1} V'_o V_{rs}.$$

The transformation matrix is then normalized by columns and may be used to obtain $V_{rs'}$ (the closest fit to V_{rs}) by:

$$V_{rs'} = V_o \lambda_x.$$

No completely satisfactory test of the goodness of fit of the transformed matrix to the hypothesis matrix has been developed, but the available procedures for matching factors and testing for the significance of a factor loading may be applied.[1]

A danger in the use of the method is that the obtained fit will be used without sufficient safeguards for accepting or re-

---

[1] If the maximum likelihood method is used to estimate the hypothesized factor matrix, the likelihood approximation to the chi square test (cf. Lawley, 905) may be used to test the significance of the difference between the obtained factor matrix and the hypothesized "simple structure" matrix, against an alternative hypothesis of any positive definite matrix. K. G. Jöreskog (*Testing a Simple Structure Hypothesis in Factor Analysis*, RB-65-1 [Princeton, N. J.: Educational Testing Service, January 1965]) has prepared a computer program for the maximum likelihood solution, using the generalized method of resultant descents, that converges rapidly.

jecting the null hypothesis. Indeed, the authors called their procedure "Procrustes" to put the user on notice that empirical results should not be "stretched" or lopped off" to fit the hypothesis matrix.

5. AN ILLUSTRATION OF TIME-SEQUENTIAL TASK COMPLEXITY ANALYSIS

To make the general type of design referred to more specific, an application of the factor regression design in a study by Fruchter and Fleishman (565) will be presented. In recent years there has been an increase in the number of studies that attempt to combine experimental and correlational methods. In analyzing correlations among some of the variables, the presence of spurious covariance due to experimental dependence frequently presents a problem. Experimental dependence may be reflected, for example, in correlations among scores obtained at successive stages of performances on the same experimental apparatus. Another example is the correlation between scores on a component of a task with total score, taken on the basis of the same performance.

If the investigator is interested in discovering the relative amounts of certain common "abilities" involved in the variance of the scores, he may be concerned that the presence of possible spurious elements in the correlations among the scores may tend to obscure the results. This was the case in a study by Fleishman (532) in which a battery of twenty-four psychomotor tests was administered to subjects who also performed on a single "criterion" psychomotor apparatus administered at several different levels of task complexity. The problem was to determine possible changes in the abilities contributing to performance on the "criterion" psychomotor task, as level of task complexity was varied. The technique of factor analysis in the conventional interdependency design was applied to analyzing the correlations among the twenty-four tests

and the seven conditions on the "criterion" task. Since the correlations among the seven intra-task conditions, at three levels of complexity, were included in this analysis, with possible experimental dependence involved, a question that needed investigation was "to what extent does inclusion of these experimentally dependent intra-task measures affect the over-all outcome of the analysis?" To investigate this question, a study by Fruchter and Fleishman (565) compared the results of two alternative methods of analyzing these data.

The results of this comparison have relevance to a variety of factor-analytic studies in which it is suspected that the effects of a few spurious correlations may influence the outcome of the analysis of the remainder of the correlations. In such analyses one can expect factors to appear which are confined to the spuriously related variables and are of doubtful communality. The relevant problem is the extent to which the other common factors are affected. This problem is also related to the general communality-estimation problem, since the original communality estimates placed in the diagonal cells are often based on the highest correlations in each column. If certain correlations are inflated, due to experimental dependence, this dependence may affect the communality estimates and the outcome of the analysis of the experimentally independent variables.

The "criterion" task, administered to 204 subjects, was a modification of the Multi-Dimensional Pursuit apparatus. The subject is confronted with a lever, stick, and footpedal controls, simulated to represent the air-speed, altitude, bank, and heading controls of an airplane. The pointers on dial indicators drift, and the subject must make appropriate control movements to keep the proper pointers at the zero point on each of the several dials. The subject received seven task conditions. In the first three, he had to use only one control at a time to keep one dial lined up (single level conditions). In the next three conditions, he was required to use two controls simultaneously to keep two dials lined up (double-level conditions). In the seventh condition he was required to use all three controls (both hands and feet) to keep three dials lined up simultaneously (triple-level condition). Each of the seven conditions was practiced for four one-minute trials. These conditions were administered successively, in the order indicated, and yielded reliable "time-on-target" scores. The obtained scores indicated that these three "levels" represented three clear-cut levels of task difficulty.

The distribution of these scores, and the scores on the 24 psychomotor tests, were transformed to normalized stanine scales and the product-moment correlations among all 31 variables were computed. Ten centroid factors were extracted from this correlation matrix and rotated orthogonally to meaningful positions consistent with simple structure. Seven of the factors were interpreted as representing psychomotor abilities identified previously; the eighth factor was specific to the seven Multi-Dimensional Pursuit scores, the ninth factor was a doublet confined to two experimentally dependent scores obtained from the Rudder Control test apparatus; and the tenth factor was a residual factor with only negligible loadings on it.

Examination of the results of this analysis indicated that there was relatively little variance in common between the performance scores of the Multi-Dimensional Pursuit test and the basic skill measures. There was, however, a strong specific factor confined to the seven component scores of the Multi-Dimensional Pursuit apparatus. The extent to which these loadings represented within-task variance and the extent to which the apparent specificity may have been inflated by experimental dependence reflected in the intercorrelations, because the seven scores were obtained from the same apparatus at a single continuous sitting, could not be determined from the results of this analysis. There was some question as to whether some of the variance, which would otherwise have shown up on some of the other common factors, might have been taken up by the specific factor. It was therefore decided to re-analyze the battery using a method that did not involve the intercorrelations among the experimentally dependent scores.

This time only the reference battery of basic psychomotor tests was factor-analyzed, with the seven "criterion" task variables omitted.[2] Using the final communality estimates and information as to how the tests would cluster from the first analysis, five factors were extracted simultaneously from the intercorrelation matrix by the multiple-group method. Two additional factors were then extracted by the centroid method from the residual correlations remaining after the first five factors. After rotation, the seven factors shown in Table 10-2 were interpreted as representing the same functions as the common factors identified in the first analysis. The loadings of the seven Multi-Dimensional Pursuit Scores on the reference factors were then estimated by a linear multiple regression technique, reported by Mosier (1080), and outlined by Fruchter (563) and by Fruchter and Jennings (566, pages 258-269), which utilizes the correlations between the set of reference variables and the set of criterion variables (the matrix R'_{12} in Table 10-1).

With regard to the factor content of the seven component scores of the Multi-Dimensional Pursuit test, the interpretations were similar to those obtained from the previous analysis. Again, little common variance was found between the performance scores of the Multi-Dimensional Pursuit apparatus and the basic skill factors. The only appreciable loadings for the Multi-Dimensional Pursuit variables were for the double-level and triple-level scores. As in the first analysis, they appeared on the "response-orientation" factor. The

[2]Variable 23, Rudder Control-Triple Target, was also omitted from this re-analysis to avoid the doublet factor for the two scores of the Rudder Control test which emerged in the first analysis.

communalities for the estimated loadings of the component scores were about the same or a little less than the communalities for these same scores obtained from the seven comparable rotated factors in the first analysis.

In general, the conclusions from both analyses concerning changes in "criterion"

TABLE 10-2

ROTATED AND ESTIMATED FACTOR LOADINGS*

	I RO	II FS	III RT	IV SAM	V AHS	VI MIC	VII Purs	h^2
Reference Variables								
1. Two-Hand Coordination	10	−10	21	−10	01	59	24	48
2. Rotary Pursuit	00	42	08	19	18	16	41	44
3. Complex Coordination	16	32	−06	−08	12	45	16	38
4. Plane Control	05	11	−02	12	02	67	96	48
5. Pursuit Confusion-T.O.T.	29	00	−17	08	27	−08	37	34
6. Pursuit Confusion-Errors	04	−04	−06	26	36	15	30	31
7. Discrimination Reaction Time	69	03	02	20	01	39	04	67
8. Motor Judgment	20	05	08	−06	21	10	49	35
9. Visual Coincidence	32	00	17	02	−02	20	06	18
10. Two-Hand Pursuit	21	16	26	−08	17	53	03	46
11. Single Dimension Pursuit	21	43	14	−05	−09	28	03	34
12. Rate Control	04	01	12	15	−15	37	30	29
13. Dial Setting	50	20	09	−06	08	20	22	40
14. Controls Adjustment	23	40	11	−14	12	27	26	40
15. Rotary Aiming	18	37	18	36	13	−14	17	39
16. Visual Reaction Time	05	20	65	23	04	−02	−04	52
17. Auditory Reaction Time	12	00	69	22	25	−08	08	62
18. Jump Visual Reaction Time	12	13	58	54	16	13	−03	70
19. Jump Auditory Reaction Time	08	−07	61	55	00	25	07	75
20. Track Tracing	08	38	07	−13	69	−08	14	67
21. Steadiness-Precision	12	−08	26	−12	60	−05	05	47
22. Rudder Control-Single Target	05	02	13	−06	−03	56	57	67
24. Printed Discrimination Reaction Time	55	27	−03	22	29	−01	00	51
Experimental Variables								
25. Multidimensional Pursuit-Bank	11	16	−08	12	02	24	04	12
26. Multidimensional Pursuit-Heading	23	14	04	05	−06	12	12	11
27. Multidimensional Pursuit-Air Speed	29	01	01	18	−03	08	19	16
28. Multidimensional Pursuit-Bank and Altitude	30	16	07	−01	04	30	22	26
29. Multidimensional Pursuit-Bank and Heading	30	25	04	07	08	29	10	26
30. Multidimensional Pursuit-Bank and Air Speed	34	13	−03	05	−02	18	03	17
31. Multidimensional Pursuit-Bank, Heading and Air Speed	32	14	−07	14	−02	22	16	22

*Decimal points omitted.
**Factors are identified as follows: I, Response Orientation; II, Fine Control Sensitivity; III, Reaction Time; IV, Speed of Arm Movement; V, Arm Hand Steadiness; VI, Multiple Limb Coordination; VII, Pursuit. See Fleishman (532).

scores as a function of changes in task complexity were similar. The presence of the high intercorrelations of the component scores, inflated somewhat owing to experimental dependence, did not materially affect the outcome of the analysis. The strong "specific" factor that emerged in the first analysis segregated and partialed out the intra-task and spurious variance associated with the Multi-Dimensional Pursuit scores without materially affecting the relationship of these component scores to the other factors.

These results are in accord with theoretical expectation. If several of the variables in a battery share unique variance, owing to experimental or linear dependence, or specificity, the rank of the correlation matrix is augmented to include factors for these unique common variances. These factors then serve to partial out the common unique variances, leaving the remaining common variances to be distributed among the other factors.

While the results from the two methods seem to be similar, the procedure of factor-analyzing the basic reference battery first and then estimating the loadings for the other variables on the basis of the rotated factor loadings may have some advantages. This is particularly true if the number of experimentally dependent scores is large and the factors in the basic reference battery are well defined without them.

First, the number of correlation coefficients to be computed is smaller, since the intercorrelations among the experimentally dependent variables are not used in the analysis and it is therefore not necessary to compute them.

Second, the size of the correlation matrix to be factored is somewhat smaller since the "criterion" variables are not included in the factoring. The resulting saving is offset to a small extent, however, by the labor of estimating the factor loadings of the criterion variables in a later step.

Third, the *number* of factors to be extracted and rotated, and the number of residual matrices to be computed, is smaller.

Finally, and most important, the structure of the basic reference battery is determined independently of the experimentally dependent variables.

This factor regression method of estimating factor loadings of the dependent variables may be especially useful in correlational studies involving experimental variations of one or more tasks, or where there is interest in changes in several kinds of scores derived from the same sample. If a suitable reference battery of "basic" skills is given to the same subjects and the factor structure of this battery is established, then the relevant experimental scores can be estimated on this structure by the described procedures.

6. AN ILLUSTRATION OF THE FACTOR-REGRESSION DESIGN, IN FLEISHMAN AND FRUCHTER'S SPEED-OF-LEARNING ANALYSIS

Another application of the factor-regression design occurred in a study where it was desired to observe shifts in the factor content of proficiency measures obtained at different stages of learning. The reference space of interest was spanned by a set of independent reference variables, and the factor content of the criterion variables was estimated on the set of common reference factors. The purpose of this type of analysis was to study *changes* in the nature of the criterion variables in the course of learning, or owing to experimental treatment or systematic variations in the criterion task, with respect to the factors in a common set of independent reference variables. The structure of the reference battery is determined independently of the influence of specific or unique variance in the criterion variables. This would *not* be the case if the independent and dependent variables were placed in a single correlation matrix and analyzed together.

The application had to do with the stages

of practice in learning Morse code. In this study by Fleishman and Fruchter (533), a battery of fourteen relevant visual and auditory aptitude tests was administered to a sample of 310 radio-operator students. Records were kept of the number of days the students required to reach four successive levels of proficiency in reception of Morse code. These four "time" measures were correlated with the fourteen reference measures, and estimates of their loadings on the five factors derived from the reference battery (as well as the multiple correlations between the proficiency time measurements and the reference battery) were obtained. These results, shown in Table 10-3, indicate that early in training, individual differences in speed of learning Morse code are, to a considerable extent, a function of two auditory ability factors, Auditory Rhythm Discrimination and Auditory Perceptual Speed. In an intermediate stage these abilities play a smaller role, with Speed of Closure (the ability to organize stimuli meaningfully) of some importance. The over-all relationship of proficiency in code learning to the reference variables decreases as learning continues and proficiency increases. This agrees with a general finding that currently used tests are valid mainly for predicting attainment of proficiency in the early periods of Morse code training. Progress at later proficiency levels appears to be less a function of general ability variables and more a function of specific habits acquired during training.

7. BECHTOLDT'S RE-ANALYSIS OF COOMBS' NUMBER ABILITY STUDY, AS AN ILLUSTRATION OF HYPOTHESIS-TESTING

The combination of multiple regression methods with factor analysis makes possible the application of tests of significance developed for multiple regression to the coefficients derived to estimate the loadings of the dependent variables on the factors. Two approaches are possible, as was previously indicated. One of them is to

TABLE 10-3

MEANS, STANDARD DEVIATIONS, FACTOR LOADINGS, AND MULTIPLE CORRELATIONS FOR FOUR PERIODS OF LEARNING TO RECEIVE CODE

Learning Period	Mean	S.D.	Factors* Vz.	Aud. Rhy.	Verb.	Speed Clos.	Aud. Speed	h^2	R**
1. Number of Days Training to Receive 4 Groups/Min.	14.53	4.57	.01	.37	.15	.23	.48	.45	.59
2. Number of Days Training to Advance from 4 to 6 Groups/Min.	4.38	4.07	−.18	.18	.07	.36	.28	.28	.39
3. Number of Days Training to Advance from 6 to 10 Groups/Min.	19.24	8.48	−.29	.26	.05	.23	.14	.22	.29
4. Number of Days Training to Advance from 10 to 14 Groups/Min.	25.49	10.53	−.20	.21	.06	.23	.21	.19	.33

*Factors were defined from the ability tests as Vz., Visualization; Aud. Rhy., Auditory Rhythm Perception; Verb., Verbal Ability; Speed Clos., Speed of Closure; Aud. Speed, Auditory Perceptual Speed.

**Multiple correlations between the 14 ability tests and the number of days to progress from one proficiency level to the next.

assemble a battery of reference variables, consisting either of established marker variables or of factor scores estimated from variables with established factor content, and to apply conventional multiple linear regression techniques. The other is to factor-analyze the intercorrelations of the reference variables derived from the sample and then to regress the dependent variables onto the factor structure of the independent reference variables.

A re-analysis by Bechtoldt (80) of some data originally published by Coombs (383) illustrates both of these procedures. The study was an investigation of two hypotheses regarding the Number Factor. The two hypotheses dealt with the effects of varying selected task dimensions and of varying amount of training in specific operations upon the number factor loadings of certain tasks. Coombs' first hypotheses (N_1) was that number factor scores represented an agility in manipulating a symbolic system according to a specified set of rules, with the restriction that the symbol system be familiar and that the rules be thoroughly practiced. His second hypothesis (N_2) was that number factor scores represented an agility with serial responses in a situation where one response to a stimulus leads to the next response. From these two hypotheses several predictions were made, as indicated in the second column of the second part of Table 10-4.

Coombs used 16 tests from the 1938 edition of the P.M.A. battery as his reference tests and 12 special tests as his experimental tests without separating these classes of variables in his analysis. Three additional cancellation tests of his battery were used in the present analysis as reference tests for the perceptual speed factor to supplement or replace the two inadequate tests of this factor from the 1938 P.M.A. battery. Table 10-4 contains a listing of the 19 reference tests and the 12 experimental tests, and 3 additional tests included in the battery.

It should be noted that the two hypotheses state nothing about six of the seven reference factors listed in Table 10-4. The hypotheses are concerned only with the Number Factor and the experimental tests. Given a definition of the Number Factor, the correlations between the defined factor and the experimental test are the relevant data. A definition of the Number Factor consistent with Thurstone's statements about the P.M.A. battery is the average of the standard scores on the two Number tests. The values in the third column of Table 10-4 are the correlations between the Number Factor, so defined, and the remaining tests of the battery; the correlations were computed by the "sum of correlation" method from values given in Coombs' paper. The notes below the table indicate the results of tests of the specific predictions. Coombs in his final analysis of the correlation with the number factor "primary" used essentially this simple procedure; his values, shown in the fourth column of the second part of Table 10-4, are not amenable to statistical tests since all of his test variables are involved in the definition of the Number primary.

It will be noted, however, that several of the reference tests have significant correlations with the defined Number Factor. For this reason, an investigation more nearly like that initially undertaken by Coombs was made by Bechtoldt. To the original hypotheses we now add the phrase "when the effects of six defined factors ($P, V, S, M, I,$ and D) are taken into consideration." The number factor predictions will be tested in terms of partial regression coefficients; partial correlations might have been used. In the first re-analysis, the results of which are shown in Table 10-5, the problem of defining the seven factors was solved by using average standard scores from the P.M.A. battery for the last five factors and from the three cancellation tests for the Perceptual Speed factor (P). A simple regression analysis of the correlations computed from Coombs' data was made. Table 10-5 contains the beta weights

TABLE 10-4

STATISTICAL TESTS OF PREDICTIONS GENERATED FROM FACTOR HYPOTHESES
Variables and selected data from Coombs (383)
(223 High School Seniors from 6 Chicago H.S. Classes in Self-Appraisal)

Code No.		Correlations with N (average)	Coombs' Correlations with N (primary)
Reference Variables	Factor		
1. Digit Cancellation	P_1 — Coombs	.44*	.47
2. Scattered X's (Rowed)	P_1 — "	.27	.25
3. Scattered X's (Pied)	P_1 — "	.16	.16
4. Identical Forms	(P) — P.M.A.	.23	.25
5. Verbal Enumeration	(P) — "	.38	.35
6. Addition	N — "	(.xx)	.66
7. Multiplication	N — "	(.xx)	.78
8. Completion	V — "	.15	.19
9. Same-Opposite	V — "	.23	.26
10. Cards	S — "	.23	.21
11. Figures	S — "	.20	.22
12. Initials	M — "	.20	.21
13. Word-number	M — "	.17	.12
14. Letter Grouping	I — "	.30	.28
15. Marks	I — "	.22	.19
16. Number Patterns	I — "	.35	.32
17. Arithmetic	D — "	.24	.25
18. Number Series	D — "	.29	.33
19. Mechanical Movements	D — "	.18	.20
Experimental Variables	N_1 or N_2 Hypotheses		
20. Two-Digit Addition	$22 > 21 > 20$	.71	.91
21. Three-Digit Addition	for N_2	.77	.94
22. Four-Digit Addition		.73	.91
23. AB	$23, 24 > 0$ for N_1	.46	.49
24. ABC	$24 > 23$ for N_2	.41	.41
25. Forms	$24 > 25$ for N_1	.36	.34
26. Alphabet I	$28 > 26$ for N_1	.34	.42
27. Alphabet II	$28 > 0$ for N_1	.36	.44
28. Alphabet III		.36	.46
29. Identical Numbers		.45	.52
30. Highest Number	(trial balloons)	.40	.47
31. Size Comparison		.28	.33
32. Substitution I	$34 > 32$ for N_1	.31	.28
33. Substitution II	$34 > 0$ for N_1	.22	.18
34. Substitution III		.28	.24

*$r \geqslant |.18|$ at 1% level

N_1 hypothesis — facility with highly practiced associations all experimental test correlations significant at the 1% level.

$r_{24} > r_{25}$, (not sig., 5%) $r_{34} > r_{32}$ (reversed)
$r_{28} > r_{26}$, (not sig., 5%)

N_2 hypothesis — chaining is involved in number performance

$r_{22} > r_{20}$, (not sig., 5%) $r_{21} > r_{20}$ ($F = 6.9$, sig., 1%)
$r_{24} > r_{23}$, (reversed) $r_{22} > r_{21}$ (reversed)

TABLE 10-5

BETA WEIGHTS FOR PREDICTING 34 VARIABLES FROM SEVEN FACTORS

(Defined as Average Standard Scores of Sets of Reference Tests, Multiple Correlation Coefficients Squared for Non-Reference Tests, and Standard Errors for N factor Beta Weights)

(Decimals at left omitted)

Code Factors No.	P	N	V	S	M	I	R	(R^2_{yp})	$S_{\beta yN}$
Reference Variables									
1. P	71	18	09	−02	00	−01	−04	x	x
2. P	85	−04	−07	09	00	02	−07	x	x
3. P	82	−14	−02	−07	00	−01	11	x	x
4. −	29	−01(NS)*	03	44	04	17	−15	40	061
5. −	24	22	41	05	01	00	−09	35	064
6. N	01	86	−03	−02	−01	07	02	x	x
7. N	−01	91	03	02	01	−07	−02	x	x
8. V	03	−03	93	04	−02	−07	03	x	x
9. V	−03	04	92	−04	02	07	−03	x	x
10. S	−02	00	−05	93	04	02	04	x	x
11. S	02	00	05	96	−04	−02	−04	x	x
12. M	01	−01	07	08	81	02	−04	x	x
13. M	−01	01	−07	−08	84	−02	04	x	x
14. I	13	−02	11	−06	07	72	−10	x	x
15. I	−10	−08	10	03	−05	76	07	x	x
16. I	−03	10	−22	03	−02	76	02	x	x
17. D	−12	03	−01	−01	09	−03	84	x	x
18. D	−01	04	04	−05	−02	04	79	x	x
19. D	13	−07	−03	06	−06	−02	70	x	x
Experimental Variables									
20.	12	66	09	02	00	−03	−02	52	054
21.	06	68	13	00	01	04	07	63	048
22.	09	63	11	−04	00	02	13	58	051
23.	17	24	26	09	09	16	00	40	061
24.	03	26	28	15	00	09	06	35	064
25.	03	18	16	15	11	28	−12	29	066
26.	10	06(NS)	28	13	11	21	17	48	057
27.	08	09(NS)	33	09	12	24	13	48	057
28.	07	10(NS)	32	08	11	23	14	47	057
29.	35	28	12	−13	07	08	00	33	064
30.	21	22	09	05	02	16	−01	26	068
31.	16	07(NS)	51	08	05	−04	10	43	059
32.	11	12(NS)	−04	08	21	19	07	23	069
33.	11	08(NS)	−04	03	13	14	03	11	074
34.	15	15(NS)	−06	04	18	12	−02	15	073

*(NS) indicates lack of significance at the 1% level on factor N only. None of the predicted *differences* in beta weights on factor N is significant at 5% level.

for predicting all variables from the seven defined factor scores. Since the "dependent" variables, as well as variables 4 and 5 are *experimentally independent* of the defined factors, the relevant predictions are now testable in terms of beta weights for 12 of these variables. The results of the test of significance are indicated in the lower portion of the table. Two things should be noted: (1) the general consistency of the results of the two analyses as well as the differences in the hypotheses tested by these two procedures, and (2) the correspondence between the patterns of the beta weights in the reference test section and the characteristics of a "simple structure" solution. No rotations were made, no communalities were estimated. Further-

TABLE 10-6

Oblique Projections and Communalities for
19 Reference Variables and Beta Weights

(Multiple Correlations Squared, and Standard Errors of Beta Weights for Factor N for 15 Experimental Variables Based on Seven Factors Defined by an Oblique Simple Structure.)

Code Factors No.	P	N	V	S	M	I	R	h^2
			(Decimals at left omitted)					
Reference Variables								
1.	43	34	13	−04	−02	08	−03	47
2.	72	04	−02	03	02	12	−01	66
3.	68	−01	−08	−06	−01	−13	26	44
4.	26	−05	03	46	09	23	−12	52
5.	18	28	46	08	−02	00	−12	43
6.	01	72	−07	−06	−03	08	12	61
7.	−02	74	03	06	03	−04	−04	54
8.	07	−08	76	07	−01	−12	12	64
9.	−06	−04	87	−08	02	13	05	81
10.	−06	00	−08	88	02	−03	11	80
11.	03	−04	03	89	−02	−09	03	77
12.	00	−03	03	06	61	03	00	39
13.	−02	03	−09	−01	61	−01	−01	36
14.	20	−03	10	−10	06	40	24	35
15.	−06	−11	15	−03	−09	50	41	45
16.	06	08	−30	04	−04	46	38	44
17.	−06	02	01	03	09	−13	76	65
18.	06	04	09	−07	−05	01	76	59
19.	20	−02	08	22	−02	−05	30	27

Code Factors No.	P	N	V	S	M	I	R	R^2_{yp}	$S_{\beta yN}$
Experimental Variables									
20.	−01	88	07	07	−09	−05	−07	69	048
21.	−02	86	07	00	−10	−03	12	79	040
22.	01	81	05	−06	−09	−04	22	73	045
23.	11	24	30	01	06	26	07	49	062
24.	−02	31	29	12	−11	06	16	40	067
25.	−06	15(NS)*	16	12	11	36	−01	37	069
26.	11	00(NS)	26	04	04	22	41	53	059
27.	07	00(NS)	31	−06	07	29	41	55	058
28.	09	00(NS)	30	−06	07	29	39	52	060
29.	29	42	18	−10	03	12	−10	46	064
30.	14	24	08	−03	00	34	07	34	070
31.	15	14(NS)	58	20	07	−14	−03	54	059
32.	11	05(NS)	−09	10	23	20	16	27	074
33.	10	03(NS)	−06	07	14	18	07	14	080
34.	09	15(NS)	−09	08	18	17	00	18	078

*(NS) indicates lack of significance at the 1% level on factor N only. The beta weights for No. 25 and No. 31 are significant at the 5% level.

more, the question of oblique and orthogonal factors is entirely a matter of the empirical results; for this sample, the factors as defined are oblique as shown in Part A of Table 10-7. It should be noted also that these beta weights can be "interpreted" in terms of "variance contributions" of factors as well as in terms of one or more hypotheses regarding factor composition. However, the definition of the seven methods and the communalities stabilized somewhat by two cycles of the multiple group procedure. The seventh factor was of doubtful significance as evaluated by four of the approximate tests of rank suggested by Thomson (1393). Graphic rotations were then made, still using only 19 tests, to a "simple structure" solution judged reasonably acceptable by the investigator. The beta weights for the 15 "experimental"

TABLE 10-7

CORRELATIONS BETWEEN FACTORS (ABOVE DIAGONAL) AND ELEMENTS OF INVERSE
(ON AND BELOW DIAGONAL) USED FOR TESTS OF SIGNIFICANCE OF
BETA WEIGHTS IN TWO ANALYSES

(Decimals omitted — 3 place nos.)

A. Factors Defined as Averages of Standard Scores

	P	N	V	S	M	I	R
P	1249	363	089	266	100	352	200
N	−333	1333	205	228	227	387	305
V	075	−072	1291	292	134	297	456
S	−169	049	−076	1498	141	454	506
M	−005	−193	−034	−032	1083	133	215
I	−267	−305	−127	−374	026	1558	451
R	024	−153	−479	−529	−153	−315	1703

B. Factors Defined by Communalities and Oblique Rotations

	P	N	V	S	M	I	R
P	1262	338	101	355	115	388	134
N	−285	1613	296	292	378	484	351
V	064	−140	1312	331	237	254	447
S	−348	237	−132	1942	164	540	530
M	−012	−387	−095	039	1228	147	331
I	−225	−605	−084	−756	092	1694	272
R	305	−387	−422	−918	−249	106	1837

$$S^2_{yp} = \left(\frac{1 - R^2_{yp}}{N - r - 1}\right)(R^{-1}_{pp})$$ where N = number of cases, r = number of predictors. R^2_{yp} is the square of the multiple correlation of the experimental variable, y, with the linear combination of the factors, p, and R^{-1}_{pp} is the diagonal value of the inverse of the matrix of intercorrelations (among the factors) corresponding to the beta weight being evaluated.

factors might be expressed in other ways; the second re-analysis is by conventional factor analysis procedures using estimates of the communalities and rotation to oblique simple structure, such as was carried out by Coombs. In the re-analysis, the factor techniques are applied to the reference tests only. Seven centroid factors were computed by the complete centroid tests were then computed by the "projection" feature of the multiple group equations; the results are shown in Table 10-6. The values for the reference variables in Table 10-6 are *not* "factor loadings" but oblique projections. They are proportional to factor loadings. The values for the 15 experimental tests are proper beta weights. Again tests of significance of the beta weights in terms of the new definitions of the factors are shown below the tabled values. Discrepancies in beta weights from the Table 10-5 values from some of the variables were found as would be expected. Such discrepancies represent the effects of changes in definition of factors from the average standard score values used in Table 10-5 to definitions by means of communality estimates and rotational procedures involving 19 reference variables.

The reader may be interested in comparing the treatment given Coombs' data in this section with that given some of Coombs' data by Guttman in Chapter 14.

8. MANIPULATIVE DESIGN ILLUSTRATED IN CATTELL AND SCHEIER'S CONDITION-RESPONSE DESIGN STUDY

In his chapter, "Structuring Variables by Combinations of Factor Analysis with Controlled Experiment," Cattell (229) outlined a number of procedures for the combination of controlled experiment and factor analysis. One of the methods, the condition-response design in multivariate experiment, in which the stimuli are randomized in relation to one another to insure orthogonality of effects, as in some analysis of variance designs, permits testing of hypotheses concerning factor content of difference scores. The differences may be due to experimental manipulation. The following quotation from Cattell and Scheier (324) gives the essence of the experimental design and procedures:

The general theory of condition-response design is given elsewhere (Cattell, 229), but its nature will be illustrated in the following account of actual experimental procedures. Essentially, it measures each subject under two conditions (which would be high and low either on situational stimulus levels, as here, or internal conditions in, say, a psychophysiological experiment). At the same time, it measures all of a

considerable variety of response variable magnitudes and then correlates changes in stimulus magnitudes with changes in response magnitudes, instead of relating significance of difference in one to difference in the other, as in analysis of variance. Upon factoring this matrix, one obtains both (*a*) evidence (or, in our case, confirmation) for what unitary response patterns, e.g., anxiety, stress, etc., may exist in the given range of dependent variables, and (*b*) the significance and magnitude of the relations of these unitary response patterns to the independent variables constituted by the stimulus conditions.

... evidence of the first can be obtained by *R* technique above, or *P* technique. Woodrow (1562) has factor analyzed increment scores in the learning and mental ability domain, and several *R* and *P* studies have recently been carried out in personality data, but to our knowledge the present study is the first to perform incremental *R* technique in personality research in a design with manipulated, randomized, independent variables in what has hitherto been a theoretical proposition for a condition-response design.

Design and Procedure

S's were 86 male undergraduates: 52 unselected in relation to anxiety, 18 of high anxiety, and 16 of low anxiety. The same 72 variables were scores for each of the 86 *S*'s on Occasion 1, and then again on Occasion 2, four weeks later. Sixty-nine of the measures entered in the matrix were *changes* in score from Occasion 1 to Occasion 2 on personality "response" variables; three scores were *changes* in the magnitude of stimuli, representing "massive" environmental "stress" conditions. The change score was always computed as Occasion 2 minus Occasion 1.

Most of the response variables are well known, collected from previous attempts to measure anxiety, stress, neurotic debility, and several other previously established general personality factor dimensions. Most readers will wish only the indication of their nature given by their title ... in the text. Those requiring more detailed descriptions can obtain them from the authors or by reference to other researches, where the rationale for selection of personality factor markers is also explained.... The main aim in the choice of variables was to make possible the distinguishing of the threat-response factors from other known personality factors.

The environmental conditions, i.e. the stimuli, were varied in a two-step, present-absent, on-off manner for the three following stimuli: Anticipation of Treadmill Run, Imminence of Academic Examinations, Questionnaire "Group Stress Interview" Probe.

It is an important part of the condition-response design . . . that the various stimuli used be randomized in relation to one another, as in an analysis of variance with several effects. Otherwise, any correlation among the stimuli would have only local meaning—an artifact of the experimenter's design—and would complicate the interpretation of the correlation with the response patterns. Accordingly, a design was set up for combining the high and low (on and off) incidences of the three stimuli with equal frequency. Actually, the essential aim is to have the *changes* from first to second occasion on each stimulus uncorrelated with changes in the other two stimuli, and to have a step down ("on" to "off") between occasion one and two just as frequent as a step up, i.e., to avoid confounding with a particular sequence effect. This requires eight combinations. . . .

The condition-response design, like analysis of variance, results in a rapid multiplication of the number of categories required (treatment subgroups) as the number of stimuli increases. Consequently, one will usually be constrained to deal with far fewer stimuli than responses, but this suits the objective of the design, which is to examine directly the relation between changes of intensity in single stimuli and changes in intensity of demonstrated response patterns. Of course, more response variables are needed to define the latter.

In the classical univariate design, one examines the significance of the difference of the dependent variable values corresponding to the two levels of the stimulus (or the two different effects). The equivalent of this in the present design is to examine the significance of the correlation of the stimulus variable with the response factor. Parenthetically, the *loading* of the stimulus on the response factor, as immediately obtained by the present proposed factoring, is not identical with the correlation when factors are oblique, and requires further calculation; but the departure is so slight with the small obliquities obtained here that we have not

considered the complex calculations justified and shall speak of the loading as the correlation.

The condition-response design gives more information than does analysis of variance (*a*) in tying down the "dependent variable" in terms of response dimensions (in groups of tests) and also (*b*) because it reveals not only whether the relation of stimulus change and response change is significant, but also how large it is. On the other hand, it says nothing about interaction effects. However, it should be noted that even if each of the several stimuli were actually perfectly related to the response (in the absence of other variables), the correlation of each therewith could not be unity. If they vary independently, . . . the summed squares of their correlations with the common-response could not exceed unity. Thus, in the present instance the three individual loadings could not exceed $\sqrt{.3}$, i.e., .58. Since our experimentally controlled, deliberate manipulation of the stimuli is not the sole variance in these stimuli, the maximum is actually lower than this. For example, if our imposed range of examination stress, between stressless periods of the semester and semester exams, is, on the average, half of the individual's actually experienced range of examination stress, a full response of the anxiety factor in our experiment to the controlled stress would still yield a correlation of only about .41. These points should be kept in mind in our subsequent examination of the stimulus loadings.

Results

Replication of the Four Threat Response Patterns. According to the above design, difference scores on all variables between the first and second occasion, including the prearranged differences on the stimuli, were computed over all 86 individuals, and product-moment intercorrelated. A centroid factor extraction from the 72×72 matrix was terminated at 14 factors, according to criteria of completeness of extraction described elsewhere (Cattell, 229) and rotated to a simple structure which, after 25 rotations, reached a plateau of 59% of variables in the hyperplane.

A separate report gives full data and general descriptive comments on all fourteen factors. . . . The four factors chosen for concentrated attention here as "threat response" factors were so chosen because (*a*) their loaded response variables most strongly suggest the character of "response to threat" as commonly conceived and (*b*) with the minor possible exception noted below, they were the only well identified factors significantly associated with at least one of the three "stress" stimuli. . . .

The Relation of Response Patterns to Stimulus Conditions. Correlations between the factors (actually, reference vectors) representing the response patterns are given in the right hand section of Table 10-8. The left hand section of Table 10-8 gives relations between each of the three stimuli and the four threat-response factors.

These results may be evaluated in terms of (*a*) the significance of a correlation on 86 cases, which must be .21 or above for significance at the $P = .05$ level, or (*b*) the significance of a loading, which is taken here as .16. We shall summarily depend on Criterion *a* to be on the safe side. On this criterion, it becomes evident, first, that *no single response factor behaves in the same way to all three threat situations;* that is, no response dimension, as a "dependent variable," is significantly affected in the same direction for all three "stress" stimuli on a given factor. There is not even a consistency in direction of sign for all three stress stimuli on a given factor. Secondly, two of the three highest relations are in the opposite direction to that which naive views might hypothesize. Thus, the anticipation of a treadmill run significantly *reduces* Neurotic Debility and the incidence of examinations significantly *reduces* anxiety. However, presence of probing questionnaire threat is significantly associated with increased Effort Stress Reaction, P.U.I. 4 (+), as would commonly be expected.

9. DEPENDENCE-INDEPENDENCE PURELY AS AN ANALYTICAL CONCEPT: FACTOR REGRESSION ANALYSES

The independent-dependent variable designs may be used either with a set of reference independent variables to determine analytical dependence, or in a time-sequence design, whether or not there is experimental manipulation of the independent variables, to establish time-related causal dependence. The studies reviewed in Sections 3 through 6 illustrate the former design, and the study reviewed in Section 7 the latter design.

For multivariate studies in which the variables fall into two classes, independent variables and dependent variables, it is more appropriate to use a dependency analysis design (e.g., the factor regression design) than an interdependency design (conventional factor analysis) in which all variables are in a single, coordinate class. In the factor-regression design, the reference factor space is determined for the independent variables, and then the dependent, experimental variables are projected onto the reference factors by linear regression analysis which uses the correlations between the reference variables and the experimental variables (Matrix R'_{12} in Table 10-1).

Some advantages of factor-regression design are:

TABLE 10-8

CORRELATIONS OF RESPONSE FACTORS WITH STIMULI AND WITH ONE ANOTHER

	Exam. Imminence	Probing Questionnaire	Anticipation of Treadmill Run	U.I. 24(+)	U.I. (23)(−)	P.U.I. 4(+)
U.I. 24(+) Anxiety	−25	00	+13			
U.I. 23(−) Neurotic Debility	+04	+06	−35	+26		
P.U.I. 4(+) Stress or General Adaptation Syndrome	+16	+28	−16	−12	+09	
U.I. 22(−) Lower Cortical Alertness or Excitation Level Lower	+20	+02	−07	+11	−04	+15

1. The factor structure of the reference battery is determined independently of the dependent variables. This yields a reference factor basis which is not influenced by the experimental variables used in a specific study, thus providing a reference space *not* partly determined by the dependent variables under investigation.

2. The use of marker reference variables and of methods for matching factors serves to increase the comparability of studies, and the generality of results over investigators, laboratories, and instruments.

3. The use of regression methods to estimate the correlations of the dependent variables with the independent variables, or the factors derived from them, makes it possible to test hypotheses by applying tests of significance to the values derived from the dependent variables.

4. The dependent variables under investigation may represent the effects of experimental conditions due to (a) experimental manipulation of the independent variables, (b) systematic changes in the construction of the experimental or dependent measure, or (c) changes in the subjects due to learning or other internal influences. The first listed is perhaps of greatest interest since it is frequently desirable to determine the effect of systematic manipulation of the experimental treatments on the dependent variables.

The notions presented here in the special context of factor analysis may be cross-referenced by the reader to Anderson's treatment of the general problems of regression in Chapter 5, as well as to Horst's treatment of canonical correlation in Chapter 4 and Harris' treatment of the study of change by canonical correlation in Chapter 12.

10. SUMMARY

(1) Factor analysis has been presented earlier as an hypothesis-generating and an hypothesis-testing design, the hypotheses being either descriptive — as a specific pattern of loadings — or interpretive, as a construct or concept. The present chapter is largely concerned with the method as incorporated in designs (a) to test hypotheses, and (b) to examine dependence-independence.

(2) In hypothesis-testing we are largely concerned with factor matching or examining the significance of loadings. Factor matching requires attention to (a) pattern, (b) correlation among factors, (c) factor loading size.

(3) An experiment by Fruchter and Fleishman (565) on task complexity analysis was taken as an example of independence-dependence design and factor regression analysis. The results from this analysis were compared with the results from the more conventional (interdependency) factor analysis design. While the conventional type of analysis was powerful enough to partial out certain sources of spuriousness due to experimental dependence among the task-complexity variables, and to give results comparable to those obtained from the factor regression analysis, certain advantages of the latter approach were cited.

(4) In another study by Fleishman and Fruchter (533), shifts in the factor content of measures of the speed of learning Morse code over the course of learning were determined by the factor regression analysis method.

(5) In a re-analysis of an investigation by Coombs (383) of two hypotheses concerning the number factor, Bechtoldt (80) demonstrated the use of operational definitions of factor variables and multiple regression analysis as an approach to test hypotheses concerning dependent variables with appropriate tests of significance.

(6) Manipulative design has so far been illustrated in practice only by what has been called the condition-response design, i.e., factoring conditions (E, E', S, S', P' in the data box) along with responses (R, R' in the data box), Cattell and Scheier (324)

performed an incremental R-technique analysis in a design with three manipulated, randomized, independent stress variables and sixty-nine personality response variables. Tests of significance of the relationship of stimulus "change" to response "change" were applied.

(7) The dependence-independence design, as applied in factor analysis through the factor-regression design, may be viewed as being appropriate for determining analytical dependence, for establishing time-related causal dependence in a time-sequence experiment, or for determining the relationship between changes in experimentally manipulated stimulus variables and associated changes in dependent response variables.

CHAPTER **11** **Patterns of Change:**
Measurement in Relation to
State-Dimension, Trait Change,
Lability, and Process Concepts

RAYMOND B. CATTELL
University of Illinois

1. THE CENTRAL PROBLEMS OF CHANGE MEASUREMENT

Among a hundred research publications taken at random from journals it is probable that more than fifty would be found to deal with measurements of change. The whole of learning theory, for example, and all that has to do with concepts of motivation, as well as vast areas of social psychology, have concerned themselves almost wholly with change measurement. Yet sophistication of concepts is lacking in many of these studies, and agreement as to what are satisfactory procedures for defining change concepts is far from widespread.[1]

This, and the ensuing two chapters, by Harris and by Brand, are devoted to the problem of measuring and conceptualizing change, especially psychological change. The present chapter aims to cover what seem to be the important models and concepts practicable at the present juncture, and to show their roots in experimental designs and familiar statistical operations. Harris' chapter follows by concentrating on the elegant canonical factor model — otherwise only lightly sketched in the chapters (4 and 5) by Horst and by Anderson — and its applications to change measurement. Brand's chapter looks at change from supplementary angles, concerned with chain processes, decision sequences, and games theory. It will be refreshing to psychologists to have this dealt with from the standpoint of a physicist and a mathe-

---

[1] Until quite recently, the neglect of growth and change, in terms of any precise formulae or models, by personality, clinical, and child development psychologists — and even by classical reflexological learning theorists — has been remarkable. It is possible to pick up a dozen standard statistical tests without finding "growth curves" in the index of any of them. Yet, as pointed out under the "time sequence" parameter of experimental designs (page 22), this parameter is vital to causal inference and to science. Indeed, expert historians of science are inclined to the view that the

idea of order and scientific law first gained explicit recognition through the Egyptian calculations of the flooding of the Nile Valley and the Sumerian observations of astronomical regularity. An area of study without technical means for formulating change is scarcely out of its scientific infancy.

matician, for our field could advantageously be cross-fertilized from this source.

In the present chapter, five major concepts are considered central to the study of most change phenomena:

(1) *Change conceived as occurring in otherwise "fixed" traits* (or profiles of traits, including measures of their integration). Such concepts of "structures normally standing stably at a particular level" are involved in most studies of growth and learning, whether of individuals or groups. We shall distinguish however, between *pure* trait change patterns which correspond one-to-one to traits, and what may be called *phasic* trait change patterns which do not.

(2) *Changes in levels on temporary states,* such as are involved in studies of mood, role, dynamic conditions, psychophysiological adjustment, drug action, etc.

(3) *Change in the environment or environmental relations of the person or group.*

(4) *Change evaluated as "tendency to change,"* i.e., as lability or instability, as in concepts of tendency to oscillate, to fluctuate, etc.

(5) *Change as a characteristic configurational sequence or process,* as in discussion of a learning conflict resolution, maturing or aging process, with a particular unfolding sequence, including the possibility of rhythmic and spiral sequences.

In all of these, we aim to deal briefly with operational concepts, scaling and calculating issues.

2. WHAT STATISTICAL AND SCIENTIFIC GROWTH LAWS RELATE TRAIT ELEMENT PATTERNS TO TRAIT CHANGE PATTERNS?

If a person or group is best defined *at a given moment* by measures on surface traits (score values on centroids of correlation clusters) or source traits (scores on simple structure or confactor rotated factors), then it is conceptually most economical to measure change — whether it be a case of learning or maturation — in terms of these same concepts. This advantage holds regardless of whether we are talking of unique traits (P-technique clusters or factors) or common traits across person populations.

Recent consolidations, such as those described by Pawlik (Chapters 18) Nesselroade and Delhees (Chapter 19), Horn (Chapter 20), Bereiter (Chapter 25.), and Cattell (Chapter 26), in the recognition of relatively invariant dimensions of abilities and dynamic traits in individuals, and of dimensions of action in small groups and national cultures, have now made possible effective substantive research in this framework. Indeed, in the individual person realm, with the availability of intelligence tests, of Thurstone's and French's primary ability batteries, of the 16 PF, the O-A Personality Battery, and MAT batteries for personality and dynamic factors, substantial progress in laws from measured change on well established source traits is now clearly in sight.

Four main issues arise in measuring such source trait change:

(1) Our capacity to distinguish change in a trait from changes in states.

(2) The adjustment of the *measure* (scaling) of a specific trait change to possibly changing patterns in the trait structure and its units of measurement. Conceivably, the weighting of manifestations (elements) should change continuously with the level.

(3) The question of the scale units in which change in general is to be measured.

(4) The development of expressions to represent *complex* change fittingly in profile pattern, e.g., integration and emergence effects from many simultaneously changing source traits.

As to the first, the distinction of a trait change from a state change can be made easily enough by arbitrary definition, but, as usual, the serious researcher will prefer to discover rather than to impose. That is to say, he would prefer to find certain consistent and coherent differences in the natural history of states and traits which permit their differentiation as two naturally distinct "types" (modes) of change manifestation. Not enough research has been done to allow this and at present we can only conjecture as to what may be found when the methods advocated here are applied.

However, the common meaning of a state connotes (a) that it is reversible, (b) that changes occur in its level more rapidly than in traits, (c) that it may modify a different pattern of variables from those involved in a trait, perhaps cutting across traits. Many psychologists would want to import other particulars into a state, e.g., that it covers the classes of moods, dynamic states, mental sets, role adoptions, etc., and that it frequently has physiological associates; but these are peripheral and perhaps accidental characteristics which should not, as ulterior conceptions, affect our primary definition.

For the present, states are defined only enough, by (a), (b), and (c) above, to set them aside from traits, and will be studied systematically in the next section. Measuring change on traits differs initially from that on states in that it presupposes the existence of a trait stable for each individual across time on which people already systematically differ in level one from another, in ways described in the chapters by Delhees, Nesselroade, Pawlik, Tucker, Horn, Coan, Thompson, and others. The trait concept presupposes an existing structure in individual difference, R-technique analysis and a characteristic individual level. As far as level is concerned, we must suppose in our model that a trait *may* suffer some small degree of function fluctuation, just like a state, but that it is of a totally smaller order of magnitude. However, if a trait fluctuates at all—and even a man's stature we are told varies slightly from day to day—then the widespread practice of

taking a single occasion measurement and calling it a trait measurement is wrong. (In practice, it may even be morally wrong, as when we measure an individual's IQ on a single occasion and allot or do not allot a scholarship to him on the basis of that result.) How many measurements are necessary for measuring a trait with a defined degree of accuracy will depend on the standard deviation of the measures over repeated occasions of measurement, due to internal and external conditions (axes P' and E' of the data box) and unreliability of measurement (axes S', R', O, and O' of the data box).

A more subtle issue concerns the possibility that the weights given to the subtests in a battery for a particular source trait factor may need to be changed as we measure change over different levels of movement. It has been demonstrated empirically since the early work of Spearman (1340) that the factor loadings, (V_{fp}), and therefore the variable weights for estimating the factor, (V_{fe}), of intelligence change appreciably with the intelligence level of the subjects, e.g., a Séguin form board is a good measure of the intelligence factor at a mental age of six, but not at a mental age of twelve. (The weights also change with the actual age, and the education of the subject, but that is a different matter from the issue of level.) The same has been shown in more detail in the recent work of Fleishman (530), Tucker (1465), and others where the factor composition of a particular learning performance is shown to change as the individual reaches higher levels or reaches a different point in the learning curve.

In Section 5, page 365, below we examine this question of relations of specification equations and factor patterns taken at different cross-section levels in more detail. But in any case it is evident that knowledge from statistical laws of how the loadings of trait elements for *changes* in a trait should differ from those for individual *differences* in a trait supplies us with another check for distinguishing trait change from state change. In the case of a pure state, such that individuals do not permanently and characteristically differ in level thereon, the weight pattern is identical for changes and for individual differences of level at a given moment; whereas in the case of traits, the nature of the growth process may well be such that the growth weight pattern at level x is significantly different from the individual difference pattern at level x, denoting that growth has previously occurred in a different way. For example, the height of the head (and presumably individual differences therein) contributes much more to the general stature factor in a young child than in an older child, and this is an important fact in the biology of growth.

On the other hand, we should be very surprised if the growth pattern in a trait bore *no* relation to its absolute pattern, as an individual difference structure, and this would throw doubt on the scientific usefulness of the concept of unitariness for the trait. A difference with a systematic and comparatively simple translation from one to the other best fits the concept of unitariness of being and of growth. A personality trait like Mobilization-vs.-Regression, U.I. 23, shows every sign of its parts growing together (as it increases through childhood) and of declining together (in neurosis) and we expect only such changes of weighting and loading patterns as statistical laws require. On the other hand, we have much to learn in this new field empirically as these questions are more accurately investigated by multivariate methods, and we know that elsewhere, as in the growth of a plant (or even the building of a house!), there are biological and learning laws, connected with the existence of distinct phases of growth, which make the individual difference weights on the final stable trait measures quite systematically different from those from incremental R technique (more generally, *differential R technique*) on the growing structure.

3. MEASURING TRANSFORMATION AND LEARNING IN PERSONALITY THROUGH TRAIT CHANGE

The last section has shown that measurement of change on a single trait is not as simple as it appears. Even granted firm scale units in the single variables, e.g., by the Simplex formula for equal interval and absolute scaling (page 109), we yet have some complications in converting this into units of *change* on the trait concept. Accepting these complications, but setting aside for Section 5 below the metric issues of "ceiling effects," effect of error on correlation, homeostatic effects, etc., — which apply to both variables and factor traits — we propose here to assume single source traits to be satisfactorily measurable by existing methods. Granted that we shall in this section pursue the further question as to how changing relations among traits, and particularly such notions as interest psychologists in "integration learning," "maturational spirals," "pattern emergents," etc., can also be brought under change measurement schemata — for they are among the most important aspects of higher learning and maturation.

Indeed, we shall take it as axiomatic that the main model necessary in learning, and change generally, is one embracing *simultaneous* change on a number of single elements (commonly source traits), so that analysis of change on a single element only is a special case. By contrast to this formulation, large areas of "learning theory" try to handle the change within the artificial abstraction not only of a single dimension but even in terms of what happens to a single variable! In quite general terms, it must be obvious that there are as many kinds of change to be considered as there are psychological entities to be recognized: personality traits, skilled habits, phobias, ergs, sentiments, perceptual habits, and role sets — to name a few. These, however, reduce to a smaller number of formal entities, which have largely been considered in Part I of this Handbook, such as surface traits (correlation clusters), source traits (simple structure factors), second-order factors, types, type derivatives, processes, state dimensions, etc. However, research on change must be prepared to recognize that certain interaction and emergent effects may be quite lost unless we are equipped, in theories and in techniques, to handle change simultaneously on many variables.

To a first approximation we can say that all change of trait, state or process can be expressed as change on either (1) a *profile* of unitary scores, or (2) a *configuration* (page 291), in which, unlike a profile, the *order* of the elements is changeable. (By order, of course, we mean not only temporal order, but order in any other dimension which is not merely that of the dimensions of measurement itself, e.g., a hierarchy of mutual influence, of control, stimulation, etc., or (3) some *emergent* or mathematical function of what is actually given in the profile or configuration, e.g., a standard deviation among, an exponential function of, etc. In Chapter 9 on types and emergents, we have recognized that at certain levels on the elements of a profile some powerful change will take place on certain criterion behavior derivable from the profile scores. These comparatively sudden "behavioral emergents" are unforeseeable by linear extrapolation from the relation of profile elements to criteria over other ranges. Some of the important psychological changes we need to study occur in just such emergents, and in these cases it is helpful to know that what we are measuring is a complex, exponential derivative from the single dimension element measures.

It would be possible, of course, to make a study of change measurement without invoking any of the five comprehensive models listed in our introduction. Such a study would deal simply with "any variable" and would confine itself to questions of scaling, of relation of absolute to change

score, and with the problem of true and error score components. Very thorough treatments along these lines have been contributed by Bechtoldt (78), Lord (946), Hammond (684), Manning and DuBois (985), Gulliksen (645), Webster and Bereiter (1505), and several of the contributors to Harris's volume (692). The alternative path of going beyond consideration of the immediate measurement of a variable is being pursued here because even in the treatment of the individual variable one cannot get very far toward matters of general psychological interest, with effective assumptions and analyses, without invoking a further model. The five basic models on forms of change used here — trait change, state change, the conception of lability, the adjustment process model of interaction with environment, and the conception of a psychological process — may be reasonably stated, from wider psychological evidence, to have probable fruitfulness.

Our concern immediately in this section will be with trait change and the model of environmental interaction (therefore, with learning). This requires a brief statement of *Adjustment process analysis,* developed elsewhere (263a, 325), which handles the formulation of (a) change simultaneously on several independent dimensions, and (b) the laws relating such transformation to environmental influences. Note that *transformation* is used as a generic term here covering the joint effects of *modification* and *learning*. Modification defines changes not primarily in the central nervous system, such as a repeated experience causing an exhaustion of the adrenal glands, a gamma globulin change, or a reduced irritability. These are important parts of the human and animal personality change with experience, and must be included in change study and environmental transformation analysis, but they are not what is commonly called learning.

Indeed, as expressed more fully in Section 1, Chapter 16, "learning theory" as intensively studied in the last generation has followed the scientifically shabby procedure of "explaining" by its narrow reflexological model without first looking at what has to be explained — namely, personality change under life experiences. There is no question that the conditioned reflex will, up to a point, predict change in highly specific behaviors. What remains to be seen is whether other or supplementary laws are needed for change in whole source traits or complex interactive changes in a configuration of source traits. Adjustment-process analysis sets out to analyze change, evaluating learning and setting it aside from modification (and, as seen below, maturation) in such a way that new laws may be sought.

Learning is now defined as "a multi-dimensional change in response to experience in a multidimensional situation." Transformation process analysis has especially the aim of analyzing change where the experimental design precludes manipulation and permits only inefficient control. The former is true of most human learning and the latter of more animal learning experiments than are recognized to be thus vulnerable. ("The animal is exposed to something more than maze learning" and seldom are all influences but one held constant.) If associations are found in humans between personality and past experience (e.g., case histories) part must be ascribed to (a) choice (personalities of certain kinds choosing certain experience paths), and part to (b) learning. In the full adjustment path analysis paradigm an experimental formulation exists for separating these, while resort to pre and post measures with control groups will further separate learning from maturation effects. The expression "path analysis" is retained rather than situation analysis because path better describes the whole situational experience and brings out the "choice" connections with decision theory. Indeed a whole development of *Adjustment path analysis* has been made (263a, 325) in

connection with the latter, but in this chapter on change we can confine ourselves specifically to transformation (modification and learning) with choice and maturation influences being considered experimentally set aside.

Now the multidimensional change in the individual is readily enough expressed as a vector of changes — absolute or percentage — on an array of personality source traits; but what are the dimensions through which the situation (path) has its dimensionality expressed? These dimensions can be either (a) physical or (b) psychological. Elsewhere it has been pointed out (256 and Chapter 19) that a situation can be given psychological meaning by the vector of behavioral indices (b's in equation 6-32) when the response is measured purely as one of recognition. Similarly here the psychological meaning of a *learning* situation can be written down as a vector expressing the typical (average population) percentage change on the total array of source traits. This is shown as a diagonal matrix (and for a single person) in Diagram 16-1, page 492, to fit the multiplication there required. Now path transformation theory provides a means of calculating this path transformation vector when we do not have controlled or manipulative experimental conditions, but only evidence of changes in persons and of the frequencies with which they have been exposed to various path situations. It assumes that within the limits concerned each successive exposure brings a similar increment, and that a path has a characteristic effect on all people — at least, a certain average effect.

Then we can set up a matrix multiplication as shown in Diagram 11-1. A column in the C matrix expresses, as a quotient, the changes on all traits in a particular person, as derived from the experimental data in Diagram 16-1 (page 492). The experience matrix, E, is the experimental record of (usually non-manipulative) frequencies (and/or intensities) of exposure to

DIAGRAM 11-1. Learning (Transformation) as a Multidimensional Change in a Multidimensional Situation (Path)(Calculation of Path Learning [Transformation] Vectors)

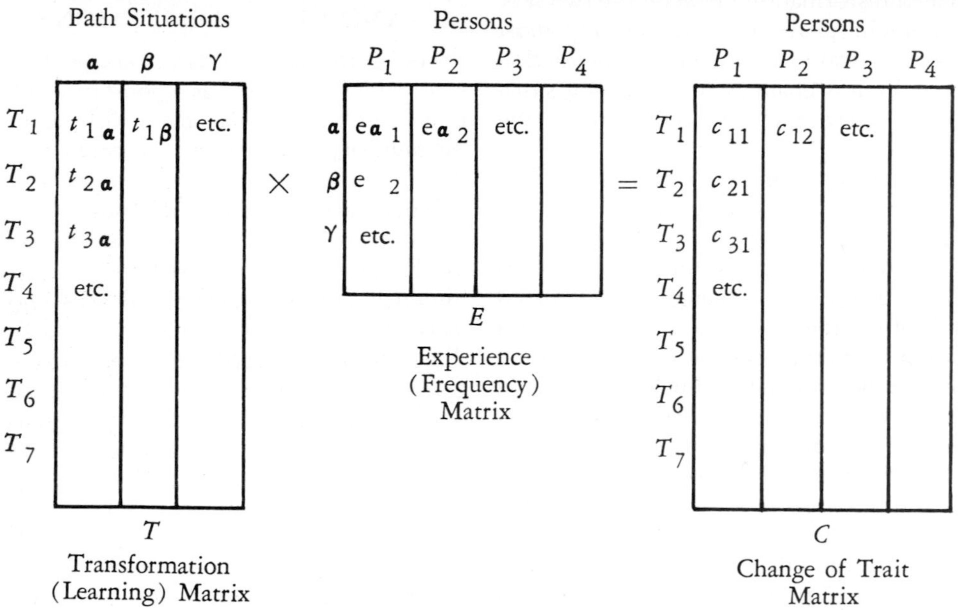

Path Situations				Persons					Persons			
α	β	γ		P_1	P_2	P_3	P_4		P_1	P_2	P_3	P_4
T_1 $t_{1\alpha}$	$t_{1\beta}$	etc.		α $e\alpha_1$	$e\alpha_2$	etc.		T_1	c_{11}	c_{12}	etc.	
T_2 $t_{2\alpha}$			$\times$	β e_2			$=$	T_2	c_{21}			
T_3 $t_{3\alpha}$				γ etc.				T_3	c_{31}			
T_4 etc.								T_4	etc.			
T_5								T_5				
T_6								T_6				
T_7								T_7				

T
Transformation
(Learning) Matrix

E
Experience
(Frequency)
Matrix

C
Change of Trait
Matrix

$t_{1\alpha}$, $t_{2\beta}$, etc. = indices of path transformation for traits.

$e\alpha_1$, $e\beta_2$, etc. = indices of frequency (and intensity) of exposure.

c_{11}, c_{21}, etc. = indices (quotients, percentages) of trait change.

certain paths (situations). By adjustment path analysis formulations it follows that:

(1) $C = TE$

whence, provided we have more persons than paths, we can solve for the unknown T by

(2a) $T = CE'(EE')^{-1}$

Obtaining the transformation quality of a particular situation would most often be the aim of basic research, though in applied psychology, e.g., clinical, one might more frequently want to discover the "case history" of experience by a different derivative from (1), namely:

(2b) $E = (T'T)^{-1}T'C$

when source traits should be more numerous than paths, to avoid a singular matrix.

The above T matrix defines (by any one column vector) the multidimensionality of the situation in *psychological* terms, by its typical learning effect on the totality of traits. By what we have called (Chapter 26) *econetics* (Cattell in 1293)—a more generalized psychophysics—it is theoretically possible, however, to relate the *physical* dimensions of situations to these *psychological* dimensions. Most commonly today the physical dimensions are related directly to learning, e.g., the intensity of a shock or the length of a runway, to increment in speed of running. In psychophysics one physical dimension is commonly related to one psychological dimension. The present econetic proposition is to take many situations whose physical and psychological dimensions are scored and, by canonical correlation or other approaches, obtain a linear transformation between the two sets. This might prove the theoretically most satisfying way of organizing prediction from physical changes in a learning situation to behavior change rates, etc., in the organism.

It remains to consider trait change from the standpoint of profile emergents. (All issues of *configuration,* i.e., of change in a profile which involves time sequence as well as quantitative changes, are deferred until after the discussion of *process,* in Section 9.) Obviously the change in some complex polynomial is much more than a change in the elements which go into it. Then it becomes possible for individuals to have different change scores on the actual trait component scores but the same score on the function. A practical example occurs in the Motivation Analysis Test (297) with respect to the integration and conflict derivatives. It is simple because a meaningful emergent is derivable merely from a difference between the integrated (I) and unintegrated (U) components, over all ten factors—which differences are added (sign regarded) to a single score. Other examples occur in obtaining change scores on a second-order factor, and in a criterion score from a linear or exponential specification equation. In the extreme case of what have been called emergents in Chapter 9, the rate and manner of change in an emergent function could be very different indeed from that in the source trait elements.

The fact that in such cases the function itself could change has already been illustrated at a simple level in this section, in the changing weights for estimating a factor at different levels, and this is pursued further in Chapter 16 by Tucker and Chapter 15 by Digman. The whole realm of change study in relation to change of functional *effect* of traits is a fascinating one, but too recent for further illustration here.

4. THE CONCEPTION OF STATE CHANGE AND STATE DIMENSIONS

Let us distinguish a *state dimension* from a *state,* which is defined as a point or level on that dimension. One may wish also to distinguish as a scientific concept the purely descriptive dimension, i.e., the list of co-varying variables, from the notion of an influence or cause, e.g., blood glucose level as the *determiner* of a state level on the dimension of hungry-vs.-satiated. Psychologists are familiar with a number of state dimensions of a *general* kind (analogous to *general* personality factors), such as elation-depression, anxiety, fatigue, activation, etc., as described in Chapter 22, and of a *dynamic* kind (analogous to dynamic traits) such as hunger, thirst, fear, lust, and other ergic tensions, discussed in Chapter 20. Our purpose here is to develop a non-arbitrary methodology for recognizing them, and a valid procedure for measuring them.

A state dimension has been initially defined as *a uniquely resolvable (simple structure or confactor) factor found in change measures, on a wide sample of variables, either observed in one typical person (P technique) or in a sample of persons (Chain P technique), and which can be shown not to be a trait change factor.* Its distinction from a trait change factor has already been made above and will now be referred to four operational tests, as follows:

(1) When the pattern is repeatedly measured over a period of weeks on a sample of individuals, the ratio of intra- to inter-individual variance is much higher on a state than on a trait. It remains to be discovered whether a line must be drawn arbitrarily in this parameter of state-trait variance differences or whether studies will reveal a bimodality in the plotted distribution of ratios among known simple structure patterns.

(2) Within the individual, trait changes

are likely to show *trends,* and perhaps to exhibit no true reversibility, whereas states should show readily reversible level changes and relatively rapid fluctuation.

(3) A trait, for reasons set out above, might be expected to show some (1) resemblance, but also (2) some significant difference between its trait change pattern and the trait level (individual difference) pattern. Its trait change pattern beginning at one level should also differ from its trait change pattern beginning at other levels. whereas a state should show a pattern relatively uniform across its range (and in the comparison of mean state level individual difference analysis and single person state level analyses). Insofar as the state pattern changes with range, it may be expected to do so according to relatively simple laws as discussed below.

(4) Conceivably, both traits and state-dimensions will show some difference of correlation of the parts when developing and when declining, or moving outward from the mean and returning to the mean. Differences between them in this respect might prove very diagnostic. For example, traits might show a difference of pattern between rise and decline, whereas states might show a difference between the pattern of outward shift from the mean position and return to the mean. Differences of pattern might be accompanied also by difference of curve of total factor score change, e.g., a cyclical sine curve form in states, but not traits.

These are all the differences we shall suggest for *preliminary* identification of the concepts. For the ultimate classification must depend on a taxonomy founded on a natural history. Philosophy, or even methodology, is no substitute for science. When enough studies of change are completed, keeping an eye on these angles of analysis, we shall perhaps find ourselves with several formally distinguishable families and species of states and traits, e.g., state-dimensions characterized by reversibility in a few

hours, similar inward and outward change patterns, etc., and state dimensions with a mean cycle of ten days, dissimilar inward and outward pattern, stronger physiological relations, analyzable into three major sine curves, etc., etc. Only one thing is certain, that it is absurd for a scientific psychologist to assume that we can subjectively name and number the varieties of human trait and state change dimensions. They have to be investigated and located, and then have their special properties discovered.

When the discussion above speaks of dimensions and factor patterns, the reader will realize, in the light of earlier chapters, particularly Chapter 6 on factor analysis, that certain technical conditions and standards, are implied. First, it will be recognized (page 365 below) that any specific, given psychological state, e.g., a complex mood, is considered representable as a combination of measurements on the complete set of functionally unitary mood dimensions, i.e., as a specific vector. Second, the reader familiar with the factor-analytic chapter will realize that the procedures for recognizing state-dimensions are specifically:

(1) P *technique*, as defined on page 68, in which an individual is measured on a suitable choice of variables repeatedly, at intervals of seconds, hours, days, etc., on a sufficient population sample of occasions, with ensuing correlation of variables across occasions and factoring to a simple structure or confactor resolution.

(2) *Differential* R *technique* (or *dR* technique referring to the analysis of *differences* over people as referees, as in *R* technique) in which a sample of persons is measured twice, and the differences on each variable are then used for correlation over people, the factors in change being located as usual by simple structure or confactor resolution.

Before proceeding, the trait change factors will, of course, need to be set aside from the state-dimension factors, according to criteria of experimental design and analysis described above. It will be noted that the designs here are regarded as proceeding to observe change either *with or without application of manipulation* of state stimuli over the change interval. The definition of a state here given makes either course acceptable. For it does not assume that *there is one and only one stimulus for change in each kind* of state. Anxiety and fatigue, for example, may be unitary *response* patterns, but each could be due to a diverse and perhaps cumulative array of *stimulus* patterns or stimuli. Discovering the unique *response pattern* is the basic undertaking. The relating of this pattern to the various situations potent to trigger it is a secondary phase of research. In what Cattell and Scheier (324) have called the condition-response design of experiment (see Chapter 10, Sections 3 and 8), one *can* factor responses and stimuli *together,* thereby making a moderate gain by collapsing the two phases of experiment into one. But manipulating stimuli, or even measuring them, is not *necessary* to the basic recognition of response patterns. Indeed, commonly one would begin by leaving the production of change in the states to the natural onslaughts of daily events, which are more powerful than the resources that the laboratory can usually apply toward disturbing human beings. The two designs should yield the same patterns, and, as experiment shows, they consistently do so.

Leaving, therefore, the issue of manipulative and non-manipulative experiment, let us next look at the mathematical model features and analysis procedures which distinguish what have been called the *P*-technique and differential *R*-technique designs for locating states. One can, as usual, also get equivalent factors, granted the right conditions, from the two corresponding *transpose* techniques (Chapter 6) known as O, and incremental Q technique, respectively. The first, which measures n variables over p conditions (which may be

internal P' or external E', stimulus background conditions) and which keep p greater than n, obviously yields what we may call *unique states*, in strict analogy to what have been called *unique traits,* i.e., patterns of variation possibly peculiar to the individual. Differential R technique (dR technique) on the other hand, takes n variables over N people on a single difference between two occasions and thus yields *common states*. However, it pays for this "superiority" over P technique by using a specific pair of occasions instead of a goodly sample of occasions. Thus whereas dR technique can claim a more typical and reliable statement of what the state-dimension pattern is in our *population of people,* P technique can claim to run across a typical sample of *occasions* and thus escape the restriction of possibly having peculiarities of an occasion or condition.

(3) *Grid P technique.* A brief referral to the data box (page 67) and the discussion of factoring grids (page 124) will remind the reader that P and dR techniques may be considered as dealing with the extreme facets of a common person-test-occasion grid matrix, the test set being the common relatives in both. Consequently there exists a grid analysis which subsumes both (except that it treats all data as absolute, not as difference, as in dR) correlating tests simultaneously across people and across occasions. By the notation fixed in Chapter 3 it can be briefly designated as $PRS.P'E$ analysis.

However, as discussed in more detail below, it does not make sense to mix inter- and intra-individual variance, and the real alternatives are to rescore all people to the same mean, which we shall call the *population P technique* approach, or to bring them both to the same mean *and* the same sigma over occasions, which we shall call *chain P technique* (because it is a *P*-technique analysis of a chain of people, each being an equivalent "link" as to mean and sigma).

Because of its great demand on data gathering to get a complete grid, grid P technique, in either population or chain P technique analyses form is rare indeed.

Despite the sampling difference of P and dR techniques (and a difference due to origin, discussed below) the substantive results have been encouragingly congruent. Indeed, one can already safely conclude that the nine *general* state dimensions (Chapter 22, Mefferd) and the ten or more *dynamic* state factors (Chapter 20, Horn) have shown up as very similar patterns in P and dR techniques. (It may be worthwhile for the reader to scan these, especially those in Chapter 22, to get a feeling for the empirical background of the present methodological chapter.) In other words, in the state-dimensions so far located, individual persons keep pretty close to the general pattern either of responsiveness or of "endogenous change" found for people in general. This fact that the state-dimension patterns are replicable and modal is the primary truth; but, second arily, they may have lesser peculiarities, idiosyncratic to the person in whom they occur and to the stimuli or occasions to which they are attached. The specialized methodological questions in conceptually handling the possibility of characteristic modification of state pattern with occasion, person, and experience are transferred, for reasons of space, to Section 5, in Mefferd's chapter on psychophysiological processes. Meanwhile, we must deal with methodological issues central to the whole approach.

5. METHODOLOGICAL ISSUES AND IMPROVEMENTS IN STATE AND TRAIT CHANGE RESEARCH

Some methodological improvements obviously needed in current researches on change of state and trait are common to P and differential R (dR) technique, and, indeed, are demanded in factor-analytic researches generally. One must mention, for instance, (1) the need for marker variables to avoid the isolation of "private space." The IPAT Seven Factor State Battery of Cattell and Nesselroade (305), and the tables given in Section 5, Chapter 22, provide the experimentalist with markers for *general* states, while Chapter 20, or the MAT battery (297), provides identifiers for *dynamic* states. One must also note (2) the need to add new variables, based on research now in progress, better to distinguish states and trait changes; and (3) the importance of avoiding push-button *orthogonal* analytic rotations which only very "approximately" yield the true oblique simple structure. For in change factors, since they are likely to be correlated with time, they are also *likely to be more highly correlated* with one another than in R technique, i.e., orthogonality is an even grosser approximation than usual.

The first really new issue which appears is that of (1) scaling, and (2) reliability effects upon change scores, and these we shall consider mainly in relation to dR technique, but with all implications indicated for P technique.

As for scaling, if we could assume that our absolute scores, from which difference and change scores are taken, are true ratio scales, no problem need arise, but, of course we can commonly claim little beyond ordinal properties for our measuring scales. This creates a problem in difference measures unknown in absolute measures. Consider a typical transformation from raw to true scale units as shown in Diagram 11-2. It is easy to see that whereas single-occasion (absolute level) scores will always place people in the *same order* in raw scores and in any true derived units, i.e., will provide a monotonic function, *the difference (two occasion) measure scores* can become quite erratic even in regard to the *order* of persons. In the case illustrated they would actually put people in the *opposite* order in true scores to their measured order in raw scores! Since ordinarily we rarely need assume anything more complicated than a *monotonic* transformation from raw to true scale scores, the correlations of single-occasion measures, pursued by a rank-order coefficient, will normally turn out exactly the same in both raw and true scores. But this is uncertain in regard to difference scores. Consequently, confused. Let us first disentangle these. The former has been most considered in the realm of artificial "achievement test" units, and there it was first clearly brought out by Woodrow (1579, 1581). The latter has cropped up more in the realm of physiological, and, indeed, largely autonomic variables. Since the beginning of work in that area, suggestions have constantly been

DIAGRAM 11-2.   The Scaling Problem in Difference Scores Contrasted with Absolute *Single*-Occasion Scores

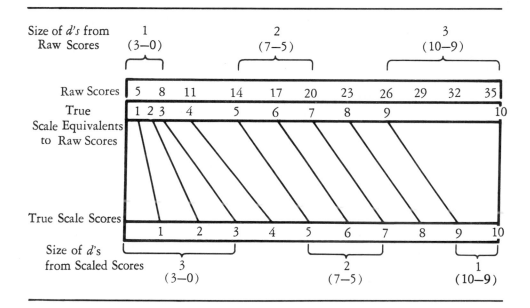

This diagram shows the transformation between raw scores values in the upper row to what are known to be the true scale scores in the lower row. (A slight difference in the lower raw scores means a lot, while equivalent differences at the top do not correspond to much real increase.) It will be seen that the rank order of three people in difference scores calculated in raw scores is exactly opposite to that from scaled scores. Such complete reversal is, of course, an extreme instance.

the whole issue of providing a rational and defensible scaling system becomes far more vital.

Before discussing this further, let us note another issue which experimenters have intuitively introduced into the change score evaluation problem. This includes: (a) "ceiling" and "floor" effects, and (b) homeostatic effects, the two effects being frequently made, e.g., by Haggard, (662), Lacey and Lacey (895, 896), and others, that the same raw score change when far out from the mean should be considered greater than an equivalent raw score change in the central range. In other words, the level from which the individual starts his reaction should enter into evaluation of the magnitude of his response. Variations of this include the notion that, from ulterior knowledge, we should change a scale by a logarithmic transformation, and so on.

These proposals have frequently dragged in for their support some quite ad hoc assumptions, the full implications of which have not been worked out. Let us take first the most restricted and specialized proposal — that for changing to "homeostasis corrected" scores. Here the implied model is that of a stretched spring, obeying Hooke's law. If the individual is already very upwardly deviant from his usual blood pressure then, it is argued, a further upward shift of x millimeters is more important than it would be it if occurred from the mean. There would be less objection to these base level correction notions if they were carried out according to a consistent model. For example, one could take the simple Hooke's law model, and more consistently make the response score equal to the work done, i.e., the distance moved multiplied by the average force over the interval, this homeostatic force being considered proportional to the baseline-to-finishing-line deviation. However, to be consistent, one would obviously then have to take into account the direction of movement — toward or away from the mean, i.e., from the equilibrium position.

Proposals for allowing for ceiling and floor effects use a similar but inverted model in which distance from the outer boundary decides the scale weight ("stretching") to be given. In this case the average upward movement from a very deviant upward position x is explained to be less than from a position y (less deviant) not only because one cannot go beyond the ceiling, but also because it becomes increasingly difficult to make a given raw score response magnitude as one *approaches* the ceiling.

In both of these instances — *limiting score* and *homeostasis* — the present writer would argue for conducting research at first *without* such assumptions, and thus establishing laws about what actually happens typically.

It could be that the average shift of people at a deviant position is *not* less than for those at central values, or that some relation more complex than Hooke's law applies. The best solution to a floor or ceiling effect, when a skewed or leptokurtic distribution shows that it exists in any *made-up* list of items, is to add other items so that the normally distributed scores no longer reach the ends, or to choose a longer interval of observation, so that a skewed distribution no longer exists. The problem of whether the raw scores need modifying to make a truer equal interval scale may still remain, and the test of this, it has been suggested in Chapter 3, Section 11, lies in the *relational simplex* principle of finding the scaling that maximizes the clarity of relations to a stratified sample of other variables. Granted such a scaling principle has been applied — or even the cruder principle of a scale to give a normal distribution where it might be reasonably expected — then the existence of homeostatic or bounding effects is something to be found out and evaluated experimentally. One can then make the decision whether one wishes to investigate further, allowing for or not allowing for this effect. For example, one can accept the Weber-Fechner law as it stands, or say that one wishes to rescale the stimulus scores logarithmically to give equal units for equal response units, and thus substitute a new, linear law.

The problem in the broader sense, i.e., not merely as a homeostatic or a boundary effect, can be illustrated by that hardy annual the galvanic skin reflex, for which a series of proposals for reformed scoring seem to go in cycles. Soon after Feré and Tarchanoff distinguished the two distinct effects, it became fashionable to score at any rate the former by expressing the drop in resistance (increase in conductance) as a percentage of the person's absolute resistance. It was shown by the present writer in 1929 (198) that taking the variation simultaneously across people and states of people, this ratio remains practically constant (or could be made constant by a slight and simple correction formula). Haggard (662) has since proposed a logarithmic transformation which would have different properties, and Lacey and Lacey (895, 896) have proposed yet another treatment. Simple though the percentage is, it may yet be hiding some law. For example, though it may be desirable to make *people* at different resistances absolutely comparable (see *ipsative scoring,* in Chapter 3, Section 11, and Chapter 20, Section 4), since the difference may arise from nothing but the thickness of their skins, or how recently they washed, it might be that within the range of one person it is a law that when his skin resistance is high (sleepy, low, P.U. 1 state) he *typically* does not react so powerfully to stimuli, and that to correct to a percentage (which gives constancy of reaction magnitude over range of resistance) is an overcorrection. Nothing we can call an adequate set of laws has yet been established in the change score field and one reason for this is that assumptions have been too confidently made which prevent the laws being recognized! It would be best to proceed whenever possible by raw scores or raw scores scaled by the Relational Simplex, or failing data for this, correction to a scale that simply gives a normal distribution. Certainly in factor analyses of difference scores, producing erratic results of the kind suggested in Diagram 11-2, clearer factor structure emerges when this simple scaling improvement by normalization is made.

Measurement problems of both scaling and error are more crucial in change than absolute scores. Although the relational simplex method of deriving meaningfully scaled scores involves intricate arguments (254), its essence is that "the proof of the pudding is the eating." A theoretically adequate account of what this proof would be in the change area, and, still more, a sufficiently exhaustive empirical determination of equal interval scale units for important variables, would be a major contribution to science. However, certain pragmatic conclusions in our own labora-tory (which, to date, has probably analyzed more change data by P and dR techniques than most) perhaps already offer rough guidance. Our main practice has been *to plot the before and after measures* (in, e.g., dR technique) *in a single distribution, which is then normalized.* The difference scores are then calculated from absolute scores already thus normalized in this sample from a broader population. By such parameters of the results—agreement of patterns from different experiments, goodness of simple structure, etc.—as running observation has offered, this yields a better approach than any other to good scaling of difference scores. (In P technique, normalization over the range is the equivalent.)

If we accept the position that, next to placing scaling on the basis of a full relational simplex analysis, one's best resort is to a normal distribution in the transformed raw scores, then the question arises, "On what population is one to ask for the normal distribution?" Logically one could answer, "The population of difference scores," yet this condition conceivably *might* be met by the obviously unsatisfactory raw score differences obtained, as in Diagram 11-2.

It is necessary to put the original absolute scores into a normal distribution (two separately or one pooled). This tends to obviate the above danger and also produces the required normal distribution in the differences. To preserve a real meaning to the algebraic sign of the change score (not + and − equally about zero), for important reasons shortly to be stated, it is better to make a single pooled distribution. The variance of this distribution will be $\frac{1}{2}\left(\sigma_1{}^2 + \sigma_2{}^2 + \frac{d^2{}_{12}}{2}\right)$ where 1 and 2 are the before and after occasions and d_{12} is the difference of means before and after. The fact that we shall now be taking a unit, and a normality of distribution, decided not only by change scores as such but by individual difference distributions may seem to deny the above logic of scaling differences according to the distribution of differences. But there is a wider and more compelling logic for keeping absolutes and change scores in the same scaling. Indeed, if the experimenter should have other samples from the same population on that same variable, beyond his experiment, they could advantageously be included to give greater stability to the normal distribution employed to scale. The scaled scores will now bring the change scores into what we may call a joint change-absolute normalization scaling, or *joint c-a scaling,* for short. Joint c-a scaling will have its differences from separate distribution scaling, i.e., scoring change as a difference between the separately standardized and normalized before and after score distributions, below. However, we may note immediately that the s-d *scaling* yields no mean change of the group from before to after. The c-a scale, on the other hand, makes the mean change score of all individuals not zero but equal to the difference of the group means. And it does this in units reflecting a normalized standardization over the whole range of our experience of measurement of that variable.

Let us next consider the effect of errors of measurement in change score calculation, as they affect *P, dR,* and other kinds of analysis. It is widely realized (Lord, 948; Webster & Bereiter, 1505; Cattell, 240, 260; and Holtzman, 740), that error introduces more serious and complex problems in change scores, and that obtained consistency of measurement indices (whether of homogeneity or reliability (*dependability,* specifically) tend to be poorer than for similar tests in ordinary individual difference research. The wisdom of alternative attempts to cope with this in experimental design needs comment.

(1) In *dR* technique can readily be seen that the lower dependability coefficients are a purely algebraic consequence of an error variance term entering both the first and the second occasion of measurement and thus appearing twice in the difference expression. Thus if d_o is the observed difference (change) score, a_1 and a_2 the true

initial and final scores, and e_1 and e_2 first and second errors, then:

$$(3a) \qquad d_o = (a_1 + e_1) - (a_2 + e_2)$$

where (b) $d = a_1 - a_2$

d being the true difference.

If, as usual, a_1 and a_2 are positively correlated, the true variance will be $\sigma^2_{a_1} + \sigma^2_{a_2} - 2r_{12}a_1a_2$ and the ratio of error to true variance will give a reliability:

$$(4) \quad r_r = 1 - \frac{2\sigma^2_e}{2(\sigma^2_a - r_{12}\sigma_{a1}\sigma_{a2})}$$

$$= 1 - \frac{\sigma^2_e}{\sigma^2_a(1 - r_{12})}$$

(assuming $\sigma_{a1} = \sigma_{a2}$ which is the most likely general tendency). This could obviously be substantially lower than $r_r = 1 - \frac{\sigma^2_e}{\sigma^2_a + \sigma^2_e}$.

(2) Similarly in P technique, the ratio of experimental error variance to true variance is larger than in the familiar R-technique situation. But in this case, the disproportion arises, instead, from the true variance being reduced. If, in the usual R technique situation a_c and a_f are respectively the score components from change of the individual from his usual value and from fixed inter-individual difference in those values (and σ^2_c and σ^2_f are the corresponding variance contributions), then the P-technique reliability, r_{r_p}, is only:

$$(5a) \qquad r_{r_p} = 1 - \frac{\sigma^2_e}{\sigma^2_c}$$

whereas r, the reliability in the familiar usage will run higher at:

$$(5b) \qquad r = 1 - \frac{\sigma^2_e}{\sigma^2_c + \sigma^2_1}.$$

A special analysis of the reliabilities over series of occasions has been made by Hoffman (733).

Observing that the reliabilities (dependability) or homogeneities in *dR* and *P* technique are frequently around 0.4 to 0.5 whereas they stand around 0.8 for single-occasion measures of the same length, some less realistic investigators have reacted with horror to factoring correlations between such less reliable measures, or have built up statistical treatments which appear to get away from this unreliability. The only realistic solution, however, is to increase the length of tests and in other ways to reduce the relative variance of error in the experimental situation itself. Such devices, discussed below, as working with a difference score from which the initial score has been partialled out introduce more disturbance of meaning than they eliminate. In this instance, eliminating $(a_1 + e_1)$ does not get rid of the e variance but of the combination—a different matter—and it removes much of whatever correlation does and should exist between a trait level and the rate of growth in that trait.

Another aspect of error effect is its potential artificial production of change factors which are actually determined by the absolute, trait factors. Thus if one subtracted an initial score from a second score which happened to be wholly error, the difference score factoring would produce factors entirely determined by the factor structure in the initial scores. This can be seen from the covariances derivable from (3) above, namely:

$$(6) \quad \text{Cov} = \Sigma \{ (a_{j1} + e_{j1}) - (a_{j2} + e_{j2}) \\ \cdot \{ (a_{k1} + e_{k1}) - (a_{k2} - e_{k2}) \} /N \\ = \Sigma a_{j1} a_{k1} + \Sigma a_{j2} a_{k2} - \Sigma a_{j1} a_{k2} \\ - \Sigma a_{j2} a_{k1} /N$$

(The implications of this in correlations are shown below.[2])

Error being uncorrelated with itself and the true measurement, all terms with error vanish. If we can conceive a situation in which the second measure were wholly error, with no trace of the real, a_2, measure, then (6) would equal $\frac{\Sigma a_{j1} a_{k1}}{N}$ and the "difference" analysis would be a "projection" of the initial structure. This is an experimental impossibility (the second scores would have to be a table of random numbers!), but one can ask whether some *degree* of this might happen if measures on one occasion were significantly greater, i.e., of greater variance than the other. The answer is that it would not: only some correlation of error and true variance could produce distortion. However (6) does remind us that if for any reason the true measurement variance on the second occasion were much smaller than the first, the first-occasion absolute structure would more largely determine the change covariance. This is an argument, granted certain assumptions, for bringing the first and second occasions (of equal reliability) to standard scores before subtracting one from the other, and indeed before pooling them as suggested above.

A lingering feeling among "individual difference" psychometrists that change scores are somehow error is probably responsible for some experimenters (Gulliksen, 644; Humphreys, 793) stating a preference for proceeding indirectly from a factoring of the first- and second-occasion correlation matrices. Granted certain con-

---

[2]The extent to which correlations among original and first- and second-occasion scores are implied by those among change scores and vice versa, admits of expression in a variety of formulae, of which the following is central:

$$(7) \quad r_{(a_2 - a_1)(b_2 - b_1)} = \frac{(r_{a_1 b_1} + r_{a_2 b_2}) - (r_{a_2 b_1} + r_{a_1 b_2})}{2 \sqrt{(1 - r_{a_1 a_2})(1 - r_{b_1 b_2})}}$$

where a_1 and a_2, etc., are first- and second-occasion measures on the same variable.

High correlations between changes arise, according to the top line, when the two variables intercorrelate more on each occasion than they do across occasions. The similarity of this term to a tetrad difference implies similar "common factor" conceptions. As the denominator shows, high correlations between change scores are assisted by high retest reliabilities. In effect, tables of the intercorrelations of change scores contain row and column corrections for non-attenuation in the raw scores. Harris (691) uses a matrix algebra equivalent of the above formula to derive the factors in change scores from the factors in raw scores.

ditions it is true that a simple algebraic equivalence permits exact inference of the difference score factors from the initial and final factors. The question is whether one needs to do two factor analyses instead of one, with resultant "fitting together" problems, and whether our model can always accept the statistical restrictions needed for some of the assumptions. However, this alternative approach suggested itself to Nesselroade (1096) and the present writer as an interesting one, and we have made a number of methodological studies comparing outcomes, discussed below. Nevertheless, if it is asserted that they avoid the error in the simple difference measurement (actually they "push it under the rug" to a different part of the analysis) or that they are intrinsically superior to dR technique, etc., then they are falsely conceived.

By a suitable "operator" it is possible to equate the results of the difference between two occasions to a derivative of the two separate testing occasions at almost any stage of a factor analysis—at the score stage, at the correlation matrix stage, and at the factor matrix stage. The mathematical equivalences are clear, and they could be programed for a computer. The algebraic transformation is implicit in Truman Kelley's well-known work on correlations of sums and differences. If we write his formula with the factor, f, as the third variable with which the correlation of the *difference* of variable a_j and a_k, i.e., a_{j-k}, is required, we can obtain it, assuming standard scores, by:

$$(7a) \qquad r_{(j-k)f} = \frac{r_{jf} - r_{kf}}{b^2_j - r_{jk} + b^2_k}$$

or, if we have the same test a, on two occasions:

$$(7b) \qquad r_{(a_1-a_2)f} = \frac{r_{a_1f} - r_{a_2f}}{b^2_{a_1} - r_{a_1a_2} + b^2_{a_2}}$$

where $r_{(a_1-a_2)f}$ is the correlation of any variable's difference score with the factor, and r_{a_1f} and r_{a_2f} are the correlations of the

original before-and-after scores with the factors given directly by factoring the two matrices R_{11} and R_{22} together (or, if desired, separately, with rotation as described below).

What is not so clear is whether the inferences we wish to make for the scientific model can be as well made from the statistical treatment of separate "before"- and-"after" matrices as they can from the factoring of differences directly. By the scientific model we mean information about trait factors, trait change factors, and state factors—their patterns and intercorrelations.

To pursue this, let us consider two experiments carried out measuring the same n variables on the same N people on two occasions, 1 and 2. The resulting three possible correlation matrices among "absolute" scores are shown in Diagram 11-3. The symbols a_1, b_1 ... n_1 stand for the tests on the first administration, and a_2, b_2 ... n_2 for the second.

Let us consider the three main ways of handling the data to get evidence on traits, trait change, and state factors:

(1) The first may be called the *Comparison of Meaningful Before-and-After Matrices*. Here one would factor R_{11} and R_{22} separately, and use formula (7) to discover the nature of trait change factors. To employ formula (7) one needs to have some sense in which the *same* factor can be recognized in V_{11} and V_{22}. This cannot be done until they are rotated to maximum congruity, which might be done by the confactor method, or, since the variables are on the same subjects, by bringing them by Kaiser's or Tucker's interbattery method to the common overlap space. Any such procedure either involves assumptions of which we are not sure at this stage of research, or it introduces some inaccuracy. These are:

(a) That we shall find the *same* number of factors in R_{11} and R_{22}. On the scientific model this is probable but not certain.

(b) That we can match the factors, in order to speak of the *same* factor. This runs

DIAGRAM 11-3. Possible Matrices and Analyses for Two-Occasion Measures

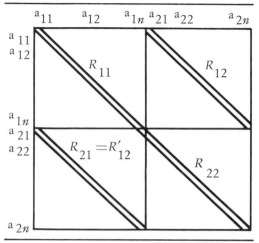

into a practical difficulty in that the matching can never be exact because the two studies have factors not strictly in the same space. One can surmise that the calculated $r_{(a_1-a_2)f}$, owing to this lack of equivalence of f in r_{a_1f} and r_{a_2f}, is likely to have more error (because it involves a new *source* of error) than any arising from the low reliability of a difference score (already present in hidden form in the $r_{a_1f} - r_{a_2f}$ term, even when f is identical). On the other hand, the trait factors, which could change somewhat in pattern, e.g., as intelligence does, between occasion 1 and occasion 2 will be more accurately represented than in some of the alternatives below.

Incidently, one should notice that the *state* factors will actually be differently correlated with other factors on the two occasions, and each will not correlate above chance with its counterparts in the second experiment. This is due to the fact that if a long enough period is allowed to intervene, the order of individual persons on their "endowment" on the state factor on occasion 1 need have no relation to that on occasion 2. Here we have the curious situation of two factors having the same loading pattern (if a_1 is considered identical with

a_2), yet the endowment of the people upon them being quite different. (This is, formally, a special case of the cooperative factor phenomenon.)

Our final expectation from Method 1, therefore, is that when rotated for simple structure, the trait factors in $V_{f_{p_{11}}}$ and $V_{f_{p_{22}}}$, namely, F_{t1} and F_{t2}, appearing as F_{t11}, F_{t12} and F_{t21}, F_{t22} in the first and second matrix, will be both similar in loading pattern *and* highly correlated as to persons. The state dimension factors, on the other hand, F_{c1} and F_{c2}, will be similar in pattern but not systematically correlated. This independence of corresponding state factors will come out more clearly when experiments 1 and 2 are "synthesized" and rotated in the same space than by correlating state factor estimates, for the latter *will* be spuriously correlated, owing to the variables from which they are estimated being the same, to a certain extent, as those for estimating the fixed traits and owing to specifics presumably remaining unaltered.

The status of trait and state factors is clear, but that of *trait change* factors in this design and others needs more detailed comment. According to habitual models and modes of thinking in this field, no trait change factor would be expected to appear directly in either $V_{f_{p_{11}}}$ or $V_{f_{p_{22}}}$, i.e., in any "absolute" factorization. Such a factor would appear only if we accepted as a model that the trait is what existed, say, twelve months before the first experiment, so that the "trait" at occasion 1 is conceived as "trait plus twelve months trait change," and on occasion 2, say, six months later, as "basic trait plus 18 months of the trait change factor." Since we have no natural zero point (unless it be birth!) for the trait in itself, it is most natural to take it as that which exists at occasion 1. If so, occasion 2 and the difference (dR) scores will include trait plus trait change factors, but occasion 1 will not. As equation (3) above suggests, the pattern of a trait change factor, at certain life stages, could be very different from that of the individual difference trait. As indicated above, this also implies that the change which has occurred on the trait between occasions 1 and 2 will show in a slightly modified loading pattern of the "absolute" traits, and some corresponding slight reduction in the near perfect correlation of F_{t1} and F_{t2} when brought to the common space.[3]

Any difference factor calculated by formula (7) between R_{11} and R_{22} (that is, between V_{fs1} and V_{fs2}, since differences must be in correlations in the factor structure) could therefore be interpreted either as a trait change or a state factor, pending additional evidence.

(2) The *Comparison in a Single Across-Occasions Matrix* is the second design to be

considered; it involves factoring at once the whole matrix[4] shown in Diagram 11-3. There are two ways of doing this, one described by Harris in the next chapter, using canonical correlation, and a second method we shall use here. In this second design, when simple structure is reached, the "before-and-after" trait 1 measures will load on the same factor, F_{t1}, not two factors, F_{t11} and F_{t12}, which one has tried to align as the same meaningful factor by rotation. The method has the advantage that formula (7) will no longer be rendered approximate in its operation by inexact alignment of two versions of the same factor, for they are now a single axis. But it has several disadvantages: (a) that the unrotated factors are no longer meaningful, so that rotation of the resulting difference score factors calculated from them has still to be carried out; (b) that, insofar as trait factor definition is part of our aim, no amount of rotation can give the clarity that Method 1 can give to the before-and-after trait factors because, if these differ appreciably, we are now compelled to take a middling compromise. (We are essentially factoring the same variables with people mixed from two different ages.) (c) Each state will now have to appear as two distinct factors (this is common to Methods 1 and 2), since there is no reason why a person high on the first occasion should be high on the second. Its first appearance will be in loadings on a_{11} to a_m and its second on variables a_{21} to a_{2n}. This creates a problem in that there may be more difference factors to be accounted for than there are absolute factors from which they could be derived. (d) This last is the most disabling of difficulties for Method 2, namely, that in any factor analysis as ordinarily pursued, the existence of a_{11} and

---

[3]Incidentally, the only really serious alternative to thus accepting a trait as the individual difference pattern on the first occasion (or as the mean of a whole series of such occasions) is to take the model that any trait should really appear as a whole set of change factors over certain natural historical phases which arose in its production. That is to say, we should have to assume in the latter model that history (not merely present structure) is written as a deposit of distinct but essentially similar factors into the factor matrix. In the case of the concepts of fluid and crystallized general intelligence (205, 240, 258) we come near to this, and it is a tenable hypothesis also by the motivation component factor field (Chapter 20) that they represent phases or contributions in the history of an interest.

But this cannot be taken as a universal model because (a) it requires that there be certain non-arbitrary periods in growth, such that each produces a "phase of growth" factor of recognizably different form from the preceding ones. The occasion 1 to 2 experimental period would normally be an arbitrary one and there is no reason to expect that it would give a different hyperplane or loading pattern from the main individual difference factor which we call the trait, and (b) the practical difficulties of separation — especially when there would be uncertainty (owing to the limitations of present techniques in deciding the number of factors to take out) extending to plus or minus two factors — would normally be an insuperable obstacle to locating such trait change factors directly in the V_{fp}. We may conclude that in general, and in practice, a trait change factor would not be located by Design 1 among change factors, i.e., such factors would remain essentially state dimension factors.

[4]Incidentally, Guttman's use of the term Simplex applies to an early relative of this factoring together of similar variables measured at different times without the special inference methods here discussed. Its roughness lies in the impossibility in continuously time-scattered measurements of arriving at clear and distinct hyperplanes.

a_{21}, etc., in pairs in the same matrix *will create as many common factors (doublets formed by the specifics entering twice) as there are variables.* In short, we shall be trying to take $k + n$ common factors from $2n$ variables, which exceeds the half necessary to iterate to exact communalities. An attempt at escape from this is to try to find communalities to insert in the R_{12} and R_{21} (Diagram 11-3) diagonals instead of the actual obtained correlations that will prevent these doublets arising. For reasons that space prevents us from discussing here, this would be an "artistic" and questionable procedure, though approximate solutions could be obtained if the number of variables were so large as to swamp error of communality estimation, and iteration were not contemplated.

(3) *The Direct Difference Factor Matrix.* Here we directly factor what we are interested in, namely, change scores to get the structure of change. However, it needs due attention to scaling questions introduced above, notably the use of either joint-absolute normalization or standardized absolute differences. These we shall focus in a more final sense below. Meanwhile it should be noted that this approach is most closely coordinate to P technique, population P technique, chain P technique, and especially differential P technique (below).

In most experimental research, although mathematically there is nothing inadequate in inferring difference structures from before-and-after structures, as in Methods 1 and 2, we prefer Method 3, the direct factoring of differences in dR technique, because it is free of those errors which come in through the assumptions and associated processes which distinguish factor analysis, as a scientific method, from component analysis, as a mathematical theorem. Methods 1 and 2 can founder on the poor basis for communality estimates (Method 2); through errors in rotation (Method 1); through smudging trait factors

from two periods together in one axis (Method 2); through the fact that it is quite possible for occasions 1 and 2 to give different numbers of factors; and through the number of variables becoming insufficient to define the number of state factors.

However, in advocating Method 3, one must recognize that it gives only state and trait change factors, but not trait factors. If one seeks the totality he will need what we shall describe shortly as the Coordinated Change Experiment design for getting maximum information on trait, trait change, and state structures from jointly planned matrices.

But first we shall try to clear up certain scaling and correlation problems in the direct difference factoring method. Measurement error has been discussed, and we recognize that its difficulties are just as great by any of the methods. As to "modifying" raw change scores, in ways different from that here proposed, there is the proposition, initially discussed by Woodrow (1579), and very thoroughly by Lord (948), of partialling out the first-occasion scores from the second-occasion scores, thus leaving zero correlation *between beginning and end scores.* Second, there is the proposition that it would be good to work with difference scores after any correlation has been similarly removed *between initial and difference* score. Third, there is the proposition that the *mean of the initial and final score* (a better estimate of the trait level than is either separately) should be rendered uncorrelated with a "corrected" difference score as finally used. Arguments have also been made, along the lines indicated by DuBois in another connection (431) for using *part correlations* (Chapter 5) in partialling, thus eliminating, for example, the variance of the second occasion from the difference score before correlating it with the initial occasion, but not eliminating it from the initial occasion.

As statistical procedures, these are clear in intent, but one may well ask how far they are "gimmicks" for some immediate seeming gain, whose appropriateness to a model meeting general scientific assumptions has been insufficiently examined. Let us consider, for example, the arguments for making gain scores uncorrelated with the first-occasion scores. Often this is based on the supposition discussed above that homeostatic or bounding ("ceiling" of scale, etc.) effects produce a spurious correlation. The answer to this has been given above (page 366). Others point out that error of measurement is likely to produce a negative correlation between the initial and the difference score, which might advantageously be removed. If we could remove the correlation due to the error alone without removing whatever may be due to the systematic, real score relations, this would be attractive!

Resort to a likely scientific model of growth or learning suggests two possibilities: (1) That insofar as we deal with concepts of trait and trait change factors, we should expect in any individual that his profile of measures on the second occasion would show more than chance resemblance to the first, with each element increased proportionally to its original absolute size (first occasion). This proportionality of change to absolute structure is apparent in the growth of a bush, possibly in some interest growths, and apparently in measures on the primary abilities. (2) That the learning or growth of a structure may, on the other hand, sometimes proceed alternatively now by an advance in this part and now by an advance in that. In such case, the trait change pattern would be expected to have little resemblance to the structure pattern over a limited time, but only if it is considered as the accumulation of growth over the total growth period.

The first model would definitely forbid us to reduce correlation of first-occasion and increment score to zero. The second

would lead to a *laissez faire* position. Both would agree with the position already reached on scaling generally, that one should work on some sound general principle, e.g., the Simplex or aiming at a normal distribution, and make no ad hoc adjustments of the kind sometimes advocated in this field, except perhaps for bounding effects *in instruments* (e.g., ceiling). Earlier (page 366) we made what seems to us the only important concession in the direction of raw score modification by saying that in difference structuring, good scaling properties are far more important than elsewhere, and suggesting that, in the absence of Simplex scaling evidence, *normalizing* would produce substantial improvements.

Finally, in regard to scaling in direct difference, dR factoring, let us first concentrate on the relative merits of *joint* c-a *scaling* and s-d *scaling*. The former, it will be recalled, throws before and after scores into a single distribution, which is normalized and standardized, and the change score is then expressed in this metric—change and absolute being thus in one scale. (Hence "joint *c-a*"). But *s-d* scaling standardizes each normalized distribution separately and takes change as a difference. If variables are next to be correlated, in terms of their difference scores, these two scaling procedures will finish up with the same end matrix result, since the correlation coefficient loses information about difference of means. However, if we use *cross products* $\left(\dfrac{\Sigma XY}{N}\right.$ instead of $\left.\dfrac{\Sigma xy}{\sqrt{\Sigma x^2 \Sigma y^2}}\right)$ as entries instead of r, which the present writer (Chapter 5) has argued to be in general superior for any more basic, comprehensive use of factor analysis, the invulnerability of the *c-a* scaling to the initial loss of information incurred in *s-d* scaling remains important. Let us see what this extra information may mean.

In joint *c-a* scaling the score tells us

whether a given individual actually rises or falls on a given variable, whereas in *s-d* scaling he might actually rise yet get a score negatively deviant (from the average change). It could be argued that since a difference score is one of the few scores in psychology where an absolute zero is meaningful and obtainable, namely, as a definitely zero change, it is somewhat cavalier to throw this luxury away! On the other hand it can be argued that since the change score on the variable is to be regarded as a composite of changes on several factors, some moving positively and others negatively during the change, the outcome, whether scored positively or negatively, cannot reflect the sign directions of all changes concerned but only a mixed outcome, and that the sign is scarcely sacred.

Indeed, there is nothing *fundamentally* wrong in using the correlation coefficient, which treats an *actual* increase as, in some cases, negative by comparison. It merely throws away information, and the question remains, "Is the distortion therefrom in any way systematic?" What the *s-d* score (or *r* with the joint *c-a* score) does is to throw away evidence on variance and covariance *due to shifts in the group as a whole* (between first and second testing) on the means of all the variables. Now if our scientific model is one of factors as determiners, this movement of the group takes place through just the same influences (determiners) as are at work in producing the covariance of scores among individuals. (Parenthetically, this statement is entirely compatible with the occasional observation that changes on variables a_j and a_k are positively correlated in the group even while the group mean rises on a_j and drops on a_k; though this must be less common than joint change.)

Consequently the difference between *dR* analysis results with *c-a* scaling (to reduce gross metric difference effects), employing cross-products, on the one hand, and *s-d* or *c-a* scaling with *r*, on the other,

should be one due to multivariate selection, through loss of the inter-occasion group mean variance and covariance effects. From Thurstone's analysis (1420) of this problem we may assume that it will not fundamentally change (obliterate) the factor structure, but will change factor loadings and, especially, the correlations among primary factors. However, when cross-products are advocated above it is with the reservation that since we do not yet know enough about the rotation problems with the factors representing the differing raw score means of the variables we should minimize such effects by bringing all variables to roughly comparable means. And this we have in fact done by the *c-a* scaling which, while it does not bring all change to exactly the same variance, brings change plus absolute variance to standard scores, and thus obviates completely any gross difference of metric among change scores.

The above argument for pursuing *dR*-technique analyses primarily through the third, *direct difference* approach, with the special improvements indicated, does not deny that the other two approaches bring some additional information. But as a best research design we would advocate obtaining this information on related traits, etc., by distinct analyses, arranged in what we shall now describe as the *Coordinated Change Experiment Design*. In its totality this calls for (1) a double *dR* analysis, (2) an *R* analysis of the corresponding before and after matrices and the mean matrix, and (3) a comparison of results with *P* and what will be defined as *dP* analyses on the same variables. If pursued under the best conditions it supposes also a broader basis of data than is usually envisaged in such work, namely, at least a three- rather than a two-occasion retest — in fact, in the ultimate ideal it should proceed to a full data box of *n* tests, *N* people and *v* occasions. The aim of this design is to yield analyses in which (a) factors can be compared across matrices, (b) the same factors reappear with predictably changed total variance contribution, and (c) especial markers have been introduced to distinguish state and trait factors (nothing can be done in this connection to separate trait and trait change). The design has the object of separating (1) state, (2) trait change and (3) trait factor patterns.

If the accompanying R-technique analyses are performed not only on the separate single occasion matrices, as in Design 2 above, but also on the mean score matrix across two or more occasions, the comparison of single- and mean-occasion analyses should contribute to recognizing trait patterns because their variance will increase, while that of states will decrease (due to their being out of phase for each individual on successive occasions). Similarly the state factors could be brought out with greater clarity and variance by using as difference measures the difference between each occasion and the *mean* of a sufficient sample of single occasion measures. The separation of state from trait change factors would be effected by referance to (a) a necessary relation of trait change to trait loading patterns, (b) the tendency of state factors over a few days, to fluctuate where trait change factors show trend across occasions.

As to variance contribution comparisons we should note that both dR and P technique have two forms. In one each occasion deviation score is taken from the mean of a whole series of occasions. (This is P technique and what we might call PdR technique.) In the other (dR technique and what we might call dP technique) each score is produced as the difference between two successive occasions. Except for the reduction of the change factor variance in the dR and dP steps, and a different behavior of error, one would expect from the model that the factor dimensions would be exactly the same, namely, the unique source state in P and the common source state in dR technique.

Diagram 11-4 may help summarize the evidence from which inferences are to be drawn in the Coordinated Change Experiment Design.

It has been suggested above that a second important means for distinguishing a trait change from a state factor — over and above the tendency of the former to show a trend and the latter to oscillate — is the existence of a necessary and systematic relation between the loading patterns of a trait and a trait change factor. For, in a general sense, a trait can be viewed as a summation of trait changes. Indeed, when we factor on occasions t_1 and t_2 do we regard t_1 as the trait plus a trait change to t_2, or conversely? Obviously the trait structure is peculiar to some point in time and has to be defined as such (in R technique), and the dR technique will define trait change (plus state change) increments or decrements therefrom.

A comprehensive model, fitting what trait theory we at present possess, must accept, however, certain statistically more awkward possibilities. The manner of an object's growth might not coincide with its own functional-structural divisions. (We speak of R technique as yielding "structure," which in psychology is generally isomorphic with function. For example, R-technique analysis of body measurements yields a head size factor, marking the head as a distinct structure, but in psychological data the factor is normally a statement of functional unity — of behaviors functioning in association — and the structure is simply an inference to something less transitory than the actual behavior, which determines it.) Now there are two kinds of differences possible between patterns of growth (or change) and patterns of finished structure which we need to examine:

(1) *Organic-vs.-Non-Organic Change Patterns.* The sets of variables which change together could be identical with or different from those which R technique shows to constitute unitary functioning sets in

DIAGRAM 11-4. Matrices Forming Basis of Inference in Coordinated Change Experiment Design

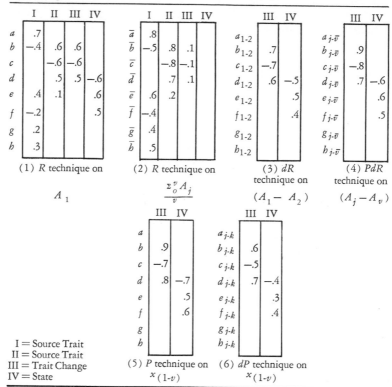

(1) R technique on A_1

(2) R technique on $\dfrac{\sum_o^v A_j}{v}$

(3) dR technique on $(A_1 - A_2)$

(4) PdR technique on $(A_j - A_v)$

(5) P technique on $x_{(1-v)}$

(6) dP technique on $x_{(1-v)}$

I = Source Trait
II = Source Trait
III = Trait Change
IV = State

The illustrative numerical entries are not intended to be exact but only to summarize the relative contributions of factors to variance hypothesized for the various experiment and measurement situations.

The corresponding *factor score* matrices would show good agreement of (1) and (2) on I and II and slight on III. Otherwise, i.e., on the III's and IV's, there would be no agreement anywhere.

the stable organism. In general, in physical organisms, growth and change operate on an organ as a whole; though, of course, second order factors may affect several organs simultaneously. On the other hand the way in which cars or houses are typically built up and demolished *may* have no relation at all to the dimensions which would be obtained from individual difference studies on the finished product. The latter would yield size of engines, of kitchens, of plumbing systems; but the manufacturer might typically put on the engine head always along with the front body work, and a house demolition process might typically

disregard all structure and begin at the roof and work down. Tentatively, one might expect psychological change more often to follow an organic pattern, as in the maturation of intelligence or the acquisition of skills in a foreign language.

(2) *Phasic-vs.-Continuous Growth.* Regardless of whether change occurs in patterns common to growth and final structure or peculiar to growth, the change over a total period, e.g., the maturation period, can be for each factor on a steady linear or non-linear curve, in the "continuous" case, or phasically, by fits and starts. And in the former case the curves can operate on the

same equations, except for constants, in all factors, or they can be characteristically very different, i.e., "continuous differential." The scant available research evidence, e.g., the work of Gesell and Ilg on early motor and cognitive development, strongly suggests that most psychological development is either "continuous differential" or thoroughly "multiphasic." These "differential" and "multiphasic" models present decidedly more complications than the "uniform continuous" model to any attempt to relate the form of growth (dR) factors to structure (R) factors.

However, in any form of organic model we can write the trait level in the final specification equation as the sum of trait change scores over periods, keeping a term T_o for the level of the trait at birth or at the origin of whatever total time period we are studying, as in equation (9).

$$(9) \quad a_{ij} = b_{j1}(T_{10i} + T_{11i} + T_{12i} \ldots + T_{1ci})$$
$$+ \ldots b_{jk}(T_{koi} + T_{k1i} + T_{k2i} \ldots + T_{kci})$$

where T_{11}, T_{12} to T_{1c} are the change scores on trait T_1 up through the last period, c, and the rest (the specific and error factors being understood) is as in the usual specification equation. (The factors, however, would need to be estimated with regard to scaling inferences and in raw scores, adjusting the b's appropriately.)

For the non-organic case the present T values would have to be constructed as functions of the change factors operating as second stratum factors.

Obviously a whole book would be needed to explore fully the relationships of growth phase and final structure in the more complex model. However, if we take the organic model we are assuming that in any given period, even when multiphasic growth obtains, the *same* factors are at work, though with different variance contributions, as in any other period. The identification of factors therefore comes within the scope of the general principles and formulae developed for confactor rotation (page 189). In the special case where we can

assume simple continuous change, however, the matching of the corresponding trait and trait change factors becomes relatively simple.

In the comparisons of R- and dR-analysis patterns we need to ask what our assumptions will be (already restricted to the organic and non-phasic continuous model) regarding (a) the form of the growth curve, (b) the equality or non-equality of age of the subjects, and (c) the similarity among (i) factors and (ii) people, as to rates of growth. One must inevitably assume that some growth constant g_d will be specific to each factor d, and that, additionally, it will be modified by some inherent rate in the person, r_i. For an initial simplicity we will write g_{di}, combining these two by some appropriate function into a single growth rate constant peculiar to factor and person. Let us first consider a group of persons all of the same age, c years, R-technique-factored at c, and dR-technique-factored for the interval c to $(c+1)$ years.

If a linear growth relation, i.e., $T_{di} = g_{di}c + k_{di}$ and if k_{di} is zero, i.e., the trait magnitude is zero at birth, it can readily be shown that R and dR should yield exactly the same factors (our organic growth principle being assumed). With greater probability, we may surely assume a growth equation known to be characteristic of many living things, namely, a logarithmic curve, thus:

$$(10) \quad c_i = g_{di}^{T_{di}} - (k+1)$$

where $(k+1)$ is simply a constant added to accommodate the likelihood that growth must be considered, with constitutional traits, to begin maturation k months before birth. (It should be noted that g, the growth rate, is inverted in relation to the usual verbal meaning, a small value corresponding to rapid growth.) If this is differentiated one obtains:

$$(11a) \quad \frac{dT}{dc} = \frac{1}{C + (k+1) \log g}$$

whence, dropping the constant by assuming for simplicity the particular case of growth from birth, the last year's increment becomes:

$$(11b) \quad T_{d(c+1)i} - T_{dci} = \frac{\log \dfrac{c+1}{c}}{\log g_{di}}$$

From this it is evident that again the last year's increment remains the same constant function for all individuals of the final individual absolute growth level. Conceivably most reasonably probable growth functions will continue to show this constant relation and to yield the answer that the R and dR patterns should therefore be the same. With unequal ages this would not be the case, but we shall leave the reader to derive the modification to be expected on the above assumption. It must be remembered also that with phasic growth this simple relation would not hold, and that the confactor analysis principle would need to be brought in to recognize corresponding factors.

Such steps to identify the trait change pattern — and thereby to resolve all known patterns into traits, trait changes and states — are contributory to a total solution only when we consider also the P-technique approach; to this we shall now turn in the next section.

One can, further, gain additional checks on the change and state factors by reference to P-technique designs now to be discussed.

6. METHODOLOGICAL ISSUES AND IMPROVEMENTS SPECIFIC TO *P* TECHNIQUE IN CHANGE STUDY

Although P technique, even in its simple form, has already done yeoman service in psychology notably by (1) checking through trait-change evidence the number and nature of trait structures independently reached by R technique (240, 325), (2) generating basic and testable concepts about the number and psychophysiological nature of psychological states (Karvonen & Kunnas, 851; Cattell, 240; H. Williams, 1547, 1548; J. Williams, 1550, 1551; Luborsky, 300) — see Chapter 23 — yet it has quickly involved methodologists in debate about fairly basic issues, and is undergoing steady technical improvement. Diagram 11-5 will remind the reader of its

DIAGRAM 11-5.   Covariation Over Time: Basis of *P*-Technique Correlations

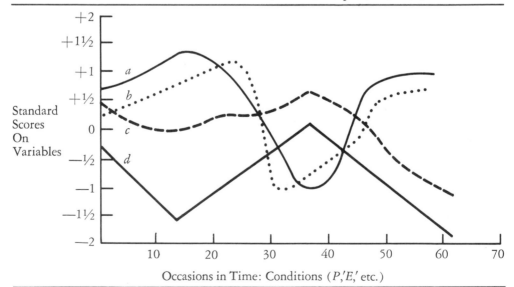

Occasions in Time: Conditions (*P,' E,'* etc.)

purpose, while Diagram 3-4 (page 93) gives perspective on the facet of scores in the DB.

Reduction of Time-Correlated Boredom and Learning Effects

By its very nature, repetitive testing introduces certain variance contributions which are irrelevant to the inherent changes and belong to the testing process instrumentation per se. This problem has been successfully attacked by (1) searching for variables equally valid as factor representatives (markers) but freer of practice effects than those at first used; (2) obtaining experimental emancipation from such spurious time correlations by the alternative method of using different but *equivalent* forms to get the repeated measures on the same variable. This is merely an extension of the familiar practice of making equivalent-standardized A and B forms, in this case to produce, say, 100 equivalent forms, as Moran (1070) has begun to do with intelligence tests, and as Mefferd illustrates in Chapter 22. Probably this is the ideal solution, but it requires more foresight and inter-researcher organization than is likely to be reached for some years. Incidentally, both (1) and (2) are more effective checks on "practice" than on "boredom." (3) Instead of trying by either of the methods mentioned to make the repeated measures *experimentally* equivalent, one can try to remove the practice or boredom effects *statistically* in the final analysis. The method advocated by economists (and uncritically copied by some psychologists) of partialling out completely *any* secular (time) trend, is, however, not the answer, and is as theoretically vicious as it is widespread. For a time trend is a basket containing many real things besides the artificial boredom, practice, etc., effects. How much of significance would be left in life if we removed everything that has been important in terms of time trend and historical change? Real factors change with time, and often as part of

some steady trend or cyclical process. Even if partialling out time-tied effects does not completely eliminate such factors, it badly distorts their correlations and reduces their variance.

The elimination of "instrument factors" expected to be generated by repeated testing, and therefore time-tied, should be made by the same principles applied to their elimination elsewhere (281). Perhaps the only thing worse than eliminating time-correlated variance is to give excessive importance to time, e.g., by choosing to place a factor through the time variable, but this will be discussed.

Control of Sampling Effects

A major practical difficulty in P technique is obtaining *enough* occasions of measurement to reduce sampling errors sufficiently. The basic estimate of the degrees of freedom in factor analysis generally, when directed to factor estimates, is the amount by which the number of people exceeds the number of variables (plus, for certain purposes, the number of factors). Obviously, the number of planned occasions, on this basis alone, should exceed the number of variables roughly by that 50, 100, or 150 degrees of freedom that the given experimenter's taste commonly considers necessary in R-technique studies. But the above-advocated maintenance of a strong foundation of marker variables in every study (to ensure a firm reference space in the final rotation and identification) itself often requires thirty variables, so that the experimenter, after adding those for his own hypothesis, may well start with, say, fifty. In such circumstances one may say that he will want to hold his subject for *at least* a hundred days in any satisfactory P-technique study. But only the most serious and determined experimentalists seem to have risen to such demands of P-technique research.

However, certain statisticians have argued that a further principle must be considered which demands even a greater

number of occasions. For example, Holtzman (739), following such economic statisticians as Quenouille (1174, 1175), maintains that the degrees of freedom in *P*
technique are further curtailed by the
presence of autocorrelation in each time
series. (Parenthetically, clarity is aided by
restricting the term "autocorrelation" to
the lagged correlation of a series *with itself,*
and by using "serial cross correlation," or
simply serial correlation, for any time-
series correlations among *different,* time-
coordinated variables. See Diagram 11-6.)

lag autocorrelation in the *Y* variable series,
and so on.

The reduction of degrees from this effect
can obviously be considerable, sufficient
possibly in some cases to lose as much as a
third of the gathered occasions data. The
present writer has discussed at more length
elsewhere (682) his reasons for disagreeing
with this apparently immaculate application
of classical sampling theory rules. Its logical
error is apparent from the fact that nowhere else does one rest the definition of
degrees of freedom upon the particular

DIAGRAM 11-6.   Serial Correlation and Autocorrelation Illustrated

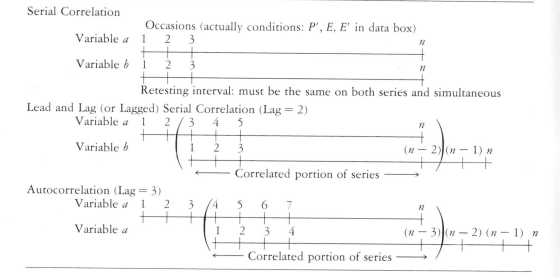

Now the autocorrelation on a short, say,
one hour, interval between testing and
retesting is often significant up to a five- or
six-lag remove, and on a one-day interval
for two or three days. The calculation for
reducing appropriately the degrees of freedom is given (Quenouille, 1174, 1175) as:

(11) $1 + 2r_{x1}r_{y1} + 2r_{x2}r_{y2} + \ldots = P + \ldots$

where $P =$ the number of paired observations necessary to equal one degree of
freedom for purposes of statistical inference and where r_{x1} is a one-lag autocorrelation in the *X* variable series, and r_{y1} is a one-

numerical outcome in the data, rather than
on the design of the experiment and the
independence of the experimental operations of
measurement. Consistent with most economists' peculiar subjectivity in believing that
they know what a trend is, and their wish to
get rid of it, Quenouille's treatment is really
asking what the degrees of freedom for
inferences and calculations should be assuming the trend is something to be
removed and ignored. But in the psychologists' thinking (and one hopes, ultimately in the economists'), time-tied
change, i.e., trend, is not something to be

taken for granted. It is part of what we are investigating. The significance of evidence on factor structure in change, *which includes factors in trends,* has to be examined by using the usual degrees of freedom, which are defined in the absence of any foreknowledge or assumption that significant serial correlation exists.

The practical problem of working with a really adequate sample, despite the social difficulties of holding one subject for a sufficient sample of occasions, can fortunately be overcome by a change in design, provided one's interest is in *common* change factors rather than in those unique to the individual. This modification consists in setting up the design I have called *population* or *chain* P *technique.* The latter can be viewed as a linking, in series, of *several* people, each person being measured on a run of occasions too short in itself to provide an adequate sample. The results are put in a single "chain" score matrix only after fully ipsatizing each person's scores. That is to say, they are brought to standard, normative scores over the sample of occasions for each person for each variable. Chain P technique may be thought of basically as factoring a grid, but bringing all the linked persons to the same mean and sigma eliminates the individual difference variance, in which we are not interested. However, for some purposes there is an argument for semi-ipsatizing only, i.e., eliminating differences of means but not of sigmas in what has been called *population* P *technique.* In either case the adequately lengthy series thus produced is then handled by the usual *P*-technique analysis.

Obvious alternatives for operating on this same grid of data with broadly the same end result are (1) to average (by z) across all persons the separate correlation matrices for the short series provided by each person (*population* P *technique* is the same as averaging covariance matrices), or (2) to average the corresponding loadings on the corresponding rotated factor matrices. However, for various reasons,

these are somewhat less satisfactory. It will be noted that chain P technique will no longer give the idiosyncratic (unique) trait expression pattern for which P technique is sometimes used. Instead, its results will approach the common pattern, such as we have seen would be obtained (with appropriate transformation) also from differential R technique or population P technique. To obtain a *unique trait* analysis there is no escape from the cost of holding one subject longer. That a chain P technique design is thoroughly practicable, and capable of yielding meaningful state patterns, consistent with other findings, has been shown by the recent try-out by Cattell and Scheier (325) on stress interview data gathered in cooperation with Grinker's laboratory.

Using a Correct Model for Factor Resolution

If we are looking for the distinct influences underlying change, the merely mathematical factor analysis will need, of course, to be brought to scientific meaning and completion in P technique just as in incremental R technique, by a unique rotational resolution. In principle, either of the two rotational resolution methods, simple structure or confactor rotation (Chapter 5), can be used. So far, only simple structure has been applied. As indicated above, it works very well, provided one recognizes, as both the psychological data and Damarin's data on disease processes have exemplified, that greater factor correlations may be expected in P technique than in R technique; which means, for example, that such programs as Promax, which start at an orthogonal position before going oblique, are less likely to work. The reasons for this greater obliquity, besides the tendency pointed out above of factors to be correlated with time and therefore with one another, must perhaps also include the more powerful influence of second-order factors, and the tendency of stimulus situations to provoke simultaneously a reaction from more than one factor.

Issues of Sampling in
P Technique and the Question
of Cycles and Trends

In connection with the last point above it has been suggested that the correlations among factors over time are smaller for short intervals, e.g., within a diurnal cycle, than over longer intervals, e.g., measured once a day at irregular times, thus covering both intra- and inter-diurnal variance. This seems likely, but it needs to be considered as part of a wider issue: the effects of sampling over time and occasions upon correlations and factor structure generally.

In practice, the sampling issues intrude themselves perhaps more imperatively in P technique than in R technique. One has a range of choice from measuring every hundredth of a second, as in EEG work, to every hour, or to every day or month. Phenomena that come out clearly at one "density" of observation are completely missed at another.

This is especially apparent in regard to trends and cycles, which may be considered here. For example, the steady upward trend of a factor in the spring months, which appeared in Luborsky's daily measures on a patient in P technique would be lost in the same number of measures at one-minute or one-year intervals, and the EEG alpha wave would be lost in measures taken every three minutes. One must distinguish between losing the perception of a trend or cycle and losing the factors (and their variances) that contribute to its variance. Gross variations in sampling interval may not lose the variance, the difference between any two occasions being a function of all processes, and the factors in short and long processes may not therefore be mutually lost (though changed in relative importance). But in the recognition of any process *form, trend,* or *cycle,* the sampling in-terval is obviously important. Finally we should remember that, in terms of the data box, we are not really sampling time, but conditions, internal and external, and, especially where the latter are concerned, sampling in P technique faces the same need for choosing comprehensively from the environment as sampling does in R technique.

As to trends, it has been mentioned, in connection with degrees of freedom, that economists and some others have very arbitrarily decided in time study to throw away the steady trend in order to study "what interests them." This can easily be done by computing devices, but to the investigator who believes that all Nature has something to teach him this rejection is a supreme example of "throwing out the baby with the bath water." Since a trend is almost certainly a trend jointly in several meaningful factors, such partialling out will not only maim the description of the primary factors, by loss of adequate variance, but also lose the typical meaning of second-order factors (Thomson & Leder-mann, 1394).

It may be, as just hinted, that some second-order structures will reflect merely situational constraints, but others may represent internal organization, as is suggested in the only psychological P-technique study yet taken to the second order, and plotted below in Diagram 22-1, page 706, which suggests stressful "coping" versus anxious "retreat."

Related to this interval sampling problem is the "paradox" pointed out many years ago by Udny Yule (1597) that if two phenomena are purely cyclical and of exactly the same frequency, they will nevertheless correlate zero if they happen to be half a cycle out of phase. (When in phase they would, of course, correlate plus one, and, when in opposite phase, minus one.) A case such as this illustrates more dramatically than most the desirability of using the exploratory lead-and-lag correlations we discuss below to unearth essential connections. If no consistent pattern of lags will bring a number of wave forms of identical frequency into perfect correlation, then we must indeed consider them causally distinct and accidentally of the same frequency; but it is surely going to be far more common that Yule's paradox will yield to insertion of appropriate lag values (see below).

Some statisticians have rather vaguely warned against sampling difficulties in P technique, and this may arise from their uncertainty as to whether they are sampling time, which could introduce some special problems, or sampling occasions. However, what we are actually sampling is a universe of *life situations,* each of which, like a person, may be considered an organic pattern. Unless some fallacy can be found in this principle, the laws of sampling for individuals of a species, as in the case of persons, should apply to the species we call situations according to classic principles.

Principles in Iterative, Factor-Lagged P Technique

The question of what have been called lead-and-lag or staggered serial correlations in factor analysis (See Diagram 11-6) requires that for its clear evaluation we hark back to the earlier discussion of causation in relation to correlation (Chapter 3) and to factor analysis (Chapter 6). There it has been suggested that the best and most likely model, in R technique as in P technique, is the assumption that factors are causes or influences operating upon the variables and that second-order factors are in turn determiners of the first-order factors.

Ordinary P technique, it will be observed, assumes no time lag between factors and variables or one variable measurement and another. If the scores for all variables for one occasion were placed on one card, and one had as many cards as occasions, the cards could be shuffled in any order and the correlations and factors

would come out the same. Incidentally, this reveals another reason for rejecting the proposal of Holtzman and Quenouille that we lose degrees of freedom when there is autocorrelation within variables, for this autocorrelation vanishes with change of order of cards, while the correlations and factors stand as before. Shuffling does not remove trend covariance, but it ensures what we have argued for above: that it be regarded as part and parcel of whatever covariance is produced by the change-producing influences we are seeking to understand.

However, if in scientific fact one variable or factor acts upon another, its causal effect will occur with *some* time lag. Let us suppose our occasions of measurement are at one-hour intervals; then the variable "amount of drink consumed" will correlate most highly with the variable "intoxicated behavior" if we lag the latter by one hour on the former. The variable "amount of hangover" will correlate best if we lag it, say, ten intervals on the first, and so on.

In first proposing lead-and-lag factor analysis in P technique, the present writer (240) thus dealt with a plan to discover by trial and error the lags of one variable on another which would maximize their correlation, on the grounds that the largest correlation represented the most organic connection between them, least attenuated by irrelevant error (intermediate influences). However, one naturally quickly reaches the end of such manipulative possibilities, since, when there are many variables, compromises have to be made between the ideal lag of a on b and on c, and what is required by the ideal lag of b on c. Obviously, with three variables and more, internal inconsistencies can rapidly develop.

But we need waste no time regretting the comparative failure of this model, for it is in any case a less adequate model than that which would lag various variables differently directly on the same factor (and various primaries differently on the same secondary). The rationale of lagging variables on factors is best perceived through describing the actual operations. One must begin by choosing a time interval appropriate to one's sampling purposes and the size of rhythms one may be interested in catching. It is, of course, *de rigueur* in P technique for lag purposes that the intervals be uniform between occasions; otherwise the staggering of one series on another (Diagram 11-6) is meaningless. A first factor analysis, proceeding to a V_{fp} for meaningfully rotated factors, is made without any lead or lag, i.e., in the normal fashion. One then estimates each factor and correlates this (or, better, obtains its loading), upon all variables, when each is lagged by intervals of say $+1, +2$, and $+3$, and -1, -2, and -3. The aim is now to find the lag *which increases the loading of those variables which this first rough estimate of the factor shows the factor indubitably to load,* and reduces more cleanly to zero the variables that appear to lie in the hyperplane. It is easy to find a simple function to check on one's success, e.g., the fourth power as used in oblimax and other analytical programs. It should be noted that this is to be reached with various variables differently led or lagged (staggered).

Now when this position is reached, we are better able to define and estimate the factor, for the first estimate was an approximation to it dictated by the fact that there were no really high correlations of the factor with the variables available in the unstaggered relations. Accordingly, a new estimate of the factor can now be made and this can again have loadings determined on the variables with freshly adjusted lags. This *iterative staggered* P *technique* would presumably converge relatively quickly (to zero change in the second decimal place) and leave us with a matrix yielding the best definition of the factors and a record of the lags of the variables on the factors which would be peculiar to each factor and each variable. The latter constitutes a "lag matrix" similar

in order to the V_{fp} and serving simultaneously to calculate factor-variable relations from the score matrix and to help interpret the factors in terms of their various lags in causal action. Naturally, the factor matrix no longer has the properties of a simple factor matrix, e.g., in restoring correlations. The lag-produced factors now have a life of their own, as concepts developed beyond simple factors. What has been described here could apply equally to what we called above population P technique, i.e., factoring the grid of scores in which variables are *relatives* and persons-by-occasions constitute the *referees.*

As a minor issue it may be asked whether the determination of a maximum correlation by lead and lag is capitalizing on chance, i.e., on error. It is, but not to the same degree that it is in computing a multiple correlation. This is a complex question, but one suspects that the shrinkage from sample to sample might be less than is customary in the latter, and, in any case, would have to be checked by repeating the study. (The situation would be different with staggering of variable on variable, which we have rejected.) However, even with the unstaggered correlations the weights of variables to estimate factors are at the mercy of the sample. The full evaluation of a state and its influences, as pursued under this Design 4, will in any case, require repeated experiments, e.g., with longer and shorter equi-interval measures, to explore the full range of influences under the control of the state response.

Yet another improvement, or, at least, extension, of state and trait change study by P technique needs discussion. In its initial form the technique is aimed, simply at discovering response patterns, i.e., consequences which vary together, as a result of endogenous and exogenous stimuli, or influences determining trait growth. However, as in the *condition-response* design (Chapter 10, page 364) in R technique, or other designs in Chapter 3, it is also possible to introduce values for stimulus situations and thus locate both the state dimension or trait-change factors and the situations in the environment which trigger them. This, of course, has the advantage over the classical bivariate approach (even when it shrewdly uses factor patterns as response measures instead of single variables) of obtaining a statement of the *relative importance* (in the life situation or an experimental situation) of the various stimuli capable of determining the response.

However, precautions are necessary to avoid possible conceptual complications. First, if the stimuli are subject to manipulative control, one would normally wish to randomize their relations, just as for treatments in analysis of variance, and leave the factor analysis uncomplicated by any meaningless correlations among the independent variables. Second, if one is simply measuring the strength of a number of *naturally occurring* stimuli, and where this randomizing therefore cannot be done, the correlations among the independent variables will now represent a real structure. But this is a structure in the situation, not in the organism's responses, and the danger then arises that the factor structure of the organism's responses may get mixed up with this factor structure of the ecology of environmental stimuli. In such circumstances it might be a better design to factor the response variables alone and then to relate the factor state scores to the stimulus factor scores. Effective instances of this are presented by the work of Cross (399) and of Sweney and May (1374), on ergic tension levels, and on the endogenous and exogenous conditions that produce them.

7. SINGLE CHANGE VARIABLES AND THEIR STANDARD STATISTICAL ANALYSIS

So far we have dealt with the organizing of change measurement and analysis with respect to a scientific psychological model. This model has been one of trait change and state change, and, in Sections 8 and 9

below, will be continued into further models of general or specific tendencies to lability and the notion of unique processes as sequences of multidimensional change. A logical reader may well ask, however, why we have not begun by asking more simply what kinds of statistical analysis can be made of change scores, regardless of any suggested for the study of change in the single variable.[5] Actually, in writing for psychologists, it has seemed best to begin with the likely models for their substantive interests and only thereafter to turn to the basic formalities of summarizing the parameters of change available from measures simply on a single variable.

If we consider a facet, face, or grid of scores, e.g., a set of people measured on a set of occasions over a set of variables and ask in what way change can be considered and measured, we can broadly divide the methods into those suitable to two occasions (a single repetition of measures) and those which analyze the additional information in a whole series, as will be studied under process, below. The parameters or characteristics of the set of measurements which can change are:

(1) Individual scores
(2) The mean or mode
(3) The standard deviation or higher moment
(4) The correlations among the scores
(5) The form of the multivariate distributions.

It is possible to assign names to the 2^5 combinations of these, and if one does so it is perhaps less confusing to call them systems than models. Thus Lord (948) has aptly called a system of change "a dynamic equilibrium process" (it is analogous to the dynamic equilibrium of a gas) if the mean and sigma remain constant but individual scores change. This would generally imply that (4), the correlations, also change. At

---

[5]The writer is much indebted to Professor Sam Hammond, of Melbourne University, for the first organization of this section on change evaluated from the standpoint of the single variable.

the extreme of combinations of (1), (2), (3), (4), and (5), as a base line for all change, is what might be called a static equilibrium, in which even the individuals do not change.

Although careful and sophisticated study of the total problem of change measurement is new, and may be said to be heralded by P-technique designs, by feedback and games theory (Chapter 13), and by the recent collection of stimulating methodological contributions edited by Harris (691), the study of change, in terms of learning, maturation, social and economic trends, etc., has, of course, gone on for a long time. The names of Burt, Coghill, Fiske, Harold Jones, Lowell Kelly, Fleishman, Freud, Gesell, Hebb, Stanley Hall, Hull, Lazarsfeld, Luria, Mowrer, Piaget, Skinner, Terman, Thomson, Tolman, Tucker, and others stand out in connection with various areas of development. Indeed, change may be said to have had the characteristic appeal of "the dynamic" to psychologists, so much so that, as the present writer suggested years ago, many researches have plunged into studying change without first asking what are the entities that change.

The concern of this section is, however, with this model-less study of change, and it can be said at least of the above researchers that they have applied almost every standard analysis tool in the statistician's tool chest available at the time they did their researches. They have used analysis of variance, with F and t tests to examine the significance of mean changes; they have examined the significance of changes in standard deviation; they have used analysis of covariance to partial out some associated variable or the initial starting level; they have examined the significance of trends, fitting linear and non-linear functions to curves, e.g., in learning, and they have analyzed for phases and cycles, as in the work of Gesell and the physiological psychologists working with the EEG. In social psychology they have examined the se-

quences of games theory and the requirements of Markov chain process (see Chapter 13).

Since it is not our purpose to repeat the contents of a standard statistical textbook we shall attempt no comprehensive recapitulation of the analysis methods, most of which can be equally applied to time-invariant and time-variant data. Comment will be made only on the basic issues of conceiving a single change score; of testing trends; of analysis of covariance; of the use of the discriminant function; and of the effect of time sequence on the concept of reliability.

Many writers, including especially Lord (945, 946, 948), Manning and DuBois (985), Humphreys (793), Lacey (896), Tucker (1465), McNemar (1015), Thurstone (1406), Campbell (181), Gulliksen (644), and Bock (120), have discussed the issues in repeated measurements. Broadly there are five possibilities:

(1) To take the difference of before-and-after measures in the raw score units of the given scale. Change $= a_{2i} - a_{1i}$.

(2) To take the difference in standard scores, standardized afresh (separately) for before and after. Change $= z_{2i} - z_{1i}$.

(3) To take the difference in standard scores for the common population sample constituted by before and after together. Change $= z_{2i} - z_{1i}$ (as advocated in dR technique).

(4) To find the regression of the first score on the second, w, and, as in analysis of covariance, subtract the regression estimate of the second score from the second score. Change $= a_{2i} - wa_{1i}$.

(5) To take the mean of the first and second scores as the better estimate of the individual's typical absolute level and measure his change *on each* occasion from that.

Each has advantages and disadvantages, as pointed out on page 370 above on dR technique, but much current discussion is apt to overemphasize, if only by its labels for "error" and "true" variance, some one of them. For example, (4) has sometimes been said to give the "true gain score," whereas Manning and DuBois' expression "residual gain score" is probably better. Incidentally, they have shown that attempts to predict the outcome of learning experience from an earlier battery are more effective when directed at estimating residual gains than simple gains. Calculations (2) and (4) obviously have the disadvantage of throwing away any information connected with the difference of the group as a whole from the first to the second occasion. Any device like (5) which makes gain independent of the conceived absolute score of the individual is suspect. This question has been discussed more thoroughly in Section 5 above, where it is pointed out that many of the acrobatics performed by certain psychometrists are an attempt to get away from the unpleasant but inevitable fact that the variance of a difference score contains the summed variance of the experimental errors of the initial and the final measurements. Partialling the first score out of the second, or the design (4) above, does not leave the difference uncorrelated with the error in the first, but only with the sum of true score and error score, which leaves error still correlated. As argued above, Method (1) is probably the best, provided one has a reasonable approach to an equal interval scale in the raw metric used, but (3) is also very useful, especially if scores are also normalized.

Turning next to the testing of trends one recognizes that it can be a fairly complicated statistical proposition, especially when, as usual, one has different numbers of cases at different time points, or suffers some selection when the same cases are carried on through a time series. The reader is referred to Thurstone (1406, 1410), Guilford (625), Quenouille (1174, 1175), Fiske and Maddi (522), Johnson and Neymann (812), and others. One has to consider purely descriptive curve fitting (30); the analysis of curves into

components (Aiken, 13); and the testing of significance of linear, quadratic, cubic, etc., components by analysis of variance and covariance (Gaito & Wiley, 572).

In applying analysis of covariance to change scores, the assumptions themselves sometimes need scrutiny. The frequent indefensibility of eliminating the level on the first occasion (or, for that matter, the second) to produce zero correlation of absolute level and gain has been sufficiently commented upon. Some other points may be illustrated by considering the case of a group of neurotics half exposed to therapy and half not exposed. The possibility has to be considered that some natural curative process is occurring in the untreated and that the regression for that group *alone* might better be applied to recognize among the treated group the true nature of the effect of treatment. Where reliability (dependability) coefficients are available, the question should also be considered of separating the regression due to error of measurement from the remaining possible influences in regression. In this connection one should consider the proposal of Webster and Bereiter (1505) that estimation of the error of the difference of two scores be based on examination of the items composing the test. Standard designs for investigating simple interactive and covariational effects will be found in Bereiter (101), Lindquist (936), and in Chapters 5, 28, and 7 by Anderson, Bock, and Jones respectively.

In any comparison of the ANOVA and ANOCVA designs here with the covariational, correlational designs of the sections above, the same general contrasting properties exist as with these methods when applied to non-time-related measurements, as brought out by Burt (Chapter 8), Cattell (Chapter 3), and Horst (Chapter 4).

For example, the use of correlations and partial correlations allow an experimenter to reach much the same conclusions as an ANOVA design here without the same trouble of getting a balanced design sample but also without a measure of error other than the standard error of a correlation. Perhaps the greatest advantage of an ANOVA design is that, if used with random assignment to treatments, it avoids the sampling biases which render many correlational studies of change indefinite in outcome. Attempts to approximate this random assignment after the event—for example, Chapin's ex post facto matching methods—do not carry conviction because there is no certainty that bias is overcome or that randomness of error is ensured.

On the other hand, the condition-response design (Chapter 6) of Cattell and Scheier does randomize, in a correlational factor-analytic setting, the independent variables in relation to one another, just as in analysis of variance. Unfortunately, follow-up of this design has been insufficient as yet to indicate what its full advantages and disadvantages may be. However, this design does remind us that what is often mentioned as the so-called elegance of the analysis of variance design—the neat balance of all frequencies with regard to variables—is actually a sort of outrage upon Nature. The independent variables, e.g., intelligence and age, in an experiment with growing children, are *not* actually independent. The fact that our experimental assignment of cases has brutally forced such an unnatural pattern is, of course, brought home by the extreme difficulty we sometimes have in getting adequate frequencies for certain combinations. In the above instance, for example, there will be a utilization of every available case of high actual age with low mental age, but an easy sampling of, say, low mental age with low actual age cases. It is necessary to remember therefore that in the typical ANOVA design we are (1) sometimes ignoring or, at least severely straining, sampling principles, and (2) not getting evidence of whatever correlational or factor structure may exist in Nature among the independent variables.

The use of the multiple discriminant function to maximize the psychological differences of two groups separated by a time change needs little comment. Bock in Chapter 28 discusses the application of the MDF to educational problems and the multivariate analysis of variance is applied by Harris (Chapter 12) to repeated measurements. The T^2 statistic generalizes student's t for the multivariate case and provides a test of the significance of the over-all difference between the two occasions. Bock further points out that both the use of the MDF to maximize difference between occasions and of canonical correlation to find function of two occasions which most agree, are, strictly, generalizations of multivariate analyses of variance, and he attributes both, initially to Hotelling.

While dealing with finding functions to yield the extreme positions of agreement and disagreement among scores on systems of occasions, it is appropriate also to mention what has sometimes been called canonical factor analysis. This aims to maximize the relationship between the factor loadings and the score matrix from which they are derived. Like so-called alpha factor analysis, it belongs in the maximum likelihood methods of factor analysis, and all these share the useful property of not being affected by scale transformations. They can be applied equally to covariances or to correlations merely by applying weights to the factor loadings arrived at. These developments are described very adequately by Harris in Chapter 12.

Finally, any statistical analysis, with or without implication of an underlying model, has to deal with the question of consistency, i.e., reliability and homogeneity, in change measurements. The comprehensive basis for noting the various types of consistency to be examined has been given in Chapter 3 above with the Basic Data Relation Matrix (particularly the contrast of the R-technique, P-technique, and T-technique concepts of reliability: see page 111). The fact that incremental R-

technique reliabilities and P-technique reliabilities are systematically lower than those most commonly thought of in connection with reliability (R-technique reliabilities) has been discussed, with the reason therefore, in the present chapter. Aspects of the same problem are also intensively discussed elsewhere by Webster and Bereiter (1505). A special issue — that of the P-technique type of reliability applied when a continuous trend exists, (as in the autocorrelation problem [page 382 above] — has been technically treated by Hoffman (733).

In retrospect, on this matter of general statistical treatments, as applied to change phenomenon, it is difficult not to comment on the hopeless gap that seems to exist at present between various theorists on change, such as Freud, Sorokin, Toynbee, Fromm, Piaget, etc., and the statisticians discussed above, who have attempted to put the instrumentality for change measurement into clear conceptualization for creating and testing specific theories of change.

8. THE EVALUATION OF LABILITY: OSCILLATION AND FLUCTUATION

So far we have discussed change as a difference on a simple variable, a defined model, e.g., a source trait, and a function, and we shall later discuss a change sequence as a pattern in itself — a process. This leaves from our original list the measurement of changeability in itself — broadly of a second level of abstraction from the change phenomena. Changeableness can be a characteristic of a trait, a state, a person, or a process. Thus it can be studied as characteristic of a process, e.g., in the observation that schizophrenics are more changeable early than late; or as characteristic of an area, e.g., that ergic drive levels are more changeable than dynamic sentiment levels; or of an individual, e.g., that delinquents are more labile than non-delinquents. These dimensions of the subject — of which the data box concept most readily reminds us — have unfortunately not been kept in mind in most lability studies up to the present. For example, many studies have assumed lability as a general personality characteristic without waiting to demonstrate this unity across cognitive, temperamental, and dynamic modalities; the role of environmental stimuli in accounting for part of the lability has been overlooked; and the assumption has been made that fluctuation in short-term rhythms is the same as in longer-term processes, etc. In short, substantive research in the field bristles with technical issues which require the space of a book and which can only be indicated in salient points here.

One of the earliest and also most systematic series of researches illustrating this area was that of Flugel and his students (540) on an alleged general factor "O" of *oscillation*, defined as short-term (5 to 10 seconds) variability in cognitive performance level. Another has been the study of dynamic structure *fluctuation* (207) defined as change, in any direction, in dynamic structure, e.g., in strength and direction of attitude and sentiment measures, over days or weeks; and yet others are studied by Fiske and Maddi (522). A special instance of this is the centering of such instability measures specifically in autonomic data, as in the work of Darrow and Heath (406) and Lacéy and Lacey (896), and on physiological measures, as in the work of Doust (425). A recent approach is that of Barratt on impulsiveness (63). The majority of these studies have conceived inconstancy as a constant characteristic of the individual (though it could also be examined conceptually as a characteristic of a trait or state), and have found moderate associations with other personality instability or pathology. However, the fixed personality dimensions which relate to it are not one but several: specifically, high fluctuation significantly loads personality factors U.I. 30 and 31, while high oscillation loads U.I. 22 (positively) and U.I. 26 (negatively), i.e., in the direction of poor will control. Renewed experimental interest in these phenomena has recently been aroused by return to the subject by Fiske and Maddi (522) and Doust (425).

Just as in P and differential R techniques, so here one has the alternative of deriving the actual measures either from a series of occasions or from a single pair. Flugel, and others since, have experimented with (1) subtracting each occasion's performance from the next in a series of occasions, neglecting sign and accumulating a total over many occasions, and, alternatively, (2) with taking simply a sigma over the same sample of occasions. Obviously the former scoring diminishes (and may miss completely) the importance of the more *long*-term trend changes; but the correlation of the two methods with each other has been high and the correlation of each with other traits very similar.

It behooves workers in this field not to cling to rule-of-thumb procedures either for experiment or scoring, but to explore possibilities of design systematically in the broader context of the BDR matrix. In regard to the computed scores themselves one can, for example, take change or change in change, in the manner of higher differentials. For example, the BDR reminds one that the topic can be studied in terms of change with a fixed stimulus or in relation to a standard variability of stimulus; on differences on the same response or on the difference of two responses; on measures on one person or averaged over many.

Whatever the measurement operation, the important question is whether we consider — as Doust (425), Lacey and Lacey (895, 896), Wenger (1515, 1516, 1518), and others seem to assume, and as Spearman (1340) and Flugel (540) set out to prove — that lability is a general tendency of the individual, or whether we theorize that

labilities are different in different areas. This remains to be settled by R- or P-technique factorings.

Naturally, if an investigator has worthwhile hypotheses or hunches about relations to personality, there is no reason why he should confine himself to the systematic treatment of factoring change measures on their own and absolute measures on their own. In fact the work of Flugel (540), Doust (425), Cattell (207, 240), and others already makes it certain that tendencies to oscillation (short term) and fluctuation (long term) are, first, reliably different over people, i.e., as "traits," and, second, significantly related to absolute measures on other variables. Furthermore, the state studies by Cattell and associates (325) include some change measures, e.g., frequency of spontaneous G.S.R. resistance changes, which show that lability measures not only associate themselves with the absolute measures which define a trait but also with those which define a *state.*

In uncommon research situations where the retest interval is very long, an issue could arise, since any lability is at least a two-occasion measure, as to whether the score attaches to the first or second point in time. Issues arise also as to the effect of fineness of occasion sampling upon the lability scores, e.g., variations in α and β wave amplitudes in the EEG are almost certainly of different meaning.

This brief section has had to be content with indicating the main concepts of changeability, some major researches thereon, under notions of oscillation and fluctuation, some common pitfalls in measurement, and some basic methods of calculation. Suffice it that for every form and model in behavioral measurement there can be conceived a "lability" measurement. For example, there can be changeability of a trait, a state, a function integrating these in some emergent criterion expression, a measure of personality integration or conflict (as in the MAT), and a process. Each of these can be expressed in parameters defining amplitude, interval-frequency, periodicity (by Fourier analysis), change of order, acceleration (second differentials), ratio of environmental stimulus fluctuation to fluctuation of behavior, etc., so that the possible varieties of lability evaluation are very great. There is evidence that particular lability levels are characteristic of certain traits, of states as contrasted with traits, and of total personalities, correlating with certain fixed traits, e.g., exvia.

9. PROCESS DESCRIPTION: COMPONENT PROCESS ANALYSIS

The history of process research is like that of many other psychological topics in showing a naïve assurance in the first place that one can arbitrarily and subjectively recognize the individual processes to be studied. When the process is an artificial one, arranged and dictated by the bivariate experimenter himself, or consisting of a known sequence of environmentally determined events, this may be approximately true. But such important processes as repression, projection, cognitive maturation, and the unfolding of desires in an ergic drive sequence may have a natural, inherent, characteristic pattern of their own. The assertion here is that any such natural, recurrent process is a "pattern over occasions," and, like a type, which is a pattern over people, needs to be discovered and defined, as a given natural entity. It cannot be defined, except as a misleading caricature of the real thing, by armchair fiat. It is, of course, possible to define a process arbitrarily, by teaching a rat to respond in sequences A, B, C, etc., and thus seemingly to create a known totality of pattern. But even such a learning process, though prescribed and arranged by the experimenter, is likely to have important integral parts unsuspected by him, e.g., as when rats learning to run a maze are also learning to react less shyly to the experimenter. And in investigating the adult human being we need means to recognize learnt processes

arising from earlier experiences of which we have no conception.

Both in learning and maturation, we are apt to talk too glibly of such things as the "toilet training process," "the process of acquiring language," or the "maturation process of the sex drive in adolescence." Often we bring an obviously all too simple model, e.g., a conditioned reflex, to explain it. Surely the understanding of anything in Nature must begin with accepting it as a fact and by carefully observing what has to be explained. The problem in studying human learning, maturation, or physiological response process is therefore first to discover, recognize, and define each single process and eventually to build an understanding of a natural taxonomy of processes. This approach is based on an assumption of possible simplifications. Just as with the individual we aim at the most useful limited set of dimensions and type groups, so here we take it as axiomatic that the infinitely varied flow of behavior as we actually witness it can be resolved into a limited number of elemental processes or types of process. Such a resolution is taken as a precondition for the scientifically economical study of laws about processes. Just as with traits, so with processes it is assumed that there will be *unique* instances but also *common* instances, in which a certain configurative sequence of behavior will be found repeating itself either (a) over and over in one person, or (b) over several persons. To check this possibility we must begin with a model of process which is broad and flexible enough to include all instances and precise enough to be used in empirical investigation.

By a process we mean that kind of pattern which is a configuration rather than a mere profile. That is to say, a sequential order is an essential part of the signatures of the numbers in the profile. Consequently we must consider the data box as now having in it, along with the condition entities (E, environment; P', internal condition; E', modes of environment; etc.), a numbering representing time. In the most general sense a process is thus a sequence of values on a variety of behavior measurements, stimulus measurements, etc. It does not mean the same thing backwards and forwards (as a profile would), as a moment's reflection on words, or melodies, or a movie film of a house on fire, will remind one. This configuration can have various restrictions put upon it to constitute sub-varieties of process. For example, a process can be in one person or in several persons, constituting in the latter case a social process. In its general form it covers magnitude changes in several variables behaving differently, but it can occur in a single variable, as a melody occurs in the dimension of pitch.

The variables can be of the all-or-nothing variety, or continuous and parametric, and so on. It can have its later phases predictable from its earlier ones, as in a Markov process, or any purely endogenous process, or its elements may contain both stimulus environment and organismic response, in which a sequence in the organism's behavior is dependent upon a sequence in the environment. Thus nest-building in spring can be defined only in terms *both* of the behavior in the bird, *and* of the unfolding of spring. In love, war, and scientific research, the description of the process is very much tied up with happenings in the social and physical world outside the organism being measured, and any attempt to describe and explain its behavior in self-contained scientific laws restricted to observation of the one abstraction — the organism — would almost certainly fail.

The formal problems needing to be solved for research on process are:

(1) The sheer description of a particular (unique) process;

(2) The discovery of "types" of processes at the "surface-process" level (definition below);

(3) The resolution of surface processes into what we shall call *component processes,*

corresponding to source traits in the individual difference analysis;

(4) The assignment of scores and time locations to processes.

The essential basis for describing any given process, in a single person or set of persons, is already available in the data box. However, it needs two additions: (a) A time coordinate which is different in nature from the ten sets, being a dimension not a series of ids. This "eleventh axis," which we shall indicate by the lower-case t (to remind us that it is not truly coordinate with the id sets, $P, S, R, E,$ etc.) will have values t_1 to t_c (c for "chronological" point) upon it (t_m for any moment). It will give time reference to ten ids, one on each set, simultaneously. (For example, the last entry will be: $a_{qq'nn'NN'vv'xx'c}$. See Notation page 153.) (b) The introduction of numerical score entries for stimuli (also for environmental conditions, etc., though it suffices for illustration to refer to stimuli) over and above the usual entries for response magnitudes. This introduces what we have called in Chapter 3 "heterogenous facets," obviously different from the more frequently used data box containing homogeneous, response measures only. Use of such a heterogeneous score matrix facet has however, already been illustrated elsewhere, in R technique, by what we defined as the *condition-response design* of experiment.

The reason for this second addition is that in all but the limiting case of a purely endogenous process, the psychologist is compelled to regard a succession of strengths of stimuli, conditions, etc., as part of the full definition of a process. A courtship process, or a dance, for example, is, to say the least, incomplete without reference to the particular succession of stimuli presented in a pattern by the partner, and even the melody succession overlearned by the oboe player has to take its cues in an orchestra from the other instruments and the conductor. It is *possible,* of course, to abstract and describe only the behavior-state part of a process, purely in terms of a response entry matrix. Indeed, whether we take an environment-tied or a purely endogenous process, we must certainly recognize that responses, either internal or overt, themselves play the part of stimuli to the next action, so that the pure response-entry matrix does not entirely ignore what are truly stimulus-strength entries. But the complete descriptive matrix needs to be of the kind shown in Diagram 11-7. The entries therein are either for a single person or are obtained as the average scores for a special set of persons.

Therein, for each successive point of measurement in time, a score can be entered for any one of the set of stimuli found (by reconnaissance studies) to be relevant at some point of the process, and for any of the distinct responses or performances known to occur and recur in the process. Most entries may turn out to be zero or near zero, with just one or two high points for each stimulus and response. The sheer description of a process occurring over

DIAGRAM 11-7.   Description of a Sequence or Specific Process

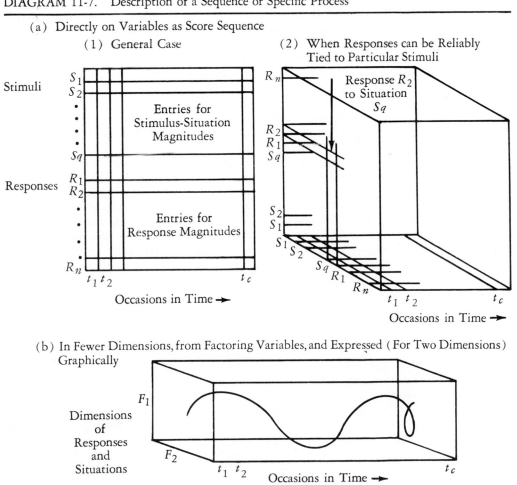

(a) Directly on Variables as Score Sequence

(1) General Case

(2) When Responses can be Reliably Tied to Particular Stimuli

(b) In Fewer Dimensions, from Factoring Variables, and Expressed (For Two Dimensions) Graphically

some particular space of time in a person or set of persons can therefore be represented by a facet or total data box of scores. Furthermore, if the latter, it can be unrolled into what we have defined in Chapter 3 as a *grid* (a form of supermatrix, partitioned into what were the successive facets of the grid, though to be handled in most processes simply as a matrix). And in either case the two-coordinate facet matrix can finally be unravelled into a single vector ($c \times n$ in length) corresponding to the person's experience in the process. (This can be done three ways in the three-dimensional data box, but all retain the same total information.)

Instead of preserving this full definition of the process in terms of particular stimulus and response variables and their scores, a condensation can be achieved by a *P*-technique analysis of the Diagram 11-7 grid, in which the series of time occasions, $t_1 - t_c$, takes the place of the usual "conditions" (E, E', etc.) axis. Then the experiment will emerge with a smaller number of dimensions — k factors — expressing (generally as distinct spaces) the k_s physico-social dimensions of the stimuli and the k_r dimensions of the stimulus ($k = k_s + k_r$). A correspondingly condensed $c \times k$ (instead of $c \times n$) matrix will now describe the "movement" of the process over time. The values can be spatially represented as a thread weaving its way through a k-dimensional space over c (for chronological) points in time. Thus, verbally, a process would be defined as "a particular succession of numerical combinations on stimulus and behavior state dimension measurements."

Description of a particular process is only the beginning, however, of the task of science in developing a taxonomy of processes and carrying out experiments with them. Just as with traits and states, we can advantageously distinguish, in developing a taxonomy, between "surface" and "source" patterns. A "typical" process, such as it is scientifically fruitful to work

upon, e.g., the diurnal fatigue process, the typical adolescent development, the process of learning to ride a bicycle, or of forgetting a language, has to be one which recurs again and again, in recognizably similar form, in contrast to any particular sequence, defined by the above matrix, which may never be seen again.

Its stereotypy, however, can exist in one of four senses:

(1) As a *common surface* process, repeating itself across different people, e.g., the process of getting up in the morning;

(2) As a *unique surface* process repeating itself in the life of one person, e.g., an air pilot's repeated taking off in a plane;

(3) As a *common component*, e.g., dancing a waltz while courting a young lady;

(4) As a *unique component* process, e.g., the process of counting roof tiles which accompanies a particular neurotic's morning walk.

The notion of *component process*, which is analogous among processes to the source trait among traits, will be defined shortly. But here we may note that the taxonomy proposed is a fourfold table from two dichotomies — common versus unique, and surface versus component — closely analogous to the concepts developed for traits (Chapter 19). Although mathematical models and experimental analysis methods have not apparently been worked out before for these concepts, they are implicit in many careful psychological and physiological studies, e.g., in embryology, and came close to being related to a sufficiency of actual data, e.g., in the work of Gesell, Amatruda and others (588, 589) on infant development processes.

Since common or unique surface processes are modal patterns the logic behind the methods for locating them is that already worked out for surface trait and types (Chapter 9). Neglecting for the moment the various refinements there described, one may state the essential method as that of setting up a Q matrix bounded by either (a) people (common surface processes) or (b) different periods from the life of the same person (unique surface processes) and entering it with either (1) correlations (covariances, etc.), i.e., r's, or (2) pattern similarity coefficients, i.e., r_p's between the *process description vectors (matrices)* described above. In the case of (1) we are ignoring the differences in process levels and basing the modal clustering only on similarity of shape, and in the case of (2) both shape and level are considered, as Chapter 9 explains.

The determination of similarity over time could in the extreme case be on scores in a single variable, but the comprehensive concept of a particular process we have developed here calls for a matrix of scores either of variables or of factors over time, as in Diagram 11-7. Unravelled, the data box, grid or facet ends as a single long vector, and, as regards the obtained correlation between grid and grid, etc., it does not matter which way it is unravelled, though, for the serial correlations we are shortly to discuss, the direction must be appropriate and conforming among the processes examined for similarity.

At this point a problem is encountered in process cluster search which does not exist in trait cluster search and which presents even greater difficulties in component than surface process analysis. Every analytical procedure so far described here assumes that the particular processes to be compared are excerpts from some continuous activity of the person which are somehow already known to be "in step," i.e., when a similar process exists it is at the same phase of its unrolling at t_1, at t_m, etc. How is this necessary prior synchronization (when similarity really exists) to be accomplished? First, if we are dealing with something not purely endogenous to behavior, but incorporating stimulus situation strengths in the process matrix, these values are known to and sometimes even arranged by the experimenter, e.g., with rats learning a maze, they are arranged. When this alignment by environmental

situation points (possibly even on a slightly different time scale) is not feasible there is no alternative but to correlate excerpts by serial correlations beginning with different leads and lags until a highly significant correlation, if it exists, is found.

This problem is, of course, tied up with the question of how we find when a process begins and ends. What we normally have before us is two (or more) random or intuitively pre-selected time sections, hopefully containing the same process, thus:

(1) DFILZOQSEQUENCEYPIZ
(2) XDPYLSEQUENCERDFUL

By trial-and-error lagged serial correlation of (1) and (2), we shall eventually find that a lag of (2) on (1) by two occasions maximizes the correlation. After such synchronization it is necessary to experiment further with dropping off early and late elements until another maximum is reached through the loss of what belongs to other processes. That is to say our model conceives a person's day (or other period) as made up of a succession of processes which can be and are arranged in different ways on different days but within each of which the situational-behavioral elements must follow the invariable, intrinsically required order of the process.

If the above procedures are successful the investigator will emerge with an array of modal, common, surface process patterns, each definitely described by a process matrix which is the centroid of the vectors found to cluster at that mode. However, except where a high degree of manipulative control can be exercised (and this latter would rule out some of the most interesting fields of investigation) it is surely unlikely that processes will be non-overlapping in time. If, for simplicity, we take a sequence pattern in a single variable, say, body temperature at the dinner table, what we plot may be a palimpsest overwriting the temperature sequence of a digestive process (ending with liqueurs) and the usual temperature effects of the characteristic social excitement of a dinner party. Perhaps Hollywood reflects the true complexity of life, at least when it depicts the hero as simultaneously recovering his breath after a life-and-death struggle, eating a large meal, and courting the heroine. The upshot in terms of, say, an EKG or EEG record, would be something that would defy visual analysis. In fact, in much natural data we may commonly expect the situation depicted in Diagram 11-8, in which a number (three, in this case) of distinct types of process are superimposed, with different starting points (differences of phase) with a resultant (in this case shown for a single variable) in the form of a unique, historical, stochastic series.

Now the most likely reaction of the pure mathematician when asked, as he would be here, to resolve an irregular curve into basic regularities is to submit the observed curve to a Fourier analysis (into sets of basic regularities is to submit the observed rhythmic sine-cosine curves, of certain frequencies and amplitudes) or some related, e.g., Taylor series, procedure. This makes sense in analyzing a melody into tones and overtones, where the model happens to fit—the nature of sound being intrinsically periodic. However, as Diagram 11-8 suggests, the basic processes in which the psychologist is interested do not consist of simple cycles.

The most likely model is surely one in which surface processes are sometimes what they appear to be, and sometimes composites of more unitary component processes. Even when the surface processes are common, frequently repeating processes, it may yet be that they are composites of synchronized component processes, potentially separable, just as a surface trait can often be resolved into more than one source trait factor. For instance, (1) experiencing late adolescent inner maturations and (2) going through the experience of a college education are similarly synchronized for a sufficient number of people to constitute a well defined surface process. This pattern is familiar in its totality to the college counselor, without his being able confidently to ascribe contributions separately to the two component processes.

However, this uniform synchronization cannot be depended upon: the most general solution has ultimately to be one capable of unravelling what we may call the *proto-processes* or *component processes* when they occur two, three or more at a time and overlap in each instance by varying degrees. In this section we cannot attempt any radical solution for the general problem, but shall assume the special case of synchronization, comforted by the reflection that this must be fairly common, and that the unity of consciousness makes more than a few components in any case uncommon. As a housewife cooks supper, knits a pullover, and goes through the process of discharging neighbor Jane's worries, intermittent attention permits this much overlap. Even in a less obviously overoccupied person we must admit simultaneous conscious, subconscious, dynamically unconscious, physiological, and simple habit processes.

A possible approach to resolution of constantly synchronized component processes is again the factor analytic one. Suppose we have measured the waking-up process in John for the first hour for two hundred mornings ($N = 200$), dividing the hour into c intervals at each of which n different stimulus and response variables are measured. These $n \times c$ measures define the particular process on any one morning, and, as pointed out in the above discussion of process description, we may simplify, after P-technique factoring, by substituting a $k \times c$ for the $n \times c$ matrix. Next we take the $(k \times c) \times N$ score matrix—call it $C \times N$—and correlate (as relatives) each of the C variables across the N referees. In this way we shall obtain K factors, each loading each C occasion by a particular amount. That is to say, each of the C points in the surface process can be viewed as standing

DIAGRAM 11-8.   Effect of Combining Proto-Processes in a Single
Process Event on a Single Response Variable

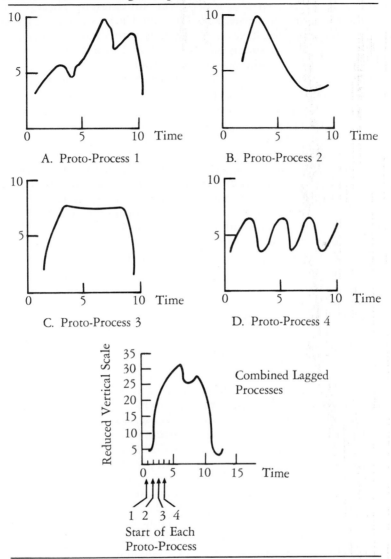

A. Proto-Process 1

B. Proto-Process 2

C. Proto-Process 3

D. Proto-Process 4

Combined Lagged
Processes

Reduced Vertical Scale

1 2 3 4
Start of Each
Proto-Process

at a level determined by the weighted sum of the levels at the same moment in the component processes. A component process, as defined by this series of factor loadings, would thus appear as a curve of its own, as shown in any one of the proto-processes in Diagram 11-8. (There are certain detailed technical points which space precludes discussing here; such as the fact that the *average* restored surface process will appear as a horizontal line, until we put the scale for each C occasion back in. Analysis of covariance and particularly of cross-product matrices will probably be preferable to correlation matrices. Also unique resolution cannot be by simple structure, but must use con-factor rotation.)

In the more generalized, but also less operational notion of proto-processes put forward in Diagram 11-8, we have sup-posed that the proto-processes simply add up with equal weight, that it is the nature of the process either to be present or absent, and that the proto-process is a quite concrete behavioral entity. In the factor analytic version of proto-processes, which we have called component processes, each can be present in all degrees, just as a source trait can in an individual, and, lack-ing further evidence, it could be said that such a component process is a mere con-venient abstraction. If confactor rotation works—there are as yet no data on re-peated process measurement analysis in an individual—it should be an argument for the "reality" (*efficacy,* page 120) of the com-ponent process, and manipulative and other experimental designs might in fact expect to confirm this by producing evidence of the proto-process appearing on its own. It should be recognized that the above main experiment would produce *unique* proto-processes (to the individual). But just as P and dR techniques produce unique and common state patterns, so here there is a corresponding design—cor-relating the c relatives across people as referees—which can produce common proto-process patterns.

The unsolved problem in this whole approach is that of possible irregular phase differences in the proto-processes in any sample period. As far as common surface processes are concerned, the repeating pat-tern can in theory be satisfactorily located by auto-correlation and staggered (lead and lag) serial correlation, with the trial-and-error lopping off of various links (elements), as sketched above. But with component processes we must at least be able to get plenty of instances of the proto-processes overlapping with exactly the same phase difference in order for the

analysis to be carried out. After that, though one analysis and another deliver them in different phases, they can be identified across studies by serial correla-tion, as with surface processes.

Although component process analysis, and indeed the above concepts and methods for process analysis generally, should pro-vide a powerful aid in the as yet only vaguely approached issues of process psychology experiment, there are both difficult and intriguing technical problems to be solved. Nevertheless, if any sub-stantial advance is to be made in, for ex-ample, the study of autonomic recovery sequences (Lacey & Lacey, 896), cognitive maturational sequences (Gesell, 588), com-plex learning processes (Skinner, 1328; Mowrer, 1084), the unfolding of ergic patterns (Cattell, 240), in humans and in animal ethology (Lorenz, 949), method-ological advances must be made in this direction.

10. SUMMARY

(1) The problems of change measure-ment are varied and of great importance for large areas of learning and maturational research, but only now are they beginning to be seriously studied. A model of five concepts is suggested to cover the chief phenomena: (1) change in a profile of traits, involving *trait-change* factor patterns, phasic and non-phasic, (2) change in tem-porary states, along state-dimension axes, (3) change in environmental *relations,* of individual or group, (4) the study of lability as such, and (5) change embodied in configurations, defining *process* study.

(2) For profile changes on measurable source traits a matrix multiplication model of *Transformation Process Analysis* is pre-sented for handling integration learning effects and learning conceived as "a multi-dimensional change related to experience of a multidimensional situation."

(3) A methodology called *Coordinated*

Change Experiment Design, using comparison of R-technique, dR-technique, and P-technique experiments, is set out for defining and recognizing state dimension factors, trait factors, and trait-change factors.

(4) Change measurement, and the calculations based thereon, make greater demands on dependable scaling concepts, and on clear recognition of assumptions, than is usually vital in individual difference studies. It is suggested that devices to eliminate correlation between absolute base line measures and difference or final measures are usually unwise, as they mask effects and laws we should be interested to discover. Eliminating accidental raw score properties, e.g., bounding effects (ceiling and floor), due to instruments, however, is highly desirable, by the Simplex or the normal distribution procedures. The lower reliabilities of difference scores are not to be avoided by any subsequent statistical acrobatics, but are intrinsic and point to the need of greater emphases on *experimental* error reduction in change studies. It is suggested that *joint change-absolute normalized* standard scores would avoid many difficulties.

(5) Besides attention to these and the usual problem of getting good marker variables, effective design in the area of P technique and differential R technique requires attention to (a) sampling of occasion intervals appropriate to the phenomenon studied, (b) recognition of unusual obliquities in P factors, (c) control of repetition effects (boredom, test sophistication) in two ways, and (d) use of factor-staggered correlations, in an iterative process.

(6) From the standpoint of statistically analyzing and evaluating change without any developed model, which has been done in generations of psychological research, one considers changes in (a) individual scores, (b) mean and modes, (c) sigmas and higher moments, (d) distribution forms, and (e) correlations, covariances, etc. Comment is made on concepts of the "true" change score, testing trends, analysis of variance and covariance, the discriminant function, and reliability measurement, showing that application of standard statistical tools to time-variant data differs at only a few minor points from their familiar use in time-invariant data. A simple relation can be worked out between loadings on trait and trait change factors in the nonphasic but not in the phasic case.

(7) Lability, in the forms of oscillation and fluctuation, needs to be analyzed as a concept relative to traits, states, processes, and persons. Measured by first- or higher-order differentials of absolute measures on a variable over time, it nevertheless shows significant relations to absolute measures on certain personality traits. However, there are at least four of these and lability is thus not a single general personality characteristic.

It is perhaps surprising that Newton's "fluxions" have not found more use in psychological change study, since the differential calculus is the main tool in change study in other sciences. However, effective use has been held up by poor definition of the traits, states and processes to which it could most appropriately be applied. With the advances here indicated in taxonomic definition a fruitful use of the calculus to establish learning and maturation laws should be increasingly evident.

(8) A single instance of a process can be defined as a configuration of changing response scores (endogenously) and of response and environment scores (totally) over time, in a grid matrix $S.EE'$, S', O, O'. This can be condensed to a factor matrix and plotted as a curve in $k+1$ space, the extra dimension being time.

(9) The recognition of a type among processes — either as a surface process or a component or proto-process — cannot be left to casual observation. A taxonomy of processes is the necessary observational beginning for most learning and matura-

tion theory. A particular sequence can be described by a heterogenous facet of stimuli and responses scored over time. By correlating "unravelled" arrays (vectors) over time, each corresponding to a particular sequence, types of "surface processes" may be located. By correlating occasions in the process matrix (for many instances in one person or many persons), component processes can be located as factors. The location of typical surface processes and component or proto-processes as configurations (profiles keyed for time sequence) is important in further work on learning, on dynamic processes, and on maturation.

CHAPTER 12

Canonical Factor Models for the Description of Change*

CHESTER W. HARRIS
University of Wisconsin

1. SCOPE OF THE TREATMENT

This paper has a limited scope and purpose. It is intended to review the relevance to change measurement analysis of the notion of canonical factor analysis, which is a development due to Rao (1179), but one that is related to the earlier development known as the maximum likelihood solution for factor analysis first presented by Lawley (903).

We shall take certain liberties with the work of Lawley and Rao, primarily by underplaying the tests of significance associated with their formulations and emphasizing the features that appear to us to be important considerations in any attempt to describe a population of persons. The point of view implied here is that a careful examination of descriptive procedures is a necessary, if primitive, step in the eventual development of generalizations about populations that are based on samples. We

do not intend to assert that the descriptive problem is the only problem; we do, however, believe that at the present time the modes of describing change need further examination in an effort to clarify alternatives and to emphasize their psychometric strengths and limitations. In this respect we are adopting a point of view that underlies certain work of Guttman (654), namely, that there is a legitimate set of problems centered around the question of how various descriptive measures behave when certain measurement procedures — rather than samples of persons — are varied. A major limitation, then, of this paper is its emphasis on psychometric problems, as distinguished from inferential problems — in the sense of sampling persons.

A long-term interest in the idea of factor analysis provides motivation for the paper, but also prompts the introduction of another limitation. It seems to be a reasonable inference from the books, monographs, and journal articles which include the words "factor analysis" somewhere in the title that this is not a unitary concept. One rather gross, but quite meaningful, distinction that can be made is the distinction between the analysis of the data in hand — either completely or incompletely in the sense of accounting for the total variance in these data — and what has often been labeled a "communality solution." It might assist us — at least in communication — to call the analysis of the data in hand "component analysis" and to leave "factor analysis" for the second category. This crude distinction does not solve all the problems of variant meanings, however. For example, Harman's recent volume (688) adequately documents the point that there are varieties (some of them probably quite trivial variations) within the second category. The limitation imposed here is that of considering only an analysis that might be classified in category two. Further, we shall focus attention on only one of the "methods," but we shall try to show that this is a distinctive method conceptually, as well as differing in computation routine. It is quite evident that the canonical factor model has not been used extensively and has not been discussed widely; however, discussion or use is not an infallible guide to methodology.

A third limitation being imposed is that of concern primarily with problems of describing change in "pattern" or "profile" as distinguished from change in "scale" or "elevation." Let us suppose that for a group of students being introduced to a particular instructional program we secure a number of measures of status, as of that time, and then at the conclusion of the instructional program we repeat these measures. This practice would make available data from a set of pretests and a comparable or possibly "identical" set of posttests for a specified group of students. Presumably these data contain at least a modest amount of information about change (or lack of change) in these students, and the question of how to extract or summarize this information arises. One distinction that can be made is between changes in elevation, as represented, say, by changes in mean score, and changes in pattern or profile.

Concern with changes in pattern or profile would be represented by a question of whether or not the abilities or achievements represented in the battery tend to become "integrated" during the period, tend to remain related in the same fashion, or tend to become more specific. That this is a question of some interest is evident in the speculations about the pattern of growth of intelligence. Let us ignore the many problems connected with the assessment of changes in elevation and focus attention on this problem of changes in pattern. Very roughly, we are slighting the question of the constancy of the IQ in order to attend to the question of whether g increases or decreases. Undoubtedly, Cattell (258) would insist on elaborating the question to include two g's.

2. THE CANONICAL FACTOR MODEL

This section merely describes the canonical factor model without particular reference to the problem of measuring change; in the following section we shall attempt to show the relevance of certain characteristics of the model to this problem. This first section therefore is somewhat abstract.

There appears to be more than one way in which the canonical factor model may be developed. Rao's approach is to consider a set of factor measurements that are uncorrelated with each other. He wishes to choose these arrays in such a way that given a certain restriction, each has a maximum possible correlation with the observed data. Define W as the set of observed data scaled and deviated so that $W'W$ yields the matrix of intercorrelations of the observed variables with units in the diagonal. Throughout we use R to symbolize this matrix of intercorrelations. If S symbolizes these factor measurements, then

$$(1) \quad \begin{bmatrix} W' \\ S' \end{bmatrix} \cdot [W \ S] = \begin{bmatrix} R & F \\ F' & I \end{bmatrix}$$

yields a supermatrix for which a canonical solution results by solving the determinantal equation:

(2) $|FF' - aR| = 0$.

The roots, a_i, of (2) are the squares of the canonical correlations between the set W and the set S. The matrix F symbolizes the correlations between the observed data, W, and the factor measurements or factor scores.

What we earlier called a component analysis can now be defined with respect to (1) and (2). Suppose we require that $FF' = R$; then (2) has a solution for which every root, a_i, equals unity when R is non-singular. (If R is of rank less than its order, then one or more a_i may be zero.) Under these conditions, the matrix S is a linear transformation of the observations, W, and consequently is a set of factor measurements, or factor scores, that can be computed rather than estimated. If, however, we require that FF' reproduce only the off-diagonal elements of R (reproduce the correlations, but not the unit diagonals), we in effect define $FF' = R - U^2$, where U^2 is a diagonal matrix of unique variances. With this definition we may modify (2) thus:

(3) $|R - U^2 - aR| = 0$,

or

$|R - bU^2| = 0$,

where $b_i = 1/(1 - a_i)$. It should be evident that (3) cannot be developed from (2) when any a_i is permitted to equal unity. One way to define a communality solution is to specify that (3) holds as well as (2). The restriction on the arrays of S that is implicit in the Rao procedure is that they be hypothetical, i.e., that W' approximate rather than equal FS'. See Harris (691). When this restriction is introduced, we also restrict the squares of the canonical correlations, a_i, to less than unity.

Another treatment of the supermatrix of (1) would yield the determinantal equation:

(4) $|F'R^{-1}F - aI| = 0$.

The roots of (4) are identical with the roots of (2); see T. W. Anderson (33, pp. 340-341). Once again, a component analysis is implied by (4) when F is the complete set of correlations yielded by a linear transformation of the elements of R. Note that (4) may be written only if R is non-singular; if so, then $FF' = R$ implies $F'R^{-1}F = I$, and each $a_i = 1$. When $FF' = R - U^2$, Equation (4), following the standard canonical analysis, indicates that the characteristic vectors of $F'R^{-1}F$ give the relative weights to be used in making linear combinations of the elements of S that will have the maximum, next to maximum, etc., correlation with the appropriate linear combinations of W.

Equation (4) may be derived in a slightly different fashion. Let us now consider a set of hypothetical factor measurements, or factor scores, S, and their least-squares approximations, $\bar{S}$. The standard procedure (Harman, 688, pp. 338-348) directs that $\bar{S}'$ be estimated by

(5) $S' = F'R^{-1}W'$,

with the result that

(6) $\bar{S}'\bar{S} = \bar{S}'S = S'\bar{S} = F'R^{-1}F$.

Therefore the supermatrix generated by the hypothetical and the estimated factor scores is

(7) $\begin{bmatrix} I & F'R^{-1}F \\ F'R^{-1}F & F'R^{-1}F \end{bmatrix}$.

A canonical solution for this matrix is given by the determinantal equation already written as (4). For the case of $FF' = R$, (7) reduces to a set of four identity matrices, each of the same order, and the roots of (4) must each be unity. The case of $FF' = R - U^2$ can be solved with $F'R^{-1}F$ equal to a diagonal matrix of the roots, a_i; for such a solution, the least-squares estimators of the hypothetical factor scores have zero covariances with each other and with all but one of the set of hypothetical factor scores. We shall show below in (13) that under the restriction $FF' = R - U^2$, a canonical factor matrix F is such that (7) becomes

$$(7a) \quad \begin{bmatrix} I & D_a \\ D_a & D_a \end{bmatrix}.$$

This point may not have been made explicit before. It is a meaningful one for those who would seek to "rotate" or transform the least-squares estimators of hypothetical factor scores into arrays that have maximum correlation with the hypothetical factor scores.

A third approach to canonical factors is by way of the relationship between factors of R itself and factors of $R - U^2$. Since this relationship has been examined in some detail elsewhere (690b), it will not be repeated here.

Let us now return to equation (3) and require that the diagonal matrix of unique variances, U^2, to be admissible, be positive-definite. This device rules out communalities of unity. Our preference is to regard an analysis that admits one or more communalities of unity as belonging to category one — component analysis — rather than category two — factor analysis. We shall also require that R be positive-definite. With both R and U^2 positive-definite (Gramian and non-singular), (3) may be transformed into

$$(3a) \quad |U^{-1}RU^{-1} - bI| = 0,$$

and we deduce that all the roots, b_i, are greater than zero. The complete set of normalized characteristic vectors of $U^{-1}RU^{-1}$ may be symbolized as Q, and we may write

$$(8) \quad U^{-1}RU^{-1} = Q[b_i]Q',$$

$$(9) \quad R = UQ[b_i]Q'U,$$

and

$$(10) \quad R^{-1} = U^{-1}Q[1/b_i]Q'U^{-1}.$$

The internal matrices, $[b_i]$ and $[1/b_i]$, are diagonal. For any positive-definite U^2, then, we may write

$$(11) \quad R - U^2 = UQ[b_i - 1]Q'U,$$

noting that some of the entries in the diagonal matrix, $[b_i - 1]$, may be negative. Equation (11) locates for us the major problem: that of choosing a matrix U^2 such that $R - U^2$ will be Gramian, with the related conditions that F is real and no b_i is less than unity.

Let us assume for a moment that we can choose a matrix U^2 such that $R - U^2$ is Gramian. If so, we can write as the factors of $R - U^2$

$$(12) \quad F = UQ[b_i - 1]^{1/2},$$

and then, using (10), observe that

$$(13) \quad F'R^{-1}F = \left[\frac{b_i - 1}{b_i}\right].$$

The relationship $b_i = 1/(1 - a_i)$, established above, shows that the right side of (13) is the diagonal matrix of roots, a_i. Equation (13) holds generally for any $R - U^2$ expressed as in (11), but when $R - U^2$ is not Gramian, some of the a_i's are negative, corresponding to imaginary canonical correlations.

One feature of the canonical factor model that may be deduced from (3a) and our operations on it to secure (11) is that the communality problem can be translated into the problem of rescaling the standardized data by a diagonal matrix, U^{-1}, to achieve roots, b_i, of (3a), none of which is less than unity. This may seem incongruous, since we typically consider communalities in the context of reducing the rank of $R - U^2$, i.e., requiring some of the b_i to be unity. The canonical factor model permits this reduction of rank, which has as a consequence that some of the a_i's are zero. However, a real F, as in (12), can be secured without rank reduction. Later we shall comment on the functional utility of the requirement that $R - U^2$ be Gramian in estimating the elements of the matrix U^2; we shall also point out that adding a requirement that $R - U^2$ be singular or of minimum rank gives no obvious assistance in this estimation process.

A second feature of the canonical factor model is its independence of the original, and possibly arbitrary, scale of the variables. Let us assume that instead of beginning the analysis with R, the correlation matrix, we began with the variance-covariance matrix CRC, say. (C is diagonal.) We could arrive by regular steps at an analog of (3):

(3b) $\quad | CRC - bCU^2C | = 0,$

which would transform into the (3a) we have already written. In other words, the roots, b_i, of (3) are invariant when the equation is premultiplied and postmultiplied by a non-singular matrix. Consequently, when we "control" our solution by specifying the desired characteristics of the roots, b_i, we need not be concerned with the original scale of the data. It may be more convenient to work with R than with CRC, though this is not necessarily true since a machine program might be written either way. Convenience is not the issue, however. This feature is extremely important in the case where we can conceive of various meaningful patterns of weightings of the variables and wish to examine the factor results for these several weighting systems. This will be considered again in the next section where we take up difference scores that vary as functions of weightings applied to the original variables and show that from one canonical factor analysis we can recover the analyses that would have been secured for the various weighting schemes. The general principle, illustrated with the covariance matrix, is that if the F of (12) is a satisfactory solution for $R - U^2$, then CF is the comparable solution based on the covariance matrix.

3. INITIAL ESTIMATION OF U^2

The mode of attack used here translates the problem of estimating communalities into the problem of rescaling the data so as to achieve a desired set of roots of (3) or

(3a). The representation given in (11) indicates that $R - U^2$ will be Gramian if, and only if, no b_i is less than unity. Translating this into a requirement on the a_i, we have $R - U^2$ Gramian when all a_i's are in the interval $1 > a_i \geq 0$, and consequently all the canonical correlations are real.

Let us manufacture a matrix whose roots are the a_i. We invert $U^{-1}RU^{-1}$, of (3a), and then write

(14) $\quad | I - UR^{-1}U - aI | = 0$

to achieve this. For $R - U^2$ to be Gramian, it is necessary that every diagonal element of $I - UR^{-1}U$ be positive, providing we have not included in the set of variables one or more that is uncorrelated with all the others. This procedural rule will be assumed in what follows. Therefore:

$$1 - u_j^2 r^{jj} > 0,$$

which is equivalent to

(15) $\quad u_j^2 < 1/r^{jj}.$

We are using u_j^2 as a symbol for the diagonal elements of U^2 and r^{jj} for the diagonal elements of R^{-1}. Inequality (15) gives the familiar squared multiple correlation of each variable with the remaining variables in the set as a lower bound to the communality of the variable. Here we have written this relation as an upper bound to the unique variance, u_j^2. Guttman (654) developed our (15) without the procedural rule and consequently allowed u_j^2 to equal $1/r^{jj}$.

Let s_j^2 designate $1/r^{jj}$, and write U_s^2 to symbolize the diagonal matrix of these upper bounds to the unique variances. If we substitute U_s^2 for the essentially unspecified U^2 of (3a), we can deduce several generalizations. One is that Guttman's "best" lower bound to the number of common factors is exactly equal to the number of roots of $U_s^{-1}RU_s^{-1}$ that equal or exceed unity. Another is that at least one of these roots must be less than unity, and consequently no F consisting only of real columns can reproduce $R - U_s^2$; this is equivalent to saying that $R - U_s^2$ cannot be Gramian. A third is that the characteristic vectors and roots of $U_s^{-1}RU_s^{-1}$ can be employed to generate the factors of Guttman's image covariance matrix (651), and that the real portion of an F that reproduces $R - U_s^2$ is in a particular sense merely an approximation to the factors of this image covariance matrix. The proofs of these statements have been given elsewhere (Harris, 691). The pertinent conclusion here is that U_s^2 is not a "proper" set of unique variances, though it may be a satisfactory set of initial estimators that can be modified in some regular manner to yield a U^2 for which $R - U^2$ is Gramian. This statement should not be misinterpreted as a criticism of the s_j^2 quantities. They are excellent numbers for certain purposes, and we are now at work collecting some empirical examples which we hope will show that the factors of the image covariance matrix, which itself depends only on R and U_s^2, have certain virtues. Our criticism is of the use of the s_j^2 as if they were equivalent to the u_j^2 short of the limit reached as the number of variables increases indefinitely.

We can manufacture another matrix whose roots are $(a_i^2 - a_i)$; this matrix is $(UR^{-1}U - I)(UR^{-1}U)$. Now if $1 > a_i \geq 0$, then every trace element of $(UR^{-1} - I)(UR^{-1}U)$ must be negative. In detail, this is the requirement that

$$u_1^2 \left[\sum_{j=1}^{j=p} (u_j r^{1j})^2 - (r^{11}) \right] < 0,$$

$$u_2^2 \left[\sum_{j=1}^{j=p} (u_j r^{2j})^2 - (r^{22}) \right] < 0,$$

$$(16) \quad \cdots\cdots\cdots\cdots\cdots\cdots,$$

$$u_p^2 \left[\sum_{j=1}^{j=p} (u_j r^{pj})^2 - (r^{pp}) \right] < 0.$$

Let us assume that U^2 is positive-definite; then the inequality

$$(17) \quad [u_j^2] \cdot [(r^{jk})^2] < [r^{jj}]$$

must hold. Here $[u_j^2]$ is a row vector of the unique variances; $[(r^{jk})^2]$ is the square matrix, of order p, whose elements consist of the *squares* of the corresponding elements of R^{-1}; and $[r^{jj}]$ is a row vector of the diagonal elements of R^{-1}. A matrix U^2 might therefore be estimated by solving (17) in some fashion. One approach would be to consider this a standard linear programming problem, subject to a restriction such as maximizing the trace of $I - UR^{-1}U$. We have not yet had time to explore this approach, first with artificial problems for which the "true" u_j^2's are known and then with empirical data that have been studied in some detail by other factoring procedures; however, we intend to.

Another approach is to modify (17) to

$$(17a) \quad [v_j^2] = [r^{jj}] \cdot [(r^{jk})^2]^{-1},$$

where we use a new symbol, v_j^2, to indicate estimates of the u_j^2. The matrix $[(r^{jk})^2]$, which was constructed from the elements of R^{-1}, is non-singular and has an inverse; therefore (17a) is possible. The results of solving (17a) can, however, present a problem of negative values for one or more v_j^2. Table 12-1 illustrates this. We took a "Heywood case" from Thomson (1393, p. 231) and made the calculations presented in Table 12-1. Note that the "true" U^2 is not positive-definite; thus (16) should hold, but not (17) or (17a). From Table 12-1 it is evident that for variable 1 we have a negative value of v_j^2 corresponding to the negative "true" u_j^2. Apparently the v_j^2's are, in some as yet unexplained fashion, sensitive to the rank of the off-diagonal elements of R. This would seem to be a good feature. However, the warning that negative values can be secured is important to keep in mind in exploring this relatively unknown territory. In contrast to the "Heywood case," we have had apparently good success with the v_j^2 for empirical data.

Although our development of the v_j^2 was independently arrived at, we find that Guttman (655a) proposed these same quantities as estimators of the unique variances earlier. He arrived at them by considering $I - UR^{-1}U$, rather than by our route. He set the requirement that the sum of squares of the elements of $I - UR^{-1}U$ be a minimum, and then by partial differentiation developed the v_j^2 of (17a) as the quantities which, when substituted for the u_j^2, achieve this minimum. The rationale is that $UR^{-1}U$ is the matrix of covariances of the estimated unique factors; the minimization secures estimated unique factors whose covariances fit the identity matrix as closely as possible. This quite different approach to the development of the v_j^2 throws additional light on them as estimators of the u_j^2.

One would like to be able to show a systematic bias of the form $v_j^2 > u_j^2$, since then it would be possible to specify the conditions necessary for the chain of inequalities of the form $0 < u_j^2 < v_j^2 < s_j^2 < 1$ to hold. A similar boundary question will arise for estimates derived from a linear programming solution to (17). At present, then, we see the Guttman-Harris v_j^2 as estimators of the unique variances that have certain desirable characteristics and certain limitations. For example, the necessary condition of (17) is not satisfied by substituting v_j^2 for u_j^2.

Further, it does not seem possible, using the techniques of analysis we are employing

TABLE 12-1

ESTIMATES OF THE UNIQUE VARIANCES FOR A "HEYWOOD CASE"*

R	1.000				
	.945	1.000			
	.840	.720	1.000		
	.735	.630	.560	1.000	
	.630	.540	.480	.420	1.000
R^{-1}	38.128395				
	−22.144176	15.504227			
	−10.387650	4.803767	5.031187		
	−6.415902	2.967033	1.391812	2.820433	
	−4.382278	2.026583	0.950652	0.587166	1.963557
$[(r^{jk})^2]^{-1}$	.004608				
	−.007680	.017551			
	−.011323	.014995	.071525		
	−.012119	.016051	.023712	.163912	
	−.011032	.014610	.021539	.023053	.291640
s_i^2	.0262	.0645	.1989	.3546	.5093
v_i^2	−.0562	.1287	.2698	.4136	.5504
"true" u_i^2	−.1025	.1900	.3600	.5100	.6400

*Matrix R from Thomson (1393, p. 231).

Another problem is buried in here. It is the question of under what conditions the v_j^2 will, individually, be upper bounds to the "true" u_j^2. We were led to the v_j^2 by an attempt to find new and more restrictive bounds than the familiar s_j^2 quantities. However, this appears to be a complicated problem that will take additional study.

here, to improve these estimates by adding a requirement that $R - U^2$ be singular or of minimum rank. The reason is that in our development we restricted the a_i to the interval $1 > a_i \geq 0$, thus permitting but not requiring singularity of $R - U^2$. The deduction of the necessary character of trace elements follows from the requirement that

$R - U^2$ be Gramian, and cannot be strengthened by adding a singularity requirement. Apparently improved estimators, if there are such that are functions of R, will have to be developed along other lines.

In summary, two different diagonal matrices might be taken as the initial estimators of U^2. One is U_s^2, whose non-zero elements are the Guttman s_j^2; the other is U_v^2, whose non-zero elements are the Guttman-Harris v_j^2. It is generally true that each v_j^2 is less than the corresponding s_j^2; consequently the v_j^2 may be better initial estimators of the u_j^2. Recall, however, that the boundary problem has not yet been solved satisfactorily. As for U_s^2, we can also show that $R - U_v^2$ is not Gramian; this follows immediately by noting that the v_j^2's, when substituted for the u_j^2's, give trace elements of zero for $(UR^{-1}U - I)(UR^{-1}U)$, and thus force at least one a_i to be negative. Both sets of estimators, therefore, should be modified in some fashion if we are to secure a canonical factor solution with a maximum number of real columns of F.

4. MODIFICATION OF THE INITIAL ESTIMATES

Rao (1179) provides a scheme for taking initial estimates of the unique variances and then converging them to a stable set for a fixed number of factors. The procedure is to introduce the initial set of estimates into (3a), solve for the roots and vectors, and then construct a new set of estimates by

$$(18) \quad {}_2u_j^{-2} = \sum_{i=1}^{i=m} ({}_1b_i - 1){}_1\hat{q}_{ji}^2 + 1,$$

where ${}_1b_i$ designates the roots of (3a) secured with the initial set of estimates, and the summation is for some fixed number, m, of roots and columns of the normalized characteristic vectors. The elements ${}_1q_{ji}$ appear in the jth row and i^{th} column of the initial Q. Repeated application of (18) for a fixed m, each time securing the new characteristic vectors and roots

associated with the new estimates of uniqueness, should, according to Rao, converge the initial estimates to a stable set of values, within some chosen tolerance range.

All this is quite easy to say; however, merely saying it does not necessarily guarantee that certain problems have been solved. As one example, it is relatively simple to show that if one fixes m as the number of roots greater than unity in the solution of (3a) when the initial estimates of the unique variances are employed, then the second set of estimates of the unique variances will each be less than the corresponding initial estimate. Thus a rule such as this for choosing m is most appropriate when it can be demonstrated that the initial estimates are each too large. Recall that this is true for the matrix U_s^2 and may be true under certain conditions for the matrix U_v^2. In the illustration given in the second section we have adopted this rule. With U_s^2 as the initial set of estimates, this rule is consistent with the fact that the number of positive roots of $R - U_s^2$, which equals the number of roots of $U_s^{-1}RU_s^{-1}$ that exceed unity, is a lower bound to the number of common factors. We have also used this rule when we take U_v^2 as the initial set of estimates of the unique variances; this use is tentative and not completely justified.

Another interesting problem arises. Even though we fix m in the fashion described above for the purpose of iteration, the "final" set of uniqueness estimates, U_f^2 say, are likely to be such that $U_f^{-1}RU_f^{-1}$ has more than m roots that are greater than unity. If we then construct our factors in the fashion outlined in (12), we may choose either m real columns for our F, or some larger number that corresponds to this number of roots greater than unity. We have done the latter, and then relied on a rotation process to identify factors that are essentially null. These procedures clearly move in the direction of extracting what ordinarily would be regarded as a very large number of factors, relative to the number of variables. We believe, however, that this is a strategy that is growing in acceptance.

These comments emphasize the point that several specifications must enter into any clear description of how a particular set of canonical factors was developed. The general need for clearer descriptions of how any particular set of factors was arrived at is evident in many of the reports of research. We can summarize here the canonical factor model as we have used it in the work reported in the next section:

Type A: We use U_s^2 as the initial set of estimates of uniqueness.

We specify m to be the number of roots of $U_s^{-1}RU_s^{-1}$ that are greater than unity, and we use (18) to converge the estimates with a .005 tolerance.

We construct, by (12), all the real columns of F, which is generally greater than m.

Type B: We use U_v^2 as the initial set of estimates of uniqueness.

We specify m to be the number of roots of $U_v^{-1}RU_v^{-1}$ that are greater than unity, and we use (18) to converge the estimates with a .005 tolerance.

We construct, by (12), all the real columns of F, which is generally greater than m.

Note that m may differ for *Type A* and *Type B*, with the m for *Type B* being larger. Following the analysis, we have used Kaiser's "normal" varimax procedure (835; 688, pp. 302-308) to yield a derived set of orthogonal factors.

5. APPLICATION TO THE DESCRIPTION OF CHANGE

Our interest in the profile or pattern problem has been stated above. Given, for the same set of individuals, the "same" battery administered on two occasions, the relationships both within and between batteries over the two occasions may be expressed as correlation coefficients, yielding the supermatrix:

$$(19) \quad \begin{bmatrix} R_{11} & R_{12} \\ R_{21} & R_{22} \end{bmatrix}.$$

The intercorrelations for the first administration appear in R_{11}, which is assumed to have units in the diagonals. R_{12} and its transpose R_{21} give the correlations across occasions. R_{22} designates the intercorrelations, with units in the diagonal, for occasion 2. If we substitute (19) for the R of equation (3a), we can develop a set of canonical factors which for convenience can be written as the supermatrix:

$$(20) \quad \begin{bmatrix} F_1 \\ F_2 \end{bmatrix},$$

with

$$(21) \quad \begin{bmatrix} F_1 F_1' & F_1 F_2' \\ F_2 F_1' & F_2 F_2' \end{bmatrix}$$

reproducing

$$(22) \quad \begin{bmatrix} R_{11} - U_1^2 & R_{12} \\ R_{21} & R_{22} - U_2^2 \end{bmatrix}$$

to a satisfactory degree of approximation.

We have taken data studied by Meyer and Bendig (1053) as an illustration of our methods. Professor Bendig kindly provided all the correlations necessary for the analysis, since the complete R_{12} matrix of (19) does not appear in the journal article; we wish to express our appreciation to him. The data are based on observations from 49 boys and 61 girls and were gathered at Grade 8 and Grade 11. The Primary Mental Abilities Test, Intermediate Form, yielded scores on V, S, R, N, and W for each of the two occasions. In addition, the Myers-Ruch High School Achievement Test was administered to the students in Grade 11. Eleven variables (five PMA measures on each of two occasions and the achievement test) were available for analysis. Meyer and Bendig used a centroid analysis, extracting five factors that were rotated to an oblique solution. Boys and girls were treated separately. Their results yield the expected first-order factors, V, S, R, N, and W, and two second-order factors.

Our analysis of the Meyer and Bendig data gives a slightly different picture. The results for girls are presented in Table 12-2 and the results for boys in Table 12-3. Both Table 12-2 and Table 12-3 give two analyses: our *Type A* and *Type B*. The varimax rotated solutions rather than the

seven factors. However, Table 12-3, the data for the boys, shows that factor 7 differs somewhat for the two types of solution. At this stage, one might have slightly more confidence in the *Type A* solution, and so it will be chosen for the interpretation below.

Factors 2, 3, and 4 have sufficient similarity for both boys and girls to be regarded as essentially the same. Factor 1

TABLE 12-2

ROTATED CANONICAL FACTORS – GIRLS

		1	2	3	4	5	6	7	h^2
				Type A solution					
Grade 8	V	.32	.25	.04	.77	.13	.10	.17	.83
	S	.11	.80	.23	.16	.04	.26	.13	.83
	R	.16	.15	.79	.18	.23	.16	.02	.81
	N	.77	−.05	.13	.25	.13	.01	.27	.76
	W	.12	.07	.18	.12	.66	.18	.01	.53
Grade 11	Ach	.01	.13	.26	.70	.08	−.13	−.09	.63
	V	.61	.27	.14	.56	.07	.07	−.01	.84
	S	−.02	.88	.11	.22	.08	.11	−.11	.87
	R	.32	.19	.76	.16	.09	.01	−.01	.77
	N	.81	.04	.26	.00	.05	−.01	−.18	.76
	W	.00	.23	.09	−.04	.18	.69	.00	.58
				Type B solution					
Grade 8	V	.25	.21	.05	.84	.11	.13	.12	.87
	S	.09	.81	.23	.18	.01	.29	.15	.87
	R	.15	.14	.81	.18	.24	.16	.03	.84
	N	.75	−.06	.12	.30	.13	.01	.33	.80
	W	.11	.06	.19	.14	.62	.19	.01	.49
Grade 11	Ach	.01	.14	.28	.65	.12	−.21	−.06	.58
	V	.57	.26	.14	.63	.03	.11	−.06	.84
	S	.02	.87	.11	.23	.09	.09	−.13	.87
	R	.32	.20	.76	.17	.08	.01	−.01	.78
	N	.83	.04	.25	.03	.07	−.02	−.14	.79
	W	−.01	.24	.09	−.03	.21	.60	.00	.47

original canonical factors are presented. In each instance eight factors were produced and rotated, and then one factor with no coefficients outside the ±.15 range was dropped. Table 12-2 indicates that the *Type A* solution, which uses U_s^2 as the initial estimate of uniqueness, and the *Type B* solution, which uses U_v^2 as the initial estimates, yield very similar results for all

differs at least slightly for the two sexes: note the differences for Grade 11, Achievement and V. For the girls, factors 5 and 6 split W into two factors: one for Grade 8 and one for Grade 11; whereas factor 5 is a single W factor for the boys. These differences are consistent with the original crosscorrelations; for girls, the first and second administrations of W correlate only .27, whereas for boys the correlation is .52. For the girls, factor 7 suggests that the first administration of N has a modest specificity; there is no such evidence for the boys. There is, for the boys, an analogous suggestion of specificity for the Grade 8, S score in factor 7; this is particularly evident in the *Type B* solution. Finally, factor 6 for the boys suggests a specific for the Achievement variable which is not evident for the girls.

Let us now propose a somewhat unorthodox mode of interpretation. First, since these are canonical factors that have been rotated by the normal varimax procedure, we might multiply any row of the factor matrix by any constant we would choose and regard these new values as the ones we would have secured by using our procedure on the weighted variables. Note that the separability of scale that characterizes the Rao procedure and the normalizing feature of the varimax rotation both are required for this to be true. Second, since we rotated all eleven variables simultaneously, we have in effect kept the factor scores the same but allowed the correlations of the variables with these hypothetical factor scores to differ for the two occasions. This procedure has in effect fixed the individuals' hypothetical measures of ability in a given factor, and then allowed variables that are indexed by the same symbol to have different correlations with the factor at different times. This may seem strange, since in effect we are stating that the individuals have not changed, but the variables may have. Under this restriction

TABLE 12-3

ROTATED CANONICAL FACTORS – BOYS

		1	2	3	4	5	6	7	h^2
					Type A solution				
Grade 8	V	.31	.25	.24	.74	.31	−.13	.09	.89
	S	.12	.71	.20	.13	−.02	.08	.24	.65
	R	.15	.11	.80	.39	−.10	−.01	−.08	.86
	N	.81	−.05	.21	.32	.11	.08	.04	.84
	W	.02	.03	.00	.22	.81	−.09	.23	.77
Grade 11	Ach	.27	.18	.29	.66	.14	.27	.02	.72
	V	.29	.23	.21	.81	.20	−.06	−.06	.89
	S	.04	.75	.02	.21	.07	−.06	−.19	.65
	R	.34	.14	.82	.14	.16	.03	.10	.87
	N	.86	.10	.23	.23	.07	−.04	−.02	.88
	W	.12	.02	.04	.09	.67	.08	−.18	.51
					Type B solution				
Grade 8	V	.29	.19	.23	.76	.33	−.22	.15	.93
	S	.10	.49	.19	.17	−.03	.00	.62	.70
	R	.15	.11	.83	.39	−.11	−.02	−.01	.92
	N	.81	−.10	.20	.33	.13	.08	.08	.89
	W	.01	−.02	.00	.19	.89	−.10	.12	.85
Grade 11	Ach	.25	.11	.28	.68	.15	.26	.15	.73
	V	.28	.24	.21	.83	.21	−.03	.00	.91
	S	−.02	.80	.04	.19	.07	.00	.13	.70
	R	.32	.03	.84	.15	.17	.04	.20	.94
	N	.90	.09	.22	.23	.07	−.05	.03	.95
	W	.12	.07	.04	.11	.59	.09	−.09	.39

of fixed factor scores it is quite legitimate to look at differences in factor coefficients for the "same" variable on the two occasions with respect to the same factor. Note that when (21) adequately reproduces (22), we can derive the difference matrix $F_2 - F_1$ (restricted, of course, to only those variables common to the two occasions) by operating on (22) with the signs of the elements of R_{21} and R_{12} all reversed. Thus, $F_2 - F_1$ reproduces $R_{11} + R_{22} - R_{21} - R_{12} - U_1^2 - U_2^2$. We are here advancing the speculation that had we begun the analysis with

doubtedly is distasteful to some. Further rotations on the derived matrices of Tables 12-4 and 12-5 might be made in the hope of nullifying at least two of the factors in each instance and thus bringing the results in line with the conventional doctrine that one should not have more *common* factors than variables. Someone may wish to do this. Here we merely present the tables and make some crude observations.

The simple differences, $F_2 - F_1$, appear in Table 12-4. For girls, variables N and W, and possibly V, appear to be measuring

TABLE 12-4

APPROXIMATE FACTORS OF COVARIANCES OF DIFFERENCES IN STANDARD SCORES

	1	2	3	4	5	6	7
				Girls			
V	.29	.02	.10	−.21	−.06	−.03	−.18
S	−.13	.08	−.12	.06	.04	−.15	−.24
R	.16	.04	−.03	−.02	−.14	−.15	−.03
N	.04	.09	.13	−.25	−.07	−.02	−.45
W	−.12	.16	−.09	−.16	−.48	.51	−.01
				Boys			
V	−.02	−.02	−.03	.07	−.11	.07	−.15
S	−.08	.04	−.18	.08	.09	−.14	−.43
R	.19	.03	.02	−.25	.26	.04	.18
N	.05	.15	.02	−.09	−.04	−.12	−.06
W	.10	−.01	.04	−.13	−.14	.17	−.41

$R_{11} + R_{22} - R_{12} - R_{21}$ as our matrix of interest, we would have secured $U_1^2 + U_2^2$ as the appropriate uniqueness estimates, and thus can regard $F_2 - F_1$ as the factors that would have resulted from taking differences in standard scores across occasions as the five variables of interest. If this is correct, we can also apply diagonal matrices of weights as premultipliers of F_2, F_1, or both of them, to secure factors of differentially weighted differences in standard scores.

It is obvious from Tables 12-4 and 12-5 that this unorthodox approach to interpretation has given us seven factors for the five variables (pairs of tests). This un-

something different on the two occasions; for boys, variables R, S, and W appear to function differently. If, as we believe, the material of Table 12-4 approximates the factors of the covariances of the differences in standard scores taken as variables, then the familiar point that factoring the covariances of such differences may not be very informative is given some support. It should be noted that the variance for a difference between standard scores can readily be calculated when one knows the correlation across occasions for the designated variable, and thus one could multiply each row of Table 12-4 by the appropriate constant to approximate the results of factoring the normalized covariances, or correlations, of these differences in standard scores. Since the variance for such a difference equals $2(1 - r_{12})$, where r_{12} designates the correlation across occasions, we note would have been secured from a factoring of the correlations of these residuals. For non-zero r^2_{12}, the variance is less than one; consequently, for the data of Table 12-5, the adjustment would consist generally of

TABLE 12-5

APPROXIMATE FACTORS OF COVARIANCES OF "RESIDUAL" GAINS

	1	2	3	4	5	6	7
				Girls			
V	.37	.08	.11	−.01	−.03	.00	−.14
S	−.11	.26	−.07	.10	.05	−.09	−.21
R	.21	.08	.20	.03	−.07	−.10	−.02
N	.32	.07	.18	−.16	−.03	−.02	−.35
W	−.03	.21	.04	−.07	.00	.64	.00
				Boys			
V	.02	.01	.00	.16	−.07	.05	−.14
S	−.02	.39	−.08	.14	.08	−.10	−.31
R	.23	.06	.21	−.16	.24	.04	.16
N	.19	−.14	.06	−.04	−.02	−.11	−.05
W	.11	.00	.04	−.02	.25	.13	−.30

that the appropriate weights (the reciprocals of the standard deviations) are unity when r_{12} equals $+.50$, and greater than unity when r_{12} exceeds $+.50$. For variables that are substantially correlated across occasions, the effect of this transformation is to increase the magnitudes of the non-zero entries in Table 12-4 but not to change sign.

In Table 12-5, we give the differences between the entries in F_2 and the entries in F_1 when these are weighted by the correlation across occasions for the designated variable. Thus Table 12-5 approximates what would have been secured had we factored not the covariances of the differences in standard scores for the two occasions, but the covariances of the portions of the variables on occasion 2 that cannot be predicted (linearly) from the data of occasion 1. In this case the variance of these "residual" scores is $1 - r_{12}$; consequently an analogous transformation of the data of Table 12-5 might be made to approximate the values that

increasing the magnitude — often substantially — of the non-zero values.

The major point of this example has been that — given a certain methodology — one can derive at least an approximate factorial description of "change" from the factorial description of the data for the two occasions. Here we illustrated with two somewhat different definitions of change; other definitions, as long as only linear combinations of the standard scores are involved, might have been used. Our methods explicitly rest upon fixing the factor measurements (factor scores) for the individuals and then observing differences (weighted in some fashion) between the correlations with the factor of the variable on the two occasions.

6. SUMMARY

(1) Canonical factor analysis is a development due to Rao, but related, however, to the maximum likelihood solution first presented by Lawley.

(2) The canonical model is first described in itself, without reference to applications to change.

(3) The problem of estimating communalities becomes here that of rescaling the data to get a desired set of roots.

(4) Certain problems are discussed in relation to converging the unique variance estimates in relation to a fixed number of factors.

(5) The method is then applied to the general problem of data gathered with the same tests and same individuals on two occasions.

(6) As an example, the data of Meyer and Bendig applying Thurstone's PMA on two occasions is analyzed, arriving at a description of the factors in change from the factor description of the data on two occasions.

CHAPTER **13**   # Games Theory,
Decision Processes, and
Man-Machine Interaction

DAVID H. BRAND*
Systems Research Laboratories, Inc.

1. INTRODUCTION

This chapter briefly presents concepts and fundamentals of man-machine interactions, game theory, and multivariate decision processes. It is divided into six technical sections and a summary which discuss conditional probability, Bayesian statistical inference, two-person game theory, n-person game theory, multivariate models of decision processes, and man-machine interaction. The sequencing of the sections allows the reader to apply basic course work and interest in statistics to the development of formal techniques and problems related to decision-making and psychological aspects of man-machine interaction.

A *decision* can be thought of as *the act of selecting one from a number of alternate courses*. A process, system, or circumstance which needs decisions is a *decision process* and will be used in this frame of reference throughout the chapter. The material

*The author expresses appreciation to Robert M. Colomb, Systems Research Laboratories, Inc., for his assistance in preparing Sections 2 and 3.

covered represents a cross-section of current decision processes ranging from relatively straightforward hypothesis tests to exceedingly complex man-machine systems. In confronting the advanced psychologist with the inherent psychological problems basic to effective, formalized man-machine interaction, and decision processes, it is hoped that mixed-discipline solutions will be shortly forthcoming.

Section 2 lifts the reader easily into the domain of conditional probabilities—probabilities of events happening knowing that other events have already happened. Markov chains and Bayesian statistics are then introduced. Section 3 continues with an exploration of subjective and personal probabilities, emphasizing their utility in Bayes' theorem. A simple example of statistical inference is presented.

Sections 4 and 5 define the basic concepts of game theory and discuss game methodology in sufficient detail for the beginner. Both two-person and n-person zero-sum and non-zero-sum games are presented with an introduction to minimax techniques.

Section 6 outlines a few important multi-

417

variate models useful in describing and characterizing decision processes. Multivariate distribution theory and adaptive control systems techniques are discussed.

Section 7 deals with probably the most significant area of interest to the psychologist in this chapter — man-machine interaction. Using previously derived notions of Bayesian statistics and decision processes, the problems of optimal man-machine system design are described and presented as significant challenges to the psychologist.

Section 8 briefly summarizes the technical sections.

2. CONDITIONAL PROBABILITY THEORY

Conditional probability[1] theory deals with questions of the type "What is the probability that event B will occur given that event A has already occurred?" This kind of problem might arise if an investigator wished to determine whether or not a subject would perform rationally[2] in an experimental environment. The investigator might suspect that the subject belongs to a particular psychological class (say, a class consists of certain psychological traits — again a justification similar to that in Footnote 2) and can derive a probability that if the subject were of a particular psychological class, he would perform rationally. Many statistical concepts can be stated in terms of *conditional probability.*

Distribution Functions of Random Variables — Dependence

A random variable has associated with it a *distribution function* which assigns to every value of the random variable a probability that that value will be taken by a given sample. It is possible to consider the distribution function of two or more random variables taken together. If X_1 and X_2 are two random variables, and $P_1(X_1=x)$, $P_2(X_2=y)$ are their respective distribution functions, then their *joint distribution* $P(X_1=x, X_2=y)$ is the probability that a sample of X_1 with the value x will be paired with a sample of X_2 with the value y.

This is defined to be

$$P(X_2=y \mid X_1=x)P_1(X_1=x)$$

where $P(X_2=y \mid X_1=x)$ is the probability that $X_2=y$ given that X_1 has already been observed to have the value x. This is the explicit form of a conditional probability.

In the example presented in the introduction to this section, we can take X_1 to be the possible psychological classes of the subject and X_2 to be whether the subject behaves rationally. We then have $P_1(X_1)$ equal to the probability of the occurrence of a given class, and $P_2(X_2)$ equal to the probability that a subject will behave rationally irrespective of his psychological class. $P(X_1 = \text{normal}, X_2 = \text{rational})$ is the probability that a given subject will both be in a "normal" class and behave rationally. $P(X_2 = \text{rational} \mid X_1 = \text{normal})$ is the probability that a normal subject will behave rationally.

The general conditional probability distribution function is

$$P(X_2 \mid X_1)$$

and

$$P(X_1, X_2) = P(X_2 \mid X_1)P_1(X_1)$$

is the joint probability distribution of two random variables.

In general, $P(X_2 \mid X_1)$ will not be equal to $P_2(X_2)$. If the two are equal, then observing X_1 gives no information about what to expect from X_2 and the two variables are said to be *independent*. Otherwise, they are said to be *dependent*. In the example, the probability of a subject's behaving rationally will be different depending on whether or not we know his psychological class. If

---

[1] This is based on the concept of probability of the occurrence of an event E in a particular situation S. If S is repeated a large number of times, the probability of E is the limiting value of the number of occurrences of E divided by the number of repetitions of S.

[2] Admittedly, the objectivity of "rationality" is somewhat vague. However, for illustrative purposes in preparing the reader for basic assumptions underlying game theory, it appears as an appropriate example.

the two probabilities are the same, then the subject's psychological class and whether he will behave rationally are unrelated and hence, independent.

Conditional probability problems are primarily concerned with cases in which $P(X_2 \mid X_1)$ is different from $P_2(X_2)$. In general, we will be dealing with situations where a number of random variables are estimated and where there is an expressed, or implied, time consideration in the estimation. The example given is of this type. $P(X_1, X_2)$, $P_1(X_1)$, and $P_2(X_2)$ describe the situation before the subject arrives; while $P(X_2 \mid normal)$ is used after the subject has been declared representative of a normal psychological class.

Two useful tools in conditional probability theory are Markov chains and Bayes' theorem. The latter is useful whenever time of observation has only two possibilities, the former whenever a probabilistic situation occurs over a relatively long period of time.

Markov Chains

When it is necessary to deal with a large number of time-ordered conditional probabilities, a *Markov chain* can be used.

Mathematically, a Markov chain is both a set of *states* $\{E_j\}$ in which a process or environment can be found and a matrix[3] M of *transition probabilities* whose elements m_{ij} are conditional probabilities that the process being in state E_i at time t will go into state E_j at time $t+1$.

A typical situation in which a Markov model is useful occurs in prediction of behavior of individuals within an organization. Say that we are interested in determining whether or not an individual will quit the organization. For a finer resolution, we set up four possible individual states: E_1 implies that the individual is satisfied with the organization; E_2 implies that he is slightly dissatisfied; E_3 implies that he is very dissatisfied; and E_4 implies that he has

[3] It is assumed that the reader is familiar with basic matrix concepts encountered in Chapters 4 and 6.

decided to quit. For the sake of simplicity, let us assume that the individual's state is derived by some means each week.

A hypothetical transition matrix is given below.

		Next State			
		E_1	E_2	E_3	E_4
	E_1	.8	.15	.04	.01
	E_2	.5	.3	.15	.05
Current State	E_3	.1	.3	.4	.2
	E_4	0	0	0	1.0

Entry m_{ij} gives the conditional probability that if the individual is in state i in a certain week, in the next week he will be in state j. For example, m_{11} is the probability that if he is satisfied this week, he will be satisfied next week; m_{24} is the probability that if he is "mildly" dissatisfied this week, he will decide to quit next week; m_{32} is the probability that if he is very dissatisfied this week, something will happen to make him less dissatisfied next week; and so on. The entries in row 4 indicate that the decision to quit is irrevocable, since the only entry in this row which is not zero is m_{44}. This means that if the individual has decided to quit this week, the probability is zero that he will be in any of the other three psychological states next week, and the probability is 1 that he will still be determined to quit next week (assuming that he is still with the organization).

In addition to the set E and matrix M, there exists a probability a_j that an individual will be in state E_j when we begin the study. We will assume that $a_1 = 1$ and $a_2 = a_3 = a_4 = 0$; in other words, the individual is assumed to be satisfied initially. It should be noted that the sum of the entries in any row is 1 since the entries are probabilities and the probability is 1 that the individual will be in some state next week if he is in some state this week. (Matrices of this sort are known as *stochastic matrices*.)

There are many properties of transition matrices which are treated in texts on this subject (e.g. Feller, 500). One particular property with application to the current example is that state 4 has no *exit,* i.e., eventually the process will get to state E_4 and terminate. State E_4 is therefore called a *persistent* state, while states E_1, E_2, and E_3 are called *transient* states.

As time increases, the probability that the process will be in state E_4 approaches 1, while the probability that it will be in one of states E_1, E_2, or E_3 approaches zero. This means that any individual in our hypothetical example will be very likely to have quit after a long period of time. The probability that he will have quit by time t can be computed in a moderately complicated recursive fashion from the transition matrix (see Feller, 500, pp. 362-363).

Bayes' Theorem

In many cases concerning two random variables, $P_1(X_1)$, $P_2(X_2)$, and $P(X_1 \mid X_2)$ are all known *a priori* and we wish to find $P(X_2 \mid X_1)$. The following relationship can be used:

$$P(X_1 \mid X_2)P(X_2) = P(X_1, X_2)$$
$$= P(X_2 \mid X_1)P(X_1)$$

or simply

$$P(X_2 \mid X_1) = \frac{P(X_1 \mid X_2)P_2(X_2)}{P_1(X_1)}.$$

This result is known as *Bayes' theorem.*

We can apply this theorem to the first example. Assume that we know the probability that a subject will be in a normal psychological class, the probability that any arbitrary subject will behave rationally, and the probability that a normal subject will behave rationally. If we observe that a given subject behaves rationally, we can determine the probability that his psychological class is normal by Bayes' theorem:

$$P(\text{normal} \mid \text{rational}) =$$
$$\frac{P(\text{rational} \mid \text{normal})P_2(\text{normal})}{P_1(\text{rational})}.$$

One major application of this theorem is thus the validation of testing procedures. There is also a branch of statistics called Bayesian statistics which makes generalized use of Bayes' theorem. This is the topic of the next section.

3. BAYESIAN STATISTICAL INFERENCE

In recent years many workers in the field of statistical decision theory have found inadequate for their needs the assumptions underlying the type of statistics used in most statistics books. They wish to deal with the uncertainty of a decision-maker concerning the state of the external world. In many cases this uncertainty takes the form of questioning the truth of a proposition such as "Will my product be acceptable to a large enough market to make it profitable to manufacture?"

This uncertainty cannot be formulated in the classical definition of probability, since only one experiment can be made and the results will show conclusively that the proposition is true or false. In practice, one would say that there is a "good chance" or "little chance" of success. The decision-maker might recommend that a pilot study be made to more clearly determine the chances of success or failure.

Bayesian statistics was developed with the intent of formalizing this intuitive notion, and it is being found to have application to many areas now served by classical statistics, including psychological hypothesis-testing procedures.

Subjective and Personal Probabilities

The basis for Bayesian statistics is subjective and personal probability. There is a distinction between the two which will be explained later.

Subjective probability is defined loosely as follows:

The subjective probability p for a decision-maker that a proposition T is true is the amount that he would bet if someone were to give him a unit return if T turns out to be true.

This definition includes the classical definition, for if you (the decision-maker) were observing the throw of a die for the number 3, you would not pay more than 1/6 for a return of 1 because the relative frequency of 3 in many throws is 1/6. It is, however, broader, for if someone were to tell you that the die had been secretly changed and was weighted so that one number would always come up, but that he did not know which number, you would still bet 1/6 on 3 for a return of 1, even though the relative frequency of 3 from then on might be 0 or might be 1. In the latter case, you are expressing your uncertainty about the proposition "the die is weighted so that 3 will always come up," which could be known with certainty with one throw of the die.

In order to treat this concept mathematically, the decision-maker is assumed to be consistent, to prevent his being trapped into making an unfavorable bet. This means that the probability of the universal event is 1 (he will bet 1 unit for a return of 1 that *something* will happen), and that the probability of the occurrence of either event A or event B, where A and B are mutually exclusive, is the sum of the probabilities of each occurring individually.

Most people are not consistent in their subjective probability assignments, so that the theory assumes an ideal consistent person, and refers to this person's probabilities as *personal* probabilities, leaving the word *subjective* to mean the possibly inconsistent behavior of an actual person.

Increasing Knowledge of the Environment — Use of Bayes' Theorem

Now that we have a method of formalizing our uncertainty about the state of the environment, we must deal with the problem of using information to update our uncertainty. We will denote by *prior probability* a personal probability about a situation before any updating is done, and by

posterior probability the updated personal probability.

Now consider the case wherein a scientist is about to perform an experiment to investigate a hypothesis H. He will have a prior probability for its truth; call it $P_1(H)$. The experiment will involve the collection of a set of data D. What the scientist desires is $P(H \mid D)$, the probability of the truth of the hypothesis given the data collected. What he has available, besides $P_1(H)$, is the probability of the data given the truth of H, $P(D \mid H)$, and the probability of the data, $P_2(D)$. Using Bayes' theorem,

$$P(H \mid D) = \frac{P(D \mid H)P_1(H)}{P_2(D)}.$$

$P_2(D)$ can be interpreted as the probability that the data would have taken its actual value under a mutually exclusive set of hypotheses, H and $\overline{H}$, stated as

$$P_2(D) = P(D \mid H)P_1(H) + P(D \mid \overline{H})P_1(\overline{H})$$

where

$$P_1(H) = 1 - P_1(\overline{H})$$

The simplicity of the first formula hides many complicated problems. The estimation of $P_1(H)$ and $P_2(D)$ are the principal two. $P_1(H)$ is, of course, a personal probability; hence, results based on this estimate may not be universally acceptable. $P_2(D)$ is based on the probability of the data on the basis of all possible hypotheses. This, too, is often difficult to estimate and, thus, may not command universal agreement.

Much work has been done on the problem of determining conditions for ignoring the precise details of these distributions, e.g., Edwards, et al. (452) and Raiffa and Schlaifer (1177). A beginning has been made on estimating subjective probabilities by Toda (1432). See also Sections 4 and 5 of this chapter.

It will be fruitful, however, to ignore these difficulties and present a simplified example of the use of this technique.

Suppose you are going to participate in a coin-tossing experiment and that you know that the coin involved is either normal or has two heads. Let H be the hypothesis that the coin has two heads. Suppose further that you do not know in advance anything which would prejudice you in favor of or against the hypothesis. $P_1(H)$ is therefore equal to .5, and $P_1(\overline{H}) = .5$ also. You then are allowed to perform an experiment to help you decide whether H is true. The coin is tossed once and the result is heads. This is the data set D. Now $P(D \mid H) = 1$, $P(D \mid \overline{H}) = \frac{1}{2}$ so that

$$P(H \mid D)$$
$$= \frac{P(D \mid H)P_1(H)}{P(D \mid H)P_1(H) + P(D \mid \overline{H})P_1(\overline{H})} = \frac{2}{3}$$

and you are now more certain that the coin has two heads.

For comparison, suppose that you think that there is but a slight chance of H being true, say $P_1(H) = .01$. With the same experiment and the same D,

$$P(H \mid D) \approx .02$$

so that even though you still doubt H very much, its chance of being true is increased.

In the latter case, if you were to run a series of experiments, re-evaluating $P_1(H)$ after every one, a long sequence of heads would convince you that H was indeed true, (If, of course, a tail is thrown, H is discredited.)

Practical applications of Bayes' theorem and subjective probabilities are presented in terms of new approaches to teaching machines and resulting psychological problems in Section 7 of this chapter.

4. GAME THEORY: TWO PERSONS

Game theory deals with those decision processes which involve two or more decision-makers (players) whose conflicting interests result in a step-wise, rational, competitive contest. The forte of game theory is simply to determine the character of the decision processes required for execution of the contest, or more formally the game, assuming that each player's per-

formance is deterministically rational within the boundaries of constraint. In other words, game theory works within the domain of "strictly rational" participants rather than within the actual world.

Rationality

Rationality is not an easy concept to grasp in view of the varying degrees with which one can declare "common sense" or "moral expectation." There are many probabilistic paradoxes[4] which tend to contaminate any real basis for predicting rational decision-making. Many approaches have been taken to formalize player behavior in terms of "utility" gain criteria in an attempt to better, and more realistically, define quantities subject to mathematical manipulation. These new dimensions of the problem only result in confounding empiricism and obscure the purposes of formulating optimal decisions and strategies.

Games and Payoff Matrices

What, then, is a game? A *game* in the sense of game theory is a sequence of plays, each of which results in a payoff (or probability of payoff) corresponding to the choices made by the players. The set of possible choices are framed within pre-determined constraints. The set of payoffs is generally represented in a matrix whose elements are the actual values (or probabilities) dispersed in some fashion to the players at the end of a play. A simple example of a two-person game payoff matrix is

Player B

$$\begin{array}{c} \\ A_1 \\ \text{Player } A \quad A_2 \\ A_3 \end{array} \begin{array}{ccc} B_1 & B_2 & B_3 \\ \left[\begin{array}{ccc} 0 & 1 & -1 \\ 1 & 4 & 3 \\ -6 & 0 & 2 \end{array}\right] \end{array} \text{payoff to } A.$$

[4]For example, the St. Petersburg Paradox (1183, 1184) demonstrates that an innocent coin-tossing game with a simple payoff rule for winning results in an *infinite* expected gain per play, and hence, can demand any amount to play!

Each element is contained in the intersection of a row and a column of the matrix. A move (A_3, B_1) would result in a -6 payoff to player A, etc. Metric of the payoff matrix is not important in understanding gaming techniques and, consequently, will not be discussed in terms of anything but dimensionless integers.[5]

ments of game design bring to light the subtle variations that exist within game classes (452, 1214). This discussion limits itself to presenting fundamentals of two-person games involving two basic payoff matrices (with and without saddle points), two kinds of strategies (pure and mixed), and both zero- and non-zero sums.

DIAGRAM 13-1.   Tree Representation of a Two-person, Zero-sum Game

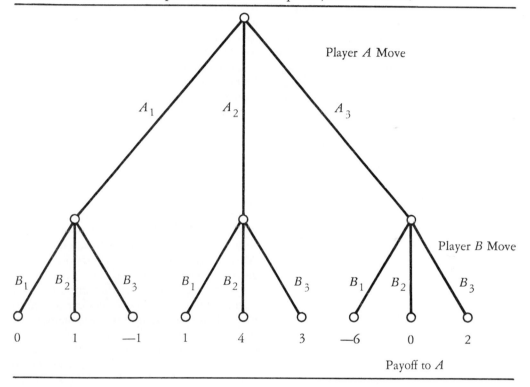

Player A Move

A_1 A_2 A_3

Player B Move

B_1 B_2 B_3 B_1 B_2 B_3 B_1 B_2 B_3

0   1 -1 1   4   3 -6 0   2

Payoff to A

Naturally there are many types of games. Principal differences lie in the number of players (this section is concerned only with games involving two persons; the next section examines n-person games, $n \geq 3$), characteristic of the payoff matrix, strategies used in playing, and zero-sum versus non-zero-sum games. More advanced treat-

Game Trees

Generally, every game can be represented by a tree, which diagrammatically expresses the possible plays in a game. Diagram 13-1 presents an example of the tree structure for a two-person, zero-sum game in which both players A and B have three possible choices. *Zero-sum* simply implies that the sum of both gains to player A and losses to player B equals zero. *Non-zero*, or *constant, sum* games are defined in an obvious parallel.

[5]In experimental situations, value is attached to the payoff matrix in order to stimulate a competitive gaming environment so necessary in validating experimental results.

The payoff matrix for this tree was given above and is called the *normalized form* of the game while the tree representation is called the *extensive form* of the game.

Saddle Points

A *saddle point* contained in a payoff matrix is an element that is both minimum in its row and maximum in its column. Clearly not all payoff matrices contain saddle points (in the payoff matrix given previously, $a_{2,1}$ is a saddle point; see also the following examples), and owing to this phenomenon, experimental divergence results in playing games with, then without, saddle points. Easily shown is the fact that if there is more than one saddle point in a payoff matrix, they are all equal and, furthermore, the rows and columns are interchangeable.

Player B

$$\begin{array}{cc} & \begin{array}{ccc} B_1 & B_2 & B_3 \end{array} \\ \begin{array}{c} A_1 \\ \text{Player } A \quad A_2 \\ A_3 \end{array} & \begin{bmatrix} 6 & 0 & -5 \\ 2 & 2 & 1 \\ -3 & 0 & -3 \end{bmatrix} \end{array}$$ payoff to A

Payoff Matrix

(a) with a saddle point

Player B

$$\begin{array}{cc} & \begin{array}{ccc} B_1 & B_2 & B_3 \end{array} \\ \begin{array}{c} A_1 \\ \text{Player } A \quad A_2 \\ A_3 \end{array} & \begin{bmatrix} 6 & 0 & -5 \\ 2 & 1 & 0 \\ 0 & -4 & 2 \end{bmatrix} \end{array}$$ payoff to A

Payoff Matrix

(b) without a saddle point

It is more or less obvious that if a payoff matrix has a saddle point, it will be selected with an increasing frequency as the game continues. As a consequence, an experiment involving saddle points should be guided by a hypothesis that this kind of player strategy will be used by alert, intelligent players. Lieberman (934) demonstrated this to be rather well substantiated when working with college students. A good standard for a control measure in experimental games might be the rate of

adeptness to a saddle-point strategy in a simple game.

Strategies

Essentially there are only two strategies which may be adopted by a player: *pure* and *mixed*. A pure strategy is a set of choices all of which are the same. Pure strategies are the least interesting by far for a player to execute even though they may guarantee him either a maximum win or a minimum loss (called a minimax solution to the game). Deviations from pure strategies are often seen as relief from boredom—again, Lieberman (934). Saddle-point strategy is a pure strategy.

Mixed strategy is a set of different choices made according to a corresponding set of relative frequencies. For example, as can be seen in the above payoff matrix without a saddle point, a best strategy for player A might be mixing his choices among A_1, A_2, and A_3 in a 1/6, 2/3, 1/6 relative frequency basis. At the same time player B might need a counter-strategy of B_1, B_2, B_3 in a 1/8, 3/8, 1/2 relative frequency basis. Mixed strategies are necessary in playing zero-sum games without saddle points.

Of interest is the fact that, theoretically, optimal mixed strategies to effect the minimax phenomenon in zero-sum games are not, in general, adopted by players, as evidenced by another Lieberman study (933). Many conjectures are presented to support these results, all of which are based on the conservative gambling attitudes, memories, and computational abilities of the players. (Considerable computation is required to derive the minimax solution.) The realized "irrational" strategies make obvious the problems in determining the predictive value of an optimal strategy solution to a real game. Indeed, the more complicated the constraints, the less conformance actually occurs to an ideal minimax solution. A zero-sum Blotto game[6]

---

[6]The game actually consisted of player A choosing a point $x = (x_1, x_2, x_3)$ such that $x_1 + x_2 + x_3 = 16$ for

devised by Sakaguchi (1249) succeeds in substantiating this point.

Frequently there exists a *dominating* strategy in the two-person game. This occurs if for every pure strategy j (jth column of the payoff matrix) selected by player B, player A selects a mixed strategy which has as high (and at least one higher) expected value $E(A, j)$ as another mixed strategy. The expected value function is given as:

$$E(A, B) = \sum_{i=1}^{m} \sum_{j=1}^{n} a_{ij}A_iB_j$$

where A_i and B_j are probabilities of selecting row i or column j in the payoff matrix and a_{ij} is the element in the payoff matrix.

Minimax. In the preceding sections, the term minimax has been used in a somewhat vague context as implying maximum gain and, at the same time, minimum loss. In the same breath the expression "optimal solution" was introduced as having the same meaning. Essentially this is the case in deriving the ideal solution to a game. The general minimax theorem is stated for a two-person, zero-sum, $m \times n$ game as follows:

$$\max_A \min_B \sum_{i=1}^{m} \sum_{j=1}^{n} a_{ij}A_iB_j =$$

$$\min_B \max_A \sum_{i=1}^{m} \sum_{j=1}^{n} a_{ij}A_iB_j = v.$$

A_i, B_j, and a_{ij} are defined as before. The meaning of this theorem follows common logic in that if A assumes that B knows his (A's) mixed strategy and will devise a strategy which will minimize A's expected return, then the maximum guaranteed return for A is

$$v_1 = \max_A \left[\min_B \sum_{i=1}^{m} \sum_{j=1}^{n} a_{ij}A_iB_j \right].$$

In the same manner if B assumes that A knows his (B's) mixed strategy, the maximum possible return for A is

$$v_2 = \min_B \left[\max_A \sum_{i=1}^{m} \sum_{j=1}^{n} a_{ij}A_iB_j \right].$$

The minimax theorem simply says that $v_1 = v_2$ for some two strategies A and B.[7] However, the computation to determine A and B is another problem, the solution of which is not trivial under actual game conditions. Little surprise is expected when hearing about mixed strategy games which, after being played, did not result in a convergence to the minimax prediction. It is reasonable, however, to accept a minimax solution as an optimum strategy (or strategies) in competitive contests between two intelligent players.

Prisoners' Dilemma and Negotiability

An interesting two-person non-zero-sum game which has been used extensively in game experiments is one called *Prisoners' Dilemma*. In essence the situation involves two prisoners who have been apprehended by the law on suspicion of committing a crime. They are separated and questioned individually. If neither of them confesses, they each receive a light, insignificant sentence on a minor charge; if they both confess, they each receive lenient, but nearly maximum punishment; however, if one confesses and the other does not, the former gets leniency for turning state's evidence and the latter gets a maximum sentence. A realistic payoff matrix might be

	Prisoner B	
	Not Confess	Confess
Not Confess	1 year each	10 years for A
Prisoner A		6 months for B
	6 months for A	8 years each
Confess	10 years for B	

---

only positive numbers. Player B chooses $y = (y_1, y_2, y_3)$ such that $y_1 + y_2 + y_3 = 12$ for only positive numbers. Payoff to A is $6 \times \max(0, x_1 - y_1) + 2 \times \max(0, x_2 - y_2) + \max(0, x_3 - y_3)$.

---

[7] In general there does not exist a minimax solution to games which involve an infinite number of moves. Rosenfeld (1218, p. 52) gives an interesting example of a non-minimax infinite game.

Naturally there are many sets of numbers which can comprise the payoff matrix according to the degree of dilemma desired. The basic model of the payoff matrix is

$$
\begin{array}{cc}
 & \text{Player } B \\
 & \begin{array}{cc} B_1 & B_2 \end{array}
\end{array}
$$

$$
\text{Player } A \begin{array}{c} A_1 \\ A_2 \end{array} \begin{bmatrix} (x_1, x_1) & (x_2, x_3) \\ (x_3, x_2) & (x_4, x_4) \end{bmatrix}
$$

payoff to both A and B

where

$$2x_1 < x_2 + x_3 < 2x_4$$
$$x_3 < x_1$$
$$x_3 < x_2$$
$$x_4 < x_2 \quad \text{are the constraints.}$$

For both players, Strategy A_2, B_2 (defection) dominates Strategy A_1, B_1 (cooperation); thus almost universal non-consistency in strategy selection exists, resulting in a mixture of rational and irrational moves. Psychologically an index of hostility, say, might well be the number of times a player selects strategy 2 over strategy 1.

Many variations of this basic model have been tried (Rapoport, 1183, pp. 13-18) by deleting some of the constraints and allowing the players an opportunity to converse, negotiate, and even reverse each other's choices. Results of these games are inconclusive; however, they do begin to substantiate the utilization of negotiation in approaching a mutually advantageous strategy. Without negotiation, (A_2, B_2) prevails, which, of course, benefits neither player.

Negotiability is an additional dimension of gaming which encourages the formation of von Neumann and Morgenstern coalition games. Intuitively and actually, these games are considerably more complex than non-negotiable games and warrant special attention in describing the nature of optimal "solutions." Solution, here, is at best a vague indicator of how coalitions may be formed to attain structural stability. Because of the enormity of the subject and the intent of this brief introduction, detail

of subtleties in negotiation is left in references (1026, 452, 1265, and 1285) and the following section.

5. GAME THEORY: N PERSONS

An extension from two-person game theory to three-person, four-person, ..., n-person game theory is now logical. In the last section we discussed the fundamentals of two-person games, presenting a few simple examples which led nicely into the Prisoners' Dilemma game model. N-person game theory can be viewed in terms of two-person games since the general assumption is made that eventually the n-persons will, by negotiations, form two opposing coalitions. All n-person games, in addition, are reduced to zero-sum if necessary simply by appending to the players an imaginary $n + 1$st player who absorbs the left-over gain or loss.

The following discussion, then, divorces itself from reiterating detail of two-person, zero-sum games and concentrates on the decisions which effect coalition formation. With a minute's thought the reader can quickly overcome the mild disappointment of not enjoying n-dimensioned plays which tax rather complicated payoff matrices in a most uninteresting way (that is, without negotiation, for which cases a generalization of the minimax solution exists in n-person, zero-sum games) by considering actualities in open-forum-like situations. Given n people, a purpose, and time, two sides will emerge which are diametrically opposite and intent on a "fight to the finish."

Coalitions

The formation of coalitions, or teams, within the boundaries of a game is conceptually interesting and at the same time vague. The idea of collusion for the purpose of increasing individual gain is certainly not earthshaking. What is earthshaking is the idea that potentially there exists an ordering in the formation of coalitions which is *most* favorable to all players during the course of a game. Remember, a game consists of a sequence of plays, after each of which the players are paid off according to the elements within the payoff matrix. In games where free negotiation is allowed, the coalition framework is potentially dynamic since new coalitions may be formed at the end of each play, or set of plays.

Independent of the game constraints, a coalition may apportion its payoff in any way it likes to maintain stability and suppress dissension among the "ranks." Important, however, is the conservation of payoff utility in terms of total game utility, which can differ from summing up the individual players' utility based on each different player utility scale. Money, for example, does not necessarily represent the same utility to all players but is probably linear, within a player, to potential payoffs and *side payments.*

Characteristic Functions

For each coalition which forms during a game, there is an expected return, or payoff, to the coalition which represents its value. If we let S be the coalition, then the function $v(S)$ is the guaranteed payoff to S under a certain presupposed set of strategies regardless of the counter-strategies employed by the remaining coalition(s). $v(S)$ is called the *characteristic function* of the game and in essence is a rule which assigns a minimum payoff to each possible coalition. If I_n is the set of n players, then clearly:

(a) $v(I_n) = 0$, for zero-sum games

(b) $v(S) = - v(-S)$, where $-S$ is the complement coalition of S and S is any subset of I_n

(c) $v(\phi) = 0$, ϕ being the null coalition.

If the game is non-zero-sum, the first and second identities are changed to:

(a') $v(I_n) = K$, the constant sum

(b') $v(S) = v(I_n) - v(-S) = K - v(-S)$.

It is conceivable, and in fact true, that in some n-person games nothing is gained in coalition formation. In other words, total payoff to the set of all players is equal to the sum of payoffs to individual players. These games are called *inessential* and are conspicuous for the lack of enthusiasm aroused by their presence. A game which is not inessential is *essential.*

The idea of characteristic functions is important in that the basis of developing optimal strategies which are used by the dynamics of the coalition structure depends on mathematical manipulations of these functions. The techniques of generating optimal strategies are left in references (452, 1295) in order not to obscure the presentation of the fundamentals.

Imputations

If we think of x_i as being the *total* payoff to player i for a game, then there should be little trouble in our generating a vector $\mathbf{X} = (x_1, x_2, \ldots, x_n)$ which represents total payoff to all players. Immediately the equality

$$(a) \quad \sum_{i=1}^{n} x_i = v(I_n)$$

should come into mind since the total sum of all payoffs would have to be exactly the value of the characteristic function if I_n were one, grand coalition. An obvious inequality which, indeed, justifies the existence of coalitions is

$$(b) \quad v(\{i\}) \leq x_i \text{ for every } i \text{ in } I_n$$

assuming, of course, that each player is rational to the point of his not joining a coalition unless the total payoff is in excess of a total payoff resulting from individual play. Any such vector $\mathbf{X}$ which satisfies both (a) and (b) is called an *imputation* and describes the outcome of the game in terms of payoff.

By ignoring the equal sign in (b), however, the issue of optimal strategy is confounded, since it is not apparent how any or all of the players can gain by coalitions while no players lose. Yet attempts have been made to clarify this in terms of an *equilibrium point* defined by a coalition S such that

$$(c) \ v(S) \leqslant \sum_{i=1}^{n} x_i \ \text{for every subset } S \text{ in } I_n.$$

The major stumbling block in including (c) with (a) and (b) is the fact that rarely does a vector $\mathbf{X}$ meet this condition. If, however, there is a set of vectors which satisfy condition (c), it is called the *core* of the game and, as a point of interest, games with non-empty cores are inessential.

The importance of imputations is stressed in establishing a solution to the n-person game.

Stability and Solution

Conceptually the solution to a game is the means by which the players obtain either maximum gain or minimum loss. In the two-person game, payoff matrices with saddle points demand pure strategies by both players. For all finite cases there exists at least minimax solution often not obvious in developing mixed strategies, particularly in games with difficult constraints.

The solution to an n-person game without negotiation can be found using an extension of the minimax theorem developed in the last section. In games which allow so-called pre-play communication, or negotiation, solutions must be defined in a less mathematical way. The concept of bargaining and side payment to persuade players to form coalitions is a complete combinatorial and psychological area of study in itself. To digress an instant within a 10-player coalition, think of how many possible ways a one-dollar payoff can be divided among the 10 players—roughly $3\frac{1}{4}$ trillion!

Classically, the details of the payoff rules which exist for a coalition are not handled in game theory, and experiments which deal with n-person games only acknowledge their presence or absence. Thus, *solutions to n-person, negotiable games are presented as*

desirable sets of imputations, rather than a single imputation, with the property that every imputation outside of the set is dominated by at least one imputation within the set in the following sense. If v is the characteristic function of a game with two imputations $\mathbf{X}$ and $\mathbf{Y}$ pertaining to a coalition S, then $\mathbf{X}$ dominates $\mathbf{Y}$ if the following inequalities are true:

$$(a) \ v(S) \geqslant \sum_{i=1}^{M} y_i, \ \text{for } M \text{ players in } S$$

(b) $y_i > x_i$, for every i in S.

Satisfaction of these conditions more or less substantiates the intuitive notion one has of domination, i.e., $\mathbf{X}$ is more rewarding than $\mathbf{Y}$. The coalition S under these circumstances is called *effective.*

Derivation of the solution set of imputations is extremely complicated, and theory leading to a *best* solution in terms of maximum payoff to each player is not yet fully developed. All is not lost on this account, however, since the addition of more rigid constraints in defining the nature of coalition-formation and the character of a useful solution has produced interesting stability phenomena.

Luce and Raiffa (968) present ψ-stability in terms of a coalition and imputation which are in balance such that no allowable changes in the coalition structure are beneficial. K-stability (Rapoport & Orwant, 1185, p. 36) also defines a coalition structure with an imputation which borders on a desirable characteristic of a solution.

It is readily seen, therefore, that in general no explicit solution is predictable for n-person negotiable games. Experimentation to validate most likely coalition structures has been done to a small degree but it is inconclusive. These experiments have dealt, by and large, with three-person games where total of possible non-trivial coalitions is only three (A and B, A and C, B and C), and considerably less attention is required than, for instance, the four-person game with 7 possible coalitions. Details of experimental n-person games and interpretation problems inherent in their playing is left in references (968, 1255), for the interested reader.

6. MULTIVARIATE MODELS OF DECISION PROCESSES

As stated in Section 1, a decision can be typically described as the act of selecting one from a number of alternate courses. Thus, any process or circumstance which requires decisions is a decision process. A block diagram showing the relational aspects of a decision to input information and output effects is given below.

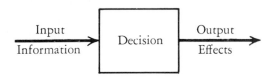

Essentially there are three basic categories of decision:

(1) decision based on strategy
(2) decision based on a rule
(3) decision based on strategies varying according to results of prior decisions.

Type 1 decisions were discussed in the previous two game theory sections. Recall that a strategy is a set of probabilities which determine the frequency of play choices during a game. The actual sequence of "decisions" affecting the strategy is assumed to be random, hence, the reader probably is not yet aware of the depth to which underlying decision theory reaches.

This section is concerned primarily with the multivariate nature of decision techniques for Types 2 and 3 decisions described in terms of their mathematical models. Since Type 3 decisions are adaptive, or perhaps learning, systems which function by decision processes, an introduction to the basic concepts of systems analysis is provided.

Multivariate Distribution Functions

Decision problems are generally presented to the statistician in a form amenable to the derivation of *joint multivariate probability distribution functions*. The joint p.d.f. gives the probability that a particular observed set of $x_1, x_2, \ldots, x_m$, the m jointly distributed random variables, can occur. For purposes of simplification let us only work with a discrete set (opposed to an infinite, continuous set) of probabilities and values of the random variables.

Obviously there are many different joint p.d.f.'s which correspond to different sets of random variables. Determining which p.d.f. fits the data best (say, in a least-squares sense) is quite a statistical computation task in itself. The analytical expression which does represent the joint p.d.f. is worth the effort in that it provides: (a) convenience in handling the data outside of manipulating an n-dimensioned data array, and (b) an abundance, in some well-known p.d.f.'s, of high-powered statistical techniques useful in hypothesis-testing and extrapolation. The most familiar joint p.d.f. is the multivariate normal (Gaussian) distribution which is

$$f(\mathbf{X}) = (2\pi)^{-\frac{n}{2}} \, |\, \sigma_{ij} \,|^{-1} \, exp$$

$$\cdot \left\{ -\frac{1}{2} \, [\mathbf{X} - \mu)'(\sigma_{ij})(\mathbf{X} - \mu)] \right\}$$

where $\mathbf{X}$ is the column vector: $\begin{pmatrix} x_1 \\ x_2 \\ \cdot \\ \cdot \\ \cdot \\ x_n \end{pmatrix}$ of random variables;

μ is the column vector: $\begin{pmatrix} \mu_1 \\ \mu_2 \\ \cdot \\ \cdot \\ \cdot \\ \mu_n \end{pmatrix}$ of individual distribution means;

(σ_{ij}) is the covariance matrix with determinant $|\, \sigma_{ij} \,|$; and $(\mathbf{X} - \mu)'$ is the transpose of vector $(\mathbf{X} - \mu)$.

Decision Rules and Minimax.

A typical problem when working with decision rules is accepting as input a set of observed random variables $\mathbf{X} = (x_1, x_2, \ldots, x_n)$ and determining a decision rule which optimizes (maximizes gain and minimizes loss) the set of observed random variables $\mathbf{Y} = (y_1, y_2, \ldots, y_m)$. A decision rule is a *list of decisions each of which corresponds to a possible set of observed values of* $\mathbf{X}$.

A quick example may be helpful at this time. Suppose a major retail sales company wanted to decide whether or not they should open a branch outlet in a chosen locality. A random poll was taken to determine an expectation of dollar sales among residents in the locality. Let us represent the m estimates by $\mathbf{X} = (x_1, x_2, \ldots, x_m)$. Then $\mathbf{Y}$ could be net profit observed over time such that y_i is the profit realized during time period i. Since the y_i's will be observed *after* the decision rule is selected, we shall not worry about their influence in the problem at this time. *The possible number of decision rules is infinite.* Two rules might be to open the branch if

$$\sum_{i=1}^{m} x_i \geq \$5,000$$

or to open the branch if over half of the x_i's exceed $50.

Let us denote by H the total number of possible joint p.d.f.'s of $x_1, x_2, \ldots, x_m, y_1, y_2, \ldots, y_n$; by x, a set of observations $x_1, x_2, \ldots, x_m$; by y, a set of observations $y_1, y_2, \ldots, y_n$; and by K, the total number of decisions which comprise a rule. Then $s(d; x)$ is the probability assigned to decision d when x is observed. The probability that the point (x, y) is observed in the joint p.d.f., θ, is given as $f(x, y; \theta)$.

Clearly, then, for each point x which is observed,

$$\sum_{d=1}^{K} s(d; x) = 1$$

since the sum of the probabilities over all possible decisions must be unity.

For each decision d and each p.d.f., θ, the *risk*, or expected value of loss, using d when θ is the true p.d.f. is $r(\theta; s)$.

To finally solve a decision rule problem we must determine the set of *admissible* decision rules from which we are to select one. A well-known theorem states that: *if* s *is an admissible decision rule, then there are* H *non-negative numbers* $N_1, N_2, \ldots, N_H$ *whose sum is one such that for each and every other decision rule* R,

$$\sum_{\theta=1}^{H} N_\theta r(\theta; s) \leq \sum_{\theta=1}^{H} N_\theta r(\theta; R).$$

Such a decision rule is called a *Bayes' decision rule* and we shall concern ourselves only with such rules. (Although the number of possible rules is infinite, this means of selection is both logical and profitable.) The reader may obtain additional detail in constructing the complete set of Bayes' decision rules under varying conditions of finiteness and infiniteness in texts dealing explicitly with the subject, e.g. Weiss (1509).

Selecting the best decision rule from the set of admissible rules is a *minimax* problem. A similar situation arose when determining an optimal strategy in playing games where a minimax solution to a game was a mixed strategy necessary to maximize gain for player A while minimizing loss to player B. A theorem which describes, in essence, the minimax decision rule is: *if* s *is a Bayes' decision rule relative to* $N_1, N_2, \ldots, N_H$, *and if* r$(\theta; s)$ *is maximum for every* θ *for which* $N_\theta > 0$, *then* s *is a minimax decision rule.*

Computation of the minimax rule is moderately complicated and can be directly constructed using techniques of *linear programming*. For a discussion of linear programming, the reader is directed to Bellman and Dreyfus (91) and Weiss (1509).

Systems Concept

A system in its entirety is *a device, procedure, or scheme which behaves according to some description, its function being to operate on information and/or energy and/or matter in a time reference to yield information and/or energy and/or matter.*[8]

Man, thus, is a system—an incredibly complex system consisting of countless subsystems connected in such a manner that it is doubtful that present analytical techniques are powerful enough to describe accurately even the simplest of biological functions. Decision theory deals with only a mere fraction of man's physical totality—his mind—and that part of decision theory which, in a sense, handles problems in relatively the same manner as man can best be presented in terms of systems concepts. That is, adaptive decision processes, sequences of decisions which are based on strategies which vary according to results of prior decisions, are closed loop systems with feedback.

A *closed loop system* with *feedback* from our viewpoint is simply a time-variant process which seeks stability by automatically correcting for variations in output using these variations as recycled input. Below is a block diagram of a simple closed loop system with feedback.

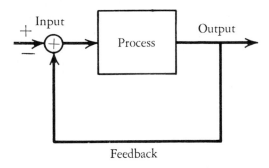

If the system possesses continually satisfactory dynamics (which includes stability), the system is called *adaptive.* The physiological adaptive systems which maintain stability in organisms are called *homeostatic mechanisms,* or in general are referred to as *homeostasis.*

[8]This definition is taken from Ellis and Ludwig (463, p. 3).

A general block diagram of an adaptive system given by Michkin and Braun (1058) and presented in Diagram 13-2 represents an expansion of a general closed loop system and is useful when *characterizing* or *identifying* adaptive decision processes.

This represents a univariate model; the multivariate model which handles many inputs and generates many outputs is essentially the same in functional context but is quite different in realization.

Adaptivity does *not* necessarily imply *learning* since the ultimate aim of an adaptive system is only to stabilize its dynamics. Learning, on the other hand, has been defined as *adaptive changes in the method of satisfying the system objectives as a result of experience.* The next discussion presents some of the more important aspects of adaptive decision processes and learning.

Adaptive Decision Processes

The idea of multivariate models useful in describing adaptive decision processes is somewhat sketchy. Truly, for each man-made decision there are numerous variables (such as psychological states, environmental factors, etc.) which can influence the outcome. Most of these, however, elude quantification because of the inability of mathematical models to describe thought processes adequately. The following discussion assumes that we can at least derive a joint p.d.f. which represents the behavior of the process at a given time *t.*

A simple two-person, non-negotiable game is a decision process in that a sequence of decisions are made over time. This decision process is analogous to an open loop system without feedback. In other words, the payoff to player *A* after a move theoretically has no influence on the next move once the strategies have been determined. In actual experiments, adaptivity occurs during the first few moves until either the saddle point is found or minimax strategies prevail.

DIAGRAM 13-2.   General Block Diagram of an Adaptive System

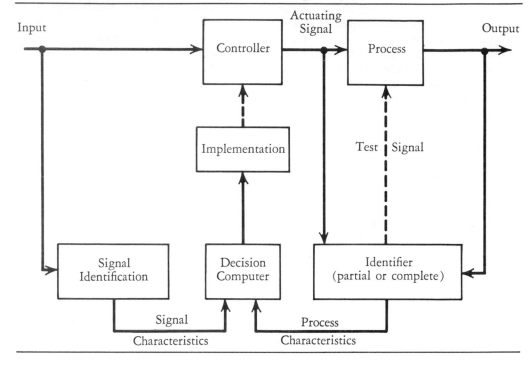

If, instead of dealing with a known payoff matrix, we select a payoff matrix some of whose elements are unknown to both players, we should expect that having uncovered some of these unknown pay-offs, the players would change strategies to maintain *minimax stability*. For example, a war game may be played between a missile-sending aggressor and an anti-missile-sending defender with a payoff matrix

$$\text{Aggressor} \begin{array}{c} \text{armed} \\ \text{decoy} \end{array} \overset{\begin{array}{cc} \text{defense} & \text{no defense} \end{array}}{\begin{bmatrix} 0 & -? \\ -? & 0 \end{bmatrix}}$$

Defender

payoff to defender.

The known elements result from either the defender successfully eliminating an armed missile or the defender not wasting the taxpayers' money on a decoy. The unknown payoffs to both sides result from: (1) the cost to the defender of sending a missile after a decoy while information is gained by the aggressor regarding anti-missile strength, and (2) the cost to the defender of letting an armed missile go undefended while he evaluates the strength and ac-curacy of the missile. In both cases the gains to the defender are considered negative.

An adaptive decision process is a closed loop adaptive system and can be described in terms of an infinite two-person game using an $n \times m$ payoff matrix with j un-known payoffs. If we assume that equal information is absorbed by both players after uncovering each unknown payoff, there exists an optimal solution to the game which guarantees a *finite* loss to player A. This optimal solution is *piecewise-stationary strategy* for both players, i.e., both players use a certain strategy until the first un-known payoff is uncovered, then change to a different strategy until the second un-known payoff is uncovered, and so on.

Minimax strategies are used by both players within the piecewise-strategy structure. In most cases involving unequal information to the players, piecewise-stationary strategy is not optimal and, in fact, no solution exists at present for unequal information.

Optimal solutions are derived computationally in a complicated manner using the joint p.d.f. which defines the strategy structure. Detail of techniques which lead to these solutions is given by Rosenfeld (1218).

Learning can be thought of as a sequence of adaptive states of a decision process whereby *efficiency* increases with experience. Efficiency, here, implies an increased output to input ratio. *Machine intelligence* is simply automated learning by an electro-mechanical device and is the cause of most work being done in areas of learning systems. Learning processes are the ultimate in adaptive decision processes.

Other attempts have been made to develop multivariate models in decision processes but they have been mostly inconclusive as to general application and utility. Excellent contributions by Adams (4), Stocklin (1353), Back (47), Zajonc (1599), Anker, et al. (37), and Johnson and Klare (811) represent a good cross-section of these efforts.

7. MAN-MACHINE INTERACTIONS

Man-machine interaction is probably the most significant topic in the design of optimal computer systems. Though many, the psychological aspects of this interaction have been the subject of surprisingly few investigations, e.g. Johnson and Kobler (808). The preceding sections have discussed techniques which require man's ability to use computers intelligently. However, none of them has considered exactly how man fits into a decision process, the details of which are left up to high-speed, automatic computation. As a concluding technical section it is natural,

therefore, to present techniques and problems of implementing decision processes in a manner suitable to both man and the machine.

Machines

We have already discussed man's complexity being conceptually describable as an adaptive system. Indeed, the psychologist knows only too well the difficulties encountered in resolving man's behavior into a static set of underlying constructs, or factors, and is beginning to rely more on the dynamics of psychological measurements which contribute to the adaptivity characteristic of the system (Chapter 11). The modeling of man's behavior becomes even more complicated when attempts are made to represent analytically the extreme, non-linear interplay inherent within the basic hydro-dynamic and electro-chemical physiological subsystems of the body.

The description of a machine, or computer, is not so difficult since basically all digital computers share the design shown below in block diagram form. Naturally

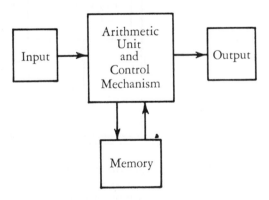

there are numerous variations of computer systems which employ this design, but these systems differ from one another mainly in techniques of input and output, memory size and accessibility, speed of computation and control, and sophistication of command repertoire. Hybrid computers which have both digital and non-digital (more specifically, analog) characteristics begin to take advantage of the relatively parallel continuum domain within which man thinks. Let us think of a machine here as a *man-made device which can be used to extend man's thought processes.*

An important assumption must be made and held fast in dealing with man-machine interactions: *man cannot outcreate himself,* i.e., never will a machine be made which is more creative than man himself. A lengthy philosophical dissertation on this point could, but will not, follow.

of a propagation of this decision dependency. The relationship between man and machine has classically been far too simple to continue to "guarantee" man significant benefit from machine's existence.

The interaction problem can be stated simply as an optimal determination of both man's and machine's roles in a man-machine system. The solution to the problem is not trivial and calls upon many research disciplines. Each discipline, of course, sees the problem differently, depending on objectivity desired. For example, engineers McRuer and Krendel (1024)

DIAGRAM 13-3.   Man-Machine Interaction Block Diagram

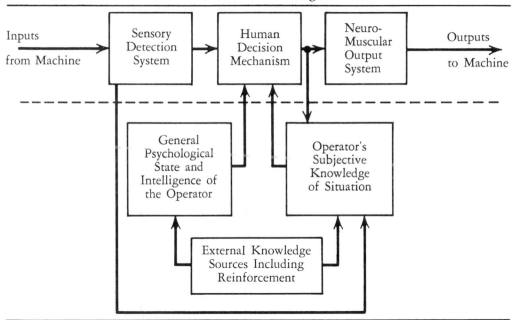

The Interaction Problem

Without man, a computer is useless. The converse (without computers, man is useless) is not yet true, and a major area of concern for psychologists is keeping this converse from becoming true. Truly, modern mankind is depending more and more on computer-made decisions without really being aware of the eventual impact

see human adaptability as a control system whose structure includes feedback and transfer function adjustments appropriate and best suited for control purposes. Behavioral scientists tend to approach the problem with tools of human engineering and models of ideal observers.

The block diagram in Diagram 13-3 presents the interaction problem in terms of a decision process. The area above the dotted line represents a simple open loop decision process without feedback. The decision made by the operator (so-called for convenience but analogous to the man in man-machine) is based on input to his sensory detection system, and consequences of output do not influence following decisions. Techniques for optimizing decisions based on both strategies and rules were presented in previous sections and fall into this category of interaction.

The area below the dotted line involves many variables, the more important of which include general psychological state and intelligence, external knowledge sources, and subjectivity of the operator. The feedback loops and other inputs below the dotted line provide for adaptivity and learning but also leave room for performance variability not necessarily desirable in adaptation.

Let us use the following representations:

$\{x_i\}$ — the set of states of the external environment which are considered by the whole system,

$\{y_i\}$ — the set of signals the machine uses to indicate its knowledge of the environment to the operator,

$\{z_i\}$ — the set of outputs of the human component.

The operator is assumed to have an estimate of the probability distribution of the x_i's, $p(x_i)$, and also a knowledge of the conditional probabilities $p(y_j \mid x_i)$ that govern the machine system. The operator's role is to decide on a particular output z_k based on his computation of $p(x_i \mid y_j)$ which minimizes the loss function r.

The effect of the adaptation is to modify both the values of $p(x_i)$ and $p(y_j \mid x_i)$ of the operator as well as the associated loss function r by the decision process. The variability of performance is a noise factor which modifies the relation between outputs and inputs without modifying the knowledge of the environment. The loss function r can be rewritten as

$$r = r_{\text{operator}} + r_{\text{noise}}$$

where r_{operator} is the known loss function of the operator and r_{noise} is the loss function related to unknown effects. The interaction problem can be looked upon as the selection of decision strategies which minimize r. However, this selection must be done using adaptive decision processes with partially known information distribution to both sides, the solution to which does not yet exist.

Attitude and Interaction

Presented in the last section was a Bayesian approach to the solution of the man-machine interaction (optimization) problem. An important aspect of this approach is that *Bayes' theorem accommodates and uses subjective (or personal) probabilities determined by man.* Too often in present man-machine systems, information is presented in an environment which reduces the human component to a questionable value and even implies redundancy. The *choiceless choice* in existing control systems which have been designed around the idea of interaction is a pathetic demonstration of man's incapability of including himself in complicated decision systems.

Gaming, on the other hand, allows man considerably more freedom in selecting moves which result in payoff. The object there, of course, is either to maximize realized return or beat (say, by taking the last move in chess or checkers) the machine with the stored decision choices. Games represent a much closer interaction between man and machine, and thus stimulate an operator attitude of importance now unparalleled by many other man-machine systems.

Recently computers have been programmed (here meaning coded in their own language) to teach methods of arriving at a decision, declaration, or diagnosis. The human component in such decision systems is certainly not redundant, since it is up to the student to ask questions which eliminate all possible alternatives but one or two. The following example which illustrates a pleasant man-machine interaction in a teaching atmosphere comes from Wallace Feurzeig (508).

> Assume that the computer is thinking of a letter of the alphabet and has broken the letter into a unique set of characteristics such as number of loose ends, horizontals, obliques, etc. The student is to identify the letter by conversing with the computer as follows. (C is computer, S is student.)
>
> C. Start when ready.
> S. CURVES?
> C. One.
> S. LOOSE ENDS?
> C. Two.
> S. OBLIQUES?
> C. Zero.
> S. C?
> C. You don't have enough information yet to get the right answer. How do you know it isn't J, for example?
> S. J?
> C. You don't have enough information yet. How do you know it isn't C, for example?
> S. HORIZONTALS?
> C. Zero. That was a wasted question. It did not eliminate any possibilities.
> S. VERTICALS?
> C. Zero. Good question.
> S. G?
> C. Wrong. Your guess is inconsistent with the information you've been given. You must have forgotten that the right letter hasn't any HORIZONTALS. The letter you guessed can't be right—it has too many LOOSE ENDS.
> S. CURVES?
> C. The answer is still one.
> S. X?
> C. Wrong. Your guess is inconsistent with the information you've been given. I think that you only made that guess to see what I would say.
> S. C?
> C. Yes, you've done it. Good work. If you want to play again, start right in.

More sophisticated examples of effective interaction have been worked out in conjunction with engineering, business, and medical schools.

Clearly the *conversational technique* in bringing the man into the man-machine system is imminent but presents many problems to the psychologist. In teaching situations, a language tone must be optimized to balance academic encouragement with academic discipline. In other words, a student must leave the computer session with an attitude of knowing something but not quite enough.

The extrapolation to other interaction environments is natural and easy. Optimization in design of the man-machine system leaves both the man and the machine with their respective fortes. However, the frailty of man bounds his forte with psychological constraints which must be considered in optimization. Over-reward can be as harmful to the decision processes as under-reward: optimism vs. pessimism. The character of the harm has not yet been determined and thus presents a significant challenge to the field of psychology.

8. SUMMARY

(1) A decision can be thought of as the act of selecting one from a number of alternate courses. A decision process is a system or circumstance which requires decisions.

(2) Conditional probability, the probability that an event will occur given that another event has already occurred, forms the basis of Bayesian statistics. Bayes' theorem relates jointly distributed variables in terms of their individual and conditional probability distribution functions. A Markov chain handles process states by means of transition matrices of conditional probabilities.

(3) Subjective and personal probabilities effectively relate past experience, couched in uncertainty, to hypothesis-testing techniques using Bayes' theorem.

(4) Game theory deals with decision processes which involve two or more decision-makers (players) whose conflicting interests result in a step-wise, rational,

competitive contest. Player rationality is assumed for the purpose of establishing order in the development of optimal solutions. Games vary in the number of players, characteristics of the payoff matrix, strategies used in playing, negotiability, total payoff, and number of moves defining the game.

(5) A payoff matrix is the normalized form of the game; a tree is the extensive form. Saddle points in payoff matrices necessitate pure strategies while minimax, mixed strategies are required in games with non-saddle point payoff matrices.

(6) *n*-person games reduce, after a while, to two-person games which involve two opposing coalitions. Coalition formation, while intuitively interesting, is exceedingly complicated; it is optimized using characteristic functions, imputations, and stability criteria. A solution to an *n*-person negotiable game is a desirable set of imputations. Minimax solutions exist for non-negotiable, finite, *n*-person games.

(7) There are three basic categories of decision: decisions based on strategy, decisions based on a rule, and decisions based on strategies varying according to results of prior decisions. A decision strategy consists of a sequence of probability distribution functions which define relative frequency of decisions, or choices. A decision rule is a list of decisions each of which corresponds to a possible set of observed values of the multivariate random variable. Decisions based on feedback comprise closed loop decision processes which may have adaptive or learning characteristics.

(8) Selecting the best decision rule from the set of admissible rules is a minimax problem. The minimax rule can be directly constructed using techniques of linear programing.

(9) Systems analysis concepts can be used to describe decision processes with feedback and characterize complicated multivariable adaptive processes. Such decision processes have, in special cases, piecewise-stationary strategies for minimax solutions. Learning can be thought of as a sequence of adaptive states of a decision process whereby efficiency increases with experience. Learning processes are the ultimate in adaptive decision processes.

(10) Man-machine interaction is a significant topic in the design of optimal computer systems and presents problems to the psychologist in determining the roles of both man and the machine. A machine is considered to be a man-made device which can be used to extend man's own thought processes.

(11) Bayesian statistical techniques can be used to describe the interaction problem in terms of operator decisions. Minimization of the system loss function is desired for optimization but cannot yet be done owing to the unknown noise influence.

(12) Examples of effective man-machine interaction can be found in conversational teaching techniques programed into computers. In teaching machines a language tone must be optimized to balance academic encouragement with academic discipline. Optimization in design of the man-machine system leaves both the man and the machine with their respective fortes.

CHAPTER 14

Order Analysis of Correlation Matrices

LOUIS GUTTMAN
The Hebrew University **and the**
Israel Institute of Applied Social Research

1. INTRODUCTION (BY THE EDITOR)

The present chapter needs to be read with cross reference to Chapter 6 on factor analysis, Chapter 3 on relational systems, Chapter 9 on types, as well as to a volume such as Torgerson's (1438) or Coombs' (384, 385) studying basic scaling problems. For in considering what Guttman has called *order analysis* (which aims to rank variables in order on various dimensions, using correlations, nevertheless, basically in a metrical sense) and *facet analysis* (as used experimentally by him [660, 660a] and by Foa [543a]), we are thrown back to a more fundamental logical examination of the concepts throughout the areas named. Indeed, the originality of Guttman's approach requires as a preparatory step a perspective on description and measurement. In several important senses we have already approached fundamentals on the description of objects, properties and systems, in pages 72 to 85 of Chapter 3 above, and elsewhere, but a further integration needs now to be made.

In Chapter 3 it was proposed that the description of the systems with which

psychologists—and, in fact, any scientists—are concerned requires attention to (a) various sets of objects (briefly and generically designated ids) and (b) various modes of properties or attributes (including inter-id relations). In the data box the Cartesian coordinates by which it is bounded are sets of *ids,* and the entries or modes are quantitative *attributes* or qualitative properties. By derivation, properties for whole systems could be derived from properties of the sets of ids. We now need to look a little more closely at the entry modes in the data box, i.e., at the possible quantitative and qualitative attributes.

The developments by Guttman require that we forsake the restrictions of ordinary, scaled, metric procedures and consider relational systems also in terms of rank orders (including also more similar and less similar) and eventually qualitative terms (though Guttman himself has not committed himself to the latter). Psychologists have been justly proud of certain advances in metric psychology in which, as Torgerson (1438) says, "many of the classificatory concepts dealing with properties tend to be replaced by quantitative concepts." He proceeds to list the advantages cited by

Hempel (713a), of greater refinement in description, precision in laws, and possibility of recourse to higher mathematics; yet here we are asked to turn about and look at rank order and qualitative approaches again.

If we agree to use "property" as the most generic of descriptive terms, then we recognize at once that properties of ids can be either qualitative or quantitative. Let us recognize also that qualities cannot be ordered as such—except in the limiting case of a dichotomy. We can place colors, for example, in the order in which they came in a procession, or in which they lose recognizability as light fades, but in so doing we borrow our order from a metric property temporarily correlated: we are really being metrical. To keep the true quality of quality to the fore it is useful to apply some such term as "a suite" to a collection of qualities with respect to which individuals are to be categorized and described. In a suite of colors, of occupations, of school subjects, etc., we generally, but not invariably, have some class concept binding them together, but there is no one way of ordering them *per se*.

By contrast to a suite of qualitative categories a property which admits of quantification can at least be ordered, and, if it has distance and origin, can progress from a rank scaling to an interval and a ratio scaling. These simple and familiar aspects of regular scales require no comment, except perhaps to add that in the most sophisticated treatment we really need two parallel sets, to cover the otherwise equivalent rank, interval, etc., concepts where progress in the continuum is not equivalent in one direction to what it is in the other, as with time. However, there would seem to be real advantages in restricting the term *scale* to a descriptive system (rank, interval, ratio) on a continuum, applying *suite* to *unorderable* categories (a so-called nominal scale). Then we could perhaps specialize *register* generically to cover *both* systems for expressing properties. A special

case for which some psychologists might wish to extend this use of scale is the dichotomous qualitative suite. Since, unlike other suites, this can be used in correlation (point biserial), one might indeed well decide to reserve "scale" for *any correlatable property,* and so define a scale operationally. In that case, the line between suite and scale would be slightly differently drawn, as shown in Table 14-1.

Incidentally, such terms as "classificatory" and "parametric or non-parametric" are irrelevant—at best supplementary and at worst confusing—in relation to any such main logical treatment as this. For one can *classify* (into groups) either on qualitative *or* on quantitative properties; consequently to speak of a suite as a "classification" does not really distinguish it from a scale. (Parenthetically, the term category is used here, in contrast to class, as having an all or nothing and therefore essentially qualitative, "categorical" character. Semantically, popularly, "category" does not stand in such an absolute contrast to "class" but for lack of a better term we will so specialize it here.) As for parametric versus non-parametric, which is often confused with quantitative versus qualitative, we need only remind ourselves that its reference is properly to the information or assumption regarding *distribution.*

Probably the second most important aspect in naming a descriptive property is whether it is just any property whatever, of any possible (and unknown) correlation with others, or whether it has the more fundamental character among properties of belonging to a set of strictly *independent* properties, sufficient to represent and comprehend all others. In metric continua, this is the difference between a variable and a dimension (such as a primary factor). In matrix terms, the set of dimensions will have relations of the same rank as their order, whereas a set of variables will have relations which admit of reduction to a lower rank. In the purist use of "Cartesian coordinates," they are assumed to have this property, not merely to be orthogonal by the experimenter's whim or conceptual assumption. Further, they are applicable in principle to qualitative as well as quantitative data, though some writers will admit this only for the dichotomous qualitative case. In many cases, it becomes useful to have qualitative terms corresponding to "variable" and to "dimension" in metric concepts. Any sensitive feeling for English would probably suggest "feature" and "aspect" as the best and most precise qualitative equivalents respectively for "variable" and "dimension." A descriptive system can then be completed by applying *attribute* to cover both "features" (qualita-

The proposal for order analysis of correlation matrices is one step from the ordinary quantitative position in factor analysis in that attributes and correlations are now handled only in rank orders. What Guttman (659, 660) has called "facet analysis" involves the statement of hypotheses mainly with respect to such a system, though Foa (543a), otherwise following him, would extend it to purely qualitative data (dichotomous). A difficulty in communication arises at this point because many psychologists, including the present writer and his colleagues, have specialized the term *facet* for any end surface of the data box, bringing it into

TABLE 14-1

CLASSIFICATION OF DESCRIPTIVE CONCEPTS FOR PROPERTIES OF SYSTEMS

			First Dichotomy		
	Adjectival: — — — — — →		Qualitative		Quantitative (metric)
	Substantive — →		SUITE (OF CATEGORIES)		CONTINUUM (OF QUANTITIES)
				← — — Definition of a Scale — →	
Second Dichotomy	Of Unspecified Interrelation	ATTRIBUTE	(Multi-Segmental) Feature	(Bi-Segmental)	Variable
	Cartesian (System of lowest rank)	CHARACTER	Aspect		Dimension

An aspect or feature is a suite of categories, segments or elements. When, as with aspects, the relation among them is that of Cartesian coordinates, the Cartesian products within a particular combination of segments (elements) are said to lie in a *cartet*.

tive attributes) and "variables" (quantitative attributes). By contrast we can reserve *character* to cover the more fundamental, independent concepts we call *aspects* (basic *qualitative* properties) and *dimensions* (basic *quantitative* properties). This conceptual analysis and the associated terminology to keep it clear are summarized in Table 14-1.

relation with *face* (for a condensed set of facets, See Chapter 3, pages 85-98). Accordingly, the present writer prefers to describe analyses of the type now to be discussed as *aspect analyses,* in accordance with the general use of aspect above, referring to any major conceptual aspect of a set of objects (ids). However, "property analysis" might do as well. The gain in clarity will perhaps become more apparent as we discuss the various possibilities and alternatives of analysis with respect to variables (quantitative) and features (qualitative) as summarized in Table 14-1.

Now, it is a historical fact regarding the evolution of ideas that the origins of property, facet, and aspect analysis happened to lie in the early quantitative factor analytic developments, though they *could* have been developed quite independently as a purely logical system. In Chapter 6, it has been pointed out that early workers in factor analysis often inferred factor structure, or checked the relations of variables to hypothesized factors by looking for specific *mosaics, i.e., ordered patterns of various kinds, among the values found in the correlation matrix.* Spearman's "hierarchical" mosaic was offered as the first evidence for a single general factor, and others have been described for Burt's bipolar structure, Holzinger's bifactor, Guttman's simplex and circumplex, and so on. Mosaics can also be (and in Burt's and Holzinger's hypotheses commonly were) designated at the factor matrix level. Matrix mosaics are naturally related to the correlation matrix mosaics, though by the time one gets to the present writer's factor *multiplex* (page 213), the complexity of relation among hypothesized factors is such that little is to be gained by bothering at all with correlation mosaics rather than by designating the alternate *factor* mosaics as the real statements of hypotheses, and testing by the Procrustes rotation (Chapter 6, page 191).

Obviously, a pattern mosaic of correlations, or a parallel pattern of distribution of people indicating the nature of covariance among them, with respect to certain axes, can be used either to generate a hypothesis or to test it. Properly, aspect, or facet analysis has stressed so strongly the hypothesis-testing function — the initial setting up of a priori conceptual categories and associated interaction assumptions — that for many students it has tended to become almost synonymous with the far wider designation of a design as "hypothesis testing." This, of course, is an unfortunate distortion — or rather lack — of perspective: all factor analysis and aspect analysis (jointly: "property analysis") procedures can be approached in *either* way. Within aspect analysis, the experimenter states clearly the number of aspects which he believes necessary to define the observed features (or, in quantitative data, including order analysis, the number of dimensions to define the observed variables). Then he indicates what combinations of aspect segments (or dimensional high and low scores) he would expect by hypothesis to occur with particularly high or low frequencies in his population (i.e., what covariation), so that the resultant correlational or associational mosaic is specified. The hypothesis can next be tested empirically by seeing, in fact, whether certain Cartesian products occur with the unusual frequency expected, as shown by the relations among the features in the relational mosaic. Naturally, in the wider sense of general property analysis, any hypothesis needs to specify, e.g., in aspect (facet) analysis, certain subsidiary hypotheses or postulates within the model, e.g., as to modes of interaction among the characters, the nature of specific elements or segments, etc. (In ordinary factor analysis, the relations are understood to be linear and without variance interaction.)

In order analysis, the specific correlational quantities, and the Euclidean properties of persons in a test space, are usually subordinated to classifying correlations as positives, negatives, zeros and non-zeros in a mosaic pattern. From this and the outcome of having variables only *ordered* on a dimension, historical developments have gone to full "aspect analysis," wherein only logical categories and segments thereof enter discussion about the characters or properties. Parenthetically, we have lacked terms for ready discussion of the technical relations which then arise, and the present writer would argue for speaking of the *segments* of an aspect and the *cartet* (from Descartes) for the particular Cartesian product formed by any particular complex *combination of segments* (or "elements" in Foa's account). For example, an important aspect (Cartesian coordinate) in classifying publications has to do with whether they are articles or books. These are two segments and one could have others in such a suite, e.g., popular books and scholarly books, survey articles and original articles. Another aspect one might hypothesize would be the nature of the reading public, divisible into segments such as student and faculty reading. A number of features, e.g., whether on reserve or open shelf, whether cited in student reading lists or not, etc., could then be named. Hypotheses could then be stated about the expected relations among these more numerous features, required by the particular set of aspects employed in the theory, and the resulting empirical mosaic of associations would test these hypotheses.

In hypothesis testing in factor analysis, as described in Chapters 6 and 10 above, the researcher first writes out the matrix of primary and second stratum factors which most exactly represents his theoretical position. He then tests the fit of the experimentally obtained *factor* matrix to the "target matrix," the particular unique rotational resolution of the experimental data used being either: (a) with the restriction that simple structure must first be obtained by blind rotation, or (b) merely the position reached in a best possible approach by the Procrustes program to the target matrix. Facet or aspect analysis tests typically by the agreement reached in the first obtained relational matrix (e.g., correlation matrix) *itself*. When the relational statement is in terms of correlations from continuous, quantitative variables, one must however remember that the mosaic seen in the R matrix could be explained by an infinite number of *other* theoretical factor resolutions than that which the facet analyst accepts. What the situation is in this respect

when one is dealing with qualitative *aspects* explaining the relations of a larger set of qualitative *features,* is something to the solution of which one confidently hopes that further work along the lines of this chapter will lead.

Finally, in reminding the student that aspect analysis and factor analysis alike (as property analysis) can proceed from a definite a priori statement of hypotheses, one must remember that in psychology we are in the peculiar position of being able to make self-fulfilling hypotheses. In most sciences the variables are given in nature, but, at least in certain areas, the psychologist can freely make them up himself—for instance when he makes up tests. This has already been commented upon in connection with Guilford's and Edwards' construction of orthogonal trait concepts by making up orthogonal scales. And since it is possible to multiply items which closely resemble one another, the charge of artificiality applies also to Tryon's rotation of factors to pass through clusters of items. The only fundamental safeguard against these fatal possibilities is, as argued elsewhere, the concept of a natural "personality sphere" or population of variables, and explicit recognition of the rules of design for representative experiment (Chapter 2 above). The reader will at this point naturally wonder how far the same objection—that items can be made up to yield an order analysis outcome as required a priori—applies to Guttman's procedures.

The difference of Tryon's and Guttman's systems may seem to a mathematician fairly large, since Guttman demands that his subsets or clusters form a correlational hierarchy, whereas Tryon is willing to put a vector through any well-defined cluster regardless of whether the correlations in this subset have further order properties. But in the sense of a general scientific model, cluster analysis and order analysis might be said to be much closer to each other than either is to factor analysis (if, as we have consistently done, we define the latter as searching for separate factors shown by simple structure to function in Nature as independent determiners).

The factor analyst's position differs from these on much more than technical issues, and goes to the roots of scientific method and philosophy. His argument is, as stated more fully on page 212 above, that it is possible to create correlation mosaics by deliberately introducing tests made up in a certain way, whereas the same is scarcely possible for the hyperplanes of factors. The latter thus offers a possibility of discovering structure in natural data, whereas the former offers a possibility of creating it in unnatural data. Thus Guttman mentions below (page 444) as an advantage of order (facet, simplex, circumplex) that "It is now possible to construct the content of batteries of variables by facet design and to predict in advance the order structures which may result from the empirical observations." Unfortunately, although Guttman is thus himself clear that he is not investigating empirically, but putting together variables which will yield desired structures, this is not always realized either by those who use order analysis or who construct Guttman scales.

Among such test constructors — if not psychological investigators — there is, indeed, a subtle misunderstanding of the hypothetico-deductive method in certain uses of order and cluster analysis. Some investigators are inclined to say that when they put in certain variables to see if a cluster or facet subset will emerge, they are testing a hypothesis. They are testing a hypothesis, but not necessarily the one they think. They are testing the hypothesis that they can choose or make up certain variables to be correlated with others, but not that a certain factor influence does or does not exist to account for these correlations. The latter, so long as simple structure or confactor rotation are our only initial tests of a natural independent function or influence, can be demonstrated only by seeing if a resolution can be found meeting the

additional and exacting conditions described earlier (Chapter 6). Mosaic analysis thus gives scope for a considerable subjectivity, in the sense that the researcher says he believes in a certain structure and then produces or selects variables in a way which will fit this. At this point the question arises whether the fit can be examined (granted no problems from selection) with the same technically good significance tests as the fit of a hypothesis to a factor solution, as discussed by Fruchter in Chapter 10.

Actually, in practice, most searchers for clustering subsets do not use any exact test of fit.[1] They follow this method of choosing their vectors, rather than by rotation, because they feel that they are "near the data." Seeing the actual clustering mosaic in a *correlation* matrix gives many psychologists not too familiar with factor analysis the feeling that they are "playing safe." But to this there arise, first, the totally disabling objections to putting source traits through surface traits, i.e., factor vectors through clusters, that the latter are characteristically ill-defined (Chapter 9, page 313), arbitrary, and unstable. Second, the whole freedom of movement of simple structure rotation to quite new scientific criteria is lost. The "safety" in sticking close to the correlation matrix reminds one of that advocated by the fond warning of a mother to her air cadet son, "Be sure to fly slowly and keep near the ground."

The reader with a sophisticated methodological view will be able to judge for himself where order analysis and factor analysis have their roles. Here Professor

---

[1] Spearman long ago worked out a reasonably satisfactory test — the tetrad difference and its standard error — for fit to a single hierarchy. When applied to bipolar, bifactor, simplex, circumplex, and other developments involving several hierarchies, some further discussion of its applicability is needed.

Parenthetically, the term Simplex as applied to a theory of *equal interval scaling* (Cattell, 254) should not be confused with simplex as a *correlation matrix mosaic,* though there are superficial resemblances in that both involve patterns in a correlation matrix. (Editor.)

Guttman examines some ability, perceptual, and attitudinal data to demonstrate that such order relations can be useful in understanding—and perhaps he implies discovering—a wide range of psychological relations. He concludes that an adequate order analysis, when it reveals the rational arrangement of the evidence, provides a possible basis for selecting the variables to be used in consolidating one's ideas.

Guttman chooses Ekman's color vision data for his second analysis. A fuller description of other multivariate methods of analyzing these same data can be found in Chapter 17.

2. PROCEDURES IN ORDER ANALYSIS

Perhaps the first example of order analysis of correlation matrices goes back to the eminent British psychologist, Charles Spearman. At the turn of this century (1336) he noticed that one could apparently arrange the rows and columns of the matrix of intercorrelation of tests of mental ability so that a certain gradient appeared. When he ordered the tests so that the highest correlations fell in the upper left-hand corner of the matrix, the smallest ones seemed to be found at the opposite (lower right-hand) corner. The coefficients tended to be smaller the farther their positions departed either to the right of or below the maximal correlations. Spearman's concept of a "general factor" of intelligence was intended to explain this type of order pattern.

Subsequent research showed that in fact such a pattern did not really hold for the mental test data then being studied, and the configural approach to the study of correlation matrices was largely abandoned. Instead, Spearman, Burt, Thurstone, and others diverted their interests to algebraic formulations of what is called today "multiple-factor analysis." In these algebraic approaches the notion of order among variables is absent. More seriously, the approximate computational procedures used actually have blinded researchers from seeing simple order patterns in their own data which may have important psychological implications.

Renewed interest in the configural approach was expressed in the 1954 work on the radex theory by Guttman (652). It is surprising how many empirical examples have since been found of simplex and the circumplex. The lists published in Guttman (656) are constantly being added to by many authors in publications on a wide variety of topics. More recently, a theory of the design of batteries of variables has been developed which attempts to get beyond blind empiricism for the study of the structure of a correlation matrix. It is now possible to construct the content of batteries of variables by facet design and to predict in advance the order structures which may result from the empirical observations.

The present paper will be devoted largely to showing two different examples of ordered structures revealed by re-analysis of data which have been treated otherwise by the original authors. Since most previous work has not been based on sufficiently systematic design of content, there may be value in re-analyzing heuristically the data of the richer published examples in order to see if some simple kind of order pattern approximately obtains. This may facilitate suggesting improved designs for obtaining clearer patterns in the future. We shall close with a third example, borrowed from one of our colleagues, where a facet design of content was made in advance; circumplexes resulted in certain submatrices, and most interesting possibilities exist for the structural pattern of the complete 128×128 correlation matrix.

The virtue of a clear order pattern is twofold. First, it helps answer the problem of sampling of variables. A clear design enables one to infer from the structure of a given sample of variables what the structure of the relationships with new variables of the same design will be. Second, one can learn best to use the given set of variables for relating them to a further set of variables (such as criteria in external prediction problems) by considering simultaneously the designs (and patterns) of both sets of variables.

A further contribution of order analysis is to the clarification of a number of issues concerning multiple-factor analysis.

3. FIRST EXAMPLE: NUMBER ABILITIES

Our first re-analysis of existing data will relate to the classical doctoral thesis of Clyde Coombs on number ability (383). This was designed to investigate certain hypotheses concerning the nature of number ability, and, secondarily, the nature of perceptual speed. A battery of thirty-four tests was given to 223 Chicago high school seniors, and the data were factored by the centroid method into ten common factors.

For the re-analysis, by a very simple process of inspection of the correlation matrix it is possible to see that half of the observed variables can have their interrelations portrayed by the simple two-dimensional plot of Diagram 14-1. Furthermore, five out of the ten common factors (including four out of the seven "primary" factors) can be plotted simultaneously with these seventeen observed variables in this two-dimensional diagram.

The position of each variable in Diagram 14-1 is indicated by the place of its number in parentheses. The numbering of the tests is Coombs'. The common factors are indicated by letters, rather than by numbers; Coombs gave them the following names:

Factor *P:* Perceptual Speed
      N: Number
      V: Verbal
      D: Deductive

Factor *A* was unnamed, but was associated with the three "Alphabet" tests.

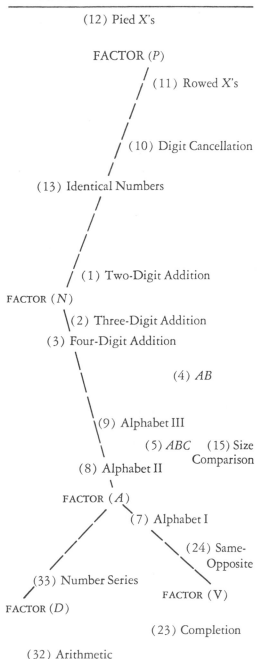

DIAGRAM 14-1. Two-Dimensional Plot of 17 Observed Tests and 5 Common Factors From Coombs' Correlational Data on Numerical Abilities

(12) Pied *X*'s

FACTOR (*P*)

(11) Rowed *X*'s

(10) Digit Cancellation

(13) Identical Numbers

(1) Two-Digit Addition

FACTOR (*N*)

(2) Three-Digit Addition

(3) Four-Digit Addition

(4) *AB*

(9) Alphabet III

(5) *ABC* (15) Size Comparison

(8) Alphabet II

FACTOR (*A*)

(7) Alphabet I

(24) Same-Opposite

(33) Number Series

FACTOR (*V*)

FACTOR (*D*)

(23) Completion

(32) Arithmetic

TABLE 14-2

INTERCORRELATIONS OF THE 17 OBSERVED TESTS AND 5 COMMON FACTORS OF DIAGRAM 14-1

(Decimal Points Omitted)

(From Coombs, 382)

Test	12	P	11	10	13	1	N	2	3	9	8	A	7	33	D	32	4	5	15	24	V	23
12. Pied X's	—	59	50	30	21	13	16	12	16	18	21	18	18	14	12	4	13	8	12	-0	09	13
Factor P	59	—	74	59	46	22	24	20	21	14	13	14	14	08	03	-07	25	01	15	-02	05	00
11. Rowed X's	50	74	—	51	37	27	25	27	24	16	14	16	18	9	03	0	32	18	22	0	07	1
10. Digit Cancellation	30	59	51	—	51	45	47	45	44	32	33	33	36	17	13	8	43	29	28	18	14	12
13. Identical Numbers	21	46	37	51	—	54	52	50	50	38	32	35	35	14	11	6	44	31	31	24	17	13
1. Two-Digit Addition	13	22	27	45	54	—	91	85	79	40	38	38	36	26	21	16	49	41	34	26	23	16
Factor N	16	24	25	47	52	91	—	94	91	46	44	44	42	33	33	25	49	41	33	26	24	19
2. Three-Digit Addition	12	20	27	45	50	85	94	—	89	49	47	48	45	36	40	30	50	46	39	33	15	27
3. Four-Digit Addition	16	21	24	44	50	79	91	89	—	51	49	48	48	36	40	33	52	47	39	32	26	25
9. Alphabet III	18	14	16	32	38	40	46	49	51	—	92	96	91	47	43	37	64	60	44	51	33	45
8. Alphabet II	21	13	14	33	32	38	44	47	49	92	—	96	92	47	44	32	59	29	45	53	34	44
Factor A	18	14	16	33	35	38	44	48	48	96	96	—	95	48	46	39	62	62	43	54	35	47
7. Alphabet I	18	14	18	36	36	36	42	45	48	91	92	95	—	48	49	41	59	60	44	48	31	49
33. Number Series	14	08	9	17	14	26	33	36	36	47	47	48	48	—	74	60	32	33	36	38	36	33
Factor D	12	03	03	13	11	21	33	40	40	43	44	46	49	74	—	72	27	35	30	28	24	29
32. Arithmetic	4	-07	0	8	6	16	25	30	33	37	32	39	41	60	72	—	27	31	29	35	31	33
4. AB	13	25	32	43	44	49	49	50	52	64	59	62	59	32	27	27	—	57	48	44	33	32
5. ABC	8	01	18	29	31	41	41	46	47	60	29	62	60	33	35	31	57	—	45	46	34	34
15. Size Comparison	12	15	22	28	31	34	33	39	39	44	45	43	44	36	30	29	48	45	—	58	64	53
24. Same-Opposite	-0	-02	0	18	24	26	26	33	32	51	53	54	48	38	28	35	44	46	58	—	80	71
Factor V	09	05	07	14	17	23	24	15	26	33	34	35	31	36	24	31	33	34	64	80	—	80
23. Completion	13	00	1	12	13	16	19	27	25	45	44	47	49	33	29	33	32	34	53	71	80	—

The distances between tests in the diagram are not intended to reflect the absolute sizes of intercorrelations, but rather the approximate *rank order* of the sizes. As a start toward understanding this, let us select a subset of the variables which are spread out along a curve which does not bend upon itself too sharply. Such a sequence is, for example: 12, *P,* 11, 10, 13, *N,* 2, 3. The matrix of intercorrelations of these nine variables is given in the first section of Table 14-2.

The pattern of the correlations in this submatrix is quite similar to that of a simplex: the largest correlations are along the main diagonal, and the correlations tend to decrease in size as their positions approach the upper right or lower left corners. The closer two variables are in their serial order, usually, the more highly they are correlated with each other.

Such a simple feature characterizing such tests has not been revealed by any technique of analysis other than the apparently simple-minded one suggested here. Surely, this simple order should throw light on the differential tasks being posed by such tests.

It is important to interpolate here that, in the years that have passed, Clyde Coombs has, of course, become one of the outstanding leaders in the field of non-metric treatment of psychometric data. Our reanalysis of his early work is actually Coombsian in the present sense of this term.

4. RETROSPECTIVE ATTEMPT TO INTERPRET THE ORDER

At the beginning of the sequence is a simple test of perceptual speed called "Pied X's," consisting of seven pages of pied letters with seven *x*'s on each page. The subjects were to find as many *x*'s on a page as they were able and then turn to the next page. At the opposite extreme of this particular sequence of nine tests is "Four-Digit Addition." Apparently, this entire sequence deals with progressively more

complex organization of perception, from disordered to ordered stimuli, culminating in a simple manipulation of ordered symbols which we call "addition." The sequence is from perception to manipulation, with other aspects involved which are subsidiary to this major emphasis so that a curve, rather than a straight line, results in Diagram 14-1.

For present purposes, it is indeed fortunate that Dr. Coombs meticulously calculated and published the correlations between the factors and the tests, as well as among the factors themselves. This enables us to include the factors both in Table 14-2 and Diagram 14-1. As has been pointed out elsewhere, a "factor" in the sense of conventional factor analysis is essentially but a weighted average of the observed tests, and can be regarded simply as an additional test (650). Diagram 14-1 shows that factor *P* was obtained by a weighting that places it within the region of tests 12, 11, 10, 13, none of which involves manipulation. In contrast, factor *N* falls within the closely grouped subset of Addition tests. Within this subset, order is determined by the number of digits to be added, or the complexity of manipulation. This time the weighting seems to have been chosen so that factor *N* falls *within* the semicircle of the variables rather than in a sequence with them. For example, test 3 correlates slightly more with *N* than it does with test 2.

Because of the high interrelations among the Addition tests (which makes them bunched so closely together in Diagram 14-1), their relative orders vis-à-vis tests outside this subsequence may sometimes be less sharply defined. Nevertheless, if we take tests distant from the subsequence, we still find the notion of order essentially maintained as indicated approximately in Diagram 14-1. Test 13 shows this most clearly, giving the sequence of correlations .54, .52, .50, .50 with tests 1, *N,* 2, 3 respectively. The other tests tend to maintain order between tests 1, 2, and 3, and behave slightly differentially with respect to the central factor N. The order relation with this subsequence stands out perhaps even more sharply with the tests in the lower part of Diagram 14-1. For example, test 9 correlates .51, .49, .46, .40 with tests 3, 2, N, 1, respectively. Similar gradients can be found in the second and third sections of Table 14-1 vis-à-vis the Addition tests.

Let us now look at another sequence of tests in Diagram 14-1: 9, 8, A, 7, 33, D, 32. These tests all deal with facility of operating according to rules. For example, test 7 (Alphabet I) gave a rule of the following sort: a pair of letters CE equals F because of the rule that if a pair is in alphabetical order, then it is equal to the letter in the alphabet following the second member of the pair. Conversely, the pair TR equals Q by the rule that a pair in backward order is equal to the letter in the alphabet preceding the second letter of the pair. Tests 8 and 9 were of the same nature as test 7, the notion being that the difference between the three tests would simply be the amount of practice the subject obtained. Thus test 7 would be facility of manipulation with the least amount of practice, and test 9 with the greatest practice. Test 7 in this sense required more reasoning, and test 9 more perception. It is interesting that in relating to the previous sequence of Addition — in which all the subjects previously had great practice and, therefore, manipulation was largely by rote — test 9 is the closest and 7 the farthest. Test 7 leads into the next sequence 33, D, 32, which requires even more facility in dealing with rules, with even less rote learning on the types of items presented.

A sequence branching off in another direction is 4, 5, 15, 24, V, 23. Tests 24 and 23 go off into the verbal domain, and it is interesting that factor V was determined to fall essentially between these two tests. Test 15 is also a verbal test, despite its name, since the pairs of objects to be compared are given only by name, such as "sardine-shark." It is interesting that 15 is closer to 24, which is also a comparison test

of a sort, than to 23, which is not a comparison test.

Tests 4 and 5 have been included in this last sequence for convenience in setting up Table 14-2. They do give a simplex-like gradient with the others in the last section of Table 14-2. In a sense, there is a verbal aspect to these tests, since they use letters of the alphabet. However, the tests actually propose problems in formal logic. Only the letters A, B, and C are used in each item of test 4, combined in various ways. The rules are that a combination of any two letters is equal to the third (remaining) letter. Thus AC equals B. Furthermore, a letter combined with itself is equal to itself. Thus BB equals B. Test 5 is of the same nature, but with larger sequences of letters.

5. CROSS-CHECKING DIAGRAM 14-1 BY AN APPROXIMATE CIRCUMPLEX

As a check on the relative adequacy of Diagram 14-1 for portraying the interrelations of the tests, let us see if we can pick an approximate circumplex out of the picture. Perhaps the closest one can get to a substantial circle involving the original tests is the following sequence: tests 1, 4, 15, 24, 23, 33, 3, 1. The corresponding submatrix of correlations for the sequence is given in Table 14-3.

The correlations in Table 14-3 do show the contiguity pattern of an approximate circumplex. The largest correlations are along the main diagonal, taper off about halfway from the main diagonal, and increase again toward the upper and lower right-hand corners.

Spacing between the tests is rather unequal, as indicated in Diagram 14-1 and verified by the correlations along the main diagonal of Table 14-3. The approximate circular pattern, however, is evident both in Diagram 14-1 and in the correlation submatrix.

The reader may wish to check other patterns in a similar fashion. It is not to be expected that complete accuracy of order-

TABLE 14-3

SUBEXAMPLE OF CIRCUMPLEX

Test	1	4	15	24	23	33	3
1. Two-Digit Addition	—	49	35	26	16	26	79
4. *AB*	49	—	48	44	32	32	52
15. Size Comparison	35	48	—	58	53	36	39
24. Same-Opposite	26	44	58	—	71	38	32
23. Completion	16	32	53	71	—	38	25
33. Number Series	26	32	36	38	38	—	36
3. Four-Digit Addition	79	52	39	32	25	36	—

ing will hold within tests bunched closely together. Not only sampling error will militate against this, but also there are problems of unequal communalities and the crudeness of our approximating technique.

6. TECHNIQUE FOR DRAWING DIAGRAM 14-1

We arrived at Diagram 14-1 by a simple trial-and-error graphic method. First, two tests where plotted as points on a blank sheet of paper. Then a third test was chosen and plotted vis-à-vis these first two points, making the relative distances equal approximately to unity minus the sizes of the corresponding correlation coefficients. Each subsequent point was plotted vis-à-vis the preceding points by the same technique, fudging the original distances when necessary to keep the rank order of the distances as similar as possible to the inverse rank order of the sizes of the correlation coefficients.

Ideally, it would be desirable to have a more exact computing technique for the plotting. A promising approach is that recently developed by Roger Shepard[2] in the context of multidimensional scaling

(1313). Since this paper was first written, the present writer has perfected a general approach for developing nonmetric computer programs for a large variety of problems.[3] Programs appropriate to the kinds of data studied in this paper are now operational on the University of Michigan IBM 7090 and on other campuses. Reanalyzing Table 14-2 by the computer calculations has turned out to give coordinates for a two-dimensional Euclidean space that precisely reproduce Diagram 14-1.

For three-dimensional and higher cases it will, of course, be difficult to operate without an analytical procedure. However, whether or not one has a computer on hand, one should not despise the quick and relatively accurate results obtainable by hand labor for the non-metric treatment of a correlation matrix.

To include in the present analysis further

[2] It is interesting that Shepard misconstrued the relation of his approach to that of conventional factor analysis. He believed his technique would give the same results, only less efficiently, as would a conventional linear factor analysis (1313, pp. 240-241). This is not at all correct; his analysis is one of *order* and in general will yield a smaller space than does factor analysis, as our present examples show.

[3] See Louis Guttman, "A General Nonmetric Technique for Finding the Smallest Euclidean Space for a Configuration of Points," *Psychometrika*, 1966, in press; James C. Lingoes, "An IBM 7090 Program for Guttman-Lingoes Smallest Space Analysis—I," *Behavioral Science*, 1965, 10, 183-184; James C. Lingoes, "New Computer Developments in Pattern Analysis and Nonmetric Techniques," *IBM Journal*, 1965, in press. For some applications see Louis Guttman, "The Structure of Interrelations Among Intelligence Tests," *Proceedings of the 1964 Invitational Conference on Testing Problems*, Princeton, N. J.: Educational Testing Service, 1965; Takako Mori, "The Structure of Motivations for Becoming a Teacher," *The Journal of Educational Psychology*, 1965, 56, 175-183. See also Ruth Guttman and Louis Guttman, "A New Approach to the Analysis of Growth Patterns: The Simplex Structure of Intercorrelations of Measurements," *Growth*, 1965, 29, 219-232.

variables of Coombs' study beyond the seventeen of Table 14-2, would require at least a three-dimensional picture in place of the two dimensions of Diagram 14-1, and so this will not be attempted here.

7. RELATIVE PARSIMONY OF AN ORDER ANALYSIS

Perhaps the most striking feature of Diagram 14-1 is that it succeeds in portraying in two dimensions the structure of the interrelations of seventeen observed tests, despite the fact that the conventional factor analysis originally made of the data prescribes five dimensions (or common factors) for these same tests. If number of dimensions is regarded as a criterion for parsimonious analysis, then surely the two-dimensional portrayal is more parsimonious than the five-dimensional.

Both of these portrayals are only approximate. The five-dimensional one attempts to reproduce the sizes of the correlation coefficients by a certain linear algebra, and does this only approximately; many more than five dimensions would be required for exact reproduction of the correlation coefficients. Similarly, the two-dimensional portrayal attempts to reproduce the essential rank order relations among the correlation coefficients, and does this only approximately.

The basic question is: Are the main features of the structure brought out by a particular analysis? In the present example, it appears to us that Diagram 14-1 does give the main features of the data; indeed so much so that it even shows the location of the five common factors within the picture. The converse seems less true: from mere conventional calculations of the five common factors, no suggestion was made as to the order pattern now obvious from Diagram 14-1 and Table 14-2.

A deeper kind of analysis would be to go into the content of the tests themselves in such a fashion as to enable prediction in advance of what the statistical structure would be. If the basic picture for the seventeen tests is essentially two-dimensional in the above non-metric sense, what are the facets of content which lead to this dimensionality? Clearly, the names of the five common factors are not sufficient to explain the two-dimensionality which reigns among these common factors and the tests of which they are averages. Why should there be a chain going from P to N to A which then divides into D in one direction and V in the other? We leave this problem for further research. It is quite conceivable that a facet design can be found for these tests which will explicate the structure of their interrelations. Furthermore, such a design would predict where further tests would fall within the picture. Our next two examples enable prediction of the structure of interrelations of tests by knowledge about their design of content.

8. SECOND EXAMPLE: A RE-ANALYSIS OF SOME COLOR VISION DATA

The first example above of a configural analysis exemplified a blind approach. No a priori theory was suggested for the structure of the correlation for the numerical ability tests. Instead, an attempt at plotting of points was made, starting directly with the correlation coefficients, with no regard for the content of the variables concerned. Our next example is to be of just the opposite approach: a theory will first be developed for the structure of the matrix on the basis of the content of the observations. Our example will again rely on data which were borrowed from another author and for which the original analysis went off in a different and less parsimonious direction.

In a study of color vision (458), Gösta Ekman had subjects compare six different colors with each other, two at a time. The colors differed primarily in wave length, from yellow to red. For each pair (C_i, C_j) of colors, the subject was asked:

"What proportion of color C_i is contained in color C_j?" The resulting data matrix is given in Table 14-4. In principle, this matrix could be asymmetric because the proportion of color C_i contained in C_j may be judged differently from the proportion of color C_j contained in C_i. The diagonal elements of Table 14-4 are non-experimental; they were set exactly equal to unity as if there were no error in judging what are closer together, the overlap will be larger. This will be true for each subject separately, and will also be true of the average of the judgments of the subjects. (A detailed analysis of this point will be published on a later occasion, together with a more complete analysis of the present example.)

Let q_{ij} be the average judgment of the proportion of C_i contained in C_j; then $1 -$

TABLE 14-4

EKMAN'S DATA MATRIX

(From Ekman, 458)

Wave Length	593	600	610	628	651	674
593	1.00	.94	.67	.22	.08	.04
600	.95	1.00	.80	.31	.16	.06
610	.63	.75	1.00	.78	.56	.38
628	.21	.37	.78	1.00	.81	.72
651	.14	.23	.61	.85	1.00	.86
674	.07	.13	.40	.80	.90	1.00

proportion of color C_i was contained in itself. Inspection of Table 14-4 shows that in fact it is close to being symmetric, so we shall regard it as such.

What kind of a theory can one develop for Table 14-4, considering the question submitted to the subjects for the paired comparisons? One suggestion is to regard each color not as a single point (say, its wave length) along a continuum, but rather as a psychological interval. Insofar as the intervals of two colors overlap on the psychological continuum, each will contain something of the other color. The proportion of color C_j contained in color C_i would be the same overlap divided by the length of C_i's interval. These proportions will be equal, then, if and only if the intervals of C_i and C_j are equal to each other.

Because of the essential symmetry of Table 14-4, we may assume all the colors to have intervals of equal length along the psychological continuum. The amount of overlap between two colors, therefore, will be a linear function of the distance between the respective midpoints, say, of their intervals. If the midpoints of the intervals

q_{ij} is the average proportion of C_i not contained in C_j. Let a_i be the midpoint of the psychological interval of C_i. Then our assumptions lead to the condition that:

$$(1) \quad 1 - q_{ij} = |a_i - a_j|,$$

whence

$$(2) \quad q_{ij} = 1 - |a_i - a_j|$$

Equation (2) clearly gives the general features of Table 14-4. For the diagonal elements, we have $i = j$; so $q_{ii} = 1$ from (2). For non-diagonal elements, the farther C_i is from C_j, the larger is the difference between a_i and a_j, and q_{ij} decreases. Thus equation (2) generates a type of simplex pattern for the observed matrix.

9. ESTIMATING THE PARAMETERS OF THE SIMPLEX STRUCTURE

Given such a parametric theory for the structure of the observed matrix, one can actually go ahead to estimate the parameters a_j. A method of obtaining least-squares estimates is to pivot on equation (1). Subtract unity from each element of Table

14-4 and reverse the signs of the elements *on one side* of the main diagonal, yielding Table 14-5. If we denote the general element of Table 14-5 by x_{ij}, then ideally:

(3) $x_{ij} = a_i - a_j$.

Notice that in the right member of (3) the absolute value sign has disappeared: x_{ij} ideally should define a skew-symmetric matrix. Clearly, the origin for the a_j is arbitrary, so that we may set the sum of the a_j equal to zero. Therefore, summing both members of (3) over j yields:

(4) $\displaystyle\sum_{j=1}^{n} x_{ij} = na_i,$

where n is the number of colors ($n = 6$ in the present case).

Equation (4) gives a simple way of estimating the a_i. One needs only the sums of the elements in each row or column inside Table 14-5 and to divide by n to obtain the corresponding a_i. Because of the slight empirical asymmetry, the row totals are not exactly equal to the column totals, so both have been added together to yield $2na_i$ (recorded in the last column of Table 14-5). Dividing this by $2n = 12$ yields the estimated a_i as recorded in the last row of Table 14-5.

How well the a_i reproduce Table 14-4 is shown in Table 14-6. The diagonals, of course, come out perfectly. The reproduced matrix is symmetric by virtue of equation (2). The fit is rather close. Indeed, the fit is closer than that given by Ekman's attempt at a factor analysis.

TABLE 14-5

THE EMPIRICAL SKEW-SYMMETRIC MATRIX (x_{ij})
DERIVED FROM TABLE 14-3

Wave Length	539	600	610	628	651	674	Total	$2na_i$
539	0	.06	.33	.78	.92	.96	3.05	−6.05
600	−.05	0	.20	.69	.84	.94	2.62	−5.08
610	−.37	−.25	0	.22	.44	.62	.66	−1.34
628	−.79	−.63	−.22	0	.19	.28	−1.17	2.51
651	−.86	−.77	−.39	−.15	0	.14	−2.03	4.32
674	−.93	−.87	−.60	−.20	−.10	0	−2.70	5.64
Total	−3.00	−2.46	−.68	1.34	2.29	2.94		
a_i	−.50	−.42	−.11	.21	.36	.47		

TABLE 14-6

EKMAN'S DATA MATRIX REPRODUCED FROM THE a_i

Wave Length	593	600	610	628	651	674	a_i
593	1.00	.92	.61	.29	.14	.03	−.50
600	.92	1.00	.69	.37	.22	.11	−.42
610	.61	.69	1.00	.68	.53	.42	−.11
628	.29	.37	.68	1.00	.85	.74	.21
651	.14	.22	.53	.85	1.00	.89	.36
674	.03	.11	.42	.74	.89	1.00	.47

10. COMPARISON OF THE ORDER ANALYSIS WITH COMMON-FACTOR ANALYSIS

As in the case of other simplex matrices, it can be shown that a matrix of the form given by equation 2 is in general non-singular, and therefore has as many linear factors as there are variables. Furthermore, the principal components of such a matrix satisfy a difference equation of the general type discussed originally in the context of scale analysis (649, 653). The oscillatory law holds again: the first principal component is essentially a constant, the second is a monotone function of the rank order of the variables, the third is a U-shaped function of the rank order, etc.

Ekman actually made a slight modification of Table 14-4 for his factor analysis and stopped at three common factors. It is interesting to see that his first three centroid factors, which are close to the first three principal components, exactly follow the oscillatory law. This indicates that he should have continued to the further three factors to find all the lawful components belonging to such a matrix. Because of the blind approach of the factor analysis, Ekman tried to stop at two factors and even regarded his third as an uninterpreted feature of the data.

When one begins with a preliminary theory for the order relation among the colors such as that in equation (2), he is not bound in advance to stop at any given number of factors; instead, he has a complete picture of the lawfulness of all the factors in the sense of factor analysis. The most important feature is that the non-Euclidean analysis given by equation (2) enables a complete reproduction of the observed matrix with only one set of coefficients a_i; this is impossible by any single set of coefficients provided by a conventional Euclidean factor analysis.

Earlier, Ekman published results of another type of experiment on color vision (456). Again, a factor analysis was performed which did not bring out the most striking feature of the data—namely that they formed a circumplex. Shepard (1314) re-analyzed these data by his non-metric computer technique, and did bring out the two-dimensional circular order of the full range of colors. Without any computing, the circular order is obvious from the data matrix itself in (456), just as the simple order in Table 14-4 above is obvious.

11. THIRD EXAMPLE: FACET DESIGN OF INTERPERSONAL RELATIONS

Our third example will be of a more complex design than the preceding one. The content will be socio-psychological. The variables were designed in advance according to a certain facet theory of social interaction (542), there being 128 variables all told. Despite the complexity of the design, the structure of the interrelationship of these many variables is easily perceived from various simple considerations.

The first large-scale research on interaction within a social dyad using a facet design was in the area of foreman-worker relations (541). From the experience gained on this project, Foa was able to focus more sharply on certain facets, leading to a second project on the dyad, namely on the husband-wife relation.

The relation could be regarded as divided into two major facets: the relater and the content of the relation. The relater facet was defined in turn in terms of three facets: actor, level, and alias, while the content of the relation was also defined by three facets: direction, object, and mode. Each of these facets was regarded as a dichotomy. All six facets and their elements are as in the following table.

The meanings of these facets and their elements are described in detail in (542) and (543) and so will not be repeated here. Our presentation will differ in emphasis and some details from that in (542) and

(543), and focus more directly on the facet design and its implications for the statistical structure.

Each observed variable had its content defined by a profile over the six facets of the form $a_i b_j c_k d_l e_m f_n$ $(i, j, k, l, m, n = 1, 2)$. Thus $2^6 = 64$ variables result for each respondent. Since there are two respondents in a dyad—the husband and the wife in this case—a total of 128 variables was observed for the dyad.

TABLE 14-7

THE MAJOR FACETS

Relater Facets	
A Actor	a_1 Non-observer a_2 Observer
B Level	b_1 Actual b_2 Ideal
C Alias	c_1 Non-actor c_2 Actor
Content Facets	
D Direction	d_1 Acceptance d_2 Rejection
E Object	e_1 Other e_2 Self
F Mode	f_1 Social f_2 Emotional

12. ORDERING CARTESIAN ELEMENTS INTO A CIRCLE

What should the structure of the statistical interrelations among the 128 variables be? The psychological theory led to considering an order relationship within each of the two major facets, relater and content. Since the relater space is defined by three dichotomous facets, it has $2^3 = 8$ different elements or profiles. The psychological theory led to an order hypothesis for these profiles, namely that of a circle, as follows.

It is an interesting fact that any Cartesian space of eight elements defined by three dichotomous facets can be regarded as a circle. Consider the following sequence of profiles:

I	$a_1 b_1 c_1$
II	$a_1 b_1 c_2$
III	$a_1 b_2 c_2$
IV	$a_1 b_2 c_1$
V	$a_2 b_2 c_1$
VI	$a_2 b_2 c_2$
VII	$a_2 b_1 c_2$
VIII	$a_2 b_1 c_1$

Each profile in the sequence differs from the preceding one in one facet only. Furthermore, the last profile VIII differs from the first profile I also in only one facet. The whole sequence could be rotated in a circular order, keeping VIII adjacent to I, without changing the contiguity property of immediate neighbors differing in only one facet.

There are several ways of determining such a circular order from an arbitrary set of three dichotomies. Notice that the facets A and B play symmetric roles vis-à-vis each other in the circular order, each consisting of two "semi-circles." Facet C behaves differently, being chopped up into four segments rather than two. The psychological problem is to decide which of the three facets should play the more chopped-up role of C, and which should play the roles of A and B. Psychological theory led to choosing the alias for the more oscillating facet C.

Similarly, the three dichotomies defining the content of relation have their profiles arranged in a circle as follows:

1	$d_1 e_1 f_1$
2	$d_1 e_1 f_2$
3	$d_1 e_2 f_2$
4	$d_1 e_2 f_1$
5	$d_2 e_2 f_1$
6	$d_2 e_2 f_2$
7	$d_2 e_1 f_2$
8	$d_2 e_1 f_1$

Again, facets D and E are divided into "semi-circles," while F is divided into quarter sections.

13. THE EMPIRICAL CIRCUMPLEXES

Accepting these semantic orders of the profiles, the contiguity metahypothesis leads to the hypothesis that, when the relater is held constant, then the eight variables of content should form a circum-

this is approximately true is verified in (543). One of the eight circumplex tables presented there is as follows:

The circumplex pattern is indicated by having the largest correlations tending to be closest to the main diagonal, tapering off as one departs somewhat from the main diagonal, and then increasing again. Eight

TABLE 14-8

AN EXAMPLE OF A CIRCUMPLEX AMONG RELATERS, HOLDING CONSTANT
THE CONTENT OF THE RELATIONSHIP

Observer Is the Husband, Content Is Profile 1:
$d_1 e_1 f_1$ (Social Acceptance of Other)

Relater	I	II	III	IV	V	VI	VII	VIII
I	—	.84	.72	.63	.35	.49	.60	.62
II	.84	—	.79	.72	.44	.50	.50	.60
III	.72	.79	—	.78	.44	.49	.49	.54
IV	.63	.72	.78	—	.39	.46	.24	.44
V	.35	.44	.44	.39	—	.62	.55	.57
VI	.49	.50	.49	.46	.62	—	.78	.69
VII	.60	.50	.49	.24	.55	.78	—	.77
VIII	.62	.60	.54	.44	.57	.69	.77	—

plex among themselves in the above order. Conversely, when the content is held constant, then the eight relaters should form a circumplex among themselves. There are eight relaters, so eight correlation matrices of content need to be studied, each of which should be a circumplex. That

such tables (one for each type of content) hold for the husband as observer, and eight also hold for the wife as observer.

Conversely, let us hold the relater constant and observe a circumplex among the eight content variables, as illustrated by Table 14-9.

TABLE 14-9

A CIRCUMPLEX AMONG EIGHT CONTENTS WHEN RELATER IS HELD CONSTANT
Observer Is Wife, Relater is $a_1 b_1 c_1$: (Non-Observer, Actual, Non-Actor)
(From Foa, 542)

Content	1	2	3	4	5	6	7	8
1	—	.74	.23	.18	.02	.06	.45	.52
2	.74	—	.15	.07	.08	.06	.56	.53
3	.23	.15	—	.62	.21	.18	−.05	.09
4	.18	.07	.62	—	.29	.25	−.13	−.10
5	.02	.08	.21	.29	—	.41	.22	.14
6	.06	.06	.18	.25	.41	—	.17	.14
7	.45	.56	−.05	−.13	.22	.17	—	.68
8	.52	.53	.09	−.10	.14	.14	.68	—

Again, eight such circumplexes were observed and reported for the wife as observer, and eight more for the husband (542).

14. GRAPHIC PORTRAYAL POSSIBILITIES FROM THE COMPLETE FACET DESIGN

To visualize the entire picture for the 128 variables, consider the following table in which to locate these variables.

Each cell in this table represents two of the variables, one for the wife and one for the husband, each of which has the relater of the given row and the content of the given column. Thus, there is a variable which can be symbolized by IV(6), indicating that it is in row IV and column 6 of the table, and so has the profile $a_1b_2c_1d_2e_2f_2$, etc.

Each cell of Table 14-10 thus names a variable for husbands and wives which can be correlated with the variables of all the remaining cells, generating a correlation matrix of order 128×128. Foa has pre-

sented until now only a small portion of this matrix, namely submatrices of the types in Tables 14-8 and 14-9. He has hypothesized a certain type of torus structure for the 64×64 matrix of the husbands separately (and for the wives separately) (543), but the data are not yet available for direct testing of this hypothesis. The present data do show that one feature of it is not correct, namely, that the apparent circumplexes of content should be of systematically differing circumference; in fact they have fairly mutually equal circumferences. Another feature is that the apparent circumplexes are more horseshoelike than circular. Always contents 4 and 5 correlate relatively little with each other, as do relaters IV and V.

The power of the idea of facet design can be illustrated here by showing how certain conclusions about the total structure can be made even on the basis of the fragmentary data now available. What we have to go on is the design of Table 14-10 and the empirical information about the horseshoelike

TABLE 14-10

THE CARTESIAN SPACE OF THE 128 VARIABLES

Content / Relater	1 $d_1e_1f_1$	2 $d_1e_1f_2$	3 $d_1e_2f_2$	4 $d_1e_2f_1$	5 $d_2e_2f_1$	6 $d_2e_2f_2$	7 $d_2e_1f_2$	8 $d_2e_1f_1$
I $a_1b_1c_1$								
II $a_1b_1c_2$								
III $a_1b_2c_2$								
IV $a_1b_2c_1$				$a_ib_jc_kd_le_mf_n$				
V $a_2b_2c_1$				(Husband, Wife)				
VI $a_2b_2c_2$								
VII $a_2b_1c_2$								
VIII $a_2b_1c_1$								

structures of submatrices of the forms of Tables 14-8 and 14-9. Since the correlations in Table 14-9 are *smaller* than in Table 14-8 on the whole — especially for the most mutually distant variables — the horseshoe representing Table 14-9 must be *larger* than for Table 14-8 (smaller correlations must be represented by larger distances graphically). All these phenomena can be well represented by a two-dimensional diagram like Diagram 14-2.

Diagram 14-2 is to be read as portraying the intercorrelations of the 64 variables for the husband (or for the wife). The smaller horseshoes are for constant content, the Arabic numeral denoting the content being placed in the middle of the horseshoe, and the Roman numerals denoting the eight

DIAGRAM 14-2. A Possible Two-Dimensional Portrayal of Foa's 16 Apparent Circumplexes of Interpersonal Behavior

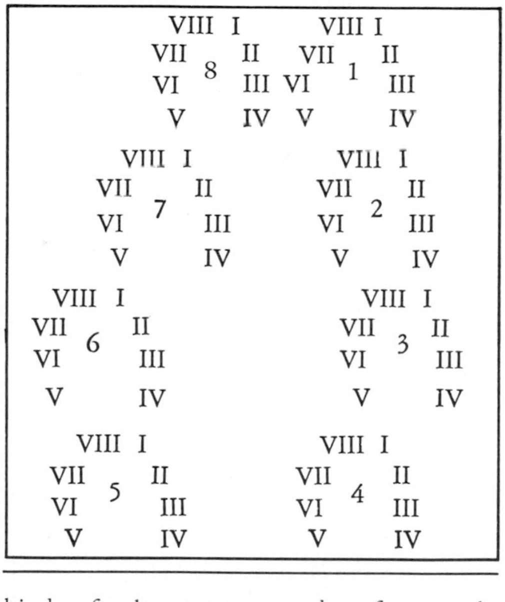

kinds of relaters go around to form each horseshoe. The larger horseshoes are obtained by holding a Roman numeral constant, and reading the eight Arabic numerals to be at the places of the respective constant Roman one.

It is premature to try to make Diagram 14-2 more exact, but the final results when all the data are available cannot deviate in any basic sense from the diagram. There is of course freedom for a number of very important details. One is the *orientations* of the horseshoes. The small ones can be completely reversed in direction and still conform to the existing data. Even more important, there is no assurance that the data will lie in a two-space. A three-space or higher may prove to be necessary when all the data are available. However, the diagram above enables visualizing what a three-space must look like: the smaller horseshoes can be twisted out of the plane to generate a three-space in a variety of ways. In particular, a certain type of torus can be generated which will conform to the data at hand. Finally, the diagram as given makes no attempt at exact presentation of distances among the 64 points; this awaits the final data.

This third example again shows how simple non-metric considerations may yield deep insight and detailed structural information about enormous correlation matrices. Such may be the road to establishing psychological laws.

15. SUMMARY (BY THE EDITOR)

The relations of order analysis to factor analysis and cluster analysis have been discussed in terms of their roles in hypothetico-deductive methods. It is pointed out that order analysis, as exemplified in Spearman's early efforts to locate a general factor and in the stereotypes or mosaics of Burt, Holzinger, and Guttman, has a different objective from factor analysis, and, like Tryon's cluster analysis or Guilford's test construction to fit orthogonal factors, keeps closer to the observed correlation matrix, and is dominated by clustering features rather than by hyperplane structure.

Its usefulness is particularly apparent in

battery construction and the understanding of relations of particular tests. Thus it is shown that the data and the factors in Coombs' study of number abilities fall into a two-space in which their intercorrelations can be clearly seen, and this appears to throw light on the differential tasks being posed by that set of tests. Further examination discloses a circumplex arrangement among seventeen tests that accounts parsimoniously for a large part of their interrelations.

An a priori theory of color intervals is used as a basis for estimating the parameters of a simplex structure to fit Ekman's data. This approach, coupled with the oscillatory law, gives a complete picture of the lawfulness of all the factors required to account for the data. In the third example a multivariable study is generated on the basis of a facet design. Again the simple non-metric formulations are shown to lead to complex tables of data and to provide insight into their arrangement.

CHAPTER 15

Interaction and Non-Linearity in Multivariate Experiment

JOHN M. DIGMAN
University of Hawaii

1. INTRODUCTION

The concept of parsimony has always had an intuitive appeal to the scientific mind. Long ago, Aristotle was convinced that Nature invariably chose the most direct path. During the high tide of English Aristotelianism, Robert Grosseteste proposed a *lex parsimoniae,* while William of Ockham phrased the principle in the way most of us remember it: "Entities are not to be multiplied unnecessarily."

Often known as Ockham's Razor, sometimes as Morgan's Canon, the notion that accounts of phenomena should be simple, direct, and free of conceptual embroidery is one of our most firmly rooted scientific principles.

This scientific preference for parsimony over needless complexity is implied by the assumptions of linearity and additivity so commonly made in psychological measurement. Probably no one who invokes these principles believes that they are sufficient to render a complete account of the linkages in the cause and effect network responsible for human behavior. Rather, they are taken as first, and conservative,

approximations of relationships between variables. If the assumptions are in error, it will be an error on the side of conservatism, one which may be corrected by taking cautious steps in the direction of complexity—but not "unnecessarily."

Investigations in the field of multivariate psychology have been characterized by an almost complete dependence on linearity and additivity. Whereas other multivariate fields, such as economics and agriculture, have been making extensive use of more complex techniques for years, the methods are scarcely mentioned in textbooks of psychological statistics. Perhaps, like the conservative farmer who is still wedded to the best tractor of the 1930's, the psychological investigator is properly suspicious of more complicated models, when the old one has served so well. Or is it simply a case of overlooking the more complicated model because of its unfamiliarity?

In this chapter, we shall examine the case for a more complex view of things, and the reader may judge for himself whether, as one recent reviewer (Lee, 915, 906) concluded, we should make greater use of complex, non-additive models, or whether

459

the simpler model will still suffice.

The question of the relevance of non-linearity and interaction will be examined with respect to three types of multivariate analysis: analysis of variance, factor analysis, and regression analysis. So far as our examination of analysis of variance is concerned, the treatment will be a review for most readers, for the topic of interaction in analysis of variance is well covered elsewhere (Lindquist, 936; Lubin, 963; McNemar, 1015). However, a brief resumé will put our concepts in better focus.

2. NON-LINEARITY AND INTERACTION IN THE ANALYSIS OF VARIANCE

Typically, in an analysis of variance, an investigator is examining the plausibility of a hypothesis of *some* kind of relationship vs. none. In this sort of analysis, the question of non-linearity is irrelevant, particularly where the experimental variables are not ordered, i.e., where they consist of qualitative categories.

Increasingly in the experimental literature, one may find use of the more sophisticated approach of trend analysis. Finding evidence for some kind of relationship between an ordered experimental variable and his observations, the investigator first tests the possibility of a linear relationship, then a quadratic, a cubic, etc. While theoretical justification of higher powers than a quadratic (i.e., a parabolic arc) may be entirely lacking, the demonstration of, say, a cubic relationship may be regarded as a genuine finding, although interpretation should be cautious. Adequate presentations of the method may be found in Lindquist (936) and McNemar (1015). More sophisticated treatment may be found in Winer (1558a).

In the case of a two-way or more complex design, interaction should always be of interest to the researcher. Unfortunately, the discovery of significant interac-

tion is all too frequently regarded as an annoyance, which implies that investigators, looking for simple answers to questions, are disappointed to find complex ones. Far from being an annoyance, the discovery of significant interaction in an analysis of variance should be regarded as an interesting and worthwhile finding.

Regardless of one's reaction to its presence, the discovery of significant interaction is a signal that the assumption of additivity is in error. This assumption is stated most clearly by

$$(1) \ \overline{X}_{ij} = f_1(A) + f_2(B)$$

where $\overline{X}_{ij}$ is a cell mean (as in a two-way analysis), and A and B are the experimental factors. Where evidence for interaction is found, we are forced to conclude that the effect of one, or both, of the variables depends on the level of the other. This is evident in Diagram 15-1, which represents a case of "ordinal interaction."

Suppose the question is asked: "Forgetting the B variable — i e., examining the main effect of A — what is the rank order of treatment effect?" In the case of Diagram 15-1, the answer is probably that, without controlling for level of B, $A_1 > A_2 > A_3$. Yet a more informative answer would be that the relationship between the effect and A exists only at the B_1 level.

Diagram 15-2 represents a more serious departure from the additivity principle. Here the relationship between X and A is

DIAGRAM 15-1. Ordinal Interaction in a Two-Way Analysis of Variance Design

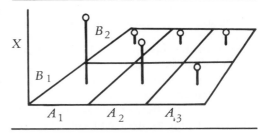

negative at the B_1 level, but positive at the B_2 level. This is an example of "disordinal interaction." In such cases, there may be no sensible answer to any question regarding main effects.

Lubin (963) points out that such results most logically imply that the investigator proceed with separate analyses at different

DIAGRAM 15-2.   Disordinal Interaction in a Two-Way Analysis of Variance Design

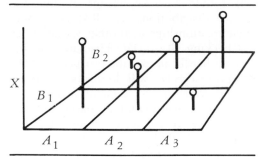

levels of B (as we shall see, there are implications here for factor analysis). Similar but more complicated interpretations attend the discovery of three-way and higher interactions. Where ordinal interactions are found, a correct but not profound answer may be given regarding a main effect. With disordinal interaction, no sensible statement about a main effect can be made.

This review of non-linearity and interaction in analysis of variance will serve as introduction to further discussion of these concepts as they apply to factor analysis and regression analysis. The notion of a curvilinear relationship between experimental and dependent variables is generally familiar to undergraduate students of statistics, although translating this concept into a quadratic or cubic function is somewhat unclear to many graduate students, which reflects the still prevalent lack of undergraduate mathematical training of many psychology majors. So far as interaction is concerned, it is the writer's experience that this concept, particularly when presented

with the use of diagrams, such as 15-1 and 15-2, is usually readily understandable.

3. FACTOR ANALYSIS: NON-LINEARITY AND INTERACTION AMONG VARIABLES

The assumptions of linearity and additivity are pervasive in factor analysis. Customarily, exposition of the rationale of factor analysis begins with the formula

$$(2)\quad z_j = b_{j1}F_I + b_{j2}F_{II} + \ldots + b_{js}F_s + b_{je}F_e,$$

which states that variability in j can be accounted for by a linear combination of hypothetical factor values, each properly weighted. If this is true, then it can be demonstrated that the inner products of the observed score matrix (when cast into standard deviate form) can be linked to the desired weighting coefficients:

$$(3)\quad 1/N\ ZZ' = V_o V_o'$$
$$\text{or}$$
$$R = V_o V_o'.$$

Knowing R, the matrix of Pearson r's between all pairs of variables, we deduce by factor analysis a value for V_o which will satisfy the above relationship with reasonable allowance for error. Further, by recalling that $z_i = r_{ij}z_j$, we see that factor analysis rests upon the assumption of simple, i.e., linear, relationships between variables. Following transformation of V_o and the obtaining of V_{fs}, the factor structure matrix, estimates of factor scores are often made from a linear combination of variables:

$$(4)\quad F_p = w_1 z_1 + w_2 z_2 + \ldots$$

A number of questions invariably arise in the mind of the student of factor analysis: Can things really be this simple? What is the evidence for such assumptions? What happens when the assumptions are violated?

There are a number of ways in which these basic assumptions of factor analysis might conceivably go awry. In this chapter we shall examine the possibility of non-linearity between variables, between variables and factors, and between factors. We shall also examine the implications of interaction: between variables, variables and factors, and factors. The reader may then draw his conclusions as to whether the method of factor analysis is unrealistically founded upon oversimplifications, or whether, as many have felt, it represents a powerful tool for the organization of a systematic theory of behavior.

Non-Linear Relationships Between Variables

In most instances, variables which are entered into a factor analysis are rather well described by the Pearson r, that is, by a linear relationship. Occasionally, one will find that this is very evidently not the case. If nothing is done about these departures from linearity, it might be supposed that the linear description of the relationships will simply err on the side of conservatism, that a variable so related to others will merely have its communality reduced, perhaps to the point of seeming to be unrelated to other variables in the study. Depending on the nature of the investigation, it may be true that "They'll none of them be missed; no, they'll none of them be missed." However, the image of a researcher as Lord High Executioner, lopping off variables here and there from his battery, hardly squares with the rest of our impressions of scientific procedure. But such simple dropping of communality is only one possibility. Another is that, in certain cases, the analysis becomes quite distorted, resulting in factors and interpretations quite different from what they would have been had the investigator considered his data more carefully.

Judging by the way in which most factor analyses are reported, one must conclude that the assumption of linearity is seldom checked. Pressed for explanation, many researchers would probably echo Thorn-dike's (1397) point: non-linear relationships are very much the exception in psychological measurement. Thorndike, however, was describing his experiences with the carefully developed tests of the Army Air Force selection program. Many variables which get into a factor-analytic study are in a far more primitive state. One implication here, perhaps, is that "rough and ready" variables ought to be polished up before factor analysis. At a minimum, one should have knowledge of their frequency distributions, as well as the form of their relationships with other variables.

Checking all $n(n-1)/2$ bivariate distributions is hardly an exciting prospect, but the careful researcher will do this before trusting his variables to a factor analysis. In addition, he will obtain all marginal distributions (i.e., frequency distributions of the variables). With data processing equipment commonly available today, this is not the herculean task it would have been a few years ago. Programs are available for the largest computers for accomplishing this with dispatch (an example of such a program is BMD X13, available to users of the Western Data Processing Center). With proper arrangement of the data, the work can also be handled by smaller machines, such as the Burroughs 220, the venerable IBM 650, or the IBM 1401. In these cases, the speed with which the problem can be done will depend on the amount of storage available. For a large problem (e.g., 50 variables), a number of passes may be required. Smaller problems (say, 15 variables) will cause no difficulties for smaller machines, and can often be accomplished with more modest equipment, such as the IBM 101 or a sorter with counter. In most instances, a common metric with no more than a dozen intervals will prove to be convenient, e.g., standard scores with nine intervals.

Suppose, having obtained all the above information, one finds the bivariate distribution $X_1 X_2$ pictured in Diagram 15-3. This distribution certainly suggests, at first glance, a non-linear relationship. The departure from linearity here is rather substantial, but this could reflect sampling error. However, let us suppose that all other pairings with X_1 give much the same results: where there is evidence of a relationship, it appears to be distinctly non-linear, with slope decreasing as X_1 increases.

DIAGRAM 15-3.   An Evident Non - Linear Relationship

```
                                    x    xx   xx    x
                            x      xx   xx   xx   xxx   xx
                    x     xx    xxx  xxx  xxx  xxx   xx
              xx    x   xxx   xxx    xx    x    x     x
              xx   xxx   xx    xx    x    x
              xxx   xx    x     x     x
              xx    x     x
        x     x
        xx
        xxx
        xx
        x
X²
                         X₁
```

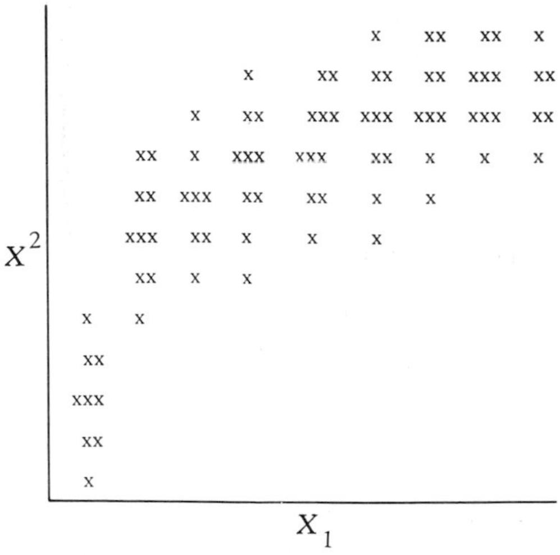

Before considering, say, a logarithmic transformation of X_1, which would tend to bring the relationships closer to linearity, the investigator should consider his knowledge of the variables in the analysis, particularly the manner in which they were scaled. As Carroll (196) has recently reminded us, there are a number of assumptions which are often implicitly made in any correlation analysis (as distinct from regression analysis): (1) the "underlying distribution" is bivariate normal; (2) the relationship is linear; (3) the scales have equal intervals. Departures from these ideal conditions will affect a factor study to the degree to which they are present. Initially, they will distort relationships between pairs of variables; beyond that they will alter the

rank of the correlation matrix and (in severe cases) cause difficulty in interpreting factors. The non-linearity evident in Diagram 15-3 could be a result of differently skewed marginal distributions, unequal scale intervals, or basic non-linearity between the characteristics of behavior which lead to the manifest variables X_1 and X_2.

In this connection, two sources of distortion are particularly worthy of comment: selection and distortion. By selection, we mean that the subjects studied in an investigation have a narrower range of scores than have the subjects in the reference population. An example would be a group of students in a "gifted" class, which would obviously be more homogeneous in many respects than an unselected group. Censoring, a serious source of distortion, refers to crudities inherent in the measuring instrument, whereby subjects with essentially different degrees of the property under consideration are given the same score. The "easy grader," who hands out A's to almost all students, provides an example: for one reason or another discriminable differences in achievement are ignored by the instrument.

Selection will always occur when some special group is selected for study, such as a group of delinquents or retardates. Obviously, because of lower variability along one or more lines, relationships between variables will be attenuated, with resulting changes in the vector configuration. The effects of selection have been extensively studied by Thurstone (1420) and Thomson (1393). Depending on the number of variables involved in the selection process, and the extent of selection, the effects will vary from moderate disturbances to severe distortions. It is evident that the problem is basically a sampling problem. If we wish to say something about the factor structure of child personality, we shall be somewhat in error to limit our investigations to subjects obtained from expensive private schools; we shall be very much in error if we limit our observations to a reform school. Of course, one may simply wish to study these atypical groups as such, in which case one should not be surprised if the analysis fails to give evidence of a factor which may characterize the group as a whole, but which fails to discriminate the members of the group one from the other.

However, our chief interest in selection concerns its bearing on the problem of non-linearity. If selection is such as to result in the inclusion in a study of only those subjects who are above average on X_1, the resulting distribution will very likely be markedly skewed. If another variable suffers the same fate, except that only below-average subjects are included, the bivariate distribution will be a considerable departure from a normal correlation surface. The relationship between the scores *as obtained* will not be linear, and, if the variables are blindly fed into a computer, one would have a factor solution which would be, among other things, an interpretation of the non-linear trends among the truncated variables. At least one, perhaps more, of the obtained factors will be factors which are needed mathematically to account for the non-linear relationships. Such factors, of course, are not factors in the psychological sense. In some cases, one may be able to recognize them as "artifactors" (as Dingman, 421, claimed), and set them aside, but one wonders whether some of them have not been "interpreted."

Carroll (196), with some good evidence to support his position, recommends dichotomization of such variables, and use of the tetrachoric coefficient, which is probably better than blind use of the Pearson *r*. Another, and generally more satisfactory, solution is to avoid getting into the problem in the first place: that is, don't restrict the investigation to a deviant group simply because it is convenient for study.

However, a comforting finding is that "natural selection," as represented by the influences responsible for institutionalization, is almost always a complex affair. Frequently the probability of a subject's selection varies with the value of the selection variable, and the result may be a distribution which is approximately normal (the distribution of batting averages of major league baseball players is a good example).

Censoring is a more serious and more prevalent source of distortion. A certain amount of this occurs in all measurement, and if it is uniform across the continuum of the property being measured, the result is simply a lack of sensitivity in the instrument employed (as occurs when scores are grouped into intervals). In some cases, however, the effects of severe censoring can be very distorting. Consider, for example, a short scale of seven items purporting to measure vocabulary. Let us suppose that this scale is administered to college freshmen and that a mode of 6 is obtained, with most of the scores at 6 and 7. Anyone with any experience with the vocabularies of freshmen would be inclined to call the test "too easy." Suppose that another seven-item test of vocabulary is constructed, and that this test yields a mode of 2 with positive skew. This is obviously "harder." The interesting thing about these tests from a factorial point of view is that if we should factor a group of such tests, we should find more than one factor. One would be a "vocabulary" factor, but at least one other would appear to be a "difficulty factor," ordering the tests from most to least difficult.

A difficulty factor does not depend on some unitary function within the individuals assessed. Rather the factor can be shown to be a result of an attempt to account for correlations based upon differently skewed marginal distributions (see Carroll, 196). If the underlying relationship between the phenomena assessed by the two instruments is high and linear (one would suppose this to be the case with two tests of vocabulary, surely), the *obtained* relationship in the above case will be artificially lowered because of non-linearity introduced by differently skewed distributions.

Many of the distortions introduced by censoring are best eliminated at the source by more careful scaling procedures. Thus, a vocabulary test of eight items with mean p of .8, *will* give a skewed distribution, but *fifty* such items will give a more symmetrical distribution. Similarly, if clinicians rate clients on a ten-point scale, but award scores of "10" to most clients, the distribution will be badly skewed. This might be avoided by requiring a ranking of clients, the ranks then being transformed to normal deviates. Of course, no flat statement can be made about the manner in which variables *must* be scaled, for this is more a concern of measurement techniques within a research area, but the plain fact of the matter is that many variables which have been included in factor analyses have been quite poor examples of the art of scaling.

Personality ratings, questionnaires, and check-lists are particularly likely to entail censoring. Regardless of whether information comes from an observer rating another, or an individual judging himself, many persons are loath to use scoring categories which imply social disapproval. One effect of this will be skewed frequency distributions, with the skewing away from the socially desirable end of the scale. Unless steps are taken to guard against this in personality measurement, the effects can be quite pervasive (Jackson & Messick, 805).

The Case for Linearity

In short, a very good case can be made for linearity. Many variables *are* related in this fashion, and most instances of non-linear relationships are more likely a result of scaling distortions than a reflection of an inherent lack of linearity. The proper way to deal with such difficulties is by correcting the scaling procedure, not by mathematical "corrections."

Finally, one would logically expect that variables which belong to the same domain are more simply related than are variables which belong to different domains. Thus, it is not surprising to find 20 measures of intelligence related in linear fashion. However, if we are dealing with 10 measures of achievement and 10 measures of motivation, we may expect things to be more complex. Since most factor-analytic investigations concern the mapping out of the structure *within* a domain, we may expect to find abundant evidence of relationships well described by Pearson r's. The exceptions to this would occur when variables from two or more domains are entered into one analysis. In such cases, we may expect departures from linearity.

The obvious solution here is to investigate the structure of each domain separately, and this is what the great majority of factor analyses restrict themselves to.

Correcting for Non-Linearity

Having entered the above caveats against quick dismissal of the linear model, let us now turn to the problem of genuine non-linear relationships. Such relationships may be expected when different sorts of variables are factored together, as in some cases of "criterion factor analysis" (Fruchter, 563). Generally, these may be classified as monotonic (increasing or decreasing throughout) or non-monotonic (as in the case of a parabolic arc). The mathematical functions invoked to account for non-linear relationships are usually either simple logarithmic functions (e.g., a power function, such as $X_1 = a + bX_2^c$) or simple polynomials (e.g., $X_1 = a + b_1X_2 + b_2X_2^2$) The great majority of cases of non-linearity can be rendered closer to linearity by simply making a logarithmic transformation of the offending variable. In the case of Diagram 15-3, the transformation of X_1 to log X_1 will result in the relationship depicted in Diagram 15-4. At this point, however, one must remember that we are, in factor analysis, interested in much more than the X_1, X_2 relationship.

We cannot use X_1 and X_3 while using log X_1 with X_2; only one form of that variable may be used, and it must be the decision of the investigator as to whether log X_1 will *generally* be the more effective form. (We will presume that our investigator has checked all bivariate distributions of X_1 and the *m*-1 other variables.) Other simple transformations—such as reciprocals—may be considered. The relationship in Diagram 15-5, for example, might be more effectively handled by transforming X_1 to $1/X_1$. The relative efficiencies of the different

all relationships with some form of X_1. While quite sophisticated methods are available for finding the best weighted polynomial, so far as the over-all relationship with the $m-1$ other variables is concerned (e.g., canonical correlation), the following procedure will probably be quite adequate in most cases: (1) select, on the basis of the $m-1$ bivariate plots involved, the one, two, or three variables with which X_1 appears to be most closely related; (2) transform the variables to standard deviate form; (3) obtain mean scores on these

DIAGRAM 15-4. Plotting of X_2 Against Log X_1

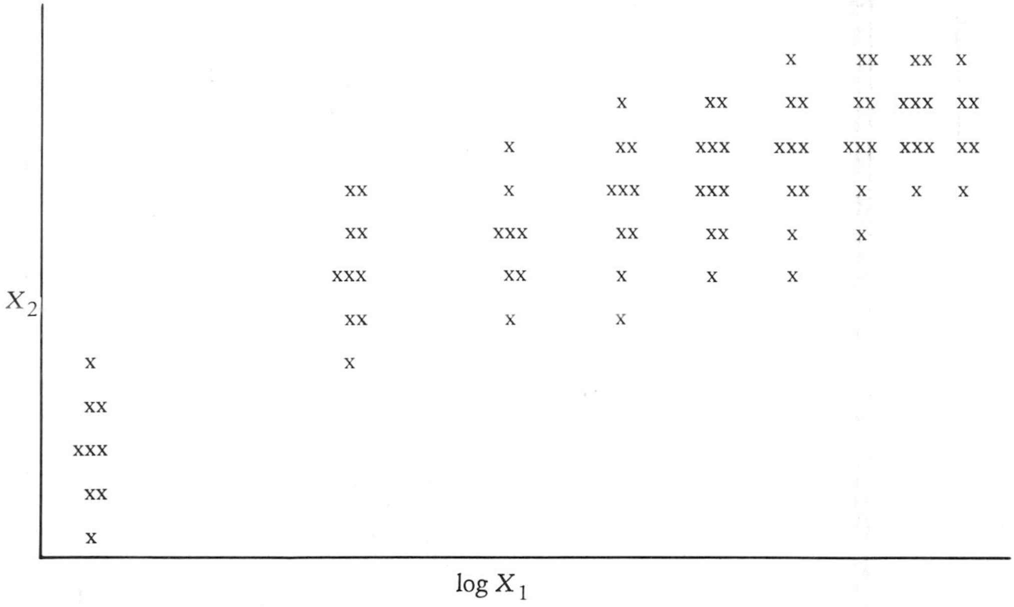

transformations can be checked by computing the correlations against the $m-1$ other variables for the two (or more) forms of the variable.

In rare cases, one may find a general non-monotonic relationship between a variable and other variables. In such cases, no simple transformation will rectify things, and the simplest type of polynomial may be examined (i.e., $X_2 = a + b_1 X_1 + b_2 X_1^2$). Here again, it is not just the relationship between X_1 and X_2 which is of concern, but

variables as a "criterion"; (4) compute the constants involved by solving for the normal equations (see discussion of non-linear regression below); (5) use these constants to transform the variable ($X_1' = b_1 X_1 + b_2 X_1^2$).

Interaction Between Variables

Interaction in the case of continuous functions is basically the same phenomenon as interaction in an analysis of variance.

DIAGRAM 15-5. A Relationship Which Might Lend Itself to Transformation by Reciprocals

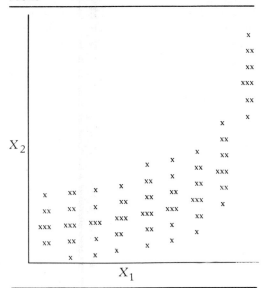

X_2

X_1

A simple example of interaction is the case:

(8) $X_1 = a + bX_2$, where $b = c_1 + c_2X_3$.

In other words, the relationship of X_2 to X_1 depends on the level, or value, of X_3. (The reader will note the *linear* assumption here; more complex interactions may exist.) With substitution, (8) becomes:

(9) $X_1 = a + c_1X_2 + c_2X_2X_3$.

In an ordinary regression analysis, such a product term may be entered into a regression equation as a "new" predictor, hopefully accounting for additional and significant variance in the criterion. Since in factor analysis we are often interested in optimal weighting of a team of variables in order to predict a factor score criterion (equation 4), it might seem reasonable to include a product term, if this is required to account for correlation among variables.

First, however, one would have to discover such cases of interaction in the data. One obviously cannot include all X_iX_j terms in an analysis. On logical grounds, it

would seem that a variable which moderates a relationship to a substantial degree is doubtless of rather large importance in the scheme of things. Further, if it is able to distort relationships to the point of turning things upside down (disordinal interaction), it is very likely a variable of considerable complexity.

Certain variables would appear to be likely candidates by the above criteria. Sex is certainly one, and social class is probably another. Even the undergraduate student would question an analysis based upon a sample of children and adults. Where the student would suspect that there must be something wrong about such procedure, the multivariate investigator would consider the moderating effects of age.

There are two logical ways of handling such interaction, although only one appears to be practical. The first is to look for interaction effects in the case of variables suspected of moderating relationships between other variables. The second procedure is to assume interaction effects in the case of certain variables, create product terms between these variables and all other variables, and include these "new" variables in the analysis.

From the point of view of maximizing prediction of a factor score criterion (equation 4), the latter might seem appropriate. However, for each moderator variable we should have $m-1$ variables added to the matrix. Most factor studies, based on samples of 150 and less, cannot have the order of the correlation matrix expanded in this fashion. At any rate, the outcome would be fairly predictable: each of the $m-1$ product variables would load on a general factor, because of common elements; in addition, each product variable would load on one or more other factors, depending on the factor relationships of the other variable in the product term. So far as interpretation of factors is concerned, it seems doubtful that this procedure would do anything but muddy the waters.

The two-way analysis of variance discussed above suggests a simpler procedure. Following the discovery of interaction in such a design, the researcher ordinarily turns his attention toward the "simple" effects: that is, the question of an experimental effect is studied at various levels of the other variable. The implication here for factor analysis is to conduct factor studies at various levels of the moderating variable. Examples of this approach are Cattell's (240) examination of personality structure at various age levels, and Hofstaetter's (735) inquiry into the changing structure of intellect during early childhood.

Studies of interaction in regression (e.g., Saunders, 1256; Ward, 1496) suggest that interaction effects are usually miniscule when most psychological scales are interrelated. On the other hand, there is abundant evidence for the moderating roles of age, sex, and social class. It will be noted that these are not psychological variables, but large rubrics for quite complex forces. A justifiable conclusion, therefore, is that interactions are very likely present where most investigators would expect them to be. Separate analyses at different levels of sex, age, occupational level, etc. will probably be much more informative than the "big factor analysis with everything in the pot."

4. FACTOR ANALYSIS: NON-LINEARITY AMONG FACTORS AND VARIABLES

From the previous discussion of non-linear relationships between variables, it is evident that a variable related to a cluster of other variables in a curvilinear fashion will have the same relationship with the factor dimension defined by the cluster. Obviously, if we can transform these variables to bring about linear relationships between the variables before analysis, we shall have a linear relationship between variable and factor.

Such non-linear cases in factor analysis have arisen chiefly in connection with the analysis of variables of differing degrees of skewness. The result of this state of affairs is that the relationships between the variables as given are not best described by a linear equation. To attempt to describe the relationships by a linear combination of factor weights will require more factors than content alone would demand. Probably the best examples of this are the well-known "difficulty" factors generated in connection with Guilford's analysis of the Seashore Pitch Discrimination Test (624), and Dingman's (421) experimental investigation of the "difficulty factor" phenomenon.

Two procedures have been suggested for dealing with this situation. One has been suggested above: i.e., eliminate these artifacts at the source by proper attention to scaling and choice of correlation coefficient. Another approach has been advanced by Gibson (597), who casts the problem into the field of latent profile analysis, a statistical relative of Lazarsfeld's (910) latent structure analysis. However, the method, while interesting and promising, is still in the experimental stage and not of use where more than two latent dimensions are involved.

Non-Linear Relationships Between Factors

The orthogonal case is occasionally encountered in factor analysis, and it is often a reasonable approximation when factors are mildly correlated. More often, and this is particularly true in personality research, factors will be substantially correlated. The usual way of expressing these interfactor relationships is in terms of the cosines of angular separation of the factor vectors, which is the geometrical representation of a correlation coefficient. These interfactor r's are given by

$$(10) \quad R_f = D \ R_r^{-1} \ D.$$

Since the vectors are the lines of intersection of the hyperplanes, and the correlation of any factor with another is in terms of the projection of the one vector on the other, we are again concerned with linear relationships.

Given present factor models and methods, the question of non-linearity between factor dimensions amounts to a contradiction of terms. The mathematical means of spanning the space of our collection of variables in a factor analysis is basically a branch of linear algebra, with n-dimensional — but Euclidean — space. Considering the present state of psychological measurement, it is probably premature to call for a non-Euclidean type of factor analysis. However, the mathematical methods are available, should they ever be required. These issues are discussed by Guttman in Chapter 14.

While it is not possible to determine non-linear relationships between factors by means of traditional factor methods, it is conceivable that the broad influences which one thinks of as factors do not interrelate in simple fashion. If this should be the case, provided the factors are monotonically related, we shall be able to make an approximation to their interrelationships by linear expressions. It should also be remembered that factor analysis does not give the final word regarding the nature of the factors which it exposes to view. Beyond the establishment of the fact that there *is* an ability, such as divergent thinking, further refinement and use of the factor dimension will tell us more about it — including a more precise account of its relationships with other important dimensions.

The complaint is sometimes heard that the "really important" factors are interrelated in most complex fashion, and that a linear model will simply not square with "facts as we know them." This, of course, has always been the complaint whenever a mathematical model has been introduced. It is interesting that in astronomy this criterion of "squaring with the facts," known as "accounting for the appearances," seemed to be one of the difficulties of the

Copernican theory: the new mathematical model for the heavens did not square with the well-known fact that the earth was stationary! Behavior theorists who employ factor analysis are not simply concerned with "facts as we know them," but seek to establish a new order in the field of human assessment, developing a taxonomy of abstract concepts of more heuristic value than the confusions of yesteryear. To accomplish this a complex — but linear — model is advanced, solely to take advantage of the powerful tools of linear algebra. The proof of a pudding, of course, is its eating. Whether this linear model of behavior is "true" depends upon its success in achieving its aims: the explication and ordering of previously confusing phenomena, and the creation of better means of assessment.

Interaction Between Factors

Let us suppose a broad determiner of behavior, X, and another, Y. Both are important and pervasive forces underlying behavior; that is, they are the sort of influences we have in mind when we think of "factors." Suppose, however, that X's influence on some bit of behavior j depends upon the level of Y. This, of course, will be recognized as simply another statement of the interaction hypothesis, this time at the factor level. Put into equation form:

$$(11) \quad z_j = b_{jX}F_X + b_{jY}F_Y$$

where

$$b_{jX} = c_1 F_Y + c_2.$$

On substitution, (11) becomes, with minor change in notation,

$$(12) \quad z_j = b_{jX}F_x + b_{jY}F_y + b_{jXY}F_{XY}.$$

The question now arises as to the practical meaning of equation (12). Perhaps we may assume that the moderating effect of F_Y on relationships with F_X is constant, regardless of variable involved. To put this another way, the joint action of $F_X F_Y$

remains the same, although variables differ with respect to the extent to which this joint effect determines their variability. Thus, if there is *any* relationship between a variable and F_X, this relationship is moderated by F_Y, but such moderation is consistent. Essentially we are saying that the broad forces symbolized by X and Y are not capricious but stable in their influence.

The effect of this on equation (12) is to link b_{jXY} to the b_{jX} term in a constant fashion across variables. Thus, if b_{jX} is .50 and b_{jXY} is .25, b_{kX} might be .40 and b_{kXY}, by the above argument, .20. So far as hypothetical factor coefficients are concerned, this means two factor columns which are in proportion, e.g.:

	F_X	F_Y	F_{XY}
1	.50	.20	.25
2	.60	.15	.30
3	. . .	. . .	. . .
		etc.	

As there are only two experimentally independent vectors in this matrix, we should expect but two factors from analysis of $R = AA'$, and such is the case. Factor Y, independent of X (in the sense of linear independence), would have its coefficients close to those entered into the original A matrix. X would be easily identifiable, but would have its loadings reflect *both* the linear *and* the joint effect. The implication, then, is that the factors would be correctly identified, but the nature of the relationships would be obscured.

An implication of the above argument is that in cases of slight to moderate interaction (i.e., ordinal interaction), factor analysis will give a rather good answer to most of the questions asked. We shall probably identify the factors correctly — provided other matters are in order — and we shall have an approximation of the "true" variable-factor relationships. Given the present state of psychometrics, it would seem unrealistic to ask for much more.

If the joint action of X and Y is such as to provide systematic disordinal interaction in the case of a number of variables in a

matrix, there is the possibility that a factor will be more a reflection of such joint action than it is a result of the simple effects of a factor. This implies that high positive z_j may reflect *either* high positive F_X and F_Y *or* high negative F_X and F_Y.

In the simplest case, where only two factors so interact, as in (12) above, the factor extracted relevant to the influence of X will actually reflect a multiplicative function of X and Y. It is almost certain that we should never make such interpretation at the conclusion of an analysis. Indeed, it is doubtful that any sensible interpretation could be made where interaction effects are chiefly responsible for the observed factor.

At this point, it seems worthwhile to raise a perennial issue: how shall we attach meaning to the factors we isolate in an analysis? If the fundamental assumption of additivity holds, factors are abstractions: so much of this variable, so much of that, etc. On this basis, factors are usually "interpreted." Not infrequently, factors turn up which defy interpretation. Sometimes, such oddities may be demonstrated to be "artifactors" — i.e., the result of such influences as extreme skewing for a few variables, or instrument characteristics shared by some of the variables (e.g., the use of paper and pencil for some of the variables in a study). In the vast majority of studies, provided they have been done with care, interpretation is not difficult.

If the additive model were generally inappropriate, this would certainly not be the case.

However, the writer would hold, with Ahmavaara (11), that some factors are probably best thought of as abstract concepts defined operationally by the variables loading them. In such cases, semantic identification will come about through experimental use of scales developed from the factors. Until then, the factor is simply "Factor X." There is so much precedence for this in the physical sciences that one may wonder why psychologists feel so compelled to identify a factor on its first appearance.

A factor which actually represents a multiplicative, i.e., joint function of two (or more) causal influences could conceivably lead to such a factor. Further, it would be a stable finding across studies. From the viewpoint of one traditional aim of science, that of understanding, such a factor would be an annoyance when it first appears, and, later, a source of confusion when it reappears. Eventually we should be goaded into both more sophisticated thinking about its nature, as well as more careful investigations of its effects and antecedents. At this point, it has surely justified its existence; there are few things which will stimulate research and thinking as much as a stable but inscrutable phenomenon.

Very likely, after refinement and experimental use of scales reflecting such oddities, we should arrive at rather different views of them, which would be quite at variance with initial "interpretations." At any rate, to write $z_j = b_{jX}F_X$, where F_X represents an abstraction for a number of interacting forces, is to come back to one of the basic arguments for the linear model: "... such linear approximation is made when a better mathematical model is unknown.... As knowledge advances and as more suitable calculation techniques are made available, linear problems will probably not dominate the field as they do now" (Dwyer, 445).

Moderator Action among Factors and Variables

The loadings of variables on factors may be changed by other factors in a number of ways. One trivial case (but not trivial so far as effects are concerned) is the distortion from absence of necessary factors, in factor under-extraction. Related to this is the change in loading which occurs when a factor fails to appear simply because of failure to include in the battery more than one variable denoting the factor.

Two kinds of moderator action in the factor realm which are more important, in the sense that they are not accidental or consequences of simple statistical relations, but part of psychological theory, are: (a) the effect of instrument factors (281, 282) and (b) role and state *modulator* action, as hypothesized by Cattell (259). The former, which considers part of the variance of personality and other real source traits to be accounted for by instrument factors, peculiar to mode of observation or measurement, has been dealt with by the present writer elsewhere (281, 282) and is treated sufficiently on pages 224-226 of this book. The latter deserves more comment.

The theory of modulator action is actually a special modification of the factor analytic model. Cattell has asked whether in a role (or dynamic state, or other "global stimulus" situation) we should consider that (a) the person (his factor scores) or (b) the loadings (situational meaning and perception) should be considered changed relative to the specification equation when there is no role identification or state. He concludes that either is a possible model and that experiment must decide between them. Also one can consider either that the role stimulus acts on the first order behavioral indices (loadings, b's), especially on a role factor, L, or that it acts on the second order factor, thus changing ("modulating") the involvement simultaneously of *several* first order factors, but especially of that dynamic factor we call the role factor. Since this theory of modulatory action presents a definite model, of considerable promise in investigating the true nature of role action, we may expect experimental checks on it in the near future.

Examples of first order role factors already exist (see page 734) in dynamic variable research in particular. An example of another kind forced itself upon the writer's attention in a recent analysis of child behavior ratings (Digman, 419). With sex of child entered into the battery, a "sex role" factor was obvious, a factor which accounted for some of the variance of "Tends toward fighting" and "Noisy." The first also loaded a "Hostility" factor, and the second an "Excitement" factor. As the correlations between these two variables would have been the same, regardless of whether sex of child had been noted or not, it is apparent that the loadings of both of these variables were moderated by the appearance of a role factor.

That performance should depend on type of instrument used or upon situational determinants is simply a fact of life. To some psychologists, seeking the philosopher's stone of uncontaminated "true" measures, this relativity of measurement is cause for despair; to others, fresh evidence of the need for a multivariate approach to the complexities of psychological assessment.

Certain conclusions seem warranted from this examination of the assumptions of linearity and additivity in factor analysis. One is that when these principles hold, or when departures from them are moderate, interpretation of the factors isolated in a carefully done study should generally prove to be straightforward and unambiguous.

Many cases of non-linear relationships between variables, and between variables and factors, will usually be well approximated by the linear model. Exceptions will most commonly be encountered in the case of poorly scaled measures, where non-linearity is probably more a function of censoring and differential skewing than of the underlying relationship. Attention to scaling matters in advance of data gathering will eliminate most of these difficulties.

The failure of the additivity principle to hold (i.e., the presence of interaction) can be a serious matter for factor analysis. The writer suggests, however, that within a domain the principles of linearity and additivity are likely to hold, but that they may often fail to hold across domains. Perhaps a reasonable corollary here is that factor analysis be used to investigate the structure of a domain, while linkages across domains be studied by the more flexible methods of regression analysis.

5. REGRESSION ANALYSIS

Where factor analysis seeks to understand relationships, regression analysis is more commonly concerned with optimal prediction, given certain predictors and criteria. However, use begets familiarity, and a better understanding of the nature of psychological variables can come from any observation of their linkages, even in the more mundane field of prediction.

As a general rule, variables which are assembled into a prediction battery should have undergone psychometric refinement before practical application is made of them. For example, the use of factor pure scales will doubtless be much more rewarding than the use of intuitively concocted measures, if only because one would have a better understanding of the nature of the predictors involved. Other sources of error and confusion should be detected and eliminated in advance, by means of item analysis and traditional techniques of improving reliability. In many cases, difficulties of prediction may be traced to insufficiently developed predictors. Logically, these sources of error should be corrected before one begins to make more sophisticated corrections for non-linearity or interaction.

Non-Linear Regression

The typical finding of many carefully done studies is that the linear model holds remarkably well (1397, 1496). However, before we assume that linearity will always characterize the prediction of human affairs, we should remember that until recent times prediction has been pretty much a case of assessing the same behavioral phenomena at different points in time (e.g., predicting "scholastic achievement" from "scholastic aptitude"). More complex regression models may be needed for studies which, say, attempt predictions of achievement from social and physiological data.

Intuitively, it would seem reasonable to suppose that relationships *within* a domain, such as the domain of intellect, are simpler than relationships *across* domains, such as the prediction of scholastic achievement from personality and motivation variables. Evidence in support of this view comes chiefly from studies of the effects of anxiety on achievement; typically, intermediate amounts of anxiety will result in highest achievement. Recently, Bronfenbrenner (148) and Becker, et al. (88) found evidence for curvilinear relationships between indicants of physical punishment and problem behavior in children. It seems likely that such non-linear functions will be found increasingly, as investigators direct their attention toward the problems of tying together such distinct domains as personality and physiology, or achievement and parental values.

Procedure in the case of non-linear multivariate regression furnishes a good illustration of the great flexibility of multivariate methods. Taking advantage of the fact that non-linear relationships may be described by higher-powered polynomials, we simply add, say, an X_1^2 term to the existing battery of predictors, and test the effect of the contribution of this "new variable." (The reader who recalls the artifacts involved when "new variables" which are *sums* of other variables are added to a battery should put his mind at rest; a powered term does not bear a *linear* relationship to the same term expressed to a different power.) Thus, if we have two predictors, both cast in quadratic form, the regression equation becomes:

$$Y = b_0 + b_1 X_1 + b_2 X_2 + b_3 X_1^2 + b_4 X_2^2.$$

Variables X_1^2 and X_2^2 may be considered as variables 3 and 4 in the regression equation, and their effects tested for significance, using either the Fisher-Doolittle method

(Walker & Lev, 1493) or an F test. For the latter the error of prediction associated with the more complex model may be compared with the error of prediction associated with some simpler model (e.g., $Y = b_0 + b_1 X_1 + b_2 X_2$). Thus:

$$F = \frac{(1 - R_s^2) - (1 - R_c^2)/df_s - df_c}{(1 - R_c^2)/df_c}$$

$$\cdot \frac{R_c^2 - R_s^2/m_c - m_s}{(1 - R_c^2)/N - (m_c + 1)}$$

Here R_c^2 and R_s^2 represent the squared multiple correlation obtained with use of the complex and simpler models, respectively; df_c and df_s, the degrees of freedom associated with these two models; m_c and m_s, the number of predictor variables in either case; and N, the size of the sample. It should be noted that a number of simpler models are possible in the above case, the simplest being either $Y = b_0 + b_1 X_1$ or $Y = b_0 + b_2 X_2$; a simpler model to test the necessity of retaining X_2^2 in the system is $Y = b_0 + b_1 X_1 + b_2 X_2 + b_3 X_1^2$. Where the number of predictors is very large, the Wherry-Doolittle (see Stead & Shartle, 1345) or Summerfield-Lubin (1366) method may be useful.

Interaction in Regression

Although the concept of joint action (interaction) of variables has a statistical history of more than thirty years (Court, 389), it has generally been ignored by psychologists. Lee's review found that "... interaction effects have not received nearly as much attention by multiple regressionists as they have by analysts of variance."

Most regression studies, however, have had predictors and criteria in the same domain (e.g., intellectual assessment by paper-and-pencil tests). Thus, the failure to find use for an interactive model probably stems largely from the fact that the few psychological investigations which have used the interaction model concerned problems in which interaction effects would not be suspected. The two best studies available (Saunders, 1256; Ward, 1496), while good expositions of method, failed to demonstrate anything but trivial interaction effects.

One reason for the general lack of interest in interactive effects in regression studies is that most investigators of cross-domain relationships are chiefly concerned with hypothesis testing: e.g., does drug X have *any* effect on "socialization"? Since measurement of the latter may be in terms of the number of times a group of hospitalized schizophrenics glances at a TV screen per observation period, it is probably premature to suggest more sophisticated models for the relationship between drug dosage and socialization.

The concept of interaction in regression is an obvious generalization from the previous discussion of interaction in analysis of variance and factor analysis. It means simply that the relationship between predictor and criterion depends on the level of some other variable. The predictors may be higher-powered variables, so that one may have a rather complex model, embodying *both* non-linearity and interaction.

Assuming that the moderating effects of a variable may be approximated by a linear function (more complex models are available; see Ezekiel & Fox, 494), we simply add a product term, $X_i X_j$, to the battery for each case of simple (two-way) interaction. Thus, if the regression of Y on X_1 depends on the level of variable X_2, the equation takes the following form:

$$Y = b_0 + b_1 X_1 + b_2 X_2 + b_3 X_1 X_2.$$

Since the term $X_1 X_2$ is simply another predictor, so far as the regression equation is concerned, its significance may be tested in the manner suggested above: obtain R_c^2, the multiple correlation squared based on the complex model, and R_s^2, the multiple correlation squared based on the simpler model (from which the $X_1 X_2$ term has been dropped). The difference in R^2 (which is related to the difference in error variance) may then be tested by the F test, as outlined above.

Should the question of higher-order interactions arise, the model provides for them in a way which may be generalized from previous discussion: a triple interaction, wherein the moderating effect of X_j on X_i depends in turn upon the level of X_k, is represented by an $X_i X_j X_k$ term.

Finally, since the choice of model reflects sample data in hand, including chance effects, the eventual equation must be tried out on a new sample. This test of cross-validation is sometimes cruel to the sophisticated but parochial model which reflects too much the vagaries of a single study, but preference for the more complex model should be based upon firm evidence. Ward (1496) furnishes an excellent example of procedure here.

6. SUMMARY

(1) There are two good reasons for the extensive use of linear computations in multivariate investigations. One is that the methods are powerful, allowing for the handling and analysis of large numbers of variables. The second is that the techniques are quite flexible, adapting to conditions of non-linearity and interaction with remarkable ease. This is particularly the case with respect to regression analysis.

(2) Factor analysis is somewhat of a special case, for here, rather than merely knitting variables together in some optimal fashion for predictive purposes, we are more concerned with the generation of new variables (factors) of greater breadth and utility than the less abstract items which enter the analysis. In most instances of factor analysis, where the analysis is made of variables belonging to a common domain, we may expect intervariable relationships to be simpler than in cross-domain studies. Therefore, in the typical application of factor analysis, where the technique is used to map out the structure

of a domain, we should expect the linear model to provide a rather reasonable approximation to reality. Most instances of departure from this simple model are probably a result of inadequate scaling. The remedy for this is not "non-linear factor analysis," but more careful scaling (or rescaling) of the variables committed to a factor analysis.

(3) However, non-linear relationships and interaction between variables are possibilities, particularly where different kinds of variables are analyzed together (as in criterion factor analysis). In such cases, provided certain information is available to the researcher, corrective steps may be taken.

(4) The interpretation of factors, together with estimation of their interrelationships, rests upon the validity of the linear model. In most instances, the factor-analytic interpretation will logically provide a reasonable first approximation to the structure of a set of relationships.

(5) Theoretically, where variability is caused more by joint action of factors than their simple (i.e., additive) effects, the interpretation of a factor analysis may be difficult, depending on the number of interacting factors. Actual plasmodes (pages 223f.) showing complex interactions, however, have not so far presented difficulties, as Bargmann's work (58, 60) shows. Interpretation of factors usually rests upon previous knowledge, and as greater use is made of factor-derived scales, the patterns and effects of unknown factors can be more clearly located by separating out the action of known factors. Thus, a factor which is originally difficult to interpret, because it is based upon interacting effects, may develop a meaning out of use in known contents.

(6) A special case of interaction effects, among factors, is that which Cattell has called modulator action, and suggested as a model for the psychologically recognized way in which roles and states apparently modify the action of the usual personality source trait profile in the usual specification equation. It can be supposed that a global situation (bringing out for example a role not stimulated by the former focal stimulus) modulates a whole set of primary product terms in the specification equation, or a single second order factor product term. This model deserves more investigation.

(7) Linear methods are usually regarded as useful in the determination of first approximations of relationships. However, their ease of accommodation to non-linearity and interaction suggests that they will be useful tools of psychological research for many years to come. Indeed, psychological measurement has only begun to take advantage of them.

CHAPTER **16** Learning Theory and
Multivariate Experiment:
Illustration by
Determination of
Generalized Learning Curves*

LEDYARD R TUCKER
University of Illinois

1. INTRODUCTION
(BY THE EDITOR)

In Mowrer's recent summary and integration of the field of learning experiment, *Learning Theory and Behavior,* he points out that "each month approximately 80 new titles appear in this field" and that "after immersing himself in this relatively immense literature, [the student] might still emerge with the feeling of having learnt very little about learning." It is indeed

*This research was jointly supported in part by Princeton University, the Office of Naval Research under Contract N6 Onr-1858-(15), and the National Science Foundation under Grant G-3407, and in part by the Educational Testing Service. Dr. Allen Gardner generously loaned his original data so that it could be analyzed by the method described in this paper. The many extremely valuable comments by Dr. Harold Gulliksen both on the developments reported and on the manuscript are greatly appreciated by the author.

written large on the face of psychological history — too large, perhaps, for those busily engaged in the details of this area to see — that something is wrong. Since it is almost impossible reliably to estimate theoretical advance itself — for realistic and bogus ideation can be inextricably mixed — our only hope of being objective, as pointed out in Chapter 2, is to look at the technological developments which the alleged theory has produced. By this standard learning theory has done far less to improve the classroom learning speeds of a hundred years ago than, say, personality theory has done to put prediction of achievement, counseling, and clinical diagnosis on a radically new footing.

Thorndike's law of effect — with all due respect to a great man, no great step beyond common-sense observation and folk wisdom — has been dressed in new "reinforcement" titles, including the useful notion of secondary reinforcement. Trial-and-error learning has been, with questionable sense, tied to conditioning by the awkward semantic trick of calling it "operant conditioning." It is questionable because a substantial proportion of learning theorists believe the facts better fitted by a two-factor learning theory, in which classical conditioning is one thing and reward learning another. Add to these simple generalizations, explored for various time intervals, etc., some evidence on gradients of reinforcement, of the effects of anticipation or "hope" of partial reinforcement, or generalization from and discrimination among stimuli, and the total is still far short of anything to give either an intellectually impressive model or a technologically effective grasp of school and clinical procedures.

Some intelligent onlookers have wondered if the difficulty lies in an obsession with simple animal learning. A recent textbook quips that a psychologist is "an individual who thinks that the human race is directly descended from the white rat." But if the present writer's position in Chapters 1 and 2 is correct, the rat is a symptom, not a cause. In those chapters it was agreed that the attempt to handle all research by classical *manipulative* experiment inevitably results in the aim slipping to one side or the other of the true target. Since major motivational and learning manipulations cannot be performed with human beings, the manipulator must either study major manipulations with the rat or minor and emotionally trivial learning situations with the human. In historical fact, this is what can be seen to have happened: on the one hand we have volumes of studies on human beings learning nonsense syllables or reacting with an eye-blink reflex, and on the other, substantial "personality learning" experiments on rats, who, unfortunately, have nothing corresponding to what a sociologist, an anthropologist, or a psychologist would, seeing beyond the over-simplified reflex model, want to call personality.

Just as planned personality study began with a taxonomic approach, asking what might be the totality of phenomena to be explained by personality theory, so, it can be argued, a healthy learning theory would have done well to ask what are the longitudinal change phenomena, i.e., what are their natural varieties and forms, which need analysis. (Chapters 11, 12, and 13 above have dealt in technical detail with what is here implied.) Instead, some psychologists—and they happened to be in positions of influence—fascinated by the reflex, a model with all the mechanical simplicity of Victorian physics, proclaimed reflexology and conditioning as a nostrum to handle any learning phenomenon anyone might bring. Imbued with high school concepts of science already obsolete with leading physicists and chemists, they concentrated on this crassly simple gadget, fit to explain learning at the reflex level, instead of asking what had to be explained. What had to be explained was a complex and fascinating array of phenomena between human birth and death, especially those of adjustment and maladjustment as seen in the clinic; of attitudes and habits vitally interacting in the social learning of groups; of abilities and aptitudes growing and changing; and, on the physiological side, the relation of learning to autonomic activity, hormones, and chemical pacemakers in the cortex.

Let us consider, for illustration, just one of these areas—that of clinical change and personality learning. To establish laws about learning we have to relate measured change to measured situational experience. To define exactly what a change is, we have first to define what exists at a given moment, technically examined in Chapters 11, 12, and 13 above. If personality is most meaningfully and economically described at a given moment by a series of source trait measurements (Chapter 18), then the change to be examined in a learning experience is that between two vectors, as implied in Table 16-1. For, although in certain cases we can be tolerably sure that the change is largely in one dimension, even the rat learning a maze learns more than the maze, e.g., he becomes more docile to handling by the experimenter.

However, a situation or stimulus (by our basic model, pages 74f.) is also a multidimensional entity, and can be so defined either in physical or psychological dimensions. What the present writer has developed elsewhere (325) as a model for *multidimensional learning theory,* therefore, assumes that *all aspects of a situation produce a learning change in all aspects of the organism's behav-*

each personality dimension, but others could be tried within the general multidimensional learning theory. Elsewhere (325) the more detailed development in relation to clinical problems has expanded the *learning vector* into a matrix of *path-personality coefficients,* expressing the effect of each of a number of trial-and-error paths upon every personality factor and then multiplying this by a *path-frequency* matrix, which is a natural development of the learning vector.

In the clinical field the whole has been called *analytical adjustment theory* (a branch of multidimensional learning theory) but, the essential concepts are (1) that learning must first be conceived and measured as a

TABLE 16-1

FIRST MODEL IN MULTIDIMENSIONAL LEARNING THEORY
(Showing matrix calculation of learning [change] vector;
illustrated on four dimensions, one situation and one person.)

	Situation S				Person P	Change in Person P	
Source Traits 1 to 4	l_{s1}				z_{p1}	c_{p1}	Source Traits 1 to 4
		l_{s2}			z_{p2}	c_{p2}	
			l_{s3}		z_{p3}	c_{p3}	
				l_{s4}	z_{p4}	c_{p4}	

($\times$ between Situation S and Person P; $=$ between Person P and Change in Person P)

L: Matrix defining general learning impact of situation s, dimensionally.

Z: Pre-learning dimensions of the personality.

C: Learning (change) vector for person p.

ior, as a single total event. The aim of learning experiment is then to find the laws relating the pre-existing dimensions of the individual and the learning dimensions of the situation to the dimensions of the individual's change, and the analysis must begin with the calculation from experiment of the *learning impact matrix,* as shown in the matrix multiplication of Table 16-1.

For simplicity we have here taken one of the simplest models—a linear relation between the dimensions of the repeated situation and the subsequent change on

multidimensional change to a multidimensional situation, and (2) that analytical procedures, on changes measured in people in the natural life situation are capable of generating learning laws for humans (or, for that matter, for animals) without the manipulative control commonly demanded in learning experiments. Actually, manipulation has its role, but the important point is that either with or without manipulation the analysis of data must be multivariate and typically in a matrix model. Parenthetically, this is a model which the new behavioral therapy could well use, though it has also tended to fall in the rut of an atomistic reflex handling of symptoms rather than of personality change. The experienced clinician naturally objects that extinguishing a symptom is a very temporary "cure." Multidimensional learning theory would resolve the dispute, giving the objectivity of measurement of change desired by the behavioral therapist and heeding the basic changes in personality structure desired by the practicing clinician.

An experimental beginning in the above direction, but in a more readily controlled and restricted situation has been made by Tucker (1463), Fleishman (531), McGee, and a few others, though it has not yet received nearly the degree of critical attention from learning theorists which such a radical advance deserves. This work examines learning as a multidimensional change, but does not treat the situation as a multidimensional term, and is thus a halfway house between the bivariate and the multivariate treatment. However, its results suffice to demonstrate the contention that a good deal of the fruitlessness of the immense labor spent in trying to arrive at firm and comprehensive laws of learning by bivariate research has been due to a great part of the relevant picture being blotted out from the experimenter's calculations. It is not unreasonable to suppose that it would be impossible to reach truly controlling, adequately predicting laws when one takes an artificial, thin slice of the data box instead of all that affects and is affected by the phenomenon in question.

This pioneer work, largely by Fleishman and Tucker, has clearly shown that the factorial structure of the learned responses changes — but in a continuous and comprehensible way — as the learning experience continues. Instead of a two-dimensional learning curve — a level of performance, X, against time, T — we now need a multidimensional curve of the various components in X against time, which can, of course, be plotted as a *set* of two-dimensional graphs.

It is surely probable that laws can be found more readily for these meaningful factorial components than for some composite of the lot of them, as has traditionally been attempted.

2. THE SHAPE AND NUMBER OF LEARNING CURVES

In a theoretical development on determination of parameters of functional relations by factor analysis, Tucker (1463) provided a possible empirical approach to the investigation of phenomena involving individual differences in the form of relations between variables. The present study is an experimental trial of this procedure and provides a concrete example of its application to a particular phenomenon: that of learning curves for a probability learning task. This example illustrates a number of intricacies that may be encountered in applications to psychological phenomena as well as indicating some of the types of results that may be expected.

Another example of the use of this procedure is the study by Ronald Weitzman (1512) in which he compared the learning functions of groups of rats and fish.

It is instructive to compare the general nature of the system used here with two traditional approaches to psychological problems. As discussed by Cattell in Chapter 1 above, and Cronbach (394) in his APA presidential address, one traditional approach attempts to discover and delineate the general attributes of psychological phenomena as applicable to all individuals, while the alternate approach deals with individual differences in the extent or quality of selected aspects of behavior. In the domain of learning behavior, for example, the first approach may attempt to develop a learning curve for a given task abstracted from individual learning curves and generalized over all individuals. The second approach might be interested in the individual differences in such things as extent of learning after some specified time, or in maximum performance obtainable by the individuals, or in time necessary for mastery of the task.

It might be said that the system to be described here combines the interests of the two traditions, an interest in general relations between variables in the behavior of individuals and an interest in individual differences in these relations. In the learning domain this implies an interest in generalized learning curves, but does not limit the consideration, necessarily, to a single general learning curve of a fixed shape. It allows, in contrast, for the possibility of a field of learning curves so constructed and related that different individual learning curves having different shapes may be represented in this field.

In the present context, two curves will be said to have the same shape when they may be superimposed after linear transformations of the scale of measurement of the dependent variable. Thus, if:

$$y = f(x)$$

$$Y = Q(x)$$

and

$$y = aY + b$$

then f and Q have the same *shape.* The concept "same shape" will be used in this paper as defined here.

In a sense, one may describe the situation on a slightly higher mathematical level by proposing that a single basic function might exist relating performance on the task to learning time such that this function takes on various forms with various values of its parameters. Each individual could be characterized by particular values of these parameters and his learning curve could be generated from the basic function. The family of possible learning curves corresponds to the field of learning curves referred to in the preceding paragraph. An important point is that each member curve of this family, or field, might not have the same shape as every other member curve. Obviously, in this case, the basic function

cannot be represented by a single learning curve: rather, some method need be adopted to indicate the various shapes existent for the function in order to obtain a more adequate description of the phenomena. This might have profound implications for conclusions as to the effects of various conditions.

Consider one of the common practices in experimental psychology, that of using the average learning curve over subjects as yielding the generalized learning curve. Such general learning curves have been obtained under a variety of conditions dependent on such matters as material to be learned, procedure employed in the learning sessions, amount of reward given to the subjects for the desired behavior, etc. If the average curve is carelessly interpreted as representing the learning law for each subject, all variations from the means are treated as errors of observation. The average learning curve will represent the learning law, or basic function, involved only when all members of the family of curves have the same shape. Otherwise, the basic function is more complex and a more complex description is indicated.

A number of authors have discussed the appropriateness of the use of the average learning curve, including Merrill (1045), Sidman (1322), Bakan (50), Estes (469), Spence (1343), and Gulliksen, (645). According to Estes (469), it is appropriate to predict the nature of an average curve from consideration of theoretical individual curves, thus arriving at evidence confirming, or not confirming, the form of the individual learning curves. We will agree that, if the observed average curve does not conform to the predicted average curve, the forms of the individual curves are not confirmed. However, conformity of observed and predicted average curves is only partial confirmation of the theoretical individual curves. In general, the same average curve can be obtained from a variety of basic functions; thus, conformity of observed and predicted average curves indicates only that the investigator has selected one of the variety of possible basic functions for his theoretical position. Stronger confirmation would occur if each individual curve was a member of the family of curves generated from the selected theoretical basic function.

Estes discussed, also, three classes of functions: "Class A. Functions unmodified by averaging," "Class B. Functions for which averaging complicates the interpretation of parameters but leaves form unchanged," and "Class C. Functions modified in form by averaging." In the first of these classes he includes functions which are linear in the parameters for the individuals. These functions have the property that the average curve is obtained by replacing the individual parameters by the mean values of these parameters over individuals in a group, thus leaving the portion of the function dependent on the trial parameters unaltered by the averaging process. This property, however, does not indicate that the various curves in the family generated by any one such function are necessarily of the same shape. Consider equation (1):

$$(1) \quad x_{ji} = b_{j1}y_{1i} + b_{j2}y_{2i} + \ldots$$

where x_{ji} is the score on trial j ($j = 1, 2, 3, \ldots, n$) for individual i ($i = 1, 2, 3, \ldots, N$); b_{j1}, b_{j2}, etc., are coefficients dependent on the trials; and y_{1i}, y_{2i}, etc., are individual parameters. There are n trials and N individuals. To obtain the average curve, the individual y's are replaced by the mean y's and the form of the function is not changed. However, even though the form of the function as expressed in equation (1) does not change, the shape of the average curve may be very different from the curves for the individuals. As an example, suppose that there are two terms in equation (1), that the series of a_{j1}'s over the set of trials tends to produce a curve that rises rapidly for early trials and soon reaches an asymptote, and that the curve for the a_{j2}'s stays near the base line for several trials

before starting to rise and then on later trials reaches an asymptote. An individual with a large value of parameter y_{1i} and zero value of y_{2i} will have a learning curve similar to the b_{j1} curve, while another individual who has a high second parameter and a zero value for the first parameter will have a learning curve similar to the b_{j2} curve. These two curves will not be similar in shape. Furthermore, if the subjects in a group have various values of the two parameters, their functions will be similar in *form* but their curves will be various combinations of the two b curves and have a variety of *shapes* as defined above. The average curve, consequently, could not have the same shape as each of the curves for members in the group.

A special case of the Class A functions occurs when all individual learning curves have the same shape so that each curve may be obtained from any other curve by a multiplication factor. This implies that only one term exists on the right side of equation (1), or that all of the b curves are proportional so that the terms on the right of equation 1 can be combined into a single term. In this case, the average curve does represent the shape of each curve.

A second special case occurs when an additive constant in addition to a multiplying factor is required to transform any one individual curve to any other individual curve. There are now, effectively, two terms on the right of equation (2) with the b_{j2}'s being a constant. The average learning curve represents the various individual learning curves in shape, this time within an additive constant.

Other than these two special cases, the average learning curve will not represent the shapes of the various individual learning curves.

Estes' Class B functions can be represented by equation (1) also, in which case, however, the coefficients y_{1i}, y_{2i}, etc., are functions of more primitive parameters for the individuals. The foregoing discussion of the shapes of the individual curves and the

TABLE 16-2

RAW SCORES BY TRIALS ON LEARNING TASK FOR GROUP 70-10-10-10

Trial	Persons 1-12 (S at 70%; L, N, and D each at 10%)												Persons 13-24 (L at 70%; S, N, and D each at 10%)												Trial Mean
	1	2	3	4	5	6	7	8	9	10	11	12	13	14	15	16	17	18	19	20	21	22	23	24	
1	09	03	01	04	06	06	09	08	05	08	14	05	05	04	02	04	13	03	00	05	02	02	08	08	05.58
2	12	09	10	07	08	18	12	14	07	14	17	11	05	09	07	08	16	11	11	05	06	02	16	17	10.50
3	12	11	16	08	11	18	13	13	10	17	17	09	07	11	10	10	11	09	11	05	10	05	14	17	11.46
4	12	14	07	08	09	13	12	13	05	15	15	09	10	16	10	05	13	11	10	09	14	04	12	14	10.83
5	10	16	07	13	11	14	14	13	09	13	15	11	17	15	11	09	16	13	15	15	14	05	13	14	12.63
6	11	18	13	16	10	15	13	10	09	16	18	13	11	18	11	11	14	14	15	16	16	03	16	17	13.33
7	11	16	15	13	11	16	15	12	13	15	16	15	15	16	15	14	14	15	16	17	17	05	14	17	14.33
8	13	20	15	19	12	17	17	13	16	16	20	14	19	17	16	15	17	16	15	16	16	04	16	20	15.75
9	13	14	16	18	14	16	12	12	14	17	18	12	15	17	11	16	15	12	12	14	16	05	16	17	14.25
10	13	18	14	13	12	15	18	14	12	15	20	17	16	16	17	13	13	15	12	16	13	12	17	20	15.13
11	12	16	16	19	15	17	13	10	12	14	20	15	16	15	16	14	13	10	15	14	14	14	15	20	14.83
12	13	16	14	20	15	16	16	12	14	16	19	16	20	15	11	12	13	14	11	16	16	17	16	20	14.79
13	12	19	17	19	15	17	16	13	14	16	20	17	20	16	16	14	12	14	14	18	15	20	17	19	16.25
14	14	18	19	20	14	17	16	15	16	17	19	15	20	18	17	13	13	14	14	16	16	19	17	20	16.38
15	13	18	18	19	12	15	16	15	13	16	18	16	15	16	18	15	12	11	12	16	14	19	18	20	16.04
16	14	18	15	20	12	17	17	14	17	16	16	19	19	15	20	14	12	13	14	14	15	19	18	20	16.42
17	11	16	17	18	15	15	15	14	14	16	20	18	16	16	20	16	12	13	12	16	14	20	18	20	15.83
18	14	17	15	20	15	14	16	13	14	16	19	17	19	15	18	16	10	13	12	16	14	19	18	20	15.96
19	15	19	15	20	14	17	19	15	14	14	20	18	16	15	17	17	12	11	14	15	15	17	19	20	16.63
20	15	18	16	20	10	16	17	13	15	16	18	15	19	16	18	14	14	13	11	17	14	17	18	20	15.79
21	14	17	19	20	16	18	18	15	15	15	16	18	20	15	18	16	15	15	14	17	18	20	16	20	16.88

average curve applies to this class. In the developments that follow, the two classes, A and B, will be treated alike. No implication will, or should be made that any parameters obtained are primitive in character.

Estes' Class C functions possess greater complexity of relation between trial parameters and individual parameters than is exhibited in equation (1). Furthermore, they are not transformable into this form without use of infinite series or transformation of the observations. For our purposes, the distinction between Classes A and B on one side and Class C on the other is very important. Equation (1) is used as the basis of the procedure to be described. Consequently, the procedure will not yield meaningful results when the basic function is of Class C and cannot be adequately approximated by a function of Classes A and B. Fortunately, the procedure will indicate those cases when it is not appropriate by indicating the need for a large number of terms on the right of equation (1) such as would be generated by an infinite series expansion of a Class C function.

While Estes' classification of functions is useful in introducing the present procedure, the mode of attack on the analysis of learning data is somewhat the opposite of Estes'. He, like many others, tends to start with a theoretically derived function and attempts confirmation by data. The procedure given here starts with data and attempts to develop empirical functions that fit the data. When such empirical functions are obtained, an attempt might be made to identify them with theoretical functions. Both of these approaches possess positive values. Insofar as the end goal is the development of a valid theoretical system, the fitting of observed data by theoretical curves is the more basic approach. The empirical approach, in comparison, may be a valuable aid in surveying the field of data and indicating the types of functions appropriate for further consideration. Systematic empirical study of data could lead to profitable hypotheses and save effort by avoidance of inappropriate hypotheses. In this empirical study it is important that the method of study have the power to represent the extent and nature of the family, or field, of individual learning curves.

3. THE RELEVANCE OF FACTOR ANALYSIS

It has been noted (1463) that equation (1) is identical with the basic linear postulate used in factor analysis. This identity leads to the possibility of empirical investigation of the family of learning curves underlying the individual learning curves of the observed performances of subjects. The b_j's are factor loadings for the trials and the y_i's are factor scores for the individuals. A common statement in factor analysis is that the observed score x_{ji} is a weighted sum of the factor scores for the individual, the weights being the factor loadings for the variable. For the present case this statement is turned around to say that the series of scores of an individual is a weighted sum of reference learning curves, the weights being the individual factor scores and the series of b's for each factor forming a reference learning curve. There are, then, questions for any particular learning situation and population of subjects as to how many reference learning curves are needed to account for the observed performances and as to the forms of these reference learning curves. Factor-analytic methods may be used to determine answers to these questions. A fairly complete documentation of the analysis of one matrix of data is given in the tables and figures to follow. Some results are given for three other related matrices in order to provide some comparisons of possible results.

Consider Table 16-2. It contains the raw data for the study used in this illustration. These data were collected by Dr. Allen

Gardner (574) of the Quartermaster Research and Development Center, who kindly supplied them for the present experimental analysis. He collected these data while located at the Army Medical Research Laboratory as part of his studies on probability learning with multiple choices. The subjects were army enlisted men. The learning session consisted of 420 presentations of letters. Just prior to each presentation, each man was to guess which letter of four letters would be presented. He could observe the accuracy of each guess when the letter was shown. For twelve of the men the letter S was presented with a probability of 70 per cent and the letters L, N, and D were presented with a probability of 10 per cent each. The 420 presentations were grouped arbitrarily into 21 "trials" of 20 presentations each, and a score for each trial for each man was the number of times he guessed the predominant letter. The subjects were not informed of the probabilities, nor of the grouping into trials, nor of the scoring method.

The situation described in the preceding paragraph will be called the 70-10-10-10 group. Comparisons of selected results will be made with three other groups, a 70-30 group for which two letters were used having probabilities of 70 per cent and 30 per cent, a 60-40 group for which two letters were used having probabilities of 60 per cent and 40 per cent, and a 60-10-10-10-10 group for which five letters were used, one of which had a probability of 60 per cent and the other four letters having a probability of 10 per cent each. A separate group of 24 subjects was used for each condition.

On the right of Table 16-2 are the means for the trials. In one of the more customary types of analysis found in the literature, these means would be used for the average learning curve. Comparisons will be made between this average learning curve and the results obtained by the factor analysis of the data in the table.

4. THE FACTORIAL FORMULATION

In form, the analysis is related to Hotelling's (771) principal components but differs in that the mean values of the variables (the trials) are not removed from the data. The formulation by Eckart and Young (447) and by Householder and Young (776) for the approximation of one matrix by another of lower rank is more appropriate for the present case in that this formulation does not imply the use of deviation scores. The Eckart-Young development provides a least-squares approximation to the raw data matrix X by a matrix $\hat{X}$ obtained from any given number of factors. In order to spell out this statement more explicitly, let $\hat{x}_{ji}$ be the approximate scores obtained from the factor system and let e_{ji} be the errors of approximation. Equation (1) is rewritten by replacing x_{ji} by $\hat{x}_{ji}$ and, using summational notation:

$$(2) \quad \hat{x}_{ji} = \sum_{f=1}^{k} b_{jf} y_{fi}$$

where $f (f = 1, 2, 3, \ldots, k)$ represents factors and k is the number of factors employed. For any given value of k, the errors of approximation obtained from equation (3) have a minimum sum of squares when the b's and y's are determined by the Eckart-Young procedure:

$$(3) \quad e_{ji} = x_{ji} - \hat{x}_{ji}$$

Equation (2) is restated in matrix form for convenience in outlining the mathematical structure of the analysis.

$$(4) \quad \hat{X}_k = B_k Y_k$$

where the capital letters represent matrices containing as their elements the corresponding lower-case letters. The subscript k is used with these matrices to indicate the number of factors involved, since they will be altered by a change in the number of factors. The Eckart-Young development consists of analyzing the given matrix into the product of three matrices containing a series of roots and vectors. It is convenient to call these principal roots and vectors to distinguish them from characteristic roots and vectors and to indicate their relation to principal components and principal factors. This analysis can be indicated by the matrix equation:

$$(5) \quad X = VGW$$

where V is an $n \times n$ orthogonal matrix $(V' = V^{-1})$, W is an $N \times N$ orthogonal matrix $(W' = W^{-1})$, and G contains the principal roots, λ_p, as diagonal entries in an upper left section and contains zeros elsewhere. Columns of V will be called the left principal vectors of X and the rows of W will be called the right principal vectors of X. Let the roots and vectors be ordered so that:

$$(6) \quad \lambda_1 \geqslant \lambda_2 \geqslant \lambda_3 \geqslant \ldots \geqslant \lambda_k > \lambda_{(k+1)} \geqslant \ldots \geqslant \lambda_n \text{ (or } \lambda_N) \geqslant 0$$

where the final term is λ_n when $n \leqslant N$ and is λ_N when $n > N$. The lower-case letter p ($p = 1, 2, 3, \ldots, n$ or N) will be used to designate principal vector or root.

The approximate matrix $\hat{X}_k$ is formed by using the first k left principal vectors in V, principal roots in G, and right principal vectors in W to form the matrices V_k, G_k, and W_k so that:

$$(7) \quad \hat{X}_k = V_k G_k W_k.$$

Note that V_k is an $n \times k$ matrix, G_k is a $k \times k$ diagonal matrix, and W_k is a $k \times N$ matrix. The matrices B^*_k and Y^*_k may be defined by equations (8) and (9).

$$(8) \quad B^*_k = (N)^{-1/2} V_k G_k$$
$$(9) \quad Y^*_k = (N)^{1/2} W_k$$

Since the sum of squares of the entries in each row of W_k equals unity, the mean square will equal $\frac{1}{N}$. The entries in each row of Y^*_k have been scaled so that their mean square is unity irrespective of the number of individuals. Then:

$$(10) \quad \hat{X}_k = B^*_k Y^*_k$$

The matrices B_k and Y_k which satisfy equation (4) are defined by

$$(11) \quad B_k = B^*_k T$$
$$(12) \quad Y_k = T^{-1} Y^*_k.$$

The matrix T is any non-singular $k \times k$ matrix. It is not defined by the least-squares fit principle used in the derivation of the preceding system, but may be fixed by auxiliary considerations so that matrices B_k and Y_k possess some desirable properties. This corresponds to the rotation of axes problem in factor analysis. Definition of the matrix T will be discussed in later paragraphs.

Several sums of squares properties of this system are of interest. Consider equations (13-16).

$$(13) \quad \sum_{j=1}^{n} \sum_{i=1}^{N} x^2_{ji} - \sum_{p=1}^{n(\text{or } N)} \lambda^2_p$$

$$(14) \quad \sum_{j=1}^{n} \sum_{i=1}^{N} \hat{x}^2_{ji} = \sum_{p=1}^{k} \lambda^2_p$$

$$(15) \quad \sum_{j=1}^{n} \sum_{i=1}^{N} e^2_{ji} = \sum_{p=k+1}^{n(\text{or } N)} \lambda^2_p$$

$$(16) \quad \sum_{j=1}^{n} \sum_{i=1}^{N} x^2_{ji} = \sum_{j=1}^{n} \sum_{i=1}^{N} \hat{x}^2_{ji} + \sum_{j=1}^{n} \sum_{i=1}^{N} e^2_{ji}.$$

The sum of squares of the observed scores, x_{ji}, is equal to the sum of squares of all principal roots, while the sum of squares of the approximate scores, $\hat{x}_{ji}$, is equal to the sum of square of the first k principal roots. The sum of squares of the errors of approximation, e_{ji}, is equal to the sum of squares of the principal roots not included in forming the approximation. Equation (16) indicates that the sum of squares of the observations has been analyzed into independent additive portions. Thus, from

TABLE 16-3

SUMS OF CROSS-PRODUCTS BETWEEN TRIALS FOR GROUP 70-10-10-10

Trials	1	2	3	4	5	6	7	8	9	10	11	12	13	14	15	16	17	18	19	20	21
1	1034	1642	1665	1578	1770	1856	1924	2188	1989	2069	2029	2032	2162	2171	2130	2172	2106	2153	2251	2121	2220
2	1642	3084	3193	2937	3284	3538	3699	4100	3719	3910	3772	3752	4071	4083	4032	4088	3988	3979	4218	3977	4191
3	1665	3193	3455	3132	3503	3806	4016	4428	4045	4244	4146	4086	4476	4522	4432	4487	4397	4379	4588	4371	4615
4	1578	2937	3132	3076	3448	3667	3839	4234	3800	4033	3900	3884	4234	4262	4173	4257	4093	4137	4323	4127	4347
5	1770	3284	3503	3448	4029	4204	4466	4944	4405	4664	4528	4531	4950	4961	4844	4974	4749	4825	5037	4796	5095
6	1856	3538	3806	3667	4204	4548	4759	5258	5010	4946	4853	4805	5248	5272	5174	5275	5072	5129	5360	5116	5386
7	1924	3699	4016	3839	4466	4759	5092	5583	5551	5293	5151	5096	5608	5638	5527	5657	5434	5479	5718	5457	5798
8	2188	4100	4428	4234	4944	5258	5583	6210	5551	5826	5700	5660	6191	6224	6084	6249	6216	6245	6563	6261	6658
9	1989	3719	4045	3800	4405	5010	5551	5551	5064	5208	5170	5120	5584	5633	5500	5610	5421	5485	5694	5445	5766
10	2069	3910	4244	4033	4664	4946	5293	5826	5208	5619	5452	5431	5963	5989	5877	6021	5811	5842	6094	5800	6158
11	2029	3772	4146	3900	4528	4853	5151	5700	5170	5452	5452	5391	5892	5949	5808	5929	5753	5803	5993	5729	6069
12	2032	3752	4086	3884	4531	4805	5096	5660	5120	5431	5391	5433	5893	5935	5784	5923	5723	5789	5997	5724	6076
13	2162	4071	4476	4234	4950	5248	5608	6191	5584	5963	5892	5893	6456	6502	6343	6498	6284	6329	6563	6261	6658
14	2171	4083	4522	4262	4961	5272	5638	6224	5633	5989	5949	5935	6502	6597	6407	6561	6342	6387	6606	6337	6715
15	2130	4032	4432	4173	4844	5174	5527	6084	5500	5877	5808	5784	6343	6407	6291	6409	6216	6245	6488	6184	6569
16	2172	4088	4487	4257	4974	5275	5657	6249	5610	6021	5929	5923	6498	6561	6409	6604	6356	6405	6637	6348	6723
17	2106	3988	4397	4093	4749	5072	5434	6216	5421	5811	5753	5723	6284	6342	6216	6356	6196	6197	6420	6173	6496
18	2153	3979	4379	4137	4825	5129	5479	6245	5485	5842	5803	5789	6329	6387	6245	6405	6197	6257	6461	6173	6544
19	2251	4218	4588	4323	5037	5360	5718	6563	5694	6094	5993	5997	6563	6606	6488	6637	6420	6461	6741	6398	6790
20	2121	3977	4371	4127	4796	5116	5457	6261	5445	5800	5729	5724	6261	6337	6184	6348	6173	6173	6398	6143	6476
21	2220	4191	4615	4347	5095	5386	5798	6658	5766	6158	6069	6076	6658	6715	6569	6723	6496	6544	6790	6476	6925

the squares of the principal roots, it is possible to judge the goodness of fit of the approximation to the data. When a small number of dimensions have large roots and the remaining roots are near zero, only a correspondingly few terms in equation (2) are indicated as necessary, and the number of learning curves needed will be correspondingly small. When only one root is large, all of the individual learning curves will be multiples of each other and have the same shape. When there are two large roots and one column of B_k is a constant, the individual learning curves can be obtained from a single reference learning curve by using an additive constant and a multiplier. These are the two special cases previously indicated. Estes' Class A and B functions include not only the preceding two special cases, but also other cases for which there are limited numbers of significant roots. When there are many significant roots, a conclusion may be reached that the basic function is of Estes' Class C.

Among the problems remaining to be discussed is that of determining the principal roots and vectors. Consider equation (17), which is derived from equation (5), and the orthogonal properties of the matrices V and W.

(17) $XX' = VG^2V'$.

Note that X' is the transpose of matrix X. The matrix XX' contains the sums of squares of scores on the trials as its diagonal entries and the sums of cross-products of scores on pairs of trials as the off-diagonal entries. This product matrix for the 70-10-10-10 group is given in Table 16-3. The formation of this product matrix transforms our problem from that of finding the principal roots and vectors of the matrix X to that of finding the characteristic roots and vectors of the product matrix V, containing the characteristic vectors of XX', and G^2 containing the characteristic roots of XX'. This solution is greatly facilitated by the use of high-speed electronic computers. The procedure is to determine

these characteristic roots and vectors, determine the number of dimensions to be employed by inspection of these roots and vectors, and then to form the matrix B_k^* by equation 8. The matrix Y_k^* can be determined by equation (18).

(18) $Y_k^* = NG^{-2}B'_kX$

5. THE ANALYSIS OF GARDNER'S DATA

The matrix of intercorrelations between trials for the 70-10-10-10 group is given in Table 16-4 for general interest although it does not enter into the analysis. For the first nine trials the high correlations appear near the diagonal, giving an appearance similar to a Guttman simplex (655). These first nine trials have low positive and negative correlations with the last nine trials. The last eleven trials tend to form a single group with high intercorrelations. It is sufficient here to indicate that a Guttman simplex structure involves a large number of factors so that if the data did follow this law of formation, it would show up in a large number of significant factors in the following analysis. Insofar as the analysis indicates a small number of factors to be adequate for the data, it may be concluded that the data do not conform to the simplex law of formation.

Table 16-5 presents the characteristic roots of the sums of cross-product matrix of Table 16-3. These are squares of the principal roots. The first root is very large. The second root, while small compared with the first one, may be significantly large. An unsolved problem exists in determining the number of factors to be used. The cumulative sum of squared principal roots following any given number of factors is listed in the third column of Table 16-5. The first entry in this column is the sum of squares of the original table of scores in Table 16-2. The second entry is the sum of squares of the errors of approximation if the first factor was used alone to approxi-

TABLE 16-4*

MATRIX OF INTERCORRELATIONS BETWEEN TRIALS FOR GROUP 70-10-10-10

Trials

Trials	1	2	3	4	5	6	7	8	9	10	11	12	13	14	15	16	17	18	19	20	21
1	100	66	44	46	32	24	02	29	34	22	19	22	−08	−11	−11	−14	−07	07	13	02	−26
2	66	100	84	61	34	51	33	39	44	42	12	09	−11	−16	−05	−20	−01	−17	13	−01	−31
3	44	84	100	54	13	48	34	35	52	43	29	08	04	09	11	−14	18	−05	09	13	−15
4	46	61	54	100	72	74	55	54	43	55	21	18	05	02	01	−06	−11	−06	00	10	−26
5	32	34	13	72	100	69	68	75	44	50	18	26	17	00	−11	00	−25	−06	00	06	−13
6	24	51	48	74	69	100	81	81	76	56	48	32	26	15	23	11	02	11	23	30	−09
7	02	33	34	55	68	81	100	81	62	62	29	04	13	03	06	07	−07	−07	−01	15	−06
8	29	39	35	54	75	81	81	100	74	60	44	32	28	17	12	23	01	18	22	15	−06
9	34	44	52	43	44	76	62	74	100	23	54	33	18	19	09	−03	03	16	06	40	03
10	22	42	43	55	50	56	62	60	23	100	45	40	52	31	44	47	42	36	50	26	−04
11	19	12	29	21	18	48	29	44	54	45	100	71	75	72	69	56	66	77	55	47	30
12	22	09	08	18	26	32	04	32	33	40	71	100	85	71	62	60	57	76	68	70	49
13	−08	−11	04	05	17	26	13	28	18	52	75	85	100	84	75	75	75	80	70	75	74
14	−11	−16	09	02	00	15	03	17	19	31	72	71	84	100	75	74	70	75	55	82	69
15	−11	−05	11	01	−11	23	06	12	09	44	69	62	75	75	100	71	84	78	79	77	71
16	−14	−20	−14	−06	00	11	07	23	−03	47	56	60	75	74	71	100	75	84	72	86	67
17	−07	−01	18	−11	−25	02	−07	01	03	42	66	57	75	70	84	75	100	82	74	68	66
18	07	−17	−05	−06	−06	11	−07	18	16	36	77	76	80	75	78	84	82	100	75	82	71
19	13	13	09	00	00	23	−01	22	06	50	55	68	70	55	79	72	74	75	100	74	58
20	02	−01	13	10	06	30	15	15	40	26	47	70	75	82	77	86	68	82	74	100	67
21	−26	−31	−15	−26	−13	−09	−06	−06	03	−04	30	49	74	69	71	67	66	71	58	67	100

*Decimal points are omitted; all values have two decimal places.

mate the observed scores. The third entry is the sum of squares of the errors of approximation if two factors were used, etc. Relations among these sums of squares and the squares of the roots are given in equations (13-16), described previously.

In order to obtain mean square ratios similar to variance ratios used in analysis of variance, degrees of freedom involved for each successive factor and for the errors of approximation for the roots beyond each factor were determined and listed in Table 16-5. The degrees of freedom assignable to factor k are $(df)_k$ and are given in equation (19).

$$(19) \quad (df)_k = n + N + 1 - 2k$$

The degrees of freedom for the errors of approximation after factor k may be designated by $(DF)_k$ and are given in equation (20).

$$(20) \quad (DF)_k = (n - k)(N - k)$$

These are equal to the cumulative sum of the degrees of freedom for the factors following factor k. Equation (21) gives the formula for the mean square ratio for factor k $(MSR)_k$.

$$(21) \quad (MSR)_k = \frac{\lambda^2{}_k (DF)_k}{(df)_k \sum\limits_{P = k+1}^{n} \lambda^2{}_P}$$

These mean square ratios are listed in the last column of Table 16-5. Mathematical investigations of these mean square ratios indicate that they are not distributed by the F ratio used in the analysis of variance. They seem to be slightly biased toward higher values. For large samples the F distribution might be an adequate approximation, but for the sample size used in the example, this approximation is not good. Inspection of the column of mean square ratios in Table 16-5 indicates that the first three are somewhat above the remaining

TABLE 16-5

PRINCIPAL ROOTS OF SCORE MATRIX FOR GROUP 70-10-10-10

Factor Number	Principal Roots, Squared Factor	Cumulative (Below)	Degrees of Freedom Factor	Cumulative (Below)	Mean Square Ratio
0	—	110306.	—	504	—
1	107634.	2672.2	44	460	421.12
2	1241.8	1430.3	42	418	8.64
3	469.1	961.3	40	378	4.61
4	238.2	723.0	38	340	2.95
5	190.5	532.6	36	304	3.02
6	123.8	408.7	34	270	2.41
7	85.12	323.6	32	238	1.96
8	74.04	249.6	30	208	2.06
9	67.28	182.3	28	180	2.37
10	50.37	131.9	26	154	2.26
11	31.63	100.3	24	130	1.71
12	28.91	71.37	22	108	1.99
13	21.32	50.05	20	88	1.87
14	17.30	32.76	18	70	2.05
15	11.74	21.02	16	54	1.88
16	7.222	13.80	14	40	1.50
17	5.577	8.223	12	28	1.58
18	4.102	4.121	10	18	1.79
19	2.193	1.928	8	10	1.42
20	1.307	.621	6	4	1.40
21	.621	—	4	0	—

values, the fourth and fifth values might be considered as questionable as to significance, and the remaining values as indicating that the factors do not account for a significant portion of the total sum of squares.

Mean square ratios are listed in Table 16-6 for all four groups investigated. Asterisks

quate for Group 60-40 while two components are required for Group 60-10-10-10-10. Again the group involving only two letters has the simpler basic learning function. This is an intriguing result. One might argue, however, that this result should have been expected in that simpler situations should involve simpler relations. A major

TABLE 16-6

MEAN SQUARE RATIOS FOR PRINCIPAL FACTORS

Factor Number	Group 70-30	Group 70-10-10-10	Group 60-40	Group 60-10-10-10-10
1	463.49*	421.12*	246.04*	461.74*
2	2.49	8.64*	3.05	3.88*
3	2.69	4.61*	2.06	2.53
4	2.34	2.95	2.23	2.13
5	2.27	3.02	1.85	2.10
6	2.44	2.41	1.97	2.14
7	2.19	1.96	2.02	1.91
8	2.08	2.06	1.79	2.19
9	2.25	2.37	1.78	1.83
10	2.31	2.26	1.91	1.88
11	2.01	1.71	1.75	1.76
12	1.80	1.99	1.34	1.43
13	1.55	1.87	1.47	1.62
14	1.58	2.05	1.43	2.01
15	1.77	1.88	1.13	1.81
16	1.50	1.50	1.32	2.27
17	1.49	1.58	1.78	2.44
18	1.18	1.79	1.71	4.01
19	1.28	1.42	1.62	6.98
20	1.18	1.40	1.22	3.60

*Interpreted as significantly large.

are used to indicate those ratios that are interpreted as being significantly large. Thus, the Group 70-30 seems to involve only one component while Group 70-10-10-10 seems to involve three components. Each component yields a reference learning curve, and the basic learning function may be thought of as having a complexity equal to the number of reference learning curves included in it. From these results we may conclude that the basic learning function for Group 70-10-10-10 seems to be more complex than the basic function for Group 70-30. One component seems to be ade-

point to be made here is that being able to investigate the complexity of a basic function is a characteristic peculiar to the present approach as compared with more traditional methods of analysis applied to data of the present kind. The author knows of no other method that would yield a conclusion on the complexity of a basic function.

While the mean square ratios presented in the previous paragraphs yield strong evidence relative to the number of reference learning curves required for the data, the absence of knowledge as to the theoretical distribution and of definite values corresponding to given confidence levels of the mean square ratios is a deficiency. It might be hoped that developments in mathematical statistics will supply the required knowledge at some future time.

In the present application of factor analysis, fortunately, a second line of evidence may be developed relevant to the number of significant dimensions. In this case the variables are consecutive trials, and the series of coefficients for any meaningful factor should form a smooth curve when plotted against the trial numbers. Table 16-7 presents the coefficients for the first four left principal vectors for the Group 70-10-10-10. These are four columns of the matrix V. Consider Diagram 16-1. It presents the curves of the left principal vectors on trials for the Group 70-30 and the Group 70-10-10-10 for the first four vectors for each group. The curve in the upper right corner is obtained from the first column of Table 16-7, the second curve on the right is obtained from the second column of Table 16-7, etc. The curves for the Group 70-30 were obtained in a similar fashion. Note that the first curve for each group is quite regular. For the Group 70-30 the second, third, and fourth curves are rather erratic, presenting a picture that might be associated with random error. For the Group 70-10-10-10, the first three curves are relatively smooth while the fourth one is quite jagged and might be associated with random error. Thus, the conclusion of one dimension for Group 70-30 and three factors for Group 70-10-10-10 is substantiated.

In order to obtain a quantitative statement of the smoothness of the left principal vector curves, the differences between consecutive coefficients of the vectors were obtained and the sum of squares of these differences computed. These sums of squares of first differences for the first four

TABLE 16-7

CoORDINATES OF LEFT PRINCIPAL VECTORS FOR GROUP 70-10-10-10

Trial	Factor Number			
	1	2	3	4
1	.08	−.26	.36	.64
2	.16	−.46	.45	−.08
3	.17	−.30	.39	−.45
4	.16	−.31	−.07	−.12
5	.19	−.21	−.35	.32
6	.20	−.27	−.27	−.12
7	.21	−.17	−.33	−.25
8	.24	−.21	−.33	.04
9	.21	−.18	−.11	−.11
10	.23	−.06	−.03	−.05
11	.22	.06	.03	.00
12	.22	.11	.05	.31
13	.24	.16	−.02	.04
14	.25	.19	.03	−.04
15	.24	.16	.08	−.12
16	.25	.20	−.02	.04
17	.24	.21	.23	−.17
18	.24	.20	.08	.15
19	.25	.12	.12	.07
20	.24	.15	.02	.01
21	.25	.20	.00	−.03

left principal vectors for each group are given in Table 16-8. The sums of squares of differences are noted on Diagram 16-1 for each curve by the Σd^2 at the lower right of each curve. Note that small values are associated with smooth curves. The maximum possible value is four. A curve with a serial correlation of zero would yield a sum of squares of differences of approximately two. Values less than .5 in Table 16-8 have been interpreted as significantly small and starred. The exactly corresponding mean square ratios in Table 16-6 are starred. This evidence tends to confirm our interpreta-

DIAGRAM 16-1.   Left Principal Vectors on Trials Curves

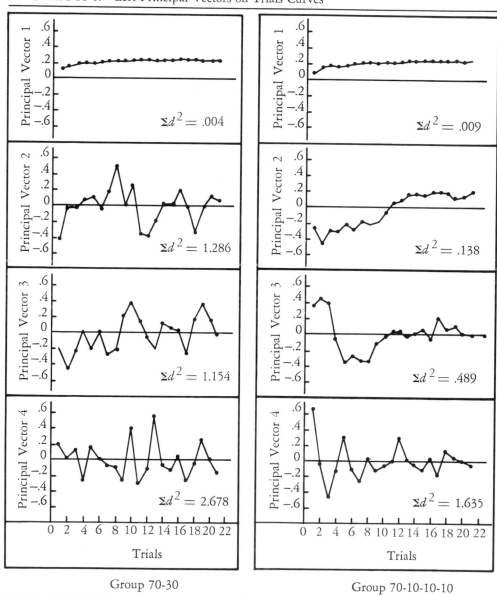

Group 70-30   Group 70-10-10-10

TABLE 16-8

SUMS OF SQUARES OF FIRST DIFFERENCES OF COORDINATES OF PRINCIPAL VECTORS

Factor Number	Group 70-30	Group 70-10-10-10	Group 60-40	Group 60-10-10-10-10
1	.004*	.009*	.014*	.011*
2	1.286	.138*	2.239	.419*
3	1.154	.489*	2.650	1.174
4	2.678	1.635	1.575	1.673

*Interpreted as significantly small.

tion as to the number of significant dimensions for each group. Again there is a complicated mathematical problem in developing a precise test of significance, and we may hope that a mathematical statistician will solve the problem.

The next steps in the analysis were the determination of the loadings of the trials and the scores of the individuals on the principal axes factors. These were accomplished by equations (8) and (18). Table 16-9 presents the loadings for Group 70-10-10-10 on the three significant principal axes factors, and Table 16-10 presents the corresponding scores for the individuals.

6. THE PROBLEM OF ROTATION

When the loadings and the scores on the significant principal axes have been obtained, the next step is the determination of the matrix T. This step is formally equivalent to the rotation of axes in factor analysis, and principles have been considered to guide this rotation, just as the principle of simple structure guides the rotation of axes in usual factor analysis. No firm suggestion has been developed. One possibility considered and discarded was that of simple structure in the factor loadings of trials space. This did not seem to be meaningful in the present context where loadings represent points on reference learning curves. Why should we look for many zeros in such curves? Another possibility was that of a simple structure in the factor score space. Maybe some individuals followed one of the factor learning curves while others followed other factor learning curves. The data were inspected for this possibility but negative results appeared. Finally a rotation was developed for which all reference learning curves had non-negative entries, non-negative slopes for smoothed curves, and all curves reached an asymptote. An orthogonal transformation given in Table 16-11 was used as the

TABLE 16-9

LOADINGS OF TRIALS ON PRINCIPAL FACTORS FOR GROUP 70-10-10-10

Trial	Factor Number 1	2	3
1	5.66	−1.90	1.59
2	10.61	−3.28	1.99
3	11.56	−2.13	1.74
4	10.94	−2.26	−.32
5	12.69	−1.53	−1.55
6	13.51	−1.94	−1.18
7	14.39	−1.21	−1.47
8	15.90	−1.50	−1.44
9	14.34	−1.30	−.50
10	15.22	−.41	−.14
11	14.99	.46	.14
12	14.93	.79	.23
13	16.34	1.12	−.08
14	16.47	1.40	.13
15	16.11	1.16	.35
16	16.49	1.47	−.10
17	15.92	1.52	1.00
18	16.05	1.47	.34
19	16.68	.88	.52
20	15.92	1.05	.10
21	16.88	1.46	.01

TABLE 16-10

SCORES ON PRINCIPAL FACTORS
GROUP 70-10-10-10

Individual	Factor Number		
	1	2	3
1	.86	−.58	.89
2	1.10	−.02	−1.31
3	1.00	.54	.64
4	1.13	1.16	−.72
5	.85	.11	.45
6	1.08	−1.02	.93
7	1.02	−.35	.34
8	.88	−.67	1.04
9	.86	.48	−.10
10	1.05	−.95	.62
11	1.22	−1.02	1.21
12	1.00	.53	.24
13	1.08	.98	−1.40
14	1.03	−.49	−1.26
15	1.01	1.02	−.24
16	.89	.41	.01
17	.89	−1.74	.14
18	.89	−.42	−.78
19	.86	−.58	−1.13
20	.97	.54	−1.67
21	.98	−.10	−1.70
22	.87	3.36	1.85
23	1.08	−.45	.96
24	1.25	−.38	.91

matrix T. The rotated factor loadings are given in Table 16-12 (for all four groups) and the rotated factor scores are given in Table 16-13.

Diagram 16-2 gives the interfactor plots for the rotated factor loadings for Group 70-10-10-10. Points for consecutive trials have been connected by lines. Note that the curve in each plot begins near one axis, progresses along this axis for some number of trials before breaking away to continue to an area in which the later trials are concentrated. In no case is there a systematic trend for the curve to have a negative slope. The foregoing seemed to be a reasonable circumstance to be utilized in selecting the location for the rotated axes.

7. DISCUSSION OF THE EXPERIMENTAL FINDINGS

Diagram 16-3 gives the rotated reference learning curves for all four groups. The dots are the mean trial scores. For Group 70-30 and Group 60-40 the single curve on each plot is for the single significant principal axis factor. Note that for these cases the mean trial scores are almost on the reference learning curve; thus, the

TABLE 16-11

ROTATION OF AXES TRANSFORMATION
MATRIX FOR GROUP 70-10-10-10

Principal Factors	Rotated Factors		
	A	B	C
1	.924	.338	.180
2	−.321	.427	.846
3	.209	−.839	.503

average learning curve would be a good representation of the learning function. For Group 60-10-10-10-10 there are two reference learning curves and for Group 70-10-10-10 there are three reference learning curves. For Group 60-10-10-10-10 the points for the trial means are quite near this group's factor A reference learning curve, while for Group 70-10-10-10 the points for the means are a little further from this group's factor A curve. Even when the trial means are on or near one of the reference learning curves, the average learning curve does not represent the learning function for the group because it does not, and cannot, represent the effects of the other reference learning curves. Thus, with few exceptions, *any single curve, average or other, cannot represent the learning function when there are two or more reference learning curves.* One exception to the foregoing proposition is when there are two reference learning curves with one of these curves being a constant. Then the form of the other reference learning curve represents the learning function within different additive constants to the scores for different

TABLE 16-12

ROTATED FACTOR MATRICES

	Group 70-30	Group 70-10-10-10			Group 60-40	Group 60-10-10-10-10	
	Factor	Factor			Factor	Factor	
Trial	1	A	B	C	1	A	B
1	8.04	6.17	−.23	.22	9.47	3.37	.75
2	9.89	11.28	.51	.14	7.97	8.59	−.02
3	11.55	11.73	1.54	1.15	10.66	10.33	.20
4	11.78	10.77	3.00	−.10	11.14	10.67	.21
5	11.63	11.89	4.93	.21	9.70	12.22	.41
6	12.62	12.86	4.72	.20	11.62	12.18	.21
7	14.23	13.38	5.58	.83	12.22	12.83	.89
8	14.33	14.87	5.94	.88	11.22	13.03	2.02
9	13.90	13.57	4.70	1.23	12.32	12.96	1.91
10	14.24	14.17	5.08	2.33	10.87	13.69	.98
11	14.00	13.73	5.14	3.16	11.95	13.76	2.19
12	14.36	13.59	5.18	3.48	12.28	12.91	2.71
13	13.93	14.72	6.06	3.86	10.58	13.60	2.55
14	14.94	14.80	6.05	4.22	11.76	13.44	3.10
15	14.17	14.59	5.64	4.06	13.39	12.73	2.97
16	14.95	14.74	6.27	4.17	10.95	14.39	2.70
17	15.00	14.44	5.18	4.66	12.74	14.23	3.65
18	15.20	14.43	5.76	4.30	13.00	13.79	3.05
19	14.17	15.24	5.57	4.01	11.67	14.52	3.06
20	14.64	14.40	5.74	3.81	12.18	13.29	2.83
21	14.78	15.13	6.32	4.28	12.56	14.09	3.58

individuals. It is an important property of the methodology presented here that it indicates when it is proper to give an interpretation based solely on an average learning curve.

Consider the reference learning curves in Diagram 16-3 for Group 70-10-10-10. These curves are generally near zero or positive and their slopes are either nearly zero or positive. These properties were the ones selected to guide the rotation of axes. Factors B and C start near zero while factor A is well above zero at all times. Factor C follows the base line for about six trials before starting to rise. All three curves seem to arrive at an asymptote by about trial 13 or 14. We might characterize A as early learning, B as middle learning, and C as late learning. The curve of factor A appears to have the shape of a negative exponential curve used extensively in learning theory while the curve of factor C appears to be more of the sigmoid shape which is also used in learning theory. Factor B lies somewhere between these two in shape. We find ourselves not on the fence between two positions in learning theory but on both sides of the fence. The data tend to support both positions, and it is not necessary to decide between the theoretical structures but to build a superstructure which encompasses both positions. It might be suggested that situations could be devised which emphasize any one of the curves; for example, the Group 70-30 curve seems to be of the negative exponential category. Some other learning situation might have a curve similar to factor C as a single factor learning curve.

Diagrams 16-4 and 16-5 present indi-

TABLE 16-13

SCORES ON ROTATED FACTORS
GROUP 70-10-10-10

| Individual | Rotated Factors | | |
	A	B	C
1	1.16	−.70	.12
2	.75	1.46	−.48
3	.88	.04	.96
4	.52	1.48	.82
5	.84	−.04	.47
6	1.52	−.86	−.20
7	1.13	−.09	.06
8	1.25	−.86	.12
9	.61	.58	.51
10	1.40	−.57	−.30
11	1.71	−1.04	−.03
12	.81	.37	.75
13	.39	1.96	.32
14	.84	1.20	−.86
15	.56	.98	.92
16	.69	.47	.52
17	1.42	−.56	−1.24
18	.79	.78	−.59
19	.74	.99	−.91
20	.38	1.96	−.21
21	.58	1.72	−.76
22	.11	.18	3.93
23	1.34	−.63	.30
24	1.47	−.50	.36

DIAGRAM 16-2. Interfactor Plots of Rotated Factor Loadings Group 70-10-10-10

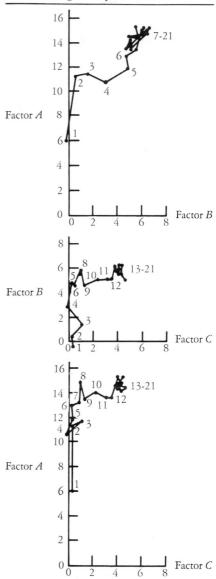

Numbers beside points indicate trials.

vidual learning curves for selected individuals. The dots are the original observations and the lines follow the fitted scores from the analysis. Individuals from Group 70-30 are given in Diagram 16-4. All of the fitted curves are proportional to the single factor learning curve, the constants of proportionality being the factor scores. The top two individuals had high factor scores, the middle two persons had middle scores, and the bottom two persons had low factor scores. Individuals from Group 70-10-10-10 are presented in Diagram 16-5. The goodness of fit of these curves is quite encouraging while, in contrast, the results from Group 70-30 seem to involve considerably greater random fluctuation. The curves in Diagram 16-5 are not only higher or lower but also of different shapes. Person 7 is almost a perfect factor A type,

Person 20 is almost a perfect factor B type, while Person 22 is almost a perfect factor C type. Persons 2, 11, and 17 are mixed types. Person 2 has significantly positive scores on factors A and B. For Person 11 a positive amount of factor A is added to a negative amount of factor B to produce a very flat curve. Person 17 has a positive score on factor A and a large negative score on factor C. It is of interest to note the negative slope over a portion of this individual's learning curve. Thus learning curves of many shapes can be produced from the limited number of reference learning curves by use of various factor scores. An array of quite diverse learning scores might be accounted for by a relatively simple system.

8. LIMITATIONS OF THE METHOD

The cases of learning functions for which the linear combining model is not appropri-

DIAGRAM 16-3.   Rotated Reference Learning Curves

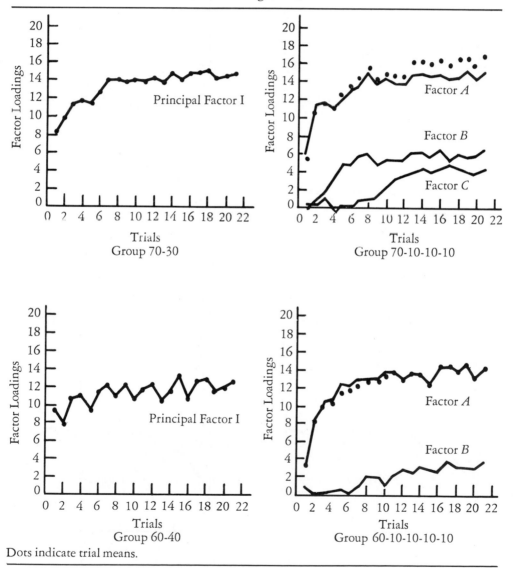

Dots indicate trial means.

DIAGRAM 16-4.   Selected Individual Learning Curves, Group 70-30

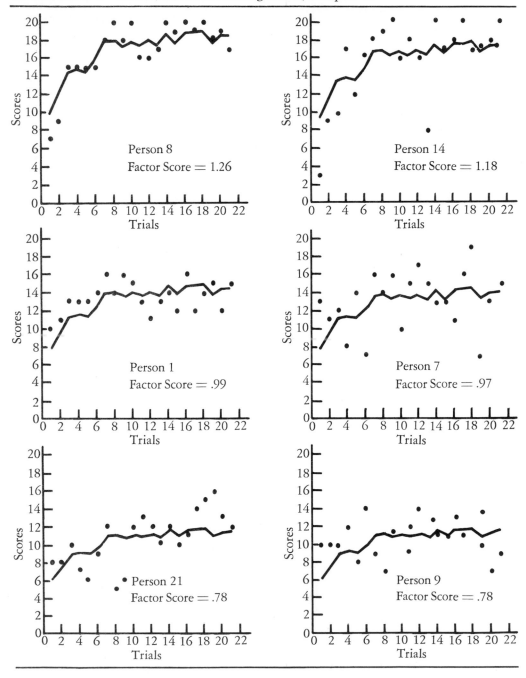

DIAGRAM 16-5.   Selected Individual Learning Curves, Group 70-10-10-10

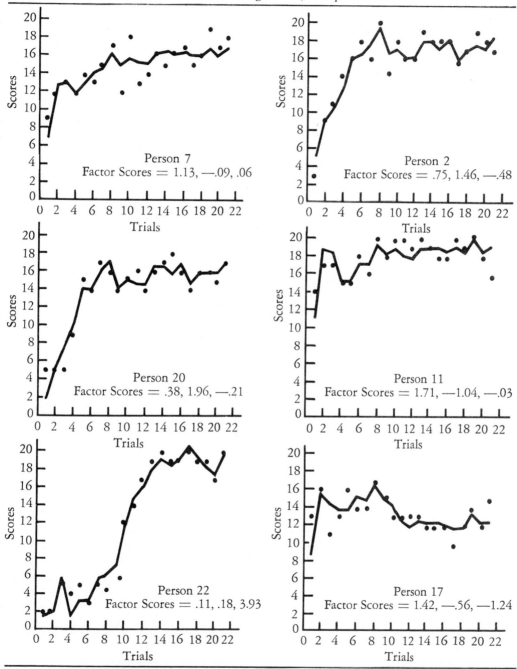

ate deserve consideration. How will the method described here treat such cases? How might we detect these cases? A suggestion is that there may be a large number of significant factors for these cases. Many complex functions can be expressed as infinite series which are linear in parameters for the individuals. Examples of such expansions are power series and the Fourier series of trigonometric functions. Each term in such a series would be a factor; consequently, a large number of factors would be required. Turning these observations around develops the conclusion that the presence of a large number of significant factors would be indicative of the inadequacy of the simple linear combining model. As a consequence, the method of analysis has the additional power of indicating those cases for which the model is not appropriate.

9. SUMMARY AND CONCLUSIONS

(1) The editor's introduction points out that the comparative slowness of development in the field of learning theory, relative to the effort expended, suggests that an adequate armory of methods and models is not being employed. The almost exclusive use of the reflexological atomistic model, dominating the training of students in this area, may be partly responsible.

It is suggested that a more basic approach is one which first asks, taxonomically, what are the kinds of change which need to be explained. In this way, in human learning, and by implication in animal learning, one begins with what has been found out about describing the total behavioral status of the organism at a given moment, by ability, personality, and dynamic factors. The difference of such a vector of factor measures for a given individual on two occasions then has to be explained by a *multidimensional learning theory*. Therein, in a matrix model, learning is conceived as a multidimensional change through experience of a multidimensional stimulus situation.

The work of Fleishman, Tucker, and a few others has opened up this field by beginning with the behavior change as multidimensional, though not as yet with that multidimensional treatment of the learning situation ·which the theory also requires. However, the advantages of this step are well shown by Tucker's clear results, based on a well-developed methodology.

(2) The problem of individual differences in learning functions is discussed for the situations when generalized learning curves are being sought. Mean learning curves are appropriate only for a limited class of special cases when the individual learning curves are linear transformations from each other on the dependent variable.

(3) Consideration is given to positions where the final mean learning curve is considered as the sum of a set of individual learning curves based on a priori theoretical considerations. Unless each of these individual curves is a member of a family of curves generated from the selected theoretical basic function, this is likely to lead to a large number of basic learning curves.

(4) It was decided to use an empirical approach, the Eckart-Young factor-analytic formulation shown to be appropriate to develop generalized learning curves, or families of curves for a much extended class of cases.

(5) This procedure is illustrated with some probability learning data. The evidence shows that only three principal factors are needed to give a good approximation to the original data and that with appropriate rotation, these factors relate in a theoretically satisfying fashion to the sequence of learning trials.

(6) The particular data and their analysis described in this report provide a first trial and example of the methods for determining parameters of functional relations by factor analysis. There are many problems in psychology and education which might be attacked profitably by the factor-analytic method. In addition to learning phenom-

ena, consideration can be given to mental development curves or to work and fatigue curves, for example. A considerable gain in information about psychological phenomena may be gained by consideration of the structure of individual differences in behavior. By such methods, leads may be obtained as to the nature of the basic functions underlying the behavior, and theories may be extended to cover more extensive domains of individual behavior.

CHAPTER 17

The Study of Perception in the Light of Multivariate Methods

HAROLD W. HAKE
University of Illinois

1. INTRODUCTION

The usefulness of a multivariate approach to the study of perception can be said to begin with the word "perception" itself. Garner, Hake, and Eriksen (577) urged that its meaning be established by operations which converge to some delimitation of the alternative concepts to which it could refer. These "converging operations" are multiple measures which serve to indicate a reasonable common meaning of the term and exclude concepts to which it should not refer.

An excellent example of the use of such operations to clear up ambiguity resulting from the use of misleading perceptual terminology was provided by Eriksen (465), who refined the meaning of the term "subception." He did so by recasting the relevant experimental results within the framework of multiple correlational analysis. The source of the term was the experiment of Lazarus and McCleary (912), who conditioned the galvanic skin response (G.S.R.) to five of ten nonsense syllables

and then exposed the syllables individually in a tachistoscope at a duration level such that verbal recognition (after each exposure the subject said which syllable he thought had been presented) was about 50 per cent correct. On trials in which the subjects incorrectly identified the syllables verbally, the G.S.R. was found to be greater for syllables to which the G.S.R. had been conditioned than for syllables to which it had not been conditioned. To this ability of the G.S.R. to discriminate between conditioned and unconditioned syllables, in cases where the verbal responses did not, Lazarus and McCleary applied the term subception: "a process by which some kind of discrimination is made when the subject is unable to make a correct conscious discrimination."

Eriksen suggested that in the recognition situation which involved two responses to each syllable, the G.S.R. and the verbal response, the obtained result consisted of a partial correlation between the syllables and the G.S.R. with the verbal response held constant. The necessary and sufficient conditions under which this is a complete description of the result are (1) that both responses are correlated less than perfectly with the syllables and less than perfectly with each other; and (2) that both the G.S.R. and the verbal responses are responses to the stimuli as perceived, rather than one being a response to the other. If these conditions are fulfilled, then there should be *both* a partial correlation between the G.S.R. and syllables, with the verbal response held constant, and a partial correlation between the verbal response and syllables, with the G.S.R. held constant. Both results have been obtained (for a review see Eriksen, 465). Hence, a concept, subception, which Lazarus and McCleary had defined in terms of other difficult and ambiguous concepts, "conscious" and "unconscious" discriminations, was defined entirely in terms of a multiple correlation model without any gratuitous or ambiguous terms or assumptions.

Similar possibilities exist for many of the specific research areas to which the term perception is applied. These areas tend to be complex and to involve the use of concepts which have been tied to measures in vague ways. Although the areas reviewed here are important areas in which the multivariate approach has been useful, this approach is unfortunately not the most common in the broad area of perceptual research. The rule of one dependent variable has been as strongly applied in the study of perception as elsewhere. Possibly, the application of this rule has done more harm in this area than in others, however, because of the complexity of tasks and concepts involved.

The importance of the essentially univariate approach to the study of perceptual topics probably derives from the importance of psychophysics to these topics. Although most perceptual research ends with speculation, it usually begins with psychophysics, and this has been traditionally univariate in nature. Even what might be called the "new" psychophysics, includ-

ing the work of Stevens (1347, 1348, 1349, 1350) bearing upon the psychophysical law, and the important methodology and concepts of the theory of signal detectability (Swets, 1376), are not multivariate in emphasis and conception.

Gulliksen (646) has written, "the one hundred years since Fechner have been marked by extensions of the psychophysical methods (1) to deal systematically with domains in which there are no relevant physical measurements, (2) to the multidimensional domain, and (3) to the systematic description of individual differences among a group of people in one-dimensional perceptions." In perception this generalization actually applies with greatest force to (1). The multivariate approach has been used most frequently where the hand on the stimulus controls has been most uncertain. Where stimulus specification is most precise, then univariate analysis and thinking tend to be the rule, whatever the topic under consideration.

In the next sections the areas of research where the multivariate approach has been most frequently and usefully applied will be covered, emphasizing those research series most strongly related to important issues in the perception and measurement areas. Following this, consideration is given to the possible contributions of multivariate analyses applied as conceptual models to current problems in perception.

2. THE DESCRIPTION OF PERCEPTUAL TRAITS AND ABILITIES

Perhaps the most familiar work consists of the older factor-analytic attempts to describe the traits and abilities underlying perceptual performance in a wide variety of complex situations. Among these are the analyses reported in Thurstone (1416), Guilford (637), and Roff (1211). The results agree in indicating the great complexities of the variety of situations assumed to involve perceptual skills. Certainly no small set of factors explains the interrelations among many tests of perceptual performance. All investigators provide a substantial list of factors (Roff lists as many as eighteen) to which reasonable names have been applied: closure, reaction time, perceptual speed, judgmental speed, directional thinking, length perception, sequential perception, complex reaction time, perception through camouflage, visual memory, paired-associates memory, reproductive memory, and memory for name-object associations. What we call visual perception is a complex of many specific talents and abilities flourishing in a variety of specific situations. In fact, one valid criticism which can be leveled at these studies is that they stretch the adjective "perceptual" over too large a variety of tasks and performances. When perceptual performance is categorized in more restrictive ways, a smaller set of factors may be sufficient to explain what is observed.

Correlational analyses have been significantly helpful in more specific areas in evaluating some older notions about perceptual traits. One of these notions concerns the important topic of perceptual continuity, or constancy: the ability of the observer to attribute fairly constant characteristics to an object although seen at a variety of viewing angles, at a variety of viewing distances, and under a variety of illumination conditions.

Thouless (1403) suggested that constancy is a unitary concept which observers possess (or which viewing situations evoke) in varying degrees. He claimed to demonstrate the presence of a general factor, using Spearman's tetrad-difference equation, among intercorrelations of measures of shape, size, and brightness constancy. This was an important claim because some type of assertion about constancy is central to most theories of perception. Without ability to maintain the apparent constancy of objects in experience we would experience the world as a most confusing environment. Hence, the description of a unitary

factor associated with this ability, and existing in varying degrees among observers, was most interesting.

Unfortunately, careful work has not supported this claim. Sheehan (1309) suggested some methodological errors in the work of Thouless and failed to find the strength of intercorrelations among different types of constancy measures that he had reported. More recent and systematic work involving many types of constancy situations is lacking, and the correlational evidence we have is not favorable to the suggestion of a general "constancy" factor, as described by Thouless, operating in the several types of perceptual constancies (e.g., see Brunswik, 152, pp. 22-23).

Within a single type of constancy situation, however, factor analysis has indicated a factor associated with the comparison of objects at different distances from the observer. Jenkin and Hyman (807) required subjects to indicate the size of a comparison triangle seen directly ahead which matched the size of a standard triangle seen to the left. Two types of judgments were required. In the first (objective) the subject was required to match the physical size of the standard and comparison triangles. In this case, apparent equality of size occurred when the subject believed the two triangles would be the same if measured with a ruler. In the second (analytical) the subject was asked to ignore distance and the information he might have about the physical sizes of the triangles. His task was to determine that size of the comparison triangle which would just be covered by the standard triangle if the latter were suspended in his forward line of vision and at its present distance. In effect, the subject under the analytical instruction was asked to determine that size of the comparison triangle at which it and the standard triangle subtended the same visual angle of regard, although seen at different distances, usually, and in different directions.

The possible commonality of judgment

under these two types of instructions is of considerable interest because it has long been thought that a basic datum for the judgment of the size of an object located at some distance is the angle which the object subtends at the retina (or, rather, the relative proportion of the visual field occupied by the object). If so, then performance under both instructions should reflect this common input datum. Under the analytical condition the relative proportion of the visual field occupied is judged directly. Under the objective condition this judgment must be combined with a distance judgment (or so the traditional statement goes) to produce a judgment of size. So the two types of judgments should have something in common.

to any impressive degree. And in only one case (A 30/15) are both factors involved in a single type of judgment. Factor B alone is involved in only those two cases in which the standard triangle is extremely close and the subject is making an analytical judgment. This may have something to do with judgments requiring conceptual changes in the line of regard. That is, the subject had to conceptually move the standard over in front of the comparison in order to make his judgment; and, since the standard was very close, perhaps the subject could do this without also subjectively altering the size or distance of the standard. All of the remaining conditions (with the exception of A 30/15) require the subject to conceptually transform the distance as well as

TABLE 17-1

CORRELATIONS AMONG MEASURES OF SIZE-DISTANCE JUDGMENT
(From Jenkin & Hyman, 807)

Measures*	O 30/15	O 30/2	O 15/1	O 15/15	A 30/15	A 30/2	A 15/1
O 30/2	.62						
O 15/1	.42	.66					
O 15/15	.23	.34	.58				
A 30/15	.14	.20	.13	.20			
A 30/2	−.02	−.17	−.12	−.12	.63		
A 15/1	−.03	−.14	−.08	−.08	.54	.88	
A 15/15	.24	.26	.19	.20	.10	−.10	−.05

*"O" signifies objective judgments and "A" signifies analytic judgments.

The important intercorrelations are presented in Table 17-1. In the table "O" stands for objective judgments, "A" stands for analytical judgments, and the numbers refer to viewing distances. The first number refers to the distance of the comparison triangle and the second to the distance of the standard triangle. The intercorrelations were factored by the centroid method and the factors rotated to orthogonal simple structure. The rotated factor loadings are plotted in Diagram 17-1.

Although factors A and B may not be precisely orthogonal, they are not related

the direction of the standard stimulus in order to follow instructions. The critical question is: Could the subjects transform distance conceptually while holding size constant? Probably not. Carlson (189) reviews the evidence to indicate that seen size and seen distance are correlated, and suggests that if a subject makes an error in transforming distance, this will show up as an error in apparent size as well. Thus, factor A appears to be important in all those cases (either under the objective conditions or where the standard triangle is located some distance away) in which errors in judging or transforming distance are reflected in errors in judged size. Factor *A*, then, reflects the fact that the subject has just one way (size estimates) in which to communicate information about apparent size and apparent distance. To say that an object appears larger (or smaller) is approximately the same as saying that it appears farther away (or closer). Perhaps factor *A* is

DIAGRAM 17-1. Location of Size-Distance Judgments in the Factor Space (after Jenkin & Hyman, 807)

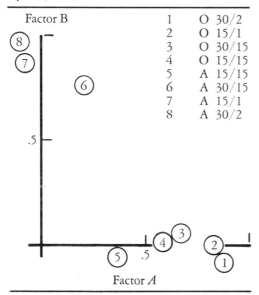

Factor B

1	O	30/2
2	O	15/1
3	O	30/15
4	O	15/15
5	A	15/15
6	A	30/15
7	A	15/1
8	A	30/2

.5

.5

Factor *A*

the constancy factor we have sought. If so, multivariate analysis has given it a more precise definition. It reflects not ability to see constant objects, but rather intercorrelations among several seen (subjective) aspects of objects. This factor could be important in all those tasks in which the subject is forced to use a single dimension in which to reflect how he locates objects in two or more conceptual dimensions. The description of this factor is, then, illustrative of the refinement in older and important perceptual concepts possible through the use of multivariate analysis.

3. THE DESCRIPTION OF THE STIMULUS FOR PERCEPTION

Although we can make many descriptive statements about the stimulus objects which are used commonly in perceptual experimentation, these descriptions seldom define the real stimulating properties of the objects — their characteristics as adequate stimuli. Hence a very useful application of multivariate methods is in the description of stimulus objects as experienced by observers.

We can, rather arbitrarily, consider two cases. One case consists of all situations in which the stimulus objects can be described rather well in terms of quantitative statements about their physical properties. This is often the case with well-controlled auditory and visual stimulation, for example. The other case, with which we begin, includes stimuli which are not easily designated in physical terms and which vary along an unspecified number of physical dimensions.

Stimuli with Unspecified Physical Dimensionality

One undertaking of this sort involves the specification of facial expressions as stimuli. The history of this effort is interesting in its own right, because of the outcome. It has, in addition, a special interest because the study of facial expression recapitulates the development of scaling concepts and techniques as well as their application to perceptual problems. In this recapitulation the conceptual advantages of multidimensional scaling over unidimensional scaling in understanding the crucial properties of complex stimuli for perception are well illustrated.

The first useful scale of facial expression was devised by Woodworth (1582). This consisted of six steps going from expressed love to expressed contempt. Schlosberg (1269), in testing this scale with a new set of photographed poses (Frois-Wittmann series), reported that the scale appeared to be recurrent. Photographs whose modes fell in the contempt category (category 6) were likely to be mis-sorted either into the disgust category (category 5) or into the love category (category 1). This appeared to be true of the Ruckmick (1239) photographs as well.

By analogy with the color surface (Woodworth & Schlosberg, 1583, p. 387), Schlosberg (1270) suggested the scale shown in Diagram 17-2. The six categories of facial expression lie on the periphery of a rough circle which has a neutral expression at its center. A point representing a photograph can be specified in terms of its distance from the center of the circle (strength of expression), and a line through that point and the center of the circle intersects the periphery at the *dominant expression.* These two measures are analogous to the *saturation* and *dominant hue* of a color plotted as a point on the color surface. Each photograph may also be plotted in terms of coordinates on the two orthogonal dimensions of the surface: the pleasantness-unpleasantness (P-U) dimension and the attention-rejection (A-R) dimension.

In a series of experiments Schlosberg tested the suggestion that photographs from the Frois-Wittmann and the Ruckmick set could be represented by points somewhere on the expression surface. In each experiment, subjects were asked to sort first a set of photographs on the P-U scale varying from maximum unpleasantness (1) to pleasantness (9). Then they were asked to sort a duplicate set along the A-R scale ranging from rejection (1) to attention (9). The ratings on the P-U scale and on the A-R scale were used as coordinates in plotting each photograph on the expression surface. Then, the *dominant expression* for each photograph was compared with the scale value for each photograph when scaled on the original Woodworth scale. The correlation between these two measures was quite high and Schlosberg concluded that the Woodworth scale values for the expressions could be accounted for in terms of judgments on two orthogonal dimensions.

At the end of this brief history this conclusion turns out to be only approximately correct, and it is instructive to look at the reasoning underlying the work. In this reasoning the strong influence of a traditional sensory model is evident. This is the color surface, with polar coordinates of hue and saturation or rectilinear red-green and yellow-blue axes. In this model the two quantities, saturation and hue, have long been considered independent of each other, observers being capable of independent judgments of colors on either scale. Logically this should mean that judgments on the two rectilinear axes, yellow-blue or red-green, are independent also; and, by analogy, it appeared reasonable to suppose at the outset that the P-U and A-R dimensions should be indepen-

DIAGRAM 17-2. The Schlosberg Two-Dimensional Representation of Facial Expression in Terms of the A-R and P-U Dimensions (from Schlosberg, 1270, Fig. 1)

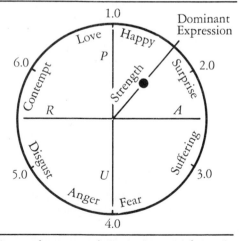

The numbers around the perimeter refer to the Woodworth scale values. The distance of a photograph from the center is the strength of expression. A line through it and the center intersects the circle at the dominant expression.

dent too in the case of facial expression. Although this conclusion comes from traditional psychophysical bias to a greater extent than from compelling logical considerations, it leads naturally to Schlosberg's supposition: if the subject rates the photographs first on one scale and then on the other and these coordinates are used in plotting points on a circular surface, the joint position of each point will adequately predict the Woodworth scale value. Subsequently, again by analogy with the psychophysics of color, a third axis was added to produce the solid figure of Diagram 17-3.

DIAGRAM 17-3. Schlosberg's First Approximation to a Solid Spatial Model Representing Facial Expressions (from Schlosberg, 1271, Fig. 1)

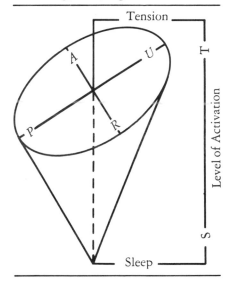

The third axis, level of activation, T-S, is analogous to the brightness dimension of the color spindle (1271).

Abelson and Sermat (2) objected that these three dimensions were not necessarily the three best dimensions or the only dimensions which could account for judgments of facial expression. They are the only three which could appear in the Schlosberg methodology, of course, be-

cause the subjects were instructed about the dimensions to be used in each case. No adequate account is taken of the dimensions which might be important for the subjects otherwise.

A more adequate statement of the problem could be the following. Can judgments of facial expressions and their mutual dissimilarities be adequately accounted for by the location of points in a two- or three-dimensional space? This question, posed in 1962 by Abelson and Sermat (2), is answerable in terms of multidimensional scaling procedures and presupposes a considerable development of theory and methodology beyond that available at the time Schlosberg first began his work with expressions.

This development crucially involves the work of many persons, including Richardson (1198), Young and Householder (1595, 1596), and others to be considered shortly. Some crucial work and the job of organizing the methods and theory in a coherent fashion are credited properly to Torgerson (1437, 1438).

Just as unidimensional scaling assumes that comparative judgments of objects varying on a unidimensional attribute can be represented by points on a line, so multidimensional scaling assumes that such comparisons can be accounted for by the locations of points in a space. In fact, one of the tasks of multidimensional scaling is just the reverse: given the comparisons (reflecting interpoint distances), determine the dimensionality of the space in which the points are located and determine the projections of these points on these dimensions. The second task is that of determining the relationship between the similarity judgments of the objects and distance in the conceptual space in which the points exist.

The first task is accomplished with the aid of three theorems of Young and Householder (1595) which can be applied in the case of stimuli whose mutual similarities have been judged. It is supposed that one of the alternative judgmental methods (see Torgerson, 1438, pp. 261-263) was used to provide estimates of the degree of similarity evident within all pairs of stimuli judged in terms of a complex attribute. In some cases these interstimulus similarities can be considered to represent directly absolute measures of interstimulus distances, the most dissimilar stimuli being separated by the greatest distance and identical stimuli being separated by no distance at all. In other cases the similarities must be related to absolute distances by a suitable transformation. This is a troublesome business, as will be indicated subsequently, because of the effects of the transformation upon the scaling result.

Given the distance measures, then, the matrix B_i may be constructed. Each element of B_i is a function of the distances existing among one stimulus, i, and two of the others. That is, the elements b_{jk} of B_i are defined by

$$(1) \quad b_{jk} = \tfrac{1}{2}(d_{ij}^2 + d_{ik}^2 - d_{jk}^2) \quad \begin{bmatrix} i,j,k = 1,2,\ldots n \\ j,k \neq i \end{bmatrix}$$

where j and k designate the rows and columns of the matrix B_i and the notation d_{ij}, for example, designates the distance between stimulus, i, and stimulus, j. Each b_{jk} is the scalar product of vectors from stimulus, i, to stimuli, j and k. In practice some method of taking all of the n B_i matrices into account must be followed in applying the three theorems.

The first theorem answers the question of whether the stimuli can be represented by points in a real Euclidean space, and states that they can if B_i is positive semidefinite. The second theorem states that the dimensionality of the set of points is given by the rank of the positive semidefinite matrix B_i. Finally, the third states that the positive semidefinite matrix B_i may be factored such that

$$(2) \quad B_i = AA'.$$

If the rank of B_i is no larger than the number of stimuli minus one, then A is a $(n-1) \times r$ rectangular matrix, where r is the rank of B_i. The elements of A are the projections of the points on r orthogonal axes with their origin at the ith point of the space. The similarity between this methodology and factor analysis is, of course, quite evident. The correlations or covariances with which factor analysis is begun can be interpreted as scalar products of vectors.

This methodology was applied by Abelson and Sermat to estimates of the similarity obtained by the use of the method of categorical judgment, in which photographs from the Lightfoot series were presented to the subjects in pairs and each subject was asked to state, on a scale running from one to nine, how much stimuli in each pair seemed to differ in the (unspecified) emotion being expressed.

These are rather simple instructions, the subjects being left free to judge the photographs in their own terms. Possibly this is a more primitive situation, relative to the case where the subject is given a restricted aspect of the stimulus to judge, but it makes possible the derivation of the nature and number of the scales underlying judgment and their interrelations (712).

As a first step in their analysis Abelson and Sermat compared their obtained interstimulus distances with those which could be derived from the Schlosberg scale for the same photographs. This was a problem in multiple regression in which weights for the coordinates of each photograph on each of the three Schlosberg scales were sought such that the relation between the Schlosberg interstimulus distances and the Abelson and Sermat interstimulus distances would be a maximum. The obtained weights were approximately 4.0 for the P-U, 3.0 for the T-S, and 2.0 for the A-R coordinates on the Schlosberg scale.

This is an outstanding result, for it demonstrates the power of similarity judgment, applied to all stimulus pairs, to calibrate component dimensions of judgment, one with another. Where the subject must first judge stimuli on one arbitrary unidimensional scale and then on another, the supposition that judgments on the first may be compared quantitatively with those on the second is highly questionable. Helm (711) has provided a set of assumptions which must be met if the results of several experiments, each involving the judgment of a single dimension or attribute, are to be meaningfully combined to indicate simultaneously the interrelations of the stimuli with respect to the several dimensions. (1) The angular displacement of each dimension with respect to the others must be assumed. (2) It must be assumed that the set of dimensions which were judged includes all of the important dimensions defining the general interstimulus relation-

calibration shows, as a fact, the extent to which each of the Schlosberg dimensions entered into the judgment of similarity of facial expression, when these are assumed to be orthogonal dimensions. Obviously, all dimensions did not have equal weights in the determination of interstimulus distances (dissimilarities).

Application of the multidimensional methodology described by Torgerson (1438) then indicated that the distances among the photographs as judged by the subjects could be accounted for by the location of points with respect to five dimensions, rather than three. The first three of these accounted for 73 per cent of the judgmental variance. Table 17-2 indicates the correlations between each of the

TABLE 17-2

CORRELATIONS BETWEEN THE ABELSON AND SERMAT DIMENSIONS
AND THE THREE SCHLOSBERG SCALES
(From Abelson & Sermat, 2)

Schlosberg Scale	Dimension					Multiple-R
	I	II	III	IV	V	
P−U	.947	.121	−.094	−.031	.061	.962
A−R	.026	.878	−.374	.210	.094	.982
T−S	−.295	.917	.011	−.041	.046	.965

ship of interest. (3) It must be assumed that dissimilarities among the stimuli with respect to any single dimension satisfy the distance axioms assumed for the multidimensional space formed by the combination of the dimensions. These are rather strong assumptions and they can be checked only if the judgmental method allows all dimensions simultaneously to enter into stimulus comparisons. For these reasons the earlier attempt of Triandis and Lambert (1443) to modify the shape (as described by the ranges of judgments on the separately explored dimensions) of the Schlosberg figure is quite meaningless. Operations to show the calibration of the separate dimensions with respect to each other were totally lacking. The Abelson and Sermat

Schlosberg scales and the dimensions of this analysis. The very high multiple correlations shown indicate that each of the Schlosberg scales can be located by suitable rotations of axes I through V.

The indication of the redundancy of the A-R and T-S scales of Schlosberg is an important contribution. Both are highly correlated with axis II and neither has a high correlation with any other. Hence, it does not appear that judgments of facial expression are adequately accounted for by three orthogonal axes, as the color model of Schlosberg demands.

The most recent development in the history of this problem is the important work of Shepard (1313) providing a computer methodology in which only a weak assumption about the relation between similarity and distance is made beforehand. Given measures of the similarity of pairs of all stimuli from a set (or some type of measure of proximity or association), the analysis provides simultaneously: (1) the minimum number of dimensions of a Euclidean space satisfying the requirement that the distances in the space separating stimulus points are monotonically related to the measures of similarity, (2) a set of orthogonal coordinates for each stimulus point in the minimum space, and (3) an actual plot of the distance function relating distances in the space to the measures of similarity. The method is iterative and produces a convergence to a final configuration of the points. The convergence involves two parameters. The first, α, controls the rate of approach to the condition of monotonicity. The second, β, controls the

rate at which the initial configuration of the analysis, an $(N-1)$-dimensional regular simplex (N is the number of stimuli judged), collapses to the space of minimum dimensionality. The final configuration can be secured by rotations of the coordinate system to principal axes, or "premature" rotations can be performed early in the analysis and the iterative procedures carried on in collapsed spaces.

Shepard applied the method to the data of Abelson and Sermat and found that two independent dimensions accounted for a large share of the judgmental variance. This two-dimensional solution provided a slightly better approximation to the Abelson and Sermat five-dimensional solution than did their own two-dimensional solution. The relation between these two-dimensional solutions is shown in Diagram 17-4. Again the result indicates that two

DIAGRAM 17-4. Changes in the Estimated Positions of Facial Expressions from the Two-Dimensional Solution of Abelson and Sermat to Shepard's Two-Dimensional Solution (from Shepard, 1313, Fig. 11)

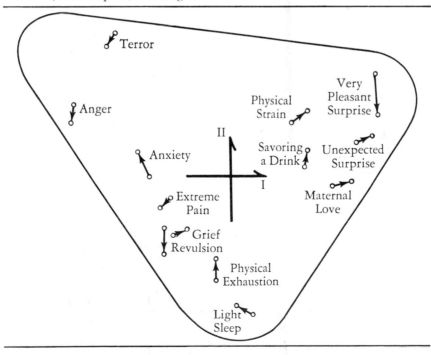

orthogonal dimensions are important in the judgment of facial expression, but that a complete accounting of judgment requires a series of additional dimensions which account for a small share of the judgmental variance.

An extremely important result of the Shepard work is shown in Diagram 17-5, which plots the function relating the dissimilarity ratings of Abelson and Sermat and distances in the Shepard configuration. This is not an assumed function. It is part of the solution produced by the method and provides assurance that no other function could permit the judgments to be accounted for by a Euclidean space of smaller dimensionality.

DIAGRAM 17-5. The Reconstructed Function Relating Mean Dissimilarity Ratings (*Y*) for 13 Facial Expressions to Latent Interstimulus Distances (*X*) in Shepard's Three-Dimensional Solution (Data from Abelson and Sermat, 2: from Shepard, 1313, Fig. 12.)

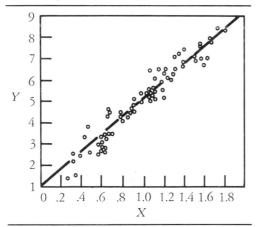

Stimuli with Specified Dimensionality

In this section the topic of the stimulus for color vision is considered at some length. Again, this choice is made because this topic highlights certain interesting methodological and conceptual developments. It is also true that the stimulus for color has been of considerable concern to

multivariate methodologists for several reasons, including the obvious one that the experience of color has so long been considered multidimensional in nature.

Certainly two physical dimensions can be demonstrated for extended sources of homogeneous light—wave-length and luminance. If the light consists of a mixture of a single wave-length and a particular white light, then a third measure is needed. This is a measure of purity reflecting the ratio of pure to white light.

Corresponding to those three dimensions of variation are the traditional dimensions of experience, the attributes of light. These are hue, brightness, and saturation. They do not, of course, bear a one-to-one relationship to the physical dimensions of light. (If they did, there would be no further problem for multivariate analysis.)

One type of helpful psychophysical analysis has been applied to the facts of color mixture. With the use of the colorimeter of Nutting (see Le Grand, 919, pp. 137-139), a subject can manage to match a heterogeneous light with a suitable mixture of a monochromatic light, λ, and a specified white light. He does so by adjusting three variables: the luminance of the white light, L_w; the wave-length of the monochromatic light, λ; and the luminance of the monochromatic light, L_λ. Then the total luminance of the mixture, $L = L_w + L_\lambda$; the colorimetric purity of the mixture, $p_c = L_\lambda/L$; and the dominant wave-length, λ, have relevance to the three traditional attributes of the experience of color.

Historically more important is the tristimulus photometry of Wright (1587) in which the subject matches a color, *C*, by adjusting the amounts of three suitably chosen primary lights to produce a fundamental equation

(3) $C = xR + yB + zG$

in which *R, B,* and *G* refer to the quality of the primary lights and *x, y,* and *z* refer to the amounts of the primary lights. If this system worked for any *C*, given a suitable (or even unique) set of primaries, an important result would be attained. We should, then, be confident of the dimensionality of color experience and perhaps also have obtained important information about the nature of the visual receptors themselves.

However, the system does not work for all C. To produce a match the subject often must add one of the primaries to the color C, thus producing negative coefficients and thwarting the goal of identifying primaries with retinal pigments. In spite of this inconvenience, we are left with the fact that just three numbers (where one may be negative) are sufficient to specify each C, and this has been used to devise a complex scale of color, the chromaticity diagram based on a "standard observer" and a standard coordinate system (see Judd, 834). This is an extremely useful multidimensional scale, although it does not answer all our basic questions about the visual system and the characteristics of the experience of color.

Other types of multivariate analysis, namely factor analysis and multidimensional scaling, have been useful also in trying to attain two objectives. The first of these is a description of the metric of the conceptual space which can represent the experience of color (and perhaps also indicate something about the mechanisms of color vision), and the second is an adequate description of individual differences in color vision.

The first has involved a good deal of factor-analytic work related to crucial questions about the number of factors required to account for color vision and about whether these factors are unipolar or bipolar. The delimitation of the factors and their polarity has been considered important because of pertinence to traditional color theory. There has been much concern about whether just three factors are sufficient, as the Young-Helmholtz theory suggests, or whether more processes are involved, as Granit has suggested. Also, the Young-Helmholtz theory implies unipolar

factors whereas the Hering theory and modern derivatives imply bipolar factors.

Much of the fire in these disputes should now be extinguished, in view of the excellent work which has been done on the retinal receptors and the visual nervous system. Marks, Dobelle, and MacNichol (988) have used a microspectrophotometer to measure the absorption spectra of individual cones in primate and human eyes and have published rather clear evidence for the existence of just three spectra in either case. Clearly, one of three pigments like those suggested by the Young-Helmholtz theory does exist in each individual cone. On the other hand, the excellent work of DeValois (417, 418) indicates the existence of three bipolar neural systems at the level of the geniculate in the primate visual system. Thus, both traditional theories have proved to be correct, depending upon whether one considers the retinal receptors themselves or the nature of the neural coding occurring above that point; and we are in the happy position of being able to take advantage of the explanatory benefits of both traditional types of theory.

It is interesting to compare the results of outstanding factor-analytic work with those developments. The first of these was the work of Jones (814), who used the data of Coblentz and Emerson (354). Flicker photometry had been used to produce measures of the relative sensitivity of the human observer to monochromatic lights. Spectra were available for 92 observers and 20 different wave-lengths. Product-moment correlations were computed for each pair of wave-lengths to produce a matrix of correlations, and this matrix was analyzed by the centroid method. The loadings on three rotated factors are shown in Diagram 17-6. Factor I was called a yellow factor, Factor II was described as a blue factor, and Factor III appears to be associated with the long wave-lengths. A subsequent analysis (815) of sensitivity spectra based upon heterochromatic luminosity matching (594) provided similar results with the exception

DIAGRAM 17-6.   Loadings on the Three Color Factors (from Jones, 814, Fig. 1)

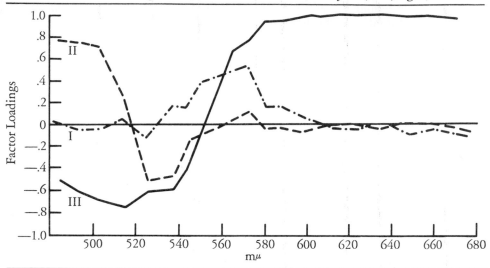

that the negative swing of the blue factor obtained in the earlier study was not found.

Much ado was made about the evident bipolarity of the "red" factor of Jones. For example, Pickford (1161) interpreted this factor and a factor of Ekman (456) as evidence for bipolar receptive systems. In both cases this interpretation is a dubious one. The bipolarity of the red factor of Jones reflects the fact that observers who showed relatively high sensitivity for long wave-lengths tended also to show relatively low sensitivity for shorter wave-lengths. This need not be interpreted as trends in the real sensitivity of the visual system. The psychophysical methods involved were rather crude, and heterochromatic luminance matching as used in the 1950 study is notoriously difficult. It is, for example, entirely reasonable to suppose that in adopting a *criterion* of judgment (that appearance of the stimulus pattern which is tolerated as a match), the observers could have adopted one which produced spuriously high sensitivity for red and spuriously low sensitivity for green light. There is in the data no means of separating this factor of judgmental criterion from basic acuity.

Ekman (456) required subjects to rate the similarity of stimuli presented in pairs. The stimuli were adjacent translucent windows illuminated from behind by light transmitted through one of 14 filters, each window being illuminated by a separate light source and filter. The mean rating of similarity for each pair of filters was then transformed to range between 0 and 1, and these values were factor-analyzed directly. The analysis indicated that five factors (violet, blue, green, yellow, and red) were required to account for the similarity measures. This multiplicity of factors appears to be clearly artifactual. For example, Mellinger (1038) compared results obtained by Ekman's analytical method with results obtained by use of the Young-Householder model. The crucial difference is that Ekman accepted the transformed similarity measures as correlations, whereas the latter model requires that similarity measures be transformed first to scalar products. Ekman's method indicated that four factors accounted for judgments of thirteen colors while the Young-Householder model indicated three factors as sufficient.

The difficulty with the Ekman result appears to be an effect of the application of factor analysis to an inappropriate set of data. Although his measures of similarity were all normalized to vary in the range between 0 and 1, they are not correlation coefficients and cannot be considered scalar products of interstimulus distances. That the result was partly due to this inappropriateness of the data can be seen in the parallel between factor analysis and multidimensional scaling methodology. As was indicated earlier, the latter methodology consists of the factor analysis of a matrix of scalar products. These scalar products derive from the distance postulates of Euclidean scaling (711).

Elements representing stimuli are located as points in the space. To each ordered pair of points, i and j, there is assignable a non-negative real number, d_{ij}, which is the distance between the points. The d_{ij} satisfy the following postulates:

I. $d_{ij} = 0$ if $i = j$
II. $d_{ij} > 0$ if $i \neq j$
III. $d_{ij} = d_{ji}$
IV. The matrix B (b_{jk}) is positive semi-definite, where $b_{jk} = \frac{1}{2}(d_{ij}^2 + d_{ik}^2 - d_{jk}^2)$, and i is a constant.

The last postulate insures that the triangular inequality, $d_{ik} + d_{kj} \geq d_{ij}$, holds for all point triples and for the corresponding relation on all higher-order sets of points. It also makes explicit the relationship between the b_{jk} and the correlation coefficient, for

(4) $\frac{1}{2}(d_{ij}^2 + d_{ik}^2 - d_{jk}^2) = d_{ij}d_{ik}\cos\theta_{jik}$

That is, b_{jk} is the scalar product of the vectors from point i to points j and k, a definition of the correlation coefficient. When the data do not satisfy the four distance postulates, the result of factor analysis is ambiguous. Certainly one expected result is the inflation of the number of factors resulting (1050).

It is often the case that measures of the similarity of stimuli do not satisfy the distance postulates, particularly the last, because the data are *relative* measures of similarity. The required absolute distances in many cases may then be obtained by the addition of a constant to all measures. This was possibly true for Ekman's data. His method, a variant of the method of equal-appearing intervals, provided measures of similarity referred to an arbitrary zero. However, the problem of selecting the appropriate constant to achieve absolute measurement was not attempted.

The problem of selecting the appropriate "additive constant" in the case of interval data is complex, generally, and possible solutions have important implications for multidimensional scaling results. The problem is involved crucially in the scaling of complex, patterned stimulation and is considered in detail in a subsequent section.

As stated earlier, the technique of Shepard makes weaker demands upon similarity measures than does the Young-Householder model. It requires, in fact, only an ordinal measurement of similarities. Thus, the use of Shepard's technique should indicate the extent to which the multidimensional methodology applied by Ekman directly to his similarity measures artifactually complicated the result obtained. Shepard provided this analysis (1313, pp. 235-237) and showed that a two-dimensional configuration accounted for 84 per cent of the variance (vs. 64 per cent for Ekman's first two axes). In addition, Shepard's solution indicated the transformation which should be applied to Ekman's similarity measures to permit a minimum-dimensionality solution by traditional analytical methods. This exponential transform is indicated in Diagram 17-7 as the reconstructed function relating Ekman's measures to distance in the obtained two-dimensional space.

In summary it must be said that factor analysis, as opposed to more traditional multivariate psychophysical analyses, has not been impressively useful in the description of color vision. It has focused interest

DIAGRAM 17-7. The Reconstructed Function Relating Ekman's Original Measures of the Similarities among 14 Colors to the Latent Interstimulus Distances of Shepard's Two-Dimensional Solution (from Shepard, 1313, Fig. 14)

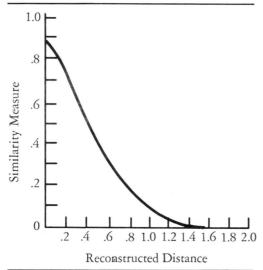

Recomstructed Distance

The Scaling of Perceivers

The contributions of multidimensional scale analysis to the study of color perception are important because a critical development in the study of individual differences was well documented in connection with judgments of color. The outstanding work is that of Tucker and Messick (1468), who provided the methodology permitting the specification of color spaces appropriate for individuals and the delimitation of the number of unique spaces required.

It cannot be said that prior to this work persons interested in the perception of color were seriously interested in a general description of individual differences. They were interested in the performance of normals, as a group, and abnormals, as classified into several groups, but not in the color spaces of all individuals. Certainly, a part of this bias reflects the underlying assumption that there is *a* general sensory or perceptual system to be understood and described. Individual differences among normals, especially, have been interpreted, in line with this bias, as being inconvenient in obscuring our view of these general and universal mechanisms.

The multidimensional scaling procedures described so far also hide individual differences, as the data from several subjects usually are combined to produce the matrix of interstimulus proximities with which the analysis begins. Analysis then produces a space in which distances separating stimulus points may be specified, and each stimulus point is characterized by its coordinates on the axes of the space. Tucker and Messick (1468) contrasted this *distance space* with a *vector space* which is the multidimensional space of stimulus objects

on the possible existence of a "bipolar" factor, indicating in some older visibility studies that subjects who showed relatively high sensitivity for long wave-lengths tended also to show relatively low sensitivity for shorter wave-lengths. This is an aspect of the visibility data which had not otherwise been noticed. Factor analysis has also, however, led to some questionable discussion about the number of color factors, discussion emphasizing work which appears to have produced a spuriously large number of factors. In any event, current sensory physiology appears close to describing the color receptors and neural mechanisms in detail.[1]

---

[1] A related issue in visual perception is the multivariate analysis of the phenomenon of binocular rivalry by Meredith and Meredith (1043). Ss described their "subjective" impressions of a *fused* (Ganzfeld) and a *rivalry* field along 30 bipolar rating dimensions, and 24 of the scales significantly differentiated the fields ($p < .01$). In an unpublished follow-up study, Ss rated two reversible fields (binocular rivalry and Necker Cube) along 33 bipolar scales, and a factor analysis of the ratings across fields revealed the operation of four Osgood "meaning" factors (e.g., *stability, receptivity, dynamism,* and *coherency*). It is anticipated that research on mediating processes in perception will lead to an understanding of the weak statistical linkage between *rate of change* measures between binocular rivalry and figure reversal.

in which each individual point of view about the similarities apparent among the objects is represented by a vector. Stimulus projections on each vector, then, represent scale values for that individual point of view. Dimensions in the *distance space* represent the attributes of stimulus variation; dimensions in the *vector space* represent consistent points of view about the properties of the stimuli.

The methodology of Tucker and Messick provides both types of spaces: a separate multidimensional configuration of the stimulus points is provided for each consistent judgmental point of view. The analysis is begun with a matrix consisting of a row for each pair of stimuli and a column for each subject. The elements of the matrix, X, are the proximity measures, $x_{(jk)i}$, where i refers to individuals and jk to a pair of stimuli. This matrix is factored into principal components to indicate possible consistent covariation among subjects. If one factor is found, then a single distance space will be sufficient to account for the judgments of all subjects. If several factors result, then a similar number of different distance spaces will be required. A rotational method then provides a matrix, Z, in which each column provides a set of measures representing distances between pairs of stimuli in terms of a consistent point of view about stimulus similarity. Each column is itself a distance matrix which may be analyzed by the Young-Householder analysis model or the Shepard technique to describe a separate multidimensional space associated with a point of view.

An especially important contribution is the description of *ideal individuals*. The analysis provides a matrix with entries which are the coordinates of points representing individuals on rotated axes. These points may be plotted graphically, and it is possible to insert points representing individuals who have not been tested but who represent persons of special interest, perhaps for theoretical reasons. Separate multidimensional distance spaces for each such ideal point in the factor space of individuals can then be derived.

An interesting instance of the application of this methodology was provided by Helm and Tucker (713). Fourteen subjects were sorted into a group of ten normal subjects and a group of four color-weak subjects according to their ability to discriminate differences among the charts prepared by the American Optical Company. These subjects judged the similarities among a set of ten color tiles, using the triads procedure in which all possible triples of the tiles were presented to each subject. Each was required to locate the three tiles of each triple on a neutral surface so that location represented similarity relations among the tiles. The tiles were separated by equal distances on the Munsell hue scale and had the same value (lightness) and chroma (saturation). Traditionally, points representing these stimuli could be expected to plot around a circle and be separated by approximately equal arcs.

Analysis of the X matrix indicated that three factors accounted for 98 per cent of the variance. The first of these, the largest characteristic root of the matrix, was associated with the very nearly constant mean interpoint distance scale value for each subject. This is an important result, providing a distance calibration factor for each subject, but it is less interesting than the second and third factors. Diagram 17-8 shows the plotting of points representing individuals in the space of the second and third factors. All color-weak subjects plot along the "B" line; all normal subjects plot along the "A" line.

Differences represented by location along the "A" line were indicated by the derivation of color spaces for *ideal* subjects plotted in Diagram 17-8 along that line. These spaces are shown in Diagram 17-9. Each space is two-dimensional, as expected, and the stimuli are arranged in rough circular form. Chief differences among these spaces is the extent to which longer distances are exaggerated relative to shor-

DIAGRAM 17-8. The Scaling of Perceivers
(from Helm & Tucker, 713, Fig. 1)

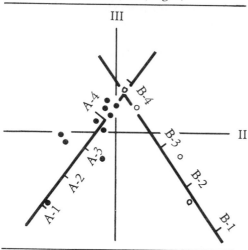

III

II

Open circles represent color-weak individuals
and closed circles represent normals.

ter interstimulus distances. The implication
of location along the "B" line is indicated
by the color spaces corresponding to *ideal*
subjects plotted at points along that line.
These spaces are shown in Diagram 17-10.
The crucial differences evident among
these color-weak spaces are related to the
extent to which certain critical stimulus
tiles were indistinguishable. Thus, the examination of the color spaces for *ideal*
individuals indicates the difference between the two types of subjects tested.
Differences among the normals along the
"A" line involve the scale of distance —
over- or under-estimation of larger dis-

tances relative to small. Differences among
color-weak individuals along the "B" line
involve the spatial model; the configuration
of points for color-weak subjects tends to
be more nearly one-dimensional. It may be
concluded that differences among the normal subjects are independent of particular
stimuli while differences among color-weak
subjects are not.

The power of this methodology to indicate the number and nature of unique
judgmental systems has not yet been exploited in traditional perceptual topics
outside of the scaling of color. Certainly,
this methodology will have great general
importance in the future. The examination
of individual differences in a wide variety of
situations, using this methodology, is certain to produce information useful to
theory. And, there is a further important
implication of the method — the indication
of the effect of changes in methodology
upon the nature of resulting multidimensional scales. That is, although the method
as described deals with individual differences among subjects treated alike, it can
be used as well to indicate real differences
between groups of subjects where judgmental method or stimulus objects differ
from group to group.

4. THE PSYCHOPHYSICS OF
SHAPE AND FORM

The problem of determining the aspects
of complex, patterned stimulation to which
the subject responds in recognizing stimuli,
making judgments of some aspect of the

DIAGRAM 17-9.   Color Spaces of "Ideal" Individuals on Line A (from
Helm & Tucker, 713, Fig. 2)

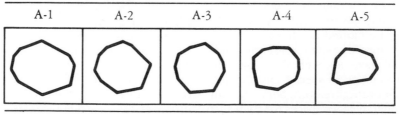

stimuli, or in making fine discriminations among stimuli has been a difficult one to solve. The psychophysics of shape and form has lagged behind the psychophysics of simple stimulation such as sounds or lights or smells, etc.

One of the problems involved is the adequate specification of forms in physical terms. In the case of natural forms (e.g., a landscape, a single tree, a face) this problem has been most acute and has attracted a lot of thought (see 46, 344, 1389, 1541). Even in the case of simple, closed geometric or nonsense forms there is usually an embarrassment of riches — there is an unmanageable number of possible physical descriptions (see Hake, 664, pp. 142-150).

DIAGRAM 17-10.   Color Spaces of "Ideal" Individuals on Line B (from Helm & Tucker, 713, Fig. 3.)

B-1	B-2	B-3	B-4

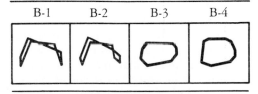

Multidimensional analysis has been useful in attempts to specify the aspects of simple forms which are psychologically relevant, i.e., those aspects or dimensions of variation which are related to judgment. The history of these attempts involves several difficult problems and the outcome is still in some doubt. It makes, however, an instructive story.

The Judged Similarity of Forms

Attneave (43) provided the first important study of its type. It was about ten years ahead of its time in its consideration of the judgment of similarity as a crucial means of accomplishing a dimensional analysis of simple forms. Because it was ahead of its time it suffered somewhat from a bias in

conception and a lack of adequate methodology.

Attneave reported several experiments designed to indicate two things: whether judgments of the similarity of forms could be accounted for by distances between points in a space defined in physical terms and whether the space was Euclidean or non-Euclidean. As it turned out, the latter question was emphasized at the expense of the former.

His first experiment (providing a typical result) involved the judgment of seven plane parallelograms varying in the angle which the vertical long side made with the shorter horizontal side and in the size of the sides. (The horizontal sides were always half the length of the vertical sides.) Parallelograms were presented to the subjects in pairs to be judged in terms of their similarity on a seven-category scale. These judgments were scaled by Attneave's Method of Graded Dichotomies (42), a variant of the method of successive intervals (Torgerson, 1438, pp. 208-210).

The question of the type of space in which these points could be represented became acute because the scaled values for the stimuli did not appear to possess distance properties along either the single dimension of size or of angle. The stimuli are represented in terms of their physical characteristics in Diagram 17-11. In the case of stimuli B, E, and G, representing parallelograms differing in area but not angle, he found that the sum of distances $(E-B)$ and $(B-G)$ was not the distance $(E-G)$, in terms of scale values. Those distances and those involving the stimuli, D and C, C and B, and D and B, on the other dimension, however, could be made to act like distances on a single dimension by the subtraction of the quantity, $c=3.4$, from all scaled distances. This transformation failed to produce distances in two dimensions which satisfied all properties of Euclidean distances, and this result led Attneave to reject the Euclidean spatial model as the appropriate model for his data.

DIAGRAM 17-11.   Schematic Arrangement of Attneave's Parallelograms on the Physical Dimensions of Size and Tilt (from Attneave, 43, Fig. 1)

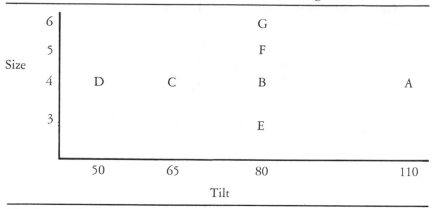

Stimulus F differed slightly in color from the remainder.

There is a set of logical statements underlying this conclusion: namely, if: (1) the judged similarities, s_{ij} (where the i and j are alternative subscripts for the stimuli) are absolute distances on either of the orthogonal physical dimensions, that is, if on each dimension

(5)
    a. $s_{ij} = 0$ if $i = j$
    b. $s_{ij} > 0$ if $i \neq j$
    c. $s_{ij} = s_{ji}$
    d. $s_{ij} + s_{ik} = s_{ik}$ for all triples on a single axis,

then (2) the defined plane in which all s_{ij} exist, including the two-dimensional distances, is a Euclidean space if

$$(6)\quad s_{ij} = \left[\sum_{m=x}^{y} (i_m - j_m)^2 \right]^{\frac{1}{2}},$$

that is, if the distance between two points representing stimuli is the square root of the sum of the squared distances as projected on the two physical axes.

Attneave concluded that his transformed scale values satisfied (1) but not (2). He suggested that all distances actually satisfied

$$(7)\quad s_{ij} = \sum_{m=x}^{y} |i_m - j_m|.$$

This says that the distance between two points representing stimuli is the sum of the absolute distances as projected on the two axes. This led him to suggest that the data indicated the appropriateness of the "city-block" spatial model. The name comes from the fact that in a city, distances are normally measured in terms of blocks traversed, and cutting diagonally across blocks is not allowed.

There are some difficulties with this conclusion. One involves the assumption that the two orthogonal physical dimensions coincide with two orthogonal dimensions of judged similarity. No method was applied to support this assumption, and later work indicates that the physical dimensions do not, in general, coincide completely with dimensions derived from multidimensional scale analysis.

A second difficulty involves Attneave's rather arbitrary choice of the additive constant, c. Criteria determining "best" methods available for this choice and the implications of these methods for subsequent scales have been considered by Messick and Abelson (1050), Torgerson (1438), and Helm, Messick, and Tucker (712).

a. The constant, c, can be selected such that the measures show absolute distance properties on the individual dimensions (1352, 711).

b. The constant, c, can be selected to minimize the number of large positive roots in the matrix of scalar products of distances (1050). This solution, suggested by Tucker, is an iterative technique seeking the value of c which produces minimal dimensionality of the measures.

c. The constant, c, can be selected such that minimum dimensionality is achieved simultaneously with a monotonic relationship between the similarity measures and distance in the space in which points represent stimuli (1313).

d. The obtained measures may be transformed by use of a rational exponential function (involving an optimum k in the exponent) to achieve ratio scaling (712).

The last three have the advantage of minimizing the dimensionality of the space in which the stimulus points may be plotted, but all three assume Euclidean space. Hence, their usage precludes a test for the nature of the space involved. The first (Attneave's choice) is a highly dubious business, however, because for any set of s_{ij} a value of c can be found to make the measures conform to Euclidean space. The constant needs simply to be large enough. In the limit, the points representing stimuli would be arrayed as the vertices of an $(n-2)$-dimensional simplex having equal distances separating vertices. The value of c determines not only whether the s_{ij} show distance properties on individual axes but also determines the dimensionality of the space in which they represent distances between stimulus points.

Thus, the arbitrary choice of c to adjust the interval data of Attneave's experiment was a questionable business. In fact, it did not produce the result required — the satisfaction of distance requirements along either single unidimensional axis. Attneave actually chose a value of c such that two equations were satisfied:

$$(8)\ (D-C)+(C-B)=(D-B)$$
$$(9)\ (E-B)+(B-G)=(E-G)$$

where, for example, $(D-C)$ is the transformed judged similarity of stimulus D and stimulus C. Each of these equations relates stimuli on one of the physical dimensions of Diagram 17-11. Given his choice of c (-3.4), the obtained transformed similarities $(D-B)$ and $(E-G)$ are approximately equal to amounts computed by adding the terms in the left sides of equations (8) and (9). Diagram 17-12 shows the relations between such obtained and computed transformed dissimilarities, with $c=-3.4$, for all the distances separating stimuli on either the size or angle dimension. The two cases tried by Attneave, equations (8) and (9) satisfy equations (5), as do two other cases, but there are two other distance relations evident in the case of distances $(C-A)$, $(E-G)$, $(D-A)$, and $(B-G)$. Attneave's choice of c did not achieve the desired result for all distances on either axis!

In fact, the best that can be done is shown in Diagram 17-13 in which a value of c has been chosen separately for the angle and size axes using Torgerson's method (1438, pp. 271-273). In this case three distance relations (L, M, and N in the figure) are again evident. Two of the distances on the angle dimension satisfy relation L and the other two satisfy relation M. Two of the distances on the size dimension satisfy relation L and the remaining two satisfy relation N. Clearly, the size and the angle dimensions of Attneave's study lack unidimensionality: stimulus A is not judged to be on the angle dimension and stimulus F is not judged to be on the size dimension. The test performed for the nature of the space involved, then, is meaningless, and the city-block model has no real support here.

This being so, why has the city-block model, which is based almost entirely on Attneave's data, persisted as a real alternative? A partial answer is that the Attneave

DIAGRAM 17-12.   Relationships Between Computed Distances and the Obtained Distances
(after Attneave, 43)

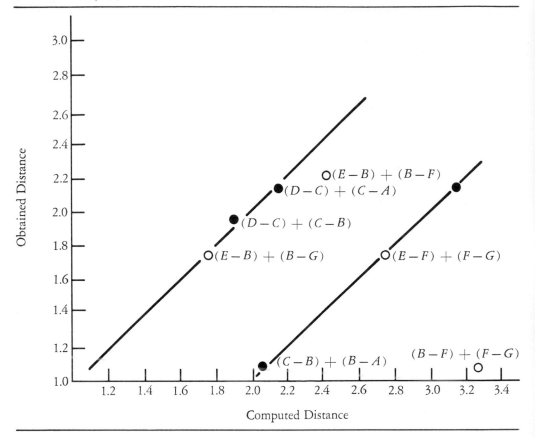

data have not been fully explored to see
whether they satisfied the critical assumptions involved. A more important answer,
probably, is that the city-block model has a
strong intuitive appeal. It seems entirely
reasonable to suppose that there are some
cases of stimuli whose similarity varies
obviously in more than one way. Torgerson
has suggested in these cases that judged
similarities could behave as though the
subject conceives of similarity in terms of
so much similarity on one of the obvious
dimensions plus so much on another (1438,
p. 254).

It would appear, intuitively, that this
should be true for some stimuli. For
example, Shepard (1314) required subjects

to judge the similarity of stimulus patterns
consisting of circles varying in size and
containing a radius line varying in orientation. His criterion for the existence of
Euclidean scaling was that all *isosimilarity
contours* (describing in the physically
defined space the locus of all stimuli having
a stated degree of similarity to a particular
stimulus) should be simultaneously transformable to circles, i.e., all should have an
elliptical shape. No definite information
was provided, however. Departures of the
isosimilarity contours from ellipses appeared
to be due to characteristic individual differences in the tendency to judge similarity
either in terms of circle size or orientation
of the radius.

The nature of the appropriate spatial model is not easily demonstrated. Lacking absolute distance measures on the separate axes of stimulus variation, the nature of the "true" space in which the points representing stimuli exist becomes indeterminate. The points will satisfy the distance properties of many spatial models, depending upon the choice of an additive constant. As long as a value of c can be chosen such that the points can be represented in a minimum Euclidean space with a manageable number of dimensions, however, this appears to be the preferable alternative.

The usefulness of that alternative approach is apparent in the work of Stilson (1352), utilizing a methodology applied earlier by Attneave in one of the experiments in the series on similarity of form (43). The subjects were trained to a rather

DIAGRAM 17-13. Relationship Between Computed Distances and Obtained Distances for Attneave's Data (Data from Attneave, 43)

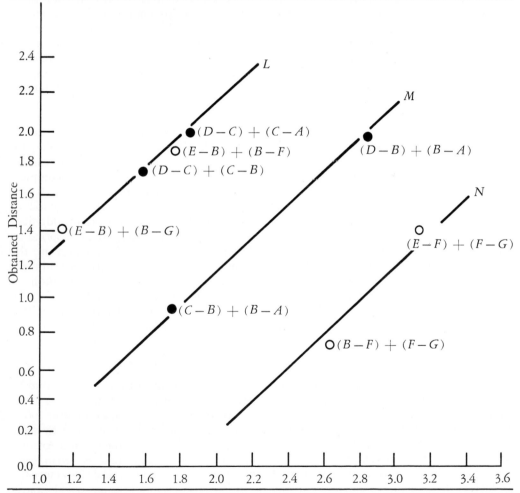

When $c_{tilt} = -3.56$ and $c_{size} = -3.73$. Evidently, neither the tilt nor the size dimension was unidimensional.

low level of proficiency in associating distinct words with each of a set of triangles. Then in a subsequent recall session the frequency with which each pair of triangles was confused was the measure of the similarity of the triangles in the pair. This is a type of scaling technique in which intrusion errors in identification learning are used as measures of proximity (see also Shepard, 1312). Two samples of 13 triangles each were used and the triangles were specified in terms of 14 physical measures.

The measures of proximity, as in the case of the data of Attneave, have an unknown relationship to an absolute scale of distance. Stilson arbitrarily adopted a transformation which forced Euclidean properties on the distances; and, hence, his results provide an interesting comparison with those of Attneave. The frequency with which each pair of triangles was confused during a test trial was recorded and arranged in a sequence matrix. From this confusion matrix two estimates of the distance between any pair of triangles were calculated, assuming Euclidean distances. An average of these two distances was found, and multidimensional scaling analysis was applied to these averages. The first five of the resulting dimensions in the "psychological space" accounted for 90.5 per cent of the variation in the interstimulus distances of the first sample of triangles and of 88.6 per cent of the variation in the second sample. Evidently the stimuli varied *apparently* in relatively a small number of ways, and certainly in fewer than the 14 physical ways devised by Stilson on intuitive grounds.

The interesting question here is: how much do these *psychological* dimensions have in common with the 14 physical measures of the stimuli? Stilson answered this question by forming a 19×19 matrix of the intercorrelations of the 14 physical measures and the 5 psychological dimensions. Principal axis factor analysis yielded 11 factors. But linear combinations of the first three factors reproduced 99 per cent of the total variance of all 14 physical measures in both samples. That is, the first

three factors in the "psychophysical space" and the set of all physical measures span the same space.

Linear combinations of the first five factors in the psychophysical space accounted for 97 per cent of the variation in the first five dimensions of the psychological space in sample 1 and for 98 per cent in sample 2. The first five factors in the psychophysical space and the first five factors in the psychological space span approximately the same space. The corresponding proportions accounted for by linear combinations of only the first three factors in the psychophysical space are 70 per cent and 68 per cent. Evidently some of the psychological components have an appreciable portion of variation which is not common to the physical measures.

The special importance of the judgment of similarity as an analogue for distance in a conceptual space locating stimulus points has been emphasized earlier here and by Helm, Messick, and Tucker (712), Shepard (1313), Torgerson (1438), and Abelson and Sermat (2). In the study of complex, patterned stimulation there is a strong convention, however, in the direction of imposing arbitrary dimensions of judgment which appear obviously to correspond to dimensions of physical variation in the stimuli. This convention has been influential in the study of the perception of complex forms; and, indeed, one of the most frequently studied judgments is that of apparent *complexity* of form.

The Complexity of Form

The pioneering work again was done by Attneave (44), who asked subjects to judge the complexity of 72 quasi-random polygons (nonsense forms) generated by techniques described by Attneave and Arnoult (46). These polygons were classified in terms of several computed physical characteristics —(G) matrix grain (the grain of the matrix in which points determining the outline of the form were located by a random process), (C) curvedness of outline, (Sy) symmetry, (*NIT*) number of independent turns in the outline of the form, (*P²/A*) ratio of square of perimeter length to area, and (*AV*) variability of the angles formed in the outline of the form. The subjects rated the forms on a seven-category scale (from "extremely simple" to "extremely complex"). Ratings were scaled by the Method of Graded Dichotomies and ranged from .82 to 5.24. Table 17-3 indicates the proportion of the scaled rating variance explained by each of the individual physical variables. A multiple regression equation involving three of the physical variables accounted for approximately 90 per cent of the rating variance:

$$(10) \quad J = 5.46 \log_{10}(NIT) + .54S + .005\,AV - 2.91$$

TABLE 17-3

CONTRIBUTIONS OF THE INDIVIDUAL PHYSICAL VARIABLES TO JUDGED COMPLEXITY
(From Attneave, 44)

Physical Variable	Percentage Variance of Complexity Ratings Explained
Matrix Grain*	—
Curvedness	—
Symmetry	3.8
Number of Turns	78.7
P^2/A	4.5**
Angular Variability	7.1

*Only statistically significant components were shown.
**P^2/A and Angular Variability are correlated, $r = .48$, and explain common variance.

in which *J* is rated complexity, *S* is a variable having value 1 for symmetrical forms or 0 for asymmetrical forms, and *NIT* and *AV* are the physical measures described. The measure *AV* was found to correlate .48 with the measure *P²/A*.

Elliott (461) demonstrated that judged complexity as scaled by Attneave's method and by a paired-comparison technique (Thurstone case V) was consistent ($r = .92$ for a set of 40 forms). Consistent results were obtained for different populations of subjects and different samples of forms as well as for the two scaling methods. Neither Attneave nor Elliott included a direct test for the dimensionality of the physical measures of the forms or of the complexity ratings.

Arnoult (39) explored three types of judgments—complexity, familiarity, and size. In addition, the meaningfulness of the forms was measured by a count of the number of associations made to each form in a one sec. interval by each subject. Table 17-4 presents the multiple correlations computed between these four psychophysical measures and the combinations of physical measures shown. No weights were reported.

The possible commonalities among the physical measures were not explored directly, but Table 17-5 from Arnoult's report indicates the pattern of intercorrelations existing among these measures. It is obvious that the eight measures provide a smaller number of independent measures of the forms.

An indication about the number of

TABLE 17-4

MULTIPLE CORRELATIONS BETWEEN PHYSICAL MEASURES AND PERCEPTUAL JUDGMENTS
(From Arnoult, 39)

Judgment	Predictors	R_{mult}	R^2_{mult}
Complexity	*Is,* *P²/A, AV, Sy*	.9335	.8715
Familiarity	*Is, AV, Sy, C*	.8485	.7200
Meaningfulness	*Is, P²/A, AV, Sy, C*	.7547	.5691
Size	*Is, A, AV*	.9616	.9246

*Independent sides.

TABLE 17-5

INTERCORRELATIONS AMONG THE PHYSICAL MEASURES
(From Arnoult, 39)

Measure	1	2	3	4	5	6	7	8
1. (*TS*)		.7927	.7537	.5579	.2824	.2755	.1472	−.0588
2. (*IS*)			.4451	.0854	.4007	.3289	−.4640˙	−.0211
3. (*P*)				.7517	.4903	.4433	.3628	−.3346
4. (*A*)					−.1233	.1189	.6566	−.0157
5. (*P²/A*)						.4059	−.2541	−.4907
6. (*AV*)							−.1489	−.0593
7. (*Sy*)								.0000
8. (*C*)								

different, independent ways in which subjects judge complex, nonsense forms was supplied by the report of Elliott and Tannenbaum (462). The forms judged were selected from the Arnoult study and described physically in terms of the measures of Attneave (44). The subjects rated each form on each of 20 bipolar, seven-point adjective scales. These scales represented factors obtained in previous research with the semantic differential (1121, 1135, pp. 1-75) and were selected as being intuitively appropriate. The resulting 20 × 20 matrix of intercorrelations among the ratings was factored (centroid method, rotation by quartimax), and extraction of factors was stopped at four factors. On the basis of other knowledge of the scales these factors were considered to be (I) an activity or complexity factor, (II) an evaluative or esthetic factor, (III) a size or potency factor, and (IV) a hardness-angularity factor. These judgmental factors were related to the physical measures and two of the factors, complexity and size, appeared to be very similar to Arnoult's size and complexity dimensions of judgment.

The results of this experimental series utilizing arbitrarily imposed dimensions of judgment and attacking the problem in small parts, using multiple regression analysis chiefly, may be compared with the information which Stilson obtained in one fell swoop. Stilson (1352) answered three important questions which in themselves provide an important model for research of

this type: (1) what is the dimensionality of the judgments or ratings used? This question concerns the spatial model (Stilson's "psychological space") appropriate for the judgments themselves and the distance model relating judgments to distance in the spatial model (2) In how many independent ways do the physical measures specify the stimuli? This question concerns the spatial and distance models appropriate for the stimuli. (3) To what extent does the dimensionality of the judgmental (psychological) and physical measure spaces correspond and what is the degree of commonality? The research series on the judgment of the very useful random polygons (nonsense forms) has provided partial answers to the first two questions but no information on the last. The research of Stilson involving the judgment of similarity, the assumption of Euclidean distances, and multidimensional scaling evidently exemplifies the more powerful methodology.

The Apparent Three-Dimensionality of Two-Dimensional Forms

There are instances, however, in which an arbitrarily imposed dimension of judgment can be as useful as the primitive judgment of similarity. This is where a particular judgment may have unique theoretical importance. An illustration of this is the study of Hochberg (730) involving the judgment of the apparent three-dimensionality of two-dimensional forms. The hypothesis tested was that apparent three-dimensionality is proportional to the geometrical complexity of plane stimuli. The stimulus forms were nine families of reversible-perspective figures (described in terms of 17 physical measures normalized on a 10-point scale) of varying complexity. When confronted with a family of forms each subject was required to place the form seemingly most solid or three-dimensional at 10 on the scale and the form seemingly least solid at 0. The remaining forms were placed appropriately in between.

The intercorrelations of judged three-dimensionality and the 17 physical measures of geometric, two-dimensional complexity were arranged in a 18×18 matrix. All correlations between judged three-dimensionality and the physical measures were positive. The largest correlation (.89) related judgment to the total number of continuous line segments of the forms.

This matrix was factor-analyzed (rotated quartimax) and eight factors extracted. The first three factors accounted for 94 per cent of the variance of the responses and were identified by loadings on physical measures as (1) angular complexity, (2) specific angular asymmetry or diversity (number of different angles divided by number of angles), and (3) number of continuous lines (or linear discontinuity).

It appears then that the apparent three-dimensionality of plane geometric forms can be accounted for quite well by three dimensions of variation of the stimuli. The nature of the dimensions, however, suggests that the judgment of the three-dimensionality of complex forms is not unlike the judgment of complexity itself.

5. MULTIVARIATE MODELS AS PERCEPTUAL MODELS

Just as the analysis of intercorrelations has led to the development of conceptual models of considerable usefulness in understanding personality, the analysis of interstimulus similarities, as judged by the observer, has led to the development of conceptual models for perceptual behavior. Multidimensional scaling itself provides a perceptual model depicting the perceptions of stimulus events as locations of points in a conceptual space whose dimensions may or may not coincide with the physical characteristics of the events. Interest in such scaling models results from their relevance to important perceptual questions. The dimensionality of perceptual judgment is certainly one such question, and the matter of type of spatial model is another. Both questions relate to how the subject selectively responds to the various aspects of stimulation and how he combines these aspects in evaluating stimulation.

The work of Tucker and Messick (1468) provides a perceptually meaningful model encompassing variation in multidimensional stimulus spaces. However, our ability to specify scaling models for certain ideal observers of theoretical or practical importance has not really been exploited. Since the ideal observers are essentially perceptual models, this methodology should be extremely important in future attempts to relate judgments to theory.

It can be said in general that the multidimensional scaling models have not yet been applied to the limit of their usefulness as a conceptual tool in the understanding of perceptual experience and behavior. In the history of the study of perception these models represent rather recent developments and in a surprising number of cases are still not significantly involved in the training of persons interested in perception as a topic.

A Non-Metric Scaling Model, Uncertainty Analysis

One particular scaling model has received a good deal of attention. This is the model derived from information theory, and it is well described by Attneave (45) and more recently by Garner (575). Both sources stress the perceptual implications of the theory.

One interesting generalization derived from the theory stresses a type of non-metric correlation. If a set of stimuli (the X_i) are presented to a subject, one stimulus at a time, and he identifies each with a unique response (the Y_j), we can after many trials form a stimulus-response matrix, the confusion matrix, like that of Table 17-6. The relation between the stimuli and responses can then be expressed as

$$(11) \quad U(Y{:}X) = U(Y) - U_x(Y)$$

where $U(Y{:}X)$ is the correlation measure, the contingent uncertainty, where $U(Y)$ is a measure of the uncertainty of the responses (row marginals),

$$(12) \quad U(Y) = -\sum_j^n p(Y_j)\log_2 p(Y_j),$$

and $U_x(Y)$ is a measure of the uncertainty of the responses with the stimulus held constant (within-column uncertainty)

$$(13) \quad U_x(Y) =$$

$$-\sum_i^n p(X_i) \sum_j^n p_x(Y_j)\log_2 p_x(Y_j).$$

The parallel between the uncertainty measure U and the variance σ^2 is indicated by these two equations:

$$(14) \quad \sigma_y^2 = \sigma_{y \cdot x}^2 + r_{y \cdot x}^2 \sigma_y^2$$
$$(15) \quad U(Y) = U_x(Y) + U(Y{:}X)$$

The first shows that the total variance of y, a continuous variable, can be partitioned into two parts: $r_{y \cdot x}^2 \sigma_y^2$, the part which represents covariation with x; and $\sigma_{y \cdot x}^2$, the average error of estimating y with x constant. Part of the variance of the measure y may be identified with the variation in x and part may not. In the second equation our total uncertainty in predicting discrete values of Y is partitioned into a part, $U(Y{:}X)$, representing a measure of the contingency between Y and X; and a part, $U_x(Y)$, the average uncertainty involved in the prediction of Y with X held constant.

Further analogies between variance and the uncertainty of continuous measures and in the multiple correlation case are provided by Ross (1225).

Although the confusion data of Table 17-6 can provide the raw data for multidimensional scaling of the stimulus inputs, the analysis of these data in uncertainty terms has certain advantages. One of these stems from the fact that no assumptions about the metric underlying stimuli and responses are made. Both are described only in terms of the uncertainty measure, and this permits statements to be made which hold for all types of stimuli and responses whose uncertainties are equivalent. Another advantage is that the description of the behavior of subjects in terms of uncertainty measures has enabled psychologists, especially, to compare the behavior of the human subject with certain ideal, as well as real, communication components.

The interesting generalization deriving

DIAGRAM 17-14. Relationships Between the Contingent Uncertainty and the Stimulus Uncertainty

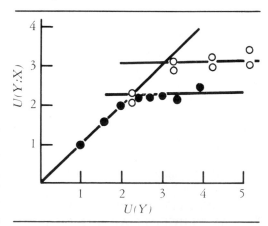

The diagonal line represents maximum possible values. Open circles based on judgments of pointer positions (665) and closed circles based on judgments of auditory pitch (1169).

TABLE 17-6

SYMBOLIC REPRESENTATION OF THE NUMBER OF JOINT OCCURRENCES OF STIMULUS CATEGORY (X_i) WITH RESPONSE CATEGORY (Y_j).

	1	2	•	i	•	n	
1	N_{11}	N_{12}	•	N_{1i}	•	N_{1n}	$N_{1\bullet}$
2	N_{21}	N_{22}	•	N_{2i}	•	N_{2n}	$N_{2\bullet}$
3	•	•	•	•	•	•	•
j	N_{j1}	N_{j2}	•	N_{ji}	•	N_{jn}	$N_{j\bullet}$
•	•	•	•	•	•	•	•
n	N_{n1}	N_{n2}		N_{ni}		N_{nn}	$N_{n\bullet}$
	$N_{\bullet 1}$	$N_{\bullet 2}$		$N_{\bullet i}$		$N_{\bullet n}$	N

$$p(Y_j) = \frac{N_{j\bullet}}{N} \qquad p(X_i) = \frac{N_{\bullet i}}{N} \qquad p_x(Y_j) = \frac{N_{ji}}{N_{\bullet i}}$$

from the non-metric measure of correlation, $U(Y{:}X)$ is that of *channel capacity*. If the number of stimuli and responses involved in the confusion matrix of Table 17-6 is fairly large, we can be sure that the contingent uncertainty computed for the matrix, $U(Y{:}X)$, will be considerably less than the uncertainty of the stimuli, $U(Y)$. If then a larger or smaller set of stimuli covering the same, or even a somewhat larger, range of variation is used and the subject is again required to identify each with a unique response (the number of stimuli and responses being equal), we may with considerable confidence make a prediction about $U(Y{:}X)$ for this new situation. The prediction follows from the general form of the data shown in Diagram 17-14. This figure combines data for the judgment of tones (1169) and data from

judgment of position of a pointer on a line (665). In both cases a limit to the size of the contingent uncertainty is indicated; and to this limit, the maximum possible value of $U(Y{:}X)$ for that type of stimulus input, the term *channel capacity* has been applied. It implies that where the number of stimuli and responses is large and where $U(Y{:}X)$ is less than $U(Y)$ for these stimuli, it is likely that no increase in the number of stimuli will produce a larger $U(Y{:}X)$ and that the antilogarithm of $U(Y{:}X)$ is actually the number of stimuli above which the contingent uncertainty will not increase (576).

This is certainly an interesting statement, and the implication is that a confusion matrix has a certain latent property. The property is that the matrix for which $U(Y{:}X) < U(Y)$ is the product of a ($n \times N$) matrix by a ($N \times n$) matrix, where n is the number of stimuli and responses and N is the antilogarithm of $U(Y:X)$. This, of course, begs questions about the significance of the number N and the matrices into which the confusion matrix could be factored. We have made very little specific progress with these questions, although some possible factors affecting the size of N can be described (see Garner, 575, pp. 62-78).

This discussion is certainly not intended to suggest that the usefulness of uncertainty analysis as a model is limited to stimuli varying on a single dimension. Appropriate analyses are available for cases where stimuli are describable in terms of more than a single dimension of variation and where the responses are multivariate. These analyses, described by Garner (575, pp. 98-112), have permitted other types of generalizations. For example, it appears that an increase in the dimensionality of stimulation increases the total contingent uncertainty measure of the relation between stimuli and responses but decreases the relative amount of relationship existing between responses and each dimension of stimulus variation.

Multivariate Models and Perceptual Theory

Current models of most interest concern the general problem of how the perceiver combines and evaluates inputs of many types in many different perceiving situations to achieve reliable and valid concepts concerning the nature of his environment, to permit accurate and/or consistent judgments of an enormous variety of stimulus objects and events, and to recognize these objects and events when transformed in a variety of ways. In this, the models are being applied to very old questions which have been highlighted by our current perceptual theories. Multivariate models have special relevance to one type of theory, probabilistic functionalism, and to one theorist, Egon Brunswik. Brunswik's

major beliefs concerning the human perceiver were that the environment of the perceiver is uncertain and describable only in probabilistic terms and that perception of that environment consists of a set of inferences made on the basis of probabilistic data. Since Brunswik's death these beliefs have been given more explicit statement and recast within the framework of multiple correlational analysis.

The general model is presented schematically in Diagram 17-15, which is taken from Hursch, Hammond, and Hursch (801). In this model, Brunswik's "lens model," a stimulus (distal variable) has a certain set of characteristics (cues), the X_i. The identity or value of the distal stimulus is not given by the value of any one cue. However, each cue is correlated with the identity of each stimulus and the cues show intercorrelations among their own values. The perceiver is in contact only with the cues and must combine and weight them, in any instance, so as to produce the highest possible correlation between his estimate of the distal variable and the identity of that variable. A complete analysis of a particular perceptual situation, then, includes the multiple correlation between the distal variable and the cues, the multiple correlation between the cues and the perceiver's estimate of the distal variable, and the correlation between the distal variable and the perceiver's estimate. Hursch, Hammond, and Hursch provide the analysis for several cases. These include cases where the correlations between the distal variable and the cues are matched by those between the cues and the perceiver's estimates, as well as cases in which they are not, and cases in which the cues are intercorrelated, as well as cases in which they are not. The method was applied in a specific and interesting way to the data of Summers (1367), who had required subjects to give a response (length of produced line) to each of a set of stimuli varying in color, angle, and area and in which each of these three cues were correlated less than perfectly

DIAGRAM 17-15. Brunswik's Lens Model (from Hursch, Hammond, & Hursch, 801, Fig.1)

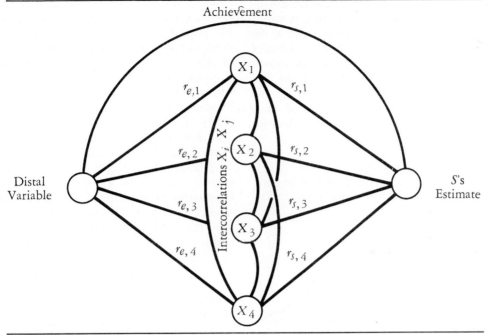

"Ecological validity" is expressed as correlations ($r_{e,i}$) between the cues and a distal variable and "cue utilization" as correlations ($r_{s,i}$) between the cues and the subjects estimate of the distal variable. Achievement refers to the correlation between the estimate and the distal variable.

with the correct response for each stimulus. The analysis indicated, for example, that subjects often began a series of trials with a large positive multiple correlation between responses and the cues and a large negative correlation between responses and the correct response for each stimulus. During the course of learning trials, the multiple correlation between cues and responses decreased, while the correlation between responses and the correct responses (achievement) became increasingly positive. That is, it appeared that subjects brought to the experimental situation the ability to demonstrate a high multiple correlation between the response and the cues, but that during a set of trials this correlation was given up in favor of increases in the correlation between response and a criterion of correctness.

This type of correlational model applies most usefully to those cases in which the "cues" to which the subject responds are explicitly defined and measured. Another type of probabilistic model of increasing importance assumes that the variables which the subject evaluates in deriving concepts and responses are implicit and not measurable directly. One such model, made explicit in the theory of signal detectability (for related papers see Swets, 1377), borrows elements from engineering and from the psychophysics of Thurstone. Where, for example, there are two stimulus events, X_1 and X_2, the immediate experience of the subject corresponding to these events is a variable along the axis depicted in Diagram 17-16. It is assumed that when stimulus X_1 is presented, the experience of the subject is sampled from the left-hand distribution of the figure, and when X_2 is presented his experience is sampled from the right-hand distribution. In the presence of a stimulus, then, the subject must infer from x, his immediate experience of the stimulus, which stimulus is present. This is equivalent to inferring from which of the two distributions x was sampled. The inference is made by adopting a criterion of judgment, as shown in the figure, and a decision rule relative to that criterion.

DIAGRAM 17-16.   A Schematic Representation of the Theory of Signal Detectability Model

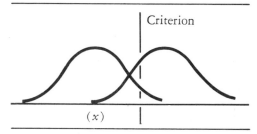

This model, as schematized in Diagram 17-16, emphasizes the fact that psychophysical judgments in the simple discrimination situation described have two independent characteristics. One of these is an indication of discrimination acuity, the normalized distance between the first moments of the distributions in the figure. This is a "sensory" aspect of judgment. The second aspect is determined by the criterion adopted by the subject. This second, "non-sensory" or "motivational" aspect of judgment is reflected by the relative use of the subject's two possible response types. These two aspects of judgment are made explicit in Diagram 17-17, which depicts the relation between the subject's "hit-rate" (the conditional proportion of the X_2 occurrences which are judged to be X_2 occurrences) and his "false-alarm rate" (the conditional proportion of the X_1 occurrences which are judged to be X_2 occurrences). This relationship has been described both as a receiver operating

characteristic (ROC), a term borrowed from engineering, and as an iso-sensitivity contour, a term with more meaning for the psychophysical situation. The shape of this curve is crucially involved in the evaluation of the theory of signal detectability as an adequate psychophysical model. This shape varies with the variances of the two distributions of Diagram 17-16, but within those limits the shape of the iso-sensitivity contour has important implications for perceptual theory. In particular, if data from a two-choice discrimination between two stimuli always yield a pair of hit-rate and false-alarm values falling on a smooth iso-sensitivity contour defined by the theory, then the status of the threshold concept is highly questionable. The signal detectability model has no such concept and this is an

DIAGRAM 17-17. The Relationship Between the Hit Rate and False-Alarm Rate

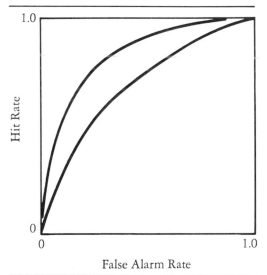

The relationship between the hit rate and false-alarm rate in the task of discriminating X_1 from X_2 occurrences depends upon the normalized distance between the hypothetical distributions of Diagram 17-16. These "receiver operating characteristics" or "iso-sensitivity curves" can be derived by integrating the left and right distributions of Diagram 17-16 to the right of the criterion.

important implication for perceptual theorizing, which historically has leaned heavily upon the notion of absolute and differential thresholds. Attempts to demonstrate that data do or do not conform to the model have yielded ambiguous results, however, because of difficulty in demonstrating that data do or do not yield iso-sensitivity contours of a specific shape (1375, 1099).

The axis of experiential variation of the signal detectability model, the horizontal line of Diagram 17-16, has little conceptual usefulness because its location and orientation are indeterminate. The model may be related easily to the linear discriminant function of Fisher (520), however, to provide a useful perceptual model. The linear discriminant function is

$$(16) \quad Y = v_1X_1 + v_2X_2 + \cdots + v_iX_i + \cdots + v_nX_n$$

in which the X_i are measurable aspects of stimulus objects or events and the v_i are weighting coefficients. The stimulus events are classifiable into two sets, and on the basis of the Y computed for each stimulus event we wish to classify each as belonging to set A or set B. Fisher's methodology permits the derivation of the weights, the v_i, such that the events can be classified on the basis of Y and that the ratio of variation *between* the two classified sets of stimuli to variation *within* the sets is a maximum.

Rodwan and Hake (1206) have suggested the discriminant function as a perceptual model applicable in all cases in which the perceiver attempts to classify stimulus events in dichotomous classes (safe or unsafe, clear or unclear, good or evil, intelligent or unintelligent, etc.). Analysis of such classification behavior indicates that subjects do act to maximize the ratio of between-class variance to within-class variance. This was demonstrated, for example, in the case where subjects classified schematic faces varying in forehead height, nose length, length of chin, and distance between the eyes. Subjects classified the schematic faces so as to maximize the "distance" between the two classes of stimuli. An important aspect of this maximization involved the fact that although the entire set of stimulus faces was an orthogonal set with respect to the four facial variables, the stimuli within each of the response classes were not. The correlations within response classes among the facial characteristics of the stimuli within each class were, in fact, opposite in sign from the correlations between the *mean* values of each characteristic for the stimuli in each response class. That is, the axis of maximum variation among the stimuli *within* each response set tended to be orthogonal to the axis of variation connecting the multidimensional means of the sets. Within each response set the maximum axis of variation was irrelevant to the variation upon which classification into sets was based.

Subjects classifying stimulus events in this way were said to be satisfying a *coherence criterion*: the two classes of stimuli formed by the classifications correspond to two classes of *experiences* which are as different as possible. This is possibly the objective of a lot of perceptual behavior. In any event, the use of this analysis permits us to learn whether the perceiver in any particular situation acted to satisfy that type of criterion or whether he acted to satisfy an accuracy criterion.

6. SUMMARY

The contributions of multivariate methodology to the study of perception were considered here, emphasizing those research trends and series which illustrate advantages, and some difficulties, of the methodology.

(1) The multivariate approach provides the converging operations which permit unambiguous definition of perceptual terms and concepts. Correlational analysis has been used, for example, in rendering the term "subception" gratuitous. This approach contrasts with the usual stronger bias toward the univariate approach in the perceptual area.

(2) The factor-analytic attempts to describe the traits and abilities underlying perceptual performance produced a longer list of perceptual factors than are involved probably in any of the more restricted perceptual situations. In one situation, the size-distance constancy experiment, the existence of a factor was suggested in judgmental situations in which the perceiver is forced to use a single dimension in which to report how he judges objects in two or more conceptual dimensions.

(3) The experimental series on the judgment of facial expression recapitulates the history of scaling methodology and illustrates well the conceptual advantages and requirements of multidimensional scaling. The older results, based upon the color-solid model of Schlosberg, are not well supported by current scaling methodology.

Several types of multivariate analyses of color vision are considered. The traditional tristimulus photometric analyses agree that there are three basic visual dimensions of judgment. Factor analysis of older visibility data indicated the possible existence of a bipolar factor. The existence of as many as five factors in the analysis of the similarity of colored stimuli is probably a spurious result of the improper use of interval data.

A new methodology permits the careful study of individual differences by providing for the scaling of perceivers, both real and ideal, as well as the scaling of stimuli.

(4) The judgment of the similarity of complex polygons and geometric forms has raised questions about which of the abundant quantitative descriptions of such forms is related to judgment and about the nature of the space in which comparative judgments of the stimuli may be represented by distances. Earlier work has suggested the "city-block" spatial model, instead of a Euclidean spatial model, but a closer look at that work failed to provide any support for the model. The problem of the "additive constant" becomes extremely important in attempts to describe a "true" spatial model.

The complete analysis of the "psychological space" (independent dimensions of similarity judgment), the "physical space" (independent dimensions of physical variation in the stimuli), and the commonality of the two spaces was provided in one instance, assuming a Euclidean spatial model. An imposed dimension of judgment which has had a lot of study is the judgment of form complexity. This may be related to the judgment of the solidity (three-dimensionality) of two-dimensional forms.

(5) Multidimensional scaling provides a conceptual model depicting the perception of stimulus events as the location of points in a conceptual space whose dimensions may or may not coincide with the dimensions of physical variation measurable in the events. The uncertainty-analysis model has provided the concept of channel capacity in absolute judgments; the implications of this concept are not yet well understood.

Multiple correlation analysis is closely related to one theoretical position, probabilistic functionalism. Current statements of the theory are framed entirely in the framework of multiple correlation.

The theory of signal detectability provides two measures of detection performance: a measure of a sensory (or acuity) aspect and a measure of a non-sensory (or motivational) aspect. The iso-sensitivity contour, which is independent of the non-sensory aspect, challenges the deep-rooted concept of the threshold in the area of perception.

A new criterion of perceptual adequacy, the coherence criterion, is defined in terms of the ability of the observer to form "clusters" of immediate experiences such that the ratio of between-cluster variation to within-cluster variation is a maximum. In achieving this coherence of experience, subjects sort stimuli such that the correlations among stimulus characteristics within response classes are opposite in sign to those between the means of response classes.

CHAPTER 18 Concepts in Human Cognition and Aptitudes

KURT PAWLIK
University of Hamburg

1. SCOPE OF THE CHAPTER (BY THE EDITOR)

A glance at the data box enables us readily to separate the concept of individual differences in structure from process structure, but in practice the treatment of what textbooks sometimes call "individual differences" is not so easily isolated. Indeed, as Chapters 11, 12, and 13 on change show, it is very questionable whether "individual differences" conceived simply in statistical operations *should* be a subject for absolutely separate study. More desirable is a functional view of process and product together, which would lead us to study abilities, temperament traits, dynamic traits, etc., using individual difference statistical analysis as *one* avenue to understanding that structure. The individual difference methodology then needs to be supplemented by the study of trait change, of states, of learning, and so on, in the interests of understanding the structure of the individual.

Thus, although the psychologist perceiving in traditional terms might want to say that this and the two following chapters comprise the area of "individual differences," it is to be hoped that they are more than that, while, in turn, other chapters, e.g., Chapters 9, 14, 23, 28, and 30, have substantial individual difference aspects.

The definition of the topic of this chapter also requires that a distinction be drawn in another direction, namely, between the *abilities* with which it is concerned, and the *personality and dynamic traits* with which Chapters 19 and 20, respectively, are concerned. Although psychologists have been happy up to a point with their capacity intuitively to separate these three modalities, they obviously must in the end have a more rigorous definition. The need for this is shown for example by Cattell and Saunders' (314) claim that some of Thurstone's perceptual factors are really the "corners" of general personality factors outcropping in a cognitive realm, as has recently been followed up, for example, by Riley Gardner, and by Cattell's early study (200) showing that Spearman's and Bernstein's "fluency" ability factor appeared to be a *general* temperament trait. A rigorous operational definition of ability, temperament, and dynamic trait distinctions has been given elsewhere (213) and on page 538 here, and will not be pursued now except to say that such traits are different abstractions from one and the same set of behaviors. The dynamic measurements and factors are those responding to goal incentives; the ability traits relate to the individual differences in reaching agreed goals in the face of varying complexities of the goal path; and the temperament traits are concerned with the remaining variance, being concerned mainly with ratios and other scores which prove independent of incentive and difficulty.

With this recognition that present approaches, as yet untouched by application of such rigorous analysis, may lead to some temperament and dynamic traits being included in the study of abilities, we may proceed. However, this theoretical analysis of the variance of a behavioral act into three parts has also a practical consequence of importance in routine psychological examinations. Except in a very lucky choice of behavioral aspects for measurement, the measurement of modality X will always be contaminated by some variance from modalities Y and Z. This will perhaps only reach its fullest meaning for the reader after studying Professor Horn's Chapter 20, where, in dynamic measurement (by objective devices) it is obvious that an appreciable part of the score is always due to the "vehicle" or manifestation through which the interest expresses itself, e.g., memory power. What has not been so widely realized is that the "correction for vehicle" developed in dynamic measurement has long needed to be reciprocally employed in the two other modalities, e.g., in partialling out the dynamic component from an intelligence test measurement, or the ability component from the score on a set of personality factor sub-tests.

Dr. Pawlik fully recognizes this present problem, admitting that several of his structures "span the three realms." He also constantly reminds us that even when there is no doubt about modality, there may be correlations of a slight but significant nature between abilities on the one hand and temperament and dynamic traits on the other. The fantastically unreal mathematical "simplification" of orthogonality is not imposed by him either on the ability factors themselves or on their relations to the two other modalities. At the same time he recognizes that the personality temperament modality is largely a "new space" beyond the ability space, just as Horn proves that the dynamic-interest modality domain is new space again beyond the ability and general personality factor spaces. This is shown, for example, by the increments — incidentally almost equal — of prediction of, for example, school achievement, which follow from the addition of trait measures ("predictors") from the three realms in succession. In this connection one may note the curious embedding of dynamic-trait-multiplied-by-time in the concept of crystallized general ability and in achieved skills, as discussed in Section 7. As the reader will note, Section 7 does not express the views of Dr. Pawlik, but is an independent statement by Professor Horn based on his recent, intensive studies in this special area.

Abilities is a wide term which, in the persisting unsettled use of terminology in this field, is used here to cover aptitudes and achievements and a variety of perceptual and motor skills. The question of which of these represent inherited capacities and which acquired capacities is left largely to Thompson's Chapter 23 on genetics. However, "common-sense" decisions are accepted between what may be relatively constitutional "aptitudes" on the one hand and abilities or "skills in being" on the other. Incidentally, those aspects of perception which largely concern individual differences in perceptual ability structure are handled systematically here and only incidentally in Hake's Chapter 17 on perception (though vision and hearing and sensory capacities are dealt with in the latter).

In regard to correlational analysis of

individual differences, Pawlik accepts the distinction between a surface trait or correlation cluster on the one hand, and a source trait or related factor on the other. In the latter he considers the unique resolution to a simple structure or confactor position essential, as in the statistical methodology of Thurstone, Tucker, Kaiser, Cattell, and others, and attempts only to align, as invariant factors, the results of those studies which reach these and other standards and scientific restrictions. Finally, since the "change" study of ability patterns, by Horn, Nesselroade, and others, is in its infancy, he has kept very largely to R-technique, individual difference results.

The treatment is on a trait-by-trait (or factor-by-factor) basis initially (though factors are "grouped" by psychological meaning later), attempting to arrive first at a truly experimentally based view of the number and nature of factors in the ability realm. The effectiveness of such an approach naturally depends upon the preciseness of factor identification between different analyses. Special care has been taken in this respect to guard against subjectivity in matching factors by their inferred psychological meaning. Available resources naturally did not allow for computing, in each case, exact coefficients of factor matching (cf. Hundleby, Pawlik, & Cattell, 796; Chapter 3); still the question whether or not a factor can be identified from one research to another has been decided on objective grounds only, viz., from the degree of similarity, over identical variables, between the respective column vectors of factor loadings. Special mention is made in those cases where the identification had to be based on less firm grounds such as by also considering inferred psychological meaning of a factor.

One has to ask himself whether this experimental approach, aimed at recognizing the number and nature of primary abilities, and then to recognize, further, the second-strata factors among them, is more or less profitable than that represented by

the attempts of Guilford (626), Piaget (1158), Roback (1202), Thorne (1401), and others to define a scheme qualitatively in descriptive terms, relative to the operations performed. It is indeed a major parting of the ways which is faced at this point, since quite different sets of concepts of ability will follow from each. Our study of classification procedures (Chapter 9) leaves little doubt that the only firm ground for classifying behavior which we possess is correlational not inspectional. In the latter direction lies the garbage dump filled with the subjective, semantic classifications of the last seventy years of "psychological schemas." On the other hand, even by quantitative methods, a serious divergence of approaches has to be recognized. Does one, as Thurstone did in this field, aim to discover the natural unities and modes of growth of abilities, as the outcome of genetic and cultural influences, or does one, as Guilford and to some extent Guttman have done, set out to construct testing devices which will break down into areas of a conceived framework of possible performances? The latter means making up tests with various trial-and-error combinations of this and that kind of item until they correlate as required by the a priori concepts of the designer's scheme to give a particular mosaic (see page 212 f.) in the obtained correlation or factor matrix. Anyone of mature experimental skill and statistical sophistication can apparently succeed in constructing clusters to fit almost any subjective concept of ability structure, though this cannot happen with representative experiment and simple structure criteria.

The present chapter has inspected this parting of the ways, with results which the reader may follow. Mainly it has taken the position that the psychologist's task is to find what structures exist, as independent simple structure factors, in existing races and cultures. Then it proceeds to apply classification and interpretation to what may be found.

2. SOME PRELIMINARY CONSIDERATIONS

Within the scope of this handbook, the purpose of this chapter and the next is to present a review and integration of the results available from applying factor analysis to individual differences in personality traits. By the latter we simply mean all reliably measurable behavior differences which are not related to dynamic or motivational components, such as interests, drives, and attitudes; these are dealt with in Chapter 20. Thus "personality" implies both temperament and aptitude traits, the latter in turn spanning the whole range from individual differences in sensory functioning and motor skills to differences in cognitive performances. However, available space does not allow for equal coverage of all areas included in this definition, and certain ones will have to be dealt with rather briefly (e.g., the field of non-cognitive aptitude factors).

In the second place this review is selective as to the individual researches considered. First of all it is restricted to factor analyses following the R-technique design (i.e., yielding test factors from intercorrelating tests over people); evidence on person factors and state factors (from Q-technique and P-technique studies, respectively) will not be reported here. Second, for the sake of comparability of results, it seemed desirable to stay within one and the same factor-analytic mode. Since Thurstone's (1420) method of multiple factor analysis (restricting the analysis to common factors, with subsequent simple structure rotation) has been used most widely, studies following different factor-analytic techniques are generally not considered in this review except for special cases.

For brevity of presentation the discussion will be on a factor-by-factor basis rather than by individual studies. The fruitfulness of such an approach naturally depends upon the preciseness of factor identification between different analyses.

Special care has been taken in this respect to guard against subjectivity in matching factors by their inferred psychological meaning. Available resources naturally did not allow for computing, in each case, exact coefficients of factor matching (see 796, Chapter 3). Still the question whether or not a factor can be identified from one research to another has been decided on objective grounds only, viz., from the degree of similarity, over identical variables, between the respective column vectors of factor loadings. Special mention will be made in those cases where the identification had to be based on less firm grounds, such as by also considering inferred psychological meaning of a factor.

In distinguishing between aptitude and ability factors (the present Chapter 18) and temperament or "personality" factors (now using the term in its more restricted sense) the two realms, however, are not assumed to be orthogonal to each other; quite to the contrary, several examples will be reported in the text of factors relating to both aptitude and temperament measures, thus spanning across the two realms. Whenever possible, factors will be clustered within a given realm into groups according to empirical evidence on their mutual interrelationships; lacking such evidence, the grouping will be in terms of operational characteristics of the respective factor salients. Other systems of presentation have been tried in the past, most notable among these Guilford's "structure of the intellect" and his schema of temperament and hormetic factors (626), to which the reader is particularly referred.

3. FACTORS OF SENSORY FUNCTIONING

Spearman, in his first provocative paper on a general intellective factor (1336), entertained the hypothesis that simple sensory performances (e.g., stimulus discrimination, stimulus identification, etc.) can be accounted for by the same single factor of "general intelligence" which also determines most of the variance in mental tests. However, subsequent research by Burt (155), Carey (186), and Walters (1495) soon rejected this proposition, already yielding a multiplicity of factors rather than one single dimension. Unfortunately this question has not been investigated yet to any larger extent by the more powerful techniques that have become available since, and the emphasis has shifted from the question of intersensory factor structure to research on individual sensory systems.

Most of these studies have been carried out in the area of *vision*. Analysis of standard vision tests yielded a factor of visual acuity or retinal resolution (1150, 1598), a factor of brightness discrimination (1150), and at least four different phoria factors (1598).

The factorial structure of *color vision* (see also Chapter 17 here) has been investigated in several analyses. Burt (164) and Pickford (1159) obtained a three-factor solution: the first factor appeared to be a general factor of color perception, the other two factors related to red-green and yellow-blue sensitivity, respectively. This result would be in support of the Hering and Ladd-Franklin theories of color vision. However, upon re-analyzing his data by the group method of factor analysis, Burt (164) arrived at a four-factor solution now yielding a "general factor," a "red" factor, a "green" factor, and a "blue" factor. Burt was also able to show that the two solutions can be mutually transformed into each other. From Burt's results the Hering and Ladd-Franklin theories of color vision should not be incompatible with trichromatic color theory; the two would only represent different rotational positions in the same factor space. But even then trichromatic color theory is more parsimonious (in Thurstone's sense): rotation of axes for simple structure, whenever applied to color data, always yielded results consistent with trichromatic theories of color vision (as well as with colorimetric

reference curves known from color matching experiments: see 814, 819, 1506).

Factor-analytic research in audition is mainly due to Karlin (842, 843, 844). In his two earlier analyses (842, 834), only the tonal sensitivity factor appears properly cross-identified. In the larger matrix of auditory tests available for the third analysis (843, 844), however, tonal sensitivity no longer yielded a single factor but was split into the components pitch discrimination, loudness discrimination, and time estimation. An interesting analogy to the three factors of color vision has been found by Henry (719) in a factor analysis of auditory sensitivity measures for selected wave-lengths of the acoustic wave spectrum: he found three factors, a low-frequency (up to 2,048 c.p.s.), an intermediate-frequency (2,048 to approximately 6,000 c.p.s.), and a high-frequency auditory sensitivity factor (beyond 6,000 c.p.s.) As Guilford (626, page 345) has pointed out, it might prove worthwhile to search the physiology of hearing for the possibility of three corresponding physiological mechanisms of audition.

Little is known about factors of semicircular canal functioning; the two studies available (74, 1010) yield conflicting results. In the kinesthetic sense domain both Bass (74) and Fleishman (530) found a factor of kinesthetic sensitivity. No studies have yet been undertaken for the sense areas of taste and smell; the evidence regarding olfaction is still highly contradictory (492, 781).

4. THE STRUCTURE IN PSYCHOMOTOR PERFORMANCES

Two comprehensive summaries on psychomotor aptitude factors have appeared within the last ten years, one by Fleishman (530) and one by Guilford (625, pages 348-359); the latter also covers factors of physical proficiency (e.g., body strength, trunk flexibility, etc.) which will not be considered in the present review. The psychomotor factors described below are all very adequately replicated, i.e., have been found consistently in several studies with good agreement in loading pattern between the studies. The factors are discussed in order of decreasing rate of replication.

Best confirmed of all psychomotor dimensions is the factor called Psychomotor Coordination, which has been identified in about 15 different analyses (637, 433, 630, 530, 714, 1054, 1209, 1212). Principal marker variables of the Psychomotor Coordination factor are: higher per cent time-on-target in rotary pursuit test, better two-hand coordination, higher speed and accuracy of hand and foot adjustments to complex stimuli in the Air Force standard Complex Coordination Test, and better coordination of foot adjustments in the Air Force standard Rudder Control Test; minor positive loadings are in finger dexterity and speed of discrimination reaction. Thus Psychomotor Coordination essentially relates to the achieved degree of adjustment of limb (finger, hand, or foot) motions in response to visual stimuli; the hypothesis is that skillful use of kinesthetic feedback information plays the most important part in it. As yet the factor has been demonstrated in military (mostly Air Force) subject populations only. It appears to be one of the most important psychomotor aptitude dimensions, in terms of criterion validities as well (538, 637).

A second factor of coordination of movements, though limited to paper-pencil tests only, has become known under the descriptive title Aiming. It has been identified by Guilford in his analysis of dexterity tests (1039), in two analyses carried out during World War II by USES (1477), and in a series of further factor analyses of psychomotor variables (618, 605, 606, 341, 530, 535, 714).[1]

Aiming is an aptitude dimension of "paper-pencil psychomotor speed and precision" (529), relating to quick and precise hand-finger movements of comparatively small extent, with the emphasis on good eye-hand coordination. Aiming and Psychomotor Coordination are factors of motor precision and control of movements; however, the two are different in that the Aiming factor also loads speed of movements (which is of little importance in the Psychomotor Coordination factor) and relates to rather small arm-hand movements only. Tests loaded highly on Aiming are: marking, dotting (the loading increases with decreasing area of the circles into which the dots are to be placed!), and tracing.[2]

If the eye-hand coordination element is reduced in typical tests of Aiming (e.g., by increasing the size of the circles into which the dots have to be put), speed of performance then no longer relates to Aiming but to a factor usually called Tapping (618); in accordance with Fleishman (530) we shall use the term Wrist-Finger Speed as a more appropriate factor title. The title "tapping factor" has been used because simple speed of tapping is one of the best markers of the factor; further loadings are in various measures of speed of wrist-finger motions (e.g., speed of simple movements of the fingers and/or the wrist, particularly repetitive movements which ask for little if any eye-hand coordination). So far the factor has been identified in at least six studies (1283, 618, 1563, 1039, 530, 535); in addition, Rimoldi (1200) found a very similar factor relating to wrist-finger tempo rather than speed.

Manual dexterity and finger dexterity originally have been treated as more or less synonymous trait terms. However, there is coercive evidence from several factor-analytic studies showing that the two "dexteri-

[1] The additional factor "Hand Aiming" found by Hempel and Fleishman (714) could be regarded as a composite of the factors Steadiness and Finger Dexterity (see below).

[2] In all tests of this type the subject has to "aim" carefully with his pencil, which led to the factor title "Aiming."

ties" are in fact two separate psychomotor aptitude factors. The Manual Dexterity factor (1477, 1563, 530, 535, 536, 714) loads speed and coordination of arm-hand movements in skillful manipulations of objects (e.g., speed and accuracy in placing or turning of objects, such as in the Minnesota Rate of Manipulation Test). In all but two of these analyses (538, 1563) a Finger Dexterity factor has been found too (see also 637, 689: the factor called "psychomotor precision ability"). Finger Dexterity relates to speed and accuracy in manipulating small objects with the fingers, whereas precision and speed of arm movements are unrelated to the factor. Typical marker tests are unit and bolt assembly and tweezer dexterity tests; the familiar pegboard tests seem to measure both Manual Dexterity and Finger Dexterity.

A Reaction Time factor accounting for speed of simple reaction to auditory or visual stimuli has been hypothesized already in several correlational studies (1248, 1285, 1286); factor-analytic evidence on such a factor is due to Seashore, et al. (1283), Thurstone (1416), Rimoldi (1200), and Fleishman (530). However, from the work of Cattell (240) this factor seems part of a much broader source trait involving, at its positive pole, fast speed of simple reaction, high alertness, an over-readiness to respond, and low endurance.

Last of the well-established factors in psychomotor aptitude tests is Steadiness, i.e., the ability to perform very precise arm-hand movements with little to no emphasis on speed.[3] Among its marker tests are the well-known tracing steadiness tests and stylus thrusting. The steadiness factor has been proved most clearly in two studies by Fleishman and Hempel (530, 714); Seashore, et al. (1284) have reported what may be three lower-order components of this

factor. According to Hempel and Fleishman (714) the Steadiness factor is uncorrelated with general static balance.

Besides these seven well-confirmed psychomotor aptitude factors several others are indicated, a few of which may be briefly mentioned: A factor interpreted as the skill in using the non-preferred hand has been found in two analyses by Greene (618) and called Ambidexterity; it has not yet been replicated by any other investigator. Carroll (193) reported a factor of Articulation Speed, loading rate of reading and speed of repeatedly articulating the same consonant. Further psychomotor speed and tempo factors found only once are: Speed of Arm Movements (530), Tempo of Large Movements of Limbs and Trunk, Tempo of Fast Movements, and Tempo of Hand Movements (1200).

According to Rimoldi's work on the factor structure of tempo measures, the various first-order tempo factors can be explained through a broad second-order factor Basic Motor Tempo which is practically uncorrelated with perceptual and intellective tempo and the Reaction Time factor. It is not known to which extent these findings on "personal tempo" can be generalized to hold for speed measures too. French (1550) has discussed some evidence on a possible speed factor involving a large variety of performances. In the case of cognitive performance measures a broad speed factor has been found by Davidson and Carroll (407); however, this may be only part of a still broader personality factor relating, besides speed of performance, to several other personality traits.

5. FACTORS IN THE REALM OF PERCEPTUAL AND INTELLECTUAL ABILITIES

The perceptual and intellectual skills constitute the oldest area of trait study and one most tied to process study. This is true not only from an historical perspective or in view of the body of accumulated results,

---

[3]The factor is different from general Psychomotor Coordination in that (1) only arm-hand movements are involved, and (2) the full stimulus pattern is known to the subject from the beginning.

but holds to an equal (if not greater) degree also in terms of the impact both fields have had on psychological theory and methodological advancement. As a matter of fact, the first instances of ever applying correlational techniques to behavioral data are found here (1090, 1556, 1336, 888), and early two-factor-analytic work took off from the study of intellective (and related) functions. Similarly, from an historical point of view, technical developments of factor-analytic methods took place with particular reference to the factorial analysis of higher-ability measures.

An excellent review of Spearman's two-factor theory of intelligence (1339) has been given by Dodd (423), and a later one by Jones (827). Early multifactor work on abilities has been summarized by Wolfle (1576) and Guilford (622); more recent reviews are those by Burt (168), Meili (1037), Vernon (1489), Guilford (626), Guilford and Merrifield (640), and Olèron (1116). A synthesis of research on ability factors up to 1950 has been presented by French (550). For the factors showing highest replicability according to French's survey, Cattell (241) has suggested a unifying reference system, the Universal Index (U.I.) of objective test factors, for convenient cross-reference. In addition, several special reviews on certain groups or "families" of intelligence factors have become available, such as Marron's (989) on reasoning abilities, Michael's (1055) on spatial orientation and visualization factors, and Thurstone's (1423) on factors involved in "visual thinking."

For simplicity and clarity of presentation the following discussion of intellective aptitude factors will be subdivided into five sections, viz.: perception; memory; semantic and symbolic proficiency; traits of fluency and flexibility; logical reasoning, problem-solving, and evaluation. As a matter of fact, no theoretical or final classificatory system shall be implied by this subdivision. In the absence of complete empirical evidence on the functional relationships between established mental ability factors, a large number of different classifications is indeed equally possible—and plausible. The sole purpose of the scheme adopted here is to facilitate presentation by employing a frame of reference directly relating to measurement operations.

FACTORS ISOLATED IN TESTS OF PERCEPTION AND "VISUAL THINKING"

Each factor confirmed in this "surface cluster" of aptitude variables can be placed in one of three fairly distinct subdomains, viz.: (1) speed of perception, (2) spatial visualization, and (3) Gestalt perception. Our discussion will proceed in this order, and brief reference to narrower group factors of perception will be made at the end.

Speed of Perception

Best confirmed among perceptual aptitude dimensions is the Perceptual Speed factor *P*. It is identical with the "Figural Identification" factor described by Guilford (626) and has been found in more than 30 factor analyses. The factor was first identified by Thurstone (1412, 1413, 1415, 1426, 561) and has since been demonstrated in practically every factor study in which speed tests of simple perceptual performances have been included (1562, 1477, 637, 1385, 433, 368, 1054, 1056). The essential characteristic of factor *P* is fast speed in comparing visual configurations. Principal marker tests are: "identical forms" (indicate which of five figures is identical to a standard), speed of mirror reading, dial and table reading, Guilford and Zimmerman's tests "spatial orientation I and II" (locate a small configuration, e.g. aerial photo, within a larger one containing the former). Thus Perceptual Speed is restricted to speed of performance on tasks emphasizing quick apprehension of a visual pattern and/or its identification among similar and therefore distracting configurations. The task in itself has to be fairly easy (given untimed conditions); otherwise the test will be loaded by one of the Closure factors (see below) rather than the Perceptual Speed factor.

A separate factor "Symbol Identification," similar to P but restricted to perceptual speed in tasks involving solely symbolic material, has been suggested by Guilford (626). In his monograph on aptitude factors, French (550) did not yet consider "Symbol Identification" a separate factor; this would be in line with Thurstone's finding of P loading both figural and symbolic identification tasks (1413, 1426) as well as with similar results obtained in the Army Air Forces analyses (637). Another possible, though very narrow, subfactor of P is "Speed of Symbol Discrimination" loading primarily standard cancellation tests (78, 382, 383). Whether this should be regarded a separate factor or simply part of P is still unclear; in some analyses P did in fact also load speed of cancellation scores (1415, 1562, 241).

Spatial Visualization

This second subdomain of visual thinking factors still presents some puzzling problems. There is ample evidence arguing for at least two separate factors of spatial reasoning; on the other hand, assuming three distinct factors provides for a much better interpretation of available results. In his review on visual thinking factors, Thurstone (1423) too distinguished between three spatial visualization factors, whereas Guilford (626, 627) still regards two of them as identical.

There is agreement between two-factor and three-factor theory of spatial reasoning as to the existence of a factor called Visualization (Vi). It has been found in nearly 30 independent analyses and corresponds to Thurstone's (1423) factor S_2. When first reported by Thurstone (1412), Vi appeared cooperative with the Spatial

Relations factor S; however, subsequent studies by Chein (343), Harrell (689), the USES (1477), Guilford and Lacey (637), and Fruchter (561: re-analysis of some of Thurstone's original data) left no doubt as to the distinctness of this factor. (See also 1209, 1056, 1057, 630, 631, 723, 1556, 1557, 857, 104.) Psychologically, Visualization represents a long-established aptitude concept, viz., the ability to imagine properly the movement or spatial displacement of a configuration or some of its parts. Its principal marker tests are: "mechanical movements" (given a drawing of a mechanism, indicate the direction of the resulting movement of one of the parts), "punched holes" (indicate what a folded and punched square sheet of paper would look like when again unfolded), Guilford-Zimmerman Spatial Visualization Test (visualize the final view of an object after its being rotated in a specified way), and the familiar paper form board and surface development tests.

The second factor in this area is the Spatial Relations factor S, Thurstone's (1423) S_1. Unlike Vi, tasks with high saturation in S do not require the subject to imagine spatial transformations of a configuration but to recognize "the identity of an object when it is seen from different angles" (1423) or in different positions. In other words: The Spatial Relations factor relates to individual differences in correctly perceiving spatial relationships between rigid configurations, whereas the Visualization factor accounts for aptitude differences in imagining, in spatial terms, the end result of a certain displacement (movement or rotation) of a configuration. The difference becomes apparent by comparing the salient variables of the two factors; for the Spatial Relations factor they are: "flags" and "cards" (indicate whether drawings show opposite or same side of a flag or card, respectively); "hands" (mark which drawings represent a left hand and which ones a right hand); "cubes" (given two drawings of a cube and assuming no cube will have two faces alike, indicate for each pair of drawings whether it shows the same or two different cubes).

Factor S was first reported by El Koussy (460) and by Thurstone (1412; cf. also Fruchter, 561), and it has been replicated since in about a dozen further analyses. (See also 1413, 1414, 1415, 1426, 382, 383, 1562, 78, 637: the factor called "Space II" in the analysis of Perceptual Battery II, 134, 387, 1147.)

The third spatial reasoning factor, Thurstone's (1423) S_3, is best called Spatial Orientation (SO). As Thurstone put it, SO relates to aptitude differences in thinking "about those spatial problems in which the body orientation of the observer is an essential part of the problem." This factor was reported for the first time by Guilford and Lacey (637) and subsequently, with good agreement in loading pattern, by Comrey (368), Michael (1054), Roff (1209), and Guilford (630, 631). Its chief markers are good performance on apparatus tasks involving complex compensatory reactions similar to those essential in navigating an airplane (Complex Coordination test, Rudder Control test; see Guilford and Lacey, 637), two-hand coordination, complex instrument comprehension, and good performance in the Guilford-Zimmerman Spatial Orientation Test (inferring one's own position in steering a boat from changes in the view one has of external reference points).

In terms of test content and psychological interpretation the three spatial reasoning factors differ markedly. In terms of objective statistical criteria, however, only Vi is established as a separate factor; S and SO may be two different factors (Thurstone's three-factor hypothesis) or one and the same (Guilford's two-factor hypothesis). The latter view is supported by four studies, each of which yielded a factor loading both S and SO markers (Michael, et al., 1056, 1057; Guilford & Lacey, 637: Perceptual Batteries I and II); secondly, no single study is known to the present reviewer in which both S and SO would have been obtained within the same matrix.

However, this does not necessarily verify the two-factor hypothesis. On the one hand, S and SO markers (which do not overlap) were never included within the same analysis but for the four studies mentioned before. So all depends upon how decisive these four analyses are in regard to the $S - SO$ question. Turning first to the results reported by Guilford and Lacey (637), we note that no Psychomotor Coordination factor has been identified in the analyses of Perceptual Batteries I and II; since SO is partly cooperative with PC, the factor found by Guilford and Lacey may well be S partly confounded with PC rather than a combined factor of Spatial Relations and Spatial Orientation. Regarding the remaining two analyses by Michael, et al. (1056, 1057), the decision is rendered somewhat difficult as rotation was not solely guided by simple structure criteria. Considering also the difference in test content between S and SO, the suggested distinction between a Spatial Relations and a Spatial Orientation factor is indeed very plausible, and ought to be tested in a crucial factor-analytic experiment.

Factors Found in Tests of Gestalt Perception

Factorization of tests of visual Gestalt perception consistently yielded two different "closure" factors, the Speed of Closure factor Cs (Thurstone's C_1) and the Flexibility of Closure Factor Cf (Thurstone's C_2).

Speed of Closure[4] loads performance on the Street Gestalt Test, speed of dark adaptation (identifying a dimly illuminated letter following light adaptation) and speed of semantic Gestalt completion ("mutilated word" test). When first isolated by Thur-

[4]Indexed as U.I.T. 3, Speed of Closure, by Cattell (241). Guilford (626) refers to the factor as "Visual Cognition," and French (550) calls it "Gestalt Perception." Note that the factor called "Speed and Strength of Closure" in Thurstone's (1416) perceptual study is not identical with factor Cs; it rather represents factor Cf confounded with S. Such confounding is easily understood from the high positive correlation between Cf and S (134, 1147).

stone (1416, 1422), it was called "speed of perception"; subsequent confirmation of the factor is due to Roff (1209), Botzum (134), Pemberton (1147), and Wilson, et al. (1557). The factor determines the speed of Gestalt organization and appears identical to Meili's factor "globalization" ("Ganzheit") (see Meili, 1036; Schaedeli, 1263).

The second closure factor, Flexibility of Closure[5] or *Cf,* accounts for differences in perceptual performance where the task is to abstract a given Gestalt from a distracting field in which it is embedded. This is in sharp contrast to factor *Cs,* which involves organizing hitherto unrelated configurations into a structured pattern exhibiting familiar Gestalt qualities. Factor *Cf* is Thurstone's factor "changing Gestalts" (Thurstone, 1416; also 1422), further confirmed by Roff (1209), Botzum (134), Pemberton (1147), and Frick, et al. (557). Chief markers of *Cf* are tests in which a familiar though hidden configuration has to be detected (hidden pictures, hidden numbers, hidden letters, Gottschaldt figures). A similar factor has been reported by Meili (1036; see also Schaedeli, 1263) and called "plasticity" (*Plastizität*).

In the two closure factors *Cs* and *Cf* we encounter another example of apparently pure ability dimensions which actually are components of considerably broader personality factors relating to both aptitude and temperament traits. According to Cattell (218, 240, 241), Speed of Closure and Flexibility of Closure each represent an aptitude component of the more comprehensive personality factors U.I.T. 17− and U.I.T. 19+, respectively. Similar results have been obtained by Pemberton (1148). Thurstone too was aware of a possible broader nature of the two closure factors (1423).

There is some evidence on what may be a subfactor of Verbal Closure[6] from a study by Pemberton (1147, 1148) and possibly also from Mooney (1067), and on a similar subfactor of Auditory Closure from the work of Karlin (843). However, these factors should not be accepted before sufficiently confirmed in new studies. Thus White's (1538) correlational study of auditory and visual closure tests does not support the notion of separate auditory and visual closure factors.

Minor Factors in Tests of Perception

Wittenborn (1562) reported an Attention factor relating to performance on tests such as "following directions," which require maintaining increased alertness ("attentiveness") over a longer period of time. A similar factor has been found in the analysis of Integration Tests in the Army Air Forces research (637) and by Roff (1209), who called it "directional thinking." Whether Attention actually represents a separate and unitary factor is still unknown; Süllwold's (1363) analysis, for example, would not support this notion.

A factor of Length (and Size) Estimation, specific to a rather narrow group of perceptual tasks, has been found repeatedly (Woodrow, 1579; Guilford & Lacey, 637; Roff, 1209; Guilford, et al., 631); its relation to other perceptual dimensions is not yet fully understood. Other narrow group factors found in perceptual tests are: a factor common to figure illusions (1416), a factor relating to rate of perceptual alternations such as in tests of reversible perspective (1416), a factor of movement detection (1209), a factor of attention to perceptual detail (e.g., 630), and a factor common to tests of sequential perception (successive exposition of the parts of a configuration; Roff, 1209).

REPRODUCTIVE ABILITIES

We owe to Spearman the fundamental distinction between merely reproductive, recall functions — or *anoegenetic* processes —

---

[5]Indexed as U.I.T. 4, Flexibility of Closure, by Cattell (241). This is Guilford's (626) factor "Figural Adaptive Flexibility" and French's (550) "Gestalt Flexibility."

[6]Called "Symbolic Cognition" by Guilford (626).

on the one hand, and judgmental processes capable of creating entirely new content — *noegenetic* abilities — on the other. Our topic in this section is the former — the abilities to call back and make available mental content already known.

Compared with other aptitude and ability areas, the multifactor analysis of memory functions has been somewhat neglected in the past; few studies (e.g., 188, 859, 1224) deal specifically with the memory domain. Tests of memory functions usually have been somewhat under-represented in factorial research on intellective abilities, and the measures utilized were mostly of the paired-associate learning type only. (The frequent emergence of a corresponding memory factor, which is best confirmed of all, may simply be attributable to this choice of memory measures.) Furthermore, available studies have been concerned in the main with "storage capacity" aspects of memory (i.e., the amount retained), and little is known about general aptitude factors involved in rate of learning.[7] This is true despite extensive multivariate research on learning processes (536, 1344, 1465), where the primary emphasis has been on discovering functions underlying the raw learning data — rather than on representing learning aptitude factors within the broader reference system of intellective ability factors.

The Associative Memory factor M (Cattell, 241: U.I.T. 7; Guilford, 626: "Rote Memory") was first reported by Anastasi (21, 22), and by Carlson (188), and has been successfully replicated since in about twenty further factor analyses. (See 193, 194, 579, 631, 859, 1224, 1412, 1413, 1414, 1426, 1562, 1564.) It primarily loads retention scores from paired-associate memory tests (memory for word-number pairs, number-number pairs, word-word pairs, figure-word pairs, etc.). Loadings in memory tests not following the paired-associate format (e.g., picture recall) are

considerably lower. Obviously M is not as broad a memory factor as it has been interpreted occasionally; it either is format-specific to paired-associate tests or, alternatively, relates to memory for non-meaningful material only.

If the latter is true, a separate factor of memory for meaningful material should exist. Such a factor has indeed been found by Roff (1209) and subsequently confirmed by Kelley (859); since both M and a Meaningful Memory factor appear within the same matrix in Kelley's results the hypothesis that M is mostly mechanical rote learning ability is given some support. From Thurstone's (1412) results, on the other hand, Meaningful Memory would appear but a component of M; however, not enough measures of memory for meaningful associations have been included in Thurstone's research to make it a crucial experiment in that respect.

A special Visual Memory factor has been reported a number of times (188, 637, 631, 859); it is restricted to memory for visual material, however, cutting across different test formats. Similarly, an Auditory Memory factor has been identified by Karlin (842).

There is some evidence on a fifth memory factor, viz. Span Memory. As yet the factor has emerged in three studies only[8] (1580, 56, 859, 1224); principal markers are memory span tests such as the familiar digit span measure. Still more specific are various scholastic and related attainment factors such as Mechanical Knowledge, Mathematics Background, and foreign language factors. Guilford (626) and French (550) have discussed their possible nature and pertinent factor analytic results.

FACTORS RELATING TO SEMANTIC AND SYMBOLIC PROFICIENCY

The two factors discussed in this section, Verbal Comprehension (V) and Numerical

---

[7]A promising start in this direction has recently been made by Allison (17).

[8]A corresponding group factor had already been reported by Moore in 1919.

Facility (N), are best confirmed of all aptitude factors known. As aptitude factors of basic proficiency in native language and figure work, respectively, V and N closely resemble achievement factors in English and arithmetic as taught in school. Their similar nature is also borne out by second-order analyses of primary aptitude factors which showed V and N to load on the same second-order factor (Botzum, 134: second-order factor B; Cattell, 258: second-order factor "crystallized ability"; see also Table 18-1).

The Verbal Comprehension Factor V^9 has been found in about 50 different factor analyses of aptitude measures. As a matter of fact, the present reviewer does not know of a single study in which verbal tests have been analyzed and V would not have been found. The Verbal Comprehension factor as defined through simple structure rotation was first reported by Thurstone (1412, 1413, 1414, 1420), Garrett (579; see also 1274, 21, 22) and Woodrow (1563). However, a similar factor was suggested as early as 1915 by Burt (156; see also 168). The factor has subsequently been found in most of the Army Air Forces analyses (637), in the USES studies (1477), and by many other investigators too numerous to be quoted individually. The chief markers of V are tests of vocabulary and reading comprehension, verbal analogies, and Thurstone's tests "reading I, II" (select two out of four statements which match a given proverb or quotation in meaning). Thus Verbal Comprehension relates to knowledge of words and their meaning as well as to application of this knowledge in understanding connected discourse. (Note that V also loads tests of grammar and spelling, e.g., 1412).

About equally confirmed is the Numerical Facility factor N (241: U.I.T. 10 (N): Number Facility) identifiable in no less than 40 analyses. It has been found in all

researches quoted above for the Verbal Comprehension factor and numerous times since. (For early group-factor-analytic results on "arithmetical ability" the reader is referred to the excellent review by Burt, 168). Factor N can best be described as the facility in performing elementary arithmetical operations (typically under speeded conditions). The factor does *not* determine higher mathematical skills or complex mathematical reasoning and only loads speed tests of elementary arithmetic (addition, subtraction, multiplication, division) and related tests. Loadings in number series or arithmetic reasoning tests, for example, are usually low to negligible.

FACTORS ISOLATED IN TESTS OF VERBAL FLUENCY AND FLEXIBILITY OF THINKING

This is the area of what Guilford (626, 628) has called "divergent thinking abilities." Tests defining these factors have an interesting common characteristic: There is no unique solution to an item but a whole class of possible responses; a subject's score is the number of different answers or some rated quality of answers he supplies out of this class (or simply the speed with which he is able to produce responses belonging to this class). This is in sharp contrast to what Guilford has called "convergent thinking abilities," in which case there is one single correct response only to each item.

(*i*) *Factors in verbal fluency tests.* Correlational and early factor-analytic work on verbal fluency dates back more than thirty years to the studies by Hargreaves (687), Cattell (261), Studman (1361), and others. Though still of a more exploratory nature, these first results already indicated a substantial correlation between verbal fluency abilities and certain temperament traits (see 239, 485). At present there is evidence of certainly two, and possibly four, distinct factors in verbal fluency tests; a brief summary of pertinent findings up to 1955 has been given in a report by Guilford and Christensen (628). Best

---

[9]Indexed as U.I.T. 13 (V), Verbal Knowledge, by Cattell (241). The factor "Eduction of Semantic Correlates" described by Guilford (626) is here considered part of V.

confirmed of all four is the Word Fluency factor W (Cattell, 241: factor U.I.T. 15). It was reported by Thurstone (1412, see also 561, 1413, 1426), and has been replicated since by several other investigators (78, 134, 193, 628, 641, 1147, 1148, 1557). The factor accounts for individual differences in the ability to rapidly produce words fulfilling specific symbolic or structural requirements. Important marker tests are: "prefixes" and "suffixes" (given a prefix or suffix, e.g., -tion, supply as many fitting words as possible), anagram tests, "four-letter words" (give as many four-letter words as possible), "first and last letters" (supply words with given first and last letter), and tests of word knowledge. Word Fluency is therefore quite different from Verbal Comprehension, although the two factors correlate positively in all obliquely rotated analyses: Verbal Comprehension accounts for individual differences in knowledge and understanding of both single words and connected discourse, whereas Word Fluency determines the ease of producing words belonging to a well-specified symbolic or structural class (with word meaning being of little if any importance). The difference between V and W thus is comparable to the distinction between "passive" and "active" vocabulary proficiency — a distinction very familiar to anyone learning a foreign language!

Psychologically related to Word Fluency is the Associational Fluency factor AF; however, it does not load simple fluency of word production performances (Thurstone's W) but concerns the facility of producing "isolated words meeting specific requirements of meaning" (628), i.e., "quality" rather than "fluency" of word production. This is readily seen from its principal markers "simile insertion" (complete similes such as: as . . . . as a fish) and "controlled associations" (supply several synonyms for a given word). The factor has as yet been identified in orthogonally rotated analyses only (561, 1556, 1557, 635, 628, 868). In two studies (1044, 1385),

Associational Fluency appears partly confounded with the Ideational Fluency factor.

The Ideational Fluency factor IF (Cattell, 241: U.I.T. 6) is the psychological equivalent of W at the level of production of ideas: it represents the ability which provides for rapid production of ideas fitting a given specification. As in W it is again the fluency (or "quantity") rather than linguistic "quality" of expression which relates to this factor. Variables with high loadings in IF are "topics" (list as many ideas as possible relating to a given topic), "brick uses" — fluency score (number of different uses of a brick listed by the subject), "plot titles" (similar fluency score). The factor has been found by Carroll (193), Bechtoldt (78, 76), Taylor (1385), Rogers (1212), and in several studies by Guilford (1556, 723, 1557, 635, 628, 104, 986, 557, 868, 1044). A factor very similar to IF in content, though presumably containing some Expressional Fluency as well, has been reported by Meili (1036) (see also 1504, 1261).

Evidence on a fourth fluency factor, called Expressional Fluency (EF), has been obtained by Carroll (193), Taylor (1385), and Guilford (628, 635, 868). In tests of EF the subject's task is not to produce ideas but to supply proper verbal expressions for ideas already stated or to find a suitable expression which would fit a given semantic frame of reference. Examples of such tests are "picture description" — quality rating (the subject is shown a picture for two minutes and subsequently has to talk about it for two minutes; score is the rated quality of verbal expression), "simile completion" (complete a given simile, e.g.: A woman's beauty is like the autumn, for it . . . . .), "four-word combinations" (given the initials of four words complete the phrase; e.g., w. . . . d. . . . y. . . . s. . . . , possible answer: *w*hat *d*id *y*ou *s*ay?).

Presumably related to Expressional Fluency, if not simply part of it, is a narrow factor common to tests in which the subject has to supply a name for an object, a concept, or a group of objects. Such a Naming factor has been found by Carroll (193), Kettner, et al. (868), and Guilford, et al. (640).

The Associational Fluency and Expressional Fluency factors are partly "cooperative"[10] in loading pattern. In the orthogonally rotated study by Johnson and Reynolds (809), for example, W, AF, and EF all contributed to the same single factor "verbal fluency." However, oblique rotation of the primaries followed by second-order analysis would place such a broad verbal fluency factor at the second-order rather than first-order factor level (see 416). Whereas Word Fluency and Associational Fluency appear more or less pure aptitude factors (1147, 416, 629), there is evidence that both Ideational Fluency and Expressional Fluency are part of broader personality dimensions involving both aptitude and non-aptitude traits (200, 213, 240, 416, 1210, 629, 796). Thus Ideational Fluency is a component of the personality factor U.I.T. 21 ("Exuberance vs. Suppressibility"[11]); similarly, Expressional Fluency related to the temperament factor F, "Surgency vs. Desurgency," found repeatedly in questionnaire data.

(ii) Factors in tests of flexibility of thinking. The factor-analytic exploration of flexibility tests is largely due to Guilford (626, 1556, 1557, 635, 557, 868, 986, 241). Two main factors have been found in this area, "Semantic Spontaneous Flexibility" and "Symbolic Adaptive Flexibility." The former may be described as the facility of producing a diversity of ideas. It differs from Ideational Fluency in that the emphasis is not on quantity but on *diversity* of ideas produced. The second factor was found to load tests in which the task is to restructure a given problem or situation. As yet, both factors appear rather narrow in content and their relationship to possibly related personality factors still remains to be investigated.

THE STRUCTURE OF PROBLEM-SOLVING, INDUCTIVE, DEDUCTIVE, AND EVALUATIVE ABILITIES

Factors of Logical Reasoning

Despite the great interest factor-analysts have shown in this area, there is still some doubt as to the true number and nature of logical reasoning factors. Of the three factors indicated, Deduction (D), Induction (I), and Reasoning (R), only D is certainly distinct, whereas I and R may or may not represent separate factors. In the following, Thurstone's (1412, 1421) three-factor resolution will be adopted. Since part of the confusion is due to inconsistent factor identifications in the past, each identification has been carefully cross-checked on the basis of all pertinent data published by the individual author.

The Deduction factor D (241: U.I. 4; 626: "Logical Evaluation") can be identified with certainty in seven analyses only (1412, 134, 630, 723, 867, 105, 557). It involves reasoning from the general to the specific, the ability to test the correctness of a meaningful conclusion by applying general principles to the individual case. Markers of Deduction are various syllogism tests in which the task is to select (rather than invent) the correct conclusion. For example: Given two premises, indicate which one of several alternative conclusions is correct. Or: Among syllogisms of meaningless word content and occasionally false reasoning, mark those in which the conclusion does not follow from the given premises. In addition, the factor shows minor loadings in tests of figure classification.

By contrast, the Induction factor I[12]

---

[10]Two factors are called "cooperative" if they have marker variables in common (240).

[11]See page 576 for a description of this factor.

[12]Indexed as factor U.I.T. 5 by Cattell (241). Guilford (626) does not regard Induction as a unitary factor (see his factors "Education of Structural Patterns" and "Education of Symbolic Patterns").

relates to reasoning from the specific to the general, in the sense of discovering a rule or principle in a given material and subsequently applying it correctly. Typical tests of I are: "series continuation" (the familiar number-series or letter-series tests), Thurstone's "marks" test (discover the rule according to which a mark has been placed in each of several rows of meaningless symbols and apply this rule by indicating in which position the mark should be placed in the next row), figure matrix tests, Thurstone's "secret writing" test (solve a letter-number code and use it subsequently), Thurstone's "pedigrees" test (answer questions about family relationships given a pedigree chart covering three generations).

The Induction factor was first reported by Thurstone (1412), and can be identified in at least fourteen further analyses[13]. Also the factor "complexity" ("Komplexität") reported by Meili (1036; see also 1504, 1261) may be largely Induction; however, the identification is tentative only since the factor also loads some tests typical of the Reasoning factor.

Although identifiable in no less than 26 different analyses, the Reasoning factor R (626: "General Reasoning") is still difficult to interpret psychologically (1412, 1421, 636). Evidence on factor R is available from the work of Thurstone (1412: the factor referred to as "restrictive task ability"; 1413: the factor called I), and Guilford (631, 630, 641, 1557, 723, 867, 628, 104, 557, 784, 1044), and from several analyses in the Army Air Forces research (637, 368, 1054). Principal marker tests of the Reasoning factor are: tests of arithmetic reasoning (which require little specific mathematical training), "mechanical movements"

(described under factor S), "numerical judgment" (select one of four alternative answers to an arithmetic problem through quickly estimating the result), "ship destination" (compute the distance of a ship from the port by considering several variables simultaneously), "necessary facts" (state missing conditions needed for solving a problem). No generally satisfactory interpretation has yet been found for the factor. It may simply represent a general convergent reasoning factor the way Thurstone (1421) conceived of it; alternatively R may constitute a principal determinant of general intelligence (Spearman's g) at the first-order level. (Such an interpretation would seem particularly applicable to some of the Army Air Forces analyses in which R appears to represent all abstract reasoning variance not accounted for by more specific factors such as N, V, and S). Several other hypotheses concerning the psychological nature of R have recently been summarized by Guilford, et al. (636).

Further research is needed in this area to clarify the nature of the Reasoning factor. As yet there are only three studies (1412, 867, 640) in which both I and R can be identified within the same matrix, and practically all instances of factorial confounding in the area of reasoning abilities are in I and R, yielding a composite "induction-reasoning" factor. The present reviewer is nevertheless inclined to regard the two factors as different; however, it should be borne in mind that no final decision is yet possible.

Further Factors in Tests of Problem-Solving and Evaluation

Analysis of tests of practical, common-sense reasoning repeatedly yielded a factor called Judgment (J), which bears a striking resemblance to the notion of "practical intelligence." Both French (550) and Guilford (626) regarded J a distinct aptitude factor. It was found first in the Army Air Forces analyses (637: analysis of Judg-

---

[13]Chein (343: the factor called "Structural"), Thurstone (1415), Thurstone and Thurstone (1426: in analyses II the factor labeled R), Coombs (383), Goodman (604), Hall and Robinson (678), Taylor (1385: the factor called R), Roff (1209), Botzum (134), Pemberton (1147: the factor called R). In Guilford's work the factor is referred to as "Eduction of Patterns" (Kettner, et al., 867, 868; Guilford, et al., 640).

ment Tests, Foresight and Planning Tests I and II); subsequent confirmation is due to Corter (387), Guilford, et al. (630), Berger, et al. (104) and Kettner, et al. (868). Chief markers are tests in which the subject has to select, on common-sense grounds, the best solution to a given predicament or has to point out deficiencies in a plan. As French (550) has put it, *J* presents the ability to make "wise judgments to practical problems where some estimation or guessing as to the most likely occurrences is necessary."

Two psychologically very interesting factors have been isolated by Guilford in research on creative thinking abilities: Originality and Sensitivity to Problems. Both have as yet been found in orthogonally rotated analyses only, and it still remains to be seen if they can be replicated in oblique solutions too. The Originality factor *O* (1556, 1557, 635, 628, 104, 557, 868, 986, 1044) loads tests in which the subject is to invent uncommon and clever responses (e.g.: suggesting clever plot titles, thinking of unusual uses of common objects, suggesting improvements for a familiar apparatus such as a telephone, imagining remote consequences of hypothetical occurrences, investing a graphic symbol to depict a phrase, etc.). The factor seems related to the more general personality factor U.I.T. 25— (called: "Tense Inflexidia vs. Less Imaginative Realism"; see 796), which in turn resembles Eysenck's (475) "Psychoticism" factor. As yet there is only indirect evidence supporting such a broader interpretation of *O* (see Guilford, et al., 629; Marks, et al., 986), but it appears an hypothesis worthwhile following up in future research.

The Sensitivity to Problems factor (1556, 1557, 868, 986, 1044) relates to recognizing the existence of a problem; it loads tests in which the individual is asked to point out problems that may occur in the use of a familiar object, in the functioning of certain social institutions, and the like. At present no direct temperament correlates of the Sensitivity to Problems factor are known, although broader personality associations seem rather likely.

A third possible factor in the area of problem-solving behavior is Integration (Guilford & Lacey, 637; see French, 550). According to French (549), it represents the ability "simultaneously to bear in mind and combine or integrate several conditions, premises, or rules." A similar factor has been found by Süllwold (1363, 1364), but further replication is still needed. Repeated factor analyses of "double performance" tests by Pawlik (1138), including also some of Sullwold's tests, did not support the notion of a single Integration factor.

Guilford (626, 640) has described several narrower group factors in tests of reasoning and evaluation, some of which may in fact be subfactors of aptitude dimensions discussed earlier in this section. The three "Eduction of Relations" factors (Eduction of Figural Relations, Eduction of Symbolic Relations, Eduction of Semantic Relations), for example, and the factor "Eduction of Symbolic Correlates" are likely to be subfactors of Induction, the factor "Symbol Manipulation" a subfactor of Deduction. Similarly, the nature of the factor called "Planning" (637, 550, 627: "Perceptual Foresight" and "Conceptual Foresight") will need further empirical clarification, particularly concerning its relationship to (or distinction from) the Judgment factor. Other group factors recognized by Guilford are "Experiential Evaluation" (appraising the aspects of a given situation in terms of their internal consistency), "Elaboration" (supplying details to complete a given outline or skeleton form), and "Ordering" (arranging steps or events in a reasonable sequence; see also French, 550).

6. ABILITY FACTORS AT THE SECOND-ORDER LEVEL

Some psychologists may feel that up to this point we have discussed the royal court without mentioning the monarch himself. For too many practicing psychologists, in particular, important issues begin and end with the king of abilities—intelligence. Granted this importance of intelligence—which lies in theory as well as practice—one recognizes that, for reasons given below, it is better approached through discussion of second-order factor analyses.

Even apart from this concern with higher-order factors one recognizes that since Thurstone's classical studies on primary mental abilities, factor analysts have been interested in knowing the correlations between aptitude factors. As a matter of fact, isolating primary factors without knowing, at the same time, the degree and direction of correlation existing between them may yield as incomplete a knowledge of mental organization as (in the case of comparative anatomy) isolated study of individual fossils, without taking into account their taxonomic, local, and historic distance, will fail to give an adequate insight into phylogenetics. As pointed out in Chapter 6 on factor analysis, there are two ways of evaluating factor intercorrelation: the empirically determined coefficient of correlation between two (fallible) factor estimates, and the cosine of the exact angle between factor vectors in multifactor space as obtained from oblique simple structure rotation. Far too little information of this latter type has accumulated, and indeed there is a greater lack for intellective factors than for personality factors. And, although it is the true factor (cosine) relations that would give us the clearest second-order information, it is on the correlations of partially valid scales or batteries that we shall often have to depend.

In the attempt to obtain a preliminary correlational picture of the mutual interrelationships, at least of the most important (and best confirmed) intellective ability factors, the present reviewer prepared a matrix of factor intercorrelations averaged over available obliquely rotated analyses (78, 134, 193, 194, 382, 383, 579, 1147, 1385, 1413, 1415, 1416, 1426, 1477). Owing to lack of results for some of the factors, this search has to be limited to the following 12 dimensions: $P, S, Cs, Cf, M, V, N, W, IF, I, D,$ and R. The resulting matrix is presented in Table 18-1. A value is put between parentheses if it is based upon one single study only. Empty cells indicate that the corresponding correlations could not be determined.

Owing to the many blank cells, the matrix in Table 18-1 cannot be factored directly, and a brief discussion of the obtained correlations will be given instead. Note that

TABLE 18-1

AVERAGED INTERCORRELATIONS OF 12 PRIMARY MENTAL ABILITY FACTORS

	P	S	Cs	Cf	M	V	N	W	IF	I	D	R
P Perceptual Speed	—	+27	(+47)	(+12)	+14	+13	+14	+21	(+08)	+08		−02
S Spatial Relations		—	+05	+60	+14	+15	+20	+15	(−07)	+28	(+28)	+10
Cs Speed of Closure			—	+13		(−06)	(−38)	−15		+08	(+05)	
Cf Flexibility of Closure				—		(−01)	(+26)	+24		+13	(+26)	
M Associative Memory					—	+15	+14	+23	−04	+12		+04
V Verbal Comprehension						—	+23	+23	+11	+26		+15
N Numerical Facility							—	+28	(−01)	+13	(−07)	−04
W Word Fluency								—	+13	+16	(−05)	+12
IF Ideational Fluency									—	(+08)		
I Induction										—	(+50)	(+18)
D Deduction											—	
R Reasoning												—

almost all correlations are positive, as Spearman originally claimed. If we disregard correlations lower than .10, there remains but one instance of negatively correlated primaries, viz., Word Fluency (*W*) and Speed of Closure (*Cs*). Most correlations are comparatively low, i.e., .20 or less. The highest *r* obtained is between Spatial Relations (*S*) and Flexibility of Closure (*Cf*), which would argue for considerable overlap between the two in terms of underlying perceptual mechanisms. The high correlation of +.50 between Induction and Deduction is in line with some theories of a single logical reasoning factor, largely a function of *D, I,* and *R.* However, not too much reliance should be placed in this one finding, which resulted in a single study only (133). The only other two factors showing substantial correlation with *I* are Spatial Relations and Verbal Comprehension. These results are in good agreement with Cattell's (258) notion of a single second-order factor of "fluid general ability." A second "cluster" of primaries seems to comprise *V, N,* and *W,* which could correspond to Cattell's "crystallized general ability." However, with blanks and no personality factors included in Table 18-1, this interpretation has to be tentative. Associative Memory apparently is more or less independent of most primary abilities; its only "significant" correlation is with Word Fluency. There is some possibility also of a third cluster of primaries, specific to perception, which contains *P, S,* and *Cf.*

Table 18-1 certainly does not support the notion of a single general ability factor like Spearman's (1339) "*g.*" As Rimoldi (1201) was able to show, "*g*" at best resembles the largest unrotated second-order factor obtained upon analyzing intercorrelations between the primaries, and this resemblance vanishes, once second-order factors are rotated for simple structure. This is in agreement with the early results of Thurstone (1416, 1423), and applied psychologists will be well advised to reconsider current intelligence testing practices on the background of these findings.

7. INTEGRATION OF STRUCTURAL AND DEVELOPMENTAL CONCEPTS IN THE THEORY OF FLUID AND CRYSTALLIZED INTELLIGENCE

(BY JOHN L. HORN, UNIVERSITY OF DENVER)

Encountering the mass of facts presented by research on primary mental abilities, the reader may be in danger of recoiling in confusion, unable to integrate the complex findings within a theoretical context. That a problem exists, through the psychometrist and statistician failing to integrate with general psychological testing, is shown by the deficient impact, despite its experimental precision, of psychometric work upon clinical, educational, and general developmental theory. For example, sixty years after Spearman's tremendous methodological contribution, fifty years after Burt's lucid refinements of statement, and thirty years after Thurstone's general structuring of the ability field, the intelligence tests still most popularly used in schools and clinics remain on relatively crude "omnibus" designs and rest on a priori subtests, factored, if at all, *after* the construction. Of course, this prolonged cultural lag may well be largely due to the failure of many psychology departments to give students training and confidence in multivariate experimental principles, such as factor analysis, upon which these vital developments hinge. But the blame must also go, in part, to the factor analytic researcher's inability or unwillingness to bring his abstractions into relation with the verbal theories and developmental viewpoints which constitute the main dialogue of his field. By and large, the factorial findings on abilities have not been linked, in theory, to the independent variables widely believed to be operating in development, to learning theory, and to the notions handled in other branches of psychology. The well-replicated findings from multivariate research have simply not been brought creatively into the arena of discussion of general psychology.

A noteworthy exception to this general stagnation is the theory of fluid and crystallized intelligence (205, 240, 258). In this, Cattell put forward integrating principles showing how, in accordance with certain major influences operating in development, primary-level abilities become organized at two distinct levels. Yet, rather ironically, until quite recently, this theory was all but ignored by factor analytic researchers, and one might say that even Cattell "left it on the shelf"! This suspended germination may have been partly due to the theory not being "pushed" and partly because its proper experimental confirmation demands analyses of such large scope that, prior to recent advances in computer technology, checking was not very practicable. For example, adequate test of the major structural provisions of the theory alone requires that not only representative samples of primary abilities be chosen for factoring, but also that primary factors other than abilities be judiciously, strategically included to define the hyperplanes against which the general abilities can be rotated.

But, no matter what the diversity of reasons for the neglect of this challenging theory may have been, it is evidently at length exciting widespread attention. First, we see in the present decade that many of the empirical implications of the fluid and crystallized theory have been spelled out and research has been aimed at testing crucial hypotheses (258, 264a, 749, 749a, 749b, 750a, 750b, 750c). Although certain intriguing vacant spots, as discussed below, still appear in the pattern of evidence generated by such researches, the available results now give some definite shape to the main concepts involved in regard to the organization of human abilities. Perhaps more importantly, this work has already gone far—and promises to go farther—toward establishing rapprochement between multivariate theories and

findings and those of, for example, developmental, physiological, educational, and animal learning areas.

The main theses of fluid and crystallized general abilities theory may be briefly stated as follows. First, structurally, it states that in a broad sampling of human abilities, there are two major dimensions, both included in the area semantically called "intelligence." In fact, because of this tie of the new with the more traditional concepts of intelligence, the term "intelligence" is used to tag both of the dimensions in question: hence, in verbal discussion the terms *fluid intelligence* (abbreviated Gf) and *crystallized intelligence* (abbreviated Gc). At a purely theoretical-verbal level, the concepts here have some resemblances to Hebb's notions about general abilities labeled simply A and B. But unlike Hebb's theory, wherein ability A is an unmeasured and unmeasurable (in behavioral terms) physiological potential, the fluid-crystallized theory specifies definite and distinct behavioral referents for the two major concepts.

At work in both the fluid and the crystallized intelligence is that relation-perceiving, correlate-educing capacity which Spearman first described as the essence of "g." This power, according to further aspects of the theory, is determined by neural and related physiological factors, as laid down initially by heredity and intrauterine influences. It is subsequently modified by injuries, dietary aids and deficiencies, physical exercise, oxygen lacks, etc., i.e., influences which directly affect structure and function at the biological level. Relation eduction becomes manifest in all areas of sensory discrimination, assists all kinds of cognitive learning, and functions in all of what come to be called intellectual abilities.

Although fluid intelligence is the most direct correlate of basic neural-physiological capacity and is the purest behavioral representation of this, it should not be mistaken for a measure of hereditary potential as such. In fact, the safest referent for *Gf* is not brain physiological capacity at all but a *pattern of behavior* resulting from the interaction of this capacity with a broad, common, environmental-developmental set of influences. The distinction between *Gf* and *Gc* is thus not conceived as a difference between physiological and experiential origin, but between two kinds of experience in which the physiological potential becomes expressed.

As was noted in Section 5, measured intelligence may be regarded as manifested through both anoegenetic and noegenetic processes. More specifically, it is manifested in the recall of concepts previously attained or discovered and in the behavior of actually attaining or discovering concepts. In either case, it is necessary to perceive relationships among stimulus elements (what Spearman called "fundaments") and to educe relational consequences. The detailed processes involved here are perhaps numerous and complex, but at a fairly general level, they may be classified as basically either (a) *anlage* functions, reflecting the perceptual limits of an individual, or (b) *generalized solution instruments,* which Cattell (258) has conveniently designated "aids."

An example of an anlage function is *span of apprehension,* as described by Spearman. An organism, it seems, can retain only a finite number of distinct elements in immediate awareness on which to exercise judgment. In the adult human, this number varies from less than four elements to around 10 or 11, as the research on what was previously described as memory span (*Ms*) has demonstrated. Other anlage functions may be what Hearnshaw has described as temporal integration, what Piaget and Elkind have discussed as de-centration, what Guilford and his co-workers have identified as adaptive flexibility, etc. Anlage functions are involved in anoegenetic processes, as noted above in reference to *Ms*, but they are also involved in the reasoning factors described in Section 6.

For example, in solving a fairly difficult matrices problem, one must keep in mind a set of relations for the horizontal array, a set for the vertical array, and a relation between these two sets of relations, indicated perhaps in the main diagonal. If one can only retain four distinct elements in immediate awareness, he may be unable to solve this kind of problem even when he can clearly perceive the relations in each separate section of the problem.

Continuing with the above example, an *aid* may be seen, from one angle, as a technique which enables one to cope, by learned codes or judgment habits, with the realities of his anlage function. If a person's span of apprehension is six elements, say, and yet the problems he encounters require him to immediately apprehend seven elements (a telephone number, for example), then the "trick" of coding elements into sets (a set of three and a set of four in the case of a telephone number, e.g., 352-4739) is an aid which enables the person to "get by," so to speak, with his limited span of apprehension. Aids may range from such simple "tricks" to highly involved procedures, such as the calculus or other procedures of mathematics, enabling us to solve problems we could not otherwise solve. Aids are what Harlow described as "learning sets," often what Piaget discusses as "operations," what Bruner and his co-workers have treated as "strategies," etc.

As the above examples illustrate, aids may be seen as ranging along a continuum from those which are one's own idiosyncratic, personally acquired techniques for dealing with problems to those which, although they were once the private inventions of individuals, have become the prized common possessions of all in a culture. These examples also illustrate that aids may be seen as along a continuum from those which virtually everyone has an opportunity to acquire to those available to only a relatively few people who have passed through a number of progressively more selective programs — notably organized educational programs — aimed at producing acculturation.

Now the principal distinction between fluid and crystallized intelligence has to do with their place in this latter continuum. Both Gf and Gc are defined in terms of awareness of concepts and use of aids. And both reflect, in some degree, anlage functions. If we think in terms of variance components, demonstrated for the factors in various tests, relatively more of the variance of Gf (compared to Gc) reflects anlage functions and use of aids in the immediate environmental situation. On the other hand, a larger proportion of variance in Gc involves recall of concepts previously acquired — through previous anlage function and use of aids. However, the major difference between Gf and Gc is that the concepts and aids involved in the former are of a kind that reflect relatively *common* experiences, acquirable anywhere in our physical world, whereas the concepts and aids which define crystallized intelligence more nearly represent degree of immersion in a particular culture.

It is apparent that level of acculturation reached indicates much more than merely neural-physiological capacity and that, at any stage in development, it is determined by factors other than those contributed by one's basic ability. Some of these factors are non-intellectual attributes of the individual, such as his motivation, his personality integration, his physical health, etc. And some of them are factors over which he has no control whatsoever, such as the competency of his teachers, the stability of his community, etc. Furthermore, the state of being advanced in acculturation tends to beget further acculturation, and for a number of reasons. In part, this can be ascribed to positive transfer in learning, as Ferguson (501a) pointed out. The Numerical Facility (N) factor described in Section 5 is an example of an ability in which positive transfer in devel-

opment has rather obviously operated, as Guttman demonstrated by precise methods. Reproduced in Diagram 18-1 is a schematic analysis showing how Cattell uses these concepts to account for the genesis of Gc from Gf plus opportunity, motivation and memory. This diagram also illustrates the development of primary abilities through the joint action of Gf directly and Gc by further positive transfer. The expected factor loading patterns are merely suggestive.

The growth of the Gc pattern is by no means only a consequence of transfer: societal and educational influences have other effects. For example, educational systems generally require that one pass elementary arithmetic before he take calculus. In general, the society requires that one pass through one level of an acculturation process before he is allowed to go on to another level. This procedure is pedagogically defended on the grounds that it ensures positive transfer in an orderly progression, although any teacher knows that the system does not always bring about the desired outcome. For present purposes, however, the point is that the level of acculturation is the effect of many influences other than neural-physiological capacity expressed in the fluid intelligence available at a given stage, as Diagram 18-1 reminds us. The upshot is, as expressed in a formula elsewhere (258), that the culturally acquired pattern crystallizes in a form common to many people and reaches relative levels different from those of the fluid ability levels possessed by these people.

One might argue that the product of progressive acculturation in the above sense is really not intelligence but something else, like achievement. But this is a quibble which does not clearly recognize the facts of measurement and the difference between judgmental achievements and those merely due to rote memory. Any ability (i.e., as a behavioral attribute) represents achievement in some sense. And, as a matter of fact, many of what are acknowledged to be "good" tests of intelligence — such as the Stanford-Binet, Lorge Thorndike, Concept Mastery, etc. — rather obviously involve substantial portions of variance due to just the kind of socially organized and individually memorized acculturation influences described above.

Moreover, it is apparent that the ability to use an aid instilled by acculturation — such as algebra, for example — is intelligence in the sense that it enables one better to cope with a wide and generalized range of problems.

It would require much more space than is available here properly to delimit and

DIAGRAM 18-1. Theoretical Statement of Relations of Fluid Intelligence (Culture Fair) to Crystallized Intelligence (Traditional Test) Sub-Tests and Factors

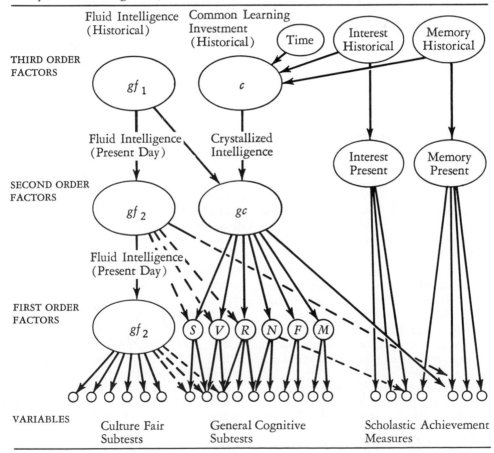

Arrows indicate direction of influence, literally loadings. Continuous arrows show major loadings.

define the above area of common growth and thus to do justice to the theory (258, 749). But perhaps enough has been said to indicate the kind of correlational and developmental organization of primary abilities which the theory predicts. Thus, mainly the primary abilities defined by the limits of anlage functioning in the immediate situation, and involving the use of aids that could have been learned by virtually all people tested, should be found covered by the factor of fluid intelligence. The fundaments or basic contents operated upon in the tasks set in these primaries should be either very novel concepts, with which no one would have had experience prior to testing, or, at the opposite extreme, perceptions, etc., so over-experienced ("overlearned" says too much) by everyone that experience, per se, contributes little to individual difference variance. On the other hand, primaries indicating the limits of the individual's acculturation, and involving the use of aids which are clearly produced by the educational process, would be hypothesized to define the crystallized general intelligence factor. In this case, the fundaments subjected to the perceptual or reasoning process could be somewhat esoteric, when viewed in a different cultural perspective. Since the tasks defining most primaries are not pure representations of either of the kinds of process here specified, it is to be expected that *Gf* and *Gc* will be *cooperative factors,* both determining *some* of the variance on many primary abilities. It is for this reason that Cattell insisted that the two would need to be identified by certain new, relatively "pure" tests, in company with non-ability primaries, to permit the broad patterns to stand out against a ground.

Perhaps an example will help to clarify the essential measurement distinction drawn here. Thus consider the following analogy subtest items and suppose that both are administered to adults 25-35 years of age.

Broom-Floor::Spoon-?
Fork   Table   Soup   Dish
Hippocrates-Galen::Aeschylus-?
Greece   Euripides   Pericles   Heraclitus

Both are to some extent ambiguous (as are all ability items) in the sense that one might defend more than one answer and yet it is evident that both require ability to perceive relations among concepts. However, the first problem rather obviously involves concepts that almost all adults aged 25-35 in this country *could,* as far as experiences are concerned, know (which is not to say that all do). On the other hand, it is reasonable to suppose that a substantial proportion of 25-35-year-old adults never met with the opportunity to acquire the concepts of the second problem.[14]

Thus, the essential task for most people in the first problem is one of working out the best relation to complete the analogy, while for many people, the task in the second problem could never get to the point of working out a relation: yet if you are aware of the meanings of the fundaments in the second problem, the analogy itself is no more difficult than the first problem. Thus both problems indicate analogic reasoning to some extent, but the second much more clearly reflects degree of acculturation as well.

Horn has brought together a wide array of evidence bearing on the above hypotheses, including factor analytic results at what can be regarded as the second stratum or, at least, a higher order than primary. Included in his summary are several factor analyses of the Wechsler scales (112, 358, 360), the WAIS and WISC (361, 362), Saunders (1256a, 1259), as well as studies, e.g., by Botzum (134), Corter (387), Denton and Taylor (416), Rimoldi (1201), Doppelt, Martin and Adkins and others, in which primary factors

---

[14]Modeled, incidentally, on the well-known Concept Mastery test which was used in Terman's study of the gifted.

(albeit rather small samples of these) were defined in accordance with the research cited in previous sections. The consensus suggested by this review indicates that: (1) fluid intelligence is most purely defined by Induction (*I*), Deduction (*D*), Figural Relations (*CFR*[15], e.g., Matrices), Figural Classifications (*CFC*) and Memory Span (*Ms*). (2) Crystallized intelligence is most purely represented by Verbal Comprehension (*V*), Mechanical Knowledge (*Mk*), Numerical Facility (*N*), Experiential Evaluation (*EMS*) and Judgment (*J*). (3) *Gf* and *Gc* are highly cooperative on General Reasoning (*R*), Logical Evaluation (*Rs*; e.g., Syllogisms), and Semantic Relations (*CMR*; e.g., Analogies). (4) Crystallized intelligence is distinct from, but highly cooperative with, a general fluency dimension involving Word Fluency (*Fw*), Ideational Fluency (*Fi*), Associational Fluency (*Fa*), Expressional Fluency (*Fe*) and Symbol Adaptive Flexibility. (5) Fluid intelligence is distinct from, but somewhat cooperative with a general visualization dimension defined by Visualization (*Vz*), Speed of Closure (*Cs*), Flexibility of Closure (*Cf*), Spatial Orientation (*S*), Figural Adaptive Flexibility (*DFT*), and Visual Memory (*MFU*). (6) None of these factors is characterized by exclusively speeded or exclusively unspeeded tasks and, in fact, although the evidence leaves much to be desired, there is suggestion of separate intellectual and non-intellectual speediness dimensions along the lines suggested by Rimoldi (1200).

Cattell's (258) study, however, was the first to be conceptually aimed and methodologically designed specifically for a check on the fluid-crystallized theory. In this, he factored split-half forms of the primaries furnished by the Science Research Associates PMA battery — viz., *I, V, S, Fw* and *N* —

along with the subtests of the Culture Fair Test, representing *CFR* and *CFC,* and split-half forms of the *HSPQ*. This splitting, providing 44 variables in all, 26 of which were non-ability variables, ensured that primaries would first be located. The sample was 277 junior high school students. The 44 variables were intercorrelated, 22 primary factors were extracted and carefully rotated to oblique simple structure, whence the intercorrelations between primaries were determined from the transformation matrix. When these correlations were factored, two general factors having the properties of fluid and crystallized dimensions were found along with the second order factors of Exvia, Anxiety, Independence and Control (Super Ego) in the questionnaire realm. The fluid dimension was defined by *CFR, CFC* and *S,* while the crystallized involved *V, N, Fw,* and *I.*

The Horn (749) and Horn-Cattell (750b) studies involved 59 ability and personality measures administered to a sample of 297 adults in an age range of from 15 to 61. Primary abilities were measured by combining the scores on two or more tests found to load a factor in previous research. In all, 31 primaries were estimated, of which 11 were non-ability dimensions. The intercorrelations between these primaries were determined in the usual manner and the second order analysis based upon these intercorrelations. The basic results from this study are shown in Table 18-2.

Most recently, Horn (749a) and Horn and Bramble (749b) have completed studies verifying the structure shown in Table 18-2 and demonstrating that fluid intelligence is subject to short-period fluctuations (as in a state defined as in Chapter 11) not found in crystallized intelligence. Tests for the various factors were administered on 10 separate occasions over a period of 5 days, and newly developed techniques (745, 750d, 1467, Chapters 11 and 20) were employed to distinguish trait and state

---

[15]Symbols here, where not coordinate with those of earlier sections, are taken from French, Ekstrom, and Price (553); French (550); or Guilford and Merrifield (640).

TABLE 18-2

OBLIQUE STRUCTURE FOR PRIMARY MENTAL ABILITY FACTORS
(after Horn, 749)

Primary Factor Symbol and Name		Second-Order Factors and Loadings[a]				
		Gf	Gc	Gv	Gs	F
I	Induction	55		28		
CFR	Figural Relations	48		43		
Ma	Associative Memory	32				
ISp	Intellectual Speed	30				
IL	Intellectual Level	47				
R	General Reasoning	26	30			
CMR	Semantic Relations	30	50			20
Rs	Formal Reasoning	29	40			
N	Number Facility	20	29		34	
V	Verbal Comprehension		69			26
Mk	Mechanical Knowledge		48	25		
EMS	Experiential Evaluation		43		23	
Fi	Ideational Fluency		25		25	42
Fa	Associational Fluency		35			60
S	Spatial Orientation			50		−20
Vz	Visualization			58		
Cs	Speed of Closure	21		36		
Cf	Flexibility of Closure			48		
DFT	Figural Adaptive Flexibility			40		
P	Perceptual Speed				48	
Sc	Speed Copying				63	
Pf	Productive Flexibility		−23		46	

[a]Factor loadings below .20 and decimal points have been omitted in order to achieve maximum clarity of presentation.

variance. Both the fluid and crystallized dimensions appeared by these analyses, as well as general visualization and fluency, and all manifested substantial trait variance. But, relatively, the fluid ability subtests showed more significant day-to-day covariation than did the crystallized abilities.

Cattell (264a) has recently completed an ability study on 150 four- and five-year-olds. The results suggest that fluid and crystallized factors are distinguishable even in early childhood. The fluid factor was defined primarily by the Culture Fair Test and a few markers from the California Test of Intelligence. Crystallized intelligence appeared in reading, vocabulary and number tasks. A dimension approximating

the general visualization function also appeared. This involved some of the subtests from the Culture Fair, Mazes, and Picture Absurdities.

The general Gf-Gc theory argues that both sets of abilities improve rapidly in childhood, though at decelerating rates, but that improvement in Gf slows to a stop at the point where physical growth ceases, whence it declines at first slowly and then more rapidly as aging continues, whereas Gc improves into adulthood, perhaps into late maturity, as long as acculturation stays ahead, so to speak, of attrition due to loss of memory, degeneration of anlage functions, etc. Horn (749) and Horn and Cattell (750a, 750c) examined this hypothesis using their sample of 297 adults aged 15 to 61, divided into 5 age groupings. In one set of analyses they used the primary abilities listed in Table 18-2, in the other they used the second-order factors and included sex, education and various factors as covariates. Their analyses of variance and covariance showed significant age differences favoring the young in pure fluid primaries and in the fluid dimension but significant differences favoring the older subjects in pure crystallized primaries and in the crystallized second-order factor.

The primaries in which (as suggested by experiment) subjects are able to use alternative mechanisms, either Gf or Gc, and which split their variance about equally between Gf and Gc (i.e., the highly cooperative primaries of Table 18-2) were found neither to decline systematically nor to improve in adulthood. Likewise, a general omnibus measure of intelligence, involving all putative measures of intelligence, neither declined nor improved. It was shown that by defining a "general intelligence test" with suitable proportions of Gf and Gc, intelligence could be made to decline somewhat with age, as had been found in the well-known studies of Miles, Conrad and Jones, and Lorge, or to improve, as in the apparently contradictory findings of Bayley and Oden, Bradway and Thompson and Owens. The general visualization skills were found to be a maximum for 20-28-year-olds and to drop off systematically on either side of this peak. There were no systematic age trends for the general speediness dimension, some of the primaries of this showing improvement with age (e.g., speediness in numerical operations), some showing decline.

In summary, we can say today that the results, over all, provide definite support for the Gf-Gc theory. In so doing, they give clearer understanding of the development and structure of intelligence. It is to be hoped that multivariate research in the next few years will be directed toward filling some of the intriguing gaps in the evidence described above.

8. SUMMARY
(BY DR. PAWLIK)

(1) The preceding review is an attempt towards a clarification of the nature and interrelationships of replicated factors of individual differences in ability and aptitude traits. Special attention is paid to careful, objective identification of factors between studies in order to arrive at a firm basis of established ability dimensions from which hypotheses can be deduced and submitted to new multivariate experiments. At the same time a number of open problems are pointed out, with regard to both matters of factor identification and factor interpretation. They should be given particular consideration in future factor analytic studies of ability traits.

(2) The survey of factor analytic findings is organized in terms of three major subdivisions: factors of sensory functioning, psychomotor performances, and intellectual abilities, the latter being further subdivided into sections on perceptual, memory, semantic and symbolic proficiency, fluency, flexibility and logical thinking factors. For each trait area the replicated factors are reviewed; in addition, respective minor or subfactors (differing from the former either in behavioral breadth or in rate of replication) are briefly discussed.

(3) Throughout the review the theoretical position is held that ability and temperamental traits, though investigated more or less independently in the past, should not be regarded as mutually orthogonal on *a priori* grounds. Thus a number of factors are described which span across these two trait modalities, i.e., account for both intellectual *and* temperamental traits.

(4) Finally, correlations among primary aptitudes are considered and the second-order structure which these generate, giving rise to at least two general intelligence factors.

(5) Space did not allow us to deal with the vast literature on educational achievement factors and on factors in specific in-

telligence test batteries. Here the following leads may be helpful:

Factor analyses of reading and spelling ability tests have been reported by Langsam (818), Davis (408), Richardson (1195), and Knoell and Harris (879), of musical aptitude tests by Tamaoka (1378), Drake (426), and Wing (1559), and of specific occupational aptitude tests by Hellfritzsch (708), Friedman (559), Hale (668), and Andrew (35), for example. Second, there exist a large number of analyses of various standard intelligence test batteries, such as of the Stanford-Binet test (175, 820, 821, 1586) or the Wechsler tests (362, 411, 866, 1199, 1257). On factor analyses of specific achievement and scholastic attainment tests, see Murray (1091), Baker, et al. (51), Beezhold (89), Edwards (451), and Bartlett, et al. (64), for example.

(6) (Summary, by Professor Horn, of Section 7) The main theoretical development with implications for intelligence test practice over the last 25 years arises

in the theory of fluid and crystallized general ability. Four specifically designed researches, as well as the re-analyses of older data, confirm two general ability factors (besides visualization and speed) across the general cognitive ability realm. Their differences are traced developmentally, physiologically, culturally, and in daily variability and age curves across the adult span. Culture Fair Test developments stand on the theoretical basis of the fluid general intelligence factor.

(7) Our review of abilities has also been restricted to factors found in adult populations and school children. Available results on pre-school children were summarized in 1960 by Myers and Dingman; aptitude factors in infants have been investigated by Richards and Nelson (1193) and Bell (90). Evidence on the controversial matter of age development of aptitude factors will be found, for example, in the studies by Balinski (56), Burt (170), and Sumita and Ichitani (1365).

CHAPTER 19 Methods and Findings in
Experimentally Based
Personality Theory

JOHN R. NESSELROADE
KARL H. DELHEES
University of Illinois

1. METHODS AND FIELDS OF OBSERVATION AND ANALYSIS (BY THE EDITOR)

No one is likely to make the error of asserting that technological development in society is a precise reflection of the level of basic science in the corresponding area. Nevertheless, as has been suggested elsewhere, the level of technological development is an acid test of whether the theory alleged to supply logical substance to a given area of science is genuine or a mass of bogus verbiage. Surely, nowhere in science has there been such a discrepancy between, on the one hand, the volumes of pseudo-theory, and, on the other, the impotence to do anything that a science should claim to do, than in the area of personality theory at the beginning of this century. This is true despite the fact that *some* of the personality theory in the early part of the century, though not experimentally based, was, like Freud's, essentially empirical in approach and thoroughly scientific in intent. It nevertheless reached a level more noted for popular interest than scientific

dependability and insight. The complete lack of experimental foundation, as we understand that foundation in other sciences, in the work of Freud, Jung, Adler, and others in the clinical area, and their equivalents in the non-clinical area of observation, is evident in two main ways. First, the ability to predict and to control behavior, as in therapy, remains at an extremely low level of effectiveness and, secondly, the various theoretical writings themselves show disagreement extending to absolute fundamentals. The clash of opinions in the early twentieth century in the area of personality theory is loud with unprovable statements and untestable concepts and theories. As to the first, namely, the capacity to make lawful prediction, the literature is now full of instances of virtually zero agreement between highly trained psychiatrists and psychotherapists in their evaluations and predictions from the same data. Another blow to this phase of verbal theory came when an era of wishful thinking regarding the practical effectiveness of psychotherapy came to an end with the thunderclap of Eysenck's demonstration (474a) of the virtual ineffectiveness of current therapy and Meehl's (1026) evidence on the very erratic nature of diagnosis. The disillusionment was completed in the follow-up of these inquiries by Colby (367b), Gilbert (597a), Gendlin (582a), Rotter (1226a), and Keislar (869a), while such ancillary approaches as that of Fiedler (509, 511) bore out the same conclusion from another angle.

By contrast, and by the same touchstone of technological effectiveness, the newer experimental developments in personality theory, from multivariate and other research approaches, have already developed a thoroughly meaningful body of theory. Indeed, if one compares personality theory with learning theory in this respect, it is probable that personality theory as now rooted in refined measurement would show the more positive contributions, in terms of practically effective predictions and procedures in education and industry and the meaningfulness of clinical diagnosis. Most sciences have made their initial real progress by weighing and measurement and by the development of taxonomy. By these standards of normal scientific growth, psychology got off to a misdirected start, but enough psychologists have had enough insight and integrity to back off from this false start, couched in verbose theoretical literature, and to readdress themselves to the problems of taxonomy and measurement. Not that anyone wants to stop at taxonomy itself, but all viable laws regarding maturation and learning in personality have to begin with a meaningful depiction of the personality at a given moment of time. Measurement is not enough, for measurement needs additionally to be organically related to structures and functions. It needs valid and central concepts, though these concepts have themselves to be developed by experimental iteration out of measurement.

The importance of a central, functional measurement is most quickly realized if one reflects how great is the number of psychologists concerned to measure this and that, and how infinite are the variables which they might conceivably measure. At first, therefore, it was not surprising that an "open season" on measurement produced only the appearance of a vast, misguided activity. One suspects that part of this was due to a systematic tendency of less mature psychologists to seek originality by measuring something different than anyone else had measured. This insured that any research would be so new that it had no connection with the body of research which had gone on before! Such shallow and perverted originality has manifested itself all too frequently in psychology and the social sciences generally. Instead of each investigator standing on the shoulders of his predecessor, as Newton described it, resulting in an architectonic growth as seen in the physical sciences, our landscape in the behavioral sciences has typically been a shanty town of cluttered, one-story efforts abandoned and unrelated to any other psychologist's developments.

As far as personality theory is concerned, we have to come to the 1940-1965 generation of effort before the isolation of meaningful functional unities by multivariate experimental methods began to provide an array of central, measureable concepts upon which developmental, social, cross-cultural, and other studies could be based. The present chapter appropriately begins with a study of these structures and the experimental evidences from which they are derived. Nesselroade and Delhees have themselves made major contributions to this field, Nesselroade in the realm of discovering and checking source traits in objective behavioral measurements among children, and Delhees in checking personality structure across joint normal and mental-hospital populations.

A valuable advance in the last decade of this phase of structural measurement has been the provision of better technical methods for deciding the number of factors, for rotation to reliably unique resolutions, and for recognizing and matching factor patterns in the light of the transformations they undergo from study to study. A high point of this last decade has thus been the integration of dozens of studies, using the most sophisticated technical methods, by Hundleby, Pawlik, and Cattell (796), following the early leads of Cattell (213, 226, 240), French (550, 551), Guilford (627), and Thurstone (1412, 1416, 1424). Since Nesselroade and Delhees properly wish to push ahead to the theoretical vistas in developmental and other fields which this opens up, they have built upon the Hundleby compendium and only briefly given independent evidence on matching principles and findings.

The number of actual measurement scales launched in the area of personality and interest, even if we take only questionnaires, is, of course, a fabulous one. Consequently, the writers have not attempted to adumbrate this tedious jungle, but have cut their way through it to functional measurement concepts. They have elsewhere examined carefully the scientific contribution of these voluminous productions, but here they have permitted themselves to penetrate quickly to measurements of functional unities based on multivariate experimental analysis. That is to say, the chapter is in no sense a catalogue of behavioral tests or even a list of laboratory experiments with all variables that have ever been used in personality research. Instead, it is a very carefully weighed, comprehensive, but ultimately evaluative and restrictive statement of what has claim to be significant in terms of established unitary patterns and functions.

Since it is not the intention of the writers to stop at the stage of structure and taxonomy, they have proceeded to developmental and general theory. But they have properly reminded the reader that the harvest of results from meaningful measurement in the area of personality change, maturation, learning, social criterion relationships, etc., is so recent and scanty that the empirical foundation of their theoretical statements bears no comparison with that underlying their structural and taxonomic

conclusions. Psychoanalysts and some more speculative theorists have often accused multivariate experimental personality theory of restricting itself to personality structure and measurement. Actually, the vision of the researchers here has been as broad as any, but by the time they have built firm foundations where they are needed, there has been no time to go out and get criterion and developmental relationships — and general developmental theorists have been extraordinarily slow to perceive and avail themselves of the advantages of functional measurement concepts. Just in the last five years, however, there has begun an exploration of personality genetics, development, and learning in terms of these meaningful concepts, and it has already shown an altogether higher return of significant regularities and laws than was obtained by the miscellany of previous measures. These longitudinal and learning theories occupy the last three sections of the present chapter.

A multivariate experimentalist with a broad approach has some four main models in terms of which he can operationally look for structure: (a) the concept of unity of action in the form of a correlation cluster or surface trait, (b) a functional unity as a simple structure factor or source trait, (c) the recognition of a modal pattern or type, (d) the entity which we call a process or repeating sequence. At various points in this handbook (Chapters 6, 10, 20, and 21) each of these concepts is examined with care, setting out more precisely the mathematical model involved and its implications for analysis procedures. Beyond these four, the experimental psychologist at present encounters no models of major importance, and rightly will not accept a verbal concept which cannot be brought to the formal experimental test of recognition variously illustrated in these four. Unless and until more complex mathematico-statistical developments occur, they represent the four cornerstones of any sound taxonomy. Any verbal taxonomy which plans to become operational and to yield substantive evidence by experiment must sooner or later find itself operating with concepts reduced formally to one of these kinds of patterns, or of one or two variations of them having some additional special properties or assumptions.

To reduce the risk that the above will be misunderstood as being narrower or more rigid than it actually is, the reader must recognize that each formal entity has several varieties. For example, all of these forms can be recognized either as patterns across individual difference data, and illustrated by a source trait in R-technique factor analysis, or as a pattern within the changes within one individual over time, as when we recognize a unique source trait by P technique. With presently available research results falling mainly in the R-technique domain, the emphasis in illustration is bound to be largely upon the source traits (simple structure factors from R technique). The isolation and reliable recognition of types, by the precise methods of Chapter 9, has barely begun, and most type concepts at the moment, as in psychopathology, whatever their alleged theoretical model, actually still rest on the work of the unaided human eye and memory. The recognition of processes, isolated as common processes by correlational and sequential methods as described in Chapter 11, is also in its infancy. Except for some fragmentary studies in Cattell's laboratory at factoring out proto-processes (Chapter 11) and the work of Tucker (Chapter 16, 1465) and Fleishman and Hempel (534, 536) on factoring learning processes, the important processes in personality change, e.g., the process of repression or projection, of adolescent development, of absorption into the group, etc., still rest on a purely observational, clinical type of judgment, and have barely been brought within the scope of true experiment. On the other hand, the fact that little more space is given to the surface trait findings than to type and process findings is *not* due to dearth of substantive research. It is due rather to the fact, brought out in Chapter 20, that the surface trait or correlation cluster is fundamentally an artificial and unstable unity, the boundaries of which are all too often consciously or unconsciously drawn by the experimenter himself. The elementary simplicity of concept and computation has nevertheless attracted many to the use of cluster analytic procedures and has been responsible for much of the confusion regarding the definition of such concepts as extraversion, introversion, intelligence, the authoritarian personality, etc.

Conceptually, therefore, a good deal of the discussion of actual substantive findings here is necessarily concerned with source traits, i.e., simple structure factors, with the higher stratum factors which can be derived from them, and with the linear and non-linear modes of interaction which occur among the traits and between the traits and environment. As a possibly helpful orientation to the general approach of Nesselroade and Delhees, one should perhaps point out, especially to the mathematical statistician, that the factor model is here used with the many additional requirements of a *scientific* model. In particular, the various factors obtained in personality data fall into several quite distinct concepts, as follows:

(1) According to the stimuli and situational conditions of the measurement of variables themselves, factors divided according to *modality* into ability traits, temperament traits, and dynamic traits, symbolized by A, T, and D in the main specification equations.

(2) A class of instrument factors connected with modes of data observation and a class of role factors which are concerned with variance contributed to the expression of a trait in a rather specialized set of environmental situations. These are commonly indicated by the symbols I and R in the specification equation.

(3) A major division of traits by combined area of expression of response and method of observation into (a) traits observed in the everyday life situations of behavior, measured by some form of life-

behavior recording or rating by observers, and symbolized as arising from L data, i.e., life-record data. (b) Traits based on introspective reaction of the individual to his own behavior, i.e., on self-evaluative responses, partly in the consulting room and partly in questionnaires. This we shall call the realm of Q data. (c) Structure based on objective behavior, which avoids the self-evaluation of Q data but retains the "test" character of a controlled experimental situation. This we shall call objective behavioral test data, or T data, for short.

(4) There are also important distinctions between common traits and unique traits, i.e., patterns unique to an individual, between traits and states, and other distinctions which will be drawn at a finer technical level in the course of this chapter.

The concept of an instrument factor is not quite to be identified with an area of observation (as defined by the L, Q, and T media), because each medium may generate several instrument factors, the set being peculiar to itself. A simple one-to-one correspondence of factor traits from the three media is also upset by a difference of stratum or order, due to differing breadth of the variables themselves, analogous to difference of "grain" size in a photograph. Fortunately, as the authors show, light is beginning to dawn here in the form of a recognition that second-order factors in the questionnaire realm are likely to be first-order factors in the T-data realm. However, these problems need not be further anticipated in this introductory section.

The main model, applied in much of the data and conceptual development available today has therefore been that of the source trait as a simple structure factor and the prediction of any specific piece of behavior from a linear and additive combination of scores on the personality and ability factors found. For the purpose of the present chapter, the general specification equation familiar from Chapter 6 and several other chapters in this handbook is written in a symbolism which helps us to remember the sense of the personality setting. The re-

sponse is symbolized by a_j (for "act"), in a response to a situation j; the traits are represented by A for abilities, T for temperament traits, D for dynamic traits, S for state, and R, for role or instrument factor. (Sometimes in more specific treatment, I is used for instrument factor.) The factor loadings are represented by b's for *behavioral indices*, since they show how the factors influence behavior in that particular setting as follows (for an individual i):

$$(1)\ a_{ji} = b_{jA_1} A_{1i} + \ldots + b_{jAx} A_{xi} + b_{jT_1} T_{1i} \\ + \ldots + b_{jTy} T_{yi} + b_{jD1} D_{1i} + \ldots \\ + b_{jDz} D_{zi} + b_{jS1} S_{1i} + \ldots + b_{jSk} S_{ki} \\ + b_{jR1} R_{1i} + \ldots + b_{jRl} R_{li}$$

Since Professor Horn's Chapter 20 makes a special study of the dynamic traits in personality, in terms of the peculiar complexities of dynamic concepts, little is said about the dynamic structure factors in the present chapter. Essentially, this chapter deals with what might be called *general* personality factor traits, i.e., factors found in the most general arrays of behavioral variables. Some of these turn out to be dynamic factors, but at present little has been done to assert a basis of distinction among the subvarieties of the general personality factors.

2. *L* DATA: PERSONALITY STRUCTURE IN LIFE RECORD AND CLINICAL OBSERVATION

As mentioned in the introduction, the basic data of personality research are obtained exclusively from three principal media—elsewhere (240, 796) designated as L, Q, and T. In this and the two succeeding sections, a brief and necessarily limited discussion of results from these sources of quantifiable concepts is presented, along with some ideas about their integration to the study of personality.

The pursuit of strategically valuable personality dimensions by multivariate experiment may lead in several directions. Their common jumping-off place is the

matrix of intercorrelations which summarizes the extent to which each of the *n* observed variables is linearly related to the
other *n*−1. For example, various cluster
search methods (240, 1016, 1017, 1454)
can be used to determine surface traits
(240), i.e., subsets of variables which covary.
There are a number of reasons why the
inquiring researcher should not form his
concepts directly from the correlation
matrix, but the one most pertinent to the
present discussion is that "surface traits,"
i.e., the sets of variables which have high
homogeneity and form a correlation cluster,
cannot be regarded as the best patterns for
study. Not only do they tend to be factorially complex, but they tend to overlap each
other in irregular patterns. While any such
correlation cluster may be initially unob-
jectionable as a *descriptive* behavioral pattern, the simple structure model considers
them only as overlapping surface traits
beneath which are source traits (240) −
simple structure factors − whose discovery
is one of the basic aims of multivariate
experimental personality research.

The initial exploratory factor analyses of
a given domain should begin with a set of
guiding hypotheses to provide some
assurance of an adequate sampling of relevant variables. Thurstone (1412), for
example, began his primary mental abilities investigation with a set of hypotheses
created from then-present knowledge of
that particular domain of performance. His
results supported some of these hypotheses
and suggested modification or discard of
others. The importance of a clear rationale
to guide the selection of variables for an
effective multivariate study cannot be overemphasized, and at the outset of research it
may be the notion of a "representation"
of the domain.

In this section, we are concerned primarily with the medium of *L* or life-criterion
data, one form of which is behavior ratings.
The behavior of ultimate concern here is
that of the subject in his life situation.
Ideally, these data would be obtained from

accurate, comprehensive life records of the
subject, but, unfortunately, the nearest we
can get to this kind of information, aside
from a comparatively few bits and pieces,
such as the number of times Jones reported
for sick call during his three years of military service and the frequency of Freddie's
being sent to the principal, is to employ an
intermediary to rate the subject on the
variables relevant to the research project.

Although substantial progress has been
made in this field by Cattell (213, 226,
240), Degan (413), Digman (419), Hammond (684a), Kelly and Fiske (858b), Lorr
and his associates (956, 957), Norman
(1100, 1101), Peterson (1153), Schaie
(1264a), Tupes and his associates (1469,
1470, 1471, 1472), and others with a substantial agreement as shown by Cattell's
1957 survey (240), it has nevertheless been
clearly recognized by Cattell and Digman
(281) and by Campbell and Fiske (183),
that instrument ("method") factors enter
to distort findings as powerfully in this
field as in *Q* data or anywhere else. In fact,
Cattell (250) has shown the presence of
"refraction factors," i.e., variance patterns
introduced into ratings, relative to *Q* data
factors, due to the behavior being refracted
through the perceptions of the rater. In
spite of this − or rather when the instrument factors are recognized and set aside −
the agreement of *L* and *Q* data factors is
good, as shown in Diagram 19-1.

L data results have often been accepted
as the criterion against which to judge the
validity of results obtained in other media.
This unfortunate tendency to assume a
"generalization of accuracy" from the true
life record to that of mere rating data,
which are a special, distorted form of it,
needs to be watched and evaluated in the
light of needed syntheses of constructs
emerging from the various observational
media.

It has been strongly urged by Cattell and
put in practice in his own work (213, 226,
240), that the multivariate experimental
analysis of personality should start un-

biased by older clinical theories. His designs have begun as deliberate representation designs, arguing that *L* data are ideal for invoking the *personality sphere* concept (240) for determining the initial domain of behaviors to be sampled, since a population of behaviors which "covers" the total domain of personality is immediately available in language. In other words, those guarantee a surer initial sampling of variables.

Taking verbal behavior as the basis, a systematic reduction of over 4,000 words found descriptive of personality by Allport and Odbert (18a) has provided a stratified sample of the parent population of personality variables. The end result has been 42 bipolar variables (36 of which

DIAGRAM 19-1. Factor Plot of *F* (Surgency) and *H* (Parmia) Obtained When Instrument Factors Are Accounted for (After Cattell, 250)

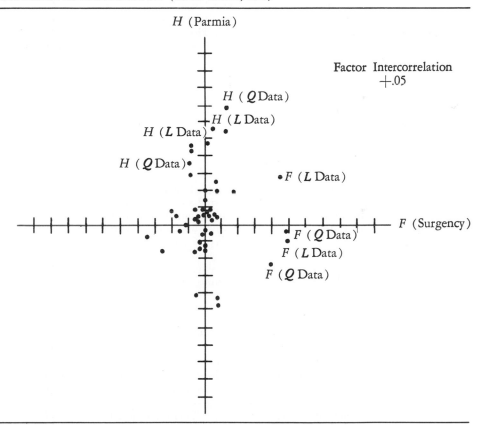

aspects of a person's behavior which affect the behavior of others can be assumed to have their verbal symbols existing in the language. Although the possibility exists in theory for developing a representative sampling in other media of behavior, e.g., miniature behavioral situations (*T* data), it seems that language and therefore ratings were centroids of correlation clusters emerging from the initial term reduction analysis) such as adaptable vs. rigid, assertive vs. submissive, and happy vs. sad, to be used in rating studies.

These bipolar variables, in a series of interrelated studies (213, 226, 240), yielded some 12 to 15 factors, which were tenta-

TABLE 19-1

SALIENT VARIABLES LOADING ON SOURCE TRAIT *A* (CYCLOTHYMIA)
(From *Personality and Motivation Structure and Measurement* by Raymond B. Cattell, © 1957
by Harcourt, Brace & World, Inc. and reproduced with their permission.)

Cyclothymic Pole		Schizothymic Pole
1. Easy-going	vs.	Obstructive, cantankerous
2. Adaptable (in habits)	vs.	Inflexible, rigid
3. Warmhearted, attentive to people	vs.	Cool, indifferent
4. Frank, placid	vs.	Close-mouthed, secretive, anxious
5. Emotional, expressive	vs.	Reserved
6. Trustful, credulous	vs.	Suspicious
7. Impulsive, generous	vs.	Close, cautious
8. Cooperative, self-effacing	vs.	Hostile, egotistical

TABLE 19-2

SALIENT VARIABLES LOADING ON SOURCE TRAIT *C* (EGO STRENGTH)
(From *Personality and Motivation Structure and Measurement* by Raymond B. Cattell, © 1957
by Harcourt, Brace & World, Inc. and reproduced with their permission.)

Ego Strength Pole		Ego Weakness Pole
1. Emotionally stable	vs.	Emotional, dissatisfied
2. Free of neurotic symptoms	vs.	Showing a variety of neurotic symptoms
3. Not hypochondriacal	vs.	Hypochondriacal, plaintive
4. Realistic about life	vs.	Evasive, immature, autistic
5. Unworried	vs.	Worrying, anxious
6. Steadfast, self-controlled	vs.	Changeable
7. Calm, patient	vs.	Excitable, impatient
8. Persevering and thorough	vs.	Quitting, careless

TABLE 19-3

SALIENT VARIABLES LOADING ON SOURCE TRAIT *E* (DOMINANCE)
(From *Personality and Motivation Structure and Measurement* by Raymond B. Cattell, © 1957
by Harcourt, Brace & World, Inc. and reproduced with their permission.)

Dominance Pole		Submissiveness Pole
1. Self-assertive, confident	vs.	Submissive, unsure
2. Boastful, conceited	vs.	Modest, retiring
3. Aggressive, pugnacious	vs.	Complaisant
4. Extrapunitive	vs.	Impunitive, intropunitive
5. Vigorous, forceful	vs.	Meek, quiet
6. Willful, egotistical	vs.	Obedient
7. Rather solemn or unhappy	vs.	Lighthearted, cheerful
8. Adventurous	vs.	Timid, retiring

tively identified and labeled *A, B, C,* etc., in decreasing order of variance magnitude. These obliquely rotated, simple-structure factors were presumed effectively to "span the space" of the personality sphere. Space precludes even a superficial examination of these source traits here except to say that they have confirmed such clinical concepts as Ego Strength, Schizothyme temperament, etc., and added a rich variety of new concepts. The reader wishing to fish in deeper waters is referred to other sources (213, 226, 240). Tables 19-1, 19-2, and 19-3, which present the salient features of *A, C,* and *E,* will, however, give the reader an idea of the characteristic flavor of *L* data source traits. These factors serve the double function of (a) providing a set of measurable personality dimensions to be integrated into a system, and (b) furnishing hypotheses to aid the systematic extension of personality research into the *Q* and *T* media.

An issue which has cut research on personality structure into two camps has grown out of the position taken by Eysenck, (472, 474, 486), Becker (85, 87), Peterson (1152), and others that three or four factors suffice to represent the important concepts of personality, and, on the other hand, that taken by Burt (159, 161), Thurstone (1424), Cattell (240), Guilford (627), and others that the statistical requirements indicate a dozen to 20 factors. Technical advance has been such that there should be no question that the first-named investigators are underfactoring, and it remains only to examine their notion that in grossly underfactoring they are somehow approximating the second-order factors which emerge from refactoring the complete set of simple structure primaries. Underfactoring, as Thurstone (1420), Cattell (261), and Guilford (625) have all pointed out, ignores valuable chunks of variance, needed to define the earlier rotated factors, which would be extracted with the later factors. This is clear to anyone who has unsuccessfully tried to carry out a clean simple-structure rotation with an insufficient number of factors, and then, with the inclusion of one or more additional factors, watched a substantially tidier resolution of axes appear.

When those using technically unacceptable underextraction claim that their first few factors are Extraversion, Anxiety, Cortertia, etc., found at the second order from rating primaries (240) or *Q* data primaries (608, 744, 848, 850, 1265), one must point out that their "pseudo-second-stratum" factors are apt to be rotationally obscure, from the standpoint of both (a) significant simple structure, and (b) precise psychological interpretation. The transformation of variable loadings by the Cattell-White (261) or Schmid-Leiman (1272) procedures directly from the second order by:

$$(2)\ V_{fpII} = V_{fp1}\, V_{fp2}$$
$$\text{(Cattell-White)}$$
$$(3)\ V_{fpII} = V_{fp1}\, (V_{fp2} : U_2)$$
$$\text{(Schmid-Leiman)}$$

(Formula 3 assumes either one second-order factor or a set of uncorrelated second-order factors.)

is quite unlikely to repeat, upon the variables, the simple structure which the second-stratum factors have on the primaries (261).

Despite the various instrument factor intrusions, most good simple structure analyses of ratings yield the same (conceptual) 10 to 20 primaries and 6 to 8 second-order factors in ratings as we shall now be concerned with in *Q* data.

3. *Q* DATA: PERSONALITY STRUCTURE DETERMINED BY FACTORING AND CLUSTERING OF QUESTIONNAIRE MEASURES

Q data (questionnaires, inventories, self-report scales, etc.), because of the ease of instrument construction and data gathering, especially with students, has occupied the center ring in personality research for the past three or so decades. We have no intention of trying to mention, let alone catalogue, the untold number of Q data *instruments* that have sprung into existence during this interval. Although many, e.g., MMPI (Minnesota Multiphasic Personality Inventory, 701) CPI (California Psychological Inventory, 610), EPPS (Edwards Personal Preference Schedule, 449), 16P.F. (16 Personality Factor Questionnaire, 329), and GZTS (Guilford-Zimmerman Temperament Survey, 642) are at least currently viable instruments, practicing psychologists have been saved much by the fact that a fair number of questionnaire scales do not survive even the first attempt at cross-validation.

At the risk of oversimplifying, one can speak broadly of two approaches to constructing questionnaires. Given a domain (unfortunately, sometimes poorly specified) of items, a subset can be brought together to form a measuring instrument either (1) because of their statistical relationships to each other or (2) by reason of their relationships to external criteria. Parenthetically, one may conceive of a third approach combining aspects of (1) and (2), as in the case, for example, of combining factor analysis and criterion rotation (473, 486), or subsequent "purification" of empirically constructed scales.

The first approach—by the inherent structure found experimentally among the item-response behaviors—can be further split into at least two procedures: (a) selecting items on the basis of their intercorrelations (homogeneity), and (b) selecting items after a factor analysis (including rotation) to measure a well-replicated factor. The difference between (a) and (b) is most briefly designated that between surface trait and source trait.

Questionnaire development oriented to outside criteria (e.g., MMPI, Strong Interest Blank) is structurally similar to that of factored scales to the extent that both seek high validity (in the one case correlation with the external criterion, in the other correlation with the factor) instead of high homogeneity. The similarity ends here, however. Any data, with or without conceptual bases, is grist for the empirical mill as long as it correlates with the criterion. Such "special purpose scales" (Cattell, 240) may be effective for their special purposes, but from the standpoint of meaning and therefore more scientific predictive use, they are unknown mixtures of factorially pure source traits. Thus, while such atheoretic devices may be useful for selection purposes, their explanatory power must, by their very nature, be sharply limited. It might be argued that a theoretical base for such a scale will gradually accumulate through its utilization in diverse projects, but its inherent complexity—like that of herbal remedies in medicine—renders such an outcome unlikely. After thousands of experiments, the Rorschach signs can be used to indicate the probability of this or that diagnosis, but no one knows why.

The factored scale, on the other hand, depends on a prior global research effort designed to (1) find a personality structure, (2) clarify and extend its interpretation, and (3) determine its predictive efficacy against various criteria. One cannot state a priori that measurements on a given factor will discriminate among specified groups. If a factor has been firmly established in a series of studies, both with respect to the stability of its loading pattern and its psychological interpretation, one can then hypothesize that it will discriminate significantly between x and y and proceed to test this empirically.

Since weighted linear combinations of factor scores have repeatedly been shown to discriminate among specified groups as significantly as scales constructed on special purpose or face validity principles, there are theoretical advantages to using the former, which can have weights adopted to circumstances and meaning. Recently, there have been attempts to understand the surface trait and special purpose scales in terms of the source trait scales, as exemplified by Specht's (1342a) factoring of the MMPI in company with the 16P.F. Several MMPI scales can be predicted substantially by the "normal" personality traits in the 16P.F., but others involve specifically pathological clusters. In either case, it has been suggested (263b) that a principle of "depth psychometry," in which individuals' scores are obtained simultaneously on the pathological surface traits and on the general personality factors which explain their variance so that an individual and dynamic understanding is gained for a particular pathological surface trait profile, would be clinically illuminating.

Lest the reader wrongly form the impression that the proponents of factor-analytic development of scales form a monolithic technical front against "barbaric" empiricism, unchecked intuition, and shortsighted "homogenization" in scale construction, it should be explicitly pointed out that there are still two, or more, sides to their psychometric street. Perhaps the Guilford-Zimmerman Temperament Survey (642) and the Cattell 16P.F. (329) best represent the two sides of one of the thorniest issues in factor analysis — orthogonal vs. oblique rotation of axes. The methodological and philosophical aspects of this controversy are dealt with in Chapter 6, where it has been argued that maximum simple structure and orthogonality strictly are incompatible goals, but that orthogonal factors are certainly simpler to use. A common factor analysis of markers from these two sets of scales (286a) shows, not surprisingly, that the personality dimensions measured by the two instruments occupy, to a marked degree, the same "space." Except in two or three instances where the orthogonal position happens not to be far from the oblique, however, the scales do not mutually align. From a purely geometric standpoint, it is obviously impossible to align a set of orthog-

onal vectors with a set of oblique ones, and as they are mathematically distinct, so are they psychologically distinct. It seems pointless to attempt to establish a conceptual isomorphism between them, though mutual transformation is readily possible.

It is argued — though much evidence from outside factor analysis needs to be gathered to check — that the oblique factors have greater constancy and generality from sample to sample, as well as closer correspondence to real psychological influences. The power and generality of oblique rotation (and surprisingly this needs to be reiterated from time to time) lies in the fact that an oblique solution is not forced upon the factors — rather it is permitted, as maximum attainment of the rotation criterion requires.

Once an oblique factor resolution has been determined, the new possibility arises of factoring the intercorrelations of these factors, i.e., of making a second-order analysis. This process is, at least theoretically, repeatable until one either has (1) only one factor or (2) several uncorrelated ones. These higher order factors, as we shall see, are very meaningful in the personality Q data realm.

Cattell (261) has recommended that a distinction be made between factor order and factor stratum, which is helpful for communication purposes. Order refers to the purely *operational* level of analysis, e.g., "first order" to factoring observed varibles, "second order" to factoring first-order factors, etc., while stratum defines a *conceptual* level, with a given data system, arrived at partly on more general considerations. The 16P.F. second-stratum factor Exvia-Invia, for example, is composed primarily of the first-stratum factors $A, E, F, H,$ and Q_2, but operationally could be called either a first- or second-order factor depending on whether the observed, correlated data are scale scores or individual item scores. Table 19-7, showing a series of second-stratum resolutions of Exvia-Invia and Anxiety, some as first-order and others as second-order solutions, demonstrates that the precision of rotation necessary for accurate second-order analyses can indeed be obtained.

It has long been recognized that Q data shares with L data (in contrast to T data, below) a possibly substantial susceptibility to instrument factors. Indeed, they could now range all the way from sabotage, through self-illusion, to specific "response set effects." A major difference of approach to these distortion phenomena has existed for years between such investigators as Chapman and Bock (340a), Cronbach (390a, 391), Edwards (450), Helmstadter (713a), Jackson and Messick (803a, 804, 805), Wiggins (1542, 1542a), and others,[1] on the one hand, and Campbell and Fiske (183), Cattell and Digman (281), and Hundleby, Pawlik, and Cattell (796) on the other. The former have conceptualized and approached the problem purely as something which happens in questionnaire responses, whereas Cattell in particular has considered response set as a personality-revealing form of behavior which he incorporated, before the recent outburst of interest in the problem by questionnaire designers, in the performance test (T data) approach. This work in the late forties showed that acquiescence responses, extremity, social desirability, etc., are predictable by such personality factors as Anxiety (U.I. 24), Comention (U.I. 20), and Extraversion (U.I. 32). In fact, measures of both social desirability and acquiescence have been used extensively in the large-scale multivariate studies reported by Hundleby, Pawlik, and Cattell (796) with the result that a substantial and highly consistent relationship has been shown to exist between both of these response sets and U.I. 24 (Anxiety). Additionally, acquiescence is loaded by U.I. 20 (Comention), U.I. 21 (Exuberance), and U.I. 28 (Asthenia), for reasons which seem ade-

quately given by the general nature of these factors. Couch and Keniston (389a), for example, found significant correlations between their acquiescence measure (OAS) and 16 P.F. factors $A+$, $C-$, $L+$, $O+$, Q_3-, and Q_4+, the last five of which constitute the second-stratum anxiety pattern. This is consistent with the personality factor explanation of acquiescence. Nesselroade (1095a) administered both the 15-item Couch and Keniston scale and the IPAT anxiety questionnaire (241b) to 94 undergraduates and repeated both measurements after a one-month interval, finding them correlated .32 and .49 on occasions 1 and 2, respectively. The stability coefficients of these two scales were .72 (Acquiescence) and .82 (Anxiety).

There is fairly diverse evidence to support the position that it is equally misleading either to elevate "acquiescence" and "social desirability" themselves to the status of source traits, i.e., factors, or to treat them merely as score-distorting habits, specific to test behavior, to be swept under a psychometric carpet! If one eliminated all variance associated with social desirability, he would throw away much of the Anxiety factor, a genuine manifestation of which is a certain degree of self-denigration.

A more comprehensive theoretical approach to the whole problem of distortion in Q data has been presented by Cattell and Digman (281), in which the actual score on a scale is viewed as a true score plus a distortion explicable in terms of loadings on all other source traits, as well as motivation and role factors, which determine such behavior. This can be formulated as follows:

$$C_T = d_{T1}T_1 + d_{T2}T_2 + \ldots + d_{Tk}T_k + d_{M_1}M_1 + \ldots + d_{M_l}M_l + d_{R_1}R_1 + \ldots + d_{R_p}R_p$$

where C_T is a correction for distortion, and the d's are weights determined by the extent to which the traits and dynamic factors distort self-perception on traits T_1 to T_k. The procedure for estimating true (undistorted) scores calls for estimating factors

[1] For a recent, critical review of this literature see Rorer (1216a).

from factoring the scale scores and role scores together.

The last point we propose to discuss in this section concerns the equivalence of Q and L data factors. Cross-media factor matching is a controversial topic (85, 250, 486, 1265, 1264a), and one which has thus far eluded a definitive resolution. Cattell maintains the position that, as concepts, there is essentially a one-to-one correspondence between 15 or so factors found in these two media. He points out that a demonstration of these relationships by correlational means requires getting at the pure factors by an analysis designed to set aside various "perturbing" influences, such as instrument and refrac-

demonstrable. Diagram 19-2 shows a plot from Schaie (1264a) indicating the relationship of E (Dominance) and G (Super Ego Strength) obtained from factoring pooled L and Q data factor scores. Nevertheless, the actual factor *estimates* between these two kinds of data remain poorly correlated because of the impossibility of getting rid of the instrument variance.

4. T DATA: OBJECTIVE, BEHAVIORAL TEST STRUCTURE IN TRAITS AND STATES

Objective test devices, with their orientation toward measuring behavior (verbal and non-verbal, social and individual) as

DIAGRAM 19-2. Factor Plot of E (Dominance) and G (Super Ego Strength) Obtained from Pooled Q and L Factor Scores (After Schaie, 1264a)

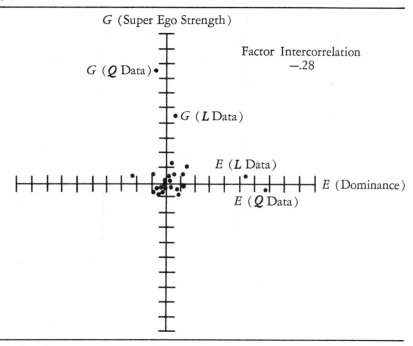

tion factors. In a recent study, Schaie (1264a) has shown that by exercising some control over technique and rater sources of variance, the concept validity of 12 of the 16 P.F. factors (against rating factors) is

such, rather than depending on evaluation by self or others, offer a radically different approach to determining personality structure. It is an approach which only a very small (though steadily increasing) percentage of personality theorists have set out upon, since the pioneer work of Berg, and his associates (102a), Brogden (140), Cattell (213, 226, 240), Coan (277), Downey (425a), Eysenck (474, 476, 486), Flugel (540), Getzels and Jackson (589a), Gibb (591), Gruen (292), Henning (718a), Hull (791a), Hundleby (796), Jaensch (805a), Kretschmer (886a), Lazarus (911a), Meeland (1037a), Pawlik (796, 1139, 1141), Peterson (310), Rethlingshafer (1191b), Rimoldi (1200), Rodnick (1205a), Stephenson (1346), Thurstone (1416), Warburton (337), Witkin and his associates (1561), Zeigarnik (1599a), and others. Probably the major obstacle to its "popularity" has not been so much the greater experimental, laboratory rigor required as the creative ingenuity demanded in producing miniature situations demonstrably expressing personality theory. That this is so is shown by the tendency of nine-tenths of the attempted inventions in the objective, T data area to "fall off" into projective tests or even virtual questionnaires, which are far easier to produce. Yet here is the true experimental approach, most completely emancipated from the snares and vaguenesses of verbal rating. It is measurement in its best and least ambiguous form, and although the man in the street may say that the thought of the novelist resorting to mere numbers to convey the essential temperament of his heroine has little, if any, more appeal than the notion that he simply enumerate her anthropometry, yet the shift from a verbal to a behaviorally defined system of personality is considered highly desirable by most behavioral scientists.

T data are the multivariate experimenter's counterpart of the laboratory data of other areas of psychology. Objective tests aim to provide information which is conceptually similar to true L data, i.e., to yield an objective record of an individual's behavior in a set of defined stimulus situations, but is more controllable.

Objective tests (not to be confused with objectively scorable tests) have many varieties and assumptions in construction, as brought out by the recent compendium of Cattell and Warburton (337). This objectivity has two main aspects: (1) constraints placed on the liability of the subject to fake or otherwise distort his responses, and (2) the manner in which his responses are scored. The first refers to the fact that the tests are constructed and administered in such a manner as to conceal from the subject what aspects of his performance are actually being measured. Instead of evaluating himself (or being evaluated by a rater), he behaves in a structured situation designed to produce a record of his acts to be assessed. The second connotation of objective, referring to the evaluation of the behavior, implies the use of an explicit set of scoring procedures such that two persons, be they psychologists or undergraduate hourly employees, arrive at the same numerical appraisal of the subject's performance. Although projection, for example, is one behavior measured in objective testing (Chapter 20), the perfect (except for carelessness) conspect reliabilities (240) of objective instruments are a far cry from the agreement of two raters of traditional projective tests such as the Rorschach. T data instruments are extremely diverse in format, type of response measured, etc., but test situations T9, T121, and T45 (Cattell & Warburton's index, 337) will serve to illustrate both the points mentioned regarding objectivity.

T9 covers a large variety of performances presented together for reasons of economy. For our purposes it is best considered with T10 (the two forming an interacting unit). The two tests are administered at different times (T9 early in a session and T10 later in the same session, or in a subsequent session), yielding a variety of difference measures which indicate behaviors such as: (1) willingness to change opinion with additional information, (2) shifts of attitude toward authority after the authority position is announced, (3) shifts of attitude toward those revealed for "successful" people, (4) shifts of attitude away from neurotics. These experimentally manipulated fluctuations have turned out to be strongly linked to U.I. 20, U.I. 21, U.I. 30, and other source traits. The measures mentioned are only a few of the possible scores obtainable, others such as short-term memory, ratio of consonant to dissonant recall, logical consistency of attitudes, severity of judgment, and personal relative to institutional values are derived from either T9 or T10 and, in some cases, the experimenter can combine scores from both instruments to yield a more stable estimate of the subjects's performance.

T121, the cursive miniature situations test, has shown itself to be one of the most important of the objective test devices. Adapted for either group or individual administration, this test requires the subject to operate at great speed, and with a complex set of rules, in a series of decision-making situations lacking in verbal content. Briefly, the subject's task is to obtain points by crossing (with a pencil) vertical and horizontal lines in a paper strip swiftly passing a window. In so doing he has to choose between alternate pathways in such a manner as to maximize his scoring opportunities with horizontal lines crossed worth one point and vertical lines worth four points. The subject is also instructed never to cross slanting lines and is given permission to use six circles (to surround a dense cluster of lines, thereby "scoring" as though he had crossed each line) in each run. After familiarizing himself with the task, he is given a run at a moderate rate of speed and then, after a short rest, one at a considerably faster pace. Besides total score, which is loaded by U.I. 16 (Assertiveness), U.I. 18 (Hypomanic Smartness), and U.I. 29 (Wholehearted Responsiveness), his performance can be scored for greater use of circles, number of slanting lines crossed,

use of excess circles, score under fast relative to slow conditions, number of correct decisions, etc., all of which are substantial marker variables of various U.I. factors.

In T45 the subject is shown pairs of lines, and for each pair is required to make a judgment as to which is longer. Without its being explicitly pointed out to the subject, some blocks of items are relatively easy and others difficult. The extent to which he changes his speed, and the extent to which he avoids a sudden increase of errors, as he hits the harder pairs, are among the measures taken. As Hundleby, Pawlik, and Cattell (796) have shown, these variables relate substantially to source traits U.I. 16 and U.I. 21.

The development of the existing large battery of objective tests (over 400 have been catalogued by Cattell and Warburton) depended directly upon the earlier advances in determining personality structure through the L and Q media. Hypotheses generated from knowledge of the major personality dimensions of these modes of observation provided a means of guaranteeing a more comprehensive coverage of the total personality sphere than would have been possible without such guidelines.

The carefully coordinated series of over 30 large-scale multivariate researches (796) over 20 years, using older marker variables constantly improved by new "recruits" to mark the concepts discovered, began with such older tests as sway suggestibility, oscillation in performance, rigidity, etc., and have moved on to attempt a wholesale coverage of the T data domain. As of 1966, these researches have developed, replicated, and constructed effective batteries for some 21 personality source traits, indexed[2] as U.I. 16 through U.I. 36. Table 19-4 presents a portion of the evidence on consistency of loading pattern for source trait U.I. 21 (Exuberance) abstracted from

[2]The U.I. is an abbreviation of Universal Index (241) proposed to aid the integration of factor-analytic results.

TABLE 19-4

SALIENT VARIABLES OF PERSONALITY DIMENSION U.I. 21: EXUBERANCE VS. SUPPRESSIBILITY

(Taken with permission from Hundleby, Pawlik, & Cattell, 796)

Factor Identification (Sample Size, Age of Subjects)

Master Index Number	Variable	200 Adult	100 Adult	100 Adult	370 Adult	410 Adult	100 Adult	100 Adult	500 Adult	250 Adult	86 Adult	86 Adult	139 Adult	184 Adult	80 Adult	164 Adult	197 Adult
271	Higher total verbal fluency on topics	+54	+55						+32	+35			+39	+13	+27	+32	+32
34	Less immaturity of opinion				−25	−42	−56	−66	−08					−43	−02		
167a	Better immediate memory	+41					+03	+47	+13	+44				+06		+20	
35	Less suggestibility to authority			+50	−23	−46	−07	−28	−08	−13				−26			
244	Faster speed of judgment in test of hard-headed realism								+48	+70				+41			
108	Less self-confidence regarding untried performance						−34	(+01)	−15	−16	−59	−30		−06		(+04)	
146b	Lower proportion correct in perceptual closure						−03	−09	−24	−13			−08	−49	−01	(+14)	
199	Higher numerical ability								+33	+35	+10	+12	+27	+09	(−03)		+00
282	Greater number of objects seen in unstructured drawings	+35							+04	+24	(−06)				+09	+73	+24
152	More tendency to agree						+15	+06	+37	+70	+05	+27	+02	+07		(−09)	
288	Faster speed of evaluating others' performance								+51	+70	+27		+44				
307	Faster speed of letter comparison								+46	+36			+44		+28		
308	Faster speed of perceptual judgment in comparing numbers								+48	+44							
13a	More oscillation				+02	+30	+21	+41						+12			
71	Fewer erroneous reactions under complex instructions						+10		(+08)					−02			
33	Larger size of myokinetic movement	+45			(−01)	−30			−08		−10	(+09)			−02	−03	
22a-c	Higher ratio of chance to purposeful observation and memory				+04	+13	+15	+24			+21	+19					
168a	Faster speed of social judgment														+48		+15
309	Faster speed of line judgment (regardless of accuracy)								+54							+11	
278	Faster reading tempo								+59								

Hundleby, Pawlik, and Cattell (796), in which a full account of each of the 21 factors including criterion relationships and questionnaire correlates is given.

Both the researches of Cattell and associates (213, 226, 240, 796) and Eysenck (472, 474, 486) have maintained contact with older factors such as "g", fluency, perseveration, rigidity, oscillation, Thurstone's perceptual factors, etc., to meet the fluency variables (both verbal and ideational), but has a dozen other aspects, ranging from higher speed of judgment on social issues to general efficiency and good memory, which clearly distinguish it from a purely fluency factor. Similar findings exist for U.I. 17 and inhibition and U.I. 23 and rigidity.

Research programs subsequent to those reported by Hundleby (796) are currently

DIAGRAM 19-3. Factor Plots of U. I. 20 (Comention) and U. I. 21 (Exuberance) Found in Samples of American and Japanese Children

AMERICAN SAMPLE ($N = 273$)   JAPANESE SAMPLE ($N = 175$)

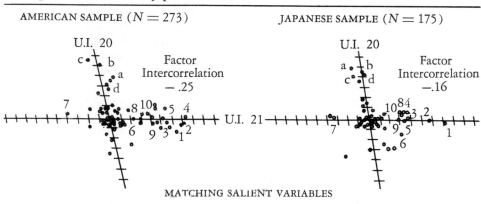

MATCHING SALIENT VARIABLES

a. Higher severity of judgment (M.I. 116a)

b. More tendency to agree (M.I. 152)

c. Greater pessimism over doing good (M.I. 100)

d. Greater susceptibility to annoyance (M.I. 211a)

1. Greater number of objects seen in unstructured drawings (M.I. 282)

2. Larger number of hidden objects seen (M.I. 171)

3. Greater numerical ability (M.I. 199)

4. Higher total fluency on topics (M.I. 271)

5. Higher total number of acquaintances recalled (M.I. 474)

6. Faster tempo of reading (M.I. 278)

7. Greater percentage correct on gestalt completion (M.I. 146b)

8. Faster speed of letter comparison (M.I. 307a)

9. Faster speed of line length judgment (M.I. 309)

10. Higher total number of friends recalled (M.I. 473)

scientific necessity of proving that newly discovered factors were not simply replications of previous ones. A case in point is U.I. 21 (see Table 19-4), a factor which has been replicated in both adult and child studies (Meredith, 1042a). It accounts for a considerable portion of the variance in investigating the constancy of these factor patterns both across age range (including 4- and 5-year-olds) and across cultures (American, Japanese, and Austrian). Diagram 19-3 shows two plots from studies presently being prepared for publication (797) which demonstrate the similarity of the U.I. 20 and U.I. 21 patterns found in American and Japanese children. The agreement, with respect to both loading pattern and factor intercorrelations is impressive, and decidedly so when one takes into account the following: (1) the American sample is composed of 273 11- to 13-year-old males and females, the Japanese sample of 175 11- to 13-year-old males only; (2) of the 69 variables represented in the American sample, only 45 were common to the 60 used in the Japanese study; and (3) both studies were rotated "blindly" and independently of each other, the final resolution of the Japanese study being made in Japan by Dr. Bien Tsujioka.

As mentioned, the concepts which emerge from scrutiny of these patterns have a lineage going back to L and Q data factors, inasmuch as the latter were important guiding hypotheses in test construction, and partly deriving from patterns found for the first time by multivariate study of laboratory tests. However, the total development of interpretations depends also on the full use of these factor measures in clinical, educational, physiological, social, and industrial psychology. And here the unfortunate situation has arisen that, after all the advanced techniques and major creativity involved in preparing the instruments, they have "stood on the shelf" for lack of "marketing."

Failing to understand the theory and mathematical-statistical reasoning involved, and excited by the pursuit of simpler and more popular fashions, the applied psychologists have, on the whole, stared uncomprehendingly at the relatively finished products cast shining before them. In these circumstances, it has fallen to the multivariate experimentalists themselves to verify the concepts by entering various fields, notably the clinical field, as has been done by Eysenck (474, 476, 493), Cattell (240, 325, 796), Dubin (285), Killian (870a), Tatro (334a), and Delhees (279a), or those of educational, physiological, and learning psychology, as has been done by

Pawlik and Cattell (1139, 1142), Scheier (320, 325), Van Egeren (1486), and others.

Both Eysenck (474, 476, 493) and Cattell (240, 325, 263b) have contributed substantially to the understanding of abnormal behavior through objective test analyses. Their fundamentally different applications of factor analytic methodology, however, manifest themselves very clearly in the study of neuroticism, for example, where Eysenck's approach has produced one major dimension of neuroticism, while Cattell's, though agreeing with the nature and meaning of the Eysenck factor, has yielded at least five other distinct personality factors which discriminate significantly between neurotics and normals (see Sections 6 and 9). Elsewhere, in questionnaires, Eysenck has arrived roughly at what were located as second-order factors by Cattell and his co-workers, after fixing the primary positions. Eysenck's argument (486) that his short-cut to secondaries reliably demonstrates the same conceptual system cannot be supported by T data research. For example, Cattell and Scheier (325) report evidence for at least five of the second-order objective test factors (presented in Table 19-5) being significantly linked to neuroticism, rather than there being a single second-order neuroticism factor. Underfactoring, as a short-cut to a few second-order factors, is scientifically not determinate, as are complete-extraction, oblique, simple-structure rotation, and higher order analysis.

The evidence for linkage of T with Q data factors has been collated by Hundleby, Pawlik, and Cattell (796), and to date centers on three putative matches: the second-stratum Q data factors Exvia-Invia, Anxiety, and Pathemia with U.I. 32, U.I. 24, and U.I. 22, respectively. Matching of factors from these two media has not received the attention that matching of L and Q factors has, but promises to do so, now that effective batteries for their measurement have been developed. At any rate, the evidence now available suggests that such correspondences as appear will occur between the *T* data factors and the second-stratum *Q* data factors.

Developments in the objective test realm have opened the door also to a systematic, rigorous examination of dimensions of intra-individual change (states, moods, etc.), long a topic of concern to students of

TABLE 19-5

SECOND-ORDER FACTORS WITH FIRST-ORDER SALIENTS FOUND IN *T* DATA RESEARCH

F(T)I   Tied Socialization vs. Absence of Cultural Introjection
    1. Comention (U.I. 20+)
    2. Rigidity of Superego (U.I. 28+)
    3. Low general intellectual ability (U.I. 1−)
    4. Subduedness (U.I. 19−)
    5. Realism (U.I. 25+)
    6. Laziness (U.I. 35+)
    7. Extraversion (U.I. 32+)

F(T)II   Expansion Ego vs. History of Difficulty in Problem Solving
    1. Assertiveness (U.I. 16+)
    2. High general intellectual ability (U.I. 1+)
    3. Critical independence (U.I. 19+)
    4. Neurotic debility (U.I. 23−)
    5. Strong self-sentiment (U.I. 36+)
    6. Thoroughness (U.I. 18−)

F(T)III   Temperamental Ardour vs. Temperamental Apathy
    1. Exuberance (U.I. 21+)
    2. Comention (U.I. 20+)
    3. Low general intellectual ability (U.I. 1−)
    4. Critical independence (U.I. 19+)
    5. Trustingness (U.I. 27−)
    6. Extraversion (U.I. 32+)

F(T)IV   High Educated Self-Consciousness vs. Low Self-Consciousness
    1. Cortertia (U.I. 22+)
    2. Smartness (U.I. 18+)
    3. Psychotic tendency (U.I. 25−)
    4. Strong self-sentiment (U.I. 36+)
    5. Tenseness (U.I. 30−)
    6. Uncooperativeness (U.I. 29−)
    7. Pessimism (U.I. 33+)

F(T)V   History of Inhibiting, Restraining Environment vs. Laxness
    1. Timidity (U.I. 17+)
    2. Ego Strength (U.I. 23+)
    3. Wariness (U.I. 31+)

F(T)VI   Narcissistic Development vs. Environmental Contact and Investment
    1. Narcissism (U.I. 26+)
    2. Grudgingness (U.I. 27+)
    3. Autism (U.I. 34+)

F(T)VII   High Tension to Achieve and Controlled Drive Tension Level vs. Low Tension to Achieve
    1. High anxiety (U.I. 24+)
    2. Smartness (U.I. 18+)
    3. Tenseness (U.I. 30−)

human personality. Hitherto, it has been mainly approached either by speculation or inadequate research design and methodology, but objective tests lend themselves excellently to multivariate techniques discussed elsewhere (Chapters 11 and 12, 692a), by means of which substantive research is now coming to grips with the complexities of change. We can pause only briefly here to indicate the nature of these developments, which have been explored more fully elsewhere (240, 345). Intraindividual difference research has yielded some nine dimensions (state factors), along which a person can vary from occasion to occasion, including Torpor vs. Excitement (P.U.I. 1), Elation vs. Depression (P.U.I. 2), Effort Stress vs. Effort Relaxation (P.U.I. 4), Mobilization vs. Regression (P.U.I. 8), and Anxiety vs. Tranquility (P.U.I. 9).

Although some of these state factors (e.g., Anxiety, Elation-Depression, and Mobilization-Regression) are similar in loading pattern to certain source traits of inter-individual differences, and thus pose the problem of experimentally separating them as distinct behavioral influences (see Chapter 11), others, such as Effort Stress, Diurnal Fatigue, and Adrenergic Response, have no known trait counterparts. Also noteworthy among the findings resulting from psychological state research are: (1) the emergence of separate anxiety and stress dimensions, and (2) decidedly more substantial physiological relationships with states than have been found with traits.

5. GENERAL THEORETICAL MODELS FOR PERSONALITY RESEARCH

Since any review of major theories of personality would require a volume (676a, 112a), we naturally confine ourselves here to those based on reasonably strict multivariate models which can be subjected to rigorous experimentation. Even then, we are reduced, if we are to be comprehensive, to rather bald statements of each.

As pointed out in the introduction, investigators attempting to delineate the structure of personality by multivariate methods converge on at least four distinct operational concepts as a basis for further superstructuring, i.e., (1) surface traits (correlation clusters), (2) source traits (factors resolved according to some general rule such as — simple structure or confactor rotation), (3) types (modal patterns in k dimensions), and (4) processes (modal sequences in k dimensions), each of which has been examined in a succession of chapters (6, 9, 11) above. Certain additional concepts, e.g., the circumplex and other order models arising from patternings found in correlation matrices (see "Mosaics in Correlation and Factor Matrices," Chapter 6, above) and notions of subdivisions in a circular spectrum of behavior dimensions, as, for example, in Leary (912a), Schaefer (1262), and Stern (1346a), are actually special instances of these models. Beyond these prototype models hinging on multivariate treatment of happenings recordable in the basic data relation matrix (data box) extend others on a mechanical basis, e.g., computer models, which are also briefly discussed here.

The superstructure which is most commonly and immediately built on the surface and source-trait foundation blocks, leads to a model (indeed, it is an integral part of the source-trait factor model) of deriving behavior predictions by a linear specification equation described briefly in the editor's introduction, which is a generalization of the basic factor analytic equation:

$$(4) \quad a_{ji} = b_{j1} T_{1i} + b_{j2} T_{2i} + \ldots + b_{jk} T_{ki}$$

where a represents the performance of individual i on test j; the b's represent factor loadings; and the T's represent factor scores (see Chapter 6). Equation (4) can be further developed by distinguishing ability (A), temperament (T), and dynamic (D)

traits and by adding terms for states (S) and role (R) factors, as in equation (1).

$$(1) \quad a_{ji} = b_{jA_1} A_{1i} + \ldots b_{jAx} A_{xi} + b_{jT_1} T_{1i}$$
$$+ \ldots + b_{jTy} T_{yi} + \ldots + b_{jD_1} D_{1i}$$
$$+ \ldots + b_{jDz} D_{zi} + b_{jS_1} S_{1i}$$
$$+ \ldots + b_{jSk} S_{ki} + b_{jR_1} R_{1i}$$
$$+ \ldots + b_{jRl} R_{li}$$

As a model from which to predict behavior, the general specification equation (1) differs from the general-purpose mathematician's linear specification in several ways. Thurstone was responsible for bringing in these more specific and boundary conditions in adapting to the field of abilities, and Cattell has been largely responsible for continuing the development of the model in further adaptations to personality theory. Indeed, one of the problems of communication which frequently arises today is that between the mathematical statistician, innocently working with the assumptions of the original bare factor-analytic concepts, e.g., as in Anderson (33), and the personality theorists, following Cattell, who have brought in several more specific conditions and operational requirements to fit it to the psychological realities of personality research. Thus, the personality theorist's specification equation now assumes: (a) terms having different properties for traits from the three modalities (ability, temperament, and dynamic), as well as terms for state, instrument, and role factors, all of which cannot practicably be obtained in a single analysis; (b) the a_{ji} represents any behavioral act, not just a particular test performance; (c) the b_j's, instead of representing regression weights, are generalized to behavioral situation indices which express the stimulating power of the situation upon the magnitude of behavior originating from the given factor (as part of "econetics" or generalized psychophysics [256b]); (d) the condition of simple structure or confactor resolution of factors, to insure objective, replicable concepts, exists.

Thus, the general specification implies that person i's performance in situation j is a linear function of his factor endowments, each weighted according to its relevance to that particular behavior in a particular situation. Among definitions of personality, Cattell's (226) "that which predicts what a person will do in a defined situation" has been conspicuous for elegance and permits a concise separation of terms in the specification equation into situation parameters and personality parameters, as shown in Equation (1) above. However, as he has recently had to admit (259, 301b), an ambiguity of definition by this model arises when terms for states—S's—as well as traits—T's—are entered. If personality is to retain the meaning of constancy with respect to an individual, his momentary states cannot be part of it. The alternatives are (a) to redefine personality as "that which predicts . . . when the state levels are defined" or (b) to consider the state levels as functions of personality under the influence of situational modulation (described below). In the latter case, we must substitute for "defined situation" "the present stimulus situation and an indefinite succession of preceding modulating situations." For example, a person's behavior will differ from situation to situation as a function of his changing level on, say, dynamic factors, determined by earlier situations of deprivation, etc. But the fixed traits and the immediate situation, of course, remain: how vigorously Smith attacks his meal depends not only on how hungry he happens to be, but also on his temperament and whether he is having dinner with his employer's family or is eating alone at home.

The b_j's, then, may be regarded as a vector supplying the psychological meaning of the situation and in this context raise a variety of questions as to their relation to perception and role as well as personality. The model of personality is inseparably tied to the model of the situation. Elsewhere, Cattell (259) has tackled these problems with the formulation of perception, role, mood, etc., as modulators which may systematically alter the behavioral indices and trait scores of the specification equation. The importance of situational determinants of behavior has long been realized (by psychologists as well as sociologists), and most theories of personality make an attempt to include them (e.g., Murray's "press," Lewin's "environment," Cattell's "focal," "ambient," and "global" stimuli, etc.) regardless of the degree of operational precision in definition. (Recently, indeed, those personality theorists who had "lost" the situation have perhaps tended to overvalue it on its return [Hunt, 798b; Sells, 1293].)

A consequence of the above development of the specification model of personality and environment has been (1) considerable substantive advance, notably by Burt, Cattell, Eysenck, Guilford, Thurstone, and their colleagues, in finding the basic or fundamental units (source traits) of personality, (2) the development of efficient instruments for factor measurement, and (3) the beginnings of systematic attention to classifying the environment and its demands. Once the instruments measuring personality and ability source traits are constructed, with demonstrated reliabilities and validities, we are no longer tied to the linear specification equation but can cast about for more powerful models in which to utilize these theoretically superior predictors. Factor analysis is then part of a general iterative research process (Chapter 6) in which a first approximation to the nature of a personality factor is made on the linear model, followed by non-linear approaches. For instance, a variety of alternative prediction models have emerged in the past few years such as moderator variables (Chapter 15; 1256, 590a), suppressor variables (1014a, 1535a), curvilinear and non-additive models (915), including developments in non-linear factor analysis (1011a, 1011b), all of which offer poten-tially useful alternatives to the linear specification equation, although the simplicity of linear equations is not to be lightly abandoned. As Cattell has pointed out (240), the whole realm of polynomials is open to us to express those more subtle relations which many psychologists believe they perceive, but he has rightly added that we should not get too intoxicated with these until we have thoroughly explored the outcome of using the linear model. Ward (1496), for example, has shown that while more complex functions may provide a better fit to a given set of data, with a new sample their predictive efficiency is actually less than that of simpler ones due to the magnitude of shrinkage occurring upon cross-validation.

The configurative, interactive, emergents, etc., models to which these considerations lead have been discussed in Chapter 9 and are not covered again here. These include models which consider effects of relative magnitudes of source traits rather than absolute level. Permissive models (240) in which one trait cannot come into play until another reaches a certain magnitude (the conjunctive model of Coombs and Kao, 386) and "permits" it to enter the specification equation are but one of the large class of mathematical models which can be expressed as polynomials of varying degrees of complexity. In passing, one should note that configurative and type-understanding models are in essentials the same. The notion of predicting from a total type "gestalt" implies that particular patterns of personality arise with modal frequency (Chapter 9) because emergents or high criterion efficiency are developed by the polynomial formula at those combinations.

So much for the third formal model, the type. Let us next consider process. Although the process model is commonly thought of as the very antithesis of individual difference models, yet it has its place in personality models, notably in the proposition of Cattell and Van Egeren

(335a) that the individuality of a person could be defined independently of traits by the peculiarities of sequence in a process, e.g., by a particular sequence of values in k states when the individual enters a standard situation. Such sequence idiosyncrasies could turn out to be related to cross-sectional trait scores, as does Flugel's demonstration of poorer character with higher oscillation (540), Das' correlation (406a) of low C (Ego Strength) with high attitude fluctuation, and Wessman's and Ricks' (1530a) showing of high elation-depression fluctuation with Extraversion as a trait. These are *general* process characters rather than specific sequences, but, in principle, either is capable of presenting a model for defining and describing personality. Possibly, a particular personality will prove susceptible to definition by its specific predominance of what Cattell has indicated to be measurable as proto-processes (Chapter 11).

Any consideration of models for personality must ask about the relevance of models used in particular areas, e.g., in attitude and social interaction research and in learning. Social interaction behavior has actually always been given its due role in the objective test devices covered in Section 4 above and has appeared strongly in some factors, e.g., U.I. 20 (Comention). Extensive examination of the relations of personality and group models has been made by Cattell (252), involving syntality, synergy, ties, and other concepts, and the work of Gibb (592), Fiedler (513, 513a, 513b), Stice (328), and Lawson (907), among others, has exemplified these personality — group dynamics interactions.

In learning, one looks to the stochastic models of Estes (468), Bush and Mosteller (177a), and Anderson (32a) eventually to give new dimensions of description to human traits of a dynamic, interest nature and those involving skills. One may anticipate some integration of this with the matrix treatment in adaptation process

analysis (Section 7). Insofar as history and change concepts are part of any good personality model, a link here becomes essential.

Games theory (see Chapter 13) also has an obvious future in personality models. Much personality learning, especially social, but also vis-à-vis the physical world, has to do with expectations of "play" on the part of a non-passive environment. Whole systems of habits constituting the personality are almost certainly explicable in terms of the nature of an environment in which the individual has played and the extent of his learning. For example, the general theory of the level of Surgency-Desurgency (F factor) as expressing the degree of "punish-ingness" of the environmental play experienced — with the resulting spread of caution and inhibition — is a case in point.

Much has been written in recent years about computer models (131a, 615, 1434a). Information-processing models are fashionable from cognitive fields (1097b) to motivation (798a) and from simulating neurotic processes (367a) to impersonating chess players (1097a). Unfortunately, there has been a lack of clarity, e.g., in the symposium of Tomkins and Messick (1434a), on the difference between *the computer as a model* in itself and the programming of a computer to express (as in a plasmode, page 223) and to try out some *mathematical model as such.* Along the lines of the latter, one might, for example, set up the model of the dynamic crossroads (page 594) as a series of choice points in the neurotic process and experiment with the cumulative effects of various decision ratios in simulating the percentages of early and late, severe and mild, neuroses found in particular cultures.

On the other hand, in terms of the computer as a general model of what goes on inside a person, we have to consider the basic mechanisms of input, output, storage, processing, and control. One difficulty which immediately strikes the personality theorist in looking at this model is the absence of any true analogue for motivation (but see Hunt, 798a). Little more than interesting talk yet appears, in any case, to have emerged from this "model." For example, it has been suggested that the Exvia-Invia factor (U.I. 32) might be explained in terms of the exviant person having relatively more neurones given to input and output, whereas the inviant has a larger ratio of his resources devoted to processing. (In fact, this has been invoked by Golovin [603a] and by Kuhn [892a] to explain the greater creativity found for inviants.)

With these varied possibilities of model development, the future for experimental attacks on personality theory is an exciting one. In terms of work accomplished and readiness for immediate attack, however, the developments proposed above in the specification equation probably offer the greatest promise to the multivariate experimenter. In what Cattell (259) has called the theory of modulators, we have a double action in which the specification equation operates first (1) to express modulation of the state and role factor levels of the individual, according to weights derivable from the *ambient* or preceding situation and specification equation, and then is invoked again (2) to predict his reaction to the *focal* stimulus according to the usual specification equation. It is just conceivable that some existing findings on second-order factors would really be more simply explained by this model. In any case, the great need in this field today is a coordination of model construction with degrees of precision in experimental work and statistical significance developments which will insure model-making the respect of being something more than a parlor game.

6. PRINCIPLES IN INTERPRETING MULTIVARIATE FINDINGS ON STRUCTURE AND PROCESS

Wider reflections on possible theoretical models in connection with multivariate research have been given in Section 5.

Proceeding now to specific psychological theories, the present section integrates with those concepts, insofar as any particular psychological interpretation also involves a general model. However, the focus here is upon psychological and general experimental principles in interpreting structure and process, assumed to be defined in the most common (linear, additive) factor-analytic model, and the model of processes as composed of proto-processes, as defined in Chapter 11.

Considerable attention has been given recently, since certain source trait factors have become well replicated, to competing hypotheses regarding their nature. For example, Cattell (325) and Eysenck (476) have offered alternative theories for the U.I. 23 (Regression or Neuroticism) and U.I. 32, Exvia (Social Inhibition or Reactive Inhibition), factors; Meredith has presented stimulating theories regarding the U.I. 21, Exuberance (1042a), and U.I. 16, Ego Strength, factors (1042b); Cattell has developed a developmental theory for the peculiar pattern of U.I. 28, Asthenia (260a); Pawlik and Cattell (1142) have presented a neurological theory (based partly on EEG) for the U.I. 22, Cortertia, pattern; Horn (743) and Gorsuch (608a) have debated the interpretation of U.I. 29 in terms of psychoanalytic super ego leads; and Scheier (1265), Cattell (325), Rickels (1198a), and Spielberger have devoted papers and books to the interpretation of the state and trait pattern of U.I. 24, as Anxiety.

These are only a few, though perhaps some of the more important, instances of the capacity and interest of psychologists to integrate factorial and other experimental evidence on structure beyond merely statistical or actuarial measurement statements. The clinical, the social, and the bivariate experimental psychologists are increasingly employing theories on the psychological nature of the structures concerned. Consequently, we should take a searching look at the procedures of inference, which include (a) drawing conclusions about the identity and matching of the factor pattern simply *as an empirical pattern,* (b) inferring the nature of the *difference* or dimension from the nature of the variables, (c) testing the hypothesis in *manipulative* experiments, and (d) looking at the actual mental *process* of perception and action which represent the factor in action, and so on.

A complete set of principles for the above stages in recognition and interpretation of factors has been set out and expanded upon in several publications, notably by Burt (161), Cattell (229, 251), Cattell and Baggaley (268), and Harman (688). The criteria and methodological procedures are as follows:

From Within the Factor Analytic Evidence Itself

(1) To examine the goodness, in terms of hyperplane count and statistical significance, of the *simple structure* itself, as reached by blind, independent and sometimes automated rotation across several related studies (59).

(2) To check the significance of *matching agreement* of the factor patterns by Burt's coefficient of congruence (688), the pattern similarity coefficient (268), or the (nonparametric) configurative matching method (263).

(3a) To consider first hypotheses as suggested by the loading pattern itself, i.e., by the *nature of the variables* that load highly positively and highly negatively, and those variables with essentially zero loadings. It becomes necessary to compare, at the same time, the pattern with that of other factors.

(3b) To analyze extension variables and their factor pattern which serve as an adjunct to the factor interpretation procedure (442a). Not only the variables that are in the factorization are crucial, but also those (extension) variables that are correlated with the included variables.

(4) To determine the rank order of general variance of the factor among factors.

(5) To inspect the correlations of the factor with questionnaire (Q), rating (L), or objective (T) factors for matches across different measurement media.

In Experiment Beyond the Initial Factor Analytic Location

(6) To look for a similar persisting pattern, with modifications of a kind that could be predicted at other ages, in other cultures, and in P and dR techniques (240, 1096).

(7) To examine the nature-nurture ratios, both between families and within families. For it would be fruitless to devote much time to a temperamental theory when this initial "sorting" points to an environmental explanation, or to go far with learning theories if the evidence points clearly to a predominantly hereditary explanation (259a).

(8) To examine age trends in the factor score.

(9) To look at the interpretations possible in second-order structures among objective-test factors, in which the given factor might be involved.

(10) To examine correlations with (or group differences on) particular life criteria, e.g., school success, clinical problems, delinquency, etc.

(11) To seek evidence of effects of manipulative experiments upon factor scores.

(12) To study, in a clinical sense, the behavior of individuals known to be extremely high or extremely low on the factor measurement.

It becomes immediately evident that many years may elapse between, on the one hand, the recognition among experimenters of an invariant, experimentally replicable pattern and, on the other, its interpretation by a correctly conceived and named source trait, i.e., its establishment theoretically. To preserve the pattern during the period of lacking a final interpretative label, Cattell (241) has suggested that each factor receive a Universal Index, with a number for each pattern (just as has been done in biochemistry, e.g., in the investigation of the vitamins and hormones, and in other sciences). These U.I. numbers and their underlying rationale have been more fully described in Section 4 above.

The practical task of developing an abstract factor concept may be illustrated by considering criterion 3, the loading pattern, on the *E* factor (240, p. 297). U.I. (L) 5, the *E* factor, is one of authoritarianism, or temperamental toughness, or extrapunitiveness, or aggressive sadism, or dominance, according to the experimenter's theoretical sensitivities. The findings that self-assertiveness has a loading of (on an average) 0.8, whereas extrapunitiveness loads only 0.6, self-conceit only about 0.5, poise or demeanor only about 0.4, and sadism nothing at all (plus many other observations, e.g., sex differences, prediction of achievement, biochemical research, manipulative experiment with frustration and aggression, etc.) favor the view that self-assertiveness, overriding others, and seeking control of the physical world are much nearer the central, essential character then, say, sadism, hostility, or narcism. "Dominance" is therefore the most likely hypothesis. The conceptual nature of all experimentally known *Q* data factors has been intensively examined in a series of independent researches. (The reader is referred to the bibliographies in the respective handbooks for the Guilford-Zimmerman Temperament Schedule, the 16 Personality Factor Questionnaire, the Thurstone Temperament Schedule, etc., for information on these researches.)

The emphasis in research on objective test (*T* data) factors has, now that the phases of discovery and confirmation of some 20 factors is complete, shifted toward the factor interpretation phase, i.e., inferences are being made as to the underlying influence of the factors. A series of hypotheses on the meaning of the known personality factors have been offered by Cattell (240) and Hundleby, Pawlik, and Cattell (796). A brief digression on the factor-hypotheses confirmation of factor U.I. (T) 23, the regressive or "neuroticism" factor, may suffice to demonstrate briefly, for

objective test factors, how a factor pattern permits a more developed theory than certain premetric or literary clinical theories have reached.

Let us take U.I. 23, variously considered "Neuroticism" (Eysenck, 476) and Regression (Cattell, 325). The latter interpretation by Cattell and Scheier (325) and Scheier, Cattell, and Horn (1266) is based on a wider array of criterion and personality context evidence than could be reviewed here. We limit ourselves to the essential ones. The objective performance measures which load most consistently on U.I.(T) 23 involve behaviors which the consensus of modern clinical opinion regards — as Eysenck has correctly stated — as neurotic, e.g., rigidity, effort intolerance, suggestibility, neurotic hesitation. (See summary by Cattell, 240; and Cattell and Scheier, 325.) However, other variables suggest that the U.I. (T) 23 factor may involve the process by which the Freudian withdrawal of libido comes about. The individual low on U.I. 23 shows an "inability to mobilize," since, despite possessing the necessary habits and skills in the same amount as others, he is unable to coordinate them to cope with any demanding situation. Descriptively, as Cattell and Scheier have indicated, it is close to a withdrawal of interest or, psychoanalytically, of "object libido." The work of Rickels (1198a) shows that this function, as shown by U.I. 23 scores, is particularly low in depressives. Yet it cannot be equated with neuroticism as such, i.e., as a total pattern, because Cattell and Scheier (325) and Tatro (334a) have shown that several other factors — U.I. 16(−), 19(−), 21(−), 22(−), 23(−), 24(+), 29(−), 32(+) — are equally significant in deviation among clinical cases, which is why their theoretical position is different from the "unitary dimension of neuroticism" proposed by Eysenck. The theoretical discussion on the two positions has been carried forward in Section 9.

It is perhaps scarcely necessary to stress, in a handbook on the experimental approach, that the interpretation of personality factors does not have to lean upon clinical concepts. Yet any survey of personality theories, such as that of Bischof (112a) will show that certainly not less than 95 per cent of what is written in general personality textbooks either disguisedly or undisguisedly confines its concepts to what is derived from clinical observation. By contrast, the writings of Burt (160), Cattell (240), Eysenck (476), Guilford (627), and Thurstone (e.g., in perception [1416]), have amply shown that an experimental personality theory, though it may sometimes confirm clinical views (as in the Ego Strength, C, and Super Ego Strength, G, factors in the 16 P.F.), can and should rest on theoretical notions of a more precise kind directly derivable from the factor-analytic and manipulative evidence. Cattell (325, 260a), Eysenck (476, 486), Meredith (1042a), and Pawlik (1142) particularly have shown how powerful and novel can be the theoretical developments directly from experimental evidence as in U.I. 28, U.I. 23, U.I. 16, U.I. 21, or U.I. 22.

7. PERSONALITY MATURATION (PSYCHOLOGICAL GENETICS) AND LEARNING

The ultimate aim of personality study is not description but explanation. It has to do with establishing laws of personality learning and with explaining how a personality matures the way it does. The difference of emphasis between the multivariate experimentalist on the one hand and the bivariate and clinical psychologist on the other has resided in the former's assertion that it is vital first to discover and measure the structures in which change and learning are to be studied. Unfortunately, this far-sighted aim has not been sufficiently recognized by the bivariate experimentalist or the clinician, who have sometimes assumed that surface and source trait structure is a descriptive end in itself. One result is, as

this section is bound painfully to reveal, that in spite of years of alleged concentration on developmental psychology, it is almost impossible to find firm experimental evidence on personality learning and laws of change rooted in those major dimensions and structures with which personality study is concerned. And this despite the fact that an army of applied psychologists are daily concerned with bringing about personality change, in clinic and school, upon what they claim to be a basis of psychological laws.

Conceptually, change phenomena can be analyzed into (a) genetic maturation, (b) learning, and (c) reversible fluctuations and instabilities. Since the last is thoroughly handled in Chapter 11, we here only give it due recognition as a source of variance. As to (a) and (b), their factual separation is a far more difficult problem than their conceptual separation! Chapter 25 below, and the recent developments (248, 259a) of the MAVA (Multiple Abstract Variance Analysis) method, as well as the surveys of Fuller and Thompson (568), or of Vandenberg (1482), have intensively examined the methodological problems and dealt with models with and without (a) correlation and (b) interaction of heredity and environment, as well as with the problem of proceeding from population genetics formulation with continuous variables to underlying Mendelian mechanisms.

As we attempt here to organize substantive findings on maturational personality development, we are forced to recognize that much of it has not been gathered by ideal methods. For example, perhaps 90 per cent comes from the very limited twin method and less than 18 per cent from the MAVA (Chapter 25) or other sophisticated approaches. The data rest not only on graded, quantitative behavioral evidence, but broadly include:

(1) Categorical qualitative features such as color blindness, taste blindness, Huntington's chorea, being in or out of jail, or Kallman's "process" schizophrenia.

(2) Attempts to relate personality to physical features which are known to be largely inherited, such as eye color, Mongolian eye fold, hypotension, split foot, Addison's disease, etc.

(3) Scores on continuous, psychometrically measurable traits, fractions of the variance of which can be associated respectively with genetic and environment influences.

Initially, (1) and (2) were investigated largely by what is briefly called the "twin method." This approach has resulted in the prefactorial research, beginning with the studies of Galton, and continuing with Dahlberg (400a), von Verschuer (1489a), Allen (16a), Kallman (841a), and others. Almost all of these accumulated data have been on illness and mental deficiency in terms of specific tests; some of them are not even in terms of measurement of any kind; others have simply attempted to give a speculative answer to the question of which is more important, heredity or environment. Such work and that by approach (2), as well as "animal personality" inheritance, is described in more detail in Chapter 25.

A recent return of interest in the interaction of hereditary and environmental influences, now concentrating upon determining nature-nurture variance ratios rather than on Mendelian analysis, is marked by the publications of Anastasi (22a), Burt (169a), Burt and Howard (174a, 174b), Cattell (250a, 259a), Gottesman (609a), Isaacs (802a), Loehlin (939b), Vandenberg (1482), and others. They reflect increased attention to methodological and conceptual improvements capable of tackling the long-recognized reality that in the phenotype, hereditary and environmental influences are thoroughly intermingled. As a result, the need for special concepts and methods for separating genetic from environmental variance, and inferring from these data the Mendelian mechanism, has become apparent.

More than a decade ago, Cattell (231a), in what is designated the MAVA method mentioned above, proposed two radical improvements in determining nature-nurture ratios: first, to substitute the measurement of unitary factors (which have been objectively located by factor analysis), in place of single, arbitrary variables, which are too numerous for the scientific aim of condensing knowledge. Second, to abandon dependence on twin study, which has been criticized for vital limitations and defects, and utilize a new method called the Multiple Abstract Variance Analysis method. The MAVA method has several advantages over the traditional twin method. It derives from a set of simultaneous equations, which are set out comprehensively in Chapter 25. They lead to determination of the fractions of the observed population variance in a trait due to (1) the between-family genetic variance, (2) the within-family genetic variance, (3) the within-family environmental variance, (4) the between-family environmental variance, and (5) the covariance between any two of these four due to the hereditary and environmental influences. As an example, the equation for the observed variance for sibs raised apart (SA) is written:

$$\sigma^2_{SA} = \sigma^2_{WH} + \sigma^2_{WE} + \sigma^2_{BE} + 2r_{WH,WE}\,\sigma_{WH}\,\sigma_{WE}$$

where

σ^2_{SA} = variance of pairs of sibs raised apart;

σ_{WH} = within-family hereditary variance component;

σ_{WE} = within-family environmental variance component;

σ_{BE} = between-family environmental variance component;

$r_{WH,WE}$ = correlation of hereditary and environmental influences (within families).

Several other equations can be set up, for pairs of siblings reared together (ST), unrelated children reared together (UT), and other diverse combinations of hereditary and environmental contributions (248).

The MAVA design has already given evidence of the nature-nurture ratios for a couple of dozen primary personality factors in Q data (270), and in objective tests (299a). As pointed out in Chapter 25, the sampling errors when only some 500 cases are taken, as in these pilot studies, are such that present evidence must be accepted only as the basis for the best hypotheses to test in further experiments. If Loehlin (940) is correct in his criticism of systematic deviations in existing results (and Cattell has in fact accepted Loehlin's ammendments, personal communication), the presently published ratios are overestimating the environmental contribution, which might account for the observed skewing of the distribution of 20 or so nature-nurture ratios to the nurture pole. Allowing for this, and for some mislabelling of factors originally found at the child level, the evidence on personality factors measured by questionnaire points to a substantial *environmental* determination of C, Ego Strength; F, Surgency; G, Super Ego; O, Guilt Proneness; Q_1, Radicalism; and Q_4, Ergic Tension Level. A fairly marked hereditary determination exists for A, Affectothymia; D, Excitability; E, Dominance; J, Asthenia; and (oddly enough) Q_3, Self-Sentiment Development. The highest *hereditary* determination, probably 80 to 90 per cent variance, occurs for B, Intelligence; and H, Parmia-vs.-Threctia (the autonomic associations of which have long been noted).

Among personality factors measured by objective tests ($4\frac{1}{2}$ hours of the O-A Battery on 647 boys and girls), the MAVA method showed most-environmental determination of Ego Strength (U.I. 16), Cortertia (U.I. 22), Regression (U.I. 23), Narcisstic Self-Concept (U.I. 26), Asthenia (U.I. 28), and Super Ego Strength (U.I. 29). Some predominance of hereditary determination occurred in Inhibition (U.I. 17), Independence (U.I. 19), and Exuberance (U.I. 21). The two source traits with highest constitutional determination were

Intelligence (Culture Fair test, U.I. 1) and Comention (U.I. 20)

These findings agree with other evidence on the meaning of these traits[3] and with twin-study results for intelligence.

There is still an appreciable step from the valuation of the final outcome of hereditary and environmental influences in the MAVA or twin methods to the description of the maturational process as such. About the latter there has been much in, e.g., Piaget (1158), Hunt (798), and other writers, which scientifically can only be regarded as speculation. (In the animal field such work as that of Hess [723a], and others *does,* however, permit firm inference about phases of maturation, imprinting effects, etc.) Only by the laborious process of determining the changing nature-nurture ratios at each age level can firm inferences eventually be made for humans about the interaction of maturation and learning at different stages of cultural and biological development. An instance where various sources of evidence have given a fairly clear picture is in the separation of the maturational curves for fluid general ability and the culturally determined curves of crystallized general ability (page 553).

Finally one should note that the MAVA method is yielding information only about the *dependent* variables. The independent variables of heredity, the genes and chromosomes, cannot, in humans, be directly manipulated. Methods for proceeding from psychological measurements to inference about genes and chromosomes have yet to be developed. Similarly, we know what final variance to ascribe to environment, but the *sources* of this en-

---

[3]An exception is U.I. 23, which Eysenck calls Neuroticism and which he and Prell (491) found to have a heavy hereditary determination. However, their result was based on the twin method and on a sample less than one-tenth of that collected in the Cattell, Kristy, and Stice (259a) study. Neuroticism conceivably has appreciable hereditary determination, but Regression, U.I. 23, is only one component (325) in neuroticism, and present results show it not to be heavily hereditary.

vironment influence still remain to be located (259a) after the MAVA determination. Nevertheless, the MAVA approach puts first things first. It follows a research strategy which first determines the nature-nurture ratio, so that guidance is given as to whether experiment should search for interpretation in terms of genetic or environmental mold hypotheses. In this connection, restricted space precludes special discussion of the genetic hypotheses, since we must now turn to environmental learning evidence.

maturational, but it is interesting and valuable to have these curves for one or two cultures as soon as possible. Fortunately, through the systematic way in which factoring has been carried out with similar variables at different age levels, and evidence of similar factors at different levels (see Sections 3 and 4 above), comparative developmental studies have become possible and evidence on trends is clear, as shown in Table 19-6 and Diagram 19-4.

Now the problem in bridging from learning theory (currently largely reflexological

TABLE 19-6

AGE TRENDS IN Q DATA PERSONALITY FACTORS, NORMALS ONLY
(From *Personality and Motivation Structure and Measurement* by Raymond B. Cattell, © 1957 by Harcourt, Brace & World, Inc. and reproduced with their permission.)

	Factor	Rate of Change per Year in S.T. Score × 100		Verbal Summary
		Age 16-34 yrs.	Age 34-60 yrs.	
A	Cyclothymia	0	0	No change
B	Intelligence	0	−5	Slight late fall
C	Ego Strength	+3	0	Slight early rise
E	Dominance	0	0	No change
F	Surgency	−3	−2.5	Continuous fall
G	Super Ego	0	0	No change
H	Parmia	+5	+3.5	Continuous rise
I	Premsia	+8	+3	Marked early rise
L	Protensia	−9	−3	Marked early fall
M	Autia	0	0	No change
N	Shrewdness	0	0	No change
O	Guilt Proneness	−9	−5	Marked fall
Q_1	Radicalism	0	−1	Very slight late fall
Q_2	Self-sufficiency	0	0	No change
Q_3	Will Control	+4	+4	Continuous rise
Q_4	Ergic Tension	−8	−4	Marked fall

After nature-nurture ratios, the next most important information for understanding personality maturation and learning is an adequate determining of age trends on personality factor measures, just as was done in the twenties of this century on the single source trait of general intelligence. Naturally, one cannot know, until comparisons are made across cultures and in other ways, how much of any trend is

and atomistic in conception) to personality theory is, as the Kentucky symposium (865a) showed, essentially that the former deals with disconnected bits of specific behavior, whereas the latter deals with concepts derived from total pattern structures. How far and in what manner can conditioning change a pattern such as that of Surgency, F, or Regression, U.I. 23(−), or Super Ego Strength (U.I. 29 and G)?

DIAGRAM 19-4. Childhood Age Trends in Objective Test Personality Factors U.I. 17, 22, and 28 (From *Personality and Motivation, Structure and Measurement* by Raymond B. Cattell, © 1957 by Harcourt, Brace & World, Inc. and reproduced with their permission.)

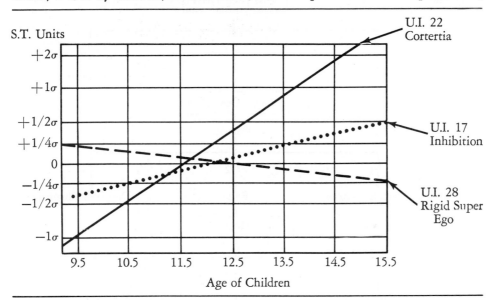

Presumably, what we call an environmental mold source trait is due to some social institution, e.g., home or church, reinforcing simultaneously a *whole set* of response patterns. If a single conditioning change is brought about, e.g., the reduction of a particular phobia by behavior therapy, does this remove only a symptom, as psychoanalysis asserts, or does it also affect the anxiety pattern and level in U.I. 24 as a whole?

At present, we do not have the beginnings of answers to these questions (except for some evidence described in Section 9 below), because learning theorists have as yet scarcely availed themselves at all of the structured concepts validated in personality theory. It is not surprising that into this vacuum there have grown some interesting developments in learning theory from personality theory. Central in these is the notion of personality change as "multidimensional change in relation to a multidimensional situation." This leads to an entirely new approach to learning theory in terms of matrix algebra, which has been discussed and illustrated in Chapters 11 and 20. Therein it is shown that by measuring a suitable sample of persons on personality factors before and after a set of complex learning experiences one can, without actual manipulative separation of the learning influences, determine the effect of each learning experience upon particular personality factors. Along with this, though separable from it theoretically and methodologically, goes the analysis of human learning influences, *in situ,* into a series of "dynamic crossroads" and "adjustment paths" schematizing the essentials which clinical observation has contributed to human personality learning, as a basis for experimental work. A brief, schematized illustration of the standard sequences of dynamic adjustment as conceived in this crossroad series is given in Diagram 19-5.

Incidentally, this new and mathematical concept of "adjustment process analysis,"

DIAGRAM 19-5. The Adjustment Process Analysis Chart (After Cattell, 262a)

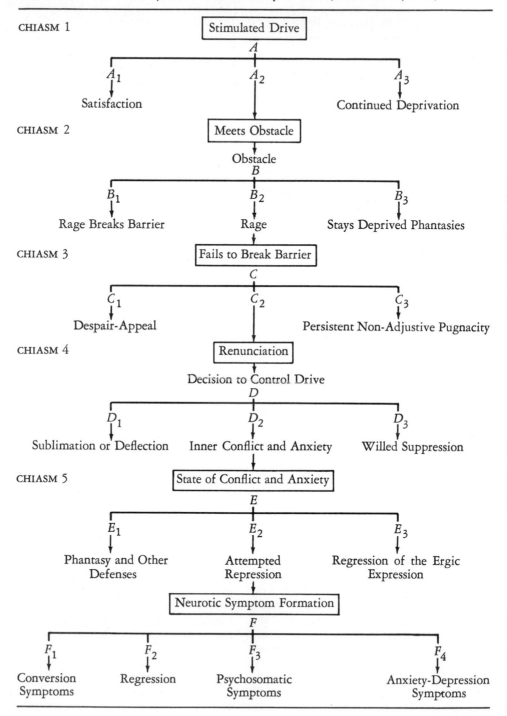

CHIASM 1

Stimulated Drive

A

A_1 — Satisfaction

A_2

A_3 — Continued Deprivation

CHIASM 2

Meets Obstacle

Obstacle
B

B_1 — Rage Breaks Barrier

B_2 — Rage

B_3 — Stays Deprived Phantasies

CHIASM 3

Fails to Break Barrier

C

C_1 — Despair-Appeal

C_2

C_3 — Persistent Non-Adjustive Pugnacity

CHIASM 4

Renunciation

Decision to Control Drive
D

D_1 — Sublimation or Deflection

D_2 — Inner Conflict and Anxiety

D_3 — Willed Suppression

CHIASM 5

State of Conflict and Anxiety

E

E_1 — Phantasy and Other Defenses

E_2 — Attempted Repression

E_3 — Regression of the Ergic Expression

Neurotic Symptom Formation
F

F_1 — Conversion Symptoms

F_2 — Regression

F_3 — Psychosomatic Symptoms

F_4 — Anxiety-Depression Symptoms

first systematically presented in Cattell and Scheier (325), also offers new light on the interaction of maturation and learning, in connection with the separation of "frequency of path choice" and "frequency of path experiences." For if a trait is fully or primarily hereditarily predetermined, it can only be a *cause* of choosing the path in the net of dynamic crossroads or successive choice points (see Diagram 19-5), not a learned *effect*. From a psychometric standpoint, a caution must be added that in this whole field allowance needs to be made for those reversible, "state" changes (e.g., age trends, seasonal cycles, physiological rhythms) considered in Chapter 11 and the variability of personality factors, discussed in the respective sections on *L, Q* and *T* data.

The Adjustment Process Analysis Chart recognizes more than any current theory of learning both the innate individual differences and the ways in which differences are acquired and essentially presents the possible history of any stimulated drive. The decisions made at the different choice points are, of course, seldom conscious. This schema has the advantage, for clinical discussions (where a diagnosis in the form of a punched-out dynamic flow chart for any clinical situation seems to be a logical consequence once an empirically derived taxonomy has been established) and experimental design, that every conceivable learning or conflict situation can be worked out empirically and quantitatively, and any individual's particular learning position can be codified.

Naturally, this matrix handling of the learning process needs to be related not only to general personality factors, as here, but also to motivation structure as discussed by Horn in Chapter 20. Much reflexological learning theory has related learning only to anxiety, and although there is no doubt that autonomic reflexes condition faster with anxiety, yet general personality learning has to be related to ergic tension levels on many ergs.

The immediate assistance which structured personality study can give to learning experiments exists, first, in defining these drives (as in the MAT) by reward on which learning can occur; secondly, in pointing out the personality structures which learning needs to explain; and, thirdly, in furnishing valid measures by which the change in these structures can be determined. This will yield the hypothetical constructs in which learning theory is primarily interested. The relationship between personality dimensions and learning effects is well demonstrated by the finding of Jensen (807a) that as much as 50 per cent of the total variance of a serial nonsense-syllable-learning experiment could be explained in terms of Extraversion (measured by Eysenck's MPI questionnaire). Similar relevance to personality traits has been shown for single speed, perception, or motivation experiments by Jensen (807a), Eysenck (489a), Weisen (1508a), and others.

We propose to take a final synoptical look at some results of empirical investigations of changes in personality traits through that learning and relearning which the clinician calls psychotherapy. Unfortunately, the evidence from controlled experiments is still sparse compared with the often questionable and conflicting results reported from premetric practice. Systematic studies of therapeutic progress and adjustment direction have been conducted in different media of observations. Thus the results on persons undergoing therapy available from pioneer studies by Hunt, Ewing, Laforge, and Gilbert (798a), with the 16 P.F. test, show that therapeutic improvement is accompanied by a rising *C* factor (increased Ego Strength), a shift toward Surgency, *F,* a shift toward Dominance (*E*), and high *H* (moving away from "Sizothyme Withdrawal" characteristic of the *H*(−) person), accompanied by a drop in the Anxiety factor. Also, the measurements of the effects of chemotherapy using the IPAT Anxiety Scale (313a), show, for the biochemical approach of therapy, that tranquilizers such as meprobamate with mild therapy lower the level of anxiety in neurotics. More substantial information on the combined effect of psychotherapy and chemotherapy on the Objective-Analytic (O-A) Battery (234) and the IPAT Eight Parallel Form Anxiety Scale (234) for the regression factor, U.I. 23, has come from the study of Cattell and his associates (313c). Here the tests give evidence of a significant two-dimensional change on Anxiety (U.I. 24) and on the U.I. 23 personality source trait, Regression. This experimental evidence strongly supports the hypothesis that the organism possesses innate unitary response patterns which, by learned behavior, may be quite variously attached to different stimuli.

8. PERSONALITY INTEGRATION AND THE SOCIO-CULTURAL GROUP

A trait, in any precise model, is by definition (240) something abstracted from the interaction of the person and his environment. Consequently, except in the special and "higher order" sense in which we can eventually reach an abstraction transcending the culture, every trait definition is bound to the culture and the environment. This cultural binding is true regardless of whether we deal with a constitutional or an environmental mold trait. Even apart from this embedding of the very definition of the trait and personality in this culture, the interaction of personality and culture is an important special aspect of personality study, and one bound up with the issue of personality integration, still undiscussed here. Accordingly, we propose very briefly to touch on the essentials of integration and of personality and culture, as they concern methods, models, and findings in personality.

A clear distinction has been drawn by Cattell (226, 240) and by Mowrer (1084) among the concepts of integration, adjust-

ment, and adaptation—the last as survival, the second as the obverse of frustration, and the first as the organization of behavior so that a minimum interference exists between one act and another, in terms of defined value goals. It is a long step, however, from verbal definitions, even of the most lucid kind, to operations and indices adequately expressing them. Such an index has, however, been defined by Horn in Chapter 20 as the inverse of a conflict measure in objective motivation measures. It remains to be seen how far, in experiment, this relates to the general personality factors with which we are here concerned, but at least in theory one would expect it to relate to the Self-Sentiment factor, U.I. 36, and possibly to U.I. 25, Reality Contact.

U.I. 36, the last of the 21 objective personality factors as yet empirically located, may nevertheless turn out to be the most important, for it relates to the structure of the self-sentiment. The chief multivariate researches explicitly directed to the structure of the self, introducing a majority of variables commonly considered theoretically important there, are those of Gorsuch (289), Gibb (593), Hofstaetter (734), Horn (743), and others. It is interesting, from the standpoint of psychoanalytic theory, that these empirical researches, starting with measured objective-test primary personality factors which represent Ego (U.I. 16) and Super Ego (U.I. 29 and 36), continue, even when carried to the second and third stratum, to show the Super Ego and the Self-Sentiment factors as distinct. There is no coalescence of the Self and Super Ego factors in a single "ideal self" (240, 262a), or ideal self-sentiment, such as that for which McDougall lucidly argued (1012). A glance at Section 4, Table 19-5 will show that at the second stratum one can recognize a factor, F(T)I, primarily concerned with the social self, and another, F(T)IV, with the factors, notably U.I. 29, having super ego meaning.

From a theoretical point of view, as Cattell has pointed out (262a), any such factor having the hypothesized function of being able to control most behavior would be expected to have high loadings on a wide array of variables (particularly those concerned with integrative, foresighted acts as contrasted with impulsive and socially objectionable behavior). For only in that way would it be able, as a factor, to veto the action of other (impulse) factors. To meet those conditions, it would necessarily have to possess a relatively limited hyperplane and consequently be hard to locate. Unfortunately, psychologists and social scientists working in group dynamics, learning theory, clinical psychology, etc., with relatively verbal concepts, and who are unfamiliar with multivariate analysis, have failed to take advantage of the theoretical and experimental possibilities which the emergence of these definite factors and their measurement in the higher strata can now bring to their work.

The concept of integration has been used with unrestrained freedom by various authors. It has sometimes been thought of as cultural integration, sometimes as life philosophy, and again as "integrating idea" (18). It is, however, reasonable to expect good integration without any highly developed ideational goal, and to expect that the single "goal" is simply the maximum expression of all ergs with the minimum of behavioral interference (240). Following this line of thinking, then, integration describes the extent to which behavior contributes harmoniously to a single goal or consistent set of goals. In the last resort, the concept of integration has to be defined operationally, by a method of covariation analysis. Such an operational definition has been given by McQuitty (1015a) as the extent of agreement, by pattern analysis (1016), of the individual's attitude system with that of the group to which he belongs. Though clear and measurable, this surely indicates conformity rather than integration.

These considerations of whether integration is integration with personal values or integration with society bring us to consider the definition of the group as "an instrumentality for the satisfactions of those who belong to it" (with or without immediate interaction). Research on groups has been largely on either small "face to face" groups ("group dynamics") or large cultural groups (civilizations, tribal cultures, etc.). In either case, as Chapter 26 shows in more detail, the most theoretically economical procedure is to determine the dimensions of group behavior, factor analytically, and to seek laws relating scores on these dimensions to (a) the personality scores (as population — membership — means and sigmas), and (b) the internal group structure.

The beginning of some laws in this area — at least of the relation of means on such personality factors as G, H, C, etc. — to performances of small groups are summarized in Chapter 26. So also are the relations of personality factors to democratic and non-democratic leadership, and to various kinds of group acts. Diagram 19-6 shows, for example, some significant relations between Q data measures of personality factors (328) and acts in the group situation.

The above results clearly indicate that certain factors, those principally associated with neuroticism, militate against effective group integration. Indeed, Cattell has argued that social psychological discussion in the psychoanalytic era has been too much concerned with what group standards do to the neurotic and insufficiently with what the neurotic does to group morale and integration. Although, as Chapter 26 substantiates, the dimensions of cultures are now well defined, at least in regard to such factors as cultural pressure, size, education-affluence and morality-integration (226, 271, 262a), the task of relating personality factors in the population to these traits in the culture is a large one, if enough instances are to be gathered to produce correlational evidence. Such correlations of mean population personality traits with culture-pattern dimension scores offer ex-

DIAGRAM 19-6. The 16 P.F. Profiles of Three Types of Leaders (from Cattell, Stice, & Eber, 329)

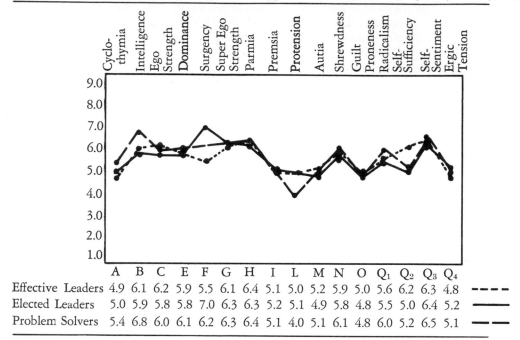

	A	B	C	E	F	G	H	I	L	M	N	O	Q_1	Q_2	Q_3	Q_4	
Effective Leaders	4.9	6.1	6.2	5.9	5.5	6.1	6.4	5.1	5.0	5.2	5.9	5.0	5.6	6.2	6.3	4.8	- - - -
Elected Leaders	5.0	5.9	5.8	5.8	7.0	6.3	6.3	5.2	5.1	4.9	5.8	4.8	5.5	5.0	6.4	5.2	——
Problem Solvers	5.4	6.8	6.0	6.1	6.2	6.3	6.4	5.1	4.0	5.1	6.1	4.8	6.0	5.2	6.5	5.1	——

citing possibilities of finding significance as shown by such results as in Table 19-7.

The similarity of factor patterns on the 16 P.F. in American (608), Brazilian, British (336), Chinese (939a), French (310a), German (305a), and Italian (301c) groups, though with divergent loading patterns, permits in principle a comparison of persons in distinct cultures on exactly the same personality factors. This allows also for an integration of personality research findings in different countries. Without doubt there will be some factors, notably in the dynamic, sentiment realm, that are unique to one culture or country. The task remains to discover and identify those personality dimensions which are essentially the same (e.g., intelligence, anxiety level, physiological factors) or alike in kind (e.g., sentiment to family and religion and super ego strength), and to separate them from factors particular to a culture (e.g., democratic versus totalitarian attitude patterns, matriarchal versus patriarchal up-

bringing, sentiment to sport or to science). The former have been called culture-free and the latter culture-bound factors (262a).

9. DEVELOPMENT AND CHECKING OF PERSONALITY THEORY BY CRITERIA IN APPLIED PSYCHOLOGY

Research using normal personality source-trait measures has been increasingly directed toward applied situations. Criterion relations for different clinical syndrome groups, occupational selection principles, educational prediction, marital compatibility, or ways of solving conflict have been established in a series of independent studies. Conceptually, the understanding of the functionally unitary personality factors and of the various criteria in applied psychology has been greatly advanced through the findings of these researches.

TABLE 19-7

Two Second-Order Personality Factors in the 16 P.F. Questionnaire Compared Across Different Cultures

Primary Personality Factor	Anxiety Second-Order Factor						Extraversion Second-Order Factor					
	American (N=1652)	Brazilian (N=2234)	British (N=112)	Chinese (N=556)	German (N=446)	Japanese (N=300)	American (N=1652)	Brazilian (N=2234)	British (N=112)	Chinese (N=556)	German (N=446)	Japanese (N=300)
A	00	−02	−01	08	11	−08	46	35	35	24	11	67
B	−06	02	−	−02	−04	02	−02	−03	−	07	−17	−10
C	−52	−33	−41	−47	−49	−65	02	05	03	08	12	−22
E	−01	03	−00	−01	−02	−09	44	53	49	56	51	24
F	05	01	14	02	−27	−00	59	60	70	69	−01	54
G	−14	−02	−24	−01	−04	−04	−08	04	−28	−05	01	−17
H	−42	−22	−18	−29	−33	−42	62	58	62	53	65	56
I	−01	02	−08	−07	10	−11	02	06	−11	07	−31	13
L	54	39	50	50	48	66	01	02	23	09	−12	24
M	21	02	40	03	05	11	−01	−02	21	26	14	−07
N	05	04	02	21	−09	12	06	02	−03	03	01	02
O	70	60	69	46	34	80	−06	−02	02	−05	16	06
Q₁	−09	−06	25	00	01	−14	02	05	−12	00	−19	−32
Q₂	04	01	20	02	−01	11	−34	−36	−35	−07	−14	−33
Q₃	−54	−39	−40	−48	−32	−82	−18	−06	−14	−05	−04	11
Q₄	76	73	62	65	12	83	02	03	18	07	14	06

Since clinical psychology informs many branches of applied psychology, we look first at the principles of diagnosis, pathological taxonomy, and therapy as affected by advances in structured personality measurement.

The power of diagnosis from such instruments as the Guilford-Zimmerman Temperament Survey (642), the Thurstone Temperament Schedule (1423a), or the 16 P.F. Questionnaire (317) has proven to be a substantial advance over that of older tests. Considering the relatively short time they have been used, the new factored questionnaires show a very high effectiveness. Thus in the recent work of Cattell and Rickels (313b) on private patients, the measures of Anxiety (U.I. 24) and Regression (U.I. 23) (the former derived from the 16 P.F. Questionnaire) each separate patients from normals at t values of the order of 10, i.e., a $P < .001$ significance. Additionally, the 16 factors (of the 16 P.F. Questionnaire) have been found valid predictors in numerous aspects of adjustment, prognosis, or success by Cattell (240), Cattell and Scheier (325), Cattell, Tatro, and Komlos (334b, 334c), Rickels and Cattell (1198a), and many others. They have clearly demonstrated the need for a redefinition of personality change and its underlying mechanisms. Changes in personality should henceforth be regarded as multidimensional in response to multidimensional changes in the environment (262a), which, conceptually, is a complete shift from the descriptive-symptomatic to the functional-dynamic approach. Emphasis in diagnosis is consequently placed on quantitative analysis of changes and differences in personality structures and dynamic source traits rather than on a description of symptoms and syndromes.

Characteristic personality profiles from questionnaire research exist for different mental hospital groups such as neurotics, psychotics, or psychopaths, and especially for distinction of such syndrome groups as anxiety hysterics, obsessionals, conversion hysterics, psychosomatics, and others (240, 325). The measurement of several hundreds of patients alternatively on the questionnaire, 16 P.F. test of such factors as Ego Strength, Sizothymia, Super Ego Strength, Ergic Tension, etc., have further demonstrated that neurotics, psychotics, psychopaths, homosexuals, psychosomatics, and various other syndrome groups, can be recognized by distinct 16 P.F. profiles. For example, Diagram 19-7 shows the profiles of anxiety neurotics, homosexuals, paranoid schizophrenics, and normals. Homosexuals differ from the neurotic profile by being more extravert, lower in Guilt Proneness and Super Ego Strength (factors O and G), somewhat more weak on the fundamental Ego Strength factor, C, and more radical in Social Outlook (factor Q_1) (303). The research of Cattell, Tatro, and Komlos (334b, 334c) on the structure of paranoid and non-paranoid schizophrenics shows, on the other hand, that paranoids are lower on C, Ego Strength; E, Dominance; F, Surgency; and higher on L, Paranoid Tendency or Protension; with, however, almost "normal" Guilt Proneness (factor O), but a strong development on Q_3, toward control by an explicit Self-Sentiment Concept, in addition to low Ergic Tension, Q_4. This one can hypothesize as being due to the employment by the paranoid of more regressive types of defenses such as projection, identification, or denial. A fuller treatment of this hypothesis is given in Delhees (414a). The Ego Weakness factor, $C(-)$, has been consistently present in all pathological groups (including drug addicts and alcoholics) as the most central subnormal condition. An interesting "by-product" of the questionnaire research (334b, 334c), which will be of special interest to investigators in the social sciences, lies in the significant differences found between men and women on factors A (women more affecto-thyme), E (men more dominant), I (women more premsic — protected emotional sensitivity) and Q_2 (men more self-sufficient). This and similar studies represent a tremendous advantage over "descriptive syndrome" observations on a patient, as obtained in quantitative form by, for example, the MMPI. The combination of source trait measures in the 16 P.F., HSPQ, Humor Test, Music Preference Test, MPI, etc., and surface-trait measures in the MMPI, TAT, and others could be peculiarly effective. Yet *Q* data remains

significant results from quantitative analyses of adjustment processes which have been measured in terms of anxiety level, ego strength, degree of contact with reality, constitutional degree of temperament dimensions (for example, the sizothyme temperament), and so on. The evidence comes primarily from experiments on changes in personality dimensions under

DIAGRAM 19-7. The 16 P.F. Profiles of Anxiety Neurotics, Homosexuals, Normals, and Paranoid Schizophrenics

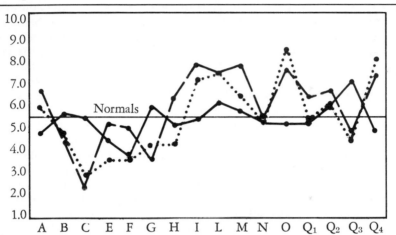

Sten Scores:	A	B	C	E	F	G	H	I	L	M	N	O	Q₁	Q₂	Q₃	Q₄	
Anxiety Neurotics	5.9	4.9	2.9	3.7	3.6	4.3	4.3	7.1	7.4	6.4	5.2	8.5	5.4	6.1	4.5	7.8	·····
Homosexuals	6.9	4.8	2.4	5.2	5.0	3.6	6.4	7.8	7.4	7.8	5.3	7.6	6.4	6.7	4.8	7.2	▬ ▬
Paranoid Schizophrenics	4.8	5.7	5.5	4.5	3.8	6.0	5.2	5.4	6.1	5.8	5.3	5.2	5.3	6.0	7.1	4.9	▬▬

only one of three media of observation. In Section 3 we have fully described the properties and distinctions of *Q* data relative to *L* data and *T* data. We may add at this point that the conceptual understanding of *L* data factors has been considerably advanced by the factoring of ratings on patients and symptom records by Degan (413), Lorr (953), and others. What remains to be done is a bringing of the *L* data factors of Lorr into a common space with the known objective test factors (325a).

Further evidence of the diagnostic value of factored questionnaires lies in the

therapy. They have been discussed in Section 8.

The application of the Objective-Analytic (O-A) source-trait measures (234) in clinical work has furnished evidence that a very high degree of agreement exists between the factor patterns found in different types of pathological syndrome groups and those found in normals, though the levels have appeared to be quite different (285, 1266, 1267, 279a). However, as Cattell and Tatro (334a) have pointed out, we cannot be sure at this stage of experiment that certain further dimensions even more important than these do not exist, and that they may be capable of contributing to the differentiation of pathological syndrome groups. It would be too early at this point to estimate how much of the variance of the particular syndrome group can be attributed to the personality factors here covered. What can be justly said, however, is that deviations among syndrome groups appear to lie in source traits of a very different nature. Intensive study is needed of the degree of association of factors with specific mental disorders. In regard to the structure and strength of *individual* unique traits, research for objectively exploring and measuring them in patient groups, notably by *P* technique (229), is in equal demand.

Only recently (334a) has the O-A Battery begun to be used as a diagnostic tool, yielding evidence on the specific kind of deviation from normality found in psychotic groups, mainly paranoid and non-paranoid schizophrenics. The Cattell and Tatro study evidenced that psychotics deviate from normal controls on no fewer than six personality dimensions beyond the $P < .01$ level of significance. Diagnostic differences were found in the direction of psychotics having lower Ego Strength (U.I. 16(−)), more Subduedness (U.I. 19(−)), lower Energy (U.I. 21 (−)), higher Regression (U.I. 23(−)), and higher Disso-frustrance (U.I. 30). The psychotic person does not differ on general Anxiety, U.I. 24, or on the factors which express merely dynamic adjustment problems (for example, U.I. 22, Cortertia-Pathemia, or U.I. 29, Responsive Will vs. Defensive Complacency) which, by contrast, differentiate neurotics (476, 325). Characteristic both of neurotics and (schizophrenic) psychotics are source-trait deviations on U.I. 16(−), Ego Weakness; U.I. 17, General Inhibition; U.I. 19(−), Subduedness; and U.I. 21(−), Restraint. A brief comment needs to be made regarding the nature of the factors which have obvious clinical associations. They have been set out in

Table 19-8. Because of limited space, we draw only upon some of the factors. A more extensive treatment of them can be read in Cattell (240), Cattell and Scheier (325), and Hundleby, Pawlik, and Cattell (796).

The role of U.I. 22 in mental health is suggested by its (negative) correlations with *O* and *L* questionnaire factors (respectively, Guilt Proneness and Protension), by its significantly lower score in neurotics, and, in addition, by its negative correlation with psychiatric rejection in air pilot training (876, 877, 235). Similarly, factor U.I. 19(−), Subduedness, has its clinical importance indicated by its consistent relation to super ego (factor *G*) measures in the questionnaire (319, 321) and by the evidence as to its diagnostic power in the O-A Battery (334a). The Cattell and Tatro study suggests that U.I. 22(−), Pathemia, represents an expression of general ergic frustration, with resulting tendency to react at the hypothalamic rather than the cortical level. On this evidence, and the evidence of high cortical alertness as shown by EEG interruption, U.I. 22(+) has been designated *Cortertia* (1142). With the physiological associations of this factor known, measures on U.I. 22 will be a guide in therapy with drugs. As to the therapeutic process, U.I. 32 (Exvia vs. Invia) gives an objective measure of the patient's position on the introversion-extraversion personality dimension which should assist the therapist in estimating the seriousness of withdrawal symptoms or the kind of adjustment that may profitably be attempted (240).

The value of the U.I. 23 factor in indicating the severity of neurotic conditions has been demonstrated independently by Eysenck and his co-workers (474, 476, 493) and by Cattell and his associates (240, 325, 796). If the hypothesis is correct in viewing U.I. 23 as a neural exhaustion produced perhaps by prolonged conflict as well as by constitutional tendencies, rather than as an immediate function of conflict per se, then this measure should indicate what reserves the individual has to take steps toward new integration (240). In terms of anticipating whether a conflict is likely to generate conversion-hysteric or emotional-anxiety symptoms, however, measures on U.I. 17 should, according to Eysenck's theory (476), be particularly valuable. What we still lack here is an intensive and comprehensive research of measured change under therapy.

Special clinical interest attaches to U.I. 25 — the personality dimension which Eysenck has referred to as Realism vs. Psychoticism, and which Cattell has described as Realism vs. Tensidia. The latter is defined in the negative (i.e., U.I. 25 direction) as a tendency to tense inner activity associated with inflexibility, upsetting adaptation to external realities. The theoretical differences between the Eysenck group at Maudsley Hospital and the Cattell group at the University of Illinois on factors U.I. 25 and U.I. 23, which to Eysenck are respectively *the* psychoticism factor and *the* neuroticism factor, are that the latter has insisted that the psychotic differs from the normal on at least five factors (240, 334a) and that the characteristic neurotic pattern consists of at least six unitary factors, one of which is the general Anxiety factor, U.I. 24 (325).

An impressive array of findings on the clinical application of the U.I. 24 personality factor has appeared in Cattell and Scheier (325), Cattell and Rickels (313b), and recently in Rickels and Cattell (1198a). The available evidence leads to the conclusion that U.I. 24 measures manifest, unbound anxiety instanced in the neurotic's increased Ergic Tension (Q_4), and his inability to integrate, shown both in Ego Weakness ($C(-)$), and in $Q_3(-)$, Low Integration. The psychotic, by contrast, does not differ on Anxiety (334a). The U.I. 24 dimension is one of the first-order objective test factors with known match among state factors. Thus it possesses a double nature as both a trait and a state dimension.

A more detailed discussion of trait and state factors has been given in Section 4.

The initial information on the extent to which primary personality factors help to predict in practical school situations has rested on the factor analysis of groups of normal children, notably by Pierson, Sweney, and Sealy in America (1165, 1371, 327a), Connor and Radcliffe in Australia, and Butcher and Warburton in Britain (336, 177a). Personality influence in backward children has been studied by O'Halloran (1113a), Wright (1586a), and others. The use of the 14 factors of the High School Personality Questionnaire or HSPQ (268a) reveals quite important differences in average school learning of children. For example, a child who is more outgoing, emotionally expressive, adaptable, and warmly related to the teacher (all aspects of the *A* factor, Affectothymia) will learn faster and easier. The same holds for the child who is more emotionally stable and less worried (*C* factor, Ego Strength). The more responsible and conscientious (*G* factor, Super Ego Strength) individual will make more progress for the same intelligence. However, the more dominant (*E* factor, Dominance) child learns more slowly than the docile, submissive absorber of examination material. The reader will realize that it would be premature to take these results as an indication of what may be predictable about (for instance) a person's later occupational success. In fact, investigation of the personality interest factors of eminent men by Cattell and Drevdahl (283) shows the productive researcher to be significantly more sizothyme (factor $A(-)$), dominant (factor $E(+)$), self-sufficient (factor Q_2) and radical (Q_1). There is thus some discrepancy between success in school and after school which should be a weighty criterion for scholarship selection and lead to more realistic testing programs in schools.

Factored questionnaires and employee ratings have been used for some time as an estimate of the adjustment and the

TABLE 19-8

THE PRINCIPAL OBJECTIVE PERSONALITY FACTORS WITH OBVIOUS CLINICAL ASSOCIATIONS

O-A Factor	Title	Psychological Description of the Positive Factor Pole and Clinical Significance
U.I. 16	Developed ego (+) vs. Unassertiveness (−)	Description: Fast speed and tempo of action; high self-assertiveness in competitive situations; less impairment of performance; "strong" body physique. Clinical Significance: Both neurotics and psychotics are significantly lower than normals; convicted criminals score significantly higher than neurotics.
U.I. 17	Timid distrust (+) vs. Trustingness (−)	Description: High cautiousness and timidity; increased tendency towards inhibiting overt behavior; less alert. Clinical Significance: Both neurotics and psychotics are significantly higher than normals.
U.I. 19	Independence (+) vs. Subduedness (−)	Description: Accurate, competent performance; less distractibility; self-complacent criticalness of others; conservative estimates of own performance; low social suggestibility. Clinical Significance: Both neurotics and psychotics are significantly lower than normals; psychiatrists' ratings of over-all anxiety and situational anxiety correlate negatively with U.I. 19(+).
U.I. 21	Exuberance (+) vs. Restraint (−)	Description: Faster speed of social and perceptual judgment, high verbal and ideational fluency; sensitivity to threat and emotional stimulation; imperviousness to social suggestion; high physiological activity. Clinical Significance: Both neurotics and psychotics are significantly lower than normals; significant negative correlation with clinical diagnosis of neurosis.
U.I. 22	Cortertia (+) vs. Pathemia (−)	Description: Fast speed performance; high immediate responsiveness, but low endurance; tense restlessness and high level of activation. Clinical Significance: Neurotics are significantly lower than normals, but psychotics do not differ on U.I. 22.
U.I. 23	Mobilization (+) vs. Regression (−)	Description: Low rigidity; less dependence on environment; less extremity of viewpoint; high endurance of stress. Clinical Significance: Neurotics are significantly lower than normals; no difference for psychotics; normals are higher than criminals.
U.I. 24	Anxiety (+) vs. Adjustment (−)	Description: High manifest anxiety; high drive tension level; insecurity, guilt, and self-depreciation; increased susceptibility to annoyance and embarrassment.

TABLE 19-8 (Continued)

THE PRINCIPAL OBJECTIVE PERSONALITY FACTORS WITH OBVIOUS CLINICAL ASSOCIATIONS

O-A Factor	Title	Psychological Description of the Positive Factor Pole and Clinical Significance
		Clinical Significance: Neurotics score significantly higher than normals; criminals score on the average higher than normals; psychotics do not differ on this factor.
U.I. 25	Realism (+) vs. Tensinflexia (−)	Description: Less imaginative cognition; high accuracy and speed in well-structured tasks; reality-directed attitudes; reduced emotional tensions.
		Clinical Significance: No difference between neurotics and normals; psychotics score significantly lower than normals; delinquents score significantly lower than sociopathic neurotics, and both groups significantly lower than non-delinquent normals.
U.I. 28	Super Ego Asthenia (+) vs. Rough Assurance (−)	Description: Low psycho-physical momentum; self-experienced insecurity; lack of self-confidence and steadfastness of opinion; increased negativistic criticalness.
		Clinical Significance: Neurotics score significantly higher than normals; both delinquents and socio-pathic neurotics (drug addicts, alcoholics) score significantly lower than non-delinquent normals; no difference between psychotics and normals.
U.I. 29	Determined Responsiveness (+) vs. Lack of Will (−)	Description: High speed and co-operativeness of responses; little effect resulting from threat and discomfort; tendency to respond too quickly.
		Clinical Significance: Important discriminator between neurotic and non-neurotic groups; no difference found between psychotics and normals.
U.I. 30	Mature Stolidness (+) vs. Dissofrustrance (−)	Description: Slow psychomotor speed and tempo; less carefulness; attitudinal independence; restricted emotionality ("dry," aloof).
		Clinical Significance: Psychotics score significantly lower than normals; neurotics and normals do not differ on this factor; criminals score lower than non-delinquent controls.
U.I. 32	Exvia (+) vs. Invia (−)	Description: Extraversion; less accurate, more fluent perception and thinking; optimistic, self-confident socio-orientedness.
		Clinical Significance: Neurotics are found to be more introverted (U.I. 32−); non-delinquents are more extraverted (U.I. 32+) than criminals; psychotics and normals do not differ significantly on this factor.

performance of a person in a particular occupation. We shall discuss them in terms of the 16 P.F. measures because far more occupational and clinical profiles and specification equations have been collected on these than on any other factored questionnaire. In terms of prediction from primary personality factors, relations between such measures and occupational criteria and selection principles have been ascertained through researches by Cattell and Stice (327b), Cattell, May, and Meeland (301a), Shotwell and Cattell (1316a), Holland (736a), and others. In addition to

pations; the details are left to the respective handbooks, but the essential industrial application is illustrated from the profile from data on 105 psychiatric technicians (taken from the handbook for the 16 P.F. Questionnaire). Shotwell (1316a) obtained reliable ratings on two criterion groups of these subjects and found significant differences between the low and high criterion group in that the former were more emotionally stable (C+), of greater super ego strength (G+), and less bewildered by irrational behavior (Q₁−). Similarly, in a study by King, several hun-

DIAGRAM 19-8. Comparison of 16 P.F. Profiles of Successful and Unsuccessful Psychiatric Technicians (from Cattell, Stice & Eber, 329)

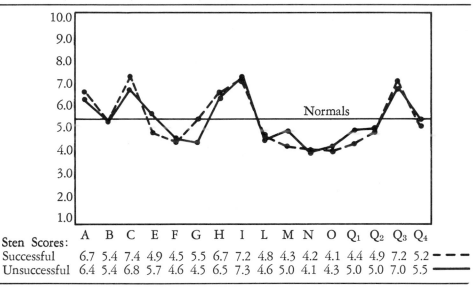

Sten Scores:	A	B	C	E	F	G	H	I	L	M	N	O	Q₁	Q₂	Q₃	Q₄	
Successful	6.7	5.4	7.4	4.9	4.5	5.5	6.7	7.2	4.8	4.3	4.2	4.1	4.4	4.9	7.2	5.2	- - -
Unsuccessful	6.4	5.4	6.8	5.7	4.6	4.5	6.5	7.3	4.6	5.0	4.1	4.3	5.0	5.0	7.0	5.5	——

the use of the general personality questionnaires (for example, the 16 P.F. Questionnaire) in industry, "special purpose" tests such as the Neurotic Personality Factor test (325), the Contact Personality Factor test (298a), or the Anxiety Scale Questionnaire (322), have been used to measure general character integration vs. neuroticism, fitness for contact jobs, anxiety level, etc. Job profiles have been constructed for a series of different occu-

dred bakery route (door-to-door) salesmen were measured on the 16 P.F. test personality factors. This study reveals that the effective salesman in this type of situation tends to be affectothyme (factor A+), surgent and talkative (F+), and of sufficient ego strength (C) not to suffer if "brushed off."

It is important to know (and future research may show) which of these personality trait scores accounts for the person fitting the occupational profile. As Cattell (262a) has pointed out, the number of source-trait scores likely to be needed to reach as good a prediction as is virtually possible may easily reach 30 to 40. The advantages in extending to the O-A Battery with it performance-test approach and to the motivation sphere become apparent here.

In examining the ways in which the quantitative theories of personality have entered the applied fields we should next, perhaps, bring out the relations of personality variables to marriage choice and stability. Several conflicting theories of mate selection and marriage compatibility have been formulated, mostly defending either the "likeness" or the "completeness" principles in marriage. However, as Tharp (1387a) has pointed out, often they suffer both from uncertainty of measurement and from insufficiently operationally defined concepts. It has been shown with remarkable success (305a) that the research design called for to remedy this shortcoming is multivariate, employing measures of pertinent relevance in the marriage field. The analysis clearly indicates that compatibility in marriage is associated with similarity on most measured personality factors. Statistically significant positive correlations have been found among stable couples with respect to eight factors (out of the 16 factors in the 16 P.F. Questionnaire); in the unstable group only two such significant positive correlations were found, and two were significantly negative (305a). This is in complete agreement with the psychological work of Fisher (519a), Kretschmer (886a), Kelly (858a), Cattell and Willson (338a), Cattell (226), and others who have demonstrated the "assortativeness of mating" (R.A. Fisher (519a): whereby like tends to choose like) in relation to physical, personality (for example, intelligence), and interest characteristics.

The question remains whether absolute as well as relative levels on personality factors contribute to a stable (happy or successful) marriage. A comparison of husbands (and wives) in the Cattell and Nesselroade study shows significant differences between those in happy and unhappy marriages. A discriminant function separates them at the $P < .001$ level, showing husbands in stable marriages to be high in H Parmia; I, Premsia; and L, Protension; and lower in E, Dominance. Correspondingly, wives in stable marriages are lower in E, Dominance; higher in L, Protension; less Radical, Q_1; and lower in Ergic Tension, Q_4. By contrast, the compensatory or completeness principle is seen to be at work more in the attempted adjustment of unstables. This suggests that an unstable person may unconsciously seek for partnership a "stabilizer." What is called for here is a study of the dynamic adjustment processes that take place in the partners in marriage. These processes are hypothesized to operate in an essentially different pattern than the likeness and the completeness principles. The latter can be stated and investigated in terms of personality and ability profiles (and eventually extended to the objective test realm of measurement); the former requires more complex reference to conflict and to ergic tension levels in the dynamic structure factors (295). The latter have been discussed in detail by Horn in Chapter 20.

The store of knowledge regarding the meaning of personality factors in the applied realms of the school, occupational guidance, leadership, mate selection, the family, etc., has so far come mostly from researches with questionnaires (notably the 16 P.F. [317] or the HSPQ [268a], the GZTS, etc.). Only in recent years (except for earlier studies by Brogden on school achievement and by Sells on military pilot proficiency) have the objective, behavioral measures been directed toward ascertaining their applied value outside the clinic and the mental hospital. This lag in use is due to the greater demands on the time and skill of the psychologist in administering the objective tests, yet there are decided advantages in the O-A Batteries. A decisive increase in the effectiveness of prediction from objective tests has already been demonstrated in the areas of elementary school achievement (140) and college achievement (1139), psychiatric screening of flying personnel (235, 326), physical fitness (1512a), and in Navy, Army, and Marine Corps settings (876, 877, 878). With the emergence of operationally shortened versions (which are currently being studied by Cattell and Hundleby) of the still complex and time-consuming O-A Battery, the objective measures of personality will be increasingly used as predictors on numerous aspects of applied criteria, selection principles, and prediction aims.

Most of our attention in this applied section has been directed to the above topics of scholastic performance, treatment of the neurotic and the abnormal, marriage, and industrial selection. They may be considered the main applications of personality measurement. There remain however, some mediate areas of effect, for example, in political issues and in personal organization. Parenthetically, a few researches are assembled which have used measures of definite factors. Thus, the study of leader personality and its relation to group success by Cattell and Stice (328) shows that leaders are significantly above average in Intelligence (factor B), high on Ego and Super Ego Strength (C and G), show higher Control (Q_3) and higher Parmia (H), and reveal lower Timidity ($O-$). Personality relations on the known 16 to 20 personality factors are very clear in relation to a wide array of political issues, consumer preferences, religious affiliations, etc. For example, coast-to-coast surveys made by the 16 P.F. Questionnaire show that in some fields buyers of different products differ significantly in personality.

With this last brief glance at personality measurement in applied situations, sufficient evidence has been presented not only to demonstrate the wealth of factual data that have been obtained by multivariate

analysis to bring about a proper taxonomy of influences, situations, and personalities, but also to offer some pragmatic proof of the suitability of the model, in general, and of the actual factor concepts isolated, in particular.

10. SUMMARY

(1) Personality theory is in transition from dependence upon mainly clinical origins to a new phase of growth from multivariate experimental roots. The beginning model is the linear, additive, specification equation, representing the situation by a vector of behavioral indices and the person by a vector of ability, temperament, and dynamic source traits. Considerable progress has been made in identifying and describing, in life-record, questionnaire, and objective test data, the primary and secondary source traits. Recently, attention has concentrated on "perturbation" sources in the simplest resolution, leading to recognition of instrument factors in the mode of observation, role, factors, and the modulation model.

(2) Analysis of L data constitutes a valuable beginning in that it (a) deals with what is commonly considered the criterion, (b) permits the operational use of the *personality sphere* concept of a stratified sample of all variables, and (c) demands attention early to the problem of instrument factors. Organization can proceed either under surface-trait (correlation clusters) or source-trait (simple structure factors) models, but the former have disabling shortcomings. The latter have yielded some 25 primary and a half dozen second-order factors. It has been argued that attempts to approach the second order directly, under an application of the parsimony principle leading to underfactoring (by known statistical criteria), does not give accurate conceptual and psychometric treatment of second-order factors.

(3) Q-data instruments (questionnaires, etc.) have been widely used in personality

research because of the relative ease with which they can be constructed and administered. Principles of construction consist essentially of three alternatives covering (a) correlation of items with some criterion or syndrome, (b) development of internal homogeneity (surface traits), and (c) development of factor validity. If simple structure is pursued "righteously," whether in test construction or large-scale analyses, it has invariably led to oblique rather than orthogonal resolution of axes. Distortion and instrument factor effects have been treated in terms of a role effect model rather than as isolated response set conceptions. There is no one-to-one correspondence of either distortion or response sets to personality factors, but personality and role factors account for response set behavior, as for any other factorially complex behavior variables.

(4) Objective behavior tests (T data), i.e., structured miniature situations designed to (a) preclude response distortion by the subject, and (b) yield objectively scored performance measures, have provided a radically different approach from those of L and Q data to the structuring of both inter- and intra-individual differences dimensions of personality. Although relying upon knowledge from L- and Q-data media to provide hypotheses to assure wide sampling of behavior in initial analyses, research with T-data instruments has since generated new concepts covering some 21 major, replicated temperament dimensions, as well as a number of ability and dynamic traits. Higher order analyses of these 20 or so factors have produced seven second-order and three third-order factors. A brief examination of the available evidence on the matching of T-data factors with those found in Q data suggests that such conceptual linkages exist between the first-stratum factors found in the former and second-stratum factors of the latter medium.

(5) Behavior can be conceptually simplified for description and measurement under four main models: surface and source traits, modal types and modal processes. The specification equation, initially linear and additive, can be applied to all of these, but also permits of development into polynomials of varying complexity, as in the phenomena covered by moderator and suppressor variables, interaction, permissive, and other factor models, modulator action and behavioral emergents. Other promising models for personality and its development exist in computer and information processing, games theory, and stochastic learning models, etc., but little in the way of substantive growth has yet transpired from these.

(6) The reflections upon psychological and experimental principles in interpreting structure and process in Section 6 show that an experimental personality theory can and should rest on theoretical notions directly derivable from factor-analytic and manipulative evidence. There have been several attempts to integrate this factorial and other experimental evidence on structure, extending the use of factor measures beyond "actuarial" procedures to include predictions and understanding from the psychological nature of the structure concerned. A number of theories regarding particular source traits have resulted from this development. The procedures of inference employed thereby have been set out in brief, and the practical task of developing an abstract factor concept has been illustrated.

(7) The most important information for understanding personality maturation and learning comes from the experimental evidence on (a) genetics, determining maturation, and (b) laws of personality learning. In attempting to organize substantive findings on personality change phenomena, the decisive advantages of recent developments in new concepts and methods have been discussed, e.g., the Multiple Abstract Variance Analysis (MAVA) for determining nature-nurture ratios, or the mathematical concept of "adjustment

process analysis" for working out empirically and quantitatively every conceivable
learning or conflict situation. These new
developments make possible a bridging
from learning theory to personality theory
and the establishing of laws of personality
learning. There is still an appreciable step
from the valuation of the final outcome of
hereditary and environmental influence,
for which we have presented evidence
from empirical investigations, to the description of the maturational process as
such and its interaction with learning.

(8) The interaction of personality and
culture is an important special aspect of
personality study, and one bound up
with the issue of personality integration.
Methods, models, and findings in regard to
this have been discussed. It has been shown
that the most theoretically economic procedure it to determine the dimensions of
group behavior, factor analytically, and
to seek laws relating scores on these dimensions to (a) the personality scores, and (b)
the internal group structure. Indications of
significant correlations of mean personality
traits with culture pattern dimension scores
open up exciting possibilities here. The
task remains to discover and identify those
personality dimensions which are essentially the same or alike in kind, and to
separate them from factors particular to
a culture.

(9) In examining the ways in which functional measurement and theories of personality based on experiment have entered
the applied fields, we have brought out the
relations of personality factors to such
areas as the diagnosis and treatment of the
neurotic and the abnormal, scholastic performance, marriage, industrial selection,
and so on. Sufficient evidence has been
presented to demonstrate the wealth of
factual data that have been obtained by
multivariate analysis to bring about a
proper taxonomy of influences, situations,
and personalities. This and the established
diagnostic power of structured measurement and its substantial advantages over
that of older tests offer some pragmatic
proof of the suitability of the model, in
general, and of the actual factor concepts
isolated, in particular. Psychologists and
social scientists working in applied situations are increasingly taking advantage of
the theoretical and experimental possibilities which the emergence of definite
personality factors and their measurement
can now bring to their work.

CHAPTER **20** Motivation and
Dynamic Calculus
Concepts from
Multivariate Experiment

JOHN L. HORN
University of Denver

1. AIMS AND RESTRICTIONS IN THE CONTENT OF THIS CHAPTER

The purpose of this chapter is to provide a broad overview of the general nature of motive measurement as it has come to be viewed in the perspective of recent developments in multivariate mathematical and statistical techniques. This chapter does not, however, as do adjacent chapters, set out a systematic review of a major portion of the results now available from empirical research. With the exception of a few very recent findings, this review has already been provided (and in more complete form than is possible here) in other easily obtained publications (40, 236, 240, 242, 246, 295, 395, 505, 627, 1005, 1144). Instead, the aim here is to present summaries of results only (or at least primarily) insofar as they typify the direction in which multivariate research on motivation seems to be heading, as they exemplify some of the major difficulties being encountered, and as they illustrate the kinds of solutions

being offered to resolve these difficulties.

Within this broad framework, other rather arbitrary restrictions have been imposed in order to meet the editor's demand that a chapter, not a book, be written. Issues developing from studies concerned almost exclusively with occupational interests (e.g., Kuder 892; Torr, 1439; Strong, 1360) have been all but ignored, for example. Neglected, also, is that large body of questions raised by what is frequently referred to as "attitude scaling," as exemplified most notably in the pioneering work of Thurstone (1405, 1406, 1408), in the refinements of this work by investigators like Ferguson (502, 503, 504, 507) and Eysenck (477, 481), and in the more recent developments of models and methods by such people as Coombs (384, 385), Guttman (648, 652), Lazarsfeld (911), Lingoes (938), Shepard (1313), Torgerson (1437) and others. Similarly ignored, except for occasional rather tangential reference, are traditional a priori listings of motives by theorists such as McDougall (1012), Murray (1090), and Maslow (997). Likewise omitted are the more operationally based but still largely a priori motive definitions provided in the tests and analyses of Allport, Vernon, and Lindzey (19), Atkinson (40), Edwards (449), McClelland (1005), and McClelland, Atkinson, Clark, and Lowell (1006). Actually most of this work — particularly the last mentioned — has already been reviewed elsewhere, as indicated by the references cited. But even if this were not true, much of it, although it may have dealt with several assumed dimensions, was based on methods that were primarily univariate (i.e., involving only one response variable and usually only a very small number of independent or stimulus variables). Where this was not the case, the researches were based on methods that are not in any basic way different from those discussed in other chapters, particularly the chapter by Pawlik on general personality traits. The emphasis in this chapter is on developments and issues that have come into being by virtue of research on motivation, and this alone.

2. OPERATIONAL DEFINITIONS FOR BASIC CONCEPTS IN MOTIVATION RESEARCH

It is customary in discussions of psychological phenomena to make a tripartite distinction between what is termed cognition, conation, and affection or, as it is worded in more modern treatments, thinking, motivation, and emotion. In the language of differential psychology, a similar distinction is represented in a separation of *ability, dynamic,* and *temperament* (or stylistic) traits. This usage need not assume, of course, that the functions and traits of one modality are necessarily and perfectly independent in an empirical probability sense from the functions and traits of another modality. Indeed, some writers have cogently argued that the traits of one modality are an outgrowth, developmentally speaking, of the traits of another modality (705, 1158). And many theorists have stressed, as has Rapaport (1182), the notion that the interaction between trait functions

of different modalities is scientifically more noteworthy than the separateness of the modalities. But to use this distinction in scientific writing, even if only as a basis for more involved developments (like the above), *does* require that different kinds of operations be specified, i.e., operations which make it clear that, whatever the empirical behavioral covariation between a motive variable and another kind of variable, the artifacts of measurement of the two are patently distinct and that, therefore, the variables represent qualitatively different attributes.

In animal research it has been customary for years to measure motivation by manipulating the environment in a way that can be assumed to set up conditions of deprivation of need or alteration of homeostasis within the organism. The strength of motive is then measured by the amount of perceptual, maze-running, intellectual, etc., "work" which the organism does. In Warden's (1500) near-classic attempt to compare the strength of different motives, for example, rats were deprived of food or water or mate, etc. — i.e., objects presumed to satisfy need — and strength of motive was then measured by counting the number of times the animals would cross an electrified grid to obtain needed objects.

This measurement approach is consistent with the usual definition of motive as a dispositional concept invoked because stimulus alone and a purely "externalized" stimulus-response history of learning do not seem adequate to explain how behavior gets started in the first place or to account for the particular quality, apparent direction, etc. of patterns of observed behavior. The observer feels that some additional conditions must be postulated, viz., conditions such as may be imagined to exist in the blood, in the viscera, in neural tissues (1115), etc. These conditions are thought to "energize" various psychological processes and thereby "force" the observed behavior.

From ancient times, of course, it has been known that some of the postulated conditions could be at least roughly controlled by merely withholding certain kinds of stimulation — withholding stimulation with food, for example. Much recent work, such as that of Lilly (935), Bexton, Heron, and Scott (109), and Berlyne (107), suggests that the absence of stimulation, per se, may set up the conditions within the organism that are needed to show motivation. In either case, deprivation of stimulation is equated with some presumed change within the organism and thus becomes the essential operational basis for the definition and measurement of motivation.

Many workers have tried to put this kind of definition to work to define motives and motive strength in humans. McClelland and his co-workers (1006), for example, have tried to use it in the measurement of what they term *n-ach* (need for achievement). They began by noting some of the behavioral effects of preventing humans from eating. In the early studies of Sanford (1251) and Atkinson and McClelland (41) it was found that as periods of food deprivation increased, there was an increase in readiness to perceive otherwise neutral stimuli as food-related, an increase in the frequency with which pictured characters were described as expressing a need for food, and in other somewhat similar behaviors. The next step was to generalize these findings to situations where conditions of deprivation were not arranged explicitly by altering the environment, but instead were assumed to exist and be represented in the individual differences that could be observed more or less "naturally" — i.e., among people who were required to write stories to TAT pictures but were otherwise in their normal walks of life. It was then reasoned that if the stories a person wrote contained many themes describing characters who were striving to overcome obstacles, etc., then conditions of deprivation of a need for achievement must exist for the person writing these stories. As will be noted in the next section, this is but one of several kinds of principles on which motivation measurement can be premised.

Motivation cannot always be studied by postulating periods of deprivation of stimulation — even if it were desirable that it should be. There may be no operations by which periods of such deprivation can be set up and it is awkward, to say the least, to have to conceptualize all motives in terms of such periods. For example, it is often difficult to talk about denying an organism the stimulation associated with an escape motive (although it can be done); it is much easier to say that the conditions which are conducive to expression of this motive may be arranged by administering shock stimulation. And, particularly when the concern is with human motivation and the approach to the problem of assessment is through the avenue of "naturally" occurring individual differences, it is desirable to, as it were, "remind" the organism of its deprived state by providing stimulation in the form of *incentives* — i.e., certain goal objects or, more generally, stimuli associated with sequences of behavior which are inferred to be directed toward goals. Several researches of McClelland, Atkinson, and their students have been designed to find TAT pictures which would be likely to "remind" subjects to write stories relating to a particular presumed motive (*cf.* Atkinson, 40, pp. 596 *ff.*), for example. Various other conditions of "arousal" have been studied by this group.

The above are very general approaches to the problem of finding operational definitions for dynamic traits. As such, they provide little basis for separating the motive variance in a set of observations from the ability or temperament variance. It appears, for example, that much (if not all) of the reliable variance in McClelland's *n-ach, n-power,* etc., measures is in fact verbal fluency (see Atkinson, 40, pp. 664 *ff.*), an attribute which most psychologists would prefer to treat as an ability (627). There is need to specify the kinds of operations needed to make the distinction implied here.

To meet this need, Cattell (213, 226) has proposed that ability traits be defined by reference to behavioral differences which arise when the tasks on which individuals perform vary principally along a dimension of complexity; that dynamic or motivational traits be defined by reference to behavior differences which show up when incentive is the principal task variable; and that temperament traits be defined with the residual variation left after ability, motive, and error variation have been removed. These definitions thus assume that the tasks which psychologists set for their subjects can be more or less accurately classified as varying primarily in complexity, in incentive value, or systematically in neither of these attributes.

Much work in psychology has implicitly assumed that this kind of classification can be made by sheer inspection, either the inspection of psychologists—in their work to sort stimuli into piles labeled "ability items," "motive items," etc., and to further classify these according to the kind of ability assumed, etc.—or the inspection implied by whatever consensus is reached among groups of "naïve" judges, as in Thurstone scaling of attitude items. Although the inspectional approach is probably always necessary as a first step—providing a rough approximation to the desired distinction—it is crude. The separation of dynamic and temperament traits has been particularly difficult to make on this basis. There are in the literature today many tests which, by inspection, are said to yield measures of motives[1], but which—in terms of the task required of subjects as well as the extent of correlational overlap—are virtually indistinguishable from tests that are reported to measure traits of temperament or, to use the thoroughly ambiguous term that is frequently preferred, traits of "personality."[2]

The crude inspectional approach is to some extent improved upon by use of factor analysis with diverse sets of a priori measures. Rather extensive results are now available from numerous investigations of this kind (summarized in 240, 550, 551, 476, 627, 796 and the present volume). In these studies, ability traits appear as factors, the high loaded variables of which clearly emphasize performance under pressure to cope with task complexities. Motivational variance is involved in the tasks as such, and no doubt some of this still resides in the factors as they can actually be estimated (173), but much of such variance cannot be assumed to be consistent from one task to another in a given factor, whereas it is apparent that the tasks are uniform with respect to varying complexity. By collating across several studies, each employing some tests that are common to two or more studies and some that vary from one study to another, it has proved possible to improve a great deal on unaided inspection and thus to partition more deftly the variance of commonly used tasks into more or less distinct ability and non-ability components.

Even by these methods, however, the separation of dynamic traits from various temperament or stylistic traits has not been clearly made. In much of this work, just as in that based on inspection alone, a satisfactory conception of incentive has not been achieved. The devices assumed to be measures of motive are in no clear sense any different from those assumed to measure temperament. Since the definition of temperament requires that variance due both to motive and ability be separated, the distinction between temperament and dynamic traits has remained obscure.

Perhaps the most significant advance on the problem of rendering distinct operational definition for dynamic traits has come about through development in what has come to be known as the *dynamic calculus* (242, 246). The hallmark of this approach to measurement is to be found in

---

[1]Inventories for assessing "interests" (892, 1360), "values" (19), "attitudes" (504, 932), "needs" (450), "hormic dimensions" (627), and the like.

[2]As assessed in, for example, the 16 P.F. (329), the CPI (610), the GAMIN and STDRC series (638, 642), and the MMPI (701).

its emphasis on use of many behavioral effects which psychologists working in various fields, with various orientations, etc., have found to be manifestations of motive. This eclecticism is based on the premise that each of numerous investigators may have seen facets of motive, but that the gem itself cannot be adequately described in terms of any one facet, or even a small number of these. Cattell has been particularly critical of motivation research that has relied exclusively on stated preferences and self-evaluations (such as most of the research mentioned above). He acknowledges that motives are expressed through ascribed-to preferences in opinionnaires, but he sees this as only one of many possible means of expression and, moreover, a means which by itself is too narrow, too susceptible to distortion, and too much contaminated by various purely questionnaire sources of variances (e.g., the "styles" implied by response sets) to give truly valid measure. He also argues that exclusive dependence on a very few misperceptive principles, as in McClelland's work, is apt to lead to narrow, distorted measures. Needed, he says, is a thoroughgoing program of analyses of the various ways in which motivation affects behavior. It is this program, insofar as it has been carried out, which constitutes what is probably the most novel feature of the dynamic calculus. And it is this which provides a basis for developing motive measurement operations which are largely distinct from the sets of operations employed to define temperament and ability traits.

3. THE PRINCIPLE OF MULTIPLE MANIFESTATIONS AS IT RELATES TO A UNIT OF MEASUREMENT

The basic measurement concept in the dynamic calculus is said to be *attitude*. This concept has some of the connotations ascribed to the same term as it is used in general psychological parlance — but by no means all such connotations! For one thing,

it is not conceived of as representing, in any simple sense, a continuum running from "for" to "against" an object, as in the polling definition (where object is usually rather narrowly limited). Rather, the full quality of an attitude is understood to involve a sensitization and activation of various sensory, perceptual, emotional, and intellectual processes which, together, constitute a readiness to follow a certain course of action with respect to an object. Cattell favors definition in terms of a paradigm, thus: "In these circumstances I want so much to do this with that" (240) where the phrase "In these circumstances" stipulates conditions of deprivation, presence of incentives, etc. which exist generally in an individual's life, including the conditions supplied by the experimenter through the testing situation; the phrase "I want so much" stipulates the organism's intensity of need or, as it is otherwise worded, strength of interest; and the phrase 'to do this with that" stipulates an object and a course of action (involving that object) which may ultimately lead to a desired end-state or goal.

Some of the salient characteristics of most motive-like concepts may be discerned in this definition. Thus attitude is a teleological-dispositional concept: an organism is said to behave *as if* it were directed toward some end-state.[3] The concept implies a variable need state: the organism is said to behave as if it were

[3]Actually, in the full development of the concept, attitude is seen to be complex with respect to a goal. It is in fact regarded as a vector in a multidimensional space, the dimensions of which are more fundamental drive patterns, termed ergs. It is the ergs which ultimately provide the energy, as it were, for all dynamic structures, including attitudes, and it is the ergs which supply the basic biological satisfactions (end-states) toward which an attitude may be said to be directed. Since an attitude would not in general lie along one of the coordinates in this ergic space, it must be seen as directed toward several goals at once. This mélange or compound of ergic end-states may be regarded as a kind of goal in itself, however, and it is in this sense that an attitude is said to have *a* (singular) goal.

aroused by internal conditions (of deprivation, of disruption of homeostasis, etc.) or external conditions of stimulation, and this state of arousal is seen to vary from quiescence upwards. The attitude is seen to be a "driving force" or "source of energy" which activates other psychological processes. But the essential and somewhat unique characteristic of this definition, as it is interpreted in actual research applications, is to be found in the emphasis that is placed on observing the ways in which various psychological processes are in fact activated.

Let us then define attitude as a kind of motive. A *principle of manifestation of motive* we will define as a statement about behavioral effects which, according to known research results, highly regarded hypotheses, etc., are said to result from arousal of motive. A *device* is a particular means for representing a principle in a set of measurement operations. Stated in terms of these definitions the main thesis of this section is that the strength of motivation inherent in an attitude can be assessed by use of any one (or all) of several principles or, since for each principle there may be many devices, by use of an even larger number of devices.

Suppose, as an example, that an attitude were defined in terms of Cattell's paradigm as: "I want Negroes in this country to have all the opportunities that are accorded to whites." Now if one favored the course of action implied by this statement, we might first of all expect him to indicate agreement with this statement itself and others like it. Our expectation is based on a belief in the utility of a preference principle—i.e., assuming honesty, awareness, etc., a person will admit to a preference for a course of action in which he is interested. This is the principle assumed in a wide variety of opinionnaire devices—i.e., forced choice, Likert, Thurstone, Guttman, etc. "scales."

One suspects, however, that if a measure were based *exclusively* on this principle, not only would it fail to represent some of the

more subtle emotional qualities which may enter into this attitude, it might yield rather grossly distorted results. For one thing a subject can rather easily "fake" his response—e.g., answer *Yes* when a more objective appraisal of a broader spectrum of behavior would suggest that *No* "should have been" his answer[4] (assuming interpretation of the referential rather than any latent meaning of the item). Even if willful distortion were not a problem, lack of awareness, ambiguity, response sets of various kinds and sheer narrowness of measure would be. Opinionnaire items do not reflect many of the less obviously conscious aspects of attitude. It is not unreasonable to suppose, on the basis of what is now known in psychology, that at a primitive, emotional level an individual might fear or despise Negroes, while at a more highly integrated, intellectual level he would ascribe sincerely to beliefs like those expressed in the above attitude statement. Rosenberg (1217) has shown how this kind of conflict between components of an attitude can be induced using hypnotic suggestion, for example. On the other hand, one might seriously question the implicit assumption that opinionnaire items provide measure of the highly conscious or integrated aspects of attitude (and, indeed, results presented below on motivational components will show that this assumption should be seriously questioned).

In fact, isn't strength of attitude regarding the Negro indicated also (and perhaps more fully) by a willingness (vs. unwillingness) to spend money and time to insure

---

[4]Strictly speaking, of course, all we can fairly say in such situations is that the questionnaire response—or the score based on a series of such responses—is inconsistent with other behavior. Such answers are not necessarily "faked," nor are they necessarily lies. Woe that each of us would be required to live up to the ideals we profess (in questionnaires and elsewhere)! No questionnaire answer or score is necessarily true or false, valid or invalid, etc.; it is merely behavior. The meaning of this behavior can be correctly gauged only when it is seen within the context of a diverse set of other behaviors.

equality of opportunity? Isn't it manifested in an unwillingness to rationalize that opportunities are already equal? Many questions of this sort come to mind. Such questions illustrate principles of motivation. A large number of such principles may be found in the psychological literature; some of these are listed in Table 20-1.

The assertion is, then, that each of these so-called principles provides a logically distinct means for assessing the strength of any attitude and that, in most cases, more than one device might be used to express a principle in concrete measurement operations.

The distinctness and validity of a few of the principles listed in Table 20-1 can be legitimately questioned. But the list is almost certainly not complete, and several of the principles could be stated in more detailed form (e.g., those dealing with purely physiological manifestations might

TABLE 20-1

SOME PRINCIPLES OF MOTIVATION MEASUREMENT APPLIED IN DEVICE CONSTRUCTION
(After Cattell, 240; Cattell & Horn, 295; and Cattell, Radcliffe, & Sweney, 313)

With increase in interest in a course of action expect increase in:

1. Preferences: Readiness to admit preference for course of action.
2. Autism: misperception. Distorted perception of objects, noises, etc., in accordance with interest (e.g., Bruner coin perception study).
3. Autism: misbelief. Distorted belief that facts favor course of action.
4. Reasoning distortion: means-ends. Readiness to argue that doubtfully effective means to goal are really effective.
5. Reasoning distortion: ends-means. Readiness to argue that ends will be easily reached by inapt means.
6. Reasoning distortion: inductive.
7. Reasoning distortion: deductive.
8. Reasoning distortion: eduction of relations in perception (e.g., analogies).
9. Utilities choice. Readiness to use land, labor, and capital for interest.
10. Machiavellism. Willingness to use reprehensible means to achieve ends favoring interest.
11. Fantasy choice. Readiness to choose interest-related topic to read about, write about, or explain.
12. Fantasy ruminations. Time spent ruminating on interest-related material.
13. Fantasy identification. Prefer to be like individuals who favor course of action.
14. Defensive reticence. Low fluency in listing bad consequences of course of action.
15. Defensive fluency. Fluency in listing good consequences of course of action.
16. Defensive fluency. Fluency listing justifications for actions.
17. Rationalization. Readiness to interpret information in a way to make interest appear more respectable, etc., than it is.
18. Naïve projection. Misperception of others as having one's own interests.
19. True projection. Misperception of others as exhibiting one's own reprehensible behavior in connection with pursuit of interest.
20. Id projection. Misperception of others as having one's own primitive desire relating to interest.
21. Superego projection. Misperception of others as having one's own righteous beliefs relating to interest.
22. Guilt sensitivity. Expression of guilt feelings for nonparticipation in interest-related activities.
23. Conflict involvement: Time spent making decision under approach-approach conflict (both alternatives favor interest).
24. Conflict involvement: Time spent making decision under avoidance-avoidance conflict (both alternatives oppose interest).
25. Threat reactivity: psychogalvanic resistance drop when interest threatened.
26. Threat reactivity: increase cardiovascular output when interest threatened.

TABLE 20-1 (Continued)

27. Physiological involvement: increase cardiovascular output when interest aroused (threatened or not).
28. Physiological involvement: finger temperature rise when interest aroused.
29. Physiological involvement: increase muscle tension when interest aroused.
30. Perceptual integration. Organize unstructured material in accordance with interest.
31. Perceptual closure. Ability to see incomplete drawings as complete when material is related to interest.
32. Selective perception. Ease of finding interest-related material imbedded in complex field.
33. Sensory acuity. Tendency to sense lights as brighter, sounds as louder, etc., when interest is aroused.
34. Attentivity. Resistance to distractive (lights, sounds, etc.) when attending to interest-related material.
35. Spontaneous attention. Involuntary movements with respect to interest-related stimuli (e.g., eye movements).
36. Involvement: Apparent speed with which time passes when occupied with interest.
37. Persistence. Continuation in work for interest in face of difficulty.
38. Perseveration. Maladaptive continuation with behavior related to interest.
39. Distractibility. Inability to maintain attention when interest-related stimuli interfere.
40. Retroactive inhibition when interest-related task intervenes.
41. Proactive inhibition by interest-related task.
42. Eagerness: effort. Anticipation of expending much effort for course of action.
43. Activity: time. Time spent on course of action.
44. Eagerness: money. Anticipation of spending much money for course of action.
45. Activity: money. Money spent on course of action.
46. Eagerness: exploration. Readiness to undertake exploration to achieve interest-related ends.
47. Impulsiveness: decisions. Speed of decisions in favor of interest (low conflict).
48. Impulsiveness: agreements. Speed of agreeing with opinions favorable to interest.
49. Decision strength. Extremeness of certainty for position favoring course action.
50. Warm-up speed: learning. Speed warming-up to learning task related to interest.
51. Learning. Speed learning interest-related material.
52. Motor skills. Apt performance to affect interest.
53. Information. Knowledge affecting and related to course of action.
54. Resistance to extinction of responses related to interest.
55. Control. Ability to coordinate activities in pursuit of interest.
56. Availability: fluency. Fluency in writing on cues related to course of action.
57. Availability: free association. Readiness to associate to interest-related material when not oriented by cue.
58. Availability: speed of free association. Number of associations when interest aroused.
59. Availability: oriented association. Readiness to associate interest-related material with given cue.
60. Availability: memory. Free recall of interest-related material.
61. Memory for rewards. Immediate recall of rewards associated with interest.
62. Reminiscence: Ward-Hovland effect. Increased recall over short interval of interest related material.
63. Reminiscence: Ballard-Williams effect. Increased recall over long intervals of interest-related material.
64. Zeigarnik recall. Tendency to recall incompleted tasks associated with interest.
65. Zeigarnik perseveration. Readiness to return to incompleted task associated with interest.
66. Defensive forgetfulness. Inability to recall interest-related material if goal not achievable.
67. Reflex facilitation. Ease with which certain reflexes are evoked when interest aroused.
68. Reflex inhibition. Difficulty in evoking certain reflexes when interest aroused.

be broken down into several more specific kinds of reactions). In sum, then, the list probably well illustrates the basic point being made, viz., that when it comes to measuring a unit of motivation, such as an attitude, there are several ways to, as it were, "skin the cat."

4. THE PROBLEM OF VEHICLES AND SOME PROPOSED SOLUTIONS BY IPSATIZATION

Although it is reasonable to suppose that devices based on the principles of Table 20-1 will indicate motive strength, it cannot be assumed that they indicate this alone. Consider, for example, an attitude about smoking cigarettes and suppose the aim is to measure this (in part) by means of a multiple-choice knowledge test (i.e., by using the so-called Information principle of Table 20-1). Acquisition of information may then be said to be the *vehicle* through which interest in smoking can be manifested. Now some of the variability between individuals on knowledge about smoking-related topics would be expected to reflect strength of interest, but some of this would almost certainly reflect differences in intelligence, amounts of education, exposure to the mass media of communication and other factors largely unrelated to expression of a particular motive. Some of these factors can be conceived of as grouped together and measured in what could be called "verbal knowledge." A raw score based on the smoking knowledge test alone could then be said to include the variance of "verbal knowledge," as well as motivational variable. Similarly, a raw score based on a preference device might include variance representing an "extremity set" (a tendency to check extreme responses in multiple-choice items) or some other extraneous, but internally consistent influence. Indeed, each device one can construct to represent one of the principles of Table 20-1 is likely to include non-error variance representing some "extraneous" influence

of the particular vehicle by which measurement is sought. Such influences, implying some perturbation or displacement of the expression of motive itself, are termed vehicle influences or merely "vehicles" or, occasionally, "vehicle factors" (although the extraneous influences may be a conglomerate of factors in the usual, in psychology, simple structure sense of this term). If relatively pure measurement of motive is to be obtained, it is necessary to get rid of vehicle influences.

The reader has probably noticed that the problem posed here is merely a rather specific example of the general problem, discussed in Chapter 3, of isolating and, where necessary, removing components of variance in any measurement. There, it will be recalled, a series of rather specific approaches to this kind of problem were described as *ipsatization* procedures (209). Now, in fact, these procedures were originally developed within the context of motivation research. Only rather recently have they been applied outside this field.

A reason for this, it seems, is that ipsatization is based upon what has been described as the "solipsistic" basis for measurement (202), and this basis has seemed particularly appropriate to motivation research. According to this view, the psychologist who wishes to comprehend a particular personality must see this person's interest in a given course of action as a "figure," so to speak, against the "ground" of this person's other interests. In other words, to say that an individual is *interested* in securing the rights of Negroes, for example, is to say that among all the other interests which this person may have, this particular interest is salient—a course of action which has harnessed a major portion of his concern, time, energy, etc. The argument is, in fact, that motive measurements should turn out to be *naturally ipsative:* the scientist should find that if he controls most of the other influences which can operate in motive measurement, then if a particular individual is found to have a very great amount of interest in one course of action, it is to be expected that he should *tend* to have smaller amounts of interest in other courses of action simply because (it is implied) he has only so much total interest, and distributing some of this in one activity precludes distributing it in other activities.

Ipsatization procedures are merely scoring devices which *require* this kind of distribution for the interest scores that are obtained with a given set of attitudes. Implicit in most of these procedures is the assumption that not only is it necessary to require that an individual distribute a finite total fund of interest through the same set of attitudes (prescribed by the experimenter), but it is also necessary to require that all individuals have the same total fund of interest over the set of attitudes sampled, for most ipsatization procedures are characterized by the fact that the ipsative scores which result must add to the same constant for all individuals.

Because ipsatization procedures have played such a very crucial role in the development of multivariate motive concepts, it is necessary to pause here, at least briefly, to review some of the ideas associated with these procedures.

In the early attempts to get rid of vehicle influences (214, 293, 301), some ipsatization procedures amounted merely to dividing a person's subscore for a given attitude by the total score he obtained in the same device for several attitudes—what was described as "fund-ipsatization" in Chapter 2. If, for example, one used an information device to measure 19 attitudes besides the above-mentioned attitude relating to smoking, then a fund-ipsative measure on the smoking attitude would be obtained by adding a person's information subscores for all 20 attitudes and dividing the raw subscore for smoking by this total. Other times in these early studies this total score was subtracted from the smoking subscore, thus effecting a linear rather than a nonlinear transformation. In still other tests,

the choices in multiple-choice items were "pitted against each other," so to speak, and all choices were scored (one for one attitude, one for another) so that, in effect, the respondent who selected one response choice, thereby obtaining a point (or points) toward score on one attitude, could not by virtue of this fact make the choice which would give him a point (or points) toward score on the other attitudes having response choices in the item in question.

A very large number of procedures now exist for accomplishing ipsatization. Many of these are discussed in Horn (746), Cattell, Radcliffe, and Sweney (313), and Radcliffe (1176). An outline of the procedures, as defined within the general Data Box, is given in Chapter 2.

Very briefly, it can be stated that ipsatization is accomplished in essentially two ways, viz. (1) at the level of gathering responses, as described above under the heading of self-ipsatization, and (2) by performing some sort of algebraic transformation on variables which would otherwise be in normative form. These latter, the analytic procedures, are the most frequently discussed. The general assumption has been that although the psychological properties of variables obtained by the two kinds of procedures may differ, the psychometric properties of the two are very similar. And since the analytic procedures usually permit somewhat easier or more direct manipulations of characteristics which might affect the psychometric properties of scores, these have been subjected to the more careful study.

It is useful for future reference to further classify the analytic methods into three broad categories, as follows: (1) computation of factor scores, (2) estimation of the vehicle by means of a test (or series of tests) external to the variables being ipsatized, and partialling this vehicle estimate (the outside partialling method), and (3) estimating the vehicle by means of a summary score obtained from the variables being ipsatized, and effecting removal of this by some linear or non-linear procedure (the inside transformation method).

The latter method includes the two techniques described earlier in which the sum score obtained over a set of 20 attitudes is either divided into each attitude subscore separately or is subtracted from each separately. It also includes the examples used to help describe incomplete and fully performative scores. Cattell and Horn (295b, 750) have recently developed still another procedure which illustrates this method. They propose to use the correlation between the total score obtained over all attitudes (excluding the one attitude in question, however) and the attitude subscore to effect a linear partialling of the former from the latter.

In contrast to this latter, the outside partialling method may be illustrated by the procedure tried out in the Cattell, Radcliffe, and Sweney (313) study. They used both Otis Beta Intelligence and Stanford Achievement Test scores to estimate the presumed vehicle in the Information device and partialled these estimates from attitude subscores.

The factor score method might not be considered an ipsatization procedure by some. But if an attitude can be identified in a clearly rotated simple structure factor coefficient solution, and if one uses a "complete" method for estimating factor scores (688, 747, 748), then scores are obtained for the attitude in such a way that all variance held in common with vehicle factors (some of which might be unique factors) is removed. The attitude factor will correlate with the vehicle factor just to that extent (approximately) found in the rotated solution. That is, assuming oblique rotation, this procedure gives correlated part scores (746). It can be quite practical when fairly good computer facilities are available, but it is not surprising that it was never seriously considered in the earlier work on ipsatization, since in this it was implicitly assumed

that ipsative scoring would generally have to be carried out by clerks.

It should be made clear that although ipsative scoring usually introduces some algebraic dependence between the resulting ipsative variables, it needn't always do this. For example, if only *one* response choice is scored in each of a set of items, the resulting variables will not be algebraically dependent even though choices are "pitted against each other." Likewise, if a semi-performative score for a smoking attitude is obtained relative to one set of 19 attitudes, and a semi-performative score for a drinking attitude is obtained from another set of 19 attitudes, then the resulting variables would be independent in the algebraic sense. In both of these cases, one variable is not predictable from (a mathematical function of) the other merely by virtue of the scoring or data-gathering procedures; in both cases, if one variable did turn out to be predictable from the other, the dependence could be interpreted as behavioral or "functional" (in the biological, not the mathematical sense) — i.e., as resulting from some commonness of function in the objects measured, not in the procedures for scoring.

In most applications of ipsative scoring, however, some algebraic dependence between the resulting ipsative scores is introduced: the examples immediately above are atypical. A problem that has very much bothered investigators working with ipsative variables has been one of determining the appropriate statistical (i.e., inferential) models to use with such scores, or, as the problem has been frequently phrased, the error (if any, and under what conditions) resulting from treating ipsative scores with the statistical procedures psychologists characteristically work with. These latter procedures are almost always based on an assumption that variables are independent in the algebraic sense, and, it is usually quite necessary, from a logical point of view, to meet this assumption before the statistical tests can be meaningful. That is, most statistical procedure contain an assumption that variables, samples, etc. are independent in the probability sense, and it is this assumption which an investigator hopes to be able to question — indeed, reject — for his data. But if independence in an algebraic sense cannot be assumed, then an hypothesis based on the assumption that variables *could be* independent (in the probability sense) is logically rather a waste of time. The problem, then, has been one of determining how failure to meet the assumption of algebraic independence affects the statistical test or, more ambitiously, one of generating the necessary density functions for various kinds of ipsatively related variables.

Although a great deal of interest has been evinced in this problem (e.g., 149, 150, 151, 281, 282, 313, 349, 455, 746, 792, 972, 1176, 1225) and some excellent formulations of basic issues have been presented (see particularly 349, 1176), it cannot be said that the problem is yet properly focused, much less solved. But some useful generalizations can be made about relationships between ipsative and normative scores and about some kinds of error which might result from using normatively based statistics with ipsative variables. In very brief form, some of the more noteworthy of these are:

(1) As noted above, scores that are ipsative with respect to each other are algebraically dependent and hence any statistical test based on an assumption of algebraic independence is biased. For example, the expected value for the correlation between two semi-performative variables derived from normative variables that are independent in the probability sense is not zero, but $\frac{-1}{n-1}$, where n is the number of variables involved in the ipsatization (349, 455, 746). The distribution for this correlation is highly skewed when n is small, less so as n becomes large, and approaches the form for non-ipsatized variables as n be-

comes very large. The standard error is a complex function of n and N (sample size), under the assumption of zero correlation, and also of rho (the population correlation) under the assumption of non-zero correlation. It can thus be assumed that the error of treating a correlation between ipsative variables as if it were a correlation between normative variables is apt to be great when n is small, and relatively smaller as n becomes larger.

(2) The variance and reliability of an ipsative variable will, generally speaking, be smaller than the variance and reliability of the variable before ipsatization (349, 1176, 746).

(3) It follows from the above that, in general, a matrix of intercorrelations between variables that are ipsative with respect to each other will tend to an average negative value ($-\frac{1}{n-1}$ if random variables were ipsatively scored) and that the matrix variance for such variables will tend to be smaller than that for a comparable set of unipsatized variables. Indeed, the matrix of intercorrelations among ipsative variables is, in a sense, a residual matrix left after extraction of certain factors. This, of course, is as it should be if ipsatization achieves removal of vehicle "factors." However, each of the possible ipsatization procedures, in effect, defines the "factors" that are removed in a somewhat different way; it is not possible to state precisely the influence of ipsatization on the rank of the covariance matrix, except to say that almost all procedures reduce maximum rank at least by 1.

(4) Because variance and covariance is generally reduced by ipsatization, the multiple correlation between a set of ipsative variables and an outside criterion is almost always lower than the R obtainable with the same variables prior to ipsatization.

(5) Although not enough work has yet been done to permit strong generalizations, present evidence (313) suggests that the

various procedures for achieving ipsatization may yield very similar results in factor-analytic and related multivariate analyses. This outcome would appear to be particularly likely if the unipsatized components are highly reliable. The evidence from this study does suggest, however, that the "outside partialling" methods suffer from a number of deficiencies associated with the fact that it is difficult, if not impossible, always to know what to partial. In particular, Cattell, Radcliffe, and Sweney concluded that the "outside partialling" methods did not get out all of the vehicle variance. In contrast, Cattell and Horn (295) argued from their results that self-ipsative and inside transformation procedures tended to remove too much variance, motive variance as well as that of the vehicle. This effect appeared to be particularly marked in variables that were, in their normative form, more reliable or more numerous than the other variables in the ipsatively scored set. This would follow from the fact that such variables would contribute relatively more variance to the total score which is then, in some sense, partialled from the variables in question.

There are many other issues pertaining to the use of ipsative scores and the general problem of controlling for vehicle influences. But with this introduction it is now possible to look more searchingly at the fundamental problems which provoked the issues on ipsatization, viz., the question of the kind of model needed to utilize information from multiple manifestations of motive in order to achieve accurate measure of motive strength.

5. MOTIVATIONAL COMPONENT RESEARCH

If, indeed, motive is manifested in the several ways listed in Table 20-1, then it follows that a measure of *total* motive strength may need to include estimates from at least several, if not all, possible manifestations. There are, theoretically, a number of ways in which information from these diverse sources might be employed in measurement. For example, it might be that an accurate estimate of motive strength would need to include estimates of exercise of this "strength" in *each* of the possible manifestations. This concept of motive is rather obviously analogous to the concept of energy in physics. In estimating the energy which a substance may produce in explosion, the physicist carefully calculates the energy expenditure which will go into heat, into various possible kinetic effects, into chemical transformations, etc. Likewise, perhaps the psychologist should aim (if he wants a measure of total motive strength) to calculate the expenditure of motivation in each possible outlet. Of course, energy from a particular source need not always be manifested in any particular one of the several possible outlets. There might be no kinetic effects, for example. But in setting up his measurement model, the physicist usually at least considers the possibility that some energy will be expended in each possible way. He usually tries to assure himself that his prediction that there are, say, no kinetic effects, is in fact borne out. Similarly, the psychologist might reason that although it's certainly conceivable that a given individual will not manifest his interest in all the ways listed in Table 20-1, the possibility that he will needs to be at least considered.

The physicist's model includes a notion of conservation in transference. In his calculations to determine amount of energy in a source, he reasons that there is only so much available and if a certain amount of this is expended in one way, it is not available to be simultaneously expended in another way. In the psychology of motivation the similar notion is found in numerous expressions of a concept of alternative mechanisms. For example, Freud's idea of sublimation implies that if a certain amount of libido is expended in translating Greek poetry, it is not available for expenditure in Latin dancing. Eriksen (465) has pointed out that the defense mechanisms, generally, may be conceived of largely in terms of this alternative mechanism model: if you use one, the chances are you don't use certain others.

When the study of motive manifestations is based upon comparisons of individual differences (different "sources of energy" by the above analogy) and when the focus is on one particular unit of measurement — as, for example, the attitude — then the above model *can imply* (it needn't, as will be seen below) that although *within a given individual* expenditure of motivation through outlet *A* tends to prevent expenditure through outlet *B* (as solipsistic theory would predict), still *between individuals* a greater expenditure through outlet *A* is associated with a greater expenditure through outlet *B*. The implication (by analogy) is that "big explosions," so to speak, spill over to give big expenditures of energy in each possible outlet, while "small explosions" produce small expenditures in all outlets. Thus, if strength of an attitude toward Negroes were assessed by use of several principles of motive manifestation, the prediction from this reasoning would be that positive manifold would obtain in an *R*-technique matrix of intercorrelations among the devices based on these principles.

It will be noted that this conclusion is premised on the implicit assumption that between-person differences in some sense "outweigh" (i.e., are more evident in behavior than) the influence by mutual exclusion (within a person) of one outlet relative to another, as implied by the alternative mechanism model. But if it were reasoned that individual differences in total attitude strength are relatively small and that the more important influence in behavior is the fact that expression of attitude strength in one way prevents (to some extent) its expression in another way, then not only would positive manifold *not* be expected in *R*-technique analyses, the prediction would be that the matrix of inter-

correlations among possible manifestations should take a form like that for variables that are ipsative with respect to each other. This reasoning implies, in fact, that manifestations will be naturally ipsative.

The general predictions above need to be conditioned by consideration for the behavioral independence, or lack of it, of the manifestations, as such, and of the vehicles which might be involved with these manifestations. For example, it might be that persons who express motivation through fantasy are, on a probabilistic basis, more likely also to express motivation in distortion of reasoning. This is, in fact, the gist of Eriksen's (466) notion that individuals "choose," as it were, their type of defense mechanism. Also, if vehicle influences are not completely removed by some sort of ipsatization procedure, then it is to be expected that persons gaining high scores through measure on one device will tend, by reason of the relationship between vehicles, to gain high scores in measures obtained with certain other devices. More specifically, since it is now well established (551, 553) that fluency and general information abilities are correlated (at least lowly), two motive measures based upon fluency and information principles (e.g., Nos. 53 and 56 in Table 20-1) will correlate by virtue of a common vehicle of ability if this is not completely removed by ipsatization. Thus, if there is behavioral dependence between ways of expressing motive or any residual vehicle influences, it is to be expected that: (1) for the positive manifold model, hierarchical order (1337, 1339) will *not* prevail, and (2) for the naturally ipsative model, there will be an inordinate number of clusters of positive correlations, more than would be expected if each of a set of variables was uniformly ipsative with respect to the other. Thus, for both general models the suggestion here is that multiple factors will be needed to account for the intercorrelations among manifestation devices. (It might be added that the same kind of generalizations apply if algebraic dependencies are allowed between device measures.)

There are, of course, several other models which could be profitably considered here[5], but these should be sufficient to suggest the major issues and provide some basis for introducing and interpreting the evidence thus far accumulated.

This evidence dates back to some rather crude studies in the 1940's and 1950's by Cattell and his co-workers (214, 294, 301); each based upon the implicit assumption that positive manifold and hierarchical order would hold. More recently, the trend has been to explore the implications of a multiple-factor model (266, 313, 334, 1372, 1380).

The procedures in both the older and the more recent investigations were similar in several respects, different in a few. The unit of measurement was in all cases an attitude, for example. A number of devices, representing a number of principles, were constructed to measure a single attitude and the resulting device-attitude variables were intercorrelated. Separate intercorrelation matrices were usually obtained in this way for several attitudes. In some studies these matrices were averaged by converting r's to Fisher z coefficients, averaging and converting the z's back to r's, the idea being that the averaging would tend to cancel out idiosyncrasies associated with any particular attitude. But in other analyses (313) the matrices for different attitudes were kept separate. In all studies ipsatization of some sort was used with the aim of eliminating (or at least reducing) vehicle influences. The semi-performative and self-ipsative procedures were the most frequently employed and the score for the attitude in

[5]Would a simplex or circumplex (652) be reasonable, for example? And suppose that some of the principles in Table 20-1 could not be actualized in measures of motivation—e.g., that a memory device could not be constructed in a way that would eliminate ability and measure only motive? The reader interested in a more detailed development of these models will surely want to consult the Cattell, Radcliffe, and Sweney (313) paper (pp. 119-146).

question was obtained by comparison with anywhere from 4 to 20 other attitudes. In the Cattell-Radcliffe-Sweney (313) study, however, various procedures for accomplishing ipsatization were tried and compared. Algebraic dependencies between the variables within a correlation matrix were generally avoided, since the entire matrix was based on scores for only the one attitude and the vehicle components were generally not the same for different variables. When correlation matrices were averaged and the attitudes for the separate correlation matrices were ipsatively scored with respect to each other, and in the few cases where the vehicle was the same, for each of two or more device-attitude scores, some (probably slight) amounts of dependency due to these procedures were introduced. The composition of the samples of subjects varied widely: the studies by Cattell, Radcliffe, and Sweney were based on samples of children aged 11 and 12. Cattell and Baggaley used young air force men. Tapp drew his sample from the introductory psychology course at the University of Illinois, and the earlier studies were based on similar samples of young adults.

It is not possible to summarize fully the results from these studies in the space allotted here, but the following conclusions appear to be justified by the data and appropriate to consider in relation to the questions asked about a measurement model for motive manifestations.

EVIDENCE

Positive manifold probably prevails among the intercorrelations for most principles in Table 20-1, assuming sample heterogeneity comparable to that in the above investigations. This is not to say that *all* correlations were in fact positive for the devices used in actual research; some of the devices tried out did not have reliabilities of a size sufficient to guarantee positive correlations; it is questionable whether some of the devices truly represented a motivational principle; the vehicle influences may not have been fully removed in all devices. For these reasons, and because sampling error would produce some negative correlations even when the population correlations were positive (and particularly so if the population values were low, as seems likely here), perfect positive manifold could not be expected in actual results. But the high amount of positiveness found among correlations in the above-mentioned research suggests that if reliabilities were improved, etc., the intercorrelations would become almost exclusively positive (although not necessarily high).

But while the results tend to support—or at least do not unequivocally rule out—a hypothesis of positive manifold, they give no support for a hypothesis of hierarchical order. A multiple-factor solution of some sort appears to be necessary, and such a solution was obtained in all of the studies mentioned above except those by Cattell, Heist, et al. (294) and Cattell, Maxwell, et al. (301).

From five to seven factors have been reported (at the first order) in available researches. These, to avoid confusing them with dynamic structure factors (to be discussed in the next section) have been labeled *motivational components* (or merely *components*). A rough summary description of these components is provided in Table 20-2, where factor loadings have been averaged for devices that have loaded fairly consistently on a given factor in two or more analyses. (The table is intended primarily as a schematic representation, not as an authoritative, definitive statement of results.)

The components have been labeled with the Greek letters used in previous study reports. The first five components were initially identified and replicated in a set of six separate studies reported by Cattell and Baggaley. The sixth factor appeared in shadowy form in some of these analyses, more substantially in the Tapp study, and with considerable clarity in the Cattell-Radcliffe-Sweney studies with children. Individual tests were not used in Tapp's study, so the factor labeled delta, which is defined almost exclusively by such tests,

TABLE 20-2

SUMMARY OF PRIMARY MOTIVATIONAL COMPONENT RESULTS TO 1963

	Alpha	Beta	Gamma	Delta	Epsilon	Zeta	Eta
Preferences	43		49				
Autism	37		30				
Reasoning distortion: means-ends, ends-means	49						
Fantasy: choice to explain and read	45		30				
Identification preference	51						
Defensive reticence	31						
Defensive fluency	27						
Naïve projection	37						
Guilt sensitivity	32						
Utilities choice	45						
Persistence: motor activity	32						
Id projection	38						
Perceptual closure	37						
Attention: auditory distraction	41	40					
Information		26					
Learning		37					
Memory for rewards		35					

TABLE 20-2 (Continued)

SUMMARY OF PRIMARY MOTIVATIONAL COMPONENT RESULTS TO 1963

	Alpha	Beta	Gamma	Delta	Epsilon	Zeta	Eta
Warm-up in learning		31					
Fantasy: time ruminating		39					
Control		21					
Availability: unoriented association	31		47				
Availability: oriented association			51				
Reasoning distortion: analogies			38				
Selective perception			38				
Expectancy: effort to be expended			23				
Perseveration: low perceptual integration			32				
Fantasy: sentence completion			38				
Superego projection			38				
Threat reactivity: cardiovascular				43			
Threat reactivity: psychogalvanic				51			
Conflict involvement: slow decisions				42			
Reminiscence					54		
Defense against recall					40		
Availability: speed association					35		
Impulsiveness: decision speed						38	
Impulsiveness: agreement speed						48	
Decision strength						52	
Fluency on cues							33
Persistence: perceptual task							43

could not be properly identified. The seventh factor was found in only the most recent studies, all based on samples of children.

The suggestion of positive manifold among devices indicates a need to look at higher-order factors. Cattell and Baggaley (266) and Cattell, Radcliffe, and Sweney (313) have carried out such analyses, with the finding that at least two and possibly three factors are required at this order. These results are shown in Table 20-3.

As to the possibility of a neat unifactor solution at the third order, Cattell, Radcliffe, and Sweney (313) conclude, after their most carefully conducted second-order analyses: "It is too early to ask how the second-orders are themselves organized, though as far as A and B are concerned it is already confirmed by three studies that they are practically uncorrelated, tending consistently to a slight positive correlation" (p. 118).

The question of the correct interpreta-

tions for these findings has stirred up considerable interest in recent years, but it cannot yet be said that investigators have reached agreement in their answers. However, some of the considerations for interpretation which have been advanced may be briefly stated as follows.

Alpha Component

Conscious Id. The seeming contradiction of terms in this interpretive title is not really a contradiction if it is granted that the blind, unconscious impulses which Freud attributed to the Id must eventually, if the psychologist is to know of them, become manifest in some conscious wishes, wants, desires, etc. And it is these latter which seem to be expressed in the devices which characterize this factor; viz., Preferences (traditional paired-choice opinionnaire), Fantasy Choice to Explain, Autism, etc.

Degree of Satisfaction Currently Obtaining. This interpretation derives from a not altogether different theory. As noted earlier, Cattell uses the term "erg" to refer to the fundamental elements of motive systems — the unlearned activators which get behavior "going," as it were, which give the first primitive directional qualities to satisfaction currently obtaining through physiological processes; and bG symbolizes the satisfaction being obtained, or being perceived as obtained, through psychological processes; K is a constant. Now, it is these latter G terms — particularly bG — which, by this interpretation, are to be

TABLE 20-3

SUMMARY OF SECOND-ORDER MOTIVATIONAL COMPONENT RESULTS TO 1963

Primary Component	Second-order Component By Study							
	A			B			C	
	C-B*	C-M**	C-R***	C-B*	C-M**	C-R***	C-M**	C-R***
Alpha	19	−07	−01	42	53	38	07	05
Beta	75	24	39	18	−07	−07	−01	−07
Gamma	35	51	22	−18	06	04	03	−22
Delta	04	−08	−04	22	−01	−02	34	49
Epsilon	−06	09	03	12	47	41	−06	−02
Zeta		08	−03		−01	−01	35	14
Eta		04	43		−64	08	−03	09

*C-B: Cattell-Baggaley (266).
**C-M: Cattell-Radcliffe-Sweney (313) Movies Attitude.
***C-R: Cattell-Radcliffe-Sweney (313) Religion Attitude.

this behavior, and which, as they are shaped by learning, supply the "push" in all subsequent behavior. He postulates that the tension resident in any erg can be analyzed into six sources, which he symbolizes as follows:

$$E = (S + K) [C + H + P - aG] - bG$$

where E is the ergic tension; S symbolizes the stimulus situation, the incentives present, etc.; C represents the constitutional capacity of the individual to derive ergic strength from this particular source (e.g., from the mating or sex erg); H summarizes the general influences of the individual's history on the erg — the imprinting influences, the extent to which conflicts in satisfaction have been avoided, etc.; P indicates the *deviation* of a present bio chemical-physiological state from that which is characteristic for the individual (as represented by the $C + H$ combination) and which might therefore be said to be his "expected" level of physiological satisfaction; G represents the amount of goal

equated with the Alpha component. In other words, it is primarily the currently felt lack of satisfaction which is being expressed in the Alpha devices.

Beta Component

Ego Expression. The Freudian notion is that primitive instinctual impulses of the Id are modified by reality-perception and thereafter expressed in gradually differentiated, reality-regulated striving termed the Ego. The interpretation here recognizes that the ability-type devices which predominate in Beta represent just this kind of striving.

Realized or Habituated Residue of Interest. This interpretation does not contradict the previous one, but puts more emphasis on the notion that the skills, knowledges, etc. which show up in this factor may be, at least in part, merely a by-product of earlier expression of reality-oriented striving.

Residue from Failure to Effect Full Removal of Ability Vehicles. As noted before, if correlated ability components in vehicles are not fully removed by ipsatization, the variance left could throw up a factor like Beta. Although this interpretation is not favored by the original investigators (or so it seems), it cannot be ruled out as a possibility on the basis of present results. The nearest attempt to eliminate this possibility was in the Cattell, Radcliffe, and Sweney (313) study, where Otis Beta Intelligence and Stanford Achievement Test scores were partialled. But the general tenor of the results there obtained left this interpretative possibility still open.

Gamma Component

Ideal Self, Ego Ideal, or Unrealized Superego Expression. Again following Freudian theory, the interpretations for this factor have stressed the idea that devices like Expectancy, Perseveration, etc., can represent a willed effort such as might result from acceptance of the commandments of parents and the dominant culture, as represented in the Superego and the Ego Ideal. The fact that this dimension shares with Alpha some of the devices (e.g, Autism and Preferences) which suggest a rather primitive, wistful expression (an "I ought" expression here) is consonant with the Freudian notion that most of the Superego sanctions are early inculcated and nearly as rigid and irrational in their demands as the Id impulses.

Delta Component

Physiological Need Expression. This is linked to the P term in the ergic tension equation (above), the term indicating the deviation of the present physiological state from the level representing homeostasis.

Residue from Failure to Effect Full Removal of Physiological Vehicles. Here, again, it could be that the factor represents what is left of a general physiological

reactivity pattern (see Cattell, 240; pp. 650-652) remaining because ipsatization did not remove all of the correlated vehicles components in physiological variables.

Epsilon Component

Expression Tied to Unconscious Memories (Arising from Complexes). The reversed loadings of memory and reminiscence are the most consistent findings in this. Speed of decisions has fluctuated a great deal. In some studies galvanic reactivity was loaded. These loadings together have suggested the workings of an unconscious complex.

Zeta Component

Unconscious Id Expression. Alpha represents Id as it is expressed in conscious (if not highly integrated) wishes, etc. Here in Zeta, however, the assumption is that Id impulses may be expressed largely in urgent impulsiveness.

Constitutional Need Expression. This interpretation equates Zeta with the C term in the ergic tension equation (above).

Residue from Failure to Effect Full Removal of Speed Vehicles.

Eta Component

Stimulation Level from Surrounding Incentives. Very tentatively this factor has been linked with the S term in the ergic tension equation.

Second-Order Component A

General Integrated Expression. The notion here is that the combination of Beta (Ego) and Gamma (Superego) manifestations indicates a collective contribution to any interest of reality-oriented, society-oriented (parent-oriented), self—ideal-oriented, largely learned and integrated strivings, together with some of the by-products of such strivings.

Second-Order Component B

General Unorganized Id. Here it is hypothesized that both the somewhat conscious but unintegrated wishes of Alpha and the less clearly conscious impulse expressions of Epsilon and Delta combine to give this general Id expression.

Second-Order Component C

General Physiological Autonomic Involvement. This hypothesis allows that present physiological need expression and the constitutional capacity for such expression tend to be functionally related at a general level.

It will be recalled that initial theoretical analyses implied that a measure of total motive strength might have to include estimates from each of the numerous possible outlets suggested by Table 20-1. But, assuming that the seven first-strata motivational components do in fact represent somewhat distinct media (defense mechanisms) through which motive is expressed, the calculations of expenditure of motive through alternative mechanisms may be considerably simplified. In particular, if none of the specific (unique factor) components left in device representations of motive principles contain motivational variance — or, if they do, the amount is trivially small — then total motive strength can be obtained quite simply from some weighted sum of the subscores representing motive expression in each component. The suggestion of positive manifold among the zero-order correlations and the slight positive correlation noted for the two major second-order components both argue that while this procedure would not greatly improve the interval consistency reliability of the resulting total strength measures, it could add to the logical, factorial, and concept validity of such measures. This, in fact, is the procedure assumed in most research based on the above findings, e g., the dynamic structure research discussed in the next section, and in most applied work, such as that based on use of the Motivational Analysis Test (MAT) (297) and the School Motivation Analysis Test (SMAT) (333).

If it turns out that some of the so-called motivational components are in fact residual vehicle components, then the above method for estimating total motive strength will give measurements that are systematically contaminated with vehicle influences. However, the breakdown into components allows for careful study of this question before finally deciding one way or the other. An investigation can obtain separate estimates of attitude strength with each of the first-strata components or at the level of the second-strata components. Then, through research with these separate attitude subscores, it can be decided whether, indeed, the Beta Component, say, should be regarded as primarily an aspect of motive strength or as primarily vehicle. Also, of course, granting that all of the components represent motivational manifestations, the breakdown of attitude strength into separate contributions allows for much more detailed research on motivation and for a more comprehensive understanding of the individual case in applied work. The trend of the research in this area is, in fact, toward making this kind of more detailed analysis (see 295, 332, 1372). This matter will be discussed more fully in a later section on conflict.

It should be noted that it is not absolutely necessary (although it may usually be desirable) to use ipsatization to remove vehicle variance in estimating total motive strength. If what has been called the "attenuation procedure" (297) is properly employed, vehicle influences can be canceled out in the over-all measure: if subscores having no single vehicle in common are added (or if vehicle influences are systematically counterbalanced), then the vehicle variance will tend to appear as random specific variance and not be systematically represented in the total score

The fact that existing results give little support for the hypothesis that devices are naturally ipsative need not be taken as evidence that this hypothesis does not have merit. The findings simply argue that in the fairly heterogeneous samples thus far studied, between-person differences have been more pronounced than within-person differences. This does not mean that the hypothesized within-persons differences do not exist, are not measurable, or are not substantial. They might be shown to be noteworthy by analyses with more homogeneous samples of subjects. Also, Horn (746) has suggested a method whereby between-person differences across time can be removed into trait dimensions, thereby leaving a residual matrix of within-person covariance, and this procedure could be appropriately used here to examine hypotheses relating to natural ipsativity.

6. DYNAMIC STRUCTURE RESEARCH

The work just reviewed focused narrowly on the problem of how best to measure the strength of a given attitude no matter how specific or trivial this attitude might be. But while it may be true that some attitudes are highly revealing of important aspects of personality, most are not; so the measurement of an attitude must usually be only a means to an end — either a means for studying the ways in which any motive can be expressed, as outlined in the previous section, or a means for studying the kinds of motives which are operative in members of a given society, the topic of this section.

If the basic premise of the argument underlying the definition of attitude is sound, then any attitude — however trivial — is bound by, and is an expression of, the laws which apply to motivation generally. From the study of representative collections of attitudes, therefore, may come information about more fundamental mo-

tives. This is the assumption upon which research on dynamic structure has been based. Specifically, this research has assumed that an attitude can be represented as a vector in a multidimensional space the axes of which are biologically based and learning-based motive patterns. It then follows that properly conducted multivariate analyses on representative samples of attitudes can disclose the nature of these more fundamental patterns.

It is not possible to give anything like a complete review of the basic studies[6] proceeding from these assumptions, but the general procedures of most of the studies can be briefly described as follows.

1. An attitude universe was conceived of and sampled from. The pioneering studies developed attitude concepts from systematic study of the hypotheses put forth by outstanding theorists such as W. James, Shand, Freud, McDougall, and Murray. Later studies expanded this "universe" by developing attitudes to assess factors adumbrated by previous research and by trying-out hypotheses emphasized in theories that were in vogue at the time. Between 20 and 60 attitudes were sampled in each study.

2. At least two (and usually more) devices were used to measure each attitude. In the early studies, before the research on motivational components had been carried out, devices were chosen merely with the idea of making them different. But after the components were discovered, devices were systematically chosen in a way to represent each component in the measure of each attitude.

3. Generally, device subscores were first transformed to standard score form and then merely added to give the total attitude measure. In the Cattell-Horn (295) study, however, four device subscores were kept separate. Similarly, in the studies by Cattell, Sweney and coworkers (see Sweney and Cattell, 1372), separate analyses were run for subscores obtained on the second-order

---

[6]226, 267, 279, 295, 296, 1317, 1372.

integrated and unintegrated components, two or three devices being used for each component. Total scores over all devices were also analyzed in these studies.

4. The attitude scores (or subscores) were correlated, factored, and carefully rotated to oblique simple structure. In the Cattell, Cross, and Shotwell, et al., studies, *P* technique was used; all other investigations were based on *R*-technique analyses.

Some of the results from this research have been summarized in Table 20-4. The coefficients, representing an attitude's correlation with a dynamic factor, are simple average factor loadings computed over at least two separate studies, usually over more than two — some over as many as six. This list should not be regarded as com-

plete: some factors were not included because marker variables were not always sufficiently overlapped from one study to another or because of inconsistency in loadings.

It must be remembered that in these studies an attitude is operationally represented by subscore measures on several quite diverse kinds of tests and that the verbal paradigm, as listed in a given study or in Table 20-4, is merely a guide to construction of subtests; it is not always an accurate indication of the attitude content. For this reason some fluctuation in loading patterns from one study to the next is to be expected. One investigator developing tests to represent the attitude: "I want to satisfy my sense of duty" might emphasize

TABLE 20-4

SUMMARY DESCRIPTIONS OF SOME DYNAMIC STRUCTURE FACTORS REPLICATED IN TWO OR MORE STUDIES WITH ADULTS AND/OR CHILDREN

Erg or Sentiment	Major Attitudes Begin Each With "I Want"	Average Loadings Adult	Children
1. Security-Fear Erg	More Protection from Nuclear Weapons	48	
	To Reduce Accidents and Diseases	33	22
	To Stop Powers that Threaten Our Nation	38	
	To Go to Mother When Things Go Wrong		43
	To Be at Home Safe		38
	To Grow Up Normally		31
2. Mating (Sex) Erg	To Love a Person I Find Attractive	52	
	To See Movies, TV Shows, etc. with Love Interest	34	
	To Satisfy Mating Needs	52	
	To Enjoy Fine Foods, Desserts, Drinks	37	
	To Spend Time with Opposite Sex		38
	To Dress to Impress Opposite Sex		38
	To Go to Parties Where Couples are Invited		32
3. Assertive Erg	To Increase Salary and Status	36	
	To Excel Fellows in Chosen Pursuits	40	
	To Dress Smartly and Command Respect	40	
	To Maintain Good Reputation	33	20
	To Read More Comics		34
	To See that My Team Wins		39
4. Protective Erg	Proud Parents Who Do not Lack Needs	47	
	To Insure that Children Get Good Education	40	
	To Help Distressed Adults and Children	40	
	To Help Spouse Avoid Drudgeries	33	
	To Take Care of Pet		38
	Siblings to Mind Me		38

TABLE 20-4 (Continued)

Erg or Sentiment	Major Attitudes, Begin Each With "I Want"	Average Loadings Adult	Children
5. Sensuality Erg (also called Narcism)	To Enjoy Drinking and Smoking	38	
	To Enjoy Fine Foods, Desserts, Delicacies	41	
	To Sleep Late, Take It Easy	31	
	To Enjoy Own Company	37	
	To Eat Well		32
	To Have More Holidays		41
6. Curosity Erg	To Listen to Music	37	
	To Know More Science	29	37
	To Enjoy Graphic Arts and Theater	40	
	To Make My Pictures Beautiful		29
7. Gregarious Erg (Sports Sentiment)	To Actively Participate in Sports	50	
	To Follow Team and Be a Rooter	48	
	To Spend Time in Companionship with Others	23	28
	To Play Games with Friends		36
	To Go to Parties Where Couples Are Invited		38
8. Pugnacity Erg	To Destroy Powers that Threaten Our Nation	42	37
	To See Violence in Movies and TV Shows	20	
	To Get Even with Others		37
9. Appeal Erg (Parental-Religious Sentiment)	To Heed Parents and Turn to Them in Need	39	
	To Feel in Touch with God or Similar Principle	55	
	Proud Parents Who Do not Lack Needs	47	
	Influence of Religion to Increase	60	
10. Construction Erg	Take Things Apart, See How They Work		38
	To Make Projects in School		33
11. Narcissism Erg	To Have Attractive Face and Figure		32
	Nice Clothes to Wear		31
12. Self Sentiment	To Control Impulses and Mental Processes	40	32
	Never To Damage Self Respect	35	27
	To Excel in My Line of Work	38	
	To Maintain Good Reputation	37	34
	Never to Become Insane	39	
	To be Responsible, in Charge of Things	31	
	To Know About Science, Art, Literature	31	
	To Know More About Myself	33	
	To Grow up Normally		28
13. Superego Sentiment	To Satisfy Sense of Duty to Church, Parents, etc.	41	
	Never to Be Selfish in My Acts	41	
	To Avoid Sinful Expression of Sex Needs	33	
	To Avoid Drinking, Gambling—i.e., "Vice"	21	
	To Maintain Good Self Control	28	31
	To Admire and Respect Father		28
14. Religious Sentiment	To Worship God		34
	To Go to Church		33
15. Career Sentiment	To Learn Skills Required for Job	34	
	To Continue with Present Career Plans	33	
	To Increase Salary and Status	27	
16. Sweetheart Sentiment	To Bring Gifts to Sweetheart	51	
	To Spend Time with Sweetheart	41	

the moral duties specified by religion, while another investigator might emphasize duties to country. If so, the attitude as measured in the first study would probably go into the religious sentiment, whereas in the second study it might load primarily on a patriotism sentiment or the pugnacity erg Usually, of course, if the same devices were employed in two studies, at least some of the items from the first were carried over and used in the second study; but when somewhat different devices were used, as was frequently the case, then this kind of continuity from one study to another could be maintained only with respect to a few, not all, of the device measures.

In view of the above-mentioned difficulties and the more usual problems raised by study of many measures, taken in a very limited amount of time on a very finite sample of individuals, the degree of confirmation thus far achieved by replication of dynamic factor patterns is encouraging. Although much more work needs to be done before the details of these structures will be clarified, the results thus far achieved indicate the fruitfulness of the general approach based on use of diverse and objective tests.

Interpretations of the dynamic structure findings have tended to emphasize recognition of two main classes of influence generally believed to affect development of motive patterns, viz., innate physiological influences and socially based, confluent learning influences. These are very complex notions requiring much more space for discussion than is available here. The best sources for a full treatment of the topics from a general standpoint are Cattell's 1950 (226) and 1966 (263a) books, and for a more psychometric orientation his 1957 treatment (280). At best, the following may give some idea of the general form which the more extended interpretations take.

Some of the dynamic factors, viz., those termed *ergs,* are believed to represent (in large measure) the particular cultural channeling of basic innate dispositions. These dispositions enable the individual to become attentive to certain classes of stimulus patterns (e.g., in the mating erg, those representing the opposite sex), to initiate certain patterns of behavior which can be seen (by inference) to be directed toward meeting bodily needs or promoting continuation of the species (e g., the primitive thrashing responses of a frustrated infant directed toward destruction of a barrier that prevents the child from obtaining food, the prototype for expression of the pugnacity erg) and to experience a certain emotion in connection with the attending and goal-directed processes (e.g., the rage accompanying frustration and arousal of the pugnacity erg). Now, of course, it is not assumed that such complex patterns of perceptual, emotional, and motor responses spring full-blown into a person's repertory of behavior, as was implied by some early concepts of instincts; nor is it assumed that the patterns are unaffected by learning. Rather, the notion is that these are the factors which underlie learning, both that of the individual and that of whole societies of people, as reflected in culture. Attitude scales then reflect the ways in which a particular culture imposes restrictions, encourages expression, etc. Of course, the goals, as such, of ergs and the quality of emotion associated with each are in the last analysis transcultural.

A second major class for dynamic structure factors is that for sentiments. These are patterns of attitudes reflecting mainly learned combinations of ergic expressions associated with a particular object-institution, such as "mother" or "religion." The object which functions as "mother" for a particular individual or the institution "mother" in a given society are both associated, through learning, with many expressions of motive, some frustrating or dissatisfying, some highly pleasurable. The sentiment is a psychological compound or conglomerate (who knows which kind of analogy is preferable, if either?) of ergic experiences associated with both the particular object which serves as one's own mother and the sets of conditions which define the concept "mother" in the culture at large.

Essentially three kinds of learning patterns are seen to underlie the formation of a sentiment, viz.: (1) The sentiment object-institution may be used simultaneously for courses of action associated with several attitudes serving several ergs. For example, the institutional church might be at once an awe-inspiring stucture, a repository for interesting books, a meeting place for sociable gatherings, a sports arena, etc., and the attitudes related to the diverse activities here implied could be learned together to constitute the sentiment. (2) The various attitudes involved in a sentiment might all be directed to a single subgoal, represented by the sentiment object. The self-sentiment, for example, may be viewed as a collection of attitudes, many of which are concerned with the preservation—in a broad mental, social, ethical, as well as physical sense—of the object self, which preservation is a condition (subgoal) necessary for the attainment of most other goals and subgoals. (3) The sentiment attitudes may reflect courses of action which become possible by virtue of attainment of a subgoal represented by a sentiment. The self-sentiment seemingly also contains attitudes which follow from the development of a controlled, responsible, respected, and confident self, for example.

Obviously, these three principles are not clearly separable. It cannot be said that existing research supports the distinction. Yet, as indications of the hypotheses implied by present interpretations of dynamic structure factors, they are worth considering.

7. SOME RELATIONSHIPS BETWEEN MOTIVATIONAL COMPONENTS AND DYNAMIC STRUCTURE FACTORS

The two previous sections imply that if we look carefully at interest expressed in a course of action via an attitude, the variance may be partitioned in two rather different ways. Looked at in terms of first-strata motivational components, the interest of person i in course of action j might be written:

$$(1) \ I_{ij} = a_{j1} C_{1i} + a_{j2} C_{2i} + \ldots + a_{j7} C_{7i}$$

where the a_{jk}'s are factor coefficients and the C_{ki}'s are component scores for individuals i ($i = 1, 2, \ldots, N$). But the same I_{ij} can, according to the analyses of the last section, be expressed as a function of various ergs and sentiments, thus

$$(2) \ I_{ij} = b_{j1} E_{1i} + \ldots + b_{jm} E_{mi} \\ + d_{j1} S_{1i} + \ldots + d_{jp} S_{pi}$$

where the b_{jk}'s and d_{jk}'s are factor coefficients for ergs and sentiments respectively and the E_{ki}'s and S_{ki}'s are the corresponding dynamic factor scores. Thus, the implication is that there is a psychological sense in which (1) might be equated with (2) and a canonical analysis made to show the correspondence between certain of the terms in (1) and the terms in (2). As yet, however, these analyses have not been carried out. All that can be considered here, therefore, are some hypotheses and cautions which might help direct such research.

First, the fact that (1) and (2) are based on somewhat different ipsative foundations needs to be considered. In the motivational component breakdown, the attitudes with which the given attitude is compared in ipsatization are quite outside the analyses leading to equation (1). By contrast, these attitudes are elsewhere found in the factor structure leading to equation (2). This latter, means, of course, that there is likely to be some algebraic dependence among the variables in dynamic structure analyses, whereas this is largely absent in the motivational component analyses. Just what this would imply for a given comparison is hard to imagine, however.

Second, it might be worth noting that factor scores would probably be the basic measures for canonical analyses and these would, for the C_{ki}'s, be combinations of device subscores and, for the S_{ki}'s, combination of attitude scores, each attitude, however, being a combination of subscores obtained on several devices. One difficulty in running a canonical analysis to compare the two kinds of factor scores would be that of avoiding spurious algebraic dependence resulting from using the same device subscores on both sides of the equation.

Third, assuming that these technical difficulties can be handled, what are the psychological hypotheses specifying the relationships between E_{ki} and S_{ki} terms on the one side, and C_{ki} terms on the other side? Cattell (246) has put forth a number of relevant suggestions, only the major of which can be reviewed here. The general hypothesis regarded as most likely to be supported specifies: (1) that since the components entering into the second-strata integrated component represent largely acculturation in some form, and the sentiments, likewise, represent learned associations of attitudes and particular social object-institutions, the former should probably tend to be equated with the latter, and (2) that since the unintegrated component indicates largely undifferentiated ergic impulses, the components entering into this second-strata factor should probably align most clearly with what are interpreted as ergs in the dynamic structure. If this reasoning be correct, then equating (1) with (2) implies a further breakdown to an equation of the unintegrated components of (1) with the $b_{jk} E_{ki}$ terms of (2) and of the integrated components of (1) with the $d_{jk} S_{ki}$ terms of (2). But, as noted, it remains for future research to determine the feasibility of this kind of hypothesis.

8. SOME APPROACHES TO THE MEASUREMENT OF CONFLICT

Traditionally, of course, it has been recognized that conflict results when satisfaction must be accompanied by some dissatisfaction, when both of two desirable courses of action cannot be simultaneously followed (as is accomplished in confluent learning [226], when one of two undesirable courses of actions must be taken, etc. But to study this phenomena by experimental means, and with motives that are significant in real-life adjustments, requires that noteworthy motive patterns be assessed. The research mentioned in previous sections may provide the basis for this kind of analysis. Several approaches based on these results have already been tried out.

A study by Williams (1550, 1551) is worth mentioning not only because it is one of the few yet conducted in this area of conflict measurement, but also because it is a pioneering attempt to show how multivariate analyses might be used routinely for diagnosis and treatment in clinical practice.

Williams used a model developed by Cattell (240) which depended on interpretation of signs in specification equation (2). It was reasoned that if the signs in (2) are opposite, i.e., some are negative, then satisfaction of certain ergs served by the course of action implied by the attitude must be obtained at the expense of dissatisfaction in other ergs. If this situation prevailed for a large and representative sample of attitudes, widespread conflict could be said to exist. Since, however, the signs for factor coefficients accompany these latter parameters and these are based on a number (N) of observations for each of a number of tests, the problem encountered by this reasoning is one of obtaining factor coefficients *for individuals* (rather than for a sample of individuals). Thus, P-technique analyses are required.

It may be anticipated that in future years, with further advance in the development of computers and computer technique, most clinical psychologists will be able routinely to carry out multivariate analyses for each of their patients. The research by Williams suggests how this could be accomplished even today. He matched a sample of 5 "normals" with 5 patients having various psychiatric diagnoses and obtained clinical judgments of the degree of conflict expressed by these people. P-technique analyses were carried out for each subject using a set of 14 attitudes representing 6 dynamic factors, and for observations extending over some 85 successive testings. From the factor coefficient matrices he then computed the ratio of the sum of the negative loadings to the sum of all loadings thus

$$(3)\quad C = \frac{b_{\bar{j}k}}{b_{\bar{j}k}^+ + b_{\bar{j}k}}.$$

This measure was found to correlate significantly with the classification "patient" vs. "not a patient," with the clinical ratings for conflict, and the 16 P.F. "ego weakness" factor $C(-)$.

In Section 5 of this chapter it was suggested that the integrated components Beta and Gamma (particularly the former) might represent realized interests or patterns of behavior rather clearly organized to achieve satisfactions, whereas Alpha, Delta, and Epsilon could represent mainly "wished for" goals for which little plan for attainment is evident in behavior. It follows from this that a measure of conflict might be obtained by contrasting the integrated and unintegrated components of any attitude or a set of attitudes. In particular, an over-all estimate of conflict can be obtained by computing the U-I (Unintegrated vs. Integrated) difference in standard scores on each component and summing this over a broad sample of attitudes. Sweney (1370) and Sweney and Cattell (1372) have presented preliminary evidence showing that this kind of measure is related as expected to various other criteria of direct conflict.

As previously noted, the work of Peak (1144) and Rosenberg (1217) shows how conflict between relatively unintegrated and relatively integrated components can be introduced by subtle suggestion that is not accompanied by relevant information.[7] The suggestion from this work is that the

integrated component is changed after, and as a function of, change of the unintegrated component. Developmentally speaking, this makes sense, for it is reasonable to suppose the ergic tension must first be expressed in rather undifferentiated form and only later rationalized, so to speak, through operation of the reality principle, in the integrated components.

The approach to conflict measurement taken by Cattell and Sweney (332) is similar in some respects to that adopted in the motivation components research. In their logical reconnoitering of the terrain of conflict they found that in order adequately to locate a conflict in personality one must take account of: (1) the degree of stabilization, the extent to which the conflict is recent or raw vs. old or scabbed-over, (2) the focus, conceived of in terms of the motive elements in conflict, from minor, as when two rather trivial attitudes are in conflict, to major, as when two powerful ergs are involved, (3) the goal distance, the affect of the goal gradient, (4) the locus with reference to the kind of dimensions involved—erg vs. erg, erg vs. sentiment, etc.

On the basis of this analysis they arranged to take a stratified sampling of kinds of conflict—some old, some recent, some between ergs, some between sentiments, etc. For each they developed device measures analogous to the devices listed in Table 20-1. For example, they reasoned that conflict might exist between the sensuousness erg and the Superego sentiment and that, if so, the extent of this might be gauged by vacillation, as this could be estimated from the number of changes made in a decision as to whether to read funnies or go to Sunday School; likewise, conflict might be indicated by an "over-rating of humor" for jokes involving the conflicting courses of action. Again, as in the motivation component research, a rather large number of hypotheses of this sort were tried out. To obtain a device score, 16 kinds of conflict were considered; three of these

---

[7]Eriksen (465) has shown clearly how complex behavioral expressions, seemingly involving a high degree of awareness, as in the Alpha component, may nevertheless be acquired and maintained at a very low level of awareness.

were selected for the main analyses; a device score for each was obtained and ipsatized with respect to the other kinds of conflict; then standard scores for the three were summed to yield an over-all device score for each of 24 devices, after which a factor analysis was carried out on the device-intercorrelation matrix.

The results from this analysis show some seven dimensions of conflict. These were given the interpretative labels: (1) Strength of Willed Suppression, (2) Restriction of Possibilities of Provocation, (3) Cautious Rigidity, (4) Fantasy from Perplexity or Frustration, (5) Passive Ignoring of Conflict, (6) Expression in Built-Up Tension, and (7) Displacement in Overactivity. The striking resemblance between the behaviors shown in these factors and those described by Anna and Sigmund Freud in their account of defense mechanisms is certainly provocative for future research. As of this writing, however, the Cattell-Sweney results must be regarded as tenuously based on only one study, although quite indicative of the kind of multivariate research on motivation which we can expect to see more of in the coming years.

9. SOME CONSIDERATIONS FOR A GENERAL MODEL FOR DYNAMICS IN PERSONALITY

What has been said about the measurement of integrated and unintegrated motivation components, and about measuring conflict by opposing signs, must be integrated now into a wider setting. Chapters 18 and 19 have described the general specification equation as one having terms for all three modalities of traits and states — ability, temperament, and dynamic modalities — thus requiring six types of factors. There it was indicated that the dynamic trait panel is in fact the most complicated, requiring the addition of role and modulator factors.

By a modulator, Cattell (259, 262) means

a psychological factor which can be temporarily raised to a new level by a particular stimulus. The factor then operates at that level with respect to a whole series of stimuli. Modulators might thus function as second-order factors, changing the level of a whole series of first-order factors. The specification equation would then show the individual's scores in all of these latter to be higher than would normally be expected for that person. An examination failure, for example, might raise an individual's level on all primary factors in the second-order anxiety dimension. Thereafter, for a while, the same factor coefficient weights, indicating the potency of various collections of stimuli for measuring anxiety, could be used to estimate the person's factor score, but his scores would be consistently higher across all primaries.

If it is convenient to define a section of personality as distinct from the role in which the person finds himself, then role can be regarded as a factor which has a modulator action. Whether a person will have a certain role factor or not will depend on his upbringing and, in particular, on whether that sentiment has been incorporated within his dynamic structure. Granted that he has it, it will be brought into action only in a certain class of stimulus situation. Among dynamic factors a role factor will thus be distinguished from broad dynamic motivation factors, such as erg, by the comparatively small number of situations in which it comes into action.

In each case of a dynamic factor — be it role, erg, or sentiment — there is a suggestion that the behaviors which define the dimension will fluctuate rather a great deal within any given individual. The general notion is that dynamic factors have much state variance. P-technique analyses by Cattell and Cross (279) and Shotwell, et al. (1317) have shown, indeed, that dynamic structure factors have substantial variation within the person; the static "snapshot" rendered by R-technique analyses is shown by these studies to be a frozen phase, so to speak, in change of intraperson functional unities.

No attempt has yet been made, however, to systematically partition the variance of representative samples of attitudes into components indicating within-person variation over global occasions and the components showing between-person variation which remains despite differences of occasion. The distinction between role, as a sort of sentiment affected largely by modulator influences, and the ergs and other sentiments can probably be made clearly only when attitude variance is thus partitioned. The expectation would be that role behaviors are "keyed off" by more or less specific, global, social stimulus situations, and that, therefore, much of the within-person variation in behaviors associated in a role factor can be rather neatly tied to such changes in the situation. On the other hand, the hypotheses underlying the interpretations of certain dynamic factors imply that the measures in these will show variation with the need satisfactions which arise in the global situation. For a factor like the mating erg, where it would generally be difficult to ask about satisfactions, the variation in measure might show rather uniform cycles, and these, on the surface, might appear to be largely unrelated to the global environmental situation. In either case, there is need to better relate the rather specific stimuli which provide measure of dynamic factors to the more nearly Life-data, global stimulus situations within which persons function in their usual day-to-day activities.

This kind of problem is crucial in motivation research, as well as in personality research, generally, and it is expected that more and more future work will be concerned with its solution. It is a difficult problem for a number of reasons, but perhaps most notably because it requires that individuals be observed over several occasions, with noteworthy change in global situation, etc., and partly because multi-variate techniques for analyzing several measures, on several occasions, for several individuals have not yet been sufficiently developed or (where they have been developed) are not yet sufficiently understood by psychologists who would use them in research.

Tucker's extension to three-way factor analysis (Chapters 6 and 16) appears to be quite appropriate for this kind of problem, but only a handful of psychologists would yet claim to understand this, and no attempt has yet been made to apply it in motivation research. Horn (746) has proposed a somewhat less ambitious scheme for analyzing attitude variance into within-person, state components and stable trait components. In this, one obtains measurements on m distinct attitudes on k occasions for N people. A "between-person — within-occasion" covariance (or correlation) matrix, W, is obtained as the pooled sum of the matrices on the separate occasions. A "between-persons — across-occasions" covariance (or correlation) matrix, B, is obtained from the total attitude scores over all occasions. It is then reasoned that trait variance is indicated primarily by the latter, but that this must be viewed relative to the within-occasion variation. On this basis, a least-squares solution is set up for a vector that will maximize the ratio of B to W. The characteristic polynomial for this has the form

$$(4) \ Det \ (W^{-1}B - ZI) = O,$$

which has nontrivial and distinct roots as long as W^{-1} exists (and this can be assured). The t vectors, say, which account for this across-occasion covariance can then be said to represent the trait components evident in a given set of data. From this basis it is then possible to partial the trait variance from the measures on each occasion and obtain a least-squares vector solution for the covariance among all attitudes over the various occasions. Since the linear component of trait variability is removed by this procedure, the factors obtained in the final analyses could be said to represent primarily the dimensions of change from one occasion to another. It is possible that a very similar outcome might be obtained by "reversing the roles," so to speak, in the above arguments in the solution for trait components, and maximizing the ratio of W to B. It's possible, too, that multivariate analyses of true gain scores (945, 946, 1015) or incremental R technique (318) would come to much the same end. The writer is now engaged in some analyses involving comparisons of these procedures, as well as Tucker's, but it will be some time before conclusions will be forthcoming.

The suggestion is, then, that besides partitioning attitude variance into (1) motivational components (representing "preferred" modes of expression of motive, defense mechanisms, or the like) and (2) dynamic structure factors (representing ergic sources and the object-institution sentiments associated in the attitude), the investigator may also identify (3) trait components (indicating the behaviors which consistently distinguish between people despite variation in global situation) and (4) state and role components (within-person variation which can, in some cases, be tied clearly to change of global situation or which shows uniform appetitive cycles). To pull out these various sources of variation is admittedly a complex task and one which may require more precision of measurement of basic variables than is now being obtained. But the problems posed by the phenomena of human motivation seem definitely to require such analyses, and the present trend in multivariate research in this area is toward providing answers for these problems.

10. SUMMARY

(1) Accurate scientific use and efficient development of concepts in motivation require clean operational distinction between the phenomena of motivation and the phenomena referred to by terms like ability, temperament, style, etc.

(2) Although we often think about motivation in terms of withholding stimulation (i.e., deprivation), measurement of human motives must usually be based on operations of administering stimulation. This has meant that stimulus situations must be characterized as varying along a dimension of incentive value. Most attempts at measuring human motivation have implicitly assumed that this characterization can be made by simple inspection of content in the construction of questionnaires and opinionnaires. But these attempts, even when coupled with factor analyses of different kinds of measures, have failed to produce a satisfactory operational distinction between motive and temperament, style, etc., and they have tended to imply an excessively narrow conception of the nature of motivation.

(3) Spurred by the availability of computers, the trend in research appears to be toward allowing—even at the elementary level of measuring interest in a simple course of action, as stipulated in an attitude —that there may be many distinct motives in man and that each of these may be expressed in many possible ways.

(4) Use of a principle of manifestation of motive in actual measurement usually introduces extraneous vehicle variance. To get rid of this and obtain more accurate measurement of motivation per se, so-called ipsatization procedures have been developed. Broadly, these may be characterized as analytic or as performed by the subject himself, so to speak, as when the scoring key requires that obtaining points toward score on one variable prevents obtaining points toward score on another variable. It is necessary to be aware of some of the difficulties of using ipsative scores with standard statistical procedures. There is suggestion that some methods of ipsatization may remove motive variance as well as vehicle; while other methods may fail to effect full removal of vehicle.

(5) Various multiple combination models might theoretically be appropriate for the measurement of an elementary unit of motivation, but neither a naturally ipsative nor a Spearman hierarchical model seems to work to describe the relationships between manifestation device measures of attitude strength. Instead, the evidence suggests that individual differences are large relative to any mutual exclusiveness of manifestation which may exist within persons, that all devices are, to a small extent, measuring the same thing, but measures overlap in groupings to suggest some seven broad components of manifestation of interest. These seven oblique components themselves resolve into two (possibly three) second-order components, representing integrated and unintegrated expressions. The approach to positive manifold among the intercorrelations of devices suggests that a single dimension is needed at the third order. More research is required to put these findings in proper perspective, but present evidence suggests that motive can, with advantage both to clinical practice and to pure research, be assessed in some seven primary modes of expression and more broadly in terms of unintegrated and integrated expression, as well as in over-all strength of interest.

(6) Replications of R-technique and P-technique analyses of the interrelationships between representative samples of attitudes, each measured by objective test devices representing several modes of expression of motivation, have indicated some 16 to 20 dynamic structure factors. Interpretations of these have stressed the biological and social-learning bases for development of motive patterns.

(7) Present evidence thus suggests that strength of interest in a course of action may be represented as a vector in two kinds of multidimensional space, one in which components of expression are axes and one in which basic kinds of motives — ergs and sentiments — are axes. Lawful relationships must exist between these two spaces but the evidence which would show this has not yet been accumulated. A reasonable hypothesis stipulates that ergs in the dynamic structure will tend toward canonical alignment with the unintegrated components, while the sentiments will be found to have most of their variance in the integrated devices. Even now, however, the evidence shows that both ergs and sentiments can be identified among device measures all of which have their principal variance in the integrated component.

(8) The resolution of attitude strength into motivational components and dynamic structure factors has opened up several possibilities for objective measurement of conflict. A method based on P-technique analysis has illustrated the application of multivariate methods to clinical diagnosis and has proved to have some validity in this application. There is suggestion that, in general, the unintegrated component is developmentally more primitive than the integrated component, and that a measure based on discrepancy between these two may be clinically useful. Preliminary analyses of the ways in which conflict can be expressed suggest that here, too, it is necessary to think in terms of multiple components. It may be anticipated that some of the components of expression of conflict will turn out to be identical with general motivational components.

(9) Dynamic structures include role and mood as well as motive patterns. Role is distinguished as a kind of sentiment, expression of which is, however, closely tied to rather specific global, social, stimulating conditions. Clear identification and separation of various kinds of dynamic patterns of behavior require repeated measurements of individuals as they move in and out of various global stimulus situations. The means for analyzing multiple measurements taken on multiple occasions with multiple individuals is now within our grasp and the future will no doubt see an increase in the use of these means for research on motivation.

CHAPTER 21 Concepts Generated in Comparative and Physiological Psychological Observations*

JOSEPH R. ROYCE
University of Alberta, Canada

1. INTRODUCTION
(BY THE EDITOR)

The division of subject matter and theme between this and the adjoining chapter by Professor Mefferd has not been too easy to arrange, despite excellent mutual cooperation by the two contributors. It rests largely on a separation of "comparative" matters, i.e., morphology, structural-neurological questions, interspecies behavior and physiology, etc., into this present chapter, and of biochemical processes, physiological functioning, etc., into the following chapter by Professor Mefferd. Such a separation is perhaps little better than some others which could be suggested, and there is

overlap necessarily in that area of emotional response patterns which has interested psychologists since the days of the James-Lange theories. However, the division otherwise can run fairly smoothly between the physiology and behavior of various species, structurally analyzed largely by R technique, individual difference methods in this chapter, and the physiology and behavior of *processes and states*, in which longitudinal P-technique methods have been fairly central, in the following chapter. Some integration of both has naturally been assigned to the second chapter.

Professor Royce, with Cattell (240), R. J. Wherry (1532), C. S. Hall (676), M. A. Wenger (1514), Van Egeren (1486), Williams (1548), and a few others, has long been an outstanding pioneer in the application of multivariate methods, especially factor analysis, to animal behavior and physiological data. Very early (1232, 1233, 1236) he perceived the indispensability of these methods to that structuring of

*Supported in part by Canadian Public Health Grant No. 608-7-82, Grant No. N6217 (A) from the U.S. National Institute of Mental Health and Grant No. 318 from the University of Alberta Research Fund.

The writer hereby acknowledges the assistance he has received from Charles Crawford in preparing this chapter for publication. Mr. Crawford was of particular help in the preparation of the material on body type and color vision.

animal behavior, of temperament and development, which should parallel what has been done with human beings. His point has been that without such precision methods a conceptually effective comparative psychology cannot be built up. The use of factor-analytic concepts of temperament dimensions, psycho-neural structures, and developmental patterns in the *animal* field has had one advantage. At least it has not suffered from confusion with a rank and weedy growth of more speculative, univariately born notions such as has confounded human behavior analysis, by reason of humans having introspective and other biased approaches to their own behavior patterns.

On the other hand, multivariate comparative methods have had to face more substantial technical difficulties, notably in finding an adequate array of diverse measurable behaviors and setting up practical, objective, experimental devices for their measurement. And when the next step is taken — that of linking the temperament patterns found in animals to related concepts in humans — it faces the great and subtle difficulties of finding some truly, precisely, comparable variables in human and lower animal behavior that are not wholly of a physiological kind, e.g., reaction time, amount of fidgeting, number of startle responses, through which markers the factor source traits can be compared across species and interpreted.

Indeed, it may be said that Royce is one of the few pioneers of factor analysis in new areas who has saved his work from futility, or at least, imprisonment in a private world, by recognizing the importance of systematically carrying marker variables for matching of factors from study to study and laboratory to laboratory. Without this the aim of finding factors which are invariant, meaningful source traits from one setting to another is a pious aspiration devoid of real implementation. And, as he rightly says "the key to the relevance of factor analysis for advancing our understanding of behav-

ior lies in the concept of invariance." He cites the compendium of French (550) as giving us evidence of invariance in the human ability field (see Pawlik, Chapter 18 above), and of Cattell (240), Eysenck (488) (chapters by Rees, Martin, Meyer, and Willett), French (551), and Guilford (626) in establishing consensus in the personality field, in objective tests and questionnaires. (Actually, the majority of these reports do not yet reach the technical dependability in the conclusions on invariance which Chapter 6 above shows to be necessary.) He then proceeds to set himself the same objective in the animal comparative field. It must be confessed at the outset, however, that while this is difficult of achievement in the human field — even where six to a score of replications with markers exist as shown in Chapter 18 on ability factors or Nesselroade's and Delhees' Chapter 19 on personality — it is virtually impossible in the, as yet, far less organized comparative psychology realm. He does best, therefore, to present the researcher with well-tabulated detailed statements instead of the condensed conclusions one would naturally like to have. For these will indicate the variables needed in the best, strategic, next steps to checking the invariance *hypotheses* here presented.

Finally, Royce has illustrated very aptly in this field the methodological generalizations made in Chapters 2 and 6 above, especially that manipulative and multivariate are not incompatible categories of design, and, second, that once a factor is well established there is no need to continue to use factor analysis in further experimentation. It can, for example, be used in simple bivariate designs once one has a battery of guaranteed validity for the factor concept. Indeed, further illumination of the concept may at that point depend vitally on manipulative experimental *use* of the factor measure in a considerable variety of situations. In the present chapter these "situations" are frequently the relation of a behavioral factor pattern to some neurological or physiological manipulative procedures.

2. SOME METHODOLOGICAL DIFFICULTIES IN THE AREA

In a period of transition, as multivariate designs begin to be more widely used, we are bound to suffer from the gathering of data being insufficiently adapted from that of bivariate designs where the number of cases and of variables has been quite insufficient to do more than give a t-test indication of a significant mean difference. For example, it may be appropriate to study brain-damaged cases and yet very difficult to find the large number of cases required for a factor analysis since, as Cattell and Pawlik (308) have shown with actual plasmodes, variables which appear to be experimentally dependent do not necessarily lead to such incidental or artifactual factors. This is true of variables involving simultaneous recording of psychological and physiological measures, and of those involving long intervening periods that permit developmental and adaptation effects. It is also true of dependent variables that involve a critical period in the development of the organism. However, partial experimental dependence results when variables that apparently are experimentally dependent are repeated at short time intervals that do not permit the operation of developmental and adaptation effects.

Problems of experimental dependence and underdetermination represent additional methodological difficulty. The criticism of underdetermination can be appropriately leveled at many of the investigations conducted in this area to date. The problem arises from the practice of obtaining dependent multiple measurements from the same behavioral event. This, in turn, leads to underdetermination. A clear example is the study by Geier, Levin, and Tolman (582), where twenty-nine measurements were obtained from two experimen-

tal setups, eleven from Hall's open field test, and eighteen from a Lashley jumping stand visual discrimination apparatus. So many measurements from such a limited sampling of behavior are bound to result in experimental dependence[1] and the identification of instrument factors (250, 282) and of artifactors (1203). Such incidental common factors have been identified frequently in the factorial literature on animal learning. However, the situation is less clear when the investigator uses both physiological and psychological measures, or when repeat measures are taken at different phases of the developmental sequence. In the only investigation on the special problems of experimental dependence in comparative physiological psychology reported to date, Royce (1234, p. 24) concluded

... (a) Apparently experimentally dependent variables involving simultaneous recording of two different levels of observation (i.e., psychological and physiological) do not necessarily identify incidental common factors. (b) Apparently experimentally dependent variables that are repeated with long intervening periods of time (i.e., that permit of developmental and/or adaptation effects) do not necessarily identify incidental common factors. (c) Apparently experimentally dependent variables that are repeated with short intervening periods of time (i.e., that do not permit of developmental and/or adaptation effects) demonstrate partial experimental dependence. (d) Apparently experimentally dependent variables that involve a "critical" period in the development of the organism (i.e., that permit of very rapid change in a very short period of time such as one week) do not necessarily identify incidental common factors.

The incompatible demands of the factorial and the physiological methodologies make

---

[1]Experimental dependence is defined as the appearance of an incidental common factor due to the sharing of the uniqueness of two or more scores derived from the same performance (Thurstone, 1420, pp. 440-441).

it mandatory that additional experimental investigations of experimental dependence be carried out, such as the one recently reported by Cattell and Pawlik (308).

The final major deterrent which has postponed the coalition of multivariate methods and comparative-physiological psychology so long needed is the sheer breadth of technical skill required for combined effort. This story will be repeated in many fields. Until psychology departments train psychologists who are both good experimentalists, conversant with the data of a given field, and good multivariate analysts and designers of experiment, futility and confusion will persist. For example, unless the comparative-physiological psychologist understands the factor-analytic experimental designs, he will continue to assemble test batteries which are factorially inadequate. And, if the mathematically oriented factor analyst is not sufficiently aware of the biological mechanisms of behavior and the technical requirements for obtaining such measurements, he will continue to analyze test batteries which are psychophysiologically meaningless.

Since the key to the relevance of factor analysis for advancing our understanding of behavior lies in the concept of invariance, the material which follows is focused on invariant factors. The possibility and, in fact, the necessity, for such study is particularly crucial in the comparative-physiological domain, for it will be possible to identify convincing biological correlates of behavioral factors only after the components of complex behavior have been sufficiently replicated. The possible relationships between genetics and behavioral factors is a good case in point. It will be impossible to identify underlying genotypes until appropriate behavioral phenotypes (i.e., factors) are well established (1235).

Although there is general agreement concerning the importance of factorial invariance and although there are now

some half-dozen proposed indices of quantitative invariance in the factor-analytic literature (see Ahmavaara, 10; Burt, 167; Cattell, 248; Wrigley & Neuhaus, 1590; Tucker, 1460; Kaiser, 836, 837; and Werdelin, 1527, 1528, 1529), it is unfortunately true that there is, at present, no adequate mathematical solution for the general case (i.e., the case which cuts across populations sampled and variables sampled). Furthermore, since quantitative indices of invariance are a relatively recent innovation, there is very little empirical data available concerning quantitative invariance.

Indeed, except for a long-range research project now underway at the University of Alberta, we know of no empirical evidence concerning the quantitative invariance of factors in the domain of comparative-physiological psychology. Hence, the invariances suggested in this chapter are based on a careful qualitative analysis of possible convergences.

The material which follows is organized under four major sections: (1) Body type and constitutional psychology; (2) The physiological basis of certain human abilities and performances; (3) The general dimensionality of animal behavior, and (4) The neuro-hormonal basis of emotional response patterns.

An initial sketch by the present writer of multivariate methods in regard to sensation, notably color vision, seemed better to belong to Chapter 17 on perception, by Hake and has therefore been incorporated there. Certain other fields were reviewed but either were eliminated from consideration or minimized because of questionable relevance. These include, for example, the elimination of a wide variety of studies on the relationships between cardiovascular variables and physical fitness (900, 1007, 1009, 1089, 1168), an analysis of the electrocardiogram by the physiologist Scher, et al. (1268), an analysis of the electroencephalogram by Hsü and Sherman (784), and Andrews' (36) study on allergies.

3. BODY TYPE AND CONSTITUTIONAL PSYCHOLOGY

For centuries man has been speculating about the relationship between physique and personality, but only in the last hundred years has an effort been made to determine empirically the nature of such relationships. From a factor-analytic point of view the first step in solving this age-old problem involves the establishment of invariant factors of body type. Once this has been achieved, an attempt can be made to relate these factors to behavior and to genetic and physiological determinants.

There have been several dozen factorial studies of body type and growth, but only those mentioned in Table 21-1 involve rotation to simple structure. There have also been attempts to define body types on what is essentially a correlation cluster basis, the best known of which is Sheldon's mesomorph, endomorph, and ectomorph trinity. The correlational evidence for these last is actually not very firm, and they rest partly on developmental evidence. Moreover, the extent to which they are supposed to be independent is unclear, since certain combinations are stated by Sheldon to have frequencies different from others. The advantage in this system, on the other hand, is that it has not confined itself to size measures but has included variables like hair distribution, etc., which many of the more "precise" studies have overlooked.

For the sake of keeping to comparable and replicated studies we shall here confine ourselves to body measurement studies which have proceeded to simple-structure— resolved factor analyses. From Table 21-1 we see that there are seven factors which have been identified in more than one study and hence show some evidence for invariance.

There is considerable evidence (see Table 21-1) for the invariance of a factor of general body size. It has been identified in five different studies (706, 778, 1009, 1069, 1418), and is most clearly identified by stature, sitting height, chest circumference, length of arms, and forearm girth. Additional support for this factor comes from the unrotated work of Burt and his students (163, 164, 165, 363, 365, 685, 686, 1187).[2] This factor is best described as a factor of simultaneous growth in all parts of the body, and may be a manifestation of what Huxley has called general or isogonic growth.

The next candidate for invariance is the fat factor (see Table 21-1), which was found by two investigators, Marshall (990) and McCloy (1009), who factored body measurements at a number of different ages. Both investigators state that this factor is loaded on measures of fat and subcutaneous tissue, but it is also loaded on other measures such as stature, sitting height, weight, chest width, and chest depth, which suggests that it may be a general body size factor such as body mass.

The evidence strongly indicates that there are two general size factors, one a factor of general skeletal size (Factor A), and the other a factor of body mass (Factor B). The suggestion that there are two body size factors is given support by Howells' (778) finding that his second-order factor of general skeletal size is related to the general body size factor (Factor A). Similar evidence is offered in a Q-technique study by Lorr and Fields (950), who report that a bi-polar factor of endomorphy-ectomorphy factor is related to the fat (or general body mass) factor, and the mesomorphy factor is related to the general size (or general skeletal size) factor.

The notion that growth in breadth and depth of the body is somewhat independent of growth in length is supported by the possible invariance of a cross-sectional

---

[2] A general size factor was also identified by Mullen (1086) using Holzinger's bi-factor method.

factor and a linear factor The cross-sectional factor can be briefly defined as a horizontal cross-section of a body taken anywhere between the neck and the hips. It is identified (see Table 21-1) by bicromial diameter,[3] chest width, chest depth, chest girth, and weight.

However, the invariance of the linear factor is not as convincing, since it is identified by only one common measurement — stature (identified in the studies of Marshall, 990, and Moore and Hsü, 1069). Evidence in support of a linear factor is also reported in the unrotated work of Burt and his students (163, 165, 363, 365, 685, 686, 1187, 1188), who have repeatedly found a bi-polar factor of length measurements opposed to cross-sectional measurements.

Table 21-1 suggests considerable support for a factor of long bone structure (Factor E), but closer inspection of the detailed data reveals a situation similar to the linear factor, namely, identification by only one variable, stature. We think it more likely that the long bone structure factor is a subentity of Factor F, size of extremities (Table 21-1), which has been identified by three different investigators (706, 1069, 1418). It is loaded on stature, calf girth, and hand length.

Four investigators, Moore and Hsü (1069), Howells (778), and Thurstone (1418), have found evidence supporting the common observation that the size of the head may vary independently of the rest of the body. The general head size factor (Table 21-1) is identified by head length, head breadth, and head height.

What can we say about the dimensionality of the human body? Guilford (626) has suggested that a three-level, hierarchical picture best describes the data: a third-order factor of general body size, several second-order factors such as head size, trunk size, and arm size, and at the first-order level, a number of narrow band factors, linear components such as head length and

foot width. Our analysis, which has focused primarily on invariance, differs from Guilford's in that we found no invariant factors comparable to his at the first-order level. Thus, on the basis of the invariant data reviewed to date, we are forced to a two-level interpretation, with two factors of general size at the second-order level, one of general skeletal size and one of general body mass, and several first-order domain factors such as cross-sectional development, general head size, and size of extremities.

Most studies to date have concentrated on the identification of factors without trying to relate them to behavior; however, there are three exceptions to this fact that are worth mentioning. Moore and Hsü (1069) factored body measurements on 99 psychotic patients, then compared different diagnostic groups by the use of multiple regression equations and t tests. They found that the mean score for paranoid schizophrenics was significantly higher on the linear factor than on either the thickness of trunk factor or the lateral muscular factor. Also, the mean score for the paranoids was significantly higher on the size of trunk factor than on the lateral muscular factor.

Rees and Eysenck (1188) derived an index of body type based on several measurements related to their factors. They then defined leptomorphs (ectomorphs) as one standard deviation to the left of the mean, mesomorphs as plus or minus one standard deviation from the mean, and meuryomorphs (endomorphs) as one standard deviation to the right of the mean of their index. An important point about this procedure is that it emphasizes the essential continuity between the different body types. Different diagnostic groups were then compared on this index. They found that: (1) leptomorphs had a marked tendency to the affective group of symptoms, (2) leptomorphs had a higher proportion of schizoid personalities than the euryomorphs, and (3) neurotics as a whole were

---

[3]Bicromial diameter refers to the measurement of the greatest breadth of the bony shoulder girdle.

TABLE 21-1

Apparently Invariant Factors of Human Body Type

Investigator and Year	Number of Ss and Species	Number and Nature of Variables and Factors	Type of Analysis
Adcock and Prior (6)	102 females, 142 females, 103 males, all Maori or part Maori	22 body measurements and blood measures. Analyzed as three studies; 5 primary and 2 second-order factors in each.	IPRAX extraction, Varimax plus Oblimax rotation.
Heath (705)	4128 women	29 circumference measurements; 5 factors	Multiple group; rotation to oblique simple structure
Howells (777)	152 paired brothers	19 physical measurements; 5 significant factors	Centroid method; rotation to oblique simple structure
Marshall (989)	850 boys; separate analyses for different ages	18 body measurements; 4 body type factors	Centroid analysis; Thurstone's logical rotation
McCloy (1008)	Boys and girls 4 days to 6 years	18 physical measurements; 4 body type factors	Centroid solution; approximate simple structure
Moore and Hsü (1068)	100 psychotics	31 anthropological measurements; 5 significant factors	Centroid solution; oblique rotation
Thurstone (1417)	140 males	12 physical measurements; 4 factors	Centroid analysis; oblique simple structure
Thurstone (1947) (1418)	200 neurotic soldiers	17 body measurements; 7 factors	Centroid solution; oblique simple structure

TABLE 21-1 (Continued)
APPARENTLY INVARIANT FACTORS OF HUMAN BODY TYPE

	Apparently Invariant Factors (Rotated)						
Factor A General Size Factor	Factor B Fat Factor	Factor C Cross-Sectional Factor	Factor D Linear Factor	Factor E Long Bone Structure Factor	Factor F Size of Extremities Factor	Factor G General Head Size Factor	Other Factors
Ectomorphy	Endomezomorphy						Blood pressure, blood content, lung capacity
General growth				Cancerous bone growth	Growth in extremities		Growth in upper half of body. Growth in lower half of body.
General size				Long bone structure		Brain size	Lateral, facial, cranial development. Facial length, Ear length (underdetermined)
	Fat factor	Cross-sectional factor (tentative)	Linear factor (tentative)				Chest factor (present between 6 mos. & 3 years).
General growth factor	Growth in fat	Growth in cross-section					Chest and shoulder (tentative). Normal growth (found only in women).
General size		Thickness of trunk	Linear factor		Lateral or circumferential factor	Cephalic factor	
		Transverse measure of girth		Bone Length	Size of Extremities	Head size	
Associated with size		Girth measurements			Limb length		Chest width, chest depth, trunk size, hand size (underdetermined)

TABLE 21-2

APPARENTLY INVARIANT COGNITIVE FACTORS WITH NEURAL OR BIOCHEMICAL CORRELATES

Investigator and Year	Number of Ss and Species	Number and Nature of Variables and Factors	Type of Analysis	Apparently Invariant Factors (Rotated)				
				Factor H Memory	Factor I Verbal Comprehension	Factor J Perceptual Closure	Factor K Number	Other Factors
Birren (112)	99 elderly Ss, aged 60 to 74; 31 senile mental patients, aged 60 to 74	2 factor analyses; 16 factor-analytic tests; 8 factors from each sample	Centroid; oblique rotation	Memory	Verbal comprehension	Perceptual closure (i.e., Thurstone C_1)		
Cohen I (358)	100 neurotics, 100 schizophrenics, and 100 brain-damaged	12 subtest scores of W-B and WAIS; 3 separate analyses; name 3 factors in all analyses	Centroid; oblique	Memory	Verbal comprehension	Perceptual organization		One second-order factor
Cohen II (360)	1152 adults of which 200 aged 18-19, 300 aged 25-34, 300 aged 45-54, 352 aged 60-75	12 subtests of WAIS; 4 separate analyses; same 3 factors in all analyses	Centroid; oblique rotation	Memory	Verbal comprehension	Perceptual organization		
de Mille (415)	150 prefrontal lobotomized schizophrenics, 150 non-lobotomized schizophrenics	2 factor analyses; 16 factor-analytic tests; 8 factors from each sample	Centroid; orthogonal rotations		Verbal comprehension		Numerical facility	General reasoning symbolic patterns sensitivity to problems, ideational fluency, experimental evaluation, spontaneous flexibility.
Halstead (682)	50 head-injured but not brain-damaged Ss	13 intelligence and sensory measures; 4 factors	Centroid oblique rotation; bifactor	Central integrative field or memory				Abstraction, power of psych. vigilance, sensory modality.
F. J. King, et al. (873)	58 children, aged 11 to 16	21 amino acid variables from urine samples; 6 uninterpreted biochem. factors, correlated with 7 intelligence factors.	Centroid; quartimax rotation	Memory	Verbal knowledge	Closure	Number	Divergent thinking, motor word fluency.

slightly more leptomorphic. However, both the Moore and Hsü study and the Rees and Eysenck study were purely empirical, and neither was able to offer a rationale for the results.

Because of its extensive coverage of relevant variables and the greater experimental control characteristic of animal studies, the study of the anthropologist G. L. Brace (135) is probably the most important factor-analytic study that has attempted to throw light on the relationship between physique and personality. Working in the Roscoe B. Jackson Memorial Laboratory at Bar Harbor, Maine, Brace factored fifty physiological, physical, and behavioral measures on 296 purebred, cross-bred and back-cross dogs. He found four factors: (1) gross physical size, (2) general reactivity, (3) heart rate, and (4) activity success.[4] Here we have behavioral, physiological, and physical factors from the same analysis, but the important point is that factors from different domains remained independent of each other. Brace concludes that

The present study has demonstrated the independence of the physical, physiological and behavioral facets of the canine biogram. Given the fact that dogs exhibit a social and behavioral level little below that of many primates, the anthropologist can infer from the present findings that a similar dimensional independence should be expected in the primates and ultimately in the human biogram.

If this interpretation proves correct, it supports Guilford's (626) conclusion that the factorial relating of physique to behavior will probably remain a will-o-the-wisp.

4. PHYSIOLOGICAL CORRELATES OF HUMAN ABILITIES

It is now three decades since a fortunate association of Charles Spearman and Karl

Lashley combined the former's theory of intelligence as "general mental energy" with the latter's conception of neural "mass action." Spearman's behavioral analysis, demonstrating correlationally the existence of a general mental ability factor, was the first firm evidence on the behavioral side of a measureable something with which neurological data could be related. Perhaps this measurable general ability would be more amenable to precise relations, but if so it looked as if some total mass of functioning cortical neurons might be the most promising correlate.

As the steady accumulation of human brain injury examinations has proceeded, it has seemed, as Cattell has claimed (258), that we may recognize a "fluid general ability factor," g_f, which is impaired to the extent of the cortical injury suffered, no matter where, as Lashley's results suggested, and a crystallized general ability factor, g_c, defects in aspects of which are associated with local injury, e.g., verbal ability defect with temporal lobe injury. Further pursuit of this plan of association of ability with brain anatomy and physiology requires clarification of the "fluid-vs.-crystallized" general ability concepts, which have grown out of the Spearman single general ability factor, as well as their relation to the concepts of Halstead. The recent work of Horn (749) has confirmed the fluid general ability factor, in its distinction from the crystallized ability factor, loading verbal, numerical, and other skills and in its loading of the perceptual, culture-fair type of intelligence test. Many of the measures used by Reitan and by Halstead clearly are principally loaded with this fluid general ability factor.

Lashley's (901) work on animal intelligence stimulated both animal and human research in this area. While the present analysis provides some evidence for invariance in animal research, such factors still have not been correlated with brain function or brain metabolism. A beginning in this direction has been made, however, in

---

[4]Activity success refers to tests where food reward provides the motivation for action.

the domain of human intellect. Since Halstead's 1947 monograph, there has been a slow trickle of research focused on identifying the cortical representation of factorially determined components of human intelligence. The relevant studies on this subject have been summarized in Table 21-2.

These six studies point to cortical and biochemical correlates for four of the many invariant factors of human intelligence. The neural evidence[5] includes three studies (Cohen, 358; de Mille, 415; Halstead, 682) which deal directly with brain-damaged subjects. The biochemical evidence[6] is reported by F. J. King (872), who performed a factor analysis on 21 biochemical variables and subsequently correlated biochemical factors with factor tests of intelligence. While the biological correlate evidence from the Birren (112) and Cohen (361) studies on old age are inferential, they are convincing. Cohen, for example,

---

[5]There is also electroencephalographic evidence linking factors and cortical function (see Mundy-Castle, 1087, 1088; and Saunders, 1257). These data are not presented in detail, however, because they can only be regarded as suggestive, having involved only two electroencephalographic measures along with the Wechsler subtests. The two EEG measures projected the major variance on each of the two factors, alpha frequency loading .77 on Saunders' factor III, and alpha index (proportion of alpha rhythm for a given period of time) loading −.97 on Saunders' factor IV. There is considerable disagreement between Saunders and Mundy-Castle regarding the interpretation of these two factors, as well as confusion concerning their possible similarity to the three Wechsler factors summarized in Table 21-2. The most likely similarity between the Saunders—Mundy-Castle factors and the previously available evidence occurs in the case of factor J, Perceptual Closure. The linkage is provided by the Picture Completion and Picture Arrangement variables of the Wechsler, and represents Saunders' alpha index factor. Unfortunately the Hsü-Sherman (784) report consists entirely of electroencephalographic measures, whereas the Mundy-Castle (1087) study is composed primarily of psychological measures. Possible interrelationships cannot be made clear until a sufficient number of measures are analyzed representing both domains.

[6]The biochemical aspects of King's research are covered in more detail in the next section (see pp. 659-662).

has demonstrated that the same three factors (memory, verbal comprehension, and perceptual organization) from the Wechsler subtests hold for brain-injured Ss as well as for normals. In fact, the invariance of these three factors extends to neurotics and schizophrenics (Cohen, 358), to lobotomized and non-lobotomized schizophrenics (de Mille), and throughout the adult life span (Birren and Cohen, 360). Furthermore, Birren's analysis of 31 senile mental patients strongly suggests a deficit in factor scores due to brain disease. Birren reports the following mean factor scores for two comparable groups of elderly senile subjects: The factor scores were determined by giving equal weights to the three most relevant subtests for each of the three factors. Thus, the Memory score was obtained by averaging the Digit Span, Arithmetic, and Digit Symbol tests; the Verbal Comprehension score by averaging the Information, Comprehension, and Vocabulary tests; and the score for Factor J included Picture Arrangement, Picture Completion, and Object Assembly. It is obvious that the senile group showed a deficit in all three factors, especially for Factor J. The force of the available evidence to date is that certain factors of mental ability are characteristic of a wide variety of normal and abnormal populations (such as neurotic, schizophrenic, brain-damaged), but that there may be a decrement in the scores of such factors as a result of organic (i.e., neural or biochemical) change.

Close study of the psychometric variables in Table 21-2 which are common to the four apparently invariant factors indicates that they come primarily from two sources: the subtests of the Wechsler intelligence scales (i e., the Wechsler-Bellevue or the WAIS) and various factored tests (i e., either from Guilford, Thurstone, or the Educational Testing Service standardized reference battery). The perceptual closure factor, for example, is identified in F. J. King's study by the ETS tests of

TABLE 21-3

MEAN FACTOR SCORES OF THE ELDERLY AND SENILE GROUPS
(Adapted from Birren, 112)

	N	Factor *H* Memory		Factor *I* Verbal Comprehension		Factor *J* Perceptual Closure	
		Mean	σ	Mean	σ	Mean	σ
Elderly	50	6.7	2.4	9.8	2.3	6.6	2.3
Senile patients	31	4.6	2.9	6.4	2.9	3.6	2.4

mutilated words, short words, and Gestalt completion. Birren and Cohen's analyses involved the non-verbal or perceptual subtests of the Wechsler-Bellevue and the WAIS, especially Picture Arrangement, Object Assembly, and Block Design. Similar findings hold for the other three factors as well, with overlap of variables being the most complete for the verbal comprehension factor. This commonality of "different investigation" variables identifying a given factor cannot be clearly seen by inspection of Table 21-2. While it would be prohibitive, and not particularly fruitful, to look at all the variables for all factors, we shall provide abbreviated summaries for selected factors in the form of simplified composite matrices. The first such matrix, summarizing the data for the verbal comprehension factor, is indicated in Table 21-4.

Here we see that Birren and Cohen

identified this factor with exactly the same four subtests of the Wechsler. Furthermore, we see that two of de Mille's measures on this factor are also from the Wechsler, even though these measures were a very small part of his total battery. The remaining three measures, Guilford's verbal comprehension, ETS vocabulary, and the California Mental Maturity verbal concepts, are all portions of composite measures of the verbal comprehension factor.

The Halstead tests, in general, do not converge with the cumulative experience of the more traditional factor tests and the Wechsler tests. In fact, only one of his factors, which he originally labeled "central integrative field factor," seems to relate to the factors summarized in Table 21-2. Inspection of his test battery indicates very little likelihood of convergence with either the verbal comprehension factor or the

TABLE 21-4

SIMPLIFIED COMPOSITE MATRIX FOR FACTOR *I*, VERBAL COMPREHENSION

Variables	Factor Loadings Birren	Cohen I	Cohen II	de Mille
Information	.57	from .59 to .68	.30 .36	
Comprehension	.40	from .49 to .58	from .33 to .45	.72 .74
Similarities	.51	from .43 to .64	.32 .42	
Vocabulary	.51	from .49 to .68	.37 .48	.76 .79

number factor, but the composition of his test battery suggests that he could identify one or two perceptual factors. I say this because eleven of the thirteen tests he factored are of a non-verbal, intellectual, sensory, or perceptual nature. Let us take a closer look at Halstead's factor matrix, reproduced here as Table 21-5.

is identified primarily by flicker-fusion and two measures involving form and color discrimination. I find it difficult to see the author's interpretation of these perceptual tasks as regulating affective or feeling forces. The interpretation of this factor as somehow related to cerebral metabolism, etc. seems forced, in spite of the argument

TABLE 21-5

OBLIQUE-FACTOR MATRIX (THURSTONE) FOR 13 NEUROPSYCHOLOGICAL INDICATORS
(From Halstead, 682, p. 41)

Indicator	Description	Factors			
		C	A	P	D
1	Carl hollow-square (IQ)	.25	.45	−.07	.04
2	Category	.49	.63	.09	−.03
3	Flicker fusion	.00	.04	.54	.05
4	Tactual performance speed	.12	−.02	.04	.61
5	Tactual incidental recall	−.02	.66	.43	−.02
6	Tactual incidental localization	.19	.34	.25	.29
9	Henmon-Nelson (IQ)	.58	.27	−.05	.23
13	Speech perception	.49	−.06	.06	.22
14	Finger oscillation	.49	−.06	.25	.18
16	Time-sense memory	.43	.11	.08	.02
17	D.V.F. form	.41	.07	.64	−.03
18	D.V.F. color	.41	−.03	.61	−.06
19	D.V.F. peripheral	−.15	.11	−.06	.54
		Σ3.60	2.51	2.81	2.04

Halstead offers us a four-factor theory, as follows. He described the first factor, C, as a memory[7] or central integrative field factor. He sees this factor as dealing with the organized habits of the individual dynamically relating the old to the new, and reflecting a coalescence of intelligence and learning. Factor A, abstraction, is concerned with concepts or universals. The key to this factor revolves around the subject's ability to group to a criterion, to see similarities embedded within differences, and vice versa. Factor P is labeled a power factor. It

which is amassed in Chapter 9 around flicker-fusion as the key to this interpretation.[8] The situation regarding Factor D, sensory modality, is even more questionable, for we are given a full-fledged interpretation in spite of the fact that the factor is identified by only two significant loadings, indicators 4 and 19. Halstead's conceptualization of this factor in terms of the

[8]Halstead's (1320) subsequent discussion of the P factor in terms of the reticular activating system provides a more explicit, as well as a more reasonable and testable, hypothesis of the neural correlate of this factor. However, this linkage has not been explicitly tested experimentally, and furthermore, Halstead's finding that the P factor follows Lashley's principle of mass action seems inconsistent with the reticular system hypothesis.

[7]In his most recent statement (1320) of the four-factor theory of biological intelligence, Halstead explicitly redesignates the C factor as a memory (M) factor.

modality or medium by which intelligence is exteriorized or manifested is insightful and possibly true, but the factor-analytic evidence is simply not convincing. This seems to be an example of a prepostulated factor which did not emerge inductively from the data, nor was this hypothesis convincingly confirmed by the two variables describing it.

The Halstead (682) study is covered in some detail in spite of its factorial shortcomings because of the author's subsequent analyses of brain-damaged patients. Although these analyses unfortunately were *not* done in terms of factor scores, 8 of the 13 factored tests were included in his 10-test impairment index for identifying cases of brain damage. These eight tests were distributed as follows: significant loadings on Factor C, indicators 2, 13, 14, 16; significant loadings on Factor A, indicators 2, 5, 6; plus 2 significant indicators for factor P (3 and 5), and one indicator for Factor D (4). In other words, two of Halstead's factors, A and C, are sufficiently (even though confounded) represented in his 10-test impairment index. A total of 237 normal controls and brain lesion patients were given different combinations of 27 neuropsychological tests. Eighty of these Ss and ten of the tests were used in a study in which three groups were compared for presence of brain damage. This study involved 30 normal controls (i.e., no evidence of brain damage), 28 frontal lobectomies, and 22 non-frontal lobectomies. Details regarding the locus and extent of brain damage are provided for each cerebral lobectomy, with damage ranging from less than 1 per cent to 32.47 per cent of the total cortex. The data clearly demonstrate higher mean impairment scores[9] for brain damage as opposed to non-brain damage cases. Furthermore, the test battery is usually able to discriminate between cases of frontal and non-frontal cerebral lobectomy. Halstead reported average impairment indices as follows:[10]

normal controls	= .13* and .23*
undifferentiated non-frontal cerebrals	= .26
temporal lobectomies	= .48* and .53
frontal lobectomies	= .78 and .86

Subsequent studies by Reitan (1189) and by Shure and Halstead (1320) were even more convincing in demonstrating the discriminatory power of the impairment index. Furthermore, the Shure-Halstead monograph provides evidence for the cortical correlate for one of Halstead's factors plus suggestive evidence for two others. Let us now examine their factorial-neurological evidence in more detail. While Halstead's original data (682) yielded zero correlations between degree of impairment and extent of lesion, thereby casting considerable doubt on Lashley's mass action principle, his second monograph (1320) provides counterevidence in favor of mass action for certain components of intelligence. In short, the combined evidence from the two monographs indicates that neither a strict localization nor a strict mass action theory will hold; the relevance of these two principles depends upon the psychological function and the cortical field in question. Both sets of data confirm the conclusion that frontal lobectomy cases, in general, do poorer on all tests of the Halstead battery. Such data led Halstead to the conclusion that while intellect is a function of the entire cortex, it is "distributed in a gradient, with its maximal

---

[9]The impairment index is based on the 10 tests of Halstead's battery which best discriminated between brain-damaged and non-brain-damaged cases. The scores vary between 0 and 1.00, depending on the proportion of tests scored above a specified cut-off value. The higher the score, the greater the probability that the S has brain damage. A score of 0 means the S shows no evidence of brain damage; a score of .5 means he manifested evidence of brain damage for 5 of the 10 tests; and a score of 1.00 means he shows brain damage for all 10 of the tests.

[10]The three values marked by an asterisk are reported in Halstead's 1958 study; the remaining values are reported in the original monograph (682).

representation occurring in the cortex of the frontal lobes" (682, p. 149). In the second monograph he goes on to show that one component, the abstraction factor, follows the same principle, namely maximal representation in the frontal lobes.[11] However, impairment of the abstraction factor is also a function of size of frontal lesion. There is no evidence for the mass action principle in other brain loci, nor is there evidence for the frontal localization of any other factorial component of intelligence.

While the evidence for the abstraction factor is based on test score analysis rather than analysis of factor scores, it is factorially convincing. It is convincing because it is based on the three tests with the highest loadings on this factor — the Halstead Category test (loading of .63), the Tactual Form Board-Recall (loading of .66), and the Carl Hollow Square (loading of .45). Unfortunately, the evidence presented for the other two factors, C (central integrative field factor) and P (power factor), is not as

convincing. The neural evidence for whatever is common to tests II (critical flicker-fusion), VII (rhythm test), and VIII (speech perception test) is convincing, but we have no evidence concerning the factorial composition of measures VII and VIII. We have only Halstead's assertion[12] that his 1958 conception of psychological vigilance, which is presumably identifiable by tests II, VII, and VIII, is essentially identical to his 1947 power factor. The only test common to the two hypotheses is variable II, CFF. Given these very severe limitations, we can say that Halstead and Shure present neurological evidence to the effect that impaired performance on the three tests which presume to measure psychological vigilance is a function of size of lesion, regardless of locus. The neural evidence relating to factor C is based on only two tests (the Henmon-Nelson and the Category Test), both of which are factorially complex. The authors suggest that the verbal-logical (or verbal learning) portion of this factor is more dependent on the cerebral functioning of the left hemisphere than the right hemisphere

Halstead's findings are of interest to us on many counts,[13] the three primary ones being: (1) that no other battery of neuropsychological indicators has been as reliable and valid in identifying cases of human brain damage, (2) that at least two factors,[14] A (abstraction) and C (central integrative field factor or memory), are represented in the battery, and (3) that there is evidence of

---

[11]This finding, combined with the Greystone Project report of W. R. King (874), provides evidence which should eventually define the limits of Goldstein's (602) and Goldstein and Sheerer's (603) claims regarding the frontal localization of abstract (as opposed to concrete) behavior. King's factor analysis of seven measures of abstract behavior indicates that Goldstein's postulation of a single general factor of abstraction will not hold up. While King's analysis is not clear on the interpretation of the factors themselves, it is clear that more than one factor is necessary to account for the observed covariation. He suggests that Goldstein's logical analysis of abstraction in terms of the three components of grouping, isolation, and shift makes more sense. When analyzed in this manner the Greystone data provide suggestive evidence which would correlate the shift factor with Brodmann's area 46 and the grouping factor with area 9. There is also minimal evidence that all components of abstract thinking follow the frontal gradient hypothesis. These conclusions are extremely tentative owing to severe methodological limitations of the factor analysis (e.g., no rotations; final conclusions regarding three components by inspection only; interpretations forced to fit Goldstein a priori), but they do suggest that Halstead's approach in this domain is on the right track. Halstead's abstraction factor is much more limited in conception than is Goldstein's. Furthermore, the evidence for its neural correlate is more specifically tied to psychometric performance.

[12]Halstead's P factor, in its operational meaning, is about identical with psychological vigilance as here defined.

[13]In addition to the findings on ablation which have been summarized in some detail in this section, Halstead's impairment index has also been correlated with such biological variations as hypo- and hyperthyroidism, adrenalectomy, hypophysectomy, vascular hypertension, and drug injections (681, 682, 683, 1320). Since none of these studies was sufficiently focused on the four biological factors per se, these findings have not been presented in detail.

[14]It is also possible that factor P, psychological vigilance or power, is adequately represented in the battery of tests.

a neural correlate for at least one of Halstead's four factors of biological intelligence. In short, this is the first convincing demonstration of cortical correlates for factorially determined components of intelligence. It is essential, however, that future research reveal a clearer psychometric interpretation of factors in combination with an analysis of impairment explicitly in terms of factor scores.

De Mille's (415) recent study is an important contribution along these lines. He administered a 16-variable factor-analytic test battery (including several Wechsler-Bellevue measures) to 150 prefrontal lobotomized schizophrenics and 150 non-lobotomized schizophrenics. Separate analyses for each sample revealed the same 8 factors: numerical facility, verbal comprehension, general reasoning, symbolic patterns, sensitivity to problems, ideational fluency, experiential evaluation, and semantic spontaneous flexibility. Comparisons of mean test scores showed that the lobotomized subjects had significantly lower scores on 9 of the 13 factor-analytic variables, as well as the various Wechsler IQs and the three Wechsler subtests. A further comparison of 50 lobotomized and 50 non-lobotomized groups, matched on the Wechsler at average IQ, also revealed significant differences on four of the factor-analytic tests.

Whereas Halstead's study suffers somewhat from insufficient factorial treatment but has strength in its neuropsychological treatment, de Mille's study suffers from neuropsychological shortcomings. For one thing, one might raise serious questions concerning the appropriateness of the non-Wechsler variables in the clinical brain-damage situation, particularly when dealing with schizophrenics. Second, prefrontal *lobotomy* cases are relatively inadequate test cases next to Halstead's prefrontal *lobectomy* cases, particularly in light of the findings of Halstead and others to the effect that prefrontal lobotomies do not result in intellectual loss, whereas prefrontal lobec-

tomies do lead to intellectual decrement. The point of these findings is that in the former case the frontal cortex remains intact, with the surgery involved merely cutting the cortico-thalamic connections, thereby removing the inhibitory effect of the frontal cortex on the thalamus and simultaneously reducing amount of manifest anxiety. The latter case, on the other hand, which leaves the cortico-thalamic projections intact, involves the elimination of frontal cortical tissue. Halstead's evidence indicates that such tissue is of optimal importance in intellectual functioning and concomitantly there is no evidence of anxiety reduction after prefrontal lobectomy. These findings, combined with the evidence from Great Britain (488, 1156) to the effect that prefrontal lobotomies lead to a reduction in anxiety, neuroticism, and introversion[15] (plus a concomitant increase in extroversion, since the introversion-extroversion factor is bi-polar) are beginning to piece together a meaningful pattern of brain function-behavior factor relationships.[16]

---

[15]Because of space limitations, personality factors can only be treated incidentally in this chapter. For more complete coverage of such factors see Chapters 19 and 24.

[16]The Bechtoldt-Benton-Fogel (83, 544) studies, although of considerable interest on methodological grounds, have not been considered in detail for several reasons, a major one being that the relevance and possible invariance of their factors is not sufficiently clear at this time. Their research involves 18 relatively simple visual-motor tasks which are associated with the Gerstmann (584, 585, 586, 587) syndrome and the parietal symptom-complex (544). The Gerstmann syndrome involves a set of agnosias and apraxias which were hypothesized as related to disease of the parietal lobes. Fogel's analyses provide factorial confirmation (i.e., a unitary factor) of this syndrome at the behavioral level. Subsequent analysis (83) indicates that five factors are necessary to account for the covariation in the 18 variable matrix, although the possible nature of such factors is not specified. There is also an implication that these factors reflect parietal-occipital functioning (since the 100 *S*s were all parietal and occipital brain-damaged cases), but the explicit relationships between factors and brain function have been deferred for future research. The Jones-Wepman (826) study of 168 aphasics (brain-damaged) will also be

In addition to the growing evidence concerning the relationships between cognitive factors and cortical or biochemical processes, there is similar empirical evidence concerning the relationships between learning and intelligence factors and heredity. The evidence on the human level comes from four studies: Thurstone, Thurstone, and Strandskov (1429), Cattell, Stice, and Kristy (330), Blewett (113), and Vandenberg (1481), involving monozygotic and dizygotic twins and the Primary Mental Abilities. The findings reported by the first study mentioned are typical, and are briefly summarized below.

From these data it is obvious that the first four factors, space, verbal comprehension, fluency, and memory, manifest a strong hereditary determination. The implication is that the performance of single-egg twins is more alike on these four factors than is the case for two-egg or fraternal twins, hence the importance of the genotype. Similar reports are made by Blewett and Vandenberg, but unfortunately the findings are discouragingly contradictory. Whereas the Thurstones report relative unimportance of genotypic determination for the reasoning factor, for example, Blewett reports a high heritability value for this factor. And whereas Vandenberg reports high heritability for the number factor, Blewett reports this factor as one of his lowest heritabilities, and Thurstone reports a chi-square value of 2.12 which is significant at the .10 level. The only factor on which there is agreement by all three

---

mentioned briefly. This investigation yielded five factors from an original matrix of 37 language tests. Four of the factors involve language inputs and outputs (i.e., factor *A* is interpreted as visual to oral transmission, factor *B* is interpreted as aural to oral transmission, factor *C* as visual to graphic transmission, and factor *D* as aural to graphic transmission); the fifth one is defined as the ability to comprehend language symbols regardless of sensory modality. The authors did not attempt to relate factor scores to brain dysfunction. The major conclusion is that aphasia is not a unitary phenomenon, and that, in fact, language impairment due to brain damage manifests itself in at least five different ways.

TABLE 21-6

THE INHERITANCE OF PRIMARY FACTORS OF MENTAL ABILITY
(Thurstone, Thurstone & Strandskov, 1429)

P.M.A. Factor	Chi Square	P
Space	14.38	.01
Verbal	12.93	.01
Fluency	5.25	.01
Memory	4.09	.05
Number	2.12	.10
Reasoning	0.40	.30

investigators is verbal comprehension! Some of these difficulties may arise from the intrinsic inferiority of the twin study method to the Multiple Abstract Variance Analysis Method (231, 248). For, as Loehlin (940) points out, the MAVA method deals with less artificial variances (including as it does data on sibs reared apart, unrelated children reared together, etc.) and is an altogether more potent design.

The MAVA method, incidentally (330), shows a higher inheritance for the fluid general ability factor, measured by Culture Fair intelligence tests, than for crystallized general ability measured by the traditional intelligence tests. If the extent to which the primary abilities divide their loading between the fluid and crystallized general ability factors is — as might be argued — an indication of the environmental implementation of the hereditary endowment, then the results of Cattell and Horn agree with Thurstone on the one hand and Blewett on the other, in showing high inheritance for spatial ability. Otherwise, it cannot be said at present that the alignment of physiological and genetic evidence regarding abilities is as clear as could be hoped.

5. THE DIMENSIONS OF ANIMAL BEHAVIOR AND LEARNING

The aforementioned difficulties in factorial-genetic relations in humans at least point to the methodological attractiveness of animal research. While there is no reason to call a halt to future efforts of this type,[17] the writer believes this question is more likely to receive a convincing answer from animal research. Significant advances have been made during the past decade in non-factorial behavior genetics (568), particularly with the availability of highly inbred strains of mice[18] and other species.

However, sooner or later, it becomes imperative in animal as in human study to find out something about the structure of the behaviors to be related and, as indicated in the introduction, this is not an easy task in animal behavior. Let us in this section consider what dimensions have been located in animal behavior, beginning with the abilities. Wherry (1535), although not rotating to a convincing simple structure, made a beginning here with his factorial analysis of Tryon's bright and dull strains of rats. He found roughly the same three factors — forward going, food pointing, and goal gradient. But he also found that dull animals make greater use of the food-pointing (or visual) factor and less use of the forward-going factor, whereas the bright animals clearly outclass the dull ones in the extent to which the goal gradient (or insight) factor is involved in maze learning. These striking results are brought out clearly in Diagrams 21-1 and 21-2.

Except for rotational principles involved,

these findings are convincing, for they involve over 500 animals in each strain, and the data were based on Tryon's 20-year selective breeding program.[19] Furthermore, one can see a likelihood of a tie-up with Krechevsky's (885) non-factorial findings to the effect that bright rats make greater use of spatial (comparable to goal gradient or insight factor) "hypotheses," while the dull rats are more likely to involve visual (comparable to forward-going or visual factor) "hypotheses." Krechevsky's (885) early studies also indicated that the spatial ability is localized in the parietal cortex and the visual ability is localized in the occipital cortex. Krech's (884) more recent studies of brains, strains (genetic, that is), and adaptive behavior provide additional evidence for the importance of biochemical processes. In particular, Krech and his associates find that there are significant differences in acetylcholine concentration between fast- and slow- (genetically determined) learning rats. This kind of evidence, combined with the well-documented findings on phenylpyruvic oligophrenia, constitute a giant step forward in providing the necessary biochemical links which intervene between underlying genotypes and factorially determined behavioral phenotype (Royce, 1235). King's (872, 873) research, in fact, constitutes a link between two decades of animal research (e.g., 787, 789, 790, 992, 993, 1601) on the effect of amino acids (e.g., glutamic acid) on learning,

---

[17]For example, Cattell's (248) recent formulation, Multiple Abstract Variance Analysis, may well provide the kind of statistical analysis which is appropriate in research situations where experimental manipulation of the relevant variables is not possible. Cattell's method involves a breakdown of the total variance into a variety of combinations of genetic and environmental variance, such as the variation due to monozygotic twins reared together, monozygotic twins reared apart, dizygotic twins reared together, apart, siblings reared together, apart, unrelated children reared together, apart, etc. Total variance requires solving for 12 unknowns which can be ascertained by way of 16 experimentally observable subvariances. Cattell (235, 240) has reported nature-nurture ratios, derived from the equations described above, for 11 personality factors. These are discussed on pp. 717-718 in Chapter 23.

[18]The writer (1237a) is presently engaged in a factorial-genetic investigation of mouse emotionality.

---

[19]Searle's (1281) simulated Q technique study also involved Tryon's bright and dull rats. He suggests that the differential maze performances of Tryon's rats are due to motivational and emotional factors rather than learning or intelligence per se. He finds the bright strain high in food drive and timidity in open field situations, and low in activity, escape from a water tank, and timidity regarding mechanical apparatus. Dull rats exhibit an opposite pattern. While the question of the relevance of Q technique vs. R technique in factorial-genetic research strategy is one which can be settled only as we gain more experience with both approaches, this particular report should be viewed with great caution since it was a purely exploratory effort based on 35 cases, with only 10 from each of the bright and dull strains.

DIAGRAM 21-1. Factors Obtained from Tryon's Maze Data: Bright (from Royce, 1233, p. 244)

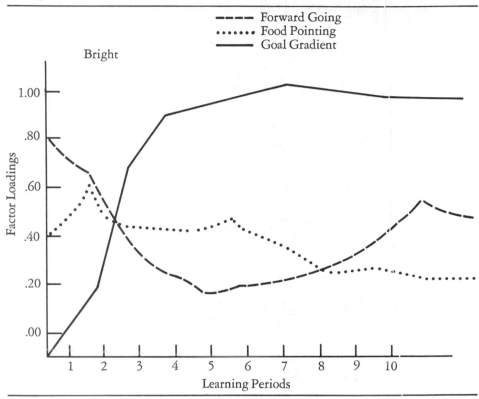

the concomitant research on biochemical feeding and mental deficiency (1214), and factorially determined components of biochemical and intellectual variability.

The evidence from these several sources is, of course, inconsistent and confusing, the major riddle being that biochemical feeding sometimes enhances adaptive behavior and sometimes it does not. Hughes and Zubek (788), for example, showed that glutamic acid feeding facilitated the maze performance of dull rats, but had no effect on brights. Similar studies (14, 1215) on the effect of glutamic acid on mentally deficient children sometimes facilitated performance on intelligence tests and sometimes had no effect. The Royce-King hypothesis, to the effect that each of several abilities (i.e., the factorially determined components of intelligence) is associated

with a different pattern of genetically determined amino acid metabolism, could well clear up the present confusion. The implication is that the effectiveness of biochemical therapy for the mentally retarded will be improved when we provide the proper matching of mental ability and biochemical variability profiles.

Unfortunately, the hypothesis in question has received only one empirical test to date (873). This study involves the correlating of seven factorially determined (the ETS factor reference battery) components of intelligence and six factorially determined amino acid complexes. While most of the individual correlations between the factorially determined variates are low, there are half a dozen in the .30 range and one at .42. Most of these statistically significant correlations involve Factor II, which is identified by the following amino acids: taurine, gamma-amino-butyric acid, glutamic acid, aspartic acid, glycine, and cysteric acid. Since brain metabolism, liver metabolism, and kidney function may all be involved in increased excretion of these

ance on the seven intellectual components (i.e., word fluency, memory, number, etc.). Similarly, the −.33 correlation between intellectual Factor I and biochemical Factor VI indicates that high excretion rates for threonine, methionine, sulfine, proline,

DIAGRAM 21-2. Factors Obtained from Tryon's Maze Data: Dull (from Royce, 1233, p. 145)

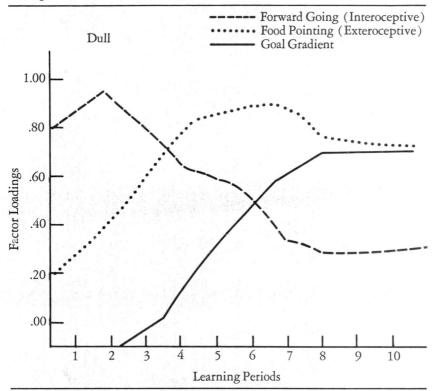

amino acids, it is impossible to offer an acceptable interpretation of this factor at this time.[20] However, since all the correlations with Factor II are negative, it is reasonable to conclude that high excretion rates for the several amino acids which define Factor II convary with low perform-

alanine, and valine covary with low performance on the tasks requiring speed of closure.

King, et al. point out that several of the relationships were curvilinear, and that linear transformations would reveal higher correlations. King's study, by itself, is inconclusive on the issue of matching intellectual-biochemical profiles, but it is clear that the Royce-King hypothesis deserves further experimental testing, for King's data revealed a canonical correlation coefficient of .60, thereby pointing to some kind of behavioral-biochemical linkage.

[20]There is a possibility that increased excretion of glutamic acid may be related to the glutamic acid "shunt." Three of the amino acids involved—gamma-amino-butyric acid, glutamic acid, and aspartic acid—have been implicated as possible non-acetylcholine transmitter substances in vertebrate and non-vertebrate nervous systems.

TABLE 21-7

APPARENTLY INVARIANT FACTORS OF ANIMAL LEARNING

Investigator and Year	Number of Ss and Species	Number and Nature of Variables and Factors	Type of Analysis	Apparently Invariant Factors (Rotated)				
				Factor L Docility or Adaptability	Factor M Visual Input	Factor N Speed	Factor O Insight	Other Factors
Anastasi, et al. (23)	73 dogs	17 behavioral measures; 5 factors, 2 cognitive	Centroid; orthogonal rotation	Docility (responsiveness to handler)	Visual observation			2 emotionality, 1 under-determined
Kawai (857)	18, 25, and 31 white rats	5 to 10 learning periods, 3 different tasks usually 3 factors	Centroid; oblique rotation	Emotional adaptability (early trials)	Reaction potential – food incentive (middle trials)		Cognitive (late trials)	Relevant reaction potential
Kawai (858)	18 albino rats	9 learning periods (10 unit T maze); 3 factors	Centroid; oblique rotation	Forward going or strangeness	Food pointing or irrelevant response tendency		Goal gradient or Hull's habit strength	
Rethlingshafer (1191)	25 rats per group, 8 groups	Light-dark discrimination task, 8 different conditions of motivation; 3 factors	Centroid; oblique rotation	Pre-solution period (early trials)			Recognition of relevant problems (late trials)	Variability of hypotheses (middle trials)
Sen (1300, 1301)	84 rats	15 temperament-learning measures; 3 bi-polar factors	Centroid; rotation				Insightful learning	
Van Steenberg (1487)	64 rats	32 behavioral measures; (Thorndike); 10 factors, 7 interpretable	Centroid; oblique rotation	Adaptability to test situation	Visual cues	Speed or motility	Visual insight – – – – cognition	Kinesthetic or alternating hypothesis
Vaughn (1488)	80 male rats	34 behavioral measures; 8 factors, 4 interpretable	Centroid; orthogonal rotation	Docility or wildness-timidity		Speed	Insight learning	Transfer
Wherry (1532)	Varying numbers of rats 30 to 150	9 or 10 learning periods; from 6 different tasks; 3 dynamic factors	Centroid; oblique rotation	Forward going (trial and error; early trials	Food pointing (middle trials)		Goal gradient (weight; late trials)	
Wherry (1534)	40-45 rats per group	14 choice point maze; 5 factors (Spearman rho)	Centroid; rotation	Forward going (trial and error; early trials)	Vision			Audition olfaction anticipation
Wherry (1535)	550 bright rats, 550 dull rats	17 alley maze; 3 factors	Centroid; oblique rotation	Forward going (trial and error; early trials)	Food pointing (middle trials)		Goal gradient (weight; late trials)	

Turning to look beyond these studies with emphasis largely on abilities, one would like to see an array of coordinated studies in animal behavior which move out into variables more like those which Cattell and his co-workers, Hundleby (796), Saunders (1257), Pawlik (see Chapter 18), and others have used in studying human temperament and personality. In fact, ideally the animal studies should contain, wherever possible, definite analogues of some of the 400 miniature situations (337) which have been found to recognize no fewer than 20 or so factor dimensions in human beings.

Unfortunately, with very few exceptions, such as in the work of Wherry (1532), Hall (676), Wenger (1514), and one or two studies by the present writer, a theoretical background of this comprehensive nature has not prevailed against the practical difficulties of conceiving diverse situations, and practically measuring them, in animals. Thus there is a gross preponderance of the studies concentrated on learning variables — since these exist already in the repertoire of animal psychologists — with neglect of more comprehensive and varied behavior. Even learning variables — handled by multivariate methods — are far from common Indeed, only four studies (1300, 23, 857, 858) have appeared in this domain since the writer reviewed the literature on the subject in 1950 (1233, see especially pp. 238-245). This is another witness to the difficulties of conducting significant factorial research in comparative-physiological psychology. The problems of size of sample, underdetermination, and experimental dependence mentioned in the introduction have served as severe deterrents. For historical and general perspective the reader is referred to the above-mentioned review. Our present concern is focused on Table 21-7, which summarizes those investigations which are most likely to identify invariant factors of animal learning.

Inspection of this table reveals that 9 of the 10 studies cited involve the rat and that none of them involves physiological measurements. In short, there are few implications here for a true comparative-physiological psychology. There are, however, four candidates for invariance which deserve brief consideration Factor L, for example, is identified by every investigator. The key to the interpretation of this factor, labeled docility or adaptability, lies in the idea of tractability or openness to alternative approaches in new situations. While the factor is primarily cognitive, as is evidenced by the major common variable of performance in mazes (common to Kawai, Van Steenberg, and all three of Wherry's studies), there is also a strong emotional or temperamental aspect to this factor. The trial-and-error nature of this factor particularly fits the cognitive aspect of Factor L as docility or adaptability. The non-cognitive aspect is less clear, but it is hinted at in such measurements as leash control and obedience in the Anastasi, et al., dog study and in Vaughn's straightaway and wildness tunnel indices. Perhaps the temperament aspect here indicated can best be described as submissiveness. There are obvious possible relationships between this factor and the emotionality factors, to be discussed in the next section, particularly the responsiveness to handling (Factor T) and aggressiveness (Factor V) factors, and possibly Factor P (autonomic balance).

Factor M, visual input, is identified by all but three investigators. It is identified by a variety of learning tasks (especially the elevated maze) where visual input is of particular importance in arriving at a solution. In terms of dynamics, this factor is dominant in the middle trials of maze learning, and is identified by Wherry as a food-pointing factor. This description literally implies a set or orientation toward the goal box, meaning that the rat will tend to enter those alleys which point toward the food and to avoid those choices which would move him away from the food. This description highlights the stimulus-bound character of the visual input factor, and is consistent with Wherry's finding that this factor is particularly characteristic of Tryon's dull rats (1534).

Factor N speed, is identified by Vaughn and Van Steenberg. It reflects time measurements in the performance of the rat on a variety of learning tasks, particularly mazes and problem boxes. Vaughn's straightaway measurement also identifies this factor. Speed factors have been identified in factorial studies of human aptitude and human learning, but the possibilities of identity with the animal speed factor have not been explored.

Factor O is the most convincing of the four apparently invariant factors of animal learning. The common variables are summarized in Table 21-8.

This factor is interpreted as insight or recognition of the relevant problem. It implies the emergence of the proper solution into the foreground after considerable trial and error. It is consistent with Gestalt thinking in that there is a figure-ground shift within a totally perceived configuration, but it does not imply an immediate insight. The slow resolution of the problem is highlighted by the consistent reports (see Kawai, Rethlingshafer, Sen, Wherry) on the importance of late trials (as opposed to early or middle trials) in the identification of this factor. The age variable (see Vaughn), an apparently irrelevant measurement, takes on significance in this context. But the crucial common variables for this factor are those indicated under maze behavior and problem solving in Table 21-

TABLE 21-8

SIMPLIFIED, COMPOSITE MATRIX FOR FACTOR O, INSIGHT
(Factor Loadings)

Common Variables	Kawai	Reth-lingshafer	Sen	Van Steenberg Visual Cognition Insight	Vaughn	Wherry (1532)	Wherry (1534)
Late Trials	from .40 to .70	from .60 to .80			Age .38	from .50 to .90	Bright = .90 Dull = .60
Maze Behavior							
Elevated (errors)				.74 .75			
Elevated (time)				.30			
Simple (Errors)						.38	
Simple (Trials)						.32 .51 .53 .31	
(Simple-water Errors, Time)			.52 .51				
Rectangular						.47 .66	
Problem Solving							
Latch Box				.43			
Multiple Platform				.31 .63	.34 .29		
Maier Reasoning							
Multiple Light' Disc			.50 .62		.47		

8. The probability that Factor O is correctly described as an insight factor is brought out most convincingly by the high loadings in such variables as Maier's reasoning problem and Jenkins' multiple platform apparatus.[21]

The studies by E. E. Anderson on rats are particularly noteworthy in that instead of using a miscellaneous collection of

This dynamic area of comparative psychology has especial strategic importance at the present juncture because these methods have turned up in human patterns of dynamic interest which strongly suggest the existence of similar innate patterns. (See Chapter 20 by Horn.) Indeed, this multivariate approach, using new objective devices to measure interest strength, as made

TABLE 21-9

INVESTIGATION OF UNITARY ERGIC PATTERNS IN THE RAT*
(Extracted from E. E. Anderson, 25)

Intercorrelations among behavior measures involving thirst or interest in drinking (51 rats)	2	3	4
1. Amount drunk (per gram body weight)	0.07	0.63	0.19
2. Readiness to face shock for drink	—	1.00	0.09
3. Drinking time	—	—	0.16
4. Readiness to jump to get water	—		

Intercorrelations among measured behavior involving sex interest (51 rats)	6	7
5. Frequency of copulation	0.57	0.44
6. Time prepared to wait at barrier to mate	—	0.15
7. Readiness to jump over obstruction to mate		

Intercorrelations among behavior measures which might be motivated by the erg of curiosity (51 rats)	9	10	11
8. Extent of exploration of Dashiell maze	0.65	0.51	0.40
9. Extent of wandering over open field	—	0.49	0.65
10. Extent of exploration among pegs on a wall	—	—	0.36
11. Extent of wandering when hungry			

Permission for reprinting this table granted by Kraus Reprint Corporation, New York.

variables they concentrate on dynamic measurements and aim at giving substance to theories of ergic ("instinctual") structure. The findings on adequate samples of white rats, by a correlation cluster search method, are shown in Table 21-9. They indicate clearly that ergic structures—in this case thirst, sex, and exploration—can be located by correlational methods as distinct entities.

by Baggaley, Cattell, Horn, Maxwell, Radcliffe, and Sweney in systematically interrelated studies (Chapters 10, 19, and 20), is the first real experimental evidence we have had (by contrast to the clinical intuitions of Freud, the semantic leanings of Murray and Edwards, or the general social observations of McDougall) as to the number and nature of drives in man. Consequently, it is of particular methodological interest at this point to see if the patterns obtained by the application of these methods, comparatively, to animals, yields ergic structures which correspond to those which ulterior evidence (ethology,

---

[21]Our present inability to determine the relative importance of two factors reported by Van Steenberg is indicated in the table with two sets of entries, one for a factor labeled visual insight, the other for a factor labeled cognition.

physiology) shows to exist. For we could then return to studies on humans with new light on the meaning of our factors.

Among the appreciable number of factor-analytic studies on animal behavior, as shown by Table 21-7, and the still larger number of studies of animal drive by traditional methods, one can at present find only two or three meeting anything like ordinary technical requirements. The Anderson pioneer studies above were initially correlation cluster studies, though later factored. Accordingly, a study was undertaken by Haverland and Cattell in 1954 (704) which measured white rats on a variety of "interest" behaviors, adding the "stimuli" (amount of water and food presented) to the correlation. The results (Table 21-10), while not extensive, sufficed to show that the extension of the Anderson type of study to true simple structure factoring could indeed be depended upon to locate drive structures. A definitive study on an adequate sample of variables, nevertheless, remains to be done on the dynamic aspects of animal behavior.

6. SOME METHODOLOGICAL QUESTIONS IN THE STUDIES ON AUTONOMIC AND EMOTIONALITY VARIABLES[22]

In a theoretically ideal treatment of comparative behavior one would separate the analysis of traits (R-technique) from the analysis of states and processes (P- $\times$ dR-techniques). Thus the last section would have been devoted to comparison of trait structures across various animal species, including man, and the present to a corresponding examination of state response patterns — anxiety, activation, depression, etc. We have already seen that the available experiments for the trait section above barely permit within any clear division into the three modalities of ability,

temperament, and dynamic traits, though the author has striven for such clarity. The design of actual experiments in the field permits still less sure division into traits and states.

The studies in this section were undertaken largely in pursuit of hunches that differences in autonomic functioning are significantly tied to general behavior. Sometimes these approaches were considered as studies of autonomic functioning pattern, sometimes as studies of emotionality, sometimes as general forays in "psychosomatics." Three problems will become very clear to the reader, however, as he surveys the collated evidence.

(1) The factor analyses are such as could yield either traits or states, in the senses defined in Chapters 11 and 12 above, and the inability to separate these leaves grave doubts about conclusions such as that which holds that an "autonomic balance" factor exists.

(2) It is probable that both the trait and the state factors, found here largely in autonomic variables, are actually parts of broader personality factors (as set out more systematically by Nesselroade and Delhees in Chapter 19), from which the more comprehensive behavioral variables in the latter are excluded by the "autonomic" preoccupations of the experimenters. The state aspects have been developed by the editor in the next chapter, by Mefferd, which deals with process and state physiology, but the links of the presumed trait factors with those in the Nesselroade and Delhees chapter are largely left to the reader.

(3) The multivariate methodology in these studies has tended, especially in its factor-analytic aspects, to be at a less developed level than in the general personality field, and certainly less uniform. For example, some years ago Cattell re-examined the factor analyses of Eysenck (211) and of Wenger (226) with different conclusions about the number of factors and demonstrably improved rotational resolution. In the latter case this led to the theory (226) of a single *general* autonomic factor,

---

[22]The following discussion was written by the editor as an introduction to the author's presentation and analysis of data commencing with Table 21-11.

TABLE 21-10

WHITE RATS MEASURED ON A VARIETY OF "INTEREST" BEHAVIORS
(E. M. Haverland, 704)

	Oblique Simple Structure		
	Factor 1 (Hunger)	Factor 2 (Thirst)	Factor 3 (Body Size)
Runway—food: median of latencies on 2nd to 10th trials	−.428	.411	−.232
Time for ten barrier crossings to food	−.443	.599	−.066
Average amount eaten (% body weight)	.631	.065	.218
Average food deprivation	.392	−.078	.887
Runway—water: median of latencies on 2nd to 10th trials	.439	−.114	−.220
Time for 10 barrier crossings to water	−.120	−.414	.344
Average amount drunk (% body weight)	−.049	.776	−.220
Average water deprivation	.056	.549	.115
Average weight loss (% original body weight)	.526	.163	.714

since adequately identified with *anxiety level,* and two more specialized autonomic factors, then named *sympathetic reaction* pattern and *parasympathetic reaction* pattern and since recognized to have broader associations as P.U.I. 5 and P.U.I. 1, or excitation level.

The reader may see for himself from the present writer's condensations of evidence in Table 21-11 that the variabilities and inadequacies of techniques, especially in the early studies, .e.g., orthogonal rotation, non-rotation, and oblique rotations, samples of only 24 and 25 students, etc., make it difficult to arrive at firm conclusions. The editor has left the author's interpretations standing just as he wishes to make them; but would strongly urge that researchers in planning further research reweight the studies (a) separating, for example, those on oblique maximum simple structure and adequate samples from orthogonal studies of non-significant hyperplane count, and (b) relating the trait factors to those surveyed in Chapter 19 in more general behavioral terms before concluding that these are specifically autonomic factors. As far as *states* are concerned, the evidence here has been considered and integrated with the general evidence on state patterns in Section 5 of the following chapter (Mefferd) on psychophysiological processes.

Both of the editorial writers (Dr. Cattell and Dr. Hammond) and the author of this chapter also question the possibility, with the lack of marker planning in past researches, as well as the above partly obsolete methodologies in researches before 1945, of cross-matching trait or state factors right across animal and human data. Any application of precise matching methods, such as the configurative method (263) or the s index (268), is impossible on such data. Furthermore many of the variables studied can only be questionably thought of as autonomic response variables. This poor foundation arises largely from a rather luxuriant speculative theoretical development here, beginning with James and Lange, and which attracted certain psychologists without broader behavioral interests by the concreteness of the physiological measures involved.

Our next table (21-11) summarizes some thirty studies in which physiological variables have been ample.

Since the three Wenger studies I, I', I'' involve a common set of variables, there are only 17 independent[23] studies, eight of

[23]There are a total of 19 studies reported but two of them, the Wenger studies labeled I' and I'', were reanalyses of data based on the same 62 children reported in Study I, but augmented by 12 Ss in Study I' and an additional 7 Ss in Study I''. Furthermore, Wenger's study labeled I' involves the deletion of certain measures included in Study I and the substitution of five additional physiological variables.

TABLE 21-11

APPARENTLY INVARIANT FACTORS OF EMOTIONALITY

Investigator and Year	No. of Ss and Species	Number and Nature of Variables and Factors	Type of Analysis
		A. Infrahuman Subjects	
Anastasi, *et al.* (23)	73 dogs	17 temperament-learning tasks; 5 factors, 3 of which are relevant to this domain	Centroid; orthogonal rotation
Billingslea (111)	40 adult female rats; 20 emotional, 20 non-emotional strain	11 behavioral variables; 3 factors	Centroid; oblique rotation
McClearn and Meredith (1004)	80 mice	25 behavioral variables; 5 factors	Principal axes; communality estimates omitted error and unique variance
Van Steenberg (1487)	64 rats	32 behavioral measures (Thorndike); 8 factors, 4 interpretable	Centroid; oblique rotation
Royce (1234)	53 dogs	32 variables, 16 physiological and 16 behavioral; 6 psychophsiological factors plus 2 partially interpreted factors.	Centroid; oblique rotation
Sen (1300, 1301)	84 rats	15 temperament-learning tasks; 3 bi-polar factors	Centroid
Willingham (1552)	114 mice	20 behavioral variables; 6 behavioral factors	Centroid; oblique rotation (Thurstone analytic)
		B. Human Subjects	
Cook (376)	88 males, Submarine Corps candidates, ages 17-26	362 variables covering biochemistry, psychology, psychiatry, physiology, anthropometry and physical fitness; 164 variables analyzed; 33 1st-order factors, 7 2nd-order factors, 3 biochemical, 3 behavioral, 1 body type	Group Centroid; oblique rotation
Darling (405)	58 children	11 variables, 6 behavioral, 5 physiological; 2 physiological factors, 2 psychological factors	Centroid; oblique rotation

TABLE 21-11 (Continued)

APPARENTLY INVARIANT FACTORS OF EMOTIONALITY

Apparently Invariant Factors (Rotated)							
Factor P autonomic balance	Factor Q motor discharge	Factor R activity level	Factor S thyroid	Factor T reactivity to avoidance conditioning	Factor U responsiveness to handling	Factor V aggressiveness	Other Factors
A. Infrahuman Subjects (continued)							
		Impulsive —active			Responsiveness to handling		Persistence or perseveration
Emotionality	Freezing timidity						
Defecation (emotionality)		Exploratory activity					Territory marking (urination), wall seeking, behavior related to barriers
				Reactivity to avoidance conditioning			
Timidity I (physiological discharge)	Timidity II (withdrawal plus motor discharge)	Activity level			Heart reactivity to social stimulation	Aggressiveness	Audiogenic reactivity
		Activity		Reactivity to to avoidance conditioning			
Elimination	Freezing				Reactivity to experimenter		Reactivity to light, grooming, emotional maturity
B. Human Subjects (continued)							
			Hormonal response				Physical stress-ketosteroid output factor psychol. stress-ketosteroid output, body type and 3 Rorschach factors
Sympathetic predominance; parasympathetic predominance	Motor activity						Attention

TABLE 21-11 (Continued)

APPARENTLY INVARIANT FACTORS OF EMOTIONALITY

Investigator and Year	No. of Ss and Species	Number and Nature of Variables and Factors	Type of Analysis
B. Human Subjects (continued)			
Duffy (434)	25 female college students	16 behavioral variables; 5 factors, only 1 of which interpretable	Centroid; rotation
Freeman and Katzoff (547)	24 male college students	30 variables, 10 physiological and 20 behavioral; 2 psychophysiological factors; 1 behavioral factor	Centroid; orthogonal rotation (Spearman rho)
Hsü (1952) (783)	100 male college students	24 variables; 2 sets of data, one for PGR response, the other for self ratings; 5 PGR factors, 4 behavioral factors	Centroid; oblique rotation (2 analyses; 1 for PGR data and 1 for self report data)
Overall and Williams (1132)	145 adults; patients suspected of thyroid disease	11 physiological variables; 1 physiol. factor 2 uninterpreted physiol. factors	Principal components; oblique rotation
Theron (1388)	50 college students; 10 female, 40 male, ages 17 to 25	12 variables, 8 psychophysiological, 2 physical, 2 behavioral, 2 psychophysiological factors	Centroid; orthogonal rotation to a priori hypothesis and simple structure (blood volume via finger plethysmograph under 4 conditions)
Wenger I (1516, 1517)	62 children; ages 6-11	20 physiological variables; 2 physiological factors	Centroid; orthogonal rotation, a priori
Wenger I' (1518, 1521)	74 children; ages 6-12	20 physiological variables (same as in I); 3 physiological factors	Centroid; orthogonal rotation, a priori
Wenger I" (1520)	81 children; ages 6-13	16 physiological variables plus 1 rating of muscular relaxation; 2 physiological factors	Centroid; orthogonal rotation, a priori
Wenger II (1523)	488 male aviation cadets, USAF	15 physiological variables; 5 physiological factors, 3 of which interpretable	Centroid; orthogonal rotation; mixture of a priori and simple structure
Wenger III (1523)	201 operational fatigue cases, USAF	12 physiological variables; 6 physiological factors, 3 of which interpretable	Centroid; orthogonal rotation, mixture of a priori and simple structure
Cattell (240, 273) Haverland (704) Karvonen (852) Williams (1548)*	5 P-technique cases (Adults)	30 physiological variables; 9 state factors of physiological-emotional nature	Centroid, blind simple structure rotation to maximum (oblique) simplicity

*The four factors in common to the studies of Cattell, Haverland, Karvonen, Williams, and others are not reproduced

TABLE 21-11 (Continued)

APPARENTLY INVARIANT FACTORS OF EMOTIONALITY

Apparently Invariant Factors (Rotated)							
Factor P autonomic balance	Factor Q motor discharge	Factor R activity level	Factor S thyroid	Factor T reactivity to avoidance conditioning	Factor U responsiveness to handling	Factor V aggressiveness	Other Factors
B. Human Subjects (continued)							
	General muscular tension level						Four specific muscle tension factors
Energy arousal	Discharge control						Self-rated emotionality
						Aggressiveness (social injustice)	Shifting responsibility passive-persecuted submissiveness
			Thyroid				2 uninterpreted physiological factors
Basic emotional tension (chronic *autonomic factor*) emotional stability-lability (phasic autonomic factor)							
Autonomic balance	Muscle tension						
Autonomic balance	Muscle tension		Thyroid				
Autonomic balance							
Autonomic balance			Thyroid				Blood sugar
Autonomic balance	Muscle tension		Thyroid				

Factors of arousal, elation-depression, general fatigue, stress, autonomic-sympathetic, general autonomic (anxiety), etc., as set out in Chapter 11.

here, but are given in several tables in the next chapter.

TABLE 21-12

SIMPLIFIED COMPOSITE MATRIX FOR FACTOR P, AUTONOMIC BALANCE

	Human Subjects							Infrahuman Subjects			
Investigator	Darling		Freeman and Katzoff	Theron		Wenger* I,I',I''	Wenger II	Wenger III	Billingslea	McClearn and Meredith	Royce	Willingham
Subjects	58 children		20 males	50 students		81 children	488 males	201 males	40 rats	80 mice	53 dogs	114 mice
Common variables	Sympathetic	Parasympathetic		Basic emotional tension	Emotional stability-lability							
Conductance Reactivity 5 different measures	.70	.70	from .58 to .90									
Palmar conductance						from .30 to .48		.41				
Log conductance change						.31						
Blood pressure (usually systolic)	.54	−.72					.30	.37			.56	
Pulse volume or pressure				from .41 to .85	from −.32 to −.47	.32 .35						
Sinus arrhythmia						.46 .62					.41	
Heart rate						from .42 to .91	.60	.36				
Oxygen consumption						.36		.35				
Sublingual temperature							.47	.45				
Emotional defecation and urination									.62	from .35 to .51		from .49 to .71
Non-aggressive or withdrawal									.39		.36	
Behavioral reactivity									.45		.35	

*The factor loadings listed in this column could have come from any one of the three analyses based on children. It should be noted that this is essentially one study with three different analyses based on augmented subjects and variables.

them using human adult *S*s, and two employing children, aged 6 to 13. The remaining five studies involved mice (2 studies), dogs (2 studies), and rats. It seems clear that the first two factors, labeled autonomic balance (Factor *P*) and motor discharge (Factor *Q*), have been independently identified most frequently. It may be further observed that their apparent (i.e., by inspection only) invariance not only transcends investigators, but also species. If it can eventually be shown more convincingly[24] that this is the case, species invariance in combination with investigator invariance would provide a strong basis for welding factor analysis and comparative-physiological psychology.

We have provided an abbreviated summary of the variables supporting factors *P, Q, R,* and *S* in Tables 21-12 through 21-16 below.

From the composite matrix designated as Table 21-12 factor *P,* whatever its ultimate interpretation, is identifiable by at least the following variables: conductance, blood pressure, sinus arrhythmia, pulse pressure and volume, heart rate, oxygen consumption, sublingual temperature, behavioral reactivity, non-agressive or withdrawal behavior, and emotional defecation and urination. The behavioral components, combined with the well-established evidence for the autonomic control of the above-mentioned physiological variables, strongly suggest that this is some kind of emotional discharge factor. The reports from Billingslea, Willingham, and McClearn and Meredith that the Hall open field (and other emotion-provoking situations) defecation and urination indices load heavily on this factor comes as no surprise. Hall conducted an extensive series of studies (669, 670, 671, 672, 673, 674, 675, 676,

677) in which he demonstrated that defecation and urination in an open field situation are valid measures of individual differences in emotion. The suggestion of timidity or wariness was brought out originally by Hall and is clearly confirmed in the table entries under Billingslea and Royce in the row labeled non-aggressive or/and withdrawal behavior.

Royce's factor *A,* in fact, was labeled Timidity I, and was described as a psychophysiological factor characterized psychologically by freezing and internally by liberation of aroused energy via physiological mechanisms. The prepotence of physiological mechanisms in the identification of this factor is clearly brought out in Table 21-12. Of the several factorial studies of physiological variables relevant to emotionality there is little doubt that Wenger's long-range studies (1514, 1516, 1517, 1518, 1519, 1520, 1521, 1522, 1523) have been the most extensive and the most convincing. Wenger sees Factor *P* as autonomic balance. Cattell, Scheier, Williams, and others, on the other hand, called it initially a "general autonomic activity" factor, not committing themselves to the "balance" notion but stressing its relation as a *general* autonomic (not reticular system) activity level, to be contrasted with two group factors, P.U.I. 5, Sympathetic activity and P.U.I. 1, Parasympathetic activity vs. Excitement. Later they obtained evidence (325) that this *general* autonomic activity corresponded very well with the by then more broadly defined general anxiety factor.

If we confine ourselves for the moment to the common physiological variables listed in Table 21-12, it is easy to conceive this as the well-known autonomic syndrome of sympathetic control of the several conductance measures reported, its probable involvement in stress situations in increasing over-all metabolic activity (i.e., oxygen consumption), including a probable rise in temperature (i e , sublingual tem-

---

[24]Presumably by some quantitative index such as those suggested by Ahmavaara (9, 10), Burt (167), Cattell (248, 257), Wrigley and Neuhaus (1591), Tucker (1460), Kaiser (835, 836), and Werdelin (1527, 1528, 1529).

TABLE 21-13*

SIMPLIFIED COMPOSITE MATRIX FOR FACTOR Q, MOTOR DISCHARGE

	Human Subjects				Infrahuman Subjects			
Investigator	Darling	Duffy	Freeman and Katzoff	Wenger I or I'	Billingslea		Royce	Willingham
Subjects	58 children	20 females	20 males	81 children	40 rats		53 dogs	114 mice
Common Variables					Freezing	Timidity		
Conductance level and recovery	.29		from .55 to .89	−.42 .74			.38	
Heart rate				.51 .62			.33 .56	
Motor activity	.58	from .31 to .91	from .65 to .73	.54		−.36	from .47 to .64	from .54 to .77
Boldness-Timidity	.30						.35	
Non-aggressive withdrawal					.50	.62	.30 .46	
Rating of well adjusted			.57		.54			

*Entries in these tables are sometimes reflected in order to make comparisons between different studies comparable (e.g., heart rate and heart period, referred to as heart rate in Tables 21-12 and 21-13).

perature), the accelerative effect of the S.N.S. on heart rate, the probability of sinus arrhythmia when heart output is activated by both the S.N.S. and the parasympathetic, and the evidence concerning the synergistic antagonistic effects of both systems on vasomotor response and blood pressure, not to mention the many more well-known autonomic effects, which have high factor loadings in several of the studies summarized in Table 21-12 but which have not yet been factorially replicated, and, have, therefore, not been included in the table. In short, there is little doubt that some kind of autonomic functioning underlies factor P but the question remains whether this is a *general* autonomic reactivity, distinct from a separately locatable P.U.I. 5 sympathetic pattern as Cattell and his associates maintain, or the sympathetic response pattern, as Wenger and others are inclined to view it.

Indeed, on the sympathetic theory, there is doubt concerning some of the details of Table 21-12. This is why we have included double entries for Darling and Theron.[25] For example, there is doubt whether Theron's factor labeled basic emotional tension or his second factor, emotional stability-lability, is the appropriate one to contribute to the identification of Factor P. Theron himself thinks his emotional tension factor is comparable to Wenger's autonomic factor, but the information summarized in Table 21-12 suggests that the argument in favor of the other factor is equally valid.

Darling reports two factors: sympathetic and parasympathetic. While it is obvious that such factors adequately reflect the anatomical-physiological situation, Wen-

ger's argument is that the final outcome should be viewed in terms of total autonomic output rather than in terms of sympathetic as opposed to parasympathetic output independently. The conception of a factor as a functional unity would fit either hypothesis, but Wenger's analysis of autonomic balance as one of several homeostatic mechanisms reflects functional significance more adequately than the alternative offered by Darling.

The most obvious characteristic of factor Q in contrast to factor P is the relative absence in Table 21-13 of physiological variables which are common to the several studies. In fact, there are only two common physiological variables, conductance and heart rate, both reflecting sympathetic control. The remaining variables are all behavioral, the bulk of them reflecting motor activity in a wide variety of situations. These include the general reactivity indices of Darling and Royce, the "reclining" movements reported by Freeman and Katzoff, the suggestion of hypoactivity in Billingslea's timidity factor, and the suggestion of non-agressiveness in the case of two Billingslea indices as well as two from Royce, and finally, the freezing pattern suggested by Willingham. Freeman suggests that this adds up to a discharge control factor. That is, he says the organism high on this factor effects a rapid recovery after sympathetic arousal (as evidenced by the high conductance loading) primarily via the motor discharge of such energy. Royce's factor H, Timidity II, is essentially in agreement with this, even to the point of including skin resistance as part of the factor syndrome. His factor is seen as a predominantly behavioral factor of timidity characterized by withdrawal and by hyperactivity. He further distinguishes this factor from the autonomic factor by the external or motor liberation of energy as opposed to the physiological energy release of factor P.

The most difficult issue concerning the interpretation of Factor Q revolves around

---

[25]An earlier report of Van der Mewre and Theron (1485) was not included in Tables 21-12 or 21-13 because of almost complete overlap with Theron's 1948 paper. The 1947 report is a preliminary version which involves few subjects ($N = 25$) and fewer variables (9 rather than 12). The findings in the two studies lead to essentially the same interpretations but are clearer in the second study.

the above-mentioned point of withdrawal or timidity as it might relate to muscle tension. The former point is brought out in the studies of Billingslea, Royce, and Willingham. The latter point is made by Wenger and Duffy. It is conceivable that the linkage between the motor discharge described in the previous paragraph and the muscle tension described by Duffy and Wenger is provided via the behavior pattern of freezing. The combination of energy available for motor discharge and the inhibitory effect which is reflected in withdrawal and freezing behavior could easily lead to a state of muscular tension. While the Duffy-Wenger hypothesis regarding Factor Q is, therefore, plausible, my interpretation is to regard it as a motor discharge factor, leaving it to subsequent evidence to determine whether the motor release is further complicated by the development of tension. Here is a case where a stringent test of invariance should eventually inform us as to whether we are dealing with two factors, one of motor release and the other covering tension, or whether we are dealing with just one factor but are confused at present as to its interpretation.[26]

Cattell's resolution of the present difficulties in interpreting factors P and Q is in terms of three factors (a general autonomic factor, plus a sympathetic and a parasympathetic factor) as given in Table 21-14, which is taken from his 1950 book, and to which some of the newer variables for the *general* autonomic factor, located by Scheier, Luborsky, Williams, Dubin, Richels, and others, have been added.

The remaining factors have not been replicated sufficiently, but they look very promising. Activity level, for example, has been identified in four investigations (Anastasi, et al., Royce, Sen, and McClearn and Meredith). There are overlapping indices, including activity in a maze situation, and the fact of decreased activity in situations

---

[26]Quantitative invariance analysis is also necessary to clarify the relevance of the two Darling factors and the two Theron factors to Factor P (see Table 21-12).

TABLE 21-14

THREE FACTORS COVERING THE ALLEGED "GENERAL" AUTONOMIC FACTOR
(From the Cattell & Luborsky 1950 P-Technique Study, 300)

	Approximate Loading
Factor 1 – P.U.I. 9.	
Anxiety ("General" Autonomic Response).	
Large P.G.R. deflection magnitude	0.70
High ratio of emotional to non-emotional words recalled	0.70
High pulse and blood pressure	0.60
Rating of "sociable"	0.50
High basal metabolic rate	0.50
Rating of "vigorous"	0.50
Large ratio of pupil to iris diameter	0.50
High skin resistance	0.40
High critical frequency of flicker fusion	0.40
Brief duration of after-images	0.40
Factor 2 – P.U.I. 5.	
Adrenergic Autonomic Response.	
Low skin resistance (high conductance)	0.70
High pulse pressure	0.60
High *pH* (alkalinity) of saliva	0.60
High irritable emotionality	0.60
Large performance upset by noise distraction	0.50
High glucose concentration in blood	0.50
High lymphocyte count	0.40
Long dark adaptation period of eye	0.40
High pulse rate	0.40
Moderately large P.G.R. deflections	0.40
Factor 3 – P.U.I. 1.	
Arousal-vs-Parasympathetic Predominance.	
High skin resistance	0.60
Rating "relaxed" (and large skin resistance rise in relaxation period)	0.60
Low cholinesterase in the blood	0.60
P.G.R. response magnitude	0.50
Briefer dark adaptation period of the eye	0.50
Frequency of urination (and volume of urine)	0.45
Small difference in upward and downward flicker fusion frequency	0.40
Slow pulse rate	0.40
Low blood sugar (glucose)	0.40

involving restraint (see Table 21-15). However, the overwhelming characteristic of
this factor is the overt activity which the
subject exhibits in a wide variety of situations. The writer regards the emergence of
this factor as a particularly happy circumstance in view of the relevance of the
concept of activity level to our understanding of normal and abnormal emotionality
states.

Factor S is most likely a thyroid factor.
It is hinted at in Wenger's studies with
significant loadings on volar conductance
and oxygen consumption, but the syndrome for this factor is brought out more

convincingly in the study of Overall and
Williams where we have included the four
additional high loadings in spite of the fact
that the variables are not shared by other
investigations. Had these studies been
given maximum simple structure by rotation to adequate obliquity, we could give
even more confidence to these variables.

It is obvious from Table 21-16 that
serum protein bound iodine and the two I-
131 uptakes revealed the highest factor
loadings. These variables, along with the
common variables of pulse rate (reported
by Cook, and Overall and Williams) and
basal metabolic rate (reported by Wenger,

TABLE 21-15

SIMPLIFIED COMPOSITE MATRIX FOR FACTOR R, ACTIVITY LEVEL
(Factor Loadings)

Investigator	Anastasi	McClearn and Meredith	Royce	Sen
Subjects Common Variables	73 dogs	80 mice	53 dogs	84 rats
Overt activity in wide variety of situations	.46 .47	from .59 to .84	from .44 to .61	.76
Activity in maze	.47	.63		
Activity level under restraint	.44 −.53		−.36	−.47

TABLE 21-16

SIMPLIFIED COMPOSITE MATRIX FOR FACTOR S, THYROID
(Factor Loadings)

Investigation	Cook	Overall and Williams	Wenger I'	Wenger II	Wenger III
Subjects Common Variables	80 males	115 persons	74 children	488 males	201 males
Basal metabolic rate (oxygen consumption)		.52	.44	.30	.35
Volar conductance			.56	.38	.34
Pulse rate	.30 .41	.48			
Protein bound iodine		.84			
Cholesterol		−.35			
6 Hour I−131 (Iodine Uptake)		.83			
24 Hour I−131 (Uptake)		.87			

and Overall and Williams), present a convincing picture of thyroid functioning. The implication is that the thyroid gland traps iodide and oxidizes it to iodine, which is later involved in the formation of thyroxine. Thyroxine is then made available via the blood in accordance with the over-all functioning of the endocrine system. The five variables mentioned above consistently reflect the changes in iodine biochemistry (i e., the two I-131 variables) and the accompanying utilization of oxygen (i.e, basal metabolic rate and possibly pulse rate). The combination of studies summarized in Table 21-11 suggests that Overall and Williams have identified the normal chemistry of the thyroid factor, while Wenger has identified its autonomic concomitants.

Overall and Williams (1132) report that their three high-loading variables were also the most effective bases for clinical diagnosis of thyroid cases. In fact, they report a canonical correlation between "thyroid factor" scores and "clinical thyroid" scores, as measured by eleven indices, at .91. The Overall-Williams study provides a very convincing demonstration of the theoretical and practical power of the factor-analytic model in dealing with a complex of physiological variables.

The remaining three factors, T, U, and V, are neither as interesting nor as convincing as the four discussed so far. Of the three, factor T, reactivity to avoidance conditioning, carries the greatest potential on the grounds of both interest and convincingness. This is the case primarily because of the volume of evidence from nonfactorial research on the importance of emotionality in avoidance conditioning (871). Whether the emotional component of Factor T does, in fact, point to the fear response, which lies at the base of the two-process theory of avoidance learning as expounded by Mowrer (1082) and Wynne and Solomon (1594), remains to be seen. The two studies which identify this factor suggest this is the case, for the central component of the variables which are

shared is hyper-reactivity and hyper-motility in the avoidance-conditioning situation. Both Sen and Van Steenberg report factor loadings around .70 on variables labeled number of responses (including both conditioned and unconditioned responses) to the conditioned stimulus. Each investigator also reports loadings of .40 to .45 in general activity as measured by standard indices such as activity. The writer (1237; Carran, Yeudall, & Royce, 191) has observed similar non-adaptive hyper-responsiveness on the part of inbred mouse strains, some of which did not reach the conditioning criterion after 700 trials. It seems clear that some kind of emotionality factor is operating under circumstances such as these.

Factors U and V, as of this writing, do not look particularly interesting. Factor U, responsiveness to handling, is identified by seventeen different indices which involve interaction between E and S. These indices involve learning, heart rate changes to threatening or quieting, and handling in the home environment. The evidence is convincing (see Anastasi, et al., Royce, and Willingham), but it is a factor which does not seem to have wide ramifications. Factor V, aggressiveness, is potentially of great interest, but the two studies (by Hsü and by Royce) identifying this factor are so disparate that we must suspend judgment and conclude that there is insufficient evidence to date concerning the invariance of this factor. There is, of course, no evidence from quantitative indices[27] concerning the invariance of any of the six factors we have discussed. But the point here is that there isn't even compelling evidence on the basis of intelligent analysis by inspection. Factor V can serve as an example of both the possibilities and the dangers involved in attempting to identify a factor. Both authors have identified a factor as aggressiveness. Have they identified the same factor? At the moment the only commonality between the two studies is the fact that the

[27]See p. 645 for a discussion of the problem of quantitative factorial invariance.

factor in question has received the same name.

One crucial and convincing indication of the validity of a factor, as pointed out in Chapter 6, is evidence of its functional unity from experimental work extending beyond its identification by factorial analysis. I have already indicated one such extension in the case of the thyroid factor. and it exists abundantly in regard to the Cattell-Scheier general anxiety factor, recognized in this area as the general autonomic activity factor. From the point of view of psychology, however, the major shortcoming of the thyroid factor extension to date is that it has remained strictly on the physiological level.[28] We are interested in extensions of psychophysiological or physiological factors in terms of behavioral significance. Such an extension has been achieved in the case of one of the factors above, namely Factor *P*. Inspection of Table 21-12 indicates that sympathetic dominance of autonomic functioning is characterized physiologically by high values on conductance, blood pressure, pulse pressure, sinus arrhythmia, blood glucose level, heart rate, oxygen consumption, and sublingual temperature. All of these measurements, plus others which are not included in Table 21-12 (e.g., salivary output and dermographic latency), have been combined by means of beta weights and the regression equation as a means of providing a best estimate of the autonomic factor score. These autonomic balance scores were then correlated ($N = 198$) with scores on Guilford's personality factor scores (i.e., factors GAMIN, STDCR, and *Co, Ag* and *O*). While the correlations reported were low, five of them were statistically significant, with the following values: depression (.31), cycloid (.27), nervousness (reflected)

(.13), subjectivity (reflected) (.23), and cooperativeness (−.26). Since high autonomic scores imply sympathetic dominance we can conclude that sympathetic imbalance is associated with a tendency toward depressiveness or moodiness, emotional instability or cyclic emotionality, nervousness or irritability, subjectivity or hypersensitiveness, and uncooperativeness or fault-finding.

An awkward methodological issue arises here, however. Even when the P.U.I. 9 general autonomic activity factor is rotationally well separated from P.U.I. 1, the parasympathetic predominance pattern, and P.U.I. 5, the sympathetic activity pattern, the number of highly loaded variables in common to the three is such that correlations of 0.7 or higher might easily be expected from *estimates* of these factors. The only hope of clarifying what is really happening in the above questionnaire correlations, for example, is either (1) to identify these factors by more variables *outside* the autonomic area, as has been most systematically done by Cattell, Scheier, and Rickels in 1964 and estimate them from a more independent set of variables, or (2) to take great pains in the factor rotation and determine the correlations of the pure factors with other factors in the matrix. For at present the above correlations supposed to be due to the sympathetic factor might indeed belong equally to the general autonomic activity level, with which measures of the former are substantially confounded in the above studies. Indeed, it is with the *general* autonomic factor (as P.U.I. 9 or U.I. 24) that Cattell and Scheier (325) find very high correlations of the questionnaire second-order anxiety factor (Factors $C(-)$, $H(-)$ O, $Q_3(-)$, and Q_4 in the 16 P.F.).

Wenger goes on to show that such sympathetic autonomic[29] imbalance is characteristic of operational fatigue cases ($N = 225$), psychoneurotics ($N = 98$), and

---

[28]In this connection it should be noted that Wenger (1523) reports zero correlations between his thyroid factor scores and the Guilford personality factor scores. He did not, of course, have the advantage of making his computations on the basis of the more adequate factor pattern which has since been reported by Overall and Williams (1132).

[29]These analyses were done with combinations of individual tests rather than factor scores.

asthma patients ($N = 16$), whereas there is no measurable autonomic imbalance in the case of normals ($N = 488$), ulcer patients ($N = 21$), or cases of neurocirculatory collapse ($N = 117$) in the decompression chamber at a simulated altitude of 18,000 feet.

All this is compatible at present either with Wenger's hypothesis that sympathetic autonomic imbalance is characteristic of the neurotic; that the neurotic, in effect, "is perpetually reacting to an emergency of greater or less seriousness" (Guilford, 625, p. 338); or with the quite different organization of evidence by Cattell and Scheier that high general autonomic activity is central to the *anxiety factor* (U. I. 24) and that these associations are found with neuroticism only because anxiety is characteristically high in neurotics. The crucial experiment to decide between these would be to obtain general autonomic activity level measures (factor 1 in Table 21-14) on (1) neurotics characteristically *low* on anxiety (Conversion hysterics according to Scheier's evidence with the IPAT Anxiety Scale), and (2) non-neurotics in a highly anxiety-provoking situation.

Other evidence, compatible as yet with either theory, shows neurotics higher on sympathetic imbalance, e.g., Theron's psychophysiological factor scores, as reported by Van der Mewre (1485). However, Van der Mewre suggests that the direction of autonomic imbalance will vary according to psychiatric nosology. While his data are based on samples which are too small to be conclusive (8 anxiety states and 12 hysterics), they indicate that cases of anxiety suffer from sympathetic imbalance while hysterics are characterized by parasympathetic imbalance. In a subsequent study, Van der Mewre (1484) presents evidence of a shift from sympathetic imbalance to autonomic balance as a result of administering two drugs, bellergal and hydergine, to a sample of 80 neurotic anxiety patients. This shift toward autonomic balance is inferred from two sources

of evidence: subjective reports of improvement regarding feelings of anxiety (i.e., less tension) combined with observations of vasodilation in previously vasoconstrictive subjects. Furthermore, Eysenck's (476) experimental program on personality structure includes a neuroticism factor, which Cattell and his colleagues have found independently and interpreted as regression (indexed as U. I. 23). The relationship between U. I. 23 and Wenger's sympathetic imbalance factor has not been investigated,[30] but Cattell's work shows anxiety (U. I. 24) to be highly correlated, to possible identity, with the general autonomic activity factor (see Table 21-14), which makes any close conceptual relation of U. I. 23 and autonomic activity very unlikely. The relation to U. I. 24, anxiety, is, however, extremely important.

Whatever the disagreement between positions such as that of Wenger, rooted in orthogonal rotation of largely autonomic data, and that of Cattell, Scheier, Williams and others based on adding psychological and physiological variables better to define hyperplanes, and rotating obliquely, it is abundantly clear that the multivariate approach, as contrasted with the single variable or measure approach, has brought greater progress and defined the issues much more clearly. This gain in insight can be documented at every phase of research in the field. For example, Wenger's work illustrates the well-known factor-analytic proposition that even when individual variables are of low reliability, e.g., through brevity of measurement, it is possible for the general patterns to emerge. Less than 5 per cent of Wenger's original matrix of 210 correlation coefficients had absolute magnitudes greater than .20. Of these 10 values, 4 were in the twenties, 5 were in the thirties,

---

[30]There is also evidence from two sources (479, 480, 833) that autonomic variability is heavily determined by inheritance. Eysenck presents similar evidence for his introversion-extroversion (479, 480) and neuroticism (491) factors.

and only 1 was above .40 (i.e., .44). The fact of the matter is, as Wenger's careful assessments of the reliability of his 26 individual physiological measures show, that in general, his variables simply are not reliable (one reliability coefficient at .88, five around .65 to .75, and the remaining twenty measures ranging from .11 to .65). This typical unreliability is undoubtedly the major cause of the low intercorrelations which have been reported to date in the comparative-physiological domain. The same is true, as Cattell points out, in *P*-technique studies in this area, where the error of measurement remains the same as in individual difference measurements while the true variance is much reduced. The fact of unreliability in Wenger's studies is also confirmed by the low communalities which have emerged from all his analyses (e.g., primarily in the range of .20 to .40).[31] Furthermore, the 125 correlations between individual physiological tests and the Guilford personality factor scores yielded only 14 significant coefficients, with the highest one at −.28. While the magnitude of correlation was not significantly higher for physiological factors as opposed to individual physiological tests, the patterning of these tests in the form of a hypothesized autonomic factor uncovered five significant correlations out of a possible thirteen, and in the case of the second-order anxiety factor in the 16 P.F. the correlation of the questionnaire factor and the objective test factor climbs to 0.8 or more. The main point, however, is that in spite of severe shortcomings in the reliability of physiological measurements as well as the validity of psychological measurements, the factor-analytic model has provided us with insight-

ful hypotheses concerning the functional relationships between autonomic discharge, personality characteristics, and psychosomatic syndromes.[32]

Let us now offer final comments regarding Table 21-11, particularly in connection with column 3 (Number and Nature of Variables and Factors) and the last column (Other factors). Column 3 indicates that the seventeen independent studies reported are about equally distributed according to type of variable involved — 7 studies involving behavioral variables only, 4 studies involving physiological variables only, and 6 involving both physiological and psychological variables in varying proportions. Omitting the Cook study (see the chapter by Mefferd for an analysis of Cook's research) a giant investigation involving 362 variables, 6 factor analyses, 33 first-order factors, and 7 second-order factors, there are a total of around 170 variables involved. These sixteen factor analyses (omitting Cook) have turned up over 50 interpretable factors, over half of them behavioral, with around 10 of the remainder physiological and 15 psycho-physiological. Up to this point we have commented on the seven factors which have manifested the greatest probability for invariance. It is important to note that these seven factors account for 37 of the 50 named factors, suggesting a considerable degree of redundancy (assuming agreement on these seven factors). The remaining factors are also likely to reveal such redundancy in the form of identities and high interrelationships. These include a half-

---

[31] The fact of low reliabilities and communalities, typical of factorial studies in comparative-physiological psychology, does not mean this must necessarily be the case. One study (1234), for example, involves a 32-variable investigation where over 80 per cent of the variables yield communalities which are .55 or higher. Similar communalities are reported by Cook (376).

[32] Although tolerable, this does not mean that unreliable measurements are desirable in factor-analytic research. It should be obvious that reductions in error variance result in increments in common factor and specific factor variances. Since the total variance or $1 = h^2 + s^2 + e^2$, where $h^2 =$ common factor variance, $s^2 =$ specific factor variance, and $e^2 =$ error variance, and since reliability or $r_{jj} = 1 - e^2$, it follows that $h^2 = r_{jj} - s^2$. Thus, reliability serves as an upper bound for community, equaling it only in the unlikely case when specific factor variance is zero.

dozen biochemical factors concerned with reactions of the organism to psychological and physiological stress. Two such factors were left uninterpreted by Overall and Williams (1132), one was reported as a blood fat factor (178), one was identified as a blood sugar factor (1523) of possible relevance to Factor Q, motor discharge, and two were reported as ketosteroid factors (376). It will be noted that only one of these researches appeared before 1961. It is not surprising, therefore, that there is little clarity concerning these factors. The possibilities for such factors were indirectly heralded by Roger Williams (1549), who has maintained that there is probably as much variation in the biochemical reactions of organisms as there is in their behavioral reactions. We should expect, therefore, that the factor-analytic model will be as fruitful in the domain of biochemical individuality as it is in other multidimensional domains.

7. SUMMARY

(1) A division in the study of the relation of physiological and anatomical variables to psychological variables is drawn between this chapter, devoted to *comparative* psychology, in the sense of comparing multivariate experimental studies, largely of individual differences, across species, and the following chapter, concerned with physiological, biochemical, and psychological relations in *processes* largely in man. No conceivable dichotomy is entirely "clean," and considerable cross-reference is necessary between the two chapters, as well as with Chapters 11, 12, 17, and 18.

(2) Body type and "constitution" have been studied by Sheldon and others in terms of correlation clusters. More precise multivariate methods, while yielding a structurally and statistically stronger and more defensible analysis into factors, have, except in rare cases, neglected to introduce an imaginative selection of variables. In terms largely of length and weight measures, with a few added somatic structural variables, one can recognize a high degree of agreement of studies in converging on five to seven factors.

(3) Study of the physiological correlates of *abilities,* begun by Lashley and Spearman and their students, has not progressed as much as might have been expected, because of the paradoxical situation that ability factors have actually not been as extensively studied and repeatedly replicated as personality factors have been in the more recent work on objective measures.

At present, psychologists can claim as tolerably certain the patterns of, as found by Thurstone and others (see Chapter 18), twelve primary abilities (U.I. 3 through 15), the fluid and crystallized general ability factors (U.I. 1 and U.I. 2) posited by Cattell and Hebb, and the factors of Halstead. Of the primaries, only four to date manifest a cortical or biochemical correlate. These are memory, verbal comprehension, perceptual closure, and number (in the universal index, U.I. (T) 7, 13, 3, and 10, respectively). The exact nature of such biological correlates is not clear, but it has been demonstrated that there is a differential decrement in factor performance as a result of organic change. Halstead reports, for example, that his C factor (which is apparently comparable to the memory factor (U.I. (T) 7) is more dependent on the cerebral functioning of the left hemisphere than the right hemisphere. Similar neural or biochemical correlates are reported for other factors, but such factors have not been checked for factorial invariance. Halstead's abstraction factor is a case in point. Halstead has presented convincing evidence of a decrement in performance on this factor as a result of lesions in the frontal lobes. He further reports that the effect of such localized lesions is a function of the mass of frontal cortical tissue. In this case we have good evidence of a neural correlate with no evidence of invariance; in the case of Halstead's C factor we have moderate evidence of invariance combined with moderate evidence regarding a neural correlate.

The recent work of Horn on fluid and crystallized ability, showing greater day-to-day function fluctuation in the former, in association with physiological variables, agrees with the general concept that fluid ability is a function of some mass action of the total cortex, whereas crystallized ability represents more local function. It is also striking that the higher inheritance of spatial and verbal ability found by Thurstone agrees with the higher loading of these primaries found by Cattell and by Horn on the fluid general ability factor. The finding of significant alpha EEG relations to U.I. 22, a form of cortical efficiency which may be regarded either as an ability or a personality trait, is discussed in the next chapter.

(4) The goal of finding the functionally unitary source traits and states in lower animals by the methods which have proved successful with human subjects is an extremely important one for comparative psychology. For one thing, if comparable temperament, etc., dimensions are found, the more potent possibilities of manipulative experiment are opened up for understanding them. Only a few pioneers have as yet attacked the matter, however, and most of these have been concerned with some special theme, e.g., animal learning, seeking a genetic pattern, looking for the dimensions of autonomic behavior, etc. Consequently, in the absence of that systematic search across the total behavior field which has characterized the human research, and of dovetailing studies by marker variables, little can yet be firmly inferred. Nevertheless, some half-dozen general behavior factors look promising, while a number of drive patterns, which could be extended by statistical treatment of ethological data, can indeed be considered established.

(5) An area which has come in for intensive study because of its interest both for psychologists and for physiologists, is that of autonomic variables and emotionality. However, the factor techniques have not been of uniform quality and finish and in any case have not made it possible to distinguish between trait and state patterns. Factors which might be tentatively called activity level, autonomic balance, motor discharge, thyroid activity, reactivity to avoidance conditioning, responsiveness to handling, and agressiveness nevertheless appear to have some degree of invariance.

In the belief that their analyses can only be methodologically convincing and satisfactory if variables *outside* the autonomic field are also included, to make clear rotational hyperplanes (and if markers, etc., are more systematically used *across* studies), Cattell, Haverland, Karvonen, Luborsky, Williams, and others have factored the same area in humans finding a general autonomic activity factor (P.U.I. 9, U.I. 24) to be identical with anxiety, and locating two other autonomic activity factors (sympathetic, P.U.I. 5, and parasympathetic, P.U.I. 1) which appear to be more states than traits. Also, they find other somatically and partly autonomically tied patterns to be better conceived as quite general personality factors, e.g., U.I. 21 and U.I. 22.

(6) Comparisons of bivariate and multivariate investigations in this area show systematic and substantial advantages, discussed above, for the multivariate approach. However, although it has been far more creative of concepts, the state of results at present is not satisfactory, because few investigators seem able to reach simultaneously the proficiency in animal and physiological experiment, and in expert and well-planned scientific use of multivariate designs, which are necessary to definitive results in this area. "Salvage" studies, by re-analysis, are indicated in several instances, while separation of lower animal from human researches, with more replication within a species before generalizing (preferably via quantitative invariance analysis) across species, are the immediate needs.

CHAPTER **22** Structuring Physiological
Correlates of
Mental Processes
and States: The Study of
Biological Correlates
of Mental Processes

ROY B. MEFFERD, JR.
Veterans Administration Hospital, Houston, and
College of Medicine, Baylor University

1. INTRODUCTION
(BY THE EDITOR)

Psychophysiological and psychosomatic relationships are discussed incidentally in several chapters of this handbook, e.g., Dr. Thompson's Chapter 23 on genetics, Dr. Nesselroade's Chapter 19 on personality, and Dr. Hake's Chapter 17 on perception. But they are concentrated largely in Dr. Royce's Chapter 21 and the present Chapter 22, which is, incidentally, the reason for their being put in tandem to form a block of three with Chapter 23.

The division between Chapters 21 and 22 is necessarily rather like an attempted administrative boundary drawn down the middle of an industrial complex, but the amicable discussions of the two authors and the editor settled upon a reasonably practical formula. Dr. Royce's Chapter 21 has concentrated more on individual differ-

ences and Dr. Mefferd's chapter on processes. Thus the former has handled more of what can be called comparative, biological psychology, somatic relationships, and the perspective which can be gained by looking at results across species, while the present chapter turns to biochemistry and physiology and particularly the changes occurring in emotional processes and psychological states.

A clear perception of the methodological and conceptual relationship of these two approaches is extremely important, and Dr. Mefferd faces it with the provocative and intensive thinking which it deserves. Sections 3, 4, and 6 especially are devoted to these issues. One particular point which has been far too little realized, but which is brought out fully in its technical aspects in Chapter 11, here, on change measurement, is that when one correlates (or examines mean differences) across different individuals as referees, e.g., by ordinary R technique, his factors will *include* state factors. For the variance covers both the between-individual and the within-individual, moment-to-moment, sources of variation. Researchers mentioned in Dr. Royce's chapter as believing they were describing patterns of traits may therefore have been describing state dimensions. Indeed, the issue becomes very real in terms of the division to be drawn between discussion of individual differences of autonomic activity in Dr. Royce's chapter and the present writer's discussion of autonomic reactivity dimensions in the outline of evidence on states in Section 5 below. Some of Dr. Royce's survey data, notably that concerning the work of Dr. Cook, has in fact been shifted to the setting of Section 5 where it belongs primarily with psychological state dimensions.

In view of the newness of the application of multivariate methods to psychophysiology, and the absolutely pioneering character of its application to physiology, Dr. Mefferd does well to devote much of the chapter to method. (Section 5 has been inserted with his approval as a substantive relaxation from method and a view of the Promised Land of applicable results.) His attention to method, though it takes stock of the statistical issues as such (which have already been treated in a more general context in Part I of the Handbook), extends to the specifically experimental, biochemical, physiological, and apparatus problems of this area. Especially in the context of longitudinal, P-technique research, the development of appropriate physiological measures has been an undertaking in itself. It is important at the present juncture to discuss the choice of variables and techniques in this area thoroughly, and to make them available to the potentially large circle of users. On the practical side, for example, these methods are much needed in the evaluation of ataractic (psychologically acting) drugs and the understanding in

psychiatry of the relation of physiology to moods and emotional states.

History may well record that we were standing at a most significant turning point in physiological methods in this decade beginning with 1960. For it is not just physiological psychology, or even physiology as a whole, but much of biology and medicine which seems about to avail itself in a comprehensive way of more potent statistical and multivariate methods. Clinical methods have long dominated medical research, and they seem to make room with extreme reluctance for the additional (and in many problems far more apt and incisive) methods of multivariate experiment and statistical analysis. The opposition is not so determined as that which met the introduction of classical experiment into medicine, e.g., in the work of Spallanzani or Pasteur, or which surrounded Harvey for twenty years in a prison of silence. But the fact is (as the present writer knows, through having been called in as an editorial consultant) that medical and physiological journals which deal with problems that could advantageously invite a 50 per cent quota of their articles employing multivariate approaches instead receive about 5 per cent and seemingly accept 1 per cent for publication. Nevertheless, especially with the shift of action and interest from infectious to systemic diseases, the medical doctor and the physiologist are unquestionably handling disorders of multiple determination and with complex feedbacks. A few pioneers in medicine, such as Mefferd and Cureton, Barnard, Wherry, and others, in America, and Uberla in Germany, however, have grasped the importance of the multivariate model in research on disease and of the electronic computer in diagnosis.

It is not so much that the doctor needs the accuracy of the multiple correlation coefficient in giving weights to different agents of treatment in a complexly produced condition, as that he needs to *think* in terms of a multiple regression, and, above all, to carry out research in terms of a design which respects multiple regression. For example, in one heart disease study (unpublished) known to the writer, quite erroneous conclusions were drawn as a result of failing to partial age out of a correlation. But even in daily practice there would be much diagnostic and prognostic gain from connecting clinical and laboratory data to a computer, since there is no reason to believe that clinical medicine is doing any better than clinical psychology proved to be doing, when it was examined by Eysenck and by Meehl. For input of information into the human mind beyond a certain very modest limit was shown to yield no increase in prediction and control like that which multivariate computation would have made possible.

Historians tell us that one of the curious facts of history is that at the great turning points in culture most of the people living at the time did not realize what was happening. Probably at the turning points of scientific history only a few pioneers realize the direction in which things are heading. Dr. Mefferd has been such a pioneer in the No Man's Land between psychology and physiology. He and others like him may, incidentally, be the means of bringing to physiology and ultimately to medicine, a flexible and comprehensive use of the multivariate research methods which have been the gift of psychology — as far as these are the gift of any single science — to biological science. But our concern here must stop with psychophysiology.

Accordingly, the remainder of this introduction is best expressed in Dr. Mefferd's own words, as follows.

Until a few years ago the documentation of the relationship between biological and mental processes rested upon meager and diverse evidence involving a handful of metabolic anomalies (i e., the inborn errors of metabolism), certain vitamin deficiencies, the influence of menses on behavior, the semi-psychotic states induced in normal persons by hallucinogenic "poisons," the effects of alcohol, and the like. It has seemed plausible to some that the dramatic natural shifts in behavior (with the sudden exacerbations and remissions frequently seen in psychotics) were due to changes in the level of some chemical at a critical site, but no evidence for this has been forthcoming. Many studies purported to have demonstrated chemical or physiological differences between psychotic, neurotic, and normal people, but these have been largely unsubstantiated in controlled experiments (869). The clearest evidence for a relationship has come from rapidly growing literature on the behavioral effects of the various drugs that are loosely classed as tranquilizers or psychic energizers (1474). These effects, however, are largely gross and non-specific. In spite of the growing volume of research aimed at demonstrating biological correlates of mental processes, we still possess no detailed understanding of any facet of such relationships.

In psychology, multivariate experiments are not uncommon. The boundaries of certain "domains" (e.g., primary mental abilities; basic personality traits; attitude, interest and value factors; behavior; etc.) already are fairly well delineated. This is not the case in biochemistry and physiology, where few studies have been concerned per se with the associations among more than two or three variables. As a result, the selection of items to represent an integrated biological system is more difficult than is the selection of appropriate variables to represent psychological functions. Relating these classes of variables is a double-barreled problem of discovering on the one hand the functional systems in which the biochemical and physiological processes are involved and on the other hand, simultaneously, of attempting to discover the role of these functional systems in psychological domains. Accordingly, much of the current multivariate experimentation in these areas is frankly and quite properly exploratory. Powerful hypothesis-generating techniques involving longitudinal experiments are being perfected (325, 342, 1035).

This chapter outlines certain inherent difficulties involved in such inter-disciplinary multivariate studies, and suggests first-approximation working solutions of some of these problems.

2. MULTIVARIATE EXPERIMENTAL PROBLEMS SPECIAL TO THE PSYCHOPHYSIOLOGICAL AREA
Considerations in the Selection of Variables

All experiments involve the sampling of two populations: subjects and variables. There is nothing inherently different between univariate and multivariate experiments in this respect. The investigator always is sampling from a population of many variables, most of which are correlated to some degree. Obviously in multivariate studies he should use the same care in selecting and measuring each item as he would were it the only one he intended to study.

In selecting specific biological variables, we attempt first to sample pertinent postulated functional systems (e.g., stress, anxiety, acclimative state, energy state, nitrogen metabolism, acid-base balance, etc.), and second to discover global systems that involve both mental-behavioral and chemical-physiological processes (e.g., stress, which has many separate interlocked simultaneous or sequential aspects from epinephrine release to increased heart rate to decreased performance on digit span and number facility tests [1033]). Thus, in an effort to relate mental and biochemical processes we measure physiological functions that we suspect are related to the chemicals we measure, as well as physiological and psychological variables that we suspect are related to specific cognitive, affective, or conative processes. In addition, extraneous factors that influence either end of the continuum are measured to facilitate interpretation of the results, e.g., time of day (666), weather conditions and season, kind (1155), quantity, and time of food and liquid intake, medication, degree of fatigue, physical condition and activity, body weight (875), body type (1310), age, intelligence (1250), education, motivation, and so on.

Eysenck (485) has discussed another aspect of variable selection which is of great importance, viz., that many measures thought of generally as "simple," such as suggestible body sway, are actually quite complex. The same applies to physiological and biochemical variables. Urinary sodium, for example, originates from all over the body where it participates in several processes, such as stress, acid-base balance, and kidney function. Thus there are several "kinds" of sodium, and such a substance is, in reality, as complex as if it were in fact two or more different variables. While the integral components of body sway may be measured separately, the direct contribution of sodium to different functional systems can be determined only after the fact by means of factor-analytic studies. For the sake of recognizing a factor more easily one will, of course, aim at a selection of variables which either general principles or exploratory simple structure factor analyses have indicated to be relatively "pure." This is an integral part of the strategy of systematically carrying marker variables from study to study, which Cattell especially has preached and practiced, and for lack of which much research in this area lies virtually on the scrap heap.

Sampling Sequence of Body Fluids Relative to the Measurement of Other Variables

A tedious problem (but one that only awaits experimentation for its solution) lies in the proper sequencing of measurements of different classes of variables. For example, should the blood sample be taken immediately before or immediately after making the psychological evaluations, or at some other interval before or after evaluation? Two factors are involved in making this decision: first, order effects caused by the measures per se, and second, the period or lag before a change in one variable is reflected in a change in another.[1]

To illustrate the first factor, the holding of a hand dynamometer under pressure will influence for some time thereafter performance on steadiness, eye-hand motor coordination, and similar measures. Examples of subtle influences of one measure upon another are replete in the psychological literature and need not be elaborated here. Drawing a blood sample even by a skilled person is a stresser for most people. This or even apprehension about it may alter materially the results of measurements of any kind made shortly thereafter.

The second factor is unexplored. Since urinary and salivary constituents arise directly from the blood, it follows that in taking these samples the lag period between them should be short. However, at present with respect to physiological or psychological evaluation this decision is based largely upon guesswork. A sample of blood reflects only the existing state at the moment it is taken. For example, the levels of some compounds change rapidly, exert their influence promptly, and then are destroyed just as promptly (e.g., epinephrine), while the levels and effects

of the other substances change more slowly (e.g., sodium). A sample taken even a few minutes after a stressful situation may be too late to detect the rise in epinephrine even though it does detect a stress-induced change in sodium levels, while the converse would occur with a sample taken immediately after the stress. A urine sample accumulated in the bladder during the stressful period and taken immediately after the stress possibly would reflect the elevated epinephrine and its metabolites (metanephrine, 3-hydroxy-4-methoxymandelic acid, etc.), but the changes are such that unless the stress were a prolonged one, it would not reflect the blood changes of the more stable constituents.

A distressing experimental complication related to these problems involves the low correlations (in addition to changes in the mean levels of all compounds) observed between urinary constituents collected from the same person at different times during the day, i.e., at different points on the diurnal cycle. Overnight (fasting) samples have been widely used, and, in many experiments there is a basic assumption that the levels in such samples are meaningful with respect to other variables whose measurement is delayed until the succeeding day. This assumption, of course, may be warranted, but any association discovered thereby is different from one that would be found in a sample collected during or immediately after the other measurements were made. We have found, for example, that the test-retest correlations of some 40 urinary constituents averaged about 0.60 for organic compounds while the electrolytes were below 0.20 between the 7-hour overnight and the succeeding 3.5-hour (both periods fasting) sample, with the highest correlation only 0.72. Furthermore, the average correlations between this 3.5-hour and the next succeeding 3.5-hour fasting samples were only slightly higher although the electrolytes now were about

---

[1]A constant problem which has come up in the various psychophysiological studies so far known is that, to obtain comparable reliability, the psychological measurements take about ten times as long as the physiological measurements. Thus it is possible in ten minutes, at one extreme, to get enough separate records on EEG, body temperature, pulse rate, pH values, etc., to make a correlatable series, whereas ten weeks may be necessary to get enough separate occasions of "simultaneous" psychological measurement for correlation. For to get reasonably reliable measurements on, say fifteen "simultaneous" behavioral variables, e.g., goodness of memory, reaction time, etc., two hours will commonly be required, whereas fifteen polygraph channels may give as many biological variables in two minutes. [Editor's note.]

0.50 (1033). Clearly, urine samples should be collected concomitantly with other measures.

Measurement of Metabolic Processes

Metabolic processes may be appraised by observing certain physiological variables such as the basal metabolic rate. These measures, however, are not only quite indirect, but they also are extremely crude over-all averages of many primary processes. More direct measures may be obtained by observing the levels of certain chemicals in the body fluids. The most convenient of these fluids and, therefore, the most thoroughly investigated are urine, blood, and saliva. There are limitations associated with each of these with which the investigator should be familiar.

Urine has been most widely studied because of its relatively large volume and ready availability. Unlike blood it may be collected with a minimum of disturbance of subsequent measures on the subject. Its ease of collection and the large number of variables that may be measured because of its relatively large volume may tend to lull investigators into a false sense of security about the meaning of these. Actually, from an analytical and interpretive viewpoint, urine is a much more complex fluid than either blood or saliva.

Body fluids are altered by the kind and quantity of food and liquid ingested. Specific substances may appear in them solely as a result of intake (e.g., several phenolic acids from coffee, salicyluric acid from aspirin, etc.) or the regular endogenous level may be increased (e.g., high sugar intake results in elevated glucose, and eating bananas results in elevated serotonin) or reduced as a result of intake (e.g., blood glycine which may become depleted as a result of its being used to detoxify ingested phenolic acids in forming the non-toxic hippuric acids). Depending on the variables measured, then, it may be impor-

tant to control the diet and medication during an experiment. Ingested materials are rapidly disposed of by metabolic, storage, or excretion processes so that throughout the day the patterns are constantly changing, (e.g., shortly after a meal the blood level of lipids is increased as the fatty material is transported to fat depots or to the liver). Obviously, samples for analysis should be taken under standardized conditions. One expeditious compromise is to have the subjects skip breakfast or lunch and then two hours before the experiment to drink a standard quantity of one of the fixed-calorie weight-control liquids or wafers now on the market. Owing to the concentrated proteins used, however, these have a high iodine content which may be reflected in the protein-bound iodine values. This would be negligible in cross-sectional experiments, but it should be watched carefully in longitudinal studies.

The Units for Expression of Biochemical Constituents

Many variables are inherently scalar quantities, i e., they involve only one parameter, such as concentration, percentage, or quantity. Blood measures are examples of this. Others are vector quantities involving two parameters, such as quantity and time. Urinary and salivary constituents are of the latter type. Meaningful measures of these involve a precise determination of both parameters. Simply collecting a urine or saliva sample and analyzing it for quantities of given compounds is inadequate unless we also know the time over which the sample was collected. The importance of starting a collection period with a completely empty bladder, and ending it with complete evacuation is evident if accurate determinations of rates are to be made. Some people, especially the elderly, have difficulty in completely emptying their bladders, and this can lead to sizable errors. Over an extended period of time the rate of excretion (or secretion in the case of saliva) may change significantly, but so long as the time intervals are the same and are constant with respect to the diurnal cycle, this poses a relatively minor problem.

3. SOME IMPORTANT PHYSIOLOGICAL VARIABLES
The Nature of Urinary Excretion Processes

The final excretion rates are the resultant of complex interactions of several processes. The first step in urine formation involves a simple filtration in the glomerulus where the diffusible constituents of blood are forced across a membrane. Physiological factors that determine the amount and pressure of the blood moving through the glomerulus influence the volume of this filtrate. The resulting filtrate then starts its course through the nephron where a series of highly complicated processes occur. Some compounds, commonly called threshold substances, are actively (enzymatically) re-absorbed from the filtrate, while others, called non-threshold substances, are more or less excreted *in toto*. However, non-active processes, e.g., diffusion, also occur which result in removal of some of these latter, as well as additional quantities of the former substances. The final fluid — urine — results from a complex interaction of hydrostatic and osmotic pressures, urine flow rate, and the "load" of waste products which must be excreted. Active re-absorption of the so-called threshold substances (such as glucose, sodium, the amino acids, and so on) is also dependent upon these factors, since before active re-absorption can occur there must be an actual physical contact between each molecule of these and its specific enzyme in the wall of the tubule. If, for example, the flow rate increases, there will be a relative "wash-out" of these materials simply because there is insufficient time to permit many of the molecules to gain such contact.

This will also occur when blood levels of these compounds are high and relatively large amounts of them are being filtered. Therefore, the quantities of the threshold substances in urine are determined by processes even more complicated than those that influence the non-threshold substances.

Characteristics of Urinary Variables

As was indicated above, some substances in urine arise from endogenous metabolism while others have an exogenous origin, but usually they arise from a combination of both sources, e.g., there is always some serotonin in blood resulting from normal metabolism (arising primarily in the intestinal mucosa), but ingestion of a banana (which contains serotonin) will increase this level. Regardless of their origin, these become mixed, and lose their identity in the blood and urine. It is impossible with ordinary techniques to tell the source in the body of a given urinary constituent, i.e., whether it entered the blood from the gastro-intestinal tract, the lymph, muscle, or elsewhere. Needless to say, this fact must be considered in interpreting the results of an experiment.

Evidence of the state of a given metabolic process may involve measurement of several constituents of urine. For example, if we attempt to evaluate the amount of epinephrine released by the body we not only will have to measure epinephrine itself, but also its major breakdown products (metabolites) including metanephrine and 3-methoxy-4-hydroxymandelic acid. Also many metabolites combine with other compounds in the blood and are excreted in this modified form, e.g., as sulfates, glucuronides, and the like. If a complete analysis of epinephrine excretion is desired, all these must be accounted for. Fortunately, at least in exploratory studies, this seldom is required, since indices of epinephrine metabolism (i.e., one of the metabolites) often may serve quite adequately for the desired purposes.

In evaluating metabolic processes, the investigator must be alert to the fact that the urine is not the only route for loss of substances from the body. Most of the calcium and magnesium are lost through the feces, and there undoubtedly is some loss of every constituent of blood and lymph by this route. Likewise, considerable quantities of diffusible materials in the blood are lost in the form of sweat. The rates of these losses vary with many factors, such as activity, temperature, amount ingested, liquids drunk, etc. Complete evaluation of the metabolism of a given substance can be made only by means of balance studies in which the quantities ingested and excreted or otherwise lost by all routes are precisely determined over a considerable period of time. Fortunately, this is seldom necessary in exploratory studies.

Preparation of Blood Samples

Blood consists of plasma in which there are a number of different kinds of cells including the oxygen-transporting red cells (erythrocytes), and five kinds of white cells (leucocytes). There are also the tiny platelets and other particles. If blood is drawn and prevented from clotting by the addition of an anticoagulant (sodium citrate, lithium oxalate, or heparin), the cells can be centrifuged and removed. The resulting plasma contains the protein involved in clotting, fibrinogen, which constitutes about 6 per cent of the total protein.

If blood is allowed to clot, the fibrinogen molecules join to form a fibrous mass in which the cells are trapped. The mass at first forms a firm jelly-like clot which shrinks on standing, leaving the clear yellowish serum. This may be decanted from the clot. The main difference between the two fluids is the presence or absence of the fibrinogen.

Non-particulate material remains in the fluid, and this includes a vast array of inorganic and organic substances including the large protein molecules. The great majority of these proteins can be placed into one of two classes — globulins and albumins. Some chemicals adhere to these protein molecules, while others are free.

Some chemicals, such as potassium and phosphate, leach from the cells rapidly after a sample is taken, while others, such as certain steroids, seem to be taken up by the cells. The concentration in the fluid of such constituents may change quite significantly in a few minutes unless the cells are promptly removed. Although they should not be left in contact with the serum any longer than required once the clot forms, some samples will clot more rapidly than others. Therefore, it is necessary to standardize the processing time so as to minimize differences due to leaching, etc. Regardless of whether plasma or serum is being used, great care should be taken to prevent rupture (hemolysis) of the red cells, since the cell contents obviously will alter the fluid significantly. Furthermore, the red color that results from the release of hemoglobin will complicate many analytical procedures. Hemolysis can be minimized by using sharp needles, clean silicon-treated glassware, and by handling the sample gently throughout. A good precaution is to divide the sample immediately after it is drawn to insure that at least one aliquot does not hemolyze.

Characteristics of Blood Variables

Approximately half the volume of a blood sample consists of the various blood cells, most of which are red blood cells (erythrocytes). Both the number of the latter and their hemoglobin content are commonly determined. Electronic counters have greatly increased the accuracy of blood cell counts, while the packed volume or percentage of the cells (the hematocrit) and their hemoglobin content can be determined quite accurately. These measures are correlated, although the cells may vary both in size and in hemoglobin content at any given cell count. Platelet numbers are sometimes determined, but these are subject at best to gross errors.

The white blood cells (leucocytes) are subject to relatively larger and more rapid changes in number than are the far more numerous red blood cells. Again automatic counting methods have increased the accuracy of their determination, but this is still below that obtained for the red blood cells. There are five kinds of white blood cells (neutrophils, lymphocytes, monocytes, eosinophils, and basophiles, in order of number), which are commonly determined by averaging the numbers in several microscopic fields and expressing these as percentages of the total white blood cell count, i.e., the differential count. A mistake commonly made in multivariate studies is to include in analyses both the total white blood cell and the differential counts — a whole-part relationship with its own built-in specific correlations.

Besides being gauges of general hemopoietic activity, white blood cells increase markedly in number during infections. Pathological conditions affect the various kinds of white cells differentially, and, since these conditions also may influence other variables, the cell counts serve as valuable markers for such effects. At one time the eosinophil count was taken as a measure of stress, but their count is so inaccurate and mutable that an elevated value should be taken only as presumptive evidence of stress.

Many compounds may exist in the blood both in free and protein-bound forms. Analytical methods usually are designed to release all the bound compound before the final determination is made, but sometimes this is not the case. For example, although copper exists in the blood mostly as a moiety of the enzyme ceruloplasmin, small but significant quantities are bound to other proteins (albumins), and some exists in the free ionic form. Which of these we

determine will depend on the analytical method selected. Although in this case we have methods to analyze for all three forms, this is not always true.

One experimental advantage in the use of blood is that it contains several important metabolic enzymes. Since each molecule of an enzyme can process thousands of molecules of its specific substrate, their quantity reflects functional capacity or capability. Measures of these provide a much more direct and meaningful gauge of metabolism than we can obtain from mere knowledge of the concentrations of various compounds.

Characteristics of Saliva

Saliva has not been widely used as an experimental tool, other than as a measure of autonomic activity (e.g., salivary flow rate and pH) and in conditioning experiments. The secretion rates of few chemicals have been definitively determined, and, indeed, little is known about the mechanisms by which most constituents are secreted in saliva. It seems clear that they do not occur as simple filtrates, although this process undoubtedly is involved, since almost every constituent of blood is found in some quantity in saliva.

Recent studies have centered upon the standardization of collection techniques, including evaluation of stimulated (by means of pilocarpin, chewing of rubber bands or various gums, etc.) and unstimulated flow rates, the influence of flow rate upon the quantity of various substances secreted, comparison of the secretion rates of various compounds in the parotid and whole mouth saliva, and so on (110, 1303, 1304, 1305). Parotid saliva may be collected directly from the orifice of the gland. There is a distinct experimental advantage to this procedure since the three pairs of salivary glands produce saliva at different rates and of different constitutions. When the conditions of collection are carefully standardized, timed samples should be most useful in multivariate experiments. Many of the problems encountered in the collection of blood and in the comparison of blood and urinary constituents do not occur in the case of saliva. For example, the correlations of salivary and blood variables are much higher than are those of urinary and blood variables (1033). This may be due in part to the fact that the formation of saliva is a more straightforward process than is that of urine, but also it is due in part to the fact that shorter time intervals for collection (3-5 minutes) are used, i.e., the saliva more nearly reflects the levels in the blood at the time of collection.

Considerations Governing the Selection of Physiological Variables for Multivariate Studies

Precise information about the interrelationship of physiological and biochemical and psychological processes is virtually non-existent. Even the interrelationship of the various physiological events themselves are only meagerly understood. With rapid advances that are being made in the development of transducers, of high fidelity equipment, and of means for the semiautomatic processing of physiological data, however, systematic factor-analytic studies of these variables may be expected to increase our understanding. Meanwhile, choice of variables must depend largely upon rational consideration. The leading variables on the Autonomic Balance Factor (derived from heart rate, blood pressure, palmor resistance, and salivary flow rate) of Wenger and his collaborators (1516, 1519) are a good starting point.

As is the case with many other body functions, the physiological processes also are ordinarily under tight homeostatic control. To be sure, there are individual differences in the equilibration levels of these, but the data we obtain from measurement of such systems during resting periods at a time that they are under effective homeostatic control are not very informative. Much more information may be obtained by deliberately pushing a system out of equilibrium by means of imposing a standardized disruptive agent (e.g., administration of drugs, exposure to a stresser or to gravity changes, etc.). We then may note how far out of equilibrium the system goes, how long it stays, whether it oscillates below, around, or above the basal or resting level before it returns to initial levels, and so on (569). Autonomic responsiveness, or autonomic lability derived from each of the separate measures reveals a great deal about autonomic function that is not manifest in the stabilized system (894, 1032).

Numerous devices designed to process data, e.g., digitalization, averaging, and the like, are appearing on the market. With most of these it is unnecessary to record the data in its original analog form, i.e., the information is processed directly. Although modern techniques of digitalization permit near-duplication of the original analog curves, information is always lost in the process. Therefore, unless the analog data is recorded per se, it can never be recouped. For this reason it is more desirable to record the basic event per se on magnetic tape, and to use this for further processing. Then at any later date new techniques of data processing may be applied, and new variables may be extracted or derived from the basic data at will.

Measurement Sequence of Physiological Processes Relative to Other Variables

The quantities of various constituents in the body fluids are determined in part by cellular metabolic rates. These rates and the quantities of the products of metabolism, in turn, are a function of various factors, including body temperature (within limits the rate increases with temperature), the quantity and balance of several hormones, the available supply at the cell level of enzyme substrates (including oxygen), and the rapidity of removal of the enzyme products and waste materials. The rate and amplitude of respiration and of the heart, the amount of hemoglobin available to transport oxygen, the number of capillaries open, and many other physiological variables condition these factors.

However, both the saliva and urine are influenced more directly by physiological processes. For example, blood pressure, heart rate, number of nephrons functional at a given time, and other factors are directly involved in the mechanical aspects of urine formation, and these in turn also modify the final concentrations of constituents by altering the flow rate, and, accordingly, the time available for re-absorption. There also is a similar influence upon salivary variables. In view of this direct and immediate effect, it appears safe to conclude that measures of autonomic function should be made immediately prior to the collection of the body fluids. They should not be made after this, since the collection per se may modify the physiological function to be measured.

Physiological processes also influence many psychological variables, such as any motor task, and many tests of cooperation and motivation. Time perception judgments are a function of body temperature and at the same time rhythmical processes well may provide subconscious cues for these estimates (727). We would expect many other perceptual functions to be influenced by the blood supply, temperature, etc. at the site (e.g., kinesthetic after-effect, and visual and auditory functions). It seems valid, therefore, to conclude that as is the case with chemical processes, physiological and psychological measurements should coincide temporally.

4. PROBLEMS AND PRINCIPLES UNIQUE TO LONGITUDINAL MULTIVARIATE STUDIES (INCLUDING *P* TECHNIQUE)

Facta non verba

It would be foolhardy to minimize the statistical problems as well as the great practical difficulty in the conduct of longi-

tudinal studies. We believe, however, that these can be solved, and that it is now time to accumulate data that will permit their solution. This is the only technique available for the elucidation of complex functional systems. We cannot learn how a motor functions without examining it at intervals as it is running. We can no more learn how the human body functions by cross-sectional experiments (where statistical criteria are understood), than we can learn how a motor functions by studying the average position of the pistons, of the cam shafts, of the size of sparkplugs, or of anything else, in 100 motors at a given instant. Yet by stopping one motor (as with a stroboscopic light) at frequent intervals as it is running, we can quickly discern how it functions. And we do not have to study 100 motors to learn how motors function.

Our statistical concern arises from the fact that in one important sense the observations are not independent of one another. As a result the number of degrees of freedom available for evaluation purposes is uncertain, and it probably is different for many of the variables. The crucial matter, however, is not resolvable strictly by consideration of serial and autocorrelations alone, for the question is not simply the degree to which subsequent observations can be predicted by preceding ones. The concept of independence of successive measures has a subtly different meaning in the case of biological variables from what it has with business data. The question at hand is whether the day-to-day variation of measurements is significant irrespective of any superimposed trends. A straight line may be predicted mathematically by two points, but depending on the error of the method used to obtain the measurements (and with most biological and chemical variables this is quite small). There may be many statistically significant points along it. We need to distinguish between those points that represent meaningful autocorrelation and those that result from mere measurement duplication. The additional contribution to trends by systematic errors must be resolved by other means.

The problems are largely statistical, and the investigator should not be discouraged thereby from conducting rigorous, rationally conceived, longitudinal experiments. Reasons for believing that certain rules often automatically applied to longitudinal data may be strictly inapplicable have been given by Cattell in Chapter 11 on change analysis (page 380 f.). The opposing viewpoints have been clearly stated by Cattell and by Holtzman in Harris (692). Certainly one must conclude that the unique power of such studies in the discovery and elucidation of functional systems far overshadows the temporary impediments posed by present statistical uncertainties. The resulting data per se form the basis for new information, and they may be reanalyzed repeatedly as mathematical techniques improve.

However, the investigator must in the meantime be conservative in his conclusions and interpretations. He can aid this by spacing his observations into rationally meaningful intervals (i.e., achieve intuitive independence), accumulate as many of these as possible (but well over 100), reduce the number of variables sampled to well below the number of occasions (remembering that a variable may be discarded after the experiment, but that it cannot then be added), pay careful attention to the distributions of values, and if he analyzes his data by factor-analytic techniques, to attend only relatively high factor loadings in making his interpretations. This author feels that we have dissuaded ourselves from the conduct of longitudinal studies long enough, and that it is now time to accumulate a body of data that will aid in the solution of these statistical problems.

Variable Selection

In longitudinal studies we are looking at a new domain of variables that are basically different from those that are most useful in cross-sectional studies. Since we can understand function only through change, we must measure "unstable" variables in the former. In the latter, on the other hand, "stable" variables are needed in which the rank-order position of subjects does not change erratically from day to day. Some measures can be classified as "either-or" (e.g., somatotype and mood) in this respect, but most occupy the middle range — somewhat unstable or more unstable in some individuals (e.g., anxiety). The latter forms the bridge between the two types of studies.

Chemical and physiological measurements may be repeated almost at will with little influence upon (or change in the meaning of) subsequent measurements of the same or other variables. This is not true of most psychological tests, e.g., there are practice effects even with a process such as dark adaptation (99). Largely as a result of such effects, coupled with an intuitive belief on the part of many psychologists that mental traits are inherently stable (i.e., that periodic differences result solely from measurement error, learning or practice, motivational changes, and the like), measures of higher mental function have been grossly neglected in longitudinal experiments. Indeed, there are almost no tests having sufficient alternate forms for such use. Modest starts in rectifying this have been made with word associations (1072, 1073), primary mental abilities (1071), memory for faces (1074),[2] and anxiety (322), but virtually no work has been done in the vast areas of formal thought processes (such as object-sorting), self-evaluation, mood, motivation, attention, and personality assessment in general. Needless to say, these latter perhaps constitute the most critical area for study if we are to develop detailed understanding of man's most important functional systems.

[2]See *Psychol. Repts,* 1966, 18, 3-10, and *Psychol. Monogr.,* 1964, 78, No. 2, for recent additions to this test battery. A Trisecting Test is in press in *Psychol. Repts.*

Sampling of Occasions

In group comparison and cross-sectional experiments we take elaborate precautions to achieve random sampling of subjects. Should we also do the same with respect to occasions in longitudinal studies? Many factors, some of which are discussed in succeeding sections, contribute to make this an undesirable procedure. Not the least of these is the existence of many periodic cycles which we must sample in phase. (See discussion in Chapter 11, page 384 on sampling of various cycles.) Random sampling would introduce considerable error variance simply because it would contain points from the entire cycle.

Differences in the Approach to Variable Measurement in Cross-Sectional and Longitudinal Experiments

Cross-sectional experiments are concerned with the accurate determination of population parameters—with the exact determination of absolute thresholds and the like. Both internal consistency and test-retest reliability are urgently desirable. Large numbers of items and repeated measurements on each subject are required to achieve "true and stable" values, i.e., we over-determine the parameter.

On the other hand, in longitudinal experiments there is a different emphasis, viz., we are interested in determining the test-retest variability in a subject. Variability in the absolute threshold of pitch would be interesting per se, but by the very nature of the determination (i.e., it is designed to yield an average value for each subject based on sufficient observations to subsume intra-individual variability), it would be difficult to demonstrate. Apart from this over-determination factor, however, longitudinal studies have quite stringent experimental restrictions. The measurements must be made as nearly concomitantly as possible, so the time allotted to each test is short. The number of tests must be limited for the same reason, but also to minimize

boredom of the subject. Since the tests cannot be spaced over several measurement periods, the sequence of their administration must be arranged to minimize saturation, carry-over, and similar effects. It is not possible to meet these requirements and at the same time to achieve the order of test reliabilities that one takes for granted in cross-sectional experiments.

This does not mean that we are advocating the use of unreliable tests, but rather that we need to understand and develop and pursue a different kind of reliability for repeated measures. We are concerned only with a special kind of internal consistency on each test which is established separately for each subject of a longitudinal experiment. To accomplish this, the subject is given on three or more occasions (after the pre-experiment learning and practice period) tests that are considerably longer than that suspected to be required for the experiment proper. Then by means of analysis of variables to estimate reliabilities (using the item and day variances for successively shorter tests), the shortest test possible is selected—a test whose length is specially tailored for the individual subject.

Natural Periodic Cycles That Influence Experiments

Periodic cycles and rhythms such as the diurnal cycle, work week, dietary cycles (e.g., fish on Fridays, etc.), menses, and seasonal changes (e.g., temperature, humidity, length of day, etc.) can have a distressingly large influence upon all variables typically measured in multivariate experiments (666, 1032, 1034). Either the measurements must be made at the same relative time with respect to the various cycles (i.e., in phase), or the effects of the cycling must be confounded in some way. Consider the diurnal cycle for a moment. It is an exceedingly complex curve, being the resultant of many factors including the action of light on the pituitary, time of sleeping, time of eating, working hours, etc.

It shifts somewhat with the seasons. Almost every body process changes during the day. Body temperature is a good example of a variable that changes continuously throughout each 24-hour period. If we measure it regularly at 8 A.M. for a period of four months, we are introducing a great deal of unnecessary error variance. In this case, as the days become progressively longer or shorter during the experiment, the measurements actually are made at different points on the daily curve, and mean changes are introduced which will inflate the correlations. Furthermore, since the means change systematically as the days lengthen, a trend is introduced which further inflates the correlations. This is a problem that warrants much more consideration than it usually is given, particularly in psychological experiments where there seems to be a tacit assumption that it makes little difference when measurements are made. The measures may be made at a standard period after sunrise, but a much more practical though less exact solution is to make the measurements around the lunch hour. This at least is equidistant between sunrise and sunset, and most activities involving sleep, eating, and work. Shorter-term cycles also pose problems. Biological processes, for example, operate under rather tight controls to maintain homeostasis. Most of these controls are servo-mechanisms and result in periodic cycling in the controlled variable. These may have periods far shorter than our sampling period so that the sampling is essentially random, or it may coincide with our sampling and become a systematic measure of trends. On the other hand if the sampling period is shorter than that of the oscillating variable, an error component is introduced consisting of the amplitude of the oscillations since we are simply sampling at different parts of the curve.

A related problem that poses considerable experimental difficulty concerns the delayed effects of various activities, procedures, treatments, and the like. Short-term lags (e.g., resulting from a cold pressor test), important as they are, may be resolved by relatively simple techniques. Long-term lags (e.g., chlorpromazine therapy where several days are required before effects upon behavior are noted, and the effects of which persist for several days after therapy is stopped) are more difficult to handle. A change in the level of some constituent of the blood, for example, sometimes must persist for hours or days before a related change is noted in a mental process or in behavior. Even a transient change may not be reflected in other events for a considerable period. Practically nothing is known about such relationships, and only through longitudinal experimentation can we learn of them. A method of analysis suitable for revealing such lagged relations has been proposed by Cattell in the factor-lagged variables method (Chapter 11, page 385). It avoids the difficulties of the earlier proposal to lead and lag variables on one another. However, systematic empirical application of the factor-lag method remains to be made, and until we see this, any conclusion on its effectiveness in handling the problems just discussed would be premature.

Long-term trends (e.g., seasonal changes, slow weight changes, persistent low-order practice effects, etc.) pose special problems. Biochemical and physiological (and undoubtedly psychological also) processes undergo acclimative changes of sometimes surprising proportions (1032, 1034, 1519). Such trends leading to changes in the mean levels of variables concern us because of the strong influence this has on the magnitude of the correlation coefficients.

Subtle Influences of Longitudinal Experimentation That May Change Interrelationship Patterns

This, of course, is one of the major concerns in the interpretation of the results of longitudinal experiments. There are obvious difficulties such as changes in motivation and cooperation, long-term practice effects, saturation effects with test items (e.g., where symbols or faces are presented daily they soon may all look alike), surreptitious practice midway in an experiment (e.g., judgments of time, distance, weights, and the like may change dramatically unless an initial practice period with feedback is provided to satisfy the subject's curiosity), a growing apprehension at repeated blood sampling, changes in the erythropoietic processes as a result of repeated sampling (e.g., the steady depletion of red blood cells may stimulate their production by the bone marrow), and so on. These may result in shifts in factor structure (537) during the course of the experiment that can only be rectified by analyzing different periods separately. This introduces two requirements of all multivariate longitudinal experiments: (1) variables designed to measure these shifting sands must be included, and (2) sufficient observations must be obtained to permit separate evaluation of portions of the experiment if there are obvious shifts in factor structure.

Less obvious changes may occur also. The subject may begin to attach special significance to the measurements made upon a given day (e.g., on Sunday), or in special periods (e.g., during Christmas). "Week-end effects" may result in large differences between Friday and Monday. The substitution of testers during illnesses or emergencies usually results in startling changes in test results. Even slight changes in the order or manner of administration of tests and measurements may upset the apple cart. The repeated special attention given a particular part of the body (e.g., if blood is always drawn from the same place) may result in changes in the subject's body image. Similarly, test objects may assume special significance (e.g., the subject may become very concerned over the difficulty he has with a particular test). With or without feedback, subjects may develop exaggerated body concern as a result of

continuous measurement, of EKG, EEG, temperature, and the like. Repeated quizzings about sleep, dreams, food intake, activity and exercise, social and sexual activities may introduce changes that can be quite distressing experimentally. The subject may develop an overpowering morbid curiosity about measures where no feedback is provided.

This is a discouraging recital of very real difficulties. They must be considered and met in some fashion. Some are transient and even desirable because variability is thereby introduced. Far from being disastrous, an illness in the subject can yield exceedingly useful information provided measurements are continued during this period. *Occasional* loss of sleep, fasting, overindulgence, fatigue, anxiety, grief, depression, boredom, and hostility likewise may be most desirable. As we become more sophisticated in the conduct of longitudinal experiments we may find that we will encourage changes of this nature in order to increase the over-all useful variability.

5. A BRIEF SURVEY OF PRESENT KNOWLEDGE AND HYPOTHESES ON PSYCHOPHYSIOLOGICAL STATE DIMENSIONS (BY THE EDITOR)

As Chapter 11 on change measurement has pointed out, we should theoretically expect *P*-technique studies to yield factor patterns unique to an individual, but these should center upon those found by differential *R* technique, expressing the common human pattern, for the reason that all human beings have certain common neural response structures. It is proposed here to condense the totality of the still rare studies existing in this area—some 8 *P* technique and 2 *dR* technique (differential *R*)—which should thus agree in essence. For the meaning of what has been discussed above in terms of choices of variables, and principles of design of longitudinal studies, as well as of what follows about interpretation of longitudinal and cross-section correlations, will become enriched by this consideration of the structure which is actually emerging.

An experimental design along the above lines may either introduce stimuli intended to produce changes in anxiety, stress, elation, activation, etc. — as in the condition-response design of Cattell and Scheier (318), or the parachutist experiment of Grinker and Spiegel (619), or the stress interviews by Grinker, Cattell, and Scheier or the submarine stress work of Cook (375, 376, 377) below — or it can leave the daily onslaught of events to produce its stress, etc. In the initial determination of state response patterns as such, the simplicity of the latter has certain advantages, but after that the introduction of stimuli helps to interpret any doubtful factors and to bring out their "natural history." Taking Cook's experiment as an example of the latter, we see a physical and psychological stress being applied (the former consisting of escapes from an escape hatch below water level).

The complete investigation involved 362 variables covering biochemistry, psychology, psychiatry, physiology, anthropometry, and physical fitness. Eight large blocks of data were formed in accordance with a priori groupings, and the relevant variables were intercorrelated. By inspection of the obtained correlations the author reduced the original number of variables to 164. These were then placed in four blocks and the appropriate variables intercorrelated. Four large matrices, labeled A, B, C, and D were then factored. Two of these four matrices, A and C, are included as the second and third entries in the first column of Table 22-1. The first three of these analyses involved some 107 variables and 26 factors. The fourth one involved 7 second-order factors related back to the original 164 variables by the usual methods (Chapter 6). Using the same criteria as in Table 22-1, we have listed those factors

which were identified in more than one analysis. The first two, ketosteroid (Factor H) and creatinine (Factor I), have been replicated at least twice, and the blood chemistry factors involve changes in the count of seven different blood components.

These factors may be best interpreted in the light of the coordinated studies in Tables 22-4 through 22-9. However, two methodological points need to be made. (1) The inclusion of stimuli does not guarantee that responses will be connected with them in the popularly expected direction. Table 22-2, which is from Cattell and Scheier (325), shows, for example, that anxiety is actually higher three weeks before an exam than during the exam itself; that anxiety falls and stress rises during the exam; and that a stressful challenge (threat of treadmill run) actually reduces the neurotic regression (see Table 22-2 below) state. There has been too much assumption that stress produces a single dimension of response, whereas the following evidence indicates that anxiety and stress are two distinct factors.

(2) In longitudinal studies, above all others, the factor-analytic techniques have to be applied with extreme patience, perfectionism, and regard to proper control of design. In the comprehensive Cook studies above, for example, the use of the group centroid tends to predetermine rotation position by clusters, and its alignment with the factors in the other studies below has been postponed pending examination of the achieved hyperplane count. The studies which follow have a similarity of technical standards and a continuous trend of old and new marker variables, which gives hope that if invariance can be achieved it will be achieved here. In particular, the rotations have been (a) very thorough, typically a dozen or more over-all rotations continued over three or four months, (b) pursued blindly, i.e., with variables as unnumbered points, so that no preconceived theories have affected the exact rotation, (c) carried, by a plot of % variables in the ±10 hyper-

plane, to a plateau which is (i) high, typically about 60-80 per cent and (ii) demonstrably the highest possible among many positions.

A survey including 4 of the 10 researches now available was made in 1957 (240); the present survey is the first since to bring the survey up to date. The indexing is by the P.U.I. numbers — Universal Index numbers for *P*-technique or state factors — intended to hold the pattern while interpretation

proceeds. At the present stage of tolerably confirmed interpretation, the names for the P.U.I. numbers are as shown in Table 22-3 (which omits factors P.U.I. 6 and P.U.I. 7 as not sufficiently confirmed).

The pattern P.U.I. 1 is given this first number because it has tended to be the largest in variance, at least in *P*-technique studies. The references for the researches summarized, which are numbered 1 through

TABLE 22-1

FACTORS IN COOK'S STUDY OF STRESS RESPONSE
(GROUP CENTROID EXTRACTION, OBLIQUE ROTATION)

Four Factor Analyses No. of *S*s and Species	Apparently Invariant Factors (Rotated)			
	Number and Nature of Variables and Factors	Factor *H* Ketosteroid	Factor *I* Creatinine	Other Factors (Blood Chemistry Factors)
K 85 male submariners	20 urine chemistry variables; 9 biochemical factors, 4 interpretable	Ketosteroid output due to psychological and physiological stress	General creatinine output factor	
A 88 male submariners	48 variables, 28 urine and blood chemistry, 20 psychological; 8 interpretable factors, 5 biochemical, 3 psychological	Ketosteroid output-physical stress Ketosteroid output-psychological stress	General creatinine output factor	Lymphocyte ratio change due to physical stress Lymphocyte ratio change due to psychological stress
C 88 male submariners	39 variables, 24 blood count ratios, 15 Rorschach scores; 9 factors, 6 blood chemistry, 2 psychological, 1 uninterpretable psychophysiological			Six different factors involving ratio changes in such polymorphonuclear leucocytes as basophils, eosinophils, and monocytes due to psychological and physical stress.
T 88 male submariners	33 variables derived from 33 1st-order factors, based on 164 variables, 1st-order factoring procedures; 7 factors, 3 biochemical, 3 behavioral, 1 body type	Ketosteroid output-physical stress Ketosteroid output-psychological stress		

TABLE 22-2

RELATION OF STATES TO STIMULUS SITUATIONS

Provocative Situations	Anxiety $F(Q)$II, U.I. 24 and P.U.I. 9	Effort Stress P.U.I. 4	Pathemia $F(Q)$III+, U.I. 22 and P.U.I. 2	Neurotic Debility U.I. 23 − P.U.I. 8
Provocation of Threatening Ideas*	.00(5)***	+.28(5)	+.02(5)	+.06(5)
	.00(9)	+.45(9)	+.43(9)	+.08(9)
Anticipation of Treadmill Run	+.13(5)	−.16(5)	−.07(5)	−.35(5)
Imminence of Academic Examinations	−.25(5)	+.16(5)	+.20(5)	+.04(5)
Therapy-Counseling** (Hunt, *et al.*)	− (Hunt, *et al.*)			
Believed Failure on Academic Examinations	+ (Tsushima)			
Anticipation of Dangerous or Challenging Flying Experience	+ (Sells)			
Removal of Parachute Training "Stress" (Several days after training)	+ (Basowitz)			

*"Provocation of Threatening Ideas" also tends to increase a dimension tentatively identified as Adrenergic Response, P.U.I. 5, in the study (9).
**Therapy also slightly reduces Introversion, $F(Q)$.
***These numbers in parentheses refer to the same independent studies as the preceding tables do.
Note.— All personality dimensions are given at their neurotic-contributory poles, except for Effort Stress, where the relation to neurosis has not been clearly established. The sign (+ or −) in any one cell of the table gives the direction of effect (association) on that dimension, at the pole described in its column heading, due to the stimulus in the intersecting row. Thus, for the Treadmill Run-Neurotic Debility cell, the −.35 value means that Anticipation of Treadmill Run lowers Neurotic Debility. Actual correlational (factor-analytic) values for the relationship are given, where available, while the appearance of a sign without a value indicates a *t*-ratio type comparison approaching or achieving significance. The study in which the data were found is given in parentheses, and more fully described in the text and Appendix I.

TABLE 22-3

LIST OF RECOGNIZED STATE CHANGE DIMENSIONS

Indexed as	Poles: Positive Pole Italicized	Similar Factor Found in R-Technique (Trait) Studies
P.U.I. 1	*Activation* (Excitement) vs. Torpor	U.I.
P.U.I. 2	*Elation* vs. Pathemia or Depression	U.I. 22
P.U.I. 3	*General Fatigue*	
P.U.I. 4	*Effort Stress*	
P.U.I. 5	*Sympathetic Autonomic (Adrenergic Response)*	
P.U.I. 8	*Mobilization* vs. Regression	U.I. 23
P.U.I. 9	*High Anxiety* vs. Low Anxiety	U.I. 24

10 at the column heads in Tables 22-4 through 22-9 are as follows: 1. Cattell, Cattell, and Rhymer, 1947 (273); 2. Cattell and Luborsky, 1950 (300); 3. Williams, 1954 (1548); 4. Haverland (703); 5. Cattell and Scheier, 1956 (318); 6. Van Egeren, 1963 (1186); 7. Connor (in press); 8. Nesselroade, 1964 (1096); 9. Cattell and Scheier (with Grinker), 1961 (325); 10. Mefferd, Moran, and Kimble, 1960 (1035). Researches 5 and 8 are incremental R-technique studies on roughly a hundred cases, and the rest are P-technique studies on normal and clinical cases running from 60 to 200 or more days. All are studies tested for number of factors, designed with marker variables (which, however, "move on" from study to study so that the set of studies covers maximum ground) and rotated for maximum simple structure.

In this case we see a pattern characterized by small G.S.R. (deflection as per cent of absolute resistance), high blood sugar, low skin resistance, low ataxia, etc. All but two of these check with significant loadings across three or more researches. It has every sign of being a dimension of excitement (not anxiety, or elation, or fear, but general excitement or activation level). Incidentally, the connection of small G.S.R. deflection size with high alertness and activation was noticed in a bivariate study long ago (Cattell, 198), but its meaning became clear only in the pattern of a multivariate study. The association noted with rating and self-rating variables is here with surgency and extraversion, but this may be because excitement or alertness as such were not rated.

The pattern of P.U.I. 2 is one of quick

TABLE 22-4

P.U.I. 1. ACTIVATION (EXCITEMENT) VS. TORPOR

Independent Researches:	1	2	3	4	5	6	7	8
Small per cent PGR deflections	−73	−68	−50	−84	—	—	—	—
Low initial PGR resistance	—	−40	−45	−67	−19	—	−06	−11
High glucose concentration in blood	—	53	40	—	—	—	36	—
Low ataxic sway suggestibility	−75	—	−15	—	−31	−51	—	—
Low ratio emotional/non-emotional recall	−65	—	−12	—	—	—	—	−14
Large lag of flicker fusion thresholds	—	—	50	—	—	—	—	—
Better immediate memory for words	—	—	—	—	35	22	30	05
F+, Surgency and extroversion	—	—	—	—	23	27	—	24*
High respiratory amplitude	—	—	—	—	—	64	—	—
High systolic blood pressure	—	—	—	—	—	29	10	20
Higher body temperature	—	—	—	—	—	(−01)	42	30

*Complete extroversion configuration rather than just F+

In Table 22-4 and subsequent tables, a— means that the variable was not used in that study. Unless a loading is put in parenthesis, it is consistent in sign of loading with other studies. A cross-comparison of the researches has always checked the matching by showing that no factors other than the one chosen could match the factor with which it is placed. (This "proof by elimination" is important.)

reaction time, fast reversible perspective, and fast large body movement tempo (Rimoldi, 1200), which check over four researches, but larger loadings actually exist for good calculating, good memorization, and high cholinesterase in the blood serum. This matches also the R-technique factor called Cortertia-vs.-Pathemia, which has been shown to be associated with much alpha rhythm EEG interruption (Pawlik &

TABLE 22-5

P.U.I. 2. Elation vs. Pathemia (Depression)

Independent Researches:	1	2	3	4	5	6	7	8
Short reaction time	−75	−35	−67	−21	—	−09	−67	−16
Fast reversible perspective	43	—	61	(−05)	—	25	16	07
Acidity of saliva (low pH)	−56	−33	−10	—	—	−44	—	—
Good memorization	45	00	61	13	—	—	—	07
Many figures added correctly in two minutes	—	—	61	49	—	—	—	—
High cholinesterase in serum	—	—	78	—	—	—	—	—
High body temperature	—	—	—	70	—	03	07	24
Fast tempo	—	—	66	—	—	—	—	—
Lengthy dream recall	—	48	—	—	—	—	—	—
Fast arm-shoulder tempo	—	—	—	—	—	55	01	64
Fast leg circling tempo	—	—	—	—	19	30	—	71
Faster ideomotor speed	—	—	—	—	—	—	41	35

Cattell, 1142) and is interpreted as high cortical alertness (hence cortertia) and effectiveness. The opposite pole is called Pathemia (see Chapter 19, Pawlik) because it is associated with feeling, generaliy of a depressive kind. In extremes it may be elation-depression, or one component therein.

P.U.I. 4 has been defined as effort stress, for reasons discussed more fully under anxiety below. The identification is partly because of fitting in with Hoagland's (729) and Grinker's (619) findings of ketosteroid output in stress. It also contains low lymphocyte and eosinophil disturbance, thus suggesting that one of Cook's (376) and one of Wenger's (1522) factors also belongs here. However, Royce points out that the latter contains significant loading on blood sugar, which suggests a rotation confounding the factor with P.U.I. 2 or P.U.I. 5.

On its first discovery P.U.I. 5 was noted to have the hallmarks of the classical adrenergic response pattern of Cannon — rapid pulse, high blood glucose, high erythrocyte count — and a theory of *three* autonomic response patterns — general, sympathetic, and parasympathetic — was put forward (Cattell, 226) with defined loading

TABLE 22-6

P.U.I. 4. Effort Stress

Independent Researches:	1	2	3	4	6	7	8	9
Low fluency (verbal and drawing)	−55	−14	−29	−44*	−31	—	—	—
Low rigidity	−51	−09	−31	−42	(05)	—	—	—
Small myokinesis	−40	−36	—	—	−38	—	−27	—
Good memory, commit, and recall	(−40)	36	44	31**	10	04	23	—
High 17−ketosteroids	—	—	97	—	—	—	—	47***
High level of anxiety (questionnaire responses only)	—	—	—	—	08	—	23	47
Faster heart rate	—	—	—	—	16	—	36	39

*Mean of three tests.
**Mean of two tests.
***In blood plasma in this case; in urine in others.

TABLE 22-7

P.U.I. 5. Sympathetic (Adrenergic) Autonomic Response

Independent Researches:	2	3	4	6	7	10
High per cent lymphocytes	48	48	—	—	—	49
Small per cent neutrophils	−30	−67	—	—	—	−52
High glucose in blood	34	54	—	—	29	—
Poor memorizing	−58	−23	−38	−15	—	—
Large PGR upward drift in relaxation	—	16	22	—	27	—
High erythrocyte count	(−05)	09	—	—	27	44
Many slanting lines on C.M.S.	—	—	50	56	—	—
Rapid pulse rate	—	—	38	(−01)	—	—
Much time used, letter-number comparison	—	—	—	57	—	—
High E-D questionnaire factor VII score (elated)	—	—	—	45	—	—
More rapid pulse rate (after startle)	—	—	—	—	30	—

patterns for the three (see P.U.I. 1 — in which Torpor may be considered parasympathetic predominance, and P.U.I. 9 below). It is associated with poor control of cognitive and other performances, excitement, and some elation in the one study in which this was rated. The impulsive performance is seen also in aspects of the cursive miniature situation test other than that listed here.

P.U.I. 9 factor was first labeled "general autonomic activity level" (having possibly the same meaning as lack of autonomic balance) because of the raised temperature, heart rate, systolic blood pressure, etc. But Cattell and Scheier's (325) research on over 800 anxiety signs and variables quickly revealed that it is indeed the general anxiety factor, which, of course, has the effect of thus generally activating the

TABLE 22-8

P.U.I. 8. Mobilization vs. Regression

Independent Researches:	2	4	5	6	7	8
Low disposition rigidity (motor)	−54	(−17)	−30	−56	—	—
Many hours of sleep previous night	51	26	—	—	—	—
Large movements in myokinesis	44	—	26	23	—	—
Fast reaction time	−41	−14	—	−43	—	—
High fluency of association	07	38	—	—	—	—
Early in day	—	−21	—	—	—	—
Higher ratio accuracy to accomplishment	—	—	40	33	—	—
C+, High Ego Strength, 16 P.F. Scale	—	—	21	—	—	—
Less errors made in complex reaction time	—	—	−21	−49	—	—
Small minimum body displacement, ataxic sway	—	—	—	−29	—	—

Nothing will be said of P.U.I. 8 except that it matches the U.I. 23 Mobilization-Regression factor in more variables than can be shown in this small table. The "overwroughtness" of the regression pole is associated with ego weakness on the 16 P.F. and insufficiency of sleep, but it is distinct from the diurnal fatigue factor P.U.I. 3.

autonomic system. The pattern has since been defined in studies other than those recorded here, as a trait-like pattern, U.I. 24, though these are to date the only complete simple structure factorings defining it as a state, using change measures.

Two patterns, this and the effort stress (Table 22-6), have more resemblance than most, and the distinction between them can

TABLE 22-9

P.U.I. 9. HIGH ANXIETY VS. LOW ANXIETY

Independent Researches:	3	5	6	9	10
Low cholinesterase in serum	-78	—	—	—	—
High pulse pressure	71	30	37	08	08
High basal metabolic (estimated)	59	—	—	—	—
Low initial PGR resistance	-25	-26	—	—	—
Fast rate of respiration	—	—	17	45	—
High plasma 17-hydroxycorticosteroids in blood	10	—	—	43	22
High level of anxiety (questionnaire responses only)	41	—	—	37	—
Faster heart rate	(-04)	—	51	30	20
Much lack of confidence in skill in untried performances	—	-35	—	22*	20
High level of psychiatrically evaluated anxiety	—	—	—	20	—
$Q4+$, Higher Ergic Tension	—	40	—	—	—
$C-$, Low Ego Strength	—	-29	—	—	—
Higher anxiety score on IPAT Verbal Anxiety scale	—	—	33	—	—
High $m-OH-$phenylhydracrylic	—	—	—	—	74
High $m-OH-$hippuric acid	—	—	—	—	74
High $p-OH-$hippuric acid	—	—	—	—	57
High histidine	—	—	—	—	52

*Scored in opposite direction in this research. Its direction is actually consistent.

only be made by attention to the loading pattern of all variables. For example, some loading on questionnaire anxiety occurs on both but is higher on P.U.I. 9 and extends across markers (Q_4, C-) for the second-order anxiety factor; loading on 17-*OH* ketosteroids occurs on both, but is higher for effort stress. The loadings on the physiological measures from the Mefferd, Moran, and Kimble study on a schizophrenic were made from a rotation and matching carried out by the present writer on their data with their permission.

A seven-state battery for measuring these state dimensions through their psychological variables is now available (322), and the factoring has been carried to the second order, where a structure as shown in Diagram 22-1 appears.

Space precludes adequate discussion of the theory which has developed around these seven to ten psychophysiological state dimensions and their associations with stimuli and other criteria. What is more important is a recognition that they stand out from an assortment of inconclusive published factor analyses in this general area as a reasonable approach to invariant structures. The justifiable doubts expressed about factor analyses having located the true functionally unitary entities in such a field can only be put aside when (1) every component study has been *independently* and blindly rotated to *truly maximum* hyperplane count, which is as much labor as all the rest of the study put together and seems to be undertaken seldom, and (2) a sufficiency of exactly similar markers measured with the precisions defined by Dr. Mefferd and other specialists, is carried with strategic sense from study to study. At the present technical stage of factor analysis there can be no such thing as the definition of a factor influence by a single experiment. Loadings vary more with sampling than correlations, since the given correlations are divided up in each experiment according to the different magnitudes with which the same factor influences interact at the given scene. Thus in Tables 22-4 through 22-9, a factor loading may vary appreciably, *but it practically never changes sign*, which is the important evidence. And when one has a pattern fixed by, say, 8 variables (the above tables are sections from larger ones), the incidence of such a sign loading pattern among the statistically possible patterns is 1 in 2^8 (1 in 256), whence an 8-element replication of signs, despite loading level changes, should be considered a very ample significance. This has been easily reached in the anxiety (general autonomic action or imbalance), the activation-torpor dimension pattern, and certain others.

It will be obvious from the tables above that to think one has identified two experimental factors as identical because "they both load pulse rate, blood pressure, and blood sugar level" ignores the whole sense in which factor analysis should be made to operate. There are (see above and references) *at least* four factors which significantly load these three variables. But they do so in a different rank order of magnitude and sometimes with different signs, and their loadings on other, e.g., psychological variables have a different pattern. For example, both anxiety and effort stress load raised pulse and respiration rates and ketosteroid output, but the rise of metabolic

DIAGRAM 22-1.   Interrelation of State Factors in Second-Order Action

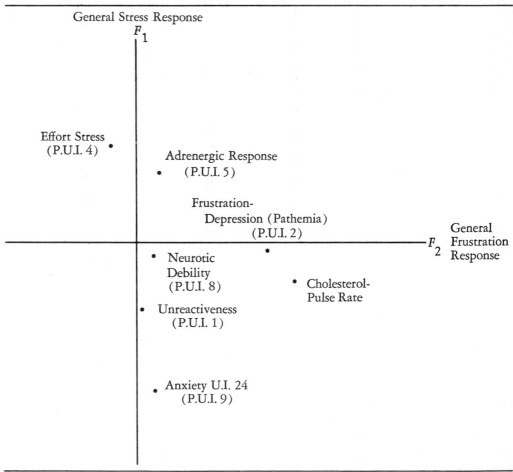

rate is large in anxiety, the steroid rise is higher in stress, electrical skin resistance fall is marked only in anxiety, while psychological variables showing strong concentration, e.g., good memorizing, low rigidity, are improved in effort stress, whereas in anxiety cognitive efficiency is lowered. By the stepwise progress of experiment we are likely to use — until our hypotheses crystallize more clearly — the same initial sets of variables to recognize several different factors. Careful, repeated, and jointly planned studies (the joint planning of P- and dR-technique (Chapter 11) studies has been part of this in the state area), pursued with independent rotations and leading to positive replications, alone can hope to define these subtle differences of pattern by which different factors show themselves in much the same variables. But today the definition of the foregoing emergent hypotheses for specific factors permits us to move on to more idiosyncratic variables for final confirmation.

With regard to substantive conclusions, it must now be recognized that much of the work that was done on the "autonomic balance" concept lacked the technical requirements noted above, and this rather gross concept ill fits the patterns which are clearly emerging above. Human states are coordinated response patterns which concern much more than the autonomic nervous system. The anxiety response pattern, P.U.I. 9, inherits the emerging concept of *general* autonomic activity level, but it includes also hormonal action (17-*OH*) steroids, serum cholinesterase change, and much upset of amino acid metabolism. The notion of a fairly independent adrenergic autonomic pattern stands up well in the P.U.I. 5 pattern. Conceivably, the notion of a parasympathetic and inhibitory action could be connected with the torpor pole of P.U.I. 1. Otherwise, in cortertia-pathemia, P.U.I. 2 (which might be considered a cortical/hypothalamic activity ratio), and other factors, we are out in "new space."

Although these seven or more independent[3] state response patterns may now be considered tolerably established at the empirical level, they are in the best sense still hypotheses to guide research. That is to say, they admit of reasonably well-crystallized but yet differently slanted hypotheses and provide a firm foundation of measurement for their testing.

6. THE NATURE OF CORRELATION COEFFICIENTS BETWEEN BIOLOGICAL VARIABLES

It is proposed in this last section to consider certain special problems regarding the form of correlation and factorization in this psychophysiological area. For a number of reasons the correlation coefficients between certain biological variables are lower than we intuitively feel they actually are in fact. Rarely, however, can this be due to low reliability in the ordinary sense, for physiological measurement errors are usually lower than those to which a psychologist is accustomed.

The reductions are due more to what we think of as low stability coefficients, not low dependability or equivalence coefficients.

---

[3]It should be noted that although they are independent influences, as shown by their distinct hyperplanes, these factors, at least when found in *P*-technique studies, are sometimes fairly substantially correlated. Diagram 22-1 clearly brings out this tendency of the state factors to become correlated over time. Some as yet unpublished *P*-technique studies on cancer, analyzed by Damarin and the present writer, show quite substantial correlations as might be expected from the coordination of an ongoing disease process. This occasionally appreciable obliquity in the state field is one reason why earlier *orthogonal* factorizations of autonomic etc., data failed to locate the invariant unities. It may well be, however, that the substantial second-order factor variances now needing investigation here will often turn out to be situational rather than inherent. For example, anxiety (P.U.I. 9), effort stress (P.U.I. 4), and pathemia (P.U.I. 2) might rise together on weekdays and fall at weekends in a child having difficulties at school. The second-order factor would then be "the situation," but others could be inherent.

To illustrate, urine formation is one of the principal means for maintaining the levels of blood constituents within narrow bounds. As the blood level of a compound increases slightly, its glomerular filtration rate also increases until the blood concentration levels off, and then as it begins to drop, the filtration rates also decrease, since, other things being equal, the volume of fluid filtered remains the same throughout. As the filtrate passes down the tubules, some of the water is re-absorbed. This leads to a net concentration of non-threshold substances (e.g., urea and creatinine) over that found in the blood, but the relationship to blood concentrations should remain the same. A high urine concentration should accompany a high blood concentration. Threshold substances (e.g., glucose, amino acids, and sodium) are re-absorbed in part along with some of the water, so that there will be no net concentration, and, indeed, the concentration may fall below that of the blood. Hence, the quantity of threshold materials excreted is more a function of flow rate than of their concentration in the blood, and the latter can be predicted from the urine concentration less reliably in the case of threshold substances than of non-threshold substances. Were we able to sample both the urine and blood frequently at short time intervals, we could ascertain the concomitant rises and falls in the concentrations of both as homeostatic adjustments occur. This is most difficult to accomplish with more than one or two compounds, because of the small volumes of both fluids that could be taken. We must be contented in multivariate experiments to allow the urine to collect over a relatively long period. Now the concentration in the bladder becomes the average of many oscillations in the concentration of the urine draining into it, and the total quantity of all substances increases at rates varying with the homeostatic adjustments. When only one blood sample is taken and the bladder is drained only once, no knowledge is obtained about these various oscillations in rates and concentrations.

Thus, here as in many measures in this area the correlations observed are based simply upon the periodic variations in the instantaneous values. Some of this variation will be due to the fact that at the instant of sample-taking the homeostatic balance was in the process of adjusting on the high side, while at other times, or in other subjects, it occurred on the low side of the cycle. This also serves to deflate correlation coefficients between the two fluids. The situation may be improved somewhat by using a short collection period, and by measuring other variables that influence excretion processes (e.g., liquid intake, urinary flow rate and specific gravity, blood pressure, heart rate, etc.) so that the correlations may be interpreted. Diuretics (such as coffee, tea, large amounts of water or other liquid, etc.) should not be drunk for two or three hours before the samples are taken, as these increase the urine flow rate.

The fact that many physiological processes, which we are certain on functional grounds are actually highly intercorrelated, often have quite low correlation coefficients, has several roots. Incidentally, this observation has an inference of importance in the opposite direction, namely, that quite low but consistent correlations (see last section above) may correspond to what the physiologist thinks of as quite substantial functional connection! Reductions occur partly from the following: some processes respond rapidly to stimuli while others have a considerable lag in response; the oscillations of some processes are marked and readily measured (e.g., G.S.R.) while others (e.g., temperature) oscillate in amplitudes below detectable limits with available practicable instruments; discrete events (e.g., heart beats and respiration) must be related to continuous variables; and some functions can at present be measured only at intervals (e.g., blood pressure), thereby reducing their degrees of freedom. There is a vast array of variables influencing each process that must be measured simultaneously if we hope to untie this Gordian knot. Comprehensive longitudinal studies of a few hours duration can aid materially in this endeavor.

Although the relation of cross-sectional and longitudinal studies has already been appreciably discussed (Chapter 11, and Section 1 above), a few comments from the standpoint of a physiologist may be added. Cross-sectional studies have the primary purpose of determining stable traits and characteristics. Longitudinal studies on the other hand are most powerful in the study of functions and states. The one inherently is static and the other dynamic. There is a strong interaction between the two, however, since it is not unusual for one individual to exhibit variation over a period of a few months as great as the "normal range" for large samples of subjects. The day chosen for evaluation of each subject in a cross-sectional study is arbitrary, and the results obtained depend upon his state or condition at the time. The results would have been different in all likelihood if another arbitrary time had been chosen, since the rank order position of the subjects may change from day to day. This is viewed as part of the error variance in cross-sectional studies, but it is upon this periodic variability in individuals that longitudinal studies capitalize. The result is, as Cattell points out, that state variance and state patterns may turn up in R-technique researches, as well as in P- and dR (incremental R) studies; though one must admit *the model* (Chapter 11) that change covers both *trait-change* factors and *state dimensions*.

We could learn a very great deal indeed about traits and states, genotypes and phenotypes, and static and dynamic conditions were we to conduct a multivariate experiment adequately sampling different aspects of many functional systems involving 100 subjects replicated 100 times, in what Chapter 3 and 11 above have defined as a "group P-technique" design, using a score grid instead of a score facet. Such a

study is not only feasible, but it is urgently needed. While we wait for an adequately heroic, visionary, and well-heeled investigator to undertake this task, however, we can begin to achieve some of its benefits by more carefully coordinating the two kinds of studies. We need adequate trait-genotype type descriptions including behavioral, personality, cognitive, anthropological, and related demographic attributes of each succeeding subject of longitudinal studies in order that he may be positioned with respect to similar cross-sectional studies. Cumulative longitudinal studies then will increase in over-all power.

7. SUMMARY

(1) The division between the present and the preceding chapter is essentially that between structural somatic and physiological associates of *traits* and the functional psychophysiological associations of *processes*. The former also covers the *comparative* psychophysiology of species and the present chapter keeps closer to *human* medical, physiological, and biochemical data. It concentrates on multivariate methodology, which, incidentally, has a considerable future in medicine generally, not only in psychophysiology.

(2) The general and specific problems of sampling variables are discussed. Many special problems of relevance and reliability arise in the physiological field owing to lag effects, the influence of taking the measurements themselves, the influence of recency of eating, urination, sleeping, and other ongoing physiological adjustments in daily life.

(3) Specific discussion is made regarding what are to be considered *important* physiological variables, particularly in terms of what is available from blood, urine, saliva, etc. samples.

(4) The problems peculiar to longitudinal study, in their statistical and physiological aspects, and the interactions of the two, are discussed, partly in relation to sampling of

occasions, cyclical processes, and the effect of the study as such upon the changes in the variables. It is shown that the field bristles with technical difficulties that can be overcome only by specialized attention to its problems.

(5) A brief survey is made (by the editor) of the unitary state change dimensions which have so far appeared from some eight P-technique and two or three incremental R-technique studies that have used adequate technical designs, checks on factor number and uniqueness of rotation, and sufficient markers for cross-matching. It is shown that centering discussion on "autonomic balance" is not particularly profitable, and that the seven or more dimensions found — anxiety, elation-depression, activation-torpor, effort stress, mobilization-regression, etc. — involve complex coordinations of autonomic, hormonal, blood chemistry, and central nervous system activities. These dimensions are sufficiently established to make most fruitful jumping-off — point hypotheses for further research in the field, and this research should now include situational stimuli and higher-order structure investigation.

(6) The fact that correlations actually found in physiological data often run much smaller than the physiologist would expect from knowledge from other experiments of the functional connections has implications in two directions. First, it points to reductions through the distance occupied by intervening variables, by lag, and by influences which come under stability coefficient rather than dependability (reliability of measurement) coefficient concepts. Second, it reminds us that the correlational expression of multivariate relations means that quite small loadings (partial correlations) can correspond to very positive and substantial functional connections, the evidence of which is partly swamped in the natural, non-constant situation by the normal operation of many other influences.

CHAPTER **23** **Multivariate Experiment in Behavior Genetics**

WILLIAM R. THOMPSON
Wesleyan University

1. INTRODUCTION

In order to understand more easily the significance of multivariate analysis for behavior genetics, it will first be necessary to explore the status and definition of this field and make explicit some of the special problems contained in it.

It can perhaps be argued that behavior genetics is simply one aspect of the science of genetics, or even, on the other hand, that it is just another aspect of psychology. Each of these views has something to commend it, but neither seems to the writer to be quite accurate. Since geneticists focus mainly on the study of the hereditary mechanism, they are not usually interested in traits as such (omitting practical considerations), but rather in traits as they can contribute to an understanding of the operation of genes. Analogously, the main problem in psychology is the scientific analysis of causal dependencies in behavior. Genes represent only one class of causes or variables out of a very large number.

To assign behavior genetics to one or another of these disciplines is to lay aside some unique and interesting problems that arise from the union of two very unlike fields. The one, genetics, has a good deal of precision and formalization. It centers on a relatively narrow range of problems. The other, psychology, is rather imprecise, is much less formalized, and deals with a great diversity of substantive issues. Out of the dialectic created by juxtaposing two such disciplines, some new and special questions are bound to arise.

In point of fact, the area of physiological psychology represents a good example of this kind of gain. The increasingly close relations between psychologists and neurophysiologists over the past thirty years have resulted in the location of new kinds of problems, new theoretical models about the brain, and even new techniques of studying brain function. It took some time, however, before there was a realization that conceptualizations in terms of function or behavior added to the understanding of structure and vice versa. The fears of Skinner (1326, Chap. 12) that adding the nervous system to behavior would simply be adding one type of ignorance to another were rather like those of the pessimist who might expect to get, from adding one half-empty glass to another half-empty glass, a completely empty glass. In fact, his pessimism has proved to be unjustified.

711

Before very long, we may expect to find that behavior genetics will develop in a similar fashion. As a field, it has had up to the present a rather spotty history, involving the amassing of a great deal of data, much of which is redundant and much of which is trivial. Some indication of the sheer quantity of material gathered can be obtained simply by glancing at the bibliography compiled by Fuller and the writer (568), one which covers almost a century of work and contains over 800 references. There are now signs that this fact-gathering phase is giving way to a theoretical phase involving the location of critical problems and the development of crucial theoretical issues. I would now like to discuss the general nature of these problems and issues.

As a character for genetic analysis, behavior has at least three properties that separate it rather sharply from the simple kinds of marker traits, such as flower color or pod shape, on whose study formal genetics was built. First, behavior traits tend to be *continuous* rather than discrete. There are some syndromes, of course, like severe forms of mental defect, that appear to show an all-or-none occurrence, but these are relatively rare. Most traits, like intelligence, introversion, or emotionality, vary along continua from high to low. This feature of behavior introduces immediately the concepts of scaling and sampling as problems of major concern. A second characteristic of behavior that must concern us is its *complexity*. Almost any behavior trait can be broken down into an almost unlimited number of components. This is essentially the validity problem in psychological measurement. It involves the isolation of underlying dimensions. As will be discussed later, current modes of isolating such underlying dimensions are rather arbitrary and seldom give unique solutions. Nonetheless, they are based on a supposition which is probably correct, namely, that behavior is not completely homogeneous, but has some kind of "grain" that we can ultimately expose by making

the right kinds of cuts. Third, behavioral traits are highly *fluid*. That is, they tend to fluctuate both randomly and systematically over time. This relates essentially to the problem of reliability or repeated measurements. All three of these features of behavior traits introduce questions of major concern both to the quantitative geneticist (495) and to the psychologist (248). In point of fact, they are questions with which behavior theory has been intimately concerned for a long time, and most formal models of behavior deal directly with them. We should, therefore, emphasize that behavior is a datum for genetics very different from most characters commonly studied by geneticists, for example, weight, height, litter-size, and others. There are no "weightologists," or "litter-sizologists"; but there are behavior theorists, and they are here to stay. Thus it is the writer's view that the three properties of behavior set forth above can pose core problems for any worker in behavior genetics and that decisions regarding them will determine the future development of the field. It will also be obvious that the kind of methodology that seems most useful to handling these three features of behavior is some kind of multivariate analysis. Let us now discuss each of them in some detail.

2. PROBLEMS ARISING FROM BEHAVIOR BEING TYPICALLY A CONTINUUM

Continuous variation is not unique to behavioral traits. In fact, most characters that are of interest to agricultural geneticists are of this sort, such as milk-yield in cattle, back-fat thickness in swine, egg-size in hens, and so on. But it is still true that the original models of Mendelian genetics were based on traits that could be handled by nominal scales, including, more specifically simple counts of occurrences and nonoccurrences of a character in differing but related generations. It took a good deal of time before the extension of such models could be made to continuous traits of the kind studied by the Pearson-Fisher school in England. The classical example of the manner in which such an extension can be made is East's analysis of size inheritance in maize. The general principle involved can be illustrated by reference to a simple two-locus system as shown in the third column of Table 23-1. As indicated in the table, quantitative values are given to each gene underlying a character, so that their assortment in an F_2 population yields a distribution of the kind indicated.

tion of each to be expected. It is clear that in the limit of n, the equation generates an approximation to a normal curve. However, an important assumption is involved. This is that each of the genes contributes an effect that is equal and additive. The assumption is violated if some genes in the system contribute disproportionately large effects to the variance of the character (major genes), and also if some genes interact in some way with each other. Interaction occurring between allelic genes at the same locus is commonly called *dominance;* that between genes at different

TABLE 23-1

THE EFFECT OF DOMINANCE AND EPISTASIS IN THE F_2 OF A CROSS
BETWEEN TWO PURE STRAINS (HYPOTHETICAL DATA)

Geno-type	Proportion of Total Group	Additive Hypothesis $A = B = 1$, $a = b = 0$	Phenotype Score Dominance Hypothesis $Aa = AA = 2$, $aa = 0, B = 1$, $b = 0$	Epistatic Hypothesis $A = 1, a = b = 0$, $AB = 2, aB - 0$
AABB	1/16	4	4	4
AABb	1/8	3	3	3
AaBB	1/8	3	4	3
AaBb	1/4	2	3	2
AAbb	1/16	2	2	2
aaBB	1/16	2	2	0
Aabb	1/8	1	2	1
aaBb	1/8	1	1	0
aabb	1/16	0	0	0

The general case of quantitative inheritance or polygenic systems may be stated in terms of a simple binomial expansion as follows:

$$(x + y)^{2n}$$

where x is one condition of a gene having a certain quantitative value, (e.g., 1), y is the allele having a different quantitative value, (e.g., o), n is the number of allelic pairs of genes underlying the character.

The expression reduces, when expanded, to the number of different genotypes. Adding the coefficients gives the propor-

loci is called *epistasis*. These two possibilities are illustrated in columns 4 and 5 of Table 23-1. It will be clear that the departure of the distribution of a character from normal then indicates that the assumption of equality and additivity of effects may not in fact have been met. To some extent, differences in size of effects of different genes may be allowed for by various scaling devices. To separate dominance from epistatic effects, however, is more difficult. In principle, it is possible, working backward from a given distribution, to obtain estimates of average dominance and/or epistatic effects occurring in a polygenic system. This allows us to partition the sources of phenotypic variance of a trait into components as shown in Table 23-2.

TABLE 23-2

GENETIC AND ENVIRONMENTAL
COMPONENTS OF PHENOTYPIC VARIANCE

Phenotypic	V_P
Genotypic	V_G
Additive	V_A
Dominance	V_D
Epistastis	V_I
Environmental	V_E
Genotype-environment interaction	V_{GE}

It should be noted that the kinds of partitioning carried out depend on the interests of the investigator. For example, we may be content to lump together all genotypic effects and separate out instead the different types of environmental variances. A good example of this is the work of Penrose and Robson on human birth weight, as cited by Falconer (495). The data are presented in Table 23-3. "Maternal genotype" refers to genetic differences

TABLE 23-3

COMPONENTS OF VARIANCE
IN HUMAN BIRTH WEIGHT
(Falconer, 495)

Causes of Variation	% of Total	
Genetic		
Additive	15	
Non-additive (approx.)	1	
Sex	2	
Total Genotypic		18
Environmental		
Maternal genotype	20	
Maternal environment, general	18	
Maternal environment, immediate	6	
Age of mother	1	
Parity	7	
Intangible	30	
Total Environmental		82

between mothers as sources of variation in infant birth weight. "Maternal environment, general," refers to non-genetic variation between mothers independent of any particular pregnancy. "Maternal environment, immediate" refers to sources of variation arising from the one maternal environment but as it differs in successive pregnancies. The other variables are self-explanatory.

Such partitioning is, of course, best accomplished in experimental populations over which control of breeding is possible. The most conventional scheme involves comparison of means and variances of pure-breeding parental strains, $F1$ and $F2$ and backcross hybrids. It is theoretically possible to obtain estimates of the several types of epistatic or non-allelic interactions, but to do so may require schemes more complex and laborious than the value of such information merits. Much the same is true for higher-order interactions between partitioned genotypic and environmental variances.

By and large, these methods have not as yet found very wide usage in behavior genetics. A notable exception is represented by the work of Broadhurst at the University of London. In collaboration with Jinks (139), he has recently summarized some of the biometrical methods of Mather and others and applied them to a number of sets of existing behavioral data. In addition, he has illustrated with his own animal data (138) the use of another different but related mode of analysis, the diallelic cross method. His papers perhaps mark the beginning of a new level of sophistication in work on animal behavior genetics.

With non-experimental, free-breeding populations, for example, human kinship groups, the possibilities of analysis are more limited. However, by calculating covariances between offspring and parents, between full sibs and between half-sibs, we may arrive at estimates of genotypic variances, including additive, dominance, and epistatic effects. Perhaps the major difficulty lies in properly isolating environmental variances. This is particularly important with environment-sensitive behavior traits. In fact, the large bulk of work done in behavior genetics using the family correlation method is of doubtful significance precisely because good estimates of environmental contribution to trait variance have not been available. Even more difficult to obtain in natural populations are estimates of genotype-environment relationships. Such relationships may be of two sorts. First, genotypes and environments may be correlated. It is highly likely, for example, that children with genetically high intelligence tend to come from more intellectually stimulating homes and that children with genetically low intelligence tend to come from intellectually restricting homes. Second, different genotypes may respond differently to the same environmental influences. An enriching environment, for example, may have a much greater effect on a bright child than on a dull child, or vice versa. An animal study by Hughes and Zubek (789) provides a ready example of this. These workers have reported that administration of glutamine markedly improves the maze-ability of dull rats but hardly affects that of bright animals. In other words, responsiveness to an environmental condition is dependent on, or interacts with, genotype. Other examples have been cited by Fuller and Thompson (568) and by Falconer (495).

The reader may well ask, at this point: just what is the point of partitioning variances in this way? What are the gains for psychology? Perhaps the answer to this question is that such a procedure allows us to locate the kinds of variables that are of major importance in molding those traits we are examining. In agriculture, this has obvious economic importance. There would be little point in breeding for desirable traits which have low heritabilities and therefore respond only very slowly to selection. Similarly, from the standpoint of basic science, it is of heuristic value to

know that some form of behavior is highly sensitive or relatively insensitive to environmental or genetic determination. Such knowledge can provide broad guidelines for future experimentation.

One of the more thorough attempts to apply the general method of partitioning variances to human behavioral data has recently been made by Cattell (248, 270, 330). Since the method involves inferring unknown or abstract variances from empirical or observed variances, he has christened the method *multiple abstract variance analysis*. As is usual in biometrical genetics, the method starts by expressing the phenotypic variance of a trait in terms of two major components plus the covariation between them:

$$V_P = V_G + V_E + 2\,cov_{GE}.$$

Further equations are then constructed by partitioning V_G and V_E in various ways and expressing them in terms of different observable variances. Cattell's so-called limited resources design contains ten such equations, his complete design involves seventeen. Table 23-4 gives his list of observable and abstract variances.

Two examples of the manner in which these are equated can be given as follows:

$$(1) \quad \sigma_{SA}^2 = \sigma_{wh}^2 + \sigma_{we}^2 + \sigma_{be}^2$$
$$+ 2r_{wh \cdot we}\,\sigma_{wh}\,\sigma_{we}$$
$$[+ 2r''_{wh \cdot be}\,\sigma_{wh}\,\sigma_{be}]$$

$$(2) \quad \sigma_{BBF}^2 = \sigma_{wh}^2 + \sigma_{we''}^2 + 2\sigma_{bh}^2$$
$$+ \sigma_{be}^2 + 2r_{wh \cdot we}\,\sigma_{wh}\,\sigma_{we}$$
$$+ 2\sqrt{2}\,r_{we \cdot bh}\,\sigma_{we}\,\sigma_{bh}$$
$$+ 2\sqrt{2}\,r''_{bh \cdot be}\,\sigma_{gh}\,\sigma_{re}$$
$$\cdot [+ 2r''_{wh \cdot be}\,\sigma_{wh}\,\sigma_{be}]$$

By using these together with the other equations, it becomes possible to solve for the unknown variances involved, plus at least some of the covariances between them. The methods available actually yield an indeterminate solution owing to the fact

TABLE 23-4

OBSERVABLE AND ABSTRACT VARIANCES USED
IN THE MULTIPLE ABSTRACT VARIANCE ANALYSIS
(Cattell, 248)

Abstract Variances	Observed Variances
1. σ^2_{we} = trait variance (between sibs) due to within-family environmental (*we*) variation. Incidentally, we assume that this variability of environment among children raised in the same family is essentially the same for all kinds of families, including normal and adoptive families. On the other hand in the special case of fraternal twins, who are of identical age, and identical, who, according to clinicians, have an urge to be more alike, or, in other opinions, more individualistic, we enter with special terms capable of discovering such differences, as follows:	1. $\sigma^2 ITT$ = variance in the trait as measured among identical twins reared together by their parents.
2. $\sigma^2_{we'}$ = trait variance within family associated with type of environmental difference peculiar to fraternal twins.	2. $\sigma^2 ITA$ = variance in the trait as measured among identical twins reared apart.
3. $\sigma^2_{we''}$ = trait variance within family associated with type of environmental difference peculiar to identical twins.	3. $\sigma^2 FTT$ = variance in the trait as measured among fraternal twins raised together by their true parents.
4. σ^2_{wh} = trait variance due to within-family heredity (*wh*) variation.	4. $\sigma^2 ST$ = variance in the trait as measured among ordinary siblings reared together by their parents.
5. σ^2_{be} = trait variance due to between-family environment (*be*) variation.	5. $\sigma^2 SA$ = variance in the trait as measured among ordinary siblings reared apart.
6. σ^2_{bh} = trait variance due to between-family hereditary (*bh*) variation.	6. $\sigma^2 UT$ = variance in the trait as measured among unrelated children reared together in one family with foster parents who are biological parents of none.
7. $r_{wh.we}$ = correlation between effects of within-family heredity and within-family environment (siblings).	7. $\sigma^2 UA$ = variance in the trait as measured among unrelated reared apart (general population).
8. $r'_{wh.we}$ = correlation of heredity and environment in adoptive families.	8. $\sigma^2 BITTF$ = variance in the trait as measured between the means of identical twin pairs in their true families.
9. $r'_{we.bh}$ = correlation of within-environment and between-heredity peculiar to adoptive families. A prime is placed on this *r* though there is no other $r_{we.bh}$ from which to distinguish it, because it helps classification to have all *r*'s peculiar to adoptive families marked with a prime.	9. $\sigma^2 BITAF$ = variance in the trait as measured between the means of identical twin pairs raised apart.
10. $r_{bh.be}$ = correlation between effects of between-family heredity and between-family environment. The frequently discussed correlation of "good" heredity with "good" environment among families is a possible instance.	10. $\sigma^2 BNF$ = variance in the trait as measured between the means of natural families, i.e., means of sib pairs (or trios, etc.) reared together.
	11. $\sigma^2 BBF$ = variance in the trait as measured between the means of biological families whose siblings are reared in different foster homes.
	12. $\sigma^2 BSF$ = variance in the trait as measured between the means of social families, i.e., adoptive families of biologically unrelated children.
	13. $\sigma^2 HST$ = variance in the trait as measured among half-siblings raised together.
	14. $\sigma^2 HSA$ = variance of half-siblings raised apart.

TABLE 23-4 (Continued)

OBSERVABLE AND ABSTRACT VARIANCES USED
IN THE MULTIPLE ABSTRACT VARIANCE ANALYSIS
(Cattell, 248)

Abstract Variances	Observed Variances
11. $r''_{wh.be}$ = placement agency correlation peculiar to sibs raised in different families, where within-family hereditary differences may become correlated with between-family environment by deliberate intention of social agencies in placing, e.g., brighter sib in more educated family.	15. $\sigma^2 BHSTF^5$ = variance in the trait as measured among means between half-siblings raised together by one true parent.
12. $r''_{bh.be}$ = placement agency correlation, through any systematic tendency to match biological family characters of adopted children to environmental characters of foster parent families.	16. $\sigma^2 BHSAF$ = variance of means between half-siblings raised apart.

of having too many unknowns. However, some of these can reasonably be dropped if they do not appear to represent any real situation. An example of such a term is the correlation between genetic deviation from family mean with genetic deviation of the family from the population mean. It does not seem likely that such a correlation would appear. Other covariance terms, however, cannot as readily be dropped. For example, the correlation between environmentally produced and genetically produced deviations within the family represents a possibility of considerable psychological importance, since it bears on the whole question of how a family tolerates, encourages, or discourages deviants.

Cattell has applied his method to the heritability of personality and intelligence using eleven source traits as measured by the Junior Personality Quiz administered to a group of 10−15-year-old children (330). The general results of this application are shown in Table 23-5.

Cattell and his co-workers have drawn several major conclusions from these data. First, most of the eleven traits showed a predominantly environmental determination both within and between families

though the correction proposed by Loehlin (940) would give a more even balance. The exceptions are A factor (sizothymia), H (now called parmia), and general intelligence, for which genetic factors are much more important determiners of variance across families than are environmental factors. This result is in line with the conclusions of Shuttleworth (1321) and of Burt (171). However, Vandenberg (1482) has recently obtained a very low heritability estimate for Cattell's general intelligence factor as measured in his Junior Personality Quiz. As Cattell and his associates have indicated (330), it is possible that the environmental variances are artificially large on account of rather low factor reliabilities. We will take up this point again later.

In the second place, variations due to within-family environment seemed to be somewhat more pronounced than those due to between-family environmental factors. According to the authors, "the results favor a psychologist's rather than a sociologist's view of the importance of environment" (Cattell, et al., 330, p. 154). Third, there appeared a tendency for deviation due to heredity to correlate negatively with deviations due to environment. The effect

TABLE 23-5

WITHIN- AND BETWEEN-FAMILY NATURE AND NURTURE VARIANCES FOR 11
PERSONALITY FACTORS

(Cattell, Stice, & Kristy, 330)

	Personality Source Traits: Universal Index Numbers										
	1	16	17	19	20	21	22	23	26	28	29
Value for $r_{be,bh}$	.25	no solution	−.51	−.28	−.53	.23	−.80	−.56	−.98	−.91	no solution
Most consistent value for r_{wewh}	.00	−.85	.10	−.20	−.60	−.10	.50	−.50	−.60	−.30	.50
σ^2_{we}	179.1	10.5	2.6	1.3	16.7	5.2	5.8	2.2	2.2	2.6	3.1
$\sigma^2_{we'}$	52.9	7.3	1.3	[0.2]*	15.1**	4.7	4.8	3.9	1.8	2.3	2.7
σ^2_{wk}	122.5	0.06	1.8	1.1	24.0	3.1	1.23	1.6	1.2	1.1	.5
σ^2_{be}	6.7	3.2	3.2	1.6	4.6	.4	2.3	5.8	3.1	3.7	3.4
σ^2_{bk}	83.3	[0]	1.0	.50	21.1	2.4	.9	1.0	.6	.7	[0]

*The only solution on this neighborhood is for $r_{be,bh}$ − 15 which is as shown.
**From 1st equation.

was somewhat less pronounced within the family and more pronounced between families. This result suggests that society exerts a pressure on genetically different individuals to conform to some kind of social mean but that the family is more permissive in this respect, relatively speaking.

In general, Cattell's work represents an interesting application of this general method of multivariate analysis to obtain estimates of the relative contribution of heredity and environment to variation in psychological traits. It is to be hoped that other workers in the field will start to follow Cattell's lead in making use of these kinds of tools.

The next problem to be considered arises from the complexity of behavior. As indicated previously, psychological traits are usually made up of an indefinite number of components. The following section will deal specifically with the question of defining such components and of deciding what kinds of genetic meaning they may have.

3. THE PROBLEM OF MEANING AND VALIDITY OF TRAIT MEASUREMENT

For the most part, classical Mendelian genetics dealt with highly stable and dis-crete characters. Interest was focused on mechanisms and their cytological basis. Consequently, it was logical enough to choose, for this purpose, marker traits whose identification and specification were easy. Thus, much of the original work done by Mendel and others and from which the basic laws of segregation and independent assortment were derived, was based on the transmission of readily available characters such as flower color, pod shape, and so on. Had complex and continuous traits been used instead, it is doubtful whether the beautifully simple and elegant basic principles of genetics would have emerged so readily.

In any case, the problem of phenotypic units never arose in early Mendelian genetics. It is, on the other hand, a central problem in behavior genetics. There are few, if any, obvious behavioral marker traits that intuitively compel our attention as does something like coloration or any other morphological character. Instead, we face a large spectrum of characteristics which vary continuously over a population and which may be taken in any one of a large number of combinations. As in much of the work on behavior, the choice of combinations seems to be quite arbitrary. Thus we may measure what we call "intelligence" or "personality" in many different ways, each of these having certain advantages or disadvantages. The axiom that most basic researchers in the field entertain, however, is that *there are basic traits underlying the complex phenotypes measured by ordinary tests.* Just as chemistry gains enormously in the economy of its explanations of matter by having the concepts of atom and molecule, so also the behavioral sciences should gain by discovering and utilizing analogous basic or natural units.

It was such an axiom that generated the technique of factor analysis. It is precisely the aim of this method to find those units out of which are compounded the complex behavior systems which we observe at a more superficial level by means of typical tests. In other terms, factor analysis is designed to reduce redundancy.

Now it is very clear that we have available very many ways of pulling out factors from a battery of tests. But it is also equally clear that we have no criteria, other than those that are purely mathematical, for deciding which of several sets of alternative factors make the "best sense," or are the most "natural" units. In the context of behavioral genetics, we may make a broad assumption about the relation between factors and genes, and hypothesize that factors will make more sense genetically than complex tests. The phrase "make sense" can be taken as meaning here—be more sensitive to manipulation by variables of a hereditary or environmental type. This

axiom has been held, at least implicitly, by Royce (1235), has been entertained by the writer (1392), and stated rather explicitly by Cattell (250). It is perhaps convenient to quote in full this last writer's statement of the case: "The position adopted in our own investigations [is] that the variance ratio for any factorially composite piece of behavior will be middling but that more clear-cut predominance of heredity or environment will be found for factor-pure source traits" (Cattell, 248, p. 370).

Royce's position can best be summarized by reference to his own diagram as shown in Diagram 23-1. Now, in point of fact, although such an axiom has a good deal of intuitive appeal, it is not one that has much empirical support, nor is it one that makes very much logical sense. Let us look at some of the empirical evidence. Table 23-6 shows a comparison between heritability estimates for (1) composite tests, (2) primary factor tests, and (3) second-order factor tests.

It may be noted in passing that not all the estimates obtained by Blewett (113) shown in the table correspond with those obtained by another worker, Vandenberg (1482). The two factors showing the greatest discrepancy are Number and Reasoning. Blewett's h^2 values for these are .07 and .64, respectively. Vandenberg, on the other hand, obtained values of .61 and .28. Consequently, there exists a good deal of ambiguity as to the heritability of different

TABLE 23-6

COMPARISON OF HERITABILITY ESTIMATES FOR COMPOSITE STANDARD TESTS, PRIMARY FACTORS, AND SECOND-ORDER FACTORS

Composite Tests		Primary Factors		Second-Order Factors*	
(Newman, et al., 1098)		(Blewett, 113)		(Blewett, 113)	
Test	h^2	P.M.A. Factor	h^2	Factor	h^2
Stanford-Binet	.73	Verbal	.68	Composite 1*	.339
Otis	.79	Space	.51	Composite 2*	.594
Stanford Achiev.	.61	Number	.07	Composite 3*	.549
		Reason	.64		
		Fluency	.64		

*The three composite factors are arrived at by slightly different methods (see Blewett, 113).

DIAGRAM 23-1. Royce's Concept of the Paths Between Genes and Behavior (from Royce, 1235)

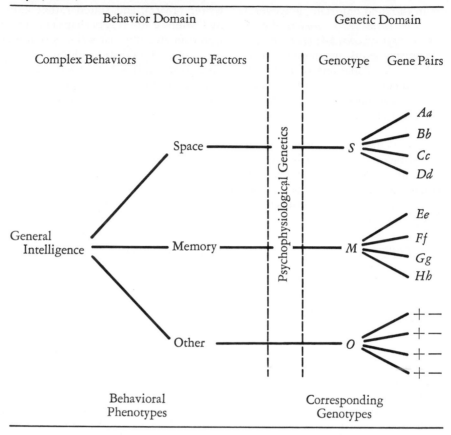

| Behavior Domain | | Genetic Domain |

| Complex Behaviors | Group Factors | Genotype Gene Pairs |

Behavioral Phenotypes

Corresponding Genotypes

factors. Some support for this action has been obtained by Eysenck and Prell, in their study (491) of the heritability of the Neuroticism factor (Cattell's U.I. 23, Regression). The evidence remains ambiguous, especially since the Cattell, Stice, and Kristy (330) study on larger samples shows lower inheritance for this factor.

If there are no empirical grounds for postulating a special kind of relation between factors and genes, neither are there any theoretical grounds. In point of fact, factors may have several kinds of meaning, as the writer has previously pointed out elsewhere (1392). Basically, factors are derived from the covariation between vari-

ables. It is assumed that two tests that correlate highly are, in some sense, measuring the same basic variable. Thus, to understand what possible meaning factors might have genetically, it is first necessary to explore the manner in which correlations between variables can be generated. There appear, in fact, to be four basic possibilities within the heredity-environment framework.

First, correlations may arise between variables if they depend on a common gene or common set of genes. There are many recorded instances of such pleiotropic effects, for example, the Ellis-Van-Crevald Syndrome in which a number of abnormalities, such as dwarfism, ectodermal defects, polydactyl, and others are all referable to one or a few genes (1051). When the genes are present, several phenotypic traits are also present. When the genes are absent, the traits also tend to be absent. In this sense, the traits are correlated and the correlation is dependent on a *genetic communality* between them. The hypothetical case is diagramed in Diagram 23-2.

In the same figure is shown the second possibility, which may be labeled *chromosomal communality*. In this case, the correlation between traits is due to the fact that each is carried by genes lying on the same chromosome, and as a consequence they tend to sort together. In large random-breeding populations, this may be of little importance, since, at equilibrium, the coupling and repulsion phases of the linked loci will usually be equally frequent, thus negat-

ing the correlation. However, effects of linkage may show up in cases where two smaller populations start to intermix. In this case, the stronger the linkage between the traits, the slower will be the approach of the loci to equilibrium frequency (495). Likewise, correlations due to linkage may be maintained where selection is occurring in respect to one of the linked traits.

The third meaning that a correlation between phenotypic units may have can be called *gametic communality*. This case arises when selection occurs for two traits simultaneously in such a way that the genes underlying certain quantities of these traits tend to be present together in gametes. Thus assortative mating in human populations might result in persons high in one type of ability mating with those high in another; for example, males high in mathematical ability might marry females high in

DIAGRAM 23-2.   Diagrammatic Representation of Genetic and Chromosomal Communality (from Fuller & Thompson, 568)

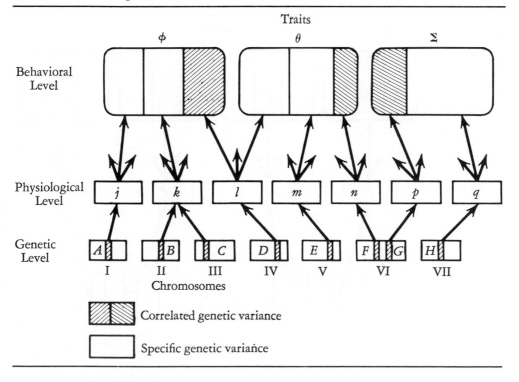

musical ability. Assuming those abilities are dependent on genes, then offspring should, on the average, show a correlation between musical and mathematical ability. In this case, the gamete would be the basis for the correlation between phenotypes, hence the designation gametic communality. The case is depicted in Diagram 23-3. It is difficult to know what influence this causal influence may have in producing correlations in natural human populations. It is known, however, that assortative mating does occur (1391), probably in respect to many traits simultaneously. Obviously, males and females are valued as mates for many reasons and not always for the same ones. Thus it is likely that in some societies strength and aggressiveness may be admired in males, beauty and grace in females. Depending on the heritability of these traits, and assuming an initial independence between them, we could expect to find a correlation arising between them over successive generations. The whole problem of genetic outcomes of different social breeding patterns in human populations is exceedingly interesting and important and has hardly been touched. One notable exception is the theoretical work of Halsey (680) on the effects of vertical social mobility in a stratified society on distribution of intellectual genotypes. A great deal of empirical work can be done here both with experimental and natural populations.

The final cause of correlation between traits is through common environment or *environmental communality*. Variation in some aspect of child-rearing practice, for example, the indulgence-severity dimension, might affect a number of variables of

DIAGRAM 23-3.   Diagrammatic Representation of Gametic Communality (from Fuller & Thompson, 568)

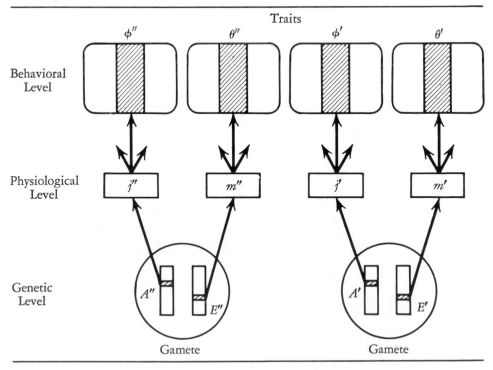

personality in such a way that correlations are generated between them. This cause may well be the most important cause of correlation in human populations. It will, of course, operate most successfully when one or both traits have low heritabilities and are thus environment-sensitive.

The four possible cases described are difficult to separate in practice. It is likely that in any given instance of two or more correlated traits, more than one causal influence contributes to the covariance. However, they can be sorted out without too much difficulty in experimental populations by manipulating assortative mating patterns, using crosses to test for linkage and pleiotropy, and, of course, by manipulating environmental influences. Sometimes, such a separation is important when a phenotypic correlation is assumed to imply some causal dependency of one trait on the other. A good case in point is the work of Krech and his co-workers (1222) showing a correlation in selected strains of rats between brightness and cholinesterase level. The authors have inferred from this that intelligence depends on this particular brain enzyme, the two being linked, presumably in a chain fashion, to genes. This would imply some kind of genetic correlation. However, analogous work with mice by Ginsburg strongly suggests that such a correlation reduces to zero in an $F2$ cross between strains high or low in each character. Such a result indicates that some caution is necessary before assuming causal relations of a genetic sort. Some may be spurious, others may be due to assortative mating or to common environmental pressures.

The general statement of the composition of a phenotypic correlation has been made by Lerner (923) as follows:

$$r_{AB} = e_A \, e_B \, r_{E_A E_B} + h_A \, h_B \, r_{G_A G_B}$$

where r_{AB} is the phenotypic correlation between traits A and B

h_A, h_B represents the degrees of hereditary determinations of A and B ($\sqrt{h^2}$)

e_A, e_B represents the degrees of environmental determinations of A and B ($\sqrt{1-h^2}$)

$r_{E_A E_B}$ is the correlation between A and B due to environmental causes

$r_{G_A G_B}$ is the correlation between A and B due to genetic causes.

It should be clear that there are no logical reasons for assuming as an axiom any particular relationship between genes and correlation, and hence between genes and factors. Consequently, we must look for possible ways of (1) uncovering the relative contribution of hereditary or environmental causes to the composition of factors; or, alternatively, (2) generating, by a particular methodology, factors in which one particular class of causes is maximally represented. Let us examine each of these possibilities.

As indicated in the equation of Lerner's given above, the covariation of two or more characters can be partitioned into components, much as in the case of the variation of single characters. The derivation of the equation is shown by Falconer (495), among others, and need not be reproduced here. Its essential feature, however, is that the contribution of the genetic covariance and the phenotypic correlation depends on the heritabilities of the two characters. The higher the heritability of each, the lower the environmental contribution; the lower the heritability of each, the higher the environmental contribution. Estimation of the component $r_{G_A G_B}$ is given by the following equation:

$$r_{G_A G_B} = \frac{Cov_{AB}}{\sqrt{Cov_{AA} \; Cov_{BB}}}.$$

Cov_{AB} is the cross-covariance of one trait in offspring with the other trait in parents; Cov_{AA} and Cov_{BB} are covariances of each trait in offspring with the same trait in parents. The regressions of trait values in offspring on their values in parents yields estimates of heritability (h^2). Knowing h^2 for each trait, we may obtain the values of e_A, e_B. The one remaining unknown, $r_{E_A E_B}$ is then estimated by subtraction.

The results of this partitioning of covariances between traits can sometimes yield surprising results. A few examples from Falconer (495) are shown in Table 23-7. It

TABLE 23-7

EXAMPLES OF PHENOTYPIC, GENETIC, AND ENVIRONMENTAL CORRELATIONS
(Falconer, 495)

Traits	Correlations		
	r_P	$r_{G_A G_B}$	$r_{E_A E_B}$
Milk Yield × Butterfat Yield in Cattle	.93	.85	.96
Body Length × Back-fat Thickness in Pigs	−.24	−.47	−.01
Fleece-weight × Body Weight in Sheep	.36	−.11	1.05
Body Weight × Egg Weight in Poultry	.16	.50	−.05

will be clear from these figures that a considerable range of variation is possible, both in respect to magnitude and direction of phenotypic, genetic, and environmental correlations. Consequently, it is equally obvious that factors extracted from a matrix of phenotypic correlations between a number of traits will not be the same as those extracted from a matrix of genotypic or environmental correlations. To the knowledge of the writer, no worker has attempted so far to compare the psychological composition of factors from such different sets of correlations. Such a project would be of importance in at least two ways. In the first place, it would represent a crucial step in defining the heritable limits of different behavioral traits. Second, it would also initiate a closer liaison between the rather abstract methods of

factor analysis and manipulable empirical variables. For too long, factor analysts have engaged themselves in endlessly extracting factors of almost limitless variety and often of strangely exotic quality. It seems high time that more concern be given to the job of relating factors to some sensible experimental frameworks. Without such an orientation, factor analysis is a dead-end pursuit.

An approach rather different from that described above, but having the same essential aim, is Eysenck's method of criterion analysis (473). This involved essentially the placement of a criterion test in a battery and the rotation of factors to maximal correlation with the criterion. In this way, the factors are made to reflect the criterion. Eysenck (473) has illustrated the method with reference to neuroticism, the criterion being defined in terms of presence or absence of psychiatric treatment. His suggestion that some criterion of heritability could be used in the same way seems a reasonable one, though this has not been tried so far. By the proper use of such a method, it should be possible to obtain factors that maximally reflect genotypic, or, on the other hand, environmental influences. However, this method does not seem to be in any way superior to the mode of analysis suggested previously. Furthermore, the latter has the additional advantage of relating to standard techniques in quantitative genetics. In either case, any attempt to relate factors to genes should probably be made, at least initially, with a limited number of tests and preferably with well-defined populations, perhaps animal ones over which a good control of genetic background and breeding patterns is possible.

4. THE FLUIDITY OF TRAITS: THE RELIABILITY AND STABILITY PROBLEM

It is characteristic of most behavioral traits that they are very likely to undergo fluctuation over time. Thus, repeated measurements of the same phenotype sometimes may give widely differing values. In any situation like this, several possibilities obtain. In the first place, an individual's score on some measure may deviate randomly over time. Such variation can be defined as error, and its estimation, in combination with the systematic variation occurring between individuals, yields the reliability coefficient. In classical test theory, the phenotypic or observed variation is thus made up of two parts as follows:

$$\sigma_x^2 = \sigma_t^2 + \sigma_e^2$$

where $\sigma_x^2 =$ observed variance, $\rightarrow$
$\qquad \sigma_t^2 =$ variance of true scores
$\qquad \sigma_e^2 =$ variance of error scores.
The reliability coefficient r_{xx} can be expressed in the form

$$r_{xx} = \frac{\sigma_t^2}{\sigma_t^2 + \sigma_e^2}$$

where the terms on the right side of the equation have the same meaning as before.

A second possibility that has been considered (248, 523, 1404), but not investigated very thoroughly, is that part of the within-individual fluctuation commonly regarded as random is actually systematic. Thus,

$$\sigma_x^2 = \sigma_t^2 + \sigma_f^2 + \sigma_e^2$$

where σ_f^2 refers to systematic fluctuations characteristic of the trait.

As Cattell has pointed out (248), there is every reason to suppose that numerous behavior traits show such "function-fluctuation," as Thouless calls it, and that this is not random but highly systematic. Biological drives, diurnal activity cycles, and perhaps even various types of personality characteristics may well be subject to such predictable temporal changes.

A third cause of deviation within the same individuals over time is the dependence of the phenotypic scores on different causal agencies at different testings. Most psychological tests are complex, as dis-cussed above, in the sense of being composed of a number of components. Time-dependent factors, such as maturational changes, or situational factors such as slightly altered conditions of testing, may produce alterations in the relative contribution of the different components to the total score, thus causing it to fluctuate over time. This happens even with physiological traits. Thus, milk yield in cattle as measured in successive lactations is not the same character, as shown by Rendel (1190). The result may be a spuriously low reliability coefficient, in spite of the fact that the actual genotypes underlying each measurement may themselves be quite stable.

In work on behavior genetics, we have the problem, in general, of separating out from each other these three possibilities, and, in particular, of relating each to genetic and environmental components of variance. Work on these problems will directly expedite the more basic aim of discovery of the paths between genes and behavior. In examining this problem we will first consider some methods commonly employed to increase accuracy of prediction by using repeated measurements. Following this, we will describe some empirical points of contact between the variability problem in genetics and in psychology.

The two major methods used in assessing reliability of measurement relate to the spatial or to the temporal aspects of the trait under consideration. Many morphological characters are represented more than once in an organism, for example, bristle length, wing venation, eye facet number, and many others. The analogue in psychological traits is the population of items being used to measure a particular trait. Thus, reliability is estimated from a comparison of two samples drawn from such a population and matched in respect to their statistical parameters. The two most commonly used methods are the method of equivalent tests and the split-half method. It is assumed — and this assumption can be tested — that the different phenotypic values are estimates of the same genotype. Similarly, many physical traits can be measured at different points in time, for example, litter sizes, ovary sizes, and many others. In psychology, this method is known as the test-retest method and is perhaps the most commonly used technique of estimating reliability.

Of main interest to our discussion here is the utility of these methods in partitioning the total variance into genetic and environmental components, and the gains in accuracy of such partitioning that may ensue from the use of multiple measurements.

The essential separation that is made by means of reliability coefficient is that between the effects of general, more permanent causes from specific local causes, for example, between the variance arising within individuals and that arising between these same individuals. The between-individuals variance is not, of course, to be assumed to be purely genetic. It represents, rather, the joint contribution of genetic and general environmental effects. The variance within individuals, unless there is reason to believe otherwise, can be identified with specific environmental effects. Sometimes, the contribution made by such local conditions can be very large, as illustrated in Table 23-8 by data cited by Falconer (495).

The most striking feature of these data is the large proportion of environmental

TABLE 23-8

RESULTS OF PARTITIONING VARIANCE OF
BRISTLE NUMBER IN DROSOPHILA,
USING ONE OR TWO
ABDOMINAL SEGMENTS
(Falconer, 495)

Point of Variance	Per Cent of Variance 1 segment	2 segments
Total phenotypic	100	100
Additive genetic	34	52
Non-additive genetic	6	9
Environmental, general	2	4
Environmental, special	58	35

effects due to specific local conditions. As Falconer (495) points out, selection has succeeded in eliminating a large part of the variation due to general environment causes, but the special environmental effects remaining still contribute over a third of the total variance. Whether the development of such environment-sensitive traits may have basic evolutionary significance presents an interesting problem to which we will return later.

A second important point shown in the data of Table 23-8 lies in the fact that the use of repeated measurements produces an increase in the relative contribution of more stable general environmental and genetic sources of variance by reducing the contribution of special environment. This represents a gain in accuracy. Falconer's equational statement of this in the terms of quantitative genetics, is as follows (495):

$$\frac{V_{p(n)}}{V_p} = \frac{1 + r(n - 1)}{r}$$

where $V_{p(n)}$ = total phenotypic variance of trait measured in a number of individuals r times.

V_p = total phenotypic variance of trait measured once in a number of individuals.

n = number of measurements.

r = correlation between measurements of the same individual.

It will be recognized that the equation is a derivation of the classical Spearman-Brown formula relating reliability and test length:

$$R = \frac{nr}{1 + (n - 1)r}$$

where R = new reliability after test length is increased n times.

n = factor by which test length is increased.

r = reliability of test when $n = 1$.

The derivation from the Spearman-Brown to Falconer's formula is as follows:

$$R = \frac{nr}{1 + (n - 1)r}$$

$$\therefore \quad \frac{r}{R} = \frac{1 + r(n - 1)}{n}$$

now $\quad r = \dfrac{V_t}{V_p}$

and $\quad R = \dfrac{V_{t(n)}}{V_{p(n)}}$

But where the variances of true scores on the test of unit length (V_t) and of true scores on the test lengthened r times ($V_{t(n)}$) are assumed to be equal,

$$rV_p = RV_{p(n)}$$

$$\therefore \quad \frac{r}{R} = \frac{V_{p(n)}}{V_p}.$$

Then, from the Spearman-Brown formula,

$$\frac{V_{p(n)}}{V_p} = \frac{1 + r(n - 1)}{n}.$$

Note that the equation of Falconer depends on the assumption that the variance is reduced by taking multiple measurements and that only the error portion (or special environmental component) of the total variance is involved in this reduction. Accuracy can also be increased by increasing the proportional contribution of the true variance, in this case, that due to general environmental or genetic factors, while keeping error constant. However, Falconer's equation does not hold true under these circumstances.

Finally, as we have already indicated, any gains in precision that accompany multiple measurements depend on the assumption that the same character is being measured. From a mensural standpoint, the sole available criterion of whether this is in fact occurring is the size of the correlation coefficient. Furthermore, even when this is high, either the genetic or general environmental components could have theoretically diminished as a result of taking the means of several measurements, provided the reduction in one is accompanied by a rise in the other. Many situations are thus possible. For example, a trait that appears to be highly heritable in one measurement, and that shows high reliability on a retest, might show, when expressed in terms of the average of more than one testing, low heritability and predominantly general environmental determination.

5. THE FLUIDITY OF TRAITS: RELATIONS TO LEARNING AND GENETIC ASSIMILATION

Whether all possibilities actually occur in nature is not known. However, at this point, we may turn to a few cases which may illustrate some of the empirical and theoretical problems arising from the fluid character of behavior traits.

My first case has to do with the relation between learning, reliability, and heritability. Learning ability can be looked on as the result of genetic selection for a trait of environment-responsiveness, but of responsiveness that is systematic rather than random. That is to say, the changes that we call learning, occurring in a population, occur in a direction common to most individuals. Thus all tend to respond more quickly, or faster, or with fewer "mistakes." Forgetting or unlearning is a similar kind of predictable change, and is one which may also have adaptive value. Thus while it may be generally useful for an organism to learn, for example, that food is not commonly present in certain parts of its territory, it is obviously disadvantageous to do so too thoroughly in an environment so changeable that the occurrence or non-occurrence of food in parts of it is not completely predictable. Under certain conditions, a combination of rapid learning and rapid forgetting may have the most adaptive value.

Now it appears to be true, at least in certain cases of learning, that reliability increases with additional trials given. In other words, error, or variation arising from environmental conditions special to each trial, seems to diminish. If this is true, we might hypothesize that *either* general environmental or genotypic contributions to variance will increase, or possibly both. We have available rather little empirical data on this point. In one experiment by Fuller and Scott (567), however, no relationship between reliability and heritability was found. Their data are shown in Diagram 23-4.

DIAGRAM 23-4. Relation Between Reliability and Heritability in a Series of Learning Trials in Five Dog Breeds (from Fuller & Thompson, 568)

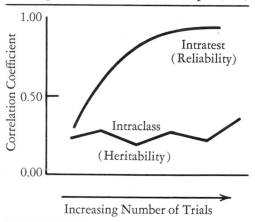

Unfortunately, it was not reported whether the relative constancy of heritability, as measured by intraclass conditions, was due to a simple lack of fluctuation in the size of both between and within variances, or was maintained by simultaneous fluctuations in both. This would be interesting to know.

Thus, more data are needed on this problem. It is an exceedingly important one theoretically, since it bears on the whole question of time-course and strength of gene expressivity. Some genetic mechanisms of adaptation (such as learning or habituation) may be slow and gradual in expressing themselves fully. But they may have, in the long run, much greater adaptive value than modes that are very rapidly

and fully expressed after minimal exposure to an environment. It seems impossible, at present, to arrive at any general conclusion about this matter. The outcome in particular species will depend presumably on the features of the ecological niche it occupies. There is room here for some truly comparative work on behavior.

The second case relevant to the problem of behavior fluidity is that of genetic assimilation. A phenomenon demonstrated by Waddington and some of his students at Edinburgh (1491), genetic assimilation involves essentially the selection of a population maximally responsive to environment in respect to the expression of a certain trait. Thus the example shown in Diagram 23-5 from Falconer (495) illustrates the transition from a base *drosophila* population, in which a character (cross-veinless) is induced only under special environmental circumstances by administering heat-shock to pupae, to a selected population in which the character appears in a large proportion "spontaneously." What has been altered is essentially the threshold of response of the genotype to environment.

So far as the writer knows, little work has been done on the degree to which such responsiveness is general or confined to particular traits. Certainly, as Mayr (1002) has pointed out, it may well be that a character like cross-veinlessness has itself little adaptive significance, but may simply be a pleiotropic side-effect arising from a more basic or general change. If this is so, then, it is possible that in higher animals the development of learning ability is also a case of genetic assimilation — that is, the evolutionary selection of a high degree of general environment-responsiveness that results in those subtle neural and chemical changes that are thought to underlie learning and memory. Thus a selected line of "maze-bright" rats may simply represent a population that contains individuals with a lower threshold of sensitivity than that characteristic of individuals in a "maze-dull" line. Such a possibility — namely, that individuals vary genetically in their responsiveness to environment—brings me to my final case. This relates to the problem of genetic homeostasis and heterosis.

It appears to be empirically true that more heterozygous genetic populations often have a survival advantage over populations that are more inbred. This advantage may be expressed in terms of various size characteristics, disease resistance, offspring viability, and others (922). It is not unreasonable to suppose that analogous gains may also occur at the behavioral level.

as large as that appearing in the $F2$. Assuming homozygosity of the parental strains, we might then suppose that the effect of heterosis was not to increase mean performance but rather to increase environment-responsiveness in the hybrids. Since we know nothing of the composition of the $F1$ variance, we cannot affirm that Caspari's suggestion is right. Only in a few other studies are there data that bear on this interesting problem. In some of these, the $F1$ variance has been smaller than that of the parents (806), but in others, it has

DIAGRAM 23-5. Diagrammatic Illustration of Genetic Assimilation of a Threshold Character (from Falconer, 495)

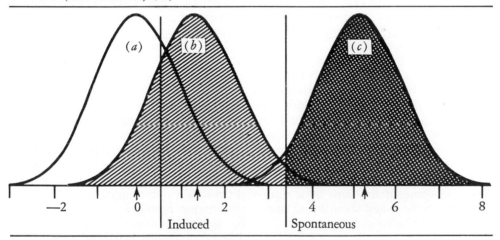

Distributions on the underlying scale, which is marked in standard deviations. The vertical lines show the positions of the induced and spontaneous thresholds, and the arrows mark the population means at three stages of selection.

(*a*) before selection: incidence—induced = 30%, spontaneous = 0%
(*b*) after some selection: incidence—induced = 80%, spontaneous = 2%
(*c*) after further selection: incidence—induced = 100%, spontaneous = 95%

However, it is not so easy to predict a priori just what form this might take in any particular case. Caspari (197) has suggested that it might well be expressed in terms of increased variability. To support this hypothesis he has cited Tryon's results on the genetics of maze-ability in rats (568). These data showed that the variability of an $F1$ cross between the dull and bright lines was

been larger (1280, 1479). Obviously, increased variability in one form of behavior may be useful, but in other forms decreased variability may be of greater advantage. Furthermore, the adaptive value of either an increase or a decrease will depend greatly on the uniformity of the niche which the genotype happens to occupy. Thus Chance (340) has argued that the highly variable, convulsive-like behavior shown by deer-mice in nature is precisely what protects them from the unpredictable attacks of predators. It is equally true, on the other hand, that the highly stereotyped chemical defense mechanisms of many insect species (454) are equally effective ways of coping with natural enemies. Clearly, the matter is as complex as it is important. At this stage of our knowledge, more empirical data will be necessary before we can start to make any very firm generalizations.

The three cases described should illustrate the richness of the general relationship between behavior fluidity and heritability that we have been exploring. It seems clear that, as with the other two problems discussed previously, many kinds of experimental possibilities lie open. Work on them will be feasible only through the close cooperation of geneticists and behavioral scientists and by the general training of researchers with interdisciplinary skills and interests. Judging from the amount of activity now going on in the field, I think we will soon see behavior genetics emerging as a very important area of study—one, in fact, in which we may well expect to find answers to some of the most basic questions that can be asked about living organisms and their behavior.

6. SUMMARY

Like other interdisciplinary fields, behavior genetics can offer unique opportunities for research and theory. If these are to be properly realized, it is essential that the fact-gathering orientation which has characterized the development of the field up to the present now be supplemented by attempts to locate crucial theoretical problems of interest both to the behavioral scientist and to the geneticist. To the writer, such problems appear to arise from precisely those properties of behavior that make it a difficult subject matter for genetic analysis. These properties are: (1) the continuous character of behavior; (2) the complexity of behavior, i.e., its potentiality for division into many different kinds and numbers of "natural" units; (3) the fluidity of behavior, i.e., its tendency to undergo both systematic and random fluctuations over time. Each of these properties generates problems that can best be handled by means of multivariate analysis.

Treatment of continuous characters focuses primarily on the goal of partitioning the total observable variance of a continuing trait into genetic and environmental components and subcomponents of each of these. This has found wide application in agricultural genetics, but rather little for behavioral traits, Cattell's work with his multiple abstract variance analysis being a significant exception in this regard.

The complexity of behavior raises questions that comes under the psychometrician's rubric of validity. One of the major techniques used in psychology for discovering these basic units that underlie complex traits is factor analysis. Several writers have accordingly entertained the notion that factors may be more suitable to genetic analysis than composite tests. However, such a postulate is not supportable either theoretically or empirically. Thus, any phenotypic correlation is generated both by genetic and environmental agencies. Therefore, factors extracted from a matrix of genetic correlations need not be the same as those extracted for a matrix of environmental correlations. On the empirical side, heritability estimates obtained from factors (e.g., P.M.A. scores) are little different from those obtained by using tests (e.g., Stanford-Binet). Accordingly, the behavior geneticist should work either with correlations known by independent criteria to reflect the operation of genetic or environmental determinants, or else, as in Eysench's criterion analysis, extract from phenotypic correlations factors obtained by rotation to pre-established criteria.

The third feature of behavior, its fluidity, or changeability over time, entails problems of reliability. Both physical and behavioral traits fluctuate both randomly and systematically over time and space. Specification of these sources of variation allows greater accuracy in estimating the genetic and environmental variance components for these traits. Aside from its methodological importance, the fluidity problem has significance and interest in its own right. Three examples of experimental work dealing directly with it are (a) the analysis of the relation between heritability and learning; (b) genetic assimilation and the inheritance of threshold characters; (c)

heterosis and variability. These and other related lines of work pose important theoretical problems for the behavior geneticist.

In conclusion, we may emphasize the notion that behavior genetics is more than simply an aspect of genetics or an aspect of psychology. Like physiological psychology, it has it own special problems created by combining two disciplines. The issues discussed in this paper are examples of these kinds of problems. Theoretical and experimental analyses of them should contribute greatly both to psychology and to genetics.

CHAPTER **24** Child Personality and
Developmental
Psychology

RICHARD W. COAN
University of Arizona

1. THE NECESSITY OF MULTIVARIATE DESIGNS FOR DERIVING DEVELOPMENTAL LAWS

In the realm of developmental psychology lie some of the most complex issues with which psychologists have ever concerned themselves. If we seek to understand the gross changes which occur in the behavior and experience of an individual, we must first gain an understanding of his behavior and experience as an organized totality. To do this, we must be able to discern both the interrelationships that provide an organic unity to the behavioral system at any point in time and those that underlie its longitudinal integrity over periods of many years. If we then seek to discover the sources of behavioral changes, we are faced with the prospect of relating these changes both to an immensely complicated system of biological processes and to an entire world of social and physical influences that impinge on the individual over a period of time. To complicate matters further, the biological and social

determinants are not strictly independent influences on behavior but may interact in a variety of ways.

If our research is to do justice to the problems of developmental psychology, it must be recognized from the outset that little can be done to clarify these problems if our methods are confined to the simple forms of experimental design that have been so successful in the older sciences. In view of the multiplicity of interacting determinants, we cannot expect to learn much about maturation or constitutional influences from research that relates specific acts or functions to specific anatomical structures, and we cannot expect to decipher the role of environmental influences on development by research that relates specific responses to specific stimuli. Special problems in developmental research arise not only from the complexity of the basic influences, but also from the difficulty in subjecting them to control. Classical experimental methods require us to hold constant all but one specific influence, which we vary systematically as an independent variable. Because of the practical realities of human development in a normal social setting, the necessary experimental control is unattainable.

These difficulties have been generally recognized by developmental psychologists, who, on the whole, have attempted in their work to retain a global picture of the behaving and experiencing organism. Thus, instead of classical experimental research, we find descriptive tabulations of behavior and the limited experimental control commonly introduced in child laboratory observation and group-comparison studies. If we consider both the work done in America and that done in Europe, we see evidence of considerable interest in gathering data on the kinds of behavior most directly important for an understanding of human development.

Unfortunately, it is not clear that all this data-collecting has yielded quite the rich harvest of theoretical insights that one might expect from the amount of effort it has entailed. Much of what passes for developmental theory is essentially inductive summarization of profusely tabulated trends. This kind of descriptive generalization is, of course, an essential part of scientific theory construction. But adequate "explanation" of developmental phenomena demands more extensive formulation of functional relationships. We find such theorizing in the developmental area, but most of it seems only remotely connected to the realm of research observation. While the theorist may have spent years collecting developmental data, it is often difficult to see what basis the data furnish for the theoretical speculation that ultimately emerges. And once the theory has been formulated, it is likely to be regarded by the theorist as a *fait accompli*, rather than something to be revised and refined in the light of tested predictions derived from it. The basic problem here is not that the basic concepts and issues of developmental theory are uniquely intangible. It is rather that, after rejecting the inappropriate techniques of classical experimentation, developmental investigators have failed generally to develop and utilize the research tools they need to form a sound bridge between observation and theory.

The kind of resistance to this requisite of progress that is all too prevalent in the developmental area is well expressed by one of the most brilliant American leaders in this area:

"It seemed to us impractical and even unprofitable to subject all these varied clinical records to statistical analysis. The variables are too numerous and diversified to be crowded into homogeneous categories" (589).

It is, of course, precisely because of the multiplicity and diversity of the variables that we must make much greater use of statistical analysis if we hope to make sense of our data. But statistical analysis does not require that our variables be "crowded into homogeneous categories" any more than does the conceptual analysis that we ultimately apply with or without statistical tools. What the developmental investigator may properly demand are research techniques that permit him to study his phenomena in their full-blown complexity, without the artificial distortion that rigid experimental controls might introduce. It is the methods of multivariate experimentation and multivariate statistical analysis that are designed to serve this purpose — that are designed to do much more systematically what the developmental investigator has been trying to do without their aid.

To this date, only a beginning has been made in the application of multivariate methods to developmental psychology. In this chapter, we shall first examine the relevant work that has been done. It can be seen that this has been confined largely to the use of designs that have proven their worth in other areas of research. We shall then consider some problems of human development that demand innovations in method. Finally, we shall examine possible lines of approach that may prove fruitful in the solution of these and other problems.

It will be evident that the topics of this

chapter require familiarity with the theory of change score measurement in Chapters 11 and 12, as well as, of course, the Data Box and factor-analytic approaches of Chapters 1, 2, 3, and 6. Links should also be made between the long-term processes studied here and the short-time process changes in the chapter by Mefferd (Chapter 22). Since so much in personality has been traced to early childhood, and to infancy, only to prove in the end to belong to pre-infancy — indeed, to genetics — it would be a good plan to include Thompson's Chapter 23 in the unit of developmental study. (The chapters are placed in succession for this reason.) Finally, of course, a thorough familiarity with Chapter 19 on personality study in general would be advantageous.

2. THE DESIGN OF CROSS-SECTIONAL STUDIES OF CHILD PERSONALITY STRUCTURE

The most extensive application of multivariate exploration to this area is that of Cattell and various colleagues, in America and abroad, who have conducted cross-sectional studies of personality structure at several levels of childhood. It is hoped that an integration of this and other work in its implications for developmental psychology will be published by Cattell and the present writer in the near future. The methods have generally followed the over-all pattern of earlier research at the adult level. The history and the results of the methods and models in relation to adult personality structure are summarized in book form (240) and in Chapter 19 by Pawlik.

The comparative ease of getting reliable measures on adults dictated that structural research should take a "downward" course. From the adult level, attention was first shifted to the 11-to-14-year range (290, 291, 292). Later, investigations were undertaken at the 6-to-8-year level (274, 275, 276, 277, 351, 352) and at the 4-to-6-year level (309, 310, 1153). Since the

completion of the original investigations at these three age levels, a considerable amount of work has been done to clarify and refine some of the findings from them, to determine relationships among findings at the three different age levels, and to provide relevant evidence at additional age levels.

In each of the three basic child research projects, there was an attempt to gain a comprehensive picture of personality structure. In each case, a large sample of children was subjected to a great variety of measurements. In an effort to cover the "personality sphere," the researchers extensively sampled personality variables in each of three measurement media: the life-record medium (via behavior ratings and time sampling), the questionnaire medium, and the objective-test medium. At each level of childhood thus studied, the basic procedure of analysis consisted of the separate application of conventional R-technique factor analysis to the data yielded by each form of measurement and a rotation of the resulting factors to oblique simple structure.

The interpretation of the rotated factors is, of course, a very crucial step. The extent to which we can derive satisfactory generalizations from this work about child personality structure, and the changes that occur in it, depends on our success in identifying the factors found at each age level and relating them to factors found at other age levels. The problem of aligning factors from different age levels is complicated by the fact that very few measurement variables — in any of the three media — can be used over a wide age range. To provide a basis for objective ratings, behavior-rating variables must be expressed in terms of concrete behavior, which changes in form with age. Questionnaire items must be gauged to fit both the level of verbal development and the characteristic activities of the age level. Most objective tests must be altered drastically as they are moved from one age level to another. Only a few of them, like the reaction-time measures, require a minimum of revision. The more distant the age levels, the greater the difficulty we will necessarily face in trying to align factors, even if the factors are psychologically identical.

It is a common practice to interpret factors simply on the basis of the apparent common content of highly loaded variables. This is undoubtedly a useful procedure, if only as a means of arriving at a first approximation to interpretation. The validity of this first approximation depends both on the perceptiveness of the interpreter and the nature of the variables. When we are dealing with factors derived from personality measurements, this procedure can yield quite erroneous interpretations. This is most obviously true in the case of questionnaire factors, since we cannot assume that the subject, in his responses to questionnaire items, is giving us a literally valid statement of his behavior. It is more likely that he is presenting a picture of himself as he perceives himself, shaded a bit to resemble the person he would like to be and the person he believes others would find most acceptable. Behavior-rating factors provide a sounder basis for direct interpretation, though we must constantly bear in mind many possible ways in which they may be affected by the values and perceptual framework of the rater. We might well expect objective-test factors to furnish the most satisfactory basis for direct interpretation, since the loaded variables are relatively free from the influence of those biases that distort the meaning of questionnaire and rating items. Even here there are difficulties, however, for going from a pattern of objective-test performances to a basic dimension running through all behavior can involve a rather sizable inductive leap, and the direction of the leap may depend on a large number of theoretical assumptions one has been forced to make in relating loaded variables to one another.

Probably the most satisfactory, though not the most economical, way of isolating stable factors and arriving at optimal interpretations of them is to conduct a series of independent factor studies, in the course of which the test battery is systematically augmented. At each stage, the investigator can assign hypothetical interpretations to the current set of factors on the basis of accumulated evidence and then select additional test variables whose predicted loadings will provide a test of the hypotheses. In the absence of such extensive replications with the measures used at any given age level, there are certain other interpretive guides which can be used and which have been used in the work of Cattell and his collaborators. First, one can check the pattern of marker variables. Marker variables are salient, or highly loaded, variables which are carried from one factor study to another as a basis for identifying recurrent factors. In the child studies, such marker variables were adapted from the adult batteries for use at the 11-to-14-year level, and from work at this level and at the adult level, marker variables were derived for use at the lower age levels.

A second guide to interpretation is provided by the relationships among factors. Within a single system of obliquely rotated factors, there are characteristic intercorrelations among factors that will tend to remain fairly fixed over a series of replicated studies. At a previously unexplored age level, these known interrelationships provide helpful clues, though one has to allow for age changes in factor intercorrelations. The correlations of one set of factors with factors derived from other media is somewhat more useful. In each medium there will be factors that are easy to interpret and factors that are difficult to interpret. The recognized cross-medium relationships provide a basis for resolving ambiguities in each medium of measurement.

A third guide that has been consistently applied to questionnaire factors in the Cattell research is provided by cross-age comparisons. At each childhood level that has been examined, a standard question-naire instrument has been constructed on the basis of the factor research to measure the factors that have emerged. Two such sets of questionnaire scales, designed for different age levels, can be administered to a group of intermediate age for the sake of comparison. The resulting correlations be-tween the two instruments provide an indirect basis for aligning the two sets of factors on which they are based.

A fully satisfactory examination of devel-opmental trends in personality structure would require longitudinal study. The same large sample of individuals would have to be tested successively at various points in the course of development. With the aid of the techniques described above, however, we can make some relevant generalizations on the basis of Cattell's cross-sectional studies. Perhaps the most outstanding find-ing is that we need about the same number of dimensions to account for personality structure at every age level that has been studied. Even in early childhood, we must deal with over a dozen factors in each measurement medium. We may find a decreasing number of clearly interpretable factors as we move to lower age levels, but the reasons for this are methodological. For reasons already noted, it is difficult to align lower-age factors with adult factors. For practical reasons, furthermore, it has been necessary to restrict the length of question-naire and objective-test batteries used at lower age levels. Thus, we are forced to interpret the resulting factors on the basis of limited sets of salient variables.

A second generalization, which rests less firmly on established fact, is that essentially the same factors appear at all age levels in each medium. Of course, there are inevita-ble changes in the forms of expression, and there is also considerable evidence that systematic changes occur for all children in the level of some of the factors. Some factors show systematic increase, as do the ability factors, while others show systematic

decrease. In a few others, there are oppo-site trends for boys and girls.

At each level, it has been found that the behavior-rating and questionnaire factors parallel each other rather closely, most of the factors appearing in either medium having counterparts in the other medium. At the same time, the objective-test factors seem to reflect something distinctly differ-ent and to bear a rather complicated relationship to the factors in the behavior-rating and questionnaire realms. This is basically the state of affairs that Cattell (240) has amply described with regard to adult factors.

3. THE MAIN FUNCTIONAL UNITIES IN BEHAVIOR FOUND AT THE CHILD LEVEL

There is not sufficient space here to describe all the factors that have appeared in child studies of personality structure. For such description, the reader must refer to other sources beginning with Chapter 19 above. But we may list, by title, the personality factors originally found at the adult level that have been isolated at all three of the childhood levels at which major studies have been conducted, noting for purposes of cross-reference the letters and numbers in terms of which they have been indexed in other publications. The following factors have been found consist-ently in either the questionnaire medium or the life-record medium or in both:

1. Affectothymia vs. sizothymia—A, U.I. (L) 1, U.I. (Q) 1
2. Ego strength vs. general emotion-ality —C, U.I. (L) 3, U.I. (Q) 3
3. Excitability-insecurity—D, U.I. (L) 4, U.I. (Q) 4
4. Dominance vs. submissiveness—E, U.I. (L) 5, U.I. (Q) 5
5. Surgency vs. desurgency—F, U.I. (L) 6, U.I. (Q) 6
6. Superego strength—G, U.I. (L) 7, U.I. (Q) 7

7. Parmia (parasympathetic immunity) vs. threctia (threat reactivity) — H, U.I. (L) 8, U.I. (Q) 8

8. Premsia (sensitive emotionality) vs. harria (toughness) — I, U.I. (L) 9, U.I. (Q) 9

9. Coasthenia (thinking neurasthenia) — J, U.I. (L) 10, U.I. (Q) 10

10. Acculturation — K, U.I. (L) 11, U.I. (Q) 11

11. Protension (paranoid trend) vs. inner relaxation — L, U.I. (L) 12, U.I. (Q) 12

12. Guilt proneness vs. confidence — O, U.I. (L) 15, U.I. (Q) 15

13. Self-sentiment strength — $Q3$, U.I. (Q) 17

14. Ergic tension — $Q4$, U.I. (Q) 18

The following factors have been found consistently in the objective-test medium:

1. Harric assertiveness — U.I. (T) 16
2. Inhibition — U.I. (T) 17
3. Hypomanic smartness — U.I. (T) 18
4. Critical practicality — U.I. (T) 19
5. Comention — U.I. (T) 20
6. Exuberance — U.I. (T) 21
7. Cortertia vs. Pathemia — U.I. (T) 22
8. Neural reserves vs. regression — U.I. (T) 23
9. Anxiety — U.I. (T) 24
10. Self-sentiment control — U.I. (T) 26
11. Asthenia — U.I. (T) 28

To see more directly some of the transformations that can appear in the expression of a factor as we compare findings from different age levels, we may examine the salient variables for one of the above factors. Below are set forth a few of the variables that are most highly loaded by the rating factor of Dominance vs. Submissiveness at each of four age levels:

Salient variables at the adult level:

1. Self-assertive, confident, vs. submissive, unsure
2. Boastful, conceited, vs. modest, retiring
3. Aggressive, pugnacious, vs. complaisant
4. Extrapunitive, vs. impunitive, intropunitive

5. Vigorous, forceful, vs. meek, quiet
6. Willful, egotistical, vs. obedient
7. Rather solemn or unhappy, vs. lighthearted, cheerful
8. Adventurous, vs. timid, retiring

Salient variables at the 11-to-14-year level:

1. Is sure of himself, vs. is not sure of himself
2. Is jealous, vs. is not jealous
3. Is selfish, vs. thinks of others
4. Wants a lot of attention, vs. does not need a lot of attention
5. Is mean when others do better, vs. never gets mean
6. Talks a lot, vs. says very little
7. Does not care what happens to his group, vs. wants to do his share for the group
8. Is only interested in himself, vs. is interested in what others think

Salient variables at the 6-to-8-year level:

1. Complains a lot, hard to satisfy, vs. rarely complains
2. Aggressive, tends toward fighting, bullying, teasing, cruelty, vs. nonaggressive, kind, considerate
3. Has practically no fears at all, vs. has many fears, for example, of the dark, of animals, strangers, doctors, etc.
4. Has no fear of the dark, vs. afraid of the dark
5. Has frequent temper tantrums, vs. seldom or never has temper tantrums
6. Adventurous, bold, willing to take a chance, vs. very retiring, cautious
7. Negativistic, stubborn, disobedient, discourteous, argumentative, "poor sport," vs. cooperative, compliant, courteous with children and adults
8. Talkative, distracting in class, vs. quiet

Salient variables at the 4-to-5-year level:

1. Shows off, vs. does not show off
2. Egotistical, vs. self-effacing
3. Unhappy unless with others, vs. prefers to be alone
4. Assertive, vs. submissive
5. Not prone to daydream, vs. prone to daydream

6. Toilet trained early, vs. toilet trained late

7. Unconscientious, vs. conscientious

8. Gregarious, vs. self-contained

The essential ontogenetic continuity of the factor represented by these lists is strongly supported by statistical evidence. In comparing them, we find a persistent theme of self-assertion that seems to emerge at the positive pole regardless of age level. Indeed, considering the evidence at all four stages, we might ask whether "self-assertion" would not be a better label for the underlying source trait than "dominance." It is apparent that at lower age levels, at least, the basic tendency of the high scorer is more likely to lead to social friction than to successful dominance. There are also some differences among the four lists that illustrate some of the difficulties we experience in trying to decipher developmental trends through comparison of cross-sectional slices. Undoubtedly, some of these differences stem directly from the underlying facts of personality development, while others are simply a function of our methods, and we must identify the latter before we can make useful generalizations about the former.

One methodological complication affecting the above data is that the 11-to-14-year variables are derived from an analysis of peer ratings, while those at the lower age levels are based on analyses of teacher ratings and parent ratings. Child peer ratings tend to yield a somewhat simplified factor structure, and there is reason to believe that this accounts for admixtures of sizothymia and protension in the 11-year factor of dominance. The effect of item selection on the apparent content of a factor is illustrated by the relatively marked aggressiveness of the 6-year factor. As it happens, the rating batteries for that age level were constructed with a view toward illuminating the basis in personality structure of various behavioral and emotional disorders. Hence, they contained a relatively rich sampling of symptomatic elements.

In addition to differences arising from variations in item selection and method of gathering data, there may be differences stemming from variations in such things as completeness of extraction and rotation. Careful work will minimize these, but complete elimination of them is a virtual impossibility, and their influence is very difficult to assess. Thus, we see that the 4-year factor is notably lacking in the aggressive element and that it contains a kind of sociability (unhappy unless with others, gregarious) not found elsewhere. Only further investigation can tell us whether such peculiarities properly indicate that in its initial expression the factor is of a relatively benign nature or whether, on the other hand, they stem from circumstances confined to the one study that has been conducted at the early-childhood level.

4. THE NATURE OF PARENTAL BEHAVIOR

Multivariate techniques have been applied to a variety of problems that border on the area of child development. There is not sufficient space here to review all these applications, but we might consider one important area that has received considerable attention—the area of parental behavior and attitudes. This is particularly basic to an understanding of the child's development because it involves the most fundamental class of social environmental determinants. During the first decade of this century, Freud came to realize that the most important social influences in personality development were not those that appeared in relatively isolated traumatic events but those which operated in the enduring parent-child relationships existing over long periods of time. Since that time, developmental theorists have shown increasing recognition of a need for a global understanding of the parent-child relationship. Sometimes this quest for global insight has led to an oversimplified treatment of the relationship in terms of a single underlying dimension of love, authoritarianism, etc., with the result that certain constellations of parental behavior have been overemphasized to the exclusion of others that are equally common.

Undoubtedly, the most thoroughly documented finding of multivariate research on this problem is that it is necessary to distinguish at least two basic dimensions of child-rearing behavior — a dimension of acceptance vs. rejection, or love vs. hostility, and a dimension of control vs. permissiveness. Since these two dimensions are essentially independent of each other, any theoretical treatment that collapses them into a single dimension of, say, rejecting authoritarianism vs. accepting permissiveness inevitably obscures the basic issues. Much of the confusion of recent years over the virtues of permissiveness and the dire consequences of "overpermissiveness" probably stems from a widespread failure to recognize the effects of various possible interactions between the control dimension and other, qualitatively different dimensions.

Most of the relevant research has dealt primarily with maternal attitudes relating to child rearing, though some data directly based on observations of mother-child interaction have also been used. The role of the father has thus far received little attention in multivariate studies. The earliest studies of immediate concern to us are apparently those dealing with the Fels Parent Behavior Rating Scales. Baldwin, Kalhorn, and Breese (52, 53) offered early attempts to distinguish dimensions underlying these scales by grouping them into clusters. Using correlations provided by Baldwin, Kalhorn, and Breese (52), Roff (1208) extracted seven multiple-group factors and rotated them to oblique simple structure. Two of the rotated factors — identified as concern for the child and

parent-child harmony — seem to relate to emotional aspects of the parent-child relationship. There are others that pertain to various aspects of behavioral control — democratic guidance, permissiveness, and non-readiness of suggestion. Two other factors are identified as sociability-adjustment of the parents and activeness of the home. From the intercorrelations among Roff's primary factors, Lorr and Jenkins (952) derived three second-order factors, which they labeled dependence-encouraging, democracy of child training, and organization and effectiveness of control in the home.

Other studies have yielded a variety of factors whose nature evidently varies with the selection of variables and method of measurement. Even the analysis by Schaefer and Bell (1263) of the attitudes of young unmarried women toward childrearing and family relationships, however, seems to reveal some trends like those that appear in more direct examinations of child-rearing behavior. In a later publication, Schaefer (1262) notes the persistent emergence of the separate dimensions of love and control, and he shows how the various maternal behaviors involving these dimensions interrelate by ordering data from three other studies (52, 1252, 1264) by Guttman's circumplex model. Milton (1061) also notes the ubiquity of these two dimensions, and they appear in his own analysis of the child-rearing data collected by Sears, Maccoby, and Levin (1282) through interviews of 379 Suburban New England mothers. Milton reports additional factors, which he identifies as general family interaction or adjustment, responsible child-training orientation, and parents' attitude toward aggressiveness and punitiveness.

There seems to be little question regarding the distinctness of love or acceptance on the one hand and behavioral control on the other, but there may be reason to question the unitariness of each of these

DIAGRAM 24-1.   Childhood Age Trends in Objective Test Personality Factors

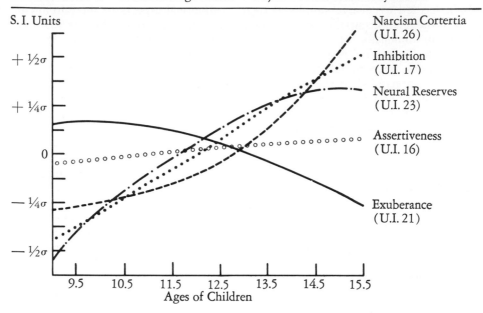

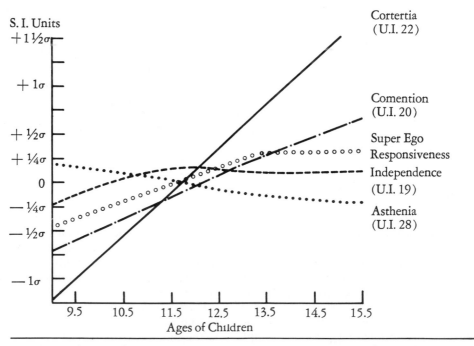

Note: S.I. (for Standard Increment) units are units of growth on change derived from standard scores in an age-homogeneous group at some agreed age — in this case 12.5 years.

dimensions. An analysis of child-training practices by Sewell, Mussen, and Harris (1302) seems to indicate that if we start with sufficiently specific variables, the control-permissiveness dimension breaks up into a number of relatively independent dimensions. In a study based on interviews of the mothers of 162 five- and six-year-old children, these workers report seven obliquely rotated factors — practices reflecting permissiveness in early feeding situations, permissive toilet-training practices, practices involving much activity of the parents with the child, non-punitive treatment of misbehaviors, practices making for early independence, practices reflecting casual attitudes of parents, and non-insistent reactions on the part of parents. To resolve the questions raised by this study and to clarify the role of the numerous poorly verified dimensions of parental behavior, we need a much more comprehensive multivariate study. Ideally, this study would involve extensive direct observation of parent-child interactions, and it would be carried on over a long period of time so as to reveal the continuities in parental action and attitude that constitute truly persistent influences in the development of the child.

5. DEVELOPMENTAL THEORY AND PROBLEMS OF RESEARCH METHODOLOGY

Hitherto it has been very difficult to extract from innumerable variables and their age plots any general laws of development. The discovery that factors retain their identity across time — with exceptions we shall discuss below — fortunately makes possible a plotting of meaningful development curves. This gives the hope of laws which, on scientific grounds, can be expected to apply to such functional unities rather than to specific, complex, and often idiosyncratic single variables. As Chapter 11 points out, however, the estimation of a factor rests on a gradually changing loading pattern from age to age, and this complication, as well as the recency of the personality theories generated by these factor researches, means that comparatively little evidence is yet available.

As pointed out above, the constancy with which certain factors appear — from 7 to 70 years — such as ego strength, C, affectothymia, A, surgency, F, parmia, H, superego strength, G, etc., holds the hope of developing age plots, for various social and racial groups, over a wide range. For example, now that the work of Tsujioka has shown the constancy of 16 P.F. factor structure as between American and Japanese, it would be interesting to make comparative studies of development with age. The recent extension of factoring to the 4-5 — year level, with the emergence of the as yet unpublished PSPQ (Pre-School Personality Questionnaire), holds out possibilities of checking on the cultural-anthropological theories of Mead and others about effects of early child-rearing methods.

When results with the objective test (O-A Battery) personality factors recently became available for middle childhood, it quickly became evident (see Diagram 24-1) that the factors indicated are distinct functional unities with a natural history of their own. For example, the factor U.I. 21, exuberance, one theory of which is that it is a physiological influence of high cortical metabolic rate, declines steeply with age, as might be expected from that theory. On the other hand, cortertia, which is the growth of cognitive alertness with decline of pure feeling reactions, rises equally steeply in the 9-15 age range. Since our object here is only to indicate areas of research, detailed discussion of the theories developing from these findings cannot be pursued.

In terms of experimental development study with questionnaire factors the evidence is at the moment better organized for the adolescent and adult than the younger child level. The work of Sealy in particular, as well as that of Cattell, Stice, and Eber (329) has gone far to pin down the nature of the essential changes. As Table 24-1 shows, there are some interesting sex differences, e.g., a greater ego strength rise in women, but otherwise the results show highly common trends.

ity, D; a rise in shrewdness, N; a decline in guilt proneness, O; and a steady slight rise in superego strength, G.

These trends have been pursued into the second-stratum realm both by Sealy, on all four main second-stratum factors—anxiety,

TABLE 24-1

AGE CHANGES ON PERSONALITY FACTORS ON THE 16 P.F.

Factor	Men and Boys		Women and Girls	
	Change Per Year	Up to Age	Change Per Year	Up to Age
C Ego Strength	+.1	45	+.2	45
E Dominance			−.1	70
F Surgency	−.3	60	−.3	60
G Superego	+.1	35	+.05	35
H Parmia	+.1	50		
L Protension	−.1	40	−.1	40
M Autia	+.1	70		
N Shrewdness	+.1	35		
O Guilt Proneness	−.1	45	−.1	45
Q_1 Radicalism	+.1	70		
Q_3 Self Sentiment	+.1	70	+.1	70
Q_4 Ergic Tension	−.2	30	−.1	30

Many of these trends agree with the wisdom of the ages about human nature and aging. For example, the growth in ego strength and capacity to cope emotionally (C factor), the natural decline in shyness (H-), and the sobering down from the high spirits of youth as shown in the desurgency (F-) trend.

The researches of Sealy on age trends on the HSPQ (High School Personality Questionnaire) are shown in more detail in Diagram 24-2. These diagrams are slightly complicated by a comparison of a high school with a college group, where some selection, social and intellectual, has separated the latter. However, this suffices to bring out an important principle, discussed below.

As far as common trends are concerned, one notes (besides the familiar rise of intelligence, B) a steep decline in excitabil-

extraversion, cortertia, and independence —and by Scheier, in an intensive study of anxiety alone. The latter results show, as would be expected from the work of G. Stanley Hall, that anxiety runs at a high level in adolescence and then drops steadily to about 35 years. There it stays steady until a rise seems to occur at retirement years.

This last result, as well as the sex differences and college-non-college differences above, remind us that the discovered trends are relative to a culture, and by no means wholly biological. This raises an important methodological point: that measures comparing different people at different ages confound personal trends with cultural trends. The preferred methodology in this area is therefore to measure a set of individuals over a wide age range and then wait two or three years and measure

DIAGRAM 24-2.   Age Trends on the High School Personality Questionnaire. Age trends: Age 11 to 17 (HSPQ); 15 to 18 (High School Students); 18 to 25 (College Students)

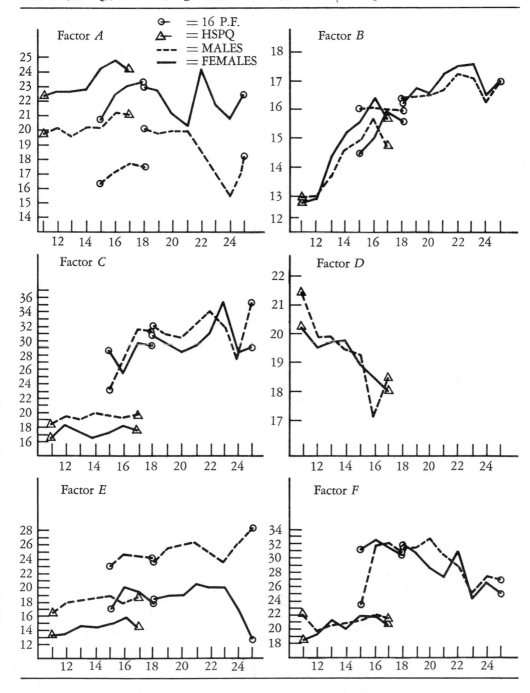

DIAGRAM 24-2 (Continued)

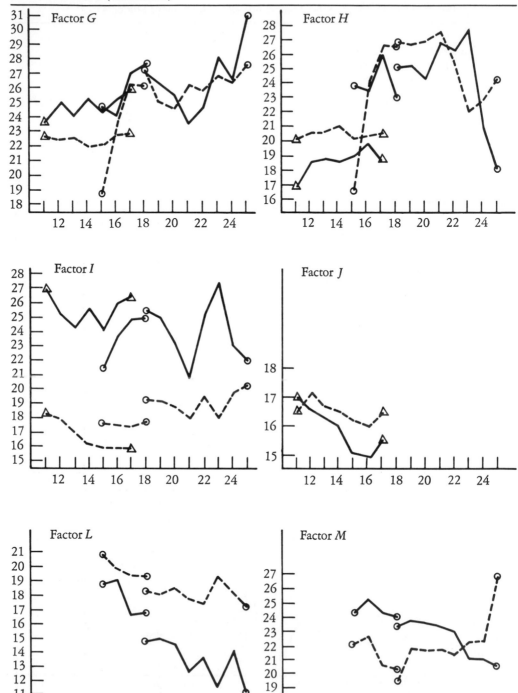

DIAGRAM 24-2 (Continued)

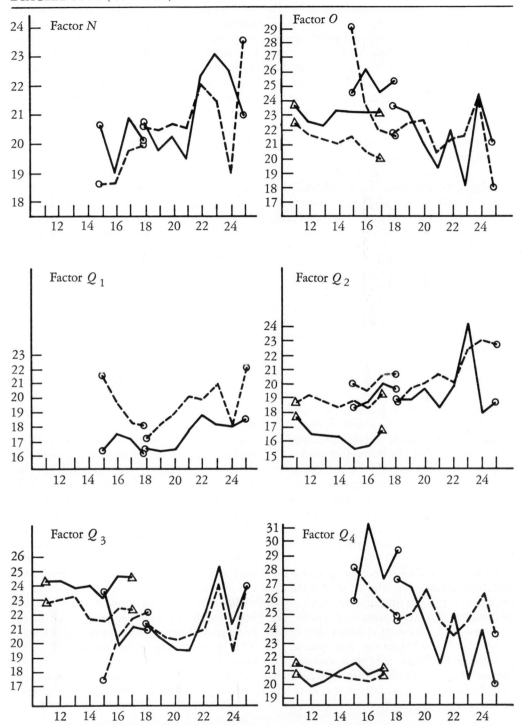

them again. Thus the differences give the trends at each age level and can be built into a single curve.

Some more subtle and debatable methodological points remain to be discussed. For example, in some factors less familiar than those above we face greater difficulty in trying to establish ontogenetic continuity. Since the universe of possible behaviors varies with age level, the behavioral expression of a factor must change even if its basic nature remains constant.

It is possible, however, to conceive of a process of *factor metamorphosis,* whereby the factor itself would gradually change in nature. Two factors appearing at widely separated age levels could then be characterized as qualitatively distinct although they represent a single historical continuity. If we regard a factor as an underlying predisposition that is represented only indirectly through its behavioral expression, there is probably nothing in our data that will enable us clearly to distinguish between a metamorphosed factor and a constant factor of shifting age-appropriate expression. Since the concept of "factor" is better regarded, in this case, as a convenient construct than as a label corresponding to a "real" entity the question is more one of the preferred mode of conceptualization than one of fact. Perhaps the choice of conceptualization should be governed by the amount of transformation seen in behavioral expression. Of course, there are many other aspects of theory construction to be considered in making such a decision, but there is not sufficient space to consider them here.

However we choose to conceptualize the transformations, we do find systematic changes with age in all the recognized personality factors. Some of these are obviously a function of changes that occur generally in behavior in the course of development. Thus, it is well known that certain features of behavior tend to become "internalized" in the course of development. Gesell notes that young children

become increasingly more "self-contained," and students of thinking have commonly explained the emergence of mental processes in terms of the inhibition of direct or outward action. It is hardly surprising, then, to find that the expression of many factors assumes an increasingly covert form with advancing age. A factor manifested in emotional outbursts in the early years, for example, will be expressed later in a disturbed feeling state that may not be obvious to others.

Another obvious facet of behavioral development in general is the process of socialization. Both the positive and the negative expressions of all personality factors seem to tend toward an increase in socially patterned and socially acceptable forms of activity. The assertiveness of the Dominance factor thus tends to shift from merely aggressive activity to successful dominance, while the emotional sensitivity of the Premsia factor may be manifested early in a self-preoccupation and later in a genuine concern for the feelings of others. In some cases, then, we may see what looks like a reversal in the direction of expression.

There are many other possible changes which could occur in a system of personality factors that need to be considered. If various aspects of behavior and experience display increasing covariation with age, we may find a group factor arising at a certain age level from what were previously uncorrelated elements. We might call this process *factor emergence.* If the elements form independent groupings that become increasingly correlated with age, we may find a single factor at one age corresponding to two or more group factors at an earlier age. Analysis at an intermediate age level might reveal a second-order factor corresponding to the later first-order factor. This process might be designated *factor convergence.*

The opposite processes, involving decreasing covariation, are equally conceivable. If a single functional unity breaks up into a great number of uncorrelated elements, we should have what might be called *factor disintegration.* If the factor splits into two or more independent factors (the original unity being preserved again at intermediate stages at the second-order level), the process might be termed *factor divergence.* This, of course, is the kind of fractionation which Garrett (580) claimed to find in the realm of mental abilities. We might well have expected to find it in the personality realm before the Cattell studies had been conducted. Something akin to this exists in personality in the "fading-out" with age, i.e., the reduction to smaller common variance of factors such as *B,* intelligence, and *D,* excitability, between the HSPQ and the 16 P.F. age ranges.

In the factor studies of personality structure in children, there are various bits of evidence suggesting the operation of each of the processes described above, but the evidence relates mostly to the more elusive factors of small variance, and it is not conclusive in any instance. It is clear, on the other hand, that none of these processes operates on a grand scale, since we find a relatively constant number of factors with much evidence of intrafactor continuities. To demonstrate more clearly the operation of any of these processes on a minor scale, we shall probably need to trace the course of factor development in the same individuals over a period of time.

There is another, more subtle kind of change that could occur in a system of factors. We might call it *factor component interchange.* As a result of a combination of increases and decreases in the correlation of ingredients, there might be considerable reassortment of the components of factors with no substantial change in the number of factors. The simplest case would be one in which each of two factors at a given age contains features of each of two earlier factors. This again is a kind of systematic change that would be difficult to detect with certainty in a comparison of cross-sectional analyses. Unfortunately, we must

recognize that the sort of cross-correspondence that it produces in the alignment of two sets of factors will sometimes occur for purely methodological reasons. There are situations in which a choice between much different rotational solutions seems arbitrary. The less adequate the sampling of variables, the more likely we are to encounter these situations and situations in which a solution that is not generally optimal looks best, with the result that we find apparent factor component interchange when we attempt a straightforward replication of a study. The simple structure criterion guarantees a certain simplicity of numerical description in the context of a given set of data. Whether it affords maximal conceptual economy for the entire observational realm that we have sampled and, correspondingly, maximal reproducibility of solution depends on the adequacy of the sampling. Thus, the two factors of size and shape may appear to fit a certain set of measurements applied to a sample of rectangles more economically than the alternative factors of length and breadth, which would generally provide more economical description. From a purely mathematical standpoint, of course, the choice is arbitrary.

In this section, we have seen that developmental changes in the over-all structure of behavior or personality can conceivably take place in quite a variety of ways. We need methods for detecting more efficiently the operation of any of the possible developmental processes. Existing cross-sectional studies provide only a preliminary glimpse of probable factor continuities and modifications. For a more adequate solution to the problem of developmental change, we shall probably have to supplement cross-sectional data with longitudinal data and apply yet untried experimental designs and modes of analysis. In the remaining section, we shall consider some possible multivariate designs that seem to hold special promise for the treatment of developmental problems.

6. POSSIBLE MULTIVARIATE TECHNIQUES FOR DEVELOPMENTAL RESEARCH

In a recent article (350), the present writer proposed a classification system for designs involving observation of covariation or correlation. This system may be regarded as a special expansion intermediate between the Covariation Chart (which has six techniques) and the full Data Box analyses (Chapter 3). The total of 24 techniques which the present analysis gives is more easily handled than the full Data Box. The techniques are distinguished on the basis of the relationships among four basic components — R, S, P, O — within the design. Design Component R is the realm of variables consisting of structural or functional manifestations on the part of the subject or subjects under investigation. It includes such things as specific responses, test scores, and attributes. Design Component S is the realm of "external stimuli," i.e., variables arising from sources outside the subject which may be expected to influence his behavior. Design Component P is the realm of "persons," or more generally, the human or animal subjects observed. Design Component O is the realm of occasions, in given time and space, on which experimental observations are made. The data of a correlational study can ordinarily be thought of as forming a score matrix in which the rows, the columns, and the elements in the body of the matrix correspond to three different design components, while the variables of the fourth component are singular or are held constant. Given these restrictions, we have the 24 possible prototypal designs shown in Table 24-2.

The designs that seem most generally suited to a treatment of developmental problems are those in which the O component is not singular or constant but is varied or is permitted to vary over a range corresponding to the age range under study. Most of the designs in the system

meet this qualification, although the ones most commonly used do not.

The designs most relevant to the problem of assessing similarities and differences among various points in development are the occasion-correlation techniques — O, T, D, F, J, and L. They provide a variety of bases for identifying stages, trends, cycles, and points of transition, within the period subjected to observation. With techniques O and D, one can do this for a single individual. The more generally applicable technique would be O, in which one correlates occasions with respect to variations in the responses elicited by a set of tests or stimulus situations common to all occasions. The R-component variable could, of course, include some response measurements and physical measurements for which no well-defined determining stimulus is immediately present. The obtained correlations among occasions might be subjected to factor analysis, cluster analysis, or some other procedure that will provide an appropriate ordering of the data. (The covariation-design classification system merely defines the form of covariation observed. The kind of statistical analysis subsequently applied is a separate issue). In any case, O technique will reveal intra-individual trends in behavior.

Technique D would be appropriate when the trends that are sought relate more to underlying sensitivities than to behavior as such. Here the response categories are fixed; hence, the acts or elicited reactions are ones that occur on all occasions. We are focally concerned not with measuring the response but with measuring the eliciting stimulus. The measurement situation common to techniques A through F is that traditionally associated with psychophysical research. Technique D might be employed in developmental research when we are concerned with trends in such things as sensory thresholds, perceptual judgments, and certain kinds of physiological functions. It should be noted, in passing, that the data within each member of the pair of columns or rows to be correlated must be expressed in a common scale. In the present instance, this means that the various stimuli must be expressed in a common physical scale or that the stimulus values must be subjected to an appropriate form of scaling.

common to the group. A study by Hofstaetter (735) illustrates the developmental application of T technique. Hofstaetter factored a matrix provided by Bayley (77) giving correlations among various age levels for a group of children whose intelligence was tested from the age of two months to eighteen years. He derived three

TABLE 24-2

Twenty-Four Covariation Techniques

Technique	Variables Correlated	Variable in Which Variation Is Noted	Series over Which Covariation Is Studied	Constant or Singular Variable
R	S	R	P	O
Q	P	R	S	O
P	S	R	O	P
O	O	R	S	P
S	P	R	O	S
T	O	R	P	S
A	R	S	P	O
B	P	S	R	O
C	R	S	O	P
D	O	S	R	P
E	P	S	O	R
F	O	S	P	R
G	R	P	S	O
H	S	P	R	O
I	R	P	O	S
J	O	P	R	S
K	S	P	O	R
L	O	P	S	R
U	R	O	S	P
V	S	O	R	P
W	R	O	P	S
X	P	O	R	S
Y	S	O	P	R
Z	P	O	S	R

Note.—The letters in the second, third, fourth, and fifth columns refer to the design components from which variables are drawn.

What we accomplish on an intra-individual basis with techniques O and D can be accomplished on a group basis for a single kind of stimulus-response relationship with techniques T and F. If, again, the O-component categories are specified in terms of meaningfully distinguishable points in development, these techniques will reveal trends in behavior or sensitivity

orthogonally rotated factors. Of these, one did not load the early age levels, while the other two did not load the later age levels. These findings thus show that the functions measured in the early years are quite different from those measured in the later years, and they provide a basis for conceptualizing the differences. The trends might be interpreted either in terms of developmental changes in the children or in terms of changes in the composition of the test battery, which, of course, cannot be held strictly constant over the entire age range. As Hofstaetter argues, the two possibilities may, in a sense, be "two sides of the same medal." The application of such a method to the personality factors yielded by cross-sectional applications of R technique could help resolve the many questions of developmental continuity.

In techniques G through L, we are primarily concerned with quantification of Component P. P-component data might be expressed in terms of the rank of a person fitting a given cell, an average rank for a number of persons, or a rank converted, with the aid of appropriate assumptions, to an interval scale value. More often the appropriate P-component values would be numbers of persons or proportions of a total sample of persons. Of the occasion-correlation techniques, J and L have least general application to the developmental area. The most likely use would be a situation in which we wish to relate age levels with respect to incidence patterns. In J, we might do this with respect to the numbers of children displaying each of a number of discrete attributes, traits, or behaviors. In L, we would relate occasions with respect to the numbers of children responding in a given way to each of a number of stimuli.

Techniques P, S, C, E, I, and K would be the transposed versions of the techniques discussed above. In these, the O component constitutes the series over which covariation is observed. Where age fluctuations occur systematically (unidirectionally or cyclically), these techniques may be used to illuminate response patterns, sensitivity patterns, and person patterns (developmental types). In each case, the pattern is one to be defined in terms of covariation over a range of development.

P and C, of course, are intra-individual techniques. In P technique, we correlate tests or stimuli with respect to response covariation over time. Thus far, P technique has been applied only to data gathered over a relatively short time span, and it has been found to yield factors similar to those found with R technique. If the time span is extended to cover several years of development, it should yield factors that are linked to developmental processes rather than to short-term situational fluctuation and physiological cycles. Technique C will yield similar information with respect to sensitivity or perceptual-judgment patterns. Here the response categories are fixed and we observe fluctuations in determining stimuli.

Of the related group-data techniques, S and E are the ones most appropriate for the identification of developmental types. With S technique, we can sort persons in terms of behavioral variation over time. With E technique, we can sort them in terms of temporal variation in the stimulus required to produce a given response. In techniques I and K, we are again dealing with the quantification of P-component data, the most likely possibility being that of incidence data. In one we can relate response categories, in the other varieties of effective stimuli, with respect to trends or cycles of associated incidence over a period of development.

Techniques U through Z present alternative ways of identifying such things as response patterns, sensitivity patterns, and person types developmentally. The primary measurement task in all these designs involves determining the occasion on which a given event occurs. For purposes of developmental study, the occasion variable might be expressed in terms of the age at which a phenomenon initially occurs, the average age at which it occurs, the length of the age range over which it occurs, etc.

The two intra-individual techniques in this case are U and V. U is similar to C in providing a basis for relating responses, though it may yield a much different kind of information. It is less pertinent to problems involving fluctuations in sensitivity, though it could be so applied. It provides more directly a way of relating responses with respect to their conjoint appearance in response to various stimuli over an age span or with respect to their parallel emergence and subsidence (as in cycles separated by a time lag). In the transposed technique, V, we perform a similar comparison of effective stimuli with respect to the points in development at which they produce various responses.

It should be noted that for the sake of simplicity we have referred to U, V, and four other techniques as intra-individual and dealt with them as though they applied only to data for individual persons. Strictly speaking, we could apply all these techniques to group data if we treated the group as a unit, using averages of O-, R-, and S-component variables as we would use single scores for individuals. The remaining techniques—W, X, Y and Z—apply only to group data.

In technique W, we correlate response categories with respect to the ages at which the responses appear in various individuals. The responses could be various effects of a controlled stimulus situation, or they could be behaviors recorded in the course of naturalistic investigation involving no deliberate stimulus manipulation. In either case, W technique provides one more way of identifying constellations of responses in terms of age of appearance. The transposed technique, X, provides a way of relating persons and, hence, of identifying types, in terms of the ages at which they display various responses.

In techniques Y and Z, it is the R component that is singular. It need not involve a single invariant act, however; it could be defined in a very general way—say, in terms of a "correct solution"—which would vary in specific form from one stimulus setting to another. In these two techniques in any case, the response must be one eventually given by every subject in response to every stimulus. Such would be the case if the stimuli are something like

problems, whether artificial or inevitably met in life, that each subject eventually masters. To follow through with this illustration, we might think of Y technique as a way of sorting problems according to the ages at which various people master them. This amounts to something much different from simply sorting them according to difficulty level, of course, for the size of a correlation here would depend on the extent to which two problems are solved relatively early or late by the same people. The correlation could be high despite a great difference in difficulty level. With technique Z, correspondingly, we could sort people according to the pattern of age levels shown in their solution of various problems.

We have described 18 of the techniques shown in Table 24-1 in terms of plausible developmental applications. These techniques may all be applied to much different kinds of problems, with appropriate changes in the specification of the occasion component. On the other hand, the remaining six techniques may be applied to various problems in the developmental area where we would deal with data gathered on a single occasion. And there are many possible variants of these techniques, such as the incremental R technique described by Cattell (240), which may have a special pertinence to developmental problems under some circumstances. In incremental R technique, the O-component variable is a pair of occasions, and the basic R-component datum is a difference between scores for the two occasions. Undoubtedly, this kind of variation could be usefully applied to many of the other techniques.

7. SUMMARY

(1) The fundamental problems of the developmental area are among the most complex in the entire field of psychology. Adequate research on these problems demands the use of multivariate experi-

mentation and multivariate statistical analysis. Thus far, however, the most appropriate tools have not been extensively used.

(2) The research of Cattell and his colleagues at various age levels furnishes a broad picture of the major components of child personality. This work is based on cross-sectional samples, but various methods have been employed to permit developmental generalizations. A sound foundation has thus been laid for future longitudinal studies.

(3) In each of the three measurement media investigated by Cattell and his co-workers, it has been found that the underlying factors remain fairly constant in number and kind from age four to adulthood. In every factor, however, there are developmental changes in level and form of expression that present a continuing challenge for research.

(4) Analyses of parental behavior and attitudes indicate a need for distinguishing at least two broad, independent dimensions — one of acceptance vs. rejection and one of control vs. permissiveness. There is a need for large-scale studies of actual parental behavior to clarify the role of additional, more specific influences on the child.

(5) The extant data on child personality structure can be conceptualized most economically in terms of a set of basic dimensions whose psychological identities are preserved through the whole course of development. Various types of progressive change in structure are conceivable, however, and future research may compel us to recognize the operation of some of these. There is a need for fresh techniques that will enable us to distinguish genuine change from effects dependent on accidents of sampling and statistical analysis.

(6) Already, however, pioneer researches have traced the age changes over childhood and adult life fairly extensively in questionnaire-measured factors and in a useful fraction of objective test-measured factors. These trends bring out clearly (a) that the factors have the functional independence we would expect from their demonstrated functional unity, (b) that their trends agree with previous clinical and general observation, and (c) that age trend data can add to our interpretation of the factors.

(7) The Data Box analyses have reminded us that there are many untried ways in which familiar multivariate methods might be applied to developmental data. These methods are most often applied to single-occasion data, but they may also be employed to analyze such things as covariation between occasions and over series of occasions. A compromise is suggested between the few techniques of the Covariation Chart and the many of the full Data Box. Through applications of these new techniques we may find ways of isolating and quantitatively specifying developmental types, stages, trends, cycles, and points of transition.

CHAPTER **25**   **Multivariate Analyses of the Behavior and Structure of Groups and Organizations**

CARL BEREITER
University of Illinois

1. INTRODUCTION

Group and organizational research has not had its Hull, but it has been favored with a number of ingenious theoreticians who, working with limited aspects of group behavior, have come up with limited theories capable of generating multitudes of testable hypotheses. This has served to stimulate a truly astounding amount of experimental activity in an area where experimentation is, to say the least, a lot of work for what comes of it. A less fortunate result, however, has been that the more elementary and logically prior business of identifying the basic variables in the field and how they relate to one another has not gone on apace. Research has tended to fixate upon a few variables or, more precisely, topics whose definitions have remained ambiguous and poorly distinguished from one another.

In the years soon to come group research is almost certain to turn more and more to factor analysis for a clarification of the variables with which it works. Present techniques are quite adequate for handling many of the questions in this area. Group performance, for instance, has been an area of long-time interest, and the number and variety of experimental group tasks has been growing steadily. The issues and problems are perfectly analogous to those in individual ability measurement, and the need for a set of clearly defined, independent group ability factors is obvious; yet only sporadic and small-scale attempts at factor analysis of group ability measures have been made.

There are other areas in the field of group behavior, however, where the failure to employ multivariate techniques is more excusable. These areas have special problems which demand new techniques or modifications of those developed for analysis of individual scores. A major aim of this chapter will be to point out the main problem areas which need such developments in the hope that specialists in multivariate methods will turn their attention to some of them.

The discussion to follow will be built around the several distinct kinds of data used in studies of groups, since each of these has its peculiar problems. The categorizations of data are roughly those set forth by Cattell (218). Part 2 deals with the characteristics of members, Part 3 with the relations of members to one another within groups, and Part 4 with characteristics of the group treated as a unit (what Cattell calls "group syntality"). Part 5 deals with the special problem of distinguishing behaviors which indicate individual personality characteristics of members from behaviors which reflect mainly structural characteristics of groups. Parts 6 and 7 deal, respectively, with practical and theoretical drawbacks to a reliance on factor analysis for the advancement of our understanding of groups.

2. MEMBER OR POPULATION CHARACTERISTICS

Practically any personality characteristic which a person may possess is likely to have some effect on his behavior in a group, to have some effect on the group as a whole, and, in turn, to be affected in some way by the person's experience in a group. Students of group and organizational behavior have therefore been interested in the full range of member characteristics, and research has suffered, along with other research on personality, from an excess of variables and trait names and a lack of replication. In a review of studies of the relationships between personality and performance in small groups, Mann (984) found 500 personality variables used in the studies he considered, with less than a quarter of them used more than once. By taking advantage of the several efforts that have been made at synthesizing factor-analytic findings in the personality field, Mann was able to assume most of these variables into seven factors and thereby to obtain some apparently well-grounded findings. It should be evident, however, that this kind of postmortem factoring, however skillful, cannot take the place of multivariate reduction of

live data, nor can inferred replications take the place of actual and deliberate ones.

A thinning out of the forest of personality variables would doubtless have a beneficial effect on the study of small groups, but researchers in that field would probably end up insisting that the woodmen spare certain favorite trees. They would be found in clusters: task-orientation, group-orientation, and self-orientation; authoritarian and democratic attitudes; needs for achievement, affiliation, and power; and so on. Variables such as these are, one may suppose, composites of more basic traits, but they are distinguished by their apparent special relevance to the kinds of group characteristics and performances in which students of group dynamics are interested.

To abolish such variables in the interests of parsimony would seem to be carrying parsimony too far. They are of a type with such variables as scholastic aptitude, mathematical aptitude, and language aptitude, which are of interest to educators: they are composites of traits which converge in independently defined kinds of criterion performance. What is needed in these cases is a specification of these complex variables in terms of more basic traits so that more generalizable interpretations can be made of results. Precise specification of these variables might lead to a reduction in their number, however, by (1) showing certain ones of them to be so closely allied with single source traits that there is no need to retain them, (2) showing that some of them are so alike in factorial composition as to be indistinguishable, or (3) showing certain ones of them to be so very complex that no meaning can be assigned to them.

There is one class of member variables that has a special relevance to group behavior. It consists of those variables which are measured in such a way that the group to which the individual belongs enters into the measurement operations. It includes such things as ratings of an individual by other members of the group, and measures of individual behavior within a group. These variables may be treated in two different ways. One approach considers the group setting as merely a convenient or appropriate way of obtaining certain personality measurements which are then treated as not substantively different from other personality variables.[1] Another approach is confined to examining relations among these group-based variables. For instance, the relation between talkativeness within a group and popularity or amount of influence might be studied. With such an approach, individual behavior within the group is viewed as a part of the group process, inextricable from it. For this reason we shall consider such treatments of individual variables in the later sections on group characteristics.

Although group-based individual characteristics may at times be treated like other personality characteristics, their fundamental difference from other characteristics shows up when they are summarized for groups. There are many ways of transforming individual scores into group scores: averages of all sorts, variances, differences, products, etc. No matter how scores on ordinary personality measures are transformed, however, they still carry information only about the members and are not in any genuine sense group characteristics. The average problem-solving ability of a group's members is not the same as the group's problem-solving ability — that is, the group's ability to solve problems jointly — which might be much greater or less than would be predicted from the average ability of its members. But group-based individual scores frequently can be transformed into meaningful group scores, by virtue of

interrelatedness. Thus, the sum of individual scores on attitudes toward the group gives a measure of the group's attractiveness to its members. The sum of ratings showing how well each member is liked by the others gives an over-all measure of the group's mutual likingness. A sum of talkativeness scores gives an indication of the over-all verbal activity of the group. (In contrast, talkativeness measures obtained outside the group or from participation in other groups, would not combine to give valid measures of a group's total talkativeness.)

The purpose in transforming ordinary personality scores into group scores is to study the relations between group characteristics and group composition (that is, the kinds of persons who make it up). Two issues are of importance so far as factor analysis of such group scores is concerned. One is the choice of transformation of individual scores, and the other is the extent to which the factors needed to account for the transformed scores are different from those needed for individual scores.

Regarding the first issue, it is important to distinguish pure from applied problems in this area because methods that are sensible for one kind of problem may be absurd when used for the other.

In applied situations the method of assigning individual characteristics to groups should be determined by the kinds of personnel decisions that are admissible. If, for instance, the only decisions that can be made concern personnel assignment — that is, you are given the people and are only free to decide which groups to assign them to — then there is no point in studying the relation between the mean scores of groups on various predictors and their performance, because nothing can be done about the mean scores. On the other hand, if one has the power to select but not assign, as might happen if assignment were voluntary or determined by the occurrence of

---

[1]There are, however, technical problems that arise when different persons' scores are obtained from different groups, so that group differences interact with individual differences. These problems are essentially the same as those that arise in other situations where not all persons are rated by the same raters, and therefore they will not be treated here.

vacancies, then mean scores on predictors are meaningful because the main effect of selection on one of the predictors would be to raise the mean score on it, and thus research could predict the gains to be achieved from such a rise in mean level.

In short, the intelligent research design for applied studies would be one that tried to approximate the kinds of groups that could be obtained through feasible alterations in personnel policies, and to gauge in this way the results to be expected from such policies. By adhering to this principle, most of the more bizarre ways of assigning individual scores to groups can be immediately rejected. Weighted averages of member scores, products of member scores, or differences – all may be excluded because there are no personnel assignment procedures to which they can correspond. If perchance one of these transformations proved to have some predictive validity it would be impossible to make anything of it for personnel selection purposes. Roby (1205) has made a penetrating analysis of problems in defining realistic functions of individual scores for studies of group composition.

When individual characteristics are assigned to groups in order to answer basic scientific questions involving cause and effect, the demands made on the scores are altered. It is no longer necessary that they be related to feasible personnel assignment practices, but it is necessary that they be interpretable. It must be remembered that no matter how the individual scores are transformed, they still carry information only about the members and not about the group as a unit. The scores of members on an anxiety scale can be reduced to a number that indicates the mean level of anxiety among the members, the extent of variation in anxiety level among members, or something of this sort; but no such number can indicate the anxiety of the group as a whole. There probably is no such thing, or if there is it would have to be measured in terms of the group's behavior.

Keeping this stricture in mind, it is again possible to eliminate most bizarre functions of individual scores. Beyond the mean, variance, and occasionally the scores of outstanding members, it is difficult to see what other ways of assigning individual scores to groups can yield results that are interpretable.

When assignment of individuals to groups is random, mean scores on different variables have the same expected correlations with each other as do individual scores on the same variables. Thus the results of factor analyses of individual scores are directly applicable to mean scores assigned to randomized groups. When assignment is not random, however, when there is some selection or self-selection, group mean scores cannot be expected to bear the same relations to one another as the corresponding individual scores. Factor analysis of group means may therefore lead to sets of factors for describing group differences which are different from those for describing individual differences. This was found, for instance, in a study of mean personality characteristics of college students in different fields of study (102).

In spite of its leading to interpretable results and to apparent parsimony (by reducing the number of variables below the number obtained through factor analysis of individual scores), the practice of factor-analyzing group means appears on theoretical grounds to be unreasonable and retrograde. Obtaining different factors for groups and for individuals implies that the mean scores relate to different conceptual entities than the individual scores, and this is absurd. Given that under special conditions of member selection, different factors can be obtained – just as they will be under special conditions of selection for factor analysis of individual scores – it follows that not one but a variety of sets of group mean factors could be obtained, depending on the basis of member selection. There might thus be different sets of factors for different clubs, teams, work groups, and what all. Such proliferation of factors can only produce confusion and is worse than having no factors at all.

The same reasoning would seem to apply to other ways of transforming individual scores into group scores. Within-group variances, for instance, cannot be expected to correlate with one another in the same ways that the corresponding individual scores do, and thus special sets of variance factors could be obtained. But what would be the use of them? What sense can be made of variances on factors whose meaning in terms of individual characteristics is not known and is perhaps non-existent?

It therefore appears that factor analysis of individual scores summarized for groups should be done sparingly, if at all, and only when the groups being studied are of such a special and interesting nature that the development of a special set of factors for their description appears warranted. In most cases, the results of factor analysis of individual scores will provide the preferred factor identifications.

3. RELATIONS AMONG MEMBERS: THE STRUCTURAL CHARACTERISTICS OF A GROUP

There are two levels at which the relations among members of a group or organization may be studied. One is at the behavioral level—who does what to whom. The other is at the level of formal representation of relationships—chains of command, status hierarchies, patterns of cliques and power, etc. The term "group structure" appears most appropriate in reference to this second level, and the term will be so used in this discussion. The other level will generally be referred to as "interactive behavior." To include both of them within the title "group structure," as is often done, is to obscure a distinction that has important methodological if not theoretical implications.

In dealing with group structure, that is,

with formal, more or less stable patterns of intragroup relationships, one has the option of abstracting the structure from its empirical context and making it an object of study in its own right. The organizational structure of a company may be represented by an idealized diagram drawn up by some administrator. On the basis of behavioral observations a different and perhaps more true-to-life structure might be inferred, but once it is diagramed, it can be subjected to the same analysis as the diagram which was arrived at purely rationally.

Much of the more sophisticated work on group structure during recent years has dealt with these formalizations of group structure. Work on communication nets, for instance, began by identifying certain basic patterns in which lines of communication may be laid down—the chain, the circle, the wheel, etc.—and then proceeded to find ways of quantifying, not communication behavior, but aspects of the formal patterns. In a more formal manner yet, graph theory has been applied to diagrams of organizational structures to yield a number of variables for describing organizations.

This sort of formalization of the internal processes of groups is, among other things, a way of describing the field in terms of limited numbers of clearly defined variables. It is a deductive procedure, however. A certain concept of power, communication, attraction, or whatever, is taken as given, and then, in an almost Euclidean fashion, various properties of it are deduced from its formal representation (1113). The approach is thus at bottom a univariate one, and this is its most serious failing. The diagrams of the communication channels, the power structure, and the status hierarchy of an organization are apt to resemble one another but not to be identical. There is obvious redundancy among the concepts, but no way of specifying or reducing it by methods of formal analysis, since the concepts are taken as postulates.

The need for factor analysis to chart the dimensions of group structural characteristics is thus increased rather than obviated by formal approaches to analysis of these characteristics. It should also be evident that factor analysis cannot very fruitfully work within the framework of these formal models, working with the properties derived from them. It needs to start at their foundations, the real-life variables from which power, status, etc. are inferred. In short, the proper subject for factor analysis is interactive behavior rather than group structure.

Much work has been devoted to systematizing the observation of interactive behavior. The task is to find, out of the limitless categorizations of behavior that are possible, a manageable set of categories that have basic psychological relevance. The systems in use were developed rationally rather than empirically, though empirical procedures have in some cases been employed to reduce the number of categories (724).

Interaction analysis has several properties that make it imperfectly amenable to ordinary multivariate techniques. In the first place, measurement is usually based on the frequency rather than the more familiar additive model (941). That is, instead of measuring a characteristic by means of a sum or average of similar measurement results, the characteristic is measured by the number of times that it is observed. A linear multivariate model provides a natural fit to additive measurements, but it is not at all obvious that linear composites of frequencies make sense.

A more basic difficulty is that a complete set of observations on a group is full of internal constraints. Categories of behavior are not independent, because emitting one kind of behavior hampers a person's emitting another at the same time. Receiving a certain behavior means that someone else had to emit it. Individuals are not independent because when one person is doing something, the other members are likely to

be prevented from acting. An extremely talkative member may make it impossible for other normally talkative persons to say much. A dominant kind of individual may show less than average dominance behavior if the leadership position has been preempted by someone else.

Wittenborn (1567) has examined the implications of what he calls "alternative responses," responses the occurrence of which precludes to some extent the occurrence of others of the same class. His solution to the problem, which consists of obtaining "derived correlations" between variables by correlating their correlations with other variables, is crude and fraught with difficulties, but his empirical findings suggest it is on the right track. His method is essentially one of powering a correlation matrix whose diagonal elements have been set at zero, and it is possible that this or some other modification of matrix powering can be developed into a method for dealing with internal constraints. This would be a valuable methodological advance as far as group dynamics is concerned, for the internal constraints in groups that hamper analysis are part of the very essence of group dynamics, and ought not to be eliminated experimentally even if they could be.

If, instead of tallying frequencies of various kinds of interactive behavior one simply has observers or other members rate individuals on the extent to which they talk, try to dominate, encourage others, etc., the technical problems just considered can be avoided, but the data are of much more doubtful validity. Borgatta, Cottrell, and Mann (129) had members rate each other on personality traits and also on behavioral characteristics within the group. The factor-analytic results show very little distinction between one kind of rating and the other. The kind of person one appears to be and the way one appears to behave are not ordinarily distinguishable in perception, so it is not surprising to find raters treating them the same. Moreover, interactive behavior is not fully represented without specifying recipients as well as emitters. This two-way arrangement presents a whole methodological issue in itself, to which we now turn.

The interactive character of group members' ratings of each other is more fully preserved in "sociometry" the study of the relationships of individuals one to another within a group. (This is the older meaning of a term which is gradually acquiring broader meaning.) Various sorts of data on these interrelationships can be obtained: members may rate each other on various dimensions, they may be asked to choose each other for this or that purpose, or they may merely be asked to state such things as which members of the group they know or like. Whatever the kind of data obtained, it can be arrayed in an N-by-N matrix where element ij indicates the response of person i with respect to person j. Depending on the sort of response called for, many or none of the cells in the matrix may be empty. The well-known sociogram records graphically the same information that may be recorded in such a matrix, with the persons being represented as points on the graph and the responses being indicated by lines connecting responder with object.

In graphical form sociometric data of simple kinds are amenable to analysis by graph theory, which can yield variables related to the centrality or isolation of individuals, to their strengthening or weakening effect on the (graphical) group structure, or in fact to almost anything which the mathematical inventiveness of the experimenter enables him to represent with points and lines.

Somewhat less flexibility has thus far been achieved through algebraic treatment of the data in matrix form. Several different techniques, excellently reviewed by Glanzer and Glaser (598), make use of successive squaring or multiplication of data matrices to explicate the more indirect interrelationships embedded in the data. For instance, by the most straightforward method a matrix is squared so that the ijth element reflects the extent to which person i chooses people who choose j. If the matrix is squared again, the ijth element would in addition reflect the extent to which i chooses people who choose people who choose j, and so on. Carried far enough, the powered matrix will reveal cliques of persons whose responses are profoundly interconnected.

This is a form of data reduction that works by reducing the number of persons. Cliques identified in this way may, as far as the response dimension that was used is concerned, be treated as equivalent.

A reduction in the number of distinct persons to be considered may also be effected by factoring the data matrix (1556, 975, 1584). The result of this approach, however, is a set of factors representing ideal types of persons as respondents and a complementary set of factors representing ideal types of persons as objects; and instead of being pigeon-holed into a certain type category, each real person will have a loading of some magnitude on each factor in both sets.

Reduction of rank in the persons mode seems at first glance to be a worthwhile goal even when groups are of modest size, because when it comes to studying interrelationships between individuals, each additional person to be considered adds greatly to the difficulty and cost. But on further thought it is not altogether clear what one might do with these factored persons. Can the factors be interpreted? Can they be meaningfully correlated with anything else? In a paper to be discussed more fully in the next section, Cattell (254) has argued plausibly for the use of a cluster rather than a vector model in problems of this type. Common sense definitely favors such a choice. A clique, after all, is a cluster of persons, not a dimension along which persons are ordered.

The graphical and algebraic approaches to analysis of sociometric data are actually much more similar than they would at first appear. Graph theory imposes a rational, a priori model on the data. Centrality, for instance, is defined mathematically and the centrality score assigned to a person is dependent upon this definition. But in the algebraic or factor-analytic approaches, cliques or degrees of association are also defined mathematically and a priori, the only difference being that a different kind of mathematics is used. There does not seem to be any basis for calling one more empirical than the other.

The univariate nature of all these approaches is an outstanding weakness. None of them provides for integrating sociometric results obtained on more than one response dimension. Suppose, for instance, that subjects are asked to choose from among their fellow members ones they would like to have with them on a problem-solving task, a picnic, and several other enterprises. Inspection of the results will probably tell us that there is some constancy of choices over the various conditions, but that there are also differences. How can such similarities and differences be assessed?

What we are dealing with is an N-by-N-by-k matrix of choosers, choices, and conditions of choice respectively. Three-way factor analysis provides a method for handling such a matrix. A three-way factor analysis would give us a set of idealized choosers, a set of idealized choices, a reduced set of conditions of choice, and a core matrix relating idealized choosers and choices to basic conditions of choice. Findings of genuine interest would now be possible, for the results, it is hoped, would show under what conditions certain types of people are chosen by certain other types. This is in effect what psychologists have been trying to read off from sociometric data by informal means.

In general it appears that the study of interpersonal behavior in groups can profit greatly from the development of three-way factor analysis, because interactive behavior becomes meaningless when viewed in less than three ways at once: there have to be at least two people and a response dimension involved.

An aspect of interpersonal relations within groups that has special applied implications is the matter of compatibility among individuals. Compatibility is obviously a relational characteristic rather than one that can be ascribed to an individual, but it is typically defined in terms of individual characteristics. If compatibility were the same as similarity it would not be so difficult to handle, since multivariate ways of dealing with similarity are well developed (see Chapter 17); but complementarity of some kind must also be recognized as a possible part of compatibility. This immediately complicates matters beyond reason: consider the number of ways that two people can be alike or different on 13 or so dimensions.

The one comprehensive attack on the issue of compatibility has been that of Schutz (1278), in which he gave an exhaustive and rigorous formulation of types of compatibility. But this was made possible only by limiting the number of dimensions on which people could differ to three and by considering even these separately rather than in combination.

A multivariate approach to compatibility would have to take into account individual characteristics, similarities and differences between members, and characteristics of the members as groups. A pair of individuals could be represented by three vectors: one a vector of mean scores on individual variables, another a vector of squared differences on the same variable, the third a vector of group variables, such as the performance of the pair on various joint tasks. The usual correlations between variables, calculated over pairs in this case, could be analyzed; but there is some appeal in the prospect of factoring pairs of persons. A separate factorization could be performed for each of the three kinds of variables. This would yield types of pairs classified in one case according to level on a set of predictors, in another case according to differences within pairs on those predictors, and in the final case according to behavior as pairs. By matching up factors obtained from these separate analyses (see Chapter 6), it might be possible to identify the types of similarities and differences within pairs that are associated with kinds of joint behavior. Compatibility and incompatibility would then be empirically determined rather than defined a priori.

4. GROUP BEHAVIOR DIMENSIONS: SYNTALITY CHARACTERISTICS

The interaction variables discussed in the preceding section describe the group as a system. The variables we turn to now may be described as output variables, describing the group's action or total effect upon someone or something. These include group actions in the form of decisions, productions, and the like, and global ratings of the group by observers, or by members when these scores are assigned to the group rather than to the members. As far as these variables are concerned, the group is treated as an individual. One can describe the group's collective behavior in terms of process variables or one can speak of the group's abilities, temperament, morale, or such special characteristics as group attractiveness, all of which ascribe states to the group. As in individual psychology, the difference is mainly one of inference from data rather than in the data itself. Whether one takes a factor to represent a certain kind of behavior or to represent a tendency or capacity to behave in a certain way is a distinction we shall not trouble to preserve in this section since its methodological implications are beyond the scope of this chapter (see, however, Chapter 2).

Not all social psychologists are content with attributing personality-like traits to groups. To them it smacks of animism, of a mystical super-personality transcending the personalities of the individual members.

Such objections, though they are largely semantic cavils, do have a point. Any system that has outputs that reflect the action of several parts of the system can be described in terms of those outputs and may thus be said to have a "personality." The catch is that not all global observations that may be made on a group truly describe its output as a system. To say that a group is happy, for instance, when all we have observed is that most of its members appear happy, is to say nothing about the group as a functional entity. A group cannot be happy, but it can have the ability to make its members happy. This would be manifested by increased signs of happiness when members enter the group. We are now describing an output from the group to its individual members, something in terms of which the group as a whole can be legitimately described.

The mere fact that numbers having psychological meanings can be assigned to groups does not guarantee that there is any conceptual entity to which they correspond. The situation is especially dangerous when it comes to observer ratings of group characteristics. Work with the semantic differential has established beyond doubt that people can rate virtually any object on virtually any dimension. Therefore the fact that observers can reliably rate groups on such attributes as "happiness," "activity," "morale," and "pleasure-seeking" does not guarantee that there is anything about the groups as entities that corresponds *literally* to these terms.

A clearer definition of what constitutes or could constitute a group characteristic is one of the needed cornerstones of a theory of group dynamics. This is not an empirical question but rather one concerning basic postulates. We have said that a group cannot be happy; only the individuals in it can be. On the other hand, we should insist that a group can be aggressive in that it can, as a group, perform aggressive actions against outside individuals or other groups. A series of basic definitions, beginning with a dynamic definition of a group is proposed systematically in Chapter 26. (The fact that aggressive groups are likely to be composed of aggressive individuals is irrelevant here; two groups composed of equally aggressive members might nevertheless differ in their aggressiveness *as groups*.) The distinction is hard to state in general yet operational terms. Loosely we can say that there are certain behaviors that can be ascribed only to groups and cannot be identified with individual members, that some of these behaviors can be described as aggressive, but that none of them can be described as happy or as indicative of happiness.

Since group syntality variables are conceptually identical to individual personality variables, they are amenable to the same kinds of factor analysis. Because of the relative lack of group syntality variables, however, factor analysis will need to be concerned much more with seeking out new dimensions than with clarifying old ones. This promises to be a slow and difficult process.

Some promising beginnings have been made. Cattell, Saunders, and Stice (316) have factor-analyzed group variables, including many objective behavioral measures of total group performance and decision as well as rated individual characteristics assigned to groups, group structure variables, and syntality variables. Among the 14 factors obtained are a number that appear to be characteristics of the group as a unit rather than of its members, including such characteristics as purposefulness, motivation, morale, procedure-orientation, and rigidity. Hemphill (715) has contributed to the vocabulary for describing group characteristics by setting forth 13 concepts derived from a categorization of 1,000 descriptive phrases. Empirical studies supported the legitimacy of these categories, but unfortunately the studies have been of a sort that could only lead to the discarding or merging of categories, not to the identification of new ones, which at present seems to be the greater need.

The present state of things with group syntality variables is not too different from that which obtained with mental ability variables at the dawn of the factor-analytic era. But we have seen a steady elaboration of concepts for dealing with mental abilities and one that has been kept pretty well within bounds by the discipline of factor analysis. On the whole, it is probably safe to say that our concepts for dealing with mental abilities are in much better shape than our concepts for dealing with non-aptitude personality traits, and that this has been due in some part to the fact that in the area of mental abilities, concepts have been built up empirically pretty much from scratch, whereas in the personality area the concepts were already there in everyday usage and the task has been to cut them down to manageable numbers and clear them up. We may therefore hope that if students of group dynamics get to work soon at building up a catalog of empirically derived group trait concepts they will in another thirty years be at the place where aptitude measurement is now.

5. DISTINGUISHING PERSONALITY FROM ROLE

As we have already noted, a person's interactive behavior in a group may be regarded as a sample of his behavior and thus may be used as a basis for inferring those behavioral dispositions which the personality psychologist recognizes as traits. These same behaviors, however, reflect the internal structure of the group and the person's role or roles within it. Observations of interactive behavior in groups thus have an intrinsic ambiguity which must be recognized if one is to avoid a spurious conceptualization of group processes.

In a recent paper Cattell (252) has dealt comprehensively with this problem, and the following discussion will build upon the formulation presented in that paper. One of Cattell's goals is an empirical definition of roles, in contrast to the a priori definition which has characterized research to date. This puts role-type definition on the same empirical footing as personality trait definition and opens up the possibility of a rational analytical procedure for distinguishing one from the other.

The approach to which Cattell devotes most attention makes use of variables which he calls "ties." Ties are defined (p. 217) as "potential, or actually intermittently recurrent, behavior patterns, representing habitual responses of a given individual learnt toward another individual or object." Ties thus include not only the interpersonal attitudes and behavioral tendencies of an individual, but also his behavioral dispositions toward non-human objects. In fact the only kinds of individual behavior that cannot be expressed in ties are those purely expressive behaviors (postures, facial expressions, tics, etc.) which have no object — and these, of course, are about the only behaviors which *prima facie* express one's personality and not one's role.

Given a sufficiently large and representative sample of tie variables, the correlation of two persons' tie scores will indicate the extent to which they tend to behave the same way in groups. A role, according to Cattell, is represented by a pattern of tie scores, and it may be unique. A *role-type,* on the other hand, is represented by a set of people whose patterns of tie scores are similar.

If a person's role is unique, then there is no way to separate it from his personality nor indeed would it be reasonable to do so (e.g., Jesus, Napoleon, etc.). It is therefore only role-types which need concern us further here.

The technique which Cattell advocates for identifying role-types is to correlate persons one with another on the basis of their tie scores and then apply his ramifying linkage method to sort out clusters (not factors) of persons. It is necessary to analyze at one time correlations between persons who are not all in the same group, because certain roles may be performed by only one person per group and yet appear in most groups. Such roles can be identified only by clusters of people from different groups.

This approach does put role definition on a much solider empirical base than it now occupies. The data are allowed to determine the number of role-types needed to describe group behavior. A particular role-type may be represented by more than one person in a group or it may not be represented in some groups at all — but this too may be determined empirically.

There is, however, a major difficulty in method which Cattell does not deal with directly. Ties, as Cattell defines them, and as they are most usefully conceived of in group dynamics, are not very general dispositions like, "Smith behaves kindly toward others," but, rather, highly specific ones like, "Smith behaves kindly to Jones," with the good possibility that Smith will not behave with equal kindness to Brown. But such ties are limited to people who are in the same group with Jones and Brown, and hence they cannot be used to identify role-types across groups, unless we are dealing with traditional groups in which the ties are traditionally or legally defined.

The consequence of restricting data to the more non-specific dispositions i.e., personality traits, like "Smith behaves kindly to others," would seem to be an analysis that yielded mostly personality-types rather than role-types, for it is just these very general dispositions that are used to define personality traits. A study by J. H. Mann (982) makes it clear that much is lost if the recipients of interactive behavior are left unspecified. Although he used questionnaire data, the items corresponded very closely to Cattell's definition of ties. They were of the form, "I dominate X," "I criticize X" etc., where X is variously specified as mother, father, girl friend, and so on. He found marked differences in the factor structure of these items depending on the specified recipient. Only in a higher-order analysis did generalized behavior tendencies emerge.

Mann's study affords a clue to an approach which might work for the kind of analysis Cattell proposes. The recipients were not specified as individuals but rather as role-types. That is, the subjects did not report behavior toward the same mother but rather toward different individuals who have in common the role-type mother. Now, although Brown may not be in Smith's group, someone of Brown's role or personality type may be. How Smith behaves toward this person (and he to Smith) gives us at least a shaky basis for inferring how Smith and Brown might relate to one another were they in the same group. This suggests a kind of iterative analysis which uses the analysis suggested by Cattell as a first approximation. One would start with a complete matrix of scores for p persons (from more than one group) on n ties which were of a sufficiently general sort that people from different groups could all be assigned comparable scores on them. Persons would be intercorrelated and then clustered into types on the basis of their intercorrelations. On the basis of these types, a different set of ties could then be scored, e.g.: "Behaves in such-and-such a way to persons of Type F." A complete data matrix would again be possible, with an augmented n of ties. A refined set of types could then be extracted, new ties scored, and so on until convergence of some sort was reached. At some point in the analysis it might become necessary to begin sampling possible ties rather than analyzing them exhaustively. It would also be possible in any iteration to "purify" the analysis by rejecting those types which were judged to be mainly personality rather than role types.

The problem of distinguishing personality from role is far from a simple sorting task. As Cattell points out (252, p. 237), circular causality is involved. People may select or attain a certain role because they have certain personality traits (e.g., dominant people becoming leaders) and, on the other hand, a role carried on for some time may modify personality.

Although common sense would lead one to expect that personality and role types would look too much alike, so that the problem is to distinguish them, it may well turn out in practice that the problem is just the opposite. Borgatta (128) factored interaction process scores along with scores from personality inventory and peer- and self-ratings. Except for one general activity factor, the interaction process variables loaded entirely different factors from the other variables. It is inconceivable that interactive behavior is that independent of personality. Rather, the results seem to replicate the depressingly familiar finding that measures of different traits by the same method tend to intercorrelate more highly than measures of the same trait by different methods (see also Hoffman, 732).

Cattell also identifies a third source of difficulty, the fact that at any given time a person may be "in" or "out of" his role to a greater or lesser extent (and may, of course, be in one role at one time and in another role at another time.)

And so the indeterminancy of intragroup behavior is confounded .... Cattell has done a valuable service by rendering these ambiguous sources of variance explicit in a proto-mathematical way. He has also tried valiantly and with great ingenuity to suggest means of rendering these sources of variance determinable. Because of the necessary and non-spurious confounding of personality variables and role-types, qualitative judgments as to whether a cluster represents a personality-type or a role-type are to be avoided. Cattell argues that role-defining variables will tend to be non-normally and multimodally distributed.

(Variables defining sex-roles in our culture would illustrate this kind of distribution. The more sharply defined the sex-role, the more discontinuous would be the distribution.) Once a role-type has been identified, a person's deviation from the personality profile associated with that role-type can be identified and used in conjunction with the role-type profile itself to predict a person's behavior in a group. The extent to which his actual behavior on a given occasion corresponds to this prediction can then be taken as a measure of the extent to which he is "in" the role.

It is difficult to be very optimistic about the possibilities of realizing the kinds of measurement of role-types, personality-types, and degrees of acceptance of role that this formulation requires. The choices required are so ambiguous, the measurements so prone to error—error which is compounded in the residuals—that there is little prospect of results in which one could place confidence. Yet it is so obvious that the variables which Cattell considers are all there and must be taken into account, that no simpler analysis, which ignored some variables and became more manageable thereby, can be accepted.

No simpler analysis can be accepted, that is, unless one is willing to forgo findings of basic theoretical import in the interests of more easily attained practical objectives. One quite plausible practical outcome which Cattell claims for his approach is that by developing separate prediction equations for different role-types, better predictions of individual behavior within groups may be attained. It seems quite reasonable that the weight given to various personality characteristics in predicting performance should depend upon the role the individual plays in the group.

This is an entirely pragmatic issue, however. The categories of role-types employed for purposes of sharpening up predictions need not have any privileged theoretical status. It is sufficient that predictions made by taking role-type into account

be more accurate than predictions which ignore it. It may well be that empirically identified role-types will yield better predictions than those arrived at by more qualitative judgments, but in a practical situation considerations of costs must enter in, and it would be surprising if the labor of identifying roles empirically would yield sufficiently superior predictions to repay the difference in cost over that of using roles identified by more direct and simple means.

6. SOME PRACTICAL CONSIDERATIONS

The matter of costs, which was alluded to in the preceding section, deserves some more detailed consideration, for it casts its shadow over the whole question of the use of multivariate methods in group and organizational research. Since the advent of high-speed computers, the cost of analysis of multivariate data, though still formidable, is no longer an insurmountable barrier. The cost of collecting data on groups and organizations, however, remains something to be reckoned with.

Recently some colleagues of the writer made the at-first-glance reasonable proposal that groups of student subjects be administered, over the course of a semester, a liberal sampling of the tasks that have been used in studies of group performance, so that independent factors of group performance, and tests suitable for measuring them, could be identified. Enthusiasm for this project waned as it was realized (1) how many subjects would be required: by well-established standards an N of 200 is needed for a large analysis, so that if three-person groups are employed, this means 600 subjects; and (2) the number of hours per subject that would be required: group tasks ordinarily take much longer to run off than individual tasks, and this is as it should be. In order for a task to be relevant to group characteristics it must be one in which the product emerges from some fairly extensive group interaction, and interaction necessarily consumes time.

Even so, this might not have been too great a price to pay for a study that could settle the issue of what are the basic dimensions of group performance and that could yield a limited set of tasks that would supply the information now obtained only from a multitude of them. But the past history of factor analysis does not permit us to suppose that one study could do this. Half a dozen, perhaps . . . . And then the findings would apply only to three-man groups, and different factors might be needed to describe four-man, five-man, and larger groups.

A more basic problem is that as these groups worked together hour after hour, they would undoubtedly change in profound and diverse ways—some going to pieces, some becoming intensely cohesive, some becoming stolidly resigned to failure, etc. Correlations between tests taken early and late in the experiment would therefore probably be low or, if not low, ambiguous. A solution, though a costly one, would be to give the groups warm-up tasks for a few hours or weeks until they had "matured," that is, until the group's structure and character had gotten pretty well fixed.

But mature groups, alas, are not what the field is interested in. The overwhelming majority of small-group experiments are carried out on what Cattell has called "neonate" groups, groups brought into being only at the commencement of the experiment. What are needed, therefore, are factors to describe the behavior and performance of neonate groups—but groups do not remain neonate long enough for such factors to be identified!

These problems are all raised by what is probably the simplest possible application of factor-analytic methods to the study of groups—factor analysis of unitary group products. The more complex types of analysis which have been noted or suggested in this chapter—three-way factorization of sociometric choice data or pair-wise

compatibility, Cattell's proposed analysis of role-types, any large multivariate experiment of factorial design—are likely to have these difficulties to an even greater degree.

What are the alternatives, then, to abandoning the effort at availing ourselves of multivariate methods in the study of groups? The most likely alternative, unfortunately, is a lowering of the standards for acceptable designs. The most ambitious factor-analytic study to date (316), though it used over 700 individual subjects, nevertheless had to use correlations based on the submarginal number of 80 groups. Most studies have been much smaller. In order to economize on the number of tasks which groups must perform, and thus keep subject time within practical bounds, investigators have tended to extract several scores from each performance. The lack of experimental independence, and even of mathematical independence, which results renders the meaningfulness of factor-analytic results and statistical tests gravely doubtful. Improvements in technique can and should be made, but it is likely to remain a bitter fact of life that knowledge about groups and organizations is based on small-scale analyses and too few of them.

Another kind of alternative is based on a more fundamental re-examination of the course of group and organizational research, its prospects and rationale. This we shall attempt in a sketchy and highly tentative manner in the next section.

7. SOME REFLECTIONS ON THE FUTURE COURSE OF GROUPS AND ORGANIZATIONAL RESEARCH

The appeal of factor-analytic methods lies in their comprehensiveness, in the notion that they take into account everything that needs to be taken into account. If we can write an equation for predicting group performance or individual behavior within a group on the basis of member characteristics, role-types and other structural variables, situational variables, and anything else deemed relevant, there comes the satisfying feeling that science has come to fruition. So appealing is this prospect that one tends to forget that there is more to science than validity coefficients of 0.60 or even 0.70.

Improved predictions are a natural consequence of scientific advances, but the actual history of these advances is written in terms of discoveries. The discovery of the conditioned reflex, of the law of effect, of shaping — these dramatically enriched the content of behavioral science so that analysis, of whatever variety, had more to work with than it did before.

The higher mission of experimental methodology, we might say, is to get Nature to reveal itself in ways that are not revealed to the common view. Multivariate analysis can serve this end, but only in a secondary role. The primary role must be played by techniques that work at the level of observation rather than analysis, and it is at this level that the study of groups is most retarded. The techniques for observing group processes have rendered observation more systematic and rigorous, but the content of the observations is just what has always been accessible to observation.

Perhaps the one area in the study of groups where genuine discoveries have been made and where knowledge has been substantially advanced is the area concerned with pressures toward conformity in groups. A perusal of the key studies in this area quickly reveals that the discoveries were made possible only by the use of clever test devices and the highly effective use of stooges. The techniques which carried this research forward have about lived out their usefulness, and one searches the horizon apprehensively for new techniques to take their place.

Lest this discussion end on too despairing a note, one use of factor analysis will be suggested which would seem to hold promise of yielding new knowledge with observational techniques already available.

Human beings are rather poor at integrating and correlating observations that are strung out over extended periods of time. Analytical methods for doing this have their difficulties, too, but progress is being made (see Harris, 692). P technique as described in Chapter 11, seems to be one of the most promising methods so far devised for examining the relations among variables as they change over time.

Group behavior has properties that make it especially promising for analysis of this kind. A group, viewed as an organism, can be said to have a developmental history much like that of any other organism. It is born, matures, and eventually, in most cases, dies, but in its early stages development proceeds at a much faster rate than it does, say, in the developing human being. Longitudinal studies of some interest can therefore be run off in a matter of days or weeks rather than years. A second advantage is that the kinds of interactions through which growth takes place are public, carried out through more or less obvious sorts of communication, whereas in the single organism many of them are internal and inaccessible to measurement. It is therefore possible that through the use of multivariate techniques for the study of change a developmental psychology of groups could be constructed that would yield valuable insights into the internal workings of groups. In this way, the sorts of change which to present-day social psychology constitute only troublesome sources of ambiguity could be made the substance of a coherent and lively science.

8. SUMMARY

This chapter has dealt mainly with potential rather than actual uses of factor-analytic methods in the study of groups and organizations. So far as member characteristics are concerned, the analytical problems are similar to those in the study of individual differences, and it was argued that analyzing group mean member characteristics as if they were properties of groups is theoretically unsound. Two approaches to the study of group structural characteristics were considered, one based on actual interactive behaviors, the other based on formal structural properties of groups. Only the former approach would seem to yield possibilities for fruitful application of factor-analytic methods, and some methods of handling the complexities of interactive behavior were examined. A special problem in the analysis of individual behavior in groups is that of determining the extent to which behavior is a function of the individual's personality and the extent to which it is a function of his role in the group. This problem was examined in the light of Cattell's formulation of it. A theoretically adequate solution would appear to be almost impossible to come by in practice, but certain suboptimal applications of the formulation can be expected to yield benefits. The most clear-cut use of multivariate methods is the factor analysis of characteristics and outputs of groups treated as unities—a development which logically parallels the factor analysis of individual personality traits.

Rather forbidding obstacles—most conspicuous of which are the enormous cost in number of subjects and in hours-per-subject—stand in the way of full exploitation of multivariate methods in the study of groups and organizations. The outstanding need in the field, however, appears to be at the level of observational rather than analytic techniques. One place where factor analysis might be able to produce important advances with available data is in the area of longitudinal studies of group development.

CHAPTER **26** Cultural and
Political-Economic
Psychology

RAYMOND B. CATTELL
University of Illinois

1. MULTIVARIATE EXPERIMENTAL DESIGN INDISPENSABLE IN THE SOCIAL SCIENCES

Social psychology, in its multivariate methodological aspects, is represented in this handbook largely by Chapters 25, 26, and 27, the first dealing with small groups, the second with large groups culturally integrated, and the third with matters of communication. Each is an ideal area for exercising multivariate methods, and it is surprising that social psychologists, sociologists, anthropologists, and political scientists have only in the last decade begun seriously to master the technicalities of multivariate designs. For, in the sense of the Data Box, with its interchange of people, situations, responses, etc. (as the bounding id sets of a matrix), the study of more than one person is necessarily multivariate from the very outset.

Researchers have in fact been far quicker to recognize the obvious truth that this area is multidisciplinary than the less obvious truth that all members of a team therein need to be competent in multivariate designs and methods. For just as the

clinical-intuitive theorists have persisted anachronistically in "qualitative" personality research, so the wildest, statistically unchecked speculations have passed as theory in cultural anthropology. Meanwhile journals of political science have lived largely on journalistic anecdotes and philosophical impressions, until the work of such researches as Rummel (1241), while the visible figures have too long been only those at the top corners of the pages!

All this is rapidly changing, but the change is too recent to permit an integrated crop of laws and discovered relations to be presented yet in the new terms. The most that can be done in a brief chapter at this time is to glance at models for formulating group behavior in relation to the individual; to consider some of the findings on cultural dimensions which enable predictions of national behavior to be made; and to glance at the new methodological possibilities in studying political and social attitudes and the behavior of politicians.

As in so many other fields of research, in the social sciences the problem of making effective advance is that of substituting a strategic for a merely tactical methodology —which incidentally is very different from the temptation to substitute premature global and cloudy theories for firm local hypotheses. The tendency has been to rely on a "living-in" observation in anthropology (as in the work of Mead, 1025; Stewart, 1351; Lewis, 929; Oeser and Hammond, 1112, and many others) instead of measurement; to work with verbal attitude measurements in sociology, instead of objective device measurements rooted in the dynamic calculus; to employ in social psychology a "sociometry" bereft of personality measurement; and to generalize, like Toynbee, in history, without the least regard to findings in psychological genetics. In place of this attachment to a local method and very limited horizon, there now grows an awareness that the social sciences are branches of behavioral science, attacking very special data and conditions, it is true, but this should not make it impossible eventually for even the most precise psychologist to label them as branches of psychology. It is an academic convenience, because of the specialized areas of observation, to separate them as sociology, anthropology, economics, and political science. But the penalty of stultified growth can be avoided only if all concerned keep in focus the fundamental fact that they deal with behavior by human beings, i.e., with the central personality dynamics of human beings, embracing the laws common to all behavior of human beings in groups. For example, the attempts to handle buying and selling motivation, or the measurement of socio-political attitudes, without embedding the design of observation in the general dynamic calculus of sentiments and drives in human beings (as approached, for example, in Chapter 20 here) are as hopeful as trying to make a machine work with substantial parts of the mechanism missing.

In what follows we shall begin by stating a general model of group and individual interaction which, being of the simplest possible form, has probability of universality. It belongs to the main system presented at the first level throughout this handbook, namely, one of multiple linear relations and additive interactions. Simple as some such formulation is, a great number of researches in social science go astray in research design or conclusions because they fail to have the implications of their formulation in this basic model clearly in mind. Bereiter's Chapter 25 on the study of groups and organizations has full regard for the implications of this model, but as his chapter does not have space to set out the model which underlies both small-group *and* national culture analyses, we shall begin by devoting the next section to the definition of the group-individual model.

2. THE CENTRAL MODEL FOR INDIVIDUAL-GROUP INTERACTION

Social science can be formulated operationally as dealing with three types of relations: (1) individual with individual, (2) group with group, and (3) individual with group—the physical environment being understood as part of the stimulus situation in all three. The model for the *individual* having been sufficiently defined (Chapters 18, 19, 20), it remains to define the *group*, psychologically and as a model in a measurement system.

For reasons which could be set out, principally having to do with defective definition of group boundaries, the writer (217) has long maintained that a group cannot be satisfactorily defined as a set of interacting people ("each the source of the stimuli affecting responses of the others"), nor as an aggregation of persons with a common (parallel, similar) pattern of interest and behavior, but only as follows:

(1) *A group is a set of persons such that the presence and action of all is necessary to certain conscious and unconscious positive satisfactions of each.*

The superiority of this dynamic definition, couched in terms of a satisfaction pattern which accounts for the cohesion of the group, i.e., referring directly to amount of ergic *goal attainment,* instead of the various tasks *instrumental* to the goals, lies in economy and lack of ambiguity. The simultaneous achievement of this conceptual economy, while still retaining an operational definition and measurement of the concepts, has actually become possible only recently through developments of the dynamic calculus which permit goal behavior to be operationally measured (240). Incidentally, since this presentation requires us to lean strongly at a number of points upon results and definitions in the dynamic calculus (246), the reader must be referred to fuller substantiation of its findings elsewhere (240, 246) and in Chapter 20. Among the important corollaries of this primary definition of a group are:

(a) That a group is an *instrument* for ergic satisfactions of individuals;

(b) That these satisfactions may be quite different in character for various members (see also Lasswell, 902);

(c) That the satisfaction patterns of the various individuals represent an equilibrium, reached by trial and error, in terms of bargaining or contract, between communal and non-communal interests of the various individuals.

(2) *Three distinct "panels" of observations are required to describe and measure a given group.* Thus the full description and measurement of a group requires *definition* of three panels, each based on a different form of observation and analysis:

(a) *Population* characteristics (217, 328), hereinafter symbolized as $\bar{P}$ measures;

(b) *Structural* characteristics (217, 328), symbolized as $\bar{R}$ measures; and

(c) *Syntality* characteristics (217, 328), symbolized as $\bar{G}$ measures, having to do with the group operations when the group acts as a unified whole. (The bar to the symbol represents a *measurement,* the simple *G* designating a group *as such.*)

(3) *By population characteristic measures,* ($\bar{P}$), *we refer to the mean and distribution, e.g., sigma, of the population, measured on those attributes of individuals which can be and are*

normally considered as individual characteristics, and are not measures of the group in its coordinated total behavior as such.

At this point, however, we must adopt a theoretically more sophisticated view of what are commonly and näively called "individual characteristics." Since "No man liveth to himself," or in John Donne's words, "No man is an island," the very structure (loading pattern) of individual personality (factor) source traits will vary from group to group. A means of conceiving and measuring a supra-group common personality trait is discussed elsewhere (240) and in Section 8 below, with the result that we recognize finally two kinds of population characteristic $\bar{P}$ measures, namely, (a) $\bar{P}'$ or group common traits, and (b) $\bar{P}''$ or group unique traits, definable as follows:

1. Quantitatively comparable, common population traits, $\bar{P}'$. In the usual situation where a person is simultaneously a member of many groups it will be possible, in addition to the individual trait level assigned to him so long as he is in a particular group, to assign to him a "group-abstracted" personality score, obtained by averaging his score on that trait over all the groups to which he belongs. Correspondingly, the mean of a group on its population characteristics can be assigned either in the "group-bound" or the "group-abstracted" values. For example, we can measure the superego strength of church members either on Sundays or weekdays. We believe that for most purposes of calculation it would be advantageous to define our $\bar{P}$ values as "group-abstracted" or true individual values, i.e., $\bar{P}'$ values. These personality scores would be retained as the individuals begin to operate as members of the group, and the changes $(\bar{P}'_1 - \bar{P}''_2)$ would remain to be explained by group structure and syntality laws.

2. Unique group traits, $\bar{P}''$, which are possessed in an all-or-nothing fashion, according as one does or does not belong to a particular group, and cannot enter into

quantitative calculations outside the group as can $\bar{P}'$ scores.

(4) *By group structure* (217, 328, 554, 1075, 1084, 1085, 1277, 1324) *characteristics we mean the patterns of interactions of individuals, out of which, by analysis, group traditions, roles, association patterns, hierarchies, cliques, status dimensions, etc. are inferred as constructs.* (This structure is symbolized by $\bar{T}$.)

These formal patterns and positions can, of course, be abstracted from the characteristics of any particular persons who occupy them, in any given concrete group, and stated as general group structure concepts. Comparatively little has yet been done to discover empirically the internal structures of groups. Sociologists, like Parsons (1136), have defined structures a priori or by the same general observation as the historian. Anthropologists like Mead (1025), and "sociometrists" like Moreno (1075), have brought out certain consistent interaction patterns. Bales (55) has contributed a valuable methodology for such interaction, and Fiedler (513, 514, 516) has shown the substantial contribution to syntality variance which occurs even from such a simple relation as that of "distance" (assumed similarity index) between leader and lieutenant.

(5) *By group syntality characteristics we mean the attributes describing the group when it acts as an organic whole* (217, 715). Syntality is used for groups in strict formal analogy to personality in individuals, thus, in personality we have:

$$(1a) \quad a_j = f.(S.P.)$$

and in groups,

$$(1b) \quad g_j = f.(\bar{S}.\bar{G}.)$$

where a_j and g_j are each a measured *response* (of the individual and the group respectively). Incidentally, when a is a response of one individual to another it will be called a *tie*. A tie is generically any relation between one person and another, e.g., an attitude, interaction, recognition

which can be inserted into a Q matrix (Chapter 9) of relations of any kind among people, for further sociometric calculations. The a response of an individual or the g response of a group are always functions of S or $\bar{S}$, the stimulus situation in which the individual or group stands, and of $\bar{P}$ and $\bar{G}$ which are, respectively, the total personality or the total syntality. Syntality, like personality, can exist only to the extent that the organism is organized. For, by definition of the variables measured therein, it deals with concerted action of the group *as a group*, through whatever organizing leadership structure exists.

That syntality, just like the personality, can in fact be experimentally measured in terms of a number of meaningful dimensions (corresponding to functional unities in group behavior discovered by simple-structure, uniquely rotated, factor analysis) was shown in 1954 by Cattell and Stice and has been conceptually incorporated in the work of Borgatta and Cottrell (130), Driver and Schuessler (429), Hemphill (715), Haas (661), Rummel (1241), and Strodt-beck (1359), among others. Naturally these dimensions must be those obtained from a stratified sample of the total ways of behaving of which a group is capable. Accordingly, the syntality $\bar{G}_i$ of a particular group, G_i, consists of a profile of scores on the syntality dimensions $f_1, f_2 \ldots f_Q$, as follows:

$$(2) \quad \bar{G}_i = f_{1i}, f_{2i} \ldots f_{Qi}.$$

Just as with personality, so the syntality presents a factor profile which can be used in the stimulus-response specification equation to estimate the response performance, g_i, of a group i, in a situation, j, thus:

$$(3) \quad g_{ji} = s_{j1}f_{1i} + s_{j2}f_{2i} \ldots + s_{jQ}f_{Qi}.$$

This is an expansion of the stimulus-response equation (1) above, familiar to all psychologists. Its contribution to formulation is that the dimensions of the syntality, $\bar{G}$, are now individually given as f_1, f_2, etc., and the dimensions of the stimulus situation, $\bar{S}$, as s_1, s_2, etc. Among the dimensions so far actually found and checked as functional factors for such prediction in small groups, are those defined as: (a) morale through leadership synergy; (b) morale of immediate synergy (cohesion), etc., while in national culture patterns the following are examples of replicated (554) dimensions: (a) cultural pressure; (b) integration; (c) affluence, etc., which will be discussed in Section 6 below.

To state the profile of scores of a given group on such a discovered set of primary dimensions is thus the most rapid and predictively potent way of characterizing it. Batteries have actually been published for thus measuring one common class of small groups, namely, neonate, leadership-structured groups, of about ten-man size (328). Naturally, the types of dimensions will differ with the types of group factored.

Before proceeding further, it may be necessary to point out that although the population, structure, and syntality panels can thus be *conceptually* and operationally separated and independently measured, this is not the same thing as stating that they are, in the normal situation, functionally and statistically independent. On the contrary, it is our assumption, formulated below, that any one of these panels should ultimately be inferable (as to the values in a particular group) from the remaining two, when the laws of group dynamics are known. For example, the performance of a group in building a house can be predicted (as yet imperfectly) from the mean intelligence of its members and the form of leadership structure, particularly in relation to intelligence distribution. But causation runs both ways, e.g., the mean population level on an information test may be a function of syntality, e.g., the national decision to require for its children an extra year of schooling.

From these basic definitions of a group as such, and its panels of description, we shall now turn to more specialized aspects of individual panels, beginning with syntality.

3. FIVE CONCEPTS CONCERNING SYNERGY AND THE DYNAMICS OF GROUPS

The remaining five of the ten basic propositions have to do with dynamics. The preliminary results on 100 groups of ten men each show that the larger of the dimensions of syntality are synergy dimensions (328). That is to say, tradition and structure being held constant, more seems to be contributed to variations in total group performance (syntality) by dynamic features of the population than by their differences in ability or personality traits. Accordingly, the dynamics of groups, in the sense of psychodynamics, remains perhaps the most important aspect of research.

To begin with this dynamics at the beginning, we need to state the proposition that the factoring of syntality can and does yield distinct dimensions of a dynamic character among the other dimensions.

(6) *A subset of all the dimensions of a group, i.e., those covering its total syntality description, will normally be of a dynamic character.*

They will describe the group's interests, the intensities of its goal strivings, the level of its dynamic integration, etc. This subspace (in factor terms), consisting of strictly dynamic dimensions, we have called the group *synergy* and shall represent symbolically by Y. This synergy, Y_i, for a group i, expresses the total energy or reactivity possessed by the group through the interest contributions of its members. Syntality dimensions that are strictly synergy dimensions will be indicated, among the f's which constitute the general syntality dimensions, by two subscripts, f_e representing the ergic coordinates, and f_m the sentiment coordinates. These correspond to two kinds of factors — (a) ergs or biological drives, and (b) sentiments or acquired unified attitude structures centered on cultural objects, e.g., home, religion — which have been repeatedly demonstrated in the structure of the dynamic measures of individuals.

Actually, no empirical results from factoring collections of purely dynamic measures obtained from the behavior of total *groups* have yet issued from research. But from our knowledge of the usual relations between factor studies on individuals and aggregates of individuals, it seems reasonably certain that the same unitary ergic structures, e.g., the escape, self-assertive, curiosity ergs, the religious, occupation, patriotic, etc., sentiments, would emerge as in individuals. Logically, this resolution of the intentions and aims of groups into the same ergs and sentiments as those of individuals must follow if our proposition, No. 1 above, is true, namely, that groups are instruments, to reach the motivational goals which first exist in individuals. Though the same ergic structure will hold for all groups, particular sentiment structures (f_m) should vary with group and culture. But in general, the synergy, Y, of a group, i, can be written as a profile in terms of a series of p ergs and q sentiments, thus:

(4) $Y_i = f_{e1i}, \ldots f_{epi}, f_{m1i} \ldots f_{mqi}$

where the f's are in standard scores on these dynamic structure factors.

(7) *The total synergy, in quantity and ergic quality, is equal to the sum of the energies which the individual members devote to the group.*

The various interest satisfactions which any one member gets from a group can be summed up in the strength of a single attitude, into which subsidiate (and are summed) all attitudes in his group activities, viz.: "In my present circumstances, I want to belong to group H." This intensity, I_h, is a vector quantity, projectable on ergic and sentiment coordinates. The sum of such attitudes, across all members, which is also a vector quantity, represents the group's total synergy, as follows:

(5) $Y_h = \overset{n}{\underset{0}{\Sigma}} I_h = \overset{n}{\underset{0}{\Sigma}} b_{e1}t_{e1} \ldots + \overset{n}{\underset{0}{\Sigma}} b_{ek}t_{ek}$

$+ \overset{n}{\underset{0}{\Sigma}} b_{m1}t_{m1} \ldots \overset{n}{\underset{0}{\Sigma}} b_{mk}t_{mk}$

where t_e and t_m are the individual trait measures on ergic and sentiment factors respectively. (When we take, as usual, the b's [behavioral indices] to be the same for all people, these can be placed before the summation sign.)

The recent development of batteries, such as the Motivational Analysis Test (297, 333), shown to measure attitude intensities and ergic tension strengths in individuals more validly than the traditional opinionnaire (employing merely conscious self-evaluation of motive), makes such measurement of group synergy a practical research possibility. It might be objected to theorem (7) above that "less the energies absorbed in internal conflict" should be added to it. This notion has been taken care of in the concepts of "effective" and "maintenance" synergies below, but, in the sense that the individual energy expresses itself in *some* group process, theorem (7) is correct as it stands.

(8) *Input and output of synergy are equal, but can be separately analyzed into different component systems.*

This states that the stimulus sources, on the one hand, and the group utilizations, on the other, of the total group synergy can be separately analyzed, conceptually and operationally. The chief, but not exhaustive *sources* of synergy, from individuals, are:

(a) Explicit group goal synergy, Y_G, i.e., motivation by the sentiments and ergs achieving satisfaction in the *expressed purposes, ideals, and activities* for which the group exists;

(b) Intrinsic synergy, Y_I, i.e., satisfactions in congenial, gregarious contacts which occur in any group, whatever its deliberate purposes;

(c) Status synergy, Y_S, e.g., ergic motivation, largely of a self-assertive nature from statuses held in the group;

(d) Occupational activity synergy, Y_O, i.e., pleasure from skills and activities as such, in the group procedures, regardless of their goal; and,

(e) Personal reward synergy, Y_R, i.e., token, e.g., money, rewards which permit reward of the individual through other than direct, situationally tied, ergic satisfactions, perhaps quite outside the group.

The main (and exhaustive) divisions in the *utilization* of synergy, on the other hand, are:

(a) Effective synergy, Y_E, i.e., energy expended in the performance of group tasks, e.g., a missionary endeavor, a war, over and above that used merely in maintaining the organic being of the group; and,

(b) Maintenance synergy, Y_M, concerned simply with keeping the group operational and in being.

Input and output will, of course, be equal, as expressed by:

$$(6) \quad Y_{E_h} + Y_{M_h}$$

$$= Y_{G_h} + Y_{I_h} + Y_{S_h} + Y_{O_h} + Y_{R_h}$$

$$= \sum_0^n I_h = Y_h$$

where the subscripts represent the divisions of the last two paragraphs.

Maintenance and effective synergies (Y_M, Y_E, etc.), on the one hand, and the intrinsic and goal (etc.) synergies (Y_G, Y_I, etc.), on the other, can be separately expressed as ergic vectors, i.e., as specific intensities of need satisfactions with specific emotional quality. Such analysis, of course, is particularly relevant to studies of group development, in which effective leadership and learning are measurable by success in changing the amounts and qualities of the ergic and sentiment satisfactions of the group's members, thus affecting total synergy.

(9) *Groups typically show interrelations in terms of subsidiation and overlap with other groups.*

Much theory and experiment over the past twenty years has unfortunately taken the ineffectual design of analyzing the dynamics of a group *as if it were an independent and self-sufficient entity,* whereas in truth the laws of its behavior can be found only when phenomena are considered in a wider context of dynamic exchanges both within and between groups. Virtually all groups have dependencies upon other groups in two senses:

(a) Groups *themselves* are arranged, as integral organisms, in dynamic subsidiations with other groups, i.e., they exist to serve, and are sometimes created by, the purposes of other groups, or enjoy symbiosis with other groups in larger functional purposes; and,

(b) Their *members* are simultaneously members of other groups, and have other responsibilities and loyalties, which affect their behavior in the given group.

There are thus two senses in which any group is in a dynamic equilibrium: (a) as a unit organism, operating in a total population of group organisms, and (b) as it is affected in structure and syntality by what goes on, even remotely in other groups which in some degree *share its population* (membership). The former equilibrium might be called an "interacting group equilibrium" and the latter a "population overlap equilibrium." A particular instance of lack of regard for the latter has been the widespread tendency in "group dynamics" experiments (of a kind which claim to attempt to establish general laws) to fail to allow for the fact that the small groups operate within a single, embracing, national culture pattern and a framework of multigroup dynamics. However, an illuminating treatment of this problem has been given more recently by Guetzkow (621) and by Simmel (1324).

Full development of formulae for these complex equilibria is not to be pursued in this space, but the more basic propositions (1) *that the synergy exchanges of a group with other groups leaves the total synergy of the total group system unchanged,* and (2) *that any individual's total interest in all group and all non-group attitudes normally remains a constant,* can be expressed as follows:

$$(7) \quad Y_j + Y_h \ldots + Y_l = C$$

where *j, h,* and *l* are groups in a single

dynamic subsidiation and C is a constant total, and

$$(8)\ \sum_0^l I_{ji} + \sum_0^z I_{ki} = K_i$$

where I_j's are attitude interest intensities with respect to all l groups to which the individual i belongs; the I_k's are his interests in z non-group attitudes, and K_i is the individual i's total constant interest-energy. Incidentally, it follows from (8) that the surest way to destroy a group is to provide outlets for a set of attitudes for group or for non-group attitudes which exactly satisfy, in ergic composition, the measured "belonging" attitudes which are found operating in, and have grown up for, this group.

(10) *Syntality is the concept at present having the greatest utility and negotiability in formulating behavioral laws of groups (both to other groups and to individuals).*

This is not a scientific "value judgment," but a proposition about the actual *frequency of use* of the concept, and formulae representing it, in calculations and predictions. Its high frequency as an intermediate term or variable results from the fact that all laws and generalizations about groups must concern either:

(a) Inter-group relations, i.e., *syntality to syntality;* or

(b) Group-to-individual relations, i.e., *syntality to personality;* or

(c) Inter-individual relations, i.e., *personality to personality;* or

(d) Group-to-environment relations, i.e., *syntality to environmental stimulus situation* formulations.

In three of these four, syntality is an indispensable term, though, incidentally, personality approaches it in frequency, even in group transactions, as a pivotal concept.

4. SOME AREAS OF EXPERIMENTAL GROWTH IN SEARCH OF CLEARER MODELS

It may be good philosophy, or even mathematics, to pursue a model to its utmost logical and experimental expression, but it is not always good science. Experiment not directed by those clear-cut theories which we call models are often asking pointless questions; but it is also true that the model maker cannot safely go far without waiting for the hints in looser experimental work to catch up with him and modify his model. The above concepts of syntality and synergy, of ties, roles, and the application of the dynamic calculus to individual and group relations have seemed very promising to many, and they have stimulated some basic experiment on small groups and personality-group relations, but it would be unrewarding to refine the model further until it has been more widely tried out.

In this section it is proposed to glance briefly over some fields of endeavor which have been the subjects of fairly sustained multivariate experiment, but which are perhaps in need of exploratory relations to such a general model. These include:

(1) Certain areas of economic behavior such as determining the dimensions of each type of business, the dimensions of spending behavior, the effects of advertising, and the phenomena of trade cycles, and intergroup relations (1216), viewed as motivational analysis by the dynamic calculus.

(2) Many areas of sociology, notably the undertakings by Warner (1502) and others to define social class; Cottrell's, Baldwin's (52, 53), and others' work on the dimensions of family atmospheres and intrafamilial behavior; Lazarsfeld's (910) studies of opinion groups; Tryon's (1456, 1457) steps to formulate the characteristics of urban subdivisions and administrative localities; and Cooley's (378) studies of primary groups.

(3) The study of values, as cultural, community, and individual values, by Morris (1077), Gouldner (612), Triandis (1445), and many others who have sought to bring order into the description of values, religious beliefs, etc., and their role in motivation.

(4) The use of games theory to study the interaction of groups, especially of the give and take of national groups in diplomacy, as in the "simulation" studies of Guetzkow (621) and the work of Zajonc (1599).

(5) The whole field of interaction (55, 328) in groups and of communicative acts (1097, 1129, 73, 913). This quickly involves the concept and measurement of roles (1359), notably in leadership (592, 516, 106).

(6) The relation of formal organization to role and interaction behavior, and the process of growth of organization in business and other units, as in the work of Bass (73), Shartle (1307), Stogdill (1354), and others.

(7) The study of political organization and voting behavior, as in the researches of Digman and Tuttle (420), Harris (690), Wrigley (1589), and others.

If we consider these and other developments from the standpoint of their effective use of, and contribution toward, theoretical models, we notice first that the work on characteristics of localities by Tryon, on primary groups by Cooley, on families by Baldwin, is well adapted to handling by syntality and synergy concepts and has to a considerable extent been so advanced, in dimensional terms, e.g., by Tryon and Baldwin and Hemphill. More detailed examination of this model will be made in Section 6 below.

The concept of social status, enriched in sociological detail by Warner and others, has nevertheless not been expressed in very precise model form. A first factor analysis of social status data in 1942 by Cattell, using occupations as entries, revealed a predominant general factor, loading prestige ratings, intelligence, occupational complexity, size of family (inversely), and a number of other variables. It was then possible to relate this dimension to psychological variables (notably with significant relations to dominance, surgency, emotional stability, and mental disorder incidence), and to use it as a means of more precisely evaluating social mobility, its

causes and effects. A lapse of nearly twenty years occurred, however, before sociologists followed this up with multivariate correlational studies along the same lines, seeking more precisely to define the dimension, and to reveal ancillary dimensions which probably exist in social status data. The model makes it possible to study more precisely the cultural differences and time changes in social status structure. For example, the intelligence level of an occupation had higher loading on social status (prestige rating being unit loading) than did income, in Cattell's 1942 study. Cultures are conceivable in which physical strength, or number of cattle owned, etc. could preempt this loading. Recent surveys show that, in the twenty-year period since that research, wealth has dropped in loading, e.g., through decline of the "banker" and rise of the "scientist" ratings. What the factor analysis showed is that social status is centrally prestige.

In the field of economics *as a specialized branch of social and dynamic psychology,* it is no exaggeration to say that all is yet chaos. The long-awaited bridging from primary drives to buying and selling behavior is, however, now rendered probable, or, at any rate possible, by the research in the dynamic calculus system having provided means for objectively measuring ergic tension levels (Chapter 20), and the development of sentiments about economic values, among other values. Psychological models have also been suggested for such economic phenomena as the business cycle. For example, if we suppose that an individual's level of education is positively correlated with his level of native intelligence (fluid general ability, g_f, see Chapter 18) sufficiently to permit us, as a first approximation, to regard an individual's final effective ability (largely crystallized intelligence, g_c) as a single entity, then we may consider that we deal for the moment with a normal distribution curve in the population in this ability. Unemployment will exist disproportionately at both ends of this curve—at the upper end because a successful rentier class "retires" or goes into non-productive, sybaritic activity in arts, etc., and at the lower end because low intelligences become virtually unemployable. (The intelligence of the destitute and chronically unemployed has been shown (203) to average significantly and distinctly below the national average.)

In a booming economy the average intelligence level of the employed group (the central ability range) will tend to drop because (1) more managerial persons will do well enough to retire, and (2) more important, industry will "scrape the bottom of the barrel," cutting into the normally borderline employable. Both of these will lead to a less efficient and intelligent production, and initiate a discrepancy between cost of product and resources to buy it, starting the ensuing swing into a down trend. These effects may be exaggerated by a birth rate trend more highly productive of borderline employable intelligence, and a change in production methods, through automation, requiring fewer persons at moderate to low intelligence levels. However, on such theories the psychologist and the economist have still to get together, for multivariate, cross-disciplinary, experimental data-gathering.

In regard to the study of formal organization in business, military, etc., units as defined by Cooley (379), Parsons (1136), Durkheim (442), and others, the interesting findings of French (554), Stogdill (1354), Shartle (1316), Bass (73), and others on "organizations in being" are likely to be linked with the interaction process analysis, and communication studies in experimental groups by Bales (54), Cattell and Stice (328), Berkowitz (106), Rohrer and Sherif (1216), Fiedler (514), Gibb (592), Hemphill (716), Schrader (1277), French and Zajonc (548), and others. However, it cannot be said that any comprehensive model has yet emerged to handle the complex interactions of communication paths, decision hierarchies, roles, lines of service, and the more "given"

personality traits, group dimensions and traditions involved. Bass has suggested the use of a longitudinal, *P*-technique type of analysis to study organizations in evolution. This would have the advantage of throwing light, through the sequential information, on the causes for the appearance of certain kinds of communication and role patterns, but it has not yet been tried.

The remaining topics above—the study of values, and the use of games and simulation experiments in international behavior—deserve separate sections. Here one must briefly refer, however, to the need for models for studying the interaction of individuals which take the total personality and role endowment into account as well as the existing group situation. The interaction of individuals has so far entered research largely through the use of the *interaction behavior categories* of Bales (54) or the slightly fuller list of Cattell and Stice (328). But this still leaves the wider model, in a stimulus-response sense, partly undefined.

5. THE STUDY OF VALUES, POLITICAL AND GENERAL

It can perhaps be shown in this section that the study of political voting behavior, religious and other value systems, and of certain cultural value comparisons, belongs to the same system of theoretical models. Countless correlational analyses have been made of value systems since the early arbitrary taxonomies of, for example, Spranger, and the interest-values test of Allport and Vernon (19), outstanding among which have been the factor analyses by Morris (1077), Eysenck (481), Gouldner and Peterson (612), Triandis and Triandis (1445), and others. But the unanswered question is "How do values and value attitudes fit into the known dynamic structure of the individual?" For the tendency has been to treat "values" as abstractions unrelated to what the clinician, for example, knows about personality dynamics, and if values are to affect behavior they must fit into that mechanism somewhere.

The term "value" is itself an extremely loose one, covering artistic taste, religious and ethical beliefs, political loyalties, economics, and almost any interest whatever, e.g., food interests. It quickly becomes apparent that if it is used as synonymous with desires or goals it is a superfluous term. To say that if I like modern pictures or enjoy playing golf I have "artistic values" or "athletic values" is a piece of unnecessary verbiage, for "interests" is adequate. The scores of an individual on a profile of dynamic traits, as in the MAT battery, state what drives are important to him and what sentiment objects have the largest investment, just as the synergy profile of a group states what goals ("values" if you please) are important to its culture. But it would better fit our reinforcement dynamics simply to call these *goals*. If one wishes to ascribe qualities of "being a goal" to an object, then it may be verbally convenient to say they have *valencies*, using valency to indicate a provoker of desire of any kind, i.e., of ergic tension level vis-à-vis an object, concrete and abstract. Then the term *value* can be given more precise meaning as being restricted to a special subclass of valencies which writers have been striving in various ways to distinguish. In the first place, values should be restricted to valencies consciously recognized by their possessors. To like pork chops is a valency, but to believe that liking pork chops is a good thing comes close to being a value. To believe in moderation in eating is undoubtedly a value, according to common usage. But if a person believes in it only for himself, then it is an ordinary attitude — part of a sentiment toward, say, physical fitness, or the ergic goal of safety (from, say, heart disease). The term value has come to have one meaning — that we believe in the thing "in the abstract" — from which it follows that it is good for everyone, no matter how much we may abstain from active evangelizing.

Values are thus evident in attitudes, or sentiments (involving several attitudes), each with the stimulus-response form "In the world as it is [this situation] I want so much to see people adopting such and such a guide to behavior." It is thus an attitude (1) very distal in the dynamic lattice from ergic goals, (2) dealing with complex "objects" which are abstractions from human behavior, such as modes of satisfaction, skills, virtues, moral inhibitions, (3) referred to a human community, or some community over and above the individual, and (4) conscious.

By this definition, typical values would be illustrated by the attitudes: "I would like to see everyone believing in God"; "I want to see more abstract art in our art galleries"; "I believe in physical fitness [for people]"; whereas, "I like to stay in bed late," or an unconscious "I like a warm room more than fresh air" would be valencies, not values. It *may* be deemed unfortunate that this definition rules out "unconscious values." The fact that a man prefers money to truth may be inferred from his conduct when he himself is unaware of it. But this kind of inference is always very difficult, requiring almost omniscient vision of what leads to what in our social life. And even if we could make it, the fact that it differs for the subject from a conscious value justifies distinguishing it as an inferred valency rather than a value.

From empirical research on values, from the above definition of value as being referred to society, and from the dynamic structure described in Chapter 20, it is evident that value attitudes have their location (by factor loadings and subsidiation studies) largely in the self-sentiment and the superego sentiment structures. *Some* variance in value attitudes, however, as in any attitudes, must come from personality factors. Thus it is clear, for example, from the loading pattern, that much of the variance in Eysenck's "tenderminded-vs.-toughminded" attitude factor is due to personality factor I, Premsia-vs.-Harria.

This is a conspicuous example of what the present writer has called the effect of "temperament as a hidden premise" in helping to determine interests and attitudes. That is to say, in the syllogisms, rationally pursued, which follow as a man argues for his beliefs, there will ultimately appear, if he is rational enough, a certain premise (of which he need not previously have been aware) that his temperamental needs are such and such. For example, an elderly person's argument for the need for a new house thermostat may ultimately trace to a low personal metabolic rate.

That temperamental personality factors contribute to the variance of acquired dynamic attitudes, each, indeed, appearing as one of several general factors calculable among them, can be readily demonstrated. But this does not mean that the greater part of the attitude variance is not of dynamic modality and learnt, acquired form. Regard must also be paid to the cognitive variance in dynamic traits, and especially in values, which comes from departures from logical connectedness, and from dissonances and inconsistencies which begin in emotional needs. These inconsistencies have been studied under Festinger's notion of *cognitive dissonance,* and were earlier studied under the tests of *general logical inconsistency* employed in personality integration research by Gruen, Coan, Cattell, Saunders, and others investigating hypotheses about personality factors (240). Objective motivation measurement research (Chapter 20) has also shown misbelief and misperception, notably as in autism and various defense mechanisms, to enter into the cognitive expression of attitudes.

These influences require reference because the term "values" is frequently associated with the term "beliefs." To say "I believe in moral restraint in sexual matters," is quite different, however, from "I believe that hydrogen is the lightest element" and is really only a figure of speech for the value attitude "I want to see moral restraint in sexual matters more widely practiced." But beliefs are, nevertheless, in a special way tied up with values. For many values, by their abstractness, are not susceptible to the kind of proof on which more concrete sentiments normally rest, and the role of autism, in everyone, is necessarily greater in all such abstract or vaguely perceptible areas. Thus to say "I believe Americans are more interested in world peace than are most nationals," or "I believe Pre-Raphaelite art creates more beauty than does Post-impressionism," or "I believe in God," is to confess a value in terms of a belief which the sophisticated speaker realizes is as uncheckable and autistic as the views of his opponent.

Such "digression" into a psychological model is essential if statistical analysis is to be carried out with proper regard to the implied mathematical model. The line between values and ordinary attitudes and valencies may not admit of being drawn with categorical sharpness by applying the definitions above concerning four main characteristics, but it is a beginning. For what are typical attitudes aimed at bringing about socially desirable ends, i.e., value attitudes, are likely to be found dynamically attached largely to the two factor structures we call the self-sentiment and the superego. They are abstract desiderata, like beauty, truth, goodness, power, comfort, etc., with which the individual has identified himself as the means of maintaining self-regard and the regard of others, together with satisfying the categorical imperatives of the superego.

To find correlation clusters or factors among checked opinionnaire items on "values" is therefore unlikely to tell us what we need to know about the dynamics of values. They need to be measured as attitudes, by objective devices, in the company of representatives of the chief dynamic structures and of general personality temperament factors which are likely to make contributions to the value variance which needs to be identified and distinguished. A movement in this direction was made by Morris's factoring (1077), across different national cultures, of value statements, along with personality and temperament measures, leading to seven value sets. But the analysis of personality dynamics by multivariate experimental measures was not at that time advanced enough to serve as a foundation, and these dimensions need to be examined by more refined methods.

The field of politics is an excellent example of the measurement of attitudes which are strictly value attitudes, in that, by definition, voting behavior is aimed at desirables for everyone—desirables of a fairly complex (not merely ergic) kind. Gosnell (609) pioneered in factoring the 1932 election returns in Chicago, finding some three "value" systems. Later researches have turned to transposed factor analysis, either under the mistaken impression that Q technique (not Q' technique, which searches for clusters) leads to a means of detecting party groupings in the votes of elected representatives, or as a means of getting the dimensions of the stimuli (political issues) when there are fewer people than issues (so that R technique cannot be used).

Carlson and Harrell (187) thus used Q technique on 17 senators and 17 representatives, finding party affiliation, New Deal values, and two uninterpretable dimensions. Alker (16) has attempted to factor the conflict interaction itself. Harris (690) took 9 issues and 95 senators in the 80th Congress and found factors of big business-vs.-bureaucracy; isolationism-vs.-internationalism; and agriculture-vs.-industry. Thurstone and Degan similarly reached three factors. Shubert (1318, 1319) has examined the methodology in relation to concrete data. An interesting variation of the Q-technique approach was made by Digman and Tuttle (420), who "rotated for political party." Recently Wrigley (unpublished) has studied United Nations General Assembly voting records by similar methods. He finished with four blocs of countries which, incidentally, have a very

suggestive resemblance to those discussed in Section 6 below, and which are derived from *total* culture pattern resemblance. From this we may hypothesize that basic similarity of culture is important in determining similarity of voting behavior, the correlation being perhaps upset secondarily by situational-historical antagonisms and alliances.

These studies have been plagued by technical difficulties and have not as yet come up with results coherent across many experiments. Possibly the need of a more comprehensive theoretical model, as discussed in Sections 2, 3, and 7 of this chapter, has also prevented a proper precision and fruitfulness of conclusion.

6. THE RECOGNITION OF CULTURE PATTERNS

After Malinowski (981) turned anthropologists from a somewhat magpie collecting of bright ethnic curiosities (which, at its best, led to Fraser's *Golden Bough*) to the "functionalist" viewpoint of a culture as a total organic pattern, a phase of mere speculation about these "functional patterns" ensued for a time. The work of Benedict (97), Mead (1025), and others, interpreting the dynamics of such patterns, was accompanied by a pseudo-scientific union between anthropology and psychoanalysis, in which there was virtually no attempt to check generalizations by measurement or careful, repeated observation.

When the concepts of syntality and synergy appeared, with accompanying defined operations for discovering the functionally unitary dimensions in the behavioral manifestations of small groups, it soon became evident that these could also be applied to large, tradition-bearing groups, e.g., national groups, as well as to the small manipulated groups of "group dynamics." Indeed, it was quickly evident that the latter yield more stable syntalities than do transient, ad hoc, experimental groups. Consequently, although comparatively few "small-group experimentalists" have yet faced up to the technical difficulties encountered in the pioneer work of Cattell, Gibb, Hemphill, Stice, and Lawson (907) in their small-group experiments (particularly in finding a means of handling the unstable variances), several systematic researchers have followed up the parallel pioneer work on national cultures with success notably in the researches of Rummel (1241), Hofstaetter (734), Driver and Schuessler (429), Gibb (593), Cattell and Gorsuch (289), Jonassen (813), and others.

Before proceeding let us note that the multivariate study of culture patterns requires two distinct stages: (1) Determination of the dimensions of syntality and (2) A Q'-technique classification into types according to pattern similarity based on profiles on these dimensions. A culture — or a culture pattern — in the standard sense, is something which pervades *several* groups. It has chiefly been used for a set of primitive, pre-literate groups, but Toynbee's "a civilization," extending across several nations, is formally the same thing, and can be recognized objectively by the same two-stage procedure.

Simply, and therefore crudely stated, the proposition of the present writer in the 1940's was to obtain scores for a sufficient sample of nations on a suitable set of psychological, sociological, economic, geographical, medical, and other variables, and to intercorrelate and factor the latter to obtain the meaningful dimensions by which any national culture can best be described — or measured for hypotheses about cultural changes, causal effects, etc.

Before one can proceed to the usual inferences from factor analysis, however, one must consider certain questions:

(1) How far can one infer necessary causal connection of behaviors within a culture if nations are not completely self-contained systems, since it is necessary, if causal dependence is to be deduced, that each should reap what it sows? This question of whether we are dealing with "organic unities," akin to personalities, becomes still more trenchant when the method is applied to cities and states as units within the U.S.A., etc.

(2) Is the total of 60 to 120 countries on which data can now be obtained to be considered a "sample," from which inference is made to a "population," or is it the whole population? Since the laws may need to be applied to the same countries at times other than the present, they are, in this sense a "sample out of history," but in another sense it can be argued that existing nations are the whole population.

(3) What period of time should be considered adequate for a behavioral measurement? "Birth rate" can be reliably taken from a year or two, but "frequency of involvement in war" requires perhaps a half century as an "observation period."

(4) Should one use ratios, such as "persons per square mile," or crude area and population, etc.? This is a dilemma in many other fields of factor analysis too (see Chapter 6 above), but the avoidance of skewed distributions and algebraic dependencies may be less powerful arguments in this realm of analysis than the need to express culture patterns in their most meaningful terms.

(5) Should one first seek dimensions from the totality of nations, old and new, pre- and post-industrial, etc., or factor members of one species of group at a time? The answer to this has been given in Chapter 9, in that one can only *know* what species exist after finding dimensions.

(6) Finally, and this is the most important, should the experimenter include in a *single* factor analysis measures from *all three* panels — syntality, structure, and population characters — of group description? Or should he factor one at a time? If we assume that relations among panels are complex and non-linear, it is probably best to factor them separately. But in a first, hypothesis-creating survey it may be fruit-

ful to take them together, as was done in the pioneer researches here. That the variables should run across sociological, psychological, medical, and other data, on the assumption that numerous causal connections pay little heed to academic organization, seems certain. (The automatic conservative resistance which delays recognition of "causes across disciplines" makes one wish for more instances of the fresh breeze across academic pedantries so vigorously introduced in the work of Ellsworth Huntington, 799.)

The first study of this nature took 72 variables on 70 nations, measures running over the years 1927-1937, except for those of low frequencies (wars, revolutions) which were taken for fifty years, 1887-1937. Although there is risk of instability in factoring with practically as many variables as entries, in this case re-factoring with two different N's of entries yielded essentially the same results (219, 231, 289). Simple structure seems as sound a resolution principle here as elsewhere, in that such obviously verifiable factors as bigness and wealth appeared, along with others, however, which were new, such as cultural pressure, morale, vigorous order, urban rationalism, etc.

This R-technique approach was followed by a P-technique approach, data being correlated over a hundred years for Britain (231), for America (265), and for Australia (593). Again simple structure gave meaningful factors consisting of functional unities existing in historical directions of change. The usual transformation of emphasis between R-technique and P-technique factors was visible, and the number of state-dimension factors was not as great as the number of trait dimensions (see Chapter 11), presumably because of permanent geographical, natural resource, race, and situational influences generating trait characters. However, the factors of cultural pressure, affluence-education, and morale which will be described below have proved

to be as visible as growth dimensions in these historical changes as they had been in the R-technique analysis of individual differences of nations.

With the emergence of these "unitary traits" in the syntalities of large national groups it became possible, as with a personality, to assign a measured profile to each. Here, at length, appeared the possibility of objectively classifying groups—tribes, nations—into larger "culture patterns" by actually calculating the resemblances by Q' technique and using the Taxonome program to sort them into families. Of course, as in all Q'-technique work, the outcome would depend partly on the areas of behavior comprehended in the choice of variables, but not so much as if variables instead of factors had been used. That the choice of variables initially made (219) hits the more basic factors is shown by the agreement of the ensuing culture pattern classification (below) with that made by historians and anthropologists. Nevertheless, as the following section brings out, there is need for refinement now in the further choice of variables.

The actual search for culture patterns was made by "correlating" by the r_p pattern similarity coefficient and applying the ramifying linkage method (Chapter 11) in the Taxonome program. This revealed ten appreciably distinct families, among which were the Catholic Mediterranean culture (Italy, Spain, Portugal—also Poland); the Scandinavian culture (Denmark, Norway, Finland, etc.—and Switzerland); the Middle East (Egypt, Iraq, Turkey, Saudi Arabia, etc.) and so on. While this determination of culture pattern areas objectively agreed in the main with the "civilizations" of Toynbee, and general cultural impressions, it also revealed some new groupings and unexpected affiliations.

On the basis of these groupings it should now be possible to determine more exactly the cultural dimensions *within* each of these relatively homogeneous groups.

7. CONCEPTS DEVELOPED IN CULTURAL DYNAMICS

The precise implications of this successful location of cultural and developmental dimensions by multivariate methods and concepts have naturally not immediately been grasped by political scientists and anthropologists accustomed to older methods. However, an appreciable activity has arisen in applying correlational methods to related data, with assumptions which now need to be examined. Some have tried a change of the type of entry constituting the set, as in Jonassen and Peres' (813) use of districts, and Hofstaetter's (734) use of states within the U.S.A. E. L. Thorndike made a classical study (1395, 1396) of American cities, in which, however, he operated with two rather arbitrary clusters, "General goodness of living" and "Moral level," rather than empirically separated clusters or factors. Driver and Schuessler have applied the methods to American Indian cultures, with results which definitely clarify some obscurities left by "intuitive" procedures. Berry (108) and Schnore (1275) have made studies on economic development of regions, and Quincy Wright (1585) has performed an "intuitive factor analysis" of international behavior variables. It was not until the last year or two, however, that any truly adequate repetition of the pioneer studies of 1949 was made, by Gorsuch (289) and by Rummel (1241), with results which in the latter's large-scale study have still to be matched, when their rotation is complete.

Although the degree of independence of cities and provinces (states of the U.S.A.) is not such as would be expected to produce as much feedback of effects within each as would lead to factors having their full quota of associated effects, yet resemblance of the emerging dimensions to those of countries is unmistakable. They are, in any case, a different species; yet some cross-species resemblance may be expected. One factor which does survive transition pretty well is that of affluence-education, to be considered shortly.

In this condensed survey the significance of the multivariate concepts discovered for cultural dynamics can be illustrated by only three instances—the dimensions of affluence-education, morale, and cultural pressure. The first has shown the following loading pattern:

Affluence-Education
(or Enlightened Affluence-vs-Narrow Poverty)

High expenditure per head on education
High real standard of living
Higher expenditure on "extras" (travel, sugar consumption)
Low death rate from tuberculosis
High musical creativity
Low government censorship of press, etc.

plus other variables showing intelligent use of resources and educational use of leisure.

A curious aspect of this pattern is the association of educational variables and wealth variables. Single pairs of correlations of education levels and wealth have been noted before, e.g., over states in the U.S.A. and cities, and the connection has been alternatively interpreted as (1) education being one more form of luxury expenditure and (2) enlightenment leading to more effective production of wealth from natural resources. It is not impossible that a higher level of native intelligence is responsible for both (204).

A dimension which seems to involve both morale and morality—which are likely to be closely bound in a group as such—has emerged now in three studies, with the following saliently loaded:

Morale and Morality

Low frequency of syphilis
Low frequency of homicides
Low death rate from alcoholism
Low death rate from typhoid fever
More eminent men eminent outside the field of politics
Small proportion of births illegitimate
Better education and civil rights for women

Fewer families per single house
No licensing of prostitution
Fewer deaths from tuberculosis
No absolute restriction on divorce
Low divorce rate
Low gross birth rate
Low gross death rate

This simple structure factor brings in most of the variables ever entered that had to do with morality (mostly judged by effects, since direct measures do not exist) of the population and morale of the national syntality. It is well confirmed on a second span of years (1927-1937 and 1953-1958) by Cattell and Gorsuch (289). Apart from the issue of the exact relation between the concept of morality in the population panel and morale in the syntality panel, we clearly have here a dimension corresponding to higher ethical values, greater self-control, and more concern with the life of the group. (Such indices as typhoid fever death rate reflect conditions which can only be improved by community conscience.)

The third example is as deliberately chosen to represent something unfamiliar as the first two were to show that factors may be common-sense concepts. Tentatively called Cultural Pressure, it loads the following:

Cultural Pressure

High ratio of tertiary to primary occupations
High frequency of political clashes with other countries
High frequency of cities over 20,000 (per 1,000,000 inhabitants)
High number of Nobel prizes in Science, Literature, Peace (per 1,000,000 inhabitants)
High frequency of participation in wars (1837-1937)
High frequency of treaties and negotiations with other countries
High expansiveness (gain in area and resources)
Many ministries maintained by government
High creativity in science and philosophy
High musical creativity
High death rate from suicide
High incidence of mental disease
High horsepower available per worker

High percentage of population in urban areas
High cancer death rate
High divorce rate
More severe industrial depression in world depression
High total foreign trade per capita
Numerous patents for inventions per capita
Higher number of women employed out of home
More riots
Lower illegitimate birth rate

The theory which the present writer has developed from this well-confirmed pattern can best be approached by noting first the four descriptive aspects involved: (1) High cultural productivity in the sense of science, art, invention; (2) High industrialization and urbanization; (3) High frustration and pugnacity as shown outwardly directed in riots, wars, etc., and inwardly directed in suicide, mental disorder and, possibly, cancer; and (4) National expansiveness and interaction on the world scene, as shown by treaties, international trade, and expansion of controlled area. Psychologically the central feature is a snowballing of the complication of living. In more exact terms, this means that ergic satisfactions are obtained by more complex, long-circuited paths, acquired with greater learning difficulty, under the influence of frustration, and the greater cognitive activity thus engendered produces additional environmental changes further complicating the adjustment. The total ergic satisfaction of needs for food, security, etc., may actually increase, but the means for attaining it become more exacting, and more frustrating to lower intelligences. The movement from direct "instinctual" ergic modes of satisfaction thus spirals into increasing aggressiveness, invention, mental illness, and national expansion.

It is not surprising that so emphatic a pattern has been dimly seen "in the rough" before its factor-analytic demonstration. But it is revealing, from a methodological standpoint, that these glimpses have been extraordinarily partial and "biased." Thus countless historians have seen it as "in-dustrialization," and Toynbee has seen it as "a time of troubles." Sociologists have con-sidered it, like Davis (410), under the con-cept of urbanization, like Merton (1047) as "stress" and "strain," and like Tarde (1381), and incidentally, Durkheim (442) and De Grazia (414), under the aspect of "anomie." Freud has touched on one aspect of it in "Civilization and its Discontents" (556), while Sorokin (1335) and Unwin (1478) have seen it as an ongoing cultural and military expansion process or phase. The latter has perhaps come nearest of all in his correlation, among preliterate peoples, of higher religious development with block-ing of simple ergic sexual expression, and his perception of the rise of tribal and national expansiveness from both.

With the theory as now defined, it should be possible to enter with more apt varia-bles, especially where resources exist for attitude measurements on actual popula-tions, to test the thesis that urbanization, industrialization, etc. are merely physical accompaniments of a fundamental psycho-logical dimension of "ergic long-circuiting" (frustration to sublimation), of which the invention, wars, riots, rising living standard, anomie (and suicide), and cultural produc-tivity are diverse expressions.

Such concepts as the above, developed at the macroscopic level in cultural dynamics, need to be related to *measurements* at the population level, testing such theories of relation to personality dynamics as have just been stated.

8. STRATEGIC EXPERIMENTAL DEVELOPMENTS IN RELATION TO MULTIVARIATE CONCEPTS

The implication of the foregoing factor-analytic approach is that a specification equation can be made out for either a syntality characteristic, such as likelihood of involvement in war, or a population characteristic, such as the percentage of marriages ending in divorce. For example,

the following has been suggested (Cattell, 219) from existing data for the former. It is a short step from prediction for a single country in isolation to a model for two or more countries in interaction, which there is no reason to treat differently from those for individuals in interaction (Chapter 25, and Section 4 above). This has been recognized by Guetzkow (621), who has allowed individuals to act as "sovereign countries' in simulated interaction, to find the new parameters of the interaction process as such. Naturally there are un-certainties as to how far this can be carried over to actual interactions of nations and rendered comparable with direct inter-action studies such as those of Alher (16, 16a) and Rummel (1241) and those sur-veyed by Merritt and Rokkan (1046a). By correlating actual international behaviors with the general culture pattern dimensions Cattell (219) obtained the following formula for the probability (frequency), W_p, of involvement in war:

$$W_p = .60F_C + .19F_I - .06F_F$$

where F_C is cultural pressure, F_I the indus-triousness factor, and F_F a dimension at present dubbed "fastidiousness."

However, the majority of researchers in this area have not yet availed themselves of the dozen or more newly definable cultural dynamics concepts but have remained with those lower-level and partially perceived entities which exist in literature and rough historical generalization. Many, for exam-ple, have concentrated on the "applied" problems of the origins of war. Even the most original and ingenious of theories on this basis, such as Richardson's profound mathematical analysis (1197), leading to a generalization of a constant sum total of pugnacious and destructive needs, is less satisfying than the tracing of war to diverse origins in the above specification equation. Haas (661) explores Merton's (1047) the-ory of stress and strain (unemployment, etc.) as causes of war and breaks down the chain of causation into steps suggested by

Bales (54). Like many working with bivariate approaches, he finds a number of moderately significant differences and correlations. But as many alternative theories are usually equally acceptable to explain a single significant relation, and the number of "valid" theories is reduced only by having a multivariate pattern of significant relations (Chapter 2 above), one may question whether this is as good a research strategy as beginning with concepts derived as above from a comprehensive array of variables. Certainly the cultural pressure concept is more than stress, or urbanization, or political expansiveness alone, and its predictive utility over a considerable range of group behavior and cultural manifestation is greater than these.

On the other hand, improvements need to be made, and assumptions need to be more sharply examined, in the cultural dimension and culture pattern approach made above. First, now that the general shape of a dozen or more dimensions (based largely on a representative design [Chapter 2]) is known, it is feasible to enter with variables more crucially chosen to test the emerging theories. This is not easy, because in the area of national action and national records the researcher is largely an onlooker, compelled to take whatever data gets compiled on as many as 80 countries. For example, the cultural pressure theory might point to schizophrenia rates, to pressure in diplomatic relations, to abruptness of the man in the street in his dealings with others, and to anxiety levels on objective tests, as more crucial variables. These are difficult to obtain in comparable form, and may require new field observation and psychological testing on the population. A list of variables more crucial to the theories above, capable of quantification but not yet recorded, has been prepared and will be made available by the present writer.

Second, the analyses of data could now be improved by factoring data separately for the three panels—syntality structure, and population characters—for it is proba-

ble that this would give a clearer definition and would leave one free to explore more complex relations (which probably exist among the panels) than the general linear ones.

A special problem foreshadowed in Proposition 3 of Section 2 above must be faced here. When population-characteristic measures are related to syntality measures, shall the national factor scores of the former be derived from the weights of the particular pattern in factoring the population in each country, or, like the syntality factor scores from weights from correlations across means of all countries? There is a sense in which a factor, such as intelligence or anxiety level, is more appropriately measured in the weights peculiar to each country. However in the statistical rather than a "logical" or conceptual sense, a comparable measure on a population characteristic is to be obtained only by factoring first over the scores consisting of the population means for each and every cultural group. This issue, ultimately of considerable practical importance in cross-cultural research, e.g., in testing the hypothesis that population anxiety level is related to syntality cultural pressure level, is discussed elsewhere (240) in more detail.

A third methodological approach which has much interest is illustrated in Rummel's "dyadic" design in which the sets to be correlated are not responses (attributes) of countries in general, nor countries, but relations between specific pairs of countries. For example, relational variables such as amount of internation trade, treaties, conflicts state visits, mutual migration, etc., are scored, as relatives over a series of paired countries—America-Britain, Belgium-China, etc. The resulting correlation clusters and factors represent distinct concepts and *dimensions of interaction.*

Such a design has general theoretical interest, and we have discussed designs encompassing it in Chapter 3 under the notion of sum, difference, and other functions constituting entries in *faces* of the

Basic Data Relation Matrix. A pattern or id — the typical bounding coordinate set number in the Data Box — is itself a set of relations, but there is no reason why relations among ids should not be used as higher-order relation sets. Indeed, there can be sets which are relations, and higher-order sets which are relations among relations, in an indefinitely extended hierarchy. For proper use of such methods it is necessary only to keep in mind the particular relational system of which one is finding the dimensionality, e.g., the dimensions of national behavior, the dimensions of relations between nations, the dimensions of relations among relations. Whereas at the first order one is discovering values — factors and loadings (behavioral indices) — for insertion in the specification equation, one is seeking, in the higher relational orders, for possible developments in the form of the equation itself. Regarding substantive findings on the dimensions of international relations (or, for that matter of interpersonal relations) by such higher relational analyses, nothing can yet be quoted.

An area which needs far more attention, in view of the several theories already in common discussion and the specific hypotheses of cultural pressure, affluence-education, and morale above, is that relating population characters structure, and syntality in an extension of Proposition 3 in Section 2 above. This states that syntality is a function of population, $\bar{P}$, and structure, $\bar{T}$ values thus: $\bar{G} = f(\bar{T}:\bar{P})$. In particular it is now becoming possible experimentally to investigate by objective measures of dynamic adjustment and expression of the typical population individual, as studied in Chapter 20 above, the relation to the synergic structure of the group. In the longitudinal studies particularly the factor-staggered P technique of Chapter 11 would get more incisively into causal connections in this and other fields. All in all, the possibilities in the next decade of moving to an altogether higher level of conceptualization and exactness of theory testing in cultural dynamics and political science multivariate methods are very great.

9. SUMMARY

(1) Social phenomena, necessarily dealing with pluralities of id entries along several sets of the Basic Data Relation Matrix (notably of S, R, P, P', and S' coordinates), are ideally adapted for investigation by multivariate experimental designs. A fortunate early recognition of this importance for concept formation and prediction has led social psychologists to be in the forefront of those developing more sophisticated multivariate designs.

On the other hand, other specialists in the social science research team such as sociologists and economists, have been slower to take in the totality of phenomena, and political scientists and anthropologists who have attacked problems appropriately with quantitative multivariate methods are still a pioneering minority.

(2) The present need is to adopt sufficiently fundamental models and develop statistical analysis methods accordingly. Since in essence social science covers three types of relation — person to person, group to group, and person to group — the simplest basic model is one of recognizing dimensions of groups and persons, and additive and linear equations for relating these dimensions to variables and to one another A series of basic formulations are proposed for this purpose.

(3) Whereas to most psychologists the general natures of personality dimensions and their interactions are familiar, the concepts and instances of group syntality dimensions are not. The concepts of (a) a group as a dynamic entity, instrumental to individual satisfactions and sustained by them; (b) the means of relating group synergy to individual dynamic structure; (c) the operational definition of tie, role, the panels of syntality structure, and population characteristics, are set out as the necessary beginning of a model.

(4) From this model some five dynamic principles logically follow for group synergy indicating experiments which need to be done to test the dynamic calculus in the group situation.

(5) A vigorous activity in the small-group research area, and in cultural psychology, has led to several areas of initial empirical integration of findings, now needing more exact models and methods for further advance in sociology, cultural anthropology and political science. The work on defining and measuring groups has encompassed primary groups, such as family and tribe, but also administrative units, living localities business organizations, and whole cultures, with rapidly developing and reasonably effective methodology.

On the other hand, social structure has largely remained in the hands of older methods. For example, only in one or two instances has the collection of data on social status structure been informed by true dimensional analysis or objective, taxonomic methods. Similarly, although economics become empirical and statistically sophisticated as a result of the work of those who forsook "armchair economics" a generation ago, the fruitfulness possible through linking it up with quantitative motivation and ability study, as in the dynamic calculus and the ability distribution theory of business cycles, has not yet been achieved.

Games theory, simulation of national interaction, and the intensive study of interaction and communication processes are yielding stimulating results, but are also in need of further model development.

(6) The study of value attitudes, social, religious, and political, and of political affiliations and voting behavior has proceeded with the impetus of applied urgency. However, a mere repetition of R-technique factoring of countless attitude value scales, or Q'-technique clustering of voting blocs, will get us little further without recognition of a general theory that value attitudes occupy a special position in

the dynamic lattice, and subsidiate particularly to the self and superego sentiments. In other words, values need to be brought into the general dynamic model of personality, their variance from temperament and dynamic traits appropriately apportioned, and their subsidiations to dynamic goals determined by multivariate experiments using a skillful choice of self and superego sentiment variables, in groups of contrasting institutional affiliations.

(7) The anthropological functional intuitive and "living in" study of culture patterns, and the historians' group consensus delineation of civilizations, can be much surpassed in analytical power and objectivity today by (a) first determining factorially the dimensions of syntality of the groups concerned and (b) applying Q' technique with r_p to determine their cultural taxonomy. The pioneer studies, which are now being followed up with more adequate choice of variables, guided by the hypotheses from these studies, yielded clear simple structure dimensions, and resulting culture pattern groupings fitting historical concepts.

(8) Variables in such studies have rightly been chosen to cut across academic disciplines, since economic, geographic, psychological, and other functions are causally connected. On the other hand, the lumping together of syntal, structural, and population characteristics in a single analysis should now be followed by more sensitive technical treatments in which they are factored separately. Three dimensions which introduce concepts of special importance are those of cultural pressure, affluence-education, and morality-morale. Attempts to explain events such as war in terms of single pairs of correlations, or the stress of particular events, seem less satisfactory than prediction from the general theoretical concepts involved in these very different dimensions. Some issues of sampling and inference are studied and proposals are made for better matching, notably of R- and P-technique studies.

CHAPTER **27** Language Behavior:
The Multivariate
Structure of
Qualification

MURRAY S. MIRON
Syracuse University
CHARLES E. OSGOOD
University of Illinois

1. INTRODUCTION

More than a decade has passed since the publication of the second author's paper (1121) proposing a multivariate technique for the measurement of meaning. The intervening years have witnessed a considerable amount of research, both by Osgood and his colleagues and by others, designed to stabilize and validate *the semantic differential technique* (henceforth in this paper to be referred to as the SD technique). A bibliography of research involving the SD has recently been compiled by the authors, (1127) and although it exceeds 200 entries, it has many lacunae and is already somewhat out of date. Much of this research is multivariate only in the sense that investigators have used some previously factored scales to assess concept meanings, or they have employed the factorial model to explore the dimensionality of the qualifying attributes of some new content domain. However, there are other studies which

probe into the nature of the theoretical model and the validity of the SD technique itself.

In a science such as ours, where measurement techniques are added and discarded from the armamentarium with amazing alacrity and where fashion often seems to rule the paths of inquiry, it is gratifying that the SD technique, so far, has outlived its initial rush of acceptance as a fad. Actually, it labored under a double handicap: first, it could be construed as simply another opinion scaling device, coupled only remotely to a theoretical rationale; second, it required reference to and some understanding of multivariate factorial models. The latter handicap alone might well have been sufficient to insure stillbirth, since experimental psychologists have traditionally viewed with distrust the multivariate methods in general and the factor-analytic models in particular. Nevertheless, the connections between mediation learning theory and the SD technique, as well as the technique itself, seem to be gaining a reasonably secure place in the growing nomological network of psycholinguistic theory.

The goal of this chapter will be to assay the extent to which the SD technique has fulfilled its promise as something more than "another test." No attempt will be made to survey all of the research employing the SD; instead, only those investigations which appear to shed light on the logic and validity of the method as a means of defining the dimensionality of semantic qualification will be treated in any detail. Relatively little theoretical exposition will be offered here (however, see 1123, 1124). This is not because the authors consider the theoretical context of the SD technique irrelevant or unimportant — indeed, we feel that it is this theoretical context which makes the SD something more than just another scaling device — but rather because this methodological approach is more consistent with the volume in which this chapter appears.

2. A REVIEW OF THE EARLY STANDARDIZATION STUDIES

The SD technique attempts to provide a method for distinguishing individuals and concepts on the basis of an efficiently small number of natural language dimensions of contrastive attributes. The extent to which such discrimination is possible is entirely dependent upon demonstration of the existence and replicability of a low-rank structure of the ways in which natural languages organize the domain of attribute terms. The domain of attribute terms, for the purposes of this technique, is made coextensive with the domain of qualifiers in a natural language. Although it is theoretically possible to enumerate the members of the set of qualifiers in any natural language and accordingly to avoid the necessity of estimating sampling error, in practice the set is too large to make such enumeration practicable. If we further assume that the

dimensionality of this set changes with the different classes of concepts to which the attributes may be applied, then, although the set of attributes for each class decreases in size, the order of the dimensionality increases.

Thus, both the attribute and concept spaces require strategies for sampling — as does, of course, the subject domain. Given equivalence of sampling strategies, if the structure of at least the qualifier domain can be shown to be relatively invariant over many such samples, while the remaining sources of sampling error are fixed, it can be inferred that there exists a potentially discriminating structure for the fixed values of the other domains. In order to demonstrate generality of such discrimination, however, it is necessary to demonstrate that this qualifier structure remains relatively invariant under varying concept and subject samples. It was because the original investigators despaired of ever finding such sweeping generality that the authors of *The Measurement of Meaning* (1129) cautiously pointed out that the semantic differential was not a test but a measurement technique.

Three primary studies served as the earliest basis for the conclusion that a stable and low rank structure could be attributed to the qualifier domain of American English. In the first of these analyses, qualifier terms were elicited from a large group of subjects as responses to a small number of stimuli selected from the Kent-Rosanoff word list in a restricted word association task. The domain of generality, in this analysis, was restricted to those qualifiers found to have highest frequency of occurrence as responses to the aggregate stimulus set. The results of this first analysis indicated that the first three centroid qualifier factors, following orthogonal rotation, accounted for approximately 50 per cent of the total subject by concept variance.[1] These factors were interpretatively

---

[1] In all of the analyses of this section, unities replace communality estimates, and each subject-concept combination is treated as a separate observation.

labeled Evaluation, Poetency, and Activity. The remaining factors had small variance contributions and were arbitrarily discarded.

Since it could be argued that this factor structure was limited to the universe of qualifiers applicable only to those concepts chosen, it follows as a next logical step that the investigators should vary the concept sample, holding the qualifier and subject samples constant.

The concepts in this second analysis were the qualifier terms themselves. Each of the 50 attribute scales was judged against all remaining scales in a dichotomous rating task. A number of criteria indicated that the results of the first and second analyses were sufficiently alike to accept the structures as being equivalent. As before, the dimensions of Evaluation, Potency, and Activity, in that order, were identified and found to account for roughly similar percentages of the total variance.

The third analysis attempted to increase the generality of the previous findings by more adequately sampling the range of possible qualification modes in the language. The primary basis for scale selection in this case was representativeness within the separate semantic domains as defined by Roget's *Thesaurus*. Within the sample of categories thus determined, a secondary criterion for selecting particular qualifiers was, again, frequency-of-usage or familiarity. Thus this analysis, like those preceding, conservatively can be said to apply only to the domain of high frequency modes of qualification. Nonetheless, the logic of generalization to high frequency qualification is sound and reasonable as a first approach to characterizing the structure of qualification in a language. However, as the investigators themselves pointed out, the sensitivity of the accomplished speaker of English is, of course, hopelessly lost in the lowest common denominator of a structure discovered for words any 10-year-old can understand. As before, the salient dimensions found in this third analysis were

qualitatively similar to those found in the previous analyses.

A study by Ware (1501) is relevant here. If the structure discovered in these three analyses is linguistically primitive, in the sense of being basic, as has been suggested, then it should be true that that structure does not differentiate among the non-primitive aspects of linguistic behavior. Ware addressed himself to this problem by inquiring whether the semantic structures of the highly intelligent could be distinguished from those of the less intelligent. Separate factor analyses were performed for individual subjects judging the same concepts against the same scales. None of six measures of the diversity of the structures of the semantic spaces was found to relate to intelligence, even though all six were highly reliable and differentiated among individuals. For example, the average cumulative per cent of total variance accounted for by the first three centroid factors of 15 individuals with IQ scores 120 or above was 48.3; for 18 individuals with IQ scores 93 or below, the average per cent was 49.8. An average of 5.9 factors was required to account for 70 per cent of the total variance for the high IQ subjects and an average of 5.8 factors for the low IQ subjects. Clearly then, whatever else the semantic structure is reflecting, it does not seem to be a correlate of variables associated with IQ scores.

In a very real sense, however, it is precisely this lack of sensitivity to intellectual variables — the basic and primitive nature of the dominant factors revealed in SD measurement — which leads to the hope that this semantic structure may be generalizable beyond a single culture or linguistic community. These early factorial studies, then, lead to the conclusion that a reasonably stable structure of qualification will be found whenever qualifiers are sampled which are applicable to and frequently used with heterogeneous concept terms. These findings led Osgood and his associates to begin probing the limits of the generality of this structure across both subject and concept domains — but before tracing this course we must take up some statistical matters.

3. STATISTICAL PROCEDURES IN ANALYZING SEMANTIC DIFFERENTIAL DATA

The SD generates a data cube containing observations on each of N subjects rating each of C concepts on each of S scales. Analyzed in terms of Abelson's (1) formulation, concepts are the objects of discrimination, the scale items are the modes of discrimination, and the subjects are the agents of discrimination. The traditional factor-analytic models may only be applied to two-mode classification data matrices. Consequently, the investigator has been forced somehow to collapse the three classification semantic differential data into two modes. A number of statistical strategies for reduction of the classifications are available.

Stringing Out

The first of these, and the one consistently employed by Osgood, Suci, and Tannenbaum in the three analyses just reported, is to string out the observations on each subject by concept combination as unique observations. By opting for this procedure the investigators were placed in the position of being unable to disentangle the subject variance from the concept variance supposedly being explained by the scale structure. The qualifier dimensions discovered in these analyses, accordingly, can be interpreted as describing either or both the concept and subject variances, depending upon the contributions to the total variance made by each. If the subject variance, as is implicitly assumed, is small or zero, the structures are then, and only then, attributable to an underlying organization of qualifiers as applied to concept terms.

Summation

The second procedure employs some variant of a summation strategy. The investigator chooses the one classification mode which is of least interest and collapses the data cube into two modes by taking sums across the unimportant mode. Since subjects are usually considered to be the instrument for assessing concept differences on scale items, and thus only contribute to instrument errors, typically the investigator sums over the individual subject replications. As in the first procedure, the subject $\times$ concept variance is unassessed and must be assumed to be negligible in order to assign the resulting structure to the action of the scale agent in concept discrimination.

Average Correlation

A third procedure, although a variant of the summation procedure, is sufficiently different in computation to warrant separate discussion. In this procedure scale correlation matrices are obtained for each of the concept replications on each subject and then averaged over the N subjects. Thus the mode reduction is obtained by calculating a series of N-scale intercorrelation matrices which are averaged to obtain a single two-dimensional scale matrix. If the correlation matrices entering into this average vary greatly from individual to individual, the same difficulties in interpretation of the final structure accrue to this method as to the others.

Thus in all instances it is necessary to justify the assumption that the subject variance is small, or at least uniform, in its effect upon the other modes of classification. Several empirical studies, heretofore unpublished, provide evidence as to the magnitude of the subject variation in the semantic differential task.

In 1963 in the first of these studies, Ware utilized 40 personality concepts as rated by 20 subjects (10 married couples) on 40

TABLE 27-1

SALIENT PRINCIPAL COMPONENT SCALES FOR (A) STRINGING-OUT, (B) SUMMATION, AND (C) SUMMATION WITH COMMUNALITY ESTIMATE METHODS

A.

Factor I (16.6%)		Factor II (6.6%)		Factor III (5.5%)		Factor IV (3.6%)	
good-bad	.77	hard-soft	.70	excitable-calm	.53	constricted-spacious	.44
kind-cruel	.69	masculine-feminine	.56	colorful-colorless	.50	awkward-graceful	.42
harmonious-dissonant	.69	strong-weak	.55	ornate-plain	.47	sensitive-insensitive	.38
beautiful-ugly	.69	severe-lenient	.50	heretical-orthodox	.45	hot-cold	.35
wise-foolish	.68	heavy-light	.49	active-passive	.44	excitable-calm	.36
reputable-disreputable	.67	tenacious-yielding	.49	changeable-stable	.44	weary-refreshed	.35
successful-unsuccessful	.66	fast-slow	.47	complex-simple	.42	small-large	.32
grateful-ungrateful	.66	angular-round	.40	rash-cautious	.40	constrained-free	.30
true-false	.63	mature-youthful	.40	fast-slow	.40	grateful-ungrateful	.28
sane-insane	.61	serious-humorous	.38	heterogeneous-homogeneous	.38	cooperative-competitive	.27

B.

Factor I (30.2%)		Factor II (15.4%)		Factor III (12.1%)		Factor IV (8.7%)	
believing-skeptical	.92	objective-subjective	.78	active-passive	.77	private-public	.76
good-bad	.91	tenacious-yielding	.76	complex-simple	.74	constricted-spacious	.67
true-false	.90	colorless-colorful	.76	pungent-bland	.72	weary-refreshed	.64
positive-negative	.88	hard-soft	.72	proud-humble	.71	awkward-graceful	.59
optimistic-pessimistic	.87	plain-ornate	.71	heterogeneous-homogeneous	.70	small-large	.54
harmonious-dissonant	.86	constrained-free	.70	hot-cold	.68	humble-proud	.53
kind-cruel	.86	stable-changeable	.70	intentional-unintentional	.63	constrained-free	.48
reputable-disreputable	.86	strong-weak	.68	excitable-calm	.60	sane-insane	.47
grateful-ungrateful	.85	mature-youthful	.63	sophisticated-naive	.56	excitable-calm	.44
sober-drunk	.82	opaque-transparent	.57	fast-slow	.56	erratic-periodic	.43

C.

Factor I (41.1%)		Factor II (20.5%)		Factor III (16.0%)		Factor IV (11.5%)	
good-bad	.92	objective-subjective	.77	active-passive	.75	private-public	.74
believing-skeptical	.91	colorless-colorful	.75	pungent-bland	.74	constricted-spacious	.65
true-false	.90	tenacious-yielding	.74	complex-simple	.73	weary-refreshed	.63
positive-negative	.88	hard-soft	.73	proud-humble	.68	awkward-graceful	.60
optimistic-pessimistic	.87	plain-ornate	.71	heterogeneous-homogeneous	.68	humble-proud	.52
kind-cruel	.86	constrained-free	.70	hot-cold	.67	small-large	.52
reputable-disreputable	.86	stable-changeable	.69	intentional-unintentional	.62	constrained-free	.48
harmonious-dissonant	.86	strong-weak	.66	excitable-calm	.60	sane-insane	.47
grateful-ungrateful	.85	mature-youthful	.62	savory-tasteless	.55	sensitive-insensitive	.43
sober-drunk	.82	opaque-transparent	.55	sophisticated-naive	.54	excitable-calm	.42

Note: — Factor percentages are proportions of total variance.

personality-relevant semantic scales. The data were analyzed by separately computing the correlations between each scale pair for each subject as in the average correlation procedure discussed above. However, instead of averaging these intercorrelations, the cross-products of the corresponding cells of each pair of the 40×40 scale matrices were computed. These cross-products formed a new matrix of order 20 summarizing the degree of similarity in the patterns of scale intercorrelations used by each of the 20 subjects. If all subjects had identical patterns of intercorrelations among the 40 scale items, the sum of these cross-products would be maximal and a factor analysis of the cross-products matrix would reveal a single subject factor. The results of a factor analysis of these cross-products, in fact, revealed a first dimension which accounted for 63 per cent of the total variance and a second factor which accounted for only 5 per cent. Thus, at least for these data, we may conclude that the subject mode has an essentially unifactorial composition, and therefore that the strategies for collapsing that dimension are justified.

Still another way to assess the contribution of subject variance to the structure of qualification is to compare the results of factor analyses of the data matrices collapsed by means of the summation and stringing out procedures. If the comparison is made using the same data matrix for both procedures, whatever change in structure is observed can be attributed to the subject variation. Table 27-1 summarizes the structures obtained by these two procedures. The data are taken from Analysis III of Section I. The factor coefficents are those obtained from unrotated principal component solutions with unities replacing communality estimates. In addition, Table 27-1 summarizes the factor structure obtained for these data when communality estimates are used. The communalities were entered into the principal diagonal of the correlation matrix calculated from the

summed individual scores. The estimates were calculated by means of an approach suggested by Tucker (see Levin, 927) utilizing what Harman (688, pp. 88ff.) has called a "complete approximation," i.e., one which utilizes all observed correlations. The communality estimates are given by the expression:

$$ h_j^2 = |r_{jk}| \frac{\sum\limits_{k'} |r_{jk'}|}{\sum\limits_{k'} |r_{kk'}|} $$

where r_{jk} is the largest correlation for variable j and $j \neq k' \neq k$.

Inspection of Table 27-1 indicates tha the structures are qualitatively very similar under all three procedures. There is ample evidence that communality estimates for correlation matrices exceeding 20 variables do not appreciably change the factor patterns (688), but it is reassuring to find that the consistent use of unities in the analyses reported has not altered the interpretations given those analyses. This observed similarity in structure for the communality and component analysis solutions (unities in the principal diagonal) can be interpreted as reflecting the relatively small unique variance of the scale items. The similarity between the structures obtained when the subject variance is manipulated indicates that subject variation does not appreciably influence the obtained structure and independently confirms the results of the Ware analysis.

4. THE THREE-WAY FACTOR SOLUTION

Obviously the analyses of the previous section are at best only indirect tests of the interactions between the modes of classification of semantic differential data. What is clearly needed is a factorial solution which does not require collapsing of any of the modes. Until recently only these indirect approaches were possible, but with the development of a three-way solution for the factor problem by Tucker (1467, 1468), it is now possible to explore each set separately and in combination with each of the other sets. As its name implies, three-mode factor analysis is an extension of the classical factor solution to matrices of three-way classification. In brief, the method treats a triple array of standardized scores X_{ijk} according to the defining formula:

$$X_{ijk} = \sum_m \sum_p \sum_q a_{im}\, b_{jp}\, c_{kq}\, g_{mpq}$$

where the $_iA_m$, $_jB_p$, and $_kC_q$ matrices are the factor-loading matrices for the I, J and K classifications and the G_{mpq} cube matrix is the set of factor scores of the J variable factors on the K variable factors (see Chapter 6 of this volume for a more detailed exposition of this method). For the semantic differential the I, J, and K variables would correspond to scales, concepts, and subjects. The solution is comparable to that which is obtained for the scale factors when the concept-by-subject observations are treated by the stringing out method, but extends the analysis to the concept, subject, and triple interaction factor matrices.

Levin (927) has employed the three-mode factor solution in a re-analysis of the Ware (1501) data. Ware had collected data from 60 high school students rating 31 concepts on 20 qualifier scales. The scales were chosen to represent 10 factors previously isolated in other studies. The concepts were chosen to sample equally the range of concept locations in the coordinate space defined by the three major dimensions of Evaluation, Potency, and Activity. Thus, both the concept and scale items were relatively heterogeneous in content. The raw rating scores were expressed as scale values varying between 3 and −3, with zero assumed to be the true scale midpoint. It was also decided to retain the differences in scale dispersion (i.e., size of scale unit differences), and thus the raw scores were considered to be both centered and standardized. Accordingly, cross-products

rather than correlations were employed throughout.

An inspection of the latent roots for the subject, concept, and scale factor matrices indicated that one subject factor, four concept factors, and four scale factors could be identified in the data. The criterion used was based upon a comparison of the ratios of the successive latent roots. All factors beyond that point for which the ratios of the ordered roots, $\dfrac{R_n}{R_{n+1}}$, can be judged to be constant, it is argued, are unique. A constant ratio of roots would be expected if the data under analysis had been drawn from a table of random numbers. A convenient method for determing this point is to plot the logarithm of each root as a function of the rank order of the root, since equal ratios will plot as a straight line after logarithmic transformation. Diagram 27-1 displays the latent roots of the factors extracted from each mode of the Levin analysis. As can be observed, there is a precipitous drop in the latent roots of the subject mode after the first value, and

DIAGRAM 27-1.   Latent Roots of Factors Extracted From Each Mode of Levin Analysis

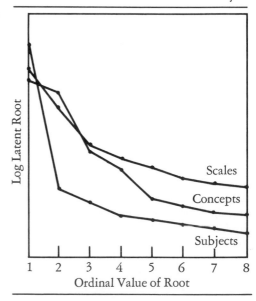

accordingly we may conclude that there is a single "idealized" subject type for these data.[2] The interaction between subjects and scales as well as subjects and concepts is minimal for this relatively homogeneous subject population. This finding confirms the conclusion drawn from the Ware anal-

analysis is readily identifiable as the Evaluative factor extracted in all the previous analyses reported. Factor II apparently represents a coalescence of the Potency and Activity dimensions previously isolated. This coalescence has been observed before (1444, 1127) and appears to occur

TABLE 27-2

SUMMARY OF HIGHEST COEFFICIENTS OF THE ROTATED SCALE FACTORS

Factor I Evaluation		Factor II Dynamism		Factor III Stability		Factor IV Warmth	
usual-unusual	.66	strong-weak	.66	even-uneven	.61	warm-cool	.54
good-bad	.61	fast-slow	.58	predictable-unpredictable	.61	hot-cold	.52
fair-unfair	.60	powerful-powerless	.55	good-bad	.46	emotional-unemotional	.38
true-false	.56	hard-soft	.46	sociable-unsociable	.43		
kind-cruel	.56			straight twisted	.28		
moral-immoral	.52			unemotional-emotional	.32		

TABLE 27-3

SUMMARY OF HIGHEST COEFFICIENTS OF THE ROTATED CONCEPT FACTORS

Factor I Human		Factor II Agitation		Factor III Slickness		Factor IV Toughness	
mother	.64	sin	.55	butter	.44	army	.45
baby	.52	anger	.54	jelly	.43	statue	.39
sex	.50	fear	.53	snow	.43	cop	.36
me	.45	sickness	.50	snail	.39	street	.35
sleep	.40	insane man	.50	dirt	.36	lamp	.33
food	.38	pain	.49	silk	.30	baby	−.20
dream	.34	grief	.43				

ysis in 1963 of an entirely independent sample of subjects using different scales and concepts. The concept and scale latent roots appear to become asymptotic after the fourth value although more clearly so for the concept roots.

Tables 27-2 and 27-3 present the most salient scale and concept items of the factor matrices for their respective modes, as determined by Levin. Factor I of the scale

whenever the Activity dimension is not well represented in the scale items chosen. When the dimension appears, it has been labeled a Dynamism factor. The third factor appears to be the Stability factor also observed in the past (1106, 1129, Analysis III). The fourth factor was identified as a Warmth factor by Levin. The concept factors were labeled Human, Agitation, Slickness, and Toughness factors in the Levin analysis. No other published factorings of the concept mode with which these can be compared are available, but they are obviously a function of the particular sample when it is small, as is the case here. The core matrix expressing the factor

[2]The interaction referred to in this analysis might better be called structural interaction. The presence of a single idealized subject type does not preclude the possibility of interaction effects between high and low scoring subjects on the same dimension, but does rule out the possibility of dimensional interaction. Intradimensional interaction effects are discussed in Section 6.

loadings of the combinations of these factors directly specifies the amount of interaction between each of the modes of the SD data. Table 27-4 displays these factor loadings for the varimax rotations of the concept and scale factors. As can be seen, the Evaluative and Warmth scales are most salient in the ratings of Human concepts. Agitation concepts are best characterized by Stability scales, Slickness concepts by Warmth scales, and Toughness concepts by Dynamism scales. These results indicate that had the concepts been drawn from any single one of the domains summarized by these four concept factors, at the very least an entirely different order of scale factor importance might have emerged. Stated in other terms, there is

TABLE 27-4

THE CORE MATRIX OF CONCEPT AND SCALE FACTOR COMBINATIONS

Concept Factors		Scale Factors			
		Evalua-tion I	Dyna-mism II	Sta-bility III	Warmth IV
Human	I	18	03	−01	18
Agitation	II	−03	10	−19	03
Slickness	III	12	−13	−06	−15
Toughness	IV	03	21	09	−14

good evidence for *concept-by-scale interaction* which is masked in the ordinary two-mode analysis of semantic differential data. The Evaluation-Potency-Activity structure apparently can be expected to obtain when a large and heterogeneous concept sample is employed, but not when the concept sample is homogeneous. A re-analysis of the data of Analysis I reported in Section I, done by Shaw (1308), for example, found significant shifts in the scale intercorrelations when the concept terms were varied. Although this indicates that the investigator must be cautious when trying to generalize the scale structure to particular content domains, nonetheless the structure of qualification when these interactions are

averaged is of considerable interest in itself. This structure represents the most general aspects of the implicit dimensionality of attribute qualification for the widest class of concept terms.

5. THE QUALIFICATION STRUCTURES FOUND IN CHILDREN

The studies so far reviewed have varied concepts, scales, and subjects. A large and practically useful concept-by-subject interaction has been found, and a limiting concept-by-scale interaction was noted. Although there is evidence for idiosyncratic use of scales in relation to concepts, there is no evidence for a subject by scale-structure interaction. We should now inquire whether there is evidence for change in scale-structure as a function of age. Is the child's increasing facility with his linguistic code reflected in the structure of qualification which he employs?

Small (1330) had a total of 275 third-, sixth-, and ninth-graders rate each of 24 heterogeneous concepts on a 23-scale form of SD. Sixteen of the scale items were chosen to represent the Evaluation-Potency-Activity structure and seven additional scales were chosen (e.g., *real — make-believe*) because of their theoretical interest. As was the case when intelligence was varied in the Ware (1501) study, there was little or no change in the total per cent of variance accounted for by the first five centroid factors when age or sex was varied. The evaluative first factor in particular showed no appreciable change as a function of age. Small had predicted that if there was to be any change in the structures of the age groups, it would appear in the relative dominance of the Evaluative factor. Younger children, it seems reasonable to predict, should utilize evaluation more than older children. This, of course, was essentially the same hypothesis Ware felt worth studying and, as in that study, the hypothesis is again unconfirmed. In all age groups of the Small study the first centroid factor, after quartimax rotations, was characterized by the scale items: *good-bad, clean-dirty, happy-sad,* and *important-unimportant* — clearly identifiable as the Evaluative factor. The second rotated factor, also similar for all age groups, had highest loadings on the scale items *strong-weak, large-small,* and *fast-slow* — appearing again to be a coalescence of Potency and Activity into a Dynamism dimension. The third factor of the Small data was characterized by the scale items *hot-cold* and *sharp-flat.* All groups evidenced a similar fourth factor characterized by *real — make-believe* and *true-pretend.* The first three factors in all age groups accounted for between 56 and 66 per cent of the total variance. Small concluded that "the similarity of the factors obtained in our children's groups as compared with adult groups suggests that the cultural use of the polar terms of the dominant semantic dimensions is adequately learned by the third grade level," a conclusion which appears to be inescapable. Of course it could be argued that the structure was at least in part forced by the choice of scales employed. The scales, after all, were chosen to represent the factors eventually isolated by Small — scales which were representative of the structure found for adults, not necessarily for children.

An extensive study by DiVesta (422) has attempted to rectify this fault. DiVesta initially had 100 school children in each of Grades 2, 3, 4, 5, and 6 supply qualifiers in a restricted word association test. A single adjective was elicited as a response to each of 100 noun stimuli. The qualifiers obtained in this manner thus represent the qualification modes actually employed by the children and provided the pool of items from which appropriate semantic scales could be drawn. The strategy for determining exactly which items would be chosen is discussed in detail in Section V since it is identical to the strategy employed in our cross-linguistic investigations. In essence, the selection procedure is designed to

choose those qualifier terms which are (1) high in over-all frequency of usage, (2) diverse in context of usage, and (3) independent in context of usage. Of the 264, 288, 306, 422, and 554 qualifiers obtained in the five increasing grade groups, 25 qualifiers maximizing the criteria above were selected for each grade level. Opposites were determined for each of these selected modifiers and semantic scales constructed. The concepts rated on these scales were the noun stimuli of the elicitation step and are identical to those used in the cross-linguistic investigations of the next section.

The factor results of these analyses essentially duplicate the findings of Small. In fact, the most interesting aspect of this research is that the qualifiers elicited from each of the grade levels are extremely similar. When the elicited qualifiers are ordered by frequency of occurrence, the correlations among the first 50 most frequently employed adjectives form a simplex ordered by age. That is, the qualifiers found at each grade level correlate highest with the qualifiers found at the nearest grade and least with those found at the furthest removed grade. Despite this orderly progression in the magnitude of the correlation coefficients as grade level is increased, the average intercorrelation between each pair of grade levels for the 50 most frequent responses is .93. Accordingly, it is not too surprising to find similar dimensions emerging from the factor analyses. We are thus again led to conclude that whatever linguistic habits these dimensions are reflecting, the dimensions are implicit in the qualification structure of even the seven-year-old.

For the sake of completeness it is of interest to examine the developmental change in concept meanings for children compared on this demonstratedly equivalent scale structure. Donahoe (424), using groups of first-, third-, sixth-grade, and college students rating concepts on three scales representing each of the major dimensions, found that the profiles for concepts with respect to Evaluative and Potency attributes stabilized to the adult level at ages 9 and 12, respectively, while the profiles for the Activity attributes of these concepts were not observed to vary across the age levels.

6. CROSS LINGUISTIC COMPARISONS OF QUALIFICATION STRUCTURE

It was out of this background that the authors began, in late 1959, to try to design a research program that would rigorously test the limits of possible cross-linguistic and cross-cultural generality of this qualification structure (cf. 1127).

A number of studies had been designed to assess the generality of affective meaning systems across different selected language and culture groups. These included a study by Kumata (893), comparing Korean bilinguals and Japanese bilinguals and monolinguals with American monolinguals, a study by Triandis and Osgood (1444), comparing Greek and American college students, one by Suci (1362), comparing several Southwest Indian cultures with Spanish-speaking Americans and Anglos, and one by Osgood (1122), comparing visual-verbal synesthetic tendencies among Navajo, Mexican-Spanish, Japanese, and American subjects.

Although these and other studies had consistently supported the hypothesis of generality in the major factors underlying affective meanings, and might have been accepted as sufficient evidence, we have been perhaps more aware than most of the possibility of methodological artifacts. Even though the details of methods varied, as did the selection of semantic scales and concepts judged, and the same factors nevertheless kept appearing, one aspect of methodology ran through all of these early studies: the samples of scales used were selected either partly or wholly on the basis of results obtained in the prior American studies, as reviewed in Section 1. Such scales were often simply translated into

languages of the other groups under investigation. Despite the care with which these translations were carried out (893), the fact that translation served as the vehicle for demonstrating structural similarities in all these investigations seemed to be the most likely source of bias, if indeed the similarities were artifactual.

To avoid the potential bias of translation, and resultant ethnocentric bias, the procedures for selecting qualifiers that would eventually serve as the dimensions of judgment in semantic differential tasks had to be entirely intracultural; each language/culture group must determine its own descriptive scales. However, the overall methodology of these *intra*culturally independent samplings had to be standardized in order to make possible the *inter*cultural comparisons required for testing the primary hypothesis of structural equivalence. In addition, it was clear that testing the limits of generality demanded as heterogeneous a sample of both languages and cultures as could be obtained practicably. If under these conditions sufficient similarities in factor structure could be demonstrated, then the shared factors could provide the basis for constructing semantically comparable instruments for measuring various aspects of "subjective culture," e.g., values, attitudes, stereotypes, and concept-meanings generally.

The group of countries participating in this research to date, the language families they represent, and the field personnel cooperating with us are given in Table 27-5. It will be noted that all of the groups represent literate "high cultures" (work with non-literate samples is just now beginning). Subjects in all cases are high-school-aged males.

Elicitation of Qualifiers

Having decided to use a restricted word-association technique for eliciting qualifiers, we faced an initial problem of finding appropriate, culturally common (so-called "culture-fair" or "culture-universal")

TABLE 27-5

Summary of Language/Culture Groups Comprising Current Project Sample

Country	Language	Language Family	Field Center	Field Staff
Afghanistan	Farsi	Indo-European	Kabul	Majrouh, Sarwari
Afghanistan	Pashto	Indo-European	Kabul	Majrouh, Ayeen
Belgium	Flemish	Indo-European	Brussels	Jansen, Nuttin
Finland	Finnish	Finno-Ugric	Helsinki	Allardt, Takala
France	French	Indo-European	Paris	Jansen, Moles
Greece	Greek	Indo-European	Athens	V. and G. Vassiliou
Hong Kong	Cantonese	Sino-Tibetan	Hong Kong	Li
India	Hindi	Indo-European	Delhi	Rastogi, Singh
India	Kannada	Dravidian	Mysore	Kuppuswamy, Shanmugam
Iran	Farsi	Indo-European	Tehran	Siassi, Minou
Japan	Japanese	Japanese	Tokyo	Obonai, Asai, Tanaka
Lebanon	Arabic	Semitic	Beirut	Prothro, Diab
Mexico	Spanish	Indo-European	Mexico City	Diaz-Guerrero
Netherlands	Dutch	Indo-European	Amsterdam	Jansen, Smolenaars
Poland	Polish	Indo-European	Warsaw	Schaff, Sarapata
Sweden	Swedish	Indo-European	Uppsala	Himmelstrand, Asplund
Turkey	Turkish	Turkic	Istanbul	Togrol, Cuceloglu
U.S.A.	English	Indo-European	Urbana	Archer, Jakobovitz, May, Miron, Osgood
Yugoslavia	Serbo-Croatian	Indo-European	Belgrade	Tomekovič, Kostić

verbal substantives to use as stimuli. An original list of some 200, derived from diverse sources (including the glottochronological investigations of Swadesh, 1369, and Lees, 918), was reduced to 100 nouns on the basis of ease and consistency of translation in pilot tests run with each of the major language families. Instructions included linguistic frames in which qualifiers are associated with substantives (e.g., in English *the* _____ *butterfly* or *the butterfly is* _____), and both the instructions and the frames were suitably modified for each language by native field personnel working with our ethnolinguist, William K. Archer. Thus, although the frames varied, Fries' (560) conception of grammatical class was uniformly followed.

Distribution Characteristics of Qualifiers

From the 10,000 (approximately) qualifiers obtained from 100 subjects of each language/culture community, we wished to extract a small subset (ultimately 50) which would be analyzed in further stages. The general criteria for selection were: (1) *over-all frequency-of-usage* (we wanted the modes of qualifying that are most characteristic of each group); (2) *diversity of usage* (we wanted modes of qualifying that are most productive across a broad range of substantive contexts); (3) *independence of usage* (we wanted to avoid redundancy in modes of qualifying, particularly evaluative modes, as much as possible). Indices for the first two criteria (total frequency of each qualifier type across all 100 nouns and number of different nouns to which it is given) can be combined conveniently into a single index — the entropy score, H, for each qualifier type. For two qualifiers with equal frequency and diversity values, that one with the more equal distribution of its frequencies will produce the greater H value.

Even at this point we begin to see similarities across language/culture communities appearing. When qualifier-types in each group are ordered according to *H*, are translated into a common language (here, English), and are then correlated in terms of *H*-rank, positive values in the .50's typically appear. Coupling these findings with those of DiVesta (422) on children of different ages, we are led to conclude that the relative importance of various modes of qualifying experiences tends to be the same regardless of the language people use, the culture they grow up in, or even how long they have been growing up (within limits, of course).

The third criterion — independence among the modes of qualifying — was applied to make our subsample of qualifiers as representative as possible of all potential dimensions of semantic differentiation and yet remain within a practically feasible total *N* for further research (about 50 scales). The numerical index adopted was the uncorrected *phi* coefficient. Given the qualifier types as rank ordered by *H,* the distribution of each lower-ranked qualifier across the 100 nouns on a presence-absence basis (cf. diversity index above) was correlated with the distribution of all higher-ranked qualifiers. If the *phi* coefficient was larger than a constant cut-off value for all languages, and positive, the lower-ranked member of that pair was dropped from the list. This process was applied iteratively until 60-70 relatively independent qualifiers had been obtained or the qualifier population exhausted. In effect, following Harris' theoretical (694) and Deese's empirical (412) definition of associative meaning, we have here postulated that the degree of similarity in meaning of any pair of terms is specified by the overlap of linguistic environments (our eliciting frames) in which they appear.

It should be noted that, although each language/culture community is free to determine its own ordering of qualifiers, the procedures are uniform for all. Furthermore, the procedures are completely objective and automatic — except for interest in what is happening, there is no need for the investigators to translate. The *H*-ordered

and reduced list of 60-70 qualifiers for each country is returned to the field staff, where about 10 independent informants, judged to be sophisticated in the mother tongue, produce opposites for these qualifiers. Where identical majority antonyms do not occur spontaneously (and they usually do), such items are re-submitted on a forced-choice basis. Fifty qualifiers and their opposites are sought on this basis for expansion into seven-step scales. Those in excess of 50 are discarded on the basis of lower *H*-rank, semantic similarity or ambiguity, or inappropriateness. These 50 polar qualification-pairs thus constitute the scale items with which we begin the second phase of the research.

Factor Analyses

The factor analyses of Phase II have as their aim the determination of the underlying structure of the modes of qualifying surviving the Phase I procedures. Our ultimate purpose is to design an efficient SD in each language that will contain scales (perhaps 12 to 18) representing factors common to all groups, thus rendering these instruments comparable across groups. The 100 substantives used to elicit qualifiers in Phase I are now used as concepts to be rated on the 50 scales derived in Phase I. At least in terms of translation equivalence, these 100 concepts are "the same" for all of the language/culture communities. The qualifier scales, on the other hand, are unique for each group, even though they may include many overlapping items when translated.

There are several ways factorial structures of scales across language/culture communities can be compared. An indirect, and necessarily somewhat subjective, method is to do separate factorizations for each group, translate as best one can the scales with high loadings on each factor for one group into the language of another, and then evaluate the similarities intuitively. This has been done, with each group's results being translated into English. On intuitive grounds, it is certain that the first and dominant factor in every language/culture community is Evaluation; the second factor may be identifiable as Potency or Activity, or a combination of these, and the third factor is usually a residual of these three. Within the limits of translation and intuition, then, we have evidence for shared factors similar to those previously described for English-speaking Americans.

A more direct and objective method would be to pool the data from all groups into the same mathematical space,[3] so that factors can be determined conjointly by correlations among between-language scales as well as among within-language scales. But to accomplish this, at least one of the three components of our data cubes —subjects, scales, or concepts—must be identical. Literally speaking, we cannot satisfy this condition; subjects are obviously different, scales are often unique, and even concepts cannot be claimed to be identical in meaning across language/culture communities. However, since the 100 concepts were originally selected as being *translation*-equivalent, they at least form the basis for pairing values and hence ordering scales into a common space— that is, we can correlate the means for any Japanese scale with any other language scale *across the 100 translation-equivalent concepts.* To the extent that these concepts are *not* identical in meaning, all this can do is lower correlations and hence work against our hypothesis of common factor structure. We have been following this logic in our recent factorial studies.

However, a practical limitation imposes itself here. Assuming an anticipated total sample of at least some 20 languages,

such a pan-language factor analysis of the total data would involve factoring a 1,000-variable correlation matrix. This is unhandy at present for even the largest of modern computers.[4] At some future date we do intend to subject *subsets* of scales from all communities, representing presumably common factors derived by some other method, to such a complete pan-cultural (and pan-language) analysis. For the present, and in lieu of such an unwieldy analysis, it was decided that each of the pairs of language groups should be jointly factored and the results of these separate analyses inspected to determine those scale items which continued to be identified with a particular factor in all or most of the joint analyses.

Beginning with the mean ratings of each concept on each scale for a pair of the language groups, intercorrelations among all scale items are computed across concepts and then factor-analyzed. Since the data domain of these bilanguage analyses is that of qualification modes, the factors discovered are interpreted as generalized aspects of experiential meaning reactions common to the two languages. If the analysis had, for example, been made for the two languages, English and Japanese, the scale items found to have salient loadings on each of the major factors in *both* English and Japanese would be said to represent the dimensions common to those two languages. If, on the other hand, we were to find that no factors were jointly determined by scale items in both of the languages, we would conclude that no scale factor appeared to be common to these two languages. In similar fashion, we then proceed jointly to analyze the bilanguage data for English and each of the other languages of the project. In each case the factors are inspected for joint language determination of the major factors, i.e., for roughly equally high

---

[3]Although other investigators (see Cattell, 246) would prefer to describe such a space in terms of oblique dimensions for which potency and activity remain distinct, it is our recognized bias to hold to the orthogonal description as better satisfying our intuitions concerning the adjectival space.

[4]As with most such statements, the pessimism was unfounded. Since this chapter was written we have successfully programmed such a pan-language analysis.

TABLE 27-6

Bilanguage Principal Component Factors

Factor I (36.5%)			Factor II (9.1%)			Factor III (6.7%)		
English	Finnish		English	Finnish		English	Finnish	
nice .94	nice	.89	big .83	sturdy	.71	fast .65	agile	.70
sweet .93	light (gloomy)	.87	powerful .70	large	.65	noisy .51	flexible	.68
heavenly .91	pleasant	.87	deep .67	heavy	.54	alive .48	fast	.67
happy .91	good	.84	strong .66	strong	.52	burning .36	lively	.56
good .91	reassuring	.79	high .64	thick	.46	young .34	lively (tired)	.50
mild .90	valuable	.78	long .61	long	.45	sharp .32	sharp	.49
beautiful .90	ripe	.78	heavy .59	old	.42	hot .32	multicolored	.47
faithful .88	clean	.78	hard .46	high	.41			
clean .88	white	.77	old .45	steady	.34			
helpful .88	happy	.77	sharp .44	brave	.33			
useful .87	honorable	.76						
sane .87	flourishing	.76						
needed .86	sweet	.76						
fine .86	right (wrong)	.75						
honest .84	smooth	.70						

Factor I (36.1%)			Factor II (9.7%)			Factor III (6.3%)		
English	Flemish		English	Flemish		English	Flemish	
nice .95	good	.91	big .77	big	.63	fast .56	quick	.69
good .93	magnificent	.90	powerful .70	deep	.61	noisy .48	active	.59
sweet .93	beautiful	.90	deep .68	strong	.58	young .47	impetuous	.55
heavenly .92	agreeable	.89	high .64	high	.54	alive .42	changeable	.50
mild .91	cozy	.87	strong .60	heavy	.53	momentary .35	violent	.50
happy .90	useful	.86	long .58	long	.53	funny .35	unequal	.49
helpful .90	clean	.84	heavy .54	sharp	.49	sharp .32	free	.47
beautiful .90	pleasant	.83	sharp .52	rare	.46		sharp	.45
clean .89	white	.79	serious .47	difficult	.40			
faithful .88	light (dark)	.75	hot .47	thick	.37			
useful .88	soft	.74	burning .42					
needed .88	necessary	.68						
sane .86	full	.67						
safe .86	colorful	.65						
fine .85	warm	.63						
honest .84								
white .81								

Factor I (37.8%)			Factor II (10.7%)			Factor III (5.4%)		
English	French		English	French		English	French	
nice .95	pleasant	.93	big .81	large	.79	fast .64	lively	.69
sweet .93	likeable	.92	powerful .70	huge	.73	noisy .50	fast	.66
good .92	good	.91	high .62	strong	.71	alive .45	living	.58
heavenly .91	nice	.90	strong .61	powerful	.61	young .44	young	.54
happy .90	proud	.89	deep .60	solid	.56	burning .37	hot	.50
beautiful .90	reassuring	.87	long .58	fat	.55	hot .33	mortal	.39
mild .89	healthy	.87	heavy .58	high	.53	known .28	modern	.35
helpful .89	gay	.87	hard .47	heavy	.53	momentary .28	red (green)	.32
faithful .88	pretty	.85	rough .47	wide	.51	funny .27	colored	.31
useful .88	useful	.84	serious .46	important	.44			
needed .88	indispensable	.82	sharp .42	heavy (sharp)	.42			
clean .87	allowed	.78	loud .40	immediate	.41			
sane .85	light (dark)	.76						
honest .84	perfect	.73						
safe .83	white	.73						
fine .82	safe	.72						

Note:—Opposites omitted in order to conserve space except where ambiguity would result.

Table 27-6 (continued)

BILANGUAGE PRINCIPAL COMPONENT FACTORS

Factor I (40.9%)				Factor II (10.9%)				Factor III (6.3%)			
English		Japanese		English		Japanese		English		Japanese	
nice	.96	pleasant	.93	powerful	.76	heavy	.72	fast	.65	cheerful	.73
good	.93	good	.92	big	.70	big	.67	noisy	.56	noisy	.68
sweet	.93	comfortable	.92	strong	.68	strong	.65	young	.46	colorful	.65
heavenly	.92	happy	.91	deep	.56	brave	.63	alive	.41	active	.55
happy	.91	elegant	.90	long	.56	sturdy	.62	burning	.38	red (blue)	.53
mild	.90	thankful	.90	heavy	.54	difficult	.61	known	.37	fast	.53
beautiful	.90	beautiful	.88	high	.51	thick	.59	hot	.36	early	.50
helpful	.90	necessary	.87	hard	.50	hard.	.53				
needed	.88	great	.86	rough	.48	complex	.48				
clean	.88	interesting	.86	serious	.48	tight	.47				
useful	.88	wise	.86								
faithful	.87	optimistic	.85								
honest	.87	skillful	.80								
sane	.86	great	.80								
safe	.86	tasty	.80								

Factor I (34.7%)				Factor II (7.5%)				Factor III (4.0%)			
English		Kannada		English		Kannada		English		Kannada	
nice	.95	merciful	.84	big	.79	big	.58	fast	.65	active	.41
good	.92	delicate	.81	powerful	.74	huge	.53	noisy	.64	noisy	.41
sweet	.92	calm	.80	strong	.69	great (light)	.49	alive	.55	fast	.39
heavenly	.90	good	.80	deep	.64	wonderful	.45	young	.49	little	.34
mild	.90	soft	.78	long	.61	many	.37	known	.40	strong	.32
happy	.89	beautiful	.77	high	.59	strong	.33	loud	.27	hasty	.30
helpful	.89	best	.72	heavy (light)	.57	magnificent	.32				
faithful	.89	useful	.72	hard	.48	plenty	.27				
sane	.88	melodious	.70	serious	.47						
beautiful	.88	safe	.70								
clean	.87	attractive	.70								

Note. — Opposites omitted in order to conserve space except where ambiguity would result.

factor coefficients on each major factor for scales in both languages. Although single factor analyses had demonstrated that qualitatively similar dimensions could be identified for all of the language groups considered separately, it still could be that a more rigorous quantitative comparison of the languages considered in pairs might reveal dimensions unique to each of the languages.

That the latter is not the case appears to be amply demonstrated by the analyses displayed in Table 27-6. For the purposes of this table, the scale items for each of the languages in each bilanguage analysis have been separated in order to facilitate comparisons. It can readily be observed, how-

ever, that for all factors displayed, there is a reasonable degree of interleafing of scales determining the factorial composition in each pair of languages. Although space does not permit the inclusion of all of the analyses, every pair of languages is or will be analyzed as the data becomes available in exactly the same manner as displayed in this table. Inspection of the table reveals an obvious set of factors common to all pairs of languages. The first factor in all pairs is clearly the Evaluative factor, the second factor can be identified as the Potency or Dynamism dimensions, and the third or fourth as Activity.

If we examine each of these analyses for which English is always the comparison language, it is possible to select those English scale items which are the most stable determiners of the factors common to each successive pair of languages. Twelve scales with their factor loadings representing each of the three major factors, selected on the basis of their reoccurrence and equivalence of loadings in all pair analyses, are displayed in Table 27-7. These scales comprise those English SD scales which would be most appropriate in any pan-cultural comparisons using the languages of this sample. The SD form *universally* applicable in all languages would be chosen by discovering those scale items in each language which continued to be found in every comparison language. Thus, the English scale items of Table 27-7 would be

available, but at the time of this writing, the results of the analysis of some six of our language groups indicate that such a semantic differential can be constructed, although we shall probably have to relax the criterion of equivalence of factor loadings somewhat for the activity factor in order to include all of the languages of our projected sample.

The factor coefficients of Table 27-8 provide evidence that the dimensions isolated in these bilanguage comparisons are present in all of the languages when considered simultaneously in anticipation of a "true" pan-cultural analysis. The data are derived from a factor analysis of the 12 "purest" scales selected to represent the first three factors of each of seven language

TABLE 27-7

STABLE AMERICAN SCALES SELECTED FROM BILANGUAGE ANALYSES

	Dutch*	Finnish	Flemish	French	Japanese	Kannada
	FI	FI	FI	FI	FI	FI
nice-awful	.94	.94	.95	.95	.96	.95
sweet-sour	.94	.93	.93	.93	.93	.92
good-bad	.89	.91	.93	.92	.93	.92
heavenly-hellish	.93	.91	.92	.91	.92	.90
happy-sad	.91	.91	.90	.90	.91	.89
	FIII	FII	FII	FII	FII	FII
powerful-powerless	.68	.70	.70	.70	.76	.74
strong-weak	.71	.66	.60	.61	.68	.69
big-little	.81	.83	.77	.81	.70	.79
long-short	.63	.61	.58	.58	.56	.61
	FII	FIII	FIII	FIII	FIII	FIV
young-old	.20	.34	.47	.44	.46	.49
fast-slow	.51	.65	.56	.64	.65	.65
noisy-quiet	.58	.51	.48	.50	.56	.64

*Varimax rotation (5 factors).

compared with the Finnish, Japanese, Dutch, etc. scale items isolated in the same way, and those common to all languages, would form the pan-language SD. That is, in the complete analysis each other language must serve as the comparison base as English has here.

As yet no such pan-language SD is

groups. Each separate factor analysis of the data supplied by a single language group was inspected for those scales which had highest factor coefficients on each of the three major factors and in addition came closest to having zero loadings on the remaining factors. Thus, for example, the American English scale *nice-awful* was found to have a loading of .96 on the first factor of the American data and loadings of −.02 and −.09 on the second and the third factors; this scale item was therefore judged to be a relatively pure measure of the first or Evaluative dimension. The remaining scales were chosen in the same manner; four scales representing each of the three factors from each language group. The 12 scales selected from each language

TABLE 27-8

PAN-CULTURAL FACTOR ANALYSIS*
(Varimax Rotation of Three Principal Axes Factors for 7 Language/Cultures)**

Factor I (29.0% TV)		Factor II (12.2% TV)		Factor III (11.6% TV)	
American English Scales					
nice-awful	.93	big-little	.83	fast-slow	.76
happy-sad	.90	long-short	.68	noisy-quiet	.57
sweet-sour	.90	strong-weak	.66	alive-dead	.47
good-bad	.88	powerful-powerless	.66	powerful-powerless	.31
Dutch Scales					
pleasant-unpleasant	.94	big-little	.76	active-passive	.78
happy-sad	.94	strong-weak	.60	absorbing-boring	.61
pretty-ugly	.92	long-short	.54	impressive-insignificant	.45
cozy-cheerless	.87	thick-thin	.45	changeable-constant	.41
		constant-changeable	.31	strong-weak	.31
Finnish Scales					
nice-awful	.91	strong-weak	.50	fast-slow	.77
light-gloomy	.86	long-short	.48	agile-clumsy	.72
happy-unhappy	.83	young-old	.42	energetic-unenergetic	.58
sweet-sour	.74	energetic-unenergetic	.28	sharp-dull	.50
				capricious-steady	.36
Flemish Scales					
agreeable-disagreeable	.92	big-small	.76	quick-slow	.84
magnificent-horrible	.91	strong-weak	.67	sharp-dull	.48
cozy-cheerless	.91	long-short	.64	shrewd-naive	.47
pleasant-unpleasant	.89	deep-shallow	.51	bloody-not bloody	.42
French Scales					
likeable-repugnant	.93	large-small	.77	lively-indolent	.79
nice-awful	.91	huge-tiny	.70	fast-slow	.75
happy-sad	.90	strong-weak	.66	living-dead	.51
proud-frightened	.90	powerful-not powerful	.51	powerful-not powerful	.37
Japanese Scales					
pleasant-unpleasant	.93	big-little	.76	fast-slow	.64
happy-sad	.93	heavy-light	.69	early-late	.57
comfortable-uncomfortable	.92	difficult-easy	.35	colorful-plain	.49
thankful-troublesome	.87			cheerful-lonely	.37
Kannada Scales					
merciful-cruel	.78	big-little	.56	fast-slow	.47
delicate-rough	.77	huge-tiny	.50	unstable-stable	.41
good-bad	.73	great-small	.48		
beautiful-ugly	.73	many-few	.31		

*Each language/culture represented by four "pure" scales from each indigenous factor.
**28 highest loadings for each factor are reported.

were intercorrelated with the 12 from each of six other languages, as well as with themselves, these correlations being taken across the means of the common 100 concepts. The reduction from 50 to 12 scales for seven groups made feasible the joint factoring of all of the languages simultaneously. The data of Table 27-8 clearly demonstrate a set of common factors which are well represented and determined more or less equally by all language/culture communities. These cross/cultural analyses as a whole, then, serve to increase our confidence that human beings share a common framework within which they allocate concepts in terms of their affective meanings — this communality over-riding gross differences in both language and culture.

7. VARIANCE ATTRIBUTABLE TO CONCEPT MEANINGS

The conclusion that human beings share a common affective framework — well supported by the evidence reported so far — in no way implies that they also share common meanings for the concepts differentiated within this framework. Not only do we have ample evidence that peoples' meanings for concepts vary both intraculturally and interculturally, but it should be recalled that the "applied" purpose behind all this research has been to devise a means of measuring such individual and cultural differences. In this section we shall present some (by no means all) evidence bearing on (1) individual differences in concept meanings, (2) cultural differences in concept meanings, and (3) evidence for concept/scale interaction.

Individual Differences in Concept Meanings

We may begin with the fact that, within a single individual, concept meanings may vary from time to time and situation to situation. A dramatic instance of this was the study by Osgood and Luria (1125) of a

case of triple personality; the emotional meanings of certain key concepts (e.g., MYSELF, MY MOTHER, and HATRED) were shown to shift both extremely and significantly in the psychotherapeutic sense as the patient assumed the "personalities" of Eve White, Eve Black, and Jane. Mogar in 1960 reported that high F-scale scorers tend to be more extreme in the SD ratings; Mitos in 1961 showed that the ratings of subjects allowed to choose their own scales also gave more extreme ratings. And, of course, all studies in which particular concept-meanings, as differentiated within the semantic structure, are associated with the characteristics of individuals or groups are relevant: Luria (971) and Endler (464) both have shown significant and predictive shifts in the meaning of the self-concept during psychotherapy; Korman (881) was able to discriminate among psychologists, social workers, and psychiatrists on the basis of their ratings of diagnostic and therapeutic terms; Cook (374) reported significant improvement in predicting academic achievement when the meanings of concepts like MYSELF AS AN IDEAL STUDENT were added to standard predictors; and Katz (855) was able to discriminate between troubled and untroubled married partners on the basis of their ratings of certain concepts. Along quite different lines, Suci was able to demonstrate marked, if not surprising, differences in the meanings of political concepts to Stevenson Democrats, Eisenhower Republicans, and Taft Republicans in the 1952 election, even though all three voting groups shared precisely the same semantic framework. *The Measurement of Meaning* (1129), in which the last study is reported, also contains many other of the earlier applications of SD technique to concept differentiation.

Cultural Differences in Concept Meanings

The factor analyses in the foregoing section clearly indicate the feasibility of constructing comparable instruments for measuring concept meanings in different cultures. The data from both Phases I and II, although primarily collected for tool-making purposes, can also be used to reflect certain differences in concept meanings. Here we will restrict our attention to three kinds of information: the H-ranks of concepts, the polarization of concepts, and the octant allocations of concepts within the affective semantic space.

It will be recalled that the H-ranks of qualifiers were obtained from their frequencies and diversities across the 100 substantives, sizable correlations among languages being found in the orderings. The *H-ranks of concepts* can be obtained by reversing this process, i.e., determining the H for each of the 100 substantives from the diversity of qualifiers given to it as a stimulus. (Note that in this case frequencies are equal, since 100 boys gave a single response to each noun.) A high H-rank for a concept indicates lack of stereotypy in a culture, in the sense that different members of the culture qualify it differently, a low H-rank suggests cultural stereotypy, since many members qualify it the same way. Do our language/culture communities agree on which concepts are stereotypical and which are not? Only slightly—correlations among H-ranks of concepts are positive, but range up to only about .20, as compared with the .50 to .70 values for H-ranks of qualifiers.

In terms of the SD measurement model, the distance of a concept from the origin of the multidimensional semantic space specifies its *polarization*—that is, its affective meaningfulness. Concepts located at the origin are said to be affectively meaningless. Table 27-9 gives the polarizations of each of the 100 concepts for each of five illustrative groups. These values were computed by summing the deviations of the means for subjects (regardless of sign) from the mid-positions of the 50 scales. These values thus reflect *cultural* meaningfulness of concepts rather than individual meaningfulness (which could be obtained by taking the average polarization values for individual subjects and then summing them). A rank of 1 was assigned to that concept which had the highest average polarity within a given language group. Thus, the high-ranking concepts in each group are those concepts for which the group means on all scales were most distant from the neutral or meaninglessness position on the scales. For purposes of comparison among these five groups, the concepts have been ordered from those having the least variance in polarization rank across all groups to those showing greatest variation in polarization. Thus, one will find both highly meaningful and meaningless substantives scattered throughout the table, the exact degree of meaningfulness being specified in the column labeled Mean Rank.

Inspection of the table indicates that the concepts MOTHER, HAND, THIEF, RIVER, WEDNESDAY, CHAIR, and BATTLE all had relatively little difference in the degree of polarization found in the five groups for which the calculations have been completed. If we examine the mean polarity ranks of these concepts, however, it can be seen that while MOTHER, THIEF, and BATTLE had *high* shared polarity, the concepts CHAIR and WEDNESDAY had *low* shared polarity. In contrast to these are the concepts GUILT, CRIME, KNOWLEDGE, GIRL, and HOPE, which show wide divergence in the degree of polarization found in each of the groups. These contrasts appear to be indicative of important aspects of the cultural descriptions of these groups. Numerous specific observations emerge from inspection of these data. Notice the provocative lessening of variance in meaningfulness across these cultures for the roles of a woman. The concept GIRL has higher variance across the cultures than does WOMAN, while MOTHER has both high meaningfulness and the least variation of any concept. There is greater intercultural agreement for the concept MAN, on the other hand, than for man as HUSBAND, and even greater agreement for man as FATHER—although, significantly, less

TABLE 27-9

THE 100 CONCEPTS RANKED BY STANDARD DEVIATION OF POLARITY RANK

	American English	Finnish	Flemish	Japanese	Kannada	Mean Rank*	Rank S. D.
			Polarity Rank				
1. mother	12	14	8	17	9	12.0 (1)	3.7
2. hand	70	63	71	60	70	66.8	
3. thief	6	4	13	1	12	7.2 (1)	
4. river	57	62	56	48	49	54.4 (	
5. Wednesday	100	99	91	100	84	94.8 (4)	
6. chair	80	73	58	75	69	71.0	
7. battle	19	3	20	5	19	13.2 (1)	
8. truth	35	47	26	25	25	31.6	
9. rope	91	70	75	84	66	77.2 (4)	
10. choice	69	98	94	82	91	82.8 (4)	11.6
11. anger	28	40	29	54	51	40.4	
12. marriage	2	7	10	21	32	14.4 (1)	
13. love	4	8	4	33	14	12.6 (1)	
14. pleasure	32	52	18	32	35	33.8	
15. freedom	1	2	31	9	6	9.8 (1)	
16. fruit	36	36	11	35	11	25.8	
17. courage	38	58	21	27	39	36.6	
18. heat	86	61	78	72	99	79.2 (4)	
19. bread	20	15	12	41	44	26.4	
20. tooth	40	34	36	65	63	47.6	15.1
21. fish	92	55	89	90	83	81.8 (4)	
22. smoke	68	37	79	67	58	61.8	
23. bird	43	24	53	43	67	46.0	
24. cat	85	45	67	81	78	71.2	
25. hair	77	94	65	85	53	74.8 (4)	
26. picture	63	42	88	66	61	64.0	
27. star	18	38	34	45	64	39.8	
28. head	81	51	46	61	37	55.2	
29. cup	72	50	70	36	76	60.8	
30. father	16	22	52	14	8	22.4 (1)	17.3
31. seed	67	43	47	87	62	61.2	
32. window	60	44	60	74	28	53.2	
33. laughter	30	68	48	58	75	55.8	
34. rain	48	72	69	94	88	74.2	
35. knot	99	56	85	99	94	86.6 (4)	
36. map	79	49	72	37	73	62.0	
37. doctor	10	35	55	26	50	35.2	
38. food	39	83	50	40	43	51.0	
39. power	56	77	92	93	54	74.4	
40. book	62	64	63	71	23	56.6	19.1
41. heart	8	5	49	30	7	19.8 (1)	
42. man	64	60	66	24	74	57.6	
43. death	73	29	32	31	56	44.2	
44. wealth	59	95	98	98	60	82.0 (4)	
45. life	52	91	35	62	52	58.4	
46. hunger	82	75	40	68	97	72.4	
47. danger	66	17	39	15	47	36.8	
48. future	55	88	97	50	89	75.8 (4)	
49. music	49	21	57	46	5	35.6	
50. work	74	79	74	52	27	61.2	21.8

TABLE 27-9 (Continued)

THE 100 CONCEPTS RANKED BY STANDARD DEVIATION OF POLARITY RANK

	American English	Finnish	Flemish	Japanese	Kannada	Mean Rank*	Rank S. D.
			Polarity Rank				
51. peace	23	59	6	11	46	29.0	22.8
52. egg	33	21	61	73	26	42.8	
53. punishment	75	16	28	51	34	40.8	
54. poison	53	39	42	6	68	41.8	
55. lake	22	48	54	16	72	42.4	
56. horse	24	13	51	57	4	29.8	
57. trust	21	46	64	38	82	50.2	
58. thunder	78	74	80	23	57	62.4	
59. purpose	80	92	100	39	71	77.0 (4)	
60. water	41	31	3	63	10	29.6	24.2
61. friend	11	10	27	64	3	23.0 (1)	
62. sun	5	1	1	7	59	14.6 (1)	
63. root	90	84	82	53	31	68.0	
64. cloud	31	67	95	69	41	60.6	
65. color	45	69	76	77	18	57.0	
66. fire	54	32	7	76	33	40.4	
67. progress	37	41	62	10	79	45.8	
68. defeat	47	26	87	55	86	60.2	
69. game	65	80	33	47	13	47.6	
70. tongue	27	57	68	96	40	57.6	26.6
71. fear	87	33	81	42	90	66.6	
72. sympathy	58	27	25	92	45	49.4	
73. money	29	54	93	91	81	69.6	
74. husband	50	96	45	22	36	49.8	
75. stone	74	23	16	78	48	47.8	
76. dog	61	9	86	59	42	51.4	
77. policeman	46	86	77	70	15	58.8	
78. respect	15	71	44	56	1	37.4	
79. story	89	78	73	79	16	67.0	
80. house	51	87	23	19	21	40.2	29.2
81. belief	13	65	42	44	93	51.4	
82. moon	26	31	90	49	12	39.6	
83. sleep	25	18	17	20	87	33.4	
84. ear	34	89	37	95	38	58.6	
85. author	88	97	83	83	20	74.2	
86. success	44	82	59	2	22	41.8	
87. woman	14	12	30	89	24	33.8	
88. pain	84	53	24	29	96	57.2	
89. snake	95	76	22	28	77	59.6	
90. luck	93	66	84	8	65	63.2	33.1
91. meat	42	91	15	86	85	63.8	
92. wind	98	81	41	91	17	65.6	
93. hope	17	93	96	34	81	64.2	
94. girl	7	11	5	88	55	33.2	
95. noise	96	85	38	18	100	67.4	
96. need	94	100	9	80	92	75.0 (4)	
97. knowledge	3	19	99	13	29	32.6	
98. tree	71	25	14	12	30	32.4	
99. crime	9	6	2	3	98	23.6 (1)	
100. guilt	97	28	19	4	95	48.6	44.1

*Numbers in parentheses indicate mean rank of first or fourth quartile.

TABLE 27-10

OCTANT ASSIGNMENTS OF 100 SUBSTANTIVE CONCEPTS*

Concept	American English	Finnish	Flemish	Japanese	Kannada
anger	V	V	V	V	VIII
author	I	IV	I	II	IV
battle	V	V	V	V	VIII
belief	I	II	II	II	IV
bird	IV	I	IV	IV	II
book	II	II	I	II	III
bread	II	II	II	III	II
cat	IV	I	I	IV	I
chair	II	II	II	III	III
choice	I	I	II	I	III
cloud	II	II	II	II	IV
color	I	I	II	IV	I
courage	I	I	I	II	IV
crime	V	VI	V	VI	VIII
cup	III	III	II	III	II
danger	V	V	V	V	VIII
death	VI	VII	V	VI	VII
defeat	V	VII	V	VI	VIII
doctor	I	I	V	II	III
dog	I	I	I	I	I,IV
ear	IV	II	III	III	I
egg	IV	III	III	III	II
father	I	II	I	II	III
fear	VI	V	V	VI	VII
fire	V	I	I	I	VII
fish	I	I	I	IV	I
food	II	II	II	I,IV	III
freedom	I	I	I	I	IV
friend	I	I	I	I	IV
fruit	II	I	III	IV	I
future	I	I	I	I	II
game	I	I	I	I	IV
girl	IV	IV	IV	III	I
guilt	V	V	V	V	V,VIII
hair	IV	IV	III	IV	IV
hand	I	I	I	IV	I
head	I	I	I	I	II
heart	I	I	I	I	I
heat	II	VI	II	V	III
hope	I	I	II	II	I
horse	I	I	I	I	IV
house	II	III	II	II	III
hunger	VII	VI	VI	VI	I,IV
husband	I	II	I	II	III
knot	II	VIII	VII	VI	V,VIII
knowledge	I	II	I	I	IV
lake	II	II	II	II	I,IV
laughter	I	I	I,II	IV	I
life	I	I	I	I	I
love	I	I	II	II	IV
luck	I	I	III	I	I

TABLE 27-10 (Continued)

OCTANT ASSIGNMENTS OF 100 SUBSTANTIVE CONCEPTS*

Concept	American English	Finnish	Flemish	Japanese	Kannada
man	I	I	I	I	III
map	II	II	II	I	III
marriage	I	I	II	I	IV
meat	II	VI	I	I,II	IV
money	II	I	III	I	III
moon	II	II	II	II	III
mother	I	I	I	I	II
music	I	I	I	I	IV
need	I	I	V	II	II
noise	I	V	V	V	IV
pain	V	V	V	V,VI	V
peace	I	IV	II	II	III
picture	II	VIII	II	II	IV
pleasure	I	I	I	IV	IV
poison	VI	V	V	V	VII
policeman	I	VI	V	VI	III
power	I	I,V	V	V	III
progress	I	I	II	I	II
punishment	V	VI	VI	VI	VIII
purpose	I	I	IV	II	III,IV
rain	I	I	VI	VIII	I
respect	II	II	II	I	III
river	II	I	II	I	III
root	I	VI	VI	II	III
rope	II	V	II	II	III
seed	IV	IV	III	III	II
sleep	II	I	II	III	III
smoke	VI	V	VI	VII	VII
snake	V	V	V	VI	VIII
star	II	II	I	III	II
stone	VI	VI	II	II	VII
story	I	I	I	IV	III
success	I	I	II	II	IV
sun	I	II	II	I	IV
sympathy	II	II	II	II	II
thief	V	V	V	VI	VIII
thunder	V	V	VI	V	VIII
tongue	I	I	IV	IV	II
tooth	I	II	I	IV	III
tree	I	II	II	II	IV
trust	II	II	I	I	III
truth	I	II	I	II	IV
water	II	I	I	II	IV
wealth	I	V	II	I	IV
Wednesday	I	IV,III	II	IV	I
wind	I	I	VI	I	IV
window	II	I	I	III	III
woman	IV	I	I	IV	III
work	I	III	V	I	IV

*Octant I = E+P+A+   Octant II = E+P+A−   Octant III = E+P−A−   Octant IV = E+P−A+
Octant V = E−P+A+   Octant VI = E−P+A−   Octant VII = E−P−A−   Octant VIII = E−P−A+

than for MOTHER. Notice that CRIME is seen to be of high meaningfulness in all countries analyzed except India. If CRIME is viewed by the Americans as being very meaningful, why is GUILT seen as relatively meaningless? If the Americans show inconsistency in their view of the meaningfulness of CRIME and GUILT, why do the Kannada subjects view them as consistently meaningless? These are only illustrative, of course, of the kinds of questions that could be put to such data in relation to external cultural information.

The scale profiles of the 100 concepts can be summarized by computing the average ratings of the concepts across a small set of scales most representative of the three major factors, such as the 12 pure scales used in the pan-language factor analysis of the previous section. In order to summarize further these concept meanings, we have arbitrarily divided the three-space defined by the major dimensions into eight regions or octants. Each octant is defined by the end points of the three dimensions taken in all possible combinations. Thus, for example, a concept would be assigned to Octant I if that concept had average ratings toward the positive ends of the composite scales of Factor I ($E+$, e.g., good), Factor II ($P+$, strong) and Factor III ($A+$, active). The *octant allocation of a concept* is thus a short-hand statement of its affective meaning.

Table 27-10 displays the specific concepts assigned to each of the octants for five illustrative language groups. These allocations reflect the basic connotation or "feeling tone" each concept has for each of the groups. For example, while the Americans see PROGRESS as being *good, strong,* and *active*,[5] as do the Finns and Japanese, the Flemish and Kannada groups assign this concept to Octant II, i.e., they see the con-

cept as being *good* and *strong,* but *passive.* The concept SYMPATHY, on the other hand, is seen by all groups as being *good, strong,* and *passive.* The concept MARRIAGE is assigned to Octant I by the Americans, Finns, and Japanese, while the Flemish- and Kannada-speaking groups assign the concept to Octants II and IV, respectively. Thus, while the Flemish apparently view marriage as being more *passive* than the Americans, the Kannada group sees marriage as being *weaker* than any of the other groups. The concept PEACE is viewed by the Americans as being *good, strong,* and *active,* while for both our NATO ally, Belgium, and our Asian cold war colleague, Japan, it is more *passive.* The south Indian Kannada group sees the same concept as being both *weaker* and more *passive,* while the Finns bordering Russia see PEACE as *good* and *active,* but *weak.* These differences in the ways our language/culture communities perceive their world — at least as it is mirrored in our 100 concepts — seem to have potential significance for a quantitative science of subjective culture.

Evidence for Concept/Scale Interaction

We have seen evidence that scale factor structure is relatively impervious to variation in subject populations, even populations differing in both language and culture. We have also seen evidence for great variations in the meanings of concepts within this common affective meaning space. A final question we must ask is this: will the factor structure of modes of qualifying prove impervious to variations in concept populations? Even on the basis of what data we have at this time, e.g., the Levin analysis of Section 3, the answer to this question seems to be clearly negative. This conclusion was foreshadowed in *The Measurement of Meaning* (1129) by the quite different structures yielded by factoring single concepts from the *Thesaurus* analysis and by Suci's finding that the usual three-

---

[5]Although we employ the shorthand notation of single adjectives to express the composite score averages, it should be recognized that the octant assignments are based on the averages of four scales representing each factor.

factor space collapsed into two (Benevolence and Dynamism) for political concepts —even though all three voting groups showed identical shifts in this respect.

In a more recent study, Osgood, Ware, and Morris (1130) had American college students rate Morris' "Ways to Live" against a form of SD; for this class of concepts—all "values"—the usual three basic factors collapse into one, termed Successfulness (i.e., a combination of *good, strong,* and *active*). Kirby collected the same kind of data (which is now being analyzed) from Hindi-speaking students in India.[6] Alexander and Husek (15) have demonstrated a unique structure for qualification when concepts tapping situational anxiety are studied. In the study by Ware already reported in Section 2 above, where 40 personality concepts were judged against 40 scales by 20 mature male and female subjects, the actual factors apparently shared across subjects are worth reporting; as given in Table 27-11 they were Morality (variant of Evaluation), Rationality, Uniqueness, Excitability (variant of Activity), Sociability, Toughness (variant of Potency), Urbanity, and Tangibility.

A study by Capell and Wohl (185) of the structure of frequently used dimensions of clinical judgment comes surprisingly close to the Evaluative-Potency-Activity structure, provided one is allowed a fair degree of leeway in the interpretation of what the clinical terms really mean. Capell and Wohl found that when the first factor dimension was forced through the evaluative qualifier scales, *pleasant-unpleasant, kind-cruel,* and *honest-dishonest,* the first factor had highest coefficients for such clinical terms as *distorted reality testing* and *orally demanding.* The second unforced dimension was characterized by such terms as *dependent, hostile,*

narcissistic, and *inadequate,* which might have as non-clinical synonyms the adjectives *weak, soft,* and *impotent.* The remaining factors lend themselves to more or less the

TABLE 27-11

VARIMAX ROTATION OF EIGHT FACTORS
OF PERSONALITY DIFFERENTIAL

Factor I	(7.9% of variance)
Morality	
moral-immoral	78
reputable-disreputable	78
wholesome-unwholesome	73
Factor II	(7.1% of variance)
Rationality	
logical-intuitive	66
objective-subjective	66
rational-irrational	60
Factor III	(6.7% of variance)
Uniqueness	
unique-typical	77
unusual-usual	74
individualistic-regular	70
Factor IV	(6.6% of variance)
Excitability	
excitable-calm	81
tense-relaxed	77
emotional-unemotional	52
Factor V	(6.5% of variance)
Sociability	
gregarious-self-contained	76
sociable-solitary	72
extroverted-introverted	66
Factor VI	(6.0% of variance)
Toughness	
tough-tender	78
insensitive-sensitive	71
rugged-delicate	63
Factor VII	(5.2% of variance)
Urbanity	
proud-humble	65
sophisticated-naive	58
deliberate-casual	53
Factor VIII	(4.0% of variance)
Tangibility	
formed-amorphous	72
predictable-unpredictable	56
tangible-intangible	42

---

[6]Incidentally, both of these studies indicate the flexibility of the "concept" to be measured in SD research; here the "concepts" were approximately 100-word statements of each "Way to Live"—which the subjects were easily able to read and then react to globally.

same kind of translation. Peterson (1152), in fact, concludes that the personality factors typically discovered are probably topical variants of the more general ways of attributing meaning to objects and accordingly should display a structure comparable to that of our own studies of ordinary qualification terms.

Finally, we have a cross-cultural study by Oyama, Tanaka, and Osgood (1133)

correlations. Thus, changing subject groups clearly affects the qualifier intercorrelations less than changing concept classes.

8. INTERPRETIVE SUMMARY

The object of concern in these studies has been *Homo Loquens.* Man is the only talking animal. He has been taught to talk by other talking men in a historical regress

TABLE 27-12

CORRELATIONS AMONG SCALE INTERCORRELATION MATRICES

		Japanese			American		
		colors	forms	words	colors	forms	words
Japanese	colors	*	.51	.33	.62	.43	.21
	forms		*	.41	.32	.52	.25
	words			*	.36	.28	.65
American	colors				*	.43	.41
	forms					*	.24
	words						*

which seems to put subject-mode variance and concept-mode variance in perspective. In this study college girls in both Japan and the United States rated three different classes of concepts — patches of color, line forms, and abstract words — against a common 35-scale form of a translation-equivalent SD. Separate scale-by-scale correlation matrices were computed for each of the six combinations of the concept and language variables. Table 27-12 displays the correlations obtained among the separate scale correlation matrices computed for these combinations. If the scale intercorrelations are more nearly similar across languages than across differing classes of concepts, the correlations between the matrices of differing concepts should be lower than those between differing languages. This is clearly the case. The italicized values of Table 27-12, the values comparing differing languages for the same concept class, are higher in every case than the off-diagonal within-language — across — concept-class

that extends back in time to our earliest inferences about man. Since language is a characteristic of the human species, and only the human species, one would expect to find massive similarities transcending language boundaries; yet the obvious differences between languages have obscured the more subtle, but certainly more fundamental, similarities from the view of language scientists and scholars. During the present decade the pendulum seems to be returning. We have, for example, the recent *Universals of Language* (617), edited by Joseph Greenberg and contributed to by anthropologists, linguists, and psychologists. In the area of psycholinguistics, our own studies clearly limit the generality of the Sapir-Whorf relativity hypothesis; at least on the matter of the structure of the affective meaning system, we find universality rather than relativity.

The researches reported here have led from the standard American college sophomore, to Americans differing in age, sex, and other characteristics, and even to peoples differing widely in both the structure of their languages and the nature of their cultures. Nevertheless, when heterogeneous samples of concepts are judged, the modes of qualifying structure themselves in the same fashion with remarkable regularity. The same three dimensions — Evaluation, Potency, and Activity — account for the largest proportions of variance and usually in that order. This system over-rides variations in subject populations, in the nature of the task, and in methods of analysis — but it does *not* over-ride variations in concept populations, a fact to which we will return momentarily. The fact that this system is common to the very young as well as the old, to the intellectually deprived as well as to the intellectually gifted, and to all humans regardless of the level of their culture, clearly suggests that this is a very fundamental and primitive aspect of meaning systems. But why this particular structure?

First, it must be confessed that when the second author began this research more than a decade ago, he rather confidently expected that the dimensions of the semantic space would correspond to the ways in which the sensory nervous system divides up the universe, i.e., the various modalities and their qualities and quantities (1121). The fact that this result would have flatly contradicted his own mediational theory of meaning — according to which meanings are identified with anticipatory portions of the reactions we make to signs — had to be forced on him by the repeated appearance of Evaluation, Potency, and Activity. These factors are clearly more *response-like* than sense-like in nature. But they are more than this. They are also *affective*, or emotive, in nature and closely related to Wilhelm Wundt's (1593) three dimensions of feeling — pleasantness, strain, and excitement. In this connection, it is interesting that when the meanings of facial expressions are factor-analyzed, similar factors typically appear, e.g., pleasantness, control, and activation (1123).

We know that the autonomic nervous system, with its organizational centers in the midbrain, is primitive neurologically and physiologically. It seems possible that affective meaning is intimately related to the functioning of the non-specific projection system, as it mediates autonomic reactions from hypothalamic, reticular, or limbic systems to the frontal lobes. Both are gross and non-discriminative, but highly generalized, systems and both are associated with the emotional, purposive, and motivational dynamics of the organism. But there is more to it than this, we think. It is precisely because this affective reaction system is so generalized — can participate equally with all of the sensory modalities and yet is independent of any of them — that its gross but pervasive structure overshadows the more discriminative semantic systems. To understand why this should be so we must inquire briefly into the nature of synesthesia and metaphor.

Early studies by the late Professor Theodore Karwoski of Dartmouth College and his associates (852, 853) made it clear that auditory-visual synesthesia is not a freak phenomenon indulged in by occasional rare individuals, but rather involves lawful translations from one modality to the other along dimensions made parallel through metaphor. When the sensory dimensions are translated into words, the translations become even more regular and lawful, e.g., *loud* goes with *near* rather than *far*, *treble* is *up* not *down*, *minor* is *dark* not *light*, and so forth. In a more recent study (1122), Navajo, Mexican-Spanish, Japanese, and American subjects related words in their own language (e.g., HAPPY, STRONG, WOMAN, WEAK, SAD, etc.) to visual alternatives displayed on cards; for example, given HAPPY, the subject might point to the *colorful* side, the *clear* side, the *up* side, the *white* side, and so forth rather than their visual opposites. Both within and between language/culture groups, agreements in the direction of synesthetic (or metaphorical) relation were far beyond chance. On a different but closely related problem, phonetic symbolism, Miron (1062) was able to demonstrate lawful within- and between-language connotations of speech sounds, when CVC syllables which were nonsense in both languages were rated against a form of SD.

Some details from the Oyama, Tanaka, and Osgood study (1133) already described seem particularly relevant here. Apart from the over-all similarities between Japanese and American factors, it was interesting to see how the particular scales connoting Evaluation, Potency, and Activity shifted as the concept-class changed from colors, to forms, to abstract words—and shifted similarly for both groups of subjects. For example, Potency is connoted by qualities like *strong* and *deep* when colors are being rated; when forms are being rated, properties like *hard, angular,* and *sharp* carry the Potency connotation; and when abstract words like LOVE, WAR, ART, and PEACE are being rated, we find that qualities like *real, distinct,* and *near* acquire Potency implications. Is it too great a leap to suggest that here we have the stuff from which metaphors are made? When we say of an abstract notion like LOVE, that it is *near* and *real,* or of a color like RED that it is *strong* and *deep,* or of a form that it is *hard* and *sharp,* we are equally conferring the feeling of power. Note that the denotative materials keep varying with the concepts being handled, yet beneath this apparent uniqueness is the common stuff of affect or feeling.

What has all this to do with the factors characteristically derived when subjects judge heterogenous concepts against samples of scales? It is a fact of factor analysis that factors will tend to go through those regions of the space where variables are most tightly clustered, i.e., through scales having high intercorrelations. If it is true that when scales are used *metaphorically* (connotatively) rather than *literally* (de-

notatively), they must rotate toward one of the gross affective dimensions which are the common coin of metaphors, then it must follow that when scales are applied to heterogeneous concepts, only a few of which are relevant denotatively, their highest over-all correlations will be with other scales having the same connotative or metaphorical meaning. Thus in the Thesaurus Study (Analysis III, Section I), the scale *masculine-feminine* is literally relevant only to the concepts MOTHER, ME, and ADLAI STEVENSON; when applied to the other 17 concepts (e.g., KNIFE, SNOW, DEBATE, DAWN, and ENGINE) it must be used metaphorically—and since metaphorically it reflects affective Potency, it has its highest correlations with scales like *strong-weak, hard-soft,* and *rugged-delicate.* Thus, the more heterogeneous the concept sample, the more likely are Evaluation, Potency, and Activity—in that order—to appear as the dominant factors. For the child, on the other hand, these metaphorical extensions may very well function as denotative synonyms. Ervin (467), for example, has shown that terms like *good, pretty* and *clean* are used as denotative synonyms by children.

Now it becomes clear why factor structures will shift when they are obtained from (1) judgments of single concepts or (2) judgments of a restricted class of concepts. First, what might be termed "denotative confounding" can operate—*masculine-feminine* will correlate positively with *pleasant-unpleasant* for ALDAI STEVENSON but negatively for MOTHER. Second, for any class of concepts (e.g., FOOD OBJECTS) certain scales will be denotatively relevant (e.g., *hot-cold, large-small, sweet-sour, hard-soft*) and hence tend to be used independently of their usual affective clusters (*hot* no longer Activity, *sweet* no longer Evaluation, *hard* no longer Potency). Third, since the affective significance of classes of concepts may differ from that for concepts in general, the *salience* (per cent variance accounted for) of factors may shift — for example, in the Oyama, Tanaka, and Osgood study, Activity is most salient for colors, Evaluation for words, and Potency for forms. And finally, since within restricted classes of concepts, dimensions which are normally independent may be correlated, or conversely dimensions normally correlated may become independent, factors may collapse together or differentiate. The Osgood, Ware, and Morris (1130) study with "Ways to Live" as concepts illustrates the former (*E, P,* and *A* all collapsing into a single Successfulness factor) and Ware's 1963 research in the domain of personality concepts illustrates the latter (*E, P,* and *A* expanding into eight more equally weighted factors). Our prediction is that if the scales representing Ware's eight Personality factors were used in the rating of an irrelevant set of concepts (e.g., colors) — and hence, of necessity, used metaphorically — they would collapse neatly into Evaluation, Potency, and Activity.

We are left with the question of why the dimensions of primitive affect should be Evaluation, Potency, and Activity. The organism's earliest, most persisting, and most significant interactions with its environment can be characterized as varying between the dichotomous states of physiological satisfaction and dissatisfaction — and this applies to the only talking organism as well. In the earliest stages, these states are induced directly by the properties of stimulus complexes encountered, but later they become associated with *signs* of such originally adequate stimuli. Still later these states come under the control of social signs produced by others, particularly linguistic signs. But in addition to this satisfaction-dissatisfaction dichotomy (which we

may identify with the Evaluation factor), stimulus complexes, and therefore their signs, can vary in at least two other respects: the amount of effort or work they demand from the organism (Potency factor) and the degree to which they arouse the organism (Activity factor). Signs of either satisfying or dissatisfying states of affairs may demand either much or little energy expenditure (e.g., shoveling through a snowbank vs. merely reaching for a gumdrop) and signs having any combination of these values may be arousing or pacifying (e.g., high arousal for holding a squirming eel vs. low for relaxing in a warm bath).

What we are suggesting is that, being constructed as we are as human organisms, we have affective reaction systems designed to react grossly in a limited number of ways — but to a very wide range of stimuli. These reactions by no means exhaust the ways in which we are capable of finely representing minute distinctions in the environment, but they are now, and always have been, fundamental for survival. While the *dimensions* of affective meaning are innate (depending upon how we are built), and hence are common to all humans regardless of differences in language or culture, the way in which this system will react to particular signs depends, equally obviously, upon learning. Thus the affective meaning of COW to an Indian vs. an American depends upon the different learning experiences provided by two different cultures, even though the ways in which these meanings can be differentiated are the same. We regard our work as contributing to an understanding of the affective meaning system, but by no means as clarifying the nature of meaning in general.

R. DARRELL BOCK
University of Chicago

1. HISTORICAL SURVEY OF MULTIVARIATE STATISTICAL METHOD DEVELOPMENT

The development of modern methods for educational research has been intimately related to the growth of multivariate analysis as a specialty within mathematical statistics. Not only has education been the field in which new multivariate methods have often found their first practical application, but some of the crucial theoretical advances in multivariate analysis were made in direct response to educational problems. The conception of factor models as descriptions of patterns of association among statistical variables, for example, was originally part of a theory contributed to educational psychology by Charles Spearman (1336, 1340). He attempted to explain the observed intercorrelations among mental tests as the effects of general and special factors of ability. His theory became a contribution to multivariate statistics when the efforts of Thomson (1393),

Burt (160), Holzinger and Harman (741), and Thurstone (1420), and others to prove or disprove it culminated in Thurstone's multiple factor model. All subsequent statistical developments of the technique of factor analysis depend directly on Thurstone's model (865).

A felicitous by-product of the investigation of mental factors was that it posed the problem of how to reduce highly multivariate data to a more limited number of variables with minimum loss of information. This purely empirical question is not involved with the theory of factors and has a solution in terms of the principal components of the original variables — a fact anticipated much earlier by Karl Pearson (1145). Truman Kelley suggested the problem to Harold Hotelling, who subsequently gave its solution in his fundamental paper on principal component analysis (771). The computational methods for component analysis which were revived by Hotelling (774) and Kelley (860) — methods for computing the latent roots and vectors of a real symmetric matrix — have since become an essential part of many multivariate procedures.

Although factor analysis was developed by the educational psychologists to prove a point about the organization of mental abilities, it did not originally include any formal statistical test of the hypothesis that the data conformed to the model. Indeed, much of the work in factor analysis antedates the modern theory of tests of hypothesis. From a statistical point of view the problem of deriving tests of hypothesis for factor analysis is difficult, and at the present time tests are available only for the hypothesis that the data can be attributed to a specified number of common factors, or that some specified factor loadings are zero (906). As a consequence, most educationists and psychologists have used factor analysis, not as a method for testing a factor theory, but as a "discovery procedure" for obtaining some intuitive grasp of the interrelationships among large sets of variables. In this use, factor analysis cannot strictly be called a formal statistical method, since the fact that the observations are random variables plays no part in it. The same can be said of component analysis; its most important application is for the simplification of the independent variables in a regression analysis (865), and the independent variables are not considered random. As a result the contribution of formal multivariate statistical methods to educational research — that is, methods involving rigorous procedures of estimation and tests of hypothesis — have come not from factor analysis, but from other sources which we now consider.

Whereas multiple factor analysis is in a sense a generalization of the correlational analysis of Karl Pearson, the other class of multivariate methods is a generalization of R. A. Fisher's methods of regression analysis. The most familiar examples of this class are (1) Hotelling's T^2 statistic, a generalization of Student's t test, (2) Fisher's discriminant analysis, (3) multivariate anal-

ysis of variance, generalizing the conventional univariate analysis of variance, and (4) canonical correlation, which is a generalization of multiple regression.

Hotelling's T^2 and the closely related technique of discriminant analysis have been widely used in educational research. The T^2 statistic provides a criterion for judging the significance of a difference between two groups with respect to a number of variables simultaneously. It may be applied, for example, to an experimental test of two curricula or teaching methods when the achievement of the subjects is measured by more than one variable. Associated with the T^2 is a "discriminant function" — a weighted sum of the original variables — which may be used to assign a new subject to the group to which he is most similar in terms of his scores on the variables. Discriminant functions have an important place in educational counseling as procedures for assigning students to programs where their chances of success are good. The computing procedure for simple applications of discriminant analysis have been described by Wert, Neidt, and Ahmann (1530).

When more than two groups are involved, discriminant analysis still may be applied, although the computations and statistical tests are slightly more complex. In this form it is usually called "multiple" discriminant analysis; it has been described by Bryan (154), Rao (1178), Jones and Bock (825), (see also Chapter 7 of this handbook), Cooley and Lohnes (381), and others (33, 1000).

Educational applications of simple and multiple discriminant analysis up to 1954 have been reviewed by Tatsuoka and Tiedeman (1384). Since then, numerous other studies have appeared in the educational literature which use the technique in a substantial way (i.e., not merely as an illustration of the computational procedure). Of special note are studies by Ahmann (8), Calia (179), Cooley (380), Ikenberry (802), Ivanoff (803), Mierzwa

(1059), and Tiedeman and Bryan (1430). As these studies illustrate, the discriminant function can be of very great utility in practical educational decisions. It enables the educational counselor to put the information from multiple test scores into a form directly relevant to the student's decision, namely, in the form of probabilities of success and failure in possible fields of study or employment. Discriminant analysis as such, however, probably should not be identified as a tool of educational research. The general research tool, which formally includes the procedures of discriminant analysis but not its purpose, is the *multivariate analysis of variance* (1331). Whereas discriminant analysis applies to practical problems of the optimal classification of subjects to groups, multivariate analysis of variance is appropriate to scientific problems of detecting and characterizing differences among experimental groups on many variables simultaneously. Combinations of the original variables which are formally equivalent to multiple discriminant functions appear in the analysis, but are of interest primarily for obtaining the so-called "canonical representation" of the effects of a way-of-classification in the experimental design (see Jones, Chapter 7 above). For historical reasons there is a tendency to use the term "multiple discriminant analysis" when the technique is applied to a purely scientific problem in which classification of subjects is not at issue. A more apt term in this case would be "one-way multivariate analysis of variance."

2. MULTIVARIATE ANALYSIS OF VARIANCE IN RELATION TO EXPERIMENTAL DESIGN

Multivariate analysis of variance has great potential for educational research because it opens the highly developed subject of design and analysis of experiments (861) to a field where research problems are inherently multivariate. Heretofore this was not possible because the statistical techniques associated with design and analysis of experiment were strictly univariate. With the advent of multivariate analysis of variance, and the availability of computers to perform the heavy computations required, a new era of progress in educational research can surely be expected.

At present the basic references for multivariate analysis of variance are the texts by Rao (1178), Kendall (865), Roy (1228), and Anderson (33). These books, particularly the latter two, are at an advanced level and may be somewhat difficult for applied workers. A good introduction to psychological applications is already given by Jones, in Chapter 7 of this handbook. Some aspects of the subject are also treated in Tatsuoka and Tiedeman (1384), Cooley and Lohnes (381), Rulon and Brooks (1240), and Bock and Haggard (124). Many important considerations in using the technique for educational experiments are not included in these papers, however, or indeed in any generally available source. To better illustrate the potential contribution of this multivariate method to educational research, the remainder of the present paper is devoted to worked examples of applications to important educational studies. Examples have been selected in which the number of variables is small and the arithmetic easy to follow. The first is drawn from a "methods" study, i.e., a study of the outcome of alternative instructional methods under actual conditions of use.

Exemplification by a Methods Study

An interesting example of a methods study has been reported by Milton Maier (980). In this study the ninth-grade algebra course developed by the School Mathematics Study Group (SMSG) was compared with a traditional algebra course in a number of schools throughout the United States. Forty-three teachers agreed to participate in the experiment and were willing to teach the new SMSG course. Twenty-one of these were selected at random and assigned to the SMSG course. The remainder continued to teach the traditional course. At the end of the experimental year, students in all forty-three classrooms were tested for achievement in algebra with a traditional test published by the Cooperative Test Division of Educational Testing Service, and with a new test devised by the School Mathematics Study Group and based on principles incorporated in the SMSG course. The experiment therefore had two dependent variables, and a multivariate analysis of variance is appropriate for comparing the achievement of the students in the two courses. Only the most simple form of analysis is required (two groups and two variates), but the main points of the general method (see Jones, Chapter 7, above) are illustrated.

In choosing a statistical model for this experiment it is important to realize that two major sources of random variation are present in the data: one arises from over-all differences between teachers and students in different classrooms and schools; the other from individual differences between students within classrooms (947). A components of variance analysis of scores from each of the tests in this study (936) shows that the variance components attributable to these sources are about equal. Call the respective components σ_b^2 and σ_w^2. Then the variance of a difference between method means, each computed from M schools and N students within schools, is

$$N(\bar{x}_1 - \bar{x}_2) = 2\left(\frac{\sigma_b^2}{M} + \frac{\sigma_w^2}{MN}\right).$$

For typical size classrooms ($N = 25$ to 50) it is apparent that this standard error is dominated by the between-classroom variation and will not be much affected by small differences in the number of students per classroom. The efficiency of our analysis will therefore not suffer appreciably if we neglect entirely the number of students in the study and consider the classroom as the primary sampling unit. In this case the classroom means constitute the observa-

tions, and the sample size for statistical purposes is the number of classrooms in each methods group.

To apply multivariate analysis of variance to these observations we must assume that the sampling covariance matrices are the same in the two methods groups. This is the analogue of the assumption of homogeneous within-cell variance in univariate analysis of variance. For a check on its tenability, a likelihood ratio test of the hypothesis of a common within-group variance matrix is available (the multivariate extension of Bartlett's test for the homogeneity of variance). This test is performed as follows (33): let S_g be the sum of squares and cross-products (briefly, "sum of products") of the test scores for group g corrected to the mean of the group (in this example $g = 1, 2$). Let $S_e = \Sigma_g S_g$ be the sum of these within-group sum of products. Similarly, let n_g be the number of degrees of freedom for group g, and $n_e = \Sigma_g n_g$ be the total within-group degrees of freedom. Let the number of tests be p and the number of groups n. Then under the hypothesis of a common population covariance matrix for the n groups the statistic

$$\chi_b^2 = -\left[1 - \left(\Sigma_g \frac{1}{n_g} - \frac{1}{n_e}\right)\left(\frac{2p^2 + 3p - 1}{6(p+1)(n-1)}\right)\right]$$

$$(\Sigma_g n_g \ln |S_g/n_g| - n_e \ln |S_e/n_e|)$$

is distributed as χ^2 on $(n-1)p(p+1)/2$ degrees of freedom in sufficiently good approximation for practical work.

In the present example the number of classrooms in the SMSG group is 21 and the number in the traditional group is 22. The within-group sums of products and their sum, the respective degrees of freedom and log determinants are as follows:[1]

---

[1] All sums of products in this paper are "over" persons. Elements above the diagonal of symmetric matrices are omitted.

$$S_1 = \begin{bmatrix} 728.38 \\ 457.82 & 323.04 \end{bmatrix}; \; n_1 = 20;$$

$$\ln |S_1/n_1| = 4.16265$$

$$S_2 = \begin{bmatrix} 527.93 \\ 170.16 & 75.22 \end{bmatrix}; \; n_2 = 21;$$

$$\ln |S_2/n_2| = 3.19421$$

$$S_e = \begin{bmatrix} 1256.31 \\ 627.98 & 398.26 \end{bmatrix}; \; n_e = 41;$$

$$\ln |S_e/n_e| = 4.14385$$

The value of the test statistic is therefore

$$\chi_b^2 = -\left[1 - \left(\frac{1}{20} + \frac{1}{21} - \frac{1}{41}\right)\left(\frac{8+6-1}{6 \times 3 \times 1}\right)\right]$$

$$(20 \times 4.16265 + 21 \times 3.19421$$
$$- 41 \times 4.14385) = 18.53,$$

on 3 degrees of freedom, and is clearly significant. A common within-group co-variance matrix cannot be assumed.

The source of this heterogeneity appears to be the relatively small variance of the SMSG scores in the group receiving traditional algebraic instruction (compare the standard deviations in Table 28-1). A likely explanation is that the distribution of item difficulties in the SMSG test is skewed toward items of greater difficulty. Thus the SMSG group, which has the higher mean, is performing at a level of difficulty where more spread among the scores is possible. The traditional algebra test, on the other hand, is a standard test which has undergone extensive item analysis and development and shows uniform variation over a wider range of scores.

Although the rejection of the hypothesis of a common covariance matrix has already demonstrated that the two methods groups could not have been sampled from the same population, let us carry through the multivariate analysis of variance with these data simply as an illustration of the calculations. All the information necessary for this purpose is contained in the group means in Table 28-1 and the partition of the sum of products in Table 28-3. The estimate of interest is the difference between the respective test means of the two groups, sometimes called the "vector contrast",

$$\begin{bmatrix} \text{Traditional test} & -5.8477 \\ \text{SMSG test} & 5.4290 \end{bmatrix}$$

When a common within-group covariance matrix can be assumed, the best unbiased estimate of the covariance matrix of this contrast is calculated from the common within-group sum of products divided by its degrees of freedom and the sum of the reciprocal of the sample sizes. In this case,

$$\frac{N_1 + N_2}{N_1 N_2 (N_1 + N_2 - 2)} (S_1 + S_2) = \frac{21 + 22}{462 \times 41}$$

$$\begin{bmatrix} 1256.31 \\ 627.98 & 398.26 \end{bmatrix} = \begin{bmatrix} 2.85193 \\ 1.42557 & .90408 \end{bmatrix}$$

Represent the contrast by the (2×1) vector $\mathbf{d}$, and its covariance matrix by V_e. Then the multivariate analogue of Student's t statistic is Hotelling's T^2,

$$(1) \quad T^2 = \mathbf{d}' V_e^{-1} \mathbf{d}$$

a quadratic form in which the variable is $\mathbf{d}$ and the matrix is the inverse of the com-

TABLE 28-1

GROUP MEANS AND STANDARD DEVIATIONS

	SMSG Group ($N = 21$)		Traditional Group ($N = 22$)	
	Mean	S.D.	Mean	S.D.
Traditional Test	11.9475	6.0349	17.7952	5.0149
SMSG Test	17.2494	4.0190	11.8204	1.8938

TABLE 28-2

GROUP MEANS AND CONTRAST

	Pretest 1	Pretest 2	Trad. Test	SMSG Test
Group 1 (Regular SMSG, $N=21$)	33.304	7.004	11.948	17.249
Group 2 (Special SMSG, $N=12$)	38.432	10.700	18.622	22.573
Contrast (Group 2 -Group 1)	5.128	3.696	6.674	5.324

mon covariance matrix. Assuming a multivariate normal distribution of d with zero mean vector and covariance matrix estimated by V_e, the distribution of T^2 may be expressed in terms of the F distribution by the change of variable

$$T^2 = n_e pF/(n_e - p + 1)$$

where the F has p degrees of freedom in the numerator and $n_e - p + 1$ in the denominator. Note that if the number of degrees of freedom for error, n_e, is large relative to the number of variates, p, critical points for T^2 are about p times larger than points on the F distribution corresponding to the same size error of the first kind. In this example

$$T^2 = [-5.8477 \ 5.4290]$$
$$\begin{bmatrix} 1.65545 \\ -2.61035 \ 5.22214 \end{bmatrix}\begin{bmatrix} -5.8477 \\ 5.4290 \end{bmatrix} = 376.27.$$

Since the .05 point for T^2 is $41 \times 2 \times 3.23/(41 - 2 + 1) = 6.62$, the vector contrast cannot be assumed zero, and could not be even with a much more conservative estimate of its covariance matrix.

If undetermined variables, say, x and y, are substituted for the components of d and (1) is set equal to say the .05 point for T^2, a quadratic equation results, the solution points of which, when added to d, describe a 95 per cent confidence region for the vector contrast. A graph of this confidence region is shown in Diagram 28-1.

When mental test scores serve as data,

the units of measurement of the variates may be arbitrary. In order to compare between-group differences of different variates in a common metric, it is convenient to divide the vector contrast by the common within-group standard deviation to obtain a "standardized contrast":

$$d = \begin{bmatrix} -5.8477/5.5355 \\ 5.4290/3.1167 \end{bmatrix} = \begin{bmatrix} -1.0564 \\ 1.7419 \end{bmatrix}.$$

In this form the contrast gives the number of standard deviations separating the group

DIAGRAM 28-1.   Confidence Region for the Mean Contrast

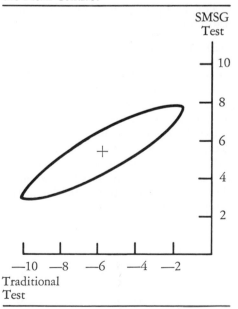

means for each test. Its variance is proportional to the within-group correlation matrix,

$$V(d) = \left(\frac{21+22}{21 \times 22}\right) \begin{bmatrix} 1.0000 & \\ .8878 & 1.0000 \end{bmatrix}.$$

3. APPLICATIONS OF THE DISCRIMINANT FUNCTION AND STEP-DOWN ANALYSIS

Multivariate analysis of variance affords other approaches to a test of the hypothesis that a vector contrast is null. One is connected with "discriminant function" analysis, which so determines the coefficients of a linear combination of the test scores as to maximize the sum of squares between groups relative to the sum of squares within groups. Represent these coefficients by the $(p \times 1)$ vector $\mathbf{a}$. Then the ratio of between- to within-group sum of squares may be expressed in quadratic forms as

$$= \mathbf{a}'S_b\mathbf{a}/\mathbf{a}'S_e\mathbf{a}.$$

The first derivatives of this expression with respect to the elements of $\mathbf{a}'$, when set equal to zero determines the required maximum

$$(2) \quad (S_b - \lambda S_e)\mathbf{a} = 0.$$

This system of homogeneous equations in $\mathbf{a}$ has a non-trivial solution if and only if the determinant $|S_b - \lambda S_e| = 0$. Expansion of this determinant leads to a polynomial in λ the largest root of which corresponds to the maximum value of the ratio of sums of squares. The coefficients of the discriminant function are the solutions of (2) when this value of λ is substituted. In the present example we have

$$\left| \begin{pmatrix} 367.402 & \\ -341.099 & 316.677 \end{pmatrix} \right.$$

$$\left. - \lambda \begin{pmatrix} 1256.31 & \\ 627.98 & 398.26 \end{pmatrix} \right| = 0$$

$$-972{,}572\,\lambda + 105.979\,\lambda^2 = 0$$

$$\lambda = 9.1770$$

for the non-zero root. A solution of (2) is

$$11{,}162a_1 + 6{,}104a_2 = 0$$
$$6{,}104a_1 + 3{,}338a_2 = 0$$
$$a_1 = 1$$
$$a_2 = -1.8286.$$

Since the unit of scale of $\mathbf{a}$ is arbitrary, it may as well be set so that the within-group variance of the discriminant scores is unity.

$$\mathbf{a}^0 = \mathbf{a}/\sqrt{\underset{N}{\mathbf{a}'V_e\mathbf{a}}} = \begin{bmatrix} 1/\sqrt{7.1062} \\ -1.8286/\sqrt{7.1062} \end{bmatrix}$$

$$= \begin{bmatrix} .3751 \\ -.6860 \end{bmatrix}.$$

Then the sum of the mean differences weighted by these coefficients is the number of standard deviations which separate the discriminant score means for the two groups.

$$v = \mathbf{a}'\mathbf{d}$$
$$= -.3751 \times 5.8477 - .6860 \times 5.4290$$
$$= 5.9178$$

If it is of interest to compare the magnitudes of the discriminant function coefficients, they must be put in standardized form by multiplying by the within-group standard deviations of the variates, i.e., the form which applies to the standardized contrasts.

$$a = \begin{bmatrix} .3751 \times 5.5357 \\ -.6860 \times 3.1167 \end{bmatrix} = \begin{bmatrix} 2.0764 \\ -2.1381 \end{bmatrix}$$

In the case of two groups, the non-zero root of the determinantal equation $|S_b - \lambda S_e| = 0$ is proportional to Hotelling's T^2,

$$T^2 = n_e\,\lambda$$
$$= 41 \times 9.1770 = 376.26,$$

and reduces to the significance test considered above.

The test of hypothesis and the confidence region for the vector contrast for all practical purposes dispose of the possibility that the observed differences in the methods means could have resulted from fortuitous assignment of the teachers to the two methods groups. The contrast demonstrates the superiority of the SMSG group on the SMSG test and the superiority of the traditional group on the traditional test. Any hope that the students could learn the new content in the SMSG course and do at least as well as the other group with traditional content was not realized.

If we were specifically interested in the possibility that the methods groups would show a converse profile of achievement on the two tests, we might have decided a priori to test a discriminant function with standardized coefficients, say,

$$ c = \begin{bmatrix} 1 \\ -1 \end{bmatrix}. $$

In this case the variance ratio, expressed in terms of non-standardized coefficients,

$$ n_e c' S_b c / n_b c' S_e c $$

or

$$ 41 \times 785.057 / 99.428 = 323.72 $$

is an F statistic on 1 and 41 degrees of freedom, and its .05 critical point is 4.07. Comparing the critical value of T^2 in this example (6.62) with this critical value of F, we see the price we have paid for fitting the coefficients of the discriminant function. T^2 is of the order of p times larger than the corresponding F statistic. This means that if we have reason to believe we can specify a priori a linear combination of variates which will discriminate between the groups, we may be rewarded by a considerably more powerful test, particularly if p is large. (See Bartlett, 70, 71, in this connection.)

The discriminant function approach generalizes to more than two groups. In the case of more than two groups, and two or more variables, the largest root of the determinantal equation

$$ |S_b - \theta(S_b + S_e)| = 0 $$

$$ |S_b - \theta S_t| = 0, $$

is Roy's criterion. Some of the critical points of its distribution have been tabled by Heck (707) in terms of the arguments

$$ s = \min(n_b, P) $$

$$ m = \frac{|p - n_b| - 1}{2} $$

$$ n = \frac{n_e - p - 1}{2} $$

(n_b is the between-group degrees of freedom). Roy's criterion may also be obtained from the largest root of $|S_b - \lambda S_e| = 0$ by the relation $\theta = \frac{\lambda}{1 + \lambda}$.

The criterion provides a test of the hypothesis that any $n_b = n - 1$ linearly independent vector contrasts among n groups are simultaneously null. Corresponding to the criterion is a single best discriminating function for the n groups; its coefficients may be obtained from the solutions of (2) or $(S_b - \theta S_t)a = 0$.

Unfortunately, Roy's criterion is presently tabulated only to $s = 5$ and $m = 10$.[1] Beyond this range only the likelihood ratio test of multivariate hypotheses is available. Bartlett's χ^2 approximation again provides a convenient test statistic for practical work (66):

$$ \chi^2 = -\left(n_e + n_b - \frac{n_b + p + 1}{2}\right) \ln \frac{|S_e|}{|S_t|} $$

The degrees of freedom are $n_b p$. In the present example, $|S_e| = 105{,}979$ and $|S_t| = |S_e + S_b| = 1{,}078{,}551$, so

$$ \chi^2 = -\left(41 + 1 - \frac{1 + 2 + 1}{2}\right) \ln .098261 $$

$$ = 92.80 \text{ on } 2 \text{ degrees of freedom.} $$

In the analysis of differences among more than two groups, questions about the

---

[1]Tables to $s = 10$ and $m = 15$ are now available. See Sreedharan Pillai, K. C., On the distribution of the largest characteristic root of a matrix in multivariate analysis, *Biometrika*, 1965, *52*, 405-414.

spatial configuration of the group means may arise. The methods of multiple discriminant analysis described by Rao (1178), and Jones and Bock (825), then apply and lead to a so-called "canonical" representation of the n group mean vectors or the $n-1$ vector contrasts. A method of factoring the likelihood ratio in order to test approximately the significance of variation in various dimensions of the canonical representation is also available (824).

Yet another approach to tests of multivariate hypotheses is the so-called "step-down" analysis of Roy and Bargmann (1230). Computationally this procedure is just a sequence of analyses of covariance (1229). It leads to a univariate test of significance of the second variate eliminating the first, of the third eliminating the first and second, and so on down to the last variate eliminating all previous variates. Roy and Bargmann have shown that under the hypothesis of no group differences, these tests of significance, including one for the first variate, are statistically independent. As a result, the probability of encountering an error of the first kind in a step-down analysis is $1 - (1 - \alpha)^p$ if the separate tests have an alpha critical level. To express the procedure generally, we can symbolize a partition of the first $i + 1$ rows and columns of S_e and S_t, respectively, as follows:

$$\begin{bmatrix} S_e^{(i)} & s_e^{(i,i+1)} \\ s_e^{(i+1,i)} & s_e^{(i+1)} \end{bmatrix}; \begin{bmatrix} S_t^{(i)} & s_t^{(i,i+1)} \\ s_t^{(i+1,i)} & s_t^{(i+1)} \end{bmatrix}.$$

The reduced sum of squares for error and total for the $i+1$ variate is, respectively,

$$s_e^{(i+1)*} = s_e^{(i+1)} - s_e^{(i+1,i)}(S^{(i)}) - 1 s_e^{(i,i+1)}$$
$$s_t^{(i+1)*} = s_t^{(i+1)} - s_t^{(i+1,i)}(S^{(i)}) - 1 s_t^{(i,i+1)}$$

and the F test of between-group differences for the $i+1$ variate, eliminating the first i variates is

$$F^{(i+1)} = \frac{(n_e - i)(s_t^{(i+1)*} - s_e^{(i+1)*})}{n_b s_e^{(i+1)*}},$$

on n_b and $n_e - i$ degrees of freedom. The two-variate case is especially simple because the inverses of $S_e^{(i)}$ and $S_t^{(i)}$ are just the reciprocals $1/s_e^{(1)}$ and $1/s_t^{(1)}$. In the present example, the F statistic for the first variate is

$$41 \times 367.402/1256.31 = 11.99 \text{ on 1 and}$$
$$41 \text{ degrees of freedom.}$$

For the second variate the reduced sum of squares for error is $398.26 - 627.98^2/1256.31 = 84.36$, and the reduced total is $714.937 - 286.881^2/1623.712 = 664.250$. The step-down F is therefore

$$40 \times (664.25 - 84.36)/84.36 = 274.95 \text{ on}$$
$$1 \text{ and 40 degrees of freedom.}$$

Unlike the other tests of multivariate hypotheses, the step-down test is not invariate under rearrangements of the variates. The order in which the variates are eliminated must be determined beforehand. It is convenient to choose this ordering so that the step-down F statistics can be used to judge the partial contribution of successive variates to discrimination between groups (in Rao's terminology, to "test the information provided by some additional characters"). Variates believed important to discrimination should appear earlier in the ordering and more dubious variables later. If the latter make no appreciable contribution, there is some empirical ground for omitting them from further consideration.

Throughout this section the multivariate analysis of variance has been represented as it applies in the one-way case. Actually, the sum of products S_b and the corresponding degrees of freedom n_b may be any sum of products and degrees of freedom for hypothesis, whether for main effects or interactions, in an analysis of variance design. Examples of this more general analysis are given by Jones (824). If the data are extensive, particularly if p is large, or the design irregular, machine computation will be necessary. Fortunately, very powerful and flexible computer programs exist for multivariate analysis of variance (121, 122), and the time or expense of the calculations is a minor consideration.

4. MULTIVARIATE ANALYSIS OF REGRESSION AND COVARIANCE

The SMSG study also included twelve classrooms in which the teacher had received special training in the content of the SMSG course. These classrooms were selected on administrative criteria and cannot be considered a well-defined sample from a statistical point of view. (For statistical purposes it must be possible to calculate the probability that a given sampling unit will enter the sample. See Cochran, 355.) The fact that the average score on each of two pretests (Table 28-2) is higher in the special group than in the regular SMSG groups suggests that they were actually drawn from somewhat better schools. Since the average scores on the measures of traditional and SMSG algebra achievement (hereafter referred to as the posttests) are also higher in the special group, the question arises whether this superior performance should be attributed entirely to superior ability of the students as measured by the pretest, or in some part to better teaching. The technique of multivariate analysis of covariance may serve to answer this question. If the data satisfy certain conditions specified below, we may estimate the difference between the posttest scores after they have been adjusted statistically for the difference in the pretest scores. These so-called "adjusted" contrasts are estimated with respect to the conditional distribution of the posttest scores given the pretest scores, and do not require the assumption that the classrooms in the two groups were originally assigned at random from the same population.

In addition to the usual multivariate

normal assumptions, the conditions which the data must satisfy if the results of the analysis of covariance are to have suitable generality are (1) the regression plane of the posttest scores on the pretest scores in one of the groups must be parallel to that in the other group, (2) residual variation about the regression planes for the two groups must be homogeneous. Since these conditions are not always met in methods experiments, a preliminary analysis of regression may be desirable. The summary statistics for both the analysis of regression and the analysis of covariance are contained in the partition of sums of squares and cross-products of the pre- and posttests shown in Table 28-3.

We first test the hypothesis that a common residual covariance matrix can be assumed for the two groups. The procedure is the same as the one used in the previous section to test the homogeneity of within-group covariance matrices, except that variation attributable to the pretests is first eliminated. For this purpose, we compute the reduced sum of products for the two groups separately, and the reduced common within-group sum of products, using a slight extension of the formula given above for step-down analysis. In general, the partition of a sum of products into submatrices associated with q pretests, x, and p posttests, y, can be represented

$$\begin{bmatrix} S^{(x)} & S^{(xy)} \\ S^{(yx)} & S^{(y)} \end{bmatrix} \begin{matrix} q \\ p \end{matrix}$$
$$ q p$$

Then the reduced sum of products is

$$S^{(y)*} = S^{(y)} - S^{(yx)} (S^{(x)})^{-1} S^{(xy)}$$

with, say, $n^* = n - q$ degrees of freedom. For example, the reduced common within-group sum of products, $S_e^{(y)*}$, shown in Table 28-5 is computed as follows:

$$\begin{bmatrix} 143.812 & \\ 73.646 & 110.296 \end{bmatrix} =$$

$$\begin{bmatrix} 1400.161 & \\ 857.934 & 612.351 \end{bmatrix}$$

$$-\begin{bmatrix} 1026.076 & 703.980 \\ 678.422 & 429.603 \end{bmatrix}$$

$$\begin{bmatrix} .00465108 & \\ -.00630068 & .0110212 \end{bmatrix}$$

$$\cdot \begin{bmatrix} 1026.076 & 678.422 \\ 703.980 & 429.603 \end{bmatrix}$$

with $n_e^* = 31 - 2 = 29$ degrees of freedom. Similarly, the reduced sum of products for the regular SMSG group (hereafter called group 1), and the special SMSG group (hereafter called group 2) is shown in Table 28-4. The corresponding log de-

terminants for the likelihood ratio tests are therefore

$$\ln_N | S_1^{(y)*}/n_1^* | = 1.58516$$

$$\ln_N | S_2^{(y)*}/n_2^* | = 3.42123$$

$$\ln_N | S_e^{(y)*}/n_e^* | = 2.51863.$$

The χ^2 approximation

$$\chi_b^2 = -\left[1 - \left(\frac{1}{18} + \frac{1}{9} - \frac{1}{29}\right)\left(\frac{8+6-1}{6 \times 3 \times 1}\right)\right]$$

$$(18 \times 1.58516 + 9 \times 3.42123 - 29 \times 2.51863)$$

$$= 12.41 \text{ on 3 degrees of freedom is}$$

clearly significant.

TABLE 28-3

PARTITION OF THE SUM OF PRODUCTS

Source of Variation	Degrees of Freedom	Pretest 1	Pretest 2	Trad. Test	SMSG Test
Within SMSG Group (Group 1)	20	568.760 293.260 564.340 389.980	216.200 372.660 242.680	728.380 457.820	323.040
Within Special Group (Group 2)	11	384.472 251.691 461.736 288.442	186.076 331.320 186.923	671.781 400.114	289.311
Common Within-Group	31	953.232 544.951 1026.076 678.422	402.276 703.980 429.603	1400.161 857.934	612.351
Between-Groups	1	200.492 144.658 261.220 208.311	104.316 188.367 150.265	340.098 271.281	216.453
Total	32	1153.724 689.609 1287.296 886.733	506.592 892.347 579.868	1740.259 1129.215	828.804

TABLE 28-4

ANALYSIS OF REGRESSION: SUM OF PRODUCTS FOR THE SEPARATE GROUPS

Source of Variation	Degrees of Freedom	SMSG Group (Group 1) Trad. Test	SMSG Test	Degrees of Freedom	Special Group (Group 2) Trad. Test	SMSG Test
		Sums of Products				
Regression	2	⎡662.606 ⎣439.232	294.025⎤	2	⎡594.127 ⎣343.814	216.567⎤
Residual	18	⎡ 65.774 ⎣ 18.091	29.015⎤	9	⎡ 77.654 ⎣ 56.300	72.744⎤
Total	20	⎡728.380 ⎣457.820	323.040⎤	11	⎡671.781 ⎣400.114	289.311⎤

The assumption of a common covariance matrix is again contradicted, and apparently for the same reason. The group with the higher average SMSG performance shows greater variation in their SMSG scores, a further indication that the SMSG test has a disproportionate number of difficult items and allows more variation in scores at higher levels. For sake of illustrating the calculations, however, let us continue with the analysis of regression.

To test whether parallel regression planes can be assumed in the two groups, we may compare the sum of products of the residuals from the separate regressions, given in Table 28-4, with the residuals from the common regression plane shown in the analysis of covariance in Table 28-5. If variation about the single common regression plane is not significantly in excess of the residual variation when two separate planes are fitted, we will consider the separate planes parallel. The likelihood ratio test of the hypothesis of parallelism is convenient. We form the ratio of the determinant of the sum of the separate residual sum of products matrices and the common residual sum of products, $| S_1^{(y)*} + S_2^{(y)*} | / | S_e^{(y)*} |$:

$$\begin{vmatrix} 143.428 \\ 74.391 & 101.759 \end{vmatrix} / \begin{vmatrix} 143.812 \\ 73.646 & 110.296 \end{vmatrix}$$

$$= 9061/10438.$$

TABLE 28-5

ANALYSIS OF COVARIANCE

Source of Variation	Degrees of Freedom	Common Within Group Trad. Test	SMSG Test	Degrees of Freedom	Total Trad. Test	SMSG Test
		Sums of Products				
Regression	2	⎡1256.349 ⎣ 784.288	502.055⎤	2	⎡1596.339 ⎣1054.290	707.849⎤
Residual	29	⎡ 143.812 ⎣ 73.646	110.296⎤	30	⎡ 143.920 ⎣ 74.924	120.955⎤
Unreduced total	31	⎡1400.161 ⎣ 857.934	612.351⎤	32	⎡1740.259 ⎣1129.215	828.804⎤

If there are q independent variables and n groups, the degrees of freedom between regressions is, say, $n_r = q(n-1)$. The degrees of freedom within-group remains $n_e^* = n_e - q$. With these degrees of freedom the χ^2 approximation applies to this criterion in the same manner as the test of group differences in the multivariate analysis of variance.

$$\chi^2 = -\left[n_e^* + n_r - \frac{n_r + p + 1}{2} \right]$$

$$\cdot \ln \left(\frac{|\Sigma_g S_g^{(y)^*}|}{|S_e^{(y)*}|} \right),$$

or in particular

$$\chi^2 = -\left(29 + 2 - \frac{2 + 2 + 1}{2} \right)$$

$$\ln (9061/10438)$$

$$= 4.03.$$

This value of χ^2 on $pn_r = 4$ degrees of freedom is not significant: the data do not contradict the assumption of parallel regression planes. The first, and perhaps more important, condition for analysis of covariance is therefore satisfied.

Before estimating the contrast between the adjusted posttest means for the two groups, let us test the hypothesis that the contrast is null, that is, that the adjusted differences for the two tests are simultaneously zero. For this purpose we perform a multivariate analysis of covariance making use of the common within-group and total sum of products from Table 28-3. We compute the corresponding reduced sums of products for the posttests shown in the residual line of Table 28-5.

$$S_e^{(y)*} = S_e^{(y)} - S_e^{(yx)}(S_e^{(x)})^{-1}S_e^{(xy)}$$

$$S_t^{(y)*} = S_t^{(y)} - S_t^{(yx)}(S_t^{(x)})^{-1}S_t^{(xy)}.$$

The first of these has already been obtained in the analysis of regression.

Any of the criteria for testing multivariate hypotheses now apply. The approximation for the likelihood ratio is

$$\chi^2 = -\left[n_b + n_e^* - \frac{n_b + p + 1}{2} \right] \ln \frac{|S_e^{(y)*}|}{|S_t^{(y)*}|}.$$

In this case

$$\chi^2 = -\left(1 + 29 - \frac{1 + 2 + 1}{2} \right)$$

$$\cdot \ln (10438/11794)$$

$$= 3.42$$

on $n_b p = 2$ degrees of freedom.

For computing Roy's criterion, we obtain the adjusted between-group sum of products by subtraction

$$S_b^{(y)*} = S_t^{(y)*} - S_e^{(y)*}$$

and find the largest root of

$$|S_b^* - \theta S_t^*| = 0.$$

For the step-down analysis, we proceed as with any other sum of products for error and total. In this example, the two step-down F statistics on 1/29 and 1/28 degrees of freedom are

$$29 \times (143.920 - 143.812)/143.812 = 0.02$$
$$28 \times (81.950 - 72.582)/72.582 \quad = 3.61.$$

These tests of significance do not contradict the hypothesis of no difference between the adjusted group means. The better performance of the classrooms taught by the teachers who had received special training could be attributed to the superior ability of their students. This can also be seen by estimating the contrast between the adjusted group means and computing its significance region. The adjustment makes use of the regression coefficients computed from the common within-group sum of products.

$$B = S_e^{(yx)}(S_e^{(x)})^{-1}.$$

The adjusted contrast is

$$\mathbf{d}^{(y)*} = \mathbf{d}^{(y)} - B\mathbf{d}^{(x)},$$

where $\mathbf{d}^{(x)}$ is the corresponding contrast for the concomitant variables.

In the data the regression coefficients computed from the within-group sum of products from Table 28-3 are

$$\begin{bmatrix} 1026.076 & 703.980 \\ 678.422 & 429.603 \end{bmatrix}$$

$$\begin{bmatrix} .00465109 \\ -.00630068 & .01102120 \end{bmatrix}$$

$$= \begin{bmatrix} .336811 & 1.293724 \\ .448606 & .460218 \end{bmatrix}.$$

The adjusted contrast for the traditional test proves to be near zero, while that for the SMSG test favors the teachers of the special groups, although not significantly so.

$$\begin{bmatrix} 6.674 \\ 5.324 \end{bmatrix} - \begin{bmatrix} .336811 & 1.293724 \\ .448606 & .460218 \end{bmatrix} \begin{bmatrix} 5.128 \\ 3.696 \end{bmatrix}$$

$$= \begin{bmatrix} 0.165 \\ 1.323 \end{bmatrix}.$$

The assumptions necessary for multivariate analysis of covariance are somewhat stronger than those for multivariate analysis of variance, and it is well to design the methods study so as to avoid analysis of covariance if possible. We have already seen in the example of the SMSG study that this can be done by a simple randomization experiment. The classrooms are assigned to the alternative methods randomly from a common group. The methods groups are then random samples from the same population initially, and equal pretest means can be assumed. The simple randomization design is quite adequate insofar as we consider the outcome or "payoff" of the methods to be proportional to the mean achievement (397). Our only concern then is to estimate the mean differences between the methods groups, and the regression of the posttest scores on any

possible pretest scores is irrelevant for this purpose.

Of course, in a more detailed analysis we may be interested in examining interactions between the pretest scores of the classes and the response to the methods. We would then want to perform the analysis of regression even when the data were obtained in a simple randomization experiment. (See Potthoff, 1170, in this connection.) More conveniently, we might choose classes which are, say, "high," "middle," and "low," according to their pretest scores and include these classifications as a factor in the multivariate analysis of variance design. In this approach we would be treating the pretest scores like the independent variables in physical experiment, which are set by the experimenter so as to best reveal an empirical relationship.

A possible disadvantage of the simple randomization experiment is that the large component variation due to teachers and schools appears in the error estimate and diminishes the sensitivity of the analysis. A better design would eliminate this component by "blocking" by teacher; that is, the experiment would be arranged so that each teacher presents two or more alternative methods. Any difficulty the teacher might experience in teaching two different methods at the same time could be avoided by having him teach them in alternate years. Counterbalancing the order in which the methods are presented in different schools would avoid confounding the method and year effect. If possible, each teacher should teach the same method in at least two sections to make available an error term for testing the important teacher by method interaction. Briefly, this type of design could be described as "methods" crossed by "sections nested within teachers, teachers nested within schools, and schools nested within orders of presentation."

A remarkably sensitive *univariate* experiment of this general type has been reported by Page (1134). An excellent example of a *multivariate* study using the principle of blocking by teacher has been carried out by Daniels and Hall (404): they experimentally compared the effectiveness of a programed textbook in elementary psychology (Holland and Skinner, *Analysis of Behavior*) with a conventional text covering the same content (Skinner, 1328). The experimental procedure was the following. Students in the general psychology course were randomly assigned to one of 24 discussion and laboratory sections, each comprised of from 21 to 26 students. Each

included as a factor. The partition of degrees of freedom, the chi-square approximations for the likelihood ratio tests, and the corresponding probability levels for this analysis are shown in Table 28-6. The sum of products for interaction between methods and instructors within sex is used to estimate the error variation and covariation for purposes of computing the likelihood ratio tests. The differences between instructors within sex are clearly significant by this (conservative) criterion, showing that the precision of the experiment is indeed improved by using the instructors as blocks. There is, however, no evidence

TABLE 28-6

MULTIVARIATE ANALYSIS OF VARIANCE FOR AN EXPERIMENTAL COMPARISON
OF A PROGRAMED AND A CONVENTIONAL TEXT

Source of Dispersion	df	Likelihood Ratio Test
Sex of instructor	1	$\chi^2 = 5.3$; df $= 6$; $p = .5$
Between instructors within sex	10	$\chi^2 = 95.7$; df $= 60$; $p < .005$
Between methods	1	$\chi^2 = 24.9$; df $= 6$; $p < .005$
Methods $\times$ sex	1	$\chi^2 = 5.6$; df $= 6$; $p > 7.25$
Residual (Methods $\times$ instructors within sex)	10	

of 12 graduate teaching assistants served as instructors for two of these sections. The programed text was assigned at random to one of the sections and the conventional text to the other. All students used their respective texts throughout the semester course and were tested by a six-part test at the end of the semester. The resulting six scores for each subject measured

(1) specific content in multiple-choice format,
(2) specific content in free recall format,
(3) concepts and principles in multiple-choice format,
(4) concepts and principles in free recall format,
(5) applications,
and (6) problem-solving.

In the multivariate analysis of variance of these data, the sex of the instructor was

of sex effect or sex by method interaction. Primary interest is, of course, in the methods effect, i.e., the difference in response to the programed text vs. the conventional text; it is clearly significant.

The nature of the methods effect is shown in Table 28-7. In each of the six tests the mean response for the programed text minus that for the conventional text is positive, favoring the programed text in all cases. Taken separately, the F statistics corresponding to each of these differences is significant at better than the .01 level. The step-down F statistics indicate, however, that when the measures of knowledge of specific content are eliminated statistically from the remaining variables, that differences in the response to the two texts are no longer significant. This suggests that achievement in tasks which require the student to generalize or apply what he has learned in the course is superior with the programed text because the student has a better command of facts upon which these generalizations and applications depend.

The result of this study cannot, of course, be considered a conclusive demonstration of the general superiority of the programed version of this psychology text, since it may depend in special ways on the population of students and on the type of course in which they were tested. It illustrates well, however, the clear and precise answer which a synthesis of principles of experimental design and multivariate analysis can provide to a problem in educational research.

to the range of errors of measurement present in test scores. Because any relationships between the test and other variables are weakened by the large proportion of error variation in the test scores, a test which is not reliable in this sense has limited value in educational research.

There are many sources of this so-called measurement error. If the test has been constructed in several alternative forms, errors will be present in the scores as a result of chance factors in the selections of items for different forms. If the same test is administered on different occasions, there will be error due to instability within individuals of the trait being measured. If

TABLE 28-7

COMPARISON OF ACHIEVEMENT WITH PROGRAMED TEXT VS. CONVENTIONAL TEXT

	Variates					
	1	2	3	4	5	6
	Specific Content		Concepts and Principles			
	Multiple Choice	Free Recall	Multiple Choice	Free Recall	Application	Problem Solving
Methods contrast (programed text vs. conventional)	.85	1.26	.35	1.79	1.63	1.70
Univariate F statistics	119.7	9.1	4.7	4.7	19.8	61.1
Step-down F statistics	119.7	12.2	1.2	<1	<1	<1

5. THE MULTIVARIATE ANALOGUE OF TEST RELIABILITY

The same multivariate methods which are used for the study of group differences in the methods experiment can be applied in the study of individual differences. An important problem connected with the description of individual differences is to determine whether a particular educational measurement is capable of making reliable discriminations among individuals. If so, the measuring instrument, usually a mental test, will produce a spread of scores in a specified population which is wide relative

the test is the multiple-choice type, some chance variation will enter the scores because of guessing. And so on. For present purposes, it will be sufficient to assume that error attributable to any or all of these sources is present and that the perturbation it introduces in the test scores of the individuals is normally distributed.

When only one test is involved, a convenient method of investigating its discriminating power is to estimate components of variance attributable to differences between individuals and to error. These estimates are calculated from the mean squares of a Type II analysis of variance in which the subjects and tests units are ways of classification (663). Call the variance component between individuals, σ_b^2, and the component for error, σ_e^2. Then an index of the discriminating power of the mean of r test units is provided by the reliability coefficient

$$\rho = \frac{\sigma_b^2}{\sigma_b^2 + \sigma_e^2/r} .$$

When variation due to individual differences is small relative to error variation, this coefficient approaches zero; when it is large relative to error the coefficient approaches unity.

In the multivariate case, i.e., when each individual is characterized by a number of test scores, the formulation of reliability in terms of components of variance has a straightforward and interesting generalization (Bock & Haggard, 123, II). As we might expect, it is based upon a Type II *multivariate* analysis of variance. Consider an experiment in which each of N individuals is administered r different forms of a test battery, possibly on different occasions. Each form of the battery is a test unit and consists of, say, p tests. Then the total sum of products can be partitioned into a sum between individuals, possibly after eliminating irrelevant group differences, and a sum within individuals. Dividing by the degrees of freedom for each, we obtain the "mean products," as represented in Table 28-8. (See Jones, 824, for the method of computing sums of products.)

To obtain a characterization of the overall discriminating power of the test battery, taking into account possible correlation among the tests, we may transform the original scores into so-called "canonical variates" which are uncorrelated both with respect to the error variation and variation between individuals. The linear combinations of the original scores which define the canonical variates are the multiple discriminant functions which maximize variation between individuals relative to the variation due to errors of measurement. The coefficients of the functions are the solutions of the homogeneous equations

(3) $(M_b - \lambda_j M_e)\mathbf{a}_j = 0,$

where the λ_j are the roots of the determinant equation

(4) $|M_b - \lambda_j M_e| = 0, j = 1, 2, \ldots, p.$

We assume the number of individuals considerably exceeds the number of tests and that each root of (4) is distinct and greater than zero.

Except for the fact that they are expressed in terms of mean products instead of sums of products, equations (3) and (4) are the same expressions which must be solved in multivariate analysis of variance. The same computer programs apply for their solution, and will be necessary when p is large because of the heavy computation involved.

The vectors $\mathbf{a}_j$ provide the coefficients which are used to compute the canonical variates from the original scores. For example, if $\mathbf{y}_{i.}$ is the mean vector for the r test units, the canonical score for the ith individual and jth canonical variate is

$$v_{ji} = \mathbf{a}_j \mathbf{y}_{i.}$$
$$= a_j^{(1)} y_{i.}^{(1)} + a_j^{(2)} y_{i.}^{(2)} + \ldots + a_j^{(p)} y_{i.}^{(p)}.$$

TABLE 28-8

PARTITION OF THE SUM OF PRODUCTS

Source of Variation	Degrees of Freedom	Sums of Products	Mean Product
Between Test Units	$n_a = r - 1$	S_a	$M_a = S_a/n_a$
Between Individuals	$n_b = N - 1$	S_b	$M_b = S_b/n_b$
Error	$n_e = (r-1)(N-1)$	S_e	$M_e = S_e/n_e$
Total	$rN - 1$	S_t	

If the canonical variates are ordered according to the magnitude of the corresponding roots of (4), they have the following properties in the sample. The first canonical variate has the maximum possible reliability of any linear combination of the original scores; the second canonical variate has the second highest reliability and is uncorrelated with the first variate; and so on, down to the last variate, which has the lowest possible reliability and is uncorrelated with all other canonical variates. The reliabilities of the canonical variates can be estimated in a simple way from the corresponding roots of (4). Suppose the units of scale of the discriminant function coefficients are chosen so that the error variance is unity, i.e., so that $a'M_ba = 1$. Then in large samples the expected value of the root associated with the jth canonical variate can be shown to be (Rao, 1178, p. 373)

$$\mathcal{E}(\lambda_j) = r\omega_b^{(j)} + (p + n_b - 2j + 1)\omega_e/n_b$$

where $\omega_b^{(j)}$ is the component of variation between individuals for the jth canonical variate and, because of the scaling convention, the error component of the canonical variate is $\omega_e = 1$. The large sample unbiased estimate of $v_b^{(j)}$ is therefore

$$\hat{\omega}_b^{(j)} = \frac{\lambda_j - (p + n_b - 2j + 1)/n_b}{r} .$$

The reliability coefficient of the canonical variate is

$$\rho_\lambda^{(j)} = \frac{\omega_b^{(j)}}{\omega_b^{(j)} + 1} .$$

Expressed in terms of λ_j this comes to

$$(5) \quad r_\lambda^{(j)} = \frac{\lambda_j - (p + n_b - 2j + 1)/n_b}{\lambda_j - (p + n_b - 2j + 1)/n_b + r} .$$

Since the canonical variates are uncorrelated in the sample, their components of variance are additive. An appropriate definition of the multivariate analogue of test reliability can therefore be defined as

$$P = \frac{\sum\limits_{j}^{p} \omega_b^{(j)}}{\sum\limits_{j}^{p} \omega_b^{(j)} + p} .$$

Substituting unbiased estimates and collecting terms gives its estimate in terms of λ_j

$$(6) \quad R = \frac{\sum\limits_{j}^{p} \lambda_j - p}{\sum\limits_{j}^{p} \lambda_j + (r - 1)p} .$$

Note that when $p = 1$, λ_j is an F statistic and (6) reduces to the formula for obtaining an intraclass correlation coefficient from an F statistic (Haggard, 663, p. 140).

An application of the multivariate analogue of reliability has been presented by Bock and Haggard (123, II). The test units were four essentially parallel forms of a battery of standard achievement tests, including reading, arithmetic, spelling, and the mechanics of language. The tests were administered to students of the University of Chicago Laboratory School as part of their achievement evaluation at the end of the fourth, fifth, sixth, and seventh year of schooling. These data were used to investigate the properties of the tests in characterizing long-term individual differences among the children tested. Since it was known from previous analyses that group differences attributable to the sex of the student were present in the data, the average sex effect was eliminated in computing the mean product between individuals shown in Table 28-9. In other words, M_b of Table 28-9 estimates the common within-sex covariance matrix. The error mean product estimates variation and covariation within individuals over the four-year period after eliminating systematic differences from year to year (each year represents one of the test units).

The computations for the canonical analysis were performed, with the results shown in Table 28-10. The discriminant function coefficients are shown in their standardized form. That is, the coefficient for each test as obtained by (3) has been multiplied by its error standard deviation. The reliabilities of each of the canonical variates have been calculated from the corresponding root by formula (5).

The reliabilities of the canonical variates show that substantially reliable discriminations among individuals can be made in only two dimensions of the test space. In the other two possible dimensions, varia-

example and are shown in Table 28-9. Even the small amount of variation in the direction of the fourth canonical variate is significant by this criterion.

The multivariate reliability coefficient of the four tests, also shown in Table 28-10, would serve as an index of all-over discriminating power in comparing the tests with some alternative battery. A battery with higher multivariate reliability could be obtained either by increasing the univariate reliability of the separate tests or decreasing their intercorrelation.

TABLE 28-9

MEAN PRODUCTS OF FOUR ACHIEVEMENT TESTS

		Test		
	Reading	Arithmetic	Spelling	Language
$M_b=$	3.36618			
	1.56160	2.50449		
$df=120$	1.62875	1.48321	3.03012	
	1.85862	1.79334	2.22091	2.58851
$M_e=$	.20664			
	.04053	.42564		
$df=363$	.01050	−.05183	.27823	
	.03891	.07726	.01374	.34793

tion between individuals is rather small relative to measurement error, although it proves to be statistically significant. A statistic for an approximate test of the variation attributable to the $p-s$ smallest roots is provided by the likelihood ratio criterion. The χ^2 approximation for this criterion can be calculated from the $p-s$ smallest roots:

$$\chi^2 = \left[n_b + n_e - \frac{n_b + p + 1}{2} \right]$$

$$\cdot \sum_{j=s+1}^{b} \ln (1 + n_b \lambda_j / n_e)$$

on $(p-s)(n_b-s)$ degrees of freedom. The χ^2 for residual variation assuming $s = 0, 1, 2,$ and 3 have been calculated for this

The canonical variates are easily interpreted in terms of the standardized coefficients in Table 28-10. The first discriminant function has all positive coefficients of similar magnitude and indicates that the individuals are most strongly discriminated by their general level of achievement. Because of the positive coefficients of the first function, the remaining functions must have both positive and negative coefficients in order to be uncorrelated with the first. In other words, they are in the form of contrasts between tests, each one contrasting one test with what is roughly the mean of the others. Four such contrasts are possible, but since only three can be independent, the analysis must exclude one of them. In this case, Spelling vs. three has been excluded. It can be obtained approximately as the sum of the three contrasts and its reliability may be calculated as .4871, simply by adding the appropriate variance components. Only the reading contrast of the second function, and very marginally the third or arithmetic

except possibly as a comprehensive test of relationship between two sets of variates. Examples of its application will be found in Bartlett (66), Anderson (33), and Cooley and Lohnes (381) and Horst (761).

Another procedure in the general area

TABLE 28-10

CANONICAL ANALYSIS OF INDIVIDUAL DIFFERENCES

Tests	Test Reliabilities r	Canonical Variates: Standardized Discriminant Function Coefficients			
		1	2	3	4
Reading	.7926	.5950	−.8163	.0918	.0938
Arithmetic	.5497	.3007	.3097	−.8934	.3183
Spelling	.7120	.5670	.5827	.3668	.4869
Language	.6168	.3146	.2839	.1039	−.9340
Roots λ_j		24.49554	8.11674	2.95933	1.60449	37.17610$=\Sigma\lambda_j$
Reliabilities $r_\lambda^{(j)}$		.8544	.6399	.3297	.1360	.6746$=R$
χ^2		1942.6	1014.1	465.9	178.9	
df		480	357	236	117	
p		<.0005	<.0005	<.0005	<.0005	

contrast are sufficiently reliable to be of some value in characterizing individual differences. The spelling contrast obtained as the sum of the other three has some reliability, but would be correlated with the reading and arithmetic contrasts.

A much more extensive canonical analysis of individual differences has been reported by Bock, *et. al.,* (125).

6. OTHER MULTIVARIATE METHODS APPLICABLE TO EDUCATION

The other important extension of a well-known univariate procedure to the multivariate domain is canonical correlation (31) due to Hotelling (772, 773). It is the generalization of multiple correlation analysis to two sets of variables, usually multiple independent and dependent variables. Although canonical correlation has great theoretical importance as the most general form of canonical analysis, so far it has not proved very useful in practical applications,

of dependence among variates which has some interesting applications, however, is the likelihood ratio test of the hypothesis that the scores on a set of tests could have been drawn from a population of uncorrelated variates. The likelihood ratio statistic for this purpose is simply the determinant of the correlation matrix (or equivalently the determinant of the covariance matrix divided by the product of the variances). For a correlation matrix R of p tests estimated on n degrees of freedom, the approximation for obtaining the percentage points of this statistic is as follows:

$$\chi^2 = -\left(n - \frac{2p+5}{6}\right) \ln |R|$$

on $p(p-1)/2$ degrees of freedom.

This test can be applied, for example, to test the hypothesis that the measurement errors of the four tests in Bock and Haggard's (123) study are uncorrelated. We compute the likelihood ratio criterion by dividing the determinant of the error mean product by the product of the error mean squares:

$$-\left(363-\frac{2\times4+5}{6}\right)$$

$$\cdot\ln\frac{.00747557}{.2664\times.42564\times.2783\times.34793}$$

$$= 20.4$$

on 6 degrees of freedom. The measurement errors evidently cannot be considered uncorrelated. This test of no association has important applications in factor analysis (68), in the analysis of repeated measurements experiments (120), and in the analysis of covariance structures (117).

7. SUMMARY (BY THE EDITOR)

(1) Technical needs in educational research have provoked some of the major theoretical advances in multivariate statistical analysis. This cannot be entirely ascribed to the admittedly multivariate determination of educational, developmental phenomena, for the same is true of agriculture, which was the birthplace of Fisher's essentially bivariate analysis of variance, or of medicine, which has contributed so little to new statistical research designs.

(2) If Spearman's interest in general intelligence can be called an educator's interest, then both the initial factor analytic model and the principal components approach of Hotelling were stimulated by educational research. So also are the developments, beginning again with Hotelling, of canonical correlation, T^2, and, as illustrated here in Chapter 7, by Lyle Jones, of multivariate analysis of variance.

(3) Long before the psychologist who followed the classical experimental design recognized that the "single case" experiment is dead, because one can never control all sources of influence, and error variance is inescapable, the educator, performing genuine experiments controlling all that could be controlled, came to terms with the need to use improved designs recognizing the many sources of "error" variance.

(4) This chapter makes no excursion into component and factor analysis, which are adequately treated elsewhere in the book. It turns first to the T^2 statistic, which is relevant to educational studies where the results from many variables are used jointly to discriminate between two groups or the outcomes of two different procedures or treatments.

(5) The related expression presented by the discriminant function has especial value in that realm of education which is concerned with student counseling. Simple and multiple discriminant procedures are to be viewed as aspects of the multivariate analysis of variance.

(6) A growing appreciation of and skill in these techniques should lead to a new era in educational research. An illustration is worked out in a methods study, with several methods and two dependent variables, different analyses being compared.

(7) A multivariate analysis of regression and covariance is particularly powerful in allowing conclusions to be reached despite some pre-experimental differences among groups.

(8) An analogue for test reliability is presented in multivariate terms. Taking a number of test scores for each individual, one can formulate reliability in terms of components of variance, basing the evaluation on a type II multivariate analysis of variance of canonical variates.

(9) A brief survey of other multivariate methods which have proved particularly apt to experiment in educational processes is given.

CHAPTER 29 Multivariate Technology in Industrial and Military Personnel Psychology

SAUL B. SELLS
Texas Christian University

1. INTRODUCTION

This chapter deals with multivariate concepts and technology applied to problems of personnel management in industrial and military settings. These applications have developed, for the most part, since World War II, although some of the most significant accomplishments were made by programs involved in that war. The extensive reference to military publications reflects not only the fact that the military services have long been the largest and most research-oriented clients of psychology, but also that their personnel problems have required the development of more advanced techniques.

The historic interdependence of science and technology are well illustrated in the development of the concepts and methods discussed here. The rise of multivariate techniques, particularly since electronic computers have become available, has implemented impressive developments in the measurement and organization of indi-vidual differences. These developments, centered around the measurement of individual characteristics and the measurement and prediction of individual performance, have in turn mediated a wide range of research and analytic procedures and practices dealing with both individual and group behavior, that have proven of immense practical value. Finally, research and development efforts in applied situations have made possible data collection on a scale not ordinarily possible in academic settings and have gathered information of major scientific importance.

2. THE NATURE OF MULTIVARIATE CONCEPTS

A fundamental methodological dichotomy has long existed in psychological research between the classical *bivariate, control* model and the *multivariate* model. Although strict observance of the bivariate model has given way to more complex analytic designs, the two models stand as

841

symbols of divergent research strategies, with zealous advocates and antagonists on both sides. Both approaches accept the principle of the multiple determination of behavior, but reflect essentially different concepts for dealing with additional sources of variance affecting the processes under investigation. The method of choice in the bivariate model is that of isolation of the dependent and independent variables, either by experimental control or by randomizing procedures, while that of the multivariate model involves simultaneous (statistical) consideration of all measurable factors, recorded usually in their normal complexity.

In current, as well as past, practice, both approaches have fallen short of ideal realization because of practical limitations on data collection and inadequate systematic knowledge concerning the universes of relevant variables to control, particularly those representing environmental sources of variance (1292). Much research remains to be done on the definition and measurement of the universe of variables representing individual characteristics (e.g., abilities, personality, and motivational variables), and systematic study of the universes of variables representing environmental sources of variance in behavior has scarcely begun (1293).

Advocates of the bivariate approach appear to regard isolation of experimental effects as advantageous and necessary to the understanding of phenomena studied, by removing the "contaminating" effects of concomitant processes, despite the fact that the phenomena in question do not occur in isolation. To what extent this position reflects attitudes of allegiance to laboratory methods as the *sine qua non* of "scientific" procedure and of distrust of statistical methods of estimation, cannot be stated. However, behavior is complex and patterned and is jointly determined by many internal and external factors whose contributions to the variance of even simple responses is essential to their understand-

ing. Experimental controls eliminate effects whose weight, in multidetermined behavior, needs to be evaluated rather than excluded or ignored.

An unfortunate traditional cleavage in psychology, in which content areas have separated along the lines of the methodological dichotomy (e.g., bivariate methods have predominated in "experimental" psychology and multivariate methods in psychometrics, personality, and social psychology), is only just beginning to break down. Multivariate analysis of variance designs, multiple discriminant analysis, factor analysis, multiple regression, canonical correlation, and other multivariate parametric and non-parametric statistical procedures have been making significant inroads over the entire field of psychological research (255; Chapters 7 and 28 of this handbook). This trend is supported by general advances in multivariate methodology and also by the fact that the more complex and expensive computation programs involved in multivariate problems have been made more feasible with the availability of computers and the increased financial support for research in recent years.

The key concept of the multivariate position is that of accounting for simultaneous joint effects of multiple events whose independence cannot be assumed. This is as true of the basic psychological processes of learning, perception, and motivation as it is of more complex behaviors, such as school and job performance, personal adjustment, and group behavior. Behavior is sequential, and temporal factors are always important. It is hierarchical and always occurs in a physical and social context, which exercises both direct and indirect influences, whose contributions need to be evaluated if explanation is to be achieved. Many of the influences are patterned and appear to covary in an organized fashion, suggesting the possibility of more parsimonious and abstract explanations, employing estimates of factors which variously represent a range of detailed manifestations of central trends or organized patterns of responses to classes of stimuli.

Multivariate concepts and methods have made significant contributions to industrial and military problems, particularly in the areas of personnel management, human factors engineering, and what is generally called industrial social psychology. In personnel management, the most spectacular applications have been made on problems of selection and classification, but important contributions have also been made on related problems, such as criterion development and performance appraisal, job analysis, training, and stress. Human factors engineering covers a wide range of problems generally related to the adaptation of the work environment, and in particular, man-machine systems, to conditions favoring optimal human performance. The applications of social psychology to industrial and military problems that have appeared most significant are those of attitude and morale measurement, the dimensions of group structure, and the prediction and measurement of group performance.

No attempt has been made to review each of the extensive problems of personnel management comprehensively. The plan of the following discussion is to analyze representative applied problems that psychologists in industrial and military settings have attempted to solve and to present illustrative solutions. Many of the solutions presented are quite recent and have not yet achieved the status of common practice. These were selected on their merits in the hope that they may serve as examples and pace-setters for future efforts in the respective areas.

3. PERSONNEL MANAGEMENT PROBLEMS

Any organization that employs a large number of persons on a variety of different kinds of jobs over long periods of time has a host of personnel management problems related to staffing, maintaining personnel productivity, and providing career opportunities for its work force. Rapid technological change and automation have increased the importance of these problems to top management, as new skill requirements have produced new jobs and made many old ones obsolete. In some cases, particularly in military and civilian aerospace specialties, manpower and personnel decisions have had to be made prior to actual experience with newly created jobs.

Determination of the kind and number of employees, according to skills required, job planning, recruiting, selection, and classification of personnel are treated here as part of the general problem of organizational staffing.

Approaches to the application of scientific methods to personnel staffing have evolved from the earliest attempts at *selection,* involving the prediction of performance criteria and decisions to hire or not hire with reference to a single job category, through a period of concern with *classification,* involving multiple job categories and the optimal utilization of available talent among several jobs, to more recent formulations in terms of complete *personnel systems.* This entire field has been actively investigated at many levels for over 50 years (506), but progress has not been uniform. The discussion is organized in terms of component problems, representing various levels of activity contributing to the over-all staffing problem.

4. PERSONNEL SELECTION AND CLASSIFICATION

Representative general discussions of the basic issues, rationales, and methodology of personnel selection are given by DuBois (430), Flanagan (526), Horst (755), McFarland (1013), Sells (1291), and Thorndike (1397). The principal technical problems include the determination of job requirements (job analysis) as a basis for planning predictor and criterion strategies, development of predictor batteries, development of criterion measures, and combination of predictors for the most valid prediction. In a large, multi-job organization there are related problems concerning job classification and structure which must be worked out prior to consideration of a selection program. Some of these, which have received attention by multivariate methods, will be discussed first.

In 1956, Travers (1442) published a highly critical review of the traditional approaches to prediction in personnel research and suggested methods of overcoming the difficulties which appeared to impose ceilings on results obtained. He pointed out that the major current effort at that time consisted of efforts to improve the metrical properties of the dependent variable. In addition to this necessary remedial research, he advocated a laboratory approach, which permits studies of many otherwise uninvestigable selection and classification problems, through experimentation on the determinants of behavior in particular job situations. Additional attention, in the writer's opinion, must also be directed to three points: (1) improvement of the original item pools from which tests are constructed, with reference to item content, range of content with reference to the universes sampled, form, and relevance to the populations tested, (2) representation of dimensions of predictors and criteria in research designs, and (3) employment of appropriate multivariate methods of analysis.

5. DETERMINATION OF JOB FAMILIES

Thorndike, Hagen, Orr, and Rosner (1399) developed and evaluated a new technique for determining profiles of qualitative personnel requirements of Air Force jobs and for grouping jobs into homogeneous job families on the basis of these requirement profiles. They con-

structed a Job Activities Blank which gave scores for 14 relatively independent aspects of job requirements. The blank was completed by 963 men working on particular jobs at 12 Air Force bases, each man indicating how often he performed the activities listed. Scores for each aspect of a job requirement were sums of credits for items related to that aspect. Profiles of job requirement aspects were then determined for 25 different Air Force specialty jobs, and profile distance measures (396) were computed between all pairs of job specialties. From these data, job clusters were defined in terms of groups of jobs that had the most similar job requirements. The basic method was reported also by Orr (1120).

This seemingly attractive method fell short of the intended goals. The analysis first separated the jobs into a mechanical and a non-mechanical cluster, but the basis for and reasonableness of further subdivision into clusters was not clear, except that there were also indications of a supervisory – non-supervisory distinction. The authors attributed the shortcomings of the method to difficulties in designing satisfactory items descriptive of job requirements. This is one of many examples in the entire field of psychological measurement in which the limits of successful practice are believed to be set by the basic item pool from which the measurement instruments were developed.

Palmer and McCormick (1135) approached a similar problem using factor-analytic methods. They coded 177 job behavior items from 250 job descriptions sampled from a large steel-producing firm and derived 14 dimensions of job behavior by multiple group factor analysis. These were reduced to four more general factors: decision-making and mental activity, a general factor, sedentary vs. physical type of work activity, and tool knowledge vs. mathematics.

Dunnette and England (438) analyzed engineering jobs by cluster analysis, and Dunnette and Kirchner (439) factor-analyzed data for sales jobs. Reeb (1186) applied a multidimensional scaling technique to a variety of skilled trades, technician, and public contact jobs.

An analysis has recently been made by Cattell and Coulter (278) of the groupings in some 40 occupations on a basis of the fifteen personality factors and the general intelligence measurement in the Sixteen Personality Factor Questionnaire. They applied the improved profile similarity coefficient to these data and obtained some useful grouping for personnel and guidance work. They raise the question whether corrections should first be made in such profiles for "inefficiency of current job selection procedures" and incomplete validity of the factor measures. Several important technical statistical issues are raised by this paper (278).

Dunnette (437), commenting on Clark's (348) statement that "people, through job experience, have broken the world of work into domains based on human aptitudes, interests, and personality traits," reminded us that, "unfortunately, the exact nature of job domains and the human capacities for each are not readily amenable to subjective judgment." They need to be replaced by empirical information based on methods such as those reviewed above.

6. JOB EVALUATION

The identification of a supervisory — non-supervisory distinction, crossing over mechanical — non-mechanical types of activity in the study by Thorndike, et al. (1399), above, suggests that the taxonomy of jobs is indeed a complex problem, involving hierarchical, as well as horizontal (content) dimensions. The problems of establishing job hierarchies and linking them with compensation plans involve techniques of job evaluation. These problems are not only fundamental for selection and classification, but have equally significant implications for the organization of career structures.

A history and annotated bibliography of the job evaluation literature are presented by Madden (977), and a description of research on job evaluation procedures by the U.S. Air Force is given by Christal and Madden (346).

Checklists and ratings, using various sources, are the basic data of job evaluation. The lack of adequate criteria for job evaluation and the difficulties introduced by the value aspect of the task have been perennial problems. Most investigators have used factor-analytic methods to identify dimensions of jobs as a basis for hierarchical rating and most have found that only a small number of factors, principally representing training and skills, is adequate for reliable placement. Madden pointed out that regardless of the number or nature of the factors employed, it is necessary to construct scales for their use, unless key reference jobs are used to define levels on factors. The latter procedure, in addition to lacking generality and flexibility, implies considerable dependence on the key jobs. Conventional unidimensional scaling methods have, for the most part, been used to rate job dimensions. Madden has proposed multidimensional scaling and demonstrated (976) that increased rating reliability is accomplished by the greater refinement achieved.

7. JOB ANALYSIS

Morsh, Madden, and Christal (1079) have classified *job analysis* as a phase of *occupational analysis,* along with *qualifications analysis, structure analysis,* and *job evaluation.* Job analysis, which involves the collection, processing, and interpretation of work performed, is also an integral aspect of personnel selection since it provides basic information to guide the development of batteries of predictor variables and also the development of measures of job performance that serve as criteria for evaluation of predictions. In relation to selection, interest centers more on qualifications analysis, the determination of characteristics of incumbents of jobs for predictor planning, and on performance measurement related to work described in job analysis, in relation to criterion development. This distinction represents a refinement of sophisticated personnel research that has not yet been generally adopted.

A comprehensive bibliography of job analysis research, covering the 50-year period from 1911 to 1961, by Morsh (1078), is a valuable reference. Rupe (1242, 1243) and Rupe and Westen (1244, 1245) carried out an important series of studies on Air Force jobs, comparing different methods of collecting job analysis data.

Gunn (647) factor-analyzed performance checklists reflecting task difficulty, frequency of performance, and task assignment of B-36 engine mechanics and supervisors and obtained five factors that suggested functional, as well as systems-related, divisions of this homogeneous job. These factors were differentially related to such variables as rank, experience, mechanical aptitude, and mechanical test performance. This study demonstrated that a presumably homogeneous job can be broken down into functional elements based on task grouping.

An impressive example of a multivariate approach to job analysis is Hemphill's (716) investigation of the dimensions of executive positions. A research form of an Executive Position Description questionnaire, containing items describing elements of positions, was completed by 93 executives representing five companies in five functional areas of business and three management levels. Each respondent utilized a seven-point scale to rate the extent to which each element applied to his position. Correlations between positions, over the 575 items, were factor-analyzed by Tucker's (1464) interbattery method applied to an off-diagonal submatrix of the intercorrelations which were defined by

designating 47 positions in the function areas of Research and Development, Manufacturing, and Industrial Relations, as Battery 1, and 46 positions in Sales, and General Administration, as Battery 2.

The ten orthogonal factors derived were designated: (1) providing a staff service in a non-operations area; (2) supervision of work; (3) business control; (4) technical: markets and products; (5) human, community, and social affairs; (6) long-range planning; (7) exercise of broad power and authority; (8) business reputation; (9) personal demands; and (10) preservation of assets.

Although the incumbent of a job may not be as appropriate a source of information in other types of positions as in the case of executives, the analytic method exemplified in this study appears applicable also to job performance data based on Flanagan's (527) critical incidence approach, as well as on more conventional methods.

Norris (1102) used a group of four professional psychologists to rate 150 Air Force enlisted jobs on 170 "qualification" attributes and intercorrelated 130 attributes that met standards of importance and reliability. This matrix was factor-analyzed by Thurstone's "diagonal" method to identify common dimensions, and residual attributes that were reliable, but not significantly loaded on the common dimensions, were identified by multiple correlation techniques. This study is distinctive for using "qualification" rather than "task" attributes and for its systematic analysis of the information collected.

8. RESEARCH RELATED TO PREDICTORS

As the methodology of personnel selection advanced, one of the most important principles that has come to be generally accepted involves the use of general dimensions of human potentialities in place of job simulation tests which predominated earlier. Research related to predictors thus includes the entire field of measurement and organization of abilities, motivational and personality traits, and other measures of individual differences, as well as methodological investigations related to test construction and assembly.

The advantages of dimensional measures for selection are increased when multipurpose batteries, for classification, are used. Properly constructed factor measures reflect general common aspects of human potentiality and are not tailored either to particular situations or tasks. Should job requirements change, regression equations, based on the same predictors, can be recomputed against new criteria, and development of new predictors need not be a pressing problem. In some cases, incremental predictive power may be achieved through the addition of supplemental predictors accounting for variance specific to certain criteria, but the importance of such increments may be expected to decline as factored measures covering greater portions of the complete universe of human traits become available.

A comprehensive summary of research on dimensions of human potentiality appears in Guilford's 1959 text. Cattell's 1957 book, although primarily a report of work in his own laboratory, supplements this in the area of personality and motivation structure and measurement. Messick's (1049) review of personality structure is an excellent independent appraisal. Although the ability area is more advanced than that of personality and motivation, Guilford, in agreement with Thurstone earlier and others, has called attention to the limited scope of presently identified ability factors. Fleishman's (530) work on the dimensions of psychomotor abilities illustrates a complex area that many psychologists formerly regarded as unitary. Guilford believes that similar attacks need to be made on mechanical abilities.

Sells (1292) has made a careful comparison of the factors of personality and motivation reported independently by Cattell and Guilford. Although a reassuring number of convergences appear, these may be regarded principally as signs of encouragement to working investigators. Indeed, on the basis of evidence, the demands of users in the applied fields for personality measurement, comparable to current ability measures, must be deferred. There are major problems ahead, in this area, of at least four general kinds: (1) improvement of measurement of personality and motivational traits in the media of observational and rating data, self-report types of instruments and objective tests (Cattell's work on objective measurement of personality and motivational traits is an important development [240]; (2) development of a replicable, generalized trait structure for personality and motivational traits that shows rational linkages and consistency across data media, among the results obtained by different laboratories, and across areas of special content, such as interests, attitudes, and stylistic personality traits; (3) elaboration of the trait structure and related measurement instruments to reflect the longitudinal growth functions of personality; and (4) integration of the measurement technology with data reflecting the effects of environmental situations on test scores Military support of research in this area has been and continues to be a major enabling factor by providing large samples of subjects, opportunities for superior criterion assessment (in comparison with other situations) and adequate data-processing facilities.

Some significant research has been done on the identification of particular trait structures related to selection problems. Tupes (1469) investigated the relationships between a number of general personality trait ratings by peers and later officer performance of officer candidates in the U.S. Air Force and found that a majority of trait variables were significantly related to a criterion based on officer effectiveness reports. The multiple correlation between trait cluster scores and the criterion was approximately equal to the reliability of the criterion. These results are superior to those commonly reported for test measures of similarly defined traits, and merit careful study as well as replication. It is suggested that both the peer rating procedure and the range and nature of the variables included in this study may have contributed to the excellence of the results. Tupes and Kaplan (1472) later reported the identification of five well-defined factors derived from peer ratings of bi-polar personality traits and of the same traits defined either by the socially acceptable and the socially unacceptable poles. These factors appeared to be the same five factors found in previous analyses.

A number of studies have focused on particular situations and criterion groups for the purpose of identifying significant trait structures for selection research. Some representative multivariate studies of this type include those of Taylor, Smith, Ghiselin, Sheets, and Cochran (1387) on the identification of communication abilities in military situations, Schmid, Morsh, and Detter (1273) on the analysis of job satisfaction, Holley (737) on isolation of traits associated with military leadership, Roff (1210), on the dimensions of spatial abilities involved in aptitude for military flight training, Holmen and Katter (738) on attitude and information patterns of OCS eligibles in the Army, Egbert, Meeland, Cline, Forgy, Spickler, and Brown (453) on the characteristics of soldiers rated as "combat fighters and non-fighters," and of Sells (1288, 1289), Cattell (235), and others on the identification of traits associated with success in military flying. McQuitty (1018) illustrated a pattern-analytic method for isolating predictor patterns associated with major criterion patterns.

Some significant work has been done on the construction of factored tests. The method of "homogeneous keying" developed by Loevinger, Gleser, and DuBois (942) was tested by Whitcomb (1537), with items measuring spatial abilities, and was found to be both feasible and productive. Cattell (213, 240) and Guilford (627) have both published factored personality questionnaires and the references to their technical papers are given in their books. Recently, Cattell, Horn, Radcliffe, and Sweney (297) have derived the MAT, giving scores on ten motivation factors, for work in industry. These ten factors are based on a dozen publications covering basic research on dynamic structure as discovered by *objective* attitude measurement devices. Extensive attention has, of course, previously been given to *verbal* attitude measurement, and useful discussions and bibliographic summaries of multivariate contributions in this area are given by Green (614) and Sells and Trites (1297).

9. CRITERION RESEARCH

The criterion problem, which is relevant to evaluation of training outcomes as well as to selection, has been viewed with alarm by reviewers for many years. As Wilson (1554) has aptly commented, criteria employed in both fields have generally been inadequate and researchers in both fields have largely neglected the problem. Jones (830) found that only 21 per cent of 2,100 selection reports published prior to 1948 even mentioned a quantitative criterion. To an overwhelming extent, criterion measures employed in selection and training research have consisted of gross indicators of over-all performance, such as membership in groups representing grades of performance, or global ratings of performance, usually by a superior in an organization.

While composite criterion measures are essential for final calibration of cutting scores and selection decisions, differentiation of specific aspects of predicted performance is integral to research and development procedures. The rationale for dimensionalization of criteria is as important as that for predictors. The ideal model for the predictor-criterion relationship is one which reveals the separate as well as joint relationship of each predictor factor to each element of the criterion, and also the relation of predictor composites to criterion composites.

Wilson (1554) has reviewed the literature on on-the-job and operational criteria in relation to training. His excellent discussion of this topic, which is equally relevant to selection, focuses on methods of collecting useful and reliable performance data and emphasizes differentiation of detail, although dimensionalization is not included. However, as noted above in another connection, the adequacy of basic data sets limits on the information that can be extracted, which cannot be overcome by elaborate statistical treatment. An earlier paper by Wherry (1536) on criteria and validity contains a valuable treatment of types of criterion contamination and also of combination of criteria into composites. Contributions to the latter problem have been made by Horst (754), Edgerton and Kolbe (448), Wherry (1533), Nagle (1092), and others.

Discussions in the literature on the relative merits of composite (not unitary, as many writers have stated) versus multiple criteria have argued at cross-purposes much of the time without recognition of specific purposes for which criterion measures are used. There are, however, cases in which components of the total criterion are either unrelated or negatively related and Wallace and Weitz (1494) observed that "to put these together in a single score would appear to make the prediction problem more difficult if not insoluble as well as to hide some important and heuristic relationships that do exist." In commenting on Rush's (1246) study of sales criteria, in which composite criterion scores were determined for four relatively uncorrelated criterion factors, Wallace and Weitz stated further, "Perhaps their rather informal combination into over-all criteria accounts for much of our lack of success in this area."

In view of the fact that performance may be evaluated at different stages of career progress, the criterion problem has hierarchical aspects as well as those related to organization at any stage. This problem has been discussed by Vallance, Glickman, and Suci (1480), Hitch (726), Ghiselli (590), and Trites and Sells (1452), among others. Ghiselli recommended longitudinal studies to evaluate the relative importance of factors contributing to job success at different stages of job experience. This approach was incorporated in the program of research on development of adaptability screening of flying personnel at the School of Aviation Medicine, USAF, and is reported in a series of papers by Kubala (897), Sells (1292, 1293, 1294), Trites (1446), Trites and Kubala (1449), Trites, Kubala, and Cobb (1450), and Trites, Kubala, and Sells (1451).

A factor-analytic study of test scores and measures of success in an Air Force Radio Operator School, by Friedman, Hempel, and Detter (558) not only indicated that over half of the variance in the code-learning phase of this course is represented by an aural ability factor, but also that the criterion of success in the school changes as the course progresses. Thorndike and Hagen (1400) correlated aptitude tests administered to applicants for flight training in 1943 with four component factors of criteria of achievement during the 12 years following testing for 873 Air Force officers. Their results showed that predicted later achievement was accounted for principally by tests of quantitative and intellectual abilities and not by tests that predict success in flight training.

Katzell (856) regards the contribution of Cronbach and Meehl (398) on "construct validity" as of particular importance to industrial psychology. "To the industrial psychologist, this concept seems to have greatest pertinence along two lines: (a) in the understanding of complex phenomena that at present cannot be adequately studied on the basis of simple two-variable designs (research on motivation and morale being a prominent example of this application) and (b) as an intermediate step in the development of more predictive tests and more predictable criteria."

A number of factor-analytic approaches to the isolation of dimensions of criterion performance have been published. Ghiselli (590) proposed the use of Q technique, transposed analysis as a means of defining significant performance dimensions. Mc-Quitty, Wrigley, and Gaier (1023) and Wrigley, Cherry, Lee, and McQuitty (1590) used the method of square-root factor analysis, developed by Wrigley and Mc-Quitty, to isolate dimensions of job success for supervisors of Air Force aircraft mechanics. Kubala (891) and Trites (1446) applied factor-analytic methods to a variety of objective and rating variables to define dimensions of military flying adaptability representing training level, post-training, and combat stages of performance. Simon (1325) reported a methodologically very careful study of the dimensions of B-25 mechanics' performance on a preflight check-list based on observation of behavior in this performance. He evaluated a variety of criterion measures on the basis of their factor loadings for the first principal component and the successive significant components, studied the relations between criterion factor scores and relevant personal data, evaluated the reliability of the factor scores with respect to observer agreement and performer consistency, and evaluated the effects on factor scores of control factors, such as Base, Observer, Flight, period of stay at the base, and time of day. Other recent methodological contributions to this problem are discussed below.

10. SELECTION AND CLASSIFICATION PROGRAMS

By far the most impressive accomplishment in the history of this problem was the aircrew selection and classification program of the U.S. Army Air Forces in World War II, directed by Flanagan (526) and described more recently by Sells (1291). In terms of magnitude of undertaking, numbers of persons tested, quality of performance, and results achieved, this is unquestionably a landmark in the progress of applied psychology and an outstanding symbol of the power of multivariate methods in industrial and military psychology.

Postwar accomplishments in the development of classification batteries for enlisted personnel have proven of at least equal importance to the United States armed services in facilitating decisions on the classification of newly inducted personnel by career field and initial skill level and on assignment to technical schools. The development of the U.S. Air Force Airman Classification Battery AC-2A, which is representative of this type of test battery, is described by Brokaw and Burgess (146). This battery, which requires one entire day for its administration, yields 11 aptitude scores and three biographical inventory scores which are differentially weighted into five aptitude indexes (Mechanical, Administrative, Radio Operator, General Aptitude, and Electronics). These have a median intercorrelation of .57 and a median reliability of .91. The battery was standardized against the scale of talent available in the World War II mobilization population and is scored in 20 percentile blocks, each designated by a number reporting the percentage of the World War II sample falling below that point.

Brokaw (145) has recently evaluated each test in the battery for its contribution to Air Force classification procedures, using success in Air Force technical training school and scores on job proficiency tests as criteria. He used a multiple regression technique, with standard beta weights and a squared multiple correlation coefficient to derive 16 predictors against both criteria for 36 criterion groups. Components for four aptitude indexes were selected by reviewing the frequency with which tests appeared among the best four predictors within each of four job clusters. Other related research includes Bechtoldt's (79) factor analysis of the Airman Classification Battery with civilian reference tests, and Humphreys' (795) investigation of the stability of classification test scores.

A more recent selection program of major importance has involved a joint effort of the United States Air Force and the Federal Aviation Agency (formerly CAA) on the selection of air traffic controllers. Brokaw (144), in 1959, administered a battery of numerical and reasoning, abstract reasoning and perceptual, verbal, clerical, and temperament tests and background questionnaires to trainees entering the CAA Air Traffic Control School and collected criterion measures (grades and ratings) at the end of the course; approximately one year later the men were identified on the job for supervisory ratings of proficiency and promotion recommendations. A battery of tests suitable for administration as a screening device was selected on the basis of the training validation. These tests displayed satisfactory validity on the job (multiple R for instructor ratings was .51 for a sample of 142 students, and for supervisor ratings, in a sample of 133 graduates, it was .34), beyond the .01 significance level. Further research and development on this problem have been reported from the Civil Aeromedical Research Institute of the FAA by Trites (1447), Cobb (353), and Trites and Cobb (1448), with additional predictors, against academic criteria. Multiple correlations of .54 with grades and .40 with passfail have been reported, and a firm basis for recommending an age limit for entry to ATC school has been obtained.

The output of selection reports, as shown by the *Annual Reviews of Psychology,* the *Psychological Abstracts,* and other bibliographic sources, is too extensive for brief summary. A few additional multivariate studies involving well-selected predictors and criteria, may be mentioned here to illustrate the work in this area. These include Flana-gan's work on selection of commercial pilots (20), Fleishman and Spratte's (539) study of prediction of radio operator success, Petrie and Powell's (1157) report on selection of nurses in England, Weitz's (1510) study of supervisor selection by peer ratings, and DuBois and Watson's (432) study of selection of policemen.

11. PERSONNEL SYSTEMS

The personnel system concept is an extension of the classification problem, which Thorndike (1398) discussed as an unresolved problem at the end of World War II, but concerning which, Votaw (1490) reported six years later, that "since that time the logical basis required has been found; furthermore, methods for computing solutions of classification problems have been developed." Votaw's report summarizes the literature on the solutions proposed up to 1954. The classification problem in personnel management evolved from personnel selection. Personnel selection involves prediction of performance criteria and hiring decisions with reference to a single job category. As Pickrel (1163) defined classification, the problem involves a number of job categories, for which there are as many or more vacancies than applicants: "The task is to assign the applicants to the vacancies in such a way that the 'average success' of the total group is at a maximum."

The personnel system is a mathematical approach to computer simulation of the operation of an organization for the purpose of estimating cost consequences of alternative selection, classification, and training policies. It is of particular importance to organizations, such as the military, which often need to develop, well in advance of delivery of the hardware, a full complement of personnel to fill new jobs associated with the operation of a new weapons system. It is important to note that the concept of cost, in this frame of reference, includes both direct financial

cost as well as cost of unproductive manpower and other waste resulting from such
factors as:

(1) training time and maintenance of
training facilities,

(2) failure to complete training satisfactorily,

(3) transfer both from job to job and
from one geographical location to another,

(4) loss of trained and experienced personnel by resignation or discharge,

(5) malassignment,

(6) unwieldy and ineffective control
procedures,

(7) personnel shortages in critical jobs,

(8) inadequate utilization of trained personnel for obsolescent jobs,

(9) failure to organize military job structures to take maximum advantage of civilian training facilities and experienced
personnel.

Several recent reports, by Kossack and
Beckwith (882), Merck and Ford (1042),
Merck (1041), Ward (1497), and Orcutt,
Greenberger, Korbel, et al. (1119), illustrate the application of Markov chains and
linear programing simulation models to
personnel systems problems. Kossack and
Beckwith applied mathematical methods of
linear programing to the development of a
Markovian simulation model of a personnel
utilization system. Such a model permits
the examination, by means of electronic
computers, of "the effects of changes in
inputs or relationships upon the simulation
model before introducing such changes
into the real situation." This model, which
is admittedly a first step, has given results
which indicate clearly the feasibility of the
approach. It includes time intervals, personnel characteristics and skills, training, assignment, and various cost factors as inputs.
It is expected that the utilization of personnel models may make an important contribution to the coordination and synthesis of
research and development in the personnel
management area, as well as the management decisions. Such an improvement is
illustrated by the contribution of Marks

(987), who developed a rationale, description, and implementation techniques for a
data organization model to be used in
connection with data for Air Force weapon
or support systems.

12. METHODOLOGICAL APPROACHES TO CLASSIFICATION

This problem involves two sets of questions that are critical in personnel research.
One concerns the discovery of discrete and
discriminating patterns among measures of
individual differences: (1) Do individuals i
and j differ, and if so, to what extent?; (2)
How homogeneous are the members of
group A?; and (3) How many discrete
subgroups are there in group A? The
second set of questions relates to the
matching or fitting of patterns: (4) To
which group is individual i most similar?;
and (5) How similar is group A to group B?

These questions were discussed by Sells,
Tiedeman, Danford, Haggard, Gupta, and
McQuitty (1296) in a symposium which
also contains detailed bibliographic references as of 1955. Tiedeman explained his
centour method for classifying patterns of
scores into discriminant types. Danford
analyzed five multivariate approaches: internal (R-technique) factor analysis, the
variance component approach, distance and
discrimination methods, external factor
analysis (involving p tests administered to N
persons at t times), and estimation of latent
structure parameters. McQuitty presented
a method for classifying individuals into
types on the basis of patterns of responses
to test items. Finally, Haggard and Gupta
used the method of intraclass correlation to
determine whether patterns exist, the
significance of individual patterns and differences between patterns, and the classification of individual profiles into known
existing patterns. McQuitty (1016) presented a more detailed discussion of his
approach, called *similarity analysis*.

Cattell has suggested (240) that the

fitting of persons to occupations should in general be handled by the "two-file system" of a profile of persons and another of occupations on a standard set of personality, ability, and motivation factors having predictive worth for *all* jobs. This also involves the concept of two distinct *kinds* of fitness evaluation: (1) *Adjustment,* i.e., how close the individual's profile is to that of a person who is adjusted to and stays in the job, and (2) *Effectiveness,* i.e., how high the person's score is on a job success criterion. The first is evaluated by the profile similarity index, r_p (Chapter 9 above), and the second by multiple regression (Chapter 5 above). Cattell, Stice, Eber, and King have presented adjustment profiles now for some forty varieties of occupations, on primary ability and personality factors.

Eber and Cattell have also discussed the statistical relation between the adjustment and the efficiency weighting systems. Their contention is that provided the occupational adjustment profile is accurate the application of a tetrachoric correlation coefficient to the estimated proportions in the occupation above and below the mean on each factor should yield correlations appropriate to give the weights for the efficiency index, — staying in the occupation being a criterion of success. However, as a basis for this they point out that the ideal profile of an occupation should deviate in the same directions from the mean as it does, but more so, since *de facto* occupational selection has various degrees of inefficiency. Possible corrections for this are discussed.

An important series of monographs on discriminatory analysis was published by the USAF School of Aviation Medicine, as a result of a research contract with the Statistical Laboratory of the University of California. These include (1) Hodges' (731), excellent survey of discriminatory analysis, with an extensive bibliography of over 250 references, (2) Fix (524), on factor analysis and discrimination, (3) Hughes (785), on

discrimination of the accident-prone individual, (4) Fix and Hodges (525), on nonparametric discrimination: consistency properties, (5) Gaffey (570), on perfect discrimination as the number of variables increases, (6) Lehmann (920), on the simultaneous classification of several individuals, (7) Lehmann (921), on the theory of selection, (8 and 9) Bates and Neyman (75, 76), on the theory of accident-proneness, and (10) Hughes (786), on two correlated bivariate non-normal distributions. The mathematical foundation and a computational routine for the generalized discriminant function were described by Bryan (154) and were treated more completely by him in his Ed.D. thesis (153). Tatsuoka and Tiedeman (1383) presented a later review of work on discriminant analysis. Price and Schatz (1171) provided a detailed guide to the programing of linear discriminant function analysis on a general-purpose digital computer.

Nunnally (1107) considered three problems in the analysis of profiles: (1) measuring profile similarity, (2) discriminating the typical profiles of two or more groups, and (3) clustering profiles into homogeneous groups. For these problems, respectively, he proposed: (1) picturing profiles as interpoint distances in Euclidean space, (2) use of the multiple discriminant function, and (3) factor analysis of profile cross-product terms.

An original contribution to discriminant grouping, which has led to some significant applications, is reported in the first three of a series of papers from the Air Force Personnel Laboratory at Lackland Air Force Base, by Ward (1498), Bottenberg and Christal (133), and Ward and Hook (1499).

Ward's basic paper is addressed to situations where it is desirable to group large numbers of persons, jobs, or objects into smaller numbers of mutually exclusive classes in which the members are as much alike as possible with respect to some criterion. When the grouping is done in a manner that establishes a taxonomy, or system of mutually exclusive clusters wherein each larger unit is a combination of subgroups, these clusters are called *hierarchical groups*. Ward emphasized the importance of hierarchical grouping for classification problems, when applied to persons and jobs. Previously this approach has not been developed for computer analysis. This report provides a general mathematical procedure for forming hierarchical groups of mutually exclusive sets such that an optimum value is obtained for the functional relation (objective function) reflecting the criterion chosen by the investigator. The number of groups need not be specified in advance. "Given k sets, this technique permits their reduction to $k-1$ mutually exclusive sets by considering the union of all possible $k(k-1)/2$ pairs that can be formed and the selection of that union which has the highest payoff with respect to the criterion chosen." The procedure can be repeated until only one set remains, thus permitting decisions on the number of groups to be used, based on knowledge of the consequences of grouping at each hierarchical stage. The report presents a computer flowchart and numerical example of the grouping procedure and explains how to determine the number of possible ways of forming groups, as well as the number of distinguishable unions possible.

Bottenberg and Christal applied the method to problems of optimal clustering of criteria, with an iterative technique, programed for a computer, that at each step reduces the number of criterion clusters and provides optimal weights for each cluster for a set of predictor tests. Ward and Hook applied the procedure to a problem of grouping test profiles so as to maximize the homogeneity of profiles within the same clusters, taking account of all profile variables and all clusters at the same time. They used 25 test profiles to which Sawrey, Keller, and Conger (1260) applied

a different technique and compared results. The hierarchical technique shows not only the order in which profiles must be grouped so as to yield the optimal value of the objective function as the number of profiles is systematically reduced, but also the costs of grouping at every stage.

Bottenberg (132) developed an iterative procedure for determining weights in a multiple regression problem, programed for an electronic computer, which permits precise tests of hypotheses, enabling the investigator to express his hunches in full detail in formulating the regression model. Ward (1496) developed three joint functional equations and compared their predictive efficiency with a conventional multiple regression equation by computing product-moment correlations between predicted and actual scores. The decrease of correlation in a validation sample was greater for the more complex joint functional equations and consequently the conventional method tends to predict more efficiently as equation complexity increases. Jones (823, 824) has contributed two important monographs, related to simplex theory, for analyzing correlations among sequentially dependent variables. Although his ideas have not yet been followed extensively in the literature, they are worthy of serious study.

13. SUMMARY

(1) In recent years multivariate concepts and methods have made significant contributions to industrial and military problems. In particular in personnel staffing the emphasis has moved from selection through classification to complete personnel systems.

(2) Factor analysis is now widely applied to the evaluative demands presented by the multiplicity of occupational descriptions in various civil and military occupations.

(3) A survey is made of the present status of factorial definition of abilities, personality, and dynamic structures. Impor-

tant advances have been made with objective tests in all three modalities. In addition to research on general structures, which might have importance for any job, work has been done on traits important for particular contexts in leadership, success in military flying, and the like.

(4) Evaluating fitness for a job can be conceived either as adjustment, i.e., fitting the profile of the typical person already in the job, or as effectiveness, i.e., scoring highly on a criterion of efficiency. The former proceeds by the discriminant function, the profile similarity index, pattern analysis methods, etc., and the latter by multiple regression, most effectively based on factor measures.

(5) The definition of the criterion has hierarchical aspects calling for longitudinal study and there is also an increased tendency to predict to components of criteria rather than simply to composite criteria.

(6) The massive aircrew selection and classification program of the USAF has been extended and similar programs for air traffic controllers are being developed.

(7) The personnel system concept has been put on a firm logical basis so that the average success of the total group is maximized. A wide range of computer use and of linear programing devices have been employed in these attempts to bring all aspects of personnel work to a common scientific basis.

(8) Multiple discriminant functions have come into wide use both to define kinds of individuals and to provide a basis for personnel assignment. Considerable power and economy come from the use of hierarchical groups.

CHAPTER **30** The Impact of
Multivariate Research
in Clinical Psychology

JACOB COHEN*
New York University

1. AIMS OF THE
PRESENT SURVEY

A multivariate metaphor describes the
concern of this chapter: what does one see
when he is set down at the intersection of
multivariate methodology, the substantive
issues of clinical psychology, and a time
line? Scientific prose permits itself to be
written in only one dimension and the
available space is woefully finite, therefore
only an overview of this locale is possible,
or (to abandon the metaphor) a sampler to
whet the appetite of the curious.

The Handbook as a whole defines multivariate method; we define clinical psychology as that which interests clinicians—
abnormal behavior, its description, understanding, and constructive modification.
Although many of the issues here may well
have their origins in general personality

*For their prompt response to my request for reprints
and references as well as their accompanying helpful
comments I wish to express my gratitude to R. B.
Cattell, H J. Eysenck, F. E. Fiedler, M. Lorr, P. E.
Meehl, H. H. Strupp, and J. R. Wittenborn. And I
acknowledge my indebtedness to my wife for her
editorial assistance and patience.

psychology, limitations of space, time, and
scholarship restrict the present discussion
to the abnormal. Even with such a limitation, the material to be covered resists
coherent organization along the unidimensional line necessary to exposition. A given
research can be classified along many
dimensions of multivariate method, clinical
content, and the source of its data. Also, the
presentation can be retrospective or prospective, primarily scholarly or primarily
pedagogical, oriented more toward the
substantive issues of clinical psychology or
more toward equally interesting issues of
method.

The problem of achieving a tight organization is insoluble and therefore unsolved.
What will be attempted is to sample across
the above dimensions through:

(1) An exposition of the major findings
to date of the two major research programs
which have attacked the abnormal area
along a broad multivariate front, namely
those of Cattell and Eysenck.

(2) A sampler of recent applications of
multivariate techniques which (hopefully)
herald a new era in clinical research.

(3) A review of features of the present clinical scene from the perspective of multivariate research findings.

2. THE THEORETICAL SYSTEM CONTRIBUTIONS OF CATTELL AND EYSENCK

Any assessment of multivariate clinical psychology is necessarily dominated by the figures of Raymond B. Cattell and Hans J. Eysenck. Each has mounted an ambitious systematic program of investigation, with accompanying theoretical developments, which has grown steadily in scope, adherence, and scientific productiveness. Both men are energetic and ingenious and show remarkable catholicity of psychological interest, having made important contributions not only to clinical psychology, but to personality, social, and genetic psychology, and to multivariate methodology.

A careful appraisal of their work thus far shows both similarities and differences in their scientific styles and findings. Their critics have rather exaggerated the latter, to which we shall turn shortly. First we consider the points at which they converge:

(1) Both value procedures in direct proportion to their objectivity. This, of course, constitutes no break with the traditions of the psychology of the laboratory, but has not been an invariant feature of the psychology of the consulting room. Both have used trait and symptom ratings in their earlier work (213, 472), and continue to use questionnaires in their current work (Cattell & Scheier, 325, Chapter 15; Eysenck, 485). Both prefer objective tests, i.e., those which involve a behavioral or physiological response whose significance is unknown to the subject or otherwise free of voluntary control and possible distortion (Cattell, 240, Chapter 7; Eysenck, 485, p. 267). Cattell and his collaborators have already published objective test batteries for personality and clinical measurement (323, 325, 339), and a compendium of some four hundred objective personality tests in

use in his laboratory has been announced (337).

(2) Both lay considerably greater stress on recognizing hereditary factors in personality than generally characterizes present-day clinical psychology, and both have contributed research findings to support this emphasis (270, 240, 479, 480, 491).

(3) Both have stressed the necessity for building a science of clinical psychology on a firm base provided by an adequate taxonomy. Thus, Eysenck's very first words in his own chapter in the valuable *Handbook of Abnormal Psychology* he recently edited are: "The importance of classification in the field of abnormal psychology is well indicated by Cattell's dictum that nosology necessarily precedes actiology" (488, p. 1). Lest this seem a truism to the reader, Cattell points out elsewhere that while the history of science shows certain sequences of development, psychology has confused these and ". . . has attempted to abort the necessary descriptive, taxonomic, and metric stages through which all healthy sciences first pass . . . [and] . . . to answer all the 'big,' theoretical, or psychologically deep questions before it had answered the small ones" (240, p. 7). Elsewhere, he comments about the multiplicity of non-standard procedures: "Indeed, the capacity of a finite number of psychologists to spread themselves over an infinite number of variables is something for sampling theorists and even mathematicians to marvel over. But the well-known upshot of this marvel is that no two studies integrate, and that where chemists make architectonic progress, by deigning to recognize the same elements, psychological research is all too frequently circular or inconclusive" (232, p. 110). Much of the research published by Cattell and Eysenck and their collaborators and students has been oriented toward the establishment of a uniform, rational, metrically based taxonomy.

Their findings also show some important areas of agreement:

(4) Both offer evidence that a concep-

tion of psychopathology that orders normality, neurosis, and psychosis along a single continuum (as, e.g., depth of regression or "degree of pathology") is demonstrably fallacious. Cattell does so by showing that the factors (questionnaire and objective, first- and second-order) which differentiate neurotics from normals do not distinguish psychotics from normals (Cattell & Scheier, 325, pp. 110-115). Eysenck points to his own works (478) and that of Sybil B. G. Eysenck (493), wherein canonical variate analysis (1329) was applied to objective test scores (e.g., visual acuity, PGR, expressive movement) for normals, neurotics, and psychotics. It was found in both these studies that at least two dimensions were necessary to account for differences among these three groups, which, upon rotation he interpreted as Neuroticism and Psychoticism (Eysenck, 488, pp. 17-20).

(5) Cattell and Eysenck, using different multivariate methods, tests, and subjects, have identified as major trait dimensions in the normal-neurosis domain, Introversion-Extraversion and Anxiety (325) or Neuroticism (472, 485), their measures of the latter correlating +.77 (90). Although this statement bridges some important differences between them (see below), it is correct as it stands.

(6) With regard to the two factors above, both investigators provide highly concordant pictures of the disposition of clinical syndrome groups, i.e., all neurotic groups and psychopaths relatively high on Anxiety-Neuroticism, normals (and psychosomatics) relatively low; psychopaths (and possibly conversion reactions) distinguished from anxiety, depressive, and obsessive-compulsive reactions on Introversion-Extraversion (325, pp. 120-135; 488, pp. 9-11).

Beyond the major similarities in style and findings detailed above, there are many minor ones. But there are also important differences between these investigators. One major difference arises from their

assumption of the factor-analytic styles of the countries of their adoption. The British school, since Spearman, has had a predilection for working with few factors, while the American school, under Thurstone's influence, has preferred relatively many. Accordingly, Eysenck in his own work and the interpretation of that of others identifies Neuroticism, Introversion-Extraversion, and Psychoticism as the three main factors operating in the clinical-personality realm. He acknowledges the existence of other factors, particularly within psychosis, but has hardly concerned himself with them. In marked contrast, Cattell claims that modern factor-analytic techniques permit objective decisions about the number of factors, and he identifies many personality trait factors: fifteen in the questionnaire realm and about twenty in the realm of objective tests.

This discrepancy closely parallels the dispute in the cognitive domain which raged a generation ago between the adherents of the single g factor of Spearman and the multiple primary ability factors of Thurstone, and turns out to have the same resolution. With Thurstone's removal of the orthogonality restriction and the admission of correlated factors, it was discovered that analysis of the correlations among the primary ability factors yielded g as a "second-order" factor, thus largely resolving the controversy (but cf. 251). Similarly, analyses of Cattell's primary personality factors in the questionnaire realm yield four "best-confirmed" second-order factors, the two largest of which are Introversion-Extraversion and Anxiety (Eysenck's Neuroticism) (325, Chapter 4). It is apparent both empirically and mathematically that when one extracts a few factors, they turn out to be the same as those which result when many factors are extracted, obliquely rotated and their correlations factored, i.e., second-order factors.

At this level, then, the discrepancy seems well on the way to resolution. But what of the status of the primaries? Eysenck (personal communication) discounts them: "Primary factors by comparison [with second-order factors] are quite impossible to reproduce; Cattell and Guilford, starting out with similar universes of questions, end up with entirely dissimilar factors.... [They] have always assumed the superiority of primary factors, but the evidence seems to be all against this.... This conclusion also seems to me to follow from simple psychological considerations. If you regard, as I do, traits (i.e. primaries) simply as habits in the Hullian sense, then clearly they must be relatively unstable, shading into each other, and extremely difficult to circumscribe in any unambiguous fashion.... [In contrast,] Extraversion-Introversion and Neuroticism ... are underlying constitutional factors which determine such things as emotional (autonomic) reactivity (neuroticism), or speed of conditioning, etc. (introversion). They are thus far more fundamental...."

Cattell would justify working at the primary level in several ways. First, he offers evidence that his primary factors can be matched (1) across different media of observation; (2) across different age and pathology groups (his response to differences pointed out by Guilford, 627, Peterson, 1151, and others is that simple structure oblique and arbitrary orthogonal factors cannot logically be expected to line up, see Chapter 6); and in some instances (3) between inter-individual or trait (R-technique) and intra-individual or state (P-technique) analyses (Cattell & Scheier, 325, Ch. 9). Second, he points out that predictive information is lost in using second-order factors, for statistical reasons, and that in any case second-order factors can be uniquely determined only through primaries, not by under extracting and rotating on variables (see Chapter 6). Thus he claims there is "wobble" in Eysenck's factors such that the latter's "Neuroticism," for example, is really the anxiety factor, U.I. 24, somewhat off center. Third, in contrast to Eysenck, he provides evidence that neurotics are discriminated from nor-

mals on many primaries: eight in questionnaire data and at least ten in objective test data, of which five are identified as "neurotic process" factors and at least five others as "neurotic-contributory." Further, not one but several questionnaire primaries distinguish among various neurotic reaction groups (Cattell & Scheier, 325, Chapter 7 and p. 459).

To descend for a moment from the heights of abstraction, following are the five objective test "neurotic process" factors described at the neurotic pole with their Universal Index numbers, names, some marker variables, and a brief verbal characterization (Cattell & Scheier, 325, Chapter 5):

U.I. 24. "General" or "Free" Anxiety. Loads willingness to admit common frailties, tendency to agree, susceptibility to annoyance, lack of self-confidence in untried performance, magnitude of cold pressor startle response, and emotionality of comment. This factor has been matched with the second order questionnaire Anxiety factor and is most consistently loaded by psychiatrists' ratings of anxiety. Interestingly, this factor "enters into neurosis but is far from accounting for the main variance in neurosis" (p. 85). Furthermore, it is sharply distinguished from "stress" response.

U.I. 22. Cortertia-vs.-Pathemia. Loads slow reaction time, particularly in the absence of a warning signal, low speed of flicker fusion, low fidgetometer frequency. It is interpreted as "a retreat to hypothalamic, emotional, and unadaptive behavior" (p. 71), is the most highly and consistently related to the normal-neurotic dichotomy, and is hypothesized as being the consequence of an upbringing favoring emotional, repressive responses to difficulties. This factor, too, is matched by a second-order questionnaire factor similarly named.

U.I. 29. Super Ego-vs.-Low Adaptation Energy. Loads variables reflecting slow ineffective handling of environmental situation demands, poor immediate memory, high impairment in performance by shock or discomfort, low basal metabolic rate, slow P.G.R. upward drift when relaxed. Ego strength and high neuroendocrinal energy reserves are competing interpretive hypotheses. No matching factor arises from questionnaire responses.

U.I. 16. Assertive Ego-vs.-Protected, Emotional Sensitivity. This factor in the negative, neurotic direction loads a pattern of variables which suggest a weak sensitivity, lack of assertiveness, lack of realism, indecisive and slow performance, and poor "taste" in social and esthetic matters. Cattell hypothesizes that this pattern is produced by an overprotective environment. It is matched by a primary questionnaire factor.

U.I. 23. Neurotic Regressive Debility or Regression. Loads motor-perceptual rigidity, poor two-hand coordination, and inability to mobilize personal habit resources generally. Cattell and Scheier (325, p. 71) offer two competing hypotheses to account for the poor energy mobilization represented by this factor: that it is a consequence of a regression of interests in the psychoanalytic sense or that it represents the debility or neurasthenia which is an outcome of prolonged conflict. This factor has no questionnaire match.

It is inevitable that brief descriptions such as the above read like a page torn from a catalogue and do not even begin to convey the rich fabric of empirical results and complex theory into which they are woven in Cattell's system. A fuller description of these source traits will be found in Pawlik's Chapter 19 above.

Eysenck and Cattell differ, more generally, in the strategy of their approaches to system building. Eysenck plows a narrow but deep furrow. He not only prefers few variables, but ties them into classical Pavlovian-Hullian learning theory. Thus, Neuroticism is hypothesized to reflect the degree of basic autonomic reactivity and Introversion the predisposition of the CNS to the production of strong excitatory and weak inhibitory potentials (with Extraversion reflecting the opposite). These hypotheses then lead to deductions about differences between introverts and extraverts in ease of conditioning, reminiscence effects, work curves, figural after-effects, and other standard experimental variables which Eysenck and his collaborators have tested and found generally confirmed (483, 488). Eysenck lays considerable stress on the necessity of moving from interdependency analyses, which lead to the discovery of factors, to dependency analyses in which factor measures are manipulated by the experimenter to afford a test of deductions from theory, including the interpretation of the factors. Thus, from the viewpoint of both content and method, Eysenck remains closer to "classical" psychology.

Cattell, in contrast, is remarkably broad. Studying many hundreds of variables of diverse kinds in both personality structure and motivation, by a variety of factor-analytic designs, using subjects varying in age and psychopathology, he has pursued the Herculean task of discovering, replicating, and integrating the dozens of resulting factor dimensions. In his program, the tie to more classical psychological theory in a manipulative experimental program must await a closer approach to completion of the map. Further, he is quite suspicious of the "classical" psychologist in "the nursery stage of methodology gained in the physical sciences and the simplicity of 'brass instrument' univariate methods . . . [who should] . . . move on to comprehensive, multivariate designs . . . in which statistical ingenuity will extract relations that cannot be separated by controlling the environmental stimuli" (325, p. 379). Thus, the general psychology Cattell would participate in writing would itself be revolutionized and enriched by insights into method and content derived from multivariate personality research (233). In particular, Cattell argues that personality theory requires, and will lead to, a development of learning theory beyond the present reflexological doctrine.

The form and necessary brevity of the above contrast does not do justice to the many innovations in method and concepts and the specific findings of these pioneering investigators—only reference to their own most recent progress reports provides adequate summaries (240, 263a, 325, 483, 485, 488). Large areas of conceptual advance provided by Cattell have not been mentioned: his *P*-technique and differential *R*-technique studies of intra-individual dimensions (states as opposed to traits), his heuristically rich integration of personality factors through the vagaries of environmental experience at "dynamic crossroads" and the resulting Adjustment Process Analysis account of the development of psychopathological phenomena, his ingenious application of multivariate methods to the analysis of drive conflicts in single patients and the resulting Conflict Index, and yet others (see Chapter 20 above). A development in this area of personality dynamics by Cattell and such colleagues as Horn (295), Sweney (332), Butcher (296), and Williams (1551) (and which has no counterpart in Eysenck's multivariate research) is the theory of the dynamic calculus leading to the recent introduction into clinical diagnostic measurement of the Motivation Analysis Test (296, 333). But any detailed appraisal of the clinical future of many of these ideas either by Cattell or by Eysenck must be omitted here.

Nor has the above account been critical; the writer has aimed for a "middle-brow" exposition, not a scholarly critique. Neither Cattell's nor Eysenck's work has escaped criticism, least of all by the other (*cf.* 483, 484, 488; 325, p. 32 *f*). Fairly comprehensive critical appraisals have been made both of Cattell (Sells, 1290) and of Eysenck (Storms & Segal, 1356).

Aside from the substantive merits of their contributions, these men have provided heuristic systems which can occupy a generation of research clinical psycholo-

gists in separating the gold from the dross, reconciling them, and building a science of clinical psychology on which preventive and restorative efforts can be securely based.

3. SPECIAL CONTRIBUTIONS: PSYCHOPATHOLOGY RATING SCHEMAS OF LORR AND OTHERS

In this section, a series of multivariate studies will be described. Their selection was made from considerations of significance and variety of content, illustration of specific multivariate models, and coverage of the subareas of content and method in clinical psychology. In order maximally to fill in the "cells" of this scheme in the limited space available, many significant contributions and contributors will necessarily be omitted.

For the past fifteen years, Maurice Lorr with a series of collaborators has been engaged in the multivariate exploration of observed psychopathologic symptoms in both inpatients and outpatients, with questionnaire data, ratings from interviews, and ward behavior observations by nurses and aides. His most intensive work has taken the form of ratings by professional personnel (usually clinical psychologists) of the interview behavior of psychiatric inpatients. Using samples of hundreds of patients and dozens of raters, he has pursued the factor-analytic study of symptom ratings. A series of such studies using progressively more refined rating instruments and cross-checking both his own and others' results has culminated in a standardized rating instrument for psychiatric hospital inpatients which yields composite rating scores on the factors which are standardized and normed (954, 955). The Inpatient Multidimensional Psychiatric Scale (IMPS) provides standard quantitative estimates of disturbance along ten primary dimensions at acceptable levels of inter-rater and internal consistency reliability with obvious utility for practical and research purposes, e.g.,

TABLE 30-1

PRIMARY FACTORS (SYNDROMES) OF THE INPATIENT MULTIDIMENSIONAL PSYCHIATRIC SCALES (IMPS)

Excitement		**Motor Disturbance**	
Hurried speech	.58	Grimacing	.68
Excess of speech	.58	Repetitive movements	.64
Dominates interview	.55	Rigid postures	.59
Elevated mood	.50	Slovenly appearance	.36
Self-dramatization	.50	Giggling	.34
Loud and boisterous	.49	Overt tension	.32
Unrestrained	.40	Startled glances	.30
Overactive	.38	Talks to self	.24
Attitude of superiority	.34		
Paranoid Projection		**Hostile Belligerence**	
Ideas of conspiracy	.53	Verbal hostility	.76
People controlling him	.53	Hostile attitude	.74
Ideas of reference	.52	Bitter and resentful	.70
Delusional beliefs	.44	Irritability	.68
Ideas of persecution	.41	Complains and gripes	.61
Forces controlling him	.38	Suspicious of people	.58
Ideas of body destruction	.20	Blames others	.54
		Attitude of contempt	.42
Disorientation		**Retardation and Apathy**	
As to state	.67	Slowed speech	.61
As to year	.67	Slowed movements	.60
As to age	.67	Fixed facies	.55
As to hospital	.60	Whispered speech	.54
As to season	.56	Failure to answer	.54
Knows no one	.55	Apathy	.50
		Speech blocking	.45
		Lack of goals	.41
		Memory deficit	.30
Anxious Intropunitiveness		**Grandiose Expansiveness**	
Self-depreciating	.80	Divine mission	.69
Blames self	.74	Great person	.59
Guilt and remorse	.71	Voices praise him	.49
Vaguely apprehensive	.68	Has unusual powers	.42
Depressed in mood	.68	Attitude of superiority	.36
Anxiety (specific)	.65		
Ideas of sinfulness	.62		
Suicidal thought	.61		
Recurring thoughts	.46		
Shows insight	−.44		
Morbid fears	.40		
Perceptual Distortion		**Conceptual Disorganization**	
Accusing voices	.72	Incoherent answers	.60
Threatening voices	.65	Irrelevant answers	.54
Hallucinatory voices	.54	Neologisms	.42
Voices order him	.52	Stereotyped speech	.42
Other hallucinations	.44	Rambling answers	.38
Visions	.42		
Ideas of change	.24		

evaluation of change as a function of therapeutic intervention, studies of prognosis, etc.

The most recent published study describes in detail the factor-analytic procedures used (954). Fortunately, Dr. Lorr has made available the results of an even more recent unpublished analysis of IMPS based on a stratified normative sample of 566 inpatients rated by pairs of observers in 44 hospitals (Lorr, Klett, McNair, & Lasky, unpublished m.s.). Following an interview of 30-45 minutes, the patient was rated on 77 scales. The intercorrelations of these scales were multiple-group factored and the ten factors subjected to blind oblique single plane rotations to a visual simple structure criterion. Table 30-1 presents the primary factors and the factor loadings of the rating scales defining each.

Factor loadings of scales on factors other than those to which they are assigned are with a single exception trivial; thus, this is a particularly "clean" simple structure solution.

There are no surprises in the identification of these factors; indeed, surprises would themselves be surprising. These represent familiar concepts to the clinical psychologist, as they must, since they are a distillation of the interaction of patient behavior and the clinician's observational system. Poorly organized rating schemes could result in factors which represented nothing more than characteristics of the implicit system. Lorr minimizes such problems by instructing his raters to consider each rating question independently of the others and to rate manifest behavior rather than "dynamic" interpretations thereof. Still, one expects the resulting factors to be familiar.

This familiarity, however, should not breed contempt. If 100 clinicians were asked to review these results, probably 95 would find them familiar and reasonable. Were they asked, however, to *predict* the outcome of such an analysis in advance, it is unlikely that as many as five would come

reasonably close to the mark. Using the "same" set of clinical concepts, they would predict more or fewer factors, fuse some and fractionate others; each clinician's results would be reasonable, but they would differ widely from each other, and what is more important, they would differ from those of Table 30-1, which represent the major primary dimensions inherent in the data.

The correlations among these primaries range between zero and about .5, and when they are factored in turn, and rotated orthogonally (since a maximal simple structure fit is virtually orthogonal), the factors of Table 30-2 result. These can be viewed as broader syndromes, accounting to some

TABLE 30-2

SECOND-ORDER FACTORS OF THE
INPATIENT MULTIDIMENSIONAL
PSYCHIATRIC SCALES (IMPS)

Excitement vs. Retardation	
Excitement	.79
Hostile belligerence	.59
Retardation and apathy	−.42
Anxious intropunitiveness	−.29
Hostile Paranoia	
Perceptual distortion	.67
Paranoid projection	.66
Grandiose expansiveness	.43
Conceptual disorganization	.22
Anxious intropunitiveness	.20
Thinking Disorganization	
Disorientation	.63
Retardation and apathy	.59
Motor disturbance	.58
Conceptual disorganization	.56
Hostile belligerence	−.26

degree for the variance in the primaries. These, too, are readily recognizable, as the reader can judge.

Thus, the IMPS provides a device which utilizes the clinician's skills as observer, and refashions his observations into standardized values in a multidimensional system of reproducible continuous variates, in place of either verbal descriptions or the more or less arbitrary Procrustean diagnostic pigeonholing. The former is unreproducible, ad hoc, and cumbersome; the latter stems from a largely irrelevant medical tradition in which disease syndromes are identified with single causes (488, pp. 1-5). Neither is sufficiently reliable. Of course, the replacement of psychiatric diagnosis by continuous measurement along empirically derived dimensions is a goal shared generally by multivariate taxonomists. IMPS has the practical advantage of transmuting the usual clinical observations into such a scheme.

How do these findings tie into larger architectonic schemes? First, no single factor of psychoticism emerges in the second order, as implied by Eysenck. Nor can it appear in the third, since the second-order factors are uncorrelated. Of course, Eysenck is not necessarily proven wrong, since the finding may not generalize to other realms of data.

A second issue arises as to whether the factors in psychosis are extreme projections of normal or neurotic personality factors or uniquely discriminating within hospitalized psychotics. Although verbal arguments can be made in favor of at least some factors being such projections (e.g., Anxious Introspectiveness, Hostile Belligerence, Grandiose Expansiveness), the issue must be considered open, pending empirical demonstration which will probably require, in order to be convincing, objective rather than rating factors.

Lorr is by no means the only investigator in the multivariate analysis of psychopathologic ratings. Wittenborn has done extensive work in this area, culminating in his Psychiatric Rating Scales (1568, 1573). Despite the crudity of the multivariate methods employed, the pioneering work of Moore (1068) is of more than historical interest. A large scale longitudinal factor-analytic study involving 1274 patients over a four year period has recently been reported by Cohen, Gurel, and Stumpf (362a).

For a comprehensive critical review and summary of this area, see Lorr, McNair, and Klett (955).

4. *Q* TECHNIQUE AND *Q'* TECHNIQUE IN CLINICAL TAXONOMY

Before we proceed with our sampler, a few words of terminological clarification. Starting with Burt's demonstration in 1926 that persons could be correlated over tests and the resultant matrix factored, a veritable alphabet soup of designations of factor-analytic designs has been contributed to by many cooks, with the inevitable result. Among Cattell's many contributions is the discovery of a series of new design possibilities, many of them peculiarly relevant to clinical psychology (228), and their logical ordering within his Covariation Chart (240, pp. 494, 835-841). In all, he has described 50 design possibilities, but his original version (230) allowed for six designs which were a function of variation over persons, variables, and occasions. Since his scheme is exhaustive, we will use his alphabetic designations. Thus, *Q* technique represents the factoring of matrices of correlations between persons over variables for a single occasion. Stephenson's pioneering researches primarily involve data arising from the "*Q*" sorting of personality-descriptive statements along a continuum of degree of descriptive adequacy or "characteristicness," which he either studies factor-analytically as above, or by analysis of variance techniques applied to the statements as sampling units (115, 1346, 1569). He offers his approach as an expression of a philosophy of scientific psychology in fundamental opposition to those of Burt, Cattell, and Eysenck in its focus on the single case and on "singular" propositions. Space limitations prohibit an exposition of his position and its criticism. The reader is referred to his 1953 book and the most outstanding application of his method in S. J. Beck's "Six Schizophrenias" (84), and Conger, et al. (372). A good general review is given by Cronbach (393) and by Mowrer (1083).

When, in Q technique, as most generally defined, one correlates persons over variables (whether by Q sorting or otherwise) instead of variables over persons (R technique), the factors which result represent ideal-types of persons, analogous to the ideal-traits or factors of R technique. Bypassing the problems of metric sampling of variables, and whether Q technique gives rise to the same factors as R technique (160, 230, 393, 1346, 477, 114), ideal-types are, in fact, the basis of any taxonomy, and therefore of immediate relevance to issues of clinical diagnosis. It may be, however, that the aims of Q technique are better reached by the modification described as Q' technique in Chapter 9 above.

From Wittenborn's varied multivariate researches, we select a modest study for illustrative purposes (1570). For his R-technique studies of rated symptomatology (1568), he had developed a set of 55 scales (e.g., difficulty in sleeping, unjustified sexual beliefs, refuses to eat, feelings of impending doom, etc.). In "The Symptoms of Involutional Psychosis" his purpose was to evaluate and compare for this diagnostic entity the descriptive adequacy of conventional psychiatric diagnosis with that provided by Q technique. Since the scales had been developed to discriminate patients over the entire spectrum of psychopathology, their application to a single diagnostic group constituted a severe test of both the scales and the Q-technique method. Selecting 20 consecutive admissions bearing the diagnosis, each patient's ratings were correlated with those of every other patient, yielding 190 r's, each based on 55 paired observations. From this matrix six centroid factors were extracted and rotated orthogonally to a simple structure criterion. The rotated factors then represent ideal symptom types, with the size of each patient's loading on a given factor indicative of his degree of resemblance to that type. Table 30-3 gives this matrix in simplified pattern form by representing loadings greater than .5 by an asterisk. The simple structure criterion serves to minimize instances in which a patient shows substantial resemblance (high loadings) to more than one type.

The psychiatric classification model has singled these patients out from patients in general as constituting a type. If this implies a general *descriptive* similarity among patients, a general type-factor should result. No such factor appears. Apparently the diagnosis is made on anamnestic considerations or a narrow segment of symptoms, not on the basis of the current total symptomatic picture.

The psychiatric model makes provisions for secondary diagnosis of "paranoid," "melancholia," and "other types." Concurrence with the Q analysis would demand a type-factor for each of the first two secondary diagnoses and two or more factors for the "other types." Factor I shows high loadings for all the "paranoids" (all of whom are women) and none of the others, and represents an excellent fit. However, the melancholias are spread over all the other five factors, and two of the three "other types" load factor III in common with four "melancholias." Despite the concurrence on factor I, the psychiatric model must be judged inadequate as a *descriptive* typology of and within involutional psychosis.

The interesting question then arises: "What is the nature of the factor types?" In Q-technique studies this question can be answered only by returning to the trait variables. For each type-factor, persons who are strongly (high loadings on the factor) and purely (near zero loadings on other factors) representative of that factor are used to define it. The type-definers' characteristics on each of the original variables are summarized (e.g., by finding means) and the resulting average profile scrutinized and interpreted. (More refined multiple regression techniques of "scoring" the variables are available.)

Since the 55 scales had previously been factor-analytically reduced to nine symptom clusters, instead of an unwieldy and less reliable average profile over 55 elements, it was possible to work with profiles over nine elements. When this was done, it was found that factor I was defined by the high paranoid cluster, II was relatively unsymptomatic, III high on both depression and excitement, interpreted as agitated depression, IV high on the hysterical and

are at all unique to patients diagnosed as involutional psychotics.

As pointed out in the methodological part of this book (Chapter 9) it is very important to distinguish between Q technique, which is a form of factor analysis, as just discussed, and Q' technique which stops short of factor analysis and classifies people into types only on the basis of correlation clusters. Some results reported as Q technique are actually Q' technique, and the

TABLE 30-3

Q-FACTOR REPRESENTATION OF 20 INVOLUTIONAL PSYCHOTICS CORRELATED OVER
55 SYMPTOM SCALES
Wittenborn and Bailey (1570)

Patient No.	Sex	Secondary Diagnosis	Rotated Type-Factors					
			I	II	III	IV	V	VI
1	F	Mel			*			
2	F	Mel				*		
3	M	Mel					*	
4	F	Mel				*		
5	M	Mel			*			*
6	M	Mel		*				
7	F	Para	*				*	
8	F	Mel			*			
9	F	Mel					*	
10	F	Mel		*				
11	M	Mel			*			
12	F	Para	*					
13	F	O.T.			*			
14	F	Para	*					
15	F	Para	*					
16	F	O.T.						
17	F	O.T.			*			
18	M	Mel					*	
19	F	Para	*					
20	F	Para	*					

anxiety clusters, V high on the anxiety and depression clusters, and VI high on both the paranoid and the excited clusters. It is noteworthy that although "melancholia" cases appeared on five factors, only factors III and IV showed a material degree of depression. One wonders how many patients with other diagnoses could be represented by the above type-factors, or more fundamentally, whether these type-factors

latter may actually have the advantage where reliable type classification, as such, is required. The above research is not offered as a definitive study of the symptomatology of involutional psychosis. But it illustrates Q technique and potentially Q' technique, as they might eventually be used (see Chapter 9 above) with adequate technical care, for a truly taxonomic classification scheme in psychiatry. Clinicians are always classifying patients, consciously in formal diagnosis, consciously or unconsciously in everyday decisions, in case disposition and in therapy. The clinical psychologist is a sensitive observer and resourceful selector of variables for study. However, as Meehl has abundantly demonstrated (1026, 1027, 1029), he is not as good an *integrator* of data as a digital computer with appropriate multivariate software. Although *Q* technique offers some methodological problems in subject and variable sampling, nevertheless for any defined sample of subjects and variables, the former can be classified on the groupings they comprise with regard to the latter *objectively*. The utility of the resultant type-constructs for etiology, treatment procedures, and prognosis are then open to exploration. Although any set of quantitative variates can thus be objectively typed, a potentially fruitful set for such investigations is provided by the objective-test factors isolated by Cattell (240, 325).

McQuitty's many methodological contributions should be noted in the present context of taxonomy. He has sought to evolve methods which are computationally far simpler than those of factor analysis and which avoid some of the latter's restrictive assumptions. The reader is particularly referred to his papers on elementary linkage analysis (1017), hierarchical syndrome analysis (1020), rank-item selection for configured scoring (1021), and rank-order typal analysis (1022). Other methods of clustering profiles on the bases of distances between objects in a multivariate space rather than on product-moment correlations have been offered (396, 1260).

5. PSYCHOTIC THOUGHT DISORDER: A MULTIVARIATE HYPOTHESIS TEST

A study from Eysenck's laboratory by Payne and Hewlett (1143) serves to illustrate simultaneously the testing of hypotheses in multivariate research, and the use of the discriminant function and the canonical analysis of discriminance, as well as factor analysis, all this apart from the intrinsic interest of its content.

Payne and Hewlett were centrally concerned with the hypothesis that schizophrenic thought is essentially and uniquely characterized by overinclusiveness. They cite prior experimental work that casts doubt on theories that offer as the fundamental character of schizophrenic thought either dissociation (Kretschmer), intellectual slowness (Babcock), or concreteness (Goldstein). Payne and Hewlett offer an hypothesis derived from Cameron: " 'Over-inclusive thinking' may be a result of the disorder of the process whereby 'inhibition' is built up to circumscribe and define the learned response (the word or 'concept'). In short, it could be an extreme degree of 'stimulus generalization'" (1143, p. 8 *f*).

Prior research had left open the possibility that overinclusiveness is not specific to schizophrenia, but generally characterizes psychosis, including depressive psychosis. Their major aim was to investigate this possibility.

Groups of 20 cases each of normals, neurotics, acute schizophrenics, and psychotic depressives were selected so as to be matched for age, vocabulary level, occupational status, and years of formal education. The 60 variables were chosen so as to be relevant to the competing hypotheses and were drawn from tests of intellectual and motor speed, concreteness and overinclusion in concept formation (Goldstein-Scheerer, proverbs, water-jar, object classification, etc.), and a miscellaneous set of tests which had distinguished psychotics from non-psychotics in previous research.

The intercorrelations for the 54 mathematically independent variables for the pooled sample of 80 cases were centroid-factored. On the hypothesis that the theoretical framework within which variables were chosen led to the expectation of three main sources of covariation (overinclusion, general retardation, and general intelligence), three centroid factors which accounted together for 39 per cent of the total variance were extracted. This study is unique in its use of a theory-dictated decision as to the number of factors to be extracted, but the writer's tendency to criticize this practice is inhibited by the rueful consideration that the solution of the communality-number of factors problem still defies the methodologists (1588). With formal significance tests of questionable utility even if they were available, it is difficult to make a completely convincing case against criteria of saliency (1457) or theoretical relevance for deciding the number of factors to accept.

Rotation was also determined by theoretical considerations, rather than as a function of the dispersion of the variable vectors in the common factor space, e.g., simple structure. This practice has its advocates; for a recent discussion, see Thompson (1390). The basis for the rotation requires a digression to discuss discriminant function analysis and the closely related canonical analysis of discriminance (1329).

Imagine a situation where scores on g groups are available on n measures. Consider first the case where only two groups are involved. Some set of n weights exists which, when used to provide a weighted sum (composite score) for each subject, will maximally discriminate between the two groups, e.g., will yield the largest possible value on a t test, or equivalently, the largest possible point biserial r between the composite score and group membership. Since it is an optimally weighted composite, the latter is properly a *multiple* point biserial correlation, and indeed, the weights and correlation solved for by applying the standard multiple linear regression technique, the dependent or "criterion" variable being group membership scored zero-one. The resulting partial regression coefficients (weights) of multiple regression applied to the measures will yield the desired optimally discriminating composite. The

weights constitute the discriminant function. Measures with relatively large weights are thus relatively more influential in the discrimination of the groups. Thus, one can obtain insight into the manifold of groups and measures from such an analysis, depending upon the meaning to be attached to the measures and the groups.

Multiple discriminant function or canonical variate analysis extends this logic to three or more groups. Here, a group's means on the n measures can be thought of as defining a single point in n dimensions, with the g groups thus defining g points. The n weights we now seek for the measures are those which will increase to a maximum the dispersion of these means relative to within-group dispersion. Instead of the weighted sum composite score yielding a maximum point biserial r as in the two-group case, we now seek a maximum between groups/within groups sum of squares for the composite, i.e., a maximum (squared) correlation ratio (eta). (Indeed, the point biserial r *is* the correlation ratio in the two-group case.) Again the size of a measure's weight indexes the degree to which it contributes to the discrimination achieved by the composite. Furthermore, it is possible to ascertain the number of significant independent dimensions in which the group means extend, e.g., five groups on ten measures may lie along a straight line or in a plane, or in three or four dimensions. The technique of analysis is discussed by Anderson in Chapter 5.

In the Payne-Hewlett study, instead of using all the 54 original test measures, it was assumed that most of their discriminating variance was contained in the first three centroids (but see Slater, 1329), and all subjects were then scored on these centroids; hence n equals three. Taking the groups a pair at a time, simple discriminant function analyses were first performed. Since the common factor 3-space was hypothesized to represent dimensions of overinclusion, retardation, and general intelligence, certain hypotheses about the outcome of these analyses could be made. Since the normals should not by theory (and matching) differ from the neurotics on any of these dimensions, a non-significant discriminant function between them was predicted. When the non-psychotic vs. psychotic pooled groups were analyzed, and similarly schizophrenics vs. depressives, they led to the expectation of significance of the respective discriminations, since the groups compared should differ on overinclusion and/or retardation (but not general intelligence, on which they had been equated by selection). These expectations were all realized.

But now the important question: in how many dimensions are the groups dispersed? If only one, this would suggest a dimension of "psychoticism," whose nature could be inferred from the heavily weighted variables. The canonical analysis of discriminance yielded two significant latent roots in the between-groups variance-covariance matrix; hence two dimensions are needed. But since the measures were centroid-factor scores not corresponding to functional or theoretical unities, their direct interpretation is not possible.

To determine the nature of these dimensions, a unique procedure for rotating the centroids was followed. From the previous discriminant function analysis of schizophrenics vs. depressives, the three weights were used as a transformation vector to rotate the centroids. On the assumption that such a difference would be a consequence of overinclusion, the factor was so provisionally labeled. The pure (unspeeded) measures of overinclusion proved to have high loadings on it, and scores on this factor separated the schizophrenics from the other groups. A "psychoticism" factor was similarly rotated, using the discriminant function weights of the psychotics vs. non-psychotics analysis. It correlated $-.48$ with the overinclusion factor and, when further rotated to minimize the distinction between depressives and schizophrenics and pass through the cluster of

speed tests, it correlated $-.38$ with the overinclusion factor and was named a retardation factor. It does not significantly discriminate depressives from schizophrenics but does discriminate both from the normals and neurotics. A general intelligence factor was found by finding an axis at right angles to the plane of the other two factors.

Thus, as hypothesized, schizophrenics were, as a group, uniquely characterized as overinclusive, while general (motor and intellectual) retardation characterized *both* forms of psychosis. Space limitations preclude detailing the many other interesting findings about the nature of the tests and evidence for the heterogeneity of the schizophrenic group, for which the reader is referred to the original report.

6. APPLICATION TO ANALYSIS OF THE SINGLE CASE: I. *P* TECHNIQUE IN A DISTURBED DEFECTIVE

That sophisticated multivariate approaches were possible in the single case has long been known (206) but little exploited as yet by practitioners. Yet the clinician as practitioner, particularly in the role of psychotherapist, is engaged at this level. Utilizing some frame-of-reference variables culled from the study of individual differences, he assumes the task of determining what pattern these variables take and their covariational flux over time for the specific patient in his charge. (That there is only one patient leads to the continually rediscovered joke among clinical students that their inferences are based on N-1 and therefore zero degrees of freedom!) The clinician then proceeds to study the *joint* concomitance of many drives, needs, symptoms, and bits of behavior over time or occasions. In this quest for regularities in the behavior of his patient, though he may be aided by a substantive theory of psychopathology and his observational skills, he is without the resources of objective measurement and the capacity for storage and multivariate simplification afforded by an appropriately programed electronic computer. In sum, he is attempting an armchair factor analysis.

The population of behavior and occasions of a single patient is very large, if not infinite, and large samples can (with some perseverance) be drawn with degrees of freedom to burn. A pair of variables determined over many occasions can be correlated, just as they can be correlated over many subjects. When a set of variables is intercorrelated over occasions, the resulting matrix of correlations can be subjected to the same forms of multivariate analysis as the more conventional kind. P technique is the name given the factor analysis of such a matrix (230). This constitutes a powerful technique, thus far largely potential (but see Cattell & Scheier, 325), for accomplishing what the therapist as diagnostician seeks to do in each case. (See Chapter 11 for method and 22 for examples, above.)

As an example of this procedure, we will briefly describe the recent case study by Shotwell, Hurley, and Cattell (1317) of a fifteen-year-old mildly mentally defective and· maladjusted girl. The variables were objective measures of motivation derived from prior factor-analytic research (for a summary, see Cattell & Scheier, 325), so that each established dynamic factor was represented by at least two marker variables. They included questions regarding activities, word association, paired comparisons, and ratings by teachers, ward technicians, and the patient herself. The dynamic factors represented by markers included the drives of sex-mating, gregariousness, appeal-dependence, escape-fear, self-assertion, parental-protective, and narcissistic play; the eighth was the self-sentiment. Of the 98 variables measured, the 42 showing sufficient variability over the 100 days were intercorrelated. Note that a high correlation between two variables indicates that they tend to be high together and low together relative to the *patient's* own

average over the 100 days, *not* to any population. The 42×42 matrix was centroid-factored and rotated to an oblique simple structure, using a modification of the oblimax method (1168) to improve upon its simple structure.

The factors which result represent sources of motivation in *this* patient which wax and wane over time. The P factors which emerge in one person need not coincide with those of another. The similarity of P factors among persons is an empirical issue. However, clinical experience would lead us to expect differences as well as similarities. Further, a motivational factor bearing the same general character and name in two patients may nevertheless differ strikingly with regard to one or two variables. The "uniqueness" of personalities lies just in such differences.

Returning to the subject of the present study, 11 dynamic factors were identified:

(1) Found in previous researches on other subjects: Sex, Fear-Anxiety, Self-Regard Sentiment, Gregariousness, Appeal-Dependence, Self-Assertion, and Narcissism.

(2) A subfactor "Good Time Yesterday," highly correlated with the Narcissism factor, and a factor which could not be plausibly interpreted.

(3) Two factors not previously found: a Menstruation-Depression factor and a Regressed Sex Component factor.

To give the reader some flavor of the results, the Fear-Anxiety and Repressed Sex Component factors are given in Table 30-4.

The interpretation of factor II, with its phobic-withdrawn quality, seems straightforward. A conflict is projected by the combination of teacher-rated shyness and the paired comparison rejection of withdrawal, "the central problem of almost any anxiety syndrome." The authors also comment, "This factor also removes any doubt as to one of the most useful functions of the television set, the poor man's Miltown" (1317, p. 425).

The unique Repressed Sex Component factor has information specific to *this* patient. Where she gives uncharacteristically many sexual responses and affirms having dreamt about her boyfriend, she gives relatively few parental responses, denies a letter from home and selects a withdrawal response on paired comparisons. "The clash of feelings for one's parents and feelings for oneself comes into sharp focus.... The rise of this factor in

they need not be restricted to such use. A therapist motivated to explore a patient's dynamic structure by these means can, after brief acquaintance with a case, delimit the variables to those of probable relevance and use them in repeated measurements for a series of occasions. With the proper data collected, their factor analysis can be effectuated quickly and economically by computer — Cattell and Scheier's computer cost estimate of $100.00 (325, p. 397) is

TABLE 30-4

TWO MOTIVATIONAL *P*-FACTORS OF A MALADJUSTED MENTAL DEFECTIVE GIRL
Shotwell, et al., (1317)

Source	Content	Loading
	Factor II: Fear-Anxiety	
PC	I want there to be fewer deaths	.54
RT	Shyness	.40
PC	I want the U. S. to have better A-bomb protection	.39
RS	Amount of worry	.35
RS	Cooperation	−.34
PC	I want time to enjoy my own company	−.33
QA	Did you watch TV yesterday? (Yes)	.21
WA	Escape-fear	.08
	Factor XI: Repressed Sex	
WA	Sex-mating	.39
WA	Parental-protective drive	−.35
PC	I want time to enjoy my own company	.34
QA	Did you dream about your boyfriend last night? (Yes)	.31
QA	Did you get a letter from home yesterday? (No)	.31

PC — paired comparison
RT — teacher's rating
RS — self-rating
QA — question about activity
WA — word association

intensity from day to day could be a signal of dammed-up sex energy looking for release" (1317, p. 425).

The authors conclude with a plea for cooperation between clinicians and psychometrists, a plea reiterated over the years by Cattell and others and fervently joined by the present writer. What *is* the role of case studies such as this? Obviously, they can contribute to our knowledge of general principles of dynamic organization. But

probably already too high, and if not, will soon be. Clinicians of the old school may well scratch their heads at the prospect of factor-analyzing a patient in the very process of psychoanalyzing him!

For another (the first published) example of *P* technique applied to a patient, the reader is referred to the Cattell and Luborsky study of a case of peptic ulcer (300). This study is also reported with greater clinical detail by Luborsky (967). In conjunction with psychotherapy, it utilized physiological variables and variables from free association and dreams, as well as the more usual objective personality and rating variables. This study is a model of fruitful clinical-psychometric collaboration.

7. APPLICATION TO THE SINGLE CASE: II. *O* TECHNIQUE APPLIED TO A NEUROTIC

O is to *P* as *Q* is to *R. R,* the traditional factor-analytic design, intercorrelates variables over subjects, while *Q* intercorrelates subjects over variables, both on a single occasion. *P*, as we have just seen, intercorrelates variables over occasions for a single subject. In *O* technique, the intercorrelations are among *occasions* over variables, also for a single subject. A high correlation here indicates that the two occasions show similarity in the ordering of the different variables, e.g., that a subject is relatively similarly described on these two occasions.

The term "occasions" need not signify simply successive days as in the previous section; it can represent different experimental conditions. Indeed, *O* technique is likely to be most productive in the latter case. A now classical example of such correlations (which did not, however, lead to factor analysis) was the correlation of "*Q* sorts" for a single individual under conditions of instruction: (1) "describe yourself," (2) "describe yourself as you would like to be," and (3) "describe people-in-general" (1214). Note that Stephenson's *Q*-sorting *method* is an attempt to solve the metric problem by having all variables used to describe an object expressed in the same unit, namely, degree of descriptive adequacy. Such data *may* be used in *Q-technique* factor-analytic designs, but they may also be used, as Stephenson himself has shown (1346), in analysis of variance designs, or as in the study about to be described, in *O*-technique factor-analytic designs.

Jum C. Nunnally (1105) approached the problem of self-concept and its change as a consequence of psychotherapy by constructing a set of 60 self-descriptive statements relative to "Miss Sun," a neurotic college student, drawn up in the light of findings from a series of interviews with her and with friends and relatives, and from Rorschach, TAT, and Szondi. A self-assessment by Miss Sun took the form of her arraying these 60 statements along a nine-point continuum from most uncharacteristic to most characteristic, using in this instance the forced frequency distribution: 2, 3, 7, 11, 14, 11, 7, 3, 2. Miss Sun assessed herself on many "occasions" during a five-month pretherapy period, but these various "occasions" represented changes in experimental conditions, specifically, instructions that she assess herself in various emotionally laden interaction situations noted during the study period. These included: as she was generally (twice), as she would like to be, as she felt she should behave, as she had been at ages 9-16 and 16-18, as she thought she was becoming, as she believed she was regarded by her friends, her father, her mother, and the psychologist assessing her, as each of her parents wanted her to be, as she acted in the presence of her aunt and uncle, and as she was when doing her music work — 15 sorts in all. Following a year of psychotherapy (with Carl Rogers), she provided during a seven-month period 19 sorts for most of the same situations as before, and some newly appropriate ones, including: as her therapist and her sister regarded her, as she behaved in her marriage, with her in-laws and on her job, and as she was regarded by each of two groups of friends.

The pretherapy situations were intercorrelated over the statements (incidentally, for *Q* sorts this can be done easily even without data-processing equipment — see Cohen, 359), centroid-factored, and rotated orthogonally to permit the testing of a series of propositions. The three factors, representing types of self-assessment called forth by the interactional situation, were interpreted by identifying invariably highly rated items for situations with high loadings on each. Factor I, a general mode of behavior highly loaded by her self-descriptions "as I am generally," was described as "aloofness, cooperativeness and imperturbability." Factor II received high loadings on "ideal" sorts and as her mother wanted her to be, and was interpreted as representing a picture of "an outgoing, striving individual . . . less idealistic and more practical than Factor I." Factor III was most highly positively loaded in "as my friends in general regard me" and negatively in "as my mother regarded me" and "as when doing my piano work" and was interpreted as a college role, "a Bohemian-like escape from the incompatibility of the modes of behavior of Factors I and II."

Nunnally formulated a series of propositions which required comparisons of the above O factors with those resulting from a similar analysis of the posttherapy assessments, as well as pre- and post-analyses of those assessments attributed by Miss Sun to others and her "owned" (non-attributed) assessments separately. One was that if one of the factors changed considerably following therapy, at least one other would also change. This was rejected for Miss Sun, when it was found that the pretherapy present-self (factor I) correlated .73 with the posttherapy present-self, while the ideal-self (factor II) correlated −.01 over the same 1½-year period. Another proposition was that if the therapy led to definite improvement (which it apparently did), the "owned" self-assessments following therapy would approach a general factor more strongly. This was supported for Miss Sun; for example, the ideal sort changed from a first centroid-factor loading of −.36 to one of .85, and others changed in the same direction. It was also anticipated that improvement would result in attributed assessments becoming incongruous with factor I of the total matrix, i.e., that she would come to believe that others regarded her differently from the way she regarded herself. Just the reverse seemed to occur; in most instances sizable increases of loading occurred on rotated factor I, e.g., "as my friends in general regard me" went from .04 to .49.

There were other interesting findings. As they waxed and waned over the total period, the correlations of the general self with those attributed to the assessing psychologist and the psychotherapist led to the interpretation that "Miss Sun uses some important person in her life as a support for her self-notions. She must feel that this person 'believes it also.' Thus, attributed assessments can be instrumental in changing present-self assessments." Another finding was that following therapy there were multiple attributed assessments where there has been only one before, a differentiation of sources of attributed selves. A finding that similarity from pre to post in the factors as defined by the pattern of assessment-situations loading them was not accompanied by item-content similarity for the second and third factors suggests the interesting conclusion that for Miss Sun, at least, O factors of the self-concept transcend their specific content. This, in turn, carries implications about non-functional implicit (perhaps unconscious) conceived similarities as a barrier to realistic self-appraisal.

It should be noted that O technique investigations using Q sorts are quite feasible in most therapeutic situations since they make quite modest demands on both patient and psychologist time in data-gathering. Data analysis, as we have seen, is relegated to the electronic computer, or short-cut methods can be resorted to (359, 1017, 1019, 1020, 1022). This type of O-technique study can, even more than P-technique studies, become a regular tool of evaluation of both the patient and the treatment in individual psychotherapy. Also, as the present writer has long advocated, it offers further interesting possibilities in group therapy, where attributed sorts can be prepared by each patient for all group members, as well as significant others in their private lives.

Another interesting example of multivariate research in psychotherapy utilizing Q sorts, this time in a Q-technique design, is provided by Apfelbaum's study of transference phenomena (38). He had therapy applicants provide Q-sort descriptions of their expectations of their therapists, prior to meeting them, and subjected these to a modified cluster analysis (1456, 1457) to isolate types of transference identified as "Nurturance," "Model," and "Critic." These were later compared with regard to demographic and MMPI characteristics and therapeutic behavior and outcome. The Q sort seems peculiarly suited for study of the psychotherapeutic process. Fiedler has actively exploited the technique by having therapist-patient pairs each sort to describe the self, the ideal self, and predict the sorts of others (72, 511, 515). From correlations among these, various measures are derived which may reflect aspects of transference and countertransference phenomena. This work has been extended to cover social perception in a variety of settings (514).

A most impressive example of O technique is provided by the Osgood and Luria blind analysis of the three personalities of "Eve" (1125). Osgood's semantic differential (1126) rivals Q sorting in its flexibility, since it makes possible the description of many kinds of concepts within one scheme. Using semantic differential ratings of a set of relevant concepts (love, child, me, mental sickness, my mother, etc.) provided by Eve in each of her three personality manifestations, analyses were performed of the distances between concepts in the three-dimensional (Evaluation, Activity, Potency) space for each personality. The resulting personality descriptions and discussion are remarkable both for their accuracy and the insights they provide. The reader is urged to become familiar with this classic.

8. A MULTIVARIATE VIEW OF PRESENT-DAY CLINICAL PROCEDURES

This chapter has been concerned with research which has broken new ground and therefore pointed in new directions, hopefully a Baedeker for the future. But multivariate methods have been abundantly applied to the diagnostic and therapeutic procedures and conceptions of clinical psychology as generally practiced today. The present section will briefly survey these findings.

The Wechsler Scales

The "pattern-analytic" interpretation of a patient's Wechsler intelligence subtest scores is a firmly rooted clinical practice. It proceeds from a rationale which assigns to each subtest a substantial specific measurement function, e.g., Similarities as a measure of "verbal concept formation," Picture Arrangement as a measure of "planning ability" (1181, pp. 129-131, 215-220). In a series of studies of Wechsler scales on psychiatric patients, normal adults, and normal children, Cohen found repeatedly that the subtests' relatively high intercorrelations and modest reliabilities led to their having subtest-specific variance amounting on the average to about one-seventh of their total variance, a proportion generally lower than that of their error variance (357, 358, 360, 361, 362). This effectively precludes material validity for rationales that are subtest-specific, although scoring for the three major (correlated) common factors and patterns of these factor scores may prove to be useful (Cohen, 360, 362).

A further difficulty with at least some Wechsler subtests lies in their factorial complexity, i.e., their measurement by their items of more than one common factor per subtest. Saunders has factor-analyzed the items of Picture Completion (1259), of Information and Arithmetic (1258), and of Comprehension and Similarities (in preparation) and finds from two to four common factors measured by each subtest, thus rendering its interpretation ambiguous. Findings such as those of Cohen and Saunders may partly account for the paucity of stable patterns from a decade of active pattern-analytic research with Wechsler subtests, particularly when taken in conjunction with the cumulated multivariate evidence for the behavioral heterogeneity within groups bearing the same diagnostic label.

Requirements of meaningfulness within a coherent theory, as well as descriptive efficiency, demand that the elements of a pattern or profile be valid measures of different functionally unitary constructs (factors). The most widely used clinical diagnostic procedures, among them the Wechsler scales, do not meet this criterion.

The Rorschach

The evidence from multivariate research on the Rorschach illustrates the point of the last paragraph. Wittenborn, in R-technique factor-analytic studies of the Rorschach response categories in college students (1564) and psychiatric patients (1565) found that the usual scoring and interpretive bases (color, movement, vista, texture) do not accord with the factors found. For example, a major factor distinguished whole and non-form—dominated responses of differing determinants. Approaching the question of differential diagnosis with the usual response categories for four cases in each of four diagnostic groups, Bendig and Hamlin (96) found that none of the resulting three type-factors were significantly related to group membership when productivity was controlled. It is interesting that Hughes (785) extracted a factor which discriminated well between organic and other patients, but Rorschach "signs" and not the usual

response categories were used and later summed, a practice eschewed by the Rorschach purist (but not by Hermann Rorschach!).

The MMPI

The writer approaches the MMPI with much ambivalence. On the one hand, it is the most thoroughly researched clinical procedure extant (1513). Moreover, this research has been marked by a high order of both statistical and clinical sophistication (1027, 1029) and a hardheaded empiricism (702, 401, 1030). On the other hand, it was originally developed by selecting items on the basis of their differentiation of each of a series of psychiatric diagnostic groups from hospital visitor controls (701). Scores on such scales do not necessarily reflect functional unities of response, but degree of response similarity to the psychiatric group in question, i.e., surface traits rather than source traits. If the group differs from the controls along more than one dimension of response, such a score is factorially complex and hence ambiguous. (Note that it may be empirically valid; indeed, there is abundant evidence that the MMPI is quite valid when properly used as a predictor of diagnostic group (1027). When factor analyses of the items on a given clinical scale have been performed, however, invariably, from 3 to as many as 14 interpretable factors have been found (370, 1109). Thus, despite its admitted concurrent diagnostic validity, it seems a roundabout strategy for attaining useful constructs for a theory of abnormal behavior. Considering the high quality and quantity of MMPI research, would that Hathaway and McKinley had begun with measures of factors, instead of diagnostic group membership!

The advent of the 16 P.F. (and its equivalents for children, the HSPQ and CPQ) into clinical work now supplies a set of instruments, however, for those who want factored measurements, either primary or second-order. Distinctive profiles have been demonstrated by Cattell and Scheier (325) for various neurotic diagnoses, and characteristic profiles have been recognized for homosexuals, delinquents (303), paranoids, and schizophrenics. The second-order anxiety measure derived from it has been shown to change significantly with psychotherapy and tranquilizers (325). However, it promises to be more useful with neurotic and other maladjusted individuals than with psychotics, in whom it may only be registering the pre-psychotic personality and missing whatever dimension exists in psychotic disorder as such. The relation of the MMPI to the 16 P.F. is obviously that which Cattell has called surface trait to source trait, i.e., a correlation cluster or syndrome "in being" to an underlying factor. Thus we should expect the 16 P.F. to (1) give more varied profiles for a given syndrome, because the causes of a disorder are more varied than the standard manifestations of the disease itself, and (2) to give clues to the best direction of therapy, insofar as the 16 P.F. factors explain in terms of normal personality structures, such as ego and superego, affectothymia and ergic tension level, the sources of the faulty adjustment.

The surface trait to source trait relation holds if one compares the traditional scales in the MMPI in what has been recently called (page 573) "depth psychometry," yielding two levels of scoring for each patient — surface and source. However, if the MMPI scales are taken to pieces, and the whole set of 560-odd items factored as such, the result, as Eber, Cattell, Fowler, and Specht have shown in a recently reported study, is some 24 factors, of which 16 correspond to those already in the 16 P.F. Following this extensive analysis, Cattell and Eber have constructed, from additional studies to this on the MMPI, a ten-factor Pathology Supplement Scale to the 16 P.F., claiming that the 16 P.F. and its supplement will more effectively cover the gamut of normal and abnormal dimensions than previous questionnaires. However, they suggest it is still desirable, by depth

psychometry simultaneously to measure syndromes, as in the MMPI and source traits, as etiological or causal entities, in the 16 P.F. and P.S.

Schools of Psychotherapy

Fiedler has explored the question of differences in therapeutic relationships among various therapeutic schools. In a series of studies of therapists' concepts and therapeutic behavior utilizing Q sorts of statements describing therapeutic relationships (509, 510), he found that factors of both concepts of an ideal therapeutic relationship and rated therapeutic behavior were organized on the basis of expertness and not therapeutic school. Within the limits set by the sample of statements, this work suggests that the substantial divergence in explanatory theory is not mirrored by like differences in actual therapeutic behavior of experienced practitioners.

9. SUMMARY

(1) This chapter aims to present (a) a brief discussion of the essence of the two most systematic clinical multivariate approaches, (b) a sampling of a diversity of substantive conceptual advances through multivariate experiment, and (c) a glance at changes consequently in progress in clinical practice and viewpoints.

(2) A system of personality measurement, leading to new theoretical views of its structure, has been contributed to independently by the systematic researches of Cattell and Eysenck and their co-workers. Their primary and second-order concepts of anxiety, ego strength, affectothymia of temperament, ergic tension, etc., have provided diagnostically significant tools for clinical practice and created a body of knowledge about neuroticism and psychoticism in quantitative terms which brings a new development of theory.

(3) Owing partly to certain methodological differences, the systematic conclusions of these two researchers show some inter-

esting disagreements as well as an over-all agreement deriving from objective experiment and subtle multivariate analysis methods. Thus Cattell points out that the second-order factors can be located accurately only after the primaries have been located, and points out that valuable predictive information is lost by working only with the broader, simpler, second-order factors such as general anxiety and extraversion. Eysenck propounds a single factor continuum for neuroticism and psychoticism, whereas Cattell's results argue for their being distinct dimensions but factorially composite. Eysenck has sought explanations in classical learning theory, whereas Cattell believes that personality theory requires and contributes a new view of dynamic laws and learning theory.

(4) Much progress has been made in the multivariate analysis of diagnostic rating and syndrome evaluation methods, by the work of Lorr, and of Wittenborn, Huffman, Cohen, and others. The resultant scales are of much practical utility.

(5) Q-technique (factoring) and Q'-technique (correlation cluster) methods have opened up another entirely new angle to the objective development of psychiatric taxonomy and to the evaluation of individual diagnosis and therapeutic change.

(6) The application of multivariate experimental methods in an entirely different way is illustrated by its use to test an hypothesis about thought disorders in psychosis, handled by canonical analysis. It suggests that schizophrenic thought is dominated by overinclusive thinking.

(7) The notion that multivariate methods supply us only with common trait measures not always penetrative of the individual case overlooks the use of P and O techniques, which are capable of giving objective evidence on the dynamic structure and specific adjustment problems of the individual. The technical skills required in these methods have unfortunately caused a lag in their application in clinical practice even when their advantages are known.

(8) A number of present clinical diagnostic and other procedures are examined from the standpoint of multivariate research concepts and found sometimes lacking in both logic and effectiveness. The Wechsler scales are often factorially complex, and the Rorschach has a limited and obscure dimensionality. The MMPI, which deals with surface traits (syndrome correlated clusters), has needed supplementation by a factored scale, now available in the 16 P.F., its Pathology Supplement, etc. These should yield, respectively, a description in terms of syndromes and an interpretation in terms of basic personality structures, normal and abnormal, according to a depth psychometry technique.

(9) The purpose of this chapter has been to describe and illustrate the contributions, both actual and potential, which multivariate methodology brings to an understanding and amelioration of abnormal behavior. It has been written in the conviction that a wider use of this methodology and the tools of thought and action it has already provided will make actual the revolution in clinical psychology which has long been heralded.

Bibliography

1. Abelson, R. P. Scales derived by consideration of variance components in multi-way tables. In H. Gulliksen and S. J. Messick (Eds.), *Psychological scaling: Theory and applications.* New York: 1960. Pp. 169-186.

2. Abelson, R. P., & Sermat, V. Multidimensional scaling of facial expressions. *J. exp. Psychol.,* 1962, 63, 546-554.

3. Abrams, E. N. A comparative factor analytic study of normal and neurotic veterans. Unpublished doctoral dissertation, Univer. of Michigan, 1949.

4. Adams, J. A. Human tracking behavior. *Psychol. Bull.,* 1961, 58, 55-79.

5. Adcock, C. J. A note on the factorial analysis of Sheldon's personality traits. *Austral. J. Psychol.,* 1950, 2, 114-115.

6. Adcock, C. J., & Prior, I. A. M. A factorial analysis of Maori physical data. 1963.

7. Adorno, T. W., Frenkel-Brunswik, E., Levinson, D. J., & Sanford, R. N. *The authoritarian personality.* New York: Harper, 1950.

8. Ahmann, J. S. Prediction of the probability of graduation of engineering transfer students. *J. exp. Educ.,* 1955, 23, 281-288.

9. Ahmavaara, Y. The mathematical theory of factorial invariance under selection. *Psychol.,* 1954, 19, 27-38.

10. Ahmavaara, Y. Transformation analysis of factoral data. *Ann. Acad. Sci. Fenn.* (Helsinki), 1954, Ser. B, 88, 2.

11. Ahmavaara, Y. On the unified factor theory of mind. *Ann. Acad. Sci. Fenn.* (Helsinki), 1957, Ser. B, 106.

12. Aiken, L. R., Jr. Mathemaphobia and mathemaphilia: An analysis of personal and social factors affecting performance in mathematics. Unpublished doctoral dissertation, Univer. of North Carolina, 1960.

13. Aiken, L. R. *Determinants and Matrices.* (2nd ed.) Edinburgh: Oliver and Boyd, 1942.

14. Albert, K., Hoch, P., & Waelsch, H. Glutamic acid and mental deficiency. *J. nerv. ment. Dis.,* 1951, 114, 471-491.

15. Alexander, S., & Husek, T. R. The anxiety differential: Initial steps in the development of a measure of situational anxiety. *Educ. psychol. Measmt,* 1962, 22, 325-348.

16. Alker, H. R. Dimensions of conflict in the general assembly. *Amer. pol. sci. Rev.,* 1964, 58.

16. (a) Alker, H. R. Supranationalism in the United Nations. *Peace Res. Soc. Papers III,* Chicago Conference, 1965.

16. (b) Allen, G. Patterns of discovery in the genetics of mental deficiency. *Amer. J. ment. Defic.,* 1958, 62, 840-849.

17. Allison, R. B., Jr. *Learning parameters and human abilities.* Office of Naval Research Tech. Rept. Princeton, N.J.: Educational Testing Service, 1960.

18. Allport, G. W. *Personality.* New York: Holt, 1937.

18. (a) Allport, G. W., & Odbert, H. S. Trait names: A psycho-lexical study. *Psychol. Monogr.,* 1936, 47, No. 211, 1-171.

19. Allport, G. W., Vernon, P. E., & Lindzey, G. *Study of values: Manual.* Boston: Houghton Mifflin, 1951.

20. American Institutes of Research. *The AIR*

stanine tests for pilot selection. Pittsburgh: American Institutes of Research, 1957.

21. Anastasi, A. A. A group factor in immediate memory. *Arch. Psychol.,* 1930, 18 (No. 120), 5-61.

22. Anastasi, A. A. Further studies on the memory factor. *Arch. Psychol.,* 1932, 22, (No. 142).

22. Anastasi, A. A. Differentiating effect of
(a) intelligence and social status. *Eugen. Quart.,* 1959, 6, 84-91.

23. Anastasi, A. A., Fuller, J. L., Scott, J. P., & Schmitt, J. R. A factor analysis of the performance of dogs on certain learning tests. *Zoologica,* 1955, p. 40.

24. Anderson, A. W. Personality traits of Western Australian University freshmen. *J. soc. Psychol.,* 1960, 51, 87-91.

25. Anderson, E. E. The interrelationship of drives in the male albino rat: III. Among measures of emotional, sexual and exploratory behavior. *J. genet. Psychol.,* 1938, 53, 335-352.

26. Anderson, H. E., Jr. A methodological comparison of factor analysis and multiple correlation analysis. Unpublished thesis, Univer. of Texas, 1958.

27. Anderson, H. E., Jr., & Fruchter, B. *Procedural studies: The computation of an inverse matrix.* Research Guide No. 1. Austin: Psychometric Lab., Dept. of Educational Psychology, Univer. of Texas, 1957. (Dittoed.)

28. Anderson, H. E., Jr., & Fruchter, B. *Statistical procedures: Multivariate analysis with the generalized distance function and canonical variates.* Research Guide No. 3. Austin: Psychometric Lab., Dept. of Educational Psychology, Univer. of Texas, 1957. (Dittoed.)

29. Anderson, H. E., Jr., & Fruchter, B. Some multiple correlation and predictor selection methods. *Psychometrika,* 1960, 25, 59-76.

30. Anderson, H. E., Jr., & Leton, D. A. Optimum grade classification with the California Achievement Test battery. *Educ. psychol. Measmt,* 1963, 23, 135-143.

31. Anderson, N. H. Scales and statistics: Parametric and non-parametric. *Psychol. Bull.,* 1961, 58, 305-316.

32. Anderson, R. L., & Bancroft, T. A. *Statistical theory in research.* New York: McGraw-Hill, 1952.

32. Anderson, T. W. Probability models for
(a) analyzing time changes in attitudes. In P. Lazarsfeld (Ed.), *Mathematical thinking in the social sciences.* Glencoe, Ill.: Free Press, 1954.

33. Anderson, T. W. *Introduction to multivariate statistical analysis.* New York: Wiley, 1958.

34. Anderson, T. W. The use of factor analysis in the statistical analysis of multiple time series. *Psychometrika,* 1963, 28, 1-25.

35. Andrew, D. M. An analysis of the Minnesota test for clerical workers. *J. appl. Psychol.,* 1937, 21, 18-47, 139-172.

36. Andrews, T. G. Statistical studies in allergy. *J. Allergy,* 1948, 19 (1), 43-46.

37. Anker, J. M., Townsend, J. C., & O'Connor, J. P. A multivariate analysis of decision making and related measures. *J. Psychol.,* 1963, 55 (1), 211-221.

38. Apfelbaum, B. *Dimensions of transference in psychotherapy.* Berkeley: Univer. of California Press, 1958.

39. Arnoult, M. D. Prediction of perceptual responses from structural characteristics of the stimulus. *Percept. mot. Skills,* 1960, 11, 261-268.

40. Atkinson, J. W. *Motives in fantasy, action and society.* New York: Van Nostrand, 1958.

41. Atkinson, J. W., & McClelland, D. C. The projective expression of needs. II. The effect of different intensities of hunger drive on thematic apperception. *J. exp. Psychol.,* 1948, 38, 643-658.

42. Attneave, F. A method of graded dichotomies for the scaling of judgments. *Psychol. Rev.,* 1949, 56, 334-340.

43. Attneave, F. Dimensions of similarity. *Amer. J. Psychol.,* 1950, 63, 516-556.

44. Attneave, F. Physical determinants of the judged complexity of shapes. *J. exp. Psychol.,* 1957, 53, 221-227.

45. Attneave, F. *Applications of information theory to psychology.* New York: Holt-Dryden, 1959.

46. Attneave, F., & Arnoult, M. D. The quantitative study of shape and pattern perception. *Psychol. Bull.,* 1956, 53, 252-271.

47. Back, K. W. Decisions under uncertainty: Rational, irrational, and nonrational. *Amer. behav. Scientist,* 1961, 6, 14-19.

48. Bacon, Francis. *Novum organum.* Trans. by Thomas Fowler. (2nd ed. rev.) Oxford: Clarendon Press, 1889.

49. Baehr, M. E. A factorial study of temperament. *Psychometrika,* 1952, 17, 107-126.

49. Baggaley, A. R., & Cattell, R. B. A com-
(a) parison of exact and approximate linear function estimates of oblique factor scores. *Brit. J. statist. Psychol.,* 1956, 9, 83-86.

50. Bakan, D. A generalization of Sidman's results on group and individual functions, and a criterion. *Psychol. Bull.,* 1954, 51, 63-64.

51. Baker, E., Baker, G. A., Roessler, E. B., & Shontz, H. B. Factor analysis of high school scholastic experience and success in the first semester at the University of California at Davis. *Coll. & Univ.,* 1955, 30, 351-358.

52. Baldwin, A. L., Kalhorn, J., & Breese, F. H. Patterns of parent behavior. *Psychol. Monogr.,* 1945, 58, No. 3 (Whole No. 268).

53. Baldwin, A. L., Kalhorn, J., & Breese, F. H. The appraisal of parent behavior. *Psychol. Monogr.,* 1949, 63, No. 4 (Whole No. 299).

54. Bales, R. F. *Interaction process analysis.* Cambridge: Addison-Wesley, 1950.

55. Bales, R. F. Some statistical problems in small group research. *J. Amer. Statist. Ass.,* 1951, 46, 311-322.

56. Balinski, B. An analysis of the mental factors of various age groups from nine to sixty. *Genet. Psychol. Monogr.,* 1941, 23, 191-234.

57. Banta, T. J. Critical note on unidimensional tests. *Psychol. Repts,* 1962, 11, 449-450.

58. Bargmann, R. A comparison of new analytic methods for the determinations of simple structure. Frankfort-Main: Hochschule fuer Internationale Paedagogische Forschung, 1953. (Mimeographed.)

59. Bargmann, R. The statistical significance of simple structure in factor analysis. Frankfurt-Main: Hochschule fuer Internationale Paedagogische Forschung, 1953. (Mimeographed.)

60. Bargmann, R. *A study of independence and dependence in multivariate normal analysis.* Mimeo. Ser., Chapel Hill: Institute of Statistics, Univer. of North Carolina, 1957.

61. Bargmann, R. Review of Ahmavaara's "On the unified factor theory of mind." *Psychometrika,* 1960, 25, 105-109.

62. Barnes, C. A. A statistical study of the Freudian theory of levels of psychosexual development. *Genet. Psychol. Monogr.,* 1952, 45, 105-175.

63. Barratt, E. S. CNS correlates of intra-individual variability of ANS activity. Symposium paper, Amer. Psychol. Ass., St. Louis, Sept. 3, 1962.

64. Bartlett, C. J., Ronning, R. R., & Hurst, J. G. A study of classroom evaluation techniques with special reference to application of knowledge. *J. educ. Psychol.,* 1960, 51, 152-158.

65. Bartlett, M. S. The statistical significance of canonical correlations. *Biometrika,* 1941, 32, 29-38.

66. Bartlett, M. S. Multivariate analysis. *J. Roy. Statist. Soc.* (Suppl.), 1947, 9, 176-197.

67. Bartlett, M. S. Internal and external factor analysis. *Brit. J. Psychol.* (Statist. Sec.), 1948, 1, 73-81.

68. Bartlett, M. S. Tests of significance in factor analysis. *Brit. J. Psychol.* (Statist. Sec.), 1948, 1, 73-81.

69. Bartlett, M. S. Tests of significance in factor analysis. *Brit. J. Psychol.* (Statist. Sec.), 1950, 3, 77-85.

70. Bartlett, M. S. The effect of standardization on a X^2 approximation in factor analysis. *Biometrika,* 1951, 38, 337-344.

71. Bartlett, M. S. The goodness of fit of a single hypothetical discriminant function in the case of several groups. *Ann. Eugenics,* 1951, 16, 199-214.

72. Bass, A. R., & Fiedler, F. E. Interpersonal perception scores and their components as predictors of personal adjustment. *J. abnorm. soc. Psychol.,* 1961, 62, 442-445.

73. Bass, B. M., & Coates, C. H. Forecasting officer potential using the leaderless group discussion. *J. abnorm. soc. Psychol.,* 1952, 47, 321-325.

74. Bass, R. I. An analysis of the components of tests of semi-circular canal function and of static and dynamic balance. *Res. Quart. Amer. Ass. Hlth phys. Educ.,* 1939, 10, 33-52.

75. Bates, G. E., & Neyman, J. *Discriminatory analysis. VIII. Contribution to the theory of accident proneness. Part I. An optimistic model of the correlation between light and severe accidents.* Randolph Field, Tex.: Air Univer. School of Aviation Medicine (Project No. 21-49-004, Rept. No. 8), 1951.

76. Bates, G. E., & Neyman, J. *Discriminatory analysis. IX. Contribution to the theory of accident proneness. Part II. True or false contagion.* Randolph Field, Tex.: Air Univer. School of Aviation Medicine (Project No. 21-49-004, Rept. No. 9), 1951.

77. Bayley, N. Consistency and variability in the growth of intelligence from birth to eighteen years. *J. genet. Psychol.,* 1949, 75, 165-196.

78. Bechtoldt, H. P. Factorial investigation of the perceptual speed factor. *Amer. Psychologist,* 1947, 2, 304-305.

79. Bechtoldt, H. P. *Factor analysis of the airman classification battery with civilian reference tests.* Res. Bull. 59-59. Lackland AFB, Tex.: Human Resources Research Center, 1953.

80. Bechtoldt, H. P. Statistical tests of predictions generated from factor hypotheses. *Amer. Psychologist,* 1960, 15, 589.

81. Bechtoldt, H. P. An empirical study of the factor analysis stability hypothesis. *Psychometrika,* 1961, 26, 405-432.

82. Bechtoldt, H. P. Factor analysis and the investigation of hypotheses. *Percept. mot. Skills,* 1962, 14, 319-342 (Monogr. Suppl. 2-V14).

83. Bechtoldt, H. P., Benton, A. L., & Fogel, M. L. An application of factor analysis in neuropsychology. *Psychol. Rec.,* 1962, 12, 147-156.

84. Beck, S. J. *The six schizophrenias.* Res. Monogr. No. 6. New York: American Orthopsychiatric Association, 1954.

85. Becker, W. C. The matching of behavior rating and questionnaire personality factors. *Psychol. Bull.,* 1960, 57, 201-212.

86. Becker, W. C. The relationship of factors in parental ratings of self and each other to the behavior of kindergarten children as rated by mothers, fathers, and teachers. *J. consult. Psychol.,* 1960, 24, 507-527.

87. Becker, W. C. A comparison of the factor structure and other properties of the 16 P.F. and the Guilford-Martin personality inventories. *Educ. psychol. Measmt,* 1961, 21, 393-404.

88. Becker, W. C., Peterson, D. R., Luria, Zella, Shoemaker, D. J., & Hellmer, L. A. Relations of factors derived from parent-interview ratings to behavior problems of five-year olds. *Child Develpm.,* 1962, 33, 509-535.

89. Beezhold, F. W. Factor analysis of language achievement tests. *J. Nat. Inst. Personnel Res.* (Johannesburg), 1956, 6, 63-73.

90. Bell, R. Q. Relations between behavior manifestation in the human neonate. *Child Develpm.,* 1960, 31, 463-477.

91. Bellman, R. & Dreyfus, S. *Applied dynamic programming.* Princeton, N.J.: Princeton Univer. Press, 1962.

92. Bendig, A. W. College norms for and concurrent validity of Cattell's IPAT anxiety scale. *Psychol. Newsltr,* 1959, 10, 263-267.

93. Bendig, A. W. Age differences in the interscale factor structure of the Guilford-Zimmerman Temperament Survey. *J. consult. Psychol.,* 1960, 24, 134-138.

94. Bendig, A. W. Item factor analyses of the scales of the Maudsley personality inventory. *J. psychol. Stud.,* 1960, 11, 104-107.

95. Bendig, A. W. Factor analyses of "anxiety" and "neuroticism" inventories. *J. consult. Psychol.,* 1960, 24, 161-168.

96. Bendig, A. W., & Hamlin, R. M. The psychiatric validity of an inverted factor analysis of Rorschach scoring categories. *J. consult. Psychol.,* 1955, 19, 183-188.

97. Benedict, R. *Patterns of culture.* Boston: Houghton Mifflin, 1934.

98. Benjamin, A. C. *An introduction to the philosophy of science.* New York: Macmillan, 1937.

99. Bennett, C. C. The drugs and I. In L. Uhr and J. G. Miller (Eds.), *Drugs and behavior.* New York: Wiley, 1960. Pp. 596-609.

100. Bennett, E. Some tests for the discrimination of neurotic from normal subjects. *Brit. J. med. Psychol.,* 1945, 20, 271.

101. Bereiter, C. Some persisting dilemmas in the measurement of change. In C. Harris (Ed.), *Problems in measuring change.* Madison: Univer. of Wisconsin Press, 1963.

102. Bereiter, C., & Freedman, M. B. Fields

of study and the people in them. In N. Sanford (Ed.), *The American college.* New York: Wiley, 1962. Pp. 563-596.

102. Berg, I. A., Hunt, W. A., & Barnes, E. H.
(a) *The perceptual reaction test.* Evanston, Ill., 1949.

103. Berge, C. *The theory of graphs and its applications.* New York: Wiley, 1962.

104. Berger, R. M., Guilford, J. P., & Christensen, P. R. A factor analytic study of planning abilities. *Psychol. Monogr.,* 1957, 71 (Whole No. 435).

105. Bergmann, G. *Philosophy of science.* Madison: Univer. of Wisconsin Press, 1957.

106. Berkowitz, L. Sharing leadership in small decision-making groups. *J. abnorm. soc. Psychol.,* 1953, 48, 231-238.

107. Berlyne, D. E. *Conflict, arousal and curiosity.* New York: McGraw-Hill, 1960.

108. Berry, B. The inductive approach to the regionalization of economic development. In N. Ginsburg (Ed.), *Essays on geography and economic development.* Chicago: Univer. of Chicago Press, 1960.

109. Bexton, W. H., Heron, W., & Scott, T. H. Effects of decreased variation in the sensory environment. *Canad. J. Psychol.,* 1954, 8, 70-76.

110. *Bibliography on Saliva.* Washington, D.C.: Office of Naval Research, Department of the Navy, ONR Rept. ACR-48, 1960, 447.

111. Billingslea, F. Y. Intercorrelational analysis of certain behavior salients in the rat. *J. comp. Psychol.,* 1942, 34, 203-211.

112. Birren, J. E. A factor analysis of the Wechsler-Bellevue Scale given to an elderly population. *J. consult. Psychol.,* 1952, 16, 399-405.

112. Bischof, L. J. *Interpreting personality*
(a) *theories.* New York: Harper & Row, 1964.

113. Blewett, D. B. An experimental study of the inheritance of intelligence. *J. ment. Sci.,* 1954, 100, 922-933.

114. Block, J. The difference between Q and R. *Psychol. Bull.,* 1955, 62, 356-358.

115. Block, J. *The Q-sort method in personality assessment and psychiatric research.* Springfield, Ill.: Charles C. Thomas, 1961.

116. Bock, R. D. A computer application of a completely general univariate and multivariate analysis of variance. Res. Memo. No. 2. Chapel Hill: Psychometric Lab., Univer. of North Carolina, 1960.

117. Bock, R. D. Components of variance analysis as a structural and discriminal analysis for psychological tests. *Brit. J. statist. Psychol.,* 1960, 13, 151.

118. Bock, R. D. Computation of solution matrices for orthogonal factorial designs. Res. Memo. No. 4. Chapel Hill: Psychometric Lab., Univer. of North Carolina, 1960.

119. Bock, R. D. Multivariate and univariate analysis of variance for any design. Res. Memo. No. 3. Chapel Hill: Psychometric Lab., Univer. of North Carolina, 1960.

120. Bock, R. D. Multivariate analysis of variance of repeated measurements. In C. W. Harris (Ed.), *Problems in measuring change.* Madison: Univer. of Wisconsin Press, 1963.

121. Bock, R. D. Programming univariate and multivariate analysis of variance. *Technometrics,* 1963, 5, 95-117.

122. Bock, R. D. A computer program for univariate and multivariate analysis of variance. In *Proceedings of scientific computing symposium on statistics.* Yorktown Heights: Thomas J. Watson Research Center, 1965.

123. Bock, R. D., & Haggard, E. A. The use of multivariate analysis of variance in psychological research: I. Group differences. II. Individual differences. (Unpublished manuscript, 1962).

124. Bock, R. D., & Haggard, E. A. The use of multivariate analysis of variance in behavioral research. In D. Whitlo (Ed.), *Handbook of measurement in education, psychology, and sociology.* Reading, Mass.: Addison-Wesley. (In press).

125. Bock, R. D., Haggard, E. A., Holtzman, W. H., Beck, S. J., & Beck, A. G. *A comprehensive psychometric study of the Rorschach and Holtzman inkblot techniques.* Chapel Hill: Psychometric Lab., Univer. of North Carolina, 1963.

126. Bolanovich, D. J. Statistical analysis of an industrial rating chart. *J. appl. Psychol.,* 1946, 30, 23-41.

127. Borgatta, E. F. The Make-a-Sentence Test (MAST): A replication study. *J. gen. Psychol.,* 1961, 65, 269-292.

128. Borgatta, E. F. A systematic study of interaction process scores, peer and self-assessments, personality and other variables. *Genet. Psychol. Monogr.,* 1962, 65, 219-291.

129. Borgatta, E. F., Cottrell, L. S., Jr., &

Mann, J. H. The spectrum of individual interaction characteristics: An inter-dimensional analysis. *Psychol. Repts.,* 1958, 4, 279-319.

130. Borgatta, E. F., Cottrell, L. S., Jr., & Meyer, H. J. On the dimensions of group behavior. *Sociometry,* 1956, 19, 223-240.

131. Borgatta, E. F., & Glass, D. C. Personality concomitants of extreme response set (ERS). *J. soc. Psychol.,* 1961, 55, 213-221.

131. Borko, H. *Computer applications in the*
(a) *behavioral sciences.* Englewood Cliffs, N.J.: Prentice-Hall, 1962.

132. Bottenberg, R. A. The exploitation of personnel data by means of a multiple linear regression model. Lackland AFB, Tex.: Personnel Lab., WADD, Rept. No. WADD-TN-60-266, 1960.

133. Bottenberg, R. A., & Christal, R. E. An iterative technique for clustering which retains optimal predictive efficiency. Lackland AFB, Tex.: Personnel Lab., WADD, Rept. No. WADD-TN-61-30, 1961.

134. Botzum, W. A. A factorial study of the reasoning and closure factors. *Psychometrika,* 1951, 16, 361-386.

135. Brace, G. L. Physique, physiology and behavior: An attempt to analyze a part of their roles in the canine biogram. Unpublished doctoral dissertation, Harvard Univer., 1962.

136. Braithwaite, R. B. *Scientific explanations.* Cambridge: Cambridge Univer. Press, 1953.

137. Broadhurst, P. S. Application of biometrical genetics to behavior in rats. *Nature,* 1959, 184, 1517-1518.

138. Broadhurst, P. S. Experiments in psychogenetics: Application of biometrical genetics to the inheritance of behavior. In H. J. Eysenck (Ed.), *Experiments in personality.* Vol. I. *Psychogenetics and psychopharmacology.* London: Routledge & Kegan Paul, 1960.

139. Broadhurst, P. L., & Jinks, J. L. Biometrical genetics and behavior: Reanalysis of published data. *Psychol. Bull.,* 1961, 58, 337-362.

140. Brogden, H. E. A factor analysis of forty character tests. *Psychol. Monogr.,* 1940, 52 (Whole No. 234).

141. Brogden, H. E. A multiple-factor analysis of the character trait intercorrelations published by Sister Mary MacDonough. *J. educ. Psychol.,* 1944, 35, 397-410.

142. Brogden, H. E. The primary personal values measured by the Allport-Vernon Test, "A Study of Values." *Psychol. Monogr.,* 1952, 66 (16) (Whole No. 348).

143. Brogden, H. E., & Thomas, W. F. The primary traits in personality items purposing to measure sociability. *J. Psychol.,* 1943, 16, 85-97.

144. Brokaw, L. D. School and job validation of selection measures for air traffic control training. Lackland AFB, Tex.: Personnel Lab., WADC, Rept. No. WADC-TN-59-39, 1959.

145. Brokaw, L. D. Suggested composition of airman classification instruments. Lackland AFB, Tex.: Personnel Lab., WADD, Rept. No. WADD-TN-60-214, 1960.

146. Brokaw, L. D., & Burgess, G. G. Development of airman classification battery AC-2A. Lackland AFB, Tex.: Air Force Personnel and Training Res. Center, Rept. No. AFPTRC-TR-57-1 (ASTIA Doc. No. 131422), 1957.

147. Brombery, N. S. Maximization and minimization of complicated multivariable functions. *Comm. & Electronics (AIEE trans. Part 1, 80).* January, 1962, 725-730.

148. Bronfenbrenner, U. Toward a theoretical model of parent-child relationships in a social context. In J. C. Glidewell (Ed.), *Parental attitudes and child behavior.* Springfield, Ill.: Charles C. Thomas, 1961.

149. Broverman, D. M. Effects of score transformations in *Q* & *R* factor analysis techniques. *Psychol. Rev.,* 1961, 68, 68-80.

150. Broverman, D. M. Normative and ipsative measurement in psychology. *Psychol. Rev.,* 1962, 69, 295-305.

151. Broverman, D. M. Comments on the vote by Mal Andrew & Forgy. *Psychol. Rev.,* 1963, 70, 119-120.

152. Brunswik, E. *Perception and the representative design of psychological experiments.* Berkeley: Univer. of California Press, 1956.

153. Bryan, J. G. A method for the exact determination of the characteristic equation and latent vectors of a matrix with applications to the discriminant function for more than two groups. Unpublished

doctoral dissertation, Harvard Univer., 1950.

154. Bryan, J. G. The generalized discriminant function: Mathematical foundation and computational routine. *Harvard educ. Rev.,* 1951, 21, 2.

155. Burt, C. L. Experimental tests of general intelligence. *Brit. J. Psychol.,* 1909, 3, 94-177.

156. Burt, C. L. Annual report of the L.C.C. Psychologist, 1915.

157. Burt, C. L. *Distribution and relations of educational abilities.* London: P. S. King, 1917.

158. Burt, C. L. Correlations between persons. *Brit. J. Psychol.,* 1937, 28, 59-96.

159. Burt, C. L. The analysis of temperament. *Brit. J. med. Psychol.,* 1938, 17, 158-188.

160. Burt, C. L. *The factors of the mind: An introduction to factor analysis in psychology.* New York: Macmillan, 1941.

161. Burt, C. L. The factorial analysis of emotional traits. *Charact. & Pers.,* 1939, 7, 238-254.

162. Burt, C. L. Factor analysis of physical growth. *Nature,* 1943, 152, 75.

163. Burt, C. L. The factorial study of physical types. *Man,* 1944, 72, 82-86.

164. Burt, C. L. The relation between eye-colour and defective colour-vision. *Eugen. Rev.,* 1946, 37, 149-156.

165. Burt, C. L. Factor analysis and physical types. *Psychometrika,* 1947, 12, 171-180.

166. Burt, C. L. Factor analysis and canonical correlations. *Brit. J. Psychol.* (Statist. Sec.), 1948, 1, 95-106.

167. Burt, C. L. The factorial study of temperament traits. *Brit. J. Psychol.* (Statist. Sec.), 1948, 1, 178-203.

168. Burt, C. L. The structure of the mind: A review of the results of factor analysis. *Brit. J. educ. Psychol.,* 1949, 19, 100-111, 176-199.

169. Burt, C. L. Tests of significance in factor studies. *Brit. J. Psychol.* (Statist. Sec.), 1952, 5, 109-133.

169. Burt, C. L. *Intelligence and fertility.*
(a) London: Cassell, 1952.

170. Burt, C. L. The differentiation of intellectual abilities. *Brit. J. educ. Psychol.,* 1954, 24, 76-90.

171. Burt, C. L. The inheritance of mental ability. *Amer. Psychologist,* 1958, 13, 1-15.

171. Burt, C. L. The factor analysis of the

(a) Wechsler scale. II. *Brit. J. statist. Psychol.,* 1960, 13, 82-87.

172. Burt, C. L. Francis Galton and his contributions to psychology. *Brit. J. statist. Psychol.,* 1962, 15, 1-49.

173. Burt, C. L. The effects of motivation on intelligence test performance. *Brit. J. statist. Psychol.,* 1963, 16.

174. Burt, C. L., & Banks, C. A factor analysis of body measurements for British adult males. *Ann. Eugenics,* 1946-47, 13, 238-256.

174. Burt, C. L., & Howard, M. The multi-
(a) factoral theory of inheritance. *Brit. J. statist. Psychol.,* 1956, 9, 115-125.

174. Burt, C. L., & Howard, M. The relative
(b) influence of heredity and environment on assessments of intelligence. *Brit. J. statist. Psychol.,* 1957, 10, 99-104.

175. Burt, C. L., & John, E. A factorial analysis of the Terman-Binet Test. *Brit. J. educ. Psychol.,* 1942, 12, 117-127, 156-161.

176. Burt, C. L., & Lewis, R. B. Teaching backward readers. *Brit. J. educ. Psychol.,* 1946, 16, 116-132.

177. Bush, R. R., & Estes, W. K. (Eds.) *Studies in mathematical learning theory.* Stanford, Calif.: Stanford Univer. Press, 1959.

177. Bush, R. R., & Mosteller, F. *Stochastic*
(a) *models for learning.* New York: Wiley, 1955.

177. Butcher, H. J., Ainsworth, M., & Nesbitt,
(b) J. E. Personality factors and school achievement: A comparison of British and American children. *Brit. J. educ. Psychol.,* 1963, 33, 276-285.

178. Cady, L. D., Gertler, M. M., Gottsch, L. G., & Woodbury, M. A. The factor structure of variables concerned with coronary disease. *Behav. Sci.,* 1961, 6, 37-41.

179. Calia, V. F. Use of discriminant analysis in the prediction of scholastic performance. *Personnel guidance J.,* 1960, 39, 184-192.

180. Campbell, D. T. Factors relevant to the validity of experiments in social settings. *Psychol. Bull.,* 1957, 54, 297-312.

181. Campbell, D. T. From description to experimentation: Interpreting trends as quasi-experiments. In C. W. Harris (Ed.), *Problems in measuring change.* Madison: Univer. of Wisconsin Press, 1963.

182. Campbell, D. T., & Clayton, K. N.

Avoiding regression effects in panel studies of communication impact. In *Studies in public communication,* No. 3. Chicago: Dept. of Sociology, Univer. of Chicago, 1961.

183. Campbell, D. T., & Fiske, D. W. Convergent and discriminant validation by the Multitrait-Multimethod Matrix. *Psychol. Bull.,* 1959, 56, 81-105.

184. Campbell, D. T., & Stanley, J. S. Experimental and quasi-experimental designs for research on teaching. In N. L. Gage (Ed.), *Handbook of research on teaching.* Chicago: Rand McNally, 1963.

185. Capell, M. D., & Wohl, J. An approach to the factor structure of clinical judgments. *J. consult. Psychol.,* 1959, 23, 51-53.

186. Carey, N. Factors in the mental processes of school children. *Brit. J. Psychol.,* 1915-1916, 7, 453-490; 8, 70-92, 170-182.

187. Carlson, A. B., & Harrell, W. Voting groups among leading congressmen obtained by means of transposed factor technique. *J. soc. Psychol.,* 1942, 16, 51-65.

188. Carlson, H. B. Factor analysis of memory ability. *J. exp. Psychol.,* 1937, 21, 477-492.

189. Carlson, V. R. Overestimation in size-constancy judgments. *Amer. J. Psychol.,* 1960, 73, 199-213.

190. Carnap, R. Foundations of logic and mathematics. In *International encyclopedia of unified science.* Chicago: Univer. of Chicago Press, 1955.

191. Carran, A. B., Yeudall, L., & Royce, J. R. Voltage level and skin resistance in avoidance conditioning of inbred strains of mice. *J. comp. physiol. Psychol.,* 1964, 58, 427-430.

192. Carrigan, P. M. Extraversion—introversion as a dimension of personality: A reappraisal. *Psychol. Bull.,* 1960, 57, 329-360.

193. Carroll, J. B. A factor analysis of verbal abilities. *Psychometrika,* 1941, 6, 279-307.

194. Carroll, J. B. The factorial representation of mental ability and academic achievement. *Educ. psychol. Measmt,* 1943, 3, 307-332.

195. Carroll, J. B. Oblimin rotation solution in factor analysis. Computing program for the IBM 704. Harvard Univer., 1958.

196. Carroll, J. B. The nature of the data, or how to choose a correlation coefficient. *Psychometrika,* 1961, 26, 347-372.

197. Caspari, E. Genetic basis of behavior. In A. Roe & G. G. Simpson (Eds.)., *Behavior and evolution.* New Haven: Yale Univer. Press, 1958.

198. Cattell, R. B. Experiments on the psychical correlate of the psychogalvanic reflex. *Brit. J. Psychol.,* 1929, 19, 357-386.

199. Cattell, R. B. Intelligence levels in schools of the South-west. *Forum Educ.,* 1930, 8, 201-205.

200. Cattell, R. B. Temperament tests: I. Temperament. *Brit. J. Psychol.,* 1933, 23, 308-329.

201. Cattell, R. B. Temperament tests: II. Tests. *Brit. J. Psychol.,* 1933, 24, 20-49.

202. Cattell, R. B. The measurement of interest. *Charact. & Pers.,* 1935, 4, 147-169.

203. Cattell, R. B. *The fight for our national intelligence.* London: King and Co., 1937.

204. Cattell, R. B. Some changes in social life in a community with a falling intelligence quotient. *Brit. J. Psychol.,* 1938, 28, 430-450.

205. Cattell, R. B. Some theoretical issues in adult intelligence testing. *Psychol. Bull.,* 1941, 38, 592.

206. Cattell, R. B. The description of personality: Basic traits resolved into clusters. *J. abnorm. soc. Psychol.,* 1943, 38, 476-506.

207. Cattell, R. B. Fluctuation of sentiments and attitudes as a measure of character integration and of temperament. *Amer. J. Psychol.,* 1943, 56, 195-216.

208. Cattell, R. B. "Parallel proportional profiles" and other principles for determining the choice of factors by rotation. *Psychometrika,* 1944, 9, 267-283.

209. Cattell, R. B. Psychological measurement: Normative, ipsative, interactive. *Psychol. Rev.,* 1944, 51, 292-303.

210. Cattell, R. B. The description of personality: Principles and findings in a factor analysis. *Amer. J. Psychol.,* 1945, 58, 69-90.

211. Cattell, R. B. The diagnosis and classification of neurotic states: A reinterpretation of Eysenck's factors. *J. nerv. ment. Dis.,* 1945, 102, 576-589.

212. Cattell, R. B. The principal trait clusters for describing personality. *Psychol. Bull.,* 1945, 42, 129-161.

213. Cattell, R. B. *Description and measurement of personality.* Yonkers-on-Hudson, N.Y.: World Book Co., 1946.

214. Cattell, R. B. The ergic theory of attitude and sentiment measurement. *Educ. psychol. Measmt,* 1947, 7, 221-246.

215. Cattell, R. B. Confirmation and clarification of primary personality factors. *Psychometrika,* 1947, 12, 197-220.

216. Cattell, R. B. The primary personality factors in women compared with those in men. *Brit. J. Psychol.* (Statist. Sec.), 1948, 1, 114-130.

217. Cattell, R. B. Concepts and methods in the measurement of group syntality. *Psychol. Rev.,* 1948, 55, 48-63.

218. Cattell, R. B. Primary personality factors in the realm of objective tests. *J. Pers.,* 1948, 16, 459-487.

219. Cattell, R. B. The dimensions of culture patterns by factorization of national characters. *J. abnorm. soc. Psychol.,* 1949, 44, 443-469.

220. Cattell, R. B. r_p and other coefficients of pattern similarity. *Psychometrika,* 1949, 14, 279-298.

221. Cattell, R. B. A note on factor invariance and the indentification of factors. *Brit. J. Psychol.* (Statist. Sec.), 1949, 2, 134-138.

222. Cattell, R. B. The discovery of ergic structure in man in terms of common attitudes. *J. abnorm. soc. Psychol.,* 1950, 45, 598-618.

223. Cattell, R. B. The fate of national intelligence: Test of a thirteen-year prediction. *Eugen. Rev.,* 1950, 42, 136-148.

224. Cattell, R. B. The principal culture patterns discoverable in the syntal dimensions of existing nations. *J. soc. Psychol.,* 1950, 32, 215-253.

225. Cattell, R. B. The main personality factors in questionnaire, self-estimate material. *J. soc. Psychol.,* 1950, 31, 3-38.

226. Cattell, R. B. *Personality: A systematical theoretical and factual study.* New York: McGraw-Hill, 1950.

227. Cattell, R. B. A factorization of tests of personality source traits. *Brit. J. Psychol.* (Statist. Sec.), 1951, 4, 165-178.

228. Cattell, R. B. On the disuse and misuse of P, Q, Qs, and O techniques in clinical psychology. *J. clin. Psychol.,* 1951, 7, 203-214.

229. Cattell, R. B. *Factor analysis.* New York: Harper, 1952.

230. Cattell, R. B. The three basic factor-analytic research designs — Their interrelations and derivatives. *Psychol. Bull.,* 1952, 49, 499-520.

231. Cattell, R. B. A quantitative analysis of the changes in the culture pattern of Great Britain 1837-1937, by P-technique. *Acta Psychol.,* 1953, 9, 99-121.

231. Cattell, R. B. Research designs in psy-
(a) chological genetics with special reference to the multiple variance analysis method. *Amer. J. hum. Genet.,* 1953, 5, 76-93.

232. Cattell, R. B. Growing points in factor analysis. *Austral. J. Psychol.,* 1954, 6, 105-140.

233. Cattell, R. B. Personality structures as learning and motivation patterns — a theme for the integration of methodologies. In *Learning theory, personality theory, and clinical research. The Kentucky Symposium.* New York: Wiley, 1954.

234. Cattell, R. B. *The objective-analytic personality factor battery.* Champaign, Ill.: Institute for Personality and Ability Testing, 1955.

235. Cattell, R. B. Psychiatric screening of flying personnel. Personality structure in objective tests — A study of 1,000 air force students in basic pilot training. Randolph Field, Tex.: Air Univer. School of Aviation Medicine (Project No. 21-0202-0007, Rept. No. 9), 1955.

236. Cattell, R. B. Personality and motivation theory based on structural measurement. In J. L. McCary, *Psychology of personality.* New York: Logos, 1956.

237. Cattell, R. B. Validation and intensification of the Sixteen Personality Factor Questionnaire. *J. clin. Psychol.,* 1956, 12, 205-214.

238. Cattell, R. B. A shortened "basic English" version (form C) of the 16 P.F. questionnaire. *J. soc. Psychol.,* 1956, 44, 257-278.

239. Cattell, R. B. Second-order personality factors in the questionnaire realm. *J. consult. Psychol.,* 1956, 20, 411-418.

240. Cattell, R. B. *Personality and motivation structure and measurement.* Yonkers-on-Hudson, N.Y.: World Book Co., 1957.

241. Cattell, R. B. A universal index for

psychological factors. *Psychologia,* 1957, 1, 74-85.

241. Cattell, R. B. The conceptual and test
(a) distinction of neuroticism and anxiety. *J. clin. Psychol.,* 1957, 13, 221-233.

242. Cattell, R. B. The dynamic calculus: A system of concepts derived from objective motivation measurement. In G. Lindzey (Ed.), *The assessment of human motives.* New York: Rinehart, 1958.

243. Cattell, R. B. Extracting the correct number of factors in factor analysis. *Educ. psychol. Measmt,* 1958, 18, 791-838.

244. Cattell, R. B. A need for alertness to multivariate experimental findings in integrative surveys. *Psychol. Bull.,* 1958, 55, 253-256.

245. Cattell, R. B. Anxiety, extraversion, and other second-order personality factors in children. *J. Pers.,* 1959, 27, 464-476.

246. Cattell, R. B. The dynamic calculus: Concepts and crucial experiments. In M. R. Jones (Ed.), *Nebraska symposium of motivation, 1959.* Lincoln: Univer. of Nebraska Press, 1959. Pp. 84-134.

247. Cattell, R. B. Personality theory growing from multivariate quantitative experiment. In S. Koch, *Psychology. A study of a science.* New York: McGraw-Hill, 1959.

248. Cattell, R. B. The multiple abstract variance analysis equations and solutions: For nature-nurture research on continuous variables. *Psychol. Rev.,* 1960, 67, 353-372.

249. Cattell, R. B. Statistical methods and logical considerations in investigating personality inheritance. *Proc. second int. Congr. hum. Genet.,* Rome, Sept. 6-12, 1961. Pp. 1712-1717.

250. Cattell, R. B. Theory of situational, instrument, second order, and refraction factors in personality structure research. *Psychol. Bull.,* 1961, 58, 160-174.

251. Cattell, R. B. The basis of recognition and interpretation of factors. *Educ. psychol. Measmt,* 1962, 22, 4, 667-697.

252. Cattell, R. B. Group theory, personality and role: A model for experimental researches. In F. A. Geldard (Ed.), *Defence psychology.* Oxford: Pergamon, 1962. Pp. 209-259.

253. Cattell, R. B. Problems and techniques of quantifying intra-individual serial measurements. Paper read at Amer. Psychol. Ass., St. Louis, Sept. 3, 1962.

254. Cattell, R. B. The relational simplex theory of equal interval and absolute scaling. *Acta Psychol.,* 1962, 20, 139-158.

255. Cattell, R. B. The task and opportunities for multivariate experimental psychologists. In C. Wrigley, Conf. Dir., Symposium on Research and Teaching Methods in Multivariate Experimental Design. Office of Naval Research Acct. No. 71-23-40, 1962. (Mimeographed.)

256. Cattell, R. B. Formulating the environmental situation, and its perception, in behavior theory. In S. B. Sells (Ed.), *Stimulus determinants of behavior.* New York: Ronald Press, 1963. Pp. 46-75.

257. Cattell, R. B. The structuring of change by *P* technique and incremental *R* technique. In C. W. Harris (Ed.), *Problems in measuring change.* Madison: Univer. of Wisconsin Press, 1963.

258. Cattell, R. B. Theory of fluid and crystallized intelligence: A critical experiment. *J. educ. Psychol.,* 1963, 54, 1-22.

259. Cattell, R. B. Personality, role, mood, and situation-perception: A unifying theory of modulators. *Psychol. Rev.,* 1963, 70, 1-18.

259. Cattell, R. B. The interaction of heredi-
(a) tary and environmental influences. *Brit. J. statist. Psychol.,* 1963, 16, 191-210.

260. Cattell, R. B. Validity and reliability: A proposed more basic set of concepts. *J. educ. Psychol.,* 1964, 55, 1, 1-22.

260. Cattell, R. B. The parental early repres-
(a) sive hypothesis for the "authoritarian" personality factor, U.I. 28. *J. genet. Psychol.,* 1964, 106, 333-349.

261. Cattell, R. B. Higher order structures: Reticular vs. hierarchical formulae for their interpretation. Chap. 14 in C. Banks & P. L. Broadhurst (Eds.), *Studies in psychology* (presented to Cyril Burt). London: Univer. of London Press, 1965.

262. Cattell, R. B. *The present status of the confactor or proportional profiles factor resolution method.* Spec. Publ. No. 20. Urbana, Ill.: Lab. of Personality Assessment and Group Behavior, 1965.

262. Cattell, R. B. *The scientific analysis of*
(a) *personality.* Harmondsworth, Eng.: Penguin, 1965.

263. Cattell, R. B. The configurative method for surer identification of personality dimensions, notably in child study. *Psychol. Repts.,* 1965, 16, 269-270.

263. Cattell, R. B. Evaluating therapy as total
(a) personality change: Theory and available instruments. *Amer. J. Psychother.,* 1966, 20 (1), 69-88.

264. Cattell, R. B. The scree test of the number of significant factors. (In press).

264. Cattell, R. B. The theory of fluid and
(a) crystallized intelligence checked at the 4-6 year-old level. (In press).

265. Cattell, R. B., & Adelson, M. The dimensions of social change in the U.S.A. as determined by *P* technique. *Soc. Forces,* 1951, 30, 190-201.

266. Cattell, R. B., & Baggaley, A. R. The objective measurement of attitude motivation: development and evaluation of principles and devices. *J. Pers.,* 1956, 24, 401-423.

267. Cattell, R. B., & Baggaley, A. R. A confirmation of ergic and engram structures in attitudes objectively measured. *Austral. J. Psychol.,* 1958, 10, 287-318.

268. Cattell, R. B., & Baggaley, A. R. The salient variable similarity index for factor matching. *Brit. J. statist. Psychol.,* 1960, 13, 33-46.

268. Cattell, R. B., & Beloff, H. *The High*
(a) *School Personality Questionnaire.* Champaign, Ill.: Institute for Personality and Ability Testing, 1960.

269. Cattell, R. B., Karson, S., & Nuttall, R. *Handbook for the I.P.A.T. High School Personality Questionnaire.* (rev. ed.) Champaign, Ill.: Institute for Personality and Ability Testing, 1962.

270. Cattell, R. B., Blewett, D. B., & Beloff, J. R. The inheritance of personality: A multiple variance analysis determination of approximate nature-nurture ratios for primary personality factors in *Q* data. *Amer. J. hum. Genet.,* 1955, 7, 122-146.

271. Cattell, R. B., Breul, H., & Hartman, H. P. An attempt at more refined definition of the cultural dimensions of syntality in modern nations. *Amer. sociol. Rev.,* 1952, 17, 408-421.

272. Cattell, R. B., & Cattell, A. K. S. Factor

rotation for proportional profiles: Analytical solution and an example. *Brit. J. statist. Psychol.,* 1955, 8, 83-92.

273. Cattell, R. B., Cattell, A. K., & Rhymer, R. M. P-technique demonstrated in determining psycho-physiological source traits in a normal individual. *Psychometrika,* 1947, 12, 267-288.

274. Cattell, R. B., & Coan, R. W. Child personality structure as revealed in teachers' behavior ratings. *J. clin. Psychol.,* 1957, 13, 315-327.

275. Cattell, R. B., & Coan, R. W. Personality factors in middle childhood as revealed in parents' ratings. *Child Develpm.,* 1957, 28, 439-458.

276. Cattell, R. B., & Coan, R. W. Personality dimensions in the questionnaire responses of six and seven-year-olds. *Brit. J. educ. Psychol.,* 1958, 28, 232-242.

277. Cattell, R. B., & Coan, R. W. Objective-test assessment of the primary personality dimensions in middle childhood. *Brit. J. Psychol.,* 1959, 50, 235-252.

278. Cattell, R. B., & Coulter, M. A. Principles of behavioral taxonomy and the taxonome program. (In press).

279. Cattell, R. B., & Cross, K. Comparison of the ergic and self-sentiment structures found in dynamic traits by R- and P-techniques. *J. Pers.,* 1952, 21, 250-271.

279. Cattell, R. B., Delhees, K. H., Tatro, D.
(a) F., & Nesselroade, J. R. Personality structure in primary objective test factors appearing in a mixed normal and psychotic sample. (In press).

280. Cattell, R. B., & Dickman, K. A dynamic model of physical influences demonstrating the necessity of oblique simple structure. *Psychol. Bull.,* 1962, 59, 389-400.

281. Cattell, R. B., & Digman, J. A theory of the structure of perturbations in observer ratings and questionnaire data in personality research. *Behav. Sci.,* 1964, 9, 341-358.

282. Cattell, R. B., & Drevdahl, J. E. A comparison of the personality profile (16 P.F.) of eminent researchers with that of eminent teachers and administrators, and of the general population. *Brit. J. Psychol.,* 1955, 46, 248-261.

283. Cattell, R. B., Dubin, S. S., & Saunders, D. R. Verification of hypothesized factors in one hundred and fifteen objective

personality test designs. *Psychometrika,* 1954, 19, 209-230.

284. Cattell, R. B., Dubin, S. S., & Saunders, D. R. Personality structure in psychotics by factorization of objective clinical tests. *J. ment. Sci.,* 1954, 100, 154-176.

285. Cattell, R. B., & Eber, H. W. *The Sixteen Personality Factor Questionnaire Test.* (rev. ed.) Champaign, Ill.: Institute for Personality and Ability Testing, 1966.

285. Cattell, R. B., Feingold, S., & Sarason, S.
(a) A culture free intelligence test: II. Evaluation of cultural influence on test performance. *J. educ. Psychol.,* 1941, 32, 81-100.

286. Cattell, R. B., & Foster, M. J. The roto-plot program for multiple single-plane, visually-guided rotation. *Behav. Sci.,* 1963, 8, 156-165.

286. Cattell, R. B., & Gibbons, B. D. The
(a) personality factor structure of the combined Cattell 16 P. F. and Guilford questionnaires. (In press).

287. Cattell, R. B., & Gorsuch, R. L. Personal communication, 1963.

288. Cattell, R. B., & Gorsuch, R. L. The uniqueness and significance of simple structure demonstrated by contrasting organic "natural structure" and "random structure" data. *Psychometrika,* 1963, 28, 55-67.

289. Cattell, R. B., & Gorsuch, R. L. The definition and measurement of national morale and morality. *J. soc. Psychol.,* 1965, 67 (2nd half), 77-96.

290. Cattell, R. B., & Gruen, W. The personality factor structure of 11 year old children in terms of behavior rating data. *J. clin. Psychol.,* 1953, 9, 255-266.

291. Cattell, R. B., & Gruen, W. Primary personality factors in the questionnaire medium for children eleven to fourteen years old. *Educ. psychol. Measmt,* 1954, 14, 50-76.

292. Cattell, R. B., & Gruen, W. The primary personality factors in 11 year old children, by objective tests. *J. Pers.,* 1955, 23, 460-478.

293. Cattell, R. B. The discovery of ergic structure in man in terms of common attitudes. *J. abnorm. soc. Psychol.,* 1950, 45, 598-618.

294. Cattell, R. B., Heist, A. B., Heist, P. A., & Stewart, R. G. The objective measure-

ment of dynamic traits. *Educ. psychol. Measmt,* 1950, 10, 224-248.

295. Cattell, R. B., & Horn, J. An integrating study of the factor structure of adult attitude interests. *Genet. Psychol. Monogr.,* 1963, 67, 89-149.

295. Cattell, R. B., & Horn, J. L. Theoretical
(a) problems in quantifying dynamic traits, with particular reference to MAT, SMAT and ipsative scoring. *Austral. J. Psychol.,* 1966.

296. Cattell, R. B., Horn, J., & Butcher, H. J. The dynamic structure of attitudes in adults: A description of some established factors and of their measurement by the Motivational Analysis Test. *Brit. J. Psychol.,* 1962, 53, 57-69.

297. Cattell, R. B., Horn, J. L., Radcliffe, J. A., & Sweney, A. B. *The motivation analysis test, MAT.* Champaign, Ill.: Institute for Personality and Ability Testing, 1964.

298. Cattell, R. B., & Howarth, E. Verification of objective test personality factor patterns in middle childhood. *J. genet. Psychol.,* 1964, 104, 331-349.

298. Cattell, R. B., & King, J. *The Contact*
(a) *Personality Factor Questionnaire.* Champaign, Ill.: Institute for Personality and Ability Testing, 1955.

299. Cattell, R. B., Knapp, R. R., & Scheier, I. H. Second-order personality factor structure in the objective test realm. *J. consult. Psychol.,* 1961, 25, 345-352.

299. Cattell, R. B., Kristy, N., & Stice, G. F.
(a) A first approximation to nature-nurture ratios for eleven primary personality factors in objective tests. *J. abnorm. soc. Psychol.,* 1952, 54, 143-159.

300. Cattell, R. B., & Luborsky, L. B. P-technique demonstrated as a new clinical method for determining personality and symptom structure. *J. gen. Psychol.,* 1950, 42, 3-24.

301. Cattell, R. B., Maxwell, E. F., Light, B. H., & Unger, M. P. The objective measurement of attitudes. *Brit. J. Psychol.,* 1949, 40, 81-90.

301. Cattell, R. B., May, M., & Meeland, T.
(a) Occupational profiles on the 16 Personality Factor Questionnaire, *Occup. Psychol.,* 1956, 30, 10-19.

301. Cattell, R. B., & Meredith, G. M. Con-
(b) temporary theories of personality: The psychologist's eye view. In A. M. Freed-

man & H. I. Kaplan (Eds.), *Comprehensive textbook of psychiatry.* Baltimore: Williams & Wilkins, 1966.

301. Cattell, R. B., & Meschieri, L. The in-
(c) ternational, cross-cultural constancy of personality factors, examined on the 16 P.F. (In press).

302. Cattell, R. B., & Miller, A. A confirmation of the ergic and self-sentiment patterns among dynamic traits (attitude variables) by *R*-technique. *Brit. J. Psychol.,* 1952, 43, 280-294.

303. Cattell, R. B., & Morony, J. H. The use of the 16 P.F. in distinguishing homosexuals, normals, and general criminals. *J. consult. Psychol.,* 1962, 26, 531-540.

304. Cattell, R. B., & Muerle, J. L. The "maxplane" program for factor rotation to oblique simple structure. *Educ. psychol. Measmt,* 1960, 20, 569-590.

305. Cattell, R. B., & Nesselroade, J. The IPAT seven factor state battery. Champaign, Ill.: Institute for Personality and Ability Testing, 1961.

306. Cattell, R. B., & Nesselroade, J. R. Untersuchung der inter-kulturellen Konstanz der Persoenlichkeitsfaktoren im 16 P.F. test. *Psychol. Beitraege,* 1965, 8, 502-515.

307. Cattell, R. B., & Nesselroade, J. R. The "fidelity" plasmode, with known higher order structure and error. *Multiv. behav. Res.* (In press).

307. Cattell, R. B., & Nesselroade, J. R.
(a) "Likeness" and "completeness" theories examined by 16 Personality Factor measures on stably and unstably married couples. (In press).

308. Cattell, R. B., & Pawlik, K. The use of algebraically mutually dependent variables in factor analytic research. (In press).

309. Cattell, R. B., & Peterson, D. R. Personality structure in 4-5-year-olds, by factoring observed, time-sampled behavior. *Ras. Psico. Gen. Clin.,* 1958, 3, 3-21.

310. Cattell, R. B., & Peterson, D. R. Personality structure in four and five year olds in terms of objective tests. *J. clin. Psychol.,* 1959, 15, 355-369.

311. Cattell, R. B., Pichot, P., & Rennes, P. Constance inter-culturelle des facteurs de personnalité mesurés par le test 16 P.F.: II. Comparaison franco-américaine. *Rev. Psychol. appl.,* 11, 165-196.

312. Cattell, R. B., & Radcliffe, J. A. Reliabilities and validities of simple and extended weighted and buffered unifactor scales. *Brit. J. statist. Psychol.,* 1962, 15, 113-128.

313. Cattell, R. B., Radcliffe, J. A., & Sweney, A. B. The nature and measurement of components of motivation. *Genet. Psychol. Monogr.,* 1963, 68, 49-211.

313. Cattell, R. B., & Rickels, K. Diagnostic
(a) power of IPAT objective analytic and motivational tests. *Arch. gen. Psychiat.,* 1964, 11, 459-465.

314. Cattell, R. B., Rickels, K., Wiese, O., Gray, B., Mallin, A., Yee, R., & Aaronson, H. G. The effects of psychotherapy on measured anxiety and regression. *Amer. J. Psychother.,* 1966, 20, 261-269.

315. Cattell, R. B., & Saunders, D. R. Interrelation and matching of personality factors from behavior rating, questionnaire, and objective test data. *J. soc. Psychol.,* 1950, 31, 243-260.

316. Cattell, R. B., & Saunders, D. R. Beitrage zur Faktoren-analyse der Persönlichkeit. *Z. exp. angew. Psychol.,* 1955, 2, 325-357.

317. Cattell, R. B., Saunders, D. R., & Stice, G. F. The dimensions of syntality in small groups. *Hum. Relat.,* 1953, 6, 331-356.

318. Cattell, R. B., & Scheier, I. H. Factors in personality change: A discussion of the condition-response incremental design and application to 69 personality response measures and three stimulus conditions. Adv. Publ. No. 9. Urbana: Univer. of Illinois, Lab. for Personality Assessment and Group Behavior, 1958.

319. Cattell, R. B., & Scheier, I. H. The nature of anxiety: A review of thirteen multivariate analyses comprising 814 variables. *Psychol. Rep.,* 1958, 4, 351-388.

320. Cattell, R. B., & Scheier, I. H. The objective test measurement of neuroticism, U.I. 23(−): A review of eight factor analytic studies. *Indian J. Psychol.,* 1958, 33, 217-236.

321. Cattell, R. B., & Scheier, I. H. Extension of meaning of objective test personality factors. Especially into anxiety, neuroticism, questionnaire, and physical factors. *J. gen. Psychol.,* 1959, 61, 287-315.

322. Cattell, R. B., & Scheier, I. H. The IPAT anxiety scale. Champaign, Ill.: Institute

for Personality and Ability Testing, 1959.

323. Cattell, R. B., & Scheier, I. H. Handbook for the objective-analytic (O-A) anxiety battery. Champaign, Ill.: Institute for Personality and Ability Testing, 1960.

324. Cattell, R. B., & Scheier, I. H. Stimuli related to stress, neuroticism, excitation, and anxiety response patterns: Illustrating a new multivariate experimental design. *J. abnorm. soc. Psychol.,* 1960, 60, 195-204.

325. Cattell, R. B., & Scheier, I. H. *The meaning and measurement of neuroticism and anxiety.* New York: Ronald Press, 1961.

325. Cattell, R. B., Scheier, I. H., & Lorr, M.
(a) Recent advances in the measurement of anxiety, neuroticism, and the psychotic syndromes. *Ann. N.Y. Acad. Sci.,* 1962, 93, 815-856.

326. Cattell, R. B., Schiff, H., et al. Psychiatric screening of flying personnel: Prediction of training criteria by objective personality test factors and development of the seven factor personality test. Randolph Field, Tex.: USAF School of Aviation Medicine, Rept. No. 10, Contract No. AF 33(038)-19569, Project No. 21-0202-0007, 1953.

327. Cattell, R. B., & Schoenemann, P. Taxonome: A computer program for determining types and cliques. (In press).

327. Cattell, R. B., & Sealy, A. P. *The general*
(a) *relations of changes in personality and interest to changes in school performance: An exploratory study.* Final Rept. to Office of Education on Coop. Res. Program Project No. 1411. Urbana, Ill.: Laboratory for Personality Assessment and Group Behavior.

327. Cattell, R. B., & Stice, G. F. Four formu-
(b) lae for selecting leaders on the basis of personality. *Hum. Relat.,* 1954, 7, 493-507.

328. Cattell, R. B., & Stice, G. F. *The behavior of small groups.* Champaign, Ill.: Institute for Personality and Ability Testing, 1960.

329. Cattell, R. B., Stice, G. F., & Eber, H. *The 16 Personality Factor Questionnaire.* Champaign, Ill.: Institute for Personality and Ability Testing, 1949.

330. Cattell, R. B., Stice, G. F., & Kristy, N. F. A first approximation to nature-nurture ratios for eleven primary personality factors in objective tests. *J. abnorm. soc. Psychol.,* 1957, 54, 143-159.

331. Cattell, R. B., & Sullivan, W. The scientific nature of factors: A demonstration by cups of coffee. *Behav. Sci.,* 1962, 7, 184-193.

332. Cattell, R. B., & Sweney, A. B. Components measurable in manifestations of mental conflict. *J. abnorm. soc. Psychol.,* 1964, 68, 479-490.

333. Cattell, R. B., & Sweney, A. B. The school motivation analysis test, SMAT. Champaign, Ill.: Institute for Personality and Ability Testing, 1964.

334. Cattell, R. B., Sweney, A. B., & Radcliffe, J. A. The objective measurement of motivation structure in children. *J. clin. Psychol.,* 1960, 16, 227-232.

334. Cattell, R. B., & Tatro, D. F. The per-
(a) sonality factors, objectively measured, which distinguish psychotics from normals. *Behav. Res. Ther.,* 1966, 4, 1-13.

334. Cattell, R. B., Tatro, D. F., & Komlos, E.
(b) The diagnosis and inferred structure of paranoid and non-paranoid schizophrenia from the 16 P.F. profile. *Indian psychol. Rev.,* 1964, 1, 52-61.

334. Cattell, R. B., Tatro, D. F., & Komlos, E.
(c) The diagnosis and inferred structure of paranoid and non-paranoid schizophrenia from the 16 P.F. profile: II. Concluding installment. *Indian psychol. Rev.,* 1965, 1, 108-115.

335. Cattell, R. B., & Tsujioka, B. The importance of factor-trueness and validity, versus homogeneity and orthogonality, in test scales. *Educ. psychol. Measmt,* 1964, 24, 3-30.

335. Cattell, R. B., & Van Egeren, L. F. Psycho-
(a) physiological states of depression: A P-technique analysis. (In preparation).

336. Cattell, R. B., & Warburton, F. W. A cross cultural comparison of patterns of extraversion and anxiety. *Brit. J. Psychol.,* 1961, 52, 3-15.

337. Cattell, R. B., & Warburton, F. W. Objective personality and motivation tests. A theoretical introduction and practical compendium. Urbana: Univer. of Illinois Press, 1967.

338. Cattell, R. B., & Willson, J. L. Contributions concerning mental inheritance: I. Of intelligence. *Brit. J. educ. Psychol.,* 1938, 8, 129-149.

339. Cattell, R. B., et al. *The objective-analytic (O-A) personality factor batteries.* Champaign, Ill.: Institute for Personality and Ability Testing, 1955.

340. Chance, M. R. A. The role of convulsions in behavior. *Behav. Sci.,* 1957, 2, 30-45.

340. Chapman, L. J., & Bock, R. D. Com-
(a) ponents of variance due to acquiescence and content in the *F*-scale measure of authoritarianism. *Psychol. Bull.,* 1958, 55, 328-333.

341. Chapman, R. L. The MacQuarrie test for mechanical ability. *Psychometrika,* 1948, 13, 175-179.

342. Chassan, J. B. Statistical inference and the single case in clinical design. *Psychiatry,* 1960, 23, 173-184.

343. Chein, I. An experimental study of verbal, numerical, and spatial factors in mental organization. *Psychol. Rec.,* 1939, 3, 71-94.

344. Cherry, C. *On human communication.* New York: Science Editions, Inc., 1961.

345. Chomsky, N. *Syntactic structures.* 's-Gravenhage: Mouton & Co., 1957.

346. Christal, R. E., & Madden, J. M. Air force research on job evaluation procedures. Lackland AFB, Tex., Personnel Lab., ASD., Rept. No. ASD-TN-61-46, 1961.

347. Claridge, G. The excitation-inhibition balance in neurotics. In H. J. Eysenck (Ed.), *Experiments in personality.* Vol. II. London: Routledge and Kegan Paul, 1960.

348. Clark, K. E. *Vocational interests of nonprofessional men.* Minneapolis: Univer. of Minnesota Press, 1961.

349. Clemans, W. V. An analytic and experimental examination of some properties of ipsative measures. Unpublished doctoral dissertation, Univer. of Washington, 1956.

350. Coan, R. W. Basic forms of covariation and concomitance designs. *Psychol. Bull.,* 1961, 58, 317-324.

351. Coan, R. W., & Cattell, R. B. Reproducible personality factors in middle childhood. *J. clin. Psychol.,* 1958, 14, 339-345.

352. Coan, R. W., & Cattell, R. B. The development of the early school personality questionnaire. *J. exp. Educ.,* 1959, 28, 143-152.

353. Cobb, B. B. Problems in air traffic management: II. Prediction of success in Air Traffic Controller school. Rept. No. 62-2. Oklahoma City, Okla.: FAA Civil Aeromedical Research Institute, 1962.

354. Coblentz, W. W., & Emerson, W. B. Relative sensitivity of the average eye to light of different colors and some practical applications to radiation problems. *Bull. Bur. Stds.,* 1918, 4 (No. 2), 167-236.

355. Cochran, W. G. *Sampling techniques.* New York: Wiley, 1963.

356. Cohen, Jacob. A comparative analysis of factors underlying intelligence test performance of different neuropsychiatric groups. *Microfilm abstract,* 1950, 10, 313-315 (see Dissertation Abstracts).

357. Cohen, Jacob. A factor-analytically based rationale for the Wechsler-Bellevue. *J. consult. Psychol.,* 1952, 16, 272-277.

358. Cohen, Jacob. Factors underlying Wechsler-Bellevue performance of three neuropsychiatric groups. *J. abnorm. soc. Psychol.,* 1952, 47, 359-365.

359. Cohen, Jacob. An aid in the computation of correlations based on Q sorts. *Psychol. Bull.,* 1957, 54, 138-139.

360. Cohen, Jacob. A factor-analytically based rationale for the Wechsler Adult Intelligence Scale. *J. consult. Psychol.,* 1957, 21, 451-457.

361. Cohen, Jacob. The factorial structure of the WAIS between early adulthood and old age. *J. consult. Psychol.,* 1957, 21, 283-290.

362. Cohen, Jacob. The factorial structure of the WISC at ages 7-6, 10-6, and 13-6. *J. consult. Psychol.,* 1959, 23, 285-299.

362. Cohen, Jacob, Gunel, L., & Stumpf, J. C.
(a) Dimensions of psychiatric symptom ratings determined at thirteen time points from hospital admission. *J. consult. Psychol.,* 1966, 30, 39-44.

363. Cohen, John. Physical types and their relation to psychotic types. *J. ment. Sci.,* 1940, 86, 602.

364. Cohen, John. Are differences in size between parts of the body due to general or specific factors? *Proc. nat. Acad. Sci.,* 1940, 26, 524-526.

365. Cohen, John. Physique, size and proportions. *Brit. J. med. Psychol.,* 1941, 18, 323-337.

366. Cohen, Jozef. Color vision and factor

analysis. *Psychol. Rev.,* 1949, 46, 224-243.

367. Cohen, M. R., & Nagel, E. *An introduction to logic and scientific method.* New York: Harcourt, Brace, 1934.

367. Colby, K. M. Computer simulation of a
(a) neurotic process. In S. S. Tomkins & S. Messick (Eds.), *Computer simulation of personality.* New York: Wiley, 1963.

367. Colby, K. M. Psychotherapeutic proces-
(b) ses. *Ann. Rev. Psychol.,* 1964, 15, 347-370.

368. Comrey, A. L. A factorial study of achievement in West Point courses. *Educ. psychol. Measmt,* 1949, 9, 193-209.

369. Comrey, A. L. A factor analysis of items on the K scale of the MMPI. *Educ. psychol. Measmt,* 1958, 18, 633-639.

370. Comrey, A. L. A study of thirty-five personality dimensions. *Educ. psychol. Measmt,* 1962, 22, 543-552.

371. Comrey, A. L., & Soufi, A. Further investigations of some factors found in MMPI items. *Educ. psychol. Measmt,* 1960, 20, 777-786.

372. Conger, J. J., Sawrey, W. L., & Krause, L. F. A reanalysis of Beck's "six schizophrenias." *J. consult. Psychol.,* 1956, 20, 83-87.

373. Connor, D. V. The effect of temperamental traits upon the group intelligence test performance of children. Unpublished doctoral dissertation, Univer. of London, 1952.

374. Cook, D. R. A study of the relationship of the meaning of selected concepts to achievement and ability. Unpublished doctoral dissertation, Indiana Univer., 1959.

375. Cook, E. B. A factor analysis of acuity measurements obtained with commercial screening devices and by standard clinical methods. New London, Conn.: Naval Res. Lab., 1948, Prog. Rept. No. 4, Proj. MN-003-011 (x-493).

376. Cook, E. B. A factor analysis of personnel selection data: Intra and inter area relationships of biochemical, physiological, psychological and anthropometric measures. Camp Lejeune, N.C.: U.S. Navy Medical Field Res. Lab., 1962, 398.

377. Cook, E. B., & Wherry, R. J. A study of the interrelationships of psychological and physiological measures on submarine enlisted men. History, experimental design and statistical treatment of data. New London, Conn.: U.S. Naval Medical Field Res. Lab., 1949, Rept. No. 1, Proj. No. NM-003-017, p. 45.

378. Cook, E. B., & Wherry, R. J. A factor analysis of MMPI and aptitude test data. *J. appl. Psychol.,* 1950, 34, 260-266.

379. Cooley, C. H. *Social organization.* New York: Scribner's, 1909.

380. Cooley, W. W. Identifying potential scientists: A multivariate approach. *School Science & Math.,* 1959, 59, 381-396.

381. Cooley, W. W., & Lohnes, P. R. *Multivariate procedures for the behavioral sciences.* New York: Wiley, 1962.

382. Coombs, C. H. A criterion for significant common factor variance. *Psychometrika,* 1941, 6, 267-272.

383. Coombs, C. H. A factorial study of number ability. *Psychometrika,* 1941, 6, 161-189.

384. Coombs, C. H. Mathematical models in psychological scaling. *J. Amer. Statist. Ass.,* 1951, 46, 480-489.

385. Coombs, C. H. The scale grid: Some interrelations of data models. *Psychometrika,* 1956, 21, 313-330.

386. Coombs, C. H., & Kao, R. C. Nonmetric factor analysis. *Bull. Dept. Engng Res., No. 38.* Ann Arbor: Univer. of Michigan, 1955.

387. Corter, H. M. Factor analysis of some reasoning tests. *Psychol. Monogr.,* 1952, 66 (Whole No. 340).

388. Cottle, W. C. A factorial study of the Multiphasic, Strong, Kuder, and Bell inventories using a population of adult males. *Psychometrika,* 1950, 15, 25-47.

389. Court, A. T. Measuring joint causation. *J. Amer. Statist. Ass.,* 1931, 25, 245-254.

389. Couch, A., & Keniston, K. Yeasayers and
(a) naysayers: Agreeing response set as a personality variable. *J. abnorm. soc. Psychol.,* 1960, 60, 151-174.

390. Courtis, S. A. *Maturation units and how to use them.* Detroit, Mich.: Author, 1950.

390. Cronbach, L. J. Response sets and test
(a) validity. *Educ. psychol. Measmt,* 1946, 6, 475-494.

391. Cronbach, L. J. Further evidence on response sets and test designs. *Educ. psychol. Measmt,* 1950, 10, 3-31.

392. Cronbach, L. J. Coefficient alpha and the internal structure of tests. *Psychometrika,* 1951, 16, 297-334.

393. Cronbach, L. J. Correlations between persons as a research tool. In O. H. Mowrer (Ed.), *Psychotherapy: Theory and research*. New York: Ronald, 1953.

394. Cronbach, L. J. The two disciplines of scientific psychology. *Amer. Psychologist*, 1957, 12, 671-684.

395. Cronbach, L. J. *Essentials of psychological testing*. New York: Harper, 1960.

396. Cronbach, L. J., & Gleser, G. C. Assessing similarity between profiles. *Psychol. Bull.*, 1953, 50, 456-473.

397. Cronbach, L. J., & Gleser, G. C. *Psychological tests and personnel decisions*. Urbana: Univer. of Illinois Press, 1957; 2nd ed., 1965.

398. Cronbach, L. J., & Meehl, P. E. Construct validity in psychological tests. *Psychol. Bull.*, 1955, 52, 281-302.

399. Cross, K. Patricia. Determination of ergic structure of common attitudes by *P*-technique. Unpublished master's thesis, Univer. of Illinois, 1951.

400. Cureton, T. K. *Physical fitness, appraisal and guidance*. St. Louis, Mo.: C. V. Mosby, 1947.

400. Dahlberg, G. *Twin births and twins from
(a) a hereditary point of view*. Stockholm: Bokförlags – A.B. Tideus Tryckeri, 1926.

401. Dahlstrom, W. G., & Welsh, G. S. *An MMPI handbook*. Minneapolis: Univer. of Minnesota Press, 1956.

402. Danford, M. B. Factor analysis and related statistical techniques. Unpublished thesis, North Carolina State College, 1953.

403. Danford, M. B., Hughes, H., & McNee, R. C. The analysis of repeated measurements experiments. *Biometrics*, 1960, 16, 547-565.

404. Daniels, W. J. Personal communication, 1963.

405. Darling, R. P. Autonomic action in relation to personality traits in children. *J. abnorm. soc. Psychol.*, 1940, 35, 246-260.

406. Darrow, C. W., & Heath, L. H. Reaction tendencies relating to personality. In K. S. Lashley, *Studies in the dynamics of behavior*. Chicago: Univer. of Chicago Press, 1932.

406. Das, Rhea S. An investigation of attitude
(a) structure and some hypothesis personality correlates. Unpublished doctoral dissertation, Univer. of Illinois, 1955.

407. Davidson, W. M., & Carroll, J. B. Speed and level components in time-limit scores: A factor analysis. *Educ. psychol. Measmt*, 1945, 5, 411-427.

408. Davis, F. B. Fundamental factors of comprehension in reading. *Psychometrika*, 1944, 9, 185-197.

409. Davis, F. B. The assessment of change. In Marquette Univer., Reading Center, *Tenth yearbook, National Reading Conference*. Milwaukee, Wis.: Marquette Univer., 1961.

410. Davis, K., et al. *Modern American society*. New York: Rinehart, 1949.

411. Davis, P. A. factor analysis of the Wechsler-Bellevue scale. *Educ. psychol. Measmt*, 1956, 16, 127-146.

412. Deese, J. On the structure of associative meaning. *Psychol. Rev.*, 1962, 69, 161-175.

413. Degan, J. W. Dimensions of functional psychosis. *Psychometr. Monogr.*, 1952, 6.

414. De Grazia, S. *Anomy*. Chicago: Univer. of Chicago Press, 1948.

414. Delhees, K. H. *Die psychodiagnostische
(a) Syndromatik der Homosexualitaet*. Bern: Huber, 1966.

415. De Mille, R. Intellect after lobotomy in schizophrenia: A factor analytic study. *Psychol. Monogr.*, 1962, 76 (Whole No. 16).

416. Denton, J. C., & Taylor, C. W. A factor analysis of mental abilities and personality traits. *Psychometrika*, 1955, 20, 75-81.

417. DeValois, R. L. Color vision mechanisms in the monkey. *J. gen. Physiol.*, 1960, 43, No. 6, Part II, 115-128.

418. DeValois, R. L., Carr, N., & Cianci, S. Physiological mechanism of successive color contrast. *Amer. Psychologist*, 1959, 14, 412 (Abstr.).

419. Digman, J. M. The principal dimensions of child personality as inferred from teachers' judgments. *Child Develpm.*, 1963, 34, 43-60.

420. Digman, J. M., & Tuttle, D. W. An interpretation of an election by means of transposed factor analysis. *J. soc. Psychol.*, 1961, 53, 183-194.

421. Dingman, H. F. The relation between coefficients of correlation and difficulty factors. *Brit. J. statist. Psychol.*, 1958, 11, 13-17.

422. Di Vesta, F. Personal communication, 1963.

423. Dodd, S. C. The theory of factors. *Psychol. Rev.,* 1928, 35, 211-234, 261-279.

424. Donahoe, J. W. Changes in meaning as a function of age. *J. gen. Psychol.,* 1961, 99, 23-28.

425. Doust, L. Spontaneous endogenous oscillatory systems in autonomic variables. *J. nerv. ment. Dis.,* October, 1960.

425. Downey, June E. *The will-temperament*
(a) *and its testing.* Yonkers, N.Y.: World, 1923.

426. Drake, R. M. Factor analysis of music tests. *Psychol. Bull.,* 1939, 36, 608-609.

427. Drevdahl, J. E., & Cattell, R. B. Personality and creativity in artists and writers. *J. clin. Psychol.,* 1958, 14, 107-111.

428. Driver, H. E. An integration of functional, evolutionary and historical theory by means of correlation. Suppl. to *Internat. J. Amer. Linguistics,* 1956, 22, 1-35.

429. Driver, H. E., & Shuessler, K. F. Factor analysis of ethnographic data. *Amer. Anthropologist,* 1957, 59, 655-663.

430. DuBois, P. H. *The classification program.* Army Air Forces Aviation Psychol. Res. Rept. No. 2. Washington, D. C.: U.S. Govt. Printing Office.

431. DuBois, P. H. *Multivariate correlational analysis.* New York: Harper, 1957.

432. DuBois, P. H., & Watson, R. I. The selection of patrolmen. *J. appl. Psychol.,* 1950, 34, 90-95.

433. Dudek, F. J. The dependence of factorial composition of aptitude tests upon population differences among pilot trainees. I. The isolation of factors. *Educ. psychol. Measmt,* 1948, 8, 613-633.

434. Duffy, E. Level of muscular tension as an aspect of personality. *J. gen. Psychol.,* 1946, 35, 161-171.

435. Duffy, E. *Activation and behavior.* New York: Wiley, 1962.

436. Du Mas, F. M. The coefficient of profile similarity. *J. clin. Psychol.,* 1949, 5, 123-131.

437. Dunnette, M. D. Personnel management. In P. R. Farnsworth, O. McNemar, and Q. McNemar (Eds.), *Annual Review of Psychology,* Vol. 13. Palo Alto, Calif.: Annual Reviews, 1962.

438. Dunnette, M. D., & England, G. W. A checklist for differentiating engineering jobs. *Personnel Psychol.,* 1957, 10, 191-198.

439. Dunnette, M. D., & Kirchner, W. K. A checklist for differentiating different kinds of sales jobs. *Personnel Psychol.,* 1959, 12, 421-430.

440. Durand, D. A note on matrix inversion by the square root method. *J. Amer. Statist. Ass.,* 1945, 40, 493-503.

441. Durkheim, E. *Suicide.* Glencoe, Ill.: Free Press, 1951.

442. Durkheim, E. *Division of labor.* Glencoe, Ill.: Free Press, 1957.

442. Dwyer, P. S. The determination of the
(a) factor loadings of a given test from the known factor loadings of other tests. *Psychometrika,* 1937, 2, 173-178.

443. Dwyer, P. S. The Doolittle technique. *Ann. math. Statist.,* 1941, 12, 449-458.

444. Dwyer, P. S. The square root method and its use in correlation and regression. *J. Amer. Statist. Ass.,* 1945, 40, 493-503.

445. Dwyer, P. S. *Linear computations.* New York: Wiley, 1951.

446. Eber, H. W. Toward oblique simple structure: A new version of Cattell's Maxplane Rotation Program for the 7094. *Multiv. behav. Res.,* 1966, 1, 112-125.

447. Eckart, C., & Young, G. The approximation of one matrix by another of lower rank. *Psychometrika,* 1936, 1, 211-218.

448. Edgerton, H. E., & Kolbe, L. E. The method of minimum variation for the combination of criteria. *Psychometrika,* 1936, 1, 183-187.

449. Edwards, A. L. *Edwards Personal Preference Schedule.* New York: Psychological Corp., 1957.

450. Edwards, A. L. *The social desirability variable in personality assessment and research.* New York: Dryden, 1957.

451. Edwards, R. M. *Factorial comparison of arithmetic performance of girls and boys in the sixth grade.* Washington, D.C.: Catholic Univer. America Press, 1957.

452. Edwards, W., Lindman, H., & Savage, L. Bayesian statistical inference for psychological research. *Psychol. Rev.,* 1963, 70(3), 193-242.

453. Egbert, R. L., Meeland, T., Cline, V. B., Forgy, E. W., Spickler, M. W., & Brown, C. *Fighter I. An analysis of combat fighters and non-fighters.* HumRRO Tech. Rept.

No. 44. Washington, D.C.: Human Resources Research Office, George Washington Univer., 1957.

454. Eisner, T., & Roth, L. M. Chemical defenses of anthropods. *Ann. Rev. Entomol.,* 1962, 7, 107-136.

455. Ekman, G. On typological and dimensional systems of reference in describing personality. *Acta Psychol.,* 1951, 8, 1-24.

456. Ekman, G. Dimensions of color vision. *J. Psychol.,* 1954, 38, 467-474.

457. Ekman, G. A note on the normal probability function in color vision. *J. Psychol.,* 1956, 41, 231-234.

458. Ekman, G. A direct method for multidimensional ratio scaling. *Psychometrika,* 1963, 28, 33-41.

459. Elfving, G., Sitgreaves, Rosedith, & Solomon, H. Item-selection procedures for item variables with a known factor structure. Chap. 4 in H. Solomon, *Studies in item analysis and prediction.* Stanford, Calif.: Stanford Univer. Press, 1961.

460. El Koussy, A. A. H. The visual perception of space. *Brit. J. Psychol. Monogr. Suppl.,* 1935, 20.

461. Elliott, L. L. Reliability of judgments of figural complexity. *J. exp. Psychol.,* 1958, 56, 335-338.

462. Elliott, L. L., & Tannenbaum, P. H. Factor-structure of semantic differential responses to visual forms and prediction of factor-scores from structural characteristics of the stimulus shapes. *Amer. J. Psychol.,* 1963, 76, 589-597.

463. Ellis, D. O., & Ludwig, F. J. *Systems philosophy.* Englewood Cliffs, N.J.: Prentice-Hall, 1962.

464. Endler, N. S., Hunt, J. McV., & Rosenstein, A. J. An S-R inventory of anxiousness. *Psychol. Monogr.,* 1962, 76 (Whole No. 536).

465. Eriksen, C. W. Discrimination and learning without awareness: A methodological survey and evaluation. *Psychol. Rev.,* 1960, 67, 279-300.

466. Eriksen, C. W. Individual differences in "choice" of defense mechanism. Personal communication, 1960.

467. Ervin, S. M., & Foster, G. The development of meaning in children's descriptive terms. *J. abnorm. soc. Psychol.,* 1960, 61, 271-275.

468. Estes, W. K. *Modern learning theory.* New York: Appleton-Century-Crofts, 1954.

469. Estes, W. K. The problem of inference from curves based on group data. *Psychol. Bull.,* 1956, 53, 134-140.

470. Estes, W. K. Of models and men. *Amer. Psychologist,* 1957, 12, 609-617.

471. Eysenck, H. J. Types of personality: A factorial study of seven hundred neurotics. *J. ment. Sci.,* 1944, 90, 851-861.

472. Eysenck, H. J. *Dimensions of personality.* London: Kegan Paul, 1947.

473. Eysenck, H. J. Criterion analysis — an application of the hypothetico-deductive method to factor analysis. *Psychol. Rev.,* 1950, 57, 38-53.

474. Eysenck, H. J. *The scientific study of personality.* London: Routledge and Kegan Paul, 1952.

474. Eysenck, H. J. The effects of psycho-
(a) therapy: an evaluation. *J. consult. Psychol.,* 1952, 16, 319-324.

475. Eysenck, H. J. Schizothymia-cyclothymia as a dimension of personality. II. Experimental. *J. Pers.,* 1952, 30, 345-384.

476. Eysenck, H. J. *The structure of human personality.* London: Methuen, 1953.

477. Eysenck, H. J. *The psychology of politics.* London: Routledge and Kegan Paul, 1954.

478. Eysenck, H. J. Psychiatric diagnosis as a psychological and statistical problem. *Psychol. Rep.,* 1955, 1, 3-17.

479. Eysenck, H. J. The inheritance and nature of extraversion. *Eugen. Rev.,* 1956, 48, 23-30.

480. Eysenck, H. J. The inheritance of extraversion-introversion. *Acta Psychol.,* (Hague), 1956, 12, 95-110.

481. Eysenck, H. J. The psychology of politics and the personality: similarities between facists and communists. *Psychol. Bull.,* 1956, 53, 431-438.

482. Eysenck, H. J. The questionnaire measurement of neuroticism and extraversion. *Riv. Psicol.,* 1956, 50, fasc. IV, 113-140.

483. Eysenck, H. J. *The dynamics of anxiety and hysteria: an experimental application of modern learning theory to psychiatry.* New York: Praeger, 1957.

484. Eysenck, H. J. The nature of anxiety and the factorial method. *Psychol. Rep.,* 1958, 4, 453-454.

485. Eysenck, H. J. *Experiments in personality.* London: Routledge and Kegan Paul, 1960.

486. Eysenck, H. J. *The structure of human personality.* (2nd ed.) London: Methuen, 1960.

487. Eysenck, H. J. A factor analysis of selected tests. In H. J. Eysenck (Ed.), *Experiments in personality.* Vol. II. London: Routledge and Kegan Paul, 1960.

488. Eysenck. H. J. (Ed.) *Handbook of abnormal psychology.* New York: Basic Books, 1961.

489. Eysenck, H. J. Classification and the problem of diagnosis. In H. J. Eysenck (Ed.), *Handbook of abnormal psychology.* New York: Basic Books, 1961.

489. Eysenck, H. J. (Ed.). *Experiments in moti-*
(a) *vation.* London: Pergamon, 1964.

490. Eysenck, H. J. Eysenck on Cattell. *Occup. Psychol.,* 1961.

491. Eysenck, H. J., & Prell, D. B. The inheritance of neuroticism. *J. ment. Sci.,* 1951, 97, 441-465.

492. Eysenck, M. D. An experimental and statistical study of olfactory preferences. *J. exp. Psychol.,* 1944, 34, 246-252.

493. Eysenck, S. B. G. Neurosis and psychosis: An experimental analysis. *J. ment. Sci.,* 1956, 102, 517-529.

494. Ezekial, M., & Fox, K. A. *Methods of correlation and regression analysis.* (3rd ed.) New York: Wiley, 1959.

495. Falconer, D. S. *Introduction to quantitative genetics.* New York: Ronald; Edinburgh: Oliver & Boyd, 1960.

496. Feather, N. T. The study of persistence. *Psychol. Bull.,* 1962, 59, 94-115.

497. Feigl, H., & Brodbeck, May. *Readings in the philosophy of science.* New York: Appleton-Century-Crofts, 1953.

498. Feigl, H., & Sellars, W. *Readings in philosophical analysis.* New York: Appleton-Century-Crofts, 1953.

499. Feldt, L. S. The use of extreme groups to test for the presence of a relationship. *Psychometrika,* 1961, 26, 307-316.

500. Feller, W. *An introduction to probability theory and its application.* New York: Wiley, 1959.

501. Ferguson, G. A. The factorial interpretation of test difficulty. *Psychol.,* 1941, 6, 323-329.

501. Ferguson, G. A. On transfer and the
(a) abilities of man. *Canad. J. Psychol.,* 1956, 10, 121-132.

502. Ferguson, L. W. The stability of the primary social attitudes. I. Religionism;

II. Humanitarianism. *J. Psychol.,* 1941, 12, 283-288.

503. Ferguson, L. W. The isolation and measurement of nationalism. *J. soc. Psychol.,* 1942, 16, 215-228.

504. Ferguson, L. W. A revision of the primary social aptitude scales. *J. Psychol.,* 1944, 17, 229-241.

505. Ferguson, L. W. *Personality measurement.* New York: McGraw-Hill, 1952.

506. Ferguson, L. W. The development of industrial psychology. In B. v. H. Gilmer, et al., *Industrial psychology.* New York: McGraw-Hill, 1961.

507. Ferguson, L. W., Humphreys, L. G., & Strong, F. W. A factorial analysis of interest and values. *J. educ. Psychol.,* 1941, 32, 197-204.

508. Feurzcig, Wallace. *Datamation* (June, 1964), pp. 39-40.

509. Fiedler, F. E. A comparison of therapeutic relationships in psychoanalytic, nondirective and Adlerian therapy. *J. consult. Psychol.,* 1950, 14, 436-445.

510. Fiedler, F. E. The concept of an ideal therapeutic relationship. *J. consult. Psychol.,* 1950, 14, 239 245.

511. Fiedler, F. E. Factor analyses of psychoanalytic, nondirective, and Adlerian therapeutic relationships. *J. consult. Psychol.,* 1951, 15, 32-38.

512. Fiedler, F. E. A method of objective quantification of certain counter-transference attitudes. *J. clin. Psychol.,* 1951, 7, 101-107.

513. Fiedler, F. E. Assumed similarity measures as predictors of team effectiveness. *J. abnorm. soc. Psychol.,* 1954, 49, 381-388.

513. Fiedler, F. E. Leadership and leadership
(a) effectiveness traits. In B. M. Bass & L. Petrullo (Eds.), *Leadership.* New York: Holt, 1960.

513. Fiedler, F. E. The leader's psychological
(b) distance and group effectiveness. In D. Cartwright & A. Zander (Eds.), *Group dynamics: Research and theory.* (2nd ed.) Evanston, Ill.: Row, Peterson, 1960.

514. Fiedler, F. E., Hutchins, E. B., & Dodge, J. S. Quasi-therapeutic relations in small college and military groups. *Psychol. Monogr.,* 1959, 73 (Whole No. 473).

515. Fiedler, F. E., & Senior, Kate. An exploratory study of unconscious feeling reactions in fifteen patient-therapist

pairs. *J. abnorm. soc. Psychol.,* 1952, 47, 446-453.

516. Fiedler, F. E., Warrington, W. G., & Blaisdell, F. J. Unconscious attitudes as correlates of sociometric choice in social groups. *J. abnorm. soc. Psychol.,* 1952, 47, 790-796.

517. Fiks, A. L. Manifold psychophysics and color perception. Unpublished manuscript, Univer. of Maryland, 1956.

518. Fillenbaum, S., & Jones, L. V. An application of "close" technique to the study of aphasic speech. *J. abnorm. soc. Psychol.,* 1962, 65, 183-189.

519. Fisher, R. A. *Statistical methods for research workers.* Edinburgh: Oliver & Boyd, 1925.

519. Fisher, R. A. *The genetical theory of*
(a) *natural selection.* Oxford: Clarendon, 1930.

520. Fisher, R. A. The use of multiple measurements in taxonomic problems. *Ann. Eugenics,* 1936, 7, 376-386.

521. Fiske, D. W. Consistency of factorial structures of personality ratings from different sources. *J. abnorm. soc. Psychol.,* 1949, 44, 329-344.

522. Fiske, D. W., & Maddi, S. *Functions of varied experience.* Homewood, Ill.: Dorsey, 1961.

523. Fiske, D. W., & Rice, L. Intra-individual response variability. *Psychol. Bull.,* 1955, 52, 217-250.

524. Fix, E. Discriminatory analysis. II. Factor analysis and discrimination. Randolph Field, Tex.: Air Univer. School of Aviation Medicine (Project No. 21-49-004, Rept. No. 2), 1950.

525. Fix, E., & Hodges, J. L. Discriminatory analysis. III. Nonparametric discrimination: Consistency properties. Randolph Field, Tex.: Air Univer. School of Aviation Medicine (Project No. 21-49-004, Rept. No. 4), 1951.

526. Flanagan, J. C. *The aviation psychology program in the Army Air Forces.* Army Air Forces Aviation Psychology Program Research Reports, No. 1. Washington, D.C.: U.S. Govt. Printing Office, 1948.

527. Flanagan, J. C. A new approach to evaluating personnel. Pittsburgh: American Institute of Research (reprinted from *Personnel,* 1949), 1949.

528. Flanagan, J. C., et al. The talents of American youth: A preliminary report. 1961.

529. Fleishman, E. A. Testing for psychomotor abilities by means of apparatus tests. *Psychol. Bull.,* 1953, 50, 241-268.

530. Fleishman, E. A. Dimensional analysis of psychomotor abilities. *J. exp. Psychol.,* 1954, 54, 437, 454.

531. Fleishman, E. A. A comparative study of aptitude patterns in unskilled and skilled motor performances. *J. appl. Psychol.,* 1957, 41, 263-272.

532. Fleishman, E. A. Dimensional analysis of movement reactions. *J. exp. Psychol.,* 1958, 55, 438-453.

533. Fleishman, E. A., & Fruchter, B. Factor structure and predictability of successive stages of learning Morse code. *J. appl. Psychol.,* 1960, 44, 97-101.

534. Fleishman, E. A., & Hempel, W. E., Jr. Changes in factor structure of a complex psychomotor task as a function of practice. *Psychometrika,* 1954, 19, 239-252.

535. Fleishman, E. A., & Hempel, W. E., Jr. A factor analysis of dexterity tests. *Personnel Psychol.,* 1954, 7, 15-32.

536. Fleishman, E. A., & Hempel, W. E., Jr. Changes in factor structure of a complex psychomotor test as a function of practice. *Psychometrika,* 1954, 19, 239-252.

537. Fleishman, E. A., & Hempel, W. E., Jr. The relationship between abilities and improvement with practice in a visual discrimination reaction task. *J. exp. Psychol.,* 1955, 49, 301-312.

538. Fleishman, E. A., & Hempel, W. E., Jr. Factorial analysis of complex psychomotor performances and related skill. *J. appl. Psychol.,* 1956, 40, 96-104.

539. Fleishman, E. A., & Spratte, J. G. The prediction of radio operator success by means of aural tests. Lackland AFB, Tex.: Air Force Personnel and Training Res. Center, Rept. No. AFPTRC-TR-54-66, 1954.

540. Flugel, J. C. Practice, fatigue and oscillation. *Brit. J. Psychol.,* Monogr. Suppl. 4, No. 13, 1929.

541. Foa, U. G. The foreman-worker interaction: A research design. *Sociometry,* 1955, 18, 226-244.

542. Foa, U. G. The structure of interpersonal

behavior in the dyad. In S. Criswell & P. Suppes (Eds.), *Mathematical methods in small group processes.* Stanford, Calif.: Stanford Univer. Press, 1962. Pp. 166-179.

543. Foa, U. G. A structural theory of interpersonal behavior. Paper read at European Conference of Experimental Social Psychologists, Sorrento, Italy, Dec., 1963.

543. Foa, U. G. New developments in facet
(a) design and analysis. *Psychol. Rev.,* 1965, 72, 262-274.

544. Fogel, M. L. The Gerstmann syndrome and the parietal symptom-complex. *Psychol. Rec.,* 1962, 12, 85-99.

545. Ford, C. F., & Tyler, L. E. A factor analysis of Terman and Miles' M-F test. *J. appl. Psychol.,* 1952, 36, 251-253.

546. Frazer, R. A., Duncan, W. J., & Collar, A. R. *Elementary matrices.* Cambridge, Eng.: Cambridge Univer. Press, 1938.

547. Freeman, G. L., & Katzoff, E. T. Individual differences in physiological reactions to stimulation and their relation to other measures of emotionality. *J. exp. Psychol.,* 1942, 31, 527-537.

548. French, J. R., Jr., & Zajonc, R. B. An experimental study of cross-cultural norm conflict. *J. abnorm. soc. Psychol.,* 1957, 54, 218-224.

549. French, J. W. The description of aptitude and achievement tests in terms of rotated factors. *Psychol. Monogr.,* No. 5, 1951.

550. French, J. W. *The description of aptitude and achievement tests in terms of rotated factors.* Chicago: Univer. of Chicago Press, 1951.

551. French, J. W. *The description of personality measurements in terms of rotated factors.* Princeton, N.J.: Educational Testing Service, 1953.

552. French, J. W. A kit for ability tests. Preliminary Report, 1961.

553. French, J. W., Ekstrom, R. B., & Price, L. A. *Manual for kit of reference tests for cognitive factors.* Princeton, N.J.: Educational Testing Service, 1963.

554. French, R. L. Morale and leadership, in human factors in undersea warfare. In National Research Council, *Human factors in undersea warfare,* 1949.

555. Freud, S. *An outline of psychoanalysis.* New York: Norton, 1949.

556. Freud, S. *Civilization and its discontents.* Garden City, N.Y.: Doubleday, 1958.

557. Frick, J. W., Guilford, J. P., Christensen, P. R., & Merrifield, P. R. A factor-analytic study of flexibility in thinking. *Educ. psychol. Measmt,* 1959, 19, 469-496.

558. Friedman, G., Hempel, W. E., Jr., & Detter, H. M. Comparative factor analyses of three radio operator training criteria. Lackland AFB, Tex.: Air Force Personnel and Training Res. Center, Rept. No. AFPTRC-TN-55-2, 1955.

559. Friedman, S. T. A factor analysis of a stenographic proficiency battery. *Psychol. Bull.,* 1941, 38, 567.

560. Fries, C. C. *The structure of English.* New York: Harcourt, Brace, 1952.

561. Fruchter, B. The nature of verbal fluency. *Educ. psychol. Measmt,* 1948, 8, 33-47.

562. Fruchter, B. Note on the computation of the inverse of a triangular matrix. *Psychometrika,* 1949, 14, 89-93.

563. Fruchter, B. *Introduction to factor analysis.* New York: Van Nostrand, 1954.

564. Fruchter, B., & Anderson, H. E., Jr. Geometrical representation of two methods of linear least squares multiple correlation. *Psychometrika,* 1961, 26, 433-442.

565. Fruchter, B., & Fleishman, E. A. A comparison of two approaches to analyzing correlations among experimentally dependent variables. *Amer. Psychologist,* 1957, 12, 438. (Abstract.)

566. Fruchter, B., & Jennings, E. E. Factor analysis. In H. Borko (Ed.), *Computer applications in the behavioral sciences.* Englewood Cliffs, N.J.: Prentice-Hall, 1962. Pp. 238-265.

567. Fuller, J. L., & Scott, J. P. Heredity and learning ability in infrahuman mammals. *Eugen. Quart.,* 1954, 1, 28-43.

568. Fuller, J. L., & Thompson, W. R. *Behavior genetics.* New York: Wiley, 1960.

569. Funkenstein, D. H., Greenblatt, M., & Solomon, H. D. Prognostic tests indicating the effectiveness of treatment. In Proc. Ass. Nerv. Ment. Dis., *Psych. Treatment,* 1953, 31, 245-266.

570. Gaffey, W. R. Discriminatory analysis. Perfect discrimination as the number of variables increases. Randolph Field, Tex.: Air Univer. School of Aviation Medicine

(Project No. 21-49-004, Rept. No. 5), 1951.

571. Gaito, J. Repeated measurements designs and counterbalancing. *Psychol. Bull.*, 1961, 58, 46-54.

572. Gaito, J., & Wiley, D. E. Univariate analysis of variance procedures in the measurement of change. In C. W. Harris (Ed.), *Problems in measuring change.* Madison: Univer. of Wisconsin Press, 1963.

573. Galton, F. Family likeness in stature. *Proc. Roy. Soc.,* 1886, XL, 49-53.

574. Gardner, R. A. Multiple-choice decision-behavior. *Amer. J. Psychol.,* 1958, 71, 710-717.

575. Garner, W. R. *Uncertainty and structure as psychological concepts.* New York: Wiley, 1962.

576. Garner, W. R., & Hake, H. W. The amount of information in absolute judgments. *Psychol. Rev.,* 1951, 58, 446-459.

577. Garner, W. R., Hake, H. W., & Eriksen, C. W. Operationism and the concept of perception. *Psychol. Rev.,* 1956, 63, 149-159.

578. Garnett, J. C. M. General ability, cleverness, and purposes. *Brit. J. Psychol.,* 1918, 9, 345-366.

579. Garrett, H. E. Differential mental traits. *Psychol. Rec.,* 1938, 2, 259-298.

580. Garrett, H. E. A developmental theory of intelligence. *Amer. Psychologist,* 1946, 1, 372-378.

581. Garside, R. F. The regression of gains upon initial scores. *Psychometrika,* 1956, 21, 67-77.

582. Geier, F. M., Levin, M., & Tolman, E. C. Individual differences in emotionality, hypothesis formation, various trial and error and visual discrimination learning in rats. *Comp. psychol. Monogr.,* 1941, 17, No. 3, 20-57.

582. Gendlin, E. T. The social significance of (a) the research. In C. R. Rogers, E. T. Gendlin, D. J. Kiesler, & C. B. Truax (Eds.), *The therapeutic relationship and its impact: A study of psychotherapy with schizophrenics.* Madison: Univer. of Wisconsin Press, 1966. (In press).

583. Gernes, E. A factorial analysis of selected items of the Strong Vocational Interest Blank for Women. Unpublished doctoral dissertation, Univer. of Nebraska, 1940.

584. Gerstmann, J. Fingeragnosie: Eine unschreibene Stoerung der Orientierung am eigenen Koerper. *Wien Klin. Wschr.,* 1924, 37, 1010-1012.

585. Gerstmann, J. Fingeragnosie und isolierte Agraphie: ein neues Syndrom. *Z. Neurol. Psychiat.,* 1927, 108, 152-177.

586. Gerstmann, J. Zur symptomatologie der Himlasionen im Vebergangsgebeit der unteren parietal — und mittheren Occipitalwindung. *Nervenaryt,* 1930, 3, 691-696.

587. Gerstmann, J. Zur symptomatologie der Herderkraukan — kungen in der' Vebergangsregion der unteren parietal — und mittheren Okzipitalwindung. *Deutsche Z. Nervenh.,* 1930, 116, 46-49.

588. Gesell, A. Human infancy and the embryology of behavior. In A. Weider, *Contributions toward medical psychology.* New York: Ronald, 1953. Pp. 51-74.

589. Gesell, A., Amatruda, C. S., Castner, B. M., & Thompson, H. *Biographies of child development: The mental growth careers of eighty-four infants and children.* New York: Hoeber, 1939.

589. Getzels, J. W., & Jackson, P. W. *Creativity* (a) *and intelligence.* New York: Wiley, 1962.

590. Ghiselli, E. E. Dimensional problems of criteria. *J. appl. Psychol.,* 1956, 40, 1-4.

590. Ghiselli, E. E. The prediction of predicta-(a) bility. *Educ. psychol. Measmt,* 1960, 20, 3-8.

591. Gibb, C. A. Personality traits by factorial analysis. *Austral. J. Psychol. Phil.,* 1942, 20, 1-15.

592. Gibb, C. A. An experimental approach to the study of leadership. *Occup. Psychol.,* 1951, 25, 233-248.

593. Gibb, C. A. Changes in the culture pattern of Australia, 1906-1946, as determined by *P*-techniques. *J. soc. Psychol.,* 1956, 43, 225-238.

594. Gibson, K. S., & Tyndall, E. P. T. Visibility of radiant energy. *U.S. Bur. Stand. Sci. Papers,* 1926, 19, 131-191.

595. Gibson, W. A. Non-linear factor analysis: Single factor case. *Amer. Psychologist,* 1955, 10, 438.

596. Gibson, W. A. Proportional profiles and latent structure. *Psychol.,* 1956, 21, 135-144.

597. Gibson, W. A. Non-linear factors in two dimensions. *Psychometrika,* 1960, 25, 381-392.

597. Gilbert, W. Counseling: Therapy and
(a) diagnosis. *Ann. Rev. Psychol.*, 1952, 3, 351-380.

598. Glanzer, M., & Glaser, R. Techniques for the study of group structure and behaviors. I. Analysis of structure. *Psychol. Bull.*, 1959, 56, 317-332.

599. Gocka, E. F., & Marks, J. B. Second-order factors in the 16 P.F. test and MMPI inventory. *J. clin. Psychol.*, 1961, 17(1), 32-35.

600. Godfrey, E. P., Fiedler, F. E., & Hall, D. M. *Boards, management, and company success.* Danville, Ill.: Interstate Printers, 1959.

601. Gold, R. Z. On comparing multinominal probabilities. USAF SAM *Rep.*, No. 62-81, 1962, 13.

602. Goldstein, K. The significance of the frontal lobes for mental performance. *J. neurol. Psychopathol.*, 1936, 17, 27-40.

603. Goldstein, K., & Scheerer, M. Abstract and concrete behavior: An experimental study with special tests. *Psychol. Monogr.*, 1941, 53, No. 2, 151.

603. Golovin, N. E. The creative person in
(a) science. In C. W. Taylor & F. Barron (Eds.), *Scientific creativity: Its recognition and development.* New York: Wiley, 1963.

604. Goodman, C. H. A factorial analysis of Thurstone's sixteen primary mental abilities tests. *Psychometrika*, 1943, 8, 3, 141-151.

605. Goodman, C. H. The MacQuarrie test for measuring mechanical ability. II. Factor analysis. *J. appl. Psychol.*, 1947, 31, 150-154.

606. Goodman, C. H. A factor analysis of Thurstone's sixteen primary mental abilities tests. *Psychometrika*, 1947, 8, 141-151.

607. Gordon, L. V. Validities of the forced-choice and questionnaire methods of personality measurement. *J. appl. Psychol.*, 1951, 35, 407-412.

608. Gorsuch, R., & Cattell, R. B. Second strata personality factors defined in the questionnaire realm in the 16 P.F. (In press).

608. Gorsuch, R. L., & Cattell, R. B. *An experi-*
(a) *mental clarification of the super ego structure.* Advance Rept. Champaign, Ill.: Lab. of Personality and Group Analysis, 1966.

609. Gosnell, H. T. *Machine politics: Chicago model.* Chicago: Univer. of Chicago Press, 1937.

609. Gottesman, I. Heritability of personality:
(a) A demonstration. *Psychol. Monogr.*, 1963, 77, No. 9 (Whole No. 572).

610. Gough, H. G. *California Psychological Inventory.* Palo Alto, Calif.: Consulting Psychologists Press, 1957.

611. Gouldner, A. W. Cosmopolitans and locals: Toward an analysis of latent social roles. *Admin. Sci. Quart.*, 1957, 2, 281-306.

612. Gouldner, A. W., & Peterson, R. A. *Notes on technology and the moral order.* Indianapolis: Bobbs-Merrill, 1963.

613. Granit, R. A physiological theory of color perception. *Nature*, 1943, 151, 11-14.

614. Green, B. F., Jr. Attitude measurement. Chap. 27 in G. Lindzey (Ed.), *Handbook of social psychology.* Cambridge, Mass.: Addison-Wesley, 1954.

615. Green, B. F., Jr. *Digital computers in research: An introduction for behavioral and social scientists.* New York: McGraw-Hill, 1963.

616. Green, B. F., Jr., & Tukey, J. W. Complex analysis of variance: general problems. *Psychometrika*, 1960, 25, 127-158.

617. Greenberg, J. H. (Ed.) *Universals of language.* Cambridge, Mass.: MIT Press, 1963.

618. Greene, E. B. An analysis of random and systematic changes with practice. *Psychometrika*, 1943, 8, 37-52.

619. Grinker, R. R., & Spiegel, J. P. *Men under stress.* Philadelphia: Blakiston, 1945.

620. Guertin, W. H. A factor analytic study of schizophrenic symptoms. *J. consult. Psychol.*, 1952, 16, 308-312.

621. Guetzkow, H. A use of simulation in the study of international relationships. *Behav. Sci.*, 1959, 4, 183-191.

622. Guilford, J. P. Human abilities. *Psychol. Rev.*, 1940, 47, 367-394.

623. Guilford, J. P. *An inventory of factors STDCR: manual of directions and norms.* Lincoln, Nebr.: Sheridan Supply, 1940.

624. Guilford, J. P. The difficulty of a test and its factor composition. *Psychometrika*, 1941, 6, 67-77.

625. Guilford, J. P. *Psychometric methods.* New York: McGraw-Hill, 1954.

626. Guilford, J. P. The three faces of intellect. *Amer. Psychologist,* 1959, 14, 469-479.

627. Guilford, J. P. *Personality.* New York: McGraw-Hill, 1959.

628. Guilford, J. P., & Christensen, P. R. *A factor analytic study of verbal fluency.* Los Angeles: Univer. of Southern California, Psychol. Lab. Rept. No. 17, 1956.

629. Guilford, J. P., Christensen, P. R., Frick, J. W., & Merrifield, P. R. *The relations of creative-thinking aptitudes to non-aptitude personality traits.* Los Angeles: Univer. of Southern California, Psychol. Lab. Rept. No. 20, 1957.

630. Guilford, J. P., Christensen, P. R., Kettner, N. W., Green, R. F., & Hertzka, A. F. A factor analytic study of Navy reasoning tests with the Air Force Aircrew Classification Battery. *Educ. psychol. Measmt,* 1954, 14, 301-325.

631. Guilford, J. P., Fruchter, B., & Zimmerman, W. S. Factor analysis of the Army Air Forces Sheppard Field Battery of experimental aptitude tests. *Psychometrika,* 1952, 17, 45-68.

632. Guilford, J. P., & Guilford, R. B. Personality factors S, E, M, and their measurement. *J. Psychol.,* 1936, 2, 109-127.

633. Guilford, J. P., & Guilford, R. B. Personality factors D, R, T, and A. *J. abnorm. soc. Psychol.,* 1939, 34, 21-36.

634. Guilford, J. P., & Guilford, R. B. Personality factors N and GD. *J. abnorm. soc. Psychol.,* 1939, 34, 239-248.

635. Guilford, J. P., Kettner, N. W., & Christensen, P. R. *The relation of certain thinking factors to training criteria in the U.S. Coast Guard Academy.* Los Angeles: Univer. of Southern California, Psychol. Lab. Rept. No. 13, 1955.

636. Guilford, J. P., Kettner, N. W., & Christensen, P. R. The nature of the general reasoning factor. *Psychol. Rev.,* 1956, 63, 169-172.

637. Guilford, J. P., & Lacey, J. I. (Eds.) *Printed classification tests.* AAF Aviation Psychol. Res. Progr. Rept. No. 5. Washington, D.C.: U.S. Govt. Printing Office, 1947.

638. Guilford, J. P., & Martin, H. G. *The Guilford-Martin inventory of factors GAMIN: Manual of directions and norms.* Beverly Hills, Calif.: Sheridan Supply, 1943.

639. Guilford, J. P., & Martin, H. G. *The Guilford-Martin Temperament Profile sheet.* Beverly Hills, Calif.: Sheridan Supply, 1945.

640. Guilford, J. P., & Merrifield, P. R. *The structure of intellect model: its uses and implications.* Los Angeles: Univer. of Southern California, Psychol. Lab. Rept. No. 24, 1960.

641. Guilford, J. P., Merrifield, P. R., Christensen, P. R., & Frick, J. W. *An investigation of symbolic factors of cognition and convergent production.* Los Angeles: Univer. of Southern California, Psychol. Lab. Rept. No. 23, 1960.

642. Guilford, J. P., & Zimmerman, W. S. *The Guilford-Zimmerman Temperament Survey: manual of directions and norms.* Beverly Hills, Calif.: Sheridan Supply, 1949.

643. Guilford, J. P., & Zimmerman, W. S. Fourteen dimensions of temperament. *Psychol. Monogr.,* 1956, 70 (Whole No. 417).

644. Gulliksen, H. *Theory of mental tests.* New York: Wiley, 1950.

645. Gulliksen, H. Mathematical solutions for psychological problems. *Amer. Scientist,* 1959, 47, 178-201.

646. Gulliksen, H. Linear and multidimensional scaling. *Psychometrika,* 1961, 26, 9-25.

647. Gunn, R. L. An empirical study of the job components check list. Lackland AFB, Tex.: Air Force Personnel and Training Res. Center, Rept. No. AFPTRC-TN-56-123, 1956.

648. Guttman, L. The Cornell technique for scale and intensity analysis. *Educ. psychol. Measmt,* 1947, 7, 247-280.

649. Guttman, L. The principal components of scale analysis. Chap. 9 in S. Stouffer, et al., *Measurement and prediction.* Princeton, N.J.: Princeton Univer. Press, 1950. Pp. 312-361.

650. Guttman, L. Multiple group methods for common-factor analysis: Their basis, computation, and interpretation. *Psychometrika,* 1952, 17, 209-222.

651. Guttman, L. Image theory for the structure of quantitative variates. *Psychometrika,* 1953, 18, 277-296.

652. Guttman, L. A new approach to factor analysis: The Radex. In P. F. Lazarsfeld (Ed.), *Mathematical thinking in the social*

sciences. Glencoe, Ill.: Free Press, 1954. Pp. 216-348.

653. Guttman, L. The principal components of scalable attitudes. In P. F. Lazarsfeld (Ed.), *Mathematical thinking in the social sciences.* Glencoe, Ill.: Free Press, 1954.

654. Guttman, L. Some necessary conditions for common-factor analysis. *Psychol.,* 1954, 19, 149-161.

655. Guttman, L. A generalized simplex for factor analysis. *Psychometrika,* 1955, 20, 173-192.

655. Guttman, L. *Communalities that maxi-*
(a) *mize determinacy.* Res. Rept. 16, Contr. No. AF 41(657)-76. Berkeley: Univer. of California, 1957.

656. Guttman, L. Empirical verification of the Radex structure of mental abilities and personality traits. *Educ. psychol. Measmt,* 1957, 17, 391-407.

657. Guttman, L. What lies ahead for factor analysis? *Educ. psychol. Measmt,* 1958, 18, 497-515.

658. Guttman, L. A structural theory for inter-group beliefs and action. *Amer. sociol. Rev.,* 1959, 24, 318-328.

659. Guttman, L. The structuring of sociological spaces. *Trans. Fourth World Congress of Sociology,* International Sociological Association, 1961, III, 315-355.

660. Guttman, L. A faceted definition of intelligence. To be published in the volume of *Scripta Hierosolymitana,* edited on behalf of the Department of Psychology of the Hebrew University.

660. Guttman, R., & Guttman, L. A new
(a) approach to the analysis of growth patterns: The simplex structure of intercorrelations of measurements. *Growth,* 1965, 29, 219-232.

661. Haas, M. *Some societal correlates of international political behavior.* Stanford, Calif.: Stanford University, 1964.

662. Haggard, A. On the application of analysis of variance to GSR data: I. The selection of an appropriate measure. *J. exp. Psychol.,* 1949, 39, 389-392.

663. Haggard, E. A. *Intraclass correlation and the analysis variance.* New York: Dryden, 1958.

664. Hake, H. W. Form discrimination and the invariance of form. In L. Uhr (Ed.), *Pattern recognition.* New York: Wiley, 1966. Pp. 142-173.

665. Hake, H. W., & Garner, W. R. The effect

of presenting various numbers of discrete steps on scale reading accuracy. *J. exp. Psychol.,* 1951, 42, 358-366.

666. Halberg, F. The 24-hour scale: A time dimension of adaptive functional organization. *Pers. Biol. Med.,* 1960, 3, 491-527.

667. Hald, A. *Statistical theory with engineering applications.* New York: Wiley, 1952.

668. Hale, J. A factor analysis of short-hand transcription ability. *Dissertation Abstr.,* 1959, 19, 2135-2136.

669. Hall, C. S. Drive and emotionality: Factors associated with adjustment in the rat. *J. comp. Psychol.,* 1934, 17, 89-108.

670. Hall, C. S. Emotional behavior in the rat. I. Defecation and urination as a measure of individaul differences in emotionality. *J. comp. Psychol.,* 1934, 18, 385-403.

671. Hall, C. S. Emotional behavior in the rat. II. The relationship between need and emotionality. *J. comp. Psychol.,* 1936, 22, 61-68.

672. Hall, C. S. Emotional behavior in the rat. III. The relationship between emotionality and ambulatory activity. *J. comp. Psychol.,* 1936, 22, 345-352.

673. Hall, C. S. The inheritance of emotionality in the rat. *Psychol. Bull.,* 1940, 37, 432. (Abstract.)

674. Hall, C. S. Measuring individual differences in emotionality. *Psychol. Bull.,* 1941, 38, 706. (Abstract.)

675. Hall, C. S., & Klein, S. J. Individual differences in aggressiveness in rats. *J. comp. Psychol.,* 1942, 33, 371-383.

676. Hall, C. S. Temperament: A survey of animal studies. *Psychol. Bull.,* 1944, 38, 909-943.

676. Hall, C. S., & Lindzey, G. *Theories of*
(a) *personality.* New York: Wiley, 1957.

677. Hall, C. S., & Martin, R. F. A standard experimental situation for the study of abnormal behavior in the rat. *J. Psychol.,* 1940, 10, 207-210.

678. Hall, W. E., & Robinson, F. P. An analytical approach to the study of reading skills. *J. educ. Psychol.,* 1945, 36, 429-442.

679. Haller, A. O., & Thomas, S. Personality correlates of the socioeconomic status of adolescent males. *Sociometry,* 1962, 25(4), 398-404.

680. Halsey, A. H. Genetics, social structure and intelligence. *Brit. J. Sociol.,* 1958, 9, 15-28.

681. Halstead, W. C. A power factor (P) in general intelligence: The effect of brain injuries. *J. Psychol.,* 1945, 20, 57-64.

682. Halstead, W. C. *Brain and intelligence: A quantitative study of the frontal lobes.* Chicago: Univer. of Chicago Press, 1947.

683. Halstead, W. C. Some fronto-temporal lobe relationships. *AMA Arch. Neurol. Psychiat.,* 1955, 74, 767.

684. Hammond, S. Some invariant factors from rating studies. Unpublished manuscript, Univer. of Melbourne, 1965.

685. Hammond, W. H. An application of Burt's multiple general factor analysis to delineation of physical types. *Man,* 1942, 52, 4-11.

686. Hammond, W. H. The constancy of physical types as determined by factor analysis. *Hum. Biol.,* 1957, 2a, 40-61.

687. Hargreaves, H. L. The "faculty" of imagination. *Brit. J. Psychol., Monogr. Suppl.,* 1927, 10, 74.

688. Harman, H. *Modern factor analysis.* Chicago: Univer. of Chicago Press, 1960.

689. Harrell, W. A factor analysis of mechanical ability tests. *Psychometrika,* 1940, 5, 17-33.

690. Harris, C. W. A factor analysis of selected Senate roll calls, 80th Congress. *Educ. psychol. Measmt,* 1948, 8, 583-591.

690. Harris, C. W. Separation of data as a
(a) principle in factor analysis. *Psychometrika,* 1955, 20, 23-28.

690. Harris, C. W. Relationships between
(b) two systems of factor analysis. *Psychometrika,* 1956, 21, 185-190.

691. Harris, C. W. Some Rao-Guttman relationships. *Psychometrika,* 1962, 27, 247-263.

692. Harris, C. W. (Ed.) *Problems in measuring change.* Madison: Univer. of Wisconsin Press, 1963.

692. Harris, C. W. Formula for the signifi-
(a) cance of a factor loading. Manuscript for private circulation, Educ. Psychol. Dept., Univer. of Wisconsin, 1965.

692. Harris, C. W., & Kaiser, H. F. Oblique
(b) factor analytic solutions by orthogonal transformations. *Psychometrika,* 1964, 29 (4), 347-362.

693. Harris, J. D. A search toward the primary auditory abilities. *USN Submar. Med. Res. Lab. Rept.,* No. 57-4, Proj. NM22 No. 0120.2.1, 1957.

694. Harris, Z. S. *Methods in structural linguistics.* Chicago: Univer. of Chicago Press, 1951.

695. Hart, H. H., Jenkins, R. L., Axelrod, S., & Sperling, P. I. Multiple factor analysis of traits of delinquent boys. *J. soc. Psychol.,* 1943, 17, 191-201.

696. Hartley, H. O. The estimation of non-linear parameters by internal least squares. *Biometrika,* 1948, 35, 32-45.

697. Hartshorne, H., & May, M. A. *Studies in deceit.* New York: Macmillan, 1928.

698. Hartshorne, H., May, M. A., & Maller, J. G. *Studies in service and self control.* New York: Macmillan, 1929.

699. Harvey, A. J. A factorial study of morphological and performance measures in pre-pubescent boys. *Dissertation Abstr.,* 17(5), 1024-1025.

700. Hathaway, S. R., & McKinley, J. C. *A multiphasic personality schedule.* (rev.) New York: Psychological Corp., 1947.

701. Hathaway, S. R., & McKinley, J. C. *The Minnesota Multiphasic Personality Inventory manual.* (rev.) New York: Psychological Corp., 1951.

702. Hathaway, S. R., & Meehl, P. E. *An atlas for the clinical use of the MMPI.* Minneapolis: Univer. of Minnesota Press, 1951.

703. Haverland, E. M. An experimental analysis by P-technique of some functionally unitary varieties of fatigue. Unpublished master's thesis, Univer. of Illinois, 1954.

704. Haverland, E. M. The application of an analytical solution for proportional profiles rotation to a box problem and to the drive structure in rats. Unpublished doctoral dissertation, Univer. of Illinois, 1954.

705. Hayes, K. J. Genes, drives and intellect. *Psychol. Rep.,* 1962, 10, 299-342.

706. Heath, H. A. A factor analysis of women's measurements taken for garment and pattern construction. *Psychometrika,* 1952, 17, 87-95.

707. Heck, D. L. Charts of some upper percentage points of the distribution of the largest characteristic root. *Ann. math. Statist.,* 1960, 31, 625-642.

708. Hellfritzsch, A. G. A factor analysis of teacher abilities. *J. exp. Educ.,* 1945, 14, 166-199.

709. Helm, C. E. *A multidimensional ratio scaling analysis of color relations.* Princeton, N.J.: Educational Testing Service, 1959.

710. Helm, C. E. *A successive intervals analysis of color differences.* Princeton, N.J.: Educational Testing Service, 1960.

711. Helm, C. E. Multidimensional ratio scaling analysis of perceived color relations. *J. Opt. Soc. Amer.*, 1964, 54, 256-262.

712. Helm, C. E., Messick, S., & Tucker, L. R. Psychological models for relating discrimination and magnitude estimation scales. *Psychol. Rev.*, 1961, 68, 167-177.

713. Helm, C. E., & Tucker, L. R. Individual differences in the structure of color perception. *Amer. J. Psychol.*, 1962, 75, 437-444.

713. Helmstadter, G. C. Procedures for ob-
(a) taining separate set and content components of a test score. *ETS res. Bull.*, 1956, RB-56-8.

713. Hempel, C. G. Fundamentals of concept
(b) formation in empirical science. In O. Neurath et al. (Eds.), *International encyclopedia of unified science.* Chicago: Univer. of Chicago Press, 1952. Vol. 2, No. /.

714. Hempel, W. E., Jr., & Fleishman, E. A. A factor analysis of physical proficiency and manipulative skill. *J. appl. Psychol.*, 1955, 39, 12-16.

715. Hemphill, J. K. Descriptions of group characteristics. *Proc. 1954 Conf. Test Problems Educ. Test Serv.*, 1955, 85-95.

716. Hemphill, J. K. *Dimensions of executive positions.* Res. Monogr. No. 98. Columbus: Ohio State Univer., Bureau of Business Research, 1960.

717. Hemphill, J. K., & Westie, C. M. The measurement of group dimensions. *J. Psychol.*, 1950, 29, 325-342.

718. Hendrickson, Donna. Personality variables: Significant departures of occupational therapists from popular norms. *Amer. J. occup. Ther.*, 1962, 16(3), 127-130.

718. Henning, H. *Die aufmerksamkeit.* Berlin,
(a) 1925.

719. Henry, S. Children's audiograms in relation to reading attainment. II: Analysis and interpretation. *J. gen. Psychol.*, 1947, 71, 3-48.

720. Henrysson, S. *Applicability of factor analysis in the behavioral sciences.* Stockholm: Almquist and Wiksell, 1957.

721. Henrysson, S. *Methods of adjustment of item-total correlations for overlapping due to unique item variance.* Stockholm: Univer. of Stockholm, Inst. Educ. Res., Bull. No. 8, 1962.

722. Heron, A. A psychological study of occupational adjustment. Unpublished doctoral dissertation, Univer. of London (quoted in Eysenck, 1952, 1951).

723. Hertzka, A. F., Guilford, J. P., Christensen, P. R., & Berger, R. M. A factor-analytic study of evaluative abilities. *Educ. psychol. Measmt*, 1954, 14, 581-597.

723. Hess, E. H. The relationship between
(a) imprinting and motivation. In M. R. Jones (Ed.), *Nebraska symposium on motivation.* Lincoln: Univer. of Nebraska Press, 1959. Pp. 47-77.

724. Heyns, R. W., & Lippitt, W. Systematic observational techniques. In G. Lindzey (Ed.), *Handbook of social psychology.* Vol. 1. Cambridge, Mass.: Addison-Wesley, 1954. Pp. 370-404.

725. Hildebrand, H. F. A factorial study of introversion-extraversion. *Brit. J. Psychol.*, 1958, 49, 1-11.

/26. Hitch, C. Sub-optimization in operations problems. *J. Oper. Res. Soc. Amer.*, 1953, 1, 87-102.

727. Hoagland, H. The physiological control of judgments of duration: Evidence for a chemical clock. *J. gen. Psychol.*, 1933, 9, 267-287.

728. Hoagland, H. Enzyme kinetics and the dynamics of behavior. *J. comp. physiol. Psychol.*, 1947, 40(3).

729. Hoagland, H. The human adrenal cortex in relation to stressful activities. *J. aviation Med.*, 1947, 18 (5).

730. Hochberg, J., & Brooks, V. The psychophysics of form: Reversible-perspective drawings of spatial objects. *Amer. J. Psychol.*, 1960, 73, 337-354.

731. Hodges, J. L. Discriminatory analysis. 1. Survey of discriminatory analysis. Randolph Field, Tex.: Air Univer. School of Aviation Medicine (Project No. 21-49-004, Rept. No. 1), 1950.

732. Hoffman, L. R. A note on ratings versus choices as measures of group attraction. *Sociometry*, 1962, 25, 313-320.

733. Hoffman, P. J. Test reliability and prac-

tice effects. *Psychometrika,* 1963, 28, 273-288.

734. Hofstaetter, P. R. Factorial study of culture patterns in the U.S. *J. Psychol.,* 1951, 32, 99-113.

735. Hofstaetter, P. R. The changing composition of "intelligence": A study in T-technique. *J. genet. Psychol.,* 1954, 85, 159-164.

735. Holland, H. L. The relation of the voca-
(a) tional preference inventory to the Sixteen Personality Factor Questionnaire. *J. appl. Psychol.,* 1960, 44, 291-296.

736. Holland, J. H. Outline for a logical theory of adaptive systems. *J. ACM,* 1962, 9, 297-314.

737. Holley, J. W. The isolation by factor analysis of personality traits in the domain of military leadership. Lackland AFB, Tex.: Air Force Personnel and Training Res. Center, Rept. No. AFPTRC-TN-56-70, 1956.

738. Holmen, M. G., & Katter, R. V. Attitude and information patterns of OCS eligibles. HumRRO Res. Memo. 2. Washington D.C.; George Washington Univer., Human Resources Res. Office, 1953.

739. Holtzman, W. H. Methodological issues in *P*-technique. *Psychol. Bull.,* 1962, 59, 248-256.

740. Holtzman, W. H. Statistical models for the study of change in the single case. In C. W. Harris (Ed.), *Problems in measuring change.* Madison: Univer. of Wisconsin Press, 1963.

741. Holzinger, K. J., & Harman, H. H. *Factor analysis.* Chicago: Univer. of Chicago Press, 1941.

742. Horn, J. L. Significance tests for use with r_p and related profile statistics. *Educ. psychol. Measmt,* 1961, 21, 363-370.

743. Horn, J. L. Structure in measures of self sentiment, ego and super ego concepts. Unpublished master's thesis, Univer. of Illinois, 1961.

744. Horn, J. L. Second-order factors in questionnaire data. *Educ. psychol. Measmt,* 1963, 23, 117-134.

745. Horn, J. L. The discovery of personality traits, *J. exp. Res.,* 1963, 56, 460-465.

746. Horn, J. L. Equations representing combinations of components in scoring psychological variables. *Acta Psychologica,* 1963, 21, 184-217.

747. Horn, J. L. On the estimation of factor scores. *Educ. psychol. Measmt,* 1964, 24 (3), 525-527.

748. Horn, J. L. An empirical comparison of methods for estimating factor scores. *Educ. psychol. Measmt,* 1965, 25 (2), 313-323.

749. Horn, J. L. Fluid and crystallized intelligence: a factor analytic and developmental study of structure among primary mental abilities. Unpublished doctoral dissertation, Univer. of Illinois, 1965.

749. Horn, J. L. *Short period changes in abili-*
(a) *ties.* Denver: Univer. of Denver, Psychol. Dept. Repts., 1966.

749. Horn J. L., & Bramble, W. J. *Second order*
(b) *ability structure revealed in rights and wrongs scores.* Denver: Univer. of Denver, Psychol. Dept. Repts., 1966.

750. Horn, J. L., & Cattell, R. B. Vehicles, ipsatization and the multiple-method measurement of motivation. *Canad. J. Psychol.,* 1965, 19 (4), 265-279.

750. Horn, J. L., & Cattell, R. B. Age differ-
(a) ences in primary mental ability factors. *J. Geront.,* 1966, 21, 210-220.

750. Horn, J. L., & Cattell, R. B. Refinement
(b) and test of the theory of fluid and crystallized general intelligences. *J. educ. Psychol.,* 1966. (In press).

750. Horn, J. L., & Cattell, R. B. Age differ-
(c) ences in fluid and crystallized intelligence. *Acta Psychol.,* 1966. (In press).

750. Horn, J. L., & Little, K. B. Isolating change
(d) and invariance in patterns of behavior. *Multiv. behav. Res.,* 1966, 1, 219-229.

751. Horowitz, M. W., & Perlmutter, H. V. The concept of the social group. *J. soc. Psychol.,* 1953, 37, 69-95.

752. Horst, P. A short method for solving for a coefficient of multiple correlation. *Ann. math. Statist.,* 1932, 3, 40-45.

753. Horst, P. Measuring complex attitudes. *J. soc. Psychol.,* 1935, 6, 369-374.

754. Horst, P. Obtaining a composite measure from a number of different measures of the same attribute. *Psychometrika,* 1936, 1, 53-60.

755. Horst, P. *The prediction of personal adjustment.* SSRC Bull. No. 48. New York: Social Science Res. Council, 1941.

756. Horst, P. Pattern analysis and configural scoring. *J. clin. Psychol.,* 1954, 10, 3-11.

757. Horst, P. A technique for the develop-

ment of a differential prediction battery. *Psychol. Monogr.*, 1954, 68 (Whole No. 380).

758. Horst, P. A technique for the development of a multiple absolute prediction battery. *Psychol. Monogr.*, 1955, 69 (Whole No. 390).

759. Horst, P. Least square multiple classification for unequal subgroups. *J. clin. Psychol.*, 1956, XII, 309-315.

760. Horst, P. Optimal estimates of multiple criteria with restrictions on the covariance matrix of estimated criteria. *Psychol., Monogr. Suppl.*, 6-V6, 1960.

761. Horst, P. Generalized canonical correlations and their application to experimental data. *J. clin. Psychol.*, Monogr. Suppl., No. 14, 1961, 331-347.

762. Horst, P. Relations among *m* sets of measures. *Psychometrika*, 1961, 26, 129-150.

763. Horst, P. *Matrix algebra for social scientists*. New York: Holt, Rinehart, and Winston, 1963.

764. Horst, P. Multivariate models for evaluating change. In C. W. Harris (Ed.), *Problems in measuring change*. Univer. of Wisconsin Press, Madison; 1963.

765. Horst, P. *Factor analysis of data matrices*. New York: Holt, Rinehart & Winston, 1965.

766. Horst, P. Relations among *m* sets of variables. *Psychometrika*, 1961, 26, 129-149.

767. Horst, P., & MacEwan, Charlotte. Optimal test length for multiple prediction: the general case. *Psychometrika*, 1957, 22, 311-324.

768. Horst, P., & MacEwan, Charlotte. Predictor elimination techniques for determining multiple prediction batteries. *Psychol. Rep.*, Monogr. Suppl., 1-V7, 1960.

769. Horst, P., et al. *Prediction of personal adjustment*. SSRC Bull. No. 48. New York: Social Science Res. Council, 1941.

770. Hotelling, H. The generalization of student's ratio. *Ann. math. Statist.*, 1931, 2, 360-378.

771. Hotelling, H. Analysis of a complex of statistical variables into principal components. *J. educ. Psychol.*, 1933, 24, 417-441, 498-520.

772. Hotelling, H. The most predictable criterion. *J. educ. Psychol.*, 1935, 26, 139-142.

773. Hotelling, H. Relations between two sets of variates. *Biometrika*, 1936, 28, 321-377.

774. Hotelling, H. Simplified calculation of principal components. *Psychometrika*, 1936, 1, 27-35.

775. Hotelling, H. A generalized *T* test and measure of multivariate dispersion. *Proc. 2nd Berkeley Symposium on Mathematical Statistics and Probability*. Berkeley: Univer. of California Press, 1951.

776. Householder, A. S., & Young, G. Matrix approximation and latent roots. *Amer. math. Monthly*, 1938, 45, 165-171.

777. Houston, R. A. *Vision and color vision*. New York: Longmans, Green, 1932.

777. Howard, K. I., & Diesenhaus, H. I. Direc-
(a) tion of measurement and profile similarity. *J. J. Res. Rept.* (Chicago), 1965, 2 (7), 1-16.

778. Howells, W. W. Factors of human physique. *Amer. J. phys. Anthropol.*, 1951, 9, 159-191.

779. Howells, W. W. A factorial study of constitutional types. *Amer. J. phys. Anthropol.*, 1952, 10, 91-118.

780. Howie, D. Aspects of personality in the classroom: A study of ratings on personal qualities for a group of schoolboys. *Brit. J. Psychol.*, 1945, 36, 15-28.

781. Hsü, E. H. A factorial analysis of olfaction. *Psychometrika*, 1946, 11, 31-42.

782. Hsü, E. H. A method for isolating presumptive personality profiles from changes in skin conductivity during word association. *Psychosom. Med.*, 1951, 13, 260-261.

783. Hsü, E. H. Comparative study of factor patterns, physiologically and psychologically determined. *J. genet. Psychol.*, 1952, 47, 105-128.

784. Hsü, E. H., & Sherman, M. The factorial analysis of the electro-encephalogram. *J. Psychol.*, 1946, 28, 189-196.

785. Hughes, H. M. Discriminatory analysis. III. Discrimination of accident-prone individuals. Randolph Field, Tex.: Air Univer. School of Aviation Medicine (Project No. 21-49-004, Rept. No. 3), 1950.

786. Hughes, H. M. Discriminatory analysis. X. On two correlated bivariate distributions. Randolph Field, Tex.: Air Univer. School of Aviation Medicine

(Project No. 21-49-004, Rept. No. 10), 1952.

787. Hughes, H. M., & Danford, M. B. Repeated measurements designs assuming equal variances and covariances. USAF Sch. Aviat. Med. Rep., No. 59-40, 1958.

788. Hughes, K. R., Cooper, R. M., & Zubek, J. P. Effect of glutamic acid on the learning behavior of bright and dull rats. III. Effect of varying dosages. *Canad. J. Psychol.*, 1957, 11, 253-255.

789. Hughes, K. R., & Zubek, J. P. Effect of glutamic acid on the learning ability of bright and dull rats. I. Administration during infancy. *Canad. J. Psychol.*, 1956, 10, 132-138.

790. Hughes, K. R., & Zubek, J. P. Effect of glutamic acid on the learning ability of bright and dull rats. II. Duration of the effect. *Canad. J. Psychol.*, 1957, 11, 182-184.

791. Hughes, R. M. A factor analysis of Rorschach diagnostic signs. *J. gen. Psychol.*, 1950, 43, 85-103.

791. Hull, C. L. *Hypnosis and suggestibility.*
(a) New York: Appleton-Century, 1933.

792. Humphreys, L. G. Characteristics of type concepts with special reference to Sheldon's typology. *Psychol. Bull.*, 1957, 54, 218-228.

793. Humphreys, L. G. Investigations of the simplex. *Psychometrika*, 1960, 25, 313-323.

794. Humphreys, L. G. The organization of human abilities. *Amer. Psychologist*, 1962, 17, 475-483.

795. Humphreys, L. G. Stability of Airman Classification Test scores. Lackland AFB, Tex.: Personnel Lab., AMD, AFSC, Rept. No. PRL-TDR-62-3, 1962.

796. Hundleby, J. D., Pawlik, K., & Cattell, R. B. *Personality factors in objective test devices.* San Diego: R. Knapp, 1965.

797. Hundleby, J. D., & Cattel, R. B. Personality structure in middle childhood and the prediction of school achievement and adjustment. *Psychol. Monogr.* (In press).

798. Hunt, J. McV. *Intelligence and experience.* New York: Ronald, 1961.

798. Hunt, J. McV. Motivation inherent in
(a) information processing and action. In O. J. Harvey (Ed.), *Motivation and social*

interaction: The cognitive determinants. New York: Ronald, 1963.

798. Hunt, J. McV. Traditional personality
(b) theory in the light of recent evidence. *Amer. Scientist,* 1965, 53, 80-96.

798. Hunt, J. McV., Ewing, T. N., LaForge, R.,
(c) & Gilbert, W. M. An integrated approach to research on therapeutic counseling with samples of results. *J. counsel. Psychol.,* 1959, 6, 46-54.

799. Huntington, E. *Mainspring of civilization.* New York: Wiley, 1945.

800. Hurley, J. R., & Cattell, R. B. The Procrustes Program: Producing direct rotation to test a hypothesized factor structure. *Behav. Sci.,* 1962, 7, 258-262.

801. Hursch, C. J., Hammond, D. R., & Hursch, J. L. Some methodological considerations in multiple-cue probability studies. *Psychol. Rev.,* 1964, 71, 42-60.

802. Ikenberry, S. O. Factors in college persistence. *J. counsel Psychol.,* 1961, 8, 322-329.

802. Isaacs, J. T. Frequency curves and the
(a) ability of nations. *Brit. J. statist. Psychol.,* 1962, 15, 76-79.

803. Ivanoff, J. M. Use of discriminant analysis for predicting freshman probationary students at one midwestern university. *Educ. psychol. Measmt,* 1961, 21, 975-986.

803. Jackson, D. N., & Messick, S. Content
(a) and style in personality assessment. *Psychol. Bull.,* 1958, 55, 243-252.

804. Jackson, D. N., & Messick, S. Acquiescence and desirability as response determinants on the MMPI. *Educ. psychol. Measmt,* 1961, 21, 771-790.

805. Jackson D. N., & Messick, S. Response style on the MMPI: Comparison of clinical and normal samples. *J. abnorm. soc. Psychol.,* 65, 285-299, 1962.

805. Jaensch, E. R. *Eidetische anlage und kind-*
(a) *liches seelenleben.* Leipzig: Bart, 1934.

806. Jakway, J. S. The inheritance of patterns of mating behavior in the male guinea pig. *Animal Behav.,* 1959, 7, 150-162.

807. Jenkin, N., & Hyman, R. Attitude and distance-estimation as variables in size-matching. *Amer. J. Psychol.,* 1959, 72, 68-76.

807. Jensen, A. R. Extraversion, neuroticism,
(a) and serial learning. *Acta Psychol.,* 1962, 20, 69-77.

808. Johnson, D. L., & Kobler, A. K. The man-computer relationship. *Science,* 1962, 138, 873-879.

809. Johnson, D. M., & Reynolds, F. A factor analysis of verbal ability. *Psychol. Rec.,* 1951, 4, 183-195.

810. Johnson, E. S. Characteristic roots and vectors of a symmetric matrix: A computer program for the LGP-30. Chapel Hill: Univer. of North Carolina, Psychometric Lab. Res. Memo. No. 1, 1960.

811. Johnson, F. C., & Klare, G. R. Feedback: Principles and analogies. *J. Commun.,* 1962, 12(3), 150-159.

812. Johnson, P. O., & Neyman, J. Tests of certain linear hypotheses and their application to some educational problems. *Statist. Res. Memoirs,* 1936, 1, 57-93.

813. Jonassen, C. T., & Peres, S. H. *Interrelationships of dimensions of community systems.* Columbus: Ohio State Univer. Press, 1960.

814. Jones, F. N. A factor analysis of visibility data. *Amer. J. Psychol.,* 1948, 61, 361-369.

815. Jones, F. N. Color vision and factor analysis: Some comments on Cohen's comments. *Psychol. Rev.,* 1950, 57, 138-139.

816. Jones, F. N. A second factor analysis of visibility data. *Amer. J. Psychol.,* 1950, 63, 206-213.

817. Jones, F. N. An analysis of individual differences in olfactory thresholds. *Amer. J. Psychol.,* 1957, 70, 227-232.

818. Jones F. N. Personal communication. 1962.

819. Jones, F. N., & Jones, M. H. A second factor analysis of visibility data. *Amer. J. Psychol.,* 1950, 63, 206-213.

820. Jones, L. V. A factor analysis of the Stanford-Binet at four age levels. *Psychometrika,* 1949, 14, 299-331.

821. Jones, L. V. Primary abilities in the Stanford-Binet, age 13. *J. genet. Psychol.,* 1954, 84, 125-147.

822. Jones, L. V. Statistical theory and research design. In C. P. Stone (Ed.), *Annual Review of Psychology,* Vol. 6. Palo Alto, Calif.: Annual Reviews, 1955.

823. Jones, L. V. Problems of devising and selecting appropriate measurement tools. *Amer. J. ment. Defic.,* 1959, 64, 384-394.

824. Jones, L. V. Some illustrations of psychological experiments designed for multivariate statistical analysis. Chapel Hill: Univer. of North Carolina, Psychometric Lab. Rept. No. 28, 1960.

825. Jones, L. V., & Bock, R. D. Multiple discriminant analysis applied to "Ways to Live" ratings from six cultural groups. *Sociometry,* 1960, 23, 162-176.

826. Jones, L. V., & Wepman, J. M. Dimensions of language performance in aphasia. *J. speech hearing Res.,* 1961, 4, 220-232.

827. Jones, L. W. Present day theories of intellectual factors (general, group, and specific). *Brit J. educ. Psychol.,* 1933, 3, 1-12.

828. Jones, M. B. *Simplex theory.* Monogr. Ser., No. 3, Pensacola, Fla.: U.S. Naval School of Aviation Medicine, 1959.

829. Jones, M. B. *Molar correlational analysis.* Monogr. Ser., No. 4, Pensacola, Fla.: U.S. Naval School of Aviation Medicine, 1960.

830. Jones, M. H. The adequacy of employee selection reports. *J. appl. Psychol.,* 1950, 34, 222-223.

831. Jones, W. S. Some correlates of the authoritarian personality in a quasi-therapeutic situation. Unpublished doctoral dissertation, Univer. of North Carolina, 1961.

832. Jost, H. The relation between certain physiological changes during learning, frustration and sensory stimulation, and personality. Unpublished doctoral dissertation, Univer. of Chicago, 1940, pp. 31-32.

833. Jost, H., & Sontag, L. W. The genetic factor in autonomic nervous system function. *Psychosom. Med.,* 1944, 6, 308-310.

834. Judd, D. B. Basic correlates of the visual stimulus. In S. S. Stevens (Ed.), *Handbook of experimental psychology.* New York: Wiley, 1951.

835. Kaiser, H. F. The varimax criterion for analytic rotation in factor analysis. *Psychometrika,* 1958, 23, 187-200.

836. Kaiser, H. F. Relating factors between studies based upon different individuals. Unpublished manuscript, Univer. of Illinois, 1960.

837. Kaiser, H. F. Alpha reliability of factors. Unpublished manuscript, 1960.

838. Kaiser, H. F. Scaling a simplex. *Psychometrika,* 1962, 27, 155-162.

839. Kaiser, H. F. Image analysis. In C. W. Harris (Ed.), *Problems in measuring change*. Madison: Univer. of Wisconsin Press, 1963.

839. Kaiser, H. F. Relating factors between
(a) studies based upon different individuals. Unpublished manuscript, Educ. Dept., Univer. of Illinois, 1960.

840. Kaiser, H. F., & Caffrey, J. Alpha factor analysis. *Psychometrika*, 1965, 30, 1-14.

841. Kaiser, H. F., & Dickman, K. W. Analytic determination of common factors. *Amer. Psychologist*, 1959, 14, 425. (Abstract.)

841. Kallman, J. W. The genetic theory of
(a) schizophrenia. *Amer. J. Psychiat.*, 1946, 103, 309-322.

842. Karlin, J. E. Music ability. *Psychometrika*, 1941, 6, 61-65.

843. Karlin, J. E. The factorial isolation of the primary auditory abilities. *Psychol. Bull.*, 1942, 39, 453-454.

844. Karlin, J. E. A factorial study of auditory function. *Psychometrika*, 1942, 7, 251-279.

845. Karlin, J. E., & Alexander, S. N. Communications between man and machine. *Proc. IRE*, 1962, 50, 1124-1128.

846. Karr, C. A comparison of EPPS scores obtained from the standard forced-choice procedure and a rating-scale procedure. Unpublished doctoral dissertation, Univer. of Washington, 1958.

847. Karson, S. Validating clinical judgments with the 16 P.F. test. *J. clin. Psychol.*, 1960, 16(4), 394-397.

848. Karson, S. Second-order personality factors in positive mental health. *J. clin. Psychol.*, 1961, 17(1), 14-19.

849. Karson, S., & Pool, K. B. The construct validity of the Sixteen Personality Factors Questionnaire. *J. clin. Psychol.*, 1957, 13, 245-252.

850. Karson, S., & Pool, K. B. Second-order factors in personality measurement. *J. consult. Psychol.*, 1958, 22, 299-303.

851. Karvonen, M. J., & Kunnas, M. Factor analysis of haematological changes in heavy, manual work. *Acta Psychol. Scand.*, 1953, 29, 220-231.

852. Karwoski, T. F., & Odbert, H. S. Color-music. *Psychol. Monogr.*, 1938, 50, No. 2.

853. Karwoski, T. F., Odbert, H. S., & Osgood, C. E. Studies in synesthetic thinking. II. The role of form in visual re-sponses to music. *J. gen. Psychol.*, 1942, 26, 199-222.

854. Kassebaum, G. G., Couch, A. S., & Slater, P. E. The factorial dimensions of the MMPI. *J. consult. Psychol.*, 1959, 23, 226-236.

855. Katz, M. Meaning as a correlate of marital success. Unpublished doctoral dissertation, Teachers Coll., Columbia Univer., 1959.

856. Katzell, R. A. Industrial psychology. In P. R. Farnsworth & Q. McNemar, (Eds.), *Annual Review of Psychology*, Vol. 8. Palo Alto, Calif.: Annual Reviews, 1957.

857. Kawai, I. An analysis of behavioral factors operating through the process of acquisition and extinction: Factorial studies on the learning process, I. *Jap. J. Psychol.*, 1957, 27, 279-284, English abstr. pp. 319-320.

858. Kawai, I. An analysis of behavioral factors operating through the learning process in the multiple T maze: Factorial studies on learning process, II. *Tohoku J. exp. Psychol.*, 1958, 2, 39-42.

858. Kelly, E. L. Marital compatibility as re-
(a) lated to personality traits of husbands and wives as rated by self and spouse. *J. soc. Psychol.*, 1941, 31, 193-198.

858. Kelly, E. L., & Fiske, D. W. *The prediction*
(b) *of performance in clinical psychology*. Ann Arbor: Univer. of Michigan, 1951.

859. Kelley, H. P. A factor analysis of memory ability. *ONR Res. Tech. Rept*. Princeton, N.J.: Princeton Univer. & Educational Testing Service, 1954.

860. Kelley, T. L. *Essential traits of mental life*. Cambridge, Mass.: Harvard Univer. Press, 1935.

861. Kempthorne, O. *The design and analysis of experiments*. New York: Wiley, 1952.

862. Kendall, M. G. *The advanced theory of statistics*. Vol. 1. London: Griffin, 1943.

863. Kendall, M. G. *The advanced theory of statistics*. Vol. 2. London: Griffin, 1948.

864. Kendall, M. G. Review of Uppsala Symposium on psychological factor analysis. *J. Roy. Statist. Soc.*, Sec. A., 1954, 107, 462-483.

865. Kendall, M. G. *A course in multivariate analysis*. New York: Hafner, 1957.

865. *The Kentucky symposium: learning theory,*
(a) *personality theory, and clinical research*. New York: Wiley, 1954.

866. Kerékjártó, M. V., & Schmidt, G. Fakto-

ren-Analysen des Hamburg-Wechsler Intelligenztests für Kinder (HAWIK). *Diagnostika,* 1962, 8, 95-110.

867. Kettner, N. W., Guilford, J. P., & Christensen, P. R. A factor-analytic investigation of the factor called general reasoning. *Educ. psychol. Measmt,* 1956, 16, 438-453.

868. Kettner, N. W., Guilford, J. P., & Christensen, P. R. A factor-analytic study across the domains of reasoning, creativity, and evaluation. *Psychol. Monogr.,* 1959, 73 (Whole No. 479).

869. Kety, S. Biochemical theories of schizophrenia. *Science,* 1959, 129, 1528-1532, 1590-1596.

869. Kiesler, D. J. Some myths of psycho-
(a) therapy research and the search for a paradigm. *Psychol. Bull.,* 1966, 65, 110-136.

870. Kilby, R. W. Personal communication, 1963.

870. Killian, L. R. The utility of objective test
(a) personality factors in diagnosing schizophrenia and the character disorders. Unpublished master's thesis, Univer. of Illinois, 1965.

871. Kimble, G. A. (Ed.) *Hilgard & Marquis' "Conditioning and Learning."* New York: Appleton-Century-Crofts, 1961.

872. King, F. J. An experimental investigation of some biochemical correlates of phenylketonuria. Unpublished doctoral dissertation, Univer. of Texas, 1960.

873. King, F. J., Bowman, Barbara, & Moreland, H. J. Some intellectual correlates of biochemical variability. *Behav. Sci.,* 1961, 6, 297-302.

874. King, W. R. *Ability to abstract.* In F. A. Mettler (Ed.), *Selective partial ablation of the frontal cortex.* New York: Columbia-Greystone Associates. Part B. New York: Hoeber, 1949.

875. Kleiber, M. Body size and metabolic rate. *Physiol. Rev.,* 1947, 27, 511-541.

876. Knapp, R. R. Criterion predictions in the Navy from the Objective Analytic Personality Test Battery. Paper read at Amer. Psychol. Ass., New York City, 1961.

877. Knapp, R. R. Objective personality test and sociometric correlates of frequency of sick bay visits. *J. appl. Psychol.,* 1961, 45, 104-110.

878. Knapp, R. R. The nature of primary personality dimensions as shown by relations of Cattell's objective personality test factors to questionnaire scales. San Diego, Calif.: U.S. Naval Personnel Res. Field Act., 1962. (Mimeographed.)

878. Knapp, R. R., & Most, J. A. *Personality*
(a) *correlates of Marine Corps helicopter pilot performance.* U.S.N. Med. Field Lab. Rept., No. 18 01 09 .1.3, 1960.

879. Knoell, D. M., & Harris, C. W. A factor analysis of spelling ability. *J. educ. Res.,* 1952, 46, 95-111.

880. Koch, H. L. A factor analysis of some measures of the behavior of pre-school children. *J. gen. Psychol.,* 1942, 27, 257-287.

881. Korman, M. Implicit personality theories of clinicians as defined by semantic structures. *J. consult. Psychol.,* 1960, 24, 180-186.

882. Kossack, C. F., & Beckwith, R. E. The mathematics of personnel utilization models. Lackland AFB, Tex., Personnel Lab., WADC, Rept. No. WADC-TR-59-359, 1959.

883. Krech, D., Rosenzweig, M. R., Bennett, E. L. Dimensions of discrimination and level of cholinesterase activity in the cerebral cortex of the rat. *J. comp. physiol. Psychol.,* 1956, 49, 261-268.

884. Krech, D., Rosenzweig, M. R., Bennett, L., & Kruckel, Barbara. Enzyme concentrations in the brain and adjustive behavior patterns. *Science,* 1954, 120, 994-996.

885. Krechevsky, I. Brain mechanisms and "hypotheses." *J. comp. Psychol.,* 1935, 19, 425-468.

886. Kremer, A. H. The nature of persistence. *Stud. Psychol. Psychiat.* (Cath. Univer. Amer.), 1942, 5, No. 8.

886. Kretschmer, E. *Körperbau und Charakter.*
(a) Berlin: Springer, 1921.

887. Kretschmer, E. *The psychology of men of genius.* Trans. by R. B. Cattell. London: Routledge and Kegan Paul, 1961.

888. Krueger, F., & Spearman, C. Die Korrelation zwischen verschiedenen geistigen Leistungsfähigkeiten. *Z. Psychol.,* 1906, 44, 50-114.

889. Krug, R. E. An analysis of the F scale. I. Item factor analysis. *J. soc. Psychol.,* 1961, 53, 285-291.

890. Krug, R. E., & Moyer, K. E. An analysis of the F scale. II. Relationships to stan-

dardized personality inventories. *J. soc. Psychol.,* 1961, 53, 293-301.

891. Kubala, A. L. Adaptability screening of flying personnel. Preliminary analysis and validation of criteria of adaptability to military flying. *U. S. Armed Forces med. J.,* 1959, 10, 815-842.

892. Kuder, G. F. *The Kuder Preference Record.* Chicago: Science Research Associates, 1948, 1953.

892. Kuhn, T. S. The essential tension: Tradi-
(a) tion and innovation in scientific research. In C. W. Taylor and F. Barron (Eds.), *Scientific creativity: Its recognition and development.* New York: Wiley, 1963.

893. Kumata, Hideya. A factor analytic investigation of the generality of semantic structures across two selected cultures. Unpublished doctoral dissertation, Univer. of Illinois, 1957.

894. Lacey, J. I. The evaluation of autonomic responses: Toward a general solution. *Ann. N.Y. Acad. Sci.,* 1956, 67, 123-164.

895. Lacey, J. I., & Lacey, B. C. The relationship of resting autonomic activity to motor impulsivity. The brain and human behavior, Chap 5 in *Proc. Ass. Res. nerv. and ment. Dis.* Baltimore: Williams & Wilkins, 1958.

896. Lacey, J. I., & Lacey, B. C. Verification and extension of the principle of autonomic response-stereotypy. *Amer. J. Psychol.,* 1958, 71, 50-73.

897. Lachman, R. The model in theory construction. *Psychol. Rev.,* 1960, 67, 113-129.

898. Landahl, H. D. Centroid orthogonal transformations. *Psychometrika,* 1938, 3, 219-223.

899. Langsam, R. S. A factorial analysis of reading abilities. *J. exp. Psychol.,* 1941, 10, 57-63.

900. Larson, L. A. A factor analysis of some cardio-vascular-respiratory variables and tests. *Res. Quart.,* 1947, 18, 109-122.

901. Lashley, K. S. Coalescence of neurology and psychology. *Proc. Amer. Phil. Soc.,* 1941, 84, No. 4, 467-469.

902. Lasswell, H. D. Person, personality, group, culture. *Psychiatry,* 1939, 2, 533-561.

903. Lawley, D. N. The estimation of factor loadings by the method of maximum

likelihood. *Proc. Roy. Soc. Edin.,* 1940, 60, 64-82.

904. Lawley, D. N. Tests of significance for the latent roots of covariance and correlation matrices. *Biometrika,* 1956, 43, 128-136.

905. Lawley, D. N. Estimation in factor analysis under various initial assumptions. *Brit. J. statist. Psychol.,* 1958, 11, 1-14.

906. Lawley, D. N., & Maxwell, A. E. *Factor analysis as a statistical method.* London: Butterworth, 1963.

907. Lawson, E., & Cattell, R. B. Sex differences in small group performance. *J. soc. Psychol.,* 1962, 58, 141-145.

908. Layman, E. M. An item analysis of the adjustment questionnaire. *J. Psychol.,* 1940, 10, 87-106.

909. Lazarsfeld, P. F. *The mutual effects of statistical variables.* New York: Bureau of Applied Social Res., Columbia Univer., 1947.

910. Lazarsfeld, P. F. The logical and mathematical foundation of latent structure analysis. In S. Stouffer, et al., *Studies on social psychology in World War II.* Vol. 4. *Measurement and Prediction.* Princeton, N.J.: Princeton Univer. Press, 1950.

911. Lazarsfeld, P. F. *Mathematical thinking in the social sciences.* Glencoe, Ill.: Free Press, 1954.

911. Lazarus, R. S. A program of research in
(a) psychological stress. In J. G. Peatman & E. L. Hartley (Eds.), *Festschrift for Gardner Murphy.* New York: Harper, 1960.

912. Lazarus, R. S., & McCleary, R. A. Autonomic discrimination without awareness: A study of subception. *Psychol. Rev.,* 1951, 58, 113-122.

912. Leary, T. F. *Interpersonal diagnosis of*
(a) *personality.* New York: Ronald, 1957.

913. Leavitt, H. J. Some effects of certain communication patterns on group performance. *J. abnorm. soc. Psychol.,* 1951, 46, 38-50.

914. Lederman, W. Note on Professor Godfrey H. Thompson's Article "The influence of univariate selection on the factorial analysis of ability." *Brit. J. Psychol.,* 1938, 29, 1-7.

915. Lee, M. C. Interactions, configurations, and non-additive models. *Educ. psychol. Measmt,* 1961, 21, 797-805.

916. Leeper, R. W. Cognitive processes. In S. S. Stevens (Ed.), *Handbook of experimental psychology.* New York: Wiley, 1951.

917. Leeper, R. W. Theoretical methodology in the psychology of personality. In M. H. Marx (Ed.), *Theories in contemporary psychology.* New York: Macmillan, 1963. Pp. 389-413.

918. Lees, R. B. The basis of glottochronology. *Language,* 1953, 29, 113-127.

919. Le Grand, Y. *Light, colour and vision.* New York: Wiley, 1957.

920. Lehmann, E. L. Discriminatory analysis, VI. On the simultaneous classification of several individuals. Randolph Field, Tex.: Air Univer. School of Aviation Medicine (Project No. 21-49-004, Rept. No. 6), 1951.

921. Lehmann, E. L. Discriminatory analysis, VII. On the theory of selection. Randolph Field, Tex.: Air University School of Aviation Medicine (Project No. 21-49-004, Rept. No. 7), 1951.

922. Lerner, I. M. *Genetic homeostasis.* New York: Wiley, 1954.

923. Lerner, I. M. *The genetic basis of selection.* New York: Wiley, 1958.

924. Leton, D. A., & Anderson, H. E., Jr. Discriminant analysis of achievement characteristics for multi-grade grouping of students. *J. exp. Educ.* (In press).

925. Lev, J. Maximizing test battery prediction when the weights are required to be non-negative. *Psychometrika,* 1956, 21, 245-252.

926. Levenson, B. *Panel analysis workbook.* New York: Planning Project of Advanced Training in Social Research, Columbia Univer., 1955.

927. Levin, J. Three-mode factor analysis. Unpublished doctoral dissertation, Univer. of Illinois, 1963.

928. Levonian, E. Personality measurement with items selected from the 16 P.F. questionnaire. *Educ. psychol. Measmt,* 1961, 21, 937-946.

929. Lewis, O. *The effects of white contact upon Blackfoot culture, with special reference to the fur trade.* Amer. Ethnological Society, Monogr. 6, 1942.

930. Lewis, O. *Life in a Mexican village.* Urbana: Univer. of Illinois Press, 1951.

931. Levonian, E. A statistical analysis of the 16 personality factor questionnaire. *Educ. psychol. Measmt,* 1961, 21, 589-596.

932. Lickert, R. A technique for the measurement of attitudes. *Arch. Psychol., N.Y.,* 1932, 22, No. 140.

933. Lieberman, B. *A failure of game theory to predict human behavior.* Memo SP-101. Cambridge, Mass.: Harvard Univer., Lab. of Social Relations, 1960.

934. Lieberman, B. Human behavior in a strictly determined 3×3 matrix game. *Behav. Sci.,* 1960, 5, 317-322.

935. Lilly, J. C. Mental effects of reduction of ordinary levels of physical stimuli on intact healthy persons. *Psychiat. res. Rept.,* 1956, 5, 1-9.

936. Lindquist, E. F. *Design and analysis of experiments in psychology and education.* Boston: Houghton Mifflin, 1963.

937. Lindsley, D. B. The reticular motivating system and perceptual integration. In D. E. Sheer (Ed.), *Electrical stimulation of the brain.* Austin: Univer. of Texas Press, 1961.

938. Lingoes, J. C. Multiple scalogram analysis. *Educ. psychol. Measmt,* 1963, 23, 501-524.

939. Lingoes, J. C. *New computer developments in pattern analysis and non-metric techniques.* Computing Center Rept. No. 4, Ann Arbor: Univer. of Michigan, 1965.

939. Liu, Phyllis Y., & Meredith, G. M. Cross
(a) cultural comparison of Chinese and American college students on the 16 Personality Factor Questionnaire. (In preparation).

939. Loehlin, J. C. Heredity, environment and
(b) personality inventory items. Paper read at Amer. Psychol. Ass., St. Louis, 1962.

940. Loehlin, J. C. Some corrections to Cattell's multiple abstract variance analysis method. (In press).

941. Loevinger, Jane. Objective tests as instruments of psychological theory. *Psychol. Rep.,* 1957, 3, 635-694.

942. Loevinger, Jane, Gleser, Goldine C., & DuBois, P. H. Maximizing the discriminating power of a multiple-score test. *Psychometrika,* 1953, 18, 809-317.

943. Lohnes, P. R. Test space and discriminant space classification models and related significance tests. *Educ. psychol. Measmt,* 1961, 21, 559-574.

944. Loos, F. M. A study of interrelationships of sense of humor with some other personality variables. Unpublished doctoral dissertation, Univer. of London, 1951 (quoted in Eysenck, 1952).

945. Lord, F. M. The measurement of growth. *Educ. psychol. Measmt,* 1956, 16, 421-437. See also Errata, *ibid.,* 1957, 17, 452.

946. Lord, F. M. Further problems in the measurement of growth. *Educ. psychol. Measmt,* 1958, 18, 437-454.

947. Lord, F. M. Test norms and sampling theory. *J. exp. Educ.,* 1959, 27, 247-263.

948. Lord, F. M. Elementary models for measuring change. In C. W. Harris (Ed.), *Problems in measuring change.* Madison: Univer. of Wisconsin Press, 1963.

949. Lorenz, K. *King Solomon's ring.* London: Macmillan, 1958.

950. Lorr, M., & Fields, V. A factorial study of body types. *J. clin. Psychol.,* 1954, 10, 182-185.

951. Lorr, M., & Jenkins, R. L. Patterns of maladjustment in children. *J. clin. Psychol.,* 1953, 9, 16-19.

952. Lorr, M., & Jenkins, R. L. Three factors in parent behavior. *J. consult. Psychol.,* 1953, 17, 306-308.

953. Lorr, M., Jenkins, R. L., & O'Connor, J. P. Factors descriptive of psychotherapy and behavior of hospitalized psychotics. *J. abnorm. soc. Psychol.,* 1955, 50, 78-86.

954. Lorr, M., Klett, C. J., McNair, D. M., & Lasky, J. J. *Manual: Impatient Multidimensional Psychiatric Scale (IMPS).* Washington, D. C.: Veterans Administration, 1962.

955. Lorr, M., McNair, D. M., & Klett, C. J. *Syndromes of psychosis.* New York: Pergamon, 1963.

956. Lorr, M., McNair, D. M., Klett, C. J., & Lasky, J. J. Evidence of ten psychotic syndromes. *J. consult. Psychol.,* 1962, 26, 185-189.

957. Lorr, M., Rubinstein, E., & Jenkins, R. L. A factor analysis of personality ratings of out-patients in psychotherapy. *J. abnorm. soc. Psychol.,* 1953, 48, 511-514.

958. Lorr, M., Schaefer, E., Rubinstein, E., & Jenkins, R. L. An analysis of an out-patient rating scale. *J. clin. Psychol.,* 1953, 9, 296-299.

959. Lorr, M., Wittman, P., & Schanberger, W. An analysis of the Elgin prognostic scale. *J. clin. Psychol.,* 1951, 7, 260-263.

960. Lovell, C. A study of the factor structure of thirteen personality variables. *Educ. psychol. Measmt,* 1945, 5, 335-350.

961. Lubin, A. Linear and non-linear discriminating functions. *Brit. J. Psychol.* (Statist. Sec.), 1950, 3, 90-104.

962. Lubin, A. *On the repeated measurements design.* Washington, D.C.: Walter Reed Army Institute of Research, 1958.

963. Lubin, A. The interpretation of significant interaction. *Educ. psychol. Measmt,* 1961, 21, 807-817.

964. Lubin, A., & Osburn, H. G. A theory of pattern analysis for the prediction of a quantitative criterion. *Psychometrika,* 1957, 22, 63-73.

965. Lubin, A. (with H. G. Osburn). The use of configural analysis for the evaluation of test scoring methods. *Psychometrika,* 1957, 22, 359-372.

966. Lubin, A., & Summerfield, A. A square root method of selecting a minimum set of variables in multiple regression. II. A worked example. *Psychometrika,* 1951, 16, 425-437.

967. Luborsky, L. B. Intraindividual repetitive measurements (*P*-technique) in understanding psychotherapeutic change. In O. H. Mowrer, *Psychotherapy: Theory and research.* New York: Ronald, 1953.

968. Luce, R. D., & Raiffa, H. *Games and decisions.* New York: Wiley, 1957.

969. Luce, R. D., and Shipley, E. F. Preference probability between gambles as a step function of event probability. *J. exp. Psychol.,* 1962, 63(1), 42-49.

970. Lunneborg, C. E. Dimensional analysis, latent structure and the problem of patterns. *Dissertation Abstr.* 1960, 20, 4186.

971. Luria, Zella. A semantic analysis of a normal and a neurotic therapy group. *J. abnorm. soc. Psychol.,* 1959, 58, 216-220.

972. MacAndrew, C., & Forgy, E. A note on the effects of score transformations in *Q* and *R* factor analysis techniques. *Psychol. Rev.,* 1963, 70, 116-118.

973. MacArthur, R. S. An experimental investigation of persistence in secondary school boys. *Canad. J. Psychol.,* 1955, 9, 42-54.

974. MacCrone, I. D., and Starfield, A. A

comparative study in multiple factor analysis of "neurotic" tendency. *Psychometrika,* 1949, 1-20.

975. MacRae, D., Jr. Direct factor analysis of sociometric data. *Sociometry,* 1960, 23, 360-371.

976. Madden, J. M. A note of the rating of multidimensional factors. Lackland AFB, Tex.: Personnel Lab., WADD, Rept. No. WADD-TN-60-258, 1960.

977. Madden, J. M. The methods and foundations of job evaluation in the United States Air Force. Lackland AFB, Tex.: Personnel Lab., ASD, Rept. No. ASD-TR-61-100, 1961.

978. Madsen, K. B. *Theories of motivation.* Cleveland: Howard Allen, 1961.

979. Mahalanobis, P. A. On the generalized distance in statistics. *Proc. National Inst. Sci. Industry,* 1936, 12, 49-55.

980. Maier, M. Evaluation of a new mathematics curriculum. *Amer. Psychologist,* 1962, 17, 336. (Abstract.)

981. Malinowski, B. *Argonauts of the western Pacific.* London: Allen and Unwin, 1922.

982. Mann, J. H. Studies of role performance. *Genet. Psychol. Monogr.,* 1961, 64, 213 317.

983. Mann, R. D. The relationships between personality characteristics and individual performance in small groups. Unpublished doctoral dissertation, Univer. of Michigan, 1958 (cf. also two further analyses quoted by Carrigan, 1960).

984. Mann, R. D. A review of the relationships between personality and performance in small groups. *Psychol. Rev.,* 1959, 56, 241-270.

985. Manning, W. H., & DuBois, P. H. Correlational methods in research on human learning perception and motor skills. *Psychol. Rep.,* Monogr. Suppl. 3-V18, 1962.

986. Marks, A., Guilford, J. P., & Merrifield, P. R. *A study of military leadership in relation to selected intellectual factors.* Los Angeles: Univer. of Southern California, Psychol. Lab. Rept. No. 21, 1959.

987. Marks, M. R. *A data organization model for the personnel subsystem.* Wright-Patterson AFB, Ohio: Behavioral Sciences Lab., ASD, ASD Tech. Rept. 61-447, 1961.

988. Marks, W. B., Dobelle, W. H., & MacNichol, E. F., Jr. Visual pigments of single primate cones. *Science,* 1964, 143, 1181-1183.

989. Marron, J. E. A search for basic reasoning abilities: A review of factor analysis. *USAF, Hum. Resour. Res. Cent. Res. Bull.,* No. 53-28, 1953.

990. Marshall, E. L. A multiple factor study of eighteen anthropometric measurements of Iowa City boys, ages 9 days to 6 years. *J. exp. Educ.,* 1938, 5, 212-228

991. Martin, R. F., & Hall, C. S. Emotional behavior in the rat. V. The incidence of behavior derangements resulting from air blast stimulations in emotional and nonemotional strains of rats. *J. comp. Psychol.,* 1941, 32, 191-204.

992. Marx, M. H. Maze learning as a function of added thiamine, *J. comp. physiol. Psychol.,* 1948, 41, 364-371.

993. Marx, M. H. Relationship between supra-normal glutamic acid and maze learning. *J. comp. psychol.,* 1949, 42, 320-327.

994. Marx, M. H. *Theories in contemporary psychology.* New York: Macmillan, 1963.

995. Marx, M. H., & Hillix, W. *Systems and theories in psychology.* New York: McGraw-Hill, 1963.

996. Marzoff, S. S., & Larsen, A. H. Statistical interpretation of symptoms illustrated with a factor analysis of problem check list items. *Educ. psychol. Measmt,* 1945, 5, 285-294.

997. Maslow, A. H. *Motivation and personality.* New York: Harper, 1954.

998. Matin, L., & Adkins, D. A second-order factor analysis of reasoning abilities. *Psychometrika,* 1954, 19, 71-78.

999. Maxwell, A. E. Statistical methods in factor analysis. *Psychol. Bull.,* 1959, 6, 141-152.

1000. Maxwell, A. E. Canonical variates when the variables are dichotomous. *Educ. psychol. Measmt,* 1961, 21, 259-271.

1001. Mayers, C. E., & Dingman, H. F. The structure of abilities at the preschool ages: Hypothesized domains. *Psychol. Bull.,* 1960, 57, 514-532.

1002. Mayr, E. *Systematics and the origin of the species.* New York: Columbia Univer. Press, 1942.

1003. McClearn, G. E. Genotype and mouse activity. *J. comp. physiol. Psychol.,* 1961, 54, 674-676.

1004. McClearn, G. E., & Meredith, W. Dimensional analysis of activity and elimination in the genetically heterogeneous group of mice (mus Musculus). Unpublished manuscript, Univer. of California, 1962.

1005. McClelland, D. C. *Personality.* New York: Dryden, 1951.

1006. McClelland, D. C., Atkinson, J. W., Clark, R. A., & Lowell, E. L. *The achievement motive.* New York: Appleton-Century-Crofts, 1953.

1007. McCloy, C. H. A factor analysis of personality traits to underlie character education. *J. educ. Psychol.,* 1936, 27, 375-387.

1008. McCloy, C. H. A study of cardiovascular variables by the method of factor analysis. *Child Develpm.,* 1936, 107-113.

1009. McCloy, C. H. An analysis for multiple factors of physical growth at different age levels. *Child Develpm.,* 1940, 11, 249-277.

1010. McCloy, C. H., & Young, N. D. *Tests and measurement in health and physical education.* (3rd ed.) New York: Appleton-Century-Crofts, 1954.

1011. McDaniel, E. D., Halter, A. N., & Hartford, D. L. Grade utility: A new noncognitive factor in academic prediction. *Educ. psychol. Measmt,* 1961, 21, 621-627.

1011. McDonald, R. P. A general approach to
(a) non-linear factor analysis. *Psychometrika,* 1962, 27, 397-415.

1011. McDonald, R. P. Difficulty factors and
(b) non-linear factor analysis. *Brit. J. math. statist. Psychol.,* 1965, 18, 11-23.

1012. McDougall, W. *Energies of men.* London: Methuen, 1932.

1013. McFarland, R. A. *Human factors in air transportation.* New York: McGraw-Hill, 1953.

1014. McNemar, Q. On the sampling errors of factor loadings. *Psychometrika,* 1941, 6, 141-152.

1014. McNemar, Q. The mode of operation of
(a) suppressant variables. *Amer. J. Psychol.,* 1945, 48, 554-555.

1015. McNemar, Q. On growth measurement. *Educ. psychol. Measmt,* 1958, 18, 47-55.

1015. McQuitty, L. L. A statistical method for
(a) studying personality. In O. H. Mowrer (Ed.), *Psychotherapy: Theory and research.* New York: Ronald, 1953. Pp. 414-462.

1016. McQuitty, L. L. A method of pattern analysis for isolating typological and dimensional constructs. Lackland AFB, Tex.: Air Force Personnel and Training Res. Center, Rept. No. AFPTRC-TN-55-62, 1955.

1017. McQuitty, L. L. Elementary linkage analysis for isolating orthogonal and oblique types and typal relevancies. *Educ. psychol. Measmt,* 1957, 17, 207-229.

1018. McQuitty, L. L. Isolating predictor patterns associated with major criterion patterns. Lackland AFB, Tex.: Air Force Personnel and Training Res. Center, Rept. No. AFPTRC-TN-57-113 (ASTIA Doc. No. 134236), 1957.

1019. McQuitty, L. L. Comprehensive hierarchical analysis. *Educ. psychol. Measmt,* 1960, 20, 805-816.

1020. McQuitty, L. L. Hierarchical syndrome analysis. *Educ. psychol. Measmt,* 1960, 20, 293-304.

1021. McQuitty, L. L. Item selection for configured scoring. *Educ. psychol. Measmt,* 1961, 21, 925-928.

1022. McQuitty, L. L. Rank-order typal analysis. *Educ. psychol. Measmt,* 1963, 23, 55-61.

1023. McQuitty, L. L., Wrigley, C., & Gaier, E. L. An approach to isolating dimensions of job success. Lackland AFB, Tex.: Air Force Personnel and Training Res. Center, Rept. No. AFPTRC-TR-54-49, 1954.

1024. McRuer, D. T., & Krendel, E. S. Man-machine system concept. *Proc. IRE,* 1962, 50, 1117-1123.

1025. Mead, Margaret. *Culture patterns and technological change.* New York: New American Library, 1955.

1026. Meehl, P. E. *Clinical versus statistical prediction.* Minneapolis: Univer. of Minnesota Press, 1954.

1027. Meehl, P. E. A comparison of clinicians with five statistical methods of identifying psychiatric MMPI profiles. *J. counsel. Psychol.,* 1959, 6, 102-109.

1028. Meehl, P. E. What can the clinician do well? Paper read at symposium Clinical skills revisited, Amer. Psychol. Ass., Sept., 1959.

1029. Meehl, P. E. The cognitive activity of the clinician. *Amer. Psychologist,* 1960, 15, 19-27.

1030. Meehl, P. E., & Dahlstrom, W. G. Objective configural rules for discriminating psychotic from neurotic MMPI profiles. *J. consult. Psychol.,* 1960, 24, 375-387.

1031. Meeland, T. An investigation of hypotheses for distinguishing personality factors A, F, and H. Unpublished doctoral dissertation, Univer. of Illinois, 1952.

1032. Mefferd, R. B., Jr. Adaptive changes to moderate seasonal heat in human subjects. *J. appl. Physiol.,* 1959, 14, 995-996.

1033. Mefferd, R. B., Jr., Hale, H. B., Kimble, J. P., Jr., Shannon, I. L., Prigmore, J. R., & Moran, L. J. Altitude-induced metabolic changes and the selection of aviation and space personnel — A baseline study. USAF SAM Repts. (In press).

1034. Mefferd, R. B., Jr., LaBrosse, E. H., Gawienowski, A. M., & Williams, R. J. Influence of chlorpromazine on certain biochemical variables of chronic male schizophrenics. *J. nerv. ment. Dis.,* 1958, 127, 167-179.

1035. Mefferd, R. B., Jr., Moran, L. J., & Kimble, J. P., Jr. Methodological considerations in the quest for a physical basis of schizophrenia. *J. nerv. ment. Dis.,* 1960, 131, 354-357.

1036. Meili, R. L'analyse de l'intelligence. *Arch. Psychol.* (Génève), 1946, 31, 1-64.

1037. Meili, R. Sur la nature des facteurs d'intelligence. *Acta Psychol.,* 1949, 6, 40-58.

1038. Mellinger, J. J. A comparison of multidimensional scaling and similarity analysis. *Amer. Psychologist,* 1958, 13, 375. (Abstract.)

1039. Melton, A. W. *Apparatus tests.* AAF Aviation Psychol. Res. Progr. Rept., No. 4: Washington, D.C.: U.S. Govt. Printing Office, 1947.

1040. Merbaum, A. D. Need for achievement in negro children. Unpublished master's thesis, Univer. of North Carolina, 1961.

1041. Merck, J. W. A mathematical model of the personnel structure of large-scale organizations based on Markov chains. Unpublished doctoral dissertation, Duke Univer., 1960.

1042. Merck, J. W., & Ford, F. B. Feasibility of a method of estimating short-term and long-term effects of policy decisions on the Airman Personnel System. Lackland AFB, Tex.: Personnel Lab., WADC, Rept. No. WADC-TR-59-38, 1959.

1042. Meredith, G. M. Contending hypotheses
(a) of ontogenesis for the exuberance-restraint personality factor, U.I. 21. *J. genet. Psychol.,* 1966. (In press).

1042. Meredith, G. M. Observations on the
(b) origins and current status of the ego assertive personality factor, U.I. 16. *J. genet. Psychol.,* 1966. (In press).

1043. Meredith, G. M., & Meredith, C. G. W. Some attributive characteristics of binocular rivalry. *Percept. mot. Skills,* 1964, 19, 511-514.

1044. Merrifield, P. R., Guilford, J. P., Christensen, P. R., & Frich, J. W. The role of intellectual factors in problem solving. *Psychol. Monogr.,* 1962, 76 (Whole No. 529).

1045. Merrill, M. A. The relationship of individual growth to average growth. *Hum. Biol.,* 1931, 3, 37-70.

1046. Merrill, M. A. *Problems of child delinquency.* New York: Macmillan, 1947.

1046. Merritt, R. L., & Rokkan, S. *Comparing*
(a) *nations: The use of quantitative data in cross national research.* New Haven: Yale Univer. Press, 1966.

1047. Merton, R. K. *Social theory and social structure.* Glencoe, Ill.: Free Press, 1959.

1048. Messick, S. Dimensions of social desirability. *J. consult. Psychol.,* 1960, 24, 279-287.

1049. Messick, S. Personality structure. In P. R. Farnsworth, O. McNemar & Q. McNemar (Eds.), *Annual Review of Psychology,* Vol. 12. Palo Alto, Calif.: Annual Reviews, 1961.

1050. Messick, S. J., & Abelson, R. P. The additive constant problem in multidimensional scaling. *Psychometrika,* 1956, 21, 1-15.

1051. Metrakos, J. D., & Fraser, F. C. Evidence for a hereditary factor in chandroectodermal dysplasia (Ellis-van Crevald Syndrome). *Amer. J. hum. Genet.,* 1954, 6, 260-269.

1052. Mettler, F. A. *Selective partial ablation of the frontal cortex.* New York: Hoeber, 1949.

1053. Meyer, W. J., & Bendig, A. W. A longitudinal study of the Primary Mental

Abilities Test. *J. educ. Psychol.*, 1961, 52, 50-60.

1054. Michael, W. B. Factor analyses of tests and criteria: A comparative study of two AAF pilot populations. *Psychol. Monogr.*, 1949, 63 (Whole No. 298).

1055. Michael, W. B. The nature of space and visualization abilities: Some recent findings based on factor analysis studies. *Trans. N.Y. Acad. Sci.*, 1949, ser. 2, 2, 275-281.

1056. Michael, W. B., Zimmerman, W. S., & Guilford, J. P. An investigation of two hypotheses regarding the nature of spatial-relations and visualization factors. *Educ. psychol. Measmt,* 1950, 10, 187-213.

1057. Michael, W. B., Zimmerman, W. S., & Guilford, J. P. An investigation of the nature of the spatial-relations and visualization factors in twin high school samples. *Educ. psychol. Measmt,* 1951, 11, 561-577.

1058. Michkin, E., & Braun, L. *Adaptive control systems.* New York: McGraw-Hill, 1961.

1059. Mierzwa, J. A. Comparison of systems of data for predicting career choice. *Personnel guid. J.,* 1963, 42, 30-34.

1060. Mill, J. S. *A system of logic.* (9th ed.) London: Longmans, Green, 1875.

1061. Milton, G. A. A factor analytic study of child-rearing behaviors. *Child Develpm.,* 1958, 29, 381-392.

1062. Miron, M. S. A cross-linguistic investigation of phonetic symbolism. *J. abnorm. soc. Psychol.,* 1961, 62, 623-630.

1063. Mitchell, J. V., Jr. Statistical relationships between score categories of the 16 P.F. and CPI inventories. Paper read at Amer. Psychol. Ass., New York, 1961 (*Amer. Psychologist,* 1961, 16, 386).

1064. Mitchell, J. V., Jr., & Pierce-Jones, J. A factor analysis of Gough's California Psychological Inventory. *J. consult. Psychol.,* 1960, 24, 453-456.

1065. Mitos, S. B. Semantic aspects of prognoses. *J. abnorm. soc. Psychol.,* 1959, 58, 137-140.

1066. Monroe, R. J. On the use of nonlinear systems in the estimation of nutritional requirements of animals. Unpublished thesis, North Carolina State College, 1949.

1067. Mooney, C. M. A factorial study of closure. *Canad. J. Psychol.,* 1954, 8, 51-60.

1068. Moore, T. V. The essential psychoses and their fundamental syndromes. *Stud. Psychol. Psychiat.* (Catholic Univ. Amer.), 1933, 3, No. 3.

1069. Moore, T. V., & Hsu, E. H. Factorial analysis of anthropological measurements in psychiatric patients. *Hum. Biol.,* 1946, 18, 133-157.

1070. Moran, L. J. *Repetitive psychological measures.* Austin: Univer. of Texas, Hogg Foundation, 1959.

1071. Moran, L. J., & Mefferd, R. B., Jr. Repetitive psychometric measures. *Psychol. Rep.,* 1959, 5, 269-275.

1072. Moran, L. J., Mefferd, R. B., Jr., & Kimble, J. P., Jr. A standardized twenty alternate form word association test for measurement of daily change in psychiatric condition. *Amer. Psychologist,* 1960, 15, 448.

1073. Moran, L. J., Mefferd, R. B., Jr., & Kimble, J. P., Jr. The objective measurement of psychopathology in longitudinal studies. *Trans. 5th Res. Conf. Chemotherapy Studies in Psychiatry and Research Approaches to Mental Illness,* 1960, 106-111.

1074. Moran, L. J., Kimble, J., Jr., & Mefferd, R. B., Jr. Repetitive psychometric measures: memory for faces. *Psychol. Rep.,* 1960, 7, 407-413.

1075. Moreno, J. L., & Jennings, H. H. Sociometric methods of grouping and re-grouping. *Sociometry,* 1944, 7, 397-414.

1076. Morgan, L. *Product semantic indices.* New York: Williams and Saylor, Inc., 1958.

1077. Morris, C. *Varieties of human value.* Chicago: Univer. of Chicago Press, 1956.

1078. Morsh, J. E. Job analysis bibliography. Lackland AFB, Tex.: Personnel Lab., AMD, AFSC, Rept. No. PRL-TDR-62-2, 1962.

1079. Morsh, J. E., Madden, M. M., & Christal, R. E. Job analysis in the United States Air Force. Lackland AFB, Tex.: Personnel Lab., WADD, Rept. No. WADD-TR-61-113, 1961.

1080. Mosier, C. I. Determining a single structure when loadings for certain tests are known. *Psychometrika,* 1936, 4, 149-162.

1081. Mosier, C. I. A factor analysis of certain neurotic tendencies. *Psychometrika,* 1937, 2, 263-287.

1082. Mowrer, O. H. On the dual nature of learning a reinterpretation of "Conditioning and Problem Solving." *Harvard educ. Rev.,* 1947, 17, 102-148.

1083. Mowrer, O. H. "*Q*-technique" — Description, history, and critique. In O. H. Mowrer (Ed.), *Psychotherapy: Theory and research.* New York: Ronald, 1953.

1084. Mowrer, O. H. *Learning theory and behavior.* New York: Wiley, 1960.

1085. Mowrer, O. H. *The new group therapy.* Princeton, N.J.: Van Nostrand, 1964.

1086. Mullen, F. A. Factors in the growth of girls. *Child Develpm.,* 1940, 11, 27.

1087. Mundy-Castle, A. C. Electrophysiological correlates of intelligence. *J. Pers.,* 1958, 26, 184-199.

1088. Mundy-Castle, A. C. Comments on Saunders' "Further implications of Mundy-Castle's correlations between EEG and Wechsler-Bellevue variables." *J. Nat. Inst. Personnel Res.* (Johannesburg), 1960, 8, 102-105.

1089. Murphy, M. A. A study of the primary components of cardiovascular tests. *Res. Quart.,* 1940, 11, 57.

1090. Murray, H. A., et al. *Explorations in personality.* New York: Oxford Univer. Press, 1938.

1091. Murray, J. E. An analysis of geometric ability. *J. educ. Psychol.,* 1949, 40, 118-124.

1092. Nagle, B. F. Criterion development. *Personnel Psychol.,* 1953, 6, 271-289.

1093. Nair, U. S. The application of the moment functions in the study of distribution laws in statistics. *Biometrika,* 1939, 30, 274-294.

1094. Nebylizin, W. D. Der Anwendung der faktor analyse bei der enforschung der struktur der hoheren nerventatigkeiten. *Problem und Ergeben der Psychologie.* Berlin, 1962.

1095. Nelson, M. D., & Shea, S. MMPI correlates of the inventory of factors STDCR. *Psychol. Rep.,* 1956, 3, 433-436.

1095. Nesselroade, J. R. An empirical examina-
(a)   tion of factor invariance with different rotational methods and indices of match-

ing. Unpublished master's thesis, Univer. of Illinois, 1965.

1096. Nesselroade, J. R. The separation of state and trait factors by *dR*-technique with special reference to anxiety, effort stress and cortertia. Unpublished doctoral dissertation, Univer. of Illinois, 1966.

1097. Newcomb, T. M. An approach to the study of communicative acts. *Psychol. Rev.,* 1953, 60, 393-404.

1097. Newell, A., Shaw, J. C., & Simon, H. A.
(a)   Chess-playing programs and the problem of complexity. *IBM J. Res. Develpm.,* 1958, 2, 320-335.

1097. Newell, A., & Simon, H. A. Computer
(b)   simulation of human thinking. *Science,* 1961, 174, 2011-2017.

1098. Newman, H. H., Freeman, F. N., & Holzinger, K. J. *Twins: A study of heredity and environment.* Chicago: Univer. of Chicago Press, 1937.

1099. Norman, D. A. Sensory thresholds, response biases, and the neural quantum theory. *J. math. Psychol.,* 1964, 1, 88-120.

1100. Norman, W. T. Validation of personality tests as measures of trait-rating factors. USAF PRL, Tech. Doc. Rept., 1962, No. 62-4.

1101. Norman, W. T. Toward an adequate taxonomy of personality attributes: Replicated factor structure in peer nomination personality ratings. *J. abnorm. soc. Psychol.,* 1963, 66, 574-583.

1102. Norris, R. C. Development of an efficient set of dimensions for description for Air Force ground crew jobs: Part I. Rating dimensions. Lackland AFB, Tex.: U. S. Air Force Personnel Training Res. Center, Rept. No. AFPTRC-TN-56-63, 1956.

1103. North, R. C., Jr. An analysis of the personality dimensions of introversion-extroversion. *J. Pers.,* 1949, 17, 352-368.

1104. Norton, D. W. An empirical investigation of some effects of non-normality and heterogeneity on the *F*-distribution. Unpublished thesis, State Univer. of Iowa, 1952.

1105. Nunnally, J. C. An investigation of some propositions of self-conception: The case of Miss Sun. *J. abnorm. soc. Psychol.,* 1955, 50, 87-92.

1106. Nunnally, J. C. *Popular conceptions of mental health.* New York: Holt, Rinehart, and Winston, 1961.

1107. Nunnally, J. C. The analysis of profile data. *Psychol. Bull.,* 1962, 59, 311-319.

1108. O'Connor, J. P. A statistical test of psychoneurotic syndromes. *J. abnorm. soc. Psychol.,* 1953, 48, 581-584.

1109. O'Connor, J. P., & Stefic, E. C. Some patterns of hypochondriasis. *Educ. psychol. Measmt,* 1959, 19, 363-371.

1110. Odbert, H. S., Karwoski, T. F., & Eckerson, A. B. Studies in synesthetic thinking. I. Musical and verbal associations of color and mode. *J. gen. Psychol.,* 1942, 26, 153-173.

1111. Oehrn, A. Experimentelle studien zur individualpsychologie. *Psychol. Arbeiten,* 1889, 1, 92-152.

1112. Oeser, O. A., & Hammond, S. B. (Eds.) *Social structure and personality in a city.* New York: Macmillan, 1954.

1113. Oeser, O. A., & Harary, F. A mathematical model for structural role theory, I. *Hum. Relat.,* 1962, 15, 89-109.

1113. O'Halloran, Ann. An investigation of
(a)   personality factors associated with achievement in arithmetic and reading. Unpublished master's thesis, Purdue Univer., 1954.

1114. O'Hare, J. J. *A factorial study of EEG and auditory functions with respect to the alpha scanning hypothesis.* Washington, D.C.: Catholic Univer. Press, 1957.

1115. Olds, J. Self-stimulation of the brain. *Science,* 1958, 127, 315-323.

1116. Olèron, P. *Les composantes de l'intelligence d'après recherches factorielles.* Paris: Presses Univer. France, 1957.

1117. Olson, H. C. A factor analysis of depth perception test scores of male subjects having normal acuity. *Amer. Psychologist,* 1950, 5, 263.

1118. O'Neil, W. M. *Introduction to method in psychology.* Melbourne: Melbourne Univer. Press, 1957.

1119. Orcutt, G. H., Greenberger, M., Korbel, J., et al. *Microanalysis of socio-economic systems: A simulation study.* New York: Harper, 1962.

1120. Orr, D. B. A new method of clustering jobs. *J. appl. Psychol.,* 1960, 44, 44-59.

1121. Osgood, C. E. The nature and measurement of meaning. *Psychol. Bull.,* 1952, 49, 197-237.

1122. Osgood, C. E. The cross-cultural generality of visual-verbal synesthetic tendencies. *Behav. Sci.,* 1960, 5, 146-179.

1123. Osgood, C. E. Studies on the generality of affective meaning systems. *Amer. Psychologist,* 1962, 17, 10-28.

1124. Osgood, C. E. On understanding and creating sentences. *Amer. Psychologist,* 1963, 18, 735-751.

1125. Osgood, C. E., & Luria, Zella. A blind analysis of multiple personality using the semantic differential. *J. abnorm. soc. Psychol.,* 1954, 59, 579-591.

1126. Osgood, C. E., & Miron, M. S. Bibliography or research using the semantic differential, 1957.

1127. Osgood, C. E., Miron, M. S., & Archer, W. K. The cross-cultural generality of meaning systems. Unpublished manuscript, Univer. of Illinois, 1963.

1128. Osgood, C. E., & Suci, G. J. A measure of relation determined by both mean difference and profile information. *Psychol. Bull.,* 1958, 49, 251-262.

1129. Osgood, C. E., Suci, G. J., & Tannenbaum, P. H. *The measurement of meaning.* Urbana: Univer. of Illinois Press, 1957.

1130. Osgood, C. E., Ware, E. E., & Morris, C. Analysis of the connotative meanings of a variety of human values as expressed by American college students. *J. abnorm. soc. Psychol.,* 1961, 62, 62-73.

1131. Overall, J. E. A common solution for transposed factor analyses. Privately circulated manuscript, 1964.

1132. Overall, J. E., & Williams, C. M. Models for medical diagnosis. *Behav. Sci.,* 1961, 6, 134-142.

1133. Oyama, T., Tanaka, Y., & Osgood, C. E. *J. verbal Learn. verbal Behav.,* 1964. (In press).

1134. Page, E. B. Teacher comments and student performance: a seventy-four classroom experiment in school motivation. *J. educ. Psychol.,* 1958, 49, 173-181.

1135. Palmer, G. J., Jr., & McCormick, E. J. A factor analysis of job activities. *J. appl. Psychol.,* 1961, 45, 289-294.

1136. Parsons, T. *The social system.* Glencoe, Ill.: The Free Press, 1938.

1137. Pauling, L. The stochastic method and the structure of proteins. *Amer. Scientist,* 1955, 43, 285.

1138. Pawlik, K. Experimentelle und theoretische Beiträge zur analyse der simultanleistung. Unpublished doctoral dissertation, Univer. of Vienna, 1958.

1139. Pawlik, K. Educational predictions from objective personality test dimensions. Paper read at Amer. Psychol. Ass., New York City, 1961.

1140. Pawlik, K. Psychologische masse der aktivierung. *Z. exp. angew. psychol.*, 1963, 10, 19-34.

1141. Pawlik, K., & Cattell, R. B. Third-order factors in objective personality tests. *Brit. J. Psychol.*, 1964, 55, 1-18.

1142. Pawlik, K., & Cattell, R. B. The relationships between certain personality factors and measures of cortical arousal. *Neuropsychology,* 1965, 3, 129-151.

1143. Payne, R. W., & Hewlett, J. H. G. Thought disorder in psychotic patients. In H. J. Eysenck (Ed.), *Experiments in personality.* Vol. 2. New York: Humanities Press, 1960.

1144. Peak, H. Attitude and motivation. In M. R. Jones (Ed.), *Nebraska Symposium on Motivation.* Lincoln: Univer. of Nebraska Press, 1955.

1145. Pearson, K. On lines and planes of closest fit to points in space. *Phil. Mag.,* 1901, 2, 557-572.

1146. Pearson, K. On the general theory of multiple contingency with special reference to partial contingency. *Biometrika,* 1915, 11, 145-158.

1147. Pemberton, C. The closure factors related to other cognitive processes. *Psychometrika,* 1952, 17, 267-288.

1148. Pemberton, C. The closure factors related to temperament. *J. Pers.,* 1952, 21, 159-175.

1149. Penrose, L. S. Some recent trends in human genetics. *Proc. 9th Int. Congr. Genet.,* Bellagio, 1953, 521-530.

1150. Personnel Research Section, Adjutant General's Office. *Studies in visual acuity.* Pers Res. Sect. Rept., No. 742. Wash., D.C.: U.S. Govt. Printing Office, 1948.

1151. Peterson, D. R. The age generality of personality factors derived from ratings. *Educ. psychol. Measmt,* 1960, 20, 461-474.

1152. Peterson, D. R. The scope and generality of verbally defined personality factors. *Psychol. Rev.,* 1965, 72 (1), 48-59.

1153. Peterson, D. R., & Cattell, R. B. Personality factors in nursery school children

as derived from parent ratings. *J. clin. Psychol.,* 1958, 14, 346-355.

1154. Peterson, D. R., & Cattell, R. B. Personality factors in nursery school children as derived from teacher ratings. *J. consult. Psychol.,* 1959, 23, 562.

1155. Peterson, W. F. *Man, weather, sun.* Springfield, Ill: Charles C. Thomas, 1947.

1156. Petrie, A. *Personality and the frontal lobes.* London: Routledge and Kegan Paul, 1952.

1157. Petrie, A., & Powell, M. B. The selection of nurses in England. *J. appl. Psychol.,* 1951, 35, 281-286.

1158. Piaget, J. *Psychology of intelligence.* Paterson, N.J.: Littlefield-Adams, 1960.

1159. Pickford, R. W. A factorial analysis of colour vision. *Nature* (London), 1946, 157, 700.

1160. Pickford, R. W. Human color vision and Garnit's theory. *Nature* (London), 1948, 162, 414-415.

1161. Pickford, R. W. *Individual differences in color vision.* London: Routledge and Kegan Paul, 1951.

1162. Pickford, R. W. A brief review of some factorial studies of color vision. *Die Farbe* (Berlin), 1962.

1163. Pickrel, E. W. Classification theory and techniques. Lackland AFB, Tex.: Human Resources Res. Center, Res. Note Pers., 1952, 52-60.

1164. Pierson, G. R. A specification equation for predicting treatment response. *J. soc. Psychol.* (In press).

1165. Pierson, G. R., et al. SMAT motivation factors as predictors of academic achievement of delinquent boys. *J. Psychol.,* 1964, 57, 243-249.

1166. Pillai, K. C. S. *Statistical tables for tests of multivariate hypotheses.* Manila: Univer. of the Philippines, Statistical Center, 1960.

1167. Pincus, G., & Hoagland, H. Steroid excretion and the stress of flying. *J. aviat. Med.,* 1943, 14, 173-193.

1168. Pinzka, C., & Saunders, D. R. Analytic rotation to simple structure. II. Extension to an oblique solution. (RB-54-31). Princeton, N.J.: Educational Testing Service, 1954. (Multilithed.)

1169. Pollack, I. The information of elementary auditory displays. *J. Acoust. Soc. Amer.,* 1952, 24, 745-749.

1169. Porter, R., Cattell, R. B., & Schaie, K. W.
(a) *Handbook for the child personality questionnaire.* (rev. ed.) Champaign, Ill.: Institute for Ability and Personality Testing, 1966.

1170. Potthoff, R. F. On the Johnson — Neyman technique and some extensions thereof. *Psychometrika,* 1964, 29, 241-256.

1171. Price, B. P., & Schatz, H. H. Application of high-speed computation to linear discriminant function operations. Lackland AFB, Tex.: Air Force Personnel and Training Res. Center, Rept. No. AFPRTC-TN-55-66, 1955.

1172. Pruitt, D. G. Pattern and level of risk in gambling decisions. *Psychol. Rev.,* 1962, 69 (3), 187-201.

1173. Quamme, H. J. A factor analysis of cardiovascular variables. Unpublished master's thesis, Springfield College (Springfield, Mass.), 1941.

1174. Quenouille, M. H. *Associated measurements.* London: Butterworth, 1952.

1175. Quenouille, M. H. *The analyses of multiple time series.* New York: Hafner, 1957.

1176. Radcliffe, J. Some properties of ipsative score matrices. *Austral. J. Psychol.,* 1963, 6, 1-10.

1177. Raiffa, H., & Schlaifer, R. *Applied statistical decision theory.* Harvard Univer., Graduate School of Business, 1961.

1178. Rao, C. R. *Advanced statistical methods in biometric research.* New York: Wiley, 1952.

1179. Rao, C. R. Estimation and test of significance in factor analysis. *Psychometrika,* 1955, 20, 93-111.

1180. Rao, C. R., & Slater, P. Multivariate analysis applied to differences between neurotic groups. *Brit. J. Psychol.* (Statist. Sec.), 1949, 2, 17-29.

1181. Rapaport, D. *Diagnostic psychological testing.* Vol. 1. Chicago: Year Book, 1945.

1182. Rapaport, D. The structure of psychoanalytic theory: A systematizing attempt. In S. Koch (Ed.), *Psychology: A study of a science.* Vol. III. New York: McGraw-Hill, 1959.

1183. Rapoport, A. *Fights, games, and debates.* Ann Arbor: Univer. of Michigan Press, 1960.

1184. Rapoport, A., Chammah, A., Dwyer, J., & Gyr, J. Three-person, non-zero-sum, non-negotiable games. *Behav. Sci.,* 1962, 7, 38-58.

1185. Rapoport, A., & Orwant, C. Experimental games: A review. *Behav. Sci.,* 1962, 7(1), 1-37.

1186. Reeb, M. How people see jobs: A multidimensional analysis. *Occup. Psychol.,* 1959, 33, 1-17.

1187. Rees, L. A factorial study of physical constitution in women. *J. ment. Sci.,* 1950, 96, 619-632.

1188. Rees, L., & Eysenck, H. J. A factorial study of some morphological and psychological aspects of human constitution. *J. ment. Sci.,* 1945, 91, 8-21.

1189. Reitan, R. M. Investigation of the validity of Halstead's measures of biological intelligence. *A.M.A. Arch. Neurol. Psychiat.,* 1955, 73, 28-35.

1190. Rendel, J. M., Robertson, A., Asker, A. A., Khishin, S. S., & Ragab, M. T. The inheritance of milk production characteristics. *J. agric. Sci.,* 1957, 48, 420-432.

1191. Rethlingshafer, Dorothy. The learning of a visual discrimination problem under varying motivating conditions. *J. comp. Psychol.,* 1941, 32, 583-591.

1191. Rethlingshafer, Dorothy. The relation of
(a) tests of persistence to other measures of continuance of action. *J. abnorm. soc. Psychol.,* 1942, 37, 71-82.

1192. Reyburn, H. A., & Taylor, J. G. Some factors of personality. A further analysis of some of Webb's data. *Brit. J. Psychol.,* 1939, 30, 151-165.

1193. Reyburn, H. A., & Taylor, J. G. Factors in introversion and extraversion. *Brit. J. Psychol.,* 1941, 31, 335-340.

1194. Richards, T. W., & Nelson, V. L. Abilities of infants during the first 18 months. *J. genet. Psychol.,* 1939, 299-318.

1195. Richardson, J. A factorial analysis of reading abilities in 10 year old primary school children. *Brit. J. educ. Psychol.,* 1950, 20, 200-201.

1196. Richardson, L. F. The distribution of wars in time. *J. Roy. Statist. Ass.,* 1946, 107, 242-250.

1197. Richardson, L. F. *Statistics of deadly quarrels.* Q. Wright and C. C. Lienan (Eds.) Pittsburgh: Boxwood Press, 1960.

1198. Richardson, M. W. Multidimensional psychophysics. *Psychol. Bull.,* 1938, 35, 659-660.

1198. Rickels, K., & Cattell, R. B. The clinical
(a) factor validity and trueness of the IPAT verbal and objective batteries for anxiety

and regression. *J. clin. Psychol.,* 1965, 21, 257-264.

1199. Riegel, R. M. Factorenanalysen des Hamburg-Wechsler-Intelligenz-Tests für erwachsene (WAWIE) für die altersstufen 20-34, 35-49, 50-64-65 jahre und älter. *Diagnostika,* 1960, 6, 41-66.

1200. Rimoldi, H. J. A. Personal tempo. *J. abnorm. soc. Psychol.,* 1951, 46, 283-303.

1201. Rimoldi, H. J. A. The central intellective factor. *Psychometrika,* 1951, 16, 75-102.

1202. Roback, A. A. *Psychology of character.* London: Kegan Paul, 1927.

1203. Roberts, A. W. H. Artifactor-analysis: Some theoretical background and practical demonstrations. *J. Nat. Inst. Personnel Res.* (Johannesburg), 1954, 7, 168-188.

1204. Robson, E. B. Birth weight in cousins. *Ann. hum. Genet.,* 1955, 19, 262-268.

1205. Roby, T. B. Problems of rational group assembly exemplified in the medium bomber crew. Lackland AFB, Tex.: Human Resources Research Center, Res. Bull., 1953, 53-58.

1205. Rodnick, E. H. The response of schizo-
(a) phrenic and normal subjects to stimulation of the autonomic nervous system. *Psychol. Bull.,* 1938, 35, 646.

1206. Rodwan, A. S., & Hake, H. W. The linear discriminant function as a model for perception. *Amer. J. Psychol.,* 1964, 77, 380-392.

1207. Roff, M. Some properties of the communality in multiple factor theory. *Psychometrika,* 1936, 1, 1-6.

1208. Roff, M. A factorial study of the Fels Parent Behavior Scales. *Child Develpm.,* 1949, 20, 29-45.

1209. Roff, M. Personnel selection and classification: Perceptual tests. A factorial analysis. Randolph Field, Tex.: USAF School of Aviation Medicine (Proj. No. 21-02-009) (cf. also: *Psychometr. Monogr.,* No. 8, 1952), 1950.

1210. Roff, M. Personnel selection and classification procedures: Spatial tests. Randolph Field, Tex.: Air Univer. School of Aviation Medicine (Proj. No. 21-29-002, Final Rept.), 1951.

1211. Roff, M. A factorial study of tests in the perceptual area. *Psychometr. Monogr.,* No. 8, 1952.

1212. Roff, M. The pilot candidate selection research program: V. A factorial study of the motor aptitudes area. Randolph

Field, Tex.: USAF School of Aviation Medicine (Proj. No. 21-29-008, Rept. No. 5), 1953.

1213. Rogers, C. A. The orectic relations of verbal fluency. *Austral. J. Psychol.,* 1956, 8, 27-46.

1214. Rogers, C. R., & Dymond, R. F. (Eds.) *Psychotherapy and personality change.* Chicago: Univer. of Chicago Press, 1954.

1215. Rogers, L. L., & Pelton, R. B. Effect of glutamine on I.Q. scores of mentally deficient children. *Tex. Repts. Biol. Med.,* 1957, 15, 1, 84-91.

1216. Rohrer, J. H., & Sherif, M. *Social psychology at the crossroads.* New York: Harper, 1951.

1216. Rorer, L. G. The great response-style
(a) myth. *Psychol. Bull.,* 1965, 63, 129-156.

1217. Rosenberg, M. Comparison of hypnotic subjects against themselves with regard to cognitive change in manipulated and non-manipulated attitudes. Adv. publication, 1959.

1218. Rosenfeld, J. L. Adaptive decision processes. Tech. Rept. 403. Cambridge, Mass.: Massachusetts Institute of Technology, Res. Lab. of Electronics, AD-287460, Sept. 1962.

1219. Rosenthal, I. A factor analysis of anxiety variables. Unpublished doctoral dissertation, Univer. of Illinois, 1955.

1220. Rosenzweig, M. R., Krech, D., & Bennett, E. L. Brain chemistry and adaptive behavior. In H. F. Harlow and C. N. Woolsey (Eds.), *Biological and biochemical basis of behavior.* Madison: Univer. of Wisconsin Press, 1958. Pp. 367-400.

1221. Rosenzweig, M. R., Krech, D., & Bennett, E. L. Brain enzymes and adaptive behavior. In *Ciba Foundation Symposium on Neurological Basis of Behavior.* London: Churchill, 1958. Pp. 337-355.

1222. Rosenzweig, M. R., Krech, D., & Bennett, E. L. A search for relations between brain chemistry and behavior. *Psychol. Bull.,* 1960, 57, 476-492.

1223. Rosenzweig, M. R., Krech, D., & Bennett, E. L. Heredity, environment, brain biochemistry and learning. In *Current trends in psychological theory.* Pittsburgh: Univer. of Pittsburgh Press, 1961. Pp. 87-110.

1224. Ross, J. *A factor test of a memory model.* (RB-61-14) Princeton, N.J.: Educational Testing Service, 1961.

1225. Ross, J. Informational coverage and correlational analysis. *Psychometrika*, 1962, 27, 297-306.

1226. The relation between test and person factors. *Psychol. Rev.*, 1963, 70 (5), 432-443.

1226. Rotter, J. B. Psychotherapy. *Ann. Rev.*
(a) *Psychol.*, 1960, 11, 381-414.

1227. Roy, S. N. On a heuristic method of test construction and its use in multivariate analysis. *Ann. math. Statist.*, 1953, 24, 220-238.

1228. Roy, J. *Some aspects of multivariate analysis*. New York: Wiley, 1957.

1229. Roy, S. N. Step-down procedure in multivariate analysis. *Ann. math. Statist.*, 1958, 29, 1177-1187.

1230. Roy, S. N., & Bargmann, R. E. Tests of multiple independence and the associated confidence bounds. *Ann. math. Statist.*, 1958, 29, 491-503.

1231. Roy, S. N., & Gnanadesikan, R. Some contributions to anova in one or more dimensions. I and II. *Ann. math. Statist.*, 1959, 30, 304-317, 318-340.

1232. Royce, J. R. A synthesis of experimental designs in program research. *J. gen. Psychol.*, 1950, 43, 295-303.

1233. Royce, J. R. The factorial analysis of animal behavior. *Psychol. Bull.*, 1950, 47, 235-259.

1234. Royce, J. R. A factorial study of emotionality in the dog. *Psychol. Monogr.*, 1955, 69 (Whole No. 407).

1235. Royce, J. R. Factor theory and genetics. *Educ. psychol. Measmt*, 1957, 17, 361-376.

1236. Royce, J. R. Factors as theoretical constructs. *Amer. Psychologist*, 1963, 18, 522-528.

1237. Royce, J. R., & Covington, M. Genetic differences in the avoidance conditioning of mice. *J. comp. physiol. Psychol.*, 1960, 53, 197-200.

1237. Royce, J. R., Carran, A. B., & Howarth,
(a) E. Factor analysis of emotionality in ten strains of inbred mice. *Multiv. behav. Res.* (In press).

1238. Rozeboom, W. W. The fallacy of the null-hypothesis significance test. *Psychol. Bull.*, 1960, 57, 416-428.

1239. Ruckmick, C. A. A preliminary study of the emotions. *Psychol. Monogr.*, 1921, 30, No. 136.

1240. Rulon, P. J., & Brooks, W. D. *On statistical tests of group differences*. Cambridge, Mass.: Educational Research Corp., 1961.

1241. Rummel, R. J. Dimensions of conflict behavior within and between nations. *General systems: Yearbook of the Soc. for Gen. Systems Res.*, 1963, 8, 1-50.

1242. Rupe, J. C. Research into basic methods and techniques of Air Force job analysis. I. Lackland AFB, Tex.: Human Resources Res. Center, Rept. No. 52-16, 1952.

1243. Rupe, J. C. Research into basic methods and techniques of Air Force job analysis. IV. Lackland AFB, Tex.: USAF Personnel and Training Res. Center, Rept. No. AFPTRC-TN-56-51, 1956.

1244. Rupe, J. C., & Westen, R. J. Research into basic methods of Air Force job analysis. II. Lackland AFB, Tex.: USAF Personnel and Training Res. Center, Rept. No. AFPTRC-TN-55-51, 1955.

1245. Rupe, J. C., & Westen, R. J. Research into basic methods of Air Force job analysis. III. Lackland AFB, Tex.: USAF Personnel and Training Res. Center, Rept. No. AFPTRC-TN-55-53, 1955.

1246. Rush, C. H., Jr. A factorial study of sales criteria. *Personnel Psychol.*, 1953, 6, 9-24.

1247. Ryans, D. G. An experimental attempt to analyze persistent behavior. *J. gen. Psychol.*, 1938, 19, 333-353.

1248. Rymert, M. L. The personal equation in motor capacities. *Scand. Sci. Rev.*, 1923, 2, 177-194.

1249. Sakaguchi, M. Reports on experimental games, *Stat. appl. Res.*, JUSE, 1960, 7, 156-165.

1250. Sanders, E. M., Mefferd, R. B., Jr., & Bown, O. H. Verbal-quantitative ability and certain personality and metabolic characteristics of male college students. *Educ. psychol. Measmt*, 1960, 20, 491-503.

1251. Sanford, R. N. The effect of abstinence from food upon imaginal processes: A preliminary experiment. *J. Psychol.*, 1936, 2, 129-136.

1252. Sanford, R. N., Adkins, M. M., Miller, R. B., & Cobb, E. Physique, personality, and scholarship. *Monogr. Soc. Res. Child Develpm.*, 1943, 8, No. 1.

1253. Saunders, D. R. Factor analysis. I. Some

effects of chance error. *Psychometrika,* 1948, 13, 251-257.

1254. Saunders, D. R. Practical methods in the direct factor analysis of psychological score matrices. Unpublished doctoral dissertation, Univer. of Ill., 1950.

1255. Saunders, D. R. A further investigation of the relation between questionnaire and behavior rating factors. Unpubl., quoted after French (1953), 1953.

1256. Saunders, D. R. Moderator variables in prediction. *Educ. psychol. Measmt,* 1956, 16, 209-222.

1256. Saunders, D. R. On the dimensionality of
(a) the WAIS battery for two groups of normal males. *Psychol. Rep.,* 1959, 5, 529-541.

1257. Saunders, D. R. Further implication of Mundy-Castle's correlation between EEG and Wechsler Bellevue variables. *J. Nat. Inst. Personnel Res.* (Johannesburg), 1960, 8, 91-101.

1258. Saunders, D. R. A factor analysis of the information and arithmetic items of the WAIS. *Psychol. Rep.,* 1960, 6, 367-383.

1259. Saunders, D. R. A factor analysis of the picture completion items of the WAIS. *J. clin. Psychol.,* 1960, 16, 146-149.

1260. Sawrey, W. L., Keller, L., & Conger, J. J. An objective method of grouping profiles by distance functions and its relation to factor analysis. *Educ. psychol. Measmt,* 1960, 20, 651-674.

1261. Schaedeli, R. Untersuchungen zur verifikation von meilis intelligenzfaktoren. *Z. exp. angew. Psychol.,* 1961, 8, 211-264.

1262. Schaefer, E. S. A circumplex model for material behavior. *J. abnorm. soc. Psychol.,* 1959, 59, 226-235.

1263. Schaefer, E. S., & Bell, R. Q. Structure of attitudes toward child-rearing and the family. *Amer. Psychologist,* 1955, 10, 319-320.

1264. Schaefer, E. S., Bell, R. Q., & Bayley, N. Development of a maternal behavior research instrument. *J. genet. Psychol.,* 1959, 95, 83-104.

1264. Schaie, K. W. Equivalence or chaos: A
(a) hypothesis testing factor analysis study of the role of behavior rating, questionnaire, and instrument factors in personality structure research. Paper read at SMEP, Boulder, Colo., 1963.

1265. Scheier, I. H., & Cattell, R. B. Confirmation of objective test factors and assessment of their relation to questionnaire factors: A factor analysis of 113 rating, questionnaire, and objective test measurements of personality. *J. ment. Sci.,* 1958, 104, 608-624.

1266. Scheier, I. H., Cattell, R. B., & Horn, J. L. Objective test factor U.I. 23: Its measurement and its relation to clinically-judged neuroticism. *J. clin. Psychol.,* 1960, 16, 135-145.

1267. Scheier, I. H., Cattell, R. B., & Mayeske, G. W. The objective-test factors of imaginative tension (U. I. 25), introversion (U. I. 32), anxiety (U. I. 24), and autistic non-conformity (U. I. 34): (1) data on new factor-measuring tests, and (2) relation of factors to clinically-judged psychosis. Urbana: Univer. of Illinois, Lab. of Personality Assessment and Group Behavior, Rept. No. 10, 1960.

1268. Scher, A. M., Young, A. C., & Meredith, W. W. A factor analysis of the electrocardiogram. *Circ. Res.,* 1960, 8, No. 3, 519-526.

1269. Schlosberg, H. A scale for the judgment of facial expressions. *J. exp. Psychol.,* 1941, 29, 497-510.

1270. Schlosberg, H. The description of facial expressions in terms of two dimensions. *J. exp. Psychol.,* 1952, 44, 229-237.

1271. Schlosberg, H. Three dimensions of emotion. *Psychol. Rev.,* 1954, 61, 81-88.

1272. Schmid, J., & Leiman, J. M. The development of hierarchical factor solutions. *Psychometrika,* 1957, 22, 53-61.

1273. Schmid, J., Jr., Morsh, J. E., & Detter, H. M. Analysis of job satisfaction. Lackland AFB, Tex.: USAF Personnel and Training Res. Center, Rept. No. AFPTRC-TN-57-30, 1957.

1274. Schneck, M. R. The measurement of verbal and numerical abilities. *Arch. Psychol.,* No. 107, 1929.

1275. Schnore, L. F. The statistical measurement of urbanization and economic development. *Land Econ.,* 1961, 37, 229-245.

1276. Schoenemann, P. H. A solution of the orthogonal Procrustes problem with applications to orthogonal and oblique rotation. Unpublished doctoral dissertation, Univer. of Illinois, 1964.

1277. Schroder, H. M. Group development and functioning. Paper read at Amer. Psychol. Ass., Sept., 1960.

1278. Schutz, W. C. *FIRO: A three-dimensional theory of interpersonal behavior.* New York: Holt, 1958.

1279. Schweiker, R. F. *Individual space models of certain statistics.* Unpublished thesis, Harvard Univer., 1954.

1280. Scott, J. P., Fuller, J. L., & King, J. A. The inheritance of animal breeding cycles in hybrid basenji-cocker spaniel dogs. *J. Hered.,* 1959, 50, 254-261.

1281. Searle, L. V. The organization of hereditary maze brightness and dullness. *Genet. Psychol. Monogr.,* 1949, 39, 279-325.

1282. Sears, R. R., Maccoby, E. E., & Levin, H. *Patterns of child rearing.* Evanston, Ill.: Row, Peterson, 1957.

1283. Seashore, R. H., Buxton, C. E., & McCollom, I. N. Multiple factorial analysis of fine motor skills. *Amer. J. Psychol.,* 1940, 53, 251-259.

1284. Seashore, R. H., Dudek, F. J., & Holtzman, W. A factorial analysis of arm-hand precision tests. *J. appl. Psychol.,* 1949, 33, 579-584.

1285. Seashore, S. H., & Seashore, R. H. Individual differences in simple auditory reaction times of hands, feet, and jaws. *J. exp. Psychol.,* 1941, 29, 342-345.

1286. Seashore, S. H., Starmann, R., Kendall, W. E., & Helmick, J. S. Group factors in simple and discrimination reaction times. *J. exp. Psychol.,* 1941, 29, 346-349.

1287. Sells, S. B. A research program on the psychiatric selection of flying personnel. I. Methodological introduction and experimental design. Randolph Field, Tex.: Air Univer. School of Aviation Medicine (Proj. No. 21-37-002, Rept. No. 1), 1951.

1288. Sells, S. B. Development of personality test battery for psychiatric screening of flying personnel. *J. aviat. Med.,* 1955, 26, 34-45.

1289. Sells, S. B. Further developments on adaptability screening of flying personnel. *J. aviat. Med.,* 1956, 27, 440-451.

1290. Sells, S. B. Structural measurement of personality and motivation: A review of contributions of Raymond B. Cattell. *J. clin. Psychol.,* 1959, 15, 3-21.

1291. Sells, S. B. Psychologic methods of air-crew selection. In H. G. Armstrong (Ed.), *Aerospace Medicine.* Baltimore: Williams and Wilkins, 1961.

1292. Sells, S. B. *Essentials of psychology.* New York: Ronald, 1962.

1293. Sells, S. B. (Ed.) *Stimulus determinants of behavior.* New York: Ronald, 1962.

1294. Sells, S. B. *Toward a taxonomy of organizations.* Fort Worth, Tex.: Texas Christian Univer. (Contract No. 3436(00), Tech. Rept. No. 2 (presented at Conference on Organizational Research, Graduate School of Industrial Administration, Carnegie Institute of Technology, Pittsburgh, Pa., June, 1962), 1962.

1295. Sells, S. B., & Manning, W. H. *Prediction of military flight adaptability criteria by personality measures. Cross-validation of Cattell factors and other predictors.* Fort Worth, Tex.: Texas Christian Univer. Contract No. AF 41 (657)-336, Final Rept., 1962.

1296. Sells, S. B., Tiedeman, D. V., Danford, M. B., Haggard, E. A., Gupta, H. C., & McQuitty, L. L. *Symposium on pattern analysis.* Randolph Field, Tex.: Air Univer. School of Aviation Medicine, 1955.

1297. Sells, S. B., & Trites, D. K. Attitudes. In C. Harris (Ed.), *Encyclopedia of educational research.* (3rd ed.) New York: Macmillan, 1960.

1298. Selye, H. *The physiology and pathology of exposure to stress.* Montreal: Acta Inc., 1950.

1299. Selye, H., & Heuser, G. (Eds.) *Fifth annual report of stress, 1955-56.* New York: M.D. Publications, 1956.

1300. Sen, N. N. An objective study of experimental neurosis. I. An historical and critical review. *Psychol. Stud.* (Mysore), 1961, 6(1), 10-29.

1301. Sen, N. N. An objective study of experimental neurosis. II. Behavioral changes during "experimental stress." *Psychol. Stud.* (Mysore), 1961, 6(2), 18-58.

1302. Sewell, W. H., Mussen, P. H., & Harris, C. W. Relationships among child training practices. *Amer. sociol. Rev.,* 1955, 20, 137-148.

1303. Shannon, I. L. *Contribution of the parotid glands to whole saliva volume.* USAF SAM Rept. 62-6, 1961.

1304. Shannon, I. L., & Prigmore, J. R. Whole

saliva volume, sodium, potassium and chloride, day to day comparisons. *J. dent. Res.*, 1959, 38, 843.

1305. Shannon, I. L., & Prigmore, J. R. *Flow rate responses of the human parotid.* USAF SAM Rept. 60-85, 1960.

1306. Shapley, L. S. Simple games: An outline of the descriptive theory. *Behav. Sci.*, 1962, 7, 59-66.

1307. Shartle, C. L. *Occupational information: Its development and application.* New York: Prentice-Hall, 1946.

1308. Shaw, D. R. Variation in inter-scale correlation on the semantic differential as a function of the concept judged. Unpublished master's thesis, Univer. of Illinois, 1955.

1309. Sheehan, M. R. A study of individual consistency in phenomenal constancy. *Arch. Psychol.*, 1938, 31, 1-95.

1310. Sheldon, W. H. *Atlas of men, a guide for somatotyping the adult male at all ages.* New York: Harper, 1954.

1311. Sheldon, W. H., & Stevens, S. S. *The varieties of temperament: A psychology of constitutional differences.* New York: Harper, 1942.

1312. Shepard, R. N. Stimulus and response generalization: Tests of a model relating generalization to distance in psychological space. *J. exp. Psychol.*, 1958, 55, 509-523.

1313. Shepard, R. N. The analysis of proximities: Multidimensional scaling with an unknown distance function, I and II. *Psychometrika*, 1962, 27, 125-140; 219-246.

1314. Shepard, R. N. Attention and the metric structure of the stimulus. *J. math. Psychol.*, 1964, 1, 54-87.

1315. Sherman, M., & Jost, H. Quantification of psycho-physiological measures. *Psychosomat. Med.*, 1945, 7, 215-219.

1316. Shortle, C. L., et al. A factorial study of administrative behavior. *Personnel Psychol.*, 1955, 8, 165-180.

1316. Shotwell, A. M., & Cattell, R. B. Per-
(a) sonality profiles of more successful and less successful psychiatric technicians. *Amer. J. ment, Defic.*, 1954, 58, 496-499.

1317. Shotwell, A. M., Hurley, J. R., & Cattell, R. B. Motivational structure of a hospitalized mental defective. *J. abnorm. soc. Psychol.*, 1961, 62, 422-426.

1318. Shubert, G. A solution to the indeterminate factor resolution of Thurstone and Degan's study of the Supreme Court. *Behav. Sci.*, 1959, 4, 183-191.

1319. Shubert, G. The 1960 term of the Supreme Court: A psychological analysis. *Amer. pol. sci. Rev.*, 1962, 56, 90-113.

1320. Shure, G. H., & Halstead, W. C. Cerebral localization of intellectual processes. *Psychol. Monogr.*, 1958, 72, 40.

1321. Shuttleworth, F. K. The nature versus nurture problem. Part II. The contributions of nature and nurture to individual differences in intelligence. *J. educ. Psychol.*, 1935, 26, 655-681.

1322. Sidman, M. A note on functional relations obtained from group data. *Psychol. Bull.*, 1952, 49, 263-269.

1323. Sidman, M. *Tactics of scientific research.* New York: Basic Books, 1960.

1324. Simmel, G. *Conflict,* trans. K. H. Wolff; *The web of group affiliations,* trans. R. Bendix. Glencoe, Ill.: Free Press, 1955.

1325. Simon, G. B. Evaluation and combination of criterion measures by factor analysis: a study of B-25 preflights by airplane and engine mechanics. Lackland AFB, Tex.: USAF Personnel and Training Res. Center, Rept. No. AFPTRC-TR-54-23, 1954.

1325. Singer, J. D. (Ed.) *Human behavior and*
(a) *international politics.* Chicago: Rand McNally, 1965.

1326. Skinner, B. F. *The behavior of organisms: An experimental analysis.* New York: Appleton-Century, 1938.

1327. Skinner, B. F. Are theories of learning necessary? *Psychol. Rev.*, 1950, 57, 193-216.

1328. Skinner, B. F. *Science and human behavior.* New York: Macmillan, 1953.

1329. Slater, P. Experiments in psychometrics. In H. J. Eysenck (Ed.), *Experiments in personality.* Vol. 2. New York: Humanities Press, 1960.

1330. Small, E. R. Age and sex differences in the semantic structure of children. *Dissertation Abstr.*, 1959, 19, 872-873.

1331. Smith, H., Gnanadesikan, R., & Hughes, J. B. Multivariate analysis of variance (MANOVA). *Biometrics,* 1962, 18, 22-41.

1332. Smith, P. A. A factor-analytic study of the self-concept. *J. consult. Psychol.*, 1960, 24, 191.

1333. Sokal, R. R. A comparison of five tests for completeness of factor extraction. *Trans. Kansas Acad. Sci.,* 1959, 62, 141-152.

1334. Sokal, R. R., & Sneath, P. H. A. *Principles of numerical taxonomy.* San Francisco: Freeman, 1964.

1335. Sorokin, P. A. *Social and cultural dynamics.* Vol. 3. New York: American Book Co., 1937.

1336. Spearman, C. General intelligence, objectively determined and measured. *Amer. J. Psychol.,* 1904, 15, 201-293.

1337. Spearman, C. The proof and measurement of association between two things. *Amer. J. Psychol.,* 1904, 15, 72-101.

1338. Spearman, C. E. *The nature of "intelligence" and the principles of cognition.* London: Macmillan, 1923.

1339. Spearman, C. *The abilities of man.* New York: Macmillan, 1927.

1340. Spearman, C. Abilities as sums of factors, or as their products. *J. educ. Psychol.,* 1937, 28, 629-631.

1341. Spearman, C. E. *Psychology down the ages.* London: Macmillan, 1937.

1342. Specht, Laura L. A comparison of the domains of the 16 P.F. items and items in the MMPI with respect to the amount of common and unique space, with a check on the magnitude of a response set factor. Unpublished bachelor's thesis, Univer. of Illinois, 1966.

1343. Spence, K. W. *Behavior theory and conditioning.* New Haven, Conn.: Yale Univer. Press, 1956.

1344. Spies, C. J. A bibliography of factor analytic studies of learning. In P. H. DuBois, W. H. Manning, and C. J. Spies (Eds.), Factor analysis and related techniques in the study of learning. ONR Tech. Rept. No. 7 (Contract No. Nonr 816(02). St. Louis, Mo.: Washington Univer., Dept. of Psychology, 1959.

1345. Stead, W. H., & Shartle, C. L. *Occupational counseling techniques.* New York: American Book Co., 1940.

1346. Stephenson, W. *The study of behavior: Q-technique and its methodology.* Chicago: Univer. of Chicago Press, 1953.

1346. Stern, G. C. The measurement of psy-
(a) chological characteristics of students and learning environment. In S. Messick & J. Ross (Eds.), *Measurement in personality and cognition.* New York: Wiley, 1962.

1347. Stevens, S. S. On the psychophysical law. *Psychol. Rev.,* 1957, 64, 163-181.

1348. Stevens, S. S. Problems and methods of psychophysics. *Psychol. Bull.,* 1958, 54, 177-196.

1349. Stevens, S. S. The psychophysics of sensory function. *Amer. Scientist,* 1960, 48, 226-253.

1350. Stevens, S. S. Toward a resolution of the Fechner-Thurstone legacy. *Psychometrika,* 1961, 26, 35-47.

1351. Stewart, J. H. *Native peoples of South America.* New York: McGraw-Hill, 1959.

1352. Stilson, D. W. A psychophysical investigation of triangular shape. Unpublished doctoral dissertation, Univer. of Illinois, 1956.

1353. Stocklin, P. L. Decision theory applications in human decision making. *Ann. N.Y. Acad. Sci.,* 1961, 89, 823-828.

1354. Stogdill, R. M. Leadership, membership and organization. *Psychol. Bull.,* 1950, 47, 1-14.

1355. Storm, T., Rosenwald, G. C., & Child, I. L. A factor analysis of self-ratings on social behavior. *J. soc. Psychol.,* 1958, 48, 45-49.

1356. Storms, L. H., & Segal, J. J. Eysenck's personality theory, with special reference to the "dynamics of anxiety and hysteria." *Brit. J. med. Psychol.,* 1958, 31, 228-246.

1357. Stott, L. H. An analytical study of self-reliance. *J. Psychol.,* 1938, 5, 107-118.

1358. Strodtbeck, F. L. The family as a three person group. *Amer. sociol. Rev.,* 1954, 19, 23-29.

1359. Strodtbeck, F. L., & Hare, A. P. Bibliography of small group research from 1900 through 1953. *Sociometry,* 1954, 17, 107-178.

1360. Strong, E. K., Jr. Strong Vocational Interest Blank for Men. Palo Alto, Calif.: Consulting Psychologists Press, 1927, 1951.

1361. Studman, L. G. Studies in experimental psychiatry. V. "W" and "f" factors in relation to traits of personality. *J. ment. Sci.,* 1935, 81, 107-137.

1362. Suci, G. J. A comparison of semantic structures in American Southwest culture groups. *J. abnorm. soc. Psychol.,* 1960, 61, 25-30.

1363. Süllwold, F. Ein beitrag zur analyse der aufmerksamkeit. *Z. exp. angew. Psychol.,* 1954, 2, 495-513.

1364. Süllwold, F. Untersuchungen über die faktorenstruktur komplexer denkprobleme. Göttingen: Hogrefe. *Ber. 20. Kongr. Deutsch. Ges. f. Psychol.,* 139f., 1956.

1365. Sumita, K., & Ichitani, T. A factor analytic study on the differentiation of intellectual abilities. *Tohoku Psychol. Folia,* 1958, 16, 51-85.

1366. Summerfield, A., & Lubin, A. A square root method of selecting a minimum set of variables in multiple regression: I. The method. *Psychometrika,* 1951, 16, 271-284.

1367. Summers, S. A. The learning of responses to multiple weighted cues. *J. exp. Psychol.,* 1962, 64, 29-34.

1368. Sundland, D. M. The construction of Q sorts: A criticism. *Psychol. Rev.,* 1962, 69, 62-64.

1369. Swadish, M. Salish internal relationships. *Int. J. Amer. Ling.,* 1950, 16, 157-167.

1370. Sweney, A. B. Faktorenanalytische methoden in der motivations-forschung Cattell. *Z. exp. angew. Psychol.,* 1961, 8, 136-148.

1371. Sweney, A. B., & Cattell, R. B. Dynamic factors in twelve year old children as revealed in measures of integrated motivation. *J. clin. Psychol.,* 1961, 4, 360-369.

1372. Sweney, A. B., & Cattell, R. B. Relationships between integrated and unintegrated motivation structure examined by objective tests. *J. soc. Psychol.,* 1962, 57, 217-226.

1373. Sweney, A. B., & Cattell, R. B. The response of ergic tension levels to environmental situations. (In press).

1374. Sweney, A. B., & May, J. The effects of electroshock therapy on repression and other related measures of motivation, personality and education. (In press).

1375. Swets, J. A. Detection theory and psychophysics: A review. *Psychometrika,* 1961, 26, 49-63.

1376. Swets, J. A. Is there a sensory threshold? *Science,* 1961, 134, 168-177.

1377. Swets, J. A. (Ed.) *Signal detection and recognition by human observers.* New York: Wiley, 1964.

1378. Tamaoka, S. Musical talent test. *Jap. J. Psychol.,* 1937, 12.

1379. Tanner, J. M., & Burt, A. W. A. Physique in the infra-human mammalia: A factor analysis of body measurements of dairy cows. *J. Genet.,* 1954, 52, 36-51.

1380. Tapp, J. An examination of hypotheses concerning the motivational components of attitude strength. Unpublished master's dissertation, Univer. of Illinois, 1958.

1381. Tarde, J. G. *Underground man.* Trans. C. Brereton. London: Duckworth, 1905.

1382. Taton, J. Translation of Ronchi, V. *Histoire de la Lumiere.* Paris, 1956.

1383. Tatsuoka, M. M., & Tiedeman, D. V. Discriminant analysis. *Rev. educ. Res.,* 1954, 24, 402-420.

1384. Tatsuoka, M. M., & Tiedeman, D. V. Statistics as an aspect of scientific method in research on teaching. In N. L. Gage (Ed.), *Handbook of research on teaching.* Chicago: Rand McNally, 1963.

1385. Taylor, C. W. A factorial study of fluency in writing. *Psychometrika,* 1947, 12, 239-262.

1386. Taylor, C. W., & Barron, F. *Scientific creativity.* New York: Wiley, 1963.

1387. Taylor, C. W., Smith, W. R., Ghiselin, B., Sheets, B. V., & Cochran, J. R. Identification of communication abilities in military situations. Lackland AFB, Tex.: Personnel Lab., WADC, Rept. No. WADC-TR-58-92, 1958.

1387. Tharp, H. G. Psychological patterning in
(a) marriage. *Psychol. Bull.,* 1963, 60, 97-117.

1388. Theron, P. A. Peripheral vasomotor reactions as indices of basic emotional tension and lability. *Psychosomat. Med.,* 1948, 10, 335-346.

1389. Thompson, D. W. *On growth and form.* Cambridge, Eng.: Cambridge Univer. Press, 1917.

1390. Thompson, J. W. Meaningful and unmeaningful rotation of factors. *Psychol. Bull.,* 1962, 59, 211-223.

1391. Thompson, W. R. The inheritance and development of intelligence. *Proc. Ass. Res. nerv. ment. Dis.,* 1954, 33, 209-231.

1392. Thompson, W. R. Traits, factors and genes. *Eugen. Quart.,* 1957, 4, 8-16.

1393. Thomson, G. H. *The factorial analysis of human ability.* Boston: Houghton Mifflin, 1939.

1394. Thomson, G. H., & Ledermann, W. The influence of multivariate selection on the factorial analysis of ability. *Brit. J. Psychol.,* 1939, 29, 288-306.

1395. Thorndike, R. L. *Your city.* New York: Harcourt, Brace, 1939.

1396. Thorndike, R. L. *Analysis of a further 300 American cities.* New York: Harcourt, Brace, 1941.

1397. Thorndike, R. L. *Personnel selection.* New York: Wiley, 1949.

1398. Thorndike, R. L. The problem of classification of personnel. *Psychometrika,* 1950, 15, 215-235.

1399. Thorndike, R. L., Hagen, E. P., Orr, D. B., & Rosner, B. An empirical approach to the determination of Air Force job families. Lackland AFB, Tex.: USAF Personnel and Training Res. Center, Rept. No. AFPTRC-TR-57-5, 1957.

1400. Thorndike, R. L., & Hagen, E. P. Long-term prediction of some officer-effectiveness measures from aptitude tests. Lackland AFB, Tex.: Personnel Lab., WADC, Rept. No. WADC-TR-58-489, 1958.

1401. Thorne, T. C. *Principles of psychological examining: A systematic textbook.* Brandon, Vt.: Journal of Clinical Psychology Press, 1955.

1402. Thornton, G. R. A factor analysis of tests to measure persistence. *Psychol. Monogr.,* 1939, 51 (Whole No. 229).

1403. Thouless, R. H. Individual differences in phenomenal regression. *Brit. J. Psychol.,* 1932, 216-241.

1404. Thouless, R. H. Test unreliability and function fluctuation. *Brit. J. Psychol.,* 1936, 26, 325-343.

1405. Thurstone, L. L. The method of paired comparisons for social values. *J. abnorm. soc. Psychol.,* 1927, 21, 384-400.

1406. Thurstone, L. L. The measurement of change in social attitude. *J. soc. Psychol.,* 1931, 2, 230-235.

1407. Thurstone, L. L. Multiple factor analysis. *Psychol. Rev.,* 1931, 38, 406-427.

1408. Thurstone, L. L. The measurement of social attitudes. *J. abnorm. soc. Psychol.,* 1931, 26, 249-269.

1409. Thurstone, L. L. A multiple factor study of vocational interests. *J. Pers.,* 1931, 10, 198-205.

1410. Thurstone, L. L. The vectors of mind. *Psychol. Rev.,* 1934, 41, 1-32.

1411. Thurstone, L. L. The isolation of 7 primary abilities. *Psychol. Bull.,* 1936, 33, 780-781.

1412. Thurstone, L. L. Primary mental abilities. *Psychometr. Monogr.,* 1938, No. 1.

1413. Thurstone, L. L. The perceptual factor. *Psychometrika,* 1938, 3, 1-17.

1414. Thurstone, L. L. Current issues in factor analysis. *Psychol. Bull.,* 1940, 37, 189-236.

1415. Thurstone, L. L. Experimental study of simple structure. *Psychometrika,* 1940, 5, 153-168.

1416. Thurstone, L. L. *A factorial study of perception.* Chicago: Univer. of Chicago Press, 1944.

1417. Thurstone, L. L. The effects of selection in factor analysis. *Psychology,* 1945, 10, 165-198.

1418. Thurstone, L. L. Factor analysis and body types. *Psychometrika,* 1946, 11, 15-21.

1419. Thurstone, L. L. Factorial analysis of body measurements. *Amer. J. phys. Anthropol.,* 1947, 5, 15-28.

1420. Thurstone, L. L. *Multiple factor analysis.* Chicago: Univer. of Chicago Press, 1947.

1421. Thurstone, L. L. Primary mental abilities. Chicago: Univer. of Chicago, Psychometric Lab. Res. Rept. No. 50, 1948.

1422. Thurstone, L. L. Mechanical aptitude. III Analysis of group tests. Chicago: Univer. of Chicago, Psychometric Lab. Res. Rept. No. 35, 1949.

1423. Thurstone, L. L. Some primary abilities in visual thinking. Chicago: Univer. of Chicago, Psychometric Lab. Rept. No. 59, 1950.

1423. Thurstone, L. L. *Thurstone Temperament*
(a) *Schedule: Examiner's manual.* Chicago: Science Research Associates, 1950.

1424. Thurstone, L. L. The dimensions of temperament: Analysis of Guilford's thirteen personality scores. *Psychometrika,* 1951, 16, 11-20.

1425. Thurstone, L. L., & Chave, E. J. *The measurement of attitude.* Chicago: Univer. of Chicago Press, 1929.

1426. Thurstone, L. L., & Thurstone T. G. Factorial studies of intelligence. *Psychometr. Monogr.,* No. 2, 1942.

1427. Thurstone, L. L., & Thurstone, T. G. *Primary mental abilities test.* Chicago: Science Research Associates, 1948.

1428. Thurstone, T. G., Thurstone, L. L., & Strandskov, H. H. A psychological study of twins: I. Distribution of absolute twin differences for identical and fraternal twins. Chapel Hill: Univer. of North Carolina, Psychometric Lab. Rept. No. 4, 1953.

1429. Thurstone, T. G., Thurstone, L. L., & Strandskov, H. H. A psychological study of twins. II. Series of one hundred and twenty-five pairs of twins on fifty-nine tests. Chapel Hill: Univer. of North Carolina, Psychometric Lab. Rept. No. 12, 1955.

1430. Tiedeman, D. V., & Bryan, J. G. Predictions of college field of concentration. *Harvard educ. Rev.,* 1958, 24, 122-139.

1431. Tinbergen, N. *The study of instinct.* Oxford: Clarendon Press, 1951.

1432. Toda, M. Measurement of subjective probability distribution. State College, Pa.: Pennsylvania State Univer., Div. Math. Psych., Inst. for Res., Rept. No. 3, 1963.

1433. Tollefson, D. Differential responses to humor and their relation to personality and motivation measures. Unpublished doctoral dissertation, Univer. of Illinois, 1959.

1434. Tolman, E. C. A psychological model. In T. Parsons and E. A. Shils (Eds.), *Toward a general theory of action.* Cambridge, Mass.: Harvard Univer. Press, 1951. Pp. 279-361.

1434. Tomkins, S. S., & Messick, S. *Computer* (a) *simulation of personality.* New York: Wiley, 1963.

1435. Toops, H. A. The selection of graduate assistants. *Personnel J.,* 1928, 6, 457-472.

1436. Torgerson, W. S. A theoretical and empirical investigation of multidimensional scaling. Unpublished doctoral dissertation, Princeton Univer., 1951.

1437. Torgerson, W. S. Multidimensional scaling: I. Theory and method. *Psychometrika,* 1952, 17, 401-419.

1438. Torgerson, W. S. *Theory and methods of scaling.* New York: Wiley, 1958.

1439. Torr, D. V. A factor analysis of 49 variables. Lackland AFB, Tex.: Hum. Resources Res. Center, Res. Bull., 1953, 53-67.

1440. Toulmin, S. *The philosophy of science.* London: Hutchinson's Universal Library, 1953.

1441. Toynbee, A. J. *War and civilization.* New York: Oxford Univer. Press, 1950.

1442. Travers, R. M. W. Personnel selection and classification research as a laboratory science. Lackland AFB, Tex.: USAF Personnel and Training Res. Center, Rept. No. AFPTRC-TN-56-96 (ASTIA Doc. No. 098872), 1956.

1443. Triandis, H. C., & Lambert, W. W. A restatement and test of Schlosberg's theory of emotion with two kinds of subjects from Greece. *J. abnorm. soc. Psychol.,* 1958, 56, 321-328.

1444. Triandis, H. C., & Osgood, C. E. A comparative factorial analysis of semantic structures in monolingual Greek and American college students. *J. abnorm. soc. Psychol.,* 1958, 57, 187-196.

1445. Triandis, H. C., & Triandis, Leigh M. Race, social class, religion and nationality as determinants of social distance. *J. abnorm. soc. Psychol.,* 1960, 61, 118.

1446. Trites, D. K. Adaptability measures as predictors of performance ratings. *J. appl. Psychol.,* 1960, 44, 349-353.

1447. Trites, D. K. Problems in air traffic management: I. Longitudinal prediction of effectiveness of air traffic controllers. Oklahoma City: FAA Civil Aeromedical Research Institute, Rept. No. 61-1, 1961.

1448. Trites, D. K., & Cobb, B. B. Problems in air traffic management: II. Implication of age for training and job performance of air traffic controllers. Oklahoma City: FAA Civil Aeromedical Research Institute, Rept. No. 62-3, 1962.

1449. Trites, D. K., & Kubala, A. L. Characteristics of successful pilots. *J. aviat. Med.,* 1957, 28, 34-40.

1450. Trites, D. K., Kubala, A. L., & Cobb, B. B. Criterion dimensions of ability to pilot training. Randolph AFB, Tex.: Air Univer. School of Aviation Medicine, Rept. No. 59-26, 1959.

1451. Trites, D. K., Kubala, A. L., & Sells, S. B. Aircraft accidents vs. characteristics of pilots. *J. aviat. Med.,* 1955, 26, 486-494.

1452. Trites, D. K., & Sells, S. B. Combat performance. *J. appl. Psychol.,* 1957, 41, 121-130.

1453. Truxal, J. G. *Automatic feedback control system synthesis.* New York: McGraw-Hill, 1955.

1454. Tryon, R. C. *Cluster analysis: Correlation profile and orthometric (factor) analysis for the isolation of unities in mind and personality.* Ann Arbor: Edwards Bros., 1939.

1455. Tryon, R. C. Genetic differences in maze-learning ability in rats. *39th Yrbk., Nat. Soc. Stud. Educ.* (Part 1) Bloomington, Ill.: Public School Pub. Co., 1940. Pp. 111-119.

1456. Tryon, R. C. Identification of social areas by cluster analysis: A general method with an application to the San Francisco Bay area. *Univer. of Calif. Publ. Psychol.,* 1955, 8(1)viii.

1457. Tryon, R. C. Cumulative communality cluster analysis. *Educ. psychol. Measmt,* 1958, 18, 3-35.

1458. Tschechtelin, S. M. A. Factor analysis of children's personality rating scale. *J. Psychol.* 1944, 18, 197-200.

1459. Tsujioka, B., Sonohara, T., & Yatabe, T. A factorial study of the temperament of Japanese college male students by the Yatabe-Guilford personality inventory. *Psychologia,* 1957, 1, 110-119.

1460. Tucker, L. R. A method for synthesis of factor analysis study. Dept. Army A.G.O. Personnel Res., Sec. Rept. No. 984, 1955.

1461. Tucker, L. R. The objective definition of simple structure in linear factor analysis. *Psychometrika,* 1955, 20, 209-225.

1462. Tucker, L. R. Factor analysis of double centered score matrices. Paper read at Division 5, Amer. Psychol. Ass. & Psychometric Soc., Sept., 1956.

1463. Tucker, L. R. Determination of parameters of a functional relation by factor analysis. *Psychometrika,* 1958, 23, 19-23.

1464. Tucker, L. R. An inter-battery method of factor analysis. *Psychometrika,* 1958, 23, 111-137.

1465. Tucker, L. R. *Determination of generalized learning curves by factor analysis.* Tech. Rept. Princeton, N.J.: Educational Testing Service, 1960.

1466. Tucker, L. R. Implications of factor analysis of three-way matrices for measurement of change. Paper presented at the Conference on Measuring Change, Univer. of Wisconsin, May 1, 1962.

1467. Tucker, L. R. Implications of factor analysis of three way matrices for measurements of change. In C. W. Harris, (Ed.), *Problems in measuring change.* Madison: Univer. of Wisconsin Press, 1963.

1468. Tucker, L. R., & Messick, S. An individual differences model for multidimensional scaling. *Psychometrika,* 1963, 28, 333-367.

1469. Tupes, E. C. Relationships between behavior trait ratings by peers and later officer performance of USAF Officer Candidate School graduates. Lackland AFB, Tex.: USAF Personnel and Training Res. Center, Rept. No. AFPTRC-TN-57-125 (ASTIA Doc. No. 134257), 1957.

1470. Tupes, E. C., & Christal, R. C. Stability of personality trait rating factors obtained under diverse conditions. Wright-Patterson AFB, Ohio: USAF WADC Tech. Note No. 58-61, 1958.

1471. Tupes, E. C., & Christal, R. C. Recurrent personality factors based on trait ratings. Lackland AFB, Tex.: Aeronaut. Syst. Dev., Personnel Lab. Rept. No. ASD-TR-61-97, 1961.

1472. Tupes, E. C., & Kaplan, M. N. Similarity of factors underlying peer ratings of socially acceptable, socially unacceptable, and bipolar personality traits. Lackland AFB, Tex.: Aeronaut. Syst. Dev., Personnel Lab. Rept. No. ASD-TN-61-48, 1961.

1473. Tyler, F. T. A factorial analysis of fifteen MMPI scales. *J. consult. Psychol.,* 1951, 15, 451-456.

1474. Uhr, L., & Miller, J. G. (Eds.) *Drugs and behavior.* New York: Wiley, 1960.

1475. Underwood, B. J., & Schultz, R. W. *Meaningfulness and verbal learning.* New York: Lippincott, 1960.

1476. United States Air Force. Randolph Field, Tex.: USAF School of Aviation Medicine, Rept. No. 10 (Contr. No. AF No. 33 (038)-19569, Proj. No. 21-0202-0007).

1477. U.S. War Manpower Commission, Division of Occupational Analysis. Factor analysis of occupational aptitude tests. *Educ. psychol. Measmt,* 1945, 5, 147-155.

1478. Unwin, J. D. *Sex and culture.* London: Oxford Univer. Press, 1934.

1479. Valenstein, E. S., Riss, W., & Young, W. C. Sex drive in genetically heterogeneous and highly inbred strains of male guinea pigs. *J. comp. physiol. Psychol.,* 1954, 47, 162-165.

1480. Vallance, T. R., Glickman, A. S., & Suci, G. J. Criterion rationale for a personnel research program. *J. appl. Psychol.,* 1953, 37, 429-431.

1481. Vandenberg, S. G. The hereditary abilities study. *Eugen. Quart.,* 1956, 3, 94-99.

1482. Vandenberg, S. G. The hereditary abilities study: Hereditary components in a psychological test battery. *Amer. J. hum. Genet.,* 1962, 14, 220-237.

1483. Vandenberg, S. G. Computers in behavioral science. *Behav. Sci.,* 1963, 8, 247-267.

1484. Van Der Mewre, A. B. The effect of bellergal and hydergine on the subjective symptoms and the peripheral vasomotor reactions in anxiety states. *South African med. J.,* 1953, 27, 84-88.

1485. Van Der Mewre, A. B., & Theron, P. A. A new method of measuring emotional stability. *J. gen. Psychol.,* 1947, 37, 109-123.

1486. Van Egeren, L. F. Experimental determination by *P*-technique of functional unities of depression and other psychological states. Unpublished master's thesis, Univer. of Illinois, 1963.

1487. Van Steenberg, N. J. Factors in the learning behavior of the albino rat. *Psychometrika,* 1939, 4, 179-200.

1488. Vaughn, C. L. Factors in the rat. *Comp. psychol. Monogr.,* 1937, 14, No. 3.

1489. Vernon, P. E. *The structure of human abilities.* London: Methuen, 1950.

1489. Von Verschuer, O. Die vererbungsbio-
(a) logische zwillingsforschung, ihre biologischen grundlagen. *Ergebn. Inr. Med. Kinderheilk,* 1957, 31, 35-120.

1490. Votaw, D. F., Jr. Review and summary of research on personnel classification techniques. Lackland AFB, Tex.: USAF Personnel and Training Res. Center, Rept. No. AFPTRC-TN-56-106 (ASTIA Doc. No. 098881), 1956.

1491. Waddington, C. H. Genetic assimilation of an acquired character. *Evolution,* 1953, 7, 118-126.

1492. Waldrop, R. S. A factorial study of the components of body build. *Psychol. Bull.,* 1940, 37, 578.

1493. Walker, Helen M., & Lev, J. *Statistical inference.* New York: Holt, 1953.

1494. Wallace, S. R., Jr., & Weitz, J. Industrial psychology. In C. P. Stone & Q. McNemar (Eds.), *Annual Review of Psychology.* Vol. 6. Palo Alto, Calif.: Annual Reviews, 1955.

1495. Walters, E. Retentivity in the special senses. In F. C. Thomas, *Ability and knowledge* (quoted after Vernon, 1950), 1935.

1496. Ward, J. H., Jr. An application of

linear and curvilinear joint functional regression in psychological prediction. Lackland AFB, Tex.: USAF Personnel and Training Res. Center, Rept. No. AFPTRC-TR-54-86, 1954.

1497. Ward, J. H., Jr. Markov models and Monte Carlo techniques. *Educ. psychol. Measmt,* 1961, 21, 219-225.

1498. Ward, J. H., Jr. Hierarchical grouping to maximize payoff. Lackland AFB, Tex.: Personnel Lab., WADD, Rept. No. WADD-TN-61-29, 1961.

1499. Ward, J. H., Jr., & Hook, M. E. A hierarchical grouping procedure applied to a problem of grouping profiles. Lackland AFB, Tex.: Personnel Lab., ASD, AFSC, Rept. No. ASD-TN-61-55, 1961.

1500. Warden, C. J. *Animal motivation studies. The albino rat.* New York: Columbia Univer. Press, 1931.

1501. Ware, E. E. Relationships of intelligence and sex to diversity of individual semantic meaning spaces. Unpublished doctoral dissertation, Univer. of Illinois, 1958.

1502. Warner, W. L., & Lunt, P. S. *The social life of a modern community.* New Haven: Yale Univer. Press, 1941.

1503. Webb, E. Character and intelligence. *Brit. J. Psychol., Monogr. Suppl.,* 1915, 1, 3.

1504. Weber, H. Untersuchungen zur faktorenstruktur numerischer aufgaben. *Z. exp. angew. Psychol.,* 1953, 3, 336-391.

1505. Webster, H., & Bereiter, C. The reliability of changes measured by mental test scores. In C. W. Harris (Ed.), *Problems in measuring change.* Madison: Univer. of Wisconsin Press, 1963.

1506. Weckroth, J. Dimensions of color sensation. *Scand. J. Psychol.,* 1961, 2, 65-70.

1507. Weil-Malherbe, H. Glutamic acid and its relation to the nervous system. In R. T. Williams, *Metabolism and function in nervous tissue.* London: Cambridge Univer. Press, 1952.

1508. Weil-Malherbe, H., & Bone, A. D. Activators and inhibitors of hexohinase in human blood. *J. ment. Sci.,* 1951, 97, 634-662.

1508. Weisen, A. Differential reinforcing
(a) effects of onset and offset of stimulation on the operant behavior of normals, neurotics, and psychopaths. Unpublished doctoral dissertation, Univer. of Florida, 1965.

1509. Weiss, L. *Statistical decision theory.* New York: McGraw-Hill, 1961.

1510. Weitz, J. Selecting supervisors with peer ratings. *Personnel Psychol.,* 1958, 11, 25-35.

1511. Weitzenhoffer, A. Hypnotic susceptibility as related to masculinity-femininity. Unpublished doctoral dissertation, Univer. of Michigan, 1956.

1512. Weitzman, R. A. *A comparison of the performance of rats and fish on a probabilistic, discriminative learning problem.* ONR Tech. Rept. and doctoral dissertation, Princeton Univer. Princeton, N.J.: Educational Testing Service, 1959.

1512. Wells, H. P. Relationships between
(a) physical fitness and psychological variables. Unpublished doctoral dissertation, Univer. of Illinois, 1958.

1513. Welsh, G. S., & Dahlstrom, W. G. (Eds.) *Basic readings on the MMPI in psychology and medicine.* Minneapolis: Univer. of Minnesota Press, 1956.

1514. Wenger, M. A. Some relations between muscular processes and personality and their factor analyses. *Child Develpm.,* 1938, 9, 261-276.

1515. Wenger, M. A. Interrelations among some physiological variables. *Psychol. Bull.,* 1940, 37, 446.

1516. Wenger, M. A. The measurement of individual differences in autonomic balance. *Psychosomat. Med.,* 1941, 3, 427-434.

1517. Wenger, M. A. The stability of measurements of autonomic balance. *Psychosomat. Med.,* 1942, 4, 94-95.

1518. Wenger, M. A. A study of physiological factors: The autonomic nervous system and the skeletal musculature. *Hum. Biol.,* 1942, 14, 69-84.

1519. Wenger, M. A. Seasonal variations in some physiological variables. *J. lab. clin. Med.,* 1943, 28, 1101-1108.

1520. Wenger, M. A. A further note on the measurement of autonomic balance. *Psychosomat. Med.,* 1943, 5, 148-151.

1521. Wenger, M. A. An attempt to appraise individual differences in muscular tension. *J. exp. Psychol.,* 1943, 32, 213-225.

1522. Wenger, M. A. A factorial appraisal of psycho-physiological relationships. *Amer. Psychologist,* 1946, 1, 454.

1523. Wenger, M. A. Studies of autonomic balance in Army Air Force personnel. *Comp. psychol. Monogr.,* 1948, 19, 1-111.

1524. Wenger, M. A. Variations in autonomic balance under nine drugs. *Amer. Psychologist,* 1949, 4, 233.

1525. Wenger, M. A., & Voos, R. B. A new factor solution for Halstead's neuropsychological tests. *Amer. Psychologist,* 1950, 5, 468.

1526. Wenig, P. The relative roles of naive, artistic, cognitive and press compatibility misperception and ego defense operations in tests of misperception. Unpublished master's thesis, Univer. of Illinois, 1952.

1527. Werdelin, I. Synthesis of factor analyses. I. The theoretical background. *Scand. J. Psychol.,* 1962, 3, 143-154.

1528. Werdelin, I. Synthesis of factor analyses. II. Application of the method on an example. *Scand. J. Psychol.,* 1962, 3, 155-164.

1529. Werdelin, I. Synthesis of factor analyses. III. Interbattery methods of synthesis of factor analyses. *Scand. J. Psychol.,* 1962, 3, 196-204.

1530. Wert, J. F., Neidt, C. O., & Ahmann, J. S. *Statistical methods in educational and psychological research.* New York: Appleton-Century-Crofts, 1954.

1530. Wessman, A. E., & Ricks, D. F. *Mood
(a) and personality.* New York: Holt, Rinehart and Winston, 1966.

1531. Wheeler, W. M., Little, K. S., & Lehner, G. F. J. The internal structure of the MMPI. *J. consult. Psychol.,* 1951, 15, 134-141.

1532. Wherry, R. J. Factorial analysis of learning dynamics in animals. *J. comp. Psychol.,* 1939, 28, 263-272.

1533. Wherry, R. J. An approximation method for obtaining a maximized multiple criterion. *Psychometrika,* 1940, 5, 109-115.

1534. Wherry, R. J. A test by factorial analysis of Honzik's exteroceptive data. *J. comp. Psychol.,* 1940, 29, 75-95.

1535. Wherry, R. J. Determination of the specific components of maze ability for Tryon's bright and dull rats by factorial analysis. *J. comp. Psychol.,* 1941, 32, 237-252.

1535. Wherry, R. J. Test selection and sup-
(a) pressor variables. *Psychometrika,* 1946, 11, 239-247.

1536. Wherry, R. J. Criteria and validity. In D. H. Fryer and E. R. Henry (Eds.), *Handbook of applied psychology*. Vol. 1. New York: Rinehart, 1950.

1537. Whitcomb, M. A. Evaluation of a method for the construction of factor-pure aptitude tests. Lackland AFB, Tex.: USAF Personnel and Training Res. Center, Rept. No. AFPTRC-TN-56-20, 1956.

1538. White, B. W. Visual and auditory closure. *J. exp. Psychol.*, 1954, 48, 234-240.

1539. White, O. The Promax Program for oblique simple structure. (In press).

1540. Whittle, P. On principle components and least square methods of factor analysis. *Skan. Aktuar.*, 1952, 35, 223-239.

1541. Whyte, L. L. (Ed.) *Aspects of form*. Bloomington: Indiana Univer. Press, 1951.

1542. Wiggins, J. S. Strategic, method and stylistic variance in the MMPI. *Psychol. Bull.*, 1962, 59, 224-242.

1542. Wiggins, J. S. Definitions of social de-
(a) sirability and acquiescence in personality inventories. In S. Messick and J. Ross (Eds.), *Measurement in personality and cognition*. New York: Wiley, 1962.

1543. Wilks, S. S. Certain generalizations of analysis of variance. *Biometrika*, 1932, 24, 109-116.

1544. Wilks, S. S. *Mathematical statistics*. Princeton, N. J.: Princeton Univer. Press, 1947.

1545. Williams. E. J. *Regression analysis*. New York: Wiley, 1959.

1546. Williams, H. V. M. A factor analysis of Berne's "social behavior patterns in young children." *J. exp. Educ.*, 1935, 4, 142-146.

1547. Williams, Henrietta V. M. A P-technique study of personality factors in the psychosomatic areas. *Microfilm Abstr.*, 1950, 9(3), 177-178.

1548. Williams, Henrietta V. M. A determination of psychosomatic functional unities in personality by means of P-technique. *J. soc. Psychol.*, 1954, 39, 25-45.

1549. Williams, J. R. *Biochemical individuality*. New York: Wiley, 1956.

1550. Williams, J. R. The definition and measurement of conflict in terms of P-technique: A test of validity. Unpublished doctoral dissertation, Univer. of Illinois, 1958.

1551. Williams, J. R. A test of the validity of the P-technique in the measurement of internal conflict. *J. Pers.*, 1959, 27, 418-437.

1552. Willingham, W. W. The organization of emotional behavior in mice. *J. comp. physiol. Psychol.*, 1956, 49, 345-348.

1553. Willner, D. *Decisions, values and groups*. Vol. 1. New York: Pergamon, 1960.

1554. Wilson, C. L. On-the-job and operational criteria. In R. Glaser (Ed.), *Training research and education*. Pittsburgh, Pa.: Univer. of Pittsburgh Press, 1962.

1555. Wilson, K. V., & Bixenstine, V. E. Forms of social control in 2-person, 2-choice games. *Behav. Sci.*, 1962, 7, 92-102.

1556. Wilson, R. C., High, W. S., Beem, H. P., & Comrey, A. L. A factor-analytic study of supervisory and group behavior. *J. appl. Psychol.*, 1954, 38, 89-92.

1557. Wilson, R. C., Guilford, J. P., Christensen, P. R., & Lewis, D. J. A factor-analytic study of creative-thinking abilities. *Psychometrika*, 1954, 19, 297-311.

1558. Windle, C. Test-retest effect on personality questionnaires. *Educ. psychol. Measmt*, 1954, 14, 617-633.

1558. Winer, B. J. *Statistical principles in experi-
(a) mental design*. New York: McGraw-Hill, 1962.

1559. Wing, H. D. A factorial analysis of musical tests. *Brit. J. Psychol.*, 1941, 31, 341-355.

1560. Wissler, C. Correlation of mental and physical tests. *Psychol. Rev., Monogr. Suppl.*, No. 16, 1901.

1561. Witkin, H. A., Lewis, H. B., Hertzman, M., Machover, K., Meissner, P. B., & Wapner, S. *Personality through perception: An experimental and clinical study*. New York: Harper, 1964.

1562. Wittenborn, J. R. Factorial equations for tests of attentions. *Psychometrika*, 1943, 8, 19-35.

1563. Wittenborn, J. R. Mechanical ability, its nature and measurement. II. Manual dexterity. *Educ. psychol. Measmt*, 1945, 5, 395-409.

1564. Wittenborn, J. R. A factor analysis of Rorschach scoring categories. *J. consult. Psychol.*, 1950, 14, 261-267.

1565. Wittenborn, J. R. Level of mental health as a factor in the implications of Rorschach scores. *J. consult. Psychol.,* 1950, 14, 469-472.

1566. Wittenborn, J. R. Symptom patterns in a group of mental hospital patients. *J. consult. Psychol.,* 1951, 15, 290-302.

1567. Wittenborn, J. R. The study of alternative responses by means of the correlation coefficient. *Psychol. Rev.,* 1955, 62, 451-460.

1568. Wittenborn, J. R. *Manual: Wittenborn Psychiatric Rating scales.* New York: Psychological Corp., 1955.

1569. Wittenborn, J. R. Contributions and current status of Q-methodology. *Psychol. Bull.,* 1961, 58, 132-142.

1570. Wittenborn, J. R., & Bailey, C. The symptoms of involutional psychosis. *J. consult. Psychol.,* 1952, 16, 13-17.

1571. Wittenborn, J. R., Bell, E. G., & Lesser, G. S. Symptom patterns among organic patients of advanced age. *J. clin. Psychol.,* 1951, 7, 328-331.

1572. Wittenborn, J. R., & Holzberg, J. D. The generality of psychiatric symptoms. *J. consult. Psychol.,* 1951, 15, 372-380.

1573. Wittenborn, J. R., Holzberg, J. D., & Simon, B. Symptom correlates for descriptive diagnosis. *Genet. Psychol. Monogr.,* 1953, 47, 237-301.

1574. Wittenborn, J. R., & Larsen, R. P. A. A factorial study of achievement in college German. *J. educ. Psychol.,* 1944, 35, 39-48.

1575. Wittenborn, J. K., Mandler, G., & Waterhouse, I. K. Symptom patterns in youthful mental hospital patients. *J. clin. Psychol.,* 1951, 7, 323-327.

1576. Wolfle, D. Factor analysis to 1940. *Psychometr. Monogr.,* 1940, No. 3.

1577. Wood, R. C. *1400 governments.* Cambridge, Mass.: Harvard Univer. Press, 1961.

1578. Woodrow, H. Quotidian variability. *Psychol. Rev.,* 1932, 39, 245-256.

1579. Woodrow, H. The relation between abilities and improvement with practice. *J. educ. Psychol.,* 1938, 29, 215-230.

1580. Woodrow, H. The common factors in fifty-two mental tests. *Psychometrika,* 1939, 4, 99-108.

1581. Woodrow, H. Intelligence and improvement in school subjects. *J. educ. Psychol.,* 1945, 36, 155-166.

1582. Woodworth, R. S. *Experimental psychology.* New York: Holt, 1938.

1583. Woodworth, R. S., & Schlosberg, H. *Experimental psychology.* New York: Holt, 1954.

1584. Wright, B., & Evitts, M. S. Direct factor analysis in sociometry. *Sociometry,* 1961, 24, 82-98.

1585. Wright, Q. *A study of war.* Chicago: Univer. of Chicago Press, 1942, 1959.

1586. Wright, R. E. A factor analysis of the original Stanford-Binet scale. *Psychometrika,* 1939, 209-220.

1586. Wright, S. Some psychological and physi-
(a) ological characteristics of certain academic underachievers. Unpublished doctoral dissertation, Univer. of Chicago, 1954.

1587. Wright, W. D. *Researches on normal and defective colour vision.* London: Henry Kimpton, 1946.

1588. Wrigley, C. Objectivity in factor analysis. *Educ. psychol. Measmt,* 1958, 18, 463-476.

1589. Wrigley, C. A multivariate study of United Nations General Assembly voting records. East Lansing: Michigan State Univer., Psychol. Dept., 1963. (Mimeographed.)

1590. Wrigley, C., Cherry, C. N., Lee, M. C., & McQuitty, L. L. Use of the square-root method to identify factors in the job performance of aircraft mechanics. Lackland AFB, Tex.: USAF Personnel and Training Res. Center, Rept. No. AFPTRC-TN-57-47 (ASTIA Doc. No. 126377), 1957.

1591. Wrigley, C., & Neuhaus, J. O. The matching of two sets of factors. *Amer. Psychologist,* 1955, 10, 418-419.

1592. Wrigley, C., Saunders, D. R., & Neuhaus, J. O. Application of the Quartimax method of rotation to Thurstone's primary mental abilities study. *Psychometrika,* 1958, 23, 151-170.

1593. Wundt, W. *Grundriss der psychologie.* Trans. C. H. Judd. Leipzig: Engelmann, 1896.

1594. Wynne, L., & Solomon, R. L. Traumatic avoidance learning: Acquisition and extinction in dogs deprived of normal peripheral autonomic function. *Genet. Psychol. Monogr.,* 1955, 52, 241-284.

1595. Young, G., & Householder, A. S. Discussion of a set of points in terms of their mutual distances. *Psychometrika,* 1938, 3, 19-22.

1596. Young, G., & Householder, A. S. A note on multidimensional psychophysical analysis. *Psychometrika,* 1941, 6, 331-333.

1597. Yule, C. U. Why we sometimes get nonsense correlations between time series. *J. Roy. Statist. Ass.,* 1926, 89, 1-64.

1598. Zachert, V. A factor analysis of vision tests. *Amer. J. Optom.,* 1951, 28, 405-416.

1599. Zajonc, R. B. The effects of feedback and probability of group success on individual and group performance. *Hum. Relat.,* 1962, 15 (2), 149-161.

1599. Zeigarnik, B. Das behalten erledigter
(a) und unerledigter handlungen. *Psychol. Forsch.,* 1927, 9, 1-85.

1600. Zigler, E., Jones, L. V., & Kafes, P. The acquisition of language abilities in first, second, and third grade boys. *Child Develpm.,* 1964, 35, 725-736.

1601. Zimmerman, F. T., & Ross, S. Effect of glutamic acid and other amino acids on maze learning in the white rat. *Arch. Neurol. Psychiat.,* 1944, 51, 446-451.

Author Index

Subject Index

C

California test of intelligence, 560
canonical correlation, 166-168, 306, 839
  significance tests in, 168, 173
canonical factor analysis,
  application to the description of change, 411
  relation to maximum likelihood solution, 415
canonical factor model, 403ff
canonical variate analysis, 836f, 868
cartet, 440, 442
Cattell's and Eysenck's systems compared, 857-861
causality, 22, 90
  plus factor analysis, 179
  causal plurality, 24
causal dependence, 331, 354
"ceiling" and "homeostatic" assumptions in scaling,
  366, 375
centour method, 852
change, five models of, 356-359
  as: configurational sequence or process, 356
  endogenons, 364
  environmental relation change, 356
  liability or instability, 356
  state change, 356
  transformation (modification and learning), 359
  trait change, 356
change factors, 403-437
  comparison in a single across-occasion matrix, 373
  derived from cross-product matrices, 375
  direct difference matrix factoring, 374
  lack of correlation over people, 372
  relation to first and second occasion factors, 370-373
change scores, 355
  and homeostasis, 367
  joint change—absolute, c-a, 369
  normalization scaling, 375
  partialling out instead and final scores, etc., 374
  relations to error of measurement, 369
  scaling effects on, 366
  separate distribution, s-d, scaling, 368, 375
channel capacity, 529
characteristic functions, 427
child personality, 732
  cross-sectionally studied, 734
  number of factors, 736
chromosomal communality, 721
circumplex, 444
  approximate, 448
  empirical, 455
civilizations of Toynbee, 783
classification battery AC-2A, 850
classification in personnel psychology, 852
clinical diagnosis and personality factors, 600, 604f
clinical method (alleged), 12
clinical practice and multivariate measurement, 636,
  856
clinical taxonomy, 864
closed loop system with feedback, 430

"closed" scientific model in factor analysis, 176
closure factors and personality, 545
cluster contiguity matrix, for delimiting aits, 319
cluster, 442, 566, 568
  phenomenal, 311, 314
coalition games, 426
coefficient of likeness or resemblance, 296
coefficient of nearness, 300
cognitive dissonance, 780
coherence criterion, 533
color vision, unipolarity or bipolarity of factors, 513
common factors, number of, 407
communality,
  in factor analysis, 182, 200, 227
  by iteration, 240
  estimated, 407, 410, 795
comparative psychology, 642
compatibility among individuals, 760
complexity of form, 524f
component analysis, vs. factor analysis, 404
  model of, 176, 179
component process analysis, 393, 398-400
  and proto-processes, 398-401
comprehensive non-trivial variance (CNTV), 204,
  209-211
computers, and theory testing, 63
concept, 42
  imported meaning in, 43
concepts, creation of, 57
  representation of in patterns, 58
  surplus, error of, 60
  strategy in pursuit of, 61
  and relevant variables, 63
concept mastery test, 557f
concern for the child, 739
concomitance or covariation, 33
conditional probability theory, 418
conditioned reflex, 7
condition-response design, 331, 334f
  example of, 350f
  in factor analysis, 231, 364
confactor resolution and rotation, 189-190, 379
confidence bounds, simultaneous, 250
configural analysis, 150
  configuration defined, 291
  configuration of change, 359
configurative method of factor matching, 196, 339
conflict, measured, 636
  dimensions of, 638
congruence, coefficient of, 196, 337, 339
  of two factor matrices, maximized, 338
constancy of factors,
  across age range, 579
  across cultures, 570, 579f, 598
construct, 42
  empirical, 45
  intermediate, 47
continuous traits in behavior genetics, 712-718
control, as a dimension of experiment, 25
conscious id, 627

PRINTED IN U.S.A.